Childcraft Dictionary

narcissus

moat

pitchfork

Childcraft

This dictionary is also published, with 16 pages of student exercises, under the title *The World Book Student Dictionary.*

musket

Pekingese

rosemary

pansy

Somali

parakeet

Dictionary

 World Book, Inc.

Chicago London Sydney Toronto

intercept

monkey

pliers

Childcraft Dictionary
Childcraft Reg. U.S. Pat. and T.M. Off. Marca Registrada
1994 printing

World Book, Inc.
525 W. Monroe
Chicago, IL 60661

ISBN 0-7166-1494-4
Library of Congress Catalog Card Number 92-64303
Printed in the United States of America

"The Magic of Words" is reprinted from *The Magic of Words—
The 1975 Childcraft Annual,* © 1975 Field Enterprises
Educational Corporation.

**This dictionary is also published, with 16 pages of student
exercises, under the title *The World Book Student Dictionary*.**

The publishers gratefully acknowledge the courtesy of the following individuals,
agencies, organizations, and corporations for permission to use the photographs
listed below. Any errors or omissions are unintentional and will be corrected in
future printings if notice is sent to World Book, Inc. All other illustrations
and photographs are the property of World Book, Inc.

Appaloosa: Appaloosa Horse Club
beagle: Hans Reinhard, Bruce Coleman, Inc.
Belgian Tervuren: Roberta Whitesides
briard: Robert L. Harris, Briard Club of America
Cardigan Welsh corgi: Walter Chandoha
Clydesdale: Anheuser-Busch, Inc.
English toy spaniel: Walter Chandoha
field spaniel: Walter Chandoha
miniature schnauzer: William P. Gilbert
Morgan: American Morgan Horse Association, Inc.
Pharaoh hound: Pharaoh Hound Club of America
Portuguese water dog: Portuguese Water Dog Club of America, Inc.
soft-coated wheaten terrier: Leprecaun from Juanita Wurzburger
Staffordshire bull terrier: Missy Yuhl
Tibetan spaniel: Tibetan Spaniel Club of America, Inc.

8 9 10 11 12 13 14 15 16 99 98 97 96 95 94

CONTENTS

STAFF

For World Book, Inc.
Publishers of
The World Book Encyclopedia,
The World Book Dictionary, and
Childcraft—The How and Why Library

For Sachem
Publishing
Associates, Inc.

President,
World Book Publishing
Daniel C. Wasp

President
Stephen P. Elliott

Publisher Emeritus
William H. Nault

EDITORIAL

Vice President
Dominic J. Miccolis

Managing Editor
Maureen Mostyn Liebenson

Associate Editor
Lisa A. Klobuchar

Contributing Editors
Mary A. Banas
Judith M. Drucker
Charles W. Olson
Michael B. Schuldt
Amy T. Taplin
Cathy Ann Tell
Mark F. Toch

EDUCATIONAL CONSULTANTS

Dolores Durkin, Ph.D.
Professor of Education
University of Illinois
at Urbana-Champaign

Joseph O'Rourke, Ph.D.
Adjunct Professor
College of Education
The Ohio State University

ART

Executive Director,
Art and Design
Roberta Dimmer

Art Director
Wilma Stevens

Senior Editorial Artist
Deirdre Wroblewski

Photography Director
John S. Marshall

Designer
Don Walkoe

Contributing Artists
Carol Brozman
Linda Kinnaman
Stanley A. Schrero
Lisa Wilkinson

Illustrators
Robert W. Addison
Seymour Fleishman
Larry Frederick
Renee Mitchell
   Advertising, Inc.
Bernard Thornton Artists
The Garden Studio
Ficho & Corley, Inc.

PRODUCT PRODUCTION

Vice President, Procurement
Daniel N. Bach

Manufacturing
Sandra Van den Broucke, director
Barbara Podczerwinski

Production Managers
Randi Park
Joann Seastrom

Proofreaders
Anne Dillon
Daniel J. Marotta

EDITORIAL

Editor
Suzanne Stone Burke

Assistant Editors
Elizabeth J. Jewell
Diane Bell Surprenant

Definition Writers
Carol O. Behrman
Kathleen L. Burns
Lisa Clyde Cassidy
Charlotte Currier
Merla C. Davies
Carol B. Dudley
Gretchen Korman Ferrante
Leah Raechel Killeen
Rebecca Lyon
Laurie M. Romanik
Gwendolyn Wilson

Chief Copy Editor
Jan Jamilkowski

Copy Editors
Patricia Charles
Christine Lindberg-Stevens
Cynthia Scott Morehouse
Michele Sensale
Adrienne V. Suddard

The *Childcraft Dictionary,* produced by the publishers of *The World Book Dictionary,* is an entirely new work. All material was selected, written, and illustrated to meet the abilities, needs, and interests of children.

The *Childcraft Dictionary* puts special emphasis on vocabulary development. Many prefixes and suffixes are entry words, and with most of these there is a *Word Power* that shows how to form and understand words that are not entries. Another kind of *Word Power* lists terms that are related by topic so as to encourage children to explore the vocabulary of a particular subject, such as music, health, government, computers, or religion.

Other entries have a *Word History* that tells the story behind the word, or a *Language Fact* that explains differences in the pronunciation of a word such as *roof;* the use of different words for the same thing, such as *bag* and *sack;* proper grammatical usage, as for *lie* and *lay;* or the difference between such words as *principal* and *principle.*

Idioms, synonyms, antonyms, and homophones all play a vital part in language development, and this dictionary has hundreds of these. A red square signals the idioms, and a blue dot signals the synonyms, antonyms, and homophones. In addition, the Word Power Exercises in the Reference Section will enable children to test their vocabulary knowledge.

The entry list includes more than fifty computer terms, as well as other terms such as acid rain, AIDS, and VCR, which reflect our changing language. There is also systematic coverage of such topics as religion and holidays.

The hundreds of full-color illustrations, both drawings and photographs, offer another kind of learning experience. Pictures, especially those that compare or contrast subjects, are both fun to look at and invaluable aids to understanding.

For quick recognition and ease of use, entry words are set as whole words, just as they would appear in any reading material. Definitions give the most commonly used meaning first. Care has been taken to ensure that definitions use simpler words than the words being defined. And sample sentences have been so constructed as to force the meaning of the defined words. Syllabication is shown by vertical rules. In the pronunciation, the syllable that gets primary stress is printed in heavy black type as an aid to young readers.

In developing the entry list and writing the definitions and sample sentences, the editors made extensive use of *The Living Word Vocabulary: A National Vocabulary Inventory,* by Edgar Dale and Joseph O'Rourke. This work proved an invaluable guide to determining the grade level at which a specific meaning of a word can be readily understood.

"How to Use Your Dictionary" (pages *8-27*) provides all the information children will need to make full use of all the features in this book. And the Reference Section (pages 837-900) offers extensive biographical and geographical information. This section also includes "The Magic of Words," which has word games, the meanings of first and last names, and the stories behind many everyday words.

HOW TO USE
YOUR DICTIONARY

**What Is a
Dictionary?**

A dictionary is a book of words listed in alphabetical order. It is also a very special kind of reference book. To get the most out of a dictionary, you need to know how to find what you want, what kind of information is provided, and how that information is organized.

This dictionary shows you how to spell words, what the words mean, what part or parts of speech they are, how to separate the words into syllables, and how to pronounce the words. In addition, you will almost always see how a word is used in a sentence or phrase. Many times you will also discover words that have the same, or nearly the same, meaning, as well as words that have the opposite meaning. And for some words you will find a special feature—a *Word History,* or a *Language Fact,* or a *Word Power.* There are also hundreds of pictures to help increase your understanding.

If you want to know something about a word, the best way to find what you want is to look the word up in your dictionary. But there are a few things you do need to know first. On the following pages you will find an explanation of all the features that make this dictionary a very useful book—how to find a word, how to understand and use all the information given about the word, and much, much more.

**Alphabetical
Order**

All the words in this dictionary are listed in alphabetical order, letter by letter. This means that all the words beginning with **a** are grouped together, all the words beginning with **b** are grouped together, and so on through **z.** Words that begin with the same letter are put in alphabetical order according to the second letter:

aisle	anywhere
ajar	aorta
akimbo	apart

If the second letters are the same, then the third letter is used to put a word in its proper alphabetical order:

abduct	alert
abhor	alfalfa
abide	algae

When the first three letters are the same, then the fourth letter is used to determine alphabetical order, and so on.

At the top of every page in the A to Z section of this dictionary, there are words printed in heavy black type:

These are called guide words because they will guide you to the word you want. The first guide word is the same as the first word listed on a page. The second guide word is the same as the last word listed on a page.

Entry Words

The words you are looking for in a dictionary are called entry words. The entry words are printed in heavy black type and stick out into the margin. There are many different kinds of entry words. Here are examples of all the kinds you will find.

■ **ONE-WORD ENTRIES**

Most of the entries in this dictionary are one-word entries. The entry words **lariat** and **lid** are examples of one-word entries.

lariat—A rope with a loop at one end; lasso. It is used to catch or tie down animals.
lar|i|at (lar′ē ət) *noun, plural* **lariats**.
● See Word History at **lasso**.

lid—**1.** A top or cover that can be removed: *She took the* lid *off the cookie jar.* **2.** A movable piece of skin that opens and closes over the eye; eyelid.
lid (lid) *noun, plural* **lids**.

■ **HYPHENATED TERMS**

Hyphenated terms are groups of two or more words that are used as one word. These terms are spelled with a hyphen or hyphens between the words in the group. In this dictionary, hyphenated terms are entered in alphabetical order, letter by letter.

jack-in-the-box—A toy consisting of a figure, usually a clown, that pops out of a small, decorated box when the top is opened.
jack-in-the-box (jak′in thə boks′) *noun, plural* **jack-in-the-boxes**.

up-to-date—Using or showing the latest developments or style; modern; current: *an* up-to-date *science book with all the recent discoveries; wearing an* up-to-date *outfit to the dance.*
up-to-date (up′tə dāt′) *adjective*.

■ **TWO-WORD ENTRIES**

Two-word entries, like hyphenated terms, are groups of words that have a special meaning when used together. Like hyphenated terms, two-word entries are entered in alphabetical order.

aircraft carrier—A naval ship with a large, flat deck on which airplanes or helicopters take off and land.
air|craft car|ri|er (ār′kraft′ kar′ē ər) *noun, plural* **aircraft carriers**.

post office—A place in the postal system where mail is received, sorted, and sent out, and where postage stamps are sold.
post of|fice (pōst awf′is) *noun, plural* **post offices**. Abbreviation: **P.O.**

■ HOMOGRAPHS

Homographs are words that are spelled the same but have different meanings. The word *homograph* comes from two Greek words meaning "same" and "writing." Sometimes, homographs are also pronounced differently. Each homograph is a separate entry and is marked by a small raised number.

lie¹—Something that is not true and is said to fool another person; false statement: *He could not tell a* lie *and confessed that he broke the window. Noun.* —To say something false or misleading: *She* lied *about having a sore throat so she would not have to read her report to the class. Verb.*
lie (lī) *noun, plural* **lies;** *verb,* **lied, lying.**
• A word that sounds the same is **lye.**

lie²—**1.** To place oneself flat on a surface: *to* lie *in bed; to* lie *on the beach.* **2.** To be in a flat position on something: *The letters* lie *on the desk.* **3.** To remain a certain way: *The dog has been* lying *asleep in front of the fire all day.* **4.** To be positioned or placed: *A bicycle path* lies *along the river.* **5.** To exist; belong: *Her success as a cook* lies *in her ability to follow recipes exactly.*
lie (lī) *verb,* **lay, lain, lying.**
• A word that sounds the same is **lye.**
• See Language Fact at **lay¹.**

■ CONTRACTIONS

A contraction is a word made by joining two words and putting an apostrophe in place of one or more of the letters. For example, the contraction **can't** is formed from the words "can not" or "cannot." The apostrophe replaces the letters *n* and *o*. All contractions are entered alphabetically, letter by letter, just as if the apostrophe were not there.

can't—The contraction of "can not" or "cannot."
can't (kant).

won't—The contraction of "will not."
won't (wōnt).

■ IRREGULAR PLURALS OF NOUNS

To change most nouns from singular to plural, you simply add *s* or *es*. But some nouns form the plural in other ways. These are called irregular plurals. In this dictionary, irregular plurals are entry words. At the entry you will see a cross-reference to the singular form:

knives—See knife.
knives (nīvz) *plural noun.*

mice—See mouse.
mice (mīs) *plural noun.*

■ IRREGULAR FORMS OF VERBS

To change the tense of most verbs, you simply add *s, ed,* or *ing.* But some verbs do not change tense in the usual way. These are called irregular verb forms. In this dictionary, irregular verb forms are separate entry words. At the entry, you will see a cross-reference to the entry where you will find all of the information you want.

knew—*See* **know.**
  knew (nū *or* nyū) *verb*.
  • Words that sound the same are **gnu** and **new.**

known—*See* **know.**
  known (nōn) *verb*.

PREFIXES AND SUFFIXES

Many words are formed by adding a prefix in front of a word or a suffix at the end of a word. Some words formed in this way are entry words in this dictionary. **Uneasy** is formed by adding the prefix *un-*. **Regardless** is formed by adding the suffix *-less*.

uneasy—**1.** Nervous or worried: *I felt* uneasy *about diving into the water.* **2.** Not comfortable: *Her anger made us* uneasy.
un|eas|y (un ē′zē) *adjective*, **uneasier, uneasiest.**

regardless—No matter what; in spite of: *The parade will be held on Saturday,* regardless *of the weather.*
re|gard|less (ri gahrd′lis) *adjective*.

This dictionary also has many prefixes and suffixes as entry words. The entry explains what the prefix or suffix means and gives examples showing how it is used to form words.

circum-—A prefix that means "around" or "in a circle." Sailors who circumnavigate the earth sail completely around it.

-able—A suffix that means "able to," or "inclined to," or "worthy of." A movable desk is able to be moved. A reasonable person is inclined to reason. A lovable pet is worthy of love.

Even if a word formed with a prefix or suffix is not an entry word, its meaning can be learned. For example, *overcautious* is not an entry word. But the prefix **over-** is an entry word and **cautious** is also an entry word. When the two meanings are combined, it is clear that *overcautious* means "too cautious" or "too careful."

ABBREVIATIONS

This dictionary includes many common abbreviations as entry words. At such entries, the full word is shown in heavy black type. Should you want more information, simply go to the entry for the full word.

km—The abbreviation for **kilometer** or **kilometers.**

kilometer—A unit of length in the metric system. One kilometer equals 1,000 meters, about five-eighths of a mile.
kil|o|me|ter (kə lom′ə tər *or* kil′ə mē′tər) *noun*, *plural* **kilometers.** Abbreviation: **km**

■ DIFFERENT SPELLINGS

Most words have only one correct spelling, but some words can be spelled in more than one way. For example, **theater** and **theatre** are both correct. If the two different spellings are next to each other alphabetically, then they both appear in the same entry—with the more common spelling first.

If the different spellings are separated alphabetically, then both spellings are entry words. The entry for the less common spelling refers you to the more common spelling. And that is where you will find the definition for the word. Note also that at the entry for the more common spelling, the alternate spelling is also given.

Moslem—*See* Muslim.
Mos|lem (moz′ləm *or* mos′ləm) *noun, plural* Moslems.

Muslim—A person who is a believer in the religion of Islam, founded by Muhammad. Mus|lim (muz′ləm) *noun, plural* **Muslims**.
• This word is also spelled **Moslem**.

■ ALTERNATE NAMES

Sometimes, there is more than one name for the same thing. Both names are correct, but one is more common. This dictionary will have entries for both. The entry for the less common name is a cross-reference to the more common name, where you will find full information.

groundhog—*See* woodchuck.
ground|hog (ground′hog′) *noun, plural* groundhogs.

woodchuck—A wild animal with short legs, brown fur, and a bushy tail. A woodchuck digs tunnels in the ground and lives in them. wood|chuck (wood′chuk′) *noun, plural* **woodchucks**.
• Another name for this animal is **groundhog**.

■ WORDS THAT AREN'T ENTRY WORDS

Not all of the words that appear in this dictionary are entry words. Many words that are formed by adding a prefix or suffix are not entry words (see page 11). Other words that are not entry words are forms of entry words.

The words **luckier** and **luckiest** are forms of the adjective **lucky**. The words **pestered** and **pestering** are forms of the verb **pester**.

lucky—**1.** Having good things happen to one; fortunate: *We were* lucky *to catch the last train home*. **2.** Causing good things to happen: *a* lucky *charm; my* lucky *day*.
luck|y (luk′ē) *adjective*, **luckier, luckiest**.

pester—To annoy, usually in order to get something; bother: *He* pestered *his father for a cookie*.
pes|ter (pes′tər) *verb*, **pestered, pestering**.
• Synonyms: **badger, harass, hound, plague**.

The definition, or meaning, of a word comes right after the entry word. Some words, such as **hammock,** have only one definition. Other words, such as **idea,** have more than one definition. If there is more than one definition, the definitions are numbered in sequence. As a general rule, the most common or most important meaning comes first.

hammock—A kind of hanging bed that is made of canvas or rope netting. It is strung between two trees or posts.
ham|mock (ham′ək) *noun, plural* **hammocks.**

idea—**1.** A thought, plan, or belief formed in one's mind: *She had an* idea *of just how she wanted the dress to look.* **2.** A central meaning; purpose: *To play a new game, you have to understand the* idea *of the game first.*
i|de|a (ī dē′ə) *noun, plural* **ideas.**

When words have more than one meaning, it is best to read all the definitions before deciding which one is right for your purpose. Suppose you want to know what the word **idea** means in the sentence "We tried to explain the plan's idea to him." Of the two definitions for **idea,** the second definition is the one that fits the sentence.

Words also have more than one definition when they are used as more than one part of speech. A word can sometimes be a noun, verb, adjective, or some other part of speech. In this dictionary, each different part of speech begins on a new line that starts with a dash. The dash tells you that the definition is for a new part of speech. The word **praise,** for example, can be a noun or a verb. The noun definition is listed first. The verb definition begins on a new line that starts with a dash.

praise—Words that express respect or approval: *The principal had nothing but* praise *for the performance of the school orchestra. Noun.*
—To express respect or approval for: *Mother* praised *my drawing and hung it on the wall. Verb.*
praise (prāz) *noun, plural* **praises;** *verb,* **praised, praising.**

instant—**1.** A certain moment in time: *Come here this* instant! **2.** A very short time; moment; flash: *The shooting star disappeared in an* instant. *Noun.*
—**1.** Immediate: *A calculator gives us an* instant *answer to difficult math problems.* **2.** Very important; urgent: *There is an* instant *need to leave the ship because it is sinking.* **3.** Able to be served quickly: instant *pudding;* instant *coffee. Adjective.*
in|stant (in′stənt) *noun, plural* **instants;** *adjective.*

When a word is used as more than one part of speech, the different parts of speech may each have more than one definition. For example, the word **instant** has two noun definitions and three adjective definitions. Again, it is best to read all the definitions, for all the parts of speech, before deciding which definition is the one you want.

Sentences and Phrases

Following most definitions you will see the entry word used in a sentence or phrase. These sample sentences or phrases will help you understand and remember the meaning or meanings of the entry word. The sentences or phrases stand out from the rest of the entry because, except for the entry word, they are printed in italics (slanted type).

Look at the two examples below. The entry for **keynote** has a complete sentence using the word **keynote**. The entry **mechanic** has two phrases using the word **mechanic**.

keynote—The main idea or theme: *The* keynote *of her speech was the need to raise money to help the poor.*
key|note (kē′nōt′) *noun, plural* **keynotes.**

mechanic—A person whose job is fixing machines or engines: *an automobile* mechanic; *a washing machine* mechanic.
me|chan|ic (mə **kan**′ik) *noun, plural* **mechanics.**

Part of Speech Labels

Some words are only one part of speech. Other words can be used as more than one part of speech. Look at the three examples:

fable—A short story that teaches a lesson, often with imaginary animals who talk: *a* fable *about a race between a rabbit and a turtle.*
fa|ble (fā′bəl) *noun, plural* **fables.**

fade—1. To decrease in brightness, color, or freshness; dim: *The old photographs* faded.
2. To lessen; disappear slowly: *With all this rain, hope is* fading *for us to go on a picnic.*
fade (fād) *verb,* **faded, fading.**

face—1. The front of the head; eyes, nose, mouth, cheeks, and chin. 2. A look that people make; an expression: *She made an ugly* face *at her brother.* 3. The front or surface of something: *Our house is wood with a brick* face. *Noun.*
—1. To look upon: *My window* faces *the garden.*
2. To meet bravely: *We must* face *the fact that we are lost. Verb.*
face (fās) *noun, plural* **faces;** *verb,* **faced, facing.**

The word **fable** can be used only as a noun and **fade** can be used only as a verb. When a word can be used as only one part of speech, the part of speech label is shown only after the pronunciation. But the word **face** can be used as a noun or a verb. When a word can be used as more than one part of speech, the part of speech labels are shown in two places. First, the part of speech label is given after the definition or the sample sentence or phrase for each part of speech. Second, the part of speech labels are repeated after the pronunciation. There, they are given in the same order as in the definitions.

Understanding the Parts of Speech

There are eight parts of speech: nouns, pronouns, verbs, adjectives, adverbs, prepositions, conjunctions, and interjections.

A **noun** is a word that names a person (John), a place (school), a thing (cup), an idea (liberty), an animal (lion), a quality (goodness), or an action (manufacture).

A **pronoun** takes the place of a noun. It stands for the noun without naming it again: "Sally could not go because *she* was sick." In this sentence, the pronoun *she* is used to avoid repeating the noun *Sally*.

Pronouns include such words as *I, we, you, he, she, it, they, mine, yours, his, hers, ours, theirs, who, which, what, this, that, each, either, neither, any, some, one, other, another,* and *none*.

A **verb** expresses an action or a state of being. *Hit,* as in "She *hit* the ball," is a verb expressing action. *Is,* as in "He *is* a fine person," is a verb expressing a state of being.

An **adjective** describes, or tells you something about, a noun or pronoun. An adjective answers one of three questions: Which one? as in "Show me *those* flowers." What kind? as in "I want the *blue* toy." or How many? as in "There are *three* cookies left."

An **adverb** is a word that describes a verb, adjective, or another adverb. An adverb answers one of five questions: How? as in "John shook the can *fiercely*." When? as in "I took the cake to him *yesterday*." Where? as in "Please take those dresses *away*." How often? as in "I *almost always* brush my teeth before I go to bed." Or, How much? as in "He was *very* surprised by the party."

A **preposition** is a word that is used to show the relation of a noun or a pronoun to some other word in a sentence. In the sentence, "We sat *under* the umbrella," the preposition *under* shows the relation between the noun *umbrella* and the verb *sat*. Prepositions include such words as *across, after, at, before, between, by, for, from, in, near, on, over, to, under, up,* and *with*.

A **conjunction** is a word that connects individual words or groups of words. The word *conjunction* means "the act of joining together." In the sentence, "I like pizza, ice cream, *and* cookies," the conjunction *and* joins the individual words. In the sentence, "I would have gone to the party, *but* I lost the address," the conjunction *but* joins the groups of words. Other conjunctions include such words as *after, although, as, because, before, for, if, nor, or, since, unless, until, when, where,* and *while*.

An **interjection** is a word or phrase that expresses emotion or strong feeling. Interjections are often followed by an exclamation point. Interjections include such words as *alas!, hurrah!, oh!,* and *wow!*

Word Division

A syllable is one part of a word and has one vowel sound. The word **ache** has one vowel sound and one syllable. The word **duty** has two vowel sounds and two syllables.

ache—A constant, dull pain. *Noun.* —**1.** To be in constant pain; hurt: *The noise made my head* ache. **2.** To want badly; long for: *We all* ached *for the circus to arrive. Verb.* ache (āk) *noun, plural* **aches;** *verb,* **ached, aching.**

duty—**1.** Something that a person should do: *a* duty *to obey the law.* **2.** The things a person does as part of his or her job; responsibilities: *A firefighter's* duties *include putting out fires and saving lives.* **3.** A tax paid on goods that are taken out of or brought into a country. du|ty (dū′tē *or* dyū′tē) *noun, plural* **duties.**

If a word has only one syllable, it cannot be divided. If a word has more than one syllable, the dictionary shows you how to divide the word. The syllables have vertical lines between them. A word can be divided where you see a vertical line—unless this would mean separating one letter from the rest of the word. So, even though words such as **adapt** (a|dapt) and **ready** (read|y) have two syllables, they should not be divided. Also, if a word has a hyphen in it, like **lady's-slipper,** the word should be divided only after the hyphen.

Pronunciation

Right after the word division, and in parentheses, you will see how to pronounce, or say, the word:

barn—A farm building used to store hay and grains and to protect farm animals and machinery.
barn (bahrn) *noun, plural* **barns.**

jacket—**1.** A short coat for the upper body, usually reaching to the hips. **2.** An outer casing or covering: *a book* jacket; *a record* jacket.
jack|et (jak′it) *noun, plural* **jackets.**

Most of the pronunciation symbols are simply letters of the alphabet. But there are some special symbols, such as ā, ē, and ə. If you don't remember what sound a symbol stands for, look at the short pronunciation key that is at the bottom of every left-hand page. There is also a full pronunciation key opposite the first page of A. In addition, you may want to look at the list of sounds in Common Spellings of English Sounds on pages *18–19.*

a at	i if	oo look	ch chalk		a in ago
ā ape	ī idle	ou out	ng sing		e in happen
ah calm	o odd	u ugly	sh ship	ə =	i in capital
aw all	ō oats	ū rule	th think		o in occur
e end	oi oil	ur turn	th their		u in upon
ē easy			zh treasure		

If a word has more than one syllable, part of the word is usually said a little more strongly than the rest of the word. If you look at **jacket,** you will see that the first syllable is shown in heavy black type and is followed by a heavy black accent mark ('). This part of the word should be said a little more strongly than the rest of the word.

If a word has a number of syllables, you will often see that one of the syllables is followed by a light accent mark ('). This syllable should be said a little more strongly than a syllable without an accent mark, but not as strongly as the syllable that is in heavy black type and has a heavy accent mark.

Knowing how to read the pronunciation symbols is always important—but sometimes it is *very* important. One such time is when the meaning of a word changes and the pronunciation also changes. Look at the entries for **perfect, progress, present**[2], and **rebel.** How you say each of these words depends upon what you mean.

perfect—1. Having no defect; containing no flaws or mistakes: *My brother did* perfect *work and got a score of 100 on his math test.* 2. Complete; lacking nothing: *Now that my best friend is back in town, my life is* perfect. 3. Exact; precise: *a* perfect *match. Adjective.*
—To remove all flaws or problems from: *The automobile manufacturer* perfected *its popular new car. Verb.*
per|fect (pur′fikt for *adjective;* pər fekt′ for *verb*) *adjective; verb,* **perfected, perfecting.**

present²—1. To supply with; hand out; give: *The coach* presented *a trophy to the best player.* 2. To introduce: *He* presented *the new student to the class.* 3. To bring into the presence of another person or other people: *The class president* presented *herself at the principal's office.* 4. To show: *She* presented *her project at the science fair. Verb.*
—Something that is given; donation; gift: *a birthday* present. *Noun.*
pre|sent (pri zent′ for *verb;* prez′ənt for *noun*) *verb,* **presented, presenting;** *noun, plural* **presents.**

progress—1. An improvement: *His health has shown steady* progress *since his operation.* 2. A forward movement: *The car's* progress *was slowed by the bumps in the road. Noun.*
—1. To improve; get better: *The new quarterback's play* progressed *as the football season went on.* 2. To move forward: *The use of computers has* progressed *greatly over the past several years. Verb.*
prog|ress (prog′res for *noun;* prə gres′ for *verb*) *noun; verb,* **progressed, progressing.**

rebel—A person who chooses to go against authority instead of obeying it: *The* rebels *were not afraid to fight for their freedom. Noun.*
—1. To go against authority, especially of one's government: *The people* rebelled *when the mayor wanted to turn the park into a shopping center.* 2. To show or feel strong dislike or unwillingness; turn away or refuse stubbornly: *The horse* rebelled *when we tried to get him into the barn. Verb.*
reb|el (reb′əl for *noun;* ri bel′ for *verb*) *noun, plural* **rebels;** *verb,* **rebelled, rebelling.**

Some homographs (words that are spelled the same but have different meanings) are also pronounced differently. Look at the difference between **sow¹** and **sow².** Say the two words aloud and listen to the difference. Do the same thing with **tear¹** and **tear².**

sow¹—To scatter and plant seeds in the ground: *They* sowed *wheat and corn this year.*
sow (sō) *verb,* **sowed, sown** or **sowed, sowing.**
● Words that sound the same are **sew** and **so.**

sow²—An adult female pig.
sow (sou) *noun, plural* **sows.**

tear¹—1. A clear drop of a salty fluid that comes from the eye. Tears form when something, such as smoke, irritates the eye or when a person is upset. 2. **tears:** The act of crying; weeping: *He broke into* tears *when he fell off his bicycle.*
tear (tēr) *noun, plural* **tears.**

tear²—1. To split or become split apart: *She* tears *up letters after she reads them.* 2. To put a hole in something: *The cat* tore *the curtains with its claws.* 3. To remove forcefully: *to* tear *a story out of a magazine.* 4. To injure by cutting: *The board he was holding slipped and* tore *his finger.* 5. To divide into sides: *The city was* torn *by riots.* 6. To move with great speed or force: *The fire engines* tore *down the street. Verb.*
—A hole caused by ripping: *She slipped on the ice and got a* tear *in her skirt. Noun.*
tear (tãr) *verb,* **tore, torn, tearing;** *noun, plural* **tears.**
■ **be torn between:** To have trouble choosing between two separate desires: *We were* torn *between going to the circus and going to the amusement park.*

Common Spellings of English Sounds

Many English words are not spelled the way they sound. For example, you write *cello*, but you say **chel'**ō. The following chart shows you how to spell different sounds. It will help you to find words you know how to say but don't know how to spell.

On the left-hand side of the chart are the pronunciation

Sound	Spellings
a	ask, plaid, calf, laugh
ā	age, rain, straight, gauge, may, café, break, vein, eight, crochet, hey
ah	father, hurrah, palm, sergeant, hearth
ār	air, aerial, prayer, tear, their, heir
aw	all, Utah, balk, cause, caught, law, recording, broad, four, sought
b	bat, rubber
ch	cello, check, Czechoslovakia, witch, righteous, question, structure
d	do, add, skilled
e	many, said, lend, lead, heifer, leopard, friend, bury
ē	algae, ecology, lean, tree, receive, key, ski, grief, actually
f	for, stiff, cough, calf, phone
g	goat, beggar, ghost, guess, vague
h	hat, who
hw	when
i	elect, it, carriage, sieve, women, busy, guild, myth
ī	aisle, kayak, aye, height, geyser, eye, ice, pie, thigh, isle, coyote, guide, guy, my, style
j	graduate, midget, ledge, soldier, gem, barge, exaggerate, region, jump
k	cat, accuse, school, ache, stack, acquit, circuit, king, khaki, talk, quite, antique, excuse
l	like, stall
m	palm, mine, comb, summer, hymn
n	gnarled, knight, nice, dinner, pneumonia
ng	link, handkerchief, strong, tongue

symbols used in this dictionary. Each symbol stands for a different sound. Opposite each symbol are words that show the different ways that the sound is spelled. The letters that show the sound are in heavy black type. The letters, or letter combinations, are listed in alphabetical order.

SOUND	SPELLINGS
o	**h**onor, **n**od, **kn**owledge
ō	**ch**auffeur, **pl**ateau, **s**ew, **c**old, **r**oach, **oh**, **p**olka, **br**ooch, **s**oul, **d**ough, **gr**ow, **owe**
oi	**b**oil, **t**oy, **bu**oy
oo	**w**olf, **t**ook, **y**our, **w**ould, **f**ull
ou	**h**our, **ab**out, **b**ough, **g**own
p	**p**iece, **l**am**p**, **co**pp**er**
r	**r**an, **rh**yme, **ma**rr**y**, **wr**ite
s	**c**ent, **h**en**c**e, **ps**alm, **s**aw, **sc**ience, **d**en**se**, **bli**ss, **li**s**ten**, **s**word, **pi**zz**a**
sh	o**c**ean, **ch**ef, vi**ci**ous, **s**ure, **sch**wa, con**sc**ience, **sh**y, pen**si**on, ti**ss**ue, fi**cti**on
t	**doub**t, decea**sed**, recei**pt**, **t**ake, **th**yme, clu**tt**er, **tw**o, pi**zz**a
th	**th**irst
<u>th</u>	**th**is, ba**the**
u	**o**ther, d**oe**s, bl**oo**d, y**ou**ng, **u**tter
ū	man**eu**ver, bl**ew**, li**eu**tenant, m**o**ve, sh**oe**, m**oo**d, gr**ou**p, thr**ough**, r**u**de, gl**ue**, s**ui**t, b**u**oy
ur	y**ear**n, **er**mine, h**er**b, g**ir**l, col**o**nel, w**or**st, w**or**ry, j**our**nal, b**ur**n, c**ur**rent, m**yr**tle
v	o**f**, **v**ase, lea**ve**
w	ch**oi**r, **qu**ote, **w**ant
y	on**i**on, piñ**a**ta, **y**et
yū	be**au**ty, f**eu**d, v**iew**, **u**nite, c**ue**, **y**outh, **y**ule
z	wa**s**, ra**sp**berry, sci**ss**ors, **x**ylophone, **z**oo, mu**zz**le
zh	mira**ge**, plea**s**ure, vi**si**on, sei**z**ure
ə	**a**bout, mount**ai**n, **au**thority, **e**ffect, dung**eo**n, pur**i**ty, parl**ia**ment, **o**ffend, porp**oi**se, prec**i**ous, foc**u**s, ox**y**gen

Plurals of Nouns

Most nouns form the plural by simply adding *s* or *es*. But some nouns have irregular plurals. In this dictionary, you will see the plural form for *all* nouns, whether regular or irregular. The plural form appears at the end of the entry in heavy black type.

wombat—An animal that looks like a small bear and lives in Australia. Female wombats carry their young in a pouch, like kangaroos. **wom│bat** (wom′bat) *noun, plural* **wombats.**

candy—A sweet food made from sugar, which often has chocolate, nuts, fruit, or other flavoring added to it. **can│dy** (kan′dē) *noun, plural* **candies.**

Verb Forms

The different verb forms appear at the end of an entry and are shown in heavy black type. The first form, which ends in *ed*, is the past tense. It is used to show that something has happened in the past. The second form, which ends in *ing*, is used to show that something is happening now. For some verbs, such as **lie,** there is another form, shown between the past and present forms, that is used with the helping verb *have*.

accept—1. To take or receive something that is offered; agree to take: *If she offers me a second helping, I will* accept *it gladly.* 2. To agree to; say yes to: *She* accepted *two invitations for the same day.* 3. To believe to be true or satisfactory: *I hope they will* accept *our reason for being absent.* **ac│cept** (ak sept′) *verb,* **accepted, accepting.**

lie²—1. To place oneself flat on a surface: *to lie in bed; to lie on the beach.* 2. To be in a flat position on something: *The letters* lie *on the desk.* 3. To remain a certain way: *The dog has been* lying *asleep in front of the fire all day.* 4. To be positioned or placed: *A bicycle path* lies *along the river.* 5. To exist; belong: *Her success as a cook* lies *in her ability to follow recipes exactly.* **lie** (lī) *verb,* **lay, lain, lying.**
● A word that sounds the same is **lye.**
● See Language Fact at **lay¹.**

Adjective Forms

Adjectives have special forms called the comparative and superlative. These appear at the end of an entry and are shown in heavy black type. The comparative form, which ends in *er*, compares one thing to another or others. The superlative form, which ends in *est*, shows the most or the least of something.

large—Bigger than the normal amount or size: *The child wanted a* large *ice cream cone.* **large** (lahrj) *adjective,* **larger, largest.** Abbreviation: **lg.**
■ **at large:** Free; not caught or shut up: *The escaped prisoner is still* at large.
● Synonyms: See Synonyms at **big.**
Antonyms: See Synonyms at **small.**

strong—1. Having great power or force: *a* strong *horse pulling a heavy wagon.* 2. Not easily damaged or changed; sturdy: *a* strong *rope.* **strong** (strawng) *adjective,* **stronger, strongest.**

Abbreviations

For some words, an abbreviation is shown at the end of the entry. Many, but not all, abbreviations end with a period. If the abbreviation is in heavy dark type, it is also an entry word.

corporal—A member of the armed forces who is above a private and below a sergeant.
cor|po|ral (kawr′pər əl) *noun, plural* **corporals.**
Abbreviation: Corp.

Fahrenheit—Having to do with the temperature scale on which water freezes at 32 degrees and boils at 212 degrees.
Fahr|en|heit (far′ən hīt) *adjective.*
Abbreviation: **F.**

An idiom is a phrase or expression whose meaning cannot be understood just from the ordinary meanings of the words in it. Did anyone ever say to you, "Has the cat got your tongue?" Of course the cat didn't have your tongue. What the expression means in plain English is "Haven't you got anything to say?"

This dictionary has many idioms. Whenever you see a red square you will find one or more idioms. If there is more than one idiom, the idioms are listed in alphabetical order. Idioms appear under the main word in the idiom. If there is more than one main word, try each one.

Idioms are printed in heavy black type. Following the meaning of the idiom there is usually an example of how it is used.

Idioms

cat—**1.** A small furry animal with whiskers, sharp claws, pointed ears, and a long tail, that is kept as a pet. **2.** Any member of the group of large animals that includes tigers, leopards, and lions.
cat (kat) *noun, plural* **cats.**
■ **cat got your tongue?** Can't you think of anything to say?
let the cat out of the bag: To tell a secret: *Someone* let the cat out of the bag *and told him about his birthday present.*
rain cats and dogs: To rain very hard: *We had to call off the game because it was* raining cats and dogs.

teeth—*See* **tooth.**
teeth (tēth) *noun.*
■ **cut (one's) teeth:** To learn or be trained by experiencing something for the first time: *The new artist was assigned to* cut *her* teeth *on a simple cartoon project.*
in the teeth of: Directly against: *He was cold when he got home, because he had walked* in the teeth of *the strong wind.*
to the teeth: Entirely; to an extreme degree: *She has furnished her new apartment* to the teeth.

Homophones are words that sound alike but have different meanings and different spellings. In this dictionary, homophones are shown at the end of entries. A blue dot calls your attention to the one or more homophones for an entry.

Homophones

sew—To fasten by stitches, using a needle and thread: *Mother* sewed *curtains for my bedroom on her new* sewing *machine.*
sew (sō) *verb,* **sewed, sewed** or **sewn, sewing.**
● Words that sound the same are **so** and **sow**[1].
sow[1]—To scatter and plant seeds in the ground: *They* sowed *wheat and corn this year.*
sow (sō) *verb,* **sowed, sown** or **sowed, sowing.**
● Words that sound the same are **sew** and **so.**

so—**1.** To this or that extent; in this or that degree: *We had never walked* so *far before.* **2.** For this or that reason; therefore: *It is late,* so *I must go now.* **3.** Also: *You like pizza, and* so *do I. Adverb.*
—In order that; with the result that: *She drove me into town* so *I could go shopping. Conjunction.*
—Such as has been said; this; that: *You told me this would be a funny movie, and it really is* so. *Pronoun.*
so (sō) *adverb, conjunction, pronoun.*
● Words that sound the same are **sew** and **sow**[1].

Cross-References

A cross-reference is a note telling you to look somewhere else in the book for further information. Cross-references appear at the end of entries and have a blue dot to call them to your attention. They may tell you to see a picture, synonyms, antonyms, or a special feature at another entry.

crocodile—A large, thick-skinned reptile with a long body, short legs, and webbed feet. It is related to the alligator but has a longer snout. It lives in rivers and marshes in the tropics.
croc|o|dile (krok′ə dīl) *noun, plural* **crocodiles.**
  ■ **crocodile tears:** Pretended or insincere sorrow: *For all his* crocodile tears, *he was actually glad I lost the election.*
  • See picture at **alligator.**

dejected—Discouraged; unhappy: *He felt* dejected *after he lost his wagon.*
de|ject|ed (di jek′tid) *adjective.*
  • See Synonyms and Antonyms at **happy.**

gladiolus—A plant with stalks of large, brightly colored flowers clustered together and long leaves that grow pointing upward.
glad|i|o|lus (glad′ē ō′ləs), *noun, plural* **gladioli** (glad′ē ō′lī) *or* **gladioluses.**
  • See Word History at **gladiator.**

immigrate—To come from the country of one's birth to live in a foreign land: *My parents* immigrated *to the United States from Mexico.*
im|mi|grate (im′ə grāt) *verb,* **immigrated, immigrating.**
  • See Language Fact at **emigrate.**

Synonyms and Antonyms

Synonyms are words that have the same or nearly the same meaning, such as big and large. Often, synonyms are part of a definition. In the entry **lair,** for example, the first part of the definition explains what a lair is. The second part of the definition is simply the word *den.* This means that den is a synonym for lair.

lair—The living place of a wild animal; den: *the lion's* lair.
lair (lār) *noun, plural* **lairs.**

Sometimes, you will see synonyms listed at the end of an entry. They are introduced by a blue dot and the word "Synonyms." In the entry for **ignore,** there are three synonyms. If the entry word is more than one part of speech, as for example **barter,** the synonym line will tell you to which part of speech the synonyms apply. Note that the synonyms are printed in heavy black type, which means that these words are entry words.

ignore—To refuse to pay attention to or take notice of: *The girls* ignored *the freezing temperature and played happily in the snow for hours.*
ig|nore (ig nawr′) *verb,* **ignored, ignoring.**
  • Synonyms: **disregard, neglect, overlook**

barter—To exchange goods for other goods without using money: *The Indians* bartered *furs for guns with the pioneers. Verb.*
  —The exchanging of goods without using money. *Noun.*
bar|ter (bahr′tər) *verb,* **bartered, bartering;** *noun.*
  • Synonyms: **swap, trade,** for *verb.*

Antonyms are words that have the opposite or nearly the opposite meaning. Sometimes, an entry has a list of antonyms. If so, the antonyms are on the line following the synonyms. As with the synonyms, antonyms are printed in heavy black type.

Sometimes, as for example in the entry for **lean²**, the synonyms and antonyms apply to only one of the definitions for the word. If so, you will see the definition number printed in heavy black type at the end of each line.

obvious—Easy to see, discover, or understand; clear: *It is* obvious *that she cares about her little brother because she worries about him a lot.* **ob|vi|ous (ob′vē əs)** *adjective.*
- Synonyms: **apparent, evident, plain**
  Antonyms: **hazy, obscure, vague**

lean²—**1.** Having very little fat: *a* lean *hamburger.* **2.** Very thin: *a* lean *young man.* **3.** Unproductive; poor: *Very slow sales made it a* lean *year for the automobile dealer.* **lean (lēn)** *adjective,* **leaner, leanest.**
- Synonyms: **gaunt, scrawny, skinny, spare,** for **2.**
  Antonyms: **fat, plump, stout,** for **2.**

At some entries there are cross-references to synonyms and antonyms that appear at another entry. So, if you want a synonym or antonym for **cheerful,** look at the entry for **happy.**

cheerful—**1.** Joyful; happy: *a smiling,* cheerful *face.* **2.** Bringing happiness: *a* cheerful *letter.* **cheer|ful (chēr′fəl)** *adjective.*
- See Synonyms and Antonyms at **happy.**

happy—Glad; pleased: *He was* happy *to see his friends again after summer vacation.* **hap|py (hap′ē)** *adjective,* **happier, happiest.**
- Synonyms: **cheerful, gay, merry**
  Antonyms: **blue, dejected, gloomy, glum, miserable, sad, unhappy**

This dictionary has a special feature called a *Word History* that appears from time to time. When you see a *Word History,* stop and read it. You will find out where the word came from, how it got into the language, and what it really means.

Word History Feature

Word History

Orient comes from a Latin word meaning "to rise." **Occident** comes from a Latin word meaning "to set." The countries of the Orient lie to the east of Europe, in the direction of the rising sun. The countries of the Occident lie to the west, the direction where the sun sets.

aardvark

Word History

Aardvark comes from two Dutch words meaning "earth pig." Dutch settlers in Africa gave the animal this name because it lives in a burrow and looks like a pig.

Word History

October comes from a Latin word meaning "eight." According to early Roman calendars, October was the eighth month of the year. Today, October is the tenth month. **Octopus** comes from two Greek words meaning "eight-footed." Anytime you see the letters "oct" in a word, the word probably has something to do with the number eight.

Language Fact Feature

A *Language Fact,* like a **Word History,** is a special feature that goes with some entry words. It may explain the use of different names for things, as at **bag;** correct English, as at **between;** the difference between two words, as at **dwarf;** or something about different pronunciations for a word, as at **roof.**

Language Fact

Bag is used to mean all kinds of containers, from grocery bags to suitcases. **Sack** commonly means a loose container made of cloth, usually burlap. But what some people call a bag, others call a sack, and the other way around, too. **Bag** is used more often in the northern part of the United States, **sack** more often in the southern part.

Language Fact

Between and **among** are often used incorrectly. **Between** should be used when only two people or things are mentioned: *I couldn't choose* between *the apple and the orange.* **Among** is used when more than two people or things are mentioned: *She divided the books* among *the three children.*

Many people say "between you and I." Careful writers and speakers always use "between you and me."

Language Fact

Dwarf and **midget** are both used for things and people that are much smaller than others. But when used for people, **dwarf** and **midget** have different meanings. A dwarf is a person with a body of normal size and very short arms and legs. A midget is a person whose body, legs, arms, and head are all much smaller than usual.

Language Fact

Roof may be pronounced in two different ways. How you pronounce the word may depend on where you live. Some people in the northern central part of the United States pronounce **roof** using the same vowel sound as in **good.** Many people in other parts of the country pronounce **roof** using the same vowel sound as in **tooth.** Both pronunciations are correct.

Word Power Feature

This dictionary has another special feature called *Word Power* that goes with certain entries. Almost every entry for a prefix and suffix has a *Word Power* feature that will help you to find the meanings of words that are not in this dictionary. The *Word Power* for **re-** shows how you can understand many words that begin with this prefix. The *Word Power* at **-ship** shows how to understand many words ending in this suffix.

re-—A prefix that means "again." A refilled glass is one that is filled again.

-ship—A suffix that means "the condition of being." Leadership is the condition of being a leader.

Word Power

You can understand the meanings of many words that begin with **re-,** if you add the meaning of the prefix to the meaning of the rest of the word.
rebuild: to build again
reoccur: to occur again

Word Power

You can understand the meaning of many words that end in **-ship,** if you add the meaning of the suffix to the meaning of the rest of the word.
friendship: the condition of being a friend
partnership: the condition of being a partner

Another kind of *Word Power* that will help you to increase your vocabulary deals with words related to a particular subject. If you have an interest in the subject, you can look up the words listed in order to learn more about the subject. Or, if you are trying to think of a word, you can look up the subject to which it is related to see if there is a *Word Power.* Suppose you are doing a paper on computers and can't remember a particular term. If you look up the *Word Power* for **computer,** you may find just what you want.

dinosaur—One of a group of reptiles that lived millions of years ago and are now all gone. Scientists have discovered more than 800 different kinds and have found them on every continent.
di|no|saur (dī′nə sawr) *noun, plural* **dinosaurs.**

computer—An electronic machine that can analyze, store, and give back information quickly.
com|put|er (kəm pyū′tər) *noun, plural* **computers.**

Word Power

There are many different types of dinosaurs. You can find descriptions of seven types in this dictionary. For each dinosaur, you'll also find a picture of what it looked like.

allosaurus	stegosaurus
anatosaurus	triceratops
ankylosaurus	tyrannosaurus
brontosaurus	

Word Power

If you are interested in computers, you can find these words in this dictionary.

BASIC	floppy disk	pixel
binary system	hard disk	printout
bit	hardware	program
bug	input	random-access memory
byte	modem	read-only memory
cursor	monitor	software
disk drive	mouse	turtle
	output	

Sometimes words are not enough. That's when pictures can be very important. Pictures are fun to look at, but they can also be tools for learning. A definition can be written very simply, but it may not be at all clear to you if it deals with an idea that is difficult to understand. Read the definition for **valve.** It tells you what a valve is and what it does—but *how* does it do it? Now look at the picture. Doesn't the picture make it much easier to understand just how a valve works?

**How Pictures Help
You to Understand**

valve—**1.** A device that opens or closes to control the flow of gas or liquid through a channel: *The valve on the water heater allows steam to escape.* **2.** One half of the hinged shell of a clam, oyster, or similar sea animal.
valve (valv) *noun, plural* **valves.**

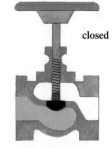
closed
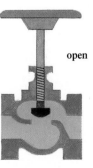
open

valve (definition 1)

Have you ever seen an Australian cattle dog? Probably not, unless you go to a lot of dog shows or live on a cattle ranch that has one of these dogs. Cover up the photograph with your hand while you read the description. Based on the description, do you think you'd recognize one of these dogs if you saw one? Almost certainly not. Now look at the photograph. Doesn't the picture add a lot to the words?

Measurements are usually defined as being equal to something or smaller than this and bigger than that. But if you don't know the "something," or the "this," or the "that," the definition is not much help. A picture, however, makes a lot of difference, as you can see by looking at the illustration for **bushel**.

Australian cattle dog—A medium-sized dog with a short, thick coat and a bushy tail. The coat is blue or red, with black, blue, red, or tan markings. This dog was originally bred in Australia to herd cattle.
Aus|tral|ian cat|tle dog (aw strāl′yən kat′əl dawg) *noun, plural* **Australian cattle dogs.**

Australian cattle dog

bushel—A unit of measurement for dry things such as vegetables, grains, and fruits. It is equal to 4 pecks or 32 quarts.
bush|el (boosh′əl) *noun, plural* **bushels.**

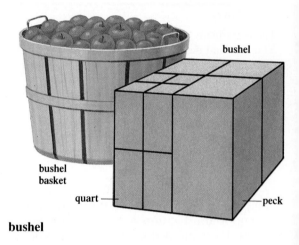

bushel basket

quart

bushel

peck

bushel

Some pictures in this dictionary compare things. That is, they note ways in which things are alike. The entry at **crane,** for instance, has two very different definitions. A crane can be a machine or a bird. The picture shows both—and makes it easy to understand why they have the same name.

Other pictures contrast things. That is, they note ways in which things are different. One example is the picture at **alligator.** It shows an alligator and a crocodile together, so that you can see the difference mentioned in the definition. (And, if you looked up **crocodile,** you'd find a cross-reference to the picture at **alligator.**) Another kind of contrast is in the pictures of dinosaurs. These pictures contrast the size of the dinosaur with the size of a human being to give you a good idea of the size of the dinosaur.

crane—**1.** A machine with a long arm for lifting and carrying heavy objects; derrick. **2.** A tall, long-legged wading bird with a long neck and bill. *Noun.*
—To stretch one's neck in order to see better: *She craned her neck to see out the window. Verb.*
crane (krān) *noun, plural* **cranes;** *verb,* **craned, craning.**

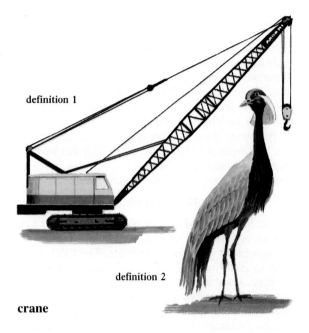

definition 1

definition 2

crane

alligator—A large reptile with a long head and tail, sharp teeth, and thick, tough skin. It looks like a crocodile but has a shorter, flatter head. *Noun.*
al|li|ga|tor (al′ə gā′tər) *noun, plural* **alligators.**

alligator

crocodile

alligator

allosaurus—A large meat-eating dinosaur that looked like a tyrannosaurus. It had short front legs and walked upright on its large hind legs.
al|lo|saur|us (al′ə sawr′əs) *noun, plural* **allosauri** (al′ə sawr′ī).

allosaurus

Full Pronunciation Key

Say aloud the words *at, ape, arch,* and *all*. Do you hear how different the sound of *a* is in each of these words? In English, there are many more sounds than there are letters. The list below gives the letters and symbols used in this dictionary to show all the different sounds.

Following the definition of each word you will see that vertical lines are used to divide the word into sound parts, or syllables, and then, in parentheses, how the word is pronounced:

flow|er (flou′ər)

If you break a word into its sound parts, it will help you to say the word. But the real help is the pronunciation given in parentheses. The "fl" is easy to understand. But the "ou" may not be quite so easy. Look at the list below and you will see that "ou" is said as in the words *out* and *house*. But what about the "ər"? The symbol (ə) is called a schwa (shwah). Look at the list and you will see

that the *e* in *flower* is pronounced like the *e* in *happen*.

When you say a word that has more than one syllable, one part of the word is usually said a little more loudly than the rest of the word. As shown in the examples, this part of the word is printed in heavy black type and is followed by a heavy black accent mark (′). When a word has a number of syllables, another part of the word may also be said more loudly than the rest, but not quite as loudly as the part in heavy black type:

fore|fin|ger (fawr′fing′gər)

In this example, the second syllable is also accented, but is not spoken quite so loudly as the first syllable.

If you have any trouble understanding the pronunciation, look at the short pronunciation key that is at the bottom of every left-hand page. If you still need help, turn to this full pronunciation key.

Sound	As In
a	at, bat, laugh
ā	ape, hate, aid, pay, wear, eight, weigh
ah	arch, calm, car, father
aw	all, author, caught, paw, coffee, oar order, adorable, more, floor
b	back, above, job
ch	chalk, pitcher, such
d	dog, puddle, bad
e	end, set, any, pleasure
ē	easy, heat, free, piano, finally
f	fond, defend, leaf, photo, rough
g	gas, juggle, fog
h	hop, ahead, who
hw	whale, what
i	if, sit, busy
ī	idle, five, by
j	join, adjective, gem, judge
k	kite, bakery, book, cat, school
l	love, million, feel
m	mark, family, am, dumb
n	note, final, on, gnaw, know
ng	sing, sink
o	odd, not
ō	oats, smoke, go, toe, row, though

Sound	As In
oi	oil, noise, toy
oo	look, wood, wolf, put, sure
ou	out, house, cow
p	pen, repair, limp
r	rain, farm, four
s	see, aside, yes, cent, scene
sh	ship, wishing, fish, sugar, tissue
t	tame, obtuse, hat
th	think, nothing, bath
th	their, mother, smooth
u	ugly, shut, oven, love, flood, rough
ū	rule, flew, move, fool
ur	ermine, fern, firm, stir, turn, word
v	veil, shiver, cave
w	wail, reward
y	yes, onion
yū	unicorn, mule, few, you
z	zone, lizard, size, jazz, rose, xylophone
zh	treasure, vision, garage, azure
ə	a in ago e in happen i in capital o in occur u in upon

About 5,000 years ago, the ancient Egyptians used a symbol of an ox's head.

About 3,500 years ago, people in the Middle East made a simpler symbol. They called it *aleph,* their word for "ox."

About 3,000 years ago, other people in the Middle East made the symbol much more simple.

About 2,600 years ago, the Greeks gave the letter this form. They called it *alpha* and made it the first letter in their alphabet.

About 1,900 years ago, the Romans gave the capital **A** its present form. The small letter **a** was first used about 1,700 years ago. It reached its present form about 500 years ago.

A or **a**[1]—**1.** The first letter of the alphabet: *The word "father" has one* a. **2.** The best of its kind or the highest mark in school: *Grade A milk; an A in math.*
A, a (ā) *noun, plural* **A's** or **As, a's** or **as.**

a[2]—**1.** Any: *Please call* a *taxi.* **2.** One; a single: *Not* a *slice was wasted.* **3.** The same: *Take three at* a *time.*
a (ā *or* ə) *indefinite article.*

aardvark—An African animal that looks like a pig but has a long tail, powerful claws, and a long sticky tongue. It eats ants and termites.
aard|vark (ahrd′vahrk′) *noun, plural* **aardvarks.**

abacus—A frame with rows of beads that are moved along wires to do arithmetic.
ab|a|cus (ab′ə kəs) *noun, plural* **abacuses.**

abandon—**1.** To give up entirely: *Rain forced us to* abandon *plans for our softball game.* **2.** To leave with no intention of returning: *The people* abandoned *their flooded town.*
a|ban|don (ə ban′dən) *verb,* **abandoned, abandoning.**

abbey—A building where monks or nuns live; a monastery or convent.
ab|bey (ab′ē) *noun, plural* **abbeys.**

abbreviate—To make shorter; shorten: *We* abbreviate *the word "Mister" as "Mr."*
ab|bre|vi|ate (ə brē′vē āt′) *verb,* **abbreviated, abbreviating.**

aardvark

Word History

Aardvark comes from two Dutch words meaning "earth pig." Dutch settlers in Africa gave the animal this name because it lives in a burrow and looks like a pig.

• Synonyms: **abridge, condense, trim**
Antonyms: **enlarge, expand, lengthen**

abbreviation—A shortened form in which a letter or group of letters stand for a whole word or phrase: *The* abbreviation *for "hour" is "hr."*
ab|bre|vi|a|tion (ə brē′vē ā′shən) *noun, plural* **abbreviations.** Abbreviation: abbr. or abbrev.

abdicate—To give up power: *The army forced the king to* abdicate.
ab|di|cate (ab′də kāt′) *verb,* **abdicated, abdicating.**

abdomen—1. The part of the body containing such digestive organs as the stomach and intestines; the belly.   2. The third and last section of the body of an insect.
ab|do|men (ab′də mən) *noun, plural* **abdomens.**
• See picture at **alimentary canal** and at **thorax.**

abduct—To carry off somebody by force; kidnap: *The robbers planned to* abduct *three people.*
ab|duct (ab dukt′) *verb,* **abducted, abducting.**

abhor—To find horrible or disgusting: *Some people* abhor *snakes.*
ab|hor (ab hawr′) *verb,* **abhorred, abhorring.**

abide—To put up with; endure: *I can* abide *loud music for just so long.*
a|bide (ə bīd′) *verb,* **abode** or **abided, abiding.**
■ **abide by:** To obey; be bound by: *Players must* abide by *the rules of the game.*
• Synonyms: **bear², stand, tolerate**

ability—1. The power or strength to do something: *An ostrich has the* ability *to run very fast.*   2. A skill: *Magicians have the* ability *to fool the eye.*
a|bil|i|ty (ə bil′ə tē) *noun, plural* **abilities.**

able—Having the ability, power, or skill to do something: *A goat is* able *to eat nearly anything. Father is an* able *clarinet player.*
a|ble (ā′bəl) *adjective,* **abler, ablest.**

Word Power

You can understand the meanings of many words that end in **-able,** if you add a meaning of the suffix to the meaning of the rest of the word.
   cleanable: able to be cleaned
   changeable: inclined to change
   questionable: worthy of question

-able—A suffix that means ''able to,'' or ''inclined to,'' or ''worthy of.'' A movable desk is able to be moved. A reasonable person is inclined to reason. A lovable pet is worthy of love.

a at	i if	oo look	ch chalk		a in ago
ā ape	ī idle	ou out	ng sing		e in happen
ah calm	o odd	u ugly	sh ship	ə =	i in capital
aw all	ō oats	ū rule	th think		o in occur
e end	oi oil	ur turn	<u>th</u> their		u in upon
ē easy			zh treasure		

abnormal—Different from the usual or ordinary; not normal: *A calf with five legs is* abnormal.
ab|nor|mal (ab nawr′məl) *adjective.*
• Synonyms: **odd, uncommon, unusual**
   Antonyms: **common, regular, typical**

aboard—On board; in or on an airplane, bus, ship, or train: *When we were* aboard, *the captain started the engine. Adverb.*
—On board of; into, in, or on (an airplane, bus, ship, or train): *He climbed* aboard *the bus. Preposition.*
—On base in baseball: *It was the last of the ninth, and we had runners* aboard *at first and third. Adjective.*
a|board (ə bawrd′) *adverb, preposition, adjective.*
■ **all aboard:** Everybody on: ''All aboard!'' *called the driver.*

abode—*See* **abide.**
a|bode (ə bōd′) *verb.*

abolish—To put an end to; do away with: *The committee voted to* abolish *the unpopular rule.*
a|bol|ish (ə bol′ish) *verb,* **abolished, abolishing.**

abolition—A putting an end to; doing away with: *Those who disliked the rule favored its* abolition.
ab|o|li|tion (ab′ə lish′ən) *noun.*

abominable—1. Hateful; disgusting: *Stealing is an* abominable *act.*   2. Disagreeable; unpleasant: *It was an* abominable *day because of sleet and high winds.*
a|bom|i|na|ble (ə bom′ə nə bəl) *adjective.*

aborigine—One of the earliest known people to live in a place, or a person descended from those people: *The settlers bought land from the* aborigines.
ab|o|rig|i|ne (ab′ə rij′ə nē) *noun, plural* **aborigines.**

abound—To be plentiful or numerous: *Trees* abound *in the jungle.*
a|bound (ə bound′) *verb,* **abounded, abounding.**

about—1. Concerning; with regard to: *a book* about *shells.*   2. Near; close to: *We should arrive* about *dinner time.*   3. On every side of; around: *Fasten the rope* about *your waist. Preposition.*
—More or less; approximately: *The bag is* about *full. Adverb.*
a|bout (ə bout′) *preposition, adverb.*
■ **about to:** Going to; ready to: *I am* about to *give up.*

above—Overhead or higher up: *The leaves fell from* above. *Adverb.*

—Higher than; over: *Hold the umbrella* above *your head. Preposition.*
a|bove (ə **buv**ʹ) *adverb, preposition.*

aboveboard—Honest; without lies or tricks: *Everything she did was completely* aboveboard.
a|bove|board (ə **buv**ʹbawrdʹ) *adjective.*

abreast—Side by side: *The children walked* abreast.
a|breast (ə **brest**ʹ) *adverb.*
■ **abreast of:** Up with: *He reads the newspaper to keep* abreast of *current events.*

abreast

abridge—To shorten by using fewer words: *The teacher asked us to* abridge *our long stories to one page.*
a|bridge (ə **brij**ʹ) *verb,* **abridged, abridging.**
● Synonyms: **abbreviate, condense, trim**
 Antonyms: **enlarge, expand, lengthen**

abroad—Outside one's own country: *We hope to go* abroad *on our vacation this summer.*
a|broad (ə **brawd**ʹ) *adverb.*

abrupt—1. Sudden; unexpected; with no warning: *With a screech of brakes, we came to an* abrupt *stop.* **2.** Not courteous; blunt: *an* abrupt *reply; an* abrupt *manner.*
a|brupt (ə **brupt**ʹ) *adjective.*
● Synonyms: **hasty, quick,** for **1.**
 Antonyms: **gradual, slow,** for **1.**

abscess—A painful sore that is a gathering of pus in some part of the body. It is caused by an infection.
ab|scess (**ab**ʹses) *noun, plural* **abscesses.**

absence—1. A being away: *Joe's latest* absence *from class caused him to miss the test.* **2.** A being without; lack: *Absence of shade made the heat unbearable.*
ab|sence (**ab**ʹsəns) *noun, plural* **absences.**

absent—1. Not present; away: *Half the class is*

absent *today.* **2.** Not existing; lacking: *Rainfall is* absent *in the desert.*
ab|sent (**ab**ʹsənt) *adjective.*

absentee—A person who is away or stays away: *There were six* absentees *at our meeting. Noun.*
—Of or having to do with an absentee or absentees: *an* absentee *ballot. Adjective.*
ab|sen|tee (ab'sən **tē**ʹ) *noun, plural* **absentees;** *adjective.*

absolute—1. Complete; whole: *He told me the* absolute *truth.* **2.** Total; unlimited: *An* absolute *ruler has* absolute *power.* **3.** Positive; certain: *You must have* absolute *proof before you accuse him.*
ab|so|lute (**ab**ʹsə lūtʹ) *adjective.*

absorb—1. To soak up or take in: *A sponge* absorbs *water.* **2.** To hold the interest of: *He was so* absorbed *in his work that he did not hear his mother call him.*
ab|sorb (ab **sawrb**ʹ *or* ab **zawrb**ʹ) *verb,* **absorbed, absorbing.**

absorption—The act of soaking up or taking in: *A tree's roots get nourishment from the soil by* absorption.
ab|sorp|tion (ab **sawrp**ʹshən *or* ab **zawrp**ʹshən) *noun.*

abstain—To hold oneself back from doing something: *We try to* abstain *from snacking before dinner.*
ab|stain (ab **stān**ʹ) *verb,* **abstained, abstaining.**

abstract—Having to do with a general idea, not with a particular object or thing: *"Truth" and "beauty" are* abstract *nouns, but "sun" and "horse" are not.*
ab|stract (**ab**ʹstrakt *or* ab **strakt**ʹ) *adjective.*

absurd—Plainly not true; against logic or good sense; silly: *It is* absurd *to say that a circle has corners.*
ab|surd (ab **surd**ʹ *or* ab **zurd**ʹ) *adjective.*
● Synonyms: **foolish, ridiculous, senseless**
 Antonyms: **reasonable, sensible**

abundance—A great amount; a quantity that is more than enough: *There is an* abundance *of books in the library.*
a|bun|dance (ə **bun**ʹdəns) *noun.*

abundant—More than enough; very plentiful: *There was* abundant *food at the picnic.*
a|bun|dant (ə **bun**ʹdənt) *adjective.*
● Synonym: **ample**
 Antonyms: **rare, scanty, scarce**

abuse—1. To make bad or wrong use of: *The privilege of using the playground will be taken away if we* abuse *it by fighting.* **2.** To treat

cruelly or badly; mistreat: *That farmer* abuses *his horse by overloading it. Verb.*
—**1.** A bad or wrong use: *The king's* abuse *of power led to his overthrow.* **2.** Cruel or harsh treatment: *The prisoner complained of beatings and other* abuse. **3.** Rude or insulting language: *The fans hurled* abuse *at the umpire. Noun.*
a|**buse** (ə byūz′ for *verb;* ə byūs′ for *noun*) *verb,* **abused, abusing;** *noun, plural* **abuses.**

abyss—A very deep hole or crack in the earth: *They stood on the edge of the volcano and gazed into the* abyss *below.*
a|**byss** (ə bis′) *noun, plural* **abysses.**

Abyssinian—A short-haired cat of medium size, with long, pointed ears and a tapering tail. Abyssinians came originally from Abyssinia (now Ethiopia), in Africa.
Ab|**ys**|**sin**|**i**|**an** (ab′ə sin′ē ən) *noun, plural* **Abyssinians.**

Abyssinian

academic—Having to do with schools or schoolwork: academic *success.*
ac|**a**|**dem**|**ic** (ak′ə dem′ik) *adjective.*

academy—**1.** A private high school. **2.** A school for the study of some special skill or subject: *a riding* academy; *a military* academy.
a|**cad**|**e**|**my** (ə kad′ə mē) *noun, plural* **academies.**

accelerate—To go faster; speed up: *When you step on the gas pedal, the car will* accelerate.
ac|**cel**|**er**|**ate** (ak sel′ə rāt) *verb,* **accelerated, accelerating.**

accelerator—A pedal or lever that adjusts the speed of a motor vehicle or machine by controlling the amount of fuel going to its engine. The harder it is pressed, the faster the speed.
ac|**cel**|**er**|**a**|**tor** (ak sel′ə rā′tər) *noun, plural* **accelerators.**

accent—**1.** A stronger tone of voice used when saying a certain word or syllable of a word: *In the word "finger," the* accent *is on the first syllable.* **2.** A mark used in writing or printing to show which syllable of a word is to be stressed. Boldface (dark) letters and the mark ′ indicate the major accent, as in the word "**base**′ball." If there are two or more accents in a word, a minor accent shows the syllable having a weaker force, as in the word "dec′o **ra**′tion." **3.** A way of saying words in different parts of a country or a way of saying words when speaking in a foreign language: *a Southern* accent; *a French* accent. *Noun.*
—To pronounce a word or syllable in a stronger way: *We* accent *"finger" on the first syllable. Verb.*
ac|**cent** (ak′sent for *noun;* ak′sent or ak **sent**′ for *verb*) *noun, plural* **accents;** *verb,* **accented, accenting.**

accept—**1.** To take or receive something that is offered; agree to take: *If she offers me a second helping, I will* accept *it gladly.* **2.** To agree to; say yes to: *She* accepted *two invitations for the same day.* **3.** To believe to be true or satisfactory: *I hope they will* accept *our reason for being absent.*
ac|**cept** (ak sept′) *verb,* **accepted, accepting.**

acceptable—Good enough; satisfactory: *Her grades were* acceptable *but not excellent.*
ac|**cept**|**a**|**ble** (ak sep′tə bəl) *adjective.*

access—**1.** The right or privilege to enter or use: *The public has* access *to the town beach at all times.* **2.** A way or means of approach: *Access to the park is through these gates. Noun.*
—To find and get information from a computer: *Please* access *and print all her grades for this year. Verb.*
ac|**cess** (ak′ses for *noun;* ak′ses or ak ses′ for *verb*) *noun, plural* **accesses;** *verb,* **accessed, accessing.**

access code—Some letters or numbers that a person enters into a computer in order to reach information in it: *The* access code *for my bank account is my birth date.*
ac|**cess code** (ak′ses kōd) *noun, plural* **access codes.**

a at	i if	oo look	ch chalk		a in ago
ā ape	ī idle	ou out	ng sing		e in happen
ah calm	o odd	u ugly	sh ship	ə =	i in capital
aw all	ō oats	ū rule	th think		o in occur
e end	oi oil	ur turn	th their		u in upon
ē easy			zh treasure		

accessory—**1.** Something extra added to a more important thing: *These shoes are a fine* accessory *to my new suit.* **2.** A person who helps to commit or hide a crime: *By hiding the stolen money, she became an* accessory *to the theft. Noun.*
—Useful but not needed; extra: *His bike has many* accessory *features, such as a tire pump. Adjective.*
ac|ces|so|ry (ak **ses′**ər ē) *noun, plural* **accessories;** *adjective.*

accident—**1.** Something that happens by chance and is not expected: *Finding the money on the sidewalk was a lucky* accident. **2.** An unexpected happening that causes sadness, damage, or loss: *I broke my leg in a skiing* accident. **3.** Chance; luck: *I found my missing necklace by* accident *when I was dusting.*
ac|ci|dent (**ak′**sə dənt) *noun, plural* **accidents.**

accidental—Happening by chance; not expected; unplanned: *an* accidental *meeting.*
ac|ci|den|tal (ak′sə **den′**təl) *adjective.*

accommodate—**1.** To have enough room for; hold: *This bus can* accommodate *60 people.* **2.** To help out; do a favor for: *When I asked for a ride, my brother* accommodated *me.* **3.** To supply with a place to sleep or stay for a time: *The hotel* accommodates *300 guests.*
ac|com|mo|date (ə **kom′**ə dāt) *verb,* **accommodated, accommodating.**

accommodation—**1.** A favor or help: *Lending her your baseball glove was an* accommodation. **2. accommodations:** A place for lodging: *hotel* accommodations.
ac|com|mo|da|tion (ə kom′ə **dā′**shən) *noun, plural* **accommodations.**

accompany—**1.** To go along with: *Please* accompany *your brother to the playground.* **2.** To happen at the same time as: *High winds* accompanied *the cold weather.* **3.** To play or sing background music for: *She will* accompany *your guitar number on her drums.*
ac|com|pa|ny (ə **kum′**pə nē) *verb,* **accompanied, accompanying.**

accomplice—A person who helps another to commit a crime: *The police are looking for the robber's* accomplice.
ac|com|plice (ə **kom′**plis) *noun, plural* **accomplices.**

accomplish—To carry out; complete; perform: *Can you* accomplish *all that work in one day?*
ac|com|plish (ə **kom′**plish) *verb,* **accomplished, accomplishing.**

accomplishment—**1.** Something that has been done successfully; achievement: *Graduating with honors is quite an* accomplishment. **2.** A special skill or ability: *Her* accomplishments *include juggling and dancing.* **3.** A carrying out; completion: *The* accomplishment *of this work will take all day.*
ac|com|plish|ment (ə kom′plish mənt) *noun, plural* **accomplishments.**
• Synonyms: deed, feat, for **1.**

accord—To agree with; be in harmony with: *My memories of the trip* accord *with yours. Verb.*
—An agreeing with; harmony: *I like your opinions, so we are in complete* accord. *Noun.*
ac|cord (ə **kawrd′**) *verb,* **accorded, according;** *noun, plural* **accords.**
■ **of (one's) own accord:** Without being asked; voluntarily: *My brother will never do the dishes of his own* accord.

accordance—A state of agreement or harmony: *I will act in* accordance *with your wishes.*
ac|cord|ance (ə **kawr′**dəns) *noun.*

according—**according to: a.** In agreement with; following: *We made the cake* according to *the recipe.* **b.** On the authority of; as said by: *According to her, you are wrong.*
ac|cord|ing (ə **kawr′**ding) *adjective.*

accordion—A musical wind instrument with a keyboard, metal reeds, and a bellows. It is played by pushing the bellows together to force air through the reeds while pressing the keys.
ac|cor|di|on (ə **kawr′**dē ən) *noun, plural* **accordions.**

accordion

account—**1.** A report; description; statement: *Can you give an* account *of where you spent the day?* **2.** Value; worth: *I fear my singing will be of little* account *in a chorus.* **3.** A record of money received and spent: *an* account *of vacation expenses.* **4.** Some money in the bank: *I have a savings* account. *Noun.*

—To regard as; consider: *We must* account *her honest unless we can prove she is not. Verb.*
ac|count (ə kount′) *noun, plural* **accounts;** *verb,* **accounted, accounting.**

■ **account for: 1.** To tell what has been done with; answer for: *You must* account for *your missing books.* **2.** To give a reason for; explain: *Heavy traffic* accounted for *the lateness of the bus.*
on no account: Under no circumstances; for no reason: On no account *can you stay up that late.*
take account of: To make allowance for; consider: *We must* take account of *the weather in making plans for our picnic.*
take into account: To make allowance for; consider: *It was a good performance, if you* take into account *the fact that the singer had a sore throat.*

accountant—A person who is trained to manage the money records of a person or a business: *An* accountant *prepared our tax returns.*
ac|count|ant (ə koun′tənt) *noun, plural* **accountants.**

accumulate—To collect or pile up little by little; gather: *Dirty dishes* accumulated *in the sink while I was sick.*
ac|cu|mu|late (ə kyū′myə lāt) *verb,* **accumulated, accumulating.**

accuracy—The state of being without errors: *The measurements must be taken with complete* accuracy, *or the wall will be crooked.*
ac|cu|ra|cy (ak′yər ə sē) *noun.*

accurate—**1.** Free from errors; correct: *I know that clock is* accurate, *because I set it this morning.* **2.** Making few or no errors; precise: *He is an* accurate *typist.*
ac|cu|rate (ak′yər it) *adjective.*

accuse—To claim that someone committed a crime or did something wrong: *The neighbors* accused *us of playing in their garden.*
ac|cuse (ə kyūz′) *verb,* **accused, accusing.**

accustom—To make familiar through habit; get used to: *I am trying to* accustom *myself to exercising every morning.*
ac|cus|tom (ə kus′təm) *verb,* **accustomed, accustoming.**

accustomed—Usual; customary: *He took his* accustomed *place at the table.*
ac|cus|tomed (ə kus′təmd) *adjective.*

■ **accustomed to:** Used to; in the habit of: *She is* accustomed to *taking this bus to school.*
● Synonyms: **familiar, habitual**
Antonyms: **odd, strange, unusual**

ace—**1.** A playing card, domino, or side of a die with one mark: *the* ace *of hearts.* **2.** An expert at something: *a basketball* ace. *Noun.*
—Having very great skill; expert: *He is an* ace *diver. Adjective.*
ace (ās) *noun, plural* **aces;** *adjective.*

■ **ace in the hole:** Something that can be a deciding factor and is held back to be used if necessary: *Our trick play is our* ace in the hole.
within an ace of: Almost; on the edge of: *I came* within an ace of *failing the test.*

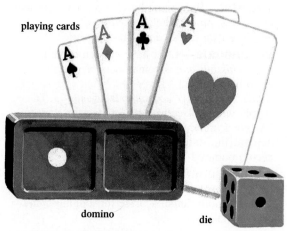

playing cards

domino   die

ace (noun, definition 1)

ache—A constant, dull pain. *Noun.*
—**1.** To be in constant pain; hurt: *The noise made my head* ache. **2.** To want badly; long for: *We all* ached *for the circus to arrive. Verb.*
ache (āk) *noun, plural* **aches;** *verb,* **ached, aching.**

achieve—**1.** To do successfully; accomplish: *He gave me more tasks than I can* achieve *in one day.* **2.** To get or reach by an effort: *She* achieved *high honors in the music contest.*
a|chieve (ə chēv′) *verb,* **achieved, achieving.**

achievement—**1.** Something done or reached by effort: *Putting a man on the moon was a great* achievement. **2.** An accomplishing; completion: *the* achievement *of a ripe old age.*
a|chieve|ment (ə chēv′mənt) *noun, plural* **achievements.**
● Synonyms: **accomplishment, deed, feat,** for **1.**

a at	i if	oo look	ch chalk		a in ago
ā ape	ī idle	ou out	ng sing		e in happen
ah calm	o odd	u ugly	sh ship	ə =	i in capital
aw all	ō oats	ū rule	th think		o in occur
e end	oi oil	ur turn	<u>th</u> their		u in upon
ē easy			zh treasure		

acid—A chemical that will change blue litmus paper to red. An acid combines with a base to form a salt. Many acids can cause burns. *Noun.* —1. Sharp or biting to the taste; sour: *Lemons and limes are* acid *fruits.* 2. Sharp or biting in speech or manner: *an* acid *remark. Adjective.*
ac|id (as′id) *noun, plural* **acids;** *adjective.*

acid rain—Rain that contains a lot of acid chemicals because of air pollution. Acid rain is suspected of killing trees and fish.
ac|id rain (as′id rān) *noun.*

acknowledge—1. To recognize or admit that something is true or exists: *I refuse to* acknowledge *that there may be ghosts.* 2. To recognize and accept: *We all* acknowledge *her as the leader.* 3. To express that something has been received: *Grandmother telephoned to* acknowledge *my birthday gift to her.*
ac|knowl|edge (ak nol′ij) *verb,* **acknowledged, acknowledging.**

acne—A skin disease common among teen-agers. Pimples form, usually on the face, because oil glands have become clogged and infected.
ac|ne (ak′nē) *noun.*

acorn—The nut of an oak tree.
a|corn (ā′kawrn *or* ā′kərn) *noun, plural* **acorns.**

oak tree

acorn

leaf

acorn

acorn squash—A small, dark-green squash that is shaped like an acorn.
a|corn squash (ā′kawrn *or* ā′kərn skwosh) *noun, plural* **acorn squashes.**
• See picture at **squash**[2].

acquaint—To make aware of, or familiar with: *Are you* acquainted *with the new neighbors?*
ac|quaint (ə kwānt′) *verb,* **acquainted, acquainting.**

acquaintance—1. A person one knows but not a close friend: *He is just an* acquaintance, *but I hope to get to know him better.* 2. An understanding of something gained from experience: *I have an* acquaintance *with music.*
ac|quaint|ance (ə kwān′təns) *noun, plural* **acquaintances.**

acquire—To get as one's own; obtain: *He* acquired *a complete set of baseball cards by careful trading.*
ac|quire (ə kwīr′) *verb,* **acquired, acquiring.**

acquit—To free from blame for a crime or an offense; declare to be not guilty: *The jury believed her story, so she was* acquitted.
ac|quit (ə kwit′) *verb,* **acquitted, acquitting.**

acre—A measure of land equal to 43,560 square feet (4,047 square meters).
a|cre (ā′kər) *noun, plural* **acres.**

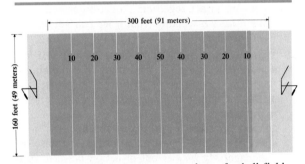

acre: An acre (dark green) compared to a football field.

Word History

Acre comes from an old English word meaning "a field," and that word came from a word meaning "to drive." A field was a place to drive cattle. When people first measured land by the acre, they said that an acre was the size of a field that a team of cattle could plow in one day.

acrobat—A person who can perform acts of great physical skill and strength, such as walking a tightrope, tumbling, or swinging on a trapeze.
ac|ro|bat (ak′rə bat) *noun, plural* **acrobats.**

acrobatics—Any acts done by or like an acrobat.
ac|ro|bat|ics (ak′rə bat′iks) *plural noun.*

across—1. From one side to the other side of: *We walked our bikes* across *the street.* 2. On the other side of: *He lives* across *the river. Preposition.*
—From one side to the other: *The lake is too wide to swim* across. *Adverb.*
a|cross (ə kraws′ *or* ə kros′) *preposition, adverb.*
■ **come across** or **run across:** To find, meet, or fall in with: *I* came across *her book today.*

act—1. Something done; a deed: *Helping that lost child was an* act *of kindness*. 2. The doing of something: *Dad caught us in the* act *of using his tools*. 3. One of the parts of a play or an opera: *The curtain fell at the end of the first* act. 4. A law: *It would take an* act *of the legislature to shorten the school year*. Noun.
—1. To do something: *We must* act *fast or it will be too late*. 2. To behave: *Sometimes he* acts *like a fool*. 3. To perform on the stage, in a movie, on television, or on the radio: *My aunt* acts *in a soap opera*. Verb.
act (akt) *noun, plural* **acts;** *verb,* **acted, acting.**
■ **act out:** To perform; show: *He could* act out *the whole story.*
act up: To behave badly: *Some children* act up *on the bus.*
get (one's) **act together:** To get organized: *We'll have a winning team if we can* get *our* act together.

action—1. Something done; an act: *Saving his life was a brave* action. 2. The doing of something: *Your quick* action *saved his life.* 3. Combat; battle; fighting: *Her father was injured in* action *in the war.*
ac|tion (ak′shən) *noun, plural* **actions.**
■ **out of action:** Not working, usually because of damage: *My bike is* out of action *because of a flat tire.*

active—1. Full of action; lively: *The kittens are so* active, *it is hard to know where they are.* 2. In operation; working: *an* active *interest; an* active *volcano.*
ac|tive (ak′tiv) *adjective.*

activity—1. The condition of being busy; movement: *There is much* activity *on the field after the game starts.* 2. A thing to do; a way to spend time: *Playing checkers is her favorite* activity.
ac|tiv|i|ty (ak tiv′ə tē) *noun, plural* **activities.**

actor—A person who acts on the stage, in a movie, on television, or on the radio.
ac|tor (ac′tər) *noun, plural* **actors.**

actress—A woman or girl who acts on the stage, in a movie, on television, or on the radio.
ac|tress (ak′tris) *noun, plural* **actresses.**

actual—Real; true: *This is the* actual *crown that was worn by the king.*
ac|tu|al (ak′chū əl) *adjective.*
● Synonyms: **authentic, genuine, original**
  Antonyms: **counterfeit, false**

acupuncture—A puncturing of the skin in a certain body area with needles. Acupuncture can relieve pain or make part of the body numb.
ac|u|punc|ture (ak′yə pungk′chər) *noun.*

acute—1. Sharp; severe: *The pain in his broken ankle was* acute. 2. Threatening; dangerous: *The dry weather caused an* acute *shortage of water.* 3. Quick to see and understand: *an* acute *person.*
a|cute (ə kyūt′) *adjective.*

acute angle—An angle that is less than a right angle.
a|cute an|gle (ə kyūt′ ang′gəl) *noun, plural* **acute angles.**

acute angle | right angle | obtuse angle

acute angle

ad—A shortened form of **advertisement**: *I saw an* ad *for skateboards in the newspaper.*
ad (ad) *noun, plural* **ads.**
● A word that sounds the same is **add.**

A.D.—An abbreviation used when giving dates after the birth of Christ. A.D. 500 is five hundred years after the birth of Christ.

Language Fact

A.D. is an abbreviation for the Latin words *anno Domini* (an′ō dom′ə nī), meaning "in the year of the Lord." It is used for dates after the birth of Christ. The abbreviation **B.C.**, meaning "before Christ," is used for dates before the birth of Christ. From 100 B.C. to A.D. 100 is two hundred years.

Adam's apple—A small lump in the front of a person's throat, made of tissue called cartilage. Everyone has an Adam's apple, but it is easier to see on men than on women.
Ad|am's ap|ple (ad′əmz ap′əl) *noun.*

adapt—To fit in with a new condition or place: *Our puppy quickly* adapted *to his new home.*
a|dapt (ə dapt′) *verb,* **adapted, adapting.**

a at	**i** if	**oo** look	**ch** chalk	⎡ a in ago
ā ape	**ī** idle	**ou** out	**ng** sing	e in happen
ah calm	**o** odd	**u** ugly	**sh** ship	ə = i in capital
aw all	**ō** oats	**ū** rule	**th** think	o in occur
e end	**oi** oil	**ur** turn	**th** their	⎣ u in upon
ē easy			**zh** treasure	

add—1. To find the sum of two or more numbers: *If you* add *3 and 4, you get 7.* 2. To say or write more: *Let me* add *to your shopping list.* 3. To put one thing with another or others: *She* added *a new record to her collection.*
ad|d (ad) *verb,* **added, adding.**
■ **add up:** To make sense; fit together: *The detective says that the clues do not* add up.
● A word that sounds the same is **ad.**

adder—A kind of snake. Some adders are harmless, while others are poisonous.
ad|der (ad'ər) *noun, plural* **adders.**

adder

Word History

Adders used to be called "nadders." But "a nadder" sounds like "an adder." Because many people said or wrote "an adder" when they meant "a nadder," the word changed, and now adder is right, not wrong.

addict—A person who has a habit that is out of control: *a drug* addict.
ad|dict (ad'ikt) *noun, plural* **addicts.**

addiction—A habit that is out of control: *Alcohol* addiction *ruins a person's health.*
ad|dic|tion (ə dik'shən) *noun, plural* **addictions.**

addition—1. The act of adding: *the* addition *of mustard to a hot dog.* 2. The adding of one number to another: *5 + 4 = 9 is an example of* addition. 3. Something that is added: *We built an* addition *onto our house.*
ad|di|tion (ə dish'ən) *noun, plural* **additions.**

address—1. A speech: *The mayor gave the Independence Day* address. 2. A place of residence or business: *The* address *of city hall is 100 Main Street.* 3. The writing on an envelope or a package that tells where it is to be delivered: *The* address *on this envelope is wrong.* 4. Any letters or numbers that say where to find information in a computer. *Noun.*
—1. To speak to a person or a group: *I would prefer to* address *him in person rather than over the telephone.* 2. To write on an envelope or a

package where and to whom it is to be delivered: *Please* address *this postcard to your brother at camp.* 3. To find information in a computer by means of letters or numbers that say where the information is. *Verb.*
ad|dress (ə dres' *or* ad'res *for noun;* ə dres' *for verb) noun, plural* **addresses;** *verb,* **addressed, addressing.**

adenoids—Small glands in the upper part of the throat, just behind the nose. Adenoids sometimes swell up and make it hard to breathe and speak.
ad|e|noids (ad'ə noidz) *plural noun.*

adequate—As much as is needed; sufficient; enough: *Deserts lack* adequate *rainfall for farming.*
ad|e|quate (ad'ə kwit) *adjective.*

adhesive—A substance, such as glue, that makes things stick together. *A postage stamp has* adhesive *on the back. Noun.*
—Having a sticky surface that will hold tightly when placed against something else: *Put an* adhesive *bandage on that cut. Adjective.*
ad|he|sive (ad hē'siv) *noun, plural* **adhesives;** *adjective.*

adios—The Spanish word for "good-by."
a|di|os (ah'dē ōs' *or* ad'ē ōs') *interjection.*

Word History

Adios is one word made by putting two words together. In Spanish, *a Dios* means "to God." It is a way of wishing for God to take care of someone when you say good-by.

adj.—The abbreviation for **adjective.**

adjacent—Near or close; next to: *My sister and I sleep in* adjacent *rooms.*
ad|ja|cent (ə jā'sənt) *adjective.*

adjective—A word that describes a noun or a pronoun. It tells which one, what kind, or how many. *That dog with the* red *collar won two* prizes. *"That," "red," and "two" are adjectives.*
ad|jec|tive (aj'ik tiv) *noun, plural* **adjectives.** Abbreviation: **adj.**

adjourn—To stop something or put it off until later: *We had to* adjourn *the meeting until next Friday.*
ad|journ (ə jurn') *verb,* **adjourned, adjourning.**

adjust—1. To change in order to make right or better: *Let me* adjust *that lamp so you can see better.* 2. To get used to something; adapt:

He found it hard to adjust *to being away from home.*

ad|just (ə **just′**) *verb,* **adjusted, adjusting.**

adlib—To make up something as one goes along: *She forgot her notes and had to* adlib *the whole speech. Verb.*

ad|lib (ad **lib′**) *verb,* **adlibbed, adlibbing.**

administer—1. To manage the operation of something; direct: *A principal* administers *a school.* 2. To give; provide: *The nurse can* administer *first aid if there is an accident.*

ad|min|is|ter (ad **min′**ə stər) *verb,* **administered, administering.**

administration—1. The managing of a business, government, school, club, or other group: *The* administration *of a big city is a difficult job.* 2. The group of people in charge of operating something: *Our town* administration *is elected every four years.* 3. The time during which a government holds office: *His* administration *lasted four years.* 4. A giving; providing: *The police handled the* administration *of food and blankets to the flood victims.*

ad|min|is|tra|tion (ad min′ə **strā′**shən) *noun, plural* **administrations.**

admiral—A navy officer of any of the four top ranks: rear admiral, vice admiral, admiral, and fleet admiral, which is the highest.

ad|mi|ral (**ad′**mər əl) *noun, plural* **admirals.**

admire—1. To feel respect for: *I* admire *your courage.* 2. To feel or express pleasure and approval: *All the neighbors came out to* admire *his new car.*

ad|mire (ad **mīr′**) *verb,* **admired, admiring.**

admission—1. The act of allowing someone or something to enter: *Good grades are important for* admission *to college.* 2. The price that one pays to enter: *The* admission *to this movie is five dollars.* 3. The act of saying that something is true; confession: *the* admission *of an error; an* admission *of defeat.*

ad|mis|sion (ad **mish′**ən) *noun, plural* **admissions.**

admit—1. To allow someone or something to enter; let in: *The club plans to* admit *two new members this year.* 2. To say that something is

true; confess: *I* admit *that I forgot to feed the dog.*

ad|mit (ad **mit′**) *verb,* **admitted, admitting.**

adobe—1. A brick made of sun-dried clay, sometimes with bits of straw mixed in. 2. A building made of such bricks.

a|do|be (ə **dō′**bē) *noun, plural* **adobes.**

adolescence—The time of youth between childhood and adulthood: *By the age of 20, he had outgrown* adolescence.

ad|o|les|cence (ad′ə **les′**əns) *noun.*

adolescent—A person who is growing from childhood to adulthood; teenager.

ad|o|les|cent (ad′ə **les′**ənt) *noun, plural* **adolescents.**

adopt—1. To take as one's own or as one's own choice: *She* adopted *her husband's last name when they married.* 2. To accept or approve: *The student council voted to* adopt *new rules for their meetings.* 3. To take a child of other parents as one's own child: *My parents plan to* adopt *an orphan.*

a|dopt (ə **dopt′**) *verb,* **adopted, adopting.**

adore—1. To love; admire; value very highly: *He* adores *his older brother.* 2. To worship: *People have many different ways of* adoring *God.*

a|dore (ə **dawr′**) *verb,* **adored, adoring.**

adorn—To add to something to increase its beauty; decorate; ornament; trim: *She* adorned *her braids with colorful ribbons.*

a|dorn (ə **dawrn′**) *verb,* **adorned, adorning.**

adrift—Floating with the wind or water current; drifting freely: *The boat had lost its anchor and was* adrift *on the lake.*

a|drift (ə **drift′**) *adjective.*

adult—1. A grown-up person. 2. A plant or an animal that has reached its full growth. *Noun.* —Grown to full size; mature: *an* adult *person. Adjective.*

a|dult (ə **dult′** *or* **ad′**ult) *noun, plural* **adults;** *adjective.*

adv.—The abbreviation for **adverb.**

advance—1. To move or push forward: *The enemy* advanced *toward the castle.* 2. To help forward; improve: *Hearing the lesson again* advanced *his understanding of it.* 3. To offer; suggest: *The principal* advanced *a new plan for longer breaks between classes.* 4. To move up in position; promote: *She* advanced *to the starting team.* 5. To supply beforehand: *Would you* advance *me part of next week's allowance? Verb.* —1. A forward movement: *The* advance *of traffic was slowed by road repairs.* 2. A

a at	i if	oo look	ch chalk		
ā ape	ī idle	ou out	ng sing		a in ago
ah calm	o odd	u ugly	sh ship	ə =	e in happen / i in capital
aw all	ō oats	ū rule	th think		o in occur
e end	oi oil	ur turn	th their		u in upon
ē easy			zh treasure		

progress; improvement: *Advances in medicine are helping to cure more and more people.* **3.** Money paid before it is due: *an advance on next week's allowance. Noun.*
ad|vance (ad vans′) *verb,* advanced, advancing; *noun, plural* advances.
■ **in advance:** Ahead of time: *We sent out the invitations two weeks* in advance.

advantage—Anything that is a useful aid in doing or getting something a person wants: *She got the job delivering papers because she had the* advantage *of owning a bicycle.*
ad|van|tage (ad van′tij) *noun, plural* advantages.
■ **take advantage of: 1.** To use to one's own good: *Take advantage of the good weather and go for a bike ride.* **2.** To make unfair use of; impose upon: *He takes advantage of her kindness by asking too many favors.*

advantageous—Giving extra benefit or help: *Being first in line was an* advantageous *position.*
ad|van|ta|geous (ad′van tā′jəs) *adjective.*

advent—**1.** The coming or arrival of something: *The whole class greeted the* advent *of summer vacation with joy.* **2. Advent: a.** The special time of devotion that begins the fourth Sunday before Christmas and ends on Christmas Eve. **b.** The coming of Christ into the world.
ad|vent (ad′vent) *noun.*

adventure—**1.** An exciting or unusual undertaking: *Their first camping trip in the woods was a big* adventure *for the Boy Scouts.* **2.** A difficult, often dangerous, undertaking: *The first space flight was a daring* adventure.
ad|ven|ture (ad ven′chər) *noun, plural* adventures.

adventurous—**1.** Fond of taking risks; bold; daring: *The men who sailed with Columbus were an* adventurous *crew.* **2.** Full of danger; risky: *Rock climbing is too* adventurous *for me.*
ad|ven|tur|ous (ad ven′chər əs) *adjective.*
● Synonyms: For **1,** see Synonyms at **brave.**
Antonyms: **afraid, fearful, timid,** for **1.**

adverb—A word that tells something about a verb, an adjective, or another adverb. An adverb tells how, when, or where something happens, or how much or how little: *He walked* slowly, *but he* finally *arrived. When he got* there, *he was somewhat* tired *but* very *happy.* The words ''slowly,'' ''finally,'' ''there,'' ''somewhat,'' and ''very'' are adverbs.
ad|verb (ad′vurb) *noun, plural* adverbs.
Abbreviation: **adv.**

advertise—To give notice of something; to announce publicly: *The company* advertised *its product on television.*
ad|ver|tise (ad′vur tiz) *verb,* advertised, advertising.

advertisement—A public announcement or a printed notice that describes a product or a service or informs of a cause or a need. Advertisements can be given on television or the radio, or they can appear in newspapers, in magazines, or on posters or billboards. On television and radio, they are also called commercials.
ad|ver|tise|ment (ad′vər tīs′mənt *or* ad vur′tiz mənt) *noun, plural* advertisements.

advice—An opinion offered about what should be done; suggestion; recommendation: *He gave me* advice *about how to solve my problem.*
ad|vice (ad vīs′) *noun.*

advisable—Being a proper and wise thing to do; smart: *It is* advisable *to carry an umbrella on rainy days.*
ad|vis|a|ble (ad vī′zə bəl) *adjective.*

advise—**1.** To offer advice; give an opinion; recommend: *I* advise *you not to play in the street.* **2.** To inform; notify: *The weather report* advised *us that a storm was coming.*
ad|vise (ad vīz′) *verb,* advised, advising.

adviser or **advisor**—Someone qualified to give advice: *I asked my* adviser *whether to take piano lessons next year.*
ad|vi|ser or ad|vi|sor (ad vī′zər) *noun, plural* advisers or advisors.

adz or **adze**—A tool somewhat like an ax, used to shape logs and heavy timbers. The blade is set at a right angle to the handle and is curved inward.
adz or adze (adz) *noun, plural* adzes.

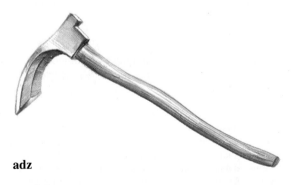

adz

aerial—A radio or television antenna. *Noun.*
—Done in or from the air: *The plane took* aerial

photographs of the city. Adjective.
aer|i|al (ār'ē əl) *noun, plural* **aerials;** *adjective.*
 • See picture at **antenna.**

aerobics—Any exercise that improves physical fitness by increasing the body's supply of oxygen and the ability of the heart to use oxygen more efficiently.
aer|o|bics (ār ō'biks) *noun.*

aeronautics—The science of designing, building, and flying aircraft.
aer|o|nau|tics (ār'ə naw'tiks) *noun.*

aerosol—Very fine particles of a solid or liquid suspended in air or some other gas. Fog and smoke are aerosols. There are many manufactured aerosols, such as hair sprays, spray paints, and insecticides.
aer|o|sol (ār'ə sol *or* ār'ə sōl) *noun, plural* **aerosols.**

aerospace—1. The science and industry dealing with rockets and other spacecraft. **2.** The earth's atmosphere and the space beyond it.
aer|o|space (ār'ə spās) *noun.*

afar—Far away: *A cloud of dust could be seen from* afar.
a|far (ə fahr') *adverb.*

affair—1. Something to do or that is done; job; task: *Starting a new job is a serious* affair.
2. Something that happens; an event or occasion: *Graduation was an* affair *to remember.*
af|fair (ə fār') *noun, plural* **affairs.**

Language Fact

Affect[1] is what you do, and **effect** is the thing that is done. If the weather affects plans and changes them, the change is the effect of the weather. Another meaning of **effect** is "to make happen." If you effect a change, you make it happen.

---

affect[1]—1. To produce a change in; have an effect on: *I hope our argument will not* affect *our friendship.* **2.** To have an effect on someone's feelings: *Reading about the lost kitten* affected *me so, I cried.*

a at	i if	oo look	ch chalk		a in ago
ā ape	ī idle	ou out	ng sing		e in happen
ah calm	o odd	u ugly	sh ship	ə =	i in capital
aw all	ō oats	ū rule	th think		o in occur
e end	oi oil	ur turn	<u>th</u> their		u in upon
ē easy			zh treasure		

af|fect (ə fekt') *verb,* **affected, affecting.**
 • A word that sounds the same is **effect.**

affect[2]—To pretend: *She* affects *a knowledge of Spanish but really speaks very few words of it.*
af|fect (ə fekt') *verb,* **affected, affecting.**
 • A word that sounds the same is **effect.**

affection—A feeling of fondness or great liking for someone or something: Affection *for each other makes our family a happy one.*
af|fec|tion (ə fek'shən) *noun, plural* **affections.**

affectionate—Feeling or showing love; fond; tender: *Her dog gave her an* affectionate *welcome.*
af|fec|tion|ate (ə fek'shə nit) *adjective.*

affenpinscher—A very small dog with a shaggy black coat. It has pointed ears, bushy eyebrows, and a mustache. Its German name means "monkey terrier."
af|fen|pin|scher (ah'fən pin'shər) *noun, plural* **affenpinschers.**

affenpinscher

afflict—To cause pain or distress to: *Fleas* afflicted *the cat so that it scratched all day.*
af|flict (ə flikt') *verb,* **afflicted, afflicting.**

afford—1. To have enough money for: *I can* afford *the movie if I baby-sit this week.* **2.** To be able to give, spare, have, or do something: *You cannot* afford *to be late again.* **3.** To provide; furnish: *These trees will* afford *us some shade.*
af|ford (ə fawrd') *verb,* **afforded, affording.**

Afghan hound—A tall hunting dog with a long, heavy, silky coat and long, drooping ears. Originally bred in Afghanistan, these dogs hunt by sight.

Afghan hound

Af|ghan hound (af′gən hound) *noun, plural* **Afghan hounds.**

afloat—Floating on the water or in the air: *Ice cubes were* afloat *in the drink. The party balloons remained* afloat *all day.*
a|float (ə flōt′) *adjective, adverb.*

afoot—**1.** On foot; by walking: *When the car broke down, we had to go the rest of the way* afoot. **2.** Moving or in progress: *Plans are* afoot *for a big party.*
a|foot (ə foot′) *adjective, adverb.*

afraid—**1.** Frightened; scared; full of fear: *I am* afraid *to dive off the high board.* **2.** Feeling sorry: *I am* afraid *I broke your bike.*
a|fraid (ə frād′) *adjective.*

 • Synonyms: **fearful, timid,** for **1.**
 Antonyms: For **1,** see Synonyms at **brave.**

African violet—A tropical plant having hairy, heart-shaped leaves and single or double purple, pink, or white flowers. It is often grown as a house plant.
Af|ri|can vi|o|let (af′rə kən vi′ə lit) *noun, plural* **African violets.**

Afro—A round, bushy hairstyle.
Af|ro (af′rō) *noun, plural* **Afros.**

aft—Toward or at the back part of a boat: *The* aft *cabin is over the rudder. If you stand* aft, *you can watch the land disappear from view.*
aft (aft) *adjective, adverb.*

after—**1.** Behind; following: *You go first and I will come* after *you.* **2.** In search of: *The police are* after *the murderer.* **3.** Later than: *School is out at ten* after *two. Preposition.*
—Later; afterward: *When I sprained my ankle, it did not hurt until two days* after. *Adverb.*
—Later than the time that: After *we eat lunch, we can go to the library. Conjunction.*
af|ter (af′tər) *preposition, adverb, conjunction.*
 ■ **forever after:** Until the end of time; always: *And they lived happily* forever after.

aftermath—Something that happens because of something else; result; consequence: *As an* aftermath *of the parade, the streets were filled with trash.*
af|ter|math (af′tər math) *noun, plural* **aftermaths.**

afternoon—The time between noon and evening.
af|ter|noon (af′tər nūn′) *noun, plural* **afternoons.**

afterthought—An idea that comes later than another thought: *I had intended to paint it solid blue, so the red stripe was an* afterthought.
af|ter|thought (af′tər thawt′) *noun, plural* **afterthoughts.**

afterward or **afterwards**—At a later time: *We will get some bait and* afterward *we can go fishing.*
af|ter|ward or **af|ter|wards** (af′tər wərd *or* af′tər wərds) *adverb.*

afterword—A section that follows the main part of a book: *The author added an* afterword *explaining what happened to the characters later.*
af|ter|word (af′tər wurd′) *noun, plural* **afterwords.**

again—One more time: *Please sing that song* again.
a|gain (ə gen′) *adverb.*

African violet

against—**1.** In opposition to; contrary to: *Stealing is* against *the law.* **2.** Opposed to; hostile to: *I am* against *walking so far.* **3.** In the opposite direction to: *Walk on the left side of the road* against *the traffic.* **4.** In contact with: *The ladder leaned* against *the wall.*
a|gainst (ə genst′) *preposition.*

age—1. The length of time someone or something has existed: *My grandfather reached the* age *of sixty last year.* 2. A period or stage of someone's life: *middle* age; *old* age. 3. A period in history: *the* age *of knighthood; the space* age. 4. **ages:** A long time: *It has been* ages *since I saw you last. Noun.*
—1. To make old: *Hardship can* age *a person.* 2. To become ready over time: *Firewood should* age *before it is burned. Verb.*
age (āj) *noun, plural* **ages;** *verb,* **aged, aging.**
■ **come of age:** To reach adulthood, often set at 18 or 21 years of age: *He will inherit a fortune when he* comes of age.

aged—1. Having lived a long time; old: *The* aged *man had a long, white beard.* 2. Of the age of: *The team will accept players* aged *ten or older.*
a|ged (ā′jid for 1; ājd for 2) *adjective.*
● For **1**, see Language Fact at **old.**

ageless—Never growing old nor looking old: *The mountains have an* ageless *beauty.*
age|less (āj′lis) *adjective.*

agency—A business firm or government department that acts for other people or groups: *A travel* agency *helps people to plan trips.*
a|gen|cy (ā′jən sē) *noun, plural* **agencies.**

agent—1. A person or company that acts for another person or company: *a real estate* agent. 2. Something that acts upon something else: *Oil and grease are lubricating* agents.
a|gent (ā′jənt) *noun, plural* **agents.**

aggravate—1. To make worse: *Scratching an insect bite will only* aggravate *the itch.* 2. To annoy; make angry: *Her constant bragging really* aggravates *me.*
ag|gra|vate (ag′rə vāt) *verb,* **aggravated, aggravating.**
● Synonyms: **bother, provoke,** for **2.**
   Antonyms: **calm, lull, soothe,** for **2.**

aggression—A forceful attack: *War starts with* aggression *by one country against another.*
ag|gres|sion (ə gresh′ən) *noun, plural* **aggressions.**

aggressive—1. Behaving as an enemy; attacking: *The* aggressive *bully picked on the younger children.* 2. Very vigorous; active: *an* aggressive

program to create more jobs.
ag|gres|sive (ə gres′iv) *adjective.*

agile—Able to move quickly and easily: *The* agile *monkeys swung gracefully through the trees.*
ag|ile (aj′əl) *adjective.*

agility—The ability to move quickly and easily: *She ran the obstacle course with great* agility.
a|gil|i|ty (ə jil′ə tē) *noun.*

agitate—1. To move or shake hard; stir up: *This machine* agitates *the popcorn by using hot air.* 2. To disturb or excite: *The sight of the bird* agitated *the cat.*
ag|i|tate (aj′ə tāt) *verb,* **agitated, agitating.**

agitator—1. A person who excites the feelings of others: *A small group of* agitators *began shouting, and soon the whole crowd was yelling.* 2. A device that shakes or stirs: *a washing-machine* agitator.
ag|i|ta|tor (aj′ə tā′tər) *noun, plural* **agitators.**

aglow—Glowing; radiant: *The sky was* aglow *with the brilliant sunrise. Their faces were set* aglow *by the light of the fire.*
a|glow (ə glō′) *adjective, adverb.*

ago—Earlier than the present time; past: *He should have been here an hour* ago. *Adjective.*
—In the past: *Long* ago, *people thought that the earth was flat. Adverb.*
a|go (ə gō′) *adjective, adverb.*

agonize—To suffer great mental or physical pain: *He* agonized *over the difficult decision.*
ag|o|nize (ag′ə nīz) *verb,* **agonized, agonizing.**

agony—Great mental or physical pain: *His infected ear caused him* agony.
ag|o|ny (ag′ə nē) *noun, plural* **agonies.**

agree—1. To have the same opinion: *I* agree *with you that the homework is too hard.* 2. To say that one is willing to do something: *She* agreed *to wait for him.*
a|gree (ə grē′) *verb,* **agreed, agreeing.**
■ **agree with:** To be good for; have a good effect on: *Don't eat food that doesn't* agree with *you.*

agreeable—1. To one's liking; pleasing: *This area has an* agreeable *climate.* 2. Willing; ready to agree: *If you want to leave now, I am* agreeable.
a|gree|a|ble (ə grē′ə bəl) *adjective.*

agreement—1. An arrangement or understanding between people or groups: *The three of us have an* agreement *to go fishing.* 2. The state of having the same opinion: *We are in* agreement *over the test answers.*
a|gree|ment (ə grē′mənt) *noun, plural* **agreements.**

a at	i if	oo look	ch chalk		⌈ a in ago
ā ape	ī idle	ou out	ng sing		e in happen
ah calm	o odd	u ugly	sh ship	ə =	i in capital
aw all	ō oats	ū rule	th think		o in occur
e end	oi oil	ur turn	th their		⌊ u in upon
ē easy			zh treasure		

agriculture—The business of raising crops and livestock; farming.
ag|ri|cul|ture (ag′rə kul′chər) *noun.*

ahead—**1.** In front; before: *The coach walked* ahead *of the team.* **2.** Forward; onward: *Set your clocks* ahead *an hour.* **3.** In advance: *It is wise to plan* ahead.
a|head (ə hed′) *adverb.*
■ **get ahead**: To succeed; to do well: *Her store is always busy, and she is really* getting ahead.

ahoy—A call or greeting used by sailors, usually to get someone's attention: *He saw a white sail and yelled, "Ship* ahoy!"
a|hoy (ə hoi′) *interjection.*

aid—To help; assist: *A map will* aid *you in finding your way. Verb.*
—**1.** Help; assistance: *The woman came to the* aid *of the lost child.* **2.** A person or thing that helps or assists. *Noun.*
aid (ād) *verb,* **aided, aiding;** *noun, plural* **aids.**
● A word that sounds the same is **aide.**

aide—A helper; assistant: *The president's* aide *arranges meetings.*
aide (ād) *noun, plural* **aides.**
● A word that sounds the same is **aid.**

AIDS—A disease in which a person's body becomes unable to defend itself against diseases and infections. A person with AIDS will often die of an infection that a healthy body can easily fight off.
AIDS (ādz) *noun.*

ail—**1.** To be wrong with: *What* ails *the dog to make it limp that way?* **2.** To have something wrong; to feel ill: *He is* ailing *with a cold.*
ail (āl) *verb,* **ailed, ailing.**
● A word that sounds the same is **ale.**

ailment—An illness: *A bad cold is a common* ailment *in winter.*
ail|ment (āl′mənt) *noun, plural* **ailments.**
● Synonyms: **disease, sickness**
Antonym: **health**

aim—**1.** To point or direct something at a target: *She* aimed *the basketball at the hoop.* **2.** To direct words or actions toward someone or something; intend for: *The pet food company* aims *its advertising at dog owners. Verb.*
—**1.** A pointing or directing of something at a target: *Is your* aim *good enough to hit that tree with this rock?* **2.** A purpose; intention; goal: *Her* aim *is to be class president. Noun.*
aim (ām) *verb,* **aimed, aiming;** *noun, plural* **aims.**

ain't—A contraction of "am not," "is not," "are not," "has not," and "have not." It is not considered good English, and careful speakers do not use it except in fun.
ain't (ānt) *verb.*

Language Fact

Ain't is a word that most people agree is wrong to use. Careful writers and speakers avoid **ain't** except when they mean to be funny.

---

air—**1.** The atmosphere that surrounds the earth. It is made up mostly of oxygen and nitrogen, with small amounts of other gases. **2.** The sky: *Birds fly through the* air. **3.** Fresh air: *I am going outdoors to get some* air. **4.** A song or melody: *He played an* air *on his flute.* **5.** The look or manner of someone or something: *She looked at the mess with an* air *of disgust.* **6. airs:** A haughty manner: *Since he became famous, he puts on* airs *and acts as if he never knew us. Noun.*
—**1.** To open to the outside: air *out a room.*
2. To make known: air *your ideas.* **3.** To broadcast on radio or television: *The cartoon show will* air *at six o'clock. Verb.*
air (âr) *noun, plural* **airs;** *verb,* **aired, airing.**
■ **clear the air**: To remove a misunderstanding, suspicion, or strain: *The argument* cleared the air, *and we are friends again.*
on the air: Being broadcast on radio or television: *The show goes* on the air *at noon.*
out of thin air: From nothing or nowhere: *She pulled a solution to the problem* out of thin air.
up in the air: Unsettled: *Our plans are still* up in the air.
walk on air: To be very happy: *He has been* walking on air *since he made the team.*
● A word that sounds the same is **heir.**

air base—A headquarters and landing area for military aircraft.
air base (âr bās) *noun, plural* **air bases.**

airborne—**1.** Off the ground: *The kite became* airborne *in a strong wind.* **2.** Carried by the air: airborne *pollution from factory smokestacks.*
air|borne (âr′bawrn′) *adjective.*

air-condition—To cool with one or more air conditioners. *The building is* air-conditioned *during the summer.*
air-con|di|tion (âr′kən dish′ən) *verb,* **air-conditioned, air-conditioning.**

air conditioner—A machine that makes the air in a place cooler and drier.
air con|di|tion|er (âr kən dish′ə nər) *noun, plural* **air conditioners.**

aircraft—Any machine made for flying in the air, such as an airplane, helicopter, glider, or dirigible.
air|craft (ār′kraft′) *noun, plural* **aircraft.**

aircraft carrier—A naval ship with a large, flat deck on which airplanes or helicopters take off and land.
air|craft car|ri|er (ār′kraft′ kar′ē ər) *noun, plural* **aircraft carriers.**

Airedale terrier—A large dog that has a wiry tan or brown coat with black markings. It is named for the Aire Valley in England.
Aire|dale ter|ri|er (ār′dāl ter′ē ər) *noun, plural* **Airedale terriers.**

Airedale terrier

airfield—The place at an airport or an air base where aircraft take off and land.
air|field (ār′fēld′) *noun, plural* **airfields.**

air force—The part of a nation's armed forces that uses aircraft.
air force (ār fawrs) *noun, plural* **air forces.**

airline—A company that uses airplanes to carry people and things from one place to another.
air|line (ār′līn′) *noun, plural* **airlines.**

airmail—Mail that is carried to other cities or countries by airplane: *If you use* airmail, *your letter will arrive in two days. Noun.*

—To send by airmail: *Please* airmail *this package to my brother. Verb.*
—Having to do with airmail: *an* airmail *letter. Adjective.*
—By airmail: *A quick reply was needed, so she sent it* airmail. *Adverb.*
air|mail (ār′māl′) *noun; verb* **airmailed, airmailing;** *adjective; adverb.*

airplane—An aircraft that is heavier than air. It has wings and propellers or jet engines to make it fly.
air|plane (ār′plān′) *noun, plural* **airplanes.**

air pocket—A downward rush of air that causes an airplane to drop suddenly and briefly: *The plane hit an* air pocket.
air pock|et (ār pok′it) *noun, plural* **air pockets.**

airport—A place for airplanes to take off and land. It usually has buildings where airplanes are stored and repaired, and other buildings for people arriving or leaving.
air|port (ār′pawrt′) *noun, plural* **airports.**

air pressure—The weight of the air as it presses on the surfaces of objects.
air pres|sure (ār presh′ər) *noun, plural* **air pressures.**

air raid—An attack by enemy airplanes, especially bombers.
air raid (ār rād) *noun, plural* **air raids.**

airship—An aircraft that is lighter than air. It has a cigar-shaped main body filled with a gas that is lighter than air, engine-driven propellers, and can be steered.
air|ship (ār′ship′) *noun, plural* **airships.**

airship

Language Fact

An **airship** can be steered. This feature led to its being called a **dirigible,** a name that comes from a Latin word meaning ''to direct.'' A **blimp** is an airship that does not have a stiff inner framework. A **Zeppelin** is a very large airship that has a stiff inner framework.

a at	i if	oo look	ch chalk		a in ago
ā ape	ī idle	ou out	ng sing		e in happen
ah calm	o odd	u ugly	sh ship	ə =	i in capital
aw all	ō oats	ū rule	th think		o in occur
e end	oi oil	ur turn	th their		u in upon
ē easy			zh treasure		

airsick—Suffering from a sick feeling caused by the movement of an aircraft.
air|sick (ār′sik′) *adjective*.

airtight—1. So tight that air cannot get in or out: *An* airtight *seal helps keep food fresh.* 2. Having no weak points: *Our football team's* airtight *defense kept the opponent from scoring a point.*
air|tight (ār′tīt′) *adjective*.

airy—1. With air coming through: *Because our kitchen has a lot of windows, it is always* airy *and cheerful.* 2. Graceful; delicate: *The clarinet played an* airy *melody.*
air|y (ār′ē) *adjective*.

aisle—A long, narrow space between two sections of something. There are aisles between the rows of seats in a movie theater and between the shelves in a grocery store.
aisle (īl) *noun, plural* **aisles**.
■ **roll in the aisles:** To laugh heartily: *The circus clowns had the audience* rolling in the aisles.
● Words that sound the same are **I'll** and **isle**.

ajar—Partly open: *The door was* ajar. *We left the bedroom door* ajar.
a|jar (ə jahr′) *adjective, adverb*.

akimbo—With hands on hips and elbows outward: *She stood with her arms* akimbo.
a|kim|bo (ə kim′bō) *adjective*.

akimbo

akin—1. Alike; of the same kind: *Alligators and crocodiles are* akin. 2. Related; belonging to the same family: *The two children are* akin *because they are cousins.*
a|kin (ə kin′) *adjective*.

Akita—A medium-sized dog with a strong body and short, rough fur that can be any of several colors. It is originally from Japan.
A|ki|ta (ah kē′tah) *noun, plural* **Akitas**.

a la mode—Served with ice cream: *apple pie* a la mode.
a la mode (ah la mōd *or* al ə mōd) *adjective*.

alarm—1. Sudden fear: *The clap of thunder made him jump in* alarm. 2. A sign of approaching danger: *The strong wind was an* alarm *that a storm was coming.* 3. A noise used to warn or wake up people: *Everyone left the building when the fire* alarm *sounded. Noun.*
—To frighten; startle: *The noise* alarmed *the rabbit. Verb.*
a|larm (ə lahrm′) *noun, plural* **alarms**; *verb,* **alarmed, alarming**.

Word History

Alarm comes from two Italian words meaning "to arms." You can see the word **arm** in **alarm**. When danger was near, people called "To arms!" so that others knew to get weapons and arm themselves for defense.

---

alas—A word that expresses sadness, regret, or disappointment: Alas, *my friend is moving away.*
a|las (ə las′) *interjection*.

Alaskan malamute—A large, powerful dog with a bushy tail and a heavy gray or black and white coat. It is originally from Alaska, where it is used to pull sleds.
A|las|kan ma|la|mute (ə las′kən mah′lə myūt) *noun, plural* **Alaskan malamutes**.

Alaskan malamute

albatross—A large, web-footed sea bird with a hooked beak. It has very long wings and can fly great distances.
al|ba|tross (**al′**bə traws *or* **al′**bə tros) *noun, plural* **albatrosses.**

albatross

albino—A person, plant, or animal that has little or no coloring. People and animals who are albinos have very pale skin, white hair, and pink eyes with dark red pupils.
al|bi|no (al **bī′**nō) *noun, plural* **albinos.**

album—1. A book with blank pages for holding postage stamps, pictures, or other things that people collect: *The whole class signed her autograph* album. **2.** A long-playing phonograph record: *the band's new* album.
al|bum (**al′**bəm) *noun, plural* **albums.**

alcohol—A kind of liquid having no color or smell, made from grains, fruits, or chemicals. It evaporates quickly and catches fire easily. It is part of drinks such as wine, beer, and whiskey. There are many kinds of alcohol. Some of them are very poisonous.
al|co|hol (**al′**kə hawl *or* **al′**kə hol) *noun, plural* **alcohols.**

alcoholic—Containing alcohol: *Wine and beer are* alcoholic *drinks. Adjective.*
—A person who has a need for drinks containing

alcohol that he or she cannot control. *Noun.*
al|co|hol|ic (al′kə **hawl′**ik *or* al′kə **hol′**ik) *adjective; noun, plural* **alcoholics.**

alcoholism—A sickness in which a person has a need for drinks containing alcohol that he or she cannot control.
al|co|hol|ism (al′kə haw liz′əm *or* al′kə ho liz′əm) *noun.*

alcove—A small room or area that opens into a larger room: *The cozy* alcove *in our library has a comfortable chair.*
al|cove (**al′**kōv) *noun, plural* **alcoves.**

alder—A tree or shrub with rough bark, roundish leaves, and small, woody cones. It grows in cool, moist places.
al|der (**awl′**dər) *noun, plural* **alders.**

ale—A strong, bitter beer.
ale (āl) *noun, plural* **ales.**
• A word that sounds the same is **ail.**

alert—1. Wide-awake; watchful: *The watchdog was* alert *to every sound.* **2.** Active; quick to learn: Alert *minds notice what happens. Adjective.*
—A signal or warning of possible danger: *The weather bureau issued a tornado* alert. *Noun.*
—To warn; tell: *The street sign* alerted *drivers to go slowly. Verb.*
a|lert (ə **lurt′**) *adjective; noun, plural* **alerts;** *verb,* **alerted, alerting.**

alfalfa—A plant that looks like clover and has bluish-purple flowers. It is used as food for cattle and horses.
al|fal|fa (al **fal′**fə) *noun.*

algae—Several very simple types of water plant that make their own food but do not have stems, roots, or leaves. Seaweeds are large algae.
al|gae (**al′**jē) *noun, singular,* **alga** (**al′**jə).

algebra—A kind of mathematics that uses both letters and numbers to find the answer to problems. The letters represent numbers that are not known.
al|ge|bra (**al′**jə brə) *noun.*

alias—A false name used by a person, usually to hide who he or she really is: *The spy's real name was Smith, but he used the* alias *of Clark when he traveled. Noun.*
—Also known as; otherwise called: *John Jones,* alias *''Diamond John,'' was a clever jewel thief. Adverb.*
a|li|as (**ā′**lē əs) *noun, plural* **aliases;** *adverb.*

alibi—1. An explanation that a person was somewhere else when a crime happened and so could not have committed that crime: *Her alibi was that she was at the movies when the bank*

a at	i if	oo look	ch chalk		a in ago
ā ape	ī idle	ou out	ng sing		e in happen
ah calm	o odd	u ugly	sh ship	ə =	i in capital
aw all	ō oats	ū rule	th think		o in occur
e end	oi oil	ur turn	th their		u in upon
ē easy			zh treasure		

was robbed.   **2.** An excuse: *What is your* alibi *for coming home so late?*
al|i|bi (al′ə bī) *noun, plural* **alibis.**

alien—A person who is not a citizen of the country in which he or she lives; a foreigner. *Noun.*
—Strange; not familiar: *Computer language was* alien *to him. Adjective.*
a|li|en (ā′lē ən) *noun, plural* **aliens;** *adjective.*

alight¹—**1.** To get down or off; dismount: *Cinderella* alighted *from her pumpkin coach.* **2.** To land or come down from flight: *The chickadee* alighted *on the bird feeder.*
a|light (ə līt′) *verb,* **alighted, alighting.**

alight²—**1.** On fire; lighted: *The dry wood was soon* alight.   **2.** Glowing; lighted up: *His face was* alight *when he saw his new bicycle.*
a|light (ə līt′) *adjective.*

align—To put into a line: *The runners* aligned *their feet on the starting line.*
a|lign (ə līn′) *verb,* **aligned, aligning.**

alike—Similar; like one another: *No two snowflakes are exactly* alike. *Adjective.*
—In the same way; similarly: *The twins enjoyed dressing* alike *to confuse their parents. Adverb.*
a|like (ə līk′) *adjective, adverb.*

alimentary canal—The parts of the body through which food passes as it is eaten and digested, and as its waste products are removed.
al|i|men|ta|ry ca|nal (al′ə men′tər ē kə nal′) *noun.*

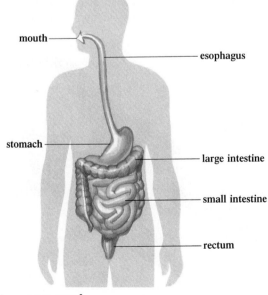

mouth

esophagus

stomach

large intestine

small intestine

rectum

alimentary canal

alimony—A certain amount of money paid to one's husband or wife after a divorce. A judge decides who must pay and how much.
al|i|mo|ny (al′ə mō′nē) *noun.*

alive—**1.** Living; having life: *The deer was still* alive *after the harsh winter.*   **2.** Active; still happening: *These pictures will always keep my memory of her* alive.
a|live (ə līv′) *adjective.*
■ **alive with:** Full of; crowded with: *The hive was* alive with *bees.*

all—**1.** Every one of: All *the campers enjoyed the forest.*   **2.** The whole of: *He lost* all *his money.* **3.** Any; every kind or sort: *He refused* all *offers of help. Adjective.*
—**1.** Everyone or everything: All *were amazed at the magic tricks.*   **2.** The whole amount or number: All *of the cookies were eaten. Pronoun.*
—A person's best try or effort: *She gave her* all *to break the school record. Noun.*
—**1.** Completely: *The puppy was* all *tired out after running home.*   **2.** Apiece; each: *The hockey game was tied at three* all. *Adverb.*
all (awl) *adjective, pronoun, noun, adverb.*
■ **above all:** Most important; before everything else: Above all, *learn reading, writing, and arithmetic.*
after all: Nevertheless; even so: *Although it was an exciting trip, she was glad to be home* after all.
all but: Almost; nearly: *He was* all but *finished mowing the lawn when it began to rain.*
all in: Exhausted; worn out: *The hikers were* all in *at the end of their climb.*
all in all: Considering everything: All in all, *it was a fine summer.*
all over: **1.** Everywhere: *After our pillow fight, feathers were* all over.   **2.** Finished; done with: *The parade was* all over *in an hour.*
all thumbs: Clumsy; not able to do well: *She was* all thumbs *when she tried to juggle.*
all told: Counting each one; altogether: All told, *he hit six home runs last year.*
at all: In any way; of any kind: *He was no help* at all.
once and for all or **once for all:** Finally; from then on: *After many arguments, the sisters agreed to stop fighting* once and for all.
● A word that sounds the same is **awl.**

Allah—The Muslim name for God.
Al|lah (al′ə *or* ahl′ə) *noun.*

all-American—**1.** Chosen as the best in the United States: *an* all-American *football player.* **2.** Made up only of Americans: *an* all-American *crew. Adjective.*

—A player picked as the best in the United States at his or her position. *Noun.*
all-A|mer|i|can (awl'ə **mer**'ə kən) *adjective; noun, plural* **all-Americans.**

all-around—Able to do many things well: *She was an* all-around *athlete who excelled in every sport.*
all-a|round (awl'ə round') *adjective.*

allegiance—1. A person's faithfulness to a country or government, a person, or an ideal: *I pledge* allegiance *to the flag.*
al|le|giance (ə lē'jəns) *noun, plural* **allegiances.**

allergic—1. Having an allergy: *I am* allergic *to cats.*   2. Of or caused by an allergy: *His rash was an* allergic *reaction to the strawberries he ate.*
al|ler|gic (ə ler'jik) *adjective.*

allergy—A reaction that a person has to something he or she ate, drank, touched, or breathed. People who have allergies may sneeze a lot, have red eyes, have headaches, or break out in a rash. Hay fever and asthma are types of allergies.
al|ler|gy (al'ər jē) *noun, plural* **allergies.**

alley—1. A narrow passageway or street between buildings.   2. A long, narrow lane down which the ball is rolled in bowling.
al|ley (al'ē) *noun, plural* **alleys.**
■ **down** (one's) **alley** or **up** (one's) **alley:** Easy or pleasant for someone to do: *Being strong, she found that sports were right* up her alley.

alliance—An agreement between two or more people, groups, or countries to work together.
al|li|ance (ə lī'əns) *noun, plural* **alliances.**

allied—Working together to help each other: *the* allied *armies.*
al|lied (ə līd' *or* al'īd) *adjective.*

alligator—A large reptile with a long head and tail, sharp teeth, and thick, tough skin. It looks like a crocodile but has a shorter, flatter head. *Noun.*
al|li|ga|tor (al'ə gā'tər) *noun, plural* **alligators.**

all-important—Extremely important: *Careful reading of directions is* all-important *when putting model airplanes together.*
all-im|por|tant (awl'im **pawr**'tənt) *adjective.*

alliteration—A repeating of the same first sound in a group of words. "Peter Piper picked a peck of pickled peppers" has alliteration of the letter *p.*
al|lit|er|a|tion (ə lit'ə rā'shən) *noun.*

allosaurus—A large meat-eating dinosaur that looked like a tyrannosaurus. It had short front legs and walked upright on its large hind legs.
al|lo|saur|us (al'ə sawr'əs) *noun, plural* **allosauri** (al'ə sawr'ī).

allosaurus

allow—1. To let someone do or have something: *Our parents do not* allow *us to cross the highway.*   2. To add or take away something for a reason: *The teacher* allowed *a longer recess because the weather was warm.*   3. To let something happen, especially through carelessness: *to* allow *the toast to burn.*
al|low (ə lou') *verb,* **allowed, allowing.**
■ **allow for:** To provide for; to realize that something will or might happen: *They left early for the new movie to* allow for *a long waiting line.*

allowance—1. A fixed sum of money given out at regular times: *Her parents gave her an*

alligator

crocodile

alligator

a at	i if	oo look	ch chalk		a in ago
ā ape	ī idle	ou out	ng sing		e in happen
ah calm	o odd	u ugly	sh ship	ə =	i in capital
aw all	ō oats	ū rule	th think		o in occur
e end	oi oil	ur turn	<u>th</u> their		u in upon
ē easy			zh treasure		

allowance *of $2 a week.*   **2.** An amount taken away for a reason; discount: *We were offered an allowance of $500 off the regular cost of the trip if we flew at night.*
al|low|ance (ə lou′əns) *noun, plural* **allowances.**
■ **make allowance for** or **make allowances for:** To consider; take into one's thinking: *Dad made allowance for the special show and let us stay up late.*

alloy—A metal made by mixing together two or more metals. Brass is an alloy of zinc and copper.
al|loy (al′oi *or* ə loi′) *noun, plural* **alloys.**

all right—**1.** Correct; without mistakes: *His spelling test was all right.*   **2.** Good enough; acceptable: *His penmanship is not perfect, but it is all right.*   **3.** Healthy: *I had the flu last week, but I'm all right now. Adjective.*
—Yes: *All right, I'll come with you. Adverb.*
all right (awl rīt) *adjective, adverb.*

all-star—Made up of the best players or performers: *baseball's yearly all-star game. Adjective.*
—A player or performer chosen as best. *Noun.*
all-star (awl′stahr′) *adjective; noun, plural* **all-stars.**

ally—A person, group, or nation that joins with another: *She befriended her opponent, and he became her ally in the club. Noun.*
—To join together: *All the people on our street allied to clean up a vacant lot. Verb.*
al|ly (al′ī *or* ə lī′ *for noun;* ə lī′ *for verb*) *noun, plural* **allies;** *verb,* **allied, allying.**

almanac—A book that has short pieces of information on many different subjects. Almanacs are usually published every year. They give facts about such things as the tides, phases of the moon, names of public officials, population figures, and the like.
al|ma|nac (awl′ mə nak) *noun, plural* **almanacs.**

almighty—All-powerful: *the nearly almighty force of a hurricane. Adjective.*
—**the Almighty:** God. *Noun.*
al|might|y (awl mī′tē) *adjective, noun.*

almond—An oval nut that is often used in candy and desserts.
al|mond (ah′mənd *or* am′ənd) *noun, plural* **almonds.**

almost—Nearly: *It is almost ten o'clock.*
al|most (awl′mōst *or* awl mōst′) *adverb.*

aloft—**1.** High above the ground: *Wind kept the balloon aloft.*   **2.** High above the deck of a ship:

The sailor climbed aloft *to fix the ship's sail.*
a|loft (ə lawft′ *or* ə loft′) *adverb.*

aloha—A Hawaiian word meaning "love" that is used to say both "hello" and "good-by."
a|lo|ha (ə lō′ə *or* ah lō′hah) *noun.*

alone—By oneself; without others: *It was frightening to be* alone *in the house during the thunderstorm. Because her brother was sick, she went trick-or-treating* alone.
a|lone (ə lōn′) *adjective, adverb.*

along—**1.** From one end to or toward the other end: *Flowers are planted* along *the sidewalks in the park.*   **2.** On or during: *We talked* along *the way to the store. Preposition.*
—**1.** On; forward; onward: *Come* along *quickly, or you'll be late.*   **2.** Together with something or someone: *Take an umbrella* along. *Adverb.*
a|long (ə lawng′) *preposition, adverb.*
■ **all along:** All the time: *The police knew who the thief was* all along.
be along: To catch up; join: *I'll be* along *in a few minutes.*
get along: **1.** To manage fairly well: *He got* along *on his own while his parents were on vacation.*   **2.** To agree: *Brothers and sisters rarely* get along *all the time.*

alongside—At the side; side by side: *She caught up with me and ran* alongside. *Adverb.*
—Beside; by the side of: *The helicopters flew* alongside *each other. Preposition.*
a|long|side (ə lawng′sīd′) *adverb, preposition.*

aloof—Not friendly; distant: *The other students could not understand the* aloof *behavior of the new girl. Adjective.*
—Apart; at a distance: *He remained* aloof *from the younger children's games. Adverb.*
a|loof (ə lūf′) *adjective, adverb.*

kernel

fruit

nut

almond

split fruit

aloud—Loud enough to be heard: *She read her poem* aloud *to her grandfather.*
a|loud (ə loud′) *adverb.*

alpaca—An animal that looks like a sheep but is related to the camel and the llama. It lives in South America and has long, silky hair.
al|pac|a (al **pak**′ə) *noun, plural* **alpacas.**

alpaca

alphabet—The set of written letters that stand for the sounds in a certain language. They are listed in a special order.
al|pha|bet (al′fə bet) *noun, plural* **alphabets.**

Word History

Alphabet comes from two Greek words, the names for the first two letters of the Greek alphabet. The Greeks used those letters to stand for all the rest, the same way that we talk about our ABC's.

---

alphabetical—Arranged in the same way as the letters of an alphabet: *Names in the telephone book are in* alphabetical *order.*
al|pha|bet|i|cal (al′fə bet′ə kəl) *adjective.*

alphabetize—To arrange in the same way as the letters of an alphabet: *The entry words in this dictionary are* alphabetized.

a at	i if	oo look	ch chalk		⌈ a in ago
ā ape	ī idle	ou out	ng sing		e in happen
ah calm	o odd	u ugly	sh ship	ə =	i in capital
aw all	ō oats	ū rule	th think		o in occur
e end	oi oil	ur turn	th their		⌊ u in upon
ē easy			zh treasure		

alphabetize—To arrange in the same way as the letters of an alphabet: *The entry words in this dictionary are* alphabetized.
al|pha|bet|ize (al′fə bə tīz) *verb,* **alphabetized, alphabetizing.**

already—Before this time: *We rushed to get there, but the movie had* already *started.*
al|read|y (awl red′ē) *adverb.*

also—Too; besides: *She is my sister and* also *my best friend.*
al|so (awl′sō) *adverb.*
• Synonyms: **furthermore, likewise, moreover**

altar—A table or raised surface used in religious services.
al|tar (awl′tər) *noun, plural* **altars.**
• A word that sounds the same is **alter.**

alter—To change; become different: *Please* alter *this skirt because it is too long for me.*
al|ter (awl′tər) *verb,* **altered, altering.**
• A word that sounds the same is **altar.**
• Synonyms: **modify, vary**
  Antonyms: **conserve, maintain, preserve**

alternate—1. To happen or be arranged by turns: *Red and black squares* alternate *on a checkerboard.* 2. To take turns: *The basketball players* alternated *taking shots. Verb.*
—1. Happening by turns, first one and then the other: *His shirt has* alternate *black and white stripes.* 2. With one in between; every other: *She waters the flowers on* alternate *days.*
3. Taking the place of another; substitute: *An* alternate *route to school might be shorter. Adjective.*
—A substitute; someone or something that takes the place of another: *If you cannot be at the meeting, send your* alternate. *Noun.*
al|ter|nate (awl′tər nāt for *verb;* awl′tər nit for *adjective* and *noun*) *verb,* **alternated, alternating;** *adjective; noun, plural* **alternates.**

alternative—A choice made between two or more things: *We had the* alternative *of going to the movies or going roller skating.*
al|ter|na|tive (awl tur′nə tiv) *noun, plural* **alternatives.**

although—Even though; in spite of the fact that: *She enjoyed reading the book,* although *parts of it were hard to understand.*
al|though (awl thō′) *conjunction.*

altimeter—An instrument that shows how high above sea level or above the ground something is. Airplanes use altimeters to show the pilot how high above the ground the airplane is flying.
al|tim|e|ter (al tim′ə tər *or* al′tə mē′tər) *noun, plural* **altimeters.**

altitude—The height of something above ground level or sea level.
al|ti|tude (al′tə tūd) *noun, plural* **altitudes.**

alto—1. The lowest female singing voice. 2. The highest male singing voice. 3. A singer with such a voice. 4. Any musical instrument with a range like that of such a voice.
al|to (al′tō) *noun, plural* **altos**.

altogether—1. Completely; entirely: *He had not* altogether *finished his sandwich when the lunch hour ended.* 2. Thinking over everything: *Altogether, it had been a good school year.* 3. Counting each one; including everything: *Altogether, there were nine players on the team.*
al|to|geth|er (awl′tə geth′ər) *adverb*.

aluminum—A strong, lightweight, silver-white metal. It does not rust or stain easily. It is used to make pots and pans for cooking and parts for cars, airplanes, and machines.
a|lu|mi|num (ə lū′mə nəm) *noun*.

always—All the time; every time: *Her grandmother was* always *glad to see her.*
al|ways (awl′wiz *or* awl′wāz) *adverb*.

am—The form of the verb **be** that is used with "I" in the present tense: *I am nine years old.*
am (am) *verb*.

a.m. or **A.M.**—Between midnight and noon: *His alarm clock goes off at 7:00 a.m.*

Language Fact

The abbreviation a.m. (or A.M.) stands for the Latin words **ante meridiem** (an′tē mə rid′ē əm), which mean "before noon." 12 a.m. is midnight. For more information, see **p.m.**

amateur—A person who does something for enjoyment, not for money: *She is only an* amateur, *but her magic tricks are very well done.* *Noun.*
—Not for money: *an* amateur *golfer. Adjective.*
am|a|teur (am′ə chər *or* am′ə tər) *noun, plural* **amateurs**; *adjective*.

amaze—To surprise greatly; astonish: *The dolphins did tricks that* amazed *us.*
a|maze (ə māz′) *verb*, **amazed, amazing**.

ambassador—A person in a government who is sent to another country to speak and act for his or her own country: *the* ambassador *of the United States to Iceland.*
am|bas|sa|dor (am bas′ə dər) *noun, plural* **ambassadors**.

amber—A hard, clear, yellow-brown substance that is used for making jewelry. Amber is a fossil that was formed from the gum of pine trees that grew millions of years ago. *Noun.*
—Yellow-brown: *Tea has an* amber *color.* *Adjective.*
am|ber (am′bər) *noun, adjective*.

ambiguous—Having more than one possible meaning; not clear. The sentence "Ann told Mary that she had won" is ambiguous, because it is not clear if "she" means Ann or Mary.
am|big|u|ous (am big′yoo əs) *adjective*.

ambition—A strong wish to succeed at something: *Her* ambition *was to be an astronaut when she grew up.*
am|bi|tion (am bish′ən) *noun, plural* **ambitions**.

ambitious—Eager; having a strong wish to succeed at something: *an* ambitious *young woman; an* ambitious *plan.*
am|bi|tious (am bish′əs) *adjective*.

ambulance—A motor vehicle used to take sick or injured people to a hospital. The people who work in the ambulance are trained to help the patients until the ambulance reaches a hospital.
am|bu|lance (am′byə ləns) *noun, plural* **ambulances**.

ambush—A surprise attack: *The soldiers caught the enemy in an* ambush. *Noun.*
—To make a surprise attack from a hidden place: *The bandits* ambushed *the travelers in the forest.* *Verb.*
am|bush (am′boosh) *noun, plural* **ambushes**; *verb*, **ambushed, ambushing**.

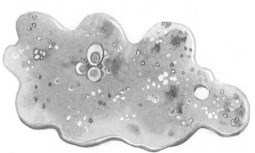

ameba

Word History

Ameba comes from a Greek word meaning "change." An ameba does not have a shape that it keeps, the way most animals have. The shape of an ameba changes all the time, so that it flows almost like water.

ameba—A very simple animal whose body is made up of only one cell. Its shape is always changing. Amebas are so tiny that they can be seen only with a microscope.

a|me|be (ə mē′bə) *noun, plural* **amebas.**

• This word is also spelled **amoeba.**

amen—"May it be true." People say **amen** at the end of a prayer, a wish, or a statement to show they agree with what has been said.

a|men (ā′men′ *or* ah′men′) *interjection.*

Word History

Amen is a Hebrew word found in the Bible and meaning "certainly" or "surely." People used the word in the same way that you might say "Right" to show that you agree with what has been said.

---

amend—To improve; make better: *He tried to amend his study habits.*

a|mend (ə mend′) *verb,* **amended, amending.**

amends—Something done to make up for doing something wrong: *When her baseball broke the window, she made* amends *by mowing the lawn.*

a|mends (ə mendz′) *noun, plural* **amends.**

American foxhound—A medium-sized dog that usually has a white coat with markings of tan or black or both. It is trained to hunt foxes by smell.

A|mer|i|can fox|hound (ə mer′ə kən foks′hound′) *noun, plural* **American foxhounds.**

American Saddle Horse—A small, light horse that was originally bred in America during colonial times. It is used both for riding and as a work horse.

A|mer|i|can Sad|dle Horse (ə mer′ə kən sad′əl hawrs) *noun, plural* **American Saddle Horses.**

American Staffordshire terrier—A medium-sized dog with a short, stiff coat that may be any of several colors.

A|mer|i|can Staf|ford|shire ter|ri|er (ə mer′ə kən staf′ərd shər ter′ē ər) *noun, plural* **American Staffordshire terriers.**

American water spaniel—A medium-sized hunting dog with a thick, curly coat. The coat is usually reddish-brown and may have white markings on the toes or chest.

a at	i if	oo look	ch chalk	⌈a in ago
ā ape	ī idle	ou out	ng sing	e in happen
ah calm	o odd	u ugly	sh ship	ə = ∣ i in capital
aw all	ō oats	ū rule	th think	o in occur
e end	oi oil	ur turn	th their	⌊u in upon
ē easy			zh treasure	

A|mer|i|can wa|ter span|iel (ə mer′ə kən waw′tər span′yəl *or* ə mer′ə kən wot′ər span′yəl) *noun, plural* **American water spaniels.**

American water spaniel

amid—Among; in the middle of: *My father was a welcome sight* amid *all those strangers.*

a|mid (ə mid′) *preposition.*

amigo—A Spanish word for "friend."

a|mi|go (ə me′gō) *noun, plural* **amigos.**

Amish—A religious group founded in the late 1600's. The Amish are farmers and lead simple lives. Today the Amish live mostly in parts of Ohio, Pennsylvania, Indiana, Iowa, Illinois, and Ontario, Canada.

Am|ish (am′ish *or* ah′mish) *noun, plural* **Amish.**

American Staffordshire terrier

amiss—Wrong; not as it should be: *We knew that something was* amiss *when the alarm rang.*
a|miss (ə **mis′**) *adjective.*

ammonia—A colorless gas with a very strong smell. It is a mixture of nitrogen and hydrogen. Many household cleansers contain ammonia.
am|mo|nia (ə **mō′**nē ə) *noun.*

ammunition—Bullets, shells, bombs, or grenades.
am|mu|ni|tion (am yə **nish′**ən) *noun.*

amnesia—A loss of the ability to remember some of the things a person knows. It can be caused by sickness, shock, or an injury to the brain.
am|ne|sia (am **nē′**zhə) *noun.*

amoeba—*See* ameba.

among—1. Part of; included in with: *Red, yellow, and green are* among *the colors of the rainbow.*
2. To each of; with a part for each: *The candy was divided* among *all the children.*
a|mong (ə **mung′**) *preposition.*
• See Language Fact at **between.**

amount—A quantity of something; the total sum: *a large* amount *of popcorn; the* amount *of the bill. Noun.*
—To add up to: *All our hard work* amounted *to nothing when the contest was canceled. Verb.*
a|mount (ə **mount′**) *noun, plural* **amounts;** *verb,* **amounted, amounting.**

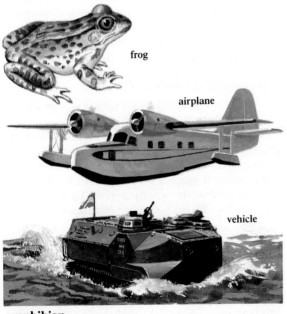

frog

airplane

vehicle

amphibian

amphibian—1. One of a group of cold-blooded animals with a backbone and moist, smooth skin. Many amphibians are born in the water and later live on land. Frogs and salamanders are amphibians. 2. An aircraft that can take off from and land on either land or water. 3. A motor vehicle that can travel on land or water.
am|phib|i|an (am **fib′** ē ən) *noun, plural* **amphibians.**

Word History

Amphibian comes from two Greek words meaning "both" and "life." Animals that are amphibians spend part of their life as air-breathing land animals, and part living in and breathing water. They have life in both places.

---

amphibious—Living or operating both on land and in water: *Toads are* amphibious *animals.*
am|phib|i|ous (am **fib′**ē əs) *adjective.*

amphitheater—An oval or circular building with rows of seats rising around an open space in the center. Sports events and concerts often take place in amphitheaters.
am|phi|the|a|ter (**am′**fə thē′ə tər) *noun, plural* **amphitheaters.**

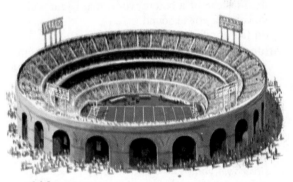

amphitheater

ample—More than enough: *We bought* ample *food for the party.*
am|ple (**am′**pəl) *adjective,* **ampler, amplest.**
• Synonyms: **abundant, plentiful**
  Antonyms: **rare, scanty, scarce**

amplifier—A device that increases the loudness of sounds: *The singer turned up the* amplifier *so we could hear her from the back row.*
am|pli|fi|er (**am′**plə fī′ər) *noun, plural* **amplifiers.**

amplify—1. To make louder, larger, or stronger: *The sound system* amplified *the band's music.*
2. To make larger, fuller, or more complete: *He*

tried to amplify *his answer by giving more details.*

am|pli|fy (am′plə fī) *verb,* **amplified, amplifying.**

amputate—To cut off by surgery: *The doctor had to* amputate *the man's injured leg after the accident.*

am|pu|tate (am′pyə tāt) *verb,* **amputated, amputating.**

amuse—To make happy; make laugh: *Make a funny face to* amuse *the baby.*

a|muse (ə myūz′) *verb,* **amused, amusing.**

amusement—**1.** The feeling of being pleased or entertained: *The new puppies caused much* amusement. **2.** Something that pleases or entertains; means of recreation: *Baseball is our favorite summer* amusement.

a|muse|ment (ə myūz′mənt) *noun, plural* **amusements.**

• Synonyms: **enjoyment, fun,** for **1; entertainment, game, pastime, play, sport,** for **2.**

Antonyms: **boredom,** for **1; chore, duty, task,** for **2.**

an—**1.** Any: *Give me* an *answer.* **2.** One: *We need* an *ounce of chocolate for the recipe.* **An** is used instead of **a** before words that begin with a vowel or a vowel sound.

an (an *or* ən) *indefinite article.*

anaconda—A very large snake, found in South America, that coils around and crushes its prey to death.

an|a|con|da (an′ə kon′də) *noun, plural* **anacondas.**

analysis—A way of learning what something is by separating it into its parts: *After a careful* analysis *of the rock, the scientist discovered silver and gold.*

a|nal|y|sis (ə nal′ə sis) *noun, plural* **analyses** (ə nal′ə sēz).

analyst—A person skilled in analysis.

an|a|lyst (an′ə list) *noun, plural* **analysts.**

analytic—Using analysis; good at analysis: *An* analytic *mind helped the policeman solve the mystery.*

an|a|lyt|ic (an′ə lit′ik) *adjective.*

analyze—To study something by separating it into parts; study closely: *We* analyzed *our project and found we needed more people to work on it.*

an|a|lyze (an′ə līz) *verb,* **analyzed, analyzing.**

• Synonyms: **examine, inspect, investigate**

anatomy—**1.** The science that examines the structure of plants and animals. Anatomy is a *branch of biology.* **2.** The structure of a plant or an animal: *The encyclopedia has a chart of a frog's* anatomy.

a|nat|o|my (ə nat′ə mē) *noun, plural* **anatomies.**

anatosaurus—A plant-eating dinosaur with a ducklike head, short forelegs, and long hind legs on which it walked upright.

a|nat|o|saur|us (ə nat′ə sawr′əs) *noun, plural* **anatosauri** (ə nat′ə sawr′ī).

anatosaurus

ancestor—Any of the people from whom one is descended: *My* ancestors *came to this country in 1875.*

an|ces|tor (an′ses tər) *noun, plural* **ancestors.**

ancestral—Coming from or having to do with ancestors: ancestral *jewels; their* ancestral *village.*

an|ces|tral (an ses′trəl) *adjective.*

ancestry—Ancestors: *Some people like to study their* ancestry.

an|ces|try (an′ses trē) *noun, plural* **ancestries.**

anchor—A heavy piece of metal fastened to a rope or chain. When lowered to the bottom of the water, it keeps a boat from drifting. *Noun.* —To hold or stay firmly in place by means of an anchor: *We* anchored *our boat in the harbor. Verb.*

an|chor (ang′kər) *noun, plural* **anchors;** *verb,* **anchored, anchoring.**

▪ **cast anchor:** To drop an anchor in the water.
weigh anchor: To pull an anchor up from the water.

anchorage—A place to anchor: *The ship's captain hoped to find an* anchorage *before the storm came.*

a at	i if	oo look	ch chalk		⌐ a in ago
ā ape	ī idle	ou out	ng sing		e in happen
ah calm	o odd	u ugly	sh ship	ə =	i in capital
aw all	ō oats	ū rule	th think		o in occur
e end	oi oil	ur turn	th their		⌐ u in upon
ē easy			zh treasure		

an|chor|age (ang′kər ij) *noun, plural* **anchorages.**

anchovy—A small, silvery fish used in salads, pizza, and sauces. It is related to the herring. an|cho|vy (an′chō vē *or* an chō′vē) *noun, plural* **anchovies.**

ancient—Belonging to times of long ago; very old: *We saw an* ancient *dinosaur skeleton at the museum.* an|cient (ān′shənt) *adjective.*
• See Language Fact at **old.**

and—1. As well as: *That girl* and *this one are new students.* 2. Added to: *Five* and *five make ten.* 3. As a result: *The man was tall* and *could get the book on the top shelf for me.* **and** (and *or* ənd *or* ən) *conjunction.*

andiron—One of the two metal supports that hold wood in a fireplace. and|i|ron (and′ī′ərn) *noun, plural* **andirons.**

android—A robot made to look like a human being. an|droid (an′droid) *noun, plural* **androids.**

anecdote—A short and usually amusing story: *The speaker told an* anecdote *to entertain the crowd before his speech.* an|ec|dote (an′ik dōt) *noun, plural* **anecdotes.**

anemia—A condition that occurs when a person loses a lot of blood or when the blood does not have enough red cells in it. Anemia causes a person to feel weak and tired and to look pale. a|ne|mi|a (ə nē′mē ə) *noun.*

anemone—A plant with small white, pink, or purple flowers that are shaped like cups. a|nem|o|ne (ə nem′ə nē) *noun, plural* **anemones.**

anesthesia—A loss of the ability to feel pain, cold, heat, or touch in part or all of the body. It is usually brought about by a drug. It can also be caused by paralysis, disease, or being hypnotized. Anesthesia is used by doctors and dentists so patients will not feel pain. an|es|the|sia (an′əs thē′zhə) *noun.*

anesthetic—A drug that causes a loss of feeling in part or all of the body. an|es|thet|ic (an′əs thet′ik) *noun, plural* **anesthetics.**

angel—1. In some religions, a beautiful and good heavenly being who helps God. Angels are often pictured with halos and wings. 2. Someone who acts or looks like an angel: *Your child is an* angel, *so quiet and calm.* an|gel (ān′jəl) *noun, plural* **angels.**

anger—The strong feeling of being mad at someone or something: *She screamed with* anger *when the dog tore her dress. Noun.*
—To make angry: *He* angered *his mother when he left the house without telling her. Verb.* an|ger (ang′gər) *noun; verb,* **angered, angering.**
• Synonyms: **fury, rage, wrath**
  Antonyms: **calm, peace**

angle—1. An amount of space between two lines that meet at a point, or between two surfaces that meet along a line: *The wall and floor form an* angle *where they meet.* 2. A point of view or a way of thinking: *Maybe we can settle our argument if we look at it from another* angle. *Noun.*
—To move away from a straight line: Angle *to the right when you reach the fork in the road. Verb.* an|gle (ang′gəl) *noun, plural* **angles;** *verb,* **angled, angling.**

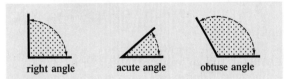

right angle   acute angle   obtuse angle

angle (noun, definition 1)

angler—A person who fishes with a line and hook. an|gler (ang′glər) *noun, plural* **anglers.**

Anglican—Having to do with the Church of England or churches elsewhere that are of the same faith. *Adjective.*
—A member of one of these churches. *Noun.* An|gli|can (ang′glə kən) *adjective; noun, plural* **Anglicans.**

Angora—A long-haired cat with a slender body. It has a wedge-shaped head, a long nose, and pointed ears. An|go|ra (ang gawr′ə) *noun, plural* **Angoras.**

angry—1. Feeling anger; mad: *He was* angry *when his sister took his toys.* 2. Painful, swollen, and red: *The nurse put medicine on my* angry *sore.* an|gry (ang′grē) *adjective,* **angrier, angriest.**

anguish—A feeling of great suffering in the body or the mind: *He felt* anguish *when his wife died.* an|guish (ang′gwish) *noun.*

angular—Having sharp angles or corners; pointed: *Snowflakes are very* angular. an|gu|lar (ang′gyə lər) *adjective.*

animal—1. Any living being that can move freely and can feel things. A turtle, a bird, a pig, and a person are all animals.   **2.** Any such living being except a human being.
an|i|mal (an′ə məl) *noun, plural* **animals.**

animosity—A feeling of great dislike; hatred: *During football season there was deep* animosity *between the rival teams.*
an|i|mos|i|ty (an′ə **mos**′ə tē) *noun.*

ankle—The joint connecting the leg and the foot.
an|kle (ang′kəl) *noun, plural* **ankles.**

ankylosaurus—A medium-sized dinosaur with a low, thick body covered with bony plates and spikes.
an|ky|lo|saur|us (an ky′lə sawr′əs) *noun, plural* **ankylosauri** (an ky′lə sawr′ī).

ankylosaurus

annex—To join to something bigger or more important: *Hawaii was* annexed *to the United States in 1898. Verb.*
—An addition to a building. *Noun.*
an|nex (ə neks′ *for verb;* an′eks *for noun*) *verb,* **annexed, annexing;** *noun, plural* **annexes.**

annihilate—To destroy: *The hurricane* annihilated *our beach house.*
an|ni|hi|late (ə nī′ə lāt) *verb,* **annihilated, annihilating.**

anniversary—A special event that is celebrated every year on the date when it first happened: *April 29th will be the first* anniversary *of our move to this town.*
an|ni|ver|sa|ry (an′ə **vur**′sər ē) *noun, plural* **anniversaries.**

anno Domini—*See* **A.D.**
an|no Dom|i|ni (an′ō **dom**′ə nī) *adverb.*

announce—To report publicly; give notice of: *The coach* announced *the date of the game.*

an|nounce (ə nouns′) *verb,* **announced, announcing.**
• Synonyms: **declare, proclaim**
  Antonyms: **conceal, hide**

annoy—To disturb; bother: *His constant talking really* annoys *me.*
an|noy (ə noi′) *verb,* **annoyed, annoying.**
• Synonyms: **aggravate, provoke**
  Antonyms: **calm, lull, soothe**

annoyance—1. The act of bothering or feeling bothered: *My mother told me of her* annoyance *at my low grades.*   **2.** A person or thing that bothers or disturbs: *That buzzing fly is an* annoyance.
an|noy|ance (ə noi′əns) *noun, plural* **annoyances.**

annual—1. Yearly; taking place once a year: *He went to the doctor for his* annual *examination.*   **2.** Within a year; for a year: annual *growth; an* annual *salary.*
an|nu|al (an′yū əl) *adjective.*

anoint—To rub or touch with a special oil in a religious ceremony.
a|noint (ə noint′) *verb,* **anointed, anointing.**

anonymous—1. Given or done by a person whose name is not known: *I received an* anonymous *Valentine's Day card.*   **2.** Not giving a name: *He did not sign the card because he wanted to remain* anonymous.
a|non|y|mous (ə non′ə məs) *adjective.*

anorexia—An illness in which a person loses the desire to eat for a long time.
an|o|rex|i|a (an′ə rek′sē ə) *noun.*

another—1. One more: *Do you want* another *piece of paper?*   **2.** Different: *I want to buy* another *type of candy. Adjective.*
—A different one; one more: *She finished one book and started reading* another. *Pronoun.*
an|oth|er (ə nuth′ər) *adjective, pronoun.*

answer—1. To respond; reply to something: *I asked the way, and he* answered.   **2.** To do something because of a signal, such as a bell: *She went to* answer *the telephone.*   **3.** To fit; serve; match: *This wood will* answer *our need. Verb.*
—1. A response; reply: *Please give an* answer *to my question.*   **2.** A solution: *Ask your mother to help you find the* answer *to that problem. Noun.*
an|swer (an′sər) *verb,* **answered, answering;** *noun, plural* **answers.**
■ **answer back:** To reply in a rude way: *Don't* answer *me* back *in that tone of voice!*
• Synonyms: **inform, tell,** for *verb* 1.
  Antonyms: **ask, inquire, question,** for *verb* 1.

ant—A small insect that belongs to the same kind

ant

of insects as wasps and bees. Most ants do not have wings. All ants live in groups.
ant (ant) *noun, plural* **ants.**
- A word that sounds the same is **aunt.**

antagonism—A feeling of great dislike; hostility: *the* antagonism *between criminals and the police.*
an|tag|o|nism (an **tag′**ə niz əm) *noun.*

antagonize—To make someone feel dislike; make an enemy of: *His constant teasing* antagonized *her.*
an|tag|o|nize (an **tag′**ə nīz) *verb,* **antagonized, antagonizing.**

antarctic—Around or from the South Pole: antarctic *penguins. Adjective.*
—**the Antarctic:** the region around the South Pole. *Noun.*
ant|arc|tic (ant **ahrk′**tik *or* ant **ahr′**tik) *adjective, noun.*

Antarctic Circle—The imaginary boundary of the antarctic region. On maps, it is shown as a line around the region near the South Pole.
Ant|arc|tic Cir|cle (ant **ahrk′**tik **sur′**kəl *or* ant **ahr′**tik **sur′**kəl) *noun.*

anteater—An animal that eats ants and termites. It has large claws, a narrow head, and a long, sticky tongue to catch its food.
ant|eat|er (**ant′**ē′tər) *noun, plural* **anteaters.**

anteater

antelope—An animal that looks like a deer but is related to goats and cows. Antelopes have horns and can run very fast.
an|te|lope (**an′**tə lōp) *noun, plural* **antelope** or **antelopes.**

antelope

antenna—1. One of a pair of long feelers on the head of an insect, a lobster, or a crab. 2. A long metal wire or rod that receives or sends television and radio signals.

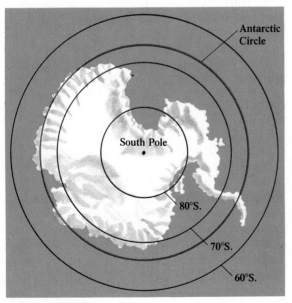

Antarctic Circle

an|ten|na (an ten′ə) *noun, plural* **antennae** (an ten′ē) for definition 1; **antennas** for definition 2.

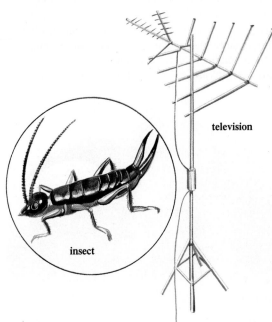

television

insect

antenna

anthem—A patriotic song of praise: *We stood to sing our national* anthem.
an|them (an′thəm) *noun, plural* **anthems.**

anther—The part of a flower that makes pollen.
an|ther (an′thər) *noun, plural* **anthers.**

anthill—A pile of dirt built up by ants when they make a nest.
ant|hill (ant′hil′) *noun, plural* **anthills.**

anthology—A collection of short stories, poems, or other writing: *an anthology of ghost stories.*
an|thol|o|gy (an thol′ə jē) *noun, plural* **anthologies.**

anthropology—The study of different groups of people and of their customs and beliefs.
an|thro|pol|o|gy (an′thrə pol′ə jē) *noun.*

anti—A prefix that means "opposed to" or "against." Antiaircraft weapons are used against aircraft. Antifreeze protects against freezing.

a at	i if	oo look	ch chalk		a in ago
ā ape	ī idle	ou out	ng sing		e in happen
ah calm	o odd	u ugly	sh ship	ə =	i in capital
aw all	ō oats	ū rule	th think		o in occur
e end	oi oil	ur turn	<u>th</u> their		u in upon
ē easy			zh treasure		

antiaircraft—Used to defend against aircraft attacks: antiaircraft *missiles.*
an|ti|air|craft (an′tē ār′kraft′) *adjective.*

antibiotic—A substance that is used as a medicine to kill germs or to slow their growth. Antibiotics are found in bacteria and fungi.
an|ti|bi|ot|ic (an′tē bī ot′ik) *noun, plural* **antibiotics.**

antibody—A substance made by a person's or an animal's body that helps the body to fight a certain disease.
an|ti|bod|y (an′tē bod′ē) *noun, plural* **antibodies.**

anticipate—To look forward to something: *He anticipates having a good time at the party.*
an|tic|i|pate (an tis′ə pāt) *verb,* **anticipated, anticipating.**
• Synonyms: **await, expect**

antidote—A cure for a poison: *The doctor gave her the* antidote *for the snake bite.*
an|ti|dote (an′tē dōt) *noun, plural* **antidotes.**

antifreeze—A substance added to a liquid to keep it from freezing: *Dad puts* antifreeze *in our car's radiator when the weather gets cold.*
an|ti|freeze (an′tē frēz′) *noun.*

antihistamine—A medicine that relieves the effects of colds and allergies.
an|ti|his|ta|mine (an′tē his′tə mēn) *noun, plural* **antihistamines.**

antique—Having to do with the distant past: Antique *jewelry from the 1800's is very popular today. Adjective.*
—Something that was made a long time ago: *Their house is full of* antiques. *Noun.*
an|tique (an tēk′) *adjective; noun, plural* **antiques.**
• See Language Fact at **old.**

antiseptic—A substance, such as iodine, that prevents infection by killing germs.
an|ti|sep|tic (an′tə sep′tik) *noun, plural* **antiseptics.**

antitoxin—A substance made by a person's or an animal's body that protects the body from a poison made by germs.

an|ti|tox|in (an'tē **tok'**sin) *noun, plural* antitoxins.

antler—One of the two horns on the head of a deer or a related animal.
ant|ler (ant'lər) *noun, plural* **antlers**.

antonym—A word that means the opposite of another word. **Love** and **hate, sick** and **well,** and **dirty** and **clean** are antonyms of each other.
an|to|nym (an'tə nim) *noun, plural* **antonyms**.

Word History

Antonym comes from two Greek words meaning "opposite" and "name." The antonym of a word names the opposite of that word. You can see the letters *ant-* in **antonym** and in **anti-,** because they both come from the same Greek word.

---

anvil—A heavy, flat block of iron or steel. Pieces of heated metal are hammered into shape on an anvil.
an|vil (an'vəl) *noun, plural* **anvils**.

anvil

anxiety—1. A worried, nervous, or uneasy feeling: *His* anxiety *about his new school kept him awake.* 2. Eagerness; desire: *Her* anxiety *to please her parents made her study hard.*
anx|i|e|ty (ang zī'ə tē) *noun, plural* **anxieties**.

anxious—1. Worried; nervous: *She is very* anxious *about tomorrow's test.* 2. Eager; willing: *He is always* anxious *to please his family.*
anx|ious (angk'shəs) *adjective*.

any—1. One of many: *Sit in* any *chair.* 2. Some: *Did you find* any *shirts you liked?* 3. Each; every: Any *bird has feathers. Adjective.*
—Some part; some one or ones: *Do you want to borrow* any *of my records? Pronoun.*
—At all: *If you run* any *faster, you may fall. Adverb.*
an|y (en'ē) *adjective, pronoun, adverb*.

anybody—Some person: *Won't* anybody *answer the telephone?*
an|y|bod|y (en'ē bod'ē) *pronoun*.

anyhow—Even so; nevertheless: *It is late, but do you want to go* anyhow?1. However the case may be: *I never liked him* anyhow.
an|y|how (en'ē hou) *adverb*.

anyone—Each person; everyone: Anyone *would love this beautiful sunset.*
an|y|one (en'ē wun) *pronoun*.

anyplace—In one of many places: *That little ring could have been lost* anyplace.
an|y|place (en'ē plās) *adverb*.

anything—Something; one of many things: *Do you need* anything *at the store? Pronoun.*
—At all; in any way: *High school is not* anything *like what I thought it would be. Adverb.*
an|y|thing (en'ē thing) *pronoun, adverb*.

anytime—At one of many times: *We can play* anytime *you like.*
an|y|time (en'ē tīm) *adverb*.

anyway—Even so; nevertheless: *Riding a horse may be hard, but I want to try it* anyway.
an|y|way (en'ē wā) *adverb*.

anywhere—In one of many places: *He would be happy living* anywhere.
an|y|where (en'ē hwãr) *adverb*.
■ **get anywhere:** To succeed; make progress: *We did not* get anywhere *in our search for our lost dog.*

aorta—The main blood vessel from the heart. It carries blood to all parts of the body except the lungs.
a|or|ta (ā awr'tə) *noun, plural* **aortas**.

apart—1. In two or more pieces: *She took her pen* apart *to clean it.* 2. Separate; not together: *She placed the chairs in rows two feet* apart. 3. From each other: *I can hardly tell those two cats* apart.
a|part (ə pahrt') *adverb*.
■ **apart from:** Other than; besides: Apart from *that chapter, it was a good book.*

apartheid—The system of strict separation of races in South Africa.
a|part|heid (ah **pahrt′**hāt *or* ah **pahrt′**hīt, *or* ah **pahrt′**hīd) *noun*.

apartment—A room or group of rooms to live in: *Their* apartment *is on the third floor.*
a|part|ment (ə **pahrt′**mənt) *noun, plural* **apartments**.

apathy—An absence of desire or interest; lack of feeling: *A week of rain left the campers in a state of* apathy.
ap|a|thy (**ap′**ə thē) *noun*.

ape—A big animal that looks like a human being but is covered with hair. Apes are related to monkeys. Gorillas, orangutans, and chimpanzees are apes. *Noun.*
—To act like; imitate: *He* aped *the way a cowboy walks. Verb.*
ape (āp) *noun, plural* **apes**; *verb*, **aped, aping**.

aphid—A tiny insect that lives by sucking juices from plants.
a|phid| (**ā′**fid *or* **af′**id) *noun, plural* **aphids**.

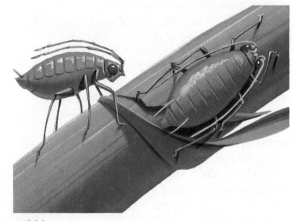

aphid

apiece—Each; for each one: *The twins got three presents* apiece.
a|piece (ə **pēs′**) *adverb*.

apologize—To make an apology; say that one is sorry: *He* apologized *for leaving a mess in the kitchen.*

a|pol|o|gize (ə **pol′**ə jīz) *verb*, **apologized, apologizing**.

apology—A statement a person makes that she or he is sorry for something: *She gave me an* apology *for calling me names.*
a|pol|o|gy (ə **pol′**ə jē) *noun, plural* **apologies**.

apostle or **Apostle**—One of the twelve followers of Christ who were chosen to preach the gospel.
a|pos|tle (ə **pos′**əl) *noun, plural* **apostles** or **Apostles**.

apostrophe—A punctuation mark that looks like this ' and has several uses: **1.** It shows that one or more letters have been left out of a word. "They'll" means "they will" or "they shall." **2.** It shows that something belongs to a person or a thing. "The dog's bowl" means "the bowl of the dog." **3.** It shows the plural of numbers or letters: There are four *i*'s in "Mississippi."
a|pos|tro|phe (ə **pos′**trə fē) *noun, plural* **apostrophes**.

appall—To fill with fear or horror; shock: *We were* appalled *to hear that robbers had broken into the house next door.*
ap|pall (ə **pawl′**) *verb*, **appalled, appalling**.

Appaloosa—A small, light horse, generally with dark brown or black spots on a white background. Appaloosas were bred by Indians in western North America.
Ap|pa|loo|sa (ap′ə **lū′** sə) *noun, plural* **Appaloosas**.

Appaloosa

a at	i if	oo look	ch chalk		a in ago
ā ape	ī idle	ou out	ng sing		e in happen
ah calm	o odd	u ugly	sh ship	ə =	i in capital
aw all	ō oats	ū rule	th think		o in occur
e end	oi oil	ur turn	th their		u in upon
ē easy			zh treasure		

apparatus—The equipment for a certain activity or job. A hairdrier, exercise machines, and a carpenter's tools are examples of apparatus.
ap|pa|ra|tus (ap′ə **rā′**təs *or* ap′ə **rat′**əs) *noun, plural* apparatus *or* **apparatuses**.

apparel—Clothing; something to wear: *sports apparel; formal* apparel.
ap|par|el (ə par′əl) *noun.*

apparent—1. Clear; easy to understand or see: *It is* apparent *when you yawn that you are sleepy.*
2. Seeming to be a certain way: *Things are smaller than their* apparent *size under a magnifying glass.*
ap|par|ent (ə par′ənt) *adjective.*
● Synonyms: **evident, obvious, plain,** for l.
Antonyms: **hazy, obscure, vague,** for l.

appeal—1. To ask for help or understanding: *He* appealed *to his friends when he needed money.*
2. To please or attract: *That style* appeals *to our customers.* 3. To ask that a law case be heard again, by a higher court: *to* appeal *a verdict. Verb.*
—1. A request for help or understanding: *Her* appeal *moved him to forgive her.* 2. A pleasing or attractive quality: *The movie actor had a special* appeal *to teenagers.* 3. A request that a law case be heard again, by a higher court: *They won the case on* appeal. *Noun.*
ap|peal (ə pēl′) *verb,* **appealed, appealing;** *noun, plural* **appeals.**
● Synonyms: **beg, entreat, plead,** for *verb* 1.

appear—1. To come into view: *The stars* appeared *after sunset.* 2. To seem to be a certain way: *She* appeared *to be sleeping, but she was really in deep thought.* 3. To be seen: *The president often* appears *on television.*
ap|pear (ə pēr′) *verb,* **appeared, appearing.**

appearance—1. The act of coming into view: *The cat made a sudden* appearance *at the window.* 2. The act of coming before the public: *The actor's* appearance *excited the audience.*
3. The way someone or something looks: *a neat* appearance.
ap|pear|ance (ə pēr′əns) *noun, plural* **appearances.**

appease—To satisfy; put at rest: *Her explanation for her sharp words* appeased *my anger.*
ap|pease (ə pēz′) *verb,* **appeased, appeasing.**

appendicitis—A disease of the appendix causing great pain.
ap|pen|di|ci|tis (ə pen′də sī′tis) *noun.*

appendix—1. The small pouch that grows next to the large intestine. 2. An addition at the end of a book. An appendix contains more information such as notes, maps, or charts.
ap|pen|dix (ə pen′diks) *noun, plural* **appendixes** or **appendices** (ə pen′də sēz′).

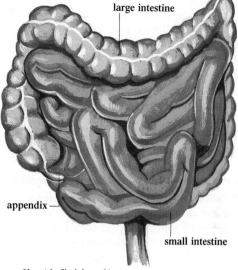

appendix (definition 1)

appetite—1. The desire for food; hunger. 2. Any great desire; liking: *Most teenagers have an* appetite *for music.*
ap|pe|tite (ap′ə tīt) *noun, plural* **appetites.**

applaud—1. To show pleasure and approval by clapping one's hands together: *We* applauded *when they finished singing.* 2. To express admiration, appreciation, or support.
ap|plaud (ə plawd′) *verb,* **applauded, applauding.**

applause—The sound made by clapping one's hands together, used to show pleasure and approval: *Loud* applause *rang through the theater when the show was over.*
ap|plause (ə plawz′) *noun.*

apple—A small, rounded fruit with red, green, or yellow skin. Apples have white flesh around a

apple

core with seeds. They grow on trees.
ap|ple (ap′əl) *noun, plural* apples.
- **the apple of** (one's) **eye:** Something very precious to someone: *That new radio is* the apple of *his* eye.

applesauce—A food made by cutting up apples and cooking them with sugar, spices, and water until they are soft and thin.
ap|ple|sauce (ap′əl saws′) *noun.*

appliance—A machine that has a special use. Most appliances are used in the home, such as refrigerators and coffeemakers.
ap|pli|ance (ə plī′əns) *noun, plural* **appliances.**

application—1. A request, usually written: *He filled out an* application *for a library card.* 2. The act of using what has been learned: *the application of rules to arithmetic problems.* 3. The act of applying something: *The* application *of paint made the walls look new.*
ap|pli|ca|tion (ap′lə kā′shən) *noun, plural* **applications.**

apply—1. To put on: *The nurse applied an ice pack to my swollen ankle.* 2. To use or put into effect: apply *the brakes.* 3. To make a request: *He is* applying *for a new job.*
ap|ply (ə plī′) *verb,* **applied, applying.**

appoint—To name; select: *She was* appointed *to collect the test papers.*
ap|point (ə point′) *verb,* **appointed, appointing.**
- Synonyms: **choose, designate**
  Antonyms: **discharge, dismiss, fire**

appointment—1. An arranged meeting time and place: *I have an* appointment *to see the dentist on Tuesday.* 2. The act of naming: *the* appointment *of a new teacher.*
ap|point|ment (ə point′mənt) *noun, plural* **appointments.**

appraise—1. To judge; rate: *The teacher* appraised *the student's essay as excellent.* 2. To set a value on: *The house was* appraised *when it was put up for sale.*
ap|praise (ə prāz′) *verb,* **appraised, appraising.**
- Synonyms: **assess, estimate, evaluate,** for **2.**

appreciate—1. To be grateful for: *I* appreciate *their help.* 2. To like: *to* appreciate *good music.* 3. To increase in value: *During the last five years, his coin collection* appreciated *greatly.*
ap|pre|ci|ate (ə prē′shē āt′) *verb,* **appreciated, appreciating.**

appreciation—1. The fact of being thankful: *She showed her* appreciation *for the dinner by helping with the dishes.* 2. A liking for something: *She has an* appreciation *of art.*
ap|pre|ci|a|tion (ə prē′shē ā′shən) *noun.*

appreciative—Grateful; thankful: *The* appreciative *audience clapped loudly.*
ap|pre|ci|a|tive (ə prē′shē ə tiv) *adjective.*

apprehend—1. To arrest someone: *The police were sent to* apprehend *the criminal.* 2. To understand: *I* apprehended *the meaning when I read the sentence over again.*
ap|pre|hend (ap′ri hend′) *verb,* **apprehended, apprehending.**
- Synonyms: For **1,** see Synonyms at **catch.**
  Antonyms: For **1,** see Antonyms at **catch.**

apprentice—A person who works with and learns from a more experienced person: *John is an* apprentice *to the carpenter. Noun.*
—To send as an apprentice: *The young man was* apprenticed *to the plumber. Verb.*
ap|pren|tice (ə pren′tis) *noun, plural* **apprentices;** *verb,* **apprenticed, apprenticing.**

approach—1. To come closer to: *Be quiet as you* approach *the bird's nest.* 2. To make a suggestion to: *The student council president* approached *the students with the idea for a dance. Verb.*
—1. A coming closer; getting nearer: *Robins announce the* approach *of spring.* 2. The way to reach a place: *The* approach *to the turnpike was an entrance ramp. Noun.*
ap|proach (ə prōch′) *verb,* **approached, approaching;** *noun, plural* **approaches.**

appropriate[1]—Proper for the occasion; suitable: *A bathing suit is* appropriate *at the beach.*
ap|pro|pri|ate (ə prō′prē it) *adjective.*

appropriate[2]—To put aside for a special reason: *The townspeople voted to* appropriate *money for a new fire engine.*
ap|pro|pri|ate (ə prō′prē āt) *verb,* **appropriated, appropriating.**

approval—1. A favorable opinion about something; praise: *Skilled athletes receive lots of* approval. 2. The permission to do something: *Our teacher gave her* approval *for a class picnic.*
ap|prov|al (ə prū′vəl) *noun, plural* **approvals.**

a at	i if	oo look	ch chalk		a in ago
ā ape	ī idle	ou out	ng sing		e in happen
ah calm	o odd	u ugly	sh ship	ə =	i in capital
aw all	ō oats	ū rule	th think		o in occur
e end	oi oil	ur turn	th their		u in upon
ē easy			zh treasure		

■ **on approval:** With the right to return a purchase if you decide not to keep it: *She bought the couch* on approval.

approve—**1.** To think well of: *The teacher* approved *of my report.*   **2.** To give consent; authorize: *The police chief* approved *the officer's promotion.*
ap|prove (ə prū̄v′) *verb,* **approved, approving.**

approximate—Almost exact: *The* approximate *population of the town is 10,000. Adjective.*
—To be close to: *The school's annual expenses* approximated *$100,000. Verb.*
ap|prox|i|mate (ə prok′sə mit for *adjective;* ə prok′sə māt′ for *verb*) *adjective; verb,* **approximated, approximating.** Abbreviation: approx.

approximately—About; almost; close to: *We are* approximately *12 miles from the ocean.*
ap|prox|i|mate|ly (ə prok′sə mit lē) *adverb.* Abbreviation: approx.
● Synonyms: **nearly, roughly, somewhat**
  Antonyms: **exactly, just, precisely**

apricot—**1.** A round, pale orange fruit that looks like a small peach.   **2.** A light orange-yellow color. *Noun.*
—Light orange-yellow. *Adjective.*
a|pri|cot (ā′prə kot′ *or* ap′rə kot′) *noun, plural* **apricots;** *adjective.*

flower

split fruit

leaf

fruit

apricot (noun, definition 1)

Apr.—The abbreviation for **April.**
April—The fourth month of the year. It has 30 days.
A|pril (ā′prəl) *noun.* Abbreviation: **Apr.**

Word History

April comes from the Latin name for the same month. Some scholars think the Latin name came from a word meaning "to open," because April is when flowers open. Other scholars think it came from the Greek name for the goddess of love, because many people feel that spring is a time for love.

April Fools' Day—April 1, a day on which people try to trick others with jokes.
A|pril Fools' Day (ā′prəl fūlz dā) *noun.*

apron—**1.** A garment tied over the front of the body to protect one's clothing.   **2.** The area for parking aircraft at an airport terminal or hangar.
a|pron (ā′prən) *noun, plural* **aprons.**

apt—**1.** Likely; inclined to: *It is* apt *to rain.*   **2.** Suitable or appropriate: *an* apt *reply.*   **3.** Quick to learn: *an* apt *student.*
apt (apt) *adjective.*

aptitude—**1.** A natural talent or ability: *an* aptitude *for computers.*   **2.** A quickness in learning: *She is a student of great* aptitude *in the arts.*
ap|ti|tude (ap′tə tūd′) *noun, plural* **aptitudes.**

aqua—A pale blue-green color. *Noun.*
—Pale blue-green. *Adjective.*
aq|ua (ak′wə) *noun, plural* **aquas;** *adjective.*

aqualung—A device used by skin divers for breathing underwater.
aq|ua|lung (ak′wə lung′) *noun, plural* **aqualungs.**

aqualung

aquarium—**1.** A water-filled tank or bowl that holds plants and animals, especially fish.   **2.** A building in which water plants and animals are kept.

a|quar|i|um (ə kwār′ē əm) *noun, plural* **aquariums** or **aquaria** (ə kwār′ ē ə).

aquatic—1. Growing or living in water: *Fish are* aquatic *animals.* 2. Taking place in or on water: *Swimming is an* aquatic *sport.*

a|quat|ic (ə kwat′ik) *adjective.*

aqueduct—A structure that carries pipes for bringing water from a distance.

aq|ue|duct (ak′wə dukt) *noun, plural* **aqueducts.**

aqueduct

Arab—A person who belongs to a group of people who mostly live in southwest Asia and north Africa.

Ar|ab (ar′əb) *noun, plural* **Arabs.**

Arabian horse—A strong, light horse that is noted for its endurance. Arabians were first bred by the Arabs for use in the desert. The Arabian is now often ridden as a saddle horse.

A|ra|bi|an horse (ə rā′bē ən hawrs) *noun, plural* **Arabian horses.**

a at	i if	oo look	ch chalk		a in ago
ā ape	ī idle	ou out	ng sing		e in happen
ah calm	o odd	u ugly	sh ship	ə =	i in capital
aw all	ō oats	ū rule	th think		o in occur
e end	oi oil	ur turn	th their		u in upon
ē easy			zh treasure		

Arabic numerals—The figures 1, 2, 3, 4, 5, 6, 7, 8, 9, 0. They are called Arabic because Europeans first learned them from Arab scholars. The figures first came from India.

Ar|a|bic nu|mer|als (ar′ə bik nū′mər əlz) *plural noun.*

arbor—A shady place, usually in a garden, formed by trees, shrubs, or vines growing on a frame.

ar|bor (ahr′bər) *noun, plural* **arbors.**

Arbor Day—A holiday that is celebrated by planting trees. Arbor Day comes at different times in different places.

Ar|bor Day (ahr′bər dā) *noun, plural* **Arbor Days.**

arc—1. Any line that curves in only one direction, especially part of a circle. 2. Anything shaped like or moving in such a curved line: *the* arc *of a rainbow. Noun.*

arc (ahrk) *noun, plural* **arcs.**

• A word that sounds the same is **ark.**

arcade—1. A passageway with an arched roof, often with shops on each side. 2. A shop with coin-operated games.

ar|cade (ahr kād′) *noun, plural* **arcades.**

arch—1. A curved structure that is able to bear the weight of the material above it: *The* arches *in the church support the roof.* 2. Anything shaped like such a structure. *Noun.*

—To curve: *The cat* arched *its back. Verb.*

arch (ahrch) *noun, plural* **arches;** *verb,* **arched, arching.**

arch (noun, definition 1)

archaeology—The study of the people, customs, and life of long ago. Students of archaeology dig to find buildings, tools, weapons, pottery, and other remains of ancient towns and cities, and study them to learn how the people lived.

ar|chae|ol|o|gy (ahr′kē ol′ə jē) *noun.*

archbishop—A bishop of the highest rank.
arch|bish|op (ahrch′bish′əp) *noun, plural*
archbishops.

archery—The skill of shooting with a bow and
arrow for sport, hunting, or fighting.
arch|er|y (ahr′chər ē) *noun.*

archipelago—A group of many islands: *The
archipelago was a hiding place for pirate ships.*
ar|chi|pel|a|go (ahr′kə **pel′**ə gō) *noun, plural*
archipelagos or **archipelagoes.**

archipelago

architect—A person who designs plans for
buildings or parts of buildings.
ar|chi|tect (ahr′kə tekt) *noun, plural* **architects.**

architecture—1. The business of designing and
building houses, churches, schools, offices, and
other buildings.   2. A special style of building:
early Greek architecture.
ar|chi|tec|ture (ahr′kə tek′chər) *noun.*

arctic—Around or from the North Pole: arctic
reindeer. Adjective.
—the Arctic: The region around the North Pole.
Noun.
arc|tic (ahrk′tik *or* ahr′tik) *adjective, noun.*

Arctic Circle—The imaginary boundary of the
arctic region. On maps, it is shown as a line
around the region near the North Pole.
Arc|tic Cir|cle (ahrk′tik sur′kl *or*
ahr′tik sur′kəl) *noun.*

are—The form of the verb **be** that is used in the
present tense with "we," "you," "they," or
any plural noun: *We* are *ready. You* are *late.
They* are *waiting. The birds* are *singing.*
are (ahr) *verb.*

area—1. The amount of surface within a certain
boundary: *The* area *of this wall is twice the* area
of that wall, because this wall is twice as long.
2. A specific region, section, or space: *From*

what area *of the country do you come?*   **3.** A
subject of study: *Which* area *of math interests
you the most?*
ar|e|a (ār′ē ə) *noun, plural* **areas.**

area code—Any of the three-number groups
given as codes for the telephone areas into which
the United States and Canada are divided. Long-
distance calls are made with the area code and
then the local number.
ar|e|a code (ār′ē ə kōd) *noun, plural* **area
codes.**

arena—A large building with a central space and
seats on all sides. Sports events and other
performances take place in arenas.
a|re|na (ə rē′nə) *noun, plural* **arenas.**

aren't—The contraction of "are not."
aren't (ahrnt *or* ahr′ənt).

argue—1. To disagree or quarrel with someone:
My brother and I argue *about sports.*   2. To give
reasons for or against something: *He* argued *for a
change in our vacation plans.*
ar|gue (ahr′gyu) *verb,* **argued, arguing.**
• Synonyms: **bicker, dispute,** for **1.**
 Antonyms: **accord, agree,** for **1.**

argument—1. A disagreement or quarrel: *The
boys had an* argument *about which show to
watch.*   2. A reason for or against something:
The good price is another argument *for buying
these shoes.*
ar|gu|ment (ahr′gyə mənt) *noun, plural*
arguments.

argumentative—Fond of quarreling;
disagreeable: *It is hard to get along with an*
argumentative *person.*
ar|gu|men|ta|tive (ahr′gyə men′tə tiv)
adjective.

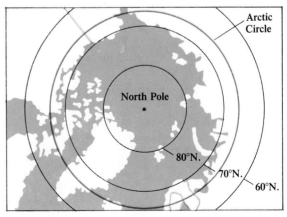

Arctic Circle

arid—Very dry; having little or no rain: *Deserts are* arid *regions.*
ar|id (ar′id) *adjective.*

arise—**1.** To get up; get out of bed: *Farmers arise early to start their chores.* **2.** To appear: *A question* arose *in my mind.* **3.** To move upward; rise: *airplanes* arising *from the ground.*
a|rise (ə rīz′) *verb,* arose, arisen, arising.

aristocracy—**1.** The group of people in a society who are of the highest class because of birth, title, or position; nobility. **2.** Any group of people who are thought to be superior because of their talents or riches.
ar|is|toc|ra|cy (ar′ə stok′rə sē) *noun, plural* aristocracies.

aristocrat—A member of an aristocracy.
a|ris|to|crat (ə ris′tə krat) *noun, plural* aristocrats.

arithmetic—**1.** The science of figuring amounts by using numbers. Arithmetic includes addition, subtraction, multiplication, and division. **2.** The act of adding, subtracting, multiplying, or dividing to calculate with numbers.
a|rith|me|tic (ə rith′mə tik) *noun.*

ark—The huge boat in a story from the Bible, in which Noah, his family, and a pair of every kind of animal survived a great flood.
ark (ahrk) *noun.*
● A word that sounds the same is **arc.**

arm¹—**1.** The part of a person's body from the shoulder to the hand. **2.** Anything used or shaped like an arm: *The boy sat on the* arm *of the chair.*
arm (ahrm) *noun, plural* arms.
■ **arm in arm:** With arms linked together: *They walked* arm in arm.
with open arms: In a warm and friendly way: *She welcomed her old friend* with open arms.

arm²—A weapon: *Soldiers need* arms *in order to fight.* Noun.
—**1.** To equip with weapons: *Each soldier is* armed *with a rifle.* **2.** To have a means of defense or attack: *The cat is* armed *with sharp claws and teeth.* Verb.
arm (ahrm) *noun, plural* arms; *verb,* armed, arming.

a at	i if	oo look	ch chalk		⎡ a in ago
ā ape	ī idle	ou out	ng sing		e in happen
ah calm	o odd	u ugly	sh ship	ə =	i in capital
aw all	ō oats	ū rule	th think		o in occur
e end	oi oil	ur turn	th their		⎣ u in upon
ē easy			zh treasure		

armada—A large group of armed ships, aircraft, or motor vehicles.
ar|ma|da (ahr mah′də) *noun, plural* armadas.

armadillo—A small animal with a hard shell of bony plates. Some kinds can roll up into a ball if attacked. Armadillos are found in some parts of southern North America and South America.
ar|ma|dil|lo (ahr′mə dil′ō) *noun, plural* armadillos.

armadillo

Word History

Armadillo comes from a Spanish word meaning "little armed one." Spanish explorers in America thought that armadillos looked as if they were wearing armor.

armament—Any military weapons, equipment, or forces.
ar|ma|ment (ahr′mə mənt) *noun, plural* armaments.

armchair—A chair having supports at both sides for a person's arms.
arm|chair (ahrm′chār′) *noun, plural* armchairs.

armed forces—The army, navy, air force, and other military services of a country.
armed forc|es (ahrmd fawr′siz) *noun.*

Armed Forces Day—A holiday honoring all branches of the armed forces of the United States. It is celebrated on the third Saturday of May.
Armed Forc|es Day (ahrmd fawr′səz dā) *noun.*

armistice—A halt to fighting; a truce: *The warring countries agreed to a month's* armistice.
ar|mi|stice (ahr′mə stis) *noun, plural* armistices.

Armistice Day—A former United States holiday in memory of the suffering caused by war, now celebrated as Veterans Day. Like Veterans Day, it was celebrated on November 11, the anniversary of the end of World War I.
Ar|mi|stice Day (ahr′mə stis dā) *noun.*

armor—1. A protective covering of metal or leather for a person's body: *a knight in* armor. 2. Any protective covering: *A turtle's shell is* armor *against attack*.
ar|mor (ahr′mər) *noun*.

armor (definition 1)

armory—A place to store weapons.
ar|mor|y (ahr′mər ē) *noun, plural* **armories**.

armpit—The hollow area under the arm at the shoulder.
arm|pit (ahrm′pit′) *noun, plural* **armpits**.

arms—Weapons: *The soldiers took up* arms *and prepared for battle*.
arms (ahrmz) *plural noun*.
■ **up in arms**: Ready to fight; very angry: *The workers were* up in arms *over plans to close their factory*.

army—1. An organization of soldiers trained and equipped for war, mainly fighting on land. 2. Any large group of people: *an army of fans at the game*.
ar|my (ahr′mē) *noun, plural* **armies**.

aroma—A pleasant odor; scent: *The* aroma *of freshly baked bread made me hungry*.
a|ro|ma (ə rō′mə) *noun, plural* **aromas**.
● Synonyms: **fragrance, smell**

arose—*See* **arise**.
a|rose (ə rōz′) *verb*.

around—1. All about in a circle: *The horse ran* around *the ring*. 2. On all sides; surrounding: *The fence went* around *the yard*. 3. About or

near: *Please stay* around *the yard today*. 4. Past; beyond: around *the corner*. *Preposition.*
—1. In a circle: *The top spun* around. 2. About: *A pen is not big* around. 3. In every direction: *The leaves blew* around. 4. In many places; here and there: *I want to shop* around. 5. In the opposite direction: *Turn* around! 6. Nearby: *He was* around *a minute ago*. *Adverb.*
a|round (ə round′) *preposition, adverb*.
■ (have) **been around**: To be experienced; to know life: *After years away at school and working in the city, she has really* been around.

arouse—1. To stir into action; excite: *His speech* aroused *the audience to cheers*. 2. To wake up: *The family was* aroused *by their barking dog*.
a|rouse (ə rouz′) *verb*, **aroused, arousing**.

arrange—1. To put into order: *to* arrange *alphabetically; to* arrange *a vase of flowers*. 2. To prepare for; plan: *Someone must* arrange *the trip for us*. 3. To adapt a piece of music so that it can be performed another way: *to* arrange *a flute piece for violin*.
ar|range (ə rānj′) *verb*, **arranged, arranging**.
● Synonyms: **compose, organize**, for 1.
Antonyms: **complicate, disturb**, for 1.

arrest—1. To seize and hold under law: *The robbers were* arrested. 2. To stop; halt: *Lack of sunlight will* arrest *a plant's growth*. *Verb.*
—The act of seizing and holding someone under law. *Noun.*
ar|rest (ə rest′) *verb*, **arrested, arresting;** *noun, plural* **arrests**.
■ **under arrest**: Held by the police: *The thief was captured and is* under arrest.
● Synonyms: For *verb* 1, see Synonyms at **catch**.
Antonyms: For *verb* 1, see Antonyms at **catch**.

arrival—1. The act of reaching someplace: *the* arrival *of the plane*. 2. A person or a thing that has come: *The newest* arrival *is this calf*.
ar|riv|al (ə rī′vəl) *noun, plural* **arrivals**.

arrive—To get to a place or a point: *The boat* arrived *at the dock*.
ar|rive (ə rīv′) *verb*, **arrived, arriving**.

arrogant—Much too proud; scornful of others; haughty: *After she won, she became* arrogant.
ar|ro|gant (ar′ə gənt) *adjective*.

arrow—1. A thin, straight stick with a point at one end and feathers at the other end. An arrow is shot from a bow. 2. A mark (→) that shows direction on signs, maps, or traffic lights, or that marks important points in print.
ar|row (ar′ō) *noun, plural* **arrows**.

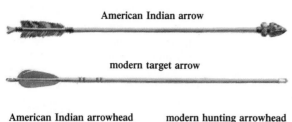

American Indian arrow

modern target arrow

American Indian arrowhead

modern hunting arrowhead

arrow (definition 1) and **arrowhead**

arrowhead—The sharp, pointed end of an arrow.
ar|row|head (ar′ō hed′) *noun, plural*
arrowheads.

arroyo—a dry stream bed or ditch formed by
running water.
ar|roy|o (ə roi′ō) *noun, plural* **arroyos.**

arson—The criminal act of purposely setting fire
to something.
ar|son (ahr′sən) *noun.*

art—1. Painting, drawing, and sculpture: *a
museum of* art; *a talent for* art.   2. The works of
an artist: *His* art *has increased in value.*   3. Any
creative work that appeals to the imagination.
Art includes painting, sculpture, drawing,
architecture, literature, drama, dance, and music.
4. Any skill or ability: *the* art *of cooking; the* art
of making conversation.
art (ahrt) *noun, plural* **arts.**

artery—1. Any of the blood vessels that carry
blood away from the heart to all parts of the
body.   2. A road or channel: *This highway is the
main* artery *into the city.*
ar|ter|y (ahr′tər ē) *noun, plural* **arteries.**

arthritis—A disease of one or more joints of the
body, often with pain, heat, swelling, and
stiffness.
ar|thri|tis (ahr thrī′tis) *noun.*

artichoke—A vegetable with thick scales like
leaves, eaten cooked. It is the flower of a plant
like the thistle.

ar|ti|choke (ahr′tə chōk) *noun, plural*
artichokes.

article—1. A piece of writing that is printed in a
magazine, newspaper, or book.   2. A part of a
formal document: *The* articles *of our constitution
are complicated.*   3. An individual thing or item;
an object: *A shirt is an* article *of clothing.*
4. The words **a, an,** or **the,** which are used with
nouns. **A** and **an** are **indefinite articles. The** is a
definite article.
ar|ti|cle (ahr′tə kəl) *noun, plural* **articles.**

artificial—1. Not found in nature; made by
people: *an* artificial *heart.*   2. False; insincere: *an*
artificial *smile.*
ar|ti|fi|cial (ahr′tə fish′əl) *adjective.*
• Synonym: **synthetic,** for **1.**
  Antonym: **natural,** for **1.**

artillery—1. Large guns that need a crew of
people to fire them.   2. The part of the army that
uses these large guns.
ar|til|ler|y (ahr til′ər ē) *noun, plural* **artillery.**

artisan—A person skilled in a craft or a trade.
Weavers, potters, and carpenters are artisans.
ar|ti|san (ahr′tə zən) *noun, plural* **artisans.**

artist—A person skilled in painting, sculpture,
music, literature, or any other art.
ar|tist (ahr′tist) *noun, plural* **artists.**

artistic—1. Having to do with artists or art:
artistic *study;* artistic *friends.*   2. Showing good
taste, skill, and an appreciation of beauty: *Her*
artistic *nature is clear by her lovely clothes.*
ar|tis|tic (ahr tis′tik) *adjective.*

as—1. Equal in amount, size, or extent: *She is as
tall as you.*   2. For example: *toys such as dolls.*
Adverb.
—1. Taking the role of; doing the work of: *She
acted as bandleader until the conductor arrived.*
2. Like: *I think of my aunt as a mother.*
Preposition.

plant   flower bud

artichoke

a at	i if	oo look	ch chalk		a in ago
ā ape	ī idle	ou out	ng sing		e in happen
ah calm	o odd	u ugly	sh ship	ə =	i in capital
aw all	ō oats	ū rule	th think		o in occur
e end	oi oil	ur turn	th their		u in upon
ē easy			zh treasure		

—**1.** When; while: As *he opened the box, a puppy jumped out.*   **2.** In the same way that: *Do as I do. Conjunction.*
—That: *He likes the same music* as *I do. Pronoun.*
as (az *or* əz) *adverb, preposition, conjunction, pronoun.*

■ **as is:** In the present condition or form: *He wants $600 for the car* as is, *or $700 with new tires.*
as well: Also; too: *Did your sister go to camp* as well?
as well as: In addition to something else: *We have to buy clothes today* as well as *groceries.*
● See Language Fact at **like.**

asbestos—A fireproof fabric made of mineral fibers. Asbestos does not burn or conduct heat.
as|bes|tos (as bes′təs *or* az bes′təs) *noun.*

ascend—**1.** To rise; go up: *The crowd watched the balloons* ascend *into the sky.*   **2.** To climb toward the top of: *The team began to* ascend *the mountain.*
as|cend (ə send′) *verb,* ascended, ascending.
● Synonyms: **climb, soar,** for **1.**
Antonyms: **descend, sink,** for **1.**

ascent—The act of rising; climbing up: *The airplane made a steep* ascent *into the clouds.*
as|cent (ə sent′) *noun, plural* ascents.

ascertain—To make sure of; determine: *It was impossible to* ascertain *what really caused the fire.*
as|cer|tain (as′ər tān′) *verb,* ascertained, ascertaining.

ash[1]—The dusty remains of a thing that has burned: *He tapped the* ash *from his cigar.*
ash (ash) *noun, plural* ashes.

ash[2]—A tree with silver-gray bark. Its tough wood is used for timber and baseball bats.
ash (ash) *noun, plural* ashes.

ashamed—Embarrassed; disgraced: *Don't be* ashamed *of admitting you were wrong.*
a|shamed (ə shāmd′) *adjective.*

ashes—The dusty remains of something that has burned: *The fireplace is full of* ashes.
ash|es (ash′iz) *plural noun.*

ashore—**1.** On the shore or on the land: *The sailor was* ashore *for three weeks visiting his family.*   **2.** To the shore or to the land: *The crew was glad to go* ashore *after our long cruise.*
a|shore (ə shawr′) *adjective, adverb.*

aside—To or on one side; away: *She did not want dinner and pushed it* aside.
a|side (ə sīd′) *adverb.*

ask—**1.** To make an inquiry about something: *Do not forget to* ask *when the party will be.*   **2.** To put a question to: Ask *her if she will play with us.*   **3.** To request: *The teacher* asked *me to show the new student our school.*   **4.** To invite: *She* asked *eight friends to her birthday party.*
ask (ask) *verb,* asked, asking.

■ **ask for it:** To do something that invites trouble: *When she made fun of my clothes, she was really* asking for it.
● Synonyms: **inquire, question,** for **1.**
Antonyms: **answer, inform, tell,** for **1.**

askew—On or to one side; twisted or turned out of position: *The curtain was* askew. *The wind blew his hat* askew.
a|skew (ə skyū′) *adjective, adverb.*

asleep—**1.** Sleeping: *Turn out the light, because the puppies are finally* asleep.   **2.** Without feeling; numb: *When he raised his leg, he discovered his foot was* asleep. *Adjective.*
—Into sleep: *The child fell* asleep *during the story. Adverb.*
a|sleep (ə slēp′) *adjective, adverb.*

asparagus—A vegetable with long, thin, green stalks. It is eaten cooked.
as|par|a|gus (ə spar′ə gəs) *noun.*

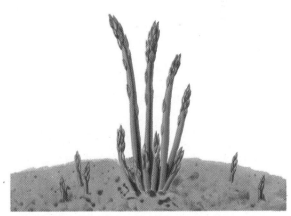

asparagus

aspect—**1.** One of the ways in which something may be looked at or thought of: *The jury must consider all* aspects *of the case before reaching a decision.*   **2.** The looks or appearance of a thing: *The castle's huge walls gave it an* aspect *of strength.*
as|pect (as′pekt) *noun, plural* aspects.

aspen—Any of several kinds of poplar trees. The **quaking aspen** has long-stemmed leaves that shake with even the lightest breeze.
as|pen (as′pən) *noun, plural* aspens.

asphalt—A tarlike material found in the ground or made from petroleum. It is used with gravel or sand to pave roads or driveways.
as|phalt (as′fawlt) *noun.*

aspire—To have an ambition; seek: *to aspire to be an artist.*
as|pire (ə spīr′) *verb,* aspired, aspiring.

aspirin—1. A drug used to relieve pain and to reduce fever.   2. A tablet of this drug.
as|pi|rin (as′pər in) *noun, plural* aspirins.

ass—An animal that looks like a small horse but has long ears and a short mane and tail; donkey.
ass (as) *noun, plural* asses.

assassin—A killer, especially of someone who is famous; murderer.
as|sas|sin (ə sas′ən) *noun, plural* assassins.

assassinate—To murder, especially someone who is famous: *The king was assassinated by his enemy.*
as|sas|si|nate (ə sas′ə nāt) *verb,* assassinated, assassinating.

assault—A sudden and violent attack. *Noun.*
—To attack suddenly and violently: *to assault the enemy. Verb.*
as|sault (ə sawlt′) *noun, plural* assaults; *verb,* assaulted, assaulting.

assemble—1. To come or bring together: collect: *The students were assembled in front of the flagpole.*   2. To put or fit parts together: *to assemble the puzzle.*
as|sem|ble (ə sem′bəl) *verb,* assembled, assembling.
• Synonyms: **congregate, gather,** for **1.**
Antonym: **scatter**

assembly—1. Any gathering of people for a special purpose; meeting: *a school* assembly. 2. **Assembly:** A group of people who make state laws; legislature.   3. A putting together of parts. An **assembly line** is a row of workers who put something together. Different parts of the work are done at different points along the row.
as|sem|bly (ə sem′blē) *noun, plural* assemblies.

assert—1. To declare firmly and positively; state clearly: *The soldiers asserted their loyalty to the government.*   2. To insist on; defend: *to assert your opinion.*

as|sert (ə surt′) *verb,* asserted, asserting.

assess—1. To set the value of something: *The land was assessed at $90,000.*   2. To require to pay; charge: *Each player was assessed one dollar for the new football.*
as|sess (ə ses′) *verb,* assessed, assessing.
• Synonyms: **appraise, estimate, evaluate,** for **1.**

asset—1. Something valuable or useful; advantage; benefit: *Good balance is an* asset *in gymnastics.*   2. **assets:** Valuable items such **as** jewelry, a car, or a house.
as|set (as′et) *noun, plural* assets.

assign—1. To give a job to someone; *to assign a book report.*   2. To name; appoint: *to assign a class messenger.*
as|sign (ə sīn′) *verb,* assigned, assigning.

assignment—1. Something that is given as a job: *a homework* assignment.   2. The act of naming; appointing: *a student's* assignment *to a homeroom.*
as|sign|ment (ə sīn′mənt) *noun, plural* assignments.

assist—To help; aid: *I assisted my sick brother into bed.*
as|sist (ə sist′) *verb,* assisted, assisting.

assistance—Some help; aid: *Dad needs our* assistance *bringing in the grocery bags.*
as|sist|ance (ə sis′təns) *noun.*

assistant—A person who helps another: *The magician's assistant held the equipment. Noun.*
—Helping someone: *the assistant principal. Adjective.*
as|sist|ant (ə sis′tənt) *noun, plural* assistants; *adjective.* Abbreviation: asst.

associate—1. To think of one thing in connection with another: *I associate spring with flowers.*
2. To join as a friend, a companion, or a business partner. *Verb.*
—A partner or companion? *Who are your* associates *in the group project? Noun.*
—Having lesser rank, rights, or privileges: *Our* associate *members cannot vote. Adjective.*
as|so|ci|ate (ə sō′shē āt *or* ə sō′sē āt for *verb;* ə sō′shē it *or* ə sō′sē it for *noun* and *adjective*) *verb,* associated, associating; *noun, plural* associates; *adjective.* Abbreviation: assoc.

association—1. A group of people formed for a special purpose: *the farmers'* association.   2. A friendship: *My* association *with the honor student helped me get better grades.*   3. The way a mind connects one idea with another: *the* association *of winter with snow.*
as|so|ci|a|tion (ə sō′sē ā′shən *or*

a at	i if	oo look	ch chalk		a in ago
ā ape	ī idle	ou out	ng sing		e in happen
ah calm	o odd	u ugly	sh ship	ə =	i in capital
aw all	ō oats	ū rule	th think		o in occur
e end	oi oil	ur turn	th their		u in upon
ē easy			zh treasure		

ə sō′shē ā′shən) *noun, plural* **associations.**
Abbreviation: **assoc.** or **assn.**

assorted—Of many different kinds; various: *Ice cream has* assorted *flavors.*
as|sort|ed (ə sawr′tid) *adjective.*
- Synonyms: **diverse, miscellaneous**
  Antonym: **uniform**

assortment—A variety of different kinds: *The library has a large* assortment *of books.*
as|sort|ment (ə sawrt′mənt) *noun, plural* **assortments.**

assume—**1.** To believe without real proof; suppose: *I* assume *that my friends are loyal to me.* **2.** To be responsible for something; undertake: *When my sister became sick, I* assumed *her chores.*
as|sume (ə sūm′) *verb,* **assumed, assuming.**

assumption—The act of believing without real proof: *Is my* assumption *that you are hungry correct?*
as|sump|tion (ə sump′shən) *noun, plural* **assumptions.**

assurance—**1.** A statement that makes someone certain; promise: *I gave my* assurance *that we would clean up after the party.* **2.** Confidence; security: *With a score of 20 to 7, we had every* assurance *of winning.*
as|sur|ance (ə shoor′əns) *noun, plural* **assurances.**
- Synonyms: **guarantee, pledge, word,** for **1.**

assure—**1.** To tell positively; convince: *The clear blue sky* assured *us that it would not rain today.* **2.** To make certain; make sure: *Our victory* assured *the championship for us.*
as|sure (ə shoor′) *verb,* **assured, assuring.**

aster—A flowering plant with a yellow center and blue, purple, white, or pink petals.
as|ter (as′tər) *noun, plural* **asters.**

asterisk—A mark like a star (*), used in printing or writing to show where added information is located on the page.
as|ter|isk (as′tər isk) *noun, plural* **asterisks.**

asteroid—Any one of thousands of small masses of rock that revolve around the sun between the orbits of Mars and Jupiter.
as|ter|oid (as′tə roid) *noun, plural* **asteroids.**

asthma—A disease that causes coughing, a tightness in the chest, and difficulty in breathing.
asth|ma (az′mə *or* as′mə) *noun.*

astir—In motion; becoming active or excited: *The class was* astir *with preparations for the party.*
a|stir (ə stur′) *adjective.*

astonish—To surprise greatly; amaze: *The lion tamer* astonished *the audience with his daring act.*
as|ton|ish (ə ston′ish) *verb,* **astonished, astonishing.**

astound—To shock; amaze: *We were* astounded *by the lion tamer's daring.*
as|tound (ə stound′) *verb,* **astounded, astounding.**

astray—Out of the right way; wandering: *Let's hold hands in this crowd so no one will go* astray.
a|stray (ə strā′) *adverb.*

astride—With a leg on each side: *I rode* astride *the horse.*
a|stride (ə strīd′) *preposition.*

astrology—The study of the power that the planets, stars, and other heavenly bodies are supposed to have on people's lives.
as|trol|o|gy (ə strol′ə jē) *noun.*

astronaut—A crew member of a spacecraft.
as|tro|naut (as′trə nawt) *noun, plural* **astronauts.**

Word History

Astronaut comes from two Greek words meaning "star sailor." An astronaut is someone who travels into outer space. You can see the letters *astro-*, for "star," in other related words such as **astrology, astronomer,** and **astronomical.**

aster

astronomer—A person who studies astronomy.
as|tron|o|mer (ə stron′ə mər) *noun, plural*
astronomers.

astronomical—1. Having to do with the science
of astronomy.   2. Extremely large or great; too
large to understand: *Grains of sand exist in*
astronomical *numbers.*
as|tro|nom|i|cal (as′trə **nom**′ə kəl) *adjective.*

astronomy—The science of studying the planets,
stars, sun, moon, and other heavenly bodies.
as|tron|o|my (ə stron′ə mē) *noun.*

asylum—1. A place that cares for people who
cannot care for themselves, such as the mentally
ill.   2. Protection or shelter for people who are
hiding or fleeing because of danger: *They found*
asylum *from the war in a neutral country.*
a|sy|lum (ə sī′ləm) *noun, plural* **asylums.**

at—1. Near, by, on, or in: at *the end of the road.*
2. Toward; to: *Throw the ball* at *me.*   3. On or
near a certain time: *Dinner is* at *six o'clock.*
at (at) *preposition.*

ate—*See* **eat.**
ate (āt) *verb.*
  • A word that sounds the same is **eight.**

atheist—A person who believes that God does
not exist.
a|the|ist (ā′thē ist) *noun, plural* **atheists.**

athlete—A person who trains to be good at sports
or exercises that take strength, speed, and skill.
ath|lete (ath′lēt) *noun, plural* **athletes.**

athletic—1. Having to do with sports or games
and the people who play them: athletic
equipment.   2. Skilled in sports: *The new student
is very* athletic.
ath|let|ic (ath let′ik) *adjective.*

atlas—A book of maps.
at|las (at′ləs) *noun, plural* **atlases.**

Word History

Atlas was a giant in old Greek stories who
carried the world on his shoulders. Long ago,
the giant's picture was often placed on the first
page of books of maps. So a book of maps came
to be known as an **atlas.**

---

a at	i if	oo look	ch chalk		a in ago
ā ape	ī idle	ou out	ng sing		e in happen
ah calm	o odd	u ugly	sh ship	ə =	i in capital
aw all	ō oats	ū rule	th think		o in occur
e end	oi oil	ur turn	th their		u in upon
ē easy			zh treasure		

atmosphere—1. the air surrounding the earth or
any other heavenly body.   2. The air in a certain
place: *the cool, damp* atmosphere *of a cellar.*
3. the feeling or emotion that surrounds a place
or thing: *the happy* atmosphere *at weddings.*
at|mos|phere (at′mə sfēr) *noun, plural*
atmospheres.

atmospheric—Of or in the air surrounding the
earth: Atmospheric *conditions produce the
weather.*
at|mos|pher|ic (at′mə sfer′ik) *adjective.*

atoll—A coral island or group of islands that
surround an area of shallow water called a
lagoon.
at|oll (at′ol *or* ə tol′) *noun, plural* **atolls.**

atoll

atom—The smallest bit of any chemical element
that has all the qualities of that element. An atom
contains a mass of protons and neutrons in a
center called a nucleus that is surrounded by
electrons. Everything is made of atoms.
at|om (at′əm) *noun, plural* **atoms.**

Word History

Atom comes from a Greek word meaning "that
cannot be divided." People first thought of atoms
as things that could not be divided into smaller
bits. But today we know this is not true. Today,
people speak of splitting the atom, although this
really means dividing what cannot be divided.

---

atomic—1. Having to do with atoms: atomic
energy.   2. Using the energy of atoms: *an atomic
bomb.*
a|tom|ic (ə tom′ik) *adjective.*

atop—On top of: *Place one block* atop *the other.*
a|top (ə top′) *preposition.*

atrocious—Very wicked; brutal; cruel: *an* atrocious *crime.*
a|tro|cious (ə trō′shəs) *adjective.*

attach—**1.** To fix in place; fasten: *We attached our drawings to the board with tacks.* **2.** To add on at the end: *I attached my name to the letter.* **3.** To draw together by love: *They are very attached to their grandparents.*
at|tach (ə tach′) *verb,* **attached, attaching.**

attack—**1.** To set upon forcefully; assault: *The fox attacked the chicken.* **2.** To harm; damage: *Poison ivy attacks the skin.* **3.** To write or talk against; criticize: *Here is a letter attacking our plan.* **4.** To go at or begin to work on eagerly: *to attack an ice cream sundae greedily. Verb.*
—**1.** An act of setting upon something forcefully; assault: *The enemy* attack *began at dawn.* **2.** A sudden illness or discomfort: *an attack of the flu. Noun.*
at|tack (ə tak′) *verb,* **attacked, attacking;** *noun, plural* **attacks.**

attain—**1.** To reach; arrive at: *to attain adulthood.* **2.** To gain by effort; achieve: *to attain first prize.*
at|tain (ə tān′) *verb,* **attained, attaining.**

attempt—To try; make an effort at: *I will now* attempt *a difficult dive. Verb.*
—**1.** An effort; a try: *The baby finally stood up after her third* attempt. **2.** An attack: *an attempt on the president's life. Noun.*
at|tempt (ə tempt′) *verb,* **attempted, attempting;** *noun, plural* **attempts.**

attend—**1.** To be present at: *to attend school.* **2.** To wait on or care for: *to attend to customers.* **3.** To go with; accompany: *A guard attended the prisoner.*
at|tend (ə tend′) *verb,* **attended, attending.**

attendance—**1.** The act or fact of being present at a place: *He won the prize for perfect* attendance *at school.* **2.** The number of people attending: *The* attendance *at my party was 12.*
at|tend|ance (ə ten′dəns) *noun.*

attention—**1.** The act of watching or listening carefully: *The story teller had everyone's complete* attention. **2.** Care; concern; consideration: *The problem was brought to the mayor's* attention. **3.** A posture, used in the armed forces, in which a person stands very straight with legs together, arms at the sides, and eyes looking straight ahead: *The soldier came to* attention *when the general entered the room.* **4. attentions:** Any acts of kindness: *When she* was sick, her brother's attentions were very comforting.
at|ten|tion (ə ten′shən) *noun, plural* **attentions.** Abbreviation: attn.

attentive—**1.** Paying attention; very observant: *An* attentive *student will do well.* **2.** Polite; considerate: *The waiter in the restaurant was very* attentive.
at|ten|tive (ə ten′tiv) *adjective.*

attic—The room directly below the roof, in many houses.
at|tic (at′ik) *noun, plural* **attics.**

attitude—A way of thinking, acting, or feeling: *Now that she plays better, her* attitude *toward sports has improved.*
at|ti|tude (at′ə tüd) *noun, plural* **attitudes.**

attorney—A person having the legal power to act for someone else; lawyer.
at|tor|ney (ə tur′nē) *noun, plural* **attorneys.** Abbreviation: atty.

attract—To draw; bring; gather: *A parade attracts a crowd.*
at|tract (ə trakt′) *verb,* **attracted, attracting.**

attraction—**1.** A thing that charms or causes interest: *The rides are the main* attraction *at the fair.* **2.** The power to draw or bring: *the* attraction *of light for moths.*
at|trac|tion (ə trak′shən) *noun, plural* **attractions.**

attractive—Pleasing; charming: *an* attractive *smile.*
at|trac|tive (ə trak′tiv) *adjective.*

auburn—A reddish-brown color. *Noun.*
—Reddish-brown: auburn *hair. Adjective.*
au|burn (aw′bərn) *noun, adjective.*

auction—A public sale at which a thing is sold to the person who offers the most money. *Noun.*
—To sell things at such a sale: *All the furniture will be* auctioned *next week. Verb.*
auc|tion (awk′shən) *noun, plural* **auctions;** *verb,* **auctioned, auctioning.**

audible—Loud enough to hear: *This whistle is* audible *from two blocks away.*
au|di|ble (aw′də bəl) *adjective.*

audience—**1.** The people gathered in a place to hear or see something. **2.** All the people who can read, hear, or see something: *the television* audience. **3.** A formal interview with an important person: *The ambassador had an* audience *with the queen.*
au|di|ence (aw′dē əns) *noun, plural* **audiences.**

audio—Having to do with sound.
au|di|o (aw′dē ō) *adjective.*

auk

audio-visual—Having to do with equipment that involves both hearing and seeing, such as films, especially in schools.
au|di|o-vis|u|al (aw′dē ō vizh′ū əl) *adjective.*

audition—A gathering at which actors, dancers, or other performers try out for a part in a show. *Noun.*
—To try out for a part in a show. *Verb.*
au|di|tion (aw dish′ən) *noun, plural* **auditions;** *verb,* **auditioned, auditioning.**

auditorium—A large hall used for performances, meetings, or other public gatherings.
au|di|to|ri|um (aw′də tawr′ē əm) *noun, plural* **auditoriums.**

Aug.—The abbreviation for **August.**

August—The eighth month of the year. August has 31 days.
Au|gust (aw′gəst) *noun.* Abbreviation: **Aug.**

Word History

August was named for the Roman emperor Augustus. After he came to power, the Romans gave the month his name to honor him.

a at	i if	oo look	ch chalk		a in ago
ā ape	ī idle	ou out	ng sing		e in happen
ah calm	o odd	u ugly	sh ship	ə =	i in capital
aw all	ō oats	ū rule	th think		o in occur
e end	oi oil	ur turn	th their		u in upon
ē easy			zh treasure		

auk—Any member of a group of arctic sea birds. They have small tails, short wings, webbed feet, and legs set back on the body like a penguin's.
auk (awk) *noun, plural* **auks.**

aunt—1. The sister of one's father or mother. 2. The wife of one's uncle.
aunt (ant *or* ahnt) *noun, plural* **aunts.**
• A word that sounds the same is **ant.**

Language Fact

Aunt may be pronounced in two different ways. How you pronounce the word may depend on where you live. Many people in the northeast part of the United States pronounce **aunt** using the same sound as in **calm.** Many people in other parts of the country pronounce **aunt** so that it sounds like **ant.** Both pronunciations are correct.

aurora borealis—The bands of colored light that sometimes appear in the night sky of the northern hemisphere; northern lights.
au|ro|ra bo|re|al|is (aw rawr′ə bawr′ē al′is) *noun.*

Australian cattle dog—A medium-sized dog with a short, thick coat and a bushy tail. The coat is blue or red, with black, blue, red, or tan markings. This dog was originally bred in Australia to herd cattle.
Aus|tral|ian cat|tle dog (aw strāl′yən kat′əl dawg) *noun, plural* **Australian cattle dogs.**

Australian cattle dog

Australian terrier—A small dog with a straight, coarse coat that is blue-black or silver-

Australian terrier

black with tan markings. This dog was originally bred in Australia.
Aus|tral|ian ter|ri|er (aw stral′yən ter′ē ər) *noun, plural* **Australian terriers.**

authentic—Real; genuine; trustworthy: *an* authentic *signature; an* authentic *antique.*
au|then|tic (aw then′tik) *adjective.*
• Synonyms: **actual, original, true**
  Antonyms: **counterfeit, false**

author—The writer of a play, book, story, poem, or article.
au|thor (aw′thər) *noun, plural* **authors.**

authoritative—1. Coming from or having proper authority: authoritative *orders.* 2. Commanding; forceful: *She gave commands to her dog in an* authoritative *voice.* 3. Having expert knowledge: *The judge wrote an* authoritative *book on law.*
au|thor|i|ta|tive (ə thawr′ə tā′tiv) *adjective.*

authority—1. The power to control or make decisions: *the* authority *of the police.* 2. **the authorities:** The officials in control; the government: *They reported the crime to the* authorities. 3. A source of good information; an expert: *The professor is an* authority *on bats.*
au|thor|i|ty (ə thawr′ə tē) *noun, plural* **authorities.**

authorization—A power or right: *The city council had* authorization *to collect the new tax.*
au|thor|i|za|tion (aw′thər ə zā′shən) *noun, plural* **authorizations.**

authorize—1. To give a power or right: *She was* authorized *to rent hotel rooms for us.* 2. To approve: *The President* authorized *the funds.*

au|thor|ize (aw′thə rīz) *verb,* **authorized, authorizing.**

auto—An automobile.
au|to (aw′tō) *noun, plural* **autos.**

autobiography—The story of a person's life, written by the person.
au|to|bi|og|ra|phy (aw′tə bī og′rə fē) *noun, plural* **autobiographies.**

autograph—A person's signature. *Noun.*
—To write one's name in or on something: *Please* autograph *this photo I have of you! Verb.*
au|to|graph (aw′tə graf) *noun, plural* **autographs;** *verb,* **autographed, autographing.**

automatic—1. Moving or working by itself: *An* automatic *elevator starts and stops itself.*
2. Done without thinking about it: *Blinking your eyes is an* automatic *motion. Adjective.*
—A type of gun that keeps firing and reloading by itself as long as the trigger is held. *Noun.*
au|to|mat|ic (aw′tə mat′ik) *adjective; noun, plural* **automatics.**

automatic teller machine—A machine that bank customers use to deposit and withdraw money without seeing a teller.
au|to|mat|ic tell|er ma|chine (aw′tə mat′ik tel′ər mə shēn′) *noun, plural* **automatic teller machines.** Abbreviation: **ATM.**

automatically—In an automatic way or manner: *The garage door opened* automatically.
au|to|mat|i|cal|ly (aw′tə mat′ ik lē) *adverb.*

automation—The use of machines that do the jobs of people and that work by themselves.
au|to|ma|tion (aw′tə mā′shən) *noun.*

automobile—A passenger vehicle with four wheels that is powered by a gasoline engine; car.
au|to|mo|bile (aw′tə mə bēl′ *or* aw′tə mə bēl′) *noun, plural* **automobiles.**

Word Power

If you are interested in automobiles, here are some useful words to know. Each is a thing that is part of an automobile or used with an automobile. You can find these words in this dictionary.

brake	headlight	spark plug
bumper	hood	speedometer
carburetor	hubcap	tire
clutch	jack	transmission
cylinder	muffler	trunk
gear	radiator	windshield

autopsy—The medical examination of a dead body to find out what caused the death.
au|top|sy (aw′top sē) *noun, plural* **autopsies.**

autumn—The season of the year that is between summer and winter; fall.
au|tumn (aw′təm) *noun, plural* **autumns.**

Language Fact

Autumn is one of two names for the season between summer and winter. People also call this season **fall,** because it is the time when leaves fall from the trees. Both names have been used for a long time, and both are correct.
• See also Word History at **harvest.**

---

auxiliary—1. Giving help; for assisting: *When the wind died, the sailboat used an* auxiliary *engine.* 2. Additional; less important: *The doctor is in her* auxiliary *office only on Fridays. Adjective.*
—A group that helps a larger organization: *Our civic club has a children's* auxiliary. *Noun.*
aux|il|ia|ry (awg zil′yər ē) *adjective; noun, plural* **auxiliaries.**

auxiliary verb—A helping verb such as "be," "can," "do," "have," "may," "must," "shall," or "will." These are used with other verbs: *I am* late. *You can* come. *She may* follow.
aux|il|ia|ry verb (awg zil′yər ē vurb) *noun, plural* **auxiliary verbs.**

avail—Help; use; benefit: *An umbrella that leaks is of no* avail *in the rain. Noun.*
—To be of use or help: *Words will not* avail *you when deeds are called for. Verb.*
a|vail (ə vāl′) *noun; verb,* **availed, availing.**

available—That one can get, have, or use: *Tickets are still* available *for the movie.*
a|vail|a|ble (ə vā′lə bəl) *adjective.*

avalanche—A great mass of snow, ice, or earth that slides quickly down the side of a mountain.
av|a|lanche (av′ə lanch) *noun, plural* **avalanches.**

avarice—A very great desire for money or property; greed for riches: *His* avarice *led him into a life of crime.*
av|ar|ice (av′ər is) *noun.*

avast—A command used by sailors that means stop; stay; hold it.
a|vast (ə vast′) *interjection.*

Ave.—The abbreviation for **avenue.**

avenge—To seek revenge for; get even for: *The basketball team* avenged *its earlier defeat with a tremendous victory.*
a|venge (ə venj′) *verb,* **avenged, avenging.**

avenue—A wide, main street.
av|e|nue (av′ə nū) *noun, plural* **avenues.**
Abbreviation: **Ave.**

aver—To say that something is true; assert positively: *The player continued to* aver *that he had not committed a foul.*
a|ver (ə vur′) *verb,* **averred, averring.**

average—1. The answer when a series of figures is added together and then divided by the number of figures. The average of 2, 3, and 10 is five (because 2 + 3 + 10 = 15, and 15 ÷ 3 = 5). 2. The usual amount: *He is short, but his brother is taller than* average. *Noun.*
—Usual or ordinary; typical: *Our house is about* average *size. Adjective.*
—1. To find out the numerical average of something: *If you* average *our ages, the answer is 11.* 2. To have or get as a usual amount: *On the* average, *I drink about three glasses of milk a day. Verb.*
av|er|age (av′ər ij) *noun, plural* **averages;** *adjective; verb,* **averaged, averaging.**
Abbreviation: **avg.**

averse—Opposed: *She is* averse *to loud noises.*
a|verse (ə vurs′) *adjective.*

aversion—A strong dislike: *He has an* aversion *to anything that has a bitter taste.*
a|ver|sion (ə vur′zhən) *noun, plural* **aversions.**

avert—1. To keep from happening; prevent: *His skillful driving* averted *an accident.* 2. To turn away part of the body: *He* averted *his face when they stared at him.*
a|vert (ə vurt′) *verb,* **averted, averting.**

avg.—The abbreviation for **average.**

aviary—A very large cage where birds, especially wild ones, are kept.
a|vi|ar|y (ā′vē är′ē) *noun, plural* **aviaries.**

aviation—The science or business of flying aircraft, particularly airplanes.
a|vi|a|tion (ā′vē ā′shən) *noun.*

aviator—A person who flies aircraft; pilot.
a|vi|a|tor (ā′vē ā′tər) *noun, plural* **aviators.**

avid—Very eager; enthusiastic: *an* avid *reader; an* avid *tennis player.*
av|id (av′id) *adjective.*

a at	i if	oo look	ch chalk		a in ago
ā ape	ī idle	ou out	ng sing		e in happen
ah calm	o odd	u ugly	sh ship	ə =	i in capital
aw all	ō oats	ū rule	th think		o in occur
e end	oi oil	ur turn	th their		u in upon
ē easy			zh treasure		

fruit

split fruit

avocado

avocado—A pear-shaped fruit with dark green or nearly black skin and a large seed. The yellow-green flesh is eaten raw.
av|o|ca|do (av′ə kah′dō) *noun, plural* **avocados.**

avocation—Something a person likes to do for pleasure; hobby: *My father works in an office, but gardening is his* avocation.
av|o|ca|tion (av′ə kā′shən) *noun, plural* **avocations.**

avoid—To stay away from: *He avoids his mother when she is angry with him.*
a|void (ə void′) *verb,* **avoided, avoiding.**

avoidance—The act of staying away; avoiding: *His* avoidance *of his old friends made us all wonder what was wrong.*
a|void|ance (ə voi′dəns) *noun.*

avow—To declare honestly or openly; admit; acknowledge: *He avowed that he did not cheat on the test.*
a|vow (ə vou′) *verb,* **avowed, avowing.**

AWACS—An airborne radar system of the U.S. Air Force that can detect low-flying aircraft at great distances.
AWACS (ā′waks) *noun.*

Word History

AWACS comes from the first letters of the words Airborne Warning and Control System.

await—1. To wait for eagerly: *I have awaited your letter for several weeks.* 2. To be ready for; be in store for: *School is over and vacation awaits us.*
a|wait (ə wāt′) *verb,* **awaited, awaiting.**
• Synonyms: **anticipate, expect,** for 1.

awake—To come out of sleep; wake up: *The campers awoke at sunrise. Verb.*

—Not asleep: *The barking dog kept me awake all night. Adjective.*
a|wake (ə wak′) *verb,* **awoke** *or* **awaked, awaking;** *adjective.*

awaken—To wake up: *I always awaken early when we are going to play baseball.*
a|wak|en (ə wā′kən) *verb,* **awakened, awakening.**

award—1. To give as something won: *I was awarded a blue ribbon for first prize in spelling.* 2. To give by deciding legally: *The judge awarded $10,000 to the accident victim. Verb.*
—A prize or honor: *She won an* award *for her painting. Noun.*
a|ward (ə wawrd′) *verb,* **awarded, awarding;** *noun, plural* **awards.**

aware—Realizing; knowing: *Be aware of your mistakes and you can learn from them.*
a|ware (ə wār′) *adjective.*

awash—Covered with water: *The land along the river was awash after the storm.*
a|wash (ə wosh′ *or* ə wawsh′) *adjective.*

away—1. From a place; to a distance: *to go away.* 2. At a distance; far: *Today the team plays away.* 3. Out of one's notice, use, or possession: *Dad took my bike away as a punishment.* 4. In another direction: *to look away.* 5. Out of being: *The snowman melted away. Adverb.*
—1. At a distance; far: *The store is two blocks away.* 2. Absent; gone: *My friend is away at camp. Adjective.*
a|way (ə wā′) *adverb, adjective.*
■ **do away with:** To put an end to something or someone: *The new government did away with several old laws.*

awe—A feeling of great wonder, fear, or respect: *They felt awe at the sight of the comet. Noun.*
—To cause someone to feel this way: *to be awed by the fireworks display. Verb.*
awe (aw) *noun; verb,* **awed, awing.**

awesome—Causing great wonder, fear, or respect: *A tidal wave is an awesome sight.*
awe|some (aw′səm) *adjective.*

awful—1. Causing fear, dread, or terror: *an awful fire.* 2. Very bad, ugly, or unusual: *They made an awful mess.* 3. Huge; great: *an awful lot of food.*
aw|ful (aw′fəl) *adjective.*
• Synonyms: **dreadful, horrible, terrible**

awfully—1. Terribly; dreadfully: *My feet hurt awfully after the long walk.* 2. Very: *I am awfully sorry.*
aw|ful|ly (aw′fə lē) *adverb.*

awhile—For a brief time: *We rested* awhile *before going swimming again.*
a|while (ə hwīl′) *adverb*.

awkward—**1.** Not having grace or skill; clumsy: *Penguins are very* awkward *on land but graceful in the water.*   **2.** Not easy to deal with; embarrassing: *He had an* awkward *moment when he forgot her name.*   **3.** Not easy to use or handle: *Three suitcases made an* awkward *load.*
awk|ward (awk′wərd) *adjective*.

awl

awl—A thin tool with a sharp point, used to make holes in leather or wood.
awl (awl) *noun, plural* **awls**.
• A word that sounds the same is **all**.

awning—A structure like a small roof, made of canvas, metal, or other material, and placed above a door or window to block the sun or rain.
awn|ing (aw′ning) *noun, plural* **awnings**.

awoke—*See* **awake**.
a|woke (ə wōk′) *verb*.

awry—**1.** Twisted or turned to one side: *Her hair was blown* awry *by the wind.*   **2.** Wrong; out of order: *My vacation plans went* awry.
a|wry (ə rī′) *adverb*.

a at	i if	oo look	ch chalk		
ā ape	ī idle	ou out	ng sing		a in ago
ah calm	o odd	u ugly	sh ship	ə =	e in happen
aw all	ō oats	ū rule	th think		i in capital
e end	oi oil	ur turn	th their		o in occur
ē easy			zh treasure		u in upon

ax or **axe**—A tool with a sharp, flat blade at the end of a long handle. It is used for chopping wood.
ax or axe (aks) *noun, plural* **axes**.
■ **get the ax:** To lose a job; be fired: *The waiter dropped so many trays, he* got the ax.
have an ax to grind: To have a strong special purpose or reason, often a selfish one: *She must* have an ax to grind *if she gave you extra punishment.*

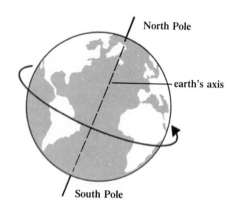

North Pole

earth's axis

South Pole

axis

axis—The straight line through an object around which the object turns or seems to turn. The earth turns around an imaginary axis running from the North Pole to the South Pole.
ax|is (ak′sis) *noun, plural* **axes** (ak′sēz).

axle—The shaft around which a wheel turns.
ax|le (ak′səl) *noun, plural* **axles**.

ayatollah—A teacher belonging to the highest rank, in a certain form of the Muslim religion.
a|ya|tol|lah (ah′yə tōl′ə) *noun, plural* **ayatollahs**.

aye—Yes: *All those in favor of the motion, say* "aye." *Adverb.*
—A "yes" vote. *Noun.*
aye (ī) *adverb; noun, plural* **ayes**.
• Words that sound the same are **eye** and **I**.

azalea—A small bush with white, pink, or red flowers.
a|zal|ea (ə zāl′yə) *noun, plural* **azaleas**.

Aztec—A member of a group of Indians that ruled a powerful empire in central Mexico about 500 years ago.
Az|tec (az′tek) *noun, plural* **Aztecs**.

azure—A sky-blue color. *Noun.*
—Having a sky-blue color. *Adjective.*
az|ure (azh′ər) *noun, adjective*.

About 1,900 years ago, the Romans gave the capital **B** its present form. The small letter **b** was first used about 1,700 years ago. It reached its present form about 500 years ago.

About 5,000 years ago, the ancient Egyptians used a symbol of a house.

About 3,500 years ago, people in the Middle East made a simpler symbol. They called it *beth*, their word for "house."

About 3,000 years ago, other people in the Middle East used a symbol of a house and a doorway.

About 2,600 years ago, the Greeks gave the letter this form. They called it *beta* and made it the second letter in their alphabet.

B or **b**—1. The second letter of the alphabet: *There are three* b's *in the word "babble."*
2. The second best of its kind, or the second highest mark in school: *a B movie; a B in reading.*
B, b (bē) *noun, plural* **B's** or **Bs, b's** or **bs.**
• Words that sound the same are **be** and **bee.**

baa—The sound a sheep makes. *Noun.*
—To make a sound like a sheep. *Verb.*
baa (ba *or* bah) *noun, plural* **baas;** *verb,* **baaed, baaing.**

babble—1. To make sounds that have no meaning or cannot be understood: *Babies* babble *until they learn how to talk.*   **2.** To chatter: *The children* babbled *for an hour about the movie.*   **3.** To make a quiet, soothing sound: *The water* babbled *as it flowed over the stones. Verb.*
—1. Any sounds that have no meaning or cannot be understood: *the* babble *of the crowd.*   **2.** A quiet, soothing sound: *the* babble *of the brook. Noun.*
bab|ble (bab′əl) *verb,* **babbled, babbling;** *noun.*

babe—A baby.
babe (bāb) *noun, plural* **babes.**
• Synonyms: **infant, newborn**

baboon—A large monkey with a short tail and a doglike face.
ba|boon (ba bün′) *noun, plural* **baboons.**

baboon

Word History

Baboon comes from an old French word meaning "stupid person." Later the word came to mean "ape." Today, people again use **baboon** to describe someone who acts silly or rude.

baby—1. An infant; a very young child.   **2.** The youngest person in a family.   **3.** A person who acts like a baby: *Take your medicine and don't be a* baby. *Noun.*

—**1.** Very young: *Look at the baby pigs in the barn.* **2.** Meant for a baby: *a baby carriage. Adjective.*

—To treat someone or something like a baby: *My father babies his plants so they will grow well. Verb.*

ba|by (bā′bē) *noun, plural* **babies;** *adjective;* *verb,* **babied, babying.**

• Synonyms: **babe, newborn,** for *noun* **1.**

baby-sit—To care for a child or children in place of the parents: *He baby-sits for the neighbors once each weekend.*

ba|by-sit (bā′bē sit′) *verb,* **baby-sat, baby-sitting.**

baby-sitter—A person who cares for a child or children in place of the parents.

ba|by-sit|ter (bā′bē sit′ər) *noun, plural* **baby-sitters.**

bachelor—A man who has never married.

bach|e|lor (bach′ə lər) *noun, plural* **bachelors.**

back—**1.** The area of the body opposite the chest. The back extends from the neck to the end of the backbone. **2.** The upper part of an animal's body. **3.** The part opposite the front: *He went around the house to the* back. *Noun.*

—**1.** To support or help. *She said she'll* back *me if I argue about the price.* **2.** To move backward: *I* backed *my bicycle into the garage. Verb.*

—**1.** Behind the front part: *the* back *seat.* **2.** Old; past: back *issues of a magazine. Adjective.*

—**1.** Toward the back; backward: *Move* back *on the bus, please.* **2.** Where something was before: *He put the pan* back *on the stove. Adverb.*

back (bak) *noun, plural* **backs;** *verb,* **backed, backing;** *adjective; adverb.*

▪ **back and forth:** In one direction and then in the opposite direction: *They threw the ball* back and forth.

back down or **back off:** To give up; surrender: *I* backed down *when he lost his temper.*

behind (someone's) **back:** Secretly; without letting someone know: *They bought her a new bicycle* behind *her* back.

get off (one's) **back:** To stop bothering; leave alone: *I did what you asked me, so get off my* back.

with (one's) **back to the wall:** In serious trouble: *Losing by two runs in the last inning, with our* backs to the wall, *we got four hits and won the game.*

backache—A pain in the back.

back|ache (bak′āk′) *noun, plural* **backaches.**

backboard—The flat surface behind a basketball hoop.

back|board (bak′bawrd′) *noun, plural* **backboards.**

backbone—**1.** The spine; the line of bones down the back. **2.** Courage; strength of character: *He has no* backbone *and cannot disagree with anyone.*

back|bone (bak′bōn′) *noun, plural* **backbones.**

backdrop—A curtain or a painted cloth hung at the rear of a stage.

back|drop (bak′drop′) *noun, plural* **backdrops.**

backfield—**1.** The players on a football team whose positions are behind the line of scrimmage.

back|field (bak′fēld′) *noun, plural* **backfields.**

backfire—A loud noise, like the sound of a gun, made by a gasoline engine that is not working right. *Noun.*

—**1.** To make such a noise. **2.** To have the opposite effect of what was expected: *Her plan* backfired, *and instead of leaving early she had to stay late. Verb.*

back|fire (bak′fīr′) *noun, plural* **backfires;** *verb,* **backfired, backfiring.**

backgammon—A game in which two players take turns throwing dice to find out how to move their pieces. The board is divided into two sections, with 12 spaces on each section.

back|gam|mon (bak′gam′ən) *noun.*

background—**1.** The most distant part of a scene or a picture: *The sunset was a nice* background *for our photograph.* **2.** Someone's experience, training, or knowledge: *You have the right* background *for this job.*

back|ground (bak′ground′) *noun, plural* **backgrounds.**

backhand—A stroke in tennis and other games using a racket or paddle. A backhand is made with the back of the hand turned forward.

back|hand (bak′hand′) *noun, plural* **backhands.**

backpack—A pack or knapsack worn on the back: *She always carries her books in a* backpack. *Noun.*

—To travel with such a pack or knapsack: *He likes to go* backpacking *in the mountains. Verb.*

a at	i if	oo look	ch chalk		a in ago
ā ape	ī idle	ou out	ng sing		e in happen
ah calm	o odd	u ugly	sh ship	ə =	i in capital
aw all	ō oats	ū rule	th think		o in occur
e end	oi oil	ur turn	th their		u in upon
ē easy			zh treasure		

back|pack (bak′pak′) *noun, plural* **backpacks;** *verb,* **backpacked, backpacking.**

backstage—In the part of a theater that is not seen by the audience: *The actors waited* backstage *for the play to begin.* **back|stage** (bak′stāj′) *adverb.*

backstop—A fence or a wall used in tennis or baseball to keep the ball in the playing court or field. **back|stop** (bak′stop′) *noun, plural* **backstops.**

backstroke—A stroke used when swimming on one's back. **back|stroke** (bak′strōk′) *noun, plural* **backstrokes.**

backward or **backwards**—**1.** Toward the back or what is behind someone: *I moved* backward *when I saw the wave rushing toward me.* **2.** With the back going first: *He put his sweater on* backward *by mistake. Adverb.* —Turned toward the back or what is behind someone: *He gave a* backward *look to make sure his sister was following. Adjective.* **back|ward** or **back|wards** (bak′wərd *or* bak′wərdz) *adverb, adjective.*
- ■ **bend over backward:** To try very hard: *They painted the walls, cleaned the rugs, and* bent over backward *trying to sell their house.*

bacon—The meat from the sides and back of a pig. **ba|con** (bā′kən) *noun.*
- ■ **bring home the bacon:** To succeed in an important way: *A college scholarship? That's* bringing home the bacon!
- • See Language Fact at **pork.**

backhand

bacteria—A kind of tiny living thing that can be seen only through a microscope. Bacteria are everywhere. Some bacteria are very useful. Others cause disease. **bac|te|ri|a** (bak′tēr′ē ə) *noun, singular* **bacterium** (bak′tēr′ē əm).

bad—**1.** Not good; not as it should be; of poor quality: *I mowed the lawn quickly and did a* bad *job.* **2.** Wicked; evil: *the big,* bad *wolf.* **3.** Harmful: bad *for your health.* **4.** Unfriendly; disagreeable: *a* bad *mood.* **5.** Causing sadness: bad *news.* **6.** Sorry or sad: *She felt* bad *when she missed the party.* **bad** (bad) *adjective,* **worse, worst.**
- • Synonyms: **naughty, wrong,** for **2.** Antonyms: **good, moral, right,** for **2.**

bade—*See* **bid.** **bade** (bad *or* bād) *verb.*

badge—A symbol that a person wears to show membership in a certain group: *a police* badge; *a sheriff's* badge. **badge** (baj) *noun, plural* **badges.**

badger (noun)

Word History

The **badger** probably got its name from the word **badge.** The markings on a badger's face are like a badge showing what animal it is.

badger—A medium-sized animal with thick gray fur, short legs, and long claws. Badgers live in holes underground but come out to hunt other animals as food. *Noun.* —To pester; annoy: *Stop* badgering *me with so many questions! Verb.* **badg|er** (baj′ər) *noun, plural* **badgers;** *verb,* **badgered, badgering.**
- • Synonyms: **harass, hound, plague,** for *verb.*

badly—1. Not well or skillfully: *He plays the piano* badly *because he seldom practices.*
2. Very much: *I* badly *want to win.*
bad|ly (bad′lē) *adverb.*

badminton—A game in which two or four players use rackets to hit a plastic object to one another over a high net.
bad|min|ton (bad′min tən) *noun.*

baffle—To confuse; bewilder: *The mystery* baffled *the detectives.*
baf|fle (baf′əl) *verb,* baffled, baffling.
  • Synonyms: perplex, puzzle
    Antonyms: enlighten, illuminate

bag—1. A soft, loose container, open at the top. Bags can be made of paper, plastic, or cloth: *She carried her Halloween candy in a* bag. 2. A suitcase or other piece of luggage: *Please put my* bags *in the car.* 3. A purse; handbag: *She took her wallet from her* bag. *Noun.*
—1. To hang loosely; droop; sag: *Pants often* bag *at the knees.* 2. To catch or kill something: *He* bagged *a duck on his first try. Verb.*
bag (bag) *noun, plural* bags; *verb,* bagged, bagging.
  ■ **hold the bag:** To suffer the results of something: *She broke the window, ran away, and left us* holding the bag.
    in the bag: Bound to succeed; certain to be favorable: *After three nights of study, the test was* in the bag.

Language Fact

Bag is used to mean all kinds of containers, from grocery bags to suitcases. **Sack** commonly means a loose container made of cloth, usually burlap. But what some people call a bag, others call a sack, and the other way around, too. **Bag** is used more often in the northern part of the United States, **sack** more often in the southern part.

---

baggage—Luggage; the suitcases, trunks, and other containers a person takes on a trip.
bag|gage (bag′ij) *noun.*

a at	i if	oo look	ch chalk		a in ago
ā ape	ī idle	ou out	ng sing		e in happen
ah calm	o odd	u ugly	sh ship	ə =	i in capital
aw all	ō oats	ū rule	th think		o in occur
e end	oi oil	ur turn	th their		u in upon
ē easy			zh treasure		

baggy—Very loose-fitting: *The clown wore* baggy *pants.*
bag|gy (bag′ē) *adjective,* baggier, baggiest.

bagpipe—A musical instrument made of five pipes and a leather bag. Air is blown into the bag through one pipe and then squeezed out the other pipes to make music.
bag|pipe (bag′pīp′) *noun, plural* bagpipes.

bagpipe

bail¹—Some money that must be paid to a court of law to get a prisoner out of jail until trial. If the person does not appear for the trial, the court keeps the money. *Noun.*
—To free (a prisoner) by paying money in this way: *She* bailed *her brother out of jail. Verb.*
bail (bāl) *noun, plural* bails; *verb,* bailed, bailing.
  • A word that sounds the same is **bale.**

bail²—To remove (water) from a boat with a bucket or other container: *I* bailed *water from the leaky canoe.*
bail (bāl) *verb,* bailed, bailing.
  ■ **bail out:** To get out of a difficult or dangerous

situation: *The pilot* bailed out *with a parachute when the airplane ran out of fuel.*
• A word that sounds the same is **bale**.

bait—Something, such as food, that attracts or tempts; lure: *Earthworms make good* bait *for fishing. Noun.*
—1. To provide with something that attracts or tempts: *They* baited *the mousetrap with cheese.* 2. To tease in a cruel way; torment: *The children* baited *the new students and called them names. Verb.*
bait (bāt) *noun, plural* **baits**; *verb,* **baited, baiting.**

bake—1. To cook food in an oven by dry heat: *We* baked *the cookies for 12 minutes.* 2. To dry or harden by heat: *Bricks are made of* baked *clay.* 3. To make very warm: *The sun* baked *them on the beach.*
bake (bāk) *verb,* **baked, baking.**

baker—A person who cooks breads, pastries, cakes, and cookies.
bak|er (bā′kər) *noun, plural* **bakers.**
■ **a baker's dozen:** Thirteen.

bakery—A store where breads, pastries, cakes, and cookies are cooked or sold.
bak|er|y (bā′kər ē) *noun, plural* **bakeries.**

balance—1. A device used to weigh things.
2. The state of having the same weight, amount, force, or effect: *The bag in her left hand and the books in her right hand were in* balance. 3. The state of being steady: *He kept his* balance *while he walked along the curb.* 4. A part that is left over: *Give me the* balance *of the money after you buy the sneakers. Noun.*
—1. To put something in a steady position: *He* balanced *a book on his head.* 2. To compare things: *She* balanced *the good and bad points of the job before she took it. Verb.*
bal|ance (bal′əns) *noun, plural* **balances;** *verb,* **balanced, balancing.**

balcony—1. A platform that is attached to the outside wall of a building. A balcony is usually

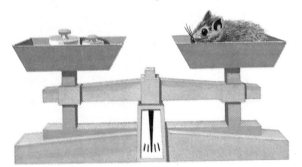
balance (noun, definition 1)

enclosed by a railing and can be reached from an inside room. 2. A large platform with seats on it that sticks out over a main floor of seats.
bal|co|ny (bal′kə nē) *noun, plural* **balconies.**

bald—1. With little or no hair: *a bald* head.
2. Having no natural cover: *The mountain was* bald *of trees after the forest fire.*
bald (bawld) *adjective,* **balder, baldest.**

bale—A large bundle of something, especially a crop, tied together: *a bale* of cotton.
bale (bāl) *noun, plural* **bales.**
• A word that sounds the same is **bail**.

Balinese cat—A long-haired cat of medium size with blue eyes and big ears. The Balinese was originally bred in the United States from Siamese cats and Persian cats.
Ba|li|nese cat (bah′lə nēz′ kat) *noun, plural* **Balinese cats.**

balk—1. To stop and refuse to do something: *He* balked *when his friends asked him to lie.* 2. To prevent something from happening: *Rain* balked *our plans for a picnic.*
balk (bawk) *verb,* **balked, balking.**

ball¹—1. A round or rounded object used in some games: *I hit the* ball *with a bat.* 2. A round object: *a* ball *of yarn.* 3. Any game played with a ball: *Let's play* ball *in the park.* 4. A baseball or softball pitch that does not pass over home plate between the batter's shoulders and knees, and at which the batter does not swing.
ball (bawl) *noun, plural* **balls.**
■ **on the ball:** Alert; aware of what is happening or what needs to be done: *She seems to daydream a lot, but she is really* on the ball.
play ball: 1. To start a ball game or go on again after it has stopped. 2. To cooperate: *If you* play ball *with me, I'll help you too.*
• A word that sounds the same is **bawl**.
• Synonyms: **globe, sphere,** for **2**.

ball²—A formal dance party.
ball (bawl) *noun, plural* **balls.**
• A word that sounds the same is **bawl**.

ballad—A song or a poem that tells a story: *She sang a* ballad *about a railroad wreck.*
bal|lad (bal′əd) *noun, plural* **ballads.**

ball bearing—One of many small metal balls, placed inside a machine part, that allow other parts of the machine to move easily.
ball bear|ing (bawl bār′ing) *noun, plural* **ball bearings.**

ballerina—A girl or a woman who performs ballet dances.
bal|le|ri|na (bal′ə rē′nə) *noun, plural* **ballerinas.**

ballet—1. A kind of dance with graceful poses, movements, and steps that follow carefully planned patterns. A ballet dance often tells a story.   2. A dance of this kind.
bal|let (bal′ā or bal ā′) *noun, plural* **ballets** for 2.

balloon—1. A large bag that is filled with heated air or another gas and then floats in the air. It may carry a cabin or a basket for passengers or equipment.   2. A plastic bag that is filled with air or another gas and then closed tightly. Balloons are used as toys and party decorations. *Noun.*
—To grow larger or fuller: *She filled her mouth with water until her cheeks* ballooned. *Verb.*
bal|loon (bə lūn′) *noun, plural* **balloons;** *verb,* **ballooned, ballooning.**
■ **like a lead balloon:** With no success; very badly: *My joke went over* like a lead balloon.

ballot—A piece of paper on which a person marks his or her vote in an election. *Noun.*
—To use a piece of paper to vote: *The voters* balloted *in the town election. Verb.*
bal|lot (bal′ət) *noun, plural* **ballots;** *verb,* **balloted, balloting.**

ballroom—A large room where formal dances are held.
ball|room (bawl′rūm′ or bawl′room′) *noun, plural* **ballrooms.**

balmy—Soothing; gentle: *a* balmy *climate.*
balm|y (bah′mē) *adjective,* **balmier, balmiest.**

baloney—1. Nonsense; foolishness: *Talk like that is just a lot of* baloney.   2. Another spelling of **bologna.**
ba|lo|ney (bə lō′nē) *noun.*

balsa—A strong wood that is very light in weight. Balsa is easy to cut and carve and is used to make toy airplanes.
bal|sa (bawl′sə) *noun.*

balsam—A North American evergreen tree. Balsams are often sold as Christmas trees.
bal|sam (bawl′səm) *noun, plural* **balsams.**

bamboo—A treelike plant with a very tall, thin, hard, hollow stem. Bamboo is used to make fishing poles, buildings, and furniture.
bam|boo (bam bū′) *noun, plural* **bamboos.**

ban—To forbid by law; not allow: *The state* bans *fishing in that lake. Verb.*
—A law or an order that forbids a certain activity: *a* ban *on smoking. Noun.*
ban (ban) *verb,* **banned, banning;** *noun, plural* **bans.**
● Synonyms: **outlaw, prohibit,** for *verb.*
 Antonyms: **license, permit,** for *verb.*

banana—A long, curved fruit with yellow or green skin and white flesh. Bananas grow in bunches on a tropical plant.
ba|nan|a (bə nan′ə) *noun, plural* **bananas.**

band¹—1. A group of people or animals: *a band of outlaws.*   2. A musical group. *Noun.*
—To join together to get something done: *They* banded *together to turn the old garage into a clubhouse.*
band (band) *noun, plural* **bands;** *verb,* **banded, banding.**
● Synonyms: **bunch, company, crew, gang, party,** for *noun* 1.

band²—A strip of cloth or other material wrapped around something: *She put a rubber* band *around her baseball cards. Noun.*
—To wrap a band on something: *They* banded *tree branches with cloth to mark the trail. Verb.*
band (band) *noun, plural* **bands;** *verb,* **banded, banding.**

bandage—A flat strip of material placed over or around an injury to protect it: *Mother wrapped my sprained ankle with a* bandage. *Noun.*
—To cover or wrap with a flat strip of material: *She* bandaged *the wound. Verb.*
band|age (ban′dij) *noun, plural* **bandages;** *verb,* **bandaged, bandaging.**

a at	i if	oo look	ch chalk		⌈ a in ago
ā ape	ī idle	ou out	ng sing		e in happen
ah calm	o odd	u ugly	sh ship	ə =	i in capital
aw all	ō oats	ū rule	th think		o in occur
e end	oi oil	ur turn	th their		⌊ u in upon
ē easy			zh treasure		

bamboo

bandanna or **bandana**—A large, colorful handkerchief, often worn on the head or around the neck.
ban|dan|na or ban|dan|a (ban dan′ə) *noun, plural* **bandannas** or **bandanas**.

bandit—An outlaw; robber.
ban|dit (ban′dit) *noun, plural* **bandits**.

bang—**1.** A sharp, loud noise: *There was a* bang *when the chair fell over.* **2.** A loud, strong blow: *We heard a* bang *on the door. Noun.*
—**1.** To make a sharp, loud noise: *The pot* banged *when it fell on the floor.* **2.** To hit noisily: *She* banged *the desk with her ruler. Verb.*
bang (bang) *noun, plural* **bangs;** *verb,* **banged, banging.**
● Synonyms: **bump, collide, jar², jolt** for *verb* **2.**

bangs—Hair cut short so as to fall over the forehead: *She brushed her* bangs *off her face.*
bangs (bangz) *plural noun.*

banish—To force to go away; exile: *The people who spilled the garbage were* banished *from the park for a month.*
ban|ish (ban′ish) *verb,* **banished, banishing.**

banjo—A musical instrument with strings, a round body, and a long neck like a guitar. A banjo's strings are plucked or strummed to make music.
ban|jo (ban′jō) *noun, plural* **banjos** or **banjoes**.

banjo

bank¹—**1.** A long pile or mound: *They plowed the snow into a* bank *next to our driveway.* **2.** The ground along a river. *Noun.*

—To make into a mound: *We* banked *snow to make a fort. Verb.*
bank (bangk) *noun, plural* **banks;** *verb,* **banked, banking.**

bank²—**1.** A place of business for people to save or borrow money. **2.** A small container used for saving money: *a coin* bank. *Noun.*
—To do business with such a place: *My sister* banks *near her office. Verb.*
bank (bangk) *noun, plural* **banks;** *verb,* **banked, banking.**
■ **bank on:** To rely on; count on: *You can* bank *on my help if you need it.*

bankbook—A small book used to record the amount of money put into a bank account or taken out.
bank|book (bangk′book′) *noun, plural* **bankbooks.**

banker—A person who manages a bank.
bank|er (bang′kər) *noun, plural* **bankers.**

banking—The business of saving or borrowing money at a bank.
bank|ing (bang′king) *noun.*

bankrupt—Unable to pay the money one owes: *The farmers were* bankrupt *after years of bad crops. Adjective.*
—To make someone unable to pay money that is owed: *Storms ruined the crops and* bankrupted *the farmer. Verb.*
bank|rupt (bangk′rupt) *adjective; verb,* **bankrupted, bankrupting.**

banner—A flag or other cloth with a design or writing on it: *The fans waved a* banner *that said, "Go, Team!"*
—Especially good: *With A's in every subject, she had a* banner *year in school. Adjective.*
ban|ner (ban′ər) *noun, plural* **banners;** *adjective.*

banquet—A formal dinner for many people: *The team held a* banquet *at the end of the season.*
ban|quet (bang′kwit) *noun, plural* **banquets.**

baptism—A ceremony performed to admit someone into the Christian church. The person is sprinkled with or dipped in water.
bap|tism (bap′tiz əm) *noun, plural* **baptisms.**

Baptist—A member of a Christian church in which a person is usually baptized by being dipped in water until covered. The church believes that people should not be baptized until they are old enough to accept the church for themselves.
Bap|tist (bap′tist) *noun, plural* **Baptists.**

baptize—1. To give baptism to; christen: *The minister* baptized *the infant.* 2. To give a name to at baptism: *The baby was* baptized *''John.''*
bap|tize (bap tīz′ *or* bap′tīz) *verb,* **baptized, baptizing.**

bar—1. A piece of some solid material that is longer than it is wide: *a bar of gold.*
2. Something that blocks the way: *His youth was a bar to entering the army.* 3. A band of color: *Her uniform has blue* bars *on the shoulders.*
4. In music, a unit of rhythm. 5. In written music, an upright line that shows the division between two units of rhythm. 6. A place where drinks are served. 7. The profession of a lawyer: *She was admitted to the* bar *last year. Noun.*
—1. To use a piece of solid material to close something: *Iron rods* barred *the jail windows.*
2. To keep out: *Automobiles are* barred *from this park. Verb.*
bar (bahr) *noun, plural* **bars;** *verb,* **barred, barring.**

barb—A sharp point that sticks out backward. Fishhooks have barbs.
barb (bahrb) *noun, plural* **barbs.**

barbarian—A person who is uncivilized, savage, or primitive: *The* barbarians *had no written language.*
bar|bar|i|an (bahr bār′ē ən) *noun, plural* **barbarians.**

barbecue—1. Some food that is cooked on an outdoor grill or fire. 2. An outdoor grill or fireplace. *Noun.*
—To cook food on an outdoor grill or fire: *We* barbecued *hamburgers at the picnic. Verb.*
bar|be|cue (bahr′bə kyū) *noun, plural* **barbecues;** *verb,* **barbecued, barbecuing.**

barbed wire—A kind of wire that has stiff, sharp points along it, often used to fence in animals.
barbed wire (bahrbd wīr) *noun.*

barbed wire

a at	i if	oo look	ch chalk		⌐a in ago
ā ape	ī idle	ou out	ng sing		e in happen
ah calm	o odd	u ugly	sh ship	ə =	i in capital
aw all	ō oats	ū rule	th think		o in occur
e end	oi oil	ur turn	th their		⌐u in upon
ē easy			zh treasure		

barbell—A piece of metal with weights on each end, used for exercise.
bar|bell (bahr′bel′) *noun, plural* **barbells.**

barber—A person whose job is to cut hair and to shave or trim beards.
bar|ber (bahr′bər) *noun, plural* **barbers.**

Word History

Barber comes from a Latin word meaning ''a beard.''

---

bare—1. Naked; uncovered: *Her* bare *arms burned in the sun.* 2. Empty: *We went shopping because the refrigerator was* bare. 3. The least necessary; smallest possible: *She does a* bare *amount of homework. Adjective.*
—To reveal; uncover: *She* bared *her feelings to her best friend. Verb.*
bare (bār) *adjective; verb,* **bared, baring.**
• A word that sounds the same is **bear.**

bareback—Without a saddle: *the* bareback *circus riders on horses; They rode the camels* bareback.
bare|back (bār′bak′) *adjective, adverb.*

barefoot—With nothing on the feet: *The* barefoot *girls walked on the beach. The boys ran* barefoot.
bare|foot (bār′foot′) *adjective, adverb.*

barely—Only just; hardly: *There was* barely *enough to eat.*
bare|ly (bār′lē) *adverb.*

bargain—1. An agreement: *Mom and I made a* bargain *that she would feed the dog and I would walk it.* 2. Something for sale at a low price: *The dress was a real* bargain *at ten dollars. Noun.*
—To try to make an agreement: *They* bargained *with the teacher for a few extra minutes of recess. Verb.*
bar|gain (bahr′gən) *noun, plural* **bargains;** *verb,* **bargained, bargaining.**

barge—A large boat with a flat bottom, used to carry freight.
barge (bahrj) *noun, plural* **barges.**

baritone—1. A male singing voice that is between the highest and the lowest male singing voices.
2. A man who has such a voice. 3. Any musical instrument with a range like that of such a voice.
bar|i|tone (bar′ə tōn) *noun, plural* **baritones.**

bark¹—The rough outer covering on the trunk and branches of a tree.
bark (bahrk) *noun, plural* **barks.**

bark²—The sharp sound made by a dog: *The little dog had a loud* bark. *Noun.*

—**1.** To make such a sound: *The dogs* barked *all day.*   **2.** To speak harshly and loudly: *The runner* barked *at the umpire who called him out. Verb.*
bark (bahrk) *noun, plural* **barks;** *verb,* **barked, barking.**

■ **bark up the wrong tree:** To be wrong about what to do or how to do it: *Looking for ice cream in a clothing store is* barking up the wrong tree.
(one's) **bark is worse than** (one's) **bite:** Someone sounds dangerous, but isn't really: *I don't worry when he threatens because his* bark is worse than *his* bite.

barley—The seeds of a grasslike plant, which are used for food and to make malt drinks.
bar|ley (bahr′lē) *noun.*

barley

bar mitzvah—The ceremony that takes place when a Jewish boy turns 13. It celebrates his becoming an adult member of that religion.
bar mitz|vah (bahr mits′və) *noun, plural* **bar mitzvahs.**

barn—A farm building used to store hay and grains and to protect farm animals and machinery.
barn (bahrn) *noun, plural* **barns.**

barnacle—A tiny animal with a hard shell, which attaches itself to boat bottoms and to underwater rocks.
bar|na|cle (bahr′nə kəl) *noun, plural* **barnacles.**
• See picture at **crustacean.**

barnyard—The area around a barn.
barn|yard (bahrn′yahrd′) *noun, plural* **barnyards.**

barometer—An instrument that measures air pressure. A barometer helps to predict changes in the weather.
ba|rom|e|ter (bə rom′ə tər) *noun, plural* **barometers.**

barracks—A large building or a group of buildings that soldiers live in.
bar|racks (bar′əks) *noun, singular or plural.*

barrel—**1.** A large wooden container with flat, circular ends and slightly curved sides. A barrel is held together by bands of metal at the top and bottom.   **2.** The tube of a gun, through which bullets are fired.
bar|rel (bar′əl), *noun, plural* **barrels.**
■ **over a barrel:** In a helpless state; forced to do as told: *They wanted to bat first, and it was their ball, so they had us* over a barrel.

barren—Unable to produce anything: *the* barren *desert; a* barren *tree.*
bar|ren (bar′ən) *adjective.*

barrette—A decorative clip that women use to hold their hair in place.
bar|rette (bə ret′) *noun, plural* **barrettes.**

barricade—Something set up to block the way: *The crowd knocked down the* barricades *and rushed up to the movie star. Noun.*
—To block the way with something: *The soldiers* barricaded *the road so the enemy could not use it. Verb.*
bar|ri|cade (bar′ə kād′) *noun, plural* **barricades;** *verb,* **barricaded, barricading.**
• Synonyms: **barrier, roadblock,** for *noun.*
  Antonyms: **entrance, entry,** for *noun.*

barrier—Something that stands in the way or that blocks progress: *His poor grades were a* barrier *that kept him from getting a job.*
bar|ri|er (bar′ē ər) *noun, plural* **barriers.**
• Synonyms: See Synonyms at **barricade.**
  Antonyms: See Antonyms at **barricade.**

barrio—**1.** A district of a town or a city in a Spanish-speaking country.   **2.** In the United States, a section of a city with a large Spanish-speaking population.
bar|ri|o (bahr′rē ō) *noun, plural* **barrios.**

barter—To exchange goods for other goods without using money: *The Indians* bartered *furs for guns with the pioneers. Verb.*
—The exchanging of goods without using money. *Noun.*
bar|ter (bahr′tər) *verb,* **bartered, bartering;** *noun.*
• Synonyms: **swap, trade,** for *verb.*

base¹—1. The part on which something stands; bottom: *The statue stood on a solid marble base.* 2. The main part of something: *This pudding has a milk base.* 3. One of the four corners of a baseball diamond. 4. A central place; headquarters: *The children made the garage their base.* 5. A chemical that will change red litmus paper to blue. A base combines with an acid to form a salt. *Noun.*
—To draw from; found: *They based the movie on the singer's life. Verb.*
base (bās) *noun, plural* **bases;** *verb,* **based, basing.**

■ **load the bases:** To have runners at first, second, and third bases at the same time in a baseball game.
● A word that sounds the same is **bass¹**.

base²—1. Mean or bad; not admirable or honorable: *Stealing from a friend is a base thing to do.* 2. Lower in quality or value than something else: *Silver is a precious metal, while iron is a base metal.*
base (bās) *adjective,* **baser, basest.**
● A word that sounds the same is **bass¹**.

baseball—1. A game played by two teams of nine players each, on a field with four bases placed in the shape of a diamond. The players take turns trying to hit a ball with a bat and to score runs by touching all the bases. Each team is allowed three outs in a turn at bat, and a turn for both teams makes an inning. The team that has the most runs at the end of nine or more innings wins the game. 2. The ball used to play the game.
base|ball (bās'bawl') *noun, plural* **baseballs.**

basement—The section of a building completely or partly below ground; cellar.
base|ment (bās'mənt) *noun, plural* **basements.**

basenji—A small dog with a smooth coat, pointed ears, and a curled tail. Originally bred in Africa, these dogs do not bark but do make a yelping sound.
ba|sen|ji (bə sen'jē) *noun, plural* **basenjis.**

bash—To hit something very hard: *I turned too quickly and bashed my elbow on the wall.*
bash (bash) *verb,* **bashed, bashing.**

bashful—Shy around other people: *The bashful girl hid behind the door when we came in.*
bash|ful (bash'fəl) *adjective.*

basic—Most important; most necessary: *Reading, writing, and arithmetic are basic school subjects.*
ba|sic (bā'sik) *adjective.*
● Synonyms: **essential, fundamental, primary**
Antonym: **trivial**

BASIC—A computer language used to introduce students to programming.
BA|SIC (bā'sik) *noun.*

Word History

BASIC is made up of the first letters of five words. It stands for **B**eginners **A**ll-purpose **S**ymbolic **I**nstruction **C**ode. It has this name because it is meant for beginning students, and because it uses mathematical symbols.

---

basically—In the most important way or ways: *basically a simple job; a basically good person.*
ba|si|cal|ly (bā'sik lē), *adverb.*

basin—1. A round dish that holds liquids, especially water. 2. An area that holds water: *The harbor basin is crowded with boats in the summer.* 3. The land that is drained by a river and its streams.
ba|sin (bā'sən) *noun, plural* **basins.**

basis—The part that something rests or stands on; foundation: *The basis for her poetry was her happy childhood.*
ba|sis (bā'sis) *noun, plural* **bases** (bā'sēz).

bask—To enjoy the warmth of something, or to enjoy something as if it were warmth: *basking in praise.*
bask (bask) *verb,* **basked, basking.**

basenji

a at	i if	oo look	ch chalk		⌈a in ago
ā ape	ī idle	ou out	ng sing		e in happen
ah calm	o odd	u ugly	sh ship	ə =	i in capital
aw all	ō oats	ū rule	th think		o in occur
e end	oi oil	ur turn	th their		⌊u in upon
ē easy			zh treasure		

basket—1. A container made of strips of wood, grass, or other material woven together: *an apple basket.* 2. A metal hoop and net used as a goal in basketball. 3. A score in basketball made by tossing the ball through this net.
bas|ket (bas′kit) *noun, plural* **baskets.**

basketball—1. A game played by two teams of five players each, on a court with a raised basket at each end. The players try to score by throwing a large inflated ball into the basket guarded by the opposing team. The team that scores the most points wins. 2. The ball used to play the game.
bas|ket|ball (bas′kit bawl′) *noun, plural* **basketballs.**

bas mitzvah—The ceremony that takes place when a Jewish girl turns 13. It celebrates her becoming an adult member of that religion.
bas mitz|vah (bahs mits′və) *noun, plural* **bas mitzvahs.**
● This phrase is also spelled **bath mitzvah** and **bat mitzvah.**

bass¹—1. The lowest male singing voice. 2. A man who has such a voice. 3. Any musical instrument with a range like that of such a voice.
bass (bās) *noun, plural* **basses.**
● A word that sounds the same is **base.**

bass²—A type of fish in North America that lives in rivers, lakes, and seas. Bass have spiny fins and are caught for food.
bass (bas) *noun, plural* **bass** or **basses.**

bass drum—A very large drum that makes a low, booming sound when struck.
bass drum (bās drum) *noun, plural* **bass drums.**
● See picture at **drum.**

basset hound—A short-legged hunting dog with a long body, a short coat, big drooping ears, and a wrinkled face. Originally bred in France, these dogs hunt by smell.
bas|set hound (bas′it hound) *noun, plural* **basset hounds.**

basset hound

bassoon—A musical instrument that has a long wooden tube and a curved metal pipe at one end. It is played by blowing into the pipe and makes a low sound.
bas|soon (bə sūn′) *noun, plural* **bassoons.**

bassoon

baste¹—To pour or brush melted butter or other liquid over food while it is roasting in order to keep the food moist or to flavor it: *The cook basted the chicken with a spicy sauce.*
baste (bāst) *verb,* **basted, basting.**

baste²—To sew something with large, loose stitches, usually to hold the cloth in place for final sewing: *Mother basted the hem of my new skirt.*
baste (bāst) *verb,* **basted, basting.**

bat¹—1. A wooden stick or club used to hit the ball in baseball or softball. 2. A turn to hit the ball: *He got a home run his first time at* bat. *Noun.*
—To hit the ball with a wooden stick or club: *I batted well today, and got four hits. Verb.*
bat (bat) *noun, plural* **bats;** *verb,* **batted, batting.**

bat²—A small, furry animal that has a mouselike body and wings of thin skin. Bats fly at night, and eat insects or fruit.
bat (bat) *noun, plural* **bats.**
■ **bats in the belfry:** Mental problems; craziness:

If you think I'll do your work, you have bats in the belfry.

blind as a bat: Unable to see well, or to see at all: *Without my glasses, I am* blind as a bat.

bat²

batch—A group of people or things: *a batch of cookies.*
bat|ch (bach) *noun, plural* **batches.**
• Synonyms: **bunch, lot, set**

bath—**1.** The washing of someone or something in water: *They gave the dog a bath in the yard.* **2.** The water used for washing: *The bath was filled with bubbles.* **3.** A room for washing: *a house with two* baths.
bath (bath) *noun, plural* **baths.**

bathe—**1.** To wash in water: *She bathed her dog in the yard.* **2.** To swim: *We bathed in the clear, cool lake.* **3.** To cover or surround as if with water: *Bright sunlight bathed the flowers in the garden.*
bathe (bāth) *verb,* **bathed, bathing.**

bathing suit—A garment worn for swimming.
bath|ing suit (ba′thing sūt) *noun, plural* **bathing suits.**

bath mitzvah—*See* bas mitzvah.
bath mitz|vah (bahth mits′və) *noun, plural* **bath mitzvahs.**

bathrobe—A long, loose garment worn before and after a bath or while relaxing.
bath|robe (bath′rōb′) *noun, plural* **bathrobes.**

bathroom—A room with a sink, a toilet, and sometimes a bathtub or shower.
bath|room (bath′rūm′ *or* bath′room′) *noun, plural* **bathrooms.**

bathtub—A large open container for taking a bath.
bath|tub (bath′tub′) *noun, plural* **bathtubs.**

bat mitzvah—*See* bas mitzvah.
bat mitz|vah (baht mits′və) *noun, plural* **bat mitzvahs.**

baton—**1.** A thin, light stick used by the leader of an orchestra or band: *The conductor raised his* baton *to begin the concert.* **2.** A metal rod that can be twirled and tossed in the air.
ba|ton (bə ton′) *noun, plural* **batons.**

battalion—A military unit made up of two or more companies or batteries. Two or more battalions make up a regiment.
ba|tal|ion (bə tal′yən) *noun, plural* **battalions.**

batter¹—To hit hard, over and over again; pound: *The angry man battered the door.*
bat|ter (bat′ər) *verb,* **battered, battering.**
• Synonyms: **beat, maul, pelt¹, thrash, whip**

batter²—Flour, liquids, and other ingredients mixed together for baking: *cake* batter.
bat|ter (bat′ər) *noun, plural* **batters.**

batter³—The person who tries to hit the ball in baseball or softball: *The next* batter *hit a home run.*
bat|ter (bat′ər) *noun, plural* **batters.**

battery—**1.** A device that uses chemicals to create electrical power: *My toy car needs two* batteries. **2.** A group of people or things that work together: *A battery of reporters waited to interview the visiting king.* **3.** A unit of artillery in the army: *All guns in the* battery *prepared to fire.*
bat|ter|y (bat′ər ē) *noun, plural* **batteries.**
• For **1,** see picture at **electromagnet.**

battle—A fight; struggle. *Noun.*
—To struggle or fight: *The two ships* battled *each other with booming guns. Verb.*
bat|tle (bat′əl) *noun, plural* **battles;** *verb,* **battled, battling.**
• Synonyms: **combat, conflict,** for *noun.*
Antonym: **peace,** for *noun.*

battle-ax or **battle-axe**—An ax with a wide, sharp edge, used in early times as a weapon.
bat|tle-ax or bat|tle-axe (bat′əl aks′) *noun, plural* **battle-axes.**

battlefield—The place where a fight happens.
bat|tle|field (bat′əl fēld′) *noun, plural* **battlefields.**

a at	i if	oo look	ch chalk		a in ago
ā ape	ī idle	ou out	ng sing		e in happen
ah calm	o odd	u ugly	sh ship	ə =	i in capital
aw all	ō oats	ū rule	th think		o in occur
e end	oi oil	ur turn	th their		u in upon
ē easy			zh treasure		

battlement—A low wall with openings, built on top of a fort or a tower. Soldiers stood behind the wall and shot through the openings. **bat|tle|ment** (bat′əl mənt) *noun, plural* **battlements**.

battlement

battleship—A ship with guns and armor, built for war. **bat|tle|ship** (bat′əl ship′) *noun, plural* **battleships**.

bawl—To shout or weep loudly: *The baby* bawled *after he fell down. Verb.*
—A loud shout or sound of weeping. *Noun.* **bawl** (bawl) *verb,* **bawled, bawling;** *noun, plural* **bawls**.
- **bawl out:** To scold loudly: *The neighbor* bawled out *the children for playing in his garden.*
- A word that sounds the same is **ball**.
- Synonyms: For *verb*, see **cry**.

bay[1]—A part of a lake or a sea that curves into the land. **bay** (bā) *noun, plural* **bays**.

bay[2]—The long, deep barking or howling of a dog. *Noun.*
—To bark or howl with long, deep sounds: *The hound was* baying *at the moon. Verb.* **bay** (bā) *noun, plural* **bays;** *verb,* **bayed, baying**.

bay[3]—Reddish-brown: *a* bay *horse.* **bay** (bā) *adjective.*

bayonet—A large knife that can be attached to the end of a rifle. It is used by soldiers for fighting. **bay|o|net** (bā′ə net′) *noun, plural* **bayonets**.

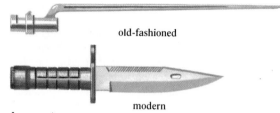
old-fashioned

modern

bayonet

bayou—A slow stream flowing through a marsh. The southern part of the United States has many bayous. **bay|ou** (bī′ū *or* bī′ō) *noun, plural* **bayous**.

bazaar—A sale of many kinds of things for a special reason: *Our class held a* bazaar *to raise money for the trip.* **ba|zaar** (bə zahr′) *noun, plural* **bazaars**.

B.C.—An abbreviation used when giving dates before the birth of Christ. 100 B.C. is one hundred years before the birth of Christ.

Language Fact

B.C. is an abbreviation for the words ''before Christ.'' It is used for dates before the birth of Christ. The abbreviation **A.D.** is used for dates after the birth of Christ. From 100 B.C. to A.D. 100 is 200 years.

---

be—**1.** To exist; live: *I remember when this problem began to* be. **2.** To happen; take place: *The first day of school will* be *next Wednesday.* **3.** To continue; remain: *We will* be *away on vacation for two weeks.* **4.** To have a certain quality; exist in a certain way: *How can I* be *happy when you are sick?* **5.** To stand for; equal: *Let the price of lemonade* be *25 cents.* **be** (bē) *verb,* **been, being**.
- Other words that sound the same are **B** and **bee**.

beach—The land along the edge of an ocean or lake. It is often covered with sand or pebbles. *Noun.*
—To pull up on the shore: *The sick whale had* beached *itself on the sand. Verb.* **beach** (bēch) *noun, plural* **beaches;** *verb,* **beached, beaching**.
- A word that sounds the same is **beech**.

beacon—A light or fire used to warn or guide: *The lighthouse* beacon *shone through the thick fog.* bea|con (bē′kən) *noun, plural* **beacons.**

bead—1. A small ball made of glass, wood, plastic, or some other material. It has a hole through it so that it can be strung on a thread with other beads to make a necklace. Beads are also sewn onto fabric as a decoration. 2. Any small, round thing, like a bubble or drop: *Beads of water formed on the outside of the glass. Noun.* —To decorate with small balls of glass, plastic, or the like. *Verb.*
bead (bēd) *noun, plural* **beads;** *verb,* **beaded, beading.**

beagle—A small dog with big, drooping ears and a curved tail. Originally bred in England, these dogs hunt rabbits by smell.
bea|gle (bē′gəl) *noun, plural* **beagles.**

beagle

beak—The pointed mouth of a bird.
beak (bēk) *noun, plural* **beaks.**

beam—1. A large, long piece of metal or wood that is used in building. 2. A ray of light: *A* beam *of sunlight broke through the clouds. Noun.* —1. To shine brightly: *Sunlight* beamed *through the clouds after the thunderstorm.* 2. To smile happily: *Dad* beamed *when he saw her good report card. Verb.*
beam (bēm) *noun, plural* **beams;** *verb,* **beamed, beaming.**

a at	i if	oo look	ch chalk		a in ago
ā ape	ī idle	ou out	ng sing		e in happen
ah calm	o odd	u ugly	sh ship	ə =	i in capital
aw all	ō oats	ū rule	th think		o in occur
e end	oi oil	ur turn	th their		u in upon
ē easy			zh treasure		

bean—1. A kind of round, narrow seed that is eaten as a vegetable. Sometimes the pods in which the seeds grow are eaten. 2. Any seed that is shaped like a bean: *coffee* beans.
bean (bēn) *noun, plural* **beans.**
■ **spill the beans:** To tell a secret: *He* spilled the beans *about the surprise party.*

beanbag—A small cloth bag filled with dry beans. Beanbags are thrown and caught as toys.
bean|bag (bēn′bag′) *noun, plural* **beanbags.**

beanstalk—The stem of any plant on which beans grow.
bean|stalk (bēn′stawk′) *noun, plural* **beanstalks.**

bear[1]—A large, heavy animal with a short tail and thick, shaggy fur.
bear (bār) *noun, plural* **bears.**
● A word that sounds the same is **bare.**

bear[2]—1. To hold up; support: *The skaters checked to see if the ice could* bear *their weight.* 2. To carry: *She* bore *the flag in the parade.* 3. To put up with: *I cannot* bear *the sound of fingernails scratching on a blackboard.* 4. To bring forth; give birth to: *a tree that* bears *fruit.*
bear (bār) *verb,* **bore, born** or **borne, bearing.**
● A word that sounds the same is **bare.**
● Synonyms: **abide, endure, stand, tolerate,** for **3.**

beard—1. The hair that grows on a man's face. 2. Something that looks like the hair on a man's face, such as the chin whiskers on a goat.
beard (bērd) *noun, plural* **beards.**

bearded collie—A large, long-haired herding dog with especially long hair around the mouth. Originally bred in Scotland, these dogs resemble Old English sheepdogs.
beard|ed col|lie (bērd′əd kol′ē) *noun, plural* **bearded collies.**

bearded collie

bearing—1. The way someone walks, acts, or stands: *She walked with the* bearing *of a dancer.* 2. A connection in thought or meaning: *The last sentence had no* bearing *on the rest of his report.* 3. A part of a machine that allows another part to move easily. 4. **bearings:** A sense of direction; knowledge of where one is or is going: *The fog caused the sailor to lose his* bearings *and turn the wrong way.*
bear|ing (bãr′ing) *noun, plural* **bearings.**

beast—1. Any four-footed animal: *The lion is the king of* beasts. 2. Any animal except a person: *The snow was so deep that neither man nor* beast *went outside.* 3. A cruel person: *He behaves like a* beast *when he is angry.*
beast (bēst) *noun, plural* **beasts.**

beat—1. To hit over and over again; pound: *Waves* beat *the shore.* 2. To flap; move up and down: *The bird* beat *its wings as it flew.* 3. To stir, mix, or whip quickly: *He* beat *the eggs.* 4. To win; defeat: *She* beat *her father at chess.* 5. To throb or thump: *She could hear and feel the drums* beating *as the parade marched by.* 6. To confuse or baffle: *It* beats *me how the monkey escaped from the cage. Verb.*
—1. A stroke or blow made over and over again: *the* beat *of the drum.* 2. A throb or thump: *the* beat *of the puppy's tail.* 3. The basic unit of time in music: *The audience clapped to the* beat *of the music.* 4. A regular round or route: *The police officer had a city* beat. *Noun.*
—Tired; exhausted: *She was* beat *after mowing the lawn. Adjective.*
beat (bēt) *verb,* **beat, beaten** or **beat, beating;** *noun, plural* **beats;** *adjective.*
■ **beat back:** To hold back or away: *The firefighters tried to* beat back *the flames.*
beat it: To go away: *He always told his little sister to* beat it *when his friends were around.*
beat up: To fight and win: *Our cat was* beaten up *by the tomcat across the street.*
● A word that sounds the same is **beet.**
● Synonyms: **batter**[1], **maul, pelt**[1], **thrash, whip,** for *verb* 1.

beaten[1]—1. Hit or mixed again and again: *The* beaten *egg whites were used for the pie.* 2. Worn out by constant use: *There was a* beaten *area under the swings where the grass would not grow.* 3. Defeated: *The* beaten *team looked sad. Adjective.*
beat|en (bē′tən) *adjective.*

beaten[2]—*See* **beat.**
beat|en (bēt′ən) *verb.*

beautiful—Very pleasant to see or hear: *a* beautiful *song.*
beau|ti|ful (byu′tə fəl) *adjective.*
● Synonyms: **gorgeous, lovely, pretty.** Antonyms: *See* Synonyms at **ugly.**

beauty—1. Something that makes a person or thing very pleasing to see or hear: *the* beauty *of a rainbow.* 2. A person or thing that is beautiful: *Her new scooter is a real* beauty!
beau|ty (byū′tē) *noun, plural* **beauties.**

beaver—An animal with soft, dark fur and a wide, flat tail. Beavers have long, strong front teeth that they use to chew through small trees. They use the branches to make dams and underwater dens.
bea|ver (bē′vər) *noun, plural* **beavers.**
■ **work like a beaver:** To work very hard: *He worked like a* beaver *to finish his science project on time.*

beaver

became—*See* **become.**
be|came (bi kam′) *verb.*

because—For the reason that; since: *We put the lights on* because *it was getting dark.*
be|cause (bi kawz′) *conjunction.*
■ **because of:** On account of: *School was closed* because of *the snowstorm.*

beckon—To signal someone by waving a hand or nodding the head: *Her friends* beckoned *her to join them.*
beck|on (bek′ən) *verb,* **beckoned, beckoning.**

become—1. To come to be; grow to be: *Caterpillars* become *butterflies*.   2. To look well on: *That red dress* becomes *her*.
be|come (bi **kum′**) *verb*, **became, become, becoming**.
 ■ **become of:** To happen to: *What has* become of *my roller skates?*

bed—1. Anything to sleep or rest on: *The hamster slept on a* bed *of cedar chips*.   2. A flat base on which something is put: *They put the swimming pool on a* bed *of sand*.   3. The ground at the bottom of a body of water: *The stream* bed *was very rocky*.   4. A piece of land used for growing plants: *a flower* bed. *Noun*.
—To provide a place for sleeping: *The farmer* bedded *the cows in the barn. Verb.*
bed (bed) *noun, plural* **beds**; *verb*, **bedded, bedding**.
 ■ **bed down:** To make a sleeping place for: *The cowboys* bedded down *around the campfire*.
 put to bed: to prepare for sleeping: *She put her child* to bed *at eight o'clock*.

bed bug—A small insect that is sometimes found in places where people sleep. Its bite is painful.
bed bug (bed bug) *noun, plural* **bed bugs**.

bedclothes—Sheets, blankets, and other coverings used on a bed.
bed|clothes (bed′klōz) *plural noun*.

bedding—1. Bedclothes used to make a bed, such as sheets, blankets, pillows, mattresses, or sleeping bags.   2. Something used to make a bed: *The pet mice used shredded newspaper as* bedding.
bed|ding (bed′ing) *noun, plural* **beddings**.

Bedlington terrier—A medium-sized dog that looks much like a lamb. It has a curly coat, long tasseled ears, and a slender body. These dogs were originally bred in England to fight badgers.
Bed|ling|ton ter|ri|er (bed′ling tən ter′ē ər) *noun, plural* **Bedlington terriers**.

bedraggled—Wet, dirty, and limp: *The dog looked* bedraggled *when he came in out of the rain*.
be|drag|gled (bi drag′əld) *adjective*.

Bedouin—A member of wandering tribes of Arabs who live in the deserts of Arabia, Syria, and northern Africa.
Bed|ou|in (bed′oo in) *noun, plural* **Bedouins**.

bedroom—A room for sleeping.
bed|room (bed′rŭm′ *or* bed′room′) *noun, plural* **bedrooms**.

bedspread—A cover that is placed over the blankets and pillows on a bed.
bed|spread (bed′spred′) *noun, plural* **bedspreads**.

bedtime—The hour at which one goes to bed: *Her* bedtime *is ten o'clock*.
bed|time (bed′tīm′) *noun, plural* **bedtimes**.

bee—1. An insect with a hairy body, four wings, and a stinger. Bees gather nectar and pollen from flowers to make honey. Some bees live in colonies, or hives.   2. A meeting for work or pleasure: *The group of women sewed and talked at the quilting* bee.
bee (bē) *noun, plural* **bees**.
 ■ **busy as a bee:** Extremely busy; busy all the time: *Since she is class president and editor of our newspaper, she has to stay* busy as a bee.
 ● Other words that sound the same are **B** and **be**.

beech—A tree with smooth, gray bark and shiny leaves. Its small, sweet nuts are good to eat.
beech (bēch) *noun, plural* **beeches**.
 ● A word that sounds the same is **beach**.

beef—Meat from a cow, steer, or bull that is used for food.   .
beef (bēf) *noun*.
 ● See Language Fact at **pork**.

a at	i if	oo look	ch chalk	⌈ a in ago
ā ape	ī idle	ou out	ng sing	e in happen
ah calm	o odd	u ugly	sh ship	ə = i in capital
aw all	ō oats	ū rule	th think	o in occur
e end	oi oil	ur turn	<u>th</u> their	⌊ u in upon
ē easy			zh treasure	

Bedlington terrier

beehive—1. A home for a colony of bees. 2. A very busy place: *The shopping mall was a beehive of activity during the sale.*
bee|hive (bē′hīv′) *noun, plural* **beehives.**

beehive (definition 1)

beeline—The shortest, straightest way between two places, like that of a bee flying to its hive: *The batter sent the baseball on a* beeline *over the fence.*
bee|line (bē′līn′) *noun, plural* **beelines.**
■ **make a beeline for:** To hurry straight toward: *She* made a beeline for *the swimming pool.*

been—*See* be.
been (bin) *verb.*
● A word that sounds the same is **bin.**

beer—An alcoholic drink.
beer (bēr) *noun, plural* **beers.**

beeswax—The yellow substance made by honeybees, which they use to build honeycombs.
bees|wax (bēz′waks′) *noun.*

beet—A plant whose long, thick roots and green leaves are eaten as a vegetable.
beet (bēt) *noun, plural* **beets.**
● A word that sounds the same is **beat.**

beetle—An insect with two hard wings that fold down over another pair of wings when the beetle is resting. Beetles have biting mouth parts and often eat plants.
bee|tle (bēt′əl) *noun, plural* **beetles.**

before—Earlier than; ahead of: *She bought some popcorn* before *the movie started. Preposition.*
—In front; ahead; already: *He had read that book* before. *Adverb.*
—1. Earlier than: *It began to rain* before *we got home.* 2. Sooner than; rather than: *I'd take the blame* before *I'd lie. Conjunction.*
be|fore (bi fawr′) *preposition, adverb, conjunction.*

beforehand—Ahead of time; in advance: *She knew about the surprise party* beforehand.
be|fore|hand (bi fawr′ hand′) *adverb.*

befriend—To act friendly toward; help: *He* befriended *the new boy in the neighborhood.*
be|friend (bi frend′) *verb,* **befriended, befriending.**

beg—To ask for: *The dog sat up and* begged *for a cookie.*
beg (beg) *verb,* **begged, begging.**
● Synonyms: **appeal, entreat, plead**

began—*See* begin.
be|gan (bi gan′) *verb.*

beggar—A person who lives by asking people for food, clothes, or money.
beg|gar (beg′ər) *noun, plural* **beggars.**

begin—1. To do the first part; start something: *We* began *to cook dinner.* 2. To start; come into being: *School* begins *on September 5th.*
be|gin (bi gin′) *verb,* **began, begun, beginning.**
● Synonyms: **commence, initiate,** for 2.
Antonyms: **end, finish, stop,** for 2.

beginner—A person who is doing something for the first time: *She took skiing lessons because she was a* beginner.
be|gin|ner (bi gin′ər) *noun, plural* **beginners.**

beet

beginning—1. The start of something: *Thursday is the* beginning *of summer vacation.* 2. The first part of something: *He came in late and missed the* beginning *of the movie.*
be|gin|ning (bi gin′ing) *noun, plural* **beginnings.**
 • Synonyms: **commencement, onset,** for **1.**
 Antonyms: **ending, finish,** for **1.**

begonia—A plant with large, beautiful flowers and leaves. It grows wild in tropical areas. People also grow them as houseplants.
be|go|nia (bi gōn′yə) *noun, plural* **begonias.**

begonia

begun—*See* **begin.**
be|gun (bi gun′) *verb.*

behave—1. To act or do: *The child* behaved *well during the long car ride.* 2. To do what is right: *Did you* behave *yourself at Grandma's?*
be|have (bi hāv′) *verb,* **behaved, behaving.**

behavior—A way of acting or behaving: *His* behavior *at the restaurant was terrible.*
be|hav|ior (bi hāv′yər) *noun, plural* **behaviors.**
 • Synonyms: **conduct, manner**

behead—To cut off the head of.
be|head (bi hed′) *verb,* **beheaded, beheading.**

behind—1. In back of: *There was a mirror* behind *the door.* 2. Helping; supporting: *Her friends were* behind *her efforts to be class president.* 3. Hidden by: *What were the real reasons* behind *his decision to quit the team?* 4. At a later time than; after: *They were an hour* behind *us in reaching the party.* 5. Not as good as: *We were* behind *by one point. Preposition.*
—1. At the back: *The cat jumped up on her from* behind. 2. Farther back: *Do not walk so fast or you will leave us* behind. 3. Late or slow: *Her watch was ten minutes* behind. *Adverb.*
be|hind (bi hind′) *preposition, adverb.*

behold—To look at; see: *The northern lights were beautiful to* behold. *Verb.*
—Look; take notice: *Behold! A shooting star streaked across the sky. Interjection.*
be|hold (bi hōld′) *verb,* **beheld, beholding;** *interjection.*

beige—A pale-brown color. *Noun.*
—Having a pale brown color: *a* beige *blouse. Adjective.*
beige (bāzh) *noun, adjective.*

being[1]—*See* **be.**
be|ing (bē′ing) *verb.*

being[2]—1. A person; living creature: *a human* being. 2. Life; existence: *to come into* being.
be|ing (bē′ing) *noun, plural* **beings.**

belfry—A tower on top of a church or other building in which a large bell or bells are hung.
bel|fry (bel′frē) *noun, plural* **belfries.**

Belgian horse—A very large, strong horse used for pulling heavy loads.
Bel|gian horse (bel′jən hawrse) *noun, plural* **Belgian horses.**

Belgian horse

a at	i if	oo look	ch chalk		a in ago
ā ape	ī idle	ou out	ng sing		e in happen
ah calm	o odd	u ugly	sh ship	ə =	i in capital
aw all	ō oats	ū rule	th think		o in occur
e end	oi oil	ur turn	th their		u in upon
ē easy			zh treasure		

Belgian Malinois

Belgian Malinois—A large herding dog with short hair and straight pointed ears. It is named for the town in Belgium where it was originally bred.
Bel|gian Mal|i|nois (bel′jən mal ə nwah′) *noun, plural* **Belgian Malinoises.**

Belgian sheepdog—A large herding dog with a long, straight, black coat and short pointed ears.
Bel|gian sheep|dog (bel′jən shēp′dawg) *noun, plural* **Belgian sheepdogs.**

Belgian Tervuren—A large herding dog with a long, straight, light-to-dark brown coat that is

Belgian Tervuren

black around the face, shoulders, and tail. It is named for the town in Belgium where it was originally bred.
Bel|gian Ter|vuren (bel′jən ter′vern) *noun, plural* **Belgian Tervurens.**

belief—1. An idea that a person thinks is true; opinion: *It is his* belief *that there is life on other planets.* 2. Faith; trust: *She had a* belief *that everything would work out.* 3. Religious faith: *Most children follow the* beliefs *of their parents.*
be|lief (bi lēf′) *noun, plural* **beliefs.**

believe—1. To think that something is true: *Do you* believe *in ghosts?* 2. To suppose; think: *I* believe *it is going to snow today.*
be|lieve (bi lēv′) *verb,* **believed, believing.**
■ **make believe:** To pretend: *My little brother likes to* make believe *that he is a scary monster.*

belittle—To treat as unimportant or minor; speak of without respect: *It was unkind of him to* belittle *her high grade by claiming the test was an easy one.*
be|lit|tle (bi lit′əl) *verb,* **belittled, belittling.**

bell—1. A hollow piece of metal that looks like an upside-down cup. It makes a musical sound when hit. 2. Anything that makes a ringing sound: *a door*bell.
bell (bel) *noun, plural* **bells.**
■ **bell the cat:** To do something that will prevent danger but that is dangerous to do: *We all agreed that someone should take the hornet nest from the tree, but no one was willing to* bell the cat *by doing it.*
ring a bell: To bring about recognition or memory: *Does her name* ring a bell?
saved by the bell: Rescued from a difficult situation by chance: *Unable to run another step, I was* saved by the bell *when a time out was called.*
with bells on: In one's finest clothes: *He was at his sister's high school graduation* with bells on.

belligerent—1. Ready to fight; hostile: *You are being* belligerent *when you talk back to your parents!* 2. At war; fighting: *Battles are fought between* belligerent *countries.*
bel|lig|er|ent (bə lij′ər ənt) *adjective.*

bellow—1. To roar; make a loud, low sound: *The cows* bellowed *with hunger.* 2. To yell loudly in anger or pain: *Dad* bellowed *when he hit his finger with the hammer. Verb.*
—A loud, deep roar. *Noun.*
bel|low (bel′ō) *verb,* **bellowed, bellowing;** *noun, plural* **bellows.**
● Synonyms: For *verb* 2, see **cry.**

bellows—A tool used to pump air at or into something.
bel|lows (bel′ōz) *plural noun.*

bellows

belly—1. The front part of the body, just below the chest; stomach; abdomen.   2. The underside of an animal's body.   3. A curved or bulging part of something: *the belly of a ship. Noun.*
—To bulge outward: *The ship's sails bellied in the wind. Verb.*
bel|ly (bel′ē) *noun, plural* **bellies;** *verb,* **bellied, bellying.**

belong—1. To have one's (or its) proper place: *The puzzle belongs in this box.*   2. To be owned by: *That watch belonged to my grandfather.*
3. To be a member of: *She belongs to a chess club.*
be|long (bi lawng′) *verb,* **belonged, belonging.**

beloved—Dear; loved very much: *his beloved daughter.*
be|lov|ed (bi luv′id *or* bi luvd′) *adjective.*

below—In, on, or to a lower place: *The flower pot fell off the window ledge to the street* below. *Adverb.*
—Lower than; under; underneath: *The subway ran* below *the city streets. Preposition.*
be|low (bi lō′) *adverb, preposition.*

belt—1. A strip of cloth, leather, or other material worn around a person's waist, usually to hold up clothing.   2. An area of a country: *the snow* belt; *the farm* belt.   3. An endless band that moves around two or more wheels or pulleys. It

transfers power or motion from one wheel or pulley to another: *The mechanic replaced the fan belt on our car's engine. Noun.*
—To hit very hard: *The batter* belted *the baseball out of the park. Verb.*
belt (belt) *noun, plural* **belts;** *verb,* **belted, belting.**
■ **below the belt:** Being very unfair: *Teasing in order to hurt other people's feelings is really hitting* below the belt.
belt out: To sing or yell very loudly: *The cheerleaders* belted out *the school song to encourage their team.*
tighten (one's) belt: To try to spend less money: *To save enough to buy a stereo, I really had to* tighten my belt.

bench—1. A long seat, usually made of wood or stone.   2. A long work table: *Dad keeps his tools on a* bench *in the garage.*   3. The judge in a courtroom: *The robber was brought before the* bench.   4. The place where team members sit during a game when they are not playing: *The player was kept on the* bench *because of an injury. Noun.*
—To keep out of a game: *The catcher was* benched *for arguing with the umpire. Verb.*
bench (bench) *noun, plural* **benches;** *verb,* **benched, benching.**

bend—1. To curve or make crooked: *The trees began to* bend *in the wind.*   2. To stoop or lean down: *She* bent *down to shake the little boy's hand. Verb.*
—A curve or turn: *a* bend *in the road. Noun.*
bend (bend) *verb,* **bent, bending;** *noun, plural* **bends.**
■ **the bends:** An illness suffered by divers who have gone too deep under water or who have come up to the surface too quickly.
bend over backwards: To make every effort: *She* bent over backwards *to please her teacher.*

beneath—1. Below; under; underneath: *The pirate buried his treasure* beneath *the rock.*
2. Unworthy of: *He is* beneath *my notice. Preposition.*
—In or to a lower place; below: *From the air, we could see the city* beneath. *Adverb.*
be|neath (bi nēth′) *preposition, adverb.*

beneficial—Helpful: *Exercise is* beneficial *to your health.*
ben|e|fi|cial (ben′ ə fish′əl) *adjective.*

benefit—Anything that helps a person or thing; advantage: *Daily practice is of great* benefit *when learning to play the piano. Noun.*
—To receive good; profit: *He could* benefit *from*

a at	i if	oo look	ch chalk		⌈ a in ago
ā ape	ī idle	ou out	ng sing		e in happen
ah calm	o odd	u ugly	sh ship	ə =	i in capital
aw all	ō oats	ū rule	th think		o in occur
e end	oi oil	ur turn	th their		⌊ u in upon
ē easy			zh treasure		

some extra help in mathematics. Verb.
ben|e|fit (ben′ə fit) *noun, plural* **benefits;** *verb,*
benefited, benefiting.

bent—*See* **bend.** *Verb.*
—**1.** Crooked or curved: *The key would not fit
into the lock because it was* bent.   **2.** Determined;
set on: *Even though it was raining, she was* bent
on riding her new bicycle. Adjective.
bent (bent) *verb, adjective.*

beret—A round, flat hat made of soft wool or
felt.
be|ret (bə rā′) *noun, plural* **berets.**

Bernese mountain dog—A large working
dog with a long, black coat and white markings
on the face, chest, feet, and tail. Originally bred
in Switzerland, these dogs were used to pull dog
carts.
Ber|nese moun|tain dog (bur nēz′ moun′tən
dawg *or* bur nēs′ mount′tən dawg) *noun, plural*
Bernese mountain dogs.

Bernese mountain dog

berry—A small, juicy fruit with many seeds.
Strawberries, raspberries, and blueberries are
berries.
ber|ry (ber′ē) *noun, plural* **berries.**
● A word that sounds the same is **bury.**

berth—**1.** A bed on a ship, train, or airplane.
2. A ship's place at a dock: *When all the sailors
were aboard, the ship left its* berth.
berth (burth) *noun, plural* **berths.**
● A word that sounds the same is **birth.**

beside—By the side of; next to; near; close to:
Her desk was beside *the window.*
be|side (bi sīd′) *preposition.*

■ **beside oneself:** Very upset: *He was* beside
himself *when his wallet was stolen.*

besides—**1.** In addition: *The television show
turned out to be boring;* besides, *she had
homework to do.*   **2.** Also: *I ate three more
cookies* besides. *Adverb.*
—In addition to; over and above: *Besides* our
*Girl Scout troop, there were fifty others at the
campout. Preposition.*
be|sides (bi sīdz′) *adverb, preposition.*

besiege—**1.** To surround and try to capture: *The
king's men* besieged *the castle.*   **2.** To crowd
around: *Fans rushed the field and* besieged *the
winning team.*
be|siege (bi sēj′) *verb,* **besieged, besieging.**

best—**1.** Of the finest quality; excellent; better
than any other: *She is the* best *swimmer on the
team.*   **2.** The most desirable: *Which is the* best
road to take?   **3.** Most; largest: *We had to wait
the* best *part of an hour. Adjective.*
—**1.** In the most excellent way; with the most
success: *Who plays the* best?   **2.** In or to the
highest degree: *I like this dress* best. *Adverb.*
—**1.** The most possible; utmost: *She did her* best
to get an A on the test.   **2.** The largest part: *His
baseball team won the* best *of seven games.
Noun.*
best (best) *adjective, adverb, noun.*
■ **all for the best:** Not as bad as it seems:
*Although she missed her old friends, moving to
a new town seemed* all for the best.
get the best of: To defeat someone or
something: *He refused to let the bad weather*
get the best of *him, and he went camping
anyway.*
make the best of: To try to make something
better than it was: *When the electricity went
off, the family* made the best of *it and ate by
candlelight.*

bet—**1.** A promise to pay someone an amount of
money or something else if the other person is
right and you are wrong. If you are right, he or
she pays you: *They made a* bet *about which team
would win the basketball game.*   **2.** The money
or thing promised: *We made the* bet *a bag of
marbles. Noun.*
—**1.** To promise to pay money or something else
to someone if you are wrong and he or she is
right: *He* bet *her that the black horse would win
the race.*   **2.** To risk; gamble: *to* bet *five
dollars.*   **3.** To be very sure: *I* bet *you can't
guess the answer to this riddle! Verb.*
bet (bet) *noun, plural* **bets;** *verb,* **bet** *or* **betted,
betting.**

betray—1. To help the enemy to: *The soldier betrayed his country by helping the enemy.* 2. To give away a secret: *She betrayed the plans for his surprise birthday party.*
be|tray (bi trā′) *verb,* **betrayed, betraying.**

better—1. Of a finer quality than another: *These are* better *gloves.* 2. More suitable: *He left for a* better *job.* 3. Improved in health: *She is feeling* better *today.* 4. Larger; greater: *We ate the* better *part of the cake. Adjective.*
—1. With greater success: *I'll try to do* better *next time.* 2. In or to a higher degree: *He likes soccer* better *than football. Adverb.*
—1. A person or thing that is better than another: *We bought the* better *of the two bicycles.* 2. A person who bets: *The* better *collected five dollars when her horse won the race. Noun.*
—To improve: *We can* better *our record if we practice more. Verb.*
bet|ter (bet′ər) *adjective; adverb; noun, plural* **betters** for 2; *verb,* **bettered, bettering.**

■ **better** (oneself): To improve a person's job or life: *He took a computer class at summer school to* better *himself.*
betters: People who are older or wiser than someone: *She listened to her* betters *when deciding what courses to take.*
for better or worse: Whether good or bad things happen: *When two people marry, they promise to love each other* for better or worse.
get the better of: To win over someone or something: *The three little pigs* got the better of *the big bad wolf.*
go (someone) **one better:** To do more than someone else has done; exceed the performance of another or others: *After I washed the dishes, she* went *me* one better *by mopping the kitchen floor.*
had better: Should: *I* had better *go home because it is almost suppertime.*
think better of: To think over and change one's mind about: *He decided to go skating, but* thought better of *it when he saw the thin ice.*

between—1. In the space or time that separates two things: *He sat* between *his parents at the movies.* 2. About; more or less: *The gorilla is* between *ten and twelve years old.* 3. From one to the other; connecting: *We hung the hammock* between *the two trees.* 4. Having to do with: *This secret is* between *friends.* 5. One or the other of: *She had to choose* between *the blue jacket and the red one.* 6. Altogether: *We had ten dollars* between *us to buy a birthday present for Dad. Preposition.*
—In the space or time that separates two things: *The baker put two layers of cake on the plate with some chocolate pudding* between. *Adverb.*
be|tween (bi twēn′) *preposition, adverb.*

Language Fact

Between and **among** are often used incorrectly. **Between** should be used when only two people or things are mentioned: *I couldn't choose* between *the apple and the orange.* **Among** is used when more than two people or things are mentioned: *She divided the books* among *the three children.*

Many people say "between you and I." Careful writers and speakers always use "between you and me."

---

beverage—A liquid for drinking. Milk, coffee, and fruit juice are beverages.
bev|er|age (bev′ər ij) *noun, plural* **beverages.**

beware—Be careful of; watch out for: Beware *of thin ice if you go skating.*
be|ware (bi wār′) *verb.*

bewilder—To confuse completely; puzzle: *The directions were so difficult that they* bewildered *her.*
be|wil|der (bi wil′dər) *verb,* **bewildered, bewildering.**

bewitch—1. To put a magic spell on: *The fairy godmother* bewitched *a pumpkin and turned it into a beautiful coach.* 2. To charm; delight: *The baby's smile* bewitched *his grandparents.*
be|witch (bi wich′) *verb,* **bewitched, bewitching.**
● Synonyms: **enchant,** for 1; **fascinate,** for 2.

beyond—1. On or to the far side of: *The lake is just* beyond *those trees.* 2. Past; later than: *The fireworks ended well* beyond *10 P.M.* 3. More than: *The price of the roller skates was* beyond *what she could pay.* 4. Not able to be understood: *How to bake a cake is* beyond *me.* 5. Besides; in addition to: *He did not do any yard work* beyond *what Dad had asked. Preposition.*
—Farther away: *The river flowed to the ocean* beyond. *Adverb.*
be|yond (bi yond′) *preposition, adverb.*

a at	i if	oo look	ch chalk		⌈ a in ago
ā ape	ī idle	ou out	ng sing		e in happen
ah calm	o odd	u ugly	sh ship	ə =	i in capital
aw all	ō oats	ū rule	th think		o in occur
e end	oi oil	ur turn	th their		⌊ u in upon
ē easy			zh treasure		

bi-—A prefix that means "two." A bicycle has two wheels. A biplane has two sets of wings.

Bible—1. A book of religious writings. The Christian Bible is the Old Testament and the New Testament. The Jewish Bible is the Old Testament. 2. **bible:** Any book that is accepted as an authority: *The Boy Scout Handbook was his bible when he went camping.*
Bi|ble (bī′bəl) *noun, plural* **Bibles.**

Biblical or **biblical**—Found in or having to do with the Bible. *There is a Biblical story about a man who is swallowed by a whale and lives.*
Bib|li|cal (bib′lə kəl) *adjective.*

bibliography—A list of books: *a bibliography of mystery books.*
bib|li|og|ra|phy (bib′lē og′rə fē) *noun, plural* **bibliographies.**

biceps—The large muscle in the front of the upper arm. It is used to bend the arm.
bi|ceps (bī′seps) *noun, plural* **biceps.**

bichon frise—A small dog with a thick, white curly coat, drooping ears, and a tail that curls over the back. The breed was first developed in Spain.
bi|chon fri|se (bē′shawn fri zā′) *noun, plural* **bichons frises.**

bicker—To argue noisily about something that is not very important: *The children bickered about whose turn it was on the swing.*
bick|er (bik′ər) *verb,* **bickered, bickering.**

bicycle—A light vehicle a person rides. A bicycle has two wheels, one behind the other, that are attached to a metal frame. There is a seat for the rider, a pair of handlebars for steering, and two foot pedals that turn the wheels.
bi|cy|cle (bī′sə kəl *or* bī′sik′əl) *noun, plural* **bicycles.**

bid—1. To tell someone what to do; order: *The queen will bid the knight to kneel.* 2. To give a greeting to: *Her father tucked her in and bid her good night.* 3. To offer a sum of money, usually at an auction: *She bid ten dollars for the painting. Verb.*
—An offer to pay a sum of money: *His bid of ten dollars for the painting was accepted. Noun.*
bid (bid) *verb,* **bid** or **bade, bidden** or **bid, bidding;** *noun, plural* **bids.**

bidden—*See* **bid.**
bid|den (bid′ən) *verb.*

bidding—1. An order; command: *The soldiers followed the king's bidding.* 2. An offer to pay a certain price for something: *The bidding went to $100 for the rare comic book.*
bid|ding (bid′ing) *noun, plural* **biddings.**

big—1. Large; great in amount or size: *a big grizzly bear; a big crowd of people.* 2. Important: *His return home was a big event.*
big (big) *adjective,* **bigger, biggest.**
• Synonyms: **colossal, enormous, gigantic, great, huge, large, massive, tremendous,** for **1.**
Antonyms: For **1,** see Synonyms at **small.**

bighorn—A large wild sheep that lives in mountainous regions. It is named for its large, curving horns.
big|horn (big′hawrn′) *noun, plural* **bighorns** or **bighorn.**

bighorn

bike—A shortened form of **bicycle** or **motorcycle.** *Noun.*
—To ride a bicycle or a motorcycle. *Verb.*
bike (bīk) *noun, plural* **bikes;** *verb,* **biked, biking.**

bilingual—1. Able to speak and understand two languages: *a bilingual* teacher.   2. Containing or written in two languages: *a bilingual* dictionary. **bi|lin|gual (bī ling′gwəl)** *adjective.*

bill¹—1. A statement, usually written, of money owed for something that was bought, for a service, or for work that was done: *a telephone* bill.   2. A piece of paper money: *Grandpa gave me a five dollar* bill.   3. A written or printed public notice, such as a large poster advertising something: *The* bill *told about the circus coming to town.*   4. A proposed law: *The legislature voted on the* bill *to control water pollution. Noun.*   5. A printed or written statement or list of things. *The* Bill *of Rights is a list of the rights of the citizens of the United States.*
—To present with a bill: *The dentist will* bill *him for filling his tooth. Verb.*
bill (bil) *noun, plural* **bills;** *verb,* **billed, billing.**

bill²—The hard part of a bird's mouth; beak.
bill (bil) *noun, plural* **bills.**

billboard—A very large outdoor sign for announcements and advertisements.
bill|board (bil′bawrd′) *noun, plural* **billboards.**

billiards—A game played with three small, hard balls on a large table that has raised, padded edges. The balls are hit with a long, thin stick called a cue.
bil|liards (bil′yərdz) *noun.*

billion—One thousand millions; 1,000,000,000. *Noun.*
—Made up of one thousand millions: *a billion stars. Adjective.*
bil|lion (bil′yən) *noun, plural* **billions;** *adjective.*

billow—A large, rolling wave of something: Billows *of fog rolled in from the sea. Noun.*
—To bulge or swell out in billows: *The strong wind* billowed *the curtains into the room. Verb.*
bil|low (bil′ō) *noun, plural* **billows;** *verb,* **billowed, billowing.**

bin—A box or enclosed place for storing things: *He put the potatoes in the vegetable* bin.
bin (bin) *noun, plural* **bins.**
• A word that sounds the same is **been.**

binary system—A way of writing numbers using only the figures 0 and 1. These two binary digits can be used in combinations to stand for any amount. The binary system is often used in computers.
bi|na|ry sys|tem (bī′nər ē sis′təm) *noun.*

bind—1. To tie or hold together; fasten: *to* bind *hair into a ponytail.*   2. To cause to stick together: *Glue is used to* bind *things together.*   3. To fasten sheets of paper between covers; put a cover on a book: *I* bind *my book reports.*
bind (bīnd) *verb,* **bound, binding.**
■ **to get into a bind:** To have a problem that is hard to solve: *She got into a bind when she bought more candy than she could pay for.*
• Synonyms: **attach, connect,** for **1.**

Word History

Binoculars comes from two Latin words meaning "two at a time" and "eyes." Binoculars are used by looking into two small telescopes with both eyes at the same time.

---

binoculars—Two small telescopes that are attached side by side so that a person can use both eyes at the same time to look at distant things. Binoculars make objects appear closer and larger.
bi|noc|u|lars (bə nok′yə lərz) *plural noun.*

bio-—A prefix that means "life" or "living things."

Word Power

You can understand the meanings of many words that begin with **bio-,** if you add the meaning of the prefix to the meaning of the rest of the word.
   bioactive: acting on living things
   biochemistry: the science of chemicals in
      living things
   bioelectricity: electricity produced by life

---

biodegradable—That can be broken down, especially by the action of bacteria: *a* biodegradable *garbage bag.*
bi|o|de|grad|a|ble (bī′ō di grā′də bəl) *adjective.*

biography—A true story of someone's life written by another person. *We read a biography of the president.*
bi|og|ra|phy (bī og′rə fē) *noun, plural* **biographies.**

biologist—A person who works or studies in the field of biology.
bi|ol|o|gist (bī ol′ə jist) *noun, plural* **biologists.**

a at	i if	oo look	ch chalk		a in ago
ā ape	ī idle	ou out	ng sing		e in happen
ah calm	o odd	u ugly	sh ship	ə =	i in capital
aw all	ō oats	ū rule	th think		o in occur
e end	oi oil	ur turn	th their		u in upon
ē easy			zh treasure		

biology—The science that studies living things; the study of plants and animals and how they live and grow.
bi|ol|o|gy (bī ol′ə je) *noun.*

birch—A hardwood tree with smooth bark that can be peeled off in strips.
birch (burch) *noun, plural* **birches.**

bird—A feathered animal that has wings and a beak. Birds walk on two legs, and most can fly. Birds have backbones, are warm-blooded, and lay eggs.
bird (burd) *noun, plural* **birds.**
■ **eat like a bird:** To eat a very small amount: *It worries us when our grandmother eats like a bird.*

Birman

Birman—A long-haired, large cat with a long body, short legs, and round ears. These cats were originally bred in Burma, where they are believed to be sacred animals.
Bir|man (bur′mən) *noun, plural* **Birmans.**

birth—1. The act of being born; the act of coming into life: *a baby's* birth.   2. The start of something: *the* birth *of a plan.*
birth (burth) *noun, plural* **births.**
• A word that sounds the same is **berth.**

birthday—1. The anniversary of the day on which a person was born: *her fifth* birthday.
2. The day on which a person is born or something begins: *July 4, 1776, was the* birthday *of the United States.*
birth|day (burth′dā′) *noun, plural* **birthdays.**

birthmark—A spot on a person's skin that is present when he or she is born.
birth|mark (burth′mahrk′) *noun, plural* **birthmarks.**

birthplace—Where a person is born.
birth|place (burth′plās′) *noun, plural* **birthplaces.**

birthstone—A gem that stands for the month of birth. Each month has a different gem. Wearing one's birthstone is supposed to bring good luck.
birth|stone (burth′stōn′) *noun, plural* **birthstones.**

biscuit—A small cake or rounded roll made from baked dough.
bis|cuit (bis′kit) *noun, plural* **biscuits.**

bisect—To cut or divide into two pieces: *A yellow line* bisects *the road for two-way traffic.*
bi|sect (bī′sekt) *verb,* **bisected, bisecting.**

bishop—1. A high-ranking member of the clergy.
2. A playing piece in the game of chess that can move only diagonally.
bish|op (bish′əp) *noun, plural* **bishops.**

bison—A big animal with a large hump and short, curved horns; buffalo. A bison is a North American wild ox.
bi|son (bī′sən *or* bī′zən) *noun, plural* **bison.**

bison

bit¹—1. A small amount: *I only want a* bit *of gravy.*   2. A little while: *I'll be with you in a* bit.
bit (bit) *noun, plural* **bits.**
■ **bit by bit:** A little at a time: *They finished the job* bit by bit.
do (one's) **bit:** To do one's share of a job or activity: *I did* my bit *by clearing the table.*

bit²—The smallest unit of information in a computer.
bit (bit) *noun, plural* **bits.**

Word History

Bit² was created by taking the first two letters from *binary* (as in *binary system*) and the last letter from *digit.*

bit³—*See* **bite.**
  bit (bit) *verb.*

bit⁴—1. The part of a drill that makes holes in wood and other materials.   2. The metal part of a bridle that is put in a horse's mouth.
  bit (bit) *noun, plural* **bits.**
  ■ **champ at the bit:** To be eager: *He's* champing at the bit *waiting for his turn.*

bit⁴ (definition 1)

bite—1. To cut into something with the teeth: *She* bit *into the meat.*   2. To wound with teeth, fangs, or a stinger: *Snakes* bite *their prey.*   3. To make something sting or smart: *The cold wind will* bite *your ears.*   4. To cut: *The tight band* bit *into my skin.*   5. To grab bait: *The fish are* biting *today.* *Verb.*
  —1. A cutting into something with the teeth: *I took a* bite *of the apple.*   2. An amount of food eaten at one time: *Try a* bite *of this apple.*   3. A wound made by biting or stinging: *a dog* bite.
  4. A sting: *the* bite *of the wind.*   5. A cutting into something: *The elastic's* bite *pinched my skin. Noun.*
  bite (bīt) *verb,* **bit, bitten, biting;** *noun, plural* **bites.**
  ■ **bite off more than (one) can chew:** To try to do too much: *When it comes to work, he always* bites off more than *he can chew.*
    bite the hand that feeds (one): To hurt someone who has been good to you: *He's the kind of person who will* bite the hand that feeds *him.*
  ● A word that sounds the same is **byte.**

a at	i if	oo look	ch chalk	⌈ a in ago
ã ape	ī idle	ou out	ng sing	e in happen
ah calm	o odd	u ugly	sh ship	ə = i in capital
aw all	ō oats	ū rule	th think	o in occur
e end	oi oil	ur turn	<u>th</u> their	⌊ u in upon
ē easy			zh treasure	

bitten—*See* **bite.**
  bit|ten (bit′ən) *verb.*

bitter—1. Having a sharp or bad taste: *a* bitter *fruit.*   2. Painful; biting: *We walked quickly in the* bitter *wind.*   3. Having strong anger or hatred: *The two boys are* bitter *enemies.*
  bit|ter (bit′ər) *adjective.*

bittern—A wading bird that lives in marshes. It is a kind of heron.
  bit|tern (bit′ərn) *noun, plural* **bitterns.**

bitterroot—A small plant with pink or white flowers and roots that can be eaten. It is the state flower of Montana.
  bit|ter|root (bit′ər rūt′ *or* bit′ər root′) *noun, plural* **bitterroots.**

bittersweet—A plant with white or colored flowers and poisonous berries. *Noun.*
  —1. Having a mix of sweet and bitter tastes.
  2. Being both painful and pleasant at the same time: *Their meeting at their aunt's funeral was* bittersweet. *Adjective.*
  bit|ter|sweet (bit′ər swēt′) *noun, plural* **bittersweets;** *adjective.*

black—1. Having the darkest color.   2. Dark; with no light: *The midnight sky was* black.   3. Having to do with people with dark skin. *Adjective.*
  —1. The darkest color; the opposite of white.
  2. A member of one of the dark-skinned races. *Noun.*
  black (blak) *adjective,* **blacker, blackest;** *noun, plural* **blacks.**

black-and-blue—Having the colors of a bruise: *Her knee is* black-and-blue *from the fall.*
  black-and-blue (blak′en blū′) *adjective.*

black and tan coonhound—A large hunting dog with a short black and tan coat and long, drooping ears. Originally bred in the United States, these dogs hunt by smell.
  black and tan coon|hound (blak and tan kūn′hound′) *noun, plural* **black and tan coonhounds.**

black and tan coonhound

blackberry—A juicy, sweet fruit. Blackberries are very dark in color and grow on vines or bushes.
black|ber|ry (blak′ber′ē) *noun, plural* **blackberries.**

blackbird—One of various kinds of birds that are mostly black in color.
black|bird (blak′burd′) *noun, plural* **blackbirds.**

blackboard—A flat sheet of material, such as slate, used for writing on with chalk.
black|board (blak′bawrd′) *noun, plural* **blackboards.**

blacken—To make or become very dark: *She used a crayon to* blacken *the white paper.*
black|en (blak′ən) *verb,* **blackened, blackening.**

black-eyed Susan—A yellow flower similar to a daisy but having a black center. The black-eyed Susan is the state flower of Maryland.
black-eyed Su|san (blak′īd sū′zən) *noun, plural* **black-eyed Susans.**

black-eyed Susan

blackhead—A tiny skin blemish with dirt in its center.
black|head (blak′hed′) *noun, plural* **blackheads.**

blackmail—The act of trying to get something from someone by threatening to reveal secrets about him or her. *Noun.*
—To try to get something from someone in such a manner: *To get her money, they* blackmailed *the rich woman with secrets from her past. Verb.*
black|mail (blak′māl′) *noun; verb,* **blackmailed, blackmailing.**

blackout—The state of having no power because of an electrical failure.
black|out (blak′out′) *noun, plural* **blackouts.**

blacksmith—Someone who makes horseshoes and other things out of iron. The iron is heated and then hammered into a desired shape.
black|smith (blak′smith′) *noun, plural* **blacksmiths.**

blacktop—A hard surface of tar or asphalt. Blacktop is used for driveways, parking lots, and roads. *Noun.*
—To make a surface of tar or asphalt. *Verb.*
black|top (blak′top′) *noun; verb,* **blacktopped, blacktopping.**

bladder—A small, thin bag in the body that holds urine received from the kidneys.
blad|der (blad′ər) *noun, plural* **bladders.**

blade—**1.** A sharp edge used for cutting or slicing. Scissors, knives, and razors all have blades.   **2.** A leaf of grass.   **3.** A flat, wide section of something: *a propeller* blade.
blade (blād) *noun, plural* **blades.**

blame—**1.** To consider someone at fault: *You cannot* blame *me for being upset after I lost my wallet.*   **2.** To consider someone or something responsible for a mistake or accident: *They* blamed *the fire on the dry weather. Verb.*
—The responsibility for a mistake or accident: *He took the* blame *for the torn page. Noun.*
blame (blām) *verb,* **blamed, blaming;** *noun.*
● Synonyms: **condemn, criticize,** for *verb* **1.**
Antonym: **praise,** for *verb* **1.**

blank—**1.** An empty space left to be completed: *Fill in the* blanks.   **2.** A form or paper with such spaces: *an application* blank.   **3.** A gun cartridge with no bullet. *Noun.*
—**1.** Having no writing or marks: *You can draw on the* blank *paper.*   **2.** With some parts left to be completed: *a* blank *line.*   **3.** Without expression or emotion: *His face went* blank *when she asked the difficult question. Adjective.*
blank (blangk) *noun, plural* **blanks;** *adjective,* **blanker, blankest.**
■ **blank out:** To lose all awareness: *The boy* blanked out *when he fainted.*
draw a blank: **1.** To have no thought or answer.   **2.** To have an unsuccessful result: *He* drew a blank *in his search for the sweater.*

blanket—**1.** A cloth cover used to keep warm.   **2.** A covering: *There was a* blanket *of dust on the table. Noun.*
—To cover something: *Leaves* blanket *the grass in the fall. Verb.*

blan|ket (blang′kit) *noun, plural* **blankets;** *verb,* **blanketed, blanketing.**

blare—To make a sudden, loud sound: *The foghorn* blared *through the mist. Verb.*
—A loud, sudden sound: *a siren's* blare. *Noun.*
blare (blãr) *verb,* **blared, blaring;** *noun, plural* **blares.**

blast—1. A sudden gust of wind, air, or heat. 2. The loud sound of a horn or whistle. 3. An explosion. *Noun.*
—1. To blow up something with an explosive: *They* blasted *the tunnel with dynamite.* 2. To do damage to; ruin: *Her bad behavior* blasted *her chances of being able to go to the movie. Verb.*
blast (blast) *noun, plural* **blasts;** *verb,* **blasted, blasting.**
■ **at full blast:** At top speed: *They ran at full* blast *down the hallway.*

blastoff—A launch of a spacecraft.
blast|off (blast′awf′) *noun, plural* **blastoffs.**

blaze[1]—1. A large, bright fire: *The house was lost in a* blaze *of fire.* 2. A bright color or light: *flowers a* blaze *of color; the* blaze *of the car's headlights.* 3. A sudden burst of feeling: *He started yelling in a* blaze *of anger. Noun.*
—1. To burn brightly: *The bonfire* blazed *in the woods.* 2. To display bright light or color: *The sun* blazed *red.* 3. To show deep feeling: *Her face* blazed *with excitement. Verb.*
blaze (blãz) *noun, plural* **blazes;** *verb,* **blazed, blazing.**
■ **blaze away:** To fire a gun or cannon without stopping: *The soldiers* blazed away *at the enemy.*

Word History

Blaze[1] comes from an old English word meaning ''a torch'' or ''a bright fire.'' **Blaze[2]** comes from an old German word meaning ''a white mark.'' The old English word and the old German word both came from a very old German word meaning ''a bright thing'' or ''a white thing.''

---

blaze[2]—A cut made on a tree or post in order to mark a trail or boundary. *Noun.*

a at	i if	oo look	ch chalk		a in ago
ā ape	ī idle	ou out	ng sing		e in happen
ah calm	o odd	u ugly	sh ship	ə =	i in capital
aw all	ō oats	ū rule	th think		o in occur
e end	oi oil	ur turn	th their		u in upon
ē easy			zh treasure		

—To make such a cut: Blaze *the path so we will know where you went. Verb.*
blaze (blãz) *noun, plural* **blazes;** *verb,* **blazed, blazing.**

blazer—A jacket of a special color, sometimes used as part of a uniform.
blaz|er (blā′zər) *noun, plural* **blazers.**

bleach—To remove color; make white: *We* bleached *the cloth to remove the spots. Verb.*
—A chemical used to remove color from something. *Noun.*
bleach (blēch) *verb,* **bleached, bleaching;** *noun, plural* **bleaches.**

bleachers—Rows of benches used by people watching an event. The rows are usually arranged one above another.
bleach|ers (blē′chərz) *plural noun.*

bleak—1. Harsh; gloomy: *a* bleak *novel about poor people.* 2. Cold and windy; raw: *the* bleak *hills bare of trees;* bleak *and rainy afternoons.*
bleak (blēk) *adjective,* **bleaker, bleakest.**

bleat—The sound made by a calf, sheep, or goat. *Noun.*
—To make such a sound: *I heard the sheep* bleating *in the field. Verb.*
bleat (blēt) *noun, plural* **bleats;** *verb,* **bleated, bleating.**

bled—*See* **bleed.**
bled (bled) *verb.*

bleed—1. To lose blood from the body: *The girl's finger* bled *when she cut it.* 2. To lose sap from a tree: *Maple* bled *from a cut in the tree.* 3. To feel sorrow or pity: *My heart* bleeds *for the poor.*
bleed (blēd) *verb,* **bled, bleeding.**

blemish—1. A flaw or mark on the skin. 2. Any flaw or lack of perfection: *Here is a* blemish *on the floor where the table fell over. Noun.*
—To damage the perfection of something: *The one low grade* blemished *her nearly perfect report card. Verb.*
blem|ish (blem′ish) *noun, plural* **blemishes;** *verb,* **blemished, blemishing.**

blend—1. To mix or combine thoroughly: *to* blend *milk, flour, sugar, and eggs to make cake.* 2. To overlap with each other slightly: *The colors of the rainbow* blend. *Verb.*
—1. A complete mixture: *The dough is a* blend *of flour and water.* 2. A slight overlapping with each other: *the* blend *of sea and sky at the horizon. Noun.*
blend (blend) *verb,* **blended, blending;** *noun, plural* **blends.**
● Synonyms: **compound, merge,** for *verb* **1.**
   Antonyms: **divide, part, separate,** for *verb* **1.**

bless—1. To make holy by a prayer or religious ceremony: *The priest* blessed *the new baby.*
2. To ask for God's help: Bless *my aunt who is ill.*   3. To give good fortune: *Our lives have been* blessed *with happy memories.*
bless (bles) *verb,* **blessed, blessing.**

blessing—1. A prayer of thanks; a religious ceremony that asks for God's favor: *Mother gave the* blessing *at Thanksgiving dinner; the* blessing *of the newborn child.*   2. Anything that brings good fortune or happiness: *Winning the contest was a* blessing *for that poor family.*
3. Approval: *The parents gave their* blessing *to the couple who wished to marry.*
bless|ing (bles′ing) *noun, plural* **blessings.**

blew—*See* **blow.**
blew (blū) *verb.*
• A word that sounds the same is **blue.**

blimp—An aircraft that is filled with a gas that is lighter than air, but that does not have a stiff frame. It carries passengers or equipment.
blimp (blimp) *noun, plural* **blimps.**
• See picture and Language Fact at **airship.**

Word History

Blimp comes from the phrase ''type-B limp.'' Because these airships do not have a stiff frame, early models were called ''limps.'' One kind was named ''type B.'' The B limp was soon known as a blimp.

---

blind—1. Unable to see.   2. Hidden or hard to see: *The car suddenly appeared from a* blind *bend in the road.*   3. Without thought or knowledge: *We had to make a* blind *choice because we had no time to think.*   4. Having only one exit: *a* blind *alley.*   5. Using instruments only, not sight: *The pilot made a* blind *landing in the storm. Adjective.*
—1. To cause to be without sight: *The robbers were* blinded *by the lights.*   2. To cause to lose clear thought: *He was* blinded *by love. Verb.*
—A window covering with thin, narrow strips of wood, plastic, or other material that can be raised and lowered. *Noun.*
blind (blīnd) *adjective,* **blinder, blindest;** *verb,* **blinded, blinding;** *noun, plural* **blinds.**

blindfold—To cover someone's eyes with a narrow piece of cloth: *The children were* blindfolded *to play ''pin the tail on the donkey.'' Verb.*
—Something placed over the eyes to prevent someone from seeing. *Noun.*

blind|fold (blīnd′fold′) *verb,* **blindfolded, blindfolding;** *noun, plural* **blindfolds.**

blink—1. To open and close the eyes rapidly: *He* blinked *at the bright light.*   2. To flash rapidly on and off: *The store sign* blinks *at night.*
blink (blingk) *verb,* **blinked, blinking.**
■ **on the blink:** Not working right; out of order: *My phone is* on the blink, *so I can't use it.*
• Synonyms: **flicker[1], glimmer, twinkle,** for *verb* 2.

bliss—Complete happiness: *Having all the cake I can eat fills me with* bliss.
bliss (blis) *noun.*
• Synonyms: **delight, joy, pleasure**
Antonyms: **misery, sorrow, woe**

blister—1. A raised sore on the skin that is filled with a watery liquid. Blisters are often a result of a burn or constant rubbing.   2. Any small swelling or bubble: *Tiny* blisters *formed on the newly painted chair. Noun.*
—To form a bubble or swelling: *My sunburned skin* blistered. *Verb.*
blis|ter (blis′tər) *noun, plural* **blisters;** *verb,* **blistered, blistering.**

blizzard—A very heavy snowstorm with strong winds.
bliz|zard (bliz′ərd) *noun, plural* **blizzards.**

bloat—To cause something to swell; expand: *Our stomachs were* bloated *after drinking too much water.*
bloat (blōt) *verb,* **bloated, bloating.**

blob—A small, shapeless mass: *He dropped a* blob *of ice cream.*
blob (blob) *noun, plural* **blobs.**

block—1. A solid piece of wood or other material: *building* blocks.   2. An area in a city or town that is enclosed by four streets.   3. A length of street that forms one side of such an area: *The store is four* blocks *from home.*
4. Anything that gets in the way or hinders: *a mental* block *against remembering that name.*
5. A group of things that are similar: *a* block *of movie tickets. Noun.*
—1. To get in the way; hinder: *That tall man is* blocking *my view. Verb.*
block (blok) *noun, plural* **blocks;** *verb,* **blocked, blocking.**
■ **knock (someone's) block off:** To hit or punch someone again and again: *She made me so mad I wanted to* knock *her* block off.

blockade—Something that shuts off or prevents passage: *The police set up a* blockade *with their cars. Noun.*

—To stop passage; close: *The army* blockaded *the borders to keep the enemy out. Verb.*
block|ade (blo′kād′) *noun, plural* **blockades;** *verb,* **blockaded, blockading.**

blockhouse—1. A small, sturdy wooden building with holes in its sides for firing weapons. Blockhouses were used in forts. 2. A strong building on the site of a rocket launch, used to protect observers.
block|house (blok′hous′) *noun, plural* **blockhouses.**

blockhouse (definition 1)

blond or **blonde**—Light yellow in color. *Adjective.*
—A person with hair that is light yellow. *Noun.*
blond or **blonde** (blond) *adjective,* **blonder, blondest;** *noun, plural* **blonds** or **blondes.**

blood—1. The red liquid that flows throughout the bodies of humans and many animals. Blood is circulated by the heart. It carries oxygen and wastes through the veins and arteries. 2. Family relationship; kinship: *All these cousins are of the same* blood.
blood (blud) *noun.*
■ **bad blood:** Unfriendly feelings between two or more people; hatred: *There has always been* bad blood *between our families.*
in cold blood: Without feeling or emotion: *She committed the crime* in cold blood.

blood bank—A place where blood is kept until it is needed for transfusions.
blood bank (blud bangk) *noun, plural* **blood banks.**

bloodhound—A large hunting dog with a short

bloodhound

coat, long drooping ears, and a wrinkled face. Originally bred in the Middle East, these dogs hunt by smell. They are often used as police dogs and as trackers.
blood|hound (blud′hound′) *noun, plural* **bloodhounds.**

bloodshed—The heavy loss of blood; the taking of life: *Wars cause* bloodshed.
blood|shed (blud′shed′) *noun.*

bloodstream—The blood flowing through the body.
blood|stream (blud′strēm′) *noun, plural* **bloodstreams.**

bloodthirsty—Eager to injure or kill; cruel: *The* bloodthirsty *criminals attacked the town.*
blood|thirst|y (blud′thurs′tē) *adjective.*
● Synonyms: **brutal, violent**
Antonyms: **gentle, kind[1], tender**

bloom—1. To flower; blossom: *The buds* bloomed *on the rose bush.* 2. To be in a time of great health, beauty, or happiness: *The students* bloomed *in high school. Verb.*
—1. A time of flowering: *In May the roses are in* bloom. 2. A time of great health, beauty, or happiness: *in the* bloom *of her life. Noun.*
bloom (blūm) *verb,* **bloomed, blooming;** *noun, plural* **blooms.**

blossom—1. A flower of a fruit tree: *cherry* blossoms. 2. The time of flowering: *The orange trees are in* blossom. *Noun.*
—1. To flower; bloom. 2. To be in a time of growth: *Her artistic talents* blossomed *in the painting class. Verb.*
blos|som (blos′əm) *noun, plural* **blossoms;** *verb,* **blossomed, blossoming.**

blot—1. A drop or stain: *an ink* blot. 2. A flaw or blemish: *A bad grade would be a* blot *on my record.*

a at	i if	oo look	ch chalk		a in ago
ā ape	ī idle	ou out	ng sing		e in happen
ah calm	o odd	u ugly	sh ship	ə =	i in capital
aw all	ō oats	ū rule	th think		o in occur
e end	oi oil	ur turn	th their		u in upon
ē easy			zh treasure		

boot—A foot covering usually made of leather, plastic, or rubber. It usually extends to the ankles or higher. *Noun.*
—To kick something: *She* booted *the ball into the goal. Verb.*
boot (būt) *noun, plural* **boots;** *verb,* **booted, booting.**

booth—1. A small place used for showing or selling things: *We were the first ones at the ticket* booth *when the theater opened.* 2. A small place, usually enclosed for privacy: *a phone* booth.
booth (būth) *noun, plural* **booths.**

border—1. An edge, side, or boundary: *The Valentine's Day card had red hearts along its* border. 2. A boundary between countries, states, provinces, or similar areas. *Noun.*
—1. To give an edge to: *She* bordered *the pillow with lace.* 2. To touch or lie alongside of: *Canada* borders *the United States. Verb.*
bor|der (bawrʹdər) *noun, plural* **borders;** *verb,* **bordered, bordering.**
• A word that sounds the same is **boarder.**

borderline—Something that divides: *The* borderline *between the two countries was drawn in red on the map. Noun.*
—Very slight; barely present: *a borderline* fever. *Adjective.*
bor|der|line (bawrʹdər līnʹ) *noun, plural,* **borderlines;** *adjective.*

border terrier

border terrier—A small hunting dog with a flat head, short folded ears, and a stiff outer coat. Originally bred in Scotland and England, these dogs were used to hunt foxes.

bor|der ter|ri|er (bawrʹdər terʹē ər) *noun, plural* **border terriers.**

bore[1]—1. To cut into with a twisting movement of a tool: *The wall was so thin that the drill* bored *all the way through it.* 2. To dig; make a hole in: *The gopher* bored *a tunnel in the ground.*
bore (bawr) *verb,* **bored, boring.**
• A word that sounds the same is **boar.**

bore[2]—To make tired or restless by being uninteresting: *His long speech* bored *the audience. Verb.*
—Someone or something that is not interesting: *Sitting around and doing nothing is a* bore. *Noun.*
bore (bawr) *verb,* **bored, boring;** *noun, plural* **bores.**
• A word that sounds the same is **boar.**

bore[3]—*See* **bear.**
bore (bawr) *verb.*

boredom—A state of feeling no interest: Boredom *caused him to fall asleep during the television show.*
bore|dom (bawrʹdəm) *noun.*

born—1. Brought into life: *The calf* born *during the storm still clings to its mother.* 2. Naturally talented: *Your child must be a* born *musician to play the piano so well. Adjective.*
—*See* **bear**[2]. *Verb.*
born (bawrn) *adjective, verb.*
• A word that sounds the same is **borne.**

borne—*See* **bear**[2].
borne (bawrn) *verb.*
• A word that sounds the same is **born.**

borough—1. Any one of the five sections of New York City that have governments of their own in addition to the city government. Manhattan and Brooklyn are two of these. 2. Any one of several sections of Alaska that are like counties in other states of the United States.
bor|ough (burʹō) *noun, plural* **boroughs.**
• Words that sound the same are **burro** and **burrow.**

borrow—1. To use something for a while that belongs to someone else: *She* borrowed *her mother's hat for the play.* 2. To get from something else: *He* borrowed *the idea for the skit from a story he had read.*
bor|row (borʹō *or* bawrʹō) *verb,* **borrowed, borrowing.**
■ **borrow trouble:** To be upset about something before it is really a problem: *Worrying if you will like your teacher, before you know who your teacher will be, is just* borrowing trouble.

borzoi—A tall, slim dog that hunts by sight. It was originally bred in Russia to hunt wolves. *Borzoi* is Russian for "swift."
bor|zoi (bawr′zoi) *noun, plural* **borzois.**
• Another name for this dog is **Russian wolfhound.**

borzoi

bosom—The chest; breast. *Noun.*
—Beloved; close: *They were* bosom *buddies and went everywhere together. Adjective.*
bos|om (booz′əm) *noun, plural* **bosoms;** *adjective.*

boss—Someone who is in charge of others. *Noun.*
—To direct others; take charge; order: *His older brother tried to* boss *him around. Verb.*
boss (baws) *noun, plural* **bosses;** *verb,* **bossed, bossing.**

Boston terrier—A small dog with short hair, a square head, pointed ears, and a short tail. These dogs were first bred in Boston as pets.
Bos|ton ter|ri|er (baws′tən ter′ē ər) *noun, plural* **Boston terriers.**

botany—The study of plants and how and where they grow.
bot|a|ny (bot′ə nē) *noun.*

both—Being two together: Both *signs said the same thing in different languages. Adjective.*
—Two things taken together: Both *of you are correct. Pronoun.*
—A word used to show that two things are to be taken together or are equal: *She was* both *happy and surprised to see us. Conjunction.*
both (bōth) *adjective, pronoun, conjunction.*

bother—1. To disturb or upset: *It really* bothers *me when my sister wears my clothes without asking.* 2. To take the trouble to do something: *Did you* bother *to pack a lunch for the trip? Verb*
—Something that is troublesome or annoying: *It is such a* bother *to have to wear a tie for the class picture. Noun.*
both|er (both′ər) *verb,* **bothered, bothering;** *noun, plural* **bothers.**
• Synonyms: **aggravate, annoy, provoke,** for *verb* **1.**
Antonyms: **calm, lull, soothe,** for *verb* **1.**

bottle—A glass or plastic container that holds liquids. *Noun.*
—To put into bottles: *The juice was* bottled *just after it was squeezed from the oranges. Verb.*
bot|tle (bot′əl) *noun, plural* **bottles;** *verb,* **bottled, bottling.**

bottom—1. The lowest or deepest part of something: *Very few people have ever gone to the* bottom *of this canyon.* 2. The foundation or base: *The* bottom *of the lamp is wood.* 3. The land under a body of water: *I could touch the* bottom *of the pond with my feet.* 4. The center or core of something: *The police hoped to get to the* bottom *of the mystery. Noun.*
—Lowest or deepest: *She started at the* bottom *step and climbed up. Adjective.*
bot|tom (bot′əm) *noun, plural* **bottoms;** *adjective.*

bough—A tree limb.
bough (bou) *noun, plural* **boughs.**
• Words that sound the same are **bow[1]** and **bow[3].**

bought—*See* **buy.**
bought (bawt) *verb.*

boulder—A large rock.
boul|der (bōl′dər) *noun, plural* **boulders.**

boulevard—A wide street or avenue, often lined with trees.
boul|e|vard (bool′ə vahrd′) *noun, plural* **boulevards.** Abbreviation: blvd.

bounce—1. To spring back, up, or away after hitting something: *The ball* bounced *down the stairs.* 2. To cause to spring: *She* bounced *the baby on her knee. Verb.*
—An act of springing: *The ball took two* bounces. *Noun.*
bounce (bouns) *verb,* **bounced, bouncing;** *noun, plural* **bounces.**
■ **bounce back:** To make a new start: *After not*

a at	i if	oo look	ch chalk		a in ago
ā ape	ī idle	ou out	ng sing		e in happen
ah calm	o odd	u ugly	sh ship	ə =	i in capital
aw all	ō oats	ū rule	th think		o in occur
e end	oi oil	ur turn	th their		u in upon
ē easy			zh treasure		

succeeding, the girl bounced back *and tried again.*

bound¹—1. Tied up: *The boxes were* bound *with rope.* 2. Required; obligated: *She was* bound *by her promise to finish the job.* 3. Most likely; certain: *The food is* bound *to spoil if it is not kept cold.*
bound (bound) *adjective.*

bound²—1. To spring back after hitting something: *The tennis ball* bounded *off the racket.* 2. To jump; leap: *The deer* bounded *across the stream. Verb.*
—A long bounce or leap: *With one* bound *he went over the fence. Noun.*
bound (bound) *verb,* **bounded, bounding;** *noun, plural* **bounds.**

bound³—The border of something; boundary: *The* bounds *of his property were marked with a fence. Noun.*
—To make boundaries; limit: *The playing field was* bounded *by white lines. Verb.*
bound (bound) *noun, plural* **bounds;** *verb,* **bounded, bounding.**

bound⁴—Heading for: *We are* bound *for the lake to cool off.*
bound (bound) *adjective.*

boundary—The edge of something, especially a piece of property: *The* boundary *of our yard is marked with a hedge.*
bound|a|ry (boun′dər ē) *noun, plural* **boundaries.**
● Synonyms: **border, limit**

bouquet—Flowers bunched together, usually for carrying: *The bride carried a* bouquet *of roses.*
bou|quet (bō kā′ *or* bū kā′) *noun, plural* **bouquets.**

bout—1. A contest of skill or strength: *The* bout *between the wrestlers ended in a tie.* 2. A period; attack: *a* bout *of illness.*
bout (bout) *noun, plural* **bouts.**

Bouvier des Flandres—A large, powerful dog with short ears, a short tail, a stiff coat, and long hair around the mouth. Originally bred in Belgium, these dogs are used as guard dogs.
Bou|vier des Flan|dres (bū vyā′ dā flahn′drə) *noun, plural* **Bouviers des Flandres.**

bow¹—1. To bend the head or body forward in order to show respect: *to* bow *the head in prayer; to* bow *before the king.* 2. To surrender; give in: *The boys* bowed *to the wishes of their older sister. Verb.*
—A bending forward of the head or upper body. *Noun.*

bow (bou) *verb,* **bowed, bowing;** *noun, plural* **bows.**
■ **bow out:** To leave; get out of something, such as an agreement: *The girl* bowed out *of the game.*
● A word that sounds the same is **bough.**

bow²—1. A weapon for shooting arrows. It is made of bent wood, metal, or spun glass with a string stretched between its ends. 2. A long stick with horsehairs attached between both ends that is used to play some stringed musical instruments. 3. A knot with loops in it: *a hair* bow; *a* bow *tie. Noun.*
bow (bō) *noun, plural* **bows.**

bow³—The front end of a ship or boat.
bow (bou) *noun, plural* **bows.**
● A word that sounds the same is **bough.**

bowels—1. The lower part of the digestive system, through which food wastes are passed out of the body; intestines. 2. The deepest or innermost part of something: *Volcanoes rise from the* bowels *of the earth.*
bow|els (bou′əlz) *plural noun.*

bowl¹—1. A rounded container or dish: *Every morning he has a* bowl *of cereal with milk.* 2. Something, such as a sports arena, that is shaped like such a container.
bowl (bōl) *noun, plural* **bowls.**
● A word that sounds the same is **boll.**

bowl²—To play a game in which a ball is rolled down an alley to knock down wooden pins set up at the other end.
bowl (bōl) *verb,* **bowled, bowling.**
● A word that sounds the same is **boll.**

bowlegged—Having legs that curve away from each other and then come together at the feet, like a bow.
bow|leg|ged (bō′leg′id) *adjective.*

bowling—A game in which a ball is rolled down an alley to knock down wooden pins set up at the other end.
bowl|ing (bō′ling) *noun.*

box¹—1. A square or rectangular container whose sides or top opens. 2. A closed-in compartment: *My father has* box *seats for the baseball game. Noun.*
—To put into such a container: *We* boxed *our toys for the movers. Verb.*
box (boks) *noun, plural* **boxes;** *verb,* **boxed, boxing.**

box²—1. To hit with the fists, as in the sport of boxing: *The two boys* boxed *for fun.* 2. To hit with the hand open; slap: *She pretended to* box *him on his head. Verb.*

—A slap with the hand: *I was so mad I wanted to give him a* box *on the ear. Noun.*
box (boks) *verb,* **boxed, boxing;** *noun, plural* **boxes.**

boxcar—An enclosed railroad car with large sliding doors. It is used to carry goods: *The freight train's* boxcars *carried crates of fruit.*
box|car (boks′kahr′) *noun, plural* **boxcars.**

boxer—1. Someone who participates in the sport of fighting with one's fists.   **2.** A medium-sized dog with a short, smooth coat, pointed ears, and a square face. Originally bred in Germany, these dogs are strong and powerful and are often used as guard dogs.
box|er (bok′sər) *noun, plural* **boxers.**

boxer (definition 2)

boxing—A sport in which two people with padded gloves fight each other in a roped-in area.
box|ing (bok′sing) *noun.*

boy—A term used for a male human being from the time he is born until he is about eighteen.
boy (boi) *noun, plural* **boys.**
  • A word that sounds the same is **buoy.**

boycott—To refuse to buy or to use the products or the services of a country, business, or person so as to show displeasure: *The town* boycotted *the store because its prices were too high. Verb.*
—The act of refusing to buy or use certain products or services.
boy|cott (boi′kot) *verb,* **boycotted, boycotting;** *noun, plural* **boycotts.**

Word History

Boycott comes from a man's name: Charles G. Boycott. During the 1800's, he demanded such high rents that people refused to have anything to do with him. When other people acted this way, later on in other places, they called it boycotting.

Boy Scouts—An organization for boys that teaches survival skills and how to be helpful to others.
Boy Scouts (boi skouts) *noun.*

Word History

The **Boy Scouts** were started in 1907 by Robert Baden-Powell of Great Britain. In 1909, a boy scout helped William D. Boyce through a London fog. In 1910, Boyce helped create the Boy Scouts of America. Today, almost 5 million people belong to the Boy Scouts of America, and over 10 million in other countries.

brace—1. Something that holds parts together or in place.   **2.** The handle of a drill.   **3.** A pair of birds.   **4.** Braces: Metal wires put on the teeth to straighten them. *Noun.*
—1. To hold things together or support them: Brace *the shelf against the wall.*   **2.** To get ready for a surprise or shock: *He* braced *himself for the long roller coaster drop. Verb.*
brace (brās) *noun, plural* **braces;** *verb,* **braced, bracing.**

bracelet—A piece of jewelry that is worn around the wrist.
brace|let (brās′lit) *noun, plural* **bracelets.**

bracket—1. A piece of wood or metal that is attached to a wall to hold up shelves.   **2.** Either of two symbols that look like this [ ] and are used to enclose numbers or words.   **3.** A group or category: *the age* bracket *of 10 to 15 years. Noun.*

a at	i if	oo look	ch chalk	⌐a in ago
ā ape	ī idle	ou out	ng sing	e in happen
ah calm	o odd	u ugly	sh ship	ə = ⎸ i in capital
aw all	ō oats	ū rule	th think	o in occur
e end	oi oil	ur turn	<u>th</u> their	⌊u in upon
ē easy			zh treasure	

—**1.** To enclose numbers or words in these symbols [ ]. **2.** To group people or things in a certain category. *Verb.*
brack|et (brak′it) *noun, plural* **brackets;** *verb,* **bracketed, bracketing.**

brag—To speak too proudly about what one has or does; boast.
brag (brag) *verb,* **bragged, bragging.**

braid—A band that is made by weaving together three or more parts of hair, cloth, or other material. *Noun.*
—To weave together three or more parts of hair, cloth, or other material. *Verb.*
braid (brād) *noun, plural* **braids;** *verb,* **braided, braiding.**

Braille or **braille**—A system of writing and printing used by blind people. Symbols for the letters of the alphabet are made by raised dots. Blind people read Braille by moving their fingers over the dots.
Braille or **braille** (brāl) *noun.*

Word History

Braille is named after the man who invented it, Louis Braille. He was a 15-year-old blind student when he developed the dot system of reading and writing in 1824.

brain—**1.** The soft mass of nerve cells and fibers inside the skulls of people and animals. The brain controls the movements of the body and allows us to think, learn, and remember.
2. brains: Intelligence: *That scientist has* brains. *Noun.*
—To give a hard hit on the head: *She* brained *the burglar with a bottle. Verb.*
brain (brān) *noun, plural* **brains;** *verb,* **brained, braining.**
■ **pick the brains of:** To get a lot of useful information from someone: *I picked the brains of my brother to learn all that he knew about cars.*
rack (one's) **brains:** To try hard to remember something: *She racked her brains but couldn't remember his name.*

brake—The part of a car, bicycle, or other machine that rubs against the wheels to slow it down or make it stop. *Noun.*
—To slow or stop a car, bicycle, or other machine. *Verb.*
brake (brāk) *noun, plural* **brakes;** *verb,* **braked, braking.**
● A word that sounds the same is **break.**

bramble—A thorny bush or vine.
bram|ble (bram′bəl) *noun, plural* **brambles.**

bran—The broken outer shell of wheat and other grains.
bran (bran) *noun.*

branch—**1.** A part of a plant that grows out from the trunk or stem. **2.** Anything that is attached to something larger: *A branch of their family lives in a neighboring town. Noun.*
—To divide like the limbs of a tree: *The highway* branches *into two roads. Verb.*
branch (branch) *noun, plural* **branches;** *verb,* **branched, branching.**
● Synonyms: **bough, limb,** for **1.**

brand—**1.** A certain kind or make of something: *a brand of film.* **2.** A mark that is burned on the skin of an animal to show who the owner is. **3.** A mark of shame or disgrace. *Noun.*
—**1.** To mark an animal with the owner's name. **2.** To label as shameful or disgraceful: *She was branded a liar. Verb.*
brand (brand) *noun, plural* **brands;** *verb,* **branded, branding.**

brand-new—Unused; totally new: *Mother traded in her used car for a brand-new one.*
brand-new (brand′nū′ *or* brand′nyū′) *adjective.*

brass—**1.** A yellowish metal that is made from copper and zinc. Brass is used to make candlesticks, musical instruments, and other things. **2.** Any of the musical instruments made of metal, such as the trumpet, trombone, or French horn. **3.** The section of the orchestra containing these instruments.
brass (bras) *noun, plural* **brasses.**

brat—A child who behaves badly.
brat (brat) *noun, plural* **brats.**

brave—Not afraid; without fear: *Adjective.*
—To face danger or pain without fear: *They* braved *the storm to find the lost dog. Verb.*
—A North American Indian warrior. *Noun.*
brave (brāv) *adjective,* **braver, bravest;** *verb,* **braved, braving;** *noun, plural* **braves.**
● Synonyms: **adventurous, bold, courageous, daring, fearless**
Antonyms: **afraid, fearful, timid**

bravery—The facing of danger or pain without fear; courage: *His acts of* bravery *during the war won him a medal.*
brav|er|y (brā′vər ē) *noun.*

brawl—A noisy, uncontrolled fight. *Noun.*
—To fight in a noisy, uncontrolled way. *Verb.*
brawl (brawl) *noun, plural* **brawls;** *verb,* **brawled, brawling.**

brawny—Strong; sturdy: *a brawny lumberjack.*
brawn|y (**braw′nē**) *adjective,* **brawnier, brawniest.**
- Synonyms: **muscular, robust**

bray—The loud, sharp sound that a donkey makes. *Noun.*
—To make a sound like a donkey. *Verb.*
bray (**brā**) *noun, plural* **brays;** *verb,* **brayed, braying.**

bread—1. A food that is made from flour mixed with milk or water and then baked in an oven.
2. The food and other things a person needs to live: *She works hard to earn her daily* bread.
bread (**bred**) *noun, plural* **breads.**
- **break bread:** To share a meal: *We invited our friends over to* break bread *with us.*
- A word that sounds the same is **bred.**

break—1. To separate forcefully into pieces: *I broke my piggy bank to get the money out.*
2. To become damaged; get ruined: *The plate will* break *if you drop it.* 3. To fail to live up to: *to* break *a promise.* 4. To change or stop: *to* break *a bad habit.* 5. To force one's way: *to* break *out of jail.* 6. To lessen the effect of: *She put out her arms to* break *her fall.* 7. To tame; teach to obey: *My uncle* breaks *horses for a living. Verb.*
—1. A forceful separation; split; crack: *a bone* break. 2. A rest period: *a coffee* break. 3. An escape: *The prison* break *worried us.* 4. A lucky or unexpected happening: *The students got a lucky* break *when the teacher was absent the day of the test. Noun.*
break (**brāk**) *verb,* **broke** or **broken, breaking;** *noun, plural* **breaks.**
- **break the ice:** To get acquainted with someone: *He* broke the ice *by saying hello to the stranger.*
  break the news: To tell someone something important: *His mother* broke the news *that the family was moving to a new city.*
- A word that sounds the same is **brake.**
- Synonyms: **crack, fracture, shatter, smash,** for *verb* 2.

breakdown—A failure to work properly: *The car had a* breakdown.
break|down (**brāk′doun′**) *noun, plural* **breakdowns.**

breaker—A wave that turns into foam when it reaches the beach or rocks.
break|er (**brā′kər**) *noun, plural* **breakers.**

breakfast—A meal usually eaten in the morning; the first meal of the day.
break|fast (**brek′fəst**) *noun, plural* **breakfasts.**

breakthrough—A useful discovery; a solution to a problem: *The doctors hope for a* breakthrough *in the search for a cure.*
break|through (**brāk′thrū′**) *noun, plural* **breakthroughs.**

breast—1. The part of the body between the neck and the stomach. 2. A gland in females that gives milk.
breast (**brest**) *noun, plural* **breasts.**
- **make a clean breast of:** To confess; tell the truth: *She made a clean breast of her misbehavior.*

breastbone—The flat, thin bone in the front of the chest. The breastbone is attached to the ribs.
breast|bone (**brest′bōn′**) *noun, plural* **breastbones.**

breaststroke—A way of swimming in which the swimmer lies face down in the water and moves the arms forward together and then to the sides and back while the legs make a frog kick.
breast|stroke (**brest′strōk′**) *noun, plural* **breaststrokes.**

breath—1. Air pulled into and pushed out of the lungs. 2. A small movement of air; breeze: *Open the windows for a* breath *of cool air.*
breath (**breth**) *noun, plural* **breaths.**
- **catch (one's) breath:** To rest: *I ran so fast that I had to* catch *my* breath.
  take (one's) breath away: To thrill; stun: *The beautiful sunset took our* breath away.
  under (one's) breath or **below (one's) breath:** In a whisper: *Talk* under *your* breath *so he won't hear you.*

breathe—1. To pull air into the lungs and then push it out: *You* breathe *faster when you run.*
2. To say; utter: *I won't* breathe *a word about your surprise party.*
breathe (**brēth**) *verb,* **breathed, breathing.**
- **breathe easy** or **breathe freely:** To feel relief: *I can* breathe easy *now that the test is over.*

breathless—1. Out of breath; winded; panting: *She was* breathless *after dancing.* 2. Unable to breathe freely because one is excited or afraid: *He was* breathless *with excitement when he saw the baseball star.*
breathless (**breth′lis**) *adjective.*

breathtaking—1. Exciting or full of action: *a* breathtaking *ride on the roller coaster.*

a at	i if	oo look	ch chalk		⌈ a in ago
ā ape	ī idle	ou out	ng sing		e in happen
ah calm	o odd	u ugly	sh ship	ə =	i in capital
aw all	ō oats	ū rule	th think		o in occur
e end	oi oil	ur turn	th their		⌊ u in upon
ē easy			zh treasure		

2. Beautiful: *The view of the mountains was* breathtaking.
breath|tak|ing (breth′tā′king) *adjective.*

bred—*See* **breed.**
bred (bred) *verb.*
• A word that sounds the same is **bread.**

breed—1. To raise plants or animals: *to breed show dogs.* 2. To give birth to; produce: *Rabbits* breed *families rapidly.*
breed (brēd) *verb,* **bred, breeding.**

breeder—1. A person who raises animals. 2. An animal that produces young.
breed|er (brē′dər) *noun, plural* **breeders.**

breeding—The manner in which a person is brought up: *Your good* breeding *shows in the kind way you treat people.*
breed|ing (brē′ding) *noun.*

breeze—A light, gentle wind: *We enjoyed the cool* breeze. *Noun.*
—To move quickly and easily: *We breezed through the audition and were hired. Verb.*
breeze (brēz) *noun, plural* **breezes;** *verb,* **breezed, breezing.**
■ **in a breeze:** With very little effort; easily: *He finished the test* in a breeze.
shoot the breeze: To spend time pleasantly in conversation: *We took a break from work and shot the breeze.*

brew—1. To make by soaking, boiling, or mixing: *to brew tea.* 2. To make beer. 3. To form: *Dark clouds are* brewing. 4. To plot; cause to happen: *When things are going well, expect him to* brew *some trouble. Verb.*
—A drink made by soaking, boiling, or mixing. *Noun.*
brew (brū) *verb,* **brewed, brewing;** *noun, plural* **brews.**

briar—*See* **brier.**
bri|ar (brī′ər) *noun, plural* **briars.**

briard—A large, tall dog with long hair, short ears, and a long body and tail. This dog was originally bred in France to herd and guard sheep.
bri|ard (brē′ahrd) *noun, plural* **briards.**

bribe—Money or a gift given to someone, to get him or her to do something that is wrong or that he or she does not want to do. *Noun.*
—To give a gift to someone, to get him or her to do something: *My sister tried to* bribe *me with candy to do her work. Verb.*
bribe (brīb) *noun, plural* **bribes;** *verb,* **bribed, bribing.**

Word History

Bribe comes from a French word meaning ''bread given to a beggar.'' Today, a bribe is still a kind of gift, but now it is a bad or illegal gift.

brick—A dried or baked block of clay used for building structures like walls and houses.
brick (brik) *noun, plural* **bricks.**

bridal—Having to do with a bride or a wedding: *a* bridal *gown.*
brid|al (brī′dəl) *adjective.*
• A word that sounds the same is **bridle.**

bride—A woman who has just married or who is about to be married.
bride (brīd) *noun, plural* **brides.**

bridegroom—A man who has just married or who is about to be married.
bride|groom (brīd′grüm′) *noun, plural* **bridegrooms.**

bridesmaid—A woman who is a special helper to the bride before and during a wedding.
brides|maid (brīdz′mād′) *noun, plural* **bridesmaids.**

bridge—1. A structure built over water, a road, or a valley so that people can easily get from one side to the other. 2. The bony part of someone's nose, just between the eyes. 3. A platform on a ship's deck. It is the place where the officer in command steers the ship. *Noun.*

briard

—To build a structure over water, a road, or a valley: *to bridge the river. Verb.*
bridge (brij) *noun, plural* **bridges;** *verb,* **bridged, bridging.**
■ **cross that bridge when** (one) **comes to it:** To act on a problem when it happens. *She decided to wait and cross that bridge when she came to it.*

bridle—A device that fits over a horse's head and is used to guide the animal. *Noun.*
—**1.** To put such a device on something: *We bridled the horses before we went riding.* **2.** To control something: *I bridle my anger by counting to ten. Verb.*
bri|dle (brī'dəl) *noun, plural* **bridles;** *verb,* **bridled, bridling.**
● A word that sounds the same is **bridal.**
● Synonyms: **check, curb, restrain,** for *verb* **2.**
Antonyms: **release, vent,** for *verb* **2.**

bridle (noun)

brief—**1.** Lasting only a short time: *a brief vacation.* **2.** Having few words: *a brief note. Adjective.*
—To give a short summary of facts or instructions. *Verb.*
brief (brēf) *adjective,* **briefer, briefest;** *verb,* **briefed, briefing.**

a at	i if	oo look	ch chalk		a in ago
ā ape	ī idle	ou out	ng sing		e in happen
ah calm	o odd	u ugly	sh ship	ə =	i in capital
aw all	ō oats	ū rule	th think		o in occur
e end	oi oil	ur turn	th their		u in upon
ē easy			zh treasure		

briefcase—A flat bag used to carry papers and books. A person carries it by a handle like a suitcase.
brief|case (brēf'kās') *noun, plural* **briefcases.**

brier—A bush or plant with thorns, such as the wild rose or the hawthorn.
bri|er (brī'ər) *noun, plural* **briers.**
● This word is also spelled **briar.**

brig—**1.** A sailing ship with two masts and square sails. **2.** A prison on a ship.
brig (brig) *noun, plural* **brigs.**

brigade—**1.** A large unit in an army. It is made up of two or more smaller units such as battalions or regiments. **2.** A group of people who work together for a certain reason: *We formed a bucket* brigade *to get water from the river to the house fire.*
bri|gade (bri gād') *noun, plural* **brigades.**

bright—**1.** Giving out much light; shining: *The morning sun is very* bright. **2.** Clear or strong in color: *The sun is a* bright *yellow.* **3.** Intelligent: *She is a* bright *math student.*
bright (brīt) *adjective,* **brighter, brightest.**
● Synonyms: **brilliant, luminous, radiant,** for **1; brilliant, clever, smart,** for **3.**
Antonyms: **dark, dim, dull,** for **1; dumb, stupid,** for **3.**

brighten—**1.** To make or become light or colorful. **2.** To make cheerful or happy: *The trip to the zoo will* brighten *the children.*
bright|en (brī'tən) *verb,* **brightened, brightening.**

brilliant—**1.** Very bright: *a brilliant sunset.* **2.** Very intelligent: *a brilliant scientist.* **3.** Excellent: *That was a brilliant performance.*
bril|liant (bril'yənt) *adjective.*
● Synonyms: For **1** and **2,** see Synonyms at **bright.**
Antonyms: For **1** and **2,** see Antonyms at **bright.**

brim—**1.** The rim of a cup, bowl, or glass. **2.** The very top: *Fill the pail to the* brim. *Noun.*
—To become filled completely: *I am* brimming *with anger. Verb.*
brim (brim) *noun, plural* **brims;** *verb,* **brimmed, brimming.**

brine—Salty water.
brine (brīn) *noun.*

bring—**1.** To carry something or someone to another place: Bring *pencils to class.* **2.** To make exist or happen: *April showers* bring *May flowers.*
bring (bring) *verb,* **brought, bringing.**
■ **bring down the house:** To receive a great deal

of applause after a performance: *Her song* brought down the house.
    bring up: To rear; raise: *to bring up children*.

brink—1. The edge of a high place: *the* brink *of a cliff*. 2. The point just before something happens: *the* brink *of success*.
    brink (bringk) *noun, plural* **brinks**.

brisk—1. Fast; active: *We took a* brisk *walk*. 2. Refreshing or sharp: *a* brisk *ocean wind*.
    brisk (brisk) *adjective*.
    • Synonyms: **energetic, lively, vigorous,** for **1.**

bristle—A stiff, short animal hair or an artificial substitute: *a boar's* bristle; *a toothbrush with white* bristles. *Noun*.
    —1. To raise the hairs on the neck or body: *The cat* bristled *when the dog growled*. 2. To become angry: *He* bristled *at the insult*. 3. To stand upright in a stiff way: *My hair was cut so short it* bristled. *Verb*.
    bris|tle (bris′əl) *noun, plural* **bristles**; *verb,* **bristled, bristling**.

Brittany—A medium-sized hunting dog with long legs, a short tail, and ears that lie flat on the sides of the head. This dog was originally bred in France to hunt by scent and point in the direction of its prey.
    Brit|ta|ny (brit′ə nē) *noun, plural* **Brittanys**.

brittle—Broken easily: *Thin ice is* brittle.
    brit|tle (brit′əl) *adjective*.

broad—1. Wide; extensive: *It took all day to cross the* broad *valley*. 2. Having a wide range; not limited: *Our teacher gave us* broad *directions for writing our book reports*. 3. Open and clear: *The fox dared to come out in* broad *daylight*.
    broad (brawd) *adjective,* **broader, broadest**.

broadcast—1. To send music, news, or other programs by radio or television. 2. To spread information widely: *Do not* broadcast *that rumor to all your friends. Verb*.
    —Something sent out by radio or television: *a* news *broadcast. Noun*.
    broad|cast (brawd′kast′) *verb,* **broadcasted, broadcasting;** *noun, plural* **broadcasts**.

broaden—To become or make wider: *The workers* broadened *the road*.
    broad|en (braw′dən) *verb,* **broadened, broadening**.

broccoli—A green vegetable whose flower buds and stems are eaten cooked or raw.
    broc|co|li (brok′ə lē) *noun*.

broil—1. To cook food over an open fire or under the heat in an oven; grill: *We* broiled *hotdogs at the barbecue*. 2. To be very hot: *We* broiled *in the desert heat*.
    broil (broil) *verb,* **broiled, broiling**.

broiler—A grill or a part of an oven that is used to cook food next to an open flame.
    broil|er (broi′lər) *noun, plural* **broilers**.

broke—*See* **break**. *Verb*.
    —Having no money: *She was* broke *after spending her allowance. Adjective*.
    broke (brōk) *verb, adjective*.
    ■ **go for broke:** To make every possible effort: *She decided to* go for broke *by speeding up early in the race*.

broken—*See* **break**. *Verb*.
    —1. Separated into pieces by force: *a* broken *leg*. 2. Not kept; not completed: *a* broken *promise*. 3. Hurt or damaged: *a* broken *heart; a* broken *radio. Adjective*.
    bro|ken (brō′kən) *verb, adjective*.

bronchial tube—A branch of the windpipe that brings air to and from the lungs to make breathing possible. Two large ones lead to the lungs, with many smaller ones inside the lungs.
    bron|chi|al tube (brong′kē əl tūb) *noun, plural* **bronchial tubes**.

Brittany

bronchitis—An inflammation of the two large bronchial tubes that go to the lungs. It causes a very deep cough.
bron|chi|tis (brong kī′tis) *noun.*

bronco—A wild or partly tamed horse; mustang.
bron|co (brong′kō) *noun, plural* **broncos.**

brontosaurus—A very large dinosaur that ate plants. It had a long neck and a long, powerful tail that it used to defend itself.
bron|to|sau|rus (bron′tə **sawr′**əs) *noun, plural* **brontosauri** (bron′tə **sawr′**ī).

brontosaurus

Word History

Brontosaurus comes from two Greek words meaning "thunder lizard." Because this dinosaur was a huge animal, people imagined that it must have made a sound like thunder when it walked.

bronze—1. A metal made from copper and tin that is often used in making jewelry and statues. It may be yellowish brown or reddish brown in color. 2. A yellowish-brown or reddish-brown color. *Noun.*
—Having a yellowish-brown or reddish-brown color. *Adjective.*
—1. To coat with a metal made from copper and tin: *His parents* bronzed *his baby shoes.* 2. To become the color of this metal: *The bathers* bronzed *in the sun. Verb.*
bronze (bronz) *noun, plural* **bronzes;** *adjective;* *verb,* **bronzed, bronzing.**

a at	i if	oo look	ch chalk		a in ago
ā ape	ī idle	ou out	ng sing		e in happen
ah calm	o odd	u ugly	sh ship	ə =	i in capital
aw all	ō oats	ū rule	th think		o in occur
e end	oi oil	ur turn	t͟h their		u in upon
ē easy			zh treasure		

brooch—A jewelry pin that is usually worn on a blouse or jacket.
brooch (brōch *or* brūch) *noun, plural* **brooches.**

brood—A group of newborn birds that is hatched by the mother from eggs laid at the same time: *Robins can have three* broods *a year. Noun.*
—1. To sit on eggs until they are hatched.
2. To worry about something for a long time: *He spent his time* brooding *about the test rather than studying. Verb.*
brood (brūd) *noun, plural* **broods;** *verb,* **brooded, brooding.**

brook—A small, natural waterway; a small stream.
brook (brook) *noun, plural* **brooks.**

broom—1. A tool used for sweeping. It has a long handle with a brush attached at one end.
2. A bush with thin branches, small leaves, and yellow flowers.
broom (brūm *or* broom) *noun, plural* **brooms.**

broth—A thin soup made from water in which meat, fish, or vegetables have been boiled.
broth (brawth) *noun, plural* **broths.**

brother—A boy or man that has the same parents as another person.
broth|er (bru̇t͟h′ər) *noun, plural* **brothers.**

brotherhood—1. The feeling of kinship between brothers. 2. A group of men with common interests or aims.
broth|er|hood (bru̇t͟h′ər hood) *noun, plural* **brotherhoods.**

brother-in-law—1. The brother of one's wife or husband. 2. The husband of one's sister.
broth|er-in-law (bru̇t͟h′ər in law′) *noun, plural* **brothers-in-law.**

brought—*See* **bring.**
brought (brawt) *verb.*

brow—1. The part of the face above the eyes; forehead. 2. The arch of hair above the eye; eyebrow. 3. The edge of a high place: *the* brow *of a hill.*
brow (brou) *noun, plural* **brows.**

brown—A dark color with many different shades. Some things having this color are dark soil, chocolate, and coffee. *Noun.*
—Having such a color or a shade of such a color. *Adjective.*
—To make or become such a color or a shade of such a color: *The leaves* browned *as they dried. Verb.*
brown (broun) *noun; adjective,* **browner, brownest;** *verb,* **browned, browning.**

brownie—1. A moist, heavy chocolate cake usually cut in squares. It often has nuts in it.

2. A fairy who does good things for people, often secretly at night.
brown|ie (brou′nē) *noun, plural* **brownies**

Brownie—A girl who is a member of the youngest age group in the Girl Scouts.
Brown|ie (brou′nē) *noun, plural* **Brownies.**
■ **Brownie points:** Honor or praise earned for doing something well: *I know she'll do it because she always wants* Brownie points.

brown thrasher—A small bird of eastern North America. It has a reddish-brown head and back. It sings like the mockingbird.
brown thrash|er (broun **thrash′**ər) *noun, plural* **brown thrashers.**

browse—**1.** To read a book, newspaper, or magazine for pleasure in bits and pieces; skim. **2.** To look in a relaxed way for items of interest in a store.
browse (brouz) *verb,* **browsed, browsing.**

bruise—**1.** A black-and-blue mark on the skin caused by a bump or blow. **2.** A dark mark on the skin of a fruit, vegetable, or plant. *Noun.*
—To cause a black-and-blue mark to appear on the skin: *I* bruised *my leg when I bumped into the table. Verb.*
bruise (brūz) *noun, plural* **bruises;** *verb,* **bruised, bruising.**

brunette or **brunet**—**1.** Dark brown in color: brunette *hair.* **2.** Having dark-brown hair and eyes. *Adjective.*
—A person who has dark-brown hair and eyes. *Noun.*
bru|nette or bru|net (brū **net′**) *adjective; noun, plural* **brunettes** or **brunets.**

brush[1]—**1.** A tool for cleaning, sweeping, scrubbing, or painting. It is made of bristles of hair or wire connected to a hard back or handle. **2.** The act of using a tool made of bristles: *She gave her hair a quick* brush. **3.** A quick, soft touch: *the gentle* brush *of the leaves against the window. Noun.*
—**1.** To clean, sweep, scrub, or paint with a tool made with bristles: *to* brush *my hair.* **2.** To wipe away; remove: *The child* brushed *the tears from her eyes.* **3.** To rub against lightly in passing: *The cat* brushed *my leg as it walked by me. Verb.*
brush (brush) *noun, plural* **brushes;** *verb,* **brushed, brushing.**
■ **brush up on:** To study again; review. *He* brushed up on *the spelling list before the test.*

brush[2]—**1.** Bushes, plants, and small trees growing close together in the woods. **2.** Branches taken or broken off bushes or trees.
brush (brush) *noun.*

Brussels griffon

Brussels griffon—A small dog with a large head, a thick body, a stiff or smooth coat, and short ears and tail. This dog was originally bred in Belgium to hunt rats.
Brus|sels grif|fon (brus′əlz grif′ən) *noun, plural* **Brussels griffons.**

Brussels sprouts—A vegetable like tiny cabbage heads, eaten cooked. Brussels sprouts grow as buds along the stalk of a plant.
Brus|sels sprouts (brus′əlz sproutz), *plural noun.*

brutal—Like a wild animal; fierce: *a* brutal *storm; a* brutal *attack.*
bru|tal (brū′təl) *adjective.*
● Synonyms: **bloodthirsty, cruel, violent**
Antonyms: **gentle, kind**[1]**, tender**

brute—**1.** An animal that cannot think clearly or show feelings as a human does. **2.** A rude, cruel person; one who acts like a wild animal.
brute (brūt) *noun, plural* **brutes.**

bubble—A tiny, ball-shaped film that encloses air or some other gas: *You can blow* bubbles *with this gum. Noun.*
—To make or rise in a ball-shaped film enclosing a gas: *Water* bubbles *when it boils. Verb.*
bub|ble (bub′əl) *noun, plural* **bubbles;** *verb,* **bubbled, bubbling.**
■ **bubble over:** To overflow with a feeling: *The child* bubbled over *with happiness at her birthday party.*
burst (one's) **bubble:** To tell a truth that makes

another feel let down: *She burst his bubble when she told him he didn't win.*

buccaneer—A pirate.
buc|ca|neer (buk′ə nēr′) *noun, plural* **buccaneers.**

buck[1]—A male deer, goat, rabbit, or sheep. *Noun.*
—**1.** To spring into the air with the head down and the back legs kicking: *The pony bucked when the child tried to climb on its back.* **2.** To go against; oppose: *to buck a bad idea. Verb.*
buck (buk) *noun, plural* **bucks;** *verb,* **bucked, bucking.**
■ **buck up:** To cheer up or endure: Buck up, *for the story has a happy ending.*
● See picture at **deer.**

buck[2]—A dollar: *He had a* buck *to spend.*
buck (buk) *noun, plural* **bucks.**
■ **pass the buck:** To turn over a job or duty to someone else: *He can't pass the buck when his younger sister isn't around.*

bucket—A container, usually having a handle, that is used to carry things; a pail.
buck|et (buk′it) *noun, plural* **buckets.**
■ **kick the bucket:** To die: *She's too lively to kick the bucket yet.*

buckeye—A tree or shrub that has flowers, large leaves, and big brown seeds.
buck|eye (buk′ī′) *noun, plural* **buckeyes.**

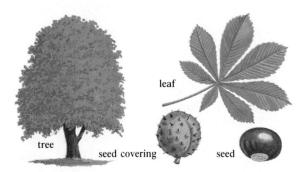

leaf

tree

seed covering

seed

buckeye

buckle—**1.** A clasp or catch used to fasten together the two ends of a belt or strap. **2.** A bend, wrinkle, or bulge: *a buckle in the sidewalk. Noun.*

—**1.** To fasten with a clasp or catch: *He buckled his belt.* **2.** To become wrinkled or bent out of shape: *Ice caused the pavement to* buckle *and crack. Verb.*
buck|le (buk′əl) *noun, plural* **buckles;** *verb,* **buckled, buckling.**
■ **buckle down:** To begin preparing oneself in a serious way: *He buckled down to study.*

buckskin—A soft, light-colored leather made from the hide of sheep or deer: *Many moccasins are made of* buckskin.
buck|skin (buk′skin′) *noun, plural* **buckskins.**

buckwheat—A plant with white flowers. Its seeds are used as food for animals and to make flour.
buck|wheat (buk′hwēt′) *noun, plural* **buckwheats.**

bud—A small growth on a plant, tree, or bush that is the beginning of a flower, leaf, or branch. *Noun.*
—To produce small growths that will become flowers, leaves, or branches: *The trees* bud *every spring. Verb.*
bud (bud) *noun, plural* **buds;** *verb,* **budded, budding.**
■ **nip (something) in the bud:** To stop something at its beginning: *Mother nipped our complaints in the bud.*

Buddha—A title given to the founder of Buddhism.
Bud|dha (bū′də) *noun.*

Buddha

a at	**i** if	**oo** look	**ch** chalk		a in ago
ā ape	**ī** idle	**ou** out	**ng** sing		e in happen
ah calm	**o** odd	**u** ugly	**sh** ship	**ə =**	i in capital
aw all	**ō** oats	**ū** rule	**th** think		o in occur
e end	**oi** oil	**ur** turn	**th** their		u in upon
ē easy			**zh** treasure		

Buddhism—A religion founded in India around 500 B.C. It is one of the world's major religions.
Bud|dhism (bū′diz əm) *noun.*

Buddhist—A person whose religion is Buddhism.
Bud|dhist (bū′dist) *noun, plural* **Buddhists.**

buddy—A close friend; chum.
bud|dy (bud′ē) *noun, plural* **buddies.**
• Synonyms: **comrade, pal**
Antonyms: **enemy, foe**

budge—To move or cause to move a little bit: *We could hardly* budge *the heavy couch.*
budge (buj) *verb,* **budged, budging.**

budget—A plan for how to use money. It is a list of how much money there is, how much is to be saved, and how the rest is to be spent. *Noun.*
—To make a plan for using money or time: *She carefully* budgets *her time among school, work, and play. Verb.*
budg|et (buj′it) *noun, plural* **budgets;** *verb,* **budgeted, budgeting.**

buff—1. A soft, yellowish-tan leather made from the skin of oxen.   2. A yellowish-tan color. *Noun.*
—To polish; rub: *She* buffed *the car until it shined. Verb.*
—Having a yellowish-tan color. *Adjective.*
buff (buf) *noun, plural* **buffs;** *verb,* **buffed, buffing;** *adjective.*

buffalo—1. A wild ox of North America that has a large, shaggy head; bison.   2. Any of several kinds of oxen in Europe, Asia, and Africa.
buf|fa|lo (buf′ə lō′) *noun, plural* **buffaloes** or **buffalos** or **buffalo.**
• See picture at **bison.**

buffet—1. A piece of furniture used to serve food. It has shelves or drawers for holding dishes, silverware, and table linens.   2. A meal set out in dishes on a table from which guests serve themselves.
buf|fet (bə fā′) *noun, plural* **buffets.**

bug—1. An insect.   2. A germ that causes a disease: *the flu* bug.   3. A flaw in a machine, computer, or plan that keeps it from working right: *The system will not work until we get the* bugs *out.*   4. A small microphone hidden in a place so someone can listen to the people talking there. *Noun.*
—1. To hide a small microphone so as to listen to people: *The spy* bugged *the general's home to get some of his top secrets.*   2. To pester; annoy: *It really* bugs *me when you talk so much. Verb.*
bug (bug) *noun, plural* **bugs;** *verb,* **bugged, bugging.**

■ **bug off** or **bug out:** To leave quickly: *My brother told me to* bug off *because he wanted to be alone.*
bug out: To bulge out; open wide: *Their eyes* bugged out *in surprise.*

buggy—1. A light carriage that is pulled by a horse.   2. A small carriage used to carry a baby: *a baby* buggy.
bug|gy (bug′ē) *noun, plural* **buggies.**

buggy (definition 1)

bugle—A musical instrument that looks like a small trumpet, but can play only a few tones.
bu|gle (byū′gəl) *noun, plural* **bugles.**

build—1. To produce something by putting materials or parts together; assemble: *Let's* build *a model airplane.*   2. To develop bit by bit: *They* built *a happy life over the years. Verb.*
—The way in which a person or animal is shaped; form: *The wrestler has a heavy* build. *Noun.*
build (bild) *verb,* **built, building;** *noun, plural* **builds.**
• Synonyms: **construct, erect,** for **1.**

building—1. A structure that is put together to provide a place where people can live or work.   2. The act or business of putting together houses, stores, bridges, and other structures: *The forest was cleared to make way for the* building *of new homes.*
build|ing (bil′ding) *noun, plural* **buildings.**
Abbreviation: bldg.

built—*See* build.
built (bilt) *verb.*

bulb—1. The round bud of some plants that is put underground and from which the plant grows.

Tulips, onions, and lilies grow from bulbs.
2. Any object that has a round shape: *a light bulb.*
bulb (bulb) *noun, plural* **bulbs.**

bulge—To swell out: *The shopping bag bulged when he put in the watermelon. Verb.*
—A swelling; bump. *Noun.*
bulge (bulj) *verb,* **bulged, bulging;** *noun, plural* **bulges.**

bulk—**1.** Size; volume: *A suitcase of such bulk is too big for you to carry.* **2.** The main or largest part: *We do the bulk of our homework after supper.*
bulk (bulk) *noun, plural* **bulks.**

bull—**1.** A grown male of cattle. **2.** The grown male of certain large animals such as a moose, whale, and elephant.
bull (bool) *noun, plural* **bulls.**
  ▪ **take the bull by the horns:** To take control of a situation: *She took the bull by the horns and told them to stop misbehaving.*
  • See picture at **moose.**

bulldog—A large dog with a big head, a flat face, and stubby legs. Originally bred in England, these dogs were trained to fight bulls.
bull|dog (bool′dawg) *noun, plural* **bulldogs.**

bulldog

bulldozer—A very powerful tractor with a wide steel blade across the front. It is used to clear land and build roads.
bull|doz|er (bool′dō′zər) *noun, plural* **bulldozers.**

bullet—A small piece of metal that is shot from a gun.
bul|let (bool′it) *noun, plural* **bullets.**
  ▪ **bite the bullet:** To act with courage; do something without complaining: *She was very nervous, but she bit the bullet and began her speech.*

bulletin—**1.** A short report of news: *The program was stopped for a news bulletin.* **2.** A brief magazine or newspaper that is put out regularly.
bul|le|tin (bool′ə tən) *noun, plural* **bulletins.**

bullfight—A fight between a person and a bull, held in an arena before spectators. It is a popular sport in Mexico and Spain.
bull|fight (bool′fīt′) *noun, plural* **bullfights.**

bullfrog—A large frog that makes a loud croaking sound.
bull|frog (bool′frawg′ *or* bool′frog′) *noun, plural* **bullfrogs.**

bullmastiff—A tall, large dog with a wrinkled head, short hair, and a dark muzzle. Originally bred in England, these dogs are used as guard dogs.
bull|mas|tiff (bool′mas′tif) *noun, plural* **bullmastiffs.**

bullmastiff

bull's-eye or **bullseye**—**1.** The center circle of a target used in such sports as archery and darts. **2.** A shot that hits the center of a target.
bull's-eye or **bulls|eye** (boolz′ī′) *noun, plural* **bull's-eyes** or **bullseyes.**

a at	i if	oo look	ch chalk		a in ago
ā ape	ī idle	ou out	ng sing		e in happen
ah calm	o odd	u ugly	sh ship	ə =	i in capital
aw all	ō oats	ū rule	th think		o in occur
e end	oi oil	ur turn	th their		u in upon
ē easy			zh treasure		

bull terrier—A medium-sized dog with a strong body, powerful jaws, and the ability to move quickly. These dogs were originally bred in England for fighting.
bull ter|ri|er (bool ter′ē ər) *noun, plural* **bull terriers.**

bull terrier

bully—Someone who threatens, teases, scares, or hurts others who are smaller or weaker. *Noun.*
—To threaten, scare, or tease another person: *My big brother* bullied *me into doing his chores for him. Verb.*
bul|ly (bool′ē) *noun, plural* **bullies;** *verb,* **bullied, bullying.**

bum—1. A person who does not do anything for a living; a lazy person. 2. A tramp.
bum (bum) *noun, plural* **bums.**

bumble bee—A large bee with a hairy, thick body that is usually banded with yellow and black stripes.
bum|ble bee (bum′bəl bē) *noun, plural* **bumble bees.**
• See picture at **insect.**

bump—1. To push, hit, or knock against: *She* bumped *her leg on the table.* 2. To move by bumping against things; move in jolts and jerks: *The red wagon* bumped *along the cracked sidewalk. Verb.*
—1. A hard hit or knock: *A bump from the person in line behind me pushed me into my friend.* 2. Any swelling or lump: *a bump on my head. Noun.*
bump (bump) *verb,* **bumped, bumping;** *noun, plural* **bumps.**
• Synonyms: **bang, collide, jar², jolt,** for *verb* 1.

bumper—The bar of metal or other sturdy material that is attached across the front and back of a vehicle. It protects against damage caused by bumping. *Noun.*
—Unusually large; abundant: *With all the rain, we will have a* bumper *crop of corn. Adjective.*
bump|er (bum′pər) *noun, plural* **bumpers;** *adjective.*

bumpy—1. Having bumps; full of bumps: *a* bumpy *road.* 2. Causing bumps: *a* bumpy *ride.*
bump|y (bum′pē) *adjective,* **bumpier, bumpiest.**

bun—A small cake or bread roll. It is often sweetened and may contain raisins or berries.
bun (bun) *noun, plural* **buns.**

bunch—1. A group of things of the same kind, often growing together in a cluster: *a* bunch *of bananas.* 2. A group of people: *There was a friendly* bunch *at the party. Noun.*
—To bring together into a group: *He* bunched *his toys in the corner. Verb.*
bunch (bunch) *noun, plural* **bunches;** *verb,* **bunched, bunching.**
• Synonyms: **batch, group, lot, set²,** for **1;** **band¹, company, crew, gang, party,** for **2.**

bundle—Many things wrapped, packaged, or fastened together: *a* bundle *of firewood. Noun.*
—To wrap things together: *Father* bundled *all his old clothes to give to charity. Verb.*
bun|dle (bun′dəl) *noun, plural* **bundles;** *verb,* **bundled, bundling.**
■ **bundle up:** To dress heavily for warmth: *You'd better* bundle up *if you're going sledding today.*

bungalow—A small, usually one-story house; cottage.
bun|ga|low (bung′gə lō′) *noun, plural* **bungalows.**

bungle—To do or make something in a clumsy, unskillful way: *When I tried to repair the broken plate, I really* bungled *the job.*
bun|gle (bung′gəl) *verb,* **bungled, bungling.**

bunk—A bed for one person, often set against a wall with a similar bed above it.
bunk (bungk) *noun, plural* **bunks.**

bunny—A rabbit.
bun|ny (bun′ē) *noun, plural* **bunnies.**

bunt—To tap a baseball lightly with the bat so that it bounces only a short distance from the batter. *Verb.*
—A baseball that is tapped lightly. *Noun.*
bunt (bunt) *verb,* **bunted, bunting;** *noun, plural* **bunts.**

bunting—1. A thin cloth from which flags are made. 2. Cloth cut in long strips that uses a flag's colors and design. It is often used in

decorating for holidays and special occasions.
bun|ting (**bun′**ting) *noun, plural* **buntings.**

buoy—**1.** A floating object anchored in the water, used to warn against hidden hazards or to show the safe way through a channel. **2.** A device filled with a light substance such as cork or foam, used to keep someone or something afloat.
buoy (boi *or* **bū′**ē) *noun, plural* **buoys.**
● A word that sounds the same is **boy.**

buoy (definition 1): There are many types of buoys.

bur—**1.** A prickly seed covering likely to stick to any fur or cloth that brushes against it. **2.** A plant with burs.
bur (bur) *noun, plural* **burs.**
● This word is also spelled **burr.**

burden—**1.** Something that is supported or carried; a load. **2.** Something that is very hard to live with: *She feared her illness made her a burden to her family. Noun.*
—To weigh down with a load: *I don't want to burden you with my problems. Verb.*
bur|den (**bur′**dən) *noun, plural* **burdens;** *verb* **burdened, burdening.**

bureau—**1.** A chest of drawers for clothes; dresser. **2.** An office or agency: *the travel bureau.* **3.** A government office: *Bureau of Indian Affairs.*
bur|eau (byoor′ō) *noun, plural* **bureaus.**

burglar—A person who breaks into a building in order to steal something.
bur|glar (**bur′**glər) *noun, plural* **burglars.**

burial—The act of putting a dead body into the ground, a tomb, or the sea.
bur|i|al (ber′ē əl) *noun, plural* **burials.**

burlap—A kind of rough cloth: *The potatoes were put into bags made of brown* burlap.
bur|lap (**bur′**lap) *noun, plural* **burlaps.**

Burmese cat—A short-haired cat of medium size with a small round head, yellow eyes, and long narrow ears. It was originally bred in the United States.
Bur|mese cat (bur mēz′ kat) *noun, plural* **Burmese cats.**

burn—**1.** To set fire to; be on fire: *A fire* burned *in the fireplace.* **2.** To injure or destroy by fire or heat: *He* burned *his leg on the radiator.* **3.** To make by fire or heat: *The iron* burned *a hole in his shirt.* **4.** To feel hot: *Her face* burned *with shame.* **5.** To use for producing heat, light, or energy: *A light bulb* burns *electricity. Verb.*
—An injury caused by fire or heat. *Noun.*
burn (burn) *verb,* **burned** *or* **burnt, burning;** *noun, plural* **burns.**
■ **burn (one's) bridges:** To destroy every chance of turning back: *He* burned *his* bridges *when he got angry.*
● Synonyms: **scorch, singe,** for *verb* **2.**

burner—**1.** The part on a stove or furnace that produces the flame. **2.** Something that makes heat by burning fuel.
burn|er (**bur′**nər) *noun, plural* **burners.**

burnt—*See* **burn.**
burnt (burnt) *verb.*

burr—*See* **bur.**
burr (bur) *noun, plural* **burrs.**

burro—A small donkey used for carrying packs and people.

a at	i if	oo look	ch chalk		⌈ a in ago
ā ape	ī idle	ou out	ng sing		e in happen
ah calm	o odd	u ugly	sh ship	ə =	i in capital
aw all	ō oats	ū rule	th think		o in occur
e end	oi oil	ur turn	<u>th</u> their		⌊ u in upon
ē easy			zh treasure		

burro

bur|ro (bur′ō) *noun, plural* **burros.**
- Words that sound the same are **borough** and **burrow.**
- Other names for this animal are **ass** and **donkey.**

burrow—A hole in the ground that an animal digs for a home or hiding place. *Noun.*
—**1.** To dig a hole in the ground: *The mole* burrowed *a tunnel under our lawn.* **2.** To search for something inside something else: *She* burrowed *in her closet for a clean shirt. Verb.*
bur|row (bur′ō) *noun, plural* **burrows;** *verb,* **burrowed, burrowing.**
- Words that sound the same are **borough** and **burro.**

burst—**1.** To break open quickly; pop: *Bubbles will* burst *if you touch them.* **2.** To act suddenly: *The horses* burst *from the starting gate.* **3.** To be completely full as if ready to break open: *The pie was* bursting *with apples. Verb.*
—**1.** The act of breaking out: *There was a* burst *of applause when she finished her speech.* **2.** A sudden output of energy: *With a* burst *of speed, she ran home. Noun.*
burst (burst) *verb,* **burst, bursting;** *noun, plural* **bursts.**

bury—**1.** To put a dead body into the ground, a tomb, or the sea: *We* buried *the dead goldfish in the back yard.* **2.** To put into the ground and cover with dirt: *They say that long ago a treasure was* buried *somewhere on this island.* **3.** To hide or conceal: *My notebook was* buried *under a pile of other books.*
bur|y (ber′ē) *verb,* **buried, burying.**
- **bury the hatchet:** To become friends after fighting: *They're always together now that they've* buried the hatchet.
- A word that sounds the same is **berry.**

bus—A vehicle larger than a car, with rows of seats for passengers. It usually runs along a regular route, stopping to pick up or let off passengers at certain places along the way. *Noun.*
—To travel or carry by such a vehicle: *The children are* bused *to school. Verb.*
bus (bus) *noun, plural* **buses** or **busses;** *verb,* **bused** or **bussed, busing** or **bussing.**

Word History

Bus is a shortened form of a Latin word meaning "for all." Buses are made to carry many passengers, and anyone who wants to may ride them. So they are "for all."

---

bush—A woody plant, smaller than a tree, with many branches starting from or near the ground; shrub.
bush (boosh) *noun, plural* **bushes.**
- **beat around the bush:** To put off getting to the main point: *Her shyness caused her to* beat around the bush *in inviting him.*

bushel—A unit of measurement for dry things such as vegetables, grains, and fruits. It is equal to 4 pecks or 32 quarts.
bush|el (boosh′əl) *noun, plural* **bushels.**

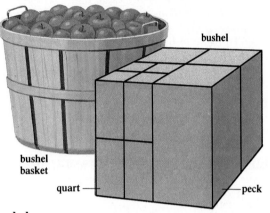

bushel

bushel basket

quart

peck

bushel

bushy—Growing out like a bush; thick: *a* bushy *beard; a* bushy *tail.*
bush|y (boosh′ē) *adjective,* **bushier, bushiest.**

business—**1.** The job a person does to make a living. **2.** A place where work is done; a store or factory. **3.** A matter; concern: *The principal talked to us about the* business *of the broken window.* **4.** The buying and selling of goods; trade: *My company has been in* business *for years.*
busi|ness (biz′nis) *noun, plural* **businesses.**
- Synonyms: **career, occupation, profession, trade,** for 1; **company, firm**[2], for 2.

businesslike—Well-run; practical: *Our teacher runs the class in a* businesslike *way.*
busi|ness|like (biz′nis līk′) *adjective.*

businessman—A man who is in trade or one who runs a company.
busi|ness|man (biz′nis man′) *noun, plural* **businessmen.**

businesswoman—A woman who is in trade or one who runs a company.
busi|ness|wom|an (biz′nis woom′ən) *noun, plural* **businesswomen.**

bust—A statue of a person's head, shoulders, and upper chest.
bust (bust) *noun, plural* **busts.**

bustle—To move busily, creating a great deal of excitement: *She* bustled *around the house getting ready for her company. Verb.*
—Busy, lively activity: *the* bustle *of the holiday season. Noun.*
bus|tle (bus′əl) *verb,* **bustled, bustling;** *noun.*

busy—**1.** Having one's time filled; having a great deal to do; active: *The cook was* busy *preparing the meal.* **2.** Having a lot of activity: *The library was a* busy *place during exam time.* **3.** Being used: *His telephone was* busy *each time I tried calling. Adjective.*
—To cause to be actively occupied: *We* busied *ourselves with the class project. Verb.*
bus|y (biz′ē) *adjective,* **busier, busiest;** *verb,* **busied, busying.**

busybody—Someone who looks closely into other people's business.
bus|y|bod|y (biz′ē bod′ē) *noun, plural* **busybodies.**

but—Yet; on the other hand: *He looked tired,* but *his mother let him stay up. Conjunction.*
—Except; save: *You may have all the candy* but *this piece of chocolate. Preposition.*
—Only; no more than: *There were* but *three people in the room. Adverb.*
but (but) *conjunction, preposition, adverb.*
• A word that sounds the same is **butt.**

Word History

Butcher comes from an old French word meaning ''one who slaughters and sells male goats.'' The word was used later to mean a person who cuts up and sells any sort of meat. Today, few butchers sell goat meat.

---

butcher—A person who prepares and sells meat. *Noun.*
—To kill or murder: *The turkeys were* butchered *at Thanksgiving time. Verb.*
butch|er (booch′ər) *noun, plural* **butchers;** *verb,* **butchered, butchering.**

a at	i if	oo look	ch chalk		⎡a in ago
ā ape	ī idle	ou out	ng sing		e in happen
ah calm	o odd	u ugly	sh ship	ə =	i in capital
aw all	ō oats	ū rule	th think		o in occur
e end	oi oil	ur turn	th their		⎣u in upon
ē easy			zh treasure		

butler—A male household servant who often is in charge of the other servants in the house.
but|ler (but′lər) *noun, plural* **butlers.**

butt¹—**1.** The blunt or bigger end of something: *The* butt *of a rifle is held against the shoulder when shooting.* **2.** A stump; all that is left of something.
butt (but) *noun, plural* **butts.**
• A word that sounds the same is **but.**

butt²—Someone or something that is the object of teasing: *I was the* butt *of the April fool's joke.*
butt (but) *noun, plural* **butts.**
• A word that sounds the same is **but.**

butt³—To bump with the head or horns: *The player* butted *the soccer ball with his head. Verb.*
—A shove made by the head or horns: *a playful* butt. *Noun.*
butt (but) *verb,* **butted, butting;** *noun, plural* **butts.**
■ **butt in:** To enter into someone's affairs without being asked. *It wasn't very nice of him to* butt in *on our conversation.*
butt out: To stop interfering in the affairs of others: *What we were doing was none of her business, so I told her to* butt out.
• A word that sounds the same is **but.**

butte—A lone hill with a flat top.
butte (byūt) *noun, plural* **buttes.**

butte

butter—**1.** A solid, yellow fat separated from cream by very fast stirring. It is used as a food spread. **2.** Any food that can be spread like butter: *peanut* butter; *apple* butter. *Noun.*
—To put a layer of such fat on: *She* buttered *her potato. Verb.*
but|ter (but′ər) *noun, plural* **butters;** *verb,* **buttered, buttering.**
■ **butter up:** To give too much praise; flatter: *She always finds the right words to* butter up *the coach.*

■ **butter wouldn't melt in** (one's) **mouth:** Someone is very sweet or coy: *She smiles so nicely, when she wants something, you'd think* butter wouldn't melt in *her mouth.*

buttercup—A plant with cup-shaped, yellow flowers. It usually grows wild.
but|ter|cup (but′ər kup′) *noun, plural* **buttercups.**

butterfingers—Someone who is clumsy or cannot hold on to things.
but|ter|fin|gers (but′ər fing′gerz) *noun.*

butterfly—An insect with a slender body and two pairs of large, colorful wings.
but|ter|fly (but′ər flī′) *noun, plural* **butterflies.**
■ **butterflies in** (one's) **stomach:** A state of being nervous; fright: *He had* butterflies in *his* stomach *when he stepped before the class.*
● See picture at **insect.**

buttermilk—The liquid remaining after butter has been separated from cream. It has a slightly sour taste.
but|ter|milk (but′ər milk′) *noun.*

butternut—1. A medium-sized tree that is related to the walnut. 2. The oily nut of this North American tree.
but|ter|nut (but′ər nut′) *noun, plural* **butternuts.**

butterscotch—A candy that is made by boiling butter and brown sugar.
but|ter|scotch (but′ər skoch′) *noun.*

button—1. A round or flat piece of plastic, metal, or other material that is used to fasten clothing together. 2. A knob that when pushed or turned makes something turn on or off. *Noun.*
—To fasten clothing with buttons: *She buttoned her sweater because it was cold. Verb.*
but|ton (but′ən) *noun, plural* **buttons;** *verb,* **buttoned, buttoning.**
■ **on the button:** Exact; precise: *His remarks had to be* on the button *in order to convince her.*

buttonhole—A hole or slit through which a button is pushed or pulled.
but|ton|hole (but′ən hōl′) *noun, plural* **buttonholes.**

buttress—A support built against a wall in order to strengthen it. *Noun.*
—To strengthen; support: *The lawyer* buttressed *his argument with evidence. Verb.*
but|tress (but′ris) *noun, plural* **buttresses;** *verb,* **buttressed, buttressing.**

buy—To obtain something by making a payment for it; purchase: *I will save my money to* buy *a new coat. Verb.*

—Something purchased, usually at a low price: *I will get a good* buy *on a coat at the end of winter. Noun.*
buy (bī) *verb,* **bought, buying;** *noun, plural* **buys.**
■ **buy off:** To bribe: *The prisoner tried to* buy off *the guard.*
● A word that sounds the same is **by.**

buyer—1. Someone who purchases something; customer. 2. The person who does the purchasing for a business: *The* buyer *for the store chose more dresses for the next season.*
buy|er (bī′ər) *noun, plural* **buyers.**

buzz—A sound like a hum: *the* buzz *of an insect. Noun.*
—1. To make a sound like a hum: *The bee* buzzed *over the flower.* 2. To talk with excitement or enthusiasm: *The crowd* buzzed *as the President's car approached.* 3. To fly low over: *The airplane pilot* buzzed *the tower. Verb.*
buzz (buz) *noun, plural* **buzzes;** *verb,* **buzzed, buzzing.**
■ **buzz about:** To move around in a busy way: *He* buzzed about *the kitchen, getting things ready for dinner.*
buzz off: To go away; leave: *You'd better* buzz off *before you're caught.*

buzzard—A large, slow-moving bird with a sharp, hooked beak and long, pointed claws. It is a type of hawk.
buz|zard (buz′ərd) *noun, plural* **buzzards.**

buzzard

buzzer—A device, usually run by electricity, that gives a signal by making a sound like a loud hum: *the alarm clock* buzzer; *the front door* buzzer.
buzz|er (buz′ər) *noun, plural* **buzzers.**

by—1. Beside; at or near: *Come and sit by me.* 2. Through the use of: *They went to the city by bus.* 3. Along; over; through: *Send the card by mail.* 4. Beyond; past: *The children walked by the school to get to the playground.* 5. Through the action of: *I enjoyed the story told by your friend.* 6. In the quantity of: *by the inch; by the truckload. Preposition.*
—Close; at hand: *Mom stays by when my baby brother is outside. Adverb.*
by (bī) *preposition, adverb.*
■ **by and by:** Eventually; soon: *We will be graduating by and by.*
by and large: Mostly: *It was a good movie, by and large.*
by fits and starts: With many stops and starts: *She did her homework by fits and starts, but finally finished it.*
by the way: Also; along with something else: *By the way, that is my book you have.*
● A word that sounds the same is **buy.**

by-—A prefix that means "secondary," or "nearby." A by-product is a secondary product. A bystander is someone who stands nearby.

Word Power

You can understand the meanings of many words that begin with **by-**, if you add a meaning of the prefix to the meaning of the rest of the word.
bylaw: a secondary law
by-play: action near the main action

---

by-and-by—In the future: *I'll get around to fixing it* by-and-by.
by-|and-|by (bī ən bī′) *noun.*

a at	i if	oo look	ch chalk		⌈ a in ago
ā ape	ī idle	ou out	ng sing		e in happen
ah calm	o odd	u ugly	sh ship	ə =	i in capital
aw all	ō oats	ū rule	th think		o in occur
e end	oi oil	ur turn	th their		⌊ u in upon
ē easy			zh treasure		

bye-bye—Good-by.
bye-|bye (bī bī) *interjection.*
bygone—Gone past; before; former: *In bygone days people did not have cars. Adjective.*
—**bygones:** What is past and over with: *Let's not worry about* bygones. *Plural noun.*
by|gone (bī′gawn′ *or* bī′gon′) *adjective; plural noun.*
■ **let bygones be bygones:** To forgive and forget: *Why don't we shake hands and* let bygones be bygones?

bylaw—A law or rule made by a corporation or a club to control its own affairs.
by|law (bī′law′) *noun, plural* **bylaws.**

byline—A line at the beginning of a news story or article giving the name of the writer.
by|line (bī′līn′) *noun, plural* **bylines.**

bypass—A road or route around something such as a town, usually in order to avoid a problem: *The* bypass *on the highway avoided the heavy city traffic. Noun.*
—To detour or go by without traveling through a place: *The train route* bypassed *the small towns. Verb.*
bypass (bī′pas′) *noun, plural* **bypasses;** *verb,* **bypassed, bypassing.**

by-product—Something of value that results from making the main product or achieving a major goal: *Self-confidence is a* by-product *of learning how to ride a bicycle.*
by-|prod|uct (bī′prod′əkt) *noun, plural* **by-products.**

bystander—Someone who stands nearby and watches but does not participate in something that is happening; spectator.
by|stand|er (bī′stan′dər) *noun, plural* **bystanders.**

byway—A road that is seldom used; side road.
by|way (bī′wā′) *noun, plural* **byways.**

byword—1. A common saying; proverb. 2. An object of scorn: *The player's name became a* byword *for cheating.*
by|word (bī′wurd′) *noun, plural* **bywords.**

byte—A computer unit of information, made up of eight bits, which are the smallest units of information in the binary system.
byte (bīt) *noun, plural* **bytes.**
● A word that sounds the same is **bite.**

About 1,900 years ago, the Romans gave the capital C its present form. The small letter c was first used about 1,400 years ago. It reached its present form about 500 years ago.

About 5,000 years ago, the ancient Egyptians used a symbol that looked like a boomerang. The letters C and G both came from this symbol.

About 3,000 years ago, people in the Middle East used a symbol that looked a bit like a hook.

About 2,600 years ago, the Greeks gave the letter this form. They called it *gamma* and made it the third letter in their alphabet.

C or **c**—1. The third letter of the alphabet: *There are two c's in the word "accent."* 2. The third best of its kind or the third highest mark in school: *a C in history.* 3. The Roman numeral for 100.
C, c (sē) *noun, plural* **C's** or **Cs, c's** or **cs.**
• Words that sound the same are **sea** and **see.**

C—The abbreviation for Celsius and for centigrade: *The temperature was 25°C, hot enough to go swimming.*

cab—1. A car with a driver that someone pays to drive him or her somewhere; taxi: *I called for a cab to take me to the airport.* 2. The front part of a train, truck, or other machine, in which an engineer or driver sits. 3. A hired carriage with a driver, which is pulled by one horse: *We rode around the park in the horse-drawn cab.*
cab (kab) *noun, plural* **cabs.**

cabbage—A vegetable that grows with its leaves tightly packed to form a round head. It is green or reddish-purple.
cab|bage (kab′ij) *noun, plural* **cabbages.**

cabin—1. A small, roughly built house sometimes made of logs: *a summer cabin in the woods.* 2. A person's room on a ship: *Our cabin was below the main deck.* 3. The place where passengers sit in an ariplane.
cab|in (kab′ən) *noun, plural* **cabins.**

cabinet—1. A piece of furniture with shelves and doors, used for storing things: *The kitchen cabinets have three shelves.* 2. A group of people who advise the head of a country: *The President's cabinet met to make plans.*
cab|i|net (kab′ə nit) *noun, plural* **cabinets.**

cable—1. A very strong rope usually made of many wires twisted together: *The bridge was held up by many cables.* 2. A covered bundle of wires that carries an electrical current. It is used to send messages: *a telephone cable.* 3. A message sent by cable: *We got a cable from overseas. Noun.*
—To send a message to someone by cable: *We cabled them our congratulations. Verb.*
ca|ble (kā′bəl) *noun, plural* **cables;** *verb,* **cabled, cabling.**

cable car—A car that is pulled up or down a hill on a moving cable: *The cable car carried skiers to the top of the mountain.*
ca|ble car (kā′bəl kahr) *noun, plural* **cable cars.**

cable car

cable television—A system for sending television programs by a special cable connected to a television set. A person pays for this service. ca|ble tel|e|vis|ion (kā′bəl tel′ə vizh′ən) *noun.*

caboose—A car on a freight train, usually the last one. It is used as living quarters for the train workers. ca|boose (kə būs′) *noun, plural* **cabooses.**

cacao—An evergreen tree grown in tropical areas. Chocolate and cocoa are made from its seeds. ca|ca|o (kə kā′ō *or* kə kah′ō) *noun, plural* **cacaos.**

cackle—A loud, sharp sound made by a hen. *Noun.*
—To make a loud, sharp sound like that of a hen: *The audience* cackled *at the clown's joke. Verb.*
cack|le (kak′əl) *noun, plural* **cackles;** *verb,* **cackled, cackling.**

cactus—A kind of thick plant usually covered with prickly spines but having no leaves. Cactuses grow well in dry, hot desert areas. cac|tus (kak′təs) *noun, plural* **cactuses** *or* **cacti** (kak′tī).

cactus

cadet—**1.** A military student training to be an officer in the army, navy, air force, or coast guard. **2.** A student at a military academy. ca|det (kə det′) *noun, plural* **cadets.**

a at	i if	oo look	ch chalk	⌐a in ago
ā ape	ī idle	ou out	ng sing	e in happen
ah calm	o odd	u ugly	sh ship	ə = i in capital
aw all	ō oats	ū rule	th think	o in occur
e end	oi oil	ur turn	th their	⌐u in upon
ē easy			zh treasure	

café—A small, cozy restaurant. ca|fé (ka fā′) *noun, plural* **cafés.**

cafeteria—A restaurant where customers choose their food while walking along a counter and carry the food to a table themselves. caf|e|te|ri|a (kaf′ə tir′ē ə) *noun, plural* **cafeterias.**

Word History

Cafeteria comes from the Mexican form of the Spanish language. It means "coffee shop." **Café** is a French word meaning "coffee." Today's cafeterias serve more than just coffee.

---

caffeine *or* **caffein**—A drug that helps keep a person alert. Coffee, tea, chocolate, and some soft drinks contain caffeine. caf|feine *or* caf|fein (kaf ēn′) *noun.*

cage—**1.** A structure closed in by bars or wire, in which animals are kept. **2.** Something that works or looks like such a structure: *The elevator* cage *carried the workers down into the coal mine. Noun.*
—To keep in an enclosed structure: *to* cage *a bird. Verb.*
cage (kāj) *noun, plural* **cages;** *verb,* **caged, caging.**
• See picture at **enclosure.**

cairn terrier—A small dog with a long, stiff coat, short legs, and a strong body. Originally bred in Scotland, these dogs were used to hunt small animals. cairn ter|ri|er (kārn ter′ē ər) *noun, plural* **cairn terriers.**

cairn terrier

cake—1. A baked product made from flour, sugar, eggs, and other ingredients. It is often covered with frosting: *a birthday* cake. 2. A thin, flat mass of dough or batter that is fried or baked: *a griddle* cake. 3. Any solid, shaped mass: *a* cake *of soap. Noun.*
—1. To cover with a hard, flat layer: *The dried mud* caked *our boots.* 2. To harden into a solid mass: *The milk* caked *as it became sour. Verb.*
cake (kāk) *noun, plural* cakes; *verb,* caked, caking.
  ■ **a piece of cake:** Something that is easy to do: *Riding a bike is* a piece of cake.
  have (one's) cake and eat it too: To do or have two desirable things that are impossible together: *She wants to* have *her* cake and eat it too *by saving her money and spending it.*
  take the cake: To be greater or better. *She* takes the cake *for telling funny stories.*

calamity—A disaster, such as a fire, flood, or earthquake: *If the flood had reached the city, it would have been a* calamity.
ca|lam|i|ty (kə lam′ə tē) *noun, plural* calamities.
  ● Synonyms: **catastrophe, tragedy**

calcium—A chemical element that is a soft metal. Teeth, bones, milk, seashells, and chalk contain calcium.
cal|ci|um (kal′sē əm) *noun.*

calculate—1. To figure out by using addition, subtraction, multiplication, or division: *They* calculated *that two boxes of cereal would cost three dollars.* 2. To estimate: *Father* calculated *that the trip would take ten hours.* 3. To intend for a specific purpose: *Her jokes were* calculated *to cheer me up.*
cal|cu|late (kal′kyə lāt) *verb,* calculated, calculating.

calculation—1. The act of using addition, subtraction, multiplication, or division to find an answer: *3 times 6, minus 4, is a simple* calculation. 2. An estimation: *Our* calculation *of our time of arrival was wrong by one hour.*
cal|cu|la|tion (kal′kyə lā′shən) *noun, plural* calculations.

calculator—A machine that solves mathematical problems.
cal|cu|la|tor (kal′kyə lā′tər) *noun, plural* calculators.

calendar—1. A chart that shows the days, weeks, and months of a year. 2. A schedule of events: *The school* calendar *lists our vacations.*
cal|en|dar (kal′ən dər) *noun, plural* calendars.

calf[1]—1. A young cow or bull. 2. A young elephant, seal, whale, or other large mammal.
calf (kaf) *noun, plural* calves.
  ● See picture at cow.

calf[2]—The thick, fleshy part of the back of the leg between the knee and ankle.
calf (kaf) *noun, plural* calves.

calico—A cotton cloth that has a small, colorful design on it: *The square dancers wore dresses of* calico. *Noun.*
—Having colorful spots: *a* calico *cat. Adjective.*
cal|i|co (kal′ə kō) *noun, plural* calicos or calicoes; *adjective.*

calico cat   calico dress

calico (noun and adjective)

call—1. To say in a loud voice: *The teacher* called *my name.* 2. To ask to come: *to* call *a plumber.* 3. To telephone: Call *me when you get home.* 4. To give a name to: *What are they going to* call *their new baby?* 5. To demand something: *to* call *the class to order.* 6. To visit briefly: *The neighbors* called *at our house yesterday. Verb.*
—1. A shout or cry: *We heard the little girl's* call *for help.* 2. The noise a bird or other animal makes: *I can do many different bird* calls. 3. The act of reaching someone by telephone: *I am expecting a* call *from my grandmother today.* 4. A short visit or stop: *Let's make a* call *at the library. Noun.*
call (kawl) *verb,* called, calling; *noun, plural* calls.
  ■ **call off:** To cancel; postpone: *The game was* called off *when it began to rain.*
  call on or **call upon: 1.** To pay a short visit to: *I* call on *Grandma every day.* 2. To ask someone to speak: *The teacher* called on *me first.*
  close call: A narrow escape from danger: *The animal trainer had a* close call *when the tiger only tore his shirt.*
  ● Synonyms: For *verb* 1, see Synonyms at cry, *verb* 2.
  Antonyms: **mumble, mutter, whisper,** for *verb* 1.

calliope—A musical instrument that is played by a keyboard. The sound comes out of steam whistles.
cal|li|o|pe (kə lī′ə pē) *noun, plural* **calliopes.**

calliope

callus—An area of thick, hardened skin, usually found on a hand or a foot: *He got* calluses *on his feet from wearing tight shoes.*
cal|lus (kal′əs) *noun, plural* **calluses.**

calm—1. Peaceful; not nervous or excited: *The first rule to follow in a fire is to stay* calm.
2. Not stirred up or moving; still: *The lake was very* calm *until the wind came. Adjective.*
—Stillness; peace: *the* calm *of the woods. Noun.*
—To make or become still; quiet: *The mother* calmed *her baby with a lullaby. Verb.*
calm (kahm) *adjective,* **calmer, calmest;** *noun;* *verb,* **calmed, calming.**
• Synonyms: **lull, soothe,** for *verb.*
Antonyms: **aggravate, annoy, bother, provoke,** for *verb.*

calorie or **calory**—1. A unit that measures the amount of energy provided by food. 2. A unit that measures the amount of heat in something.
cal|o|rie or cal|o|ry (kal′ər ē) *noun, plural* **calories.**

calves—*See* **calf.**
calves (kavz) *plural noun.*

came—*See* **come.**
came (kām) *verb.*

camel—A large, four-legged animal with a long neck and one or two humps on its back. Camels are used to carry loads and people in the deserts of Africa and Asia because they are very strong and can go a long time without drinking water. The African camel has one hump, and the Asian camel has two.
cam|el (kam′əl) *noun, plural* **camels.**

Asian camel   African camel

camel

camellia—A waxy red, white, or pink flower that smells sweet and is shaped like a rose. It is the state flower of Alabama. Camellias grow on trees.
ca|mel|lia (kə mēl′yə) *noun, plural* **camellias.**

camera—1. A device for taking photographs or motion pictures. Cameras use film or tape to record images that are formed by a lens. 2. A device that takes pictures for television.
cam|er|a (kam′ər ə) *noun, plural* **cameras.**

camouflage—A way something looks that causes it to resemble its surroundings: *A polar bear's fur is a natural* camouflage *because it is white like snow and ice. Noun.*
—To conceal something by an appearance that resembles its surroundings: *The burglar wore black clothes to* camouflage *himself at night. Verb.*
cam|ou|flage (kam′ə flahzh) *noun, plural* **camouflages;** *verb,* **camouflaged, camouflaging.**

camp—A group of tents or cabins where people live for a time: *The Girl Scouts used their new sleeping bags at the* camp. *Noun.*
—To live outdoors for a time: *This past summer the boys* camped *in the forest for a week. Verb.*
camp (kamp) *noun, plural* **camps;** *verb,* **camped, camping.**
■ **break camp:** To pack up tents and other belongings: *We* broke camp *and left for home.*

a at	i if	oo look	ch chalk		a in ago
ā ape	ī idle	ou out	ng sing		e in happen
ah calm	o odd	u ugly	sh ship	ə =	i in capital
aw all	ō oats	ū rule	th think		o in occur
e end	oi oil	ur turn	<u>th</u> their		u in upon
ē easy			zh treasure		

campaign—A set of actions carried out to make a certain thing happen: *a campaign to raise money; a campaign to be elected president.* Noun.
—To take part in such a set of actions: *My family campaigned for our neighbor when she ran for mayor. Verb.*
cam|paign (kam pān′) *noun, plural* **campaigns;** *verb,* **campaigned, campaigning.**

camper—1. A person who lives outdoors for a time: *The camper put up his tent by the lake.* 2. A vehicle that is used to travel and live in: *We drove the camper across the country last summer.*
camp|er (kam′pər) *noun, plural* **campers.**

campfire—A fire made outside for cooking and for keeping people warm.
camp|fire (kamp′fīr′) *noun, plural* **campfires.**

Camp Fire Boys and Girls—A United States organization for girls and boys that encourages personal growth and social responsibility. Founded as Camp Fire Girls, Inc., it became Camp Fire, Inc., in 1979.
Camp Fire Boys and Girls (kamp fīr boiz and gurlz) *noun.*

camphor—A white substance used to protect clothes from moths and in some medicines. Camphor has a strong smell.
cam|phor (kam′fər) *noun.*

campus—The grounds and buildings of a college or other school: *We went to campus to use the school library and gym.*
cam|pus (kam′pəs) *noun, plural* **campuses.**

can[1]—1. To be able to: *My sister can run fast.* 2. To know how to: *He can speak French and German.* 3. To be permitted to: *You can see a movie if you promise to behave.*
can (kan) *verb,* **could.**

Language Fact

Can[1] usually refers to power or ability, but **may** refers to the possibility that something will happen. If you can run well, you may win a race. A meaning that both **can** and **may** share is "to have permission": *Can she go? Yes, she may.*

can[2]—1. A rounded metal container, usually with a lid or cover: *a can of beans; a trash can. Noun.*
—To put into such a container; preserve: *Food that is canned lasts a long time. Verb.*

can (kan) *noun, plural* **cans;** *verb,* **canned, canning.**
 ■ **can it:** To stop; be quiet: *The man at the movie theater told the loud girl in front of him to can it.*

Canada Day—Canada's national holiday, July 1, which celebrates the country's independence from Great Britain in 1867.
Can|a|da Day (kan′ə də dā) *noun.*

canal—1. An artificial waterway that connects bodies of water for boats and ships to pass through. 2. A ditch made to carry water to dry areas.
ca|nal (kə nal′) *noun, plural* **canals.**

canary—A small, yellow songbird that is kept as a pet. Noun.
—Having a bright yellow color: *a canary raincoat. Adjective.*
ca|nar|y (kə nār′ē) *noun, plural* **canaries;** *adjective.*

canary (noun)

Word History

Canary comes from the name of a place, the Canary Islands. That is where these birds were first found. The islands got their name from a Latin word meaning "dog," because of the large dogs that also lived there.

cancel—1. To stop; call off: *School was canceled because of snow.* 2. To cross out something so that it cannot be used again: *The post office cancels the stamps on letters.*
can|cel (kan′səl) *verb,* **canceled, canceling.**

cancer—A very harmful disease that speeds up the growth of certain cells. Cancer often spreads through the body and can cause death.
can|cer (kan′sər) *noun.*

candidate—A person who is suggested by others for a position or an honor, or a person who seeks a position or an honor: *The coach selected her as a* candidate *for the school's athletic award.*
can|di|date (kan′də dāt) *noun, plural* **candidates.**

candle—A stick of wax formed around a piece of string that is burned to give light.
can|dle (kan′dəl) *noun, plural* **candles.**
■ **burn the candle at both ends:** To use up one's energy too fast: *Our neighbor is* burning the candle at both ends *by holding two full-time jobs.*

candlestick—A holder for a candle.
can|dle|stick (kan′dəl stik′) *noun, plural* **candlesticks.**

candy—A sweet food made from sugar, which often has chocolate, nuts, fruit, or other flavoring added to it.
can|dy (kan′dē) *noun, plural* **candies.**

cane—1. A stick with a handle used to help someone walk. 2. The long, hollow stem of certain plants, such as bamboo or sugar cane. Cane is used to make some types of furniture.
cane (kān) *noun, plural* **canes.**
• See picture at **bamboo** and **sugar cane.**

canine—1. A dog. 2. Any doglike animal, such as wolves and foxes. *Noun.*
—Like a dog: *A wolf is a* canine *animal. Adjective.*
ca|nine (kā′nīn) *noun, plural* **canines;** *adjective.*

canister—A small container with a lid, for storing powdery food, especially coffee, tea, sugar, or flour.
can|is|ter (kan′ə stər) *noun, plural* **canisters.**

cannibal—A person who eats the flesh of other human beings.
can|ni|bal (kan′ə bəl) *noun, plural* **cannibals.**

cannon—A big, heavy gun mounted on a base or pulled on wheels.
can|non (kan′ən) *noun, plural* **cannons.**

cannot—Can not; be unable: *I* cannot *play with you today because I am sick.*
can|not (kan′ot *or* ka not′) *verb.*
Contraction: **can't.**

canoe—A light boat, pointed at both ends and moved by hand with a paddle: *Indians used* canoes *to travel across rivers hundreds of years ago. Noun.*
—To travel in such a boat: *The campers* canoed *down the river. Verb.*
ca|noe (kə nū′) *noun, plural* **canoes;** *verb,* **canoed, canoeing.**
■ **paddle (one's) own canoe:** To achieve something by oneself: *Since no one can help you with this project, you'll have to* paddle *your* own canoe.

canoe (noun)

canopy—A cloth or vinyl covering that is hung over a bed, entrance, or throne.
can|o|py (kan′ə pē) *noun, plural* **canopies.**

can't—The contraction of "can not" or "cannot."
can't (kant).

cantaloupe or **cantaloup**—A type of melon that has a rough, hard skin and orange flesh that is sweet and juicy.
can|ta|loupe or can|ta|loup (kan′tə lōp) *noun, plural* **cantaloupes** or **cantaloups.**
• See picture at **melon.**

canteen—1. A small metal container used to carry liquids for drinking. 2. A store in a school or factory, or on a military base where food and supplies are sold.
can|teen (kan tēn′) *noun, plural* **canteens.**

canter—To gallop slowly: *The horse* cantered *playfully through the field. Verb.*
—A slow gallop: *The horse slowed to a* canter *after the race. Noun.*
can|ter (kan′tər) *verb,* **cantered, cantering;** *noun, plural* **canters.**
• A word that sounds the same is **cantor.**

cantor—The person who leads church members or the choir in singing or in chanting prayers.
can|tor (kan′tər) *noun, plural* **cantors.**
• A word that sounds the same is **canter.**

a at	i if	oo look	ch chalk		a in ago
ā ape	ī idle	ou out	ng sing		e in happen
ah calm	o odd	u ugly	sh ship	ə =	i in capital
aw all	ō oats	ū rule	th think		o in occur
e end	oi oil	ur turn	th their		u in upon
ē easy			zh treasure		

canvas—A strong, rough cloth. Canvas is used to make tents, sails, covers for boats, and some clothing. Oil paintings are often done on canvas.
can|vas (kan′vəs) *noun, plural* **canvases.**

canyon—A deep valley with high, steep sides. There is usually a stream or river running through a canyon.
can|yon (kan′yən) *noun, plural* **canyons.**

cap—1. A covering for the head that is soft and snug. Many caps have a brim in front.   2. The top of a jar, bottle, tube, or pen.   3. A piece of paper containing a small amount of explosive: *When he shoots his toy gun, the caps make a popping sound. Noun.*
—To cover something: *Remember to cap the toothpaste tube when you are through with it.*
cap (kap) *noun, plural* **caps;** *verb,* **capped, capping.**
■ **cap in hand:** Meekly; humbly: *He went* cap in hand *to beg her forgiveness.*

capable—Having the ability to do something: *The well-trained swimmer was very* capable *of winning the race.*
ca|pa|ble (kā′pə bəl) *adjective.*
● Synonyms: **competent, skilled**
   Antonyms: **incompetent, unqualified**

capacity—The amount of something that can be held in a container or a space: *My big new fish tank has twice the* capacity *of my old smaller one.*
ca|pac|i|ty (kə pas′ə tē) *noun, plural* **capacities.**

cape[1]—A piece of clothing with no sleeves that is worn loosely over the shoulders and fastened at the neck.
cape (kāp) *noun, plural* **capes.**

cape[2]—A point of land that extends from a coastline into a body of water.
cape (kāp) *noun, plural* **capes.**

capital—1. The city where the government of a state or country is located: *Washington, D.C., is the* capital *of the United States.*   2. The large form of a letter of the alphabet: *The word "TV" contains two* capitals.   3. All of the money or property that a person or business owns: *The business needs more* capital *to open new stores. Noun.*
—1. Extremely important: *The invention of the airplane was a* capital *advance in transportation.*
2. Involving the death penalty: capital *punishment. Adjective.*
cap|i|tal (kap′ə təl) *noun, plural* **capitals;** *adjective.* Abbreviation: cap.
● A word that sounds the same is **capitol.**

capitalize—To write with a large letter: *The first word of a sentence is always* capitalized.
cap|i|tal|ize (kap′ə tə līz) *verb,* **capitalized, capitalizing.**
■ **capitalize on:** To take advantage of: *The girl* capitalized on *her brother's mistake, and she won the card game.*

capitol—1. The building in which a state legislature meets.   2. Capitol: The building in Washington, D.C., in which the Congress of the United States meets.
cap|i|tol (kap′ə təl) *noun, plural* **capitols.**
● A word that sounds the same is **capital.**

capsize—To turn upside down: *The sailboat* capsized *in the stormy sea.*
cap|size (kap′ sīz *or* kap sīz′) *verb,* **capsized, capsizing.**

capsule—1. The thin covering that holds some medicines and makes them easier to swallow.
2. A part of a spacecraft that separates from the rocket after launching. The capsule holds crew members.
cap|sule (kap′səl) *noun, plural* **capsules.**

captain—1. The leader of a group: *the* captain *of the football team.*   2. The person in charge of a ship.   3. An officer in the army, navy, air force, or marines. *Noun.*
—To lead; command: *to* captain *a ship. Verb.*
cap|tain (kap′tən) *noun, plural* **captains;** *verb,* **captained, captaining.** Abbreviation: Capt.
● Synonyms: **chief, director, head,** for *noun* 1.
   Antonym: **follower,** for *noun* 1.

caption—The word or words that explain a picture.
cap|tion (kap′shən) *noun, plural* **captions.**

cape[2]

captive—A person or an animal held as a prisoner: *The pirates locked the* captives *below the ship's deck. Noun.*
—Held as a prisoner: *The captive monkeys were locked in a cage. Adjective.*
cap|tive (kap′tiv) *noun, plural* **captives;** *adjective.*

captivity—The condition of being held as a prisoner: *Jails keep criminals in* captivity.
cap|tiv|i|ty (kap tiv′ə tē) *noun.*

capture—To catch and hold as a prisoner: *We* captured *wild rabbits with a special cage. Verb.*
—The act of catching and holding as a prisoner: *The* capture *of the escaped tiger made the neighborhood safe again. Noun.*
cap|ture (kap′chər) *verb,* **captured, capturing;** *noun, plural* **captures.**
• Synonyms: **apprehend, arrest, detain,** for *verb.*
Antonyms: **free, liberate, release,** for *verb.*

car—1. An automobile. 2. Any vehicle that moves on wheels and rails: *a railroad* car; *a trolley* car.
car (kahr) *noun, plural* **cars.**
• See Word Power at **automobile.**

caramel—1. Sugar that is cooked and browned to give color or flavor to foods. 2. A light-brown, chewy candy made from this sugar.
car|a|mel (kahr′məl *or* kar′ə məl) *noun, plural* **caramels.**

caravan—A group of people and animals or vehicles traveling together, usually for safety: *The* caravan *went across the desert on camels.*
car|a|van (kar′ə van) *noun, plural* **caravans.**

carbohydrate—Any substance made up of carbon, hydrogen, and oxygen. Carbohydrates are made by green plants and are a source of food for animals. Sugars and starches are carbohydrates.
car|bo|hy|drate (kahr′bō hī′drāt) *noun, plural* **carbohydrates.**

carbon—A chemical element found in all living things. Both diamonds and coal are forms of carbon.
car|bon (kahr′bən) *noun.*

carbonate—To add carbon dioxide to something. Soda bubbles and fizzes because it is carbonated.
car|bon|ate (kahr′bə nāt) *verb,* **carbonated, carbonating.**

carbon dioxide—A gas made of carbon and oxygen. It has no color and no smell. When we breathe out, we put carbon dioxide into the air. Plants use carbon dioxide from the atmosphere to grow.
car|bon di|ox|ide (kahr′bən dī ok′sīd) *noun.*

carbon monoxide—A poisonous gas made of carbon and oxygen. It has no color or smell. The exhausts of cars and trucks contain this gas, which is made when carbon burns with too little air.
car|bon mon|ox|ide (kahr′bən mə nok′sīd) *noun.*

carburetor—The part of an engine that combines air with gasoline to make the engine run.
car|bu|re|tor (kahr′be rā′tər) *noun, plural* **carburetors.**

carcass—The body of a dead animal.
car|cass (kahr′kəs) *noun, plural* **carcasses.**

card—A piece of flat, stiff paper or plastic that has words, numbers, or a design on it: *a membership* card; *a deck of playing* cards; *a greeting* card; *report* cards.
card (kahrd) *noun, plural* **cards.**
■ **card up (one's) sleeve:** Another secret plan or method: *If this excuse doesn't work, I still have a* card up *my sleeve.*
hold all the cards: To have control: *My dad* holds all the cards *where he works because he's the boss.*
put (one's) cards on the table: To be honest; not hide anything: *If you tell me openly what's bothering you, I'll* put *my* cards on the table *too.*
stack the cards: To do something unfair that improves one's chances: *She* stacked the cards *in her favor by sneaking a look at the test.*
• See picture at **ace.**

cardboard—A kind of heavy, stiff paper made from layers of paper pressed together. Cardboard is used to make boxes and cards.
card|board (kahrd′bawrd′) *noun.*

Cardigan Welsh corgi—A small dog with short legs, a long body, rough hair, and a foxlike face. Originally bred in Wales, these hardy dogs were used to herd cattle and sheep.
Car|di|gan Welsh cor|gi (kahr′ də gən welsh kawr′gē) *noun, plural* **Cardigan Welsh corgis.**
• See also **Pembroke Welsh corgi.**

a at	i if	oo look	ch chalk		⎡ a in ago
ā ape	ī idle	ou out	ng sing		e in happen
ah calm	o odd	u ugly	sh ship	ə =	i in capital
aw all	ō oats	ū rule	th think		o in occur
e end	oi oil	ur turn	th their		⎣ u in upon
ē easy			zh treasure		

cardinal (noun, definition 1)

cardinal—1. A North American songbird that has a crest of feathers on its head. The male is bright red with a black patch around its bill. The female is brownish-red.   2. A rich, bright red color. 3. One of the highest officials in the Roman Catholic Church, who rank just below the Pope. Cardinals wear bright red robes and hats. *Noun.*
—1. Of the highest importance: *Being kind to others is a* cardinal *rule in our house.*
2. Having a rich, bright red color: *We could see his* cardinal *uniform a block away. Adjective.*
car|di|nal (**kahr′**də nəl) *noun, plural* **cardinals**; *adjective.*

cardinal number—A number used in counting. One, four, ten, and thirty are cardinal numbers. Numbers that show the order of something, such as first, fourth, tenth, and thirtieth, are called ordinal numbers.
car|di|nal num|ber (**kahr′**də nəl **num′**bər) *noun, plural* **cardinal numbers.**

Cardigan Welsh corgi

care—1. A feeling of worry; concern: *We forgot all our* cares *while we were on vacation.*
2. Serious attention; caution: *Take* care *not to fall when you go skiing.*   3. Watchful protection; keeping: *The child was under the babysitter's* care *while the parents were away. Noun.*
—1. To have an interest in someone or something: *I bought my girlfriend a gift to show I* care *about her.*   2. To have a feeling against: *Do you* care *if it rains today?*   3. To watch over; protect: *My mother* cared *for my dog while I was at camp. Verb.*
care (kār) *noun, plural* **cares;** *verb,* **cared, caring.**

career—The work that a person chooses to do throughout much of his or her life: *My sister is studying for a* career *as a lawyer.*
ca|reer (kə **rēr′**) *noun, plural* **careers.**
● Synonyms: **occupation, profession, vocation**

carefree—Having no worries; happy: *After the boy finished his chores he had a* carefree *day.*
care|free (**kār′**frē′) *adjective.*

careful—Paying close attention to what one says or does: *You should be very* careful *when you ride your bike to town.*
care|ful (**kār′**fəl) *adjective.*
● Synonyms: **attentive, cautious**
Antonyms: **careless, reckless**

careless—Not paying close enough attention to what one says or does: *Don't be* careless *when you do the dishes, or you might break one.*
care|less (**kār′**lis) *adjective.*

caress—To touch lightly and with affection: *The mother* caressed *her son's arm to comfort him after he was hurt. Verb.*
—A loving touch: *The girl's* caress *made the frightened cat stop trembling. Noun.*
ca|ress (kə **res′**) *verb,* **caressed, caressing;** *noun, plural* **caresses.**

caretaker—A person who attends to another person, place, or thing: *Mom hired a* caretaker *for the house when we went away for the summer.*
care|tak|er (**kār′**tā′kər) *noun, plural* **caretakers.**

carfare—The money charged for riding on a bus, on a subway, or in some other public vehicle.
car|fare (**kahr′**fār′) *noun.*

cargo—The freight carried by a truck, train, ship, airplane, or other vehicle: *The train carried a* cargo *of wool and cotton from one town to another.*
car|go (**kahr′**gō) *noun, plural* **cargoes** or **cargos.**

caribou—A type of large deer that lives in Canada and Alaska.
car|i|bou (kar′ə bū) *noun, plural* **caribou** or **caribous.**

caribou

carnation—A red, white, or pink flower with ruffled petals.
car|na|tion (kahr nā′shən) *noun, plural* **carnations.**

carnival—A fair that has games and rides.
car|ni|val (kahr′nə vəl) *noun, plural* **carnivals.**

carnivore—1. An animal that feeds mainly on meat.   2. A plant that eats insects.
car|ni|vore (kahr′ nə vawr) *noun, plural* **carnivores.**
• Antonym: **herbivore,** for **1.**

carnivorous—Feeding on the flesh of other animals. Dogs, cats, eagles, and sharks are carnivorous animals.
car|niv|o|rous (kahr niv′ər əs) *adjective.*
• Antonym: **herbivorous**

carol—A joyful song, especially one sung at Christmastime. *Noun.*
—To sing joyful songs: *The children* carol *at all the houses on our street each Christmas. Verb.*

car|ol (kar′əl) *noun, plural* **carols;** *verb,* **caroled, caroling.**

carp—A bony, edible fish that lives in freshwater ponds and streams.
carp (kahrp) *noun, plural* **carps** or **carp.**

carpenter—A person who builds and repairs houses, furniture, and other wooden items.
car|pen|ter (kahr′pən tər) *noun, plural* **carpenters.**

carpet—A heavy fabric for covering floors and stairs. Carpets are fastened to the floor, while rugs are not. *Noun.*
—To cover with such a fabric: *Mom wants to* carpet *our bedroom floor. Verb.*
car|pet (kahr′pit) *noun, plural* **carpets;** *verb,* **carpeted, carpeting.**
■ **sweep under the carpet:** To deny; pretend that (a problem) doesn't exist: *Although still angry, they* swept *their quarrel under the carpet.*

carriage—1. A vehicle that moves on wheels and does not have an engine: *a horse and* carriage; *a baby* carriage.   2. A movable machine part that holds up another part: *a typewriter* carriage.
car|riage (kar′ij) *noun, plural* **carriages.**
• See picture at **buggy.**

carrier—A person or thing that carries something: *a mail* carrier; *a passenger* carrier.
car|ri|er (kar′ē ər) *noun, plural* **carriers.**

carrot—A long, thin, orange vegetable that is the root of a garden plant. It is eaten raw or cooked.
car|rot (kar′ət) *noun, plural* **carrots.**

carrot

a at	i if	oo look	ch chalk			a in ago
ā ape	ī idle	ou out	ng sing			e in happen
ah calm	o odd	u ugly	sh ship	ə =		i in capital
aw all	ō oats	ū rule	th think			o in occur
e end	oi oil	ur turn	th their			u in upon
ē easy			zh treasure			

carry—1. To take something or someone from one place to another: *Please* carry *the baby back to her crib.*   2. In arithmetic, to move a number from one column to the next: *If you forget to* carry *the 1 when you add 12 and 8, you will get*

10 instead of 20.   **3.** To have something for sale: *That store* carries *the best clothes.*   **4.** To hold the head and body in a certain way: *He* carried *himself stiffly.*   **5.** To go a distance: *The sound of the whistle* carried *a long way.*   **6.** To sing right: *to* carry *a tune.*   **7.** To support; help to put up with: *A sense of humor* carried *him through difficult times.*
car|ry (kar′ē) *verb,* **carried, carrying.**

■ **carry away:** To cause strong feeling in, often beyond reason: *He was* carried away *by the sad movie and cried for hours.*

carry on: **1.** To continue: *The coach told us to* carry on *with our practice while she talked to a student.* **2.** To misbehave; act foolishly: *The boy* carried on *so much that the teacher told him to leave the classroom.*

carry out or **carry through:** To complete: *My sister* carried out *her promise to clean her room before dinner.*

cart—**1.** A sturdy, two-wheeled wagon that is used to carry heavy loads.   **2.** A light, four-wheeled vehicle that is moved by hand: *a shopping* cart. *Noun.*
—To carry something in such a vehicle: *My father* carted *the dirt to our garden. Verb.*
cart (kahrt) *noun, plural* **carts;** *verb,* **carted, carting.**

■ **put the cart before the horse:** To do something backward: *If you go outside and then put your coat on, you'll be* putting the cart before the horse.

● See picture at **oxcart.**

cartilage—A tough, stretchy tissue that is softer and more flexible than bone. The ears and part of the nose are made of cartilage.
car|ti|lage (kahr′tə lij) *noun.*

carton—A box made of cardboard: *a milk* carton.
car|ton (kahr′tən) *noun, plural* **cartons.**

cartoon—A drawing made to amuse people. Cartoons can be drawn on paper or on film. A cartoon can be a single drawing or a series of drawings: *a newspaper* cartoon; *a television* cartoon.
car|toon (kahr tūn′) *noun, plural* **cartoons.**

cartridge—**1.** A metal or paper tube that holds gunpowder and a bullet or shot.   **2.** A small plastic or metal case that holds something, usually made to be inserted into something else: *a film* cartridge; *a tape* cartridge *for a tape recorder.*
car|tridge (kahr′trij) *noun, plural* **cartridges.**

cartwheel—**1.** The wheel of a cart.   **2.** A sideways handspring in which the arms and legs

are held straight. A cartwheel gives a person the appearance of a turning wheel.
cart|wheel (kahrt′hwēl′) *noun, plural* **cartwheels.**

carve—**1.** To cut meat into slices or pieces: *to* carve *the turkey.*   **2.** To make something by cutting: *to* carve *a design into a piece of wood.*
carve (kahrv) *verb,* **carved, carving.**

cascade—A small waterfall that flows over steep rocks. *Noun.*
—To flow or fall like a waterfall: *Her long hair* cascaded *down her back. Verb.*
cas|cade (kas kād′) *noun, plural* **cascades;** *verb,* **cascaded, cascading.**

cascade (noun)

case¹—**1.** An example or instance of something: *The accident was a* case *of the man's driving too fast.*   **2.** The true state of things: *She thought the test would be easy, but this was not the* case. **3.** An instance of a disease: *a bad* case *of the flu.* **4.** A person being treated for an injury or disease: *The doctor's next* case *was a woman with a broken arm.*   **5.** A matter to be decided by a court of law: *The jury reached a verdict on the murder* case.
case (kās) *noun, plural* **cases.**

■ **get off** (one's) **case:** To stop bothering; leave alone: *He told you he doesn't have it, so* get off *his* case.

in case: If it should happen that; in the event that: *We brought an umbrella* in case *it rains.*

case²—A box, crate, or other container: *a case of soda; a pencil* case.
case (kās) *noun, plural* **cases.**

cash—Money; bills and coins: *I have no* cash, *so will you take a check? Noun.*
—To give or get money for: *The bank will* cash *your check. Verb.*
cash (kash) *noun; verb,* **cashed, cashing.**

cashew—A small, curved nut that grows on a tree found in parts of tropical America.
cash|ew (kash′ū) *noun, plural* **cashews.**

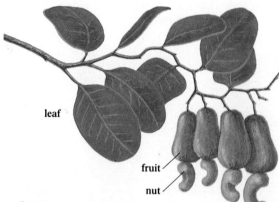

leaf
fruit
nut

cashew

cashier—The person whom customers pay for purchases in a store or other business.
cash|ier (ka shēr′) *noun, plural* **cashiers.**

cashmere—A soft, fine wool that is made from the long hair of Asian goats: *a sweater woven of* cashmere.
cash|mere (kazh′mēr) *noun, plural* **cashmeres.**

casket—A box in which a dead body is placed for burial; coffin.
cas|ket (kas′kit) *noun, plural* **caskets.**

casserole—1. A baking dish in which food is both cooked and served. Casseroles are usually made of pottery or glass. **2.** The food that is cooked in such a dish: *a tuna* casserole.
cas|se|role (kas′ə rōl) *noun, plural* **casseroles.**

cassette—A small case or cartridge that holds camera film, recording tape, or videotape.
cas|sette (kə set′) *noun, plural* **cassettes.**

cast—1. To throw; fling: *The fishermen* cast *their nets into the sea.* **2.** To place a vote: *to* cast *a ballot.* **3.** To send; direct: *She* cast *a smile of approval my way.* **4.** To choose someone for a role in a play or movie: *The director* cast *me in the part of the villain.* **5.** To shape something by pouring it into a mold and letting it harden: *We* cast *our own candles by pouring melted wax into milk cartons.* **6.** To cause to fall on something: *The building* cast *a tall shadow. Verb.*
—**1.** The act of throwing something: *a* cast *of the net into the stream.* **2.** A stiff mold applied to support and protect a broken bone: *The doctor put a* cast *on her broken arm.* **3.** All the actors in a play or a movie. **4.** A thing made by molding: *This mask is made from a* cast *of my face. Noun.*
cast (kast) *verb,* **cast, casting;** *noun, plural* **casts.**
• Synonyms: **fling, heave, hurl, toss,** for *verb* **1.**

castanet—A small wooden musical instrument that is shaped like two shells. Its halves are clicked together by the fingers to make a sharp sound.
cas|ta|net (kas′tə net′) *noun, plural* **castanets.**

castanet

cast iron—A hard, brittle kind of iron that has been shaped by melting and pouring into a mold: *a pot made of* cast iron.
cast i|ron (kast′ ī′ərn) *noun.*

castle—1. A large old building or group of buildings with high, thick stone walls and towers that protected the people inside against attack. **2.** A chess piece that is shaped like a castle tower; rook.
cas|tle (kas′əl) *noun, plural* **castles.**

casual—1. Happening by chance or without planning: *Our friendship began with a* casual *meeting at school.* **2.** Not formal: *Fancy*

a at	i if	oo look	ch chalk		⌈ a in ago
ā ape	ī idle	ou out	ng sing		e in happen
ah calm	o odd	u ugly	sh ship	ə =	i in capital
aw all	ō oats	ū rule	th think		o in occur
e end	oi oil	ur turn	th their		⌊ u in upon
ē easy			zh treasure		

restaurants do not allow casual *clothes.*
cas|u|al (**kazh′ū əl**) *adjective.*

casualty—A person who has been hurt or killed as the result of a battle or an accident.
cas|u|al|ty (**kazh′ū əl tē**) *noun, plural* **casualties.**

cat—**1.** A small furry animal with whiskers, sharp claws, pointed ears, and a long tail, that is kept as a pet. **2.** Any member of the group of large animals that includes tigers, leopards, and lions.
cat (**kat**) *noun, plural* **cats.**

■ **cat got your tongue?** Can't you think of anything to say?
let the cat out of the bag: To tell a secret: *Someone* let the cat out of the bag *and told him about his birthday present.*
rain cats and dogs: To rain very hard: *We had to call off the game because it was* raining cats and dogs.

catalog or **catalogue**—A list that describes items for purchase or use: *a library* catalog *of books; store sales* catalogs. *Noun.*
—To make such a list: *She* cataloged *the books that were on the shelf. Verb.*
cat|a|log or **cat|a|logue** (**kat′ə lawg**) *noun, plural* **catalogs** or **catalogues;** *verb,* **cataloged** or **catalogued, cataloging** or **cataloguing.**

catamaran—A small, lightweight boat with two narrow hulls.
cat|a|ma|ran (**kat′ə mə ran′**) *noun, plural* **catamarans.**

catapult

catapult—A large ancient weapon like a slingshot, for throwing stones or arrows.
cat|a|pult (**kat′ə pult**) *noun, plural* **catapults.**

cataract—**1.** A large, steep waterfall. **2.** A large, sudden flow of water; flood: *A pipe burst and* cataracts *ran down the stairs.* **3.** A change in the lens of an eye that causes it to become less clear. Cataracts can cause blindness or partial blindness.
cat|a|ract (**kat′ə rakt**) *noun, plural* **cataracts.**

catastrophe—A sudden disaster: *The earthquake was the worst* catastrophe *in the state's history.*
ca|tas|tro|phe (**kə tas′trə fē**) *noun, plural* **catastrophes.**

● Synonyms: **calamity, tragedy**

catbird—A dark gray North American songbird that sounds like a cat meowing.
cat|bird (**kat′burd′**) *noun, plural* **catbirds.**

catamaran

catbird

catboat—A sailboat that has one mast with a single sail set well forward.
cat|boat (kat′bōt′) *noun, plural* **catboats.**

catboat

catch—1. To get hold of a moving object: *Cats catch mice.* 2. To trap or entangle: *a fly caught in a spider's web.* 3. To surprise; come upon suddenly: *The teacher caught the girl passing notes in class.* 4. To be in time for: *to catch a bus.* 5. To get: *to catch the flu.* 6. To hear; understand: *I did not catch what you said.* 7. To attract: *to catch a person's attention. Verb.*
—1. The act of getting hold of a moving object: *She made a fine catch of the ball.* 2. A game in which two or more people toss a ball back and forth. 3. Something that holds or locks things together, such as a hook or latch: *The catch on my bracelet broke.* 4. Something that is taken or trapped: *a catch of fish.* 5. A hidden difficulty; trick: *There was a catch to the offer. Noun.*
catch (kach) *verb,* **caught, catching;** *noun, plural* **catches.**
■ **catch it:** To be blamed or punished: *I am sure to catch it when he finds out I lost his book.*
catch up: 1. To overtake someone or something: *Let's catch up with the others.*

2. To make up for lost time: *I can catch up on my sleep.*
● Synonyms: **apprehend, arrest, capture, detain,** for *verb* **1.**
Antonyms: **free, liberate, release,** for *verb* **1.**

catcher—1. Someone or something that gets hold of a moving object. 2. A baseball player who stands behind the batter to get hold of the balls the batter does not hit.
catch|er (kach′ər) *noun, plural* **catchers.**

catching—Likely to spread from one person to another: *I hope your cold is not catching.*
catch|ing (kach′ing) *adjective.*

category—A group of similar things; sort; kind: *Birds and insects are two categories of animals.*
cat|e|go|ry (kat′ə gawr′ē) *noun, plural* **categories.**
● Synonyms: **class, type, variety**

cater—1. To provide food and supplies: *to cater a party.* 2. To provide what someone wants or demands: *Her mother caters to her.*
ca|ter (kā′tər) *verb,* **catered, catering.**

cater-corner—diagonal. *His house is cater-corner to ours. Adjective.*
—diagonally. *Cross the park cater-corner. Adverb.*
cat|er-cor|ner (kat′ər kawr′ nər) *adjective, adverb.*
● Other names for this are **catty-corner** and **kitty-corner.**

caterpillar—The furry, wormlike insect that is the first stage in the life of a butterfly or moth.
cat|er|pil|lar (kat′ər pil′ər) *noun, plural* **caterpillars.**

caterpillar

catfish—A fish that has a large head and long feelers around its mouth that look like a cat's whiskers.
cat|fish (kat′fish′) *noun, plural* **catfish** *or* **catfishes.**

cathedral—A large church, especially one that is the official church of a bishop.
ca|the|dral (kə thē′drəl) *noun, plural* **cathedrals.**

a at	i if	oo look	ch chalk		a in ago
ā ape	ī idle	ou out	ng sing		e in happen
ah calm	o odd	u ugly	sh ship	ə =	i in capital
aw all	ō oats	ū rule	th think		o in occur
e end	oi oil	ur turn	th their		u in upon
ē easy			zh treasure		

catholic—Covering a wide variety; including everything; *Her* catholic *taste in music ranges from rock 'n' roll to opera.*
cath|o|lic (kath′lik) *adjective.*

Catholic—Concerning the Christian church that is led by the Pope; Roman Catholic: *The* Catholic *Bible. Adjective.*
—A member of the Catholic Church: *A Roman* Catholic. *Noun.*
Cath|o|lic (kath′lik) *adjective; noun, plural* **Catholics.**

Catholic Church—*See* **Roman Catholic Church.**
Cath|o|lic Church (kath′lik church) *noun.*

catnap—A short sleep: *He took a* catnap. *Noun.*
—To take a short sleep: *She* catnapped *while waiting for her friends. Verb.*
cat|nap (kat′nap) *verb,* **catnapped, catnapping;** *noun, plural* **catnaps.**

catnip—A plant of the mint family. Its leaves have a strong scent that cats enjoy.
cat|nip (kat′nip) *noun.*

catsup—See **ketchup.**
cat|sup (kat′səp *or* kech′əp) *noun.*
• See Word History at **ketchup.**

cattail—A tall plant found in marshy places. It has a long, thin stalk with a fuzzy, brown tip that looks like a cat's tail.
cat|tail (kat′tāl′) *noun, plural* **cattails.**

cattle—Cows, bulls, steers, and calves that are raised for meat, milk, or other products.
cat|tle (kat′əl) *plural noun.*

catty-corner—See **cater-corner.**
cat|ty-cor|ner (kat′ē kawr′nər) *adjective, adverb.*

caught—*See* **catch.**
caught (kawt) *verb.*

cauliflower—A garden plant that has a round, solid, white head surrounded by large leaves. The head is used as a vegetable, raw or cooked.
cau|li|flow|er (kaw′lə flou′ər *or* kol′ē flou′ər) *noun.*

cause—1. Someone or something that makes something happen: *Matches can* cause *a fire.* 2. Something a person believes in enough to do something for: *Stray pets are her* cause. *Noun.*
—To make happen; bring about: *The rain* caused *her to get wet. Verb.*
cause (kawz) *noun, plural* **causes;** *verb,* **caused, causing.**

caution—1. Carefulness; attention to safety: *Use* caution *when crossing a busy street.* 2. A warning: *The danger sign is a* caution. *Noun.*

—To tell to be careful; warn: *The teacher* cautioned *us about running in the halls. Verb.*
cau|tion (kaw′shən) *noun, plural* **cautions;** *verb,* **cautioned, cautioning.**
■ **throw caution to the winds:** To take a chance without concern for what happens: *She threw* caution to the winds *and spent her life savings.*

cautious—Avoiding risks; not taking chances: *Be* cautious *about petting strange dogs.*
cau|tious (kaw′shəs) *adjective.*
• Synonyms: **attentive, careful**
Antonyms: **careless, reckless**

cavalry—Soldiers who fight on horseback or from armored vehicles, such as tanks.
cav|al|ry (kav′əl rē) *noun, plural* **cavalries.**

cave—A hollow place in the ground. Caves usually have an opening on the side of a hill or mountain. *Noun.*
—To fall; collapse: *Our sand castle* caved *in when a wave hit it. Verb.*
cave (kāv) *noun, plural* **caves;** *verb,* **caved, caving.**

cave-in—1. A falling in; collapse: *The* cave-in *nearly buried the men in the tunnel.* 2. A place where there has been a collapse.
cave-in (kāv′in) *noun, plural* **cave-ins.**

cavern—A big cave.
cav|ern (kav′ərn) *noun, plural* **caverns.**

cavity—A hollow place; hole: *The* cavity *in his tooth was caused by decay.*
cav|i|ty (kav′ə tē) *noun, plural* **cavities.**

caw—The loud, harsh cry of a crow or raven.
caw (kaw) *noun, plural* **caws.**

CD—The abbreviation for **compact disc.**

cease—To stop: *I will not* cease *playing the tuba.*
cease (sēs) *verb,* **ceased, ceasing.**
• Synonyms: **end, finish, halt, quit**
Antonyms: **begin, commence initiate, start**

cedar—An evergreen tree with wide-spreading branches and sweet-smelling, reddish wood.

cauliflower

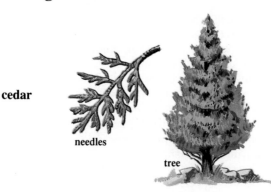

cedar

needles

tree

Cedar wood is often used to line storage chests and closets and to make pencils.
ce|dar (sē′dər) *noun, plural* **cedars.**

ceiling—1. The overhead covering of a room. 2. The distance between the ground and the lowest clouds: *Our airplane can't take off until the storm ends and the* ceiling *lifts.* 3. The top limit of something: *Mom set a* ceiling *on how much television I can watch.*
ceil|ing (sē′ling) *noun, plural* **ceilings.**
■ **hit the ceiling:** To become very angry: *Dad hit the ceiling when I got home late.*

celebrate—1. To honor or observe an occasion with special activities: *Our town celebrates the Fourth of July with a parade.* 2. To perform a religious ceremony: *to celebrate Mass; to celebrate holy days.*
cel|e|brate (sel′ə brāt′) *verb,* **celebrated, celebrating.**

celebration—1. Special activities to observe or honor a day or an event: *All the bells in town were rung for the New Year* celebration. 2. The act of observing a special day or event: *The wedding* celebration *lasted all day.*
cel|e|bra|tion (sel′ə brā′shən) *noun, plural* **celebrations.**

celebrity—A famous or well-known person: *That popular actress is a* celebrity.
ce|leb|ri|ty (sə leb′rə tē) *noun, plural* **celebrities.**

celery—A garden plant with long, crisp, green or white stalks. It is eaten as a vegetable, either raw or cooked.
cel|er|y (sel′ər ē) *noun.*

a at	i if	oo look	ch chalk	⌈ a in ago
ā ape	ī idle	ou out	ng sing	e in happen
ah calm	o odd	u ugly	sh ship	ə = i in capital
aw all	ō oats	ū rule	th think	o in occur
e end	oi oil	ur turn	th their	⌊ u in upon
ē easy			zh treasure	

cell—1. A small room, especially in a prison. 2. The tiny unit of living matter that makes up all animals and plants. A cell has a nucleus near its center, surrounded by protoplasm and enclosed by a cell wall or membrane. 3. A small space or hole: *Honeycombs have many* cells *where bees store honey.* 4. A container that holds materials that react chemically to make electricity. A battery has one or more cells.
cell (sel) *noun, plural* **cells.**
• A word that sounds the same is **sell.**
• See picture at **nucleus.**

cellar—A room or rooms located under a building and often used for storage; basement.
cel|lar (sel′ər) *noun, plural* **cellars.**

cello—A musical instrument that looks like a large violin but has a lower tone. It is held upright between the knees and is played with a bow.
cel|lo (chel′ō) *noun, plural* **cellos.**

cello

cellophane—A clear, flexible plastic material that is made from a plant substance called cellulose. It is used as a wrapping to keep food and other products fresh.
cel|lo|phane (sel′ə fān′) *noun.*

cellulose—A material that forms the walls of plant cells. The woody part of plants and trees contains cellulose. It is used to make paper, cellophane, and other products.
cel|lu|lose (sel′yə lōs) *noun.*

Celsius scale—The temperature scale used in centigrade thermometers. On this scale, water freezes at 0 degrees and boils at 100 degrees.
Cel|si|us scale (sel′sē əs skāl) *noun.*
Abbreviation: **C**
• See picture at **Fahrenheit.**

Word History

The **Celsius scale** is named after the man who invented it, Anders Celsius. He was a famous Swedish astronomer. Although Celsius developed this temperature scale in 1742, it was called a centigrade scale until 1948, because it has 100 degrees between the freezing and boiling temperatures of water.

Word Power

You can understand the meanings of many words that begin with **centi-**, if you add a meaning of the prefix to the meaning of the rest of the word.
   centigram: a measure of weight equal to one hundredth of a gram
   centiliter: a measure of a liquid or dry substance equal to one hundredth of a liter

cement—1. A powder made from clay and limestone. Adding water, crushed stones, sand, and other substances to cement makes a paste that becomes hard when it dries. Cement is used to make sidewalks, buildings, and streets.
2. Anything soft that will harden to hold things together: *The photograph was stuck to paper with rubber cement. Noun.*
—1. To spread such a paste: *to cement a sidewalk.* 2. To stick two things together with such a paste: *He cemented the doll's broken arm back into place. Verb.*
ce|ment (sə ment′) *noun, plural* **cements;** *verb,* **cemented, cementing.**

cemetery—A place for burying dead people; graveyard.
cem|e|ter|y (sem′ə ter′ē) *noun, plural* **cemeteries.**

census—An official count of the population of a place. The census lists how many people live there, their ages, sex, what kind of work they do, and other useful information.
cen|sus (sen′səs) *noun, plural* **censuses.**

cent—A coin of the United States and Canada that is worth one hundredth of a dollar; penny.
cent (sent) *noun, plural* **cents.**
   • Words that sound the same are **scent** and **sent.**

center—1. The middle point of a circle or sphere. It is an equal distance from all points on the surface. 2. The middle part of anything: *the center of the street.* 3. A main person, place, or thing: *the center of attention; a shopping center.*
4. In sports, a player who stays in or near the middle of a playing area. *Noun.*
—To place in the middle: Center *your name at the top of the page. Verb.*
cen|ter (sen′tər) *noun, plural* **centers;** *verb,* **centered, centering.**

centi-—A prefix that means "one hundred" or "one hundredth." A centipede is thought to have one hundred legs. A centimeter is one hundredth of a meter.

centigrade—Divided into one hundred degrees: *the centigrade temperature scale.*
cen|ti|grade (sen′tə grād) *adjective.*
Abbreviation: **C**
   • See picture at **Fahrenheit.**

centimeter—In the metric system, a measure of length equal to one hundredth of a meter. A centimeter is about one third of an inch.
cen|ti|me|ter (sen′tə mē′tər) *noun, plural* **centimeters.** Abbreviation: **cm**
   • See picture at **inch.**

centipede—A wormlike insect with a long, flat body and many pairs of legs.
cen|ti|pede (sen′tə pēd) *noun, plural* **centipedes.**

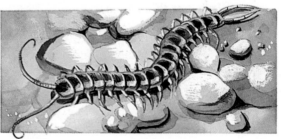
centipede

central—1. At, in, or near the middle: *The central part of the apple is the core.* 2. Most important; main: *The heroine was the central character in the story.*
cen|tral (sen′trəl) *adjective.*
   • Synonyms: **chief, major, principal,** for 2.
   Antonym: **minor,** for 2.

century—A period of one hundred years: *From 1800 to 1900 is a century.*
cen|tu|ry (sen′chər ē) *noun, plural* **centuries.**

ceramics—1. The art of making things out of baked clay: *I took a class in ceramics and made a bowl.* 2. Things made from baked clay: *There were many ceramics at the craft show.*
ce|ram|ics (sə ram′iks) *plural noun.*

cereal—1. Any grasslike plant that produces grain used for food. Wheat, rye, and corn are cereals. 2. A food made from such grain.
ce|re|al (sēr′ē əl) *noun, plural* **cereals.**
• A word that sounds the same is **serial.**

ceremony—1. A formal act that is performed on a special occasion: *a wedding* ceremony; *a graduation* ceremony. 2. Formal or very polite behavior: *The waiter bowed with great* ceremony.
cer|e|mo|ny (ser′ə mō′nē) *noun, plural* **ceremonies.**

certain—1. Sure; having no doubt: *She is* certain *that tomorrow is Friday.* 2. Some; known but not named: Certain *students will be excused early.* 3. Agreed upon; set: *The library is open only during* certain *hours.*
cer|tain (sur′tən) *adjective.*

certainly—1. Surely; positively: *It is* certainly *a beautiful day.* 2. Without fail: *The package will* certainly *arrive by Tuesday.*
cer|tain|ly (sur′tən lē) *adverb.*

certainty—Something that is sure or without doubt: *It is a* certainty *that one plus one is two.*
cer|tain|ty (sur′tən tē) *noun, plural* **certainties.**

certificate—Written proof of something: *a birth* certificate.
cer|tif|i|cate (sər tif′ə kit) *noun, plural* **certificates.**

certify—To guarantee in writing that something is true or is of a certain quality or value: *Her driver's license* certifies *that she passed the driving test.*
cer|ti|fy (sur′tə fī) *verb,* **certified, certifying.**

chain—1. A row of links or rings joined together: *a bicycle* chain. 2. A series of related things: *a* chain *of stores; a* chain *of people holding hands. Noun.*
—To hold or join together with such an object: *The boat is* chained *to the dock. Verb.*
chain (chān) *noun, plural* **chains;** *verb,* **chained, chaining.**

chair—1. A piece of furniture on which one person can sit. A chair has a back, a seat, usually four legs, and sometimes arms: *a kitchen* chair. 2. A person who leads a meeting or a committee; chairwoman or chairman.
chair (chār) *noun, plural* **chairs.**

■ **get the chair:** To be sentenced to die in the electric chair: *The murderer* got the chair.
take the chair: To start or lead a meeting: *The principal* took the chair *at the teachers' meeting.*

chairman—A man who leads a meeting or a committee; chair.
chair|man (chār′mən) *noun, plural* **chairmen.**

chairperson—A man or woman who leads a meeting or a committee; chair.
chair|per|son (chār′pur′sən) *noun, plural* **chairpersons.**

chairwoman—A woman who leads a meeting or a committee; chair.
chair|wom|an (chār′woom′ən) *noun, plural* **chairwomen.**

chalk—1. A soft, powdery limestone, made up mostly of tiny fossil sea shells. 2. A piece of this material used for marking on a blackboard or other surface. *Noun.*
—To write, draw, or mark with this substance: *She* chalked *a hopscotch board on the sidewalk. Verb.*
chalk (chawk) *noun, plural* **chalks;** *verb,* **chalked, chalking.**

challenge—1. To call someone to a fight or a game: *He* challenged *his father to a tennis match.* 2. To stop and ask for identification: *The police officer* challenged *the speeding driver. Verb.*
—1. A call to fight or take part in a contest: *One boxer accepted the other's* challenge.
2. Something that takes much thought or effort: *Trying to grow vegetables in this poor soil is a real* challenge. *Noun.*
chal|lenge (chal′ənj) *verb,* **challenged, challenging;** *noun, plural* **challenges.**

chamber—1. A room in a house, especially a bedroom: *At bedtime we climbed to our* chambers *on the top floor.* 2. A meeting hall for a legislature or other lawmaking group: *the Senate* chamber. 3. A legislature or other lawmaking group: *Congress has two* chambers, *the Senate and the House of Representatives.* 4. An enclosed space in the body of an animal or a plant: *The human eye has two* chambers. 5. The part of a gun that holds the bullet.
cham|ber (chām′bər) *noun, plural* **chambers.**

chameleon—A small lizard that can change its skin color to blend with its surroundings.
cha|me|le|on (kə mēl′yən) *noun, plural* **chameleons.**

a at	i if	oo look	ch chalk		a in ago
ā ape	ī idle	ou out	ng sing		e in happen
ah calm	o odd	u ugly	sh ship	ə =	i in capital
aw all	ō oats	ū rule	th think		o in occur
e end	oi oil	ur turn	th their		u in upon
ē easy			zh treasure		

champion—A person, animal, or thing that wins first place in a competition: *a racing* champion. *Noun.*
cham|pi|on (cham′pē ən) *noun, plural* **champions.**

championship—First place in a competition: *Our team won the state basketball* championship *this year.*
cham|pi|on|ship (cham′pē ən ship) *noun, plural* **championships.**

chance—1. An opportunity: *Will you give me a* chance *to explain?* 2. A possibility or likelihood of something happening: *There is no* chance *that my mother will let me go with you.* 3. Luck; fate: *He found the dime by* chance *on the sidewalk.* 4. A risk: *She took a big* chance *by staying out so late. Noun.*
—1. To happen or come about by accident: *I* chanced *to find just what I wanted at a garage sale.* 2. To take the risk of: *Do not* chance *making the dog angry by teasing it. Verb.*
—Not planned for or expected; accidental: *Our friendship resulted from a* chance *meeting in the lunchroom. Adjective.*
chance (chans) *noun, plural* **chances;** *verb,* **chanced, chancing;** *adjective,* **chancier, chanciest.**
▪ **on the off chance:** An unlikely possibility: *She called him* on the off chance *that he might be home.*

chancellor—A title given in some countries to high government officials and to important judges.
chan|cel|lor (chan′sə lər) *noun, plural* **chancellors.**

chandelier—A lighting fixture with branches

chameleon

containing lights. A chandelier hangs from the ceiling.
chan|de|lier (shan′də lēr′) *noun, plural* **chandeliers.**

change—1. To make different in some way: *to* change *a hairstyle.* 2. To put in place of another; substitute: *to* change *clothes; to* change *a dime for ten pennies. Verb.*
—1. The act of becoming different: *a* change *from caterpillar to butterfly.* 2. A substitution: *a* change *of clothes.* 3. The money returned when a person gives a larger amount than the price of something: *I received two dollars in* change *from my ten dollar bill.* 4. Money in the form of coins: *The* change *in his pocket included pennies and dimes. Noun.*
change (chānj) *verb,* **changed, changing;** *noun, plural* **changes.**
▪ **change hands:** To be transferred from one person to another: *That old coat* changed hands *twice.*
● Synonyms: **alter, modify, vary,** for *verb* **1.**
Antonyms: **conserve, maintain, preserve,** for *verb* **1.**

channel—1. A narrow strip of water that connects two larger bodies of water. 2. The deepest part of a waterway. 3. The electronic frequencies that allow television pictures and radio sound to be transmitted: *My radio has several* channels. *Noun.*
—To form such a strip of water: *The river* channeled *to the sea. Verb.*
chan|nel (chan′əl) *noun, plural* **channels;** *verb,* **channeled, channeling.**

chant—A song or tune with words that are repeated again and again: *the* chant *of baseball fans. Noun.*
—To sing or say over and over again: *The crowd* chanted *the hero's name. Verb.*
chant (chant) *noun, plural* **chants;** *verb,* **chanted, chanting.**

Chanukah—*See* **Hanukkah.**
Cha|nu|kah (hah′nū kah) *noun, plural* **Chanukahs.**

chaos—Total disorder; extreme confusion.
cha|os (kā′os) *noun.*

chap¹—To become dry, cracked, and rough: *My skin* chaps *from the cold.*
chap (chap) *verb,* **chapped, chapping.**

chap²—*Informal.* A man or a boy; fellow: *He was a good* chap *to help us.*
chap (chap) *noun, plural* **chaps.**

chapel—A small church. A chapel is sometimes a room in a church or other larger building.
chap|el (chap′əl) *noun, plural* **chapels.**

Word History

Chapel comes from a Latin word meaning "cloak." One of the world's first chapels contained the cloak of a famous French saint, St. Martin of Tours.

chaplain—A priest, minister, or rabbi who performs religious duties for a special group, such as a school or a prison.
chap|lain (chap′lin) *noun, plural* **chaplains.**

chaps—Strong leather pants without a seat. They are worn over trousers for protection, usually by cowboys.
chaps (chaps *or* shaps) *plural noun.*

chapter—1. A main section of a book: *For homework, I have to read* Chapter *3.* 2. A section of a larger organization: *Our town's* chapter *of the club has fifty members.*
chap|ter (chap′tər) *noun, plural* **chapters.**

character—1. All of the traits or qualities of someone or something: *The character of the landscape changes with the seasons.* 2. A person's true nature; disposition: *How he treats others shows his* character. 3. Moral strength or weakness: *People of good* character *don't lie.* 4. A person in a book, story, movie, or play: *The most important* character *in the book is a soldier.* 5. Someone who is odd or unusual: *The boy who clowns around in class is quite a* character. 6. A symbol used in printing or in writing: *The number 10 has two* characters.
char|ac|ter (kar′ik tər) *noun, plural* **characters.**

characteristic—Making one thing different from another; typical of a certain kind: *A characteristic summer day is sunny, warm, and clear. Adjective.*
—A quality or item that makes a person or thing different from another: *Her most pleasant* characteristic *is her lovely smile. Noun.*
char|ac|ter|is|tic (kar′ik tə ris′tik) *adjective; noun, plural* **characteristics.**
• Synonyms: **feature, trait,** for *noun.*

charade—1. Behavior that is false or fake: *All her boasting of being so popular was only a* charade. 2. **charades:** a game in which a person tries to guess the word or phrase another person acts out without speaking.
cha|rade (shə rād′) *noun, plural* **charades.**

charcoal—A soft, black carbon that is made by partly burning wood or other plant or animal material in an airtight place. Charcoal is used for fuel and for drawing.
char|coal (chahr′kōl′) *noun, plural* **charcoals.**

charge—1. To ask a certain price: *The babysitter charged three dollars an hour.* 2. To arrange to pay for later: *I had no cash, so I charged the dress.* 3. To be given the responsibility for: *She was charged with calling all the club members.* 4. To accuse; blame: *The police charged him with stealing the money.* 5. To attack: *to charge the enemy.* 6. To load: *to charge a car's battery with electricity. Verb.*
—1. The price of something: *The charge for the ticket is five dollars.* 2. An accusation: *The charge was for driving too fast.* 3. Care or protection: *The patient was under the charge of a doctor.* 4. An attack: *The woman escaped the lion's* charge. *Noun.*
charge (chahrj) *verb,* **charged, charging;** *noun, plural* **charges.**
■ **get a charge out of:** To find something funny or delightful: *We get a charge out of our kitten's cute behavior.*

charger—A type of horse trained for battle: *a knight's charge..*
charg|er (chahr′jər) *noun, plural* **chargers.**

chariot—A two-wheeled cart in which the rider stands. It is pulled by two or more horses. In ancient times, chariots were used for races, in parades, and in war.
char|i|ot (char′ē ət) *noun, plural* **chariots.**

a at	i if	oo look	ch chalk		a in ago
ā ape	ī idle	ou out	ng sing		e in happen
ah calm	o odd	u ugly	sh ship	ə =	i in capital
aw all	ō oats	ū rule	th think		o in occur
e end	oi oil	ur turn	th their		u in upon
ē easy			zh treasure		

chariot

charity—1. The giving of one's money or time to help poor or needy people: *She showed* charity *by preparing food for the homeless family.* 2. Kindness: *She had* charity *for all living things.* 3. An organization that helps those in need: *That* charity *raises money for people with handicaps.*
char|i|ty (char′ə tē) *noun, plural* **charities.**

charm—1. The quality of being attractive and pleasing: *The* charm *of the song is that it soothes listeners.* 2. A small piece of jewelry attached to a bracelet or necklace. 3. Something that is supposed to be magic: *A horseshoe is said to be a lucky* charm. *Noun.*
—To make happy; to please: *She* charmed *the audience with her song. Verb.*
charm (chahrm) *noun, plural* **charms;** *verb,* **charmed, charming.**

chart—1. A sheet with lists, diagrams, or tables that show specific information: *I made a* chart *showing all my school grades for the year.* 2. A map used in navigation to show the coast and dangerous places. *Noun.*
—To draw up or map out; plan: *Dad* charted *the best route on the map for his trip. Verb.*
chart (chahrt) *noun, plural* **charts;** *verb,* **charted, charting.**

charter—1. A written permit that gives someone or something the right to organize under certain rules: *The king issued a* charter *to establish a colony in the new land.* 2. A renting or leasing, usually of a vehicle: *The small company had buses for* charter. *Noun.*
—1. To establish by written permit; issue a permit to: *The state* chartered *the new bank.* 2. To rent or hire; lease: *They* chartered *a guide to take them through the jungle. Verb.*
char|ter (chahr′tər) *noun, plural* **charters;** *verb,* **chartered, chartering.**

chase—1. To run after and try to catch: *The dog* chases *the cat around the yard.* 2. To force to leave: *Rain* chased *the people from the beach. Verb.*
—The act of running after and trying to catch: *The runaway horse gave the cowboys quite a* chase. *Noun.*
chase (chās) *verb,* **chased, chasing;** *noun, plural* **chases.**

chasm—A deep opening or crack in the earth's surface.
chasm (kaz′əm) *noun, plural* **chasms.**

chat—A friendly, informal conversation: *I had a long* chat *on the phone with my friend. Noun.*
—To talk informally: *We* chatted *on the way to class. Verb.*

chat (chat) *noun, plural* **chats;** *verb,* **chatted, chatting.**

chatter—1. To talk constantly, usually about unimportant things. 2. To make rapid, noisy sounds: *The birds* chatter *in the trees. He was so cold that his teeth were* chattering. *Verb.*
—A constant talking: *the* chatter *of children in the playground. Noun.*
chat|ter (chat′ər) *verb,* **chattered, chattering;** *noun.*

chauffeur—Someone who drives a car for someone else as an occupation.
chauf|feur (shō′fər *or* shō fur′) *noun, plural* **chauffeurs.**

cheap—1. Not expensive; low-priced: *Corn is very* cheap *in the summer.* 2. Low quality; not well made: *This comb is so* cheap *that nearly all its teeth have broken off.* 3. Charging low prices: *a* cheap *store.*
cheap (chēp) *adjective,* **cheaper, cheapest.**
■ **talk is cheap:** It is easier to say something than to do it.

cheat—To trick or fool someone; act dishonestly: *She* cheated *by looking at the other players' cards. Verb.*
—Someone who is dishonest: *The* cheat *never paid back the money he owed. Noun.*
cheat (chēt) *verb,* **cheated, cheating;** *noun, plural* **cheats.**

check—1. To stop quickly or suddenly: *We* checked *our talking when the performance started.* 2. To look over or examine; test: *She* checked *her answers before handing in her paper. Check your bike's brakes before you go.* 3. To use a mark that looks like this √: *We* checked *each wrong answer on the spelling test.* 4. To leave something in another's care, usually in a public place: *We* checked *our coats at the restaurant door while we ate dinner.* 5. To hold back; curb: *I tried to* check *my tears but could not help crying during the sad movie. Verb.*
—1. A quick stop: *His sad news put a* check *to her happy mood.* 2. A holding back: *I keep a* check *on my temper when things go wrong.* 3. The act of examining or comparing: *Make a quick* check *of the house to see if we locked the doors.* 4. A mark (√) used to indicate something. 5. A written form a person makes out that tells a bank to pay money from his or her account to another person or business: *We pay our telephone bill by* check. 6. A bill for a meal in a restaurant: *The waiter handed me the* check. 7. A pattern of squares: *This tablecloth has red and white* checks. *Noun.*

check (chek) *verb*, **checked, checking;** *noun*, *plural* **checks.**

■ **check in:** To let someone know you have arrived or are all right: *The children* checked in *with their parents before going out.*

check off: To mark as completed or as done well enough: *We* checked off *each job on the list as we finished it.*

check up: To investigate; examine; make sure everything is right: *The babysitter* checked up *on what the children were doing.*

in check: To keep under control; hold back: *He kept his temper* in check.

● Synonyms: **bridle, curb, restrain,** for *verb* **1.** Antonyms: **release, vent,** for *verb* **1.**

checkerboard—A game board for playing checkers and chess. It has 64 squares that are usually red and black.
check|er|board (chek′ər bawrd′) *noun, plural* **checkerboards.**

checkers—A game played on a checkerboard by two players. Each player gets twelve flat, round game pieces to move in turn. The game ends when one player's pieces are all captured or are blocked from moving to another space.
check|ers (chek′ərz) *noun.*

checkout counter—A counter in a store where people pay for what they wish to buy.
check|out count|er (chek′out koun′tər) *noun, plural* **checkout counters.**

checkup—An examination or inspection: *She went to the doctor for a* checkup.
check|up (chek′up′) *noun, plural* **checkups.**

cheek—**1.** The part of the face under each eye and to each side of the nose. **2.** Rude boldness: *He had the* cheek *to tell me to get out.*
cheek (chēk) *noun, plural* **cheeks.**

■ **turn the other cheek:** To not fight back or protest when insulted or injured: *He* turned the other cheek *and walked away when she yelled at him.*

cheer—**1.** A yell of encouragement or praise: *Her friends gave a loud* cheer *when she won the award.* **2.** A sense of happiness: *The family was full of* cheer *during the holidays. Noun.*
—**1.** To yell encouragement or praise: *The crowd* cheered *for the basketball team during the close game.* **2.** To make or become happy: *The sight of our house* cheered *us after our long drive. Verb.*
cheer (chēr) *noun, plural* **cheers;** *verb,* **cheered, cheering.**

■ **cheer up:** To make someone feel better: *I* cheered *him* up *when he was in the hospital.*

cheerful—**1.** Joyful; happy: *a smiling,* cheerful *face.* **2.** Bringing happiness: *a* cheerful *letter.*
cheer|ful (chēr′fəl) *adjective.*
● See Synonyms and Antonyms at **happy.**

cheerleader—A person who leads a group in cheering, especially at athletic games.
cheer|lead|er (chēr′lē′dər) *noun, plural* **cheerleaders.**
● See picture at **enthusiasm.**

cheese—A food made from the curd of milk. It is solid and is usually yellow or white.
cheese (chēz) *noun, plural* **cheeses.**

cheetah—A wild, spotted cat that is a very fast runner. It is found in Africa and parts of Asia.
chee|tah (chē′tə) *noun, plural* **cheetahs.**

cheetah

chef—The chief cook in a restaurant.
chef (shef) *noun, plural* **chefs.**

chemical—Having to do with chemistry: *The teacher wrote the* chemical *formula for water on the blackboard. Adjective.*
—Any substance used in chemistry or made by chemistry. *Noun.*
chem|i|cal (kem′ə kəl) *adjective; noun, plural* **chemicals.**

chemist—A person trained in chemistry. Chemists work in many fields, including medicine and agriculture.
chem|ist (kem′ist) *noun, plural* **chemists.**

chemistry—The science that involves the study of simple substances or elements. It examines the way elements act, change, and combine with each other and other things.
chem|is|try (kem′ə strē) *noun.*

cherish—To value very highly: *She* cherished *her baby.*
cher|ish (cher′ish) *verb,* **cherished, cherishing.**

a at	i if	oo look	ch chalk	ə =	a in ago
ā ape	ī idle	ou out	ng sing		e in happen
ah calm	o odd	u ugly	sh ship		i in capital
aw all	ō oats	ū rule	th think		o in occur
e end	oi oil	ur turn	th their		u in upon
ē easy			zh treasure		

cherry—1. A small, red, round, smooth fruit that has a pit in it. Cherries grow on trees that bear lovely pink and white flowers in the spring. 2. A bright red color.
cher|ry (cher′ē) *noun, plural* **cherries.**

Chesapeake Bay retriever—A large hunting dog with an oily outer coat that sheds water. Originally bred in the United States in the Chesapeake Bay region, these dogs are used for hunting ducks and other water fowl.
Ches|a|peake Bay re|triev|er (ches′ə pēk bā ri trē′vər) *noun, plural* **Chesapeake Bay retrievers.**

Chesapeake Bay retriever

chess—A game played on a checkerboard by two players. Each player gets sixteen game pieces, one of which is called a king. The player who captures the other person's king is the winner.
chess (ches) *noun.*

chest—1. The front part of the human body between the neck and the stomach. 2. A strong, large box with a lid used to store things: *a tool* chest.
chest (chest) *noun, plural* **chests.**
■ **to get** (something) **off** (one's) **chest:** To tell others about something that is troubling oneself: *I felt better after I got it off my chest that I had lied.*

chestnut—1. A sweet nut that grows inside a prickly shell. 2. The tree that bears these nuts. 3. A reddish-brown color. *Noun.*
—Having a reddish-brown color: *the* chestnut *horse. Adjective.*
chest|nut (ches′nut) *noun, plural* **chestnuts;** *adjective.*

chestnut (noun, definitions 1 and 2)

chew—To crush with one's teeth: *Food should be* chewed *well before it is swallowed.*
chew (chū) *verb,* **chewed, chewing.**
■ **chew out:** bawl out: *His parents* chewed *him* out *for being late for dinner again.*

Chicana—A girl or woman whose home is in the United States but who was born in Mexico or whose parents or ancestors were born there; a Mexican-American girl or woman.
Chi|ca|na (chē kah′nah) *noun, plural* **Chicanas.**

Chicano—A boy or man whose home is in the United States but who was born in Mexico or whose parents or ancestors were born there; a Mexican-American boy or man.
Chi|ca|no (chē kah′nō) *noun, plural* **Chicanos.**

chick—1. A baby chicken. 2. Any baby bird.
chick (chik) *noun, plural* **chicks.**

chickadee—A small bird that has a black head and gray, black, and white feathers. It makes a sound like its name.
chick|a|dee (chik′ə dē) *noun, plural* **chickadees.**

chickadee

chicken—1. A hen or rooster.   2. The meat from a hen or rooster that is used as food. 3. Someone who is thought to be afraid of something: *His friends called him a* chicken *for not sledding down the steep hill. Noun.*
—Cowardly; being afraid of something: *I guess I am just* chicken *when it comes to climbing trees. Adjective.*
chick|en (chik′ən) *noun, plural* **chickens;** *adjective.*

chicken pox—An illness, usually of children, in which a fever occurs and red, itchy bumps appear on the body. It is easy to catch, but a person can only get it once.
chick|en pox (chick′ən poks) *noun.*

chief—One who leads a group of people: *the fire* chief; *the Indian* chief. *Noun.*
—1. Leading; at the head: *The* chief *class officer is the president.*   2. Most important; first: *Your* chief *duty as a babysitter is to watch the children. Adjective.*
chief (chēf) *noun, plural* **chiefs;** *adjective.*
• Synonyms: **captain, director, head, leader,** for *noun;* **central, main, major, principal,** for *adjective* 2.
Antonyms: **follower,** for *noun;* **minor,** for *adjective* 2.

chieftain—The head of a tribe; leader.
chief|tain (chēf′tən) *noun, plural* **chieftains.**

Chihuahua—A very small dog of the toy group with large round eyes and big ears. Originally bred in Mexico, it is the smallest kind of dog.
Chi|hua|hua (chē wah′wah) *noun, plural* **Chihuahuas.**

child—1. A young boy or girl.   2. A daughter or son.
child (chīld) *noun, plural* **children.**

childhood—The time period when a person is a youngster.
child|hood (chīld′hood) *noun, plural* **childhoods.**

childish—1. Like a youngster: childish *babble.* 2. Silly; babyish: *Losing your temper was a* childish *thing to do.*
child|ish (chīl′dish) *adjective.*
• Synonyms: **immature, juvenile,** for **2.**
Antonyms: **adult, grown-up, mature,** for **2.**

children—*See* **child.**
chil|dren (chil′drən) *plural noun.*

chili—1. A red pepper that is used as a spicy seasoning for certain foods.   2. A Spanish food containing beans and meat. It is often spicy.
chil|i (chil′ē) *noun, plural* **chilies.**
• A word that sounds the same is **chilly.**

chill—1. A feeling of coldness: *a* chill *in the air.* 2. A sudden shivering and feeling of being cold: *I got a* chill *when you opened the window. Noun.*
—Very cold: *a* chill *wind. Adjective.*
—To make something cold; refrigerate: *We* chilled *the juice before we drank it. Verb.*
chill (chil) *noun, plural* **chills;** *adjective; verb,* **chilled, chilling.**

chilly—1. Cool or cold: *It was so* chilly *last night that I slept with an extra blanket over me.* 2. Unpleasant or unfriendly: *Our neighbor was* chilly *toward us after our dog chased her cat.*
chill|y (chil′ē) *adjective,* **chillier, chilliest.**
• A word that sounds the same is **chili.**

chime—1. Any of a set of musically tuned bells, often shaped like pipes, that are played by tapping with a small hammer.   2. The ringing sound of musical bells: *The* chime *of the church bells welcomed them to the wedding. Noun.*
—To ring out: *The bells* chime *every day at noon. Verb.*
chime (chīm) *noun, plural* **chimes;** *verb,* **chimed, chiming.**

a at	i if	oo look	ch chalk		a in ago
ā ape	ī idle	ou out	ng sing		e in happen
ah calm	o odd	u ugly	sh ship	ə =	i in capital
aw all	ō oats	ū rule	th think		o in occur
e end	oi oil	ur turn	th their		u in upon
ē easy			zh treasure		

Chihuahua

chimney—A structure that connects to a fireplace, furnace, or stove. It has an air passage to carry the smoke from the fire to the outside.
chim|ney (chim′nē) *noun, plural* **chimneys.**

chimpanzee—A small ape about 4½ feet (1.5 meters) tall. It is found in Africa, where it lives mainly in trees.
chim|pan|zee (chim′pan zē′ *or* chim pan′zē) *noun, plural* **chimpanzees.**

chimpanzee

chin—The front part of the lower jaw below the lips. *Noun.*
—To hang from a bar and use one's arms to pull the body up so that the chin touches the bar. *Verb.*
chin (chin) *noun, plural* **chins;** *verb,* **chinned, chinning.**
■ **keep (one's) chin up:** To remain hopeful no matter how bad things are: *He kept his chin up even though his team was losing.*

china—1. A white clay pottery that is very shiny and hard, yet very delicate. China can have designs and colors baked into it. **2.** A set of dishes made of china: *We use our best china for holiday dinners.*
chi|na (chī′nə) *noun.*

chinchilla—A small animal that looks like a squirrel. It has soft, silvery, blue-gray fur. It belongs to the rodent family and is found in South America.
chin|chil|la (chin chil′ə) *noun, plural* **chinchillas.**

chip—1. A small, thin piece of something that has been broken or cut off: chips *of wood;* paint chips.

chinchilla

2. The place where something has broken off; nick: *The* chip *in my tooth needs to be fixed. Noun.*
—To cause a small piece to break off; to nick something: *He* chipped *the glass when he put it on the table. Verb.*
chip (chip) *noun, plural* **chips;** *verb* **chipped, chipping.**
■ **chip away at:** To keep at something steadily: *She* chipped away at *her homework and finished in time to go to the dance.*
chip in: To join with others in giving help or money: *They all* chipped in *and painted the garage in one day.*
chip off the old block: A child who is like one parent: *They told him he was a* chip off the old block *in the way he laughed.*
chip on (one's) shoulder: A state of being eager to argue or fight; bad attitude: *He had a* chip on *his* shoulder *about not making the team.*

chipmunk—A small animal that belongs to the squirrel family. It has dark stripes along its back from its head to its tail.
chip|munk (chip′mungk) *noun, plural* **chipmunks.**

chipmunk

chirp—A short, piercing sound that is made by some birds and insects. *Noun.*
—To make such a sound. *Verb.*
chirp (churp) *noun, plural* **chirps**; *verb,* **chirped, chirping.**

chisel—A strong, metal tool with a sharp edge. It is struck with a hammer to carve wood, metal, or stone. *Noun.*
—To carve or shape something by using such a tool: *He* chiseled *a toy boat from a piece of wood. Verb.*
chis|el (**chiz′əl**) *noun, plural* **chisels**; *verb,* **chiseled, chiseling.**

chivalry—The characteristics of an ideal knight of the Middle Ages. They included politeness, courage, and respect for women.
chiv|al|ry (**shiv′əl rē**) *noun.*

chives—The long, slender green leaves of a plant of the onion family. They are often cut up and used as a seasoning.
chives (chīvz) *noun, singular* **chive.**

chlorine—A yellow-green gas that has a bad smell and is poisonous. It is a chemical element.
chlo|rine (**klawr′ēn**) *noun.*

chlorophyll or **chlorophyl**—The substance that makes the green color in plants. With the help of light, it makes food for the plant by changing water and carbon dioxide into sugar.
chlo|ro|phyll or **chlo|ro|phyl** (**klawr′ə fil**) *noun.*

chocolate—1. A food made from roasted and ground-up cacao beans. Chocolate is used in many candies and drinks.   2. A drink made from this food: *hot* chocolate.   3. Candy that is made from or with this food: *We gave our mother a box of* chocolates.   4. A dark-brown color. *Noun.*
—1. Made from or with chocolate: chocolate *milk.*   2. Having a dark-brown color: *a* chocolate *sweater. Adjective.*
choc|o|late (**chawk′lit, chok′lit,** *or* **chawk′ə lit**) *noun, plural* **chocolates**; *adjective.*

choice—1. The act of deciding or selecting: *He made a* choice *between the red and the blue bicycles.*   2. The ability or chance to choose: *You have the* choice *of guests for your birthday party.*

3. Someone or something chosen: *She is my* choice *for class president.*   4. A variety of things from which to choose: *The carnival had a large* choice *of rides. Noun.*
—Having the best quality: *They had* choice *seats for the concert. Adjective.*
choice (chois) *noun, plural* **choices**; *adjective,* **choicer, choicest.**

choir—A group of people who sing together, usually in a school or church.
choir (kwīr) *noun, plural* **choirs.**

choke—1. To stop up the air passages of someone or something: *The chicken bone the dog tried to eat nearly* choked *it.*   2. To be unable to breathe easily; gag: *The fumes from the paint made me* choke.   3. To block or clog up: *Rust is* choking *the old pipes.*   4. To stop the growth of; check: *Weeds* choked *the vegetables in the garden.*
choke (chōk) *verb,* **choked, choking.**
■ **choke down:** To swallow against one's will; force down: *She* choked down *the awful dinner.*
  choke up: To be close to tears: *I* choked up *when they gave me a present.*

cholesterol—A fatty substance found in the body and in some foods.
cho|les|ter|ol (**kə les′tə rōl** *or* **kə les′tə rawl**) *noun.*

choose—1. To select from a variety; pick: *Which kind of cookie did you* choose?   2. To decide: *He* chose *to go to the movie.*   3. To select for a job or office: *She was* chosen *class president.*
choose (chūz) *verb,* **chose, chosen, choosing.**
■ **choose up:** To pick the players on a team: *to* choose up *sides for a basketball game.*
● Synonyms: **appoint, designate, name,** for 3.
  Antonyms: **discharge, dismiss, fire,** for 3.

chop¹—1. To cut by striking with an ax or other sharp tool: *We* chopped *trees into logs to build a cabin.*   2. To cut up into small pieces: *to* chop *onions. Verb.*
—1. A hard blow with a sharp tool.   2. A slice of meat: *a pork* chop. *Noun.*
chop (chop) *verb,* **chopped, chopping**; *noun, plural* **chops.**
● Synonyms: **hash, mince,** for *verb* 2.

chop²—The jaw.
chop (chop) *noun, plural* **chops.**
■ **chops:** The jaws, mouth, and cheeks: *The boxer took a blow to the* chops.
  lick (one's) chops over: To look forward to something: *I* licked *my* chops over *the thought of having dinner soon.*

a at	i if	oo look	ch chalk		
ā ape	ī idle	ou out	ng sing		a in ago
ah calm	o odd	u ugly	sh ship	ə =	e in happen
aw all	ō oats	ū rule	th think		i in capital
e end	oi oil	ur turn	<u>th</u> their		o in occur
ē easy			zh treasure		u in upon

chopsticks—A pair of long, thin sticks that are used for eating. Chopsticks are used in the Orient and are made of wood or ivory.
chop|sticks (chop′stiks′) *plural noun.*

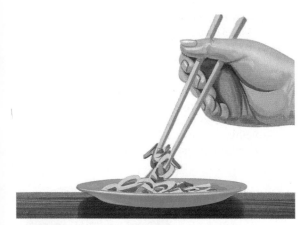

chopsticks

chord—Two or more notes of music that are played together.
chord (kawrd) *noun, plural* **chords.**
• A word that sounds the same is **cord.**

chore—A job or responsibility.
chore (chawr) *noun, plural* **chores.**
• Synonyms: **duty, task**
Antonyms: *See* Synonyms at **amusement, 2.**

chorus—**1.** A group of singers; choir. **2.** A part of a song that is repeated at the end of verses during the song. *Noun.*
—To say or sing together or at the same time: *The new members* chorused *the club oath at the start of the meeting. Verb.*
cho|rus (kawr′əs) *noun, plural* **choruses;** *verb,* **chorused, chorusing.**

chose—*See* **choose.**
chose (chōz) *verb.*

chosen—*See* **choose.**
cho|sen (chō′zən) *verb.*

chow chow—A medium-sized dog, commonly called chow, with a large head, thick hair around the neck, a square muzzle, and tiny ears. Originally bred in China, chows are the only breed of dog with a blue-black tongue.
chow chow (chou chou) *noun, plural* **chow chows.**

chowder—A soup made with seafood or vegetables or both: *clam* chowder; *corn* chowder.
chow|der (chou′dər) *noun, plural* **chowders.**

Word History

Chowder comes from a French word meaning "pot." Fish, biscuits, and other ingredients were mixed together in a pot to make a tasty food. This food became popular in the United States, and today **chowder** means not the pot but the food inside it.

Christ—*See* **Jesus.**
Christ (krīst) *noun.*

christen—**1.** To baptize; give a name to during the ceremony of baptism. **2.** To name a ship: *The ship was* christened *"Queen Elizabeth."*
chris|ten (kris′ən) *verb,* **christened, christening.**

Christian—A person who follows a religion based on a belief in Jesus Christ and His teachings. *Noun.*
—**1.** Having to do with Christ or Christianity: *the* Christian *way of life.* **2.** Following the teachings of Christ: *the* Christian *people. Adjective.*
Chris|tian (kris′chən) *noun, plural* **Christians;** *adjective.*

Christianity—The group of religions based on a belief in Jesus Christ and His teachings. It is one of the major religious movements in the world.
Chris|ti|an|i|ty (kris′chē an′ə tē) *noun.*

Christian Science—A religion founded by Mary Baker Eddy in 1866. It teaches that a

chow chow

strong belief in the power of God enables people to overcome sin and heal sickness.
Chris|tian Sci|ence (kris′chən sī′əns) *noun.*

Christian Scientist—A person who belongs to the Christian Science religion.
Chris|tian Sci|en|tist (kris′chən sī′ən tist) *noun, plural* **Christian Scientists.**

Christmas—The day on which the birth of Jesus Christ is celebrated. The date of this celebration is December 25. *Noun.*
—Having to do with Christmas: Christmas *carols. Adjective.*
Christ|mas (kris′məs) *noun, plural* **Christmases;** *adjective.*

chromium—A hard, silvery metal that does not rust or tarnish easily; chrome.
chro|mi|um (krō′mē əm) *noun.*

chrysanthemum—A round flower that blooms in the fall. Chrysanthemums have tiny petals and grow in many different colors and sizes.
chry|san|the|mum (krə san′thə məm) *noun, plural* **chrysanthemums.**

chubby—Slightly fat; plump: *The elf had a* chubby, *happy face.*
chub|by (chub′ē) *adjective.*

chuckle—To laugh softly: *I chuckled to myself when I read your cute note. Verb.*
—A soft laugh. *Noun.*
chuck|le (chuk′əl) *verb,* **chuckled, chuckling;** *noun, plural* **chuckles.**
● Synonyms: For *verb,* **giggle, laugh, snicker.** Antonyms: For *verb,* see Synonyms at **cry,** *verb* **1.**

chum—A good friend; pal.
chum (chum) *noun, plural* **chums.**
● Synonyms: **buddy, comrade** Antonyms: **enemy, foe**

chunk—A thick piece of something; hunk: *Mom cut a* chunk *of sausage for me.*
chunk (chungk) *noun, plural* **chunks.**

church—1. A building where Christians come together for religious services. **2.** A group of people who hold the same religious beliefs: *the Lutheran* Church.
church (church) *noun, plural* **churches.**

Church of England—The national church of England; Anglican Church. It is the mother church of the worldwide Anglican communion. In the United States, the Episcopal Church is part of this communion.
Church of Eng|land (church ov ing′glənd) *noun.*

churn—A container in which cream is stirred to make butter. *Noun.*
—**1.** To stir cream in such a container. **2.** To shake or move roughly: *The stormy ocean* churned *our little boat. Verb.*
churn (church) *noun, plural* **churns;** *verb,* **churned, churning.**
■ **churn out:** to produce a great deal of something without a lot of thought: *The artist* churned out *pictures she knew would sell.*

churn (noun)

chute—An inclined passageway through which things slide or drop: *mail chute; clothes* chute.
chute (shūt) *noun, plural* **chutes.**
■ **chute the chute** (*or* **chute the chutes**): to ride a chute in a playground or an amusement park.
● A word that sounds the same is **shoot.**

cicada—A large insect that makes a very loud humming sound during the summer; locust.
ci|ca|da (sə kā′də *or* sə kah′də) *noun, plural* **cicadas.**

cider—Apple juice. When cider ages, it becomes vinegar.
ci|der (sī′dər) *noun.*

cigar—Tobacco leaves that are rolled tightly for smoking.
ci|gar (sə gahr′) *noun, plural* **cigars.**

cigarette or **cigaret**—Finely chopped tobacco leaves that are rolled in paper so they can be smoked.
cig|a|rette or cig|a|ret (sig′ə ret′ *or* sig′ə ret) *noun, plural* **cigarettes** or **cigarets.**

cinch—1. A strong belt that holds a saddle or pack on a horse or donkey. **2.** Something easily

a at	i if	oo look	ch chalk		⌈ a in ago
ā ape	ī idle	ou out	ng sing		e in happen
ah calm	o odd	u ugly	sh ship	ə =	i in capital
aw all	ō oats	ū rule	th think		o in occur
e end	oi oil	ur turn	th their		⌊ u in upon
ē easy			zh treasure		

done: *Riding a bicycle is a* cinch *once you know how.*

cinch (sinch) *noun, plural* **cinches.**

cinder—A small, hot piece of wood or other material that is blackened and almost completely burned. A cinder glows, but it does not have a flame.

cin|der (sin′dər) *noun, plural* **cinders.**
 • Synonyms: **coal, ember**

cinema—A movie theater.

cin|e|ma (sin′ə mə) *noun, plural* **cinemas.**

cinnamon—1. A spice made from the reddish-brown bark of a certain tree that grows in tropical countries. 2. A reddish-brown color like cinnamon. *Noun.*
—Reddish brown in color. *Adjective.*

cin|na|mon (sin′ə mən) *noun; adjective.*

circle—1. A curved line whose ends meet to form a round shape. 2. Something in the shape of such a curved line; ring: *We stood in a* circle *to sing.* 3. A group of friends with common interests: *The boys and girls in my* circle *joined the book club. Noun.*
—1. To draw a line around something: Circle *the word that fits the picture.* 2. To move in a circle around something: *The helicopter* circled *the people waiting below.* 3. To surround; close in by making a ring around: *The firemen* circled *the burning building. Verb.*

cir|cle (sur′kəl) *noun, plural* **circles;** *verb,* **circled, circling.**
 ■ **come full circle:** Having gone through the complete process and returned to the starting point: *Dress styles have* come full circle *since then.*

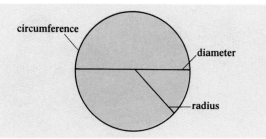

circle (noun, definition 1)

circuit—1. The act of going around; movement in a circle: *The racers made one* circuit *around the track.* 2. The path on which an electrical current flows.

cir|cuit (sur′kit) *noun, plural* **circuits.**

circular—1. Shaped like a circle; rounded: *Most coins have a* circular *shape.* 2. Turning in a circle: *A top spins in a circular motion. Adjective.*
—An advertisement or a letter that is mailed or handed out to many people. *Noun.*

cir|cu|lar (sur′kyə lər) *adjective; noun, plural* **circulars.**

circulate—To travel around: *Blood circulates through the body.*

cir|cu|late (sur′kyə lāt) *verb,* **circulated, circulating.**

circulation—1. The act of moving around: *The* circulation *of air from the kitchen brought the smell of cookies to the living room.* 2. The number of copies a newspaper or magazine distributes on a daily, weekly, or monthly basis: *If the magazine increases its* circulation, *it will make more money.*

cir|cu|la|tion (sur′kyə lā′shən) *noun, plural* **circulations.**

circum-—A prefix that means "around" or "in a circle." Sailors who circumnavigate the earth sail completely around it.

Word Power

You can understand the meanings of many words that begin with **circum-,** if you add the meaning of the prefix to the meaning of the rest of the word.
 circumlunar: around the moon
 circumrotate: to rotate around

---

circumference—1. The outside line that forms the edge of a circle. 2. The distance around the edge of something: *the* circumference *of the island.*

cir|cum|fer|ence (sər kum′fər əns) *noun, plural* **circumferences.**
 • See picture at **circle.**

circumstance—A condition, fact, or event that accompanies something and affects it: *The two* circumstances *that caused the accident were a slippery road and a careless driver.*

cir|cum|stance (sur′kəm stans) *noun, plural* **circumstances.**

circus—A show in which clowns, acrobats, trained animals, and other acts perform. A circus travels from town to town and is usually held under a big tent or in a large arena.

cir|cus (sur′kəs) *noun, plural* **circuses.**

citizen—1. A person who is a member of a country or state. A citizen has special rights and responsibilities: *Since she is a* citizen *of the*

United States, she has the right to vote.
2. Someone who lives in a certain city or town; resident: *The citizens of our city put on a parade.*
cit|i|zen (sit′ə zən *or* sit′ə sən) *noun, plural* **citizens.**

citizenship—**1.** The responsibilities and rights involved in being a member of a country, city, or town: *I have American citizenship.* **2.** The behavior of a member of a country, city, or town: *His teacher gave him a star for good citizenship.*
cit|i|zen|ship (sit′ə zən ship *or* sit′ə sən ship) *noun, plural* **citizenships.**

citrus—A type of tree on which fruits such as oranges, grapefruits, and lemons grow.
cit|rus (sit′rəs) *noun, plural* **citruses.**

city—An area larger than a village or a town where many people work and live. It usually has a mayor as the head of its government.
cit|y (sit′ē) *noun, plural* **cities.**

civic—**1.** Having to do with a city: *Our civic club works to keep the city beautiful.* **2.** Involving the responsibilities of citizenship: *Paying taxes is a civic responsibility.*
civ|ic (siv′ik) *adjective.*
● Synonyms: **municipal, urban,** for **1.**

civics—The study of how government works and of the responsibilities of citizenship.
civ|ics (siv′iks) *noun.*

civil—**1.** Pertaining to citizens: *The law protects our civil rights.* **2.** Having to do with the general public; not related to military or religious matters: *They were married in a civil ceremony.* **3.** Well-mannered: *He looked angry but answered us in a civil way.*
civ|il (siv′əl) *adjective.*

civilian—A person who is not a member of the military forces. *Noun.*
—Having to do with civilians: *The civilian visitors left the ship before it sailed. Adjective.*
ci|vil|ian (sə vil′yən) *noun, plural* **civilians;** *adjective.*

civilization—**1.** Those societies that are highly developed, especially in their systems of government, trade, agriculture, and the arts and sciences: *We study Western civilization in our history class.* **2.** The modern conveniences of

highly developed societies: *Cable television and computers are part of modern* civilization.
civ|i|li|za|tion (siv′ə lə zā′shən) *noun, plural* **civilizations.**

civilize—To introduce the ways of highly developed civilizations to less developed societies.
civ|i|lize (siv′ə līz) *verb,* **civilized, civilizing.**

civil rights—The rights guaranteed by law to a citizen.
civ|il rights (siv′əl rīts) *noun, singular* **civil right.**

claim—**1.** To act so that others know one has a right to or is the owner of something: *She claimed her book from the lost-and-found box.* **2.** To maintain that something is fact: *He claims that his bicycle was stolen. Verb.*
—**1.** A demand for something that is owed that person: *She filed a claim with the insurance company for property damaged by fire.* **2.** A statement that something is fact: *His claim about his cooking ability was true. Noun.*
claim (klām) *verb,* **claimed, claiming;** *noun, plural* **claims.**

clam—A saltwater or freshwater animal with a soft body that is covered by a shell. The shell has two connected halves. Many kinds of clams can be eaten, either raw or cooked. *Noun.*
—To gather clams: *Let's go clamming at the beach. Verb.*
clam (klam) *noun, plural* **clams;** *verb,* **clammed, clamming.**
■ **clam up:** To refuse to talk: *She clammed up when the teacher asked who was yelling.*
happy as a clam: Extremely happy.

clam (noun)

clammy—Cool, wet, and sticky: *My hands felt clammy after the walk in the rain.*
clam|my (klam′ē) *adjective,* **clammier, clammiest.**

clamor—**1.** A loud, constant noise: *We could hardly hear her talk because of the* clamor *in the*

a at	i if	oo look	ch chalk		a in ago
ā ape	ī idle	ou out	ng sing		e in happen
ah calm	o odd	u ugly	sh ship	ə =	i in capital
aw all	ō oats	ū rule	th think		o in occur
e end	oi oil	ur turn	th their		u in upon
ē easy			zh treasure		

cafeteria.   **2.** A public protest: *The citizens of our town started a* clamor *for cleaner water.* Noun.
—To make a lot of noise about something: *The dogs were* clamoring *to be let out.* Verb.
clam|or (**klam′**ər) *noun, plural* **clamors;** *verb,* **clamored, clamoring.**
• Synonyms: **commotion, din, racket, uproar,** for *noun* 1.
Antonyms: **quiet, silence, still,** for *noun* 1.

clamp—A tool used to press things together securely; vise. *Noun.*
—To press together securely: *The baby* clamped *her teeth and would not let go of the bottle.* Verb.
clamp (**klamp**) *noun, plural* **clamps;** *verb,* **clamped, clamping.**
■ **clamp down:** To become strict: *Mother* clamped down *on us when our grades dropped.*

clan—A family group that can trace its beginnings back in history to the same person.
clan (**klan**) *noun, plural* **clans.**

clap—**1.** To hit together loudly or with great force: *The boy* clapped *the erasers together to knock off the chalk.*   **2.** To show approval by hitting one's hands together; applaud.   **3.** To slap or pat in a friendly way: *My teacher* clapped *me on the shoulder when I won the spelling bee.* Verb.
—**1.** A loud, sudden noise like a slap: *a thunder* clap.   **2.** A friendly hit or pat. *Noun.*
clap (**klap**) *verb,* **clapped, clapping;** *noun, plural* **claps.**

clarify—To explain in clear terms: *I couldn't understand why Dad wouldn't let me go on the trip, but Mom* clarified *his reasons.*
clar|i|fy (**klar′**ə fī) *verb,* **clarified, clarifying.**

clarinet—A musical instrument shaped like a long pipe. It is played by covering its holes or pressing its keys while blowing into the mouthpiece.
clar|i|net (klar′ə **net′**) *noun, plural* **clarinets.**

clarinet

clarity—The state of being clear: *You explained your complicated science project with great* clarity.
clar|i|ty (**klar′**ə tē) *noun.*

clash—**1.** A loud sound like that of two hard objects crashing together: *We heard a great* clash *of pots and pans in the kitchen.*   **2.** A dispute; disagreement: *My sister and I have many* clashes *over using each other's things.* Noun.
—**1.** To make such a loud sound.   **2.** To have very different opinions: *We* clashed *over the rules of the game.* Verb.
clash (**klash**) *noun, plural* **clashes;** *verb,* **clashed, clashing.**

clasp—**1.** Something that fastens things together: *Many necklaces have* clasps *at the back.*   **2.** A tight hold with the arms or hands: *The baby was safe in the* clasp *of his father's arms.* Noun.
—**1.** To fasten something together: *She* clasped *her ponytail with a gold band.*   **2.** To hold tightly: *He fell asleep with the teddy bear* clasped *in his arms.* Verb.
clasp (**klasp**) *noun, plural* **clasps;** *verb,* **clasped, clasping.**
• Synonyms: **clutch, grasp, grip,** for *noun* 2.

class—**1.** A group of people or things that have certain things in common: *Human beings are the highest* class *of animals.*   **2.** A group that studies together: *Our art* class *went outside to draw.*   **3.** A certain rank or level of quality: *Only those drawings of the highest* class *will be displayed.* Noun.
—To group together; give a rank to: *She* classed *the shells by color.* Verb.
class (**klas**) *noun, plural* **classes;** *verb,* **classed, classing.**
• Synonyms: **category, form, kind², sort, type, variety,** for *noun* 1.

classic—**1.** Something that is the model of excellence: *These books are the* classics *of that time.*   **2. classics:** The literature of ancient Greece and Rome. *Noun.*
—Excellent; of the best quality: *This is a* classic *piece of furniture.* Adjective.
clas|sic (**klas′**ik) *noun, plural* **classics;** *adjective.*

classical—**1.** Having to do with the literature and art of ancient Greece and Rome: *Latin is a* classical *language.*   **2.** Excellent; outstanding: *That is a* classical *example of a western movie.*   **3.** Having to do with a certain kind of music, such as symphonies.
clas|si|cal (**klas′**ə kəl) *adjective.*

classification—**1.** A grouping together by classes: *The* classification *of the book collection will be according to subject.*   **2.** The result of grouping together: *In which insect* classification *does this bug belong?*
clas|si|fi|ca|tion (klas′ə fə **kā′**shən) *noun, plural* **classifications.**

classify—To organize into groups: *The coins were* classified *according to the year they were made.*
clas|si|fy (klas′ə fī) *verb,* **classified, classifying.**

classmate—A fellow member of a school class.
class|mate (klas′māt′) *noun, plural* **classmates.**

classroom—A room arranged especially for teaching and learning; schoolroom.
class|room (klas′rūm′ *or* klas′room′) *noun, plural* **classrooms.**

clatter—A loud noise made by things rattling together: *The* clatter *from the kitchen drowned out the sound of the television. Noun.*
—To make such a loud noise: *The pots and pans* clattered *in the sink. Verb.*
clat|ter (klat′ər) *noun, plural* **clatters;** *verb,* **clattered, clattering.**

clause—1. A part of a sentence that has a subject and a verb. In the sentence "I studied before I relaxed," "I studied" is a main clause, and "before I relaxed" is a subordinate clause that depends on the main clause for its meaning. 2. A part of a written agreement: *A* clause *in the sales agreement states that we can return the bicycle within ten days.*
clause (klawz) *noun, plural* **clauses.**

claw—1. A very sharp, hooked nail on the foot of an animal or a bird; talon. 2. A similar sharp part of a crab or lobster. 3. Something like the hooked nail on the foot of an animal or a bird: *A hammer has a* claw *to pull out nails. Noun.*
—To scratch, tear, or slash at something: *The kitten* clawed *at the toy. Verb.*
claw (klaw) *noun, plural* **claws;** *verb,* **clawed, clawing.**

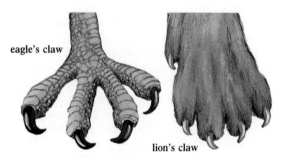

eagle's claw

lion's claw

claw (noun, definition 1)

a at	i if	oo look	ch chalk		a in ago
ā ape	ī idle	ou out	ng sing		e in happen
ah calm	o odd	u ugly	sh ship	ə =	i in capital
aw all	ō oats	ū rule	th think		o in occur
e end	oi oil	ur turn	th their		u in upon
ē easy			zh treasure		

clay—A kind of soil that can be molded into different shapes when it is wet. When clay is dried by baking, it becomes very hard.
clay (klā) *noun, plural* **clays.**

clean—1. Without dirt or spots: *The washing machine got the clothes* clean. 2. Decent; honorable; wholesome: *The family led a* clean *life.* 3. Complete: *He made a* clean *break with his past by moving to a new town. Adjective.*
—To free of dirt; make tidy: *Please* clean *your messy room. Verb.*
clean (klēn) *adjective,* **cleaner, cleanest;** *verb,* **cleaned, cleaning.**
■ **clean out:** To use up completely: *The hungry children* cleaned out *the peanut butter.*
come clean: To be truthful: *He decided to* come clean *and admit that he broke the vase.*

cleaner—1. A person who removes dirt and spots from things for a living: *a window* cleaner; *clothes* cleaners. 2. Anything that removes dirt and spots.
clean|er (klē′nər) *noun, plural* **cleaners.**

cleanliness—The state of being neat and tidy: *Our neighbor, whose house is spotless, is known for his* cleanliness.
clean|li|ness (klen′lē nis) *noun.*

cleanly[1]—Always free from dirt; neat: *a* cleanly *hospital room.*
clean|ly (klen′lē) *adjective,* **cleanlier, cleanliest.**

cleanly[2]—In a tidy manner; neatly: *The sharp knife cut* cleanly *through the apple.*
clean|ly (klēn′lē) *adverb.*

cleanse—To wash; make free of dirt: *She* cleansed *her face with soap and water.*
cleanse (klenz) *verb,* **cleansed, cleansing.**

cleanser—A liquid or powder that is used to get rid of dirt and stains: *We washed the dirty bathtub with* cleanser.
cleans|er (klen′zər) *noun, plural* **cleansers.**

clear—1. Free from clouds or darkness: *The day was bright and* clear. 2. Clean; easy to see through: *The newly washed windows were prefectly* clear. 3. Easy to hear, see, or understand; obvious: *Her meaning was* clear. *Adjective.*
—1. To make clean; remove a mess: *Please* clear *the table.* 2. To become bright or free from clouds: *The sky* cleared *after the storm ended.* 3. To get over or past something without touching it: *The runner* cleared *the hurdle. Verb.*
—In a way that can be easily heard: *Talk loud and* clear. *Adverb.*
clear (klēr) *adjective,* **clearer, clearest;** *verb,* **cleared, clearing;** *adverb.*

■ **clear the air:** To get rid of anger or conflict, especially between two people: *The two friends did not want their anger to come between them, so they* cleared the air.
in the clear: Free from guilt: *The boy was* in the clear *once the real thief was caught.*

● Synonyms: **apparent, evident, plain,** for *adjective* **3.**
Antonyms: **hazy, obscure, vague,** for *adjective* **3.**

clearance—**1.** The act of getting rid of something: Clearance *of the dead trees began in summer.*   **2.** The space between things: *The movers had only inches of* clearance *between the table and the doorway.*
clear|ance (klēr'əns) *noun, plural* **clearances.**

clearing—An open piece of land, without trees or brush: *A cabin stood in a* clearing *in the forest.*
clear|ing (klēr'ing) *noun, plural* **clearings.**

cleaver—A tool with a short handle and a wide, heavy blade that is used for cutting. A cleaver is usually used to cut large, thick pieces of meat.
cleav|er (klē'vər) *noun, plural* **cleavers.**

cleaver

clef—A musical symbol placed on the left side of a staff. It shows the pitch of the notes.
clef (klef) *noun, plural* **clefs.**

cleft—A crack; space made by splitting: *a cleft in a rock; a cleft in a log. Noun.*
—Divided; indented: *a cleft chin. Adjective.*
cleft (kleft) *noun, plural* **clefts;** *adjective.*

clench—**1.** To close firmly together; tighten: *She* clenches *her teeth when she is nervous.*   **2.** To hold onto tightly: *We* clenched *each other's hands during the horror movie.*
clench (klench) *verb,* **clenched, clenching.**

clergy—People who do religious work. Priests, ministers, and rabbis are members of the clergy.
cler|gy (klur'jē) *noun, plural* **clergies.**

clerical—**1.** Having to do with keeping records, filing, and doing other general office work. **2.** Having to do with the clergy: *Part of a minister's* clerical *work is visiting the sick. Adjective.*
cler|i|cal (kler'ə kəl) *adjective.*

clerk—**1.** A person who sells things in a store. **2.** A person who does general office work such as filing. *Noun.*
—To work at simple tasks in an office or store: *He* clerks *at the drugstore. Verb.*
clerk (klurk) *noun, plural* **clerks;** *verb,* **clerked, clerking.**

Cleveland Bay—A strong horse, originally used for pulling coaches. It was first bred in England.
Cleve|land Bay (klēv'lənd bā) *noun, plural* **Cleveland Bays.**

Cleveland Bay

clever—**1.** Smart, quick, and able: *He is very* clever *at fixing things.*   **2.** Inventive; creative: *Her drawings are very* clever.
clev|er (klev'ər) *adjective,* **cleverer, cleverest.**
● Synonyms: **bright, brilliant,** for **1.**
Antonyms: **dumb, stupid,** for **1.**

click—A sharp sound like a snap: *The channel dial on the television makes a* click *when I turn it. Noun.*
—To make a short, sharp sound: *The radio* clicked *on. Verb.*
click (klik) *noun, plural* **clicks;** *verb,* **clicked, clicking.**

client—A customer who uses someone's professional services: *My mother is a banker and has many* clients.
cli|ent (klī'ənt) *noun, plural* **clients.**

cliff—A steep slope of rock or dirt: *Mountain* cliffs *surround the lake.*
cliff (klif) *noun, plural* **cliffs.**

climate—Weather that is typical for a certain place. Climate includes the average temperature,

wetness or dryness, winds, and other conditions of an area: *a tropical* climate.
cli|mate (klī′mit) *noun, plural* **climates**.

climax—The peak or best part of something: *The* climax *of our vacation was the boat ride*.
cli|max (klī′maks) *noun, plural* **climaxes**.

climb—To go up and up: *We* climbed *to the top of the mountain. Verb*.
—**1**. A steady movement upward: *a* climb *up a ladder*. **2**. A thing that one goes up: *That hill looks like an easy* climb. *Noun*.
climb (klīm) *verb,* **climbed, climbing;** *noun, plural* **climbs**.
● Synonyms: **ascend, rise, soar**, for *verb*. Antonyms: **descend, sink**, for *verb*.

cling—To hold onto tightly; stick: *The shipwrecked sailors* clung *to life preservers*.
cling (kling) *verb,* **clung, clinging**.

clinic—A place that provides medical help: *When she cut her finger, she went to the* clinic *for stitches*.
clin|ic (klin′ik) *noun, plural* **clinics**.

clink—A sharp, ringing sound: *the* clink *of glass touching glass. Noun*.
—To make a sharp, ringing sound: *The keys* clinked *when he put them on the table. Verb*.
clink (klingk) *noun, plural* **clinks;** *verb,* **clinked, clinking**.

clip[1]—**1**. To trim by cutting: *Let me* clip *your hair*. **2**. To cut out: *to* clip *coupons from a newspaper. Verb*.
—A rate of speed: *She walked into town at a fast* clip. *Noun*.
clip (klip) *verb,* **clipped, clipping;** *noun, plural* **clips**.

clip[2]—To fasten or hold things together: *He* clipped *his report together with a staple. Verb*.
—Something that fastens or holds things together: *a paper* clip. *Noun*.
clip (klip) *verb,* **clipped, clipping;** *noun, plural* **clips**.

clipper—**1**. A very fast sailing ship. **2. clippers**: A cutting tool, such as scissors: *nail* clippers.
clip|per (klip′ər) *noun, plural* **clippers**.

cloak—A loose coat, often with no sleeves. *Noun*.

—To hide by covering: *Snow* cloaked *the lawn. Verb*.
cloak (klōk) *noun, plural* **cloaks;** *verb,* **cloaked, cloaking**.

clock—A device that measures and shows time in hours, minutes, and sometimes seconds. Clocks are usually kept in one place, not carried around like watches. *Noun*.
—To use a device that measures time to see how fast something is moving: *The coach* clocked *the speed of the relay team with his watch. Verb*.
clock (klok) *noun, plural* **clocks;** *verb,* **clocked, clocking**.
■ **around the clock**: 24 hours without stopping: *They drove* around the clock *to get there in time*.
turn the clock back: To return to an earlier time: *If only she could* turn the clock back, *she could take back her mean words*.

Word History

Cloak and **clock** both come from a French word meaning "bell." When spread out, a cloak looks like a bell. The first clocks told time by ringing a bell.

---

clockwise—Going around from left to right, in the same direction as a clock's hands move: *We walked* clockwise *around the chairs. The wheel spun in a* clockwise *direction*.
clock|wise (klok′wīz′) *adverb, adjective*.

clockwise

clog—To block; close up: *The water backed up because the drain was* clogged *with food. Verb*.
—A heavy shoe with a wooden sole. It is often open at the heel. *Noun*.
clog (klog) *verb,* **clogged, clogging;** *noun, plural* **clogs**.

a at	i if	oo look	ch chalk		a in ago
ā ape	ī idle	ou out	ng sing		e in happen
ah calm	o odd	u ugly	sh ship	ə =	i in capital
aw all	ō oats	ū rule	th think		o in occur
e end	oi oil	ur turn	th their		u in upon
ē easy			zh treasure		

clone—An exact copy of something. In science, a clone is an identical copy of another living being made by laboratory methods: *The dogs look so much alike, they could be* clones.
clone (klōn) *noun, plural* **clones.**

close[1]—**1.** To shut: *to* close *a window; to* close *a book.*   **2.** To join; connect: *Mother* closed *the rip in my pants by sewing it.*   **3.** To end: *The ceremony* closed *with a speech by the mayor. Verb.*
—The last part; end: *The* close *of the movie was exciting. Noun.*
close (klōz) *verb,* **closed, closing;** *noun.*

close[2]—**1.** Nearby: *We live* close *to a store.*
2. Very friendly: *The two sisters were* close *and did everything together.*   **3.** Thorough or careful: *Please pay* close *attention to what the teacher says.*   **4.** Almost the same: *The twins were so* close *in looks that their friends could not tell them apart. Adjective.*
—Near: *Do not ride your bicycles too* close *together. Adverb.*
close (klōs) *adjective,* **closer, closest;** *adverb.*

closet—A small room for storing clothes or other things.
clos|et (kloz′it) *noun, plural* **closets.**

close-up—A photograph taken very near to the thing or person shown: *The* close-up *showed her tears running down her cheeks. Noun.*
—Very near: *We sat in front for a* close-up *view of the movie. Adjective.*
close-up (klōs′up′) *noun, plural* **close-ups;** *adjective.*

clot—A soft lump that is solid enough to stay together; a thick mass: *a blood* clot; *a* clot *of sour milk. Noun.*
—To clump together; become thick: *The blood* clotted *and closed up the wound. Verb.*
clot (klot) *noun, plural* **clots;** *verb,* **clotted, clotting.**

cloth—**1.** Material woven of cotton, wool, or other fibers.   **2.** A piece of this material used for some special purpose: *a dust* cloth; *a* cloth *for washing. Noun.*
cloth (klawth) *noun, plural* **cloths.**

clothe—To dress: *I* clothed *myself in a heavy coat.*
clothe (klōth) *verb,* **clothed** or **clad, clothing.**

clothes—Things that are worn to cover the body, such as a dress, a shirt, or pants.
clothes (klōthz) *noun.*

clothespin—A wood or plastic fastener for hanging clothes on a line, usually to dry them after washing.

clothes|pin (klōthz′pin′) *noun, plural* **clothespins.**

clothing—Coverings for the body; clothes.
cloth|ing (klō′thing) *noun.*

cloud—**1.** A white or gray mass of water drops or bits of ice seen in the sky. Rain and snow come from clouds.   **2.** A mass of dust or smoke: *A* cloud *of smoke came from the burning house. Noun.*
—To cover up; make foggy: *The steam* clouded *my eyeglasses and I could not see. Verb.*
cloud (kloud) *noun, plural* **clouds;** *verb,* **clouded, clouding.**
■ **on cloud nine:** Perfectly happy: *Now that she's found her lost dog, she's* on cloud nine.

Word History

Cloud comes from an Old English word meaning "rock." It also is related to an Old English word meaning "lump." Many clouds look like large floating lumps of rock.

---

cloudburst—A sudden storm with heavy rains.
cloud|burst (kloud′burst′) *noun, plural* **cloudbursts.**

cloudy—**1.** Filled with clouds: *Cloudy skies can mean that it will rain.*   **2.** Unclear; hazy: *We did not want to drink the* cloudy *water.*
cloud|y (klou′dē) *adjective,* **cloudier, cloudiest.**

clove[1]—A spice made by drying the flower of a type of tropical evergreen tree. Cloves are used as a seasoning in cooking.
clove (klōv) *noun, plural* **cloves.**

clove[2]—A part of a garlic bulb.
clove (klōv) *noun, plural* **cloves.**

clover—A short plant having leaves divided into three leaflets and having many small clumps of flowers. It is used as food for cows.
clo|ver (klō′vər) *noun, plural* **clovers.**
■ **in clover:** Having a wonderful life; without worries: *We would be* in clover *if we won the lottery.*

clown—A person who wears funny clothes and makeup and does things to make people laugh. He or she is usually a member of a circus. *Noun.*
—To joke and act silly like such a person: *Stop* clowning *and settle down to work.*
clown (kloun) *noun, plural* **clowns;** *verb,* **clowned, clowning.**

club—**1.** A thick stick of wood that is narrow on one end and used as a weapon.   **2.** A stick used in certain sports: *a golf* club.   **3.** A group of

people who meet regularly because of a shared interest: *a chess* club; *a sewing* club. **4.** A playing card with a black, three-leafed design on it: *the six of* clubs. *Noun.*
—To hit with a thick stick: *He* clubbed *the rat to death. Verb.*
club (klub) *noun, plural* **clubs;** *verb,* **clubbed, clubbing.**

clue—Something that helps solve a problem or a mystery: *The footprint was our only* clue *that someone had been there.*
clue (klū) *noun, plural* **clues.**

Clumber spaniel—A large hunting dog with short legs, a heavy body, and a long, soft coat that is mostly white. Originally bred in England, these dogs are easy to train but hunt very slowly.
Clum|ber span|iel (klum′bər span′yəl) *noun, plural* **Clumber spaniels.**

Clumber spaniel

clump—**1.** A cluster; bunch: *The flowers grew close together in a* clump. **2.** A thick mass; lump: *a* clump *of dirt.* **3.** A sound like a sharp thump. *Noun.*
—To make a sharp, heavy thumping sound: *Their shoes* clumped *across the wood floor. Verb.*
clump (klump) *noun, plural* **clumps;** *verb,* **clumped, clumping.**

clumsy—Lacking in grace; awkward: *The child was very* clumsy *as he learned to walk.*
clum|sy (klum′zē) *adjective,* **clumsier, clumsiest.**

cluster—A group of similar things; bunch: *a* cluster *of stores; a* cluster *of trees. Noun.*
—To bunch together: *The children* clustered *around their babysitter to hear the story. Verb.*
clus|ter (klus′tər) *noun, plural* **clusters;** *verb,* **clustered, clustering.**

clutch—To hold onto something tightly; grip: *The child* clutched *her father's hand. Verb.*
—**1.** A tight, strong hold: *He got a good* clutch *on the ball and ran for a touchdown.* **2.** A device that connects or disconnects the motor in a machine, making it stop or go. *Noun.*
clutch (kluch) *verb,* **clutched, clutching;** *noun, plural* **clutches.**

clutter—A number of objects left in a mess: *He couldn't find his book in the* clutter *of his room. Noun.*
—To mess things up; litter: *After the game, the stands were* cluttered *with empty cups and candy wrappers. Verb.*
clut|ter (klut′ər) *noun, plural* **clutters;** *verb,* **cluttered, cluttering.**

Clydesdale—A strong, large horse with long hair on the lower part of each leg. It is used for pulling heavy loads and is often seen in parades.
Clydes|dale (klīdz′dāl) *noun, plural* **Clydesdales.**

Clydesdale

a at	i if	oo look	ch chalk		a in ago
ā ape	ī idle	ou out	ng sing		e in happen
ah calm	o odd	u ugly	sh ship	ə =	i in capital
aw all	ō oats	ū rule	th think		o in occur
e end	oi oil	ur turn	th their		u in upon
ē easy			zh treasure		

cm—The abbreviation for **centimeter** or **centimeters.**

co-—A prefix that means "with," "equal," or "together." Co-workers do jobs together.

coach—1. A closed-in carriage that is pulled by horses. 2. A railroad passenger car. 3. A low-priced passenger section of an airplane, bus, or train. 4. A person who teaches or trains athletes, actors, singers, and other performers: *a football* coach; *a voice* coach. *Noun.*
—To teach or train: *She* coached *the singer in a new style of music. Verb.*
coach (kōch) *noun, plural* **coaches;** *verb,* **coached, coaching.**

Word History

The **coach** was invented in Hungary in a village named Kocs. The word **coach** comes from an old Hungarian word meaning "vehicle made in Kocs."

---

coal—1. A black substance that forms in the earth from matter that has decayed. It is brought out from the earth by miners and is burned as fuel. 2. Any wood or other material that is burned until glowing.
coal (kōl) *noun, plural* **coals.**
• Synonyms: **cinder, ember,** for **2.**

coarse—1. Rough and scratchy; not smooth: *The* coarse *wood needed sanding to make it smooth.* 2. Made up of large pieces: *The* coarse *gravel on the road made our ride bumpy.* 3. Crude; without manners: *The teacher does not allow* coarse *speech in the classroom.*
coarse (kawrs) *adjective,* **coarser, coarsest.**
• A word that sounds the same is **course.**

coast—The edge of land; seashore: *The storm hit the* coast, *but did not go inland. Noun.*
—To slide or glide: *He stopped pedaling his bicycle and* coasted *down the hill. Verb.*
coast (kōst) *noun, plural* **coasts;** *verb,* **coasted, coasting.**
■ **the coast is clear:** No one is around; there is no danger: *After everyone went to bed, the* coast was clear *to raid the refrigerator.*

Coast Guard—A branch of the United States military forces whose responsibility is to guard the country's coasts.
Coast Guard (kōst gahrd) *noun.*

coastline—The outline of the edge of land: *The map showed how the* coastline *looks.*
coast|line (kōst′līn′) *noun, plural* **coastlines.**

coat—1. An outer covering for the body. 2. An animal's outer covering: *a dog's furry* coat. 3. A covering or layer: *a* coat *of paint. Noun.*
—To cover with a layer: *He* coated *the car with wax. Verb.*
coat (kōt) *noun, plural* **coats;** *verb,* **coated, coating.**

coat of arms—A symbol for a family, country, state, or organization. It is a shield with a design that shows something about the group it represents.
coat of arms (kōt ov ahrmz *or* kōt uv ahrmz) *noun, plural* **coats of arms.**

coat of arms

coax—To convince someone to do something: *We* coaxed *my parents into letting us have a party.*
coax (kōks) *verb,* **coaxed, coaxing.**

cob—1. The inner part of an ear of corn on which the kernels grow. 2. A male swan.
cob (kob) *noun, plural* **cobs.**

cobalt—A chemical element that is silver-white in color, very hard, and used to make steel and other metals. It is usually found with the elements nickel and iron.
co|balt (kō′bawlt) *noun.*

cobble—1. To repair or make shoes or boots. 2. To put together in a clumsy way.
cob|ble (kob′əl) *verb,* **cobbled, cobbling.**

cobbler—1. A person who makes or repairs shoes for a living. 2. A baked dessert made of fruit and topped with a crust.
cob|bler (kob′lər) *noun, plural* **cobblers.**

cobblestone—A round, smooth stone once used in paving roads.
cob|ble|stone (kob′əl stōn′) *noun, plural* **cobblestones.**

cobra

Word History

Cobra comes from a Portuguese word meaning
"the snake with the hood." When bothered, a
cobra expands the skin around its head and neck
and looks as though it is wearing a hood.

cobra—A long poisonous snake found mainly in
Africa and Asia.
co|bra (kō′brə) *noun, plural* **cobras.**

cobweb—A network of thin threads spun by a
spider.
cob|web (kob′web′) *noun, plural* **cobwebs.**

cock¹—A male bird, especially a male chicken;
rooster. *Noun.*
—To pull back on the firing pin or hammer of a
gun to prepare for shooting: *The policeman* cocked
his pistol, ready to shoot at the target. Verb.
cock (kok) *noun, plural* **cocks;** *verb,* **cocked,
cocking.**

cock²—To tilt or raise up, usually in response to
a signal or noise: *The rabbit* cocked *its ears
when it heard the dog coming.*
cock (kok) *verb,* **cocked, cocking.**

cockatoo—A large, brightly colored bird with a
tuft of feathers on its head. It is found especially
in Australia.
cock|a|too (kok′ə tū′) *noun, plural* **cockatoos.**

cocker spaniel—A small dog that has a soft,
thick coat, drooping ears, and long hairs on its
ears, chest, and legs. Originally bred to hunt,
today these dogs are mainly kept as pets and
show dogs.

a at	i if	oo look	ch chalk		a in ago
ā ape	ī idle	ou out	ng sing		e in happen
ah calm	o odd	u ugly	sh ship	ə =	i in capital
aw all	ō oats	ū rule	th think		o in occur
e end	oi oil	ur turn	th their		u in upon
ē easy			zh treasure		

cock|er span|iel (kok′ər span′yəl) *noun,
plural* **cocker spaniels.**

cocker spaniel

cockpit—The place in an airplane or boat where
the pilot or operator sits.
cock|pit (kok′pit′) *noun, plural* **cockpits.**

cockroach—An insect that lives in damp, dark
places. It has a flat, oval-shaped body that is
yellow-brown or black.
cock|roach (kok′rōch′) *noun, plural*
cockroaches.

cocktail—1. An iced drink made with liquor and
other ingredients. 2. A nonalcoholic drink or a

cockatoo

food served before the main course of a meal; appetizer: *a tomato juice* cocktail; *shrimp* cocktail.

cock|tail (kok′tāl′) *noun, plural* **cocktails.**

cocky—Overly confident in one's ability to do something: *They were sorry they had been* cocky *after they lost the game.*

cock|y (kok′ē) *adjective,* **cockier, cockiest.**

cocoa—1. A powder made from the ground-up, roasted seeds of the cocoa tree. 2. A hot drink made from cocoa powder, milk, and sugar.

co|coa (kō′kō) *noun, plural* **cocoas.**

coconut—A large, brown, tropical nut that grows on a type of palm tree. Its hard shell surrounds a layer of white meat that can be eaten and a sweet liquid center that can be drunk.

co|co|nut (kō′kə nut′) *noun, plural* **coconuts.**

whole coconut

split coconut

tree

coconut

cocoon—A soft covering that a caterpillar builds around itself while it changes into a moth or butterfly.

co|coon (kə kūn′) *noun, plural* **cocoons.**

cod—A fish that is caught for food in the northern, colder waters of the Atlantic and Pacific oceans.

cod (kod) *noun, plural* **cods** or **cod.**

coddle—To treat in a very gentle way; pamper: *Our mother* coddles *us when we are sick.*

cod|dle (kod′əl) *verb,* **coddled, coddling.**
 • Synonyms: **humor, indulge, spoil**

code—1. Any system of symbols used in the place of letters or words to send messages, especially those that are secret: *Our club has a secret* code

that only members know. **2.** Rules that one is expected to follow in specific situations or places: *The fire safety* codes *in our school required one fire drill a month. Noun.*
—To put into a secret or special language: *The message was* coded *so only we knew what it meant. Verb.*

code (kōd) *noun, plural* **codes;** *verb,* **coded, coding.**

coffee—A brown liquid that is made from roasted and ground coffee beans. The beans grow on short trees in tropical areas.

cof|fee (kaw′fē) *noun.*

coffin—A box in which a dead person is buried.

cof|fin (kaw′fin) *noun, plural* **coffins.**

cog—One of many notches on the edge of a wheel that fits into a notch on a similar wheel. When the first wheel turns, it transfers motion to the second wheel. A spring often activates the first wheel, as in a clock or a watch.

cog (kog) *noun, plural* **cogs.**

coil—1. Something that is wound up in circles: *a* coil *of rope.* **2.** A wire made into a spiral for carrying electricity. *Noun.*
—To circle around and around: *I* coiled *the clay around to make a vase. Verb.*

coil (koil) *noun, plural* **coils;** *verb,* **coiled, coiling.**
 • Synonyms: **curl, twine, twist, wind,** for *verb.*

coin—Money cut out of metal; change. It is usually round and has its value and the country's symbols stamped on it. *Noun.*
—To make money out of metal: *Money can only be* coined *by governments. Verb.*

coin (koin) *noun, plural* **coins;** *verb,* **coined, coining.**

coincide—1. To happen at the same time: *My birthday* coincides *with Christmas, so we always have a double celebration.* **2.** To be in

cocoon

agreement: *I like her because our ways of thinking* coincide.   **3.** To come together: *The two streets* coincide *just before the bridge.*
co|in|cide (kō'in sīd') *verb,* **coincided, coinciding.**

• Synonyms: **correspond, match²,** for **2.**
Antonym: **differ,** for **2.**

coincidence—A chance happening: *It is a coincidence that we have the same birthday.*
co|in|ci|dence (kō in'sə dəns) *noun, plural* **coincidences.**

coke—A solid substance that results from burning coal. It is used as a fuel.
coke (kōk) *noun.*

cold—**1.** Lacking warmth: *My hands are* cold *without my mittens.*   **2.** Very chilly; having little or no heat: *Our climate is hot in the summer and* cold *in the winter.*   **3.** Unfriendly; unfeeling: *She gave me a* cold *hello. Adjective.*
—**1.** A low temperature condition: *Because of the* cold, *we put on extra blankets.*   **2.** An illness that usually causes a sore throat, coughing, and a stuffed-up nose. *Noun.*
cold (kōld) *adjective,* **colder, coldest;** *noun, plural* **colds.**

■ **catch cold:** To have a cold: *Bundle up outside or you'll* catch cold.
get cold feet: To be unsure or nervous about doing something: *On the first day of practice, I* got cold feet *about being head coach.*
out in the cold: Alone; left out: *I was* out in the cold *because I did not know their language.*

cold-blooded—**1.** Having a blood temperature that depends on the outside surrounding temperature: *Snakes like to lie in the warm sun because they are* cold-blooded *animals.*
2. Having little feelings for others; cruel: *He seemed so* cold-blooded *when he did not ask me to his party.*
cold-blood|ed (kōld blud'id) *adjective.*

coleslaw—A cold salad made of chopped cabbage and other ingredients.
cole|slaw (kōl'slaw') *noun.*

coliseum—A large stadium or arena in which events are held.
col|i|se|um (kol' ə sē' əm) *noun, plural* **coliseums.**

collage—A picture made by pasting a mixture of many things, such as pictures and words, bits of paper, fabric, and string on a piece of paper.
col|lage (kə lahzh') *noun, plural* **collages.**

collapse—**1.** To fall down or cave in; break apart: *The house made of toy blocks* collapsed *when I touched it.*   **2.** To fold in order to take up less space: *We can* collapse *the folding chairs. Verb.*
—The act of falling down or caving in. *Noun.*
col|lapse (kə laps') *verb,* **collapsed, collapsing;** *noun, plural* **collapses.**

collar—**1.** A part of clothing that circles the neck: *I turned my* collar *up to keep my neck warm.*
2. A leather, plastic, or metal strap that buckles around an animal's neck: *a dog* collar. *Noun.*
—**1.** To put a strap around the neck: *All dogs must be* collared *and leashed in this park.*   **2.** To catch by a strap around the neck; to grab: *The stray dog was* collared *by the dogcatcher. Verb.*
col|lar (kol'ər) *noun, plural* **collars;** *verb,* **collared, collaring.**

■ **hot under the collar:** Very angry: *He got* hot under the collar *when I lost his skateboard.*

collarbone—The bone that is between the shoulder blade and the breastbone.
col|lar|bone (kol'ər bōn') *noun, plural* **collarbones.**

collard—**1.** A green leafy vegetable: *a* collard *plant.*   **2.** collards: The green leaves of the collard, eaten cooked: *The* collards *were flavored with ham.*
col|lard (kol'ərd) *noun, plural* **collards.**

colleague—A partner; someone who works with another.
col|league (kol'ēg) *noun, plural* **colleagues.**

collect—**1.** To get together; gather: *We* collected *money to get our teacher a present.*   **2.** To receive payment for what is owed: *I will* collect *my pay after I have mowed the grass.*
col|lect (kə lekt') *verb,* **collected, collecting**
• Synonyms: **keep, hoard, store,** for **1.**

collection—**1.** Things gathered together: *My baseball card* collection *gets bigger every day.*
2. A gathering together of money for a special cause: *They took up a* collection *for the party.*
col|lec|tion (kə lek'shən) *noun, plural* **collections.**

collector—Someone who gathers things together: *I am a coin* collector.
col|lec|tor (kə lek'tər) *noun, plural* **collectors.**

college—A school after high school where students can concentrate on a particular field of study.
col|lege (kol'ij) *noun, plural* **colleges.**

a at	i if	oo look	ch chalk		a in ago
ā ape	ī idle	ou out	ng sing		e in happen
ah calm	o odd	u ugly	sh ship	ə =	i in capital
aw all	ō oats	ū rule	th think		o in occur
e end	oi oil	ur turn	th their		u in upon
ē easy			zh treasure		

collide—To crash together: *We* collided *on our bicycles because we were riding too close to each other.*
col|lide (kə līd′) *verb,* **collided, colliding.**
• Synonyms: **bang, bump, jar², jolt**

collie—A large dog with long or short hair, a slender body, a long nose, and ears that lie close to the head. Originally bred in Scotland, these dogs herded sheep.
col|lie (kol′ē) *noun, plural* **collies.**

collie

collision—A crashing together; accident: *The ice on the road caused a car* collision.
col|li|sion (kə lizh′ən) *noun, plural* **collisions.**

colon¹—A punctuation mark that looks like this : and has two major uses: **1.** It separates a list, quotation, or explanation from the rest of a sentence: *I have three favorite colors: blue, orange, and red.* **2.** It is used at the end of the greeting in a business letter: *Dear Mr. Smith:.*
co|lon (ko′lən) *noun, plural* **colons.**

colon²—The last section of the large intestine. Food passes through the colon before it leaves the body.
co|lon (ko′lən) *noun, plural* **colons.**

colonel—An officer's rank in the armed services that is above a major and below a general.
colo|nel (kur′nəl) *noun, plural* **colonels.**
Abbreviation: Col.
• A word that sounds the same is **kernel.**

Word History

Colonel comes from a French word that was spelled two different ways: coronel and colonel. Today we write the word as colonel, but we pronounce it as **kur′nəl**, because of the coronel spelling.

colonial—Concerning a colony: Colonial *America was under British law until its independence in 1776.*
co|lo|ni|al (kə lō′nē əl) *adjective.*

colonist—One of a group of people who settle in an area away from their own country and government.
col|o|nist (kol′ə nist) *noun, plural* **colonists.**

colony—**1.** A group of people who settle in an area away from their own country and government. **2.** A place where such a group settles: *This country was once a* colony *but is now independent.* **3.** Any group living together: *a* colony *of ants.*
col|o|ny (kol′ə nē) *noun, plural* **colonies.**

color—**1.** A tint of shade that is not black or white. Red, blue, and yellow are the main colors from which all other colors are made. **2.** The shade of one's skin: *People of all* colors *are equal under our laws. Noun.*
—To apply a tint or shade to: *The clown* colored *her cheeks red. Verb.*
col|or (kul′ər) *noun, plural* **colors;** *verb,* **colored, coloring.**
■ **with flying colors:** Very successfully: *You passed this exam* with flying colors.

color-blind—Not able to see the difference between some colors or among all colors. Many color-blind people cannot see the difference between red and green; others, between blue and yellow.
col|or-blind (kul′ər blīnd′) *adjective.*

colored—Having a tint or shade; not just black and white: *Comic books have brightly* colored *pictures.*
col|ored (kul′ərd) *adjective.*

colorful—**1.** Having many colors: *a* colorful *poster.* **2.** Exciting; interesting: *The sailor told many* colorful *stories about his trip around the world.*
col|or|ful (kul′ər fəl) *adjective.*

coloring—**1.** The way in which something is colored: *The parrot had beautiful* coloring. **2.** A

substance used to give or make color: *He used purple* coloring *to dye the Easter eggs.*
col|or|ing (**kul′**ər ing) *noun, plural* **colorings.**

colossal—Huge; gigantic: *Some dinosaurs were colossal, while others were tiny.*
co|los|sal (kə **los′**əl) *adjective.*
 • Synonyms: *See* Synonyms at **big.**
  Antonyms: *See* Synonyms at **small.**

colt—A young horse, especially a male.
colt (kōlt) *noun, plural* **colts.**

colt

Columbus Day—A holiday celebrated in the United States on the second Monday in October. It recognizes Christopher Columbus's landing in America on October 12, 1492.
Co|lum|bus Day (kə **lum′**bəs dā) *noun.*

column—1. A tall, strong support; pillar. Columns are used to hold up or decorate a building. They are made of wood, stone, or metal.   2. Something shaped like a column: *a column of numbers.*   3. A long line of people: *A column of police officers marched in the parade.*
4. A narrow section of printed words running from the top to the bottom of a page.   5. A part of a newspaper or magazine that is regularly used for a certain subject or is written by a certain person: *the sports* column.
col|umn (**kol′**əm) *noun, plural* **columns.**

coma—A long period of unconsciousness that is usually caused by an illness or an injury, such as a very hard blow to the head. A person in a coma appears to be sleeping but cannot wake up.
co|ma (**kō′**mə) *noun, plural* **comas.**

comb—1. A plastic or metal object with many points that is used to arrange or untangle a person's hair or to hold it in place.   2. A thick, red piece of skin on the top of the head of a rooster, a chicken, or some other birds. *Noun.*
—1. To arrange or untangle with such a pointed object: *He combed his hair before breakfast.*
2. To search: *She combed the house looking for her lost library book. Verb.*
comb (kōm) *noun, plural* **combs;** *verb* **combed, combing.**

comb
(noun, definition 2)

combat—To fight or struggle against: *The people worked to* combat *the rising flood waters. Verb.*
—A fight; struggle: *The knight was brave in* combat. *Noun.*
com|bat (**kom′**bat *or* kəm **bat′** for *verb;* **kom′**bat for *noun*) *verb,* **combated, combating;** *noun, plural* **combats.**
 • Synonyms: **battle, conflict,** for *noun.*
  Antonym: **peace,** for *noun.*

combination—1. The act of joining or mixing together: *Mud comes from the* combination *of water and dirt.*   2. Something that is made by joining or mixing different things: *A milk shake is a* combination *of ice cream and milk.*   3. A series of numbers or letters that are dialed to open a lock: *I couldn't get into my locker because I forgot the* combination.
com|bi|na|tion (kom′bə **nā′**shən) *noun, plural* **combinations.**

combine—To mix; join together: *He combined yellow and blue paint to make green. Verb.*
—A machine used for harvesting grain. *Noun.*
com|bine (kəm **bīn′** for *verb;* **kom′**bīn for *noun*) *verb,* **combined, combining;** *noun, plural* **combines.**
 • Synonyms: **blend, compound, merge,** for *verb.*
  Antonyms: **divide, part, separate,** for *verb.*

a at	i if	oo look	ch chalk			a in ago
ā ape	ī idle	ou out	ng sing			e in happen
ah calm	o odd	u ugly	sh ship	ə =		i in capital
aw all	ō oats	ū rule	th think			o in occur
e end	oi oil	ur turn	th their			u in upon
ē easy			zh treasure			

combustion—The process of catching fire and burning: *Homes are heated by the energy created from the* combustion *of fuel.*
com|bus|tion (kəm bus′chən) *noun, plural* **combustions.**

come—**1.** To move in the direction of someone or something: Come *and sit down next to me.*
2. To arrive: *Her aunt is* coming *for a visit.*
3. To appear: *She watched the butterflies* come *and go among the flowers.* **4.** To happen at a certain time or place: *Thanksgiving* comes *in November.* **5.** To reach: *The skirt* comes *down past her knees.* **6.** To be taken; follow: *My last name* comes *from a French word.* **7.** To be born; originate: *She* comes *from a large family.*
8. To end up being; turn out to be: *He hoped that his wish would* come *true.* **9.** To be available: *Ice cream* comes *in many flavors.*
come (kum) *verb,* **came, come, coming.**
- **come about:** To happen: *How did the accident* come about?
come around: **1.** To get better; recover: *She was quite ill, but she's* coming around *now.*
2. To become agreeable: *At first Dad said no, but he finally* came around *and let me have a puppy.*
come by: To get: *How did she* come by *that new skateboard?*
come down on: To be very angry with; scold: *Her parents really* came down on *her when she got poor grades again.*
come down with: To become ill with: *He* came down with *a bad cold.*
come off it: To stop something: *She acted very proud until her friends told her to* come off it.
come out with: To tell; speak: *He knew who broke the window, so I told him to* come out with *it.*
come through: To succeed; do what is necessary: *The football team* came through *in the last minute to win the game.*
come to: **1.** To become conscious again: *She* came to *an hour after the accident.* **2.** To have a total of: *The bill for repairing the bike* came to *$20.*
come up: to arise; develop: *The question is not likely to* come up *at tonight's meeting.*
come upon: To find unexpectedly: *He* came upon *a dollar bill lying in the parking lot.*
how come: What is the reason; how does it happen: How come *there's no milk in the refrigerator?*

comedian—**1.** Someone whose business is to tell jokes or funny stories: **2.** An actor in a comedy.

co|me|di|an (kə mē′dē ən) *noun, plural* **comedians.**

comedienne—**1.** A woman whose business is to tell jokes or funny stories. **2.** An actress in a comedy.
co|me|di|enne (kə mē′dē en′) *noun, plural* **comediennes.**

comedy—A funny play, movie, or other work.
com|e|dy (kom′ə dē) *noun, plural* **comedies.**

comet—An object in outer space, like a star, but with a long tail of light. A comet is a frozen ball of ice, gas, and dust that travels around the sun. Most comets can be seen only with a telescope.
com|et (kom′it) *noun, plural* **comets.**

Word History

Comet comes from a Greek word meaning "wearing long hair." When a comet appears in the sky, it has a tail of bright light. The bright light looks like long, shiny hair.

---

comfort—To help to feel better; cheer up: *Mother* comforted *the little girl after she fell off her bicycle. Verb.*
—**1.** A person or thing that helps someone to feel better or more cheerful: *His dog is a* comfort *when he feels lonely.* **2.** The conditions needed to live easily or happily: *He does not like to go camping because he misses the* comfort *of home. Noun.*
com|fort (kum′fərt) *verb,* **comforted, comforting;** *noun, plural* **comforts.**
- **cold comfort:** Something that fails to help; sadness or grief: *When I broke my leg, being able to stay home from school was* cold comfort.

comfortable—**1.** Giving ease; causing good feelings: *a* comfortable *chair.* **2.** At ease: *She felt* comfortable *telling her father her troubles.*
com|fort|a|ble (kumf′tə bəl *or* kum′fər tə bəl) *adjective.*

comforter—A padded or quilted bed covering.
com|fort|er (kum′fər tər) *noun, plural* **comforters.**

comic—**1.** Causing smiles or laughter; funny: *The baby's attempt to eat an ice-cream cone was a* comic *sight.* **2.** Having to do with comedy: *a* comic *play full of jokes.*
—**1.** Someone who makes people laugh for a living. **2.** comics: Drawings in a newspaper that tell a story or joke: *He always opens the paper to the* comics *first. Noun.*
com|ic (kom′ik) *adjective; noun, plural* **comics.**

comical—Funny; amusing: *The monkey's tricks were* comical *to watch.*
com|i|cal (kom′ə kəl) *adjective.*
　● Synonyms: **hilarious, humorous**
　　Antonyms: **earnest, serious, solemn**

comic book—A magazine of comic strips.
com|ic book (kom′ik book) *noun, plural* **comic books.**

comic strip—A series of cartoon drawings that tell adventures or a funny story.
com|ic strip (kom′ik strip) *noun, plural* **comic strips.**

comma—The punctuation mark that looks like this , and has several uses: **1.** It is used between things in a list: *lions, tigers, elephants, and bears.* **2.** It shows that there is a pause in a sentence: *He looked for the jar of peanut butter, but it was empty.* **3.** To separate parts of a date, address, or name: *January 27, 1988; 30 Main Street, Pittstown.*
com|ma (kom′ə) *noun, plural* **commas.**

command—**1.** To give an order to: *The king commanded his knights to attack the castle.* **2.** To have control over: *The captain commands a crew of twelve sailors. Verb.* —**1.** An order: *She gave her dog the* command *"Stay!"* **2.** The power to control: *She is in* command *of the park rangers.* **3.** The ability to do something or use something well: *His* command *of chess made him hard to beat.* **4.** An order given to a computer to begin, end, or continue an operation. *Noun.*
com|mand (kə mand′) *verb,* **commanded, commanding;** *noun, plural* **commands.**
　● Synonyms: **direct, instruct,** for *verb* **1.**
　　Antonyms: **follow, obey,** for *verb* **1.**

commander—**1.** A person who is in control; leader; ruler. **2.** An officer in the navy who is below a captain and above a lieutenant.
com|mand|er (kə man′dər) *noun, plural* **commanders.**

commandment—**1.** A law; order: *The colonists did not obey the king's* commandment *to pay tax on tea.* **2.** **Commandments:** The ten laws that, according to the Bible, God gave to Moses.
com|mand|ment (kə mand′ment) *noun, plural* **commandments.**

commence—To begin: *Our school day* commences *when the bell rings.*
com|mence (kə mens′) *verb,* **commenced, commencing.**
　● Synonyms: **initiate, start**
　　Antonyms: **end, finish, stop**

commencement—**1.** The act or time of beginning; onset: *I came in after the* commencement *of the play.* **2.** The ceremonies of graduation for students who have finished their studies at a school or college.
com|mence|ment (kə mens′mənt) *noun, plural* **commencements.**

comment—A statement that explains or gives an opinion about something: *The teacher wrote some helpful* comments *on the last page of my book report. Noun.* —To make such a statement: *His uncle* commented *on his improved tennis skills. Verb.*
com|ment (kom′ent) *noun, plural* **comments;** *verb,* **commented, commenting.**
　● Synonyms: **remark, observation** for *noun.*

commentator—A person who reports and comments on the news on television or the radio. Commentators may also talk about sports, music, or other subjects.
com|men|ta|tor (kom′ən tā′tər) *noun, plural* **commentators.**

commerce—The buying and selling of things; business: *An increase in* commerce *often means more jobs and more money for people.*
com|merce (kom′ərs) *noun.*

commercial—Having to do with business: *The* commercial *area is at the center of our town. Adjective.* —A message on television or the radio that advertises a product or service; advertisement. *Noun.*
com|mer|cial (kə mur′shəl) *adjective; noun, plural* **commercials.**

commission—**1.** A group of people who have been officially chosen to do a job: *The mayor formed a* commission *to study the plans for the new bridge.* **2.** The act of doing something: *the* commission *of a crime.* **3.** An amount of money paid to someone who sells something: *Our school band gets a* commission *of a quarter for every dollar earned selling candy bars.* **4.** A position as a military officer: *He received his* commission *as a lieutenant. Noun.* —**1.** To appoint, hire, or order a person to do something: *The city* commissioned *an architect to design a new library.* **2.** To give a military

a at	i if	oo look	ch chalk		⎡a in ago
ā ape	ī idle	ou out	ng sing		e in happen
ah calm	o odd	u ugly	sh ship	ə =	i in capital
aw all	ō oats	ū rule	th think		o in occur
e end	oi oil	ur turn	th their		⎣u in upon
ē easy			zh treasure		

officer's position to: *to be* commissioned *as a captain. Verb.*

com|mis|sion (kə **mish′**ən) *noun, plural* **commissions;** *verb,* **commissioned, commissioning.**

■ **out of commission:** Not working; not in proper condition: *We had the washing machine repaired because it was* out of commission.

commissioner—A person who is the head of a department of a government: *a police* commissioner.

com|mis|sion|er (kə **mish′**ə nər) *noun, plural* **commissioners.**

commit—1. To carry out or do, usually something that is wrong: *to commit a crime.*
2. To pledge; dedicate: *The children committed themselves to keeping the school grounds clean.*

com|mit (kə **mit′**) *verb,* **committed, committing.**

commitment—A promise; pledge: *She made a commitment to practice the piano for an hour every day.*

com|mit|ment (kə **mit′**ment) *noun, plural* **commitments.**

committee—A group of people who are chosen to do a certain job: *The refreshments committee provided juice and doughnuts for the meeting.*

com|mit|tee (kə **mit′**ē) *noun, plural* **committees.**

commodity—Anything that can be bought and sold: *Diamonds are an expensive* commodity.

com|mod|i|ty (kə **mod′**ə tē) *noun, plural* **commodities.**

common—1. Shared equally by all; joint: *The three classrooms shared a* common *computer.*
2. Usual; familiar: *Flowers are a* common *sight in the spring.* 3. Ordinary; average: *the* common *cold.*

com|mon (**kom′**ən) *adjective,* **commoner, commonest.**

■ **in common:** Done, owned, or shared equally: *The three boys had a love of basketball* in common.

● Synonyms: **regular, typical,** for **3.**
Antonyms: **abnormal, different, odd, uncommon, unusual,** for **3.**

common denominator—A number that can be evenly divided by each of the bottom numbers of several fractions. For example, 18 is a common denominator of 1/3, 1/6, and 1/9, because 18 can be divided evenly by 3, 6, or 9. These fractions can also be expressed as 6/18, 3/18, and 2/18.

com|mon de|nom|i|na|tor

(kom′ən di nom′ə nā′tər) *noun, plural* **common denominators.**

commonplace—Happening regularly; ordinary: *Rain is* commonplace *in the tropics but not in the desert.*

com|mon|place (**kom′**ən plās′) *adjective.*

common sense—Good judgment in everyday life: *Her* common sense *told her to dress warmly in cold weather.*

com|mon sense (**kom′**ən sens) *noun.*

commonwealth—A country or state whose people make the laws that govern them. The United States and Canada are commonwealths.

com|mon|wealth (**kom′**ən welth′) *noun, plural* **commonwealths.**

commotion—Noisy activity; uproar: *There was a* commotion *at the zoo when the snake escaped from its cage.*

com|mo|tion (kə **mō′**shən) *noun, plural* **commotions.**

● Synonyms: **clamor, din, racket**
Antonyms: **quiet, silence, still**

communicate—To share feelings, thoughts, or information: *The easiest way to* communicate *with my brother is by telephone.*

com|mu|ni|cate (kə **myū′**nə kāt′) *verb,* **communicated, communicating.**

communication—1. A sharing of feelings, thoughts, or information: *Our lack of* communication *caused the misunderstanding.*
2. **communications:** A system for sending messages by telephone, telegraph, radio, television, or the like: *The earthquake left the town cut off from all* communications.

com|mu|ni|ca|tion (kə myū′nə **kā′**shən) *noun, plural* **communications.**

communion—1. A sharing of thoughts and feelings; a close relationship: *Even though they were far apart in age, she had a steady* communion *with her grandmother.*
2. **Communion:** A Christian ceremony in which bread and wine are blessed, eaten, and drunk in memory of the death of Jesus Christ.

com|mun|ion (kə **myūn′**yən) *noun, plural* **communions.**

communism—A social system in which all or most property and goods are owned by the government and are shared equally by the people.

com|mu|nism (**kom′**yə niz′ əm) *noun.*

communist—A person who favors a social system in which all or most property and goods are owned by the government.

com|mu|nist (**kom′**yə nist) *noun, plural* **communists.**

community—A group of people who live in the same area; the people in a town or district.
com|mu|ni|ty (kə **myū'**nə tē) *noun, plural* **communities.**

commute—To travel regularly to and from work: *It takes my mother an hour to* commute *to work each day.*
com|mute (kə **myūt'**) *verb,* **commuted, commuting.**

commuter—A person who travels regularly to and from work.
com|mut|er (kə **myū'**tər) *noun, plural* **commuters.**

compact[1]—1. Closely packed together; dense: *He tied the sleeping bag into a* compact *bundle.*
2. Taking up very little space: *a* compact *car. Adjective.*
—To pack closely together; compress: *The garbage truck has a machine that* compacts *the trash. Verb.*
—A small container of makeup for the face: *an eye shadow* compact. *Noun.*
com|pact (**kom'**pakt *or* kəm **pakt'** *for adjective;* kəm **pakt'** *for verb;* **kom'**pakt *for noun*) *adjective; verb,* **compacted, compacting;** *noun.*

compact[2]—An agreement between people; contract: *My best friend and I made a* compact *to stay friends forever.*
com|pact (**kom'**pakt) *noun, plural* **compacts.**

compact disc—A device on which sound is recorded. It is smaller than a phonograph record and does not have grooves.
com|pact disc (**kom'**pakt disk) *noun, plural* **compact discs.** Abbreviation: CD.

Word History

Companion comes from two Latin words meaning "with" and "bread." It originally meant a person who eats a meal with someone. Today, a companion is a friend who joins someone in many activities, not just a meal.

---

companion—A person who goes along with someone; friend: *The boy and his dog were constant* companions.

companion—(kəm **pan'**yən) *noun, plural* **companions.**

companionship—The fact of being with another or others; the relationship between friends: *She enjoyed the* companionship *of the other girls at camp.*
com|pan|ion|ship (kəm **pan'**yən ship) *noun.*

company—1. A guest or guests: *We are having* company *tonight, so set an extra place at the table.* 2. A business; firm: *That* company *builds swimming pools.* 3. Companionship: *His cat sat on the desk as* company *while he did his homework.* 4. A group of people joined together for some purpose: *a* company *of actors; a* company *of soldiers.*
com|pa|ny (**kum'**pə nē) *noun, plural* **companies.** Abbreviation: co. or Co.
• Synonyms: For **4,** see Synonyms at **band**[1].

comparative—1. Having to do with likenesses or differences: *Our teacher showed us a* comparative *chart of fishes and whales.* 2. Showing difference: *"Better" is the* comparative *form of "good." "Worse" is the* comparative *form of "bad." Adjective.*
—The form of an adjective or adverb that shows difference. *Noun.*
com|par|a|tive (kəm **par'**ə tiv) *adjective; noun, plural* **comparatives.**

compare—1. To examine how two or more people or things are alike or different: *The two friends* compared *the sand castles that each had built.* 2. To tell how one thing is like something else: *The poet* compared *the fog rolling in to a blanket.*
com|pare (kəm **pār'**) *verb,* **compared, comparing.**

comparison—1. The finding of likenesses and differences: *Our* comparison *of the two games showed that one was easier to play than the other.* 2. A telling of how one thing is like another: *a* comparison *of a beautiful girl to a rose.*
com|par|i|son (kəm **par'**ə sən) *noun, plural* **comparisons.**

compartment—A separate part or section: *The silverware drawer has* compartments *for knives, forks, and spoons.*
com|part|ment (kəm **pahrt'**mənt) *noun, plural* **compartments.**

compass—1. A device with a magnetic needle that points north. 2. A device that is used to draw circles or to measure distances. It has two arms which are connected at the top. One arm

a at	i if	oo look	ch chalk		ə =	a in ago
ā ape	ī idle	ou out	ng sing			e in happen
ah calm	o odd	u ugly	sh ship			i in capital
aw all	ō oats	ū rule	th think			o in occur
e end	oi oil	ur turn	th their			u in upon
ē easy			zh treasure			

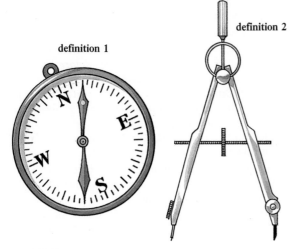

definition 1

definition 2

compass

has a pointed end and the other end holds a pencil.
com|pass (**kum′**pəs) *noun, plural* **compasses.**

compassion—A feeling of sympathy for someone; desire to help with someone's problems or suffering: *I felt* compassion *for my neighbor when her cat died.*
com|pas|sion (kəm **pash′**ən) *noun.*

compel—To force; require: *The bitter cold* compelled *us to stay home.*
com|pel (kəm **pel′**) *verb,* **compelled, compelling.**
• Synonyms: **drive, oblige**

compete—To try to win: *Four teams* competed *in the relay races.*
com|pete (kəm **pēt′**) *verb,* **competed, competing.**

competent—Able; having enough skill to do something: *I am ready to take the test to prove that I am a* competent *driver.*
com|pe|tent (**kom′**pə tənt) *adjective.*
• Synonyms: **capable, skilled**
  Antonyms: **incompetent, unqualified**

competition—1. The process of trying to win: *We were in* competition *for first place.* 2. A contest; match: *She won three ribbons at the gymnastics* competition.
com|pe|ti|tion (kom′pə **tish′**ən) *noun, plural* **competitions.**

competitive—1. Having to do with trying to win: *A race is a* competitive *kind of running.* 2. Wanting to win: *He is a very* competitive *hockey player and always plays hard.*
com|pet|i|tive (kəm **pet′**ə tiv) *adjective.*

competitor—A person who tries to win: *She is a tough* competitor *on the tennis court.*
com|pet|i|tor (kəm **pet′**ə tər) *noun, plural* **competitors.**

compile—To put together: *The nurse* compiled *a list of all the students absent from school that day.*
com|pile (kəm **pīl′**) *verb,* **compiled, compiling.**

complain—To say that something is wrong; express unhappiness: *He* complained *that his dinner was cold.*
com|plain (kəm **plān′**) *verb,* **complained, complaining.**
• Synonyms: **fuss, gripe, grumble, whine**

complaint—The act of saying that something is wrong; expression of unhappiness: *She made a* complaint *to the manager about the terrible service at the restaurant.*
com|plaint (kəm **plānt′**) *noun, plural* **complaints.**

complement—Something that completes or makes better: *Hot fudge is a perfect* complement *to vanilla ice cream. Noun.*
—To make something complete or better: *That red shirt nicely* complements *those navy blue pants. Verb.*
com|ple|ment (**kom′**plə ment′) *noun, plural* **complements;** *verb,* **complemented, complementing.**
• A word that sounds the same is **compliment.**

complete—1. Whole; having all its parts: *I have a* complete *set of all the records that band made.* 2. Finished; ended: *The building of our house is* complete, *so we can move in.* 3. Perfect; total: *a* complete *success. Adjective.*
—1. To make whole; add all the missing parts: *She needed just a few more pieces to* complete *the jigsaw puzzle.* 2. To finish; end: *We cheered when she* completed *the song.* 3. To make perfect: *A telephone call from his grandfather* completed *his birthday celebration. Verb.*
com|plete (kəm **plēt′**) *adjective; verb,* **completed, completing.**

completion—The act or condition of being complete or finished: *The students looked forward to the* completion *of the new playground.*
com|ple|tion (kəm **plē′**shən) *noun, plural* **completions.**

complex—1. Made up of many parts: *A jet engine is a* complex *machine.* 2. Hard to understand: *The rules of baseball are so* complex *that it is hard for a beginner to follow them.*
com|plex (kəm **pleks′** *or* **kom′**pleks) *adjective.*

complexion—1. The color and texture of a person's skin, especially of the face: *She has a pale* complexion *and gets sunburn easily.* 2. The general appearance or character of something: *The whole* complexion *of the neighborhood changed when some houses were torn down to build a parking garage.*
com|plex|ion (kəm **plek′**shən) *noun, plural* **complexions.**

complicate—To make something more difficult to do or understand: *Adding more twists and turns will* complicate *the dance.*
com|pli|cate (**kom′**plə kāt′) *verb,* **complicated, complicating.**

complicated—Difficult to do or understand: *We got lost trying to follow the* complicated *directions to her house.*
com|pli|cat|ed (**kom′**plə kā′tid) *adjective.*

complication—Something that causes confusion or difficulty: *The rain was a* complication *at the class picnic.*
com|pli|ca|tion (kom′plə **kā′**shən) *noun, plural* **complications.**

compliment—Something nice or good said about someone or something: *His coach gave him a* compliment *about his performance during the game. Noun.*
—To say something nice or good about someone or something: *The guard* complimented *us on our good behavior at the museum. Verb.*
com|pli|ment (**kom′**plə mənt for *noun;* **kom′**plə ment′ for *verb*) *noun, plural* **compliments;** *verb,* **complimented, complimenting.**
• A word that sounds the same is **complement.**

compose—1. To make up: *The inside of the pillow is* composed *of goose feathers.* 2. To make; create: *He* composed *a poem for his mother's birthday card.* 3. To make calm: *She tried to* compose *herself so that no one would know that she had been crying.* 4. To put in order: *a carefully* composed *flower arrangement.*
com|pose (kəm **poz′**) *verb,* **composed, composing.**
• Synonyms: **arrange, organize,** for 4.
   Antonyms: **complicate, disturb,** for 4.

a at	i if	oo look	ch chalk		a in ago
ā ape	ī idle	ou out	ng sing		e in happen
ah calm	o odd	u ugly	sh ship	ə =	i in capital
aw all	ō oats	ū rule	th think		o in occur
e end	oi oil	ur turn	th their		u in upon
ē easy			zh treasure		

composer—A person who writes music.
com|pos|er (kəm **pō′**zər) *noun, plural* **composers.**

composite—Made up of several different parts: *We gave the teacher a* composite *picture showing each student as a baby. Adjective.*
—Something that is made up of several different parts: *The picture was a* composite *of different types of leaves. Noun.*
com|pos|ite (kəm **poz′**it) *adjective; noun, plural* **composites.**

composition—1. The making of something: *The* composition *of the song took three days.* 2. What something is made of: *The* composition *of water is two atoms of hydrogen and one atom of oxygen.* 3. A short piece of writing; essay: *He wrote a* composition *about his trip to the zoo.*
com|po|si|tion (kom′pə **zish′**ən) *noun, plural* **compositions.**

compound—Having two or more parts: *"Houseboat" is a* compound *word because it is made up of two words. Adjective.*
—A mixture; combination: *Brass is a* compound *of copper and zinc. Noun.*
—To mix; blend together: *The chemist* compounded *the chemicals according to the experiment instructions. Verb.*
com|pound (**kom′**pound′ for *adjective* and *noun;* kəm **pound′** for *verb*) *adjective; noun, plural* **compounds;** *verb,* **compounded, compounding.**
• Synonyms: **combine, merge,** for *verb.*
   Antonyms: **divide, part, separate,** for *verb.*

comprehend—To understand: *He could not* comprehend *the complicated directions to the assignment.*
com|pre|hend (kom′pri **hend′**) *verb,* **comprehended, comprehending.**

comprehension—Understanding: *The teacher helped the student to improve her reading* comprehension.
com|pre|hen|sion (kom′pri **hen′**shən) *noun, plural* **comprehensions.**

compress—To make smaller by squeezing; press together: *He tried to* compress *his clothes so that the suitcase would shut. Verb.*
—A soft pad that is applied to a part of the body to lessen pain or swelling or to stop bleeding. *Noun.*
com|press (kəm **pres′** for *verb;* **kom′**pres′ for *noun*) *verb,* **compressed, compressing;** *noun, plural* **compresses.**

compromise—To settle an argument by agreeing that each side will give up some of what it

wants: *Each child wanted to fly the kite, so they* compromised *and took turns. Verb.*
—The settlement of differences by making an agreement. *Noun.*
com|pro|mise (kom′prə mīz′) *verb,* **compromised, compromising;** *noun, plural* **compromises.**

computer—An electronic machine that can analyze, store, and give back information quickly.
com|put|er (kəm pyū′tər) *noun, plural* **computers.**

Word Power

If you are interested in computers, you can find these words in this dictionary.

BASIC	floppy disk	pixel
binary system	hard disk	printout
bit	hardware	program
bug	input	random-access memory
byte	modem	read-only memory
cursor	monitor	software
disk drive	mouse	turtle
	output	

---

computerize—To solve, organize, or deal with something by means of a computer: *to* computerize *the scoring of the tests.*
com|put|er|ize (kəm pyū′tə rīz′) *verb,* **computerized, computerizing.**

computer language—A system of words, numbers, and symbols used to operate a computer.
com|put|er lan|guage (kəm pyū′tər lang′gwij) *noun, plural* **computer languages.**

computer literacy—The ability to understand and use computers.
com|put|er lit|er|a|cy (kəm pyū′tər lit′ər ə sē) *noun.*

comrade—A friend or companion, especially one who works with or has the same hobbies as another person: *an army* comrade.
com|rade (kom′rad) *noun, plural* **comrades.**
● Synonyms: **buddy, chum, pal**
  Antonyms: **enemy, foe**

Word History

Comrade comes from a Spanish word meaning "roommate." Because a person usually spends a lot of time with a roommate, **comrade** came to mean a close friend.

---

concave—Rounded inward: *The inside of a bowl is* concave.
con|cave (kon kāv′ *or* kon′kāv) *adjective.*
● Antonym: **convex**

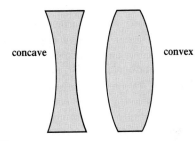

concave   convex

concave

conceal—To cover up; hide: *The magician* concealed *the playing cards in his sleeve.*
con|ceal (kən sēl′) *verb,* **concealed, concealing.**

conceited—Thinking too proudly of oneself or one's skills: *The* conceited *actor was always admiring his own acting ability.*
con|ceit|ed (kən sē′tid) *adjective.*

concentrate—**1.** To gather or collect into one area: *The town's population* concentrates *around the downtown area.* **2.** To make less weak; make thicker and stronger: *Maple sap is boiled and* concentrated *to make maple syrup.* **3.** To focus on; pay close attention to: *He did not hear the telephone ringing because he was* concentrating *on reading. Verb.*
—Something that has been made thicker and stronger: *grape juice* concentrate. *Noun.*
con|cen|trate (kon′sən trāt′) *verb,* **concentrated, concentrating;** *noun, plural* **concentrates.**

concentration—**1.** The act or process of gathering or collecting into one area: *The* concentration *of people at the fair made moving around difficult.* **2.** Strength: *The* concentration *of chlorine in the swimming pool stung her eyes.* **3.** Close attention: *The crying baby broke the actor's* concentration, *and he forgot his lines.*
con|cen|tra|tion (kon′sən trā′shən) *noun, plural* **concentrations.**

concern—**1.** To relate to; involve: *The special meeting* concerned *only those interested in computers.* **2.** To have a care or a worry about: *The nurse was* concerned *about my fever. Verb.*
—**1.** Something that involves or is important to a person: *Knowing his secret is not her* concern. **2.** Worry; care: *She felt* concern *for her lost kitten. Noun.*
con|cern (kən surn′) *verb,* **concerned, concerning;** *noun, plural* **concerns.**

concerning—About; having to do with: *Several people spoke to our class* concerning *careers in science.*
con|cern|ing (kən sur′ning) *preposition.*

concert—A public performance given by one or more musicians or singers.
con|cert (kon′sərt) *noun, plural* **concerts.**

concerto—A piece of music for one or more musical instruments and an orchestra.
con|cer|to (kən cher′tō) *noun, plural* **concertos.**

concession—1. The act of allowing to have or do: *As a* concession, *I let her borrow my favorite shoes.* 2. Something a person is allowed to have or do: *Since it was raining, Mother made a* concession *and let us play in the house.* 3. A right, usually to sell something, given by a town or business: *We were given a* concession *to sell ice cream at the parade.*
con|ces|sion (kən sesh′ən) *noun, plural* **concessions.**

conch—A large, spiral-shaped seashell. The animal that lives inside the shell is also called a conch and can be cooked and eaten.
conch (konch *or* kongk) *noun, plural* **conches** or **conchs.**

conch

conclude—1. To bring to a close; end: *The Fourth of July picnic* concluded *with a fireworks display.* 2. To decide after careful thought; judge: *After studying the fossils, the scientist* concluded *that the dinosaur had been very large.*
con|clude (kən klūd′) *verb,* **concluded, concluding.**

conclusion—1. The ending of something: *We waited until the* conclusion *of his speech to clap.* 2. A decision reached after careful thought: *The teacher came to the* conclusion *that the class*

needed more practice with multiplication.
con|clu|sion (kən klū′zhən) *noun, plural* **conclusions.**

■ **jump to conclusions:** To make a quick guess about something; assume: *When Dad saw the broken window, he* jumped to conclusions *and blamed me.*

concrete—Real; that can be seen or touched: *My mom wanted* concrete *evidence that I had been to the movies. Adjective.*
—A hard building material made by mixing cement, sand, gravel, and water. *Noun.*
con|crete (con′krēt *or* kon krēt′) *adjective, noun.*

concussion—1. A sharp, sudden blow or shaking: *The* concussion *caused by the earthquake uprooted one of our trees.* 2. An injury to the brain caused by a fall, sudden blow, or other shock.
con|cus|sion (kən kush′ən) *noun, plural* **concussions.**

condemn—1. To declare to be wrong; state strong feelings against: *Most people* condemn *the pollution of our environment.* 2. To convict someone for a crime or a wrong: *The jury* condemned *the man for the robberies.* 3. To declare unsafe or not fit to use: *Many badly damaged buildings were* condemned *after the fire.*
con|demn (kən dem′) *verb,* **condemned, condemning.**
● Synonyms: **blame, criticize,** for 1.
Antonym: **praise,** for 1.

condensation—1. The act of making something shorter: *the* condensation *of a long book into a play.* 2. The change of a substance from a gas into a liquid through cooling: *Rain is a result of* condensation *of water in the air.*
con|den|sa|tion (kon′den sā′shən) *noun, plural* **condensations.**

condense—1. To make or become shorter; reduce: *Can you* condense *your long report into a short article for the newspaper?* 2. To change from a gas into a liquid.
con|dense (kən dens′) *verb,* **condensed, condensing.**
● Synonyms: **abbreviate, abridge, trim,** for 1.
Antonyms: **enlarge, expand, lengthen,** for 1.

condition—1. The state or quality of someone or something: *He checked the* condition *of the used bicycle before he bought it.* 2. A thing on which something else depends: *Having a flexible body is one of the* conditions *for being a good gymnast.* 3. **conditions:** The circumstances

a at	i if	oo look	ch chalk		a in ago
ā ape	ī idle	ou out	ng sing		e in happen
ah calm	o odd	u ugly	sh ship	ə =	i in capital
aw all	ō oats	ū rule	th think		o in occur
e end	oi oil	ur turn	th their		u in upon
ē easy			zh treasure		

about something: *Pollution in the lake caused poor swimming* conditions. *Noun.*
—**1.** To put into a proper state: *to* condition *one's body with exercise.*   **2.** To become used to; accustom: *Because she lived near a busy street, she was* conditioned *to the sound of traffic. Verb.*
con|di|tion (kən dish′ən) *noun, plural* conditions; *verb,* conditioned, conditioning.

condominium—An apartment that is individually owned, rather than rented.
con|do|min|i|um (kon′də min′ē əm) *noun, plural* condominiums.

condor—A large bird that has no feathers on its head or neck. Condors belong to the vulture family and live in the mountains of California and South America.
con|dor (kon′dər) *noun, plural* condors.

condor

conduct—Behavior; manners: *He won an award for good* conduct *because he is always helpful to others. Noun.*
—**1.** To behave: *She* conducts *herself well when meeting new people.*   **2.** To manage; direct: *The band leader* conducted *a lively march. Our class* conducted *a paper drive.*   **3.** To serve as a route for; carry; transfer: *to* conduct *heat or electricity. Verb.*
con|duct (kon′dukt for *noun;* kən dukt′ for *verb) noun; verb,* conducted, conducting.

conductor—**1.** A person who directs: *the* conductor *of a tour; an orchestra* conductor.
2. A person on a train or bus who collects the tickets or fares from passengers and announces the names of the stops.   **3.** Something that carries heat, electricity, or another form of energy: *Rubber is a poor* conductor *of electricity.*
con|duc|tor (kən duk′tər) *noun, plural* conductors.

cone—**1.** A solid object that has a circular base and sides that come together to a pointed top.
2. Something that has a shape like such an object: *an ice-cream* cone.   **3.** The part of an evergreen tree that contains the seeds: *a pine* cone.
cone (kōn) *noun, plural* cones.

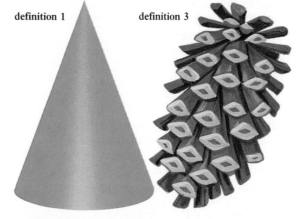

definition 1   definition 3

cone

confederacy—**1.** A group of people, states, or countries that join together for a special reason; alliance.   **2. the Confederacy:** The group of eleven Southern states that broke away from the United States in 1860 and 1861 to form their own government.
con|fed|er|a|cy (kən fed′ər ə sē) *noun, plural* confederacies.

confederate—**1.** A person or group that joins with another person or group for a special reason: *Who were your* confederates *in your plot to take over the government?*   **2. Confederate:** Someone who lived in the Confederacy, supported it, or fought for it.
con|fed|er|ate (kən fed′ər it) *noun, plural* confederates.

Confederate Memorial Day—A holiday celebrated in the Southern states that honors the men who died for the South in the Civil War. Different states celebrate it on different dates.
Con|fed|er|ate Me|mo|ri|al Day (kən fed′ər it mə mawr′ē əl dā) *noun.*

confer—**1.** to talk together; consult: *Her parents* conferred *with her teacher about her poor grades.*   **2.** To give; grant: *A merit badge was* conferred *on the Girl Scout for selling the most cookies.*
con|fer (kən fur′) *verb,* conferred, conferring.

conference—A meeting for sharing views or ideas: *a doctors' conference to discuss new treatments for a disease.*
con|fer|ence (kon′fər əns) *noun, plural* **conferences.**

confess—1. To admit; disclose: *He confessed that he had knocked over the vase.* 2. To admit one's sins to God or to a priest.
con|fess (kən fes′) *verb,* **confessed, confessing.**

confession—1. The act of admitting something: *She felt much better after her confession that she had lied.* 2. The act of admitting one's sins to God or to a priest.
con|fes|sion (kən fesh′ən) *noun, plural* **confessions.**

confetti—Tiny, colorful pieces of paper or ribbon thrown into the air in celebration: *We threw confetti at the bride and groom.*
con|fet|ti (kən fet′ē) *noun.*

confide—To entrust someone with a secret: *I always feel safe confiding in you.*
con|fide (kən fīd′) *verb,* **confided, confiding.**

confidence—1. Trust; belief: *He has confidence in my abilities.* 2. A feeling of complete certainty: *She gave the answer with total confidence.* 3. Trust that a person will keep a secret: *The information was given to the police in confidence.*
con|fi|dence (kon′fə dəns) *noun, plural* **confidences.**
• Synonyms: **assurance, security,** for 2.

confident—Certain; sure: *My mother is confident that she will pass the driving test.*
con|fi|dent (kon′fə dənt) *adjective.*

confidential—Private; secret: *The mayor had a confidential meeting with the police chief.*
con|fi|den|tial (kon′fə den′shəl) *adjective.*

confine—To limit; restrict: *We confine our spending to necessities so we can save money.* Verb.
—**confines:** a boundary; limit: *The prisoner could not leave the confines of his cell.* Noun.
con|fine (kən fīn′ for *verb;* kon′fīn for *noun*) *verb,* **confined, confining;** *noun, plural* **confines.**

confirm—1. To make sure that something is true; prove: *The doctor's test confirmed that I am allergic to milk.* 2. To approve; agree to: *Congress confirmed her appointment as a judge.* 3. To admit formally into full membership in a church or synagogue.
con|firm (kən furm′) *verb,* **confirmed, confirming.**
• Synonyms: **establish, verify,** for 1.

confirmation—1. The act of making sure that something is true, or the act of approving something: *She called the airport for confirmation of her flight.* 2. The ceremony in which a person is admitted into full membership in a church or synagogue.
con|fir|ma|tion (kon′fər mā′shən) *noun, plural* **confirmations.**

conflict—1. A battle; war: *The conflict between the two countries lasted for ten years.* 2. A difference of opinion: *They always have a conflict over who gets to sit in the front seat.* Noun.
—To disagree: *Your description of the house conflicts with hers.* Verb.
con|flict (kon′flikt for *noun;* kən flikt′ for *verb*) *noun, plural* **conflicts;** *verb,* **conflicted, conflicting.**
• Synonyms: **combat, fight,** for *noun* 1.
Antonym: **peace,** for *noun* 1.

confront—To face up to; deal face-to-face with: *If you confront your problems, they are easier to solve.*
con|front (kən frunt′) *verb,* **confronted, confronting.**

confuse—1. To mix up; make unclear: *Don't confuse me with too many instructions.* 2. To be unable to tell apart: *The boys look so much alike that people always confuse them.*
con|fuse (kən fyūz′) *verb,* **confused, confusing.**
• Synonyms: **baffle, perplex, puzzle,** for 1.
Antonyms: **enlighten, illuminate,** for 1.

confusion—The state of being mixed up; bewildered: *We took the wrong maps, so our trip was full of confusion.*
con|fu|sion (kən fyū′zhən) *noun, plural* **confusions.**

congratulate—To express praise for good fortune or success: *The coach congratulated me when I hit the home run.*
con|grat|u|late (kən grach′ə lāt) *verb,* **congratulated, congratulating.**

congratulation—1. The act of expressing praise for another's good fortune or success: *My aunt sent me her congratulations for my winning the*

a at	i if	oo look	ch chalk		a in ago
ā ape	ī idle	ou out	ng sing		e in happen
ah calm	o odd	u ugly	sh ship	ə =	i in capital
aw all	ō oats	ū rule	th think		o in occur
e end	oi oil	ur turn	th their		u in upon
ē easy			zh treasure		

writing contest. **2. Congratulations:** Praise given for another's good fortune or success: Congratulations *on your new job!*
con|grat|u|la|tion (kən grach′ə lā′shən) *noun, plural* **congratulations.**

congregate—To come together; meet: *The friends* congregated *in the room for the party.*
con|gre|gate (kong′grə gāt) *verb,* **congregated, congregating.**
• Synonyms: **assemble, gather**
  Antonym: **scatter**

congregation—A group of people gathered together: *The church* congregation *opened a kitchen to feed the poor.*
con|gre|ga|tion (kong′grə gā′shən) *noun, plural* **congregations.**

Congregationalist—A member of a Protestant church in which each individual church congregation governs itself.
Con|gre|ga|tion|al|ist (kong′grə gā′shə nə list) *noun, plural* **Congregationalists.**

congress—**1.** Those people in government who make the laws of a country, especially a republic. **2. Congress:** The House of Representatives and Senate of the United States, which together make the country's laws.
con|gress (kong′gris) *noun, plural* **congresses.**

congressman—A member of the United States Congress, particularly a member of the House of Representatives.
con|gress|man (kong′gris mən) *noun, plural* **congressmen.**

congresswoman—A woman member of the United States Congress, particularly a member of the House of Representatives.
con|gress|wom|an (kong′gris woom′ən) *noun, plural* **congresswomen.**

conjunction—**1.** A word that joins together words, clauses, phrases, or sentences. The words **and, but, if, or,** and **though** are conjunctions. **2.** A connection or joining of things; union: *The firefighters worked in* conjunction *with the police.* Abbreviation: conj.
con|junc|tion (kən jungk′shən) *noun, plural* **conjunctions.**

connect—**1.** To join; link: *A lamp must be* connected *to an electrical socket before it will work.* **2.** To associate in one's mind; relate: *I enjoy any television program* connected *with dance.*
con|nect (kə nekt′) *verb,* **connected, connecting.**

connection—**1.** The act or fact of being joined: *The loose* connection *of the hose to the pipe let*

the water leak out. **2.** A relationship of two things; association: *There is a* connection *between good health and eating healthy foods.* **3.** Something that joins together: *an electrical* connection.
con|nec|tion (kə nek′shən) *noun, plural* **connections.**

conquer—**1.** To win in war; gain by force: *to* conquer *new land.* **2.** To overcome: *The little boy learned to* conquer *his fear of the dark.*
con|quer (kong′kər) *verb,* **conquered, conquering.**

conqueror—A person who is victorious, especially in war: *The* conqueror *was proud of his winning troops.*
con|quer|or (kong′kər ər) *noun, plural* **conquerors.**

conquest—**1.** The act of overcoming or gaining by force: *Many people left the country after its* conquest *by invaders.* **2.** A person or thing gained by force: *The small town became a* conquest *of the enemy soldiers.*
con|quest (kon′kwest *or* kong′kwest) *noun, plural* **conquests.**

conscience—A person's feelings about what is right and wrong: *His* conscience *made him tell the truth.*
con|science (kon′shəns) *noun, plural* **consciences.**

conscious—**1.** Aware; knowing: *Her parents were* conscious *of the fact that she was lying.* **2.** Awake; able to see, hear, and feel: *He became* conscious *again a few seconds after falling asleep.* **3.** Done on purpose; intended: *She made a* conscious *decision to lose weight.*
con|scious (kon′shəs) *adjective.*

consecutive—Following one right after another: *April, May, and June are* consecutive *months.*
con|sec|u|tive (kən sek′yə tiv) *adjective.*

consent—To give approval; agree: *Her parents* consented *to her plans for the weekend. Verb.*
—Approval; permission: *I could not leave until I received her* consent. *Noun.*
con|sent (kən sent′) *verb,* **consented, consenting;** *noun, plural* **consents.**

consequence—**1.** A result: *He failed the test as a* consequence *of not studying.* **2.** Value; importance: *Her opinion is of great* consequence *to me.*
con|se|quence (kon′sə kwens) *noun, plural* **consequences.**
• Synonyms: **effect, outcome,** for **1.**

consequently—As a result: *I slept late, and* consequently, *I missed the bus.*
con|se|quent|ly (kon′sə kwent′lē) *adverb.*
• Synonyms: **hence, therefore, thus**

conservation—The careful use of something, especially a natural resource, to protect it from waste: *Too little rain makes the* conservation *of water important.*
con|ser|va|tion (kon′sər vā′shən) *noun.*

conservative—1. Wanting things to remain the way they are or used to be: *My* conservative *aunt does not like the new hair styles.* 2. Cautious; not risky or extreme: *A* conservative *estimate often results in a low number. Adjective.*
—A person who is against change. *Noun.*
con|serv|a|tive (kən sur′və tiv) *adjective; noun,* plural **conservatives.**

conserve—To keep from loss or waste; protect: *I try to* conserve *energy by turning off lights that I'm not using.*
con|serve (kən surv′) *verb,* **conserved, conserving.**
• Synonyms: **maintain, preserve**
Antonyms: **alter, change, modify, vary**

consider—1. To think about before making a decision: *Let me* consider *the facts before I make up my mind.* 2. To think that something or someone is a certain way; regard as: *She* considers *me her best friend.* 3. To be thoughtful of: *That nice man always* considers *the feelings of others.*
con|sid|er (kən sid′ər) *verb,* **considered, considering.**
• Synonyms: **contemplate, ponder,** for **1.**

Word History

Consider comes from a Latin word meaning ''to look at closely.'' The Latin word comes from another Latin word meaning ''star.'' People used to believe that they could tell the future by studying the stars.

---

considerable—Important; significant: *The weather will have a* considerable *effect on our camping trip.*
con|sid|er|a|ble (kən sid′ər ə bəl) *adjective.*

considerate—Thoughtful of others: *A* considerate *person will not call on the telephone late at night.*
con|sid|er|ate (kən sid′ər it) *adjective.*

consideration—1. Careful thought: *Let me give your question some* consideration *before I answer.* 2. Something to keep in mind: *How other people will feel is always a* consideration *when he makes a decision.* 3. Thoughtfulness of others: *Letting others go ahead of you in a line shows* consideration.
con|sid|er|a|tion (kən sid′ə rā′shən) *noun,* plural **considerations.**

consist—To be composed of; be made of: *An hour* consists *of sixty minutes.*
con|sist (kən sist′) *verb,* **consisted, consisting.**

consistency—1. Thickness or firmness: *This salad dressing has the* consistency *of jello.* 2. A keeping to the same way of thinking or behaving: *There is no* consistency *between what you say today and what you said yesterday.*
con|sist|en|cy (kən sis′tən sē) *noun,* plural **consistencies.**

consistent—Keeping to the same way of thinking or behaving: *A* consistent *person always tends to do the same quality of work.*
con|sist|ent (kən sis′tənt) *adjective.*

console[1]—To comfort; soothe the sorrow of: *The kindness of friends* consoled *us when our grandfather was sick.*
con|sole (kən sōl′) *verb,* **consoled, consoling.**

console[2]—A cabinet that holds a television, phonograph, radio, or computer.
con|sole (kon′sōl) *noun,* plural **consoles.**

consolidate—To unite into a whole; combine: *I* consolidated *all the books and magazines onto one shelf.*
con|sol|i|date (kən sol′ə dāt) *verb,* **consolidated, consolidating.**

consonant—A letter of the alphabet other than the vowels *a, e, i, o,* and *u.* The letters *b, c,* and *d* are the first three consonants in the alphabet.
con|so|nant (kon′sə nənt) *noun,* plural **consonants.**

conspicuous—Easy to see; noticeable: *She wore a* conspicuous *color so I could find her in the crowd.*
con|spic|u|ous (kən spik′yū əs) *adjective.*

conspiracy—A secret agreement among several people to do something that is wrong or illegal: *the* conspiracy *to overthrow the government.*
con|spir|a|cy (kən spēr′ə sē) *noun,* plural **conspiracies.**

a at	i if	oo look	ch chalk		a in ago
ā ape	ī idle	ou out	ng sing		e in happen
ah calm	o odd	u ugly	sh ship	ə =	i in capital
aw all	ō oats	ū rule	th think		o in occur
e end	oi oil	ur turn	th their		u in upon
ē easy			zh treasure		

conspirator—A person who is part of a secret agreement to do something that is wrong or illegal.
con|spir|a|tor (kən spēr′ə tər) *noun, plural* **conspirators.**

conspire—To take part in a secret agreement with others to do something that is wrong or illegal: *to conspire to rob a bank.*
con|spire (kən spīr′) *verb,* **conspired, conspiring.**
• Synonyms: **plot, scheme**

Word History

Conspire comes from Latin words meaning ''to breathe together.'' People who conspire join so closely to plan their evil deed that they almost breathe together.

---

constable—A police officer in England.
con|sta|ble (kon′stə bəl) *noun, plural* **constables.**

constant—Continuous; unchanging: *The nurse's* constant *care helped the patient recover quickly.*
con|stant (kon′stənt) *adjective.*

constellation—A group of stars that form a pattern in the sky. The constellation called the Great Bear, or Ursa Major (ur′sə mā′jər) includes the stars known as the Big Dipper.
con|stel|la|tion (kon′stə lā′shən) *noun, plural* **constellations.**

constellation: This is the constellation known as the Great Bear.

constitute—To make up; form: *Three teaspoons* constitute *one tablespoon.*
con|sti|tute (kon′stə tūt *or* kon′stə tyūt) *verb,* **constituted, constituting.**

constitution—1. The structure or makeup of someone or something: *He has a strong* constitution *and can run for miles without tiring.* 2. The primary laws for governing a group, state, or nation: *The country's* constitution *guarantees freedom of religion.*
con|sti|tu|tion (kon′stə tū′shən *or* kon′stə tyū′shən) *noun, plural* **constitutions.**

construct—To put together; make: *We* constructed *a house for our new dog.*
con|struct (kən strukt′) *verb,* **constructed, constructing.**
• Synonyms: **build, erect**

construction—1. The act of building something: *the* construction *of a new road.* 2. The way in which something is built: *Buildings have a special* construction *in places where there might be earthquakes.*
con|struc|tion (kən struk′shən) *noun, plural* **constructions.**

constructive—Helpful; useful: *Her* constructive *advice enabled me to solve the multiplication problems quickly.*
con|struc|tive (kən struk′tiv) *adjective.*

consul—A person who is appointed by a government to live in a foreign country in order to take care of the government's interests and its citizens traveling or living there.
con|sul (kon′səl) *noun, plural* **consuls.**

consult—To go to someone or something to get information or advice: Consult *the dictionary for the meaning of a word.*
con|sult (kən sult′) *verb,* **consulted, consulting.**

consultant—One who offers advice or information on a special subject.
con|sult|ant (kən sul′tənt) *noun, plural* **consultants.**

consume—1. To use up: *Watching television* consumes *all his spare time.* 2. To eat or drink up: *The children* consumed *all the spaghetti that had been cooked.* 3. To destroy: *The fire* consumed *everything in its path.*
con|sume (kən sūm′) *verb,* **consumed, consuming.**

consumer—A person who purchases and uses things and services.
con|sum|er (kən sū′mər) *noun, plural* **consumers.**

consumption—The act of using something: *We must cut down on the* consumption *of energy in our country.*
con|sump|tion (kən sump′shən) *noun, plural* **consumptions.**

contact—A connection or touching between people or things: *The shirt was ruined after it came into* contact *with the hot iron. Noun.*
—To communicate with: *We have to* contact *our parents when it's time to be picked up. Verb.*
con|tact (kon′takt) *noun, plural* **contacts;** *verb,* **contacted, contacting.**

contagious—Going easily from one person to another: *Her cheerfulness was* contagious, *and soon everyone was smiling.*
con|ta|gious (kən tā′jəs) *adjective.*

contain—1. To hold; enclose: *That closet* contains *my sister's clothes.* 2. To consist of; be made from: *Lemonade* contains *lemon juice, sugar, and water.* 3. To restrain; hold back: *I* contained *myself even though I felt like crying.*
con|tain (kən tān′) *verb,* **contained, containing.**

container—Anything used to hold things: *A trash can, a cereal box, and a truck body are* containers.
con|tain|er (kən tā′nər) *noun, plural* **containers.**

container: containers aboard a ship

contaminate—To make unfit for use; pollute: *We could not drink the water because it was* contaminated *by harmful chemicals.*
con|tam|i|nate (kən tam′ə nāt) *verb,* **contaminated, contaminating.**

contemplate—To think about something carefully over a period of time: *She* contemplated *the problem before finally writing down her answer.*

con|tem|plate (kon′təm plāt) *verb,* **contemplated, contemplating.**
• Synonyms: **consider, ponder**

contemporary—Living or happening during the same time, especially the present time: *Modern music and* contemporary *painting are my favorites. Adjective.*
—Those who are about the same age: *My* contemporaries *and I like the same kind of television shows. Noun.*
con|tem|po|rar|y (kən tem′pə rer′ē) *adjective; noun, plural* **contemporaries.**

contempt—The feeling that someone or something is wrong, shameful, or disgusting: *She has great* contempt *for people who steal.*
con|tempt (kən tempt′) *noun.*

content[1] or **contents**—1. Everthing that is contained in something: *the lead* content *of gasoline; the* contents *of the drawer.* 2. The topic discussed: *The* content *of his report was limited to what he had seen himself.*
con|tent or con|tents (kon′tent or kon′tents) *noun, plural* **contents.**

content[2]—Pleased; happy; satisfied: *The falling snow made the skiers feel very* content. *Adjective.*
—To make pleased or happy, satisfy: *When I'm hungry, it takes a big meal to* content *me. Verb.*
—A feeling of being pleased or satisfied: *After winning the game, I stretched out on the couch in complete* content. *Noun.*
con|tent (kən tent′) *adjective; verb,* **contented, contenting;** *noun.*

contented—Satisfied: *He did his best and was* contented *with the results.*
con|tent|ed (kən ten′tid) *adjective.*

contest—1. A competition: *a* contest *to choose the company motto.* 2. A battle; dispute: *A* contest *between the settlers and the American Indians took place long ago near this town. Noun.*
—To challenge; object to: *The player* contested *the call made by the umpire. Verb.*
con|test (kon′test for *noun;* kən test′ for *verb*) *noun, plural* **contests;** *verb,* **contested, contesting.**

contestant—Someone involved in a competition.
con|test|ant (kən tes′tənt) *noun, plural* **contestants.**

continent—A very large piece of land. There are seven continents: Africa, Asia, Antarctica, Australia, Europe, North America, and South America.

a at	i if	oo look	ch chalk		a in ago
ā ape	ī idle	ou out	ng sing		e in happen
ah calm	o odd	u ugly	sh ship	ə =	i in capital
aw all	ō oats	ū rule	th think		o in occur
e end	oi oil	ur turn	<u>th</u> their		u in upon
ē easy			zh treasure		

con|ti|nent (kon'tə nənt) *noun, plural* **continents.**

continental—Having to do with a continent: *The state of Hawaii is not a part of the* continental *United States.*
con|ti|nen|tal (kon'tə **nen**'təl) *adjective.*

continual—Never ending; unbroken: *The* continual *talking of the students gave their teacher a headache.*
con|tin|u|al (kən **tin**'yū əl) *adjective.*

continue—1. To keep on; go on without stopping: *Her fever* continued *for three days.* 2. To start again after stoppping: *We will* continue *our art project after lunch.*
con|tin|ue (kən **tin**'yū) *verb,* **continued, continuing.**

continuous—Going without stop: *The* continuous *sound of the clock's ticking lulled the baby to sleep.*
con|tin|u|ous (kən **tin**'yo͞o əs) *adjective.*

contour—A shape or form; outline: *The farmer makes* contours *in the field with his plow.*
con|tour (kon'to͝or) *noun, plural* **contours.**

contour: contour plowing

contract—1. To become shorter or smaller; shrink: *The balloon* contracted *as the air leaked out.* 2. To make a legal agreement: *We* contracted *to have the garbage picked up weekly. Verb.*
—A legal agreement: *She signed a* contract *to work for six weeks in the summer. Noun*
con|tract (kən **trakt**' for *verb;* kon'trakt for *noun) verb,* **contracted, contracting;** *noun, plural* **contracts.**

contraction—1. A process of becoming shorter or smaller: *As a sponge grows dry,* contraction *occurs, and it shrinks.*
—2. A shorter way of saying or writing something: *"I've" is a* contraction *for "I have."*
con|trac|tion (kən **trak**'shən) *noun, plural* **contractions.**

contradict—To disagree with; state the opposite of: *The eyewitnesses to the accident* contradict *each other.*
con|tra|dict (kon'trə **dikt**') *verb,* **contradicted, contradicting.**

contradiction—A disagreement; statement of the opposite: *His side of the story is a* contradiction *of everything I said.*
con|tra|dic|tion (kon'trə **dik**'shən) *noun, plural* **contradictions.**

contrary—1. Opposite; against: *To steal is* contrary *to everything I have been taught.* 2. Stubborn or fault-finding: *Her* contrary *attitude caused people to avoid her. Adjective.*
—The opposite: *Hot is the* contrary *of cold. Noun.*
con|tra|ry (kon'trār ē for *adjective* 1 and *noun;* kən **trār**'ē for *adjective* 2) *adjective; noun, plural* **contraries.**

contrast—A difference; unlikeness: *There was little* contrast *in the looks of the twins. Noun.*
—To show differences: *The bright red umbrella* contrasted *with her green raincoat. Verb.*
con|trast (kon'trast for *noun;* kən **trast**' for *verb) noun, plural* **contrasts;** *verb,* **contrasted, contrasting.**

contribute—1. To donate; give as one's share: *We* contributed *one decoration each for our Christmas tree.* 2. To be part of; assist in bringing about: *Homework* contributes *to the final grade.*
con|trib|ute (kən **trib**'yo͞ot) *verb,* **contributed, contributing.**

contribution—1. A donation; gift: *If everyone makes a* contribution, *we can afford to rent a movie.*
con|tri|bu|tion (kon'trə **byū**'shən) *noun, plural* **contributions.**

control—1. To have charge of; direct: *The stop-and-go lights* control *the flow of traffic.* 2. To limit; hold back: *Please* control *your talking in class. Verb.*
—1. Direction; power to rule: *I lost* control *of my bicycle and it fell over.* 2. A holding back; limiting: *We were asked to use* control *and applaud only at the end of the show.* 3. controls: Devices for operating machinery,

especially airplanes and cars: *The captain was at the* controls *during the entire flight. Noun.*
con|trol (kən **trol′**) *verb,* **controlled, controlling;** *noun, plural* **controls.**

controversial—Likely to cause disagreement; questionable: *My uncle discusses* controversial *topics that start arguments.*
con|tro|ver|sial (kon′trə **vur′**shəl) *adjective.*

controversy—A debate; argument: *The umpire's decision was a matter of much* controversy.
con|tro|ver|sy (kon′trə vur′sē) *noun, plural* **controversies.**
* Synonyms: **disagreement, dispute**

convenience—Something that saves work or time: *Home delivery of the newspaper is a* convenience *that saves my father a trip to the store.*
con|ven|ience (kən **vēn′**yəns) *noun, plural* **conveniences.**
■ **at (one's) convenience:** At a time that is easy for someone: *Please get me some milk* at *your* convenience.

convenient—Saving work and time; easy: *He took the most* convenient *route home and arrived before everyone else.*
con|ven|ient (kən **vēn′**yənt) *adjective.*

convent—The building in which nuns live.
con|vent (kon′vent) *noun, plural* **convents.**

convention—1. A large gathering of people for a particular reason; conference: *Teachers attend* conventions *to learn more about their jobs.* 2. A standard for doing things; a custom: *It is a* convention *in the United States to celebrate the Fourth of July with fireworks.*
con|ven|tion (kən ven′shən) *noun, plural* **conventions.**

conventional—1. Accepted by custom; traditional: *The* conventional *Thanksgiving dinner is turkey with all the trimmings.* 2. Ordinary; commonplace: *A camel is not a* conventional *pet.*
con|ven|tion|al (kən ven′shə nəl) *adjective.*

conversation—An informal talk: *a* conversation *on the telephone.*
con|ver|sa|tion (kon′vər sā′shən) *noun, plural* **conversations.**

converse—To talk informally: *The two mothers* converse *every day in the park.*

con|verse (kən **vurs′**) *verb,* **conversed, conversing.**

conversion—A change; transformation: *The* conversion *of a caterpillar into a butterfly takes place in stages.*
con|ver|sion (kən **vur′**zhən) *noun, plural* **conversions.**

convert—To change into something else: *He* converted *his Mexican money into American dollars when he returned from his vacation. Verb.*
—A person who changes what he or she thinks or believes: *She is a* convert *to the new church in town. Noun.*
con|vert (kən **vurt′** for *verb;* **kon′**vurt for *noun*) *verb,* **converted, converting;** *noun, plural* **converts.**

convertible—That changes easily: *My* convertible *jacket becomes a vest when I remove the sleeves. Adjective.*
—A car with a top that can be lowered or removed. *Noun.*
con|vert|i|ble (kən **vur′**tə bəl) *adjective; noun, plural* **convertibles.**

convex—Shaped in an outward curve: *The lenses on my eyeglasses are* convex *on one side.*
con|vex (kon **veks′** *or* **kon′**veks) *adjective.*
* Antonym: **concave**
* See picture at **concave.**

convey—1. To transport; carry: *Trains* convey *people from city to city.* 2. To tell; deliver a message: *Please* convey *my best wishes to your mother.*
con|vey (kən **vā′**) *verb,* **conveyed, conveying.**
* Synonyms: **communicate, express,** for 2.

convict—To find someone guilty: *to be* convicted *of stealing. Verb.*
—A prisoner. *Noun.*
con|vict (kən **vikt′** for *verb;* **kon′**vikt for *noun*) *verb,* **convicted, convicting;** *noun, plural* **convicts.**

conviction—1. The act of finding someone guilty, especially in a court. 2. A strong belief: *The explorer set sail with a strong* conviction *that the earth was round.*
con|vic|tion (kən vik′shən) *noun, plural* **convictions.**

convince—To win someone over to one's opinion or belief; persuade: *I* convinced *them that playing the game was more important than winning it.*
con|vince (kən **vins′**) *verb,* **convinced, convincing.**

a at	i if	oo look	ch chalk		a in ago
ā ape	ī idle	ou out	ng sing		e in happen
ah calm	o odd	u ugly	sh ship	ə =	i in capital
aw all	ō oats	ū rule	th think		o in occur
e end	oi oil	ur turn	th their		u in upon
ē easy			zh treasure		

convulsion—1. A violent shaking. 2. An outburst of laughter: *The joke had everyone in the room in* convulsions.
con|vul|sion (kən vul′shən) *noun, plural* **convulsions.**

cook—To prepare food so that it can be eaten: *We* cooked *the hot dogs on the grill. Verb.*
—A person who prepares food. *Noun.*
cook (kook) *verb,* **cooked, cooking;** *noun, plural* **cooks.**

cookie or **cooky**—A small cake, usually flat.
cook|ie or cook|y (kook′ē) *noun, plural* **cookies.**
■ **how the cookie crumbles:** How life is; the way things are: *She was sick on her birthday, but that's* how the cookie crumbles.

Word History

Cookie comes from a Dutch word meaning "cake." When a cake is very small, we call it a cookie.

---

cookout—An outdoor meal prepared on a grill or over a campfire.
cook|out (kook′out′) *noun, plural* **cookouts.**

cool—1. Not warm; slightly cold: *The* cool *day was a relief after the hot weather.* 2. Calm; showing no emotion: *Her* cool *manner helped quiet the excited children.* 3. Showing no emotion; indifferent: *After the argument, the men were* cool *toward each other. Adjective.*
—To make or become less hot: *I* cooled *my cocoa by adding more milk. Verb.*
—1. The condition of being slightly cold: *The* cool *of the night after the heat of the day was a welcome change.* 2. A good control of one's emotions: *He kept his* cool *during the game and let nothing upset him. Noun.*
cool (kūl) *adjective,* **cooler, coolest;** *verb,* **cooled, cooling;** *noun.*
■ **cool (one's) heels:** To be kept waiting a long time: *He* cooled *his* heels *for two hours at the dentist's office.*

coop—An enclosed area in which small animals are kept; cage: *a chicken* coop. *Noun.*
—To close in; confine to an area: *The storm kept us* cooped *up in our cabins. Verb.*
coop (kūp) *noun, plural* **coops;** *verb,* **cooped, cooping.**
■ **fly the coop:** To run away; escape: *We told her to stay home, but she* flew the coop *and left.*

cooperate—To work together: *If everyone* cooperates, *the work will be finished quickly.*

co|op|er|ate (kō op′ə rāt) *verb,* **cooperated, cooperating.**

cooperation—The act of working together: *Our* cooperation *got the job done.*
co|op|er|a|tion (kō op′ə rā′shən) *noun.*

coordinate—1. To organize; arrange: *We must* coordinate *our plans if Class Day activities are to finish by three o'clock.* 2. To cause to work well together: *A good drummer must learn to* coordinate *the movement of hands and feet. Verb.*
—Equal in rank or importance: *the cold, wet snow. The words "cold" and "wet" are* coordinate *adjectives. Adjective.*
co|or|di|nate (kō awr′də nāt for *verb;* kō awr′də nit for *adjective*) *verb,* **coordinated, coordinating;** *adjective.*

cope—To deal with something successfully; work to overcome: *The truck driver* coped *with long hours on the road by taking frequent breaks.*
cope (kōp) *verb,* **coped, coping.**

copilot—The pilot who assists the senior pilot in an airplane.
co|pi|lot (kō′pī′lət) *noun, plural* **copilots.**

copper—1. A metal that has a reddish-brown color and is a chemical element. It is used to make wire because it is a good conductor of heat and electricity and does not rust. 2. A reddish-brown color. *Noun.*
—Having a reddish-brown color: copper *hair. Adjective.*
cop|per (kop′ər) *noun, adjective.*

copperhead—A snake whose head is a reddish-brown color and whose body is light brown with dark rings. It is poisonous.
cop|per|head (kop′ər hed′) *noun, plural* **copperheads.**

copperhead

copy—1. An exact likeness of something: *He wants a* copy *of the report for himself.* 2. One

of a quantity of something published, as of a book, newspaper, or magazine: *Where is my copy of the new science textbook? Noun.*
—**1.** To make an exact likeness of: *I had to copy the arithmetic problem.* **2.** To imitate something or someone: *She learned to dance quickly because she copied her instructor's every move. Verb.*
cop|y (kop′ē) *noun, plural* **copies;** *verb,* **copied, copying.**
• Synonyms: **duplicate, replica, reproduction,** for *noun* **1.**

copycat—Someone who imitates someone else: *Some* copycat *made a poster just like mine.*
cop|y|cat (kop′ē kat′) *noun, plural* **copycats.**

copyright—The right to publish a book or produce a work of art. It is given by a government for a number of years.
cop|y|right (kop′ē rīt′) *noun, plural* **copyrights.**

coral—**1.** A colorful, stonelike material that forms from the skeletons of small sea animals. Many reefs and islands are made of coral. **2.** A reddish-pink color. *Noun.*
—Having a reddish-pink color. *Adjective.*
cor|al (kawr′əl) *noun, adjective.*

coral (noun, definition 1)

coral snake—Any of several small, poisonous tropical snakes that have brilliant rings of red, black, yellow, or white. The coral snake is found in South and Central America and in the southern part of the United States.

coral snake

cor|al snake (kawr′əl snāk) *noun, plural* **coral snakes.**

cord—**1.** A heavy string made of several strands woven together. **2.** A casing for electrical wires that attaches on one end to a plug and on the other end to an electric appliance. **3.** A part of the body that resembles a string: *the spinal* cord; *the vocal* cords. **4.** A cubic measure usually for cut wood. A cord of wood is 4 feet deep, 4 feet wide, and 8 feet long (1.2 × 1.2 × 2.4 meters), a total of 128 cubic feet (3.625 cubic meters). *Noun.*
—To tie with heavy string: *We* corded *the newspapers so they could be picked up for recycling. Verb.*
cord (kawrd) *noun, plural* **cords;** *verb,* **corded, cording.**
• A word that sounds the same is **chord.**

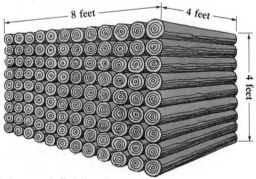

cord (noun, definition 4)

cordial—Very friendly; welcoming sincerely and warmly: *Our hostess was very* cordial *in greeting us.*
cor|dial (kawr′jəl) *adjective.*

corduroy—A thick, cotton fabric that has narrow ridges in it.
cor|du|roy (kawr′də roi) *noun, plural* **corduroys.**

core—1. The center part of some fruits, containing the seeds. 2. The most important part: *We must get to the* core *of the problem before we can solve it. Noun.*
—To cut so as to remove the center of a fruit: *Mother* cored *the apples before adding them to the salad. Verb*
core (kawr) *noun, plural* **cores;** *verb,* **cored, coring.**
• A word that sounds the same is **corps.**

cork—1. The bark from a type of oak tree, often used for making bottle stoppers and insulation. Cork is very light and floats. 2. A bottle stopper made of this substance or something similar. *Noun.*
—To put a stopper in something: *She* corked *the bottle to keep the juice fresh. Verb.*
cork (kawrk) *noun, plural* **corks;** *verb* **corked, corking.**

corkscrew—A device with a long screw, used for removing corks from bottles.
cork|screw (**kawrk'**skrū') *noun, plural* **corkscrews.**

corkscrew

corn¹—A vegetable that grows as small kernels, usually yellow, on a long, thin plant part called an ear. Corn is eaten cooked.
corn (kawrn) *noun.*

corn²—A small section of skin, usually on the toe, that becomes hard and thick and may cause pain.
corn (kawrn) *noun, plural* **corns.**

corncob—The hard, inner part of an ear of corn. Kernels of corn grow in rows on the corncob.
corn|cob (**kawrn'**kob') *noun, plural* **corncobs.**

cornea—The clear outer covering of the eye.
cor|ne|a (**kawr'**nē ə) *noun, plural* **corneas.**

corner—1. The angle formed by the meeting of two sides or lines: *the four* corners *of my desk.* 2. The place where two roads join. *Noun.*
—On a corner: *the* corner *restaurant. Adjective.*

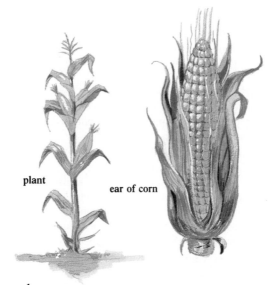
plant   ear of corn

corn¹

—To put in a position that is hard or impossible to get out of: *The police* cornered *the bank robber, and he surrendered. Verb.*
cor|ner (**kawr'**nər) *noun, plural* **corners;** *adjective; verb,* **cornered, cornering.**
■ **cut corners:** To limit in order to save money, time, or effort: *If we* cut corners *on expenses, we will have money for a holiday.*

cornerstone—1. A special stone built into the corner of a building. 2. The main or basic part of something: *The* cornerstones *of education are reading, writing, and arithmetic.*
cor|ner|stone (**kawr'**nər stōn') *noun, plural* **cornerstones.**

cornet—A musical instrument that is made of brass and looks like a wide trumpet.
cor|net (kawr **net'**) *noun, plural* **cornets.**

cornet

coronation—A ceremony in which a ruler is crowned: *The new king bowed his head to receive the crown during his* coronation.
cor|o|na|tion (kawr′ə nā′shən) *noun, plural* **coronations.**

corporal—A member of the armed forces who is above a private and below a sergeant.
cor|po|ral (kawr′pər əl) *noun, plural* **corporals.** Abbreviation: Corp.

corporation—An organization, usually a business, that exists in certain ways controlled by law. A corporation can act as if it were a single person, and it can own and sell property, make contracts, and borrow and lend money.
cor|po|ra|tion (kawr′pə rā′shən) noun, plural **corporations.** Abbreviation: corp.

corps—1. A group of specially trained soldiers: *The soldiers in the signal* corps *were trained to send radio and telegram messages.* 2. A team; crew: *A* corps *of 30 engineers designed and built the bridge.*
corps (kawr) *noun, plural* **corps** (kawrz).
• A word that sounds the same is **core.**

corpse—A dead human body.
corpse (kawrps) *noun, plural* **corpses.**

corpuscle—A red or white blood cell.
cor|pus|cle (kawr′pus əl) *noun, plural* **corpuscles.**

corral—A place to fence in large animals, especially horses and cows. *Noun.*
—1. To catch and direct into such a place: *The cowboy* corralled *the wild horse.* 2. To capture; catch; seize: *The fans* corralled *the rock musician for autographs before he could get away. Verb.*
cor|ral (kə ral′) *noun, plural* **corrals;** *verb,* **corralled, corralling.**

correct—1. Accurate; right: *We must have the* correct *measurements of the room before we can order the carpet.* 2. Suitable; acceptable: *We are expected to act in a* correct *way when company comes. Adjective.*
—1. To make accurate; fix: *I have marked where you need to* correct *the errors in your report.* 2. To discipline; punish: *They* corrected *the rude child by sending her to her room. Verb.*
cor|rect (kə rekt′) *adjective; verb,* **corrected, correcting.**

• Synonyms: **courteous, fit**[1]**, polite, proper,** for *adjective* 2.
Antonym: **rude,** for *adjective* 2.

correction—1. A change to make something right: *One* correction *will make this spelling paper perfect.* 2. The act of disciplining: *Some children need constant* correction *to help them behave.*
cor|rec|tion (kə rek′shən) *noun, plural* **corrections.**

correspond—1. To match; agree: *She believed us because our stories* corresponded. 2. To exchange letters with each other: *The two girls* corresponded *weekly.*
cor|re|spond (kawr′ə spond′) *verb,* **corresponded, corresponding.**
• Synonyms: **coincide, match**[2]**,** for *verb* 1.
Antonym: **differ,** for *verb* 1.

correspondence—1. A resemblance; condition of matching: *There is little* correspondence *in their appearance even though they are brothers.* 2. An exchange of letters between two writers.
cor|re|spond|ence (kawr′ə spon′dəns) *noun.*

correspondent—1. A person who writes letters to another person. 2. A person whose job is to gather news in a certain place and report it back to a newspaper, magazine, or radio or television station.
cor|re|spond|ent (kawr′ə spon′dənt) *noun, plural* **correspondents.**

corridor—A long hall that usually has rooms opening onto either side of it.
cor|ri|dor (kawr′ə dər) *noun, plural* **corridors.**

corrode—To wear away slowly: *Rust will* corrode *iron.*
cor|rode (kə rōd′) *verb,* **corroded, corroding.**

corrupt—Dishonest; bad: Corrupt *people will even lie and steal to get what they want. Adjective.*
—To make someone bad: *Gambling and drinking* corrupted *him, and he lost all his friends. Verb.*
cor|rupt (kə rupt′) *adjective; verb,* **corrupted, corrupting.**

corsage—Some flowers worn on the wrist or on a woman's dress or coat.
cor|sage (kawr sahzh′) *noun, plural* **corsages.**

cosmetic—A substance applied to the skin, hair, or other parts of the body to make them look better. Lipstick, nail polish, and skin cream are cosmetics. *Noun.*
cos|met|ic (koz met′ik) *noun, plural* **cosmetics.**

a at	i if	oo look	ch chalk		a in ago
ā ape	ī idle	ou out	ng sing		e in happen
ah calm	o odd	u ugly	sh ship	ə =	i in capital
aw all	ō oats	ū rule	th think		o in occur
e end	oi oil	ur turn	th their		u in upon
ē easy			zh treasure		

cottontail

cosmic—Having to do with the universe: *We have learned a lot about outer space from the* cosmic *experiments made in recent years.*
cos|mic (koz′mik) *adjective.*

cost—1. The money necessary to buy something; price: *The* cost *of a pencil is ten cents.*
2. Something sacrificed; penalty: *She told the truth at the* cost *of her friendship with the other girls. Noun.*
—1. To have a price; be worth: *This coat* costs *more money than I have.* 2. To cause to lose or suffer: *His pushing and shoving* cost *him his place in line. Verb.*
cost (kawst) *noun, plural* costs; *verb,* cost, costing.

costly—Very expensive: *It is too* costly *to take the whole family out to dinner.*
cost|ly (kawst′lē) *adjective,* costlier, costliest.

costume—1. Clothing worn to imitate something: *She dressed in a clown* costume *for Halloween.*
2. A type of outfit that represents an activity, a country, or another time in history: *The festival had* costumes *and dances from many countries.*
cos|tume (kos′tūm *or* kos′tyūm) *noun, plural* costumes.

cot—A small folding bed. It is often made of canvas stretched over a lightweight frame.
cot (kot) *noun, plural* cots.

cottage—A small house, often in the country, that is sometimes near a main house or a resort; bungalow.
cot|tage (kot′ij) *noun, plural* cottages.

cotton—1. The fluffy bunches of white fiber that grow on the cotton plant. 2. Fabric or thread made from cotton.
cot|ton (kot′ən) *noun, plural* cottons.

cottonmouth—*See* water moccasin.
cot|ton|mouth (kot′ən mouth′) *noun, plural* cottonmouths.

cottontail—A white-tailed rabbit found in North America. It has a gray or brown body.
cot|ton|tail (kot′ən tāl′) *noun, plural* cottontails.

cottonwood—A North American tree whose seeds have fluffy bunches of silky white fiber that resemble cotton.
cot|ton|wood (kot′ən wood′) *noun, plural* cottonwoods.

leaf

fruit and seeds

tree

cottonwood

couch—A long, upholstered seat for two or more people; sofa.
couch (kouch) *noun, plural* couches.

cougar—*See* mountain lion.
cou|gar (kū′gər) *noun, plural* cougars.

cough—To make a short, sharp noise by suddenly forcing air from the lungs: *I coughed when I swallowed the juice too quickly. Verb.*
—1. The sound or act of forcing air from the lungs with a short, sharp noise: *He tried to get my attention with a loud* cough. 2. The type of short, hacking sounds one makes when ill: *Mother took me to the doctor because my* cough *kept me awake all night. Noun.*
cough (kawf) *verb,* coughed, coughing; *noun, plural* coughs.
■ cough up: To give up; deliver: *We had to* cough up *five dollars for each ticket to the game.*

could—*See* can.
could (kood) *verb.*

couldn't—The contraction of "could not."
could|n't (kood′ənt).

council—1. A gathering of people to give advice or to make a decision about a specific issue or

problem.   **2.** A governing group: *The student council met to talk about the noise in the halls.*
coun|cil (koun′səl) *noun, plural* **councils.**
● A word that sounds the same is **counsel.**

counsel—1. Guidance; advice: *Her counsel was to take lessons to improve my singing ability.*
2. A person whose job is to give legal advice; lawyer. *Noun.*
—To give guidance; advise: *The teacher counseled the student on which books to use for the term paper. Verb.*
coun|sel (koun′səl) *noun, plural* **counsels;** *verb,* **counseled, counseling.**
■ **keep (one's) own counsel:** To avoid talking about one's own opinions and plans: *She kept her own counsel because she didn't trust anyone there.*
● A word that sounds the same is **council.**

counselor—Someone whose job is to guide or advise: *our school's guidance counselor.*
coun|se|lor (koun′sə lər *or* koun′slər) *noun, plural* **counselors.**

count—1. To say numbers in order: *My little brother can count to ten.*   **2.** To find the total number: *Please count the desks in the classroom.*
3. To take into account; include: *There are twenty people on my school bus if you do not count the driver. Verb.*
—The total when everything has been added up: *The count of children at the party is higher than we expected. Noun.*
count (kount) *verb,* **counted, counting;** *noun, plural* **counts.**
■ **count for:** Have a value of: *Working fast does not count for much here.*
count off: To use numbers in a way that allows groups to be divided: *The teacher asked us to count off by ones and twos and then asked all the ones to line up by the door.*
count on: To rely on: *You can count on my mother to drive us home.*

countdown—The act of saying numbers in backward order, usually from ten to zero. Those people involved then know how much time is left before the beginning or end of something: *The fans started the countdown ten seconds before the game ended.*

count|down (kount′down′) *noun, plural* **countdowns.**

counter¹—1. A long, narrow table along which many people can stand or sit. Restaurants, stores, offices, and banks have counters.   **2.** A device used to keep track of the amount of something.
3. Someone who keeps track of the amount of something by adding numbers.
count|er (koun′tər) *noun, plural* **counters.**
■ **under the counter:** In a sneaky, often illegal way: *Tickets to the game are now available only under the counter at very high prices.*

counter²—In an opposite way: *He went counter to the directions by making a left turn instead of a right. Adverb.*
—Against; opposite: *Because Bill's ideas were counter to those of his friend, the boys started to argue. Adjective.*
—To go or act in an opposite way; oppose: *After I said no, my sister countered my wishes by borrowing my book anyway. Verb.*
count|er (koun′tər) *adverb; adjective; verb,* **countered, countering.**

counter-—A prefix that means "opposite" or "against." A counterattack is one made against or in return for a first attack. To go counterclockwise is to go opposite the movement of a clock's hands.

Word Power

You can understand the meanings of many words that begin with **counter-,** if you add a meaning of the prefix to the meaning of the rest of the word.
counterproductive: achieving results opposite to those desired
counterspy: a spy who works against enemy spies

---

counterclockwise—Going around in the direction opposite to the movement of a clock's hands: *To open that jar, turn the cap counterclockwise. Adverb.*
—Being opposite the direction a clock's hands move: *a counterclockwise spin. Adjective.*
coun|ter|clock|wise (koun′tər klok′wīz′) *adverb; adjective.*
● See picture at **clockwise.**

counterfeit—Not genuine or real: *The counterfeit jewelry looked so real that we were completely fooled. Adjective.*
—To fake; imitate; copy: *The criminals*

a at	i if	oo look	ch chalk		a in ago
ā ape	ī idle	ou out	ng sing		e in happen
ah calm	o odd	u ugly	sh ship	ə =	i in capital
aw all	ō oats	ū rule	th think		o in occur
e end	oi oil	ur turn	th their		u in upon
ē easy			zh treasure		

counterfeited *money and tried to spend it. Verb.*
—A forgery; fake; imitation: *The watch was a* counterfeit *of a more expensive, well-known brand. Noun.*
coun|ter|feit (koun′tər fit) *adjective; verb,* **counterfeited, counterfeiting;** *noun, plural* **counterfeits.**
• Synonyms: **fake, false,** for *adjective.*
Antonyms: For *adjective,* see Synonyms at **actual.**

countless—Endless in numbers; unable to be counted: *the* countless *fish in the sea.*
count|less (kount′lis) *adjective.*

country—1. Any region or land area: *The* country *around the lake is beautiful.* 2. The territory of a nation: *From what* country *did your ancestors come?* 3. Land with few buildings, away from cities and towns; rural area: *My grandparents live in a farmhouse in the* country. *Noun.*
—Of or like a rustic, rural, natural area: *He prefers quiet* country *living. Adjective.*
coun|try (kun′trē) *noun, plural* **countries;** *adjective.*

countryside—An area outside a city or a town: *To escape the summer heat in the city they took a ride through the* countryside.
coun|try|side (kun′trē sīd′) *noun, plural* **countrysides.**

county—A division of a state or a country. A county has its own local government and usually includes the cities, towns, and villages within its boundaries.
coun|ty (koun′tē) *noun, plural* **counties.**

couple—1. Two of a kind; pair. 2. A man and a woman who are married or engaged; two people who join together to do something: *To perform this dance, we need eight* couples. *Noun.*
—To attach; connect: *The railroad freight cars were* coupled *together. Verb.*
cou|ple (kup′əl) *noun, plural* **couples;** *verb,* **coupled, coupling.**

coupon—A ticket or other official paper that can be traded for money, a gift, or a reduced price on something.
cou|pon (cū′pon *or* kyū′pon) *noun, plural* **coupons.**

courage—Ability to overcome despair or fear; bravery: *She showed great* courage *by admitting her mistake in public.*
cour|age (kur′ij) *noun.*
■ **have the courage of** (one's) **convictions:** To do what one thinks is right, even if it is not the way everyone else feels.
• Synonyms: See Synonyms at **grit.**

courageous—Showing no fear; brave and bold: *Saving a drowning person is a* courageous *act.*
cou|ra|geous (kə rā′jəs) *adjective.*
• Synonyms: See Synonyms at **brave.**
Antonyms: **afraid, fearful, timid**

course—1. Movement in a forward direction; progress: *His marks improved over the* course *of the school year.* 2. The path or direction taken; route: *The birds flew south on a straight* course. 3. A way of carrying on; procedure: *The easiest* course *is to wait and see what happens.* 4. A group of lessons taught over a period of time: *She took a* course *in woodworking.* 5. A part of a meal served at one time: *The first* course *was soup and the main* course *was meat loaf.* 6. A place where certain sports are played or races are held: *golf* course; *a race* course.
course (kawrs *or* kors) *noun, plural* **courses.**
■ **in due course:** After a while; at the right time: *Your birthday will come* in due course.
of course: Certainly: *Of course I will come.*
to run its course: To finish completely what is being done: *The machine must be allowed* to run its course *once it has been turned on.*
• A word that sounds the same is **coarse.**

courseware—Teaching materials used with computers or stored in computers.
course|ware (kawrs′war′ *or* kors′war′) *noun.*

court—1. A place where cases are tried and decisions are made regarding matters of law: *He got a traffic ticket and had to appear in* court. 2. A place where a king and queen and their attendants live; royal palace. 3. A place marked off for games in a certain sport: *tennis* court; *basketball* court. 4. An outdoor space enclosed by walls or buildings; courtyard: *The apartments were grouped around a grassy* court. *Noun.*
—To try to win someone's love: *to* court *her with candy and flowers. Verb.*
court (kawrt *or* kort) *noun, plural* **courts;** *verb,* **courted, courting.**

courteous—Polite; well-mannered; correct: *A* courteous *person is considerate of others.*
cour|te|ous (kur′te əs) *adjective.*

courtesy—Behavior based on good manners and thoughtfulness of others: *Carrying the heavy package for her mother was an act of* courtesy.
cour|te|sy (kur′tə sē) *noun, plural* **courtesies.**

courthouse—1. A building in which matters of the law are decided. 2. A building which has the offices of a county government and usually a court.
court|house (kawrt′hous′ *or* kort′hous′) *noun, plural* **courthouses.**

courtyard—An area with no roof that is enclosed by walls or buildings: *In the middle of the apartment building is a lovely* courtyard.
court|yard (kawrt′yahrd′ *or* kōrt′yahrd′) *noun, plural* **courtyards.**

courtyard

cousin—A child of one's aunt or uncle. People who are cousins and have the same grandparents are first cousins. People with the same great-grandparents but different grandparents are second cousins.
cous|in (kuz′ən) *noun, plural* **cousins.**

Word History

Cousin comes from a Latin word meaning ''the child of a mother's sister.'' If your mother's sister has a child, you and that child are cousins. Later the word changed to mean any child of a father's or mother's sister or brother.

---

cove—A small inlet or bay sheltered from strong winds by surrounding high land.
cove (kōv) *noun, plural* **coves.**

a at	i if	oo look	ch chalk		a in ago
ā ape	ī idle	ou out	ng sing		e in happen
ah calm	o odd	u ugly	sh ship	ə =	i in capital
aw all	ō oats	ū rule	th think		o in occur
e end	oi oil	ur turn	<u>th</u> their		u in upon
ē easy			zh treasure		

cover—**1.** To place over or upon: *He covered his toast with jam.* **2.** To occupy the surface of: *Snow covered the ground.* **3.** To hide or protect: *to cover a mistake with an excuse.* **4.** To travel; go over thoroughly: *We covered the whole neighborhood looking for him.* **5.** To include; take in: *This chapter covers plants and animals. Verb.*
—**1.** Something put over or upon something else: *a jar cover, a book cover.* **2.** Something that hides, protects, or shelters: *Some animals hunt under cover of darkness. Noun.*
cov|er (kuv′ər) *verb,* **covered, covering;** *noun, plural* **covers.**
▪ **from cover to cover:** From beginning to end: *She read the book from cover to cover in one day.*
under cover: Secretly: *The police worked under cover to catch the thief.*

covering—Anything that is placed over to protect or keep from sight: *A bedspread is a bed covering.*
cov|er|ing (kuv′ər ing) *noun, plural* **coverings.**

covert—Secret; hidden: *She gave me a covert wink when the others were not looking.*
co|vert (kō′vərt *or* kuv′ərt) *adjective.*

covet—To greatly desire something that belongs to another: *I coveted her wristwatch from the moment I first saw it.*
cov|et (kuv′it) *verb,* **coveted, coveting.**

cow—**1.** The adult female of cattle: *Farmers raise dairy cows for milk.* **2.** The adult female of some large mammals other than cattle, such as the moose, buffalo, and elephant.
cow (kou) *noun, plural* **cows.**
▪ **till the cows come home:** For a very long time: *She'll say no till the cows come home.*

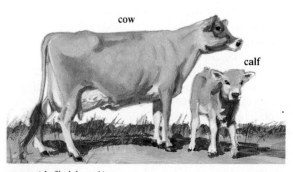

cow (definition 1)

coward—A person who lacks courage and is afraid to face danger or hardship.
cow|ard (kou′ərd) *noun, plural* **cowards.**

Word History

Coward comes from an old French word meaning "tail." When an animal is very frightened, it lowers its tail between its legs.

---

cowboy—A man who takes care of cattle on a ranch.
cow|boy (kou′boi′) *noun, plural* **cowboys.**

cowgirl—A woman who takes care of cattle on a ranch.
cow|girl (kou′gurl′) *noun, plural* **cowgirls.**

cowhand—a person who takes care of cattle on a ranch.
cow|hand (kou′hand′) *noun, plural* **cowhands.**

coy—Acting bashful in order to appear cute; pretending to be shy: *He really wanted to sing, but he acted* coy *and waited to be asked.*
coy (koi) *adjective.*

coyote—A small wolf living mostly on the prairies of western North America but now often seen in eastern parts of the continent as well.
coy|ote (kī′ōt *or* kī ō′tē) *noun, plural* **coyotes.**

coyote

cozy—Giving warmth and comfort; snug: *I took off my wet boots and put on my* cozy *slippers.*
co|zy (kō′zē) *adjective,* **cozier, coziest.**
■ **cozy up to:** to try to get on the good side of; make an effort to please: *Cozying up to* me *now won't do a bit of good.*

crab—An animal with a hard, flat shell, eight legs, and two claws in front. It moves sideways to go from one place to another. It lives in water and is often caught for food.
crab (krab) *noun, plural* **crabs.**

crab

crab apple—A small, hard apple with a sour taste. It is often used for making jelly.
crab ap|ple (krab ap′əl) *noun, plural* **crab apples.**

flower

tree

fruit

crab apple

crab grass—A thick, fast-growing grass. It is considered a weed because it quickly spreads out of control and looks unruly.
crab grass (krab gras) *noun.*

crack—**1.** A small opening or break that causes something to separate or split but not come apart: *The vase leaks because it has a* crack *in it.* **2.** A sudden noise with a sharp, snapping sound: *the* crack *of a whip.* **3.** A sharp blow: *I felt the* crack *on my arm when the ball hit me. Noun.*
—**1.** To break; split: *The ice* cracked *when we walked on it.* **2.** To make a sudden noise that has a sharp, snapping sound: *Thunder* cracked *and lightning flashed last night.* **3.** To hit

something with a sharp blow: *I cracked my head on the low beam. Verb.*

crack (krak) *noun, plural* **cracks;** *verb,* **cracked, cracking.**

■ **crack down:** To take action that is stronger than before; increase control: *The store is cracking down on shoplifters.*

crack up: To laugh or make someone laugh: *She acted so funny that I cracked up.*

take a crack at: give something a try: *You'll never know if you can succeed unless you take a crack at it.*

● Synonyms: **fracture, shatter, smash,** for *verb* **1.**

cracker—A dry, crisp biscuit or wafer: *an animal* cracker.

crack|er (krak′ər) *noun, plural* **crackers.**

crackle—To make a series of small, sharp, snapping noises: *The newpaper crackled as he turned the page. Verb.*

—A series of small, sharp, snapping noises: *We heard the* crackle *of dry leaves under our feet. Noun.*

crack|le (krak′əl) *verb,* **crackled, crackling;** *noun, plural* **crackles.**

cradle—**1.** A baby's bed, usually set on rockers. **2.** A frame or support that looks somewhat like a baby's bed on rockers and is used to hold something. The part of a phone that holds the receiver is called a cradle. *Noun.*

—To hold or support something in a baby's bed or something that looks or acts like one. *He* cradled *the injured bird in his hands. Verb.*

cra|dle (krā′dəl) *noun, plural* **cradles;** *verb,* **cradled, cradling.**

■ **rob the cradle:** to marry or have as a companion a person much younger than oneself: *He robbed the cradle when he married someone half his age.*

craft—**1.** A special ability to make or do something with one's hands: *It takes great* craft *to build furniture.* **2.** A job or kind of work that requires a special skill; trade: *Many plumbers are experts at their* craft. **3.** Skill used to trick someone or something; cunning; deceit: *She used* craft *to lure the kitten from the tree with a bowl of milk.* **4.** A boat, airplane, or spacecraft: *The*

pilot guided the huge craft *safely to earth.*

craft (kraft) *noun, plural* **crafts.**

crag—A steep cliff or rocky point: *After hours of climbing, we reached the highest* crag.

crag (krag) *noun, plural* **crags.**

cram—To pack tightly; fill; stuff: *I cannot* cram *another thing into this suitcase.*

cram (kram) *verb,* **crammed, cramming.**

cramp¹—To limit from moving; close; confine: *Six of us were* cramped *in a one-room cabin.*

cramp (kramp) *verb,* **cramped, cramping.**

■ **cramp (one's) style:** To keep someone from acting freely or from doing one's best: *Having to follow the rules really* cramps *my style.*

cramp²—**1.** A sharp, painful tightening of a muscle: *As she crossed the finish line, she felt a* cramp *in her leg. Noun.*

—To cause a painful tightening of a muscle: *Drinking the ice water too fast made his stomach* cramp. *Verb.*

cramp (kramp) *noun, plural* **cramps;** *verb,* **cramped, cramping.**

cranberry—A sour, dark red berry used for making juice, jelly, or sauce. It grows on a low plant found in marshes and bogs.

cran|ber|ry (kran′ber′ē) *noun, plural* **cranberries.**

crane—**1.** A machine with a long arm for lifting and carrying heavy objects; derrick. **2.** A tall, long-legged wading bird with a long neck and bill. *Noun.*

a at	i if	oo look	ch chalk		a in ago
ā ape	ī idle	ou out	ng sing		e in happen
ah calm	o odd	u ugly	sh ship	ə =	i in capital
aw all	ō oats	ū rule	th think		o in occur
e end	oi oil	ur turn	th their		u in upon
ē easy			zh treasure		

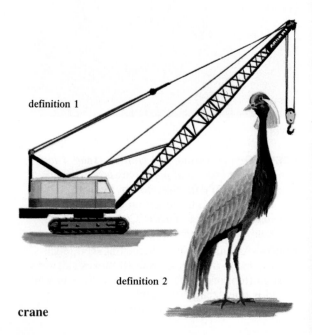

definition 1

definition 2

crane

—To stretch one's neck in order to see better: *She craned her neck to see out the window.* Verb.
crane (krān) *noun, plural* **cranes;** *verb,* **craned, craning.**

crank—1. A grouchy or bad-tempered person. 2. A device with a handle attached to one end of a rod. When the handle is turned, the rod also turns, and the device works: *Window awnings, pencil sharpeners, and many car windows are operated by use of a* crank. *Noun.*
—To operate something by turning such a device: *She has an old-fashioned ice-cream maker that she* cranks *by hand.*
crank (krangk) *noun, plural* **cranks;** *verb,* **cranked, cranking.**

cranky—Bad-tempered; grouchy, cross: *If the baby gets* cranky, *let her take a nap.*
cranky (krang'kē) *adjective,* **crankier, crankiest.**

crash—1. A sudden, loud sound as of things smashing: *the* crash *of the flower pot on the brick path.* 2. A colliding; smashing against something: *an airplane* crash. *Noun.*
—1. To make a sudden, loud sound: *The tree branch snapped in the wind and* crashed *to the ground.* 2. To collide: *He could not turn his bicycle and* crashed *into the tree.* Verb.
crash (krash) *noun, plural* **crashes;** *verb,* **crashed, crashing.**

crate—A large container made from strips of wood, used to ship or store things. *Noun.*
—To pack things into such a container: *The china vase was* crated *carefully before it was shipped.* Verb.
crate (krāt) *noun, plural* **crates;** *verb,* **crated, crating.**

crater—A large hollow in the ground shaped like a bowl: *The meteor left a huge* crater *in the desert.*
cra|ter (krā'tər) *noun, plural* **craters.**

crave—To want or need something very much: *The hungry dog* craved *food.*
crave (krāv) *verb,* **craved, craving.**
● Synonyms: **long**[2], **yearn**

crawl—1. To move along slowly, either by drawing the body along the ground or by creeping on hands and knees: *The soldiers* crawled *under the barbed wire.* 2. To be covered with slow-moving things: *The rotten fruit* crawled *with flies.* Verb.
—1. A very slow pace: *The traffic moved at a* crawl *because of the snow.* 2. A fast swimming stroke in which the arms move over the head one after the other and the legs are kicked rapidly up and down. *Noun.*

crawl (krawl) *verb,* **crawled, crawling;** *noun, plural* **crawls.**

crayfish or **crawfish**—A shellfish that looks like a small lobster, lives in fresh water, and can be eaten.
cray|fish or **craw|fish** (krā'fish' *or* kraw'fish') *noun, plural* **crayfish** or **crayfishes, crawfish** or **crawfishes.**

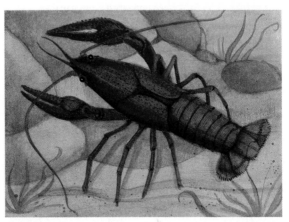

crayfish

crayon—A stick made of a colored, waxy material, used for coloring, drawing, or writing.
cray|on (krā'on) *noun, plural* **crayons.**

crazy—1. Sick in the mind; insane. 2. Very upset with anger, fear, or grief; frantic: *Mother was* crazy *with worry when we arrived three hours late.* 3. Silly; not practical: *Only a* crazy *person would go out in this storm.* 4. Eager or excited about something: *I am* crazy *about pizza and order it every chance I get.*
cra|zy (krā'zē) *adjective,* **crazier, craziest.**

creak—To make a loud, squeaking noise: *The barn door* creaked *on its rusty hinges.* Verb.
—A loud, squeaking noise: *We heard the* creak *of her rocking chair.* Noun.
creak (krēk) *verb,* **creaked, creaking;** *noun, plural* **creaks.**
● A word that sounds the same is **creek.**

cream—1. The thick, yellowish part of milk. Cream is rich in fat and is used to make butter. 2. A soft, thick substance that is put on the skin: *shaving* cream; *hand* cream.
cream (krēm) *noun, plural* **creams.**
■ **cream of the crop:** The best of something: *The students in the advanced mathematics class are the* cream of the crop.

crease—1. A line created by folding something: *I unfolded the letter and smoothed out the* creases.

2. A wrinkle: *The old woman's face was covered with creases. Noun.*
—To make a fold or a wrinkle in something: *The baby* creased *up its face and began to cry. Verb.*
crease (krēs) *noun, plural* creases; *verb,* creased, creasing.

create—To make something that did not exist before; produce; cause: *The accident* created *a huge traffic jam.*
cre|ate (krē āt′) *verb,* created, creating.

creation—**1.** A making of something that did not exist before: *The creation of new laws is the job of the legislature.* **2.** Anything that is made: *The scrapbook was her own* creation.
cre|a|tion (krē ā′shən) *noun, plural* creations.

creationism—The belief that God made the universe and everything in it at the same time and that it looks much the same now as it did then.
cre|a|tion|ism (krē ā′shə niz əm) *noun.*

creative—Able to make something that did not exist before: *The artist had a* creative *mind.*
cre|a|tive (krē ā′tive) *adjective.*

creator—**1.** Someone or something that brings something new into being. **2.** **The Creator:** God.
cre|a|tor (krē ā′tər) *noun, plural* creators.

creature—Any person or animal: *The mouse is a tiny* creature.
crea|ture (krē′chər) *noun, plural* creatures.

crèche—A Christmas display showing statues of the baby Jesus in a manger with Mary and Joseph. Shepherds, wise men, angels, and animals are also often shown.
crèche (kresh) *noun, plural* crèches.

credit—**1.** Belief; faith: *I never give* credit *to gossip.* **2.** A person's reputation concerning money: *The bank will lend you money if your* credit *is good.* **3.** The money in a person's account: *I have a $20* credit *at the clothing store.* **4.** Recognition; praise: *He got* credit *for scoring the winning goal. Noun.*
—**1.** To believe; trust in; accept: *We cannot* credit *everything we see on television.* **2.** To put money in someone's account: *The bank* credited *the $5 deposit to his savings account. Verb.*

cred|it (kred′it) *noun, plural* credits; *verb,* credited, crediting.

credit card—A small plastic card that identifies the owner as having the right to buy things and pay for them later.
cred|it card (kred′it kahrd) *noun, plural* credit cards.

creed—An explanation of the basic beliefs of a person or a group, especially religious beliefs: *the Apostles'* Creed.
creed (krēd) *noun, plural* creeds.

creek—A stream that is smaller than a river and larger than a brook.
creek (krēk) *noun, plural* creeks.
■ **up the creek:** In trouble: *When I lost my locker key, I was really* up the creek.
● A word that sounds the same is **creak.**

creep—**1.** To move slowly, timidly, or carefully; crawl: *I watched a caterpillar* creep *across a leaf.* **2.** To grow along the ground or over something: *Vines* crept *over the abandoned building.* **3.** To have the feeling as though things were crawling over one's skin; shiver: *The horror movie made my skin* creep. *Verb.*
—**the creeps:** The shivers: *Spiders give me* the creeps. *Noun.*
creep (krēp) *verb,* crept, creeping; *noun, plural* creeps.

crèche

crepe—A thin, finely crinkled fabric.
crepe (krāp) *noun.*

crepe paper—A thin, finely crinkled paper used for making decorations.
crepe pa|per (krāp pā′pər) *noun.*

crept—*See* **creep.**
crept (krept) *verb.*

crescent—The thin, curved shape of the moon when it is smallest.
cres|cent (kres′ənt) *noun, plural* crescents.

a at	i if	oo look	ch chalk		a in ago
ā ape	ī idle	ou out	ng sing		e in happen
ah calm	o odd	u ugly	sh ship	ə =	i in capital
aw all	ō oats	ū rule	th think		o in occur
e end	oi oil	ur turn	th their		u in upon
ē easy			zh treasure		

crescent

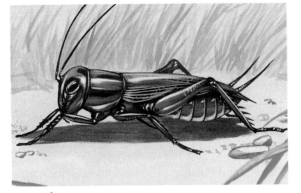

cricket¹

cricket¹—A small, dark-colored insect that is similar to a grasshopper.
crick|et (**krik′**it) *noun, plural* **crickets.**

Word History

Crescent comes from a Latin word meaning ''to grow.'' When the moon appears to be growing larger, it begins as a crescent shape.

crest—1. The pointed tuft of feathers or hair on the head of a bird or other animal: *The cardinal has a bright red crest.* 2. An ornament on the top of a helmet. 3. The top or highest part; peak: *The crowd reached a crest of excitement when the band played the national anthem.*
crest (krest) *noun, plural* **crests.**

crest
(definition 1)

cricket²

Word History

Cricket¹ comes from an old French word meaning ''to click.'' Crickets make a clicking sound. Cricket² comes from another old French word, for a stake used as a goal in a bowling game. A goal in cricket is made of three stakes.

crevice—A narrow opening; crack: *We must patch that crevice in the wall.*
crev|ice (**krev′**is) *noun, plural* **crevices.**

crew—A group, especially of people who work together on a job; team: *the crew of the ship.*
crew (krū) *noun, plural* **crews.**
• Synonyms: See Synonyms at **band¹.**

crib—1. A baby's bed with high sides that can usually be moved up and down. 2. An open box or manger for feeding farm animals. 3. A farm building used to store grain.
crib (krib) *noun, plural* **cribs.**

cricket²—An outdoor game played with a ball and bat by two teams of eleven players each, on a field with a goal called a wicket at each end.
crick|et (**krik′**it) *noun.*

cried—See **cry**.
cried (krīd) *verb*.

crime—An act that is against the law: *A person convicted of a* crime *can be sent to prison*.
crime (krīm) *noun, plural* **crimes**.

criminal—A person who breaks the law: *The police caught the* criminal *who robbed the store*. *Noun*.
—Connected with crime and its punishment: *The police officer checked the files to see if the man had any* criminal *record*. *Adjective*.
crim|i|nal (krim′ə nəl) *noun, plural* **criminals**; *adjective*.

crimson—A deep purplish-red color. *Noun*.
—Having a deep purplish-red color: *a* crimson *sweater*. *Adjective*.
crim|son (krim′zən) *noun, plural* **crimsons**; *adjective*.

cringe—To crouch in fear of pain or danger: *The child* cringed *in his father's arms during the storm*.
cringe (krinj) *verb*, **cringed, cringing**.

crinkle—To wrinkle or crush: *She* crinkled *the paper into a ball*. *Verb*.
—A wrinkle or ripple: *The cloth had many* crinkles *after it got wet*. *Noun*.
crin|kle (kring′kəl) *verb*, **crinkled, crinkling**; *noun, plural* **crinkles**.

cripple—A person or animal who is not able to fully use some part of the body, usually because of injury or disease; lame or disabled person or animal. *Noun*.
—**1**. To make lame or disabled: *Our dog was* crippled *in an accident, so we take special care of her*. **2**. To damage or weaken something so that it will not work properly: *A shortage of good players* crippled *the team*. *Verb*.
crip|ple (krip′əl) *noun, plural* **cripples**; *verb*, **crippled, crippling**.

crisis—**1**. A very difficult or troublesome situation: *Selling the farm caused a* crisis *in his life*. **2**. The point at which things turn either better or worse: *The* crisis *came when the store had to borrow money to increase its business*.
cri|sis (krī′sis) *noun, plural* **crises** (krī′sēz).

crisp—**1**. Thin and hard but easily broken; brittle: *a* crisp *potato chip*. **2**. Clear, cool, and fresh;

brisk: *a* crisp *autumn day*. **3**. Decisive and short; not wordy: *He has a* crisp *manner on the telephone and gets his business done quickly*.
crisp (krisp) *adjective*, **crisper, crispest**.

crisscross—To mark with lines that pass back and forth over each other: *Tire tracks* crisscrossed *the muddy field*. *Verb*.
—Having crossed lines: *The fence made a* crisscross *shadow on the snow*. *Adjective*.
—A pattern made of crossed lines: *The map showed a* crisscross *of roads and highways*. *Noun*.
criss|cross (kris′kraws′) *verb*, **crisscrossed, crisscrossing**; *adjective; noun, plural* **crisscrosses**.

critic—**1**. A person who states publicly what is good or bad about movies, books, music, plays, and the like. **2**. Someone who finds fault or disapproves: *My sister is a* critic *of everything I do*.
crit|ic (krit′ik) *noun, plural* **critics**.

critical—**1**. Finding fault or disapproving: *His mother was* critical *of the way his room looked*. **2**. Having to do with the work of a critic: *a* critical *review of the artist's paintings*. **3**. Highly important, especially because of danger or difficulty: *The* critical *point of the election campaign is the primary*.
crit|i|cal (krit′ə kəl) *adjective*.

criticism—**1**. The act of judging something good or bad: *Her sharp* criticism *of my new dress hurt my feelings*. **2**. A judgment; review: *The dance instructor provides helpful* criticism *to improve the students' skills*.
crit|i|cism (krit′ə siz əm) *noun, plural* **criticisms**.

criticize—**1**. To find fault with something; disapprove: *The teacher* criticized *her poor study habits*. **2**. To judge; evaluate: *I asked him to* criticize *my drawing so I can do it better*.
crit|i|cize (krit′ə sīz) *verb*, **criticized, criticizing**.
• Synonyms: **blame, condemn**, for **1**.
  Antonym: **praise**, for **1**.

croak—A hoarse noise like that of a frog or crow. *Noun*.
—To make a hoarse noise: *Her sore throat made her* croak *when she talked*. *Verb*.
croak (krōk) *noun, plural* **croaks**; *verb*, **croaked, croaking**.

crochet—To make cloth from thread by a process similar to knitting, except that a single hooked rod is used.
cro|chet (krō shā′) *verb*, **crocheted, crocheting**.

a at	i if	oo look	ch chalk		a in ago
ā ape	ī idle	ou out	ng sing		e in happen
ah calm	o odd	u ugly	sh ship	ə =	i in capital
aw all	ō oats	ū rule	th think		o in occur
e end	oi oil	ur turn	th their		u in upon
ē easy			zh treasure		

crocodile—A large, thick-skinned reptile with a long body, short legs, and webbed feet. It is related to the alligator but has a longer snout. It lives in rivers and marshes in the tropics.
croc|o|dile (krok′ə dīl) *noun, plural* **crocodiles.**
■ **crocodile tears:** Pretended or insincere sorrow: *For all his* crocodile tears, *he was actually glad I lost the election.*
● See picture at **alligator.**

crocus—A small plant with narrow leaves and white, purple, or yellow flowers. It grows from a small underground bulb and blooms early in the spring.
cro|cus (krō′kəs) *noun, plural* **crocuses.**

crocus

crook—To bend, curve, or twist: *He* crooked *his arm to carry his books. Verb.*
—**1.** A bend; curve: *We live just around this* crook *in the road.* **2.** A dishonest person; thief: *A* crook *stole her wallet. Noun.*
crook (krook) *verb,* **crooked, crooking;** *noun, plural* **crooks.**

crooked—**1.** Bent, curved, or twisted: *The dentist put on braces to straighten her* crooked *teeth.* **2.** Dishonest: *Cheating is a* crooked *way to win.*
crook|ed (krook′id) *adjective.*

crop—**1.** Any plant grown for food or other uses: *The farmer raised a* crop *of hay to feed his cattle.* **2.** A group or batch of something: *There is a large* crop *of new television shows this autumn.* **3.** A short riding whip. **4.** A pouch in a bird's throat; part of the bird's digestive system. *Noun.*
—To remove the tops of: *A lawn mower* crops *the grass short. Verb.*
crop (krop) *noun, plural* **crops;** *verb,* **cropped, cropping.**

croquet—An outdoor lawn game in which players use wooden mallets to hit wooden balls through wire arches.
cro|quet (krō kā′) *noun.*

croquet

cross—**1.** A design or structure formed by placing one bar, line, or post on top of another. The cross is a symbol of the Christian religion. **2.** A mix of different kinds: *My dog is a* cross *between a collie and a German shepherd. Noun.*
—**1.** To draw a line through: *She* crossed *out the wrong answer.* **2.** To put one thing across another: *He* crossed *his fingers for good luck.* **3.** To go from one side of something to the other: *The bus* crossed *the entire city. Verb.*
—**1.** Lying or going across: *There are two* cross *streets between your house and mine.* **2.** Having a bad temper; grumpy. *Adjective.*
cross (kraws) *noun, plural* **crosses;** *verb,* **crossed, crossing;** *adjective,* **crosser, crossest.**
● See picture at **crucifix.**

crossbow—A weapon used during the Middle Ages for shooting arrows. It had a bow-shaped piece that lay across a wooden stock.
cross|bow (kraws′bō′) *noun, plural* **crossbows.**

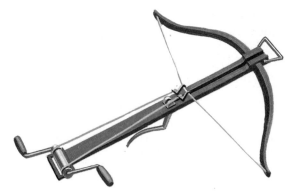

crossbow

cross-country—**1.** Moving across fields and through woods instead of by road: *We took a* cross-country *hike, following a beautiful trail through the woods.* **2.** From one side of a country to the other: *The singer's* cross-country *tour took her from New York to California.*
cross-coun|try (kraws′**kun**′trē) *adjective.*

cross-eyed—Having both eyes turned in toward the nose.
cross-eyed (kraws′īd′) *adjective.*

crossing—**1.** An intersection: *Cars must always wait at the railroad* crossing *until the train passes.* **2.** A point at which a road or a river can be crossed: *A guard at the* crossing *helped the children across the street.*
cross|ing (kraws′ing) *noun, plural* **crossings.**

cross-reference—A statement that tells a reader to look in another part of the book to find more information: *The* cross-reference *said that a picture appeared on another page.*
cross-ref|er|ence (kraws′ref′ər əns) *noun, plural* **cross-references.**

crossroad—**1.** A road that has an intersection with another road or that connects main roads. **2. crossroads:** The place where two or more roads meet: *There is a stop sign at the* crossroads.
cross|road (kraws′rōd′) *noun, plural* **crossroads.**

crosswalk—A path marked with lines where people can walk safely across a street.
cross|walk (kraws′wawk′) *noun, plural* **crosswalks.**

crotch—**1.** The place where a tree divides into two branches. **2.** The point at which the human body divides into two legs.
crotch (kroch) *noun, plural* **crotches.**

crouch—To lower the body close to the ground by bending the knees and stooping over: *She* crouched *behind the fence so no one could see her.*
crouch (krouch) *verb,* **crouched, crouching.**

crow[1]—A large black bird that has a loud, harsh call.
crow (krō) *noun, plural* **crows.**

■ **as the crow flies:** The shortest route; as if following the straight flight of a bird: *The school is not very far away* as the crow flies, *but it is much longer by way of the road.*
eat crow: To be embarrassed; accept shame: *I guess I'll have to* eat crow *and tell them that my instructions were wrong.*

crow[1]

crow[2]—**1.** To make a loud, shrill sound: *The rooster's* crowing *woke me up.* **2.** To make a pleased or happy sound: *The baby* crowed *when I tickled him.*
crow (krō) *verb,* **crowed, crowing.**

crowbar—A strong metal bar that is curved at one end. Crowbars are used to lift heavy things or to pry two things apart.
crow|bar (krō′bahr′) *noun, plural* **crowbars.**

crowbar

crowd—A large group of people together: *The police officer kept the* crowd *away from the accident. Noun.*
—**1.** To come together in large numbers: *The fans* crowded *around the team when they won the game.* **2.** To fill something so that it is too full: *Several people stepped in and* crowded *the small elevator. Verb.*

a at	i if	oo look	ch chalk		
ā ape	ī idle	ou out	ng sing		a in ago
ah calm	o odd	u ugly	sh ship	ə =	e in happen
aw all	ō oats	ū rule	th think		i in capital
e end	oi oil	ur turn	<u>th</u> their		o in occur
ē easy			zh treasure		u in upon

crowd (kroud) *noun, plural* **crowds;** *verb,*
crowded, crowding.
- Synonyms: **crush, multitude, throng,** for
noun.

crown—1. The head covering worn by a king or
queen. It is usually made of gold or silver and
decorated with jewels.   **2.** The highest part; top:
the crown *of his head; the* crown *of the hill.*
3. The part of a tooth that can be seen, not
hidden beneath the gums. *Noun.*
—1. To make king or queen: *The prince was*
crowned *king when he was only 16 years old.*
2. To honor in a ceremony; reward: *The runner
was* crowned *winner of the marathon. Verb.*
crown (kroun) *noun, plural* **crowns;** *verb,*
crowned, crowning.

crow's-nest—A small platform high on the mast
of a ship. It is used by sailors as a watching
place.
crow's-nest (krōz′nest′) *noun, plural*
crow's-nests.

crucifix—A figure of the crucified Jesus Christ
on a cross.
cru|ci|fix (krū′sə fiks) *noun, plural* **crucifixes.**

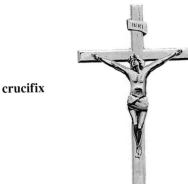

crucifix

crucifixion—1. The act of putting to death by
nailing or binding one's hands and feet to a
cross.   **2. Crucifixion:** The putting to death of
Jesus Christ on a cross.
cru|ci|fix|ion (krū′sə fik′shən) *noun, plural*
crucifixions.

crucify—To put someone to death by nailing or
binding the hands and feet to a cross: *Criminals
were sometimes* crucified *in ancient Rome.*
cru|ci|fy (krū′sə fī) *verb,* **crucified, crucifying.**

crude—1. In a natural state; raw: *The tanker ship
was filled with* crude *oil.*   **2.** Made without
attention to detail; rough: *The hikers made a*
crude *shelter of branches when the storm began.*

3. Rude; impolite: *His* crude *manners offended
everyone.*
crude (krūd) *adjective,* **cruder, crudest.**

cruel—1. Wanting to cause someone or something
to suffer: *A person can be arrested for* cruel
treatment of animals.   **2.** Causing suffering:
Cruel *weather ruined the farmers' crops.*
cru|el (krū′əl) *adjective,* **crueler, cruelest.**
- Synonyms: **bloodthirsty, brutal, violent,** for **1.**
Antonyms: **gentle, kind[1], tender,** for **1.**

cruelty—1. A desire to cause others to suffer.
2. A cruel act.
cru|el|ty (krū′əl tē) *noun, plural* **cruelties.**

cruise—1. To sail or travel about at an easy,
leisurely pace: *We* cruised *to several islands
during the summer.*   **2.** To drive or move about
at random: *She* cruised *around the library
looking for something interesting to read. Verb.*
—A boat trip taken for pleasure: *I would love to
go on a* cruise *around the world. Noun.*
cruise (krūz) *verb,* **cruised, cruising;** *noun,
plural* **cruises.**

cruiser—1. A warship that has fewer guns than a
battleship but goes faster.   **2.** A motorboat that
has living quarters and other equipment needed to
live on board: *The fishermen rented a cabin*
cruiser *and set out on a three-day trip.*   **3.** A
police car.
cruis|er (krū′zər) *noun, plural* **cruisers.**

crumb—A small fragment of food, particularly
bread, cake, or the like: *My mother uses bread*
crumbs *when she makes meat loaf.*
crumb (krum) *noun, plural* **crumbs.**

crumble—1. To break into small fragments:
Crumble *the bread so we can feed the birds.*
2. To decay or fall apart; break down: *The sand
castle* crumbled *when the waves hit it.*
crum|ble (krum′bəl) *verb,* **crumbled,
crumbling.**

crumple—1. To crush into wrinkles: *The boy had*
crumpled *the note by keeping it in his pocket.*
2. To fall down; collapse: *The sick woman fainted
and* crumpled *to the floor.*
crum|ple (krum′pəl) *verb,* **crumpled,
crumpling.**

crunch—To chew noisily: *The children* crunched
on celery and carrots at snack time. Verb.
—A crushing sound: *We heard the* crunch *of
Dad's boots on the gravel road. Noun.*
crunch (krunch) *verb,* **crunched, crunching;**
noun, plural **crunches.**

crusade—1. A campaign to change something
considered bad or to help something considered
good: *a* crusade *to stop drug abuse.*   **2. Crusade:**

Any of the European Christian military campaigns between the years 1096 and 1291. The purpose of the Crusades was to take the Middle East from the Muslims. *Noun.*
—To participate in a campaign to change something considered bad or to help something considered good: *We are* crusading *against racial injustice. Verb.*
cru│sade (krū sād′) *noun, plural,* **crusades;** *verb,* **crusaded, crusading.**

crusader—A person who takes part in a campaign to change something considered bad or to help something considered good: *She is a* crusader *for women's rights.*
cru│sad│er (krū sā′dər) *noun, plural* **crusaders.**

crush—**1.** To squeeze with force, causing something to break or get out of shape: *The garbage truck* crushed *the big bags of trash inside it.* **2.** To grind or pound into small pieces: *First we need to* crush *the tomatoes before we make the sauce.* **3.** To defeat; put down: *The revolution was* crushed *by soldiers who were loyal to the king. Verb.*
—**1.** A strong pressure: *I felt the* crush *of his fingers as he squeezed my hand tightly.* **2.** A large group of people in a small area: *We were caught in the* crush *of holiday shoppers at the mall.* **3.** A strong liking for someone: *All the girls had a* crush *on the new boy. Noun.*
crush (krush) *verb,* **crushed, crushing;** *noun, plural* **crushes.**
• Synonyms: **mash, squash,** for *verb* **2; crowd, multitude, throng,** for *noun* **2.**

crust—**1.** The hard outside surface of bread or rolls. **2.** The flaky dough used in making a pie. **3.** Any hard outer layer; covering: *The winter storm left a* crust *of ice on the lawn. Noun.*
—To form a hard outer layer: *After a volcano erupts, the hot lava* crusts *as it cools. Verb.*
crust (krust) *noun, plural* **crusts;** *verb,* **crusted, crusting.**

crustacean—Any of a group of animals that have a hard outer shell and mostly live in water. Lobsters, crabs, shrimps, and barnacles are crustaceans.
crus│ta│cean (krus tā′shən) *noun, plural* **crustaceans.**

crutch—A supporting device to help a person who has trouble walking. A crutch has a padded top that fits under the arm so a person can lean on it comfortably.
crutch (kruch) *noun, plural* **crutches.**

cry—**1.** To shed tears; weep: *The little boy* cried *when he lost his bicycle.* **2.** To call loudly; shout: *The children* cried *for help when their boat tipped over. Verb.*
—**1.** A shout: *The fire fighter heard a* cry *for help.* **2.** The noise or call of an animal: *We heard the* cries *of birds in the forest but could not see them. Noun.*
cry (krī) *verb,* **cried, crying;** *noun, plural* **cries.**
■ **cry over spilt milk:** To be sad about something that has happened and can't be changed: *The plate is broken so there is no sense in* crying over spilt milk.
cry wolf: To call for help without reason: *The boy* cried wolf *so many times that no one believed him when he really was sick.*
• Synonyms: **bawl, sob, wail,** for *verb* **1; bellow, roar, scream, yell, yowl,** for *verb* **2.** Antonyms: **chuckle, giggle, laugh, snicker,** for *verb* **1.**

crystal—**1.** A clear, shiny form of certain minerals with smooth surfaces and straight edges. Quartz occurs in crystals. **2.** A tiny particle formed when certain substances become solids. Crystals contain many angles and flat surfaces that repeat over and over. Snowflakes and salt are crystals. **3.** A very fine, clear glass used to make things such as drinking glasses and vases.
crys│tal (kris′təl) *noun, plural* **crystals.**

cub—A young bear, lion, wolf, fox, tiger, or certain other young wild animal.
cub (kub) *noun, plural* **cubs.**

a at	i if	oo look	ch chalk		⎡ a in ago
ā ape	ī idle	ou out	ng sing		e in happen
ah calm	o odd	u ugly	sh ship	ə =	i in capital
aw all	ō oats	ū rule	th think		o in occur
e end	oi oil	ur turn	th their		⎣ u in upon
ē easy			zh treasure		

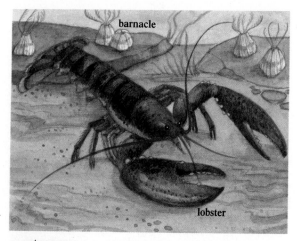

barnacle

lobster

crustacean

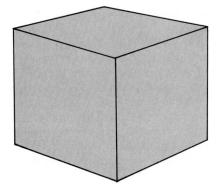

cube (noun, definition 1)

cube—1. A solid object with six square sides, all the same size. 2. Something shaped like such an object: *an ice cube; sugar cubes.* 3. The result of multiplying a number by itself two times. The cube of 4 is 64 because $4 \times 4 \times 4 = 64$. *Noun.*
—1. To cut or make something into small pieces with square sides: *The recipe says to cube the meat before frying it. Verb.*
cube (kyūb) *noun, plural* **cubes;** *verb,* **cubed, cubing.**

cubic—1. Having the shape of a cube: *the cubic shape of dice.* 2. Having three dimensions: length, width, and height. One cubic inch is the size of a cube with sides that are one inch long.
cu|bic (kyū′bik) *adjective.* Abbreviation: cu.

Cub Scouts—The junior division of the Boy Scouts. Members of the Cub Scouts are between eight and ten years old.
Cub Scouts (kub skouts) *noun, singular* **Cub Scout.**
• See Word History at **Boy Scouts.**

cuckoo—A bird that has a cry that sounds like its name. Some lay their eggs in the nests of other birds.
cuck|oo (kū′kū or koo′kū) *noun, plural* **cuckoos.**

cuckoo

cucumber—A plant with a long fruit that has firm, green skin and crisp, white flesh with many seeds in it. Cucumbers grow from vines and are eaten as vegetables in salads or used for making pickles.
cu|cum|ber (kyū′kum bər) *noun, plural* **cucumbers.**
■ **cool as a cucumber:** Calm; confident: *She was cool as a cucumber when she sang.*

cud—The partly digested food that is brought up again into the mouth of a cow, camel, or sheep after being swallowed. The food comes up so that it can be chewed again more slowly.
cud (kud) *noun, plural* **cuds.**

cuddle—1. To hug lovingly in one's arms: *She was cuddling her new doll.* 2. To lie close and comfortably: *The puppies cuddled together.*
cud|dle (kud′əl) *verb,* **cuddled, cuddling.**
• Synonyms: **nestle, snuggle,** for *verb* 2.

cue[1]—A word or signal that tells someone when to do something: *The actor's cue to come on stage was the sound of the doorbell. Noun.*
—To give a word or signal to tell a person when to do something: *I will cue you when it is time to begin your speech. Verb.*
cue (kyū) *noun, plural* **cues;** *verb,* **cued, cuing.**
• Other words that sound the same are **Q** and **queue.**

cue[2]—The long, slender stick used to hit the ball in the games of pool or billiards.
cue (kyū) *noun, plural* **cues.**
• Other words that sound the same are **Q** and **queue.**

cuff[1]—1. A strip of cloth attached to the end of a sleeve. 2. The material folded up at the bottom of a pants leg.
cuff (kuf) *noun, plural* **cuffs.**

cuff[2]—To hit, usually with the open hand; slap: *The cowboy cuffed his horse on its neck as a signal to run faster.*
cuff (kuf) *verb,* **cuffed, cuffing.**

culprit—A person guilty of doing something wrong: *I hope they find the culprits who robbed the bank.*
cul|prit (kul′prit) *noun, plural* **culprits.**

Word History

Culprit comes from two old French words meaning "deserving punishment" and "ready for trial." The first word was abbreviated "cul." The second word was abbreviated "prit." Putting these together made **culprit.**

cultivate—1. To make an area of land ready for raising crops. Cultivating land involves plowing, weeding, and planting seeds, and then caring for the growing plants.   2. To improve; encourage the growth of; train: *She cultivates her mind by reading a lot.*
cul|ti|vate (**kul′**tə vāt) *verb,* **cultivated, cultivating.**
   • Synonyms: **grow, raise,** for 1.

cultural—Having to do with customs, arts, laws, and beliefs: *The cultural life of people who lived a long time ago is very interesting to study.*
cul|tur|al (**kul′**chər əl) *adjective.*

culture—1. An appreciation of music, art, literature, and the like: *A person of culture visits museums and goes to concerts.*   2. The customs, arts, laws, and beliefs of a group of people at a certain time in history: *Animal spirits played an important part in the culture of the American Indians.*   3. The raising of animals or plants: *Some oysters are raised for the culture of pearls.*
cul|ture (**kul′**chər) *noun, plural* **cultures.**

cunning—Very skilled in fooling others: *The cunning thieves dug a tunnel underneath the bank and avoided the alarm system. Adjective.*
—Skill in getting what one desires or in avoiding one's enemies: *The cunning of the fox helps him stay away from hunters. Noun.*
cun|ning (**kun′**ing) *adjective, noun.*

cup—1. A small, round open-topped container with a handle.   2. Anything shaped like such a container: *The cup formed by the hollow tree stump collected rain water.*   3. A half pint: *The recipe calls for a cup of milk. Noun.*
—To form into a round open shape: *The coach cupped his hands around his mouth and yelled to the team. Verb.*
cup (kup) *noun, plural* **cups;** *verb,* **cupped, cupping.**
   ■ **cup of tea:** Something one likes or does well: *Sewing is my cup of tea.*

cupboard—A storage cabinet with shelves for holding food or dishes.
cup|board (**kub′**ərd) *noun, plural* **cupboards.**

cupcake—A small cake baked in a pan that has several cup-shaped molds.
cup|cake (**kup′**kāk′) *noun, plural* **cupcakes.**

curb—1. A raised stone or concrete edge along the side of a paved road or walkway: *We waited by the curb for the bus.*   2. Something that holds back an action; restraint: *We had to put a curb on our desire for sweets when we went past the candy store.*   3. A chain or strap attached to a horse's bit and to the reins. It helps to control the horse when the reins are pulled. *Noun.*
—To hold back; control: *Curb your temper, or you will be sent to your room! Verb.*
curb (kurb) *noun, plural* **curbs;** *verb,* **curbed, curbing.**
   • Synonyms: **bridle, check, restrain,** for *verb.*
     Antonyms: **release, vent,** for *verb.*

cure—1. To restore to health: *The woman was cured after spending months in the hospital.*
2. To be the remedy of; get rid of: *My grandmother told me that chicken soup will cure a cold.*   3. To treat by a process that preserves something for later use. Drying, salting, and smoking are several ways to cure things: *Hams are cured before they are cooked. Verb.*
—Something that restores health: *The cure for cancer has not been discovered yet. Noun.*
cure (kyoor) *verb,* **cured, curing;** *noun, plural* **cures.**

curfew—A set time at night when a person or group of people must be indoors or at home: *In the summer I have a curfew of nine o'clock, but during the school year it's eight o'clock.*
cur|few (**kur′**fyū) *noun, plural* **curfews.**

Word History

Curfew comes from two old French words meaning ''cover'' and ''fire.'' At curfew time in the Middle Ages, people were supposed to cover the fires that they were using for heating or cooking. This was done as a safety precaution, to keep buildings from catching fire during the night.

---

curiosity—1. A strong desire to explore and learn more about things: *He has a great curiosity about what may be in outer space.*   2. A thing that is strange; oddity: *At the circus, one can see curiosities such as the tallest man in the world.*
cu|ri|os|i|ty (kyoor′ē os′ə tē) *noun, plural* **curiosities.**

curious—1. Having a strong desire to explore and learn more about things: *The curious children were able to see and touch the armadillo at the*

a at	i if	oo look	ch chalk		a in ago
ā ape	ī idle	ou out	ng sing		e in happen
ah calm	o odd	u ugly	sh ship	ə =	i in capital
aw all	ō oats	ū rule	th think		o in occur
e end	oi oil	ur turn	th their		u in upon
ē easy			zh treasure		

zoo. **2.** Strange; unusual: *How* curious *to have snow in May!*
cu|ri|ous (**kyoor′**ē əs) *adjective.*
• Synonyms: **peculiar, queer, weird,** for **2.**

curl—To form or shape into a curve or coil: *She* curls *her hair every morning. Verb.*
—**1.** A curved or coiled portion of hair: *Mother kept one of my baby* curls *after my first haircut.* **2.** Anything having the shape of a curve or coil: *a* curl *of smoke; the* curl *of a wave. Noun.*
curl (kurl) *verb,* **curled, curling;** *noun, plural* **curls.**
• Synonyms: **twine, twist, wind²,** for *verb.*

curly-coated retriever—A large hunting dog with a tightly curled outer coat that sheds water. Originally bred in England, these dogs are used to hunt water birds.
curl|y-coat|ed re|triev|er (**kur′**lē kō′tid ri trē′vər) *noun, plural* **curly-coated retrievers.**

curly-coated retriever

currant—**1.** A small, seedless raisin that is often added to baked goods. **2.** A small red, white, or black berry with a sour taste, used chiefly in jellies and pies.
cur|rant (**kur′**ənt) *noun, plural* **currants.**
• A word that sounds the same is **current.**

currency—The money in use by a country.
cur|ren|cy (**kur′**ən sē) *noun, plural* **currencies.**

current—**1.** A flow of water or air; stream: *The Gulf Stream is a warm* current *that flows in the Atlantic Ocean.* **2.** A flow of electricity: *The wire carries the* current. *Noun.*
—Happening now; at the present time: *He kept up on* current *events by reading the newspaper. Adjective.*

cur|rent (**kur′**ənt) *noun, plural* **currents;** *adjective.*
• A word that sounds the same is **currant.**

curse—**1.** To call for a divine power to bring harm to someone or something: *The travelers* cursed *the blizzard that stranded them overnight.* **2.** To swear; use bad words. *Verb.*
—**1.** The words used by a person to wish harm to someone or something: *The witch muttered a* curse *as she stirred her brew. Noun.*
curse (kurs) *verb,* **cursed, cursing;** *noun, plural* **curses.**

cursor—A flashing, movable dot of light on a computer screen. It shows where data may be inserted or removed.
cur|sor (**kur′**sər) *noun, plural* **cursors.**

curtain—**1.** A piece of cloth or other material hung in a window or door for decoration or privacy. **2.** The movable cloth that separates the stage in a theater from the audience: *The* curtain *was lowered when the play was over. Noun.*
—To shut out; to screen something: *The cabin was* curtained *by the tall trees in front of it. Verb.*
cur|tain (**kur′**tən) *noun, plural* **curtains;** *verb,* **curtained, curtaining.**

curtsy—A gesture of respect or greeting that women and girls make by bending the knees and lowering the body. *Noun.*
—To make such a gesture: *The little girls* curtsied *as they gave her their flowers. Verb.*
curt|sy (**kurt′**sē) *noun, plural* **curtsies;** *verb,* **curtsied, curtsying.**

curve—**1.** A line that bends in one direction and has no straight parts. **2.** A bend: *There is a sudden* curve *in the road ahead. Noun.*
—To move in a bending direction: *The rainbow* curved *across the sky. Verb.*
curve (kurv) *noun, plural* **curves;** *verb,* **curved, curving.**

cushion—**1.** A pad to sit or lie on; pillow: *the* cushions *of a chair.* **2.** Anything that softens or protects: *The pile of hay acted as a* cushion *when he fell from the top of the barn. Noun.*
—**1.** To put pads on: *We* cushioned *my grandfather's old wooden chair.* **2.** To make softer: *The snow* cushioned *my fall. Verb.*
cush|ion (**koosh′**ən) *noun, plural* **cushions;** *verb,* **cushioned, cushioning.**

custard—A type of pudding made from sugar, eggs, and milk.
cus|tard (**kus′**tərd) *noun, plural* **custards.**

custodian—**1.** A person who takes care of another person or thing; guardian: *When the boy's parents died, his grandmother became his*

custodian.   2. A person who takes care of a building; a janitor: *The custodian keeps the school clean and fixes anything that breaks.*
cus|to|di|an (kus tō′dē ən) *noun, plural* **custodians.**

custody—1. The care of another person or thing: *The children are in their father's* custody.
2. The condition of being held captive, especially in prison: *The escaped convicts were soon back in police* custody.
cus|to|dy (**kus′**tə dē) *noun, plural* **custodies.**

custom—1. A habit; usual practice: *It was her* custom *to walk several miles each morning.*
2. The way a large number of people normally do something; tradition: *It is a Japanese* custom *to sit on the floor to eat.*   3. **customs:** The tax that is paid for something purchased in one country and brought into another: *We had to pay* customs *on the perfume we bought in France.*
cus|tom (**kus′**təm) *noun, plural* **customs.**

customary—Set by habit; usual: *It is* customary *in my family to eat Sunday dinner at one o'clock.*
cus|tom|ar|y (**kus′**tə mer′ē) *adjective.*

customer—A person who buys something from a business: *The store wanted more* customers, *so it had a sale each week.*
cus|tom|er (**kus′**tə mər) *noun, plural* **customers.**

cut—1. To divide, open, or remove with a knife or something sharp: *to* cut *the cake; to* cut *the wood for the fireplace.*   2. To make by using something sharp: *They* cut *a path through the woods.*   3. To shorten; trim: cut *your hair;* cut *the grass.*   4. To cross: *The new road* cuts *through the farm.*   5. To reduce: *The mayor wants to* cut *taxes, not raise them. Verb.*
—1. An opening made by something sharp: *The* cut *on his foot was deep.*   2. A decrease; reduction: *The voters favor a tax* cut. *Noun.*
cut (kut) *verb,* **cut, cutting;** *noun, plural* **cuts.**
▪ **cut down:** To decrease or reduce something: *Our family* cut down *on salt in our food.*
cut up: To show off; play tricks. *The twins always* cut up *in gym class.*

cute—Charming; pretty: *Her friends told her she looked* cute *in her new coat and hat.*
cute (kyūt) *adjective,* **cuter, cutest.**

cuticle—The tough layer of skin at the base of a fingernail or toenail.
cu|ti|cle (**kyū′**tə kəl) *noun, plural* **cuticles.**

cutlass—A short sword with a curved blade, once used as a weapon by sailors and pirates.
cut|lass (**kut′**ləs) *noun, plural* **cutlasses.**

cutlass

cycle—A group of actions or events that is repeated in the same order. *Noun.*
—To ride a tricycle, bicycle, or motorcycle: *The two boys spent the weekend* cycling. *Verb.*
cy|cle (**sī′**kəl) *noun, plural* **cycles;** *verb,* **cycled, cycling.**

cyclone—A strong, violent storm with rotating winds that can cause much damage. Typhoons, hurricanes, and tornadoes are cyclones.
cy|clone (**sī′**klōn) *noun, plural* **cyclones.**

cylinder—1. An object shaped like a tube, with two flat ends parallel to each other: *A soup can is a* cylinder.   2. A part of an automobile engine, in which gasoline burns and a piston moves.
cyl|in|der (**sil′**ən dər) *noun, plural* **cylinders.**

cymbal—A musical instrument that is made of metal and shaped like a large plate. Cymbals make a ringing sound when struck with a stick or smashed together.
cym|bal (**sim′**bəl) *noun, plural* **cymbals.**
● A word that sounds the same is **symbol.**

cymbal

a at	i if	oo look	ch chalk		⎡ a in ago
ā ape	ī idle	ou out	ng sing		e in happen
ah calm	o odd	u ugly	sh ship	ə =	i in capital
aw all	ō oats	ū rule	th think		o in occur
e end	oi oil	ur turn	th their		⎣ u in upon
ē easy			zh treasure		

cypress—Any of several evergreen trees that have small leaves.
cy|press (**sī′**prəs) *noun, plural* **cypresses.**

About 1,900 years ago, the Romans gave the capital **D** its present form. The small letter **d** was first used about 1,500 years ago. It reached its present form about 500 years ago.

About 5,000 years ago, the ancient Egyptians used a symbol of a door with panels. People living in the Middle East used the same symbol. They called it *daleth*, their word for "door."

About 3,000 years ago, other people in the Middle East used a triangle as their symbol for this letter.

About 2,600 years ago, the Greeks used an equilateral triangle. They called this letter *delta*.

D or **d**—**1.** The fourth letter of the English alphabet: *There are two* d's *in the word "decide."* **2.** The Roman numeral for 500. **D, d** (dē) *noun, plural* **D's** *or* **Ds, d's** *or* **ds.**

dab—**1.** To pat gently: *Mother* dabbed *her eyes with a tissue to wipe the tears away.* **2.** To apply gently: *He* dabbed *some butter on his potatoes. Verb.*
—**1.** A gentle pat. **2.** A small quantity: *I want just a* dab *of mustard on my hot dog. Noun.* **dab** (dab) *verb,* **dabbed, dabbing;** *noun, plural* **dabs.**

dabble—**1.** To splash up and down playfully: *Sitting on the dock, the children* dabbled *their feet in the lake.* **2.** To do something in a casual way; work on something but not regularly or seriously: *She does not take lessons but just* dabbles *at painting.* **dab|ble** (dab′əl) *verb,* **dabbled, dabbling.**

dachshund—A small or medium-sized hound dog with a long, low body, short legs, and long, drooping ears. There are three varieties of both small and medium-sized dachshunds: those with short, smooth hair; those with long, silky hair; and those with rough, wiry hair. Originally bred in Germany, these dogs were used for hunting. **dachs|hund** (dahks′hoond, daks′hoond, *or* dash′hoond) *noun, plural* **dachshunds.**

dachshund

Word History

Dachshund got its name from two German words meaning "badger dog." Dachshunds were widely used for hunting badgers and other underground animals, because the dog's body fits into the burrows of these animals.

dad—A name for a father. **dad** (dad) *noun, plural* **dads.**

daddy—A name for a father. **dad|dy** (dad′ē) *noun, plural* **daddies.**

daddy longlegs

daddy longlegs or **daddy-longlegs**—An insect that has a tiny, rounded body and very long, slender legs. It is related to the spider, but it does not bite.
dad|dy long|legs or **dad|dy-long|legs** (dad′ē lawng′legz) *noun, plural* **daddy longlegs** or **daddy-longlegs**.

daffodil—A yellow or white flower that is shaped like the end of a trumpet. The plant it grows on has long, narrow, green leaves.
daf|fo|dil (daf′ə dil) *noun, plural* **daffodils**.

daffodil

dagger—A knife used to stab something or someone. It has a short blade.
dag|ger (dag′ər) *noun, plural* **daggers**.
■ **look daggers:** To give someone or something

an angry or fierce look: *My sister* looked daggers *at me when I told her secret.*

daily—Happening, used, or done each day or every day: *Brushing your teeth is a* daily *event. Adjective.*
—Each day; any day: *The drugstore delivers medicines* daily. *Adverb.*
—A newspaper that is published each day, or each day except Sunday. *Noun.*
dai|ly (dā′lē) *adjective; adverb; noun, plural* **dailies**.

dainty—Delicate and pretty: *small* dainty *flowers.*
dain|ty (dān′tē) *adjective,* **daintier, daintiest**.

dairy—**1.** A place that sells milk and milk products. **2.** A place where cows are raised for milk and milk products, such as cheese, cream, and butter. **3.** A place where milk is treated to make milk products. *Noun.*
—Having to do with milk products: *a* dairy *farm;* dairy *cattle. Adjective.*
dair|y (dār′ē) *noun, plural* **dairies**; *adjective.*

daisy—A flower with a round, yellow center surrounded by white, yellow, or pink petals.
dai|sy (dā′zē) *noun, plural* **daisies**.

daisy

Word History

Daisy comes from two old English words meaning "day's eye." A daisy closes up at night and opens at dawn. In this way, it is like an eye.

a at	i if	oo look	ch chalk		a in ago
ā ape	ī idle	ou out	ng sing		e in happen
ah calm	o odd	u ugly	sh ship	ə =	i in capital
aw all	ō oats	ū rule	th think		o in occur
e end	oi oil	ur turn	th their		u in upon
ē easy			zh treasure		

Dalmatian—A large dog that has a white coat with black spots. It is able to run very fast for long periods of time. Originally bred in Austria, these dogs are usually pictured in the United States as riding on fire engines and living in firehouses.
Dal|ma|tian (dal mā′shən) *noun, plural* **Dalmatians.**

Dalmatian

dam—A barrier put across a river or stream to limit or prevent the water's flow. *Noun.*
—To block or hold back with a barrier: *The farmer* dammed *the brook and made a pond for his cattle. Verb.*
dam (dam) *noun, plural* **dams;** *verb,* **dammed, damming.**

damage—Injury; harm: *The* damage *to the desk was so great that it could not be repaired. Noun.*
—To injure; harm: *Did you* damage *the book when you dropped it? Verb.*
dam|age (dam′ij) *noun, plural* **damages;** *verb,* **damaged, damaging.**

dame—1. An older woman. 2. A woman with a high social rank.
dame (dām) *noun, plural* **dames.**

damp—Moist but not completely wet: *Although I finished my shower an hour ago, my hair is still* damp. *Adjective.*
—Moisture; humidity: *The* damp *of the early morning made us feel chilly. Noun.*
damp (damp) *adjective,* **damper, dampest;** *noun.*

dampen—1. To wet with a little bit of water: Dampen *the shirt before ironing it.* 2. To limit or lessen the full effect or enjoyment of something: *The noise from the fan* dampened *our enjoyment of the movie.*
damp|en (dam′pən) *verb,* **dampened, dampening.**

dance—1. To step, glide, or move in time to music: *The couples* danced *to both fast and slow music during the evening.* 2. To jump around because of excitement: *She* danced *with joy when she won the award. Verb.*
—1. Certain steps or motions done in time to music: *She learned a special* dance *for her performance.* 2. A period of dancing: *the last* dance *of the party.* 3. A social gathering for dancing: *Everyone attended the* dance *at the end of the school year. Noun.*
dance (dans) *verb,* **danced, dancing;** *noun, plural* **dances.**

dandelion—A yellow flower with many thin parts. It turns into a fluffy white ball.
dan|de|li|on (dan′də lī′ən) *noun, plural* **dandelions.**

dandelion

Word History

Dandelion comes from an old French phrase meaning ''lion's tooth.'' Dandelion plants have notched leaves that look like lion's teeth.

Dandie Dinmont terrier—A small dog with a long body, short legs, big eyes, drooping ears, and tufts of hair about the head and face. Originally bred in England and Scotland, these dogs were used to hunt small animals.

Dandie Dinmont terrier

Word History

Dandie Dinmont terrier got its name from a book by the Scottish writer Sir Walter Scott. In Scott's novel *Guy Mannering*, a character named Dandie Dinmont raised a group of terriers that were skilled at hunting. A new breed of dogs was later called Dandie Dinmont for the character in the book.

Dan|die Din|mont ter|ri|er (dan′dē din′mont ter′ē ər) *noun, plural* **Dandie Dinmont terriers.**

dandruff—1. Small flakes of dried skin: *He brushed the* dandruff *off his shoulder.* 2. A skin condition of the scalp that produces small white flakes of dried skin.
dan|druff (dan′drəf) *noun.*

dandy—1. A man who cares too much about his appearance; a very fashionable man. 2. An excellent or beautiful thing: *His new sports car is a* dandy. *Noun.*
—Terrific; great; excellent: *a* dandy *idea. Adjective.*
dan|dy (dan′dē) *noun, plural* **dandies;** *adjective,* **dandier, dandiest.**

danger—1. A risk; possibility that something bad or harmful might happen: *The sign warned of the* danger *of swimming after dark.* 2. Something possibly bad or harmful: *If a campfire is not put out properly, it can be a* danger *to the forest.*
dan|ger (dān′jər) *noun, plural* **dangers.**

a at	i if	oo look	ch chalk		a in ago
ā ape	ī idle	ou out	ng sing		e in happen
ah calm	o odd	u ugly	sh ship	ə =	i in capital
aw all	ō oats	ū rule	th think		o in occur
e end	oi oil	ur turn	th their		u in upon
ē easy			zh treasure		

• Synonyms: **hazard, peril,** for **1.**
Antonyms: **safety, security,** for **1.**

dangerous—Possibly bad or harmful; unsafe; risky: *Crossing the road without looking both ways is* dangerous.
dan|ger|ous (dān′jər əs) *adjective.*

dangle—1. To hang with a loose, free motion; swing: *The charm* dangled *from her bracelet.* 2. To let something hang down and float or swing: *I* dangled *my fishing line over the side of the dock.*
dan|gle (dang′gəl) *verb,* **dangled, dangling.**

dappled—Spotted: *The horse's coat was* dappled *with dark markings.*
dap|pled (dap′əld) *adjective.*

dappled

dare—1. To have enough courage to do something: *She* dared *to sing in front of the entire class.* 2. To challenge: *I* dare *you to try out for the play. Verb.*
—A challenge: *I took his* dare *and did a somersault in the snow. Noun.*
dare (dār) *verb,* **dared, daring;** *noun, plural* **dares.**

daring—Courage; bravery: *Explorers are famous for their* daring. *Noun.*
—Brave; eager for adventure: *The* daring *pilot did stunts with his airplane. Adjective.*
dar|ing (dār′ing) *noun, adjective.*
• For *adjective,* see Synonyms and Antonyms at **brave.**

dark—1. Having little or no light: *The inside of the cave was so* dark *that we could not even see each other.* 2. Not light or bright; deep in color: *The mud was a* dark *brown. Adjective.*
—1. An absence of light: *The wind blew the candle out, and I found myself in the* dark.

2. Nighttime: *We must try to finish the baseball game before* dark. *Noun.*
dark (dahrk) *adjective,* **darker, darkest;** *noun.*
■ **in the dark:** Ignorant of; not knowing: *She was in the dark about her surprise birthday party.*
● Synonyms: **dim, dull,** for *adjective* 1.
Antonyms: **bright, brilliant, luminous, radiant,** for *adjective* 1.

darken—To grow or make less bright: *The room darkened as night approached.*
dark|en (dahr′kən) *verb,* **darkened, darkening.**

darkness—The condition of being with little or no light.
dark|ness (dahrk′nis) *noun.*

darkroom—A room that is protected from light and that is used to develop film.
dark|room (dahrk′rūm′ *or* dahrk′room′) *noun, plural* **darkrooms.**

darling—Someone who is dearly loved by another person: Darling, *I am so happy we are married. Noun.*
—**1.** Beloved; precious: *My* darling *niece is going to be seven years old.* **2.** Cute; adorable: *My mother bought me a* darling *dress. Adjective.*
dar|ling (dahr′ling) *noun, plural* **darlings;** *adjective.*

darn—To fix a rip or hole by sewing.
darn (dahrn) *verb,* **darned, darning.**

darning needle—*See* **dragonfly.**
darn|ing nee|dle (dahrn′ing nē′dəl) *noun, plural* **darning needles.**

dart—A small, pointed object that is thrown at a target. *Noun.*
—**1.** To cast with a quick, sudden movement: *My friend* darted *an angry look my way when I interrupted him.* **2.** To dash; rush from a place: *I* darted *from the chair when I heard the telephone ring. Verb.*
dart (dahrt) *noun, plural* **darts;** *verb,* **darted, darting.**

dash—**1.** To slam; throw: *The high wind* dashed *the tree branches against the windows.* **2.** To destroy; spoil: *The team's hopes of winning the game were* dashed *when the star player was injured.* **3.** To hurry; rush: *The deer* dashed *for cover at the sound of our footsteps. Verb.*
—**1.** A rush; run: *She made a* dash *through the rain to the car.* **2.** A slight amount: *a* dash *of salt.* **3.** A short foot race: *Who won the* dash? **4.** The punctuation mark that looks like this —. It is used to set a thought apart from the rest of a sentence. *Noun.*

dash (dash) *verb,* **dashed, dashing;** *noun, plural* **dashes.**
● Synonyms: **foil**[1], **frustrate, ruin,** for *verb* 2.

dashboard—The control panel in the front of an automobile, truck, airplane, or boat.
dash|board (dash′bawrd′) *noun, plural* **dashboards.**

dashing—Daring; bold; lively: *The* dashing *hero rescued the ship from the pirates.*
dash|ing (dash′ing) *adjective.*

data—Facts and figures; information: *Please gather all the* data *you can find on the subject for your class report.*
da|ta (dā′tə *or* dat′ə) *noun, singular* **datum.**

databank—Large amounts of information on a subject stored in a computer system.
da|ta|bank (dā′tə bangk′ *or* dat′ə bangk′) *noun, plural* **databanks.**

data processing—The use of computers to keep, get, and treat information.
da|ta proc|ess|ing (dā′tə pros′əs ing *or* dat′ə pros′əs ing) *noun.*

date[1]—**1.** The day, month, or year when an event takes place: *The teacher writes the* date *on the board each day.* **2.** An appointment; agreement to meet: *My friend and I have a* date *to play at her house after school.* **3.** A companion for a social event: *He is my* date *for the prom. Noun.*
—**1.** To mark something with the day, month, or year: *I* dated *my letter so my friend would know when I wrote it.* **2.** To be a companion of someone: *She and I have been* dating *since March. Verb.*
date (dāt) *noun, plural* **dates;** *verb,* **dated, dating.**
■ **out of date:** Old-fashioned; not modern: *The clothes Mother once wore are* out of date *now.*

Word History

The words **date**[1] and **data** are more closely related than are the words **date**[1] and **date**[2]. Date[1] comes from the first word of a Latin phrase meaning "given at Rome." This phrase was put on letters to show when they were written or given to a messenger. For example, a letter might have been "given at Rome on January 2." **Data** comes from the same Latin word for "given." It means all the information "given" about a certain subject. **Date**[2], on the other hand, originally comes from a Greek word meaning "finger." The ancient Greeks thought dates looked like fingers.

date²—A brown, sticky, sweet fruit with a pit in its center. Dates grow in bunches on a palm tree.
date (dāt) *noun, plural* **dates.**

dates

date palm

date²

daughter—A female child.
daugh|ter (daw′tər) *noun, plural* **daughters.**

daughter-in-law—The wife of one's son.
daugh|ter-in-law (daw′tər in law′) *noun, plural* **daughters-in-law.**

dawdle—To waste time: *He dawdled over his breakfast and missed the school bus.*
daw|dle (daw′dəl) *verb,* **dawdled, dawdling.**
● Synonyms: **delay, dilly-dally, loiter**
Antonyms: **hasten, hurry, rush, speed**

dawn—1. The time of the sunrise; the first part of daylight; daybreak. **2.** The birth or first appearance; beginning: *the dawn of the computer age. Noun.*
—1. To become light after the dark of night: *The day dawned in rays of sunlight.* **2.** To start to be understood or realized; become clear: *It slowly dawned on the boys that they were lost in the forest. Verb.*
dawn (dawn) *noun, plural* **dawns;** *verb,* **dawned, dawning.**

day—1. The time between sunrise and sunset: *He worked in the garden all* day. **2.** The 24-hour period from one midnight to the next. **3.** A special date on the calendar: *Memorial* Day, *Labor* Day. **4.** The hours that are set apart for work: *Our school* day *is from 8:30 A.M. to 3 P.M.* **5.** A time in history: *in the* days *of the dinosaurs.*
day (dā) *noun, plural* **days.**
■ **call it a day:** To stop doing something: *The house painters* called it a day *when it began to rain.*
day in, day out: Every day; day after day: *The farmer milked his cows* day in, day out.

daybreak—The time of the sunrise; dawn.
day|break (dā′brāk′) *noun, plural* **daybreaks.**

day-care—Having to do with the supervision and teaching of children, especially those whose parents are at work: *The father drove his daughter to the* day-care *center on his way to work.*
day-care (dā′kãr′) *adjective.*

daydream—To imagine pleasant things: *She* daydreamed *about being a gymnast. Verb.*
—An act of imagining things: *He had a* daydream *about becoming a world-famous singer. Noun.*
day|dream (dā′drēm′) *verb,* **daydreamed** or **daydreamt, daydreaming;** *noun, plural* **daydreams.**

daylight—1. The hours of the day when the sun is up; daytime: *The owl slept during* daylight. **2.** Dawn; daybreak: *We woke up early but waited until* daylight *to go fishing.*
day|light (dā′līt′) *noun.*

daytime—The hours between sunrise and sunset; day: *I sleep in the* daytime *and work at* night. *Noun.*
—Of the daytime; taking place during the day: daytime *TV. Adjective.*
day|time (dā′tīm′) *noun; adjective.*

daze—To confuse; make unable to think clearly: *She was* dazed *by the fall from her bicycle. Verb.*
—A state of confusion; inability to think clearly: *He was in a* daze *after the volleyball hit him on the head. Noun.*
daze (dāz) *verb,* **dazed, dazing;** *noun, plural* **dazes.**
● A word that sounds the same is **days.**

dazzle—1. To make someone confused or blinded by light: *The flashbulb* dazzled *her when the photograph was taken.* **2.** To bewilder or impress: *The sights and sounds of the carnival* dazzled *us.*
daz|zle (daz′əl) *verb,* **dazzled, dazzling.**

a at	i if	oo look	ch chalk			a in ago
ã ape	ī idle	ou out	ng sing			e in happen
ah calm	o odd	u ugly	sh ship	ə =		i in capital
aw all	ō oats	ū rule	th think			o in occur
e end	oi oil	ur turn	th their			u in upon
ē easy			zh treasure			

de-—A prefix that means "to do the opposite of" or "to remove." To decode a message means to do the opposite of putting it into code. To defrost a refrigerator is to remove the frost from it.

Word Power

You can understand the meanings of many words that begin with **de-**, if you add a meaning of the prefix to the rest of the word.
  deemphasize: do the opposite of emphasize
  deice: remove the ice from

---

dead—1. Not living any more: *We saw many* dead *trees where the forest fire had occurred.* 2. Not working or active: *The flashlight went out because the batteries were* dead. 3. Exact; perfect: *The arrow hit the target at* dead *center.* 4. Total; complete: *There was* dead *silence during the lion tamer's act.* 5. Not lively; dull: *The party was* dead *after my friends left. Adjective.*
—1. The time of greatest darkness, quiet, or coldness: *the* dead *of the night; the* dead *of winter.* 2. People who are no longer living: *the honored* dead. *Noun.*
—1. Absolutely; utterly: *John was* dead *tired after raking the leaves.* 2. Straight; directly: *The skier swerved to avoid the tree* dead *ahead. Adverb.*
dead (ded) *adjective,* **deader, deadest;** *noun; adverb.*
  ▪ **be caught dead:** To be seen or discovered as being involved with: *He would* not *be caught* dead *riding a girl's bicycle.*
  dead duck: A person who is in trouble: *She knew that if she came home late again she was a* dead duck.
deaden—To lessen: *This medicine is supposed to* deaden *the pain of a headache.*
dead|en (ded′ən) *verb,* **deadened, deadening.**
dead end—A road or passageway that has no exit: *We need to turn back because this is a* dead end.
dead end (ded end) *noun, plural* **dead ends.**
deadline—A certain time by which something must be finished; a time limit: *Next Monday is the* deadline *for entering the contest.*
dead|line (ded′līn′) *noun, plural* **deadlines.**
deadly—Threatening or causing death; fatal: *The bite of that snake is* deadly.
dead|ly (ded′lē) *adjective,* **deadlier, deadliest.**
deaf—1. Unable to hear well or at all. 2. Unwilling to listen; ignoring: *The lifeguard*

was deaf *to the children's request for permission to go back into the pool.*
deaf (def) *adjective,* **deafer, deafest.**
deafen—To make unable to hear well or at all: *The roar of the jet engines* deafened *him.*
deaf|en (def′ən) *verb,* **deafened, deafening.**
deal—1. To be about; be concerned with: *This show* deals *with the adventures of a doctor.* 2. To treat; act: *The umpire* deals *fairly with all the players.* 3. To buy and sell as a business: *That book store* deals *only in used books.* 4. To pass out or give: *to* deal *the cards. Verb.*
—1. An agreement: *My brother and I made a* deal *that he would wash the dishes and I would dry them.* 2. One's turn at passing out cards: *Whose* deal *is it?* 3. A large amount: *It matters to me a great* deal *that you are unhappy. Noun.*
deal (dēl) *verb,* **dealt, dealing;** *noun, plural* **deals.**
dealt—*See* **deal.**
dealt (delt) *verb.*
dear—Loved very much; valued highly: *a* dear *friend.* The word "dear" is used in writing letters as a polite way of addressing someone: Dear *Sir;* Dear *Madam. Adjective.*
—A much-loved person: *"How are you, my* dear?*" asked her grandfather. Noun.*
—An exclamation showing surprise or trouble: *"Oh,* dear!*" she cried, as she took the batch of burnt brownies out of the oven. Interjection.*
dear (dēr) *adjective,* **dearer, dearest;** *noun, plural* **dears;** *interjection.*
  ● A word that sounds the same is **deer.**
dearly—Very much: *She would* dearly *like to go to the amusement park.*
dear|ly (dēr′lē) *adverb.*
death—1. The end of life. 2. An ending that is like the end of a life: *the* death *of a friendship.*
death (deth) *noun, plural* **deaths.**
  ▪ **at death's door:** Near dying: *The rabbit was at* death's door *when the boy brought it home.*
debate—To discuss by considering both sides of an idea: *The boys* debated *about whether the ice was thick enough to skate on safely. Verb.*
—1. A talk about the reasons for and against an idea: *The family had a* debate *about whether to go on vacation to the seashore.* 2. A public discussion of both sides of a certain topic. 3. A public discussion between two or more political candidates. *Noun.*
de|bate (di bāt′) *verb,* **debated, debating;** *noun, plural* **debates.**
debris or **débris**—The scattered bits and pieces of something that has been broken; rubbish: *It*

Language Fact

Debris may be pronounced and spelled in two different ways. It comes from an old French word. Some people pronounce the word in the French way so that the e rhymes with the a in **day.** They write the word with an accent mark—**débris.** Others pronounce the word so that the e rhymes with the e in **happen.** They write the word without an accent mark—**debris.** Both pronunciations are correct.

took us a while to clean up the debris *that was left after the storm.*
de|bris *or* dé|bris (də brē′ *or* dā′brē) *noun.*

debt—**1.** Something owed, especially money: *The library held a raffle to pay off the* debt *for the new books.* **2.** The state of owing something: *She was in* debt *to her brother for the price of the movie ticket.*
debt (det) *noun, plural* **debts.**

debug—*Computer.* To fix what is wrong or does not work, especially in a computer program.
de|bug (dē bug′) *verb,* **debugged, debugging.**

Dec.—The abbreviation for **December.**

decade—A time of ten years: *She is the best pianist of this* decade.
dec|ade (dek′ād) *noun, plural* **decades.**

decaffeinated—With the chemical called caffeine removed: decaffeinated *coffee.*
de|caf|fein|at|ed (dē kaf′ə nā təd) *adjective.*

decal—A small, printed picture or design that is especially made to stick securely to glass, wood, or similar material.
de|cal (dē′kal) *noun, plural* **decals.**

decathlon—A sports competition that requires athletes to perform in ten different track and field events.
de|cath|lon (di kath′lon) *noun, plural* **decathlons.**

decay—To rot slowly: *The fallen apples in the orchard* decayed *and turned brown. Verb.*
—The state of being rotten: *tooth* decay. *Noun.*
de|cay (di kā′) *verb,* **decayed, decaying;** *noun, plural* **decays.**
• Synonyms: **decompose, spoil,** for *verb.*

deceased—Dead; no longer living: *The* deceased *woman had not left a will. Adjective.*
—A dead person or persons: *The* deceased *had been the mayor for twenty years. Noun.*
de|ceased (di sēst′) *adjective, noun.*

deceit—The act of making someone believe something that is not true: *His promises of friendship turned out to be nothing but* deceit.
de|ceit (di sēt′) *noun, plural* **deceits.**

deceive—To make a person believe something that is not true; cheat: *The spy wore a disguise to* deceive *the enemy.*
de|ceive (di sēv′) *verb,* **deceived, deceiving.**
• Synonyms: **bluff², mislead, trick**

December—The twelfth month of the year. December has 31 days.
De|cem|ber (di sem′bər) *noun.* Abbreviation: **Dec.**

Word History

December comes from the Latin word for "ten." In the early Roman calendar, December was the tenth and last month of the year.

decent—**1.** Right and proper: *It was* decent *of her to help the elderly man cross the street.* **2.** Good enough; adequate: *Do you know a restaurant where I can get a* decent *meal?*
de|cent (dē′sənt) *adjective.*

deception—The act of fooling or tricking someone: *The quarterback ran with such* deception *that he scored a touchdown.*
de|cep|tion (di sep′shən) *noun, plural* **deceptions.**

deceptive—Meant to fool or trick someone: *The magician's card trick was so* deceptive *that the entire audience was fooled.*
de|cep|tive (di sep′tiv) *adjective.*

decide—**1.** To make up one's mind: *Have you* decided *what you want for your birthday?* **2.** To settle a question or disagreement; judge: *Mother* decided *who would wash the dishes.*
de|cide (di sīd′) *verb,* **decided, deciding.**

decimal—A fraction whose denominator is 10 or a multiple of 10, such as 100. For example, 0.7 (7/10) and 0.32 (32/100) are decimals. *Noun.*
—Based on the number 10; counting by tens: *In the* decimal *system used for United States coins, 100 pennies = 10 dimes = 1 dollar. Adjective.*
dec|i|mal (des′ə məl) *noun, plural* **decimals;** *adjective.*

a at	i if	oo look	ch chalk		a in ago
ā ape	ī idle	ou out	ng sing		e in happen
ah calm	o odd	u ugly	sh ship	ə =	i in capital
aw all	ō oats	ū rule	th think		o in occur
e end	oi oil	ur turn	th their		u in upon
ē easy			zh treasure		

decimal point—A period that is placed in front of a fraction whose denominator is 10 or a multiple of 10. For example, the periods in 0.2 and 4.95 are decimal points.
dec|i|mal point (des′ə məl point) *noun, plural* **decimal points.**

decipher—**1.** To figure out the meaning of something that is not clear: *She tried to* decipher *the tiny letters on the old coin.* **2.** To figure out the meaning of writing that is in a secret code; decode: *The pirate* deciphered *the mixed-up letters that gave directions to the treasure.*
de|ci|pher (di sī′fər) *verb,* **deciphered, deciphering.**

decision—A judgment or conclusion; choice: *Have you reached a* decision *about trying out for the swimming team?*
de|ci|sion (di sizh′ən) *noun, plural* **decisions.**

deck—**1.** The floor of a boat or ship. Larger ships often have several decks, similar to the levels or stories of a house. **2.** Any surface area like a ship's deck: *a* sundeck; *the upper* deck *at a baseball stadium.* **3.** A pack of playing cards. *Noun.*
—To dress up; decorate: *She was* decked *out in her fancy clothes. Verb.*
deck (dek) *noun, plural* **decks;** *verb,* **decked, decking.**
■ **on deck: 1.** On hand and ready to do something: *The whole family was* on deck *to rake leaves on Saturday morning.* **2.** Baseball. The next person up at bat: *The player who was* on deck *took several practice swings.*

declaration—**1.** A public statement or announcement: *The mayor made a* declaration *that Thursday would be a day to honor the city's fire fighters.* **2.** A written or printed announcement: *the* Declaration *of Independence.*
dec|la|ra|tion (dek′lə rā′shən) *noun, plural* **declarations.**

declare—**1.** To state publicly; make known: *The principal* declared *that there would be no school today because of the snow.* **2.** To say with strong feeling: *After the scary ride, he* declared *he'd never get on that roller coaster again.*
de|clare (di klār′) *verb,* **declared, declaring.**
● Synonyms: **announce, proclaim, report,** for **1.**

decline—**1.** To refuse: *She* declined *a second piece of chocolate cake because she was full.* **2.** To become slowly weaker; decrease: *As the dog grew older, its keen eyesight* declined. **3.** To bend or slope downward: *This path* declines *from the hill to the valley. Verb.*
—A gradual lessening or weakening: *As the team*

continued to lose, there was a decline *in attendance at games. Noun.*
de|cline (di klīn′) *verb,* **declined, declining;** *noun, plural* **declines.**

decode—To change a secret message into understandable language.
de|code (dē kōd′) *verb,* **decoded, decoding.**

decompose—To rot: *The fallen leaves* decomposed *over the winter and became fertilizer for the spring garden.*
de|com|pose (dē′kəm pōz′) *verb,* **decomposed, decomposing.**
● Synonyms: **decay, spoil**

decorate—**1.** To make more attractive; spruce up: *He* decorated *his bicycle with red, white, and blue streamers for the parade.* **2.** To give a medal, badge, ribbon, or similar honor to: *The police officer was* decorated *for bravery.*
dec|o|rate (dek′ə rāt) *verb,* **decorated, decorating.**
● Synonyms: **adorn, ornament, trim,** for **1.**

decoration—**1.** Something added to make an object more attractive; ornament: *We admired the holiday* decorations *on the city streets.* **2.** The act of making more attractive: *The whole family joined in the* decoration *of the birthday cake.* **3.** An honor, such as a medal, badge, or ribbon: *The Girl Scout wore her merit badge* decorations *on the sash of her uniform.*
dec|o|ra|tion (dek′ə rā′shən) *noun, plural* **decorations.**

Decoration Day—*See* **Memorial Day.**
Dec|o|ra|tion Day (dek′ə rā′shən dā) *noun.*

decoy—**1.** A model of a bird that is used to trick a real bird into coming near someone, usually a hunter. **2.** Someone who leads another person into a trap or into danger: *The police officer who was disguised as an elderly woman was a* decoy *for catching the purse snatcher. Noun.*
—To lure into a trap; attract by fooling: *He*

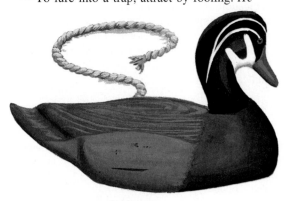

decoy (noun, definition 1)

decoyed *her to the surprise birthday party by arranging to do homework together. Verb.*
de|coy (dē′koi *or* di koi′) *noun, plural* **decoys;** *verb,* **decoyed, decoying.**

decrease—To become or make less: *He hoped that the teacher would* decrease *the amount of homework that had to be done over spring vacation. Verb.*
—**1.** A lessening: *There was a* decrease *in the number of traffic accidents after the road was straightened.* **2.** The amount by which something becomes or is made less: *The* decrease *in membership from last year came to only three Scouts. Noun.*
de|crease (di krēs′ *for verb;* dē′krēs *or* di krēs′ *for noun*) *verb,* **decreased, decreasing;** *noun, plural* **decreases.**
• Synonyms: **diminish, dwindle, reduce,** for *verb.*

decree—An official order or decision: *The mayor issued a* decree *that all city offices would be closed because of the storm. Noun.*
—To order or settle officially; command: *The judge* decreed *that the man was not guilty. Verb.*
de|cree (di krē′) *noun, plural* **decrees;** *verb,* **decreed, decreeing.**

dedicate—**1.** To set aside or use for a special purpose: *That section of the museum is* dedicated *to the dinosaur exhibit.* **2.** To open a store, park, bridge, or the like by holding a celebration: *The mayor will* dedicate *the new park at 2 P.M.* **3.** To offer (something) for a special purpose: *He* dedicated *his life to helping poor people.*
ded|i|cate (ded′ə kāt) *verb,* **dedicated, dedicating.**

dedication—**1.** The act of using or setting (something) apart for a special reason: *the* dedication *of all his spare time to practicing the piano.* **2.** The opening of a store, park, bridge, or the like by holding a celebration: *the* dedication *of the new playground.* **3.** The act or state of giving up (something) for a special reason: *The doctor was honored for her* dedication *to finding a cure for cancer.*
ded|i|ca|tion (ded′ə kā′shən) *noun, plural* **dedications.**

deduct—To take away from; subtract: *The cashier will* deduct *the value of the coupons from the cost of your groceries.*
de|duct (di dukt′) *verb,* **deducted, deducting.**

deduction—**1.** The act of taking away from a total; subtraction: *After the* deduction *of $5 for the coupons, the grocery bill totaled $36.* **2.** The amount taken away: *The* deduction *came to $5.*
de|duc|tion (di duk′shən) *noun, plural* **deductions.**
• Synonyms: **discount, reduction,** for **1.**

deed—**1.** An act or action: *He did a good* deed *when he returned the lost wallet.* **2.** A written legal agreement that shows ownership of something: *the* deed *to a house.*
deed (dēd) *noun, plural* **deeds.**
• Synonyms: **accomplishment, achievement, feat,** for **1.**

deep—**1.** Going a long way down or back: *a* deep *river; the* deep *woods.* **2.** In amount of depth: *several feet* deep. **3.** Low in musical range or sound: *a* deep *voice.* **4.** Hard to understand: *The complicated computer program was too* deep *for him.* **5.** Great; strong: *a* deep *sadness; a* deep *sleep.* **6.** Dark in color: deep *purple.* **7.** Very involved in something: *She was* deep *in her book and did not notice the time. Adjective.*
—**1.** Far back or down: *The bears lived* deep *in the forest.* **2.** Far in time; late: *The old friends talked* deep *into the night. Adverb.*
deep (dēp) *adjective,* **deeper, deepest;** *adverb.*
■ **in deep water:** In great trouble: *He was in* deep *water for breaking the window.*
the deep: The ocean or sea: *Whales and dolphins live in* the deep.

deer—A hoofed animal that can run quickly and gracefully. A male deer, which is called a buck, grows a pair of antlers that shed and grow back each year. A female deer is called a doe. Most does do not have antlers. Elk, moose, and reindeer are members of the deer family.
deer (dēr) *noun, plural* **deer.**
• A word that sounds the same is **dear.**

deface—To spoil or put marks on the surface of something: *Someone had* defaced *the wall by writing on it.*
de|face (di fās′) *verb,* **defaced, defacing.**

defeat—To cause (someone) to lose; win a victory over: *Our soccer team* defeated *the best team in the league by a score of 3 to 1. Verb.*
—The act or state of losing; loss: *The army surrendered after its* defeat. *Noun.*
de|feat (di fēt′) *verb,* **defeated, defeating;** *noun plural* **defeats.**

a at	i if	oo look	ch chalk		a in ago
ā ape	ī idle	ou out	ng sing		e in happen
ah calm	o odd	u ugly	sh ship	ə =	i in capital
aw all	ō oats	ū rule	th think		o in occur
e end	oi oil	ur turn	th their		u in upon
ē easy			zh treasure		

defect—An imperfection; flaw: *The flashlight had a* defect *that caused it to keep going out.*
de|fect (dē′fekt) *noun, plural* **defects.**

defective—Having a flaw; faulty; not perfect: *The* defective *calculator did not add correctly.*
de|fec|tive (di fek′tiv) *adjective.*

defend—1. To protect; keep from harm: *The mother chicken* defended *her young from the attacking hawk.* 2. To do, say, or write in favor or support of: *In his social studies report, the student* defended *those who took part in the revolt.*
de|fend (di fend′) *verb,* **defended, defending.**
• Synonyms: **guard, shelter, shield,** for **1.**
Antonym: **attack,** for **1.**

defendant—A person who is accused of a crime in a court of law: *The* defendant *said she was not guilty of stealing the money.*
de|fend|ant (di fen′dənt) *noun, plural* **defendants.**

defense—1. The act of guarding or protecting: *The farmer fenced in his gardens as a* defense *against hungry animals.* 2. A person or thing that guards or protects: *Bug spray is a camper's* defense *against mosquitoes.* 3. The side that supports someone in a court of law. 4. A team or group of players that try to stop the opposing team from scoring: *The football team's strong* defense *kept the other team from scoring.*
de|fense (di fens′) *noun, plural* **defenses.**

buck

doe

deer

defensive—Used to protect or guard: *She chained her bicycle to the fence as a* defensive *action against theft.*
de|fen|sive (di fen′siv) *adjective.*

defiance—A bold refusal to respect or obey someone or something; challenge: *He refused to use seatbelts in* defiance *of the new state law.*
de|fi|ance (di fī′əns) *noun, plural* **defiances.**

defiant—Showing bold refusal to respect or obey someone or something: *The* defiant *child refused to listen to his parents.*
de|fi|ant (di fī′ənt) *adjective.*

define—1. To explain the meaning of: *to* define *a word.* 2. To make clear by fixing the limits of or marking exactly: *Speed limits* define *how fast an automobile is allowed to go.*
de|fine (di fīn′) *verb,* **defined, defining.**

definite—Exact; certain: *We agreed on a* definite *time to meet for lunch.*
def|i|nite (def′ə nit) *adjective.*

definite article—The word *the* is called the definite article in English. It tells exactly the person or thing that is being named: *the* clock on the *table.*
def|i|nite ar|ti|cle (def′ə nit ahr′tə kəl) *noun, plural* **definite articles.**

definition—An explanation of the meaning of a word or phrase: *There are several* definitions *for the word "bark" in this dictionary.*
def|i|ni|tion (def′ə nish′ən) *noun, plural* **definitions.**

deform—To change so as to ruin the shape or appearance of: *The fire* deformed *the house.*
de|form (di fawrm′) *verb,* **deformed, deforming.**

deformity—A part of something that is not shaped normally, such as the body: *Her leg has a* deformity *because it is twisted outward.*
de|form|i|ty (di fawr′mə tē) *noun, plural* **deformities.**

defrost—To thaw something that is frozen; make free from ice: *to* defrost *frozen meat; to* defrost *a refrigerator freezer.*
de|frost (dē frawst′) *verb,* **defrosted, defrosting.**

defy—To boldly refuse to obey someone or something; challenge: *She* defied *her parents and came home late for dinner.*
de|fy (di fī′) *verb,* **defied, defying.**

degrade—To lower in character; bring shame to: *People who gossip* degrade *themselves.*
de|grade (di grād′) *verb,* **degraded, degrading.**

degree—1. A unit for measuring temperature: *The thermometer registered 100* degrees *during the heat wave.* **2.** Amount; extent: *He showed a high* degree *of skill in playing the video game.* **3.** A stage or a step in a process or series: *We learn by* degrees. **4.** A unit for measuring the angles or the curves of a circle: *A circle has 360* degrees.
de|gree (di grē') *noun, plural* **degrees**.
Abbreviation: deg.
■ **to the nth degree:** To the greatest extent or degree: *I will try to succeed to the nth degree.*

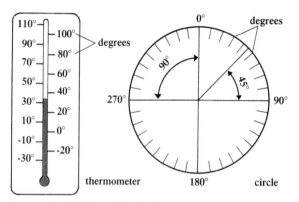

degree (definitions 1 and 4)

dehumidifier—A machine that is used to remove moisture from the air in a damp place, such as a basement.
de|hu|mid|i|fi|er (dē'hyū mid'ə fī'ər) *noun, plural* **dehumidifiers**.

dehydrate—To remove the water or moisture from; dry out: *The sun* dehydrates *grapes and turns them into raisins.*
de|hy|drate (dē hī'drāt) *verb,* **dehydrated, dehydrating**.

deity—A god or a goddess: *Athena was the Greek* deity *of wisdom.*
de|i|ty (dē'ə tē) *noun, plural* **deities**.

dejected—Discouraged; unhappy: *He felt* dejected *after he lost his wagon.*
de|ject|ed (di jek'tid) *adjective.*
● See Synonyms and Antonyms at **happy**.

delay—1. To put off until a later time: *The flight was* delayed *for an hour because of the storm.*

2. To slow or hinder so as to make late: *Heavy traffic* delayed *Dad on his way to work.* **3.** To wait too long; go too slowly: *Do not* delay *sending in your entry to the contest. Verb.*
—The act of putting something off or making late: *The* delay *in buying a ticket caused her to miss the beginning of the movie. Noun.*
de|lay (di lā') *verb,* **delayed, delaying**; *noun, plural* **delays**.
● Synonyms: For *verb* **3,** see Synonyms at **dawdle.**
  Antonyms: For *verb* **3,** see Antonyms at **dawdle.**

delegate—Someone who is chosen to speak or act for other people: *Each homeroom elected a* delegate *to the student council. Noun.*
—To appoint or send someone to speak or act for other people: *Mother* delegated *me to thank our uncle for the gift he gave our family. Verb.*
del|e|gate (del'ə git *or* del'ə gāt for *noun;* del'ə gāt for *verb*) *noun, plural* **delegates**; *verb,* **delegated, delegating**.

delegation—One or more persons chosen to speak or act for others: *A* delegation *of Boy Scouts from our state attended the national meeting.*
del|e|ga|tion (del'ə gā'shən) *noun, plural* **delegations**.

delete—To take out or cross out anything written or printed; remove; omit.
de|lete (di lēt') *verb,* **deleted, deleting**.

deli—See delicatessen.
del|i (del'ē) *noun, plural* **delis**.

deliberate—1. Said or done on purpose after careful thought; intentional: *His breaking of the plate was* deliberate. **2.** Careful and slow in deciding: *His movements were* deliberate *as he tried to sneak up on the rabbit. Adjective.*
—To think over carefully: *She* deliberated *about whether to ask for a bicycle or a radio for her birthday. Verb.*
de|lib|er|ate (di lib'ər it for *adjective;* di lib'ə rāt' for *verb*) *adjective; verb,* **deliberated, deliberating**.

delicacy—1. The fineness in the way in which something is made: *the* delicacy *of a snowflake.* **2.** Something pleasing to eat because it is rare or of very high quality: *Some people think of a dandelion salad as a* delicacy.
del|i|ca|cy (del'ə kə sē) *noun, plural* **delicacies**.

delicate—1. Finely made: *The frost made a* delicate *pattern on the windowpane.* **2.** Pleasing to smell, taste, hear, see, or feel: *a* delicate

a at	i if	oo look	ch chalk		⌈ a in ago
ā ape	ī idle	ou out	ng sing		e in happen
ah calm	o odd	u ugly	sh ship	ə =	i in capital
aw all	ō oats	ū rule	th think		o in occur
e end	oi oil	ur turn	<u>th</u> their		⌊ u in upon
ē easy			zh treasure		

breeze; a delicate *tune from the music box.*
3. Easily damaged or broken: *a* delicate *statue.*
4. Very sensitive: *The world-famous chef had a*
delicate *sense of taste.*
del|i|cate (del′ə kit) *adjective.*
- Synonyms: **fragile, frail,** for **3.**
  Antonym: **sturdy,** for **3.**

delicatessen—A store that sells ready-to-eat
foods, such as salads, meats, cheeses,
sandwiches, soups, and the like.
del|i|ca|tes|sen (del′ə kə **tes**′ən) *noun, plural*
delicatessens.
- This store is also called a **deli.**

delicious—Very pleasant to eat or smell: *a*
delicious *cup of hot chocolate.*
de|li|cious (di **lish**′əs) *adjective.*

delight—Pleasure; joy; satisfaction: *The baby*
clapped her hands in delight *when the*
jack-in-the-box popped up. Noun.
—**1.** To give pleasure or joy; satisfy: *The*
juggler's tricks delighted *the audience.* **2.** To
have pleasure or joy; be satisfied: *The boy was*
delighted *when he won first prize. Verb.*
de|light (di **līt**′) *noun, plural* **delights;** *verb,*
delighted, delighting.
- Synonyms: **bliss, happiness,** for *noun.*
  Antonyms: **misery, sorrow, woe,** for *noun.*

delightful—Very pleasing: *Spring is a* delightful
time of year.
de|light|ful (di **līt**′fəl) *adjective.*
- Synonyms: **heavenly, marvelous, sensational,**
  terrific

delirious—Wildly excited: *The fans were*
delirious *at the rock concert.*
de|lir|i|ous (di **lir**′ē əs) *adjective.*

deliver—**1.** To hand over; convey: *to* deliver *a*
message. **2.** To say: *The president* delivers *many*
speeches. **3.** To hit or throw: *The batter*
delivered *a home run.*
de|liv|er (di **liv**′ər) *verb,* **delivered, delivering.**

delivery—**1.** The act of bringing something to a
place or giving it to a person: *a mail* delivery.
2. A way of singing or speaking in public: *His*
delivery *of the oral book report earned him an*
''A.''
de|liv|er|y (di **liv**′ər ē) *noun, plural* **deliveries.**

dell—A small valley that is often sheltered by trees.
dell (del) *noun, plural* **dells.**

delphinium—A garden plant that has tall stems
topped by purple, white, or blue flowers with
large pointed petals.
del|phin|i|um (del **fin**′ē əm) *noun, plural*
delphiniums.
- Another name for this plant is **larkspur.**

delta

Word History

Delta is the fourth letter of the Greek alphabet.
The large, or capital, form of this letter is
shaped like a triangle. River deltas also are
shaped like triangles. They look like the Greek
letter **delta.** See the picture at **D.**

delta—The land at the mouth of a river, usually
shaped like a triangle. It is formed by sand,
stone, and mud that have been carried
downstream by the water current.
del|ta (del′tə) *noun, plural* **deltas.**

delphinium

deluxe or **de luxe**—Of outstanding quality; elegant: *A limousine is* deluxe *transportation.* de|luxe or de luxe (də **looks′** or də **luks′**) *adjective.*

demand—1. To ask for with strong feeling or as one's right: *She demanded to know who took her doll.* 2. To need; call for: *Being a good skier demands a lot of practice. Verb.*
—1. The act of asking for something with strong feelings or as one's right: *The store made a demand that he pay his bill.* 2. Something that is needed or called for: *The* demand *for swimsuits goes down in the winter months. Noun.*
de|mand (di **mand′**) *verb,* **demanded, demanding;** *noun, plural* **demands.**
■ **in demand:** Popular; wanted: *The famous singer is* in demand *all over the country.*

democracy—1. A type of government that is ruled by the people who live under it. A democracy is run either directly by the people themselves through public meetings or by representatives elected by the people. 2. A country, state, or town whose government is ruled by the people who live under it: *The United States is a* democracy.
de|moc|ra|cy (di **mok′**rə sē) *noun, plural* **democracies.**

democrat—1. A person whose belief is that a government should be ruled by the people who live under it. 2. **Democrat:** A member of the Democratic Party.
dem|o|crat or Dem|o|crat (dem′ə krat) *noun, plural* **democrats** or **Democrats.**

democratic—1. Of or like a government ruled by the people who live under it: *Settling the question in a* democratic *way, we voted on where to go for our field trip.* 2. Treating all people as equals: *Dad was* democratic *and let us discuss whether we should move to a new house.*
dem|o|crat|ic (dem′ə **krat′**ik) *adjective.*

Democratic Party—One of the two main political parties in the United States.
Dem|o|crat|ic Par|ty (dem′ə **krat′**ik **pahr′**tē) *noun.*

demolish—To knock down; tear down: *The bulldozer* demolished *the old building.*

de|mol|ish (di **mol′**ish) *verb,* **demolished, demolishing.**

demon—1. A devil; evil spirit: *In the story,* demons *chased the scared little girl.* 2. Someone having a lot of energy or enthusiasm: *He ran like a* demon *to get home in time.*
de|mon (dē′mən) *noun, plural* **demons.**

demonstrate—1. To show, explain, or prove something: *to* demonstrate *how a machine works; to do an experiment to* demonstrate *the temperature at which water boils.* 2. To be part of a meeting, parade, or other public action to speak out for or against something: *The children paraded to* demonstrate *against the closing of their neighborhood park.*
dem|on|strate (dem′ən strāt) *verb,* **demonstrated, demonstrating.**

demonstration—1. A showing, explanation, or proof of something: *He gave a* demonstration *of how to use the computer.* 2. A meeting, parade, or other public action held to speak out for or against something: *The parents held a* demonstration *to support the building of a new school.*
dem|on|stra|tion (dem′ən **strā′**shən) *noun, plural* **demonstrations.**

demote—To lower in grade, position, or rank: *The boy was* demoted *from second grade to first grade.*
de|mote (di **mōt′**) *verb,* **demoted, demoting.**

den—1. The home of a wild animal: *a fox's* den. 2. A small, comfortable room usually used for reading, studying, or watching television. 3. A small group of Cub Scouts.
den (den) *noun, plural* **dens.**

den (definition 1)

a at	i if	oo look	ch chalk		a in ago
ā ape	ī idle	ou out	ng sing		e in happen
ah calm	o odd	u ugly	sh ship	ə =	i in capital
aw all	ō oats	ū rule	th think		o in occur
e end	oi oil	ur turn	th their		u in upon
ē easy			zh treasure		

denial—1. The act of stating that something is not true: *He said that he did not break the plate, and his parents believed his* denial. **2.** The act of refusing something: *Dad explained his* denial *of our request for another television set.*
den|ni|al (di nī′əl) *noun, plural* **denials.**

denim—1. A heavy cotton fabric that is used to make work clothes or casual clothes. It is often dyed blue. **2. denims:** Overalls or pants that are made of this fabric.
den|im (den′əm) *noun, plural* **denims.**

Word History

Denim comes from a French phrase meaning "cloth from Nimes." The cloth used for denim was once woven in the French city of Nimes. Cloth "de [from] Nimes" became known as denim.

---

denomination—1. A religious group: *We belong to a Protestant* denomination. **2.** A class or kind of something: *Some of the* denominations *of United States paper money are $1, $5, $10, and $20.*
de|nom|i|na|tion (di nom′ə nā′shən) *noun, plural* **denominations.**

denominator—The number that is below the line in a fraction. For example, in the fractions 1/2 and 1/4, the denominators are 2 and 4.
de|nom|i|na|tor (di nom′ə nā′tər) *noun, plural* **denominators.**

denounce—To speak out strongly against; accuse of wrongdoing: *The mayor* denounced *the factory for polluting the river.*
de|nounce (di nouns′) *verb,* **denounced, denouncing.**

dense—Thick; closely packed or crowded together; *a dense fog; a dense crowd.*
dense (dens) *adjective,* **denser, densest.**

density—Thickness: *The* density *of the snow made driving dangerous.*
den|si|ty (den′sə tē) *noun, plural* **densities.**

dent—A small hollow place made by hitting or pressing down on the surface of something: *When the lamp fell over, it left a* dent *in the desk. Noun.*
—To make a small hollow place: *She missed the nail and* dented *the wall with the hammer. Verb.*
dent (dent) *noun, plural* **dents;** *verb,* **dented, denting.**

dental—1. Of or for the teeth: *Eating too many sweets can cause* dental *decay.* **2.** Used in a dentist's work: *a* dental *drill.*
den|tal (dent′təl) *adjective.*

dentist—A doctor who helps people take care of their teeth, gums, and mouth. A dentist cleans teeth, repairs or replaces damaged teeth, straightens teeth, and checks the mouth and gums for signs of disease.
den|tist (den′tist) *noun, plural* **dentists.**

deny—1. To state that something is not true: *He* denied *that he had eaten the last cookie.* **2.** To refuse to give or allow: *Our parents* denied *our request to stay up past midnight.*
de|ny (di nī′) *verb,* **denied, denying.**

deodorant—A substance or preparation that masks, destroys, or prevents odors: *a* deodorant *for under the arms; a room* deodorant.
de|o|dor|ant (dē ō′dər ənt) *noun, plural* **deodorants.**

depart—1. To leave; go away: *They will* depart *for summer vacation in July.* **2.** To change one's ways: *She* departed *from her usual habit of walking and took the bus.*
de|part (di pahrt′) *verb,* **departed, departing.**

department—A separate part of something; section: *Mother and I shopped for clothes in the children's* department *of the store.* Abbreviation: dept.
de|part|ment (di pahrt′mənt) *noun, plural* **departments.**

departure—1. The act of going away; a leaving: *The* departure *of the train is scheduled for 8:00 A.M.* **2.** A change or difference from the usual: *A ham sandwich was a* departure *from his usual lunch of soup.*
de|par|ture (di pahr′chər) *noun, plural* **departures.**

depend—1. To trust; rely on: *You can* depend *on him to tell the truth.* **2.** To be affected by, caused by, or based on: *Playing outside after supper will* depend *on getting my chores done first.* **3.** To get help, care, or support from: *The dog* depended *on its owner for food.*
de|pend (di pend′) *verb,* **depended, depending.**

dependable—Able to be trusted or relied on: *She is a very* dependable *person and will do the job right.*
de|pend|a|ble (di pen′də bəl) *adjective.*

dependence or **dependance**—1. The state of being influenced or affected by something: *the* dependence *of a picnic on good weather.* **2.** Trust or reliance on some person or thing for help: *Learning to drive a car ended his* dependence *on his bicycle for transportation.*
de|pend|ence or de|pend|ance (di pen′dəns) *noun.*

dependent or **dependant**—1. Relying on or trusting a person or thing to help: *The little girl was* dependent *on her mother to tie her shoes.* 2. Influenced or affected by something: *Receiving your allowance is* dependent *on doing your chores. Adjective.*
—A person who relies on someone else for support or help: *That boy is a* dependent *of his parents. Noun.*
de|pend|ent or de|pend|ant (di pen′dənt) *adjective; noun, plural* **dependents** or **dependants.**

deport—To force a person to leave a country, usually because of activities that are not legal or acceptable: *The spy was* deported *from the country because he stole secret government information.*
de|port (di **pawrt′** *or* di **pōrt′**) *verb,* **deported, deporting.**

deposit—1. To put or place; lay down: *She* deposited *the books she was returning on the librarian's desk.* 2. To put in a bank for safe keeping: *He* deposited *his money in his savings account. Verb.*
—1. Something that has been put in a safe place, such as a bank: *He made a $10* deposit *in his checking account.* 2. An amount of money given to hold or reserve something that will be paid for in the future: *Dad put down a* deposit *of $500 on a new car.* 3. Something left or collected by natural cause: *a* deposit *of snow from the storm.* 4. A large amount of a mineral that is found inside rocks or in the ground: *The miners found a* deposit *of gold in the cave. Noun.*
de|pos|it (di **poz′**it) *verb,* **deposited, depositing;** *noun, plural* **deposits.**

depot—A bus or railroad station.
de|pot (dē′pō) *noun, plural* **depots.**

depress—To sadden or discourage: *Her aunt's illness* depressed *her.*
depress (di **pres′**) *verb,* **depressed, depressing.**

depression—1. A state of feeling sad or discouraged. 2. A hollowed-out or lowered part: *A footprint is a* depression *in the ground.* 3. A period of time when business is slow and jobs are hard to find. Such a period in the 1930's became known as the Great Depression because

so many people were out of work.
de|pres|sion (di **presh′**ən) *noun, plural* **depressions.**

deprive—To take something away from someone; stop someone from having or doing something: *She was* deprived *of a new coat because her parents couldn't afford it.*
de|prive (di **prīv′**) *verb,* **deprived, depriving.**

depth—1. The distance from top to bottom or from front to back: *No one knows the* depth *of that lake. My bookcase does not have enough* depth *to hold large books.* 2. The intensity of something, such as feelings: *She thought no one could understand the* depth *of her sorrow.*
depth (depth) *noun, plural* **depths.**
■ **beyond (one's) depth:** Beyond a person's ability to understand something: *That foreign language is* beyond *my* depth.
in depth: Thoroughly; completely: *The police investigated the crime* in depth.

deputy—Someone appointed to act for or in place of someone else: *The mayor sent a* deputy *to the meeting because she couldn't be there.*
dep|u|ty (dep′yə tē) *noun, plural* **deputies.**

derail—To cause a train or other vehicle to run off its rails or tracks.
de|rail (dē rāl′) *verb,* **derailed, derailing.**

derby—1. A race or contest: *I am training for the bicycle* derby. 2. A man's stiff felt hat that has a dome-shaped crown and a narrow brim.
der|by (dur′bē) *noun, plural* **derbies.**

derby (definition 2)

derive—To receive or come from a source: *I* derived *much satisfaction from learning to dance. The name of my town* derives *from an Indian word.*
de|rive (di **rīv′**) *verb,* **derived, deriving.**

derrick—1. A machine for lifting heavy objects; crane. It has a long arm that swings from a tall

a at	i if	oo look	ch chalk		a in ago
ā ape	ī idle	ou out	ng sing		e in happen
ah calm	o odd	u ugly	sh ship	ə =	i in capital
aw all	ō oats	ū rule	th think		o in occur
e end	oi oil	ur turn	th their		u in upon
ē easy			zh treasure		

derrick

Word History

The **derrick** is named after a man named Derrick. He invented this device to hang criminals in London, England, during the early 1600's. Today, derricks dangle objects, not people.

steel post. **2.** A tower over an oil well that supports machinery used for lifting and drilling.
der|rick (der′ik) *noun, plural* **derricks.**

descend—**1.** To go from a higher to a lower place: *The elevator* descended *from the fifth to the first floor*. **2.** To have as one's ancestors; derive: *She is* descended *from a famous king*.
de|scend (di send′) *verb*, **descended, descending.**

descendant or **descendent**—A person who comes from a certain group or family: *I am a* descendant *of Indians*.
de|scend|ant or de|scend|ent (di sen′dənt) *noun, plural* **descendants** or **descendents.**

descent—**1.** A movement from a higher to a lower place: *the airplane's* descent. **2.** A downward slope: *The roller coaster ride has a steep* descent. **3.** Ancestry: *Our mother is of Italian* descent.
de|scent (di sent′) *noun, plural* **descents.**
• A word that sounds the same is **dissent.**

describe—To tell or write about something so that the hearer or reader will have a clear picture of it: *Can you* describe *your lost dog so we can help you look for it?*
de|scribe (di skrīb′) *verb*, **described, describing.**

description—**1.** The act of using words to give a clear picture of something: *Your* description *of your birthday cake is so good that I can almost taste the chocolate*. **2.** Kind; type: *Birds of every* description *came to our bird feeder*.
de|scrip|tion (di skrip′shən) *noun, plural* **descriptions.**

descriptive—Giving a picture of something by using words: *Mother sent away for a* descriptive *folder that tells all about the summer camp we want to attend*.
de|scrip|tive (di skrip′tiv) *adjective*.

desegregate—To put an end to the practice of having separate places for different racial groups, especially for black people and white people: *The city* desegregated *our school by allowing people of all races to attend classes*.
de|seg|re|gate (dē seg′rə gāt) *verb*, **desegregated, desegregating.**

desert[1]—A land area that is so dry, hot, and sandy that very few plants can grow there. *Noun.*
—Not supporting plant or animal life; wild and uncultivated: *The shipwrecked sailor was alone on the* desert *island. Adjective.*
des|ert (dez′ərt) *noun, plural* **deserts;** *adjective*.

desert[2]—To leave or go away from someone or something that requires one's help or protection; abandon: *The woman* deserted *her family*.
de|sert (di zurt′) *verb*, **deserted, deserting.**
• A word that sounds the same is **dessert.**

Word History

Both forms of the word **desert** come from a Latin word meaning "abandon." A desert is usually not a good place to live, so most such places remain abandoned. People who desert someone or something abandon their duty.

deserve—To be worthy of; earn or want as one's right: *You* deserve *my thanks for being so helpful*.
de|serve (di zurv′) *verb*, **deserved, deserving.**

design—**1.** A plan or sketch used as a guide to make something: *This* design *shows how to build a doghouse*. **2.** An arrangement of colors or details; a decorative pattern: *My dress has a* design *of blue stripes. Noun.*
—**1.** To make such a plan or sketch: *An architect* designed *our house*. **2.** To plan; think of: *Can*

you design *a method to keep this door shut? Verb.*

de|sign (di **zīn′**) *noun, plural* **designs;** *verb,* **designed, designing.**

● Synonyms: **devise, invent,** for *verb* 2.

designate—**1.** To point out; indicate; show: *An "X" on the map* designated *the spot where the pirates buried their treasure.* **2.** To call by a special name or title: *The queen of England is* designated *"your majesty."* **3.** To choose for a special purpose: *She was* designated *captain of the soccer team.*

des|ig|nate (**dez′**ig nāt) *verb,* **designated, designating.**

● Synonyms: **appoint, name, select,** for 3.
Antonyms: **discharge, dismiss, fire,** for 3.

desirable—Attractive; worth having: *Making the team is a* desirable *goal.*

de|sir|a|ble (di **zīr′**ə bəl) *adjective.*

desire—A longing; craving; strong wish: *I have a sudden* desire *for ice cream. Noun.*
—To long for; wish for eagerly: *Her parents give her everything she* desires. *Verb.*

de|sire (di **zīr′**) *noun, plural* **desires;** *verb,* **desired, desiring.**

desk—A piece of furniture with a flat or slanted top that is used for writing or reading. Desks often have drawers for storing things.

desk (desk) *noun, plural* **desks.**

desolate—**1.** Ruined; lifeless: *The countryside was left* desolate *by the flood.* **2.** Deserted; not lived in or visited: *The abandoned house stood empty and* desolate. **3.** Very unhappy; gloomy: *He was* desolate *at the thought of moving away from his friends.*

des|o|late (**des′**ə lit) *adjective.*

despair—A feeling of hopelessness; a total loss of hope: *The farmer was filled with* despair *when his crops failed. Noun.*
—To be without any hope: *The lost campers* despaired *of ever finding their way out of the forest. Verb.*

de|spair (di **spār′**) *noun; verb,* **despaired, despairing.**

desperate—**1.** Ready to take dangerous risks because of a loss of hope: *The* desperate *woman*

prepared to jump from the roof of the burning building. **2.** Extremely serious or hopeless: *He suffered from a* desperate *illness.*

des|per|ate (**des′**pər it) *adjective.*

despise—To dislike a great deal; think of as being worthless: *She* despises *people who cheat.*

de|spise (di **spīz′**) *verb,* **despised, despising.**

despite—In spite of: Despite *the cheerful fire in the fireplace, the room was cold.*

de|spite (di **spīt′**) *preposition.*

dessert—The last course of a meal: *Pie is a popular* dessert.

des|sert (di **zurt′**) *noun, plural* **desserts.**

● A word that sounds the same is **desert.**[2]

Word History

Dessert comes from a French word meaning "clear the table." Most people do not eat dessert until all the dishes from the main meal have been cleared away.

---

destination—A place to which someone or something is going or being sent: *The rocket's* destination *is Mars.*

des|ti|na|tion (des′tə **nā′**shən) *noun, plural* **destinations.**

destiny—What will happen to a person or thing; fate: *She believes it is her* destiny *to be a television star.*

des|ti|ny (**des′**tə nē) *noun, plural* **destinies.**

destroy—To wreck; ruin: *The fire* destroyed *the house.*

de|stroy (di **stroi′**) *verb,* **destroyed, destroying.**

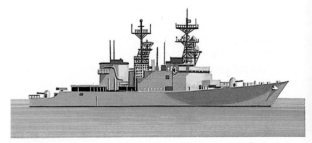

destroyer

destroyer—A small, fast ship that is used in a war to attack submarines and to escort other ships.

de|stroy|er (di **stroi′**ər) *noun, plural* **destroyers.**

destruction—**1.** The act of ruining or tearing down: *A wrecking crew began the* destruction *of*

a at	i if	oo look	ch chalk	⌐ a in ago
ā ape	ī idle	ou out	ng sing	e in happen
ah calm	o odd	u ugly	sh ship	ə = i in capital
aw all	ō oats	ū rule	th think	o in occur
e end	oi oil	ur turn	th their	⌐ u in upon
ē easy			zh treasure	

the building.   **2.** The condition of being ruined: *A flood caused the* destruction *of the farm crops.*
de|struc|tion (di **struk′**shən) *noun, plural* **destructions.**

destructive—Causing or able to cause ruin: *Many trees blew down in the* destructive *storm.*
de|struc|tive (di **struk′**tiv) *adjective.*

detach—To separate one thing from another: *He* detached *the swing from its rope.*
de|tach (di **tach′**) *verb,* **detached, detaching.**

detail—**1.** A small part of something; item: *She remembered every* detail *on the list.*   **2.** A handling of something one by one: *This book does not go into* detail *about the life of each president.*   **3.** A small group of people that is given a special task or duty: *The general sent a* detail *of soldiers to spy on the enemy. Noun.*
—**1.** To tell everything, even the small or less important parts: *The coach* detailed *the game plan to the team.*   **2.** To give someone a special task or duty: *The teacher* detailed *two students to hand out the test papers. Verb.*
de|tail (di **tāl′** *or* **dē′**tāl) *noun, plural* **details;** *verb,* **detailed, detailing.**

detain—**1.** To hold back from going; delay: *Our airplane flight was* detained *by fog.*   **2.** To jail; hold in custody: *The soldiers* detained *the enemy spy.*
de|tain (di **tān′**) *verb,* **detained, detaining.**
• For **2,** see Synonyms and Antonyms at **catch.**

detect—To find out; discover the presence or existence of something: *The pilot's radar* detected *where the other airplanes were located.*
de|tect (di **tekt′**) *verb,* **detected, detecting.**

detective—A person whose job is to find out who committed a crime by searching for and uncovering proof of the crime; a type of police officer. *Noun.*
—Using hard-to-find clues, as such a person does: *Through clever* detective *work, we found Mother's lost sweater. Adjective.*
de|tec|tive (di **tek′**tiv) *noun, plural* **detectives;** *adjective.* Abbreviation: Det.

detention—**1.** The act of holding back or state of being delayed: *She received an hour's* detention *for talking in class.*   **2.** The act of being kept in custody: *The city has a kennel for the* detention *of lost and stray dogs.*
de|ten|tion (di **ten′**shən) *noun, plural* **detentions.**

detergent—A substance used for cleaning that is stronger than soap: *We add* detergent *to the washing machine to clean our clothes.*

de|ter|gent (di **tur′**jənt) *noun, plural* **detergents.**

determination—**1.** Firmness of purpose: *His* determination *to have his own way makes it useless to argue with him.*   **2.** The act of deciding something in advance: *Her* determination *to leave came after much thought.*
de|ter|mi|na|tion (di tur′mə **nā′**shən) *noun, plural* **determinations.**
• Synonyms: **resolution, resolve,** for **1.**

determine—**1.** To decide very firmly; resolve: *She* determined *to do her very best.*   **2.** To decide or settle in advance: *We* determined *the things we would need to take with us on vacation.*   **3.** To find out about something by obtaining first-hand information: *I* determined *the warmth of the bath water by feeling it.*   **4.** To influence; be the cause of: *The number of seats on the bus will* determine *how many can go on the trip.*
de|ter|mine (di **tur′**mən) *verb,* **determined, determining.**

determined—Firm; filled with purpose: *She made a* determined *effort to improve her grades.*
de|ter|mined (di **tur′**mənd) *adjective.*

detest—To dislike very much; hate: *Some people* detest *loud music.*
de|test (di **test′**) *verb,* **detested, detesting.**

detour—A way or route that is used when another cannot be used: *We took a* detour *because the road was closed. Noun.*
—To cause to take a longer way or route: *The traffic was* detoured *around the fallen tree. Verb.*
de|tour (**dē′**toor) *noun, plural* **detours;** *verb,* **detoured, detouring.**

detract—To lessen the worth, appearance, or quality of something: *That small crack in the vase* detracts *from its beauty.*
de|tract (di **trakt′**) *verb,* **detracted, detracting.**

deuce—A playing card, domino, or side of a die with two marks: *the* deuce *of clubs.*
deuce (dūs) *noun, plural* **deuces.**

develop—**1.** To come into being: *to* develop *an interest in something.*   **2.** To grow: *An acorn* develops *into a tree.*   **3.** To improve or strengthen: *to* develop *muscles through exercise.*   **4.** To treat a film with chemicals to make the picture appear.
de|vel|op (di **vel′**əp) *verb,* **developed, developing.**

development—**1.** The process of growing, improving, or inventing: *the* development *of a child's abilities; the* development *of the telephone.*   **2.** An event or outcome: *The police reported no new* developments *in solving the*

crime. **3.** A large group of similar houses or other buildings that are usually constructed by the same builder.
de|vel|op|ment (di **vel**′əp mənt) *noun, plural* **developments.**

device—**1.** An invention or piece of equipment made for a particular purpose: *A pencil sharpener is a useful* device. **2.** A scheme or plan, usually meant to fool someone; trick: *So he could play longer, he used the* device *of pretending not to hear his mother calling.*
de|vice (di **vīs**′) *noun, plural* **devices.**
■ **leave to (one's) own devices:** To allow to do as one pleases: *When our parents weren't home, we were* left to *our* own devices.
• Synonyms: **gadget, machine,** for 1.

devil—**1.** A demon; evil spirit. **2.** The Devil: Satan, the spirit of evil that is said to be the ruler of hell. **3.** A very wicked or cruel person: *That boy is a* devil *for teasing her.*
dev|il (**dev**′əl) *noun, plural* **devils.**
■ **speak of the devil:** To say someone's name and suddenly see that person appear, as if by magic: Speak of the devil, *here comes the neighbor we were just talking about.*
the devil to pay: Trouble; serious problems because of one's actions: *You'll have* the devil to pay *if you break your promise.*

devise—To think of; plan: *See if you can* devise *a way to keep this door open.*
de|vise (di **vīz**′) *verb,* **devised, devising.**
• Synonyms: **design, invent**

devote—To set aside one's time, attention, or effort for some particular purpose: *He* devotes *all his spare time to reading.*
de|vote (di **vōt**′) *verb,* **devoted, devoting.**

devoted—Very loyal, loving, or faithful: *a* devoted *friend; a* devoted *football fan.*
de|vot|ed (di **vō**′tid) *adjective.*

devotion—Loyalty; love; faithfulness: *The two brothers show great* devotion *to each other.*
de|vo|tion (di **vō**′shən) *noun, plural* **devotions.**

devour—**1.** To eat with great hunger; gulp: *He* devoured *what was on his plate and asked for more.* **2.** To destroy completely by surrounding: *The stormy lake* devoured *the boat.*
de|vour (di **vour**′) *verb,* **devoured, devouring.**

devout—**1.** Religious; godly: *The* devout *young man talked of becoming a priest.* **2.** Sincere; deeply felt: *She gave* devout *thanks to the lifeguard who saved her from drowning.*
de|vout (di **vout**′) *adjective.*
• Synonyms: **holy, pious,** for 1.

dew—Moisture from the air that forms tiny drops on cool surfaces during the night: *The grass is covered with* dew.
dew (dū) *noun, plural* **dews.**
• Words that sound the same are **do** and **due.**

dewdrop—A drop of dew.
dew|drop (**dū**′drop *or* **dyū**′drop) *noun, plural* **dewdrops.**

dewlap—The loose fold of skin under the throat of cattle, certain dogs, and some other animals.
dew|lap (**dū**′lap *or* **dyū**′lap) *noun, plural* **dewlaps.**

dexterity—Skill in using the hands, body, or mind: *The acrobat showed great* dexterity *when doing a series of back flips.*
dex|ter|i|ty (dek **ster**′ə tē) *noun.*

Word History

Dexterity comes from a Latin word meaning ''right.'' Originally, it referred to right-handedness, which was associated with skill and ability.

---

di-—A prefix that means ''twice'' or ''two.'' Carbon dioxide has two atoms of oxygen.

Word Power

You can understand the meanings of many words that begin with **di-**, if you add the meaning of the prefix to the meaning of the rest of the word.
dipolar: having two poles
dipole antenna: a radio or television antenna having two separated conducting rods.

---

diabetes—A disease in which a person's body cannot properly use sugar and starch. Sugar collects in the blood, making the person ill.
di|a|be|tes (dī′ə **bē**′tis *or* dī′ə **bē**′tēz) *noun.*

diagnose—To examine a person or thing and to study symptoms to find out what is causing a problem, such as illness: *My doctor* diagnosed *my illness as chicken pox.*
di|ag|nose (dī′əg **nōs**′) *verb,* **diagnosed, diagnosing.**

a at	i if	oo look	ch chalk	a in ago
ā ape	ī idle	ou out	ng sing	e in happen
ah calm	o odd	u ugly	sh ship	ə = i in capital
aw all	ō oats	ū rule	th think	o in occur
e end	oi oil	ur turn	th their	u in upon
ē easy			zh treasure	

diagnosis—The act of finding out what type of problem someone or something has by actual examination and by study of its symptoms. di|ag|no|sis (dī′əg nō′sis) *noun, plural* diagnoses (dī′əg nō′sēz).

diagonal—A straight line that runs in a slanting direction, often from corner to corner of a square or rectangle. *Noun.*
—Running in a slanting direction: *An X is made of two* diagonal *lines. Adjective.*
di|ag|o|nal (dī ag′ə nəl) *noun, plural* diagonals; *adjective.*

diagram—A chart or sketch that makes something easier to understand by showing its parts and how they are arranged or put together. *Noun.*
—To explain by making such a chart or sketch: *The carpenter* diagramed *the table he planned to build. Verb.*
di|a|gram (dī′ə gram) *noun, plural* diagrams; *verb,* diagramed *or* diagrammed; diagraming *or* diagramming.

dial—1. A surface that is marked with lines, letters, or numbers over which a pointer moves to keep track of time, direction, degree, or amount of something. Clocks, meters, and compasses all have dials. 2. The knob on a radio or television that one turns to listen to or watch certain stations or programs. 3. The disk on some telephones that one turns to make calls. *Noun.*
—1. To tune in a radio or television station by using a knob: Dial *Channel 4 to get cartoons.* 2. To make a telephone call by using a disk: *He* dialed *his grandfather's number. Verb.*
di|al (dī′əl) *noun, plural* dials; *verb,* dialed, dialing.
• See picture at **compass.**

dialect—A way of speaking used in a certain area or by a certain group of people. A dialect may differ from other forms of the same language in such ways as special words used, special ways of pronouncing certain sounds, or special ways of putting phrases or sentences together: *a Southern* dialect; *black* dialect.
di|a|lect (dī′ə lekt) *noun, plural* dialects.

dialogue—A conversation; discussion: *The two men carried on a rapid* dialogue *on the telephone.*
di|a|logue (dī′ə lawg) *noun, plural* dialogues.

dial tone—The humming sound that a telephone makes when the receiver is lifted. It indicates to the caller that he or she may dial a number.
di|al tone (dī′əl tōn) *noun, plural* dial tones.

diameter—1. A straight line passing through the center of a circle, sphere, or other round object. It divides things in half. 2. The thickness or width of something: *The* diameter *of a tree trunk.*
di|am|e|ter (dī am′ə tər) *noun, plural* diameters.
• For 1, see picture at **circle.**

diamond—1. A very hard mineral that is made from pure carbon crystals. It usually has no color and is the hardest natural substance known: *a* diamond *necklace.* 2. A playing card with one or more red markings that have this shape: (◇). 3. The part of a baseball field that is marked by bases, forming this shape (◇).
dia|mond (dī′mənd *or* dī′ə mənd) *noun, plural* diamonds.
■ **diamond in the rough:** A person who has many good qualities or skills but needs some improvement: *Until she improves her backstroke, she's still a* diamond in the rough *as a swimmer.*

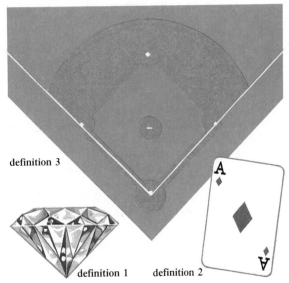

definition 3

definition 1   definition 2

diamond

diaper—A piece of soft material that absorbs moisture and is worn by babies as underpants.
di|a|per (dī′ə pər *or* dī′pər) *noun, plural* diapers.

diaphragm—1. The wall of muscles and tendons that separates the chest from the abdomen. It helps the lungs to control breathing. 2. A thin disk or cone that vibrates when sound hits it. It is used in telephones, earphones, loudspeakers, and other devices.
di|a|phragm (dī′ə fram) *noun, plural* diaphragms.

Word History

Diary comes from a Latin word meaning
"day." People who keep diaries usually write in
them each day. People record the important
events and thoughts that occurred to them on a
certain day.

diary—A written account of a person's thoughts
and activities: *I write secrets in my* diary.
di|a|ry (dī′ər ē) *noun, plural* **diaries.**

dice—Small plastic or wood cubes marked with
one to six spots on each side. They are usually
used in pairs and are shaken or tossed to play
certain games. *Noun.*
—To chop into small cubes: *We* diced *some
onions to put on our hamburgers. Verb.*
dice (dīs) *plural noun; verb,* **diced, dicing.**
■ **load the dice:** To arrange unfairly beforehand
for certain things to happen: *She failed the test
because he* loaded the dice *against her by
giving her the wrong answers.*
no dice: Definitely not: *My friend wanted me
to cheat, but I said* no dice.
● See picture at **ace.**

dictate—1. To speak or read something aloud so
that another person can write it down or a
machine can record it: *to* dictate *a homework
assignment to the class; to* dictate *a letter to a
secretary.* 2. To command by one's authority;
give orders: *I would rather be asked nicely to do
something than be* dictated *to. Verb.*
—A command; order; rule: *the* dictates *of the
king. Noun.*
dic|tate (dik′tāt *or* dik tāt′ for *verb;* dik′tāt for
noun) verb, **dictated, dictating;** *noun, plural*
dictates.

dictator—A person who rules absolutely, usually
using his or her power and authority unfairly.
dic|ta|tor (dik′tā tər *or* dik tā′tər) *noun, plural*
dictators.

dictionary—A book that lists and explains the
words of a language in alphabetical order, giving
their spellings, meanings, and pronunciations.
dic|tion|ar|y (dik′shə ner′ē) *noun, plural*
dictionaries.

Word History

Dictionary comes from a Latin word meaning
"word." Dictionaries are filled with many
thousands of words. It's no surprise then that
someone would go to a dictionary to find a
word.

did—*See* do.
did (did) *verb.*

didn't—The contraction of "did not."
did|n't (did′ənt).

die[1]—1. To stop living; become dead: *The plant
died because he didn't water it.* 2. To lessen in
strength; come to an end: *Talking in the audience
died down when the actor came on stage.* 3. To
long for very much: *I am* dying *to tell you my
secret.*
die (dī) *verb,* **died, dying.**
■ **die off:** To die one after another until all have
died: *When the water became polluted in that
pond, the fish* died off.
● A word that sounds the same is **dye.**
● Synonyms: **expire, perish,** for 1.
Antonyms: **live**[1], **survive,** for 1.

die[2]—1. A single small plastic or wood cube
marked with one to six spots on each side; one of
a pair of dice, usually used to play certain
games: *She threw the* die *to see which player
would go first.* 2. A tool made of metal that is
used to shape or stamp things, such as coins.
die (dī) *noun, plural* **dice** for 1, **dies** for 2.
■ **the die is cast:** The decision is made and can't
be changed: *The die is cast—the criminal must
go to jail.*
● See picture at **ace.**

diesel *or* **Diesel**—1. An engine in which fuel oil
is set on fire by heat from the compression of
air. 2. A vehicle run by such an engine.
die|sel *or* Die|sel (dē′zəl *or* dē′səl) *noun, plural*
diesels *or* **Diesels.**

Word History

Diesel is named after the man who invented it,
Rudolf Diesel. He was an engineer in Germany
in the 1890's when he designed this powerful
engine. Today it moves trains, trucks, tractors,
and other large vehicles.

diet—1. The food and drink a person or an animal
usually eats and drinks. 2. Any special foods

a at	i if	oo look	ch chalk		a in ago
ā ape	ī idle	ou out	ng sing		e in happen
ah calm	o odd	u ugly	sh ship	ə =	i in capital
aw all	ō oats	ū rule	th think		o in occur
e end	oi oil	ur turn	th their		u in upon
ē easy			zh treasure		

eaten for health reasons or to gain or lose weight: *a low-fat* diet. *Noun.*
—To eat special food for health reasons or to gain or lose weight: *He* dieted *and exercised and lost ten pounds. Verb.*
di|et (dī′ət) *noun, plural* **diets**; *verb,* **dieted, dieting.**

dietitian—A person trained to plan meals that provide good nutrition or meet a specific need.
di|e|ti|tian (dī′ə tish′ən) *noun, plural* **dietitians.**

differ—1. To be not the same; be unlike: *Rain* differs *from snow.* 2. To disagree: *Dad and I* differ *on what television programs we like.*
dif|fer (dif′ər) *verb,* **differed, differing.**

difference—1. The state or quality of being not alike: *There is an obvious* difference *between the colors black and white.* 2. A way of being not alike: *The only* difference *between my hat and yours is the color.* 3. The amount left after subtracting one number from another: *The* difference *between 10 and 6 is 4.* 4. The state of having unlike opinions; disagreement: *My brother and I had a* difference *over who should get the last slice of pie.*
dif|fer|ence (dif′ər əns *or* dif′rəns) *noun, plural* **differences.**

different—1. Unlike: *Salt and pepper are* different. 2. Not the same; separate: *We eat and sleep in* different *rooms.* 3. Odd; uncommon: *A car with pink wheels is really* different.
dif|fer|ent (dif′ər ənt *or* dif′rənt) *adjective.*
• Synonyms: **abnormal, unusual,** for **3.**
Antonyms: **common, regular, typical,** for **3.**

difficult—1. Hard to do, make, or understand: *Learning to drive a car is* difficult *at first.* 2. Not easy to deal with or please: *His bad temper makes him* difficult.
dif|fi|cult (dif′ə kult) *adjective.*

difficulty—1. The fact of being hard to do, make, or understand; difficult nature: *I got a low mark because of the* difficulty *of the test.* 2. Something that is hard to deal with; obstacle: *The pioneers faced many* difficulties *in their new land.*
dif|fi|cul|ty (dif′ə kul′tē) *noun, plural* **difficulties.**

dig—1. To turn up, loosen, or hollow out soil or some other substance: *Don't* dig *the dirt with your hands.* 2. To form, get, or make by digging: *We had to* dig *our way out of the snowdrift.* 3. To search: *I found an article on bears by* digging *through old magazines.* 4. To thrust; poke: *Cats* dig *their claws into the wood when they climb trees.*
dig (dig) *verb,* **dug, digging.**
• Synonyms: **excavate, scoop,** for **1.**

digest—To break down food in the mouth, stomach, and intestines so that it can be used by the body. *Verb.*
—A short summary of a longer book, article, or statement: *The television guide has a* digest *of the week's programs. Noun.*
di|gest (də **jest**′ *or* dī **jest**′ for *verb*; **di**′jest for *noun*) *verb,* **digested, digesting;** *noun, plural* **digests.**

digestion—The process of breaking down food so that it can be used by the body: *Chewing your food well helps in* digestion.
di|ges|tion (də **jes**′chən *or* dī **jes**′chən) *noun, plural* **digestions.**

digestive system—The parts of the body that break down food so that it can be used by the body. The mouth, stomach, liver, intestines, and certain glands and other organs make up the digestive system.
di|ges|tive sys|tem (də **jes**′tiv **sis**′təm *or* dī **jes**′tiv **sis**′təm) *noun, plural* **digestive systems.**

digit—1. Any of the numbers 1, 2, 3, 4, 5, 6, 7, 8, and 9. Sometimes 0 is included as a digit. 2. A finger or a toe.
dig|it (dij′it) *noun, plural* **digits.**

digital—1. Having to do with one or more of the numbers 0 through 9. 2. Having to do with information that is stored, recovered, and changed in the form of numbers. Most computers work with digital information. A digital phonograph record is made by turning sound into numbers.
dig|it|al (dij′ə təl) *adjective.*

dignified—Having or showing respect or honor; noble: *The graduating class marched in a* dignified *procession.*
dig|ni|fied (dig′nə fīd) *adjective.*

dignify—To give honor to; make noble or important: *The tall pillars* dignify *the old mansion.*
dig|ni|fy (dig′nə fī) *verb,* **dignified, dignifying.**

dignitary—A person who holds a high rank of honor: *The state governor and other* dignitaries *rode in the parade.*
dig|ni|tar|y (dig′nə ter′ē) *noun, plural* **dignitaries.**

dignity—The quality of being noble, respected, or honored: *Although our team lost, we kept our* dignity *and congratulated the winners.*
dig|ni|ty (dig′nə tē) *noun, plural* **dignities.**

dike—A high ridge of ground built to prevent flooding by a river or the sea.
dike (dīk) *noun, plural* **dikes.**

dilly-dally—To waste time; be idle: *Do not dilly-dally, or we shall miss the bus.*
dil|ly-dal|ly (dil′ē dal′ē) *verb,* **dilly-dallied, dilly-dallying.**
 • Synonyms: **dawdle, delay, loiter**
 Antonyms: **hasten, hurry, rush, speed**

dilute—To lessen the strength or thickness of something by mixing it with a liquid: *If you dilute the paint, it will spread more evenly.*
di|lute (də lūt′ *or* dī lūt′) *verb,* **diluted, diluting.**

dim—**1.** With little or no light: *a dim, rainy day; the small lamp's dim glow.* **2.** Not clear; faint: *The painting showed only the dim outline of a mountain.* **3.** Not able to see, hear, or understand clearly: *Our old dog's eyesight is very dim. Adjective.*
—To become or make less bright: *The theater lights were dimmed when the movie started. Verb.*
dim (dim) *adjective,* **dimmer, dimmest;** *verb,* **dimmed, dimming.**
 • Synonyms: **dark, dull,** for **1.**
 Antonyms: **bright, brilliant, luminous, radiant,** for **1.**

dime—A United States or Canadian coin that is worth ten cents.
dime (dīm) *noun, plural* **dimes.**

dimension—Length, width, or height, or any combination of these: *I measured the dimensions of the box to see if the gift would fit in it.*
di|men|sion (də men′shən) *noun, plural* **dimensions.**

length

length and width

length, width, and height

dimension

a at	i if	oo look	ch chalk		┌ a in ago
ā ape	ī idle	ou out	ng sing		e in happen
ah calm	o odd	u ugly	sh ship	ə =	i in capital
aw all	ō oats	ū rule	th think		o in occur
e end	oi oil	ur turn	th their		└ u in upon
ē easy			zh treasure		

diminish—To become or make smaller; lessen: *His interest in sports diminished after he started working.*
di|min|ish (də min′ish) *verb,* **diminished, diminishing.**
 • See Synonyms at **decrease.**

dimple—A small dent in the skin or any surface: *He has dimples in his cheeks when he smiles.*
dim|ple (dim′pəl) *noun, plural* **dimples.**

din—A loud, continuing noise; racket: *I can't hear myself over the din of this cafeteria. Noun.*
—To say repeatedly: *She dinned the rules into us. Verb.*
din (din) *noun, plural* **dins;** *verb,* **dinned, dinning.**
 • Synonyms: **clamor, commotion, uproar,** for *noun.*
 Antonyms: **quiet, silence, still,** for *noun.*

dine—To eat a meal, especially dinner.
dine (dīn) *verb,* **dined, dining.**

diner—**1.** A person who is eating a meal. **2.** A small restaurant that serves a wide variety of foods.
din|er (dī′nər) *noun, plural* **diners.**

dinghy—A small rowboat.
din|ghy (ding′ē) *noun, plural* **dinghies.**

dingy—Dull in appearance; dirty-looking: *This old blouse is too dingy to wear.*
din|gy (din′jē) *adjective,* **dingier, dingiest.**

dinky—Very small. *She had never seen such a dinky bedroom.*
dink|y (ding′kē) *adjective,* **dinkier, dinkiest.**

dinner—**1.** The main meal of the day: *We eat dinner every evening at 6:30.* **2.** A formal meal given in honor of a person or occasion: *The dinner was given to celebrate their parents' anniversary.*
din|ner (din′ər) *noun, plural* **dinners.**

dinosaur—One of a group of reptiles that lived millions of years ago and are now all gone. Scientists have discovered more than 800 different kinds and have found them on every continent.
di|no|saur (dī′nə sawr) *noun, plural* **dinosaurs.**

Word History

Dinosaur comes from two Greek words meaning ''terrible lizard.'' When dinosaur fossils were first discovered, their large size made scientists believe that these reptiles were terribly fierce creatures. In fact, some dinosaurs were very small plant-eating animals and no dinosaurs were actually lizards.

diocese—A church district that is directed by a bishop.
di|o|cese (dī′ə sis *or* dī′ə sēs) *noun, plural* **dioceses.**

diorama—A scene showing lifelike figures of people, animals, or other objects in front of a painted background: *The* diorama *at the museum showed an Indian village of long ago.*
di|o|ram|a (dī′ə ram′ə) *noun, plural* **dioramas.**

dip—1. To put into a liquid and then lift out again quickly: *I* dipped *my doughnut into the hot chocolate.* 2. To reach into a container to take something out: *She* dipped *her hand into the jar of coins.* 3. To lower and raise again quickly: *The pilot* dipped *the plane's wings in a salute.* 4. To drop; go down: *The afternoon sun* dipped *below the hill. Verb.*
—1. The act of quickly going in and out of liquid: *a* dip *in the pool.* 2. A creamy mixture in which to dunk foods: *vegetable* dip. 3. A lowering; drop: *Our stomachs fluttered as we went over the* dips *in the road. Noun.*
dip (dip) *verb,* **dipped, dipping;** *noun, plural* **dips.**

diphtheria—A serious, infectious disease of the throat.
diph|the|ri|a (dif thēr′ē ə *or* dip thēr′ē ə) *noun.*

diphthong—A sound made up of two vowel sounds pronounced in one syllable. The *oi* in *poise* is a diphthong.
diph|thong (dip′thawng *or* dif′thawng) *noun, plural* **diphthongs.**

diploma—A certificate given to a graduating student stating that he or she has completed a course of study at a school.
di|plo|ma (də plō′mə) *noun, plural* **diplomas.**

diplomat—A person whose job is to represent his or her country: *The* diplomats *from the different countries discussed world peace.*
dip|lo|mat (dip′lə mat) *noun, plural* **diplomats.**

diplomatic—1. Having to do with the relations between countries. 2. Skillful at dealing with people: *Her* diplomatic *approach helped to solve the problems between the children.*
dip|lo|mat|ic (dip′lə mat′ik) *adjective.*

dipper—1. A cup with a long handle, used to scoop up liquids. 2. **Dipper.** Either one of two groups of stars in the northern sky that are in the shapes of dippers. One is the Big Dipper, and the other is the Little Dipper.
dip|per (dip′ər) *noun, plural* **dippers.**
• See picture at **constellation.**

dipper (definition 1)

direct—1. To manage; control: *to* direct *the making of a movie.* 2. To give an order: *The teacher* directed *us to put our books on the floor before the test.* 3. To tell or show someone the way; guide: *The signs* directed *us to the hospital.* 4. To aim; point: *He* directed *his flashlight at the noise in the bushes. Verb.*
—1. Straight; the shortest possible way: *We took the* direct *route home.* 2. Truthful; straightforward: *She gave a* direct *answer to the question. Adjective.*
di|rect (də rekt′ *or* dī rekt′) *verb,* **directed, directing;** *adjective.*
• Synonyms: **command, instruct,** for *verb* 2. Antonyms: **follow, obey,** for *verb* 2.

direction—1. Management; guidance: *The fire department is under the* direction *of a new chief.* 2. An order or instruction: *I followed the* directions *in the recipe.* 3. A way that something faces or points: *That house faces in a northern* direction.
di|rec|tion (də rek′shən *or* dī rek′shən) *noun, plural* **directions.**

directly—1. In a straight line or manner: *I went* directly *home from school.* 2. Exactly; right: *Our house is* directly *opposite the church.* 3. Immediately; without delay: *She will see you* directly *after her next appointment.*
di|rect|ly (də rekt′lē *or* dī rekt′lē) *adverb.*
• Synonyms: **instantly, presently,** for 3.

direct object—The person or thing in a sentence that receives the action of the verb: *I hit the ball.* The direct object of the verb *hit* is *ball.* di|rect ob|ject (də rekt′ ob′jikt) *noun, plural* **direct objects.**

director—A manager; leader: *the director of the sales department.* di|rec|tor (də rek′tər *or* dī rek′tər) *noun, plural* **directors.**
 * Synonyms: **captain, chief, head** Antonym: **follower**

directory—A list of names and addresses: *a telephone directory.* di|rec|to|ry (də rek′tər ē *or* dī rek′tər ē) *noun, plural* **directories.**

dirigible—A large, gas-filled balloon that can be steered. It is a kind of airship. dir|i|gi|ble (dēr′ə jə bəl *or* də rij′ə bəl) *noun, plural* **dirigibles.**
 * See picture and Language Fact at **airship.**

dirt—1. Something that soils things, such as mud or dust. 2. Soil; earth: *Our garden needs more rain because the dirt is very dry.* dirt (durt) *noun.*

dirty—Not clean; soiled: *Please put those dirty clothes into the washing machine.* dirt|y (dur′tē) *adjective,* **dirtier, dirtiest.**

dis-—A prefix that means "the opposite of," or "the lack of," or "to undo." To disappear is the opposite of appear. Disbelief is the lack of belief. To disconnect is to undo a connection.

Word Power

You can understand the meaning of many words that begin with **dis-** if you add a meaning of the prefix to the meaning of the rest of the word.
 disinform: the opposite of inform
 discomfort: lack of comfort
 disentangle: to undo a tangle

---

disability—A condition that makes one unable to function as before or in a usual way: *Growing blindness was a disability to the painter.* dis|a|bil|i|ty (dis′ə bil′ə tē) *noun, plural* **disabilities.**

disable—To make unable; cripple: *Disabled by her leg injury, she will have to drop out of the dance recital.* dis|a|ble (dis ā′bəl) *verb,* **disabled, disabling.**

disadvantage—1. An unfavorable condition; something that makes it harder to do well: *It is a disadvantage for anyone not to know how to read.* 2. Loss; harm: *When people found out his lie, it worked to his disadvantage.* dis|ad|van|tage (dis′əd van′tij) *noun, plural* **disadvantages.**
 * Synonyms: **drawback, hindrance,** for **1.**

disagree—1. To have a different opinion; differ: *Dad and I disagreed over whether I should go to the party.* 2. To be unlike: *Our descriptions of the movie disagreed.* 3. To have a bad effect on: *Milk disagrees with my stomach, so I don't drink it.* dis|a|gree (dis′ə grē′) *verb,* **disagreed, disagreeing.**
 * Synonyms: For **1,** see Synonyms at **argue.** Antonyms: **accord, agree,** for **1.**

disagreement—A difference of opinion; dispute: *We had a disagreement over which movie to see.* dis|a|gree|ment (dis′ə grē′mənt) *noun, plural* **disagreements.**

disappear—1. To vanish; go out of sight: *The magic ink disappeared, leaving the page blank once more.* 2. To stop existing or happening: *The warm nights of summer disappear when autumn comes.* dis|ap|pear (dis′ə pēr′) *verb,* **disappeared, disappearing.**

disappearance—The act of going out of sight: *The bird's sudden disappearance from the window surprised the little boy.* dis|ap|pear|ance (dis′ə pēr′əns) *noun, plural* **disappearances.**

disappoint—To fall short of one's hopes: *It disappointed us that our soccer team's record was so poor.* dis|ap|point (dis′ə point′) *verb,* **disappointed, disappointing.**

disappointment—1. The feeling of being unsatisfied or let down: *When she did not get the part in the play, she could not hide her disappointment.* 2. Something or someone that fails to satisfy: *Having the bus trip canceled was a disappointment to everyone.* dis|ap|point|ment (dis′ə point′mənt) *noun, plural* **disappointments.**

disapprove—To be against; object: *Dad disapproves when we stay up too late.*

a at	i if	oo look	ch chalk		⌈ a in ago
ā ape	ī idle	ou out	ng sing		e in happen
ah calm	o odd	u ugly	sh ship	ə =	i in capital
aw all	ō oats	ū rule	th think		o in occur
e end	oi oil	ur turn	th their		⌊ u in upon
ē easy			zh treasure		

dis|ap|prove (dis'ə prūv') *verb*, **disapproved, disapproving.**

disarm—To take weapons away from: *The police disarmed the bank robber.*
dis|arm (dis ahrm') *verb*, **disarmed, disarming.**

disaster—A sudden event that causes much destruction or suffering. Blizzards, floods, and hurricanes are disasters.
dis|as|ter (də zas'tər) *noun, plural* **disasters.**
• Synonyms: **calamity, catastrophe**

disbelief—A lack of belief: *His eyes widened in disbelief when I told what the car had cost.*
dis|be|lief (dis'bi lēf') *noun, plural* **disbeliefs.**

disc—*See* **disk.**
disc (disk) *noun, plural* **discs.**

discard—To throw away or give up something that is useless: *She discards magazines after she reads them.*
dis|card (dis kahrd') *verb*, **discarded, discarding.**

discharge—1. To let go; release: *He was discharged from his job when he was late four days in a row.* 2. To shoot: *He discharged the gun by accident.* 3. To give off: *The chimney discharged a column of smoke into the air.* 4. To unload from a ship, plane, truck, or car. *Verb.*
—The act of being let go; releasing: *My uncle received a medical* discharge *from the army because of his wound. Noun.*
dis|charge (dis **chahrj**' for *verb*, dis **chahrj**' or dis'chahrj for *noun*) *verb*, **discharged, discharging;** *noun, plural* **discharges.**
• Synonyms: **dismiss, fire,** for *verb* 1.
Antonyms: **appoint, choose, designate,** for *verb* 1.

disciple—1. A person who follows the teachings of a leader. 2. A follower of Jesus Christ.
dis|ci|ple (də sī'pəl) *noun, plural* **disciples.**

discipline—1. Any instruction that encourages orderly, obedient behavior: *His polite manners are a result of good* discipline *by his parents.* 2. Punishment. *Noun.*
—1. To train to be obedient. 2. To punish: *She disciplined her dog when it barked at the mail carrier. Verb.*
dis|ci|pline (dis'ə plin) *noun, plural* **disciplines;** *verb*, **disciplined, disciplining.**

disconnect—To separate; break a connection: *Our telephone was disconnected during the storm.*
dis|con|nect (dis'kə nekt') *verb*, **disconnected, disconnecting.**

discontent—The state of not being satisfied; unhappiness and desire for change: *Her discontent caused her to want to work elsewhere.*
dis|con|tent (dis'kən tent') *noun, plural* **discontents.**

discontinue—To stop: *My mother discontinued her teaching job for the summer.*
dis|con|tin|ue (dis'kən tin'yū) *verb*, **discontinued, discontinuing.**

discord—1. A difference of opinion; disagreement: Discord *spoiled our club meeting.* 2. A lack of harmony in notes that are played together: *The wrong notes they played made a terrible* discord.
dis|cord (dis'kawrd) *noun, plural* **discords.**

discount—An amount off the regular price: *We bought the coat at a 20 percent discount.*
dis|count (dis'kount) *noun, plural* **discounts.**
• Synonyms: **deduction, reduction**

discourage—1. To take away one's courage, confidence, or hopes: *The boy discouraged his friend when he laughed at her drawing.* 2. To try to prevent someone from doing something: *Dad discouraged us from skating in the rain.*
dis|cour|age (dis kur'ij) *verb*, **discouraged, discouraging.**

discover—To find or learn something for the first time: *I discovered a new route to the playground.*
dis|cov|er (dis kuv'ər) *verb*, **discovered, discovering.**

discovery—1. The act of finding or learning something for the first time: *The doctor's discovery of a new treatment led to a cure for the disease.* 2. Something found or learned for the first time: *Many scientific discoveries are the result of space exploration.*
dis|cov|er|y (dis kuv'ər ē *or* dis kuv'rē) *noun, plural* **discoveries.**

discreet—Showing tact; speaking and acting carefully. *She was discreet in saying what she thought of the play we had written.*
dis|creet (dis krēt') *adjective.*

discriminate—To behave toward someone differently than toward others because of his or her race, sex, age, religion, appearance, income, or any other quality: *That company discriminates against women because it pays them less than men for the same work.*
dis|crim|i|nate (dis krim'ə nāt) *verb*, **discriminated, discriminating.**

discrimination—The act of treating people unequally because of their differences: *Racial discrimination is against the law.*
dis|crim|i|na|tion (dis krim'ə nā'shən) *noun.*

discus—A heavy, flat, round plate thrown by athletes as a test of strength and coordination. dis|cus (dis′kəs) *noun, plural* **discuses**.

discus

discuss—To talk about various sides of an issue: *The child's parents* discussed *her test results.* dis|cuss (dis kus′) *verb,* **discussed, discussing**.

discussion—A talk about different views on a subject: *The mention of summer vacation started a long* discussion *at our house.* dis|cus|sion (dis kush′ən) *noun, plural* **discussions**.

disease—A sickness that affects people, animals, or plants: *After Mary got the measles, others in the class came down with the* disease. dis|ease (də zēz′) *noun, plural* **diseases**.
   • Synonyms: **ailment, illness**
     Antonym: **health**

disgrace—1. Loss of other people's respect; shame; dishonor: *Our new puppy was sent to his bed in* disgrace *when Dad found the chewed slipper.* 2. Something or someone that is shameful: *That old run-down house is a* disgrace *to the neighborhood. Noun.*

—To cause shame: *The way he acted at the party* disgraced *his family. Verb.* dis|grace (dis grās′) *noun, plural* **disgraces**; *verb,* **disgraced, disgracing**.

disguise—1. To make oneself look like something or someone else: *The masks we wore* disguised *our faces so well that even our parents didn't know us.* 2. To make a thing seem like something else: *I* disguised *my voice on the telephone to fool my sister. Verb.*

—Makeup, face covering, clothing, or anything else used to change the way one looks so as to fool others: *The thief wore a wig as a* disguise *when he robbed the bank. Noun.* dis|guise (dis gīz′) *verb,* **disguised, disguising**; *noun, plural* **disguises**.

disgust—A strong dislike: *She felt* disgust *at the thought of touching the cold, wet frog. Noun.*

—To cause a sickening feeling of dislike: *The smell of sour milk* disgusts *me. Verb.* dis|gust (dis gust′) *noun; verb,* **disgusted, disgusting**.

dish—1. A shallow container for serving food, such as a plate or bowl. 2. Food prepared in a certain way: *Baked chicken is my favorite* dish. *Noun.*

—To put food into a shallow serving container: *He* dished *the ice cream into a bowl. Verb.* dish (dish) *noun, plural* **dishes**; *verb,* **dished, dishing**.

dishonest—Unfair; not truthful: *It is* dishonest *to make a promise that you know you cannot keep.* dis|hon|est (dis on′ist) *adjective.*

dishonor—A loss of good standing; shame: *News of the thief's crimes brought* dishonor *to his family. Noun.*

—To bring shame or disgrace: *The actions of those few who littered in the park* dishonored *everyone who was there at the school picnic. Verb.* dis|hon|or (dis on′ər) *noun, plural* **dishonors**; *verb,* **dishonored, dishonoring**.

disinfect—To kill germs to protect against disease; sterilize: *The cafeteria* disinfects *the drinking glasses after each use.* dis|in|fect (dis′in fekt′) *verb,* **disinfected, disinfecting**.

disinherit—To take away a person's right to an inheritance: *The angry parents said they would* disinherit *their daughter if she quit school.* dis|in|her|it (dis′in her′it) *verb,* **disinherited, disinheriting**.

a at	i if	oo look	ch chalk		a in ago
ā ape	ī idle	ou out	ng sing		e in happen
ah calm	o odd	u ugly	sh ship	ə =	i in capital
aw all	ō oats	ū rule	th think		o in occur
e end	oi oil	ur turn	th their		u in upon
ē easy			zh treasure		

disintegrate—To break or fall apart into many tiny pieces: *The sand at the seashore was formed from rocks that had* disintegrated.
dis|in|te|grate (dis in′tə grāt) *verb,* **disintegrated, disintegrating.**

disk—1. A thin, round object that has the same general shape as a pancake: *The chocolate mints were shaped like* disks. 2. A flat, thin, round magnetic object that stores information used by a computer.
disk (disk) *noun, plural* **disks.**
• This word is also spelled **disc.**

disk drive—The part of a computer that spins, like a record, a flat, thin, round magnetic object so as to get the information stored on it: *Be sure the* disk drive *is empty before you begin.*
disk drive (disk drīv) *noun, plural* **disk drives.**

diskette—A small, floppy disk that is used to store information on a computer.
disk|ette (dis′ket *or* dis ket′) *noun, plural* **diskettes.**

dislike—To take little pleasure in: *I* dislike *studying for tests. Verb.*
—A feeling of not enjoying someone or something: *She has a strong* dislike *for cold weather. Noun.*
dis|like (dis līk′) *verb,* **disliked, disliking;** *noun, plural* **dislikes.**

dislocate—To cause a bone to come out of its joint: *He* dislocated *his thumb when he tried to catch the ball.*
dis|lo|cate (dis′lō kāt) *verb,* **dislocated, dislocating.**

dislodge—To force out of place: *We* dislodged *the car from the ditch only after an hour of pushing.*
dis|lodge (dis loj′) *verb,* **dislodged, dislodging.**

disloyal—Not being true to someone or something; unfaithful: *You were* disloyal *to your friend when you talked about her behind her back.*
dis|loy|al (dis loi′əl) *adjective.*

dismal—Dark and dreary; depressing: *After the funeral, he went back to the* dismal *house alone.*
dis|mal (diz′məl) *adjective.*

dismay—To make afraid, sad, or troubled: *She* dismayed *her father when she said she couldn't continue her lessons. Verb.*
—A feeling of fear and sadness about what is to happen: *She was filled with* dismay *at the thought of moving to a new school. Noun.*
dis|may (dis mā′) *verb,* **dismayed, dismaying;** *noun.*

dismiss—1. To send away or release: *The principal* dismissed *school early because of the heavy snow.* 2. To be let go from a job or office: *He was late so often, his boss* dismissed *him.*
dis|miss (dis mis′) *verb,* **dismissed, dismissing.**
• Synonyms: **discharge, fire,** for 2.
Antonyms: For 2, see Antonyms at **discharge.**

dismount—To get off or down from something, such as a horse or a bicycle: *They* dismounted *their horses in order to guide the animals across the stream.*
dis|mount (dis mount′) *verb,* **dismounted, dismounting.**

disobedient—Failing to obey orders or rules: *He is usually well behaved, but today he was* disobedient.
dis|o|be|di|ent (dis′ə bē′dē ənt) *adjective.*

disobey—To fail to obey; violate orders or rules of: *She* disobeyed *her parents by coming home late.*
dis|o|bey (dis′ə bā′) *verb,* **disobeyed, disobeying.**

disorganize—To destroy the order of: *The breeze from the window* disorganized *the papers on my desk.*
dis|or|gan|ize (dis awr′gə nīz) *verb,* **disorganized, disorganizing.**

dispatch—To send something or someone off: *He* dispatched *a thank-you note to his aunt. Verb.*
—A printed or written message that is sent or delivered: *The general received the* dispatch *from headquarters early today. Noun.*
dis|patch (dis pach′) *verb,* **dispatched, dispatching;** *noun, plural* **dispatches.**

dispense—To pass out something; give out: *The school nurse* dispenses *aspirins to students with headaches.*
dis|pense (dis pens′) *verb,* **dispensed, dispensing.**
■ **dispense with:** To finish off; to do away with: *The computer* dispensed with *the need to keep so many written records.*
• Synonyms: **distribute, issue**

displace—1. To move into the position or place of; replace: *Our new microwave oven* displaced *our toaster.* 2. To move from the usual location or place: *The building of that large factory* displaced *many of the town's families.*
dis|place (dis plās′) *verb,* **displaced, displacing.**

display—To set forth for the public; show: *The way she played at the recital* displayed *a real talent for music. Verb.*

—An exhibition, demonstration, or show: *The display of toy trains drew a large crowd. Noun.*
dis|play (dis plā′) *verb,* **displayed, displaying;** *noun, plural* **displays.**

displease—To annoy; make unhappy: *It displeases me when I miss a bus.*
dis|please (dis plēz′) *verb,* **displeased, displeasing.**

displeasure—The feeling of being annoyed or unhappy: *Dad did not try to hide his* displeasure *at losing his wallet.*
dis|pleas|ure (dis plezh′ər) *noun.*

disposable—Intended to be thrown away after being used: *a disposable razor.*
dis|pos|a|ble (dis pō′zə bəl) *adjective.*

dispose—To place in a particular order or arrangement: *The general disposed the troops for a surprise attack.*
dis|pose (dis pōz′) *verb,* **disposed, disposing.**
■ **dispose of: 1.** To deal with or resolve: *He disposed of the argument by giving each child half of the apple.* **2.** To get rid of or throw away: dispose of *the garbage.*

disposition—The way a particular person usually acts or thinks: *a pleasant disposition.*
dis|po|si|tion (dis′pə zish′ən) *noun, plural* **dispositions.**
● Synonyms: **character, nature**

dispute—To make an argument against; challenge or oppose: *He disputed my claim that I am the best player on the team. Verb.*
—A quarrel; disagreement: *We settled our* dispute *about whether to go bowling or skating by flipping a coin. Noun.*
dis|pute (dis pyūt′) *verb,* **disputed, disputing;** *noun, plural* **disputes.**
● Synonyms: **argue, bicker, disagree, quarrel,** for *verb.*
　　Antonyms: **accord, agree,** for *verb.*

disqualify—To make unable to do something: *Her poor eyesight disqualifies her from becoming a pilot.*
dis|qual|i|fy (dis kwol′ə fī) *verb,* **disqualified, disqualifying.**

disregard—To give no consideration to; ignore: *Please* disregard *how the kitchen looks. Verb.*
—A lack of respect: *Their loud talking showed a* disregard *for others in the library. Noun.*
dis|re|gard (dis′ri gahrd′) *verb,* **disregarded, disregarding;** *noun.*
● Synonyms: **neglect, overlook,** for *verb.*

disrupt—To cause upset; break apart: *The sudden buzz of the fire alarm* disrupted *the meeting.*
dis|rupt (dis rupt′) *verb,* **disrupted, disrupting.**

dissatisfied—Having the attitude that someone or something is not adequate or acceptable; discontent: *I am* dissatisfied *with my grades.*
dis|sat|is|fied (dis sat′is fīd) *adjective.*

dissect—To cut apart something in order to study it: *The student's biology assignment is to* dissect *a frog.*
dis|sect (di sekt′ *or* dī sekt′) *verb,* **dissected, dissecting.**

dissent—To disagree; have a different opinion: *Most of us wanted to go to the movies, but two of our group* dissented. *Verb.*
—A disagreement; difference of opinion: Dissent *among the club members caused the meeting to break up. Noun.*
dis|sent (di sent′) *verb,* **dissented, dissenting;** *noun.*
● A word that sounds the same is **descent.**

dissolve—**1.** To make something liquid, usually by mixing with a liquid: *I* dissolved *the cocoa in warm milk.* **2.** To end; discontinue: *He* dissolved *the friendship when he learned that she had lied.*
dis|solve (di zolv′) *verb,* **dissolved, dissolving.**

distance—**1.** The space between two things or places: *It takes three hours to travel the* distance *between the two cities.* **2.** A place or point far away: *The farmer raced to his truck when he saw smoke in the* distance.
dis|tance (dis′təns) *noun, plural* **distances.**
■ **keep (one's) distance:** To be not too friendly: *A child should be taught that it is necessary to* keep *one's* distance *from strangers.*

distant—**1.** Far away or apart in space, time, or relationship; remote: *a* distant *city; the* distant *past; a* distant *cousin.* **2.** Lacking warmth; unfriendly: *My neighbor has been very* distant *toward me since our quarrel.*
dis|tant (dis′tənt) *adjective.*

distinct—**1.** Different; separate: *The salad dressing is a blend of several* distinct *flavors.* **2.** Plain and clear; easily seen, heard, or sensed: *The difference in quality becomes more* distinct *when you look closely. His behavior shows a* distinct *improvement from last week.*
dis|tinct (dis tingkt′) *adjective.*

a at	i if	oo look	ch chalk		⎡ a in ago
ā ape	ī idle	ou out	ng sing		e in happen
ah calm	o odd	u ugly	sh ship	ə =	i in capital
aw all	ō oats	ū rule	th think		o in occur
e end	oi oil	ur turn	th their		⎣ u in upon
ē easy			zh treasure		

distinction—1. The act of telling things apart: *He made a* distinction *between natural forest fires and those caused by careless campers.* 2. A difference: *Can you see the* distinction *between the two shades of blue?* 3. Known for one's achievements; excellence: *The author is a woman of* distinction.
dis|tinc|tion (dis **tingk′**shən) *noun, plural* **distinctions.**

distinctive—Having one or more unique or unusual characteristics: *I would know her anywhere because of her* distinctive *laugh.*
dis|tinc|tive (dis **tingk′**tiv) *adjective.*

distinguish—1. To tell or show a difference: *Please* distinguish *between the nouns and the verbs on this list.* 2. To make out clearly: *I could* distinguish *my friends' faces in the crowd.* 3. To set apart; mark as unique: *Her excellent record in school* distinguished *her from the others applying for the job.* 4. To make well known or outstanding: *He* distinguished *himself as a trumpet player.*
dis|tin|guish (dis **ting′**gwish) *verb,* **distinguished, distinguishing.**
● Synonyms: **identify, recognize,** for **2.**

distinguished—1. Widely known for excellence; famous; prominent: *a* distinguished *author.* 2. Elegant or important in appearance: *His new suit gives him a* distinguished *look.*
dis|tin|guished (dis **ting′**gwisht) *adjective.*

distort—To cause to become out of shape: *The years* distorted *her appearance so much I hardly recognized her.*
dis|tort (dis **tawrt′**) *verb,* **distorted, distorting.**

distract—To take one's attention away from that which he or she is doing: *Do not* distract *the student next to you by talking.*
dis|tract (dis **trakt′**) *verb,* **distracted, distracting.**

distraction—A thing that takes away one's attention to something else; diversion: *The radio was a* distraction *while she was trying to talk on the phone.*
dis|trac|tion (dis **trak′**shən) *noun, plural* **distractions.**
■ **to distraction:** To the point of frustration: *His frequent interruptions are driving her* to distraction.

distress—1. Suffering, pain, or sadness: *Her broken leg caused her much* distress. 2. Extreme difficulty or danger: *The plane reported being in* distress *just after takeoff. Noun.*
—To cause suffering, pain, or sadness: *My dog's illness greatly* distresses *me. Verb.*
dis|tress (dis **tres′**) *noun; verb,* **distressed, distressing.**

distribute—1. To give out; divide something and pass out the shares: *The director* distributed *the scripts to the actors.* 2. To spread out and cover more of a surface: Distribute *the glue evenly on the paper so there will be no lumps.* 3. To separate into groups; arrange; classify: *The teacher* distributed *workbooks to the groups according to reading level.*
dis|trib|ute (dis **trib′**yūt) *verb,* **distributed, distributing.**
● Synonyms: **dispense, issue,** for **1.**

distribution—The act of giving out something: *The* distribution *of Valentine cards will come first at our class party.*
dis|tri|bu|tion (dis′trə **byū′**shən) *noun, plural* **distributions.**

district—A section within a larger area; neighborhood; region: *the business* district *of the city.*
dis|trict (dis′trikt) *noun, plural* **districts.**

distrust—To be not able to believe in; suspect: *He* distrusted *her promises because she had kept so few in the past. Verb.*
—Doubt; suspicion: *I have a* distrust *of him even though people tell me he is honest. Noun.*
dis|trust (dis **trust′**) *verb,* **distrusted, distrusting;** *noun.*

disturb—1. To annoy or cause to worry: *The child's behavior* disturbed *his mother.* 2. To interrupt: *Do not* disturb *people when they are talking on the telephone.* 3. To disrupt; put out of normal order: *The fire drill* disturbed *our play rehearsal.*
dis|turb (dis **turb′**) *verb,* **disturbed, disturbing.**

disturbance—1. The act or state of being bothered; interruption: *Mother warned us that there would be no* disturbance *of the baby's nap.* 2. Something that interrupts or bothers: *Telephone calls can be a* disturbance *when I am trying to get something done.*
dis|turb|ance (dis **tur′**bəns) *noun, plural* **disturbances.**

ditch—A long, narrow trench in the ground that allows water to flow to or from something.
ditch (dich) *noun, plural* **ditches.**

dive—1. To plunge, usually headfirst, into something, such as water. 2. To plunge down steeply: *The plane* dived *a long way before it straightened out.* 3. To move down or out of sight suddenly: *The freezing temperature made him want to* dive *under the blankets. Verb.*
—1. The act of plunging headfirst into

something, such as water.   **2.** A steep, downward plunge: *The kite took a* dive. *Noun.*
dive (dīv) *verb,* **dived** *or* **dove, diving;** *noun, plural* **dives.**

dive and **diver** (definition 1)

diver—**1.** One who performs the act of plunging headfirst into water.   **2.** One who goes under water to search for something or to explore. Divers wear special suits with air hoses or oxygen tanks to breathe underwater.
div|er (dī′vər) *noun, plural* **divers.**

diverse—Not alike; different: *The used book store has a box of* diverse *novels.*
di|verse (də vurs′ *or* dī vurs′) *adjective.*
  • Synonyms: **assorted, miscellaneous, various**
    Antonym: **uniform**

divert—**1.** To turn aside: *This ditch* diverts *water from the river to the fields.*   **2.** To entertain: *The tumblers and clowns* diverted *the children.*
di|vert (də **vurt**′ *or* dī **vurt**′) *verb,* **diverted, diverting.**

divide—**1.** To separate into two or more parts: *The audience* divided *into four groups to discuss the speech.*   **2.** In mathematics, to find out how many times a number goes into another number: *When you* divide *twelve by four, the answer is*

three.   **3.** To share; separate into parts and distribute: *to* divide *my time between work and play.*   **4.** To split apart into sides opposing each other; disagree: *The jury* divided *on the question of whether the man is guilty or not. Verb.*
—Land that separates two waterways, each with its own system of drainage. *Noun.*
di|vide (də vīd′) *verb,* **divided, dividing;** *noun, plural* **divides.**
  • Synonyms: **part, separate,** for *verb* **1.**
    Antonyms: For *verb* **1,** see Synonyms at **mix.**

dividend—**1.** A number to be divided by some other number in the process of division in mathematics: *When twelve is divided by four, twelve is the* dividend.   **2.** Profit that is divided among owners or shareholders of a company.
div|i|dend (div′ə dend) *noun, plural* **dividends.**

divine—**1.** Coming from or having to do with God: *Kings once believed they had a* divine *right to rule.*   **2.** Having a holy quality; sacred: *I believe it is important to attend* divine *services regularly.*
di|vine (də vīn′) *adjective.*

divinity—**1.** A god; deity: *The Romans worshiped several* divinities.   **2.** The state of being divine; holiness.   **3.** The study of religion: *She attended a school of* divinity *for a while.*
di|vin|i|ty (də vin′ə tē) *noun, plural* **divinities.**

divisible—Able to be divided, usually evenly: *That number is not* divisible *by three.*
di|vis|i|ble (də viz′ə bəl) *adjective.*

division—**1.** The act of dividing; separation: *The calendar marks the* division *of a year into twelve months.*   **2.** A part of something that has been divided; partition: *Social studies is a* division *of science.*   **3.** A thing that separates someone or something from another: *This hedge is the* division *between the two properties.*   **4.** A military unit composed of brigades or regiments. **5.** Department; section: *the repair* division *of an automobile agency.*   **6.** Disagreement: *There are* divisions *among doctors on how to treat a cold.*
di|vi|sion (də vizh′ən) *noun, plural* **divisions.**

divisor—A number in mathematics that is used to divide another number: *When four is used as the* divisor *of twelve, three is the answer.*
di|vi|sor (də vī′zər) *noun, plural* **divisors.**

divorce—The act of ending a marriage in a court of law. *Noun.*
—To end a marriage in a court of law.
di|vorce (də vawrs′) *noun, plural* **divorces;** *verb,* **divorced, divorcing.**

dizzy—Feeling unsteady and as if on the point of falling: *The high fever made him* dizzy.
diz|zy (diz′ē) *adjective.*

a at	i if	oo look	ch chalk	a in ago
ā ape	ī idle	ou out	ng sing	e in happen
ah calm	o odd	u ugly	sh ship	ə = i in capital
aw all	ō oats	ū rule	th think	o in occur
e end	oi oil	ur turn	th their	u in upon
ē easy			zh treasure	

do—1. To carry out; perform, often to completion: *We* did *our work before we were allowed to play games.*   2. To make; produce: *I* did *a poster about the school fair.*   3. To put in order; take care of: *We* do *the chalkboards each day after school.*   4. To be satisfactory; serve: *This blue pencil will* do, *although I'd rather have a red one.*   5. To solve: *to* do *a multiplication problem.*   6. To fare; manage: *The substitute teacher* did *very well on such short notice.*   7. A helping verb used when asking a question: *Do you want to go to the game?*   8. A helping verb used when the main verb in a sentence needs emphasizing: *I* do *want you to come with us.*   9. A helping verb used instead of repeating another verb: *Step where she* does *to avoid falling into the brook.*   10. A helping verb used with "not": *He* does *not have to answer.*
do (dü) *verb,* **did, done, doing.**
  ■ **do in:** To kill; ruin: *You'll* do in *that car in no time the way you drive it.*
  do (one's) **thing:** To take part in an activity that one finds satisfying: *Taking a bicycle trip around the state is an example of her* doing *her thing.*
  do or die: To give one's utmost effort: *We will win this game,* do or die.
  do out of: To take something by cheating or being dishonest. *He* did *her* out of *her share of the candy by convincing her that it was his.*
  ● Words that sound the same are **dew** and **due.**

Doberman pinscher—A large, slim, black or brown dog with short, straight, smooth hair. This dog was originally bred in Germany to assist in police work.
Do|ber|man pin|scher (dō′bər mən **pin′**shər) *noun, plural* **Doberman pinschers..**

dock—A platform that is built along the shore or extends out over the water. It is used for boats to come alongside and unload or be tied up for a time. *Noun.*
  —1. To tie up a boat to a platform at or over the water.   2. To join together two vehicles while in space. *Verb.*
dock (dok) *noun, plural* **docks;** *verb,* **docked, docking.**

doctor—1. A person who is trained to treat people or animals for illness and disease; physician. A doctor must be legally permitted, or licensed, to practice medicine. Some doctors specialize in certain diseases or conditions.   2. A person who has earned a university's highest degree.
doc|tor (dok′tər) *noun, plural* **doctors.**
Abbreviation: **Dr.**
  ● See Language Fact at **surgeon.**

doctrine—A principle that is a part of the beliefs of a group or religion; a teaching that is followed by a believer: *Our Constitution is based on the doctrines of democracy.*
doc|trine (dok′trən) *noun, plural* **doctrines.**

document—An official paper that provides information about or proof of something: *I keep my important* documents *in a safe place.*
doc|u|ment (dok′yə mənt) *noun, plural* **documents.**

dodge—1. To stoop, step aside quickly, or swerve to avoid something: *She* dodged *to get out of the way of the ball.*   2. To avoid an issue by being tricky or bringing up another topic; evade: *He* dodged *talking about school by creating a big fuss about his lost book. Verb.*
  —1. A jump to the side to get out of the way of something or someone: *She made a* dodge *to the left when the snowball was just inches away.*
  2. A trick to avoid something: *His sudden headache is just a* dodge *to avoid visiting the dentist. Noun.*
dodge (doj) *verb,* **dodged, dodging;** *noun, plural* **dodges.**

dodo—A large, awkward-looking bird with small wings that could not fly. It once made its home

Doberman pinscher

Word History

Doberman pinscher comes from two words that were put together. The first word is a shorter spelling of the last name of the man who developed this animal in the 1800's, a German dog breeder named Ludwig Dobermann. *Pinscher* is the German word for "terrier."

on a particular island in the Indian Ocean, but it has not been seen alive for over 300 years. Its name has come to mean outdated or clumsy.
do|do (dō′dō) *noun, plural* **dodos** *or* **dodoes.**

■ **dead as a dodo:** Out of fashion; no longer in use: *That style of music is* dead as a dodo *these days.*

dodo

Word History

Dodo comes from a Portuguese word meaning ''silly.'' The bird that was given this name was strange in appearance, having a head that seemed too little for its body, an unusually hooked bill, and small wings that were useless for flying. Sometimes a person who is foolish or clumsy is called by this name.

doe—The adult female of the deer, antelope, goat, rabbit, and other mammals of which the male is called a buck.
doe (dō) *noun, plural* **does.**
● A word that sounds the same is **dough.**
● See picture at **deer.**

does—*See* **do.**
does (duz) *verb.*

doesn't—The contraction of ''does not.''
does|n't (duz′ənt).

dog—A domestic, four-legged animal that is trained to be a pet, to guard people and property,

or to hunt. There are many different breeds of dogs, and they range widely in size. The dog belongs to the same family as the wolf and the fox. *Noun.*
—To keep after or follow closely as a dog would track; hound: *He* dogged *his friend for days until the money he had loaned her was repaid. Verb.*
dog (dawg *or* dog) *noun, plural* **dogs;** *verb,* **dogged, dogging.**

■ **dog days:** Spells of hot, humid summer weather: *the* dog days *of August.*
dog's life: A miserable way of living: *When you're very poor, it must be a* dog's life.
go to the dogs: To wreck one's life; go to ruin: *He got in a wild group, and soon he went to* the dogs.
in the dog house: In trouble with someone: *She is* in the dog house *with the coach for missing practice.*
let sleeping dogs lie: To avoid changing things so as to keep the peace: *It's wise to* let sleeping dogs lie *when an argument has been forgotten.*

dogwood—A flowering tree that has white or pink flowers in the spring and red berries in the fall. It is found in North America. The state flower of Virginia is the dogwood.
dog|wood (dawg′wood′) *noun, plural* **dogwoods.**

dogwood

doll—A toy that is made to look something like a person.
doll (dol) *noun, plural* **dolls.**

dollar—A unit of money worth one hundred cents in the United States. A dollar is also a unit of

a at	i if	oo look	ch chalk		a in ago
ā ape	ī idle	ou out	ng sing		e in happen
ah calm	o odd	u ugly	sh ship	ə =	i in capital
aw all	ō oats	ū rule	th think		o in occur
e end	oi oil	ur turn	th their		u in upon
ē easy			zh treasure		

money in some other countries, including Canada and Australia. Its symbol is $.

dol|lar (dol′ər) *noun, plural* **dollars.**

■ **dollars to doughnuts:** Absolutely certain; very likely: *It's dollars to doughnuts she'll get a hit when she comes to bat.*

dolphin—A sea mammal related to the porpoise and the whale that is very smart. It has a long nose, or snout, and two small flippers.

dol|phin (dol′fən) *noun, plural* **dolphins.**

dolphin

-dom—1. A suffix that means "the rank of" or "the realm of" when added to a noun: *slave*dom; *king*dom. 2. A suffix that means "the condition of being" when added to an adjective: *free*dom. 3. A suffix that means "all those who have the title of" when added to a noun: *official*dom.

Word Power

You can understand the meanings of many words that end in **-dom,** if you add a meaning of the suffix to the meaning of the rest of the word.

dukedom: the rank of a duke

heathendom: the condition of being heathen

Christendom: all those who have the title of Christian

---

dome—1. A high, rounded roof or ceiling curved like a bowl that has been turned wrong side up. Some government buildings, like the White House and a number of state capitals, have domes.

dome (dōm) *noun, plural* **domes.**

domestic—1. Of or relating to the family or household: *We help Mom and Dad with* domestic *chores such as making beds and mowing the lawn.* 2. Bred to live in a tame condition with human beings; not wild: *Dogs are* domestic *animals.* 3. Of or relating to the country in which one lives: *I prefer to buy* domestic *goods rather than products made in other countries.*

do|mes|tic (də mes′tik) *adjective.*

domesticate—To tame something, usually an animal, so that it can live among humans: *The cowboys tried to* domesticate *wild horses.*

do|mes|ti|cate (də mes′tə kāt′) *verb,* **domesticated, domesticating.**

dominant—Major or most important: *The* dominant *reason for going to school is to learn.*

dom|i|nant (dom′ə nənt) *adjective.*

dominate—To have controlling power or rank over; rule: *The club president* dominated *the discussion about the new rules. The tall church* dominated *the one-story buildings around it.*

dom|i|nate (dom′ə nāt′) *verb,* **dominated, dominating.**

dominion—A ruler's territory; domain: *The king's* dominion *includes all the land from coast to coast.*

do|min|ion (də min′yən) *noun, plural* **dominions.**

domino—A small, flat piece shaped like a rectangle that is used to play a game called dominos. It is black, and each of its flat sides has from one to six white dots.

dom|i|no (dom′ə nō′) *noun, plural* **dominos** *or* **dominoes.**

domino

donate—To give something, usually to a charitable cause; contribute: *She* donated *toys to needy children during the holidays.*

do|nate (dō′nāt) *verb,* **donated, donating.**

donation—Something given as a gift; contribution: *Everyone was asked for a donation of food for the class dinner.*
do|na|tion (dō nā′shən) *noun, plural* **donations.**

done—*See* **do.** *Verb.*
—**1.** Finished; ended: *My homework was* done *in time to watch television.* **2.** Cooked and ready to eat: *The cake is* done, *so we can have it for dessert. Adjective.*
done (dun) *verb; adjective.*
■ **done in:** Completely tired out; exhausted: *The runners were* done in *by the end of the race.*
done for: Used up; ruined: *My jeans were* done for *after I played in the mud.*

donkey—A four-legged animal that is like a horse but smaller. It has long ears and is thought of as being slow and stubborn.
don|key (dong′kē *or* dung′kē *or* dawng′kē) *noun, plural* **donkeys.**
● Other names for this animal are **ass** and **burro.**

donkey

donor—A person who gives or donates something as a gift.
do|nor (dō′nər) *noun, plural* **donors.**

don't—The contraction of ''do not.''
don't (dōnt).

donut—*See* **doughnut.**
do|nut (dō′nut′) *noun, plural* **donuts.**

a at	i if	oo look	ch chalk	⌈a in ago
ā ape	ī idle	ou out	ng sing	e in happen
ah calm	o odd	u ugly	sh ship	ə = ⎸ i in capital
aw all	ō oats	ū rule	th think	o in occur
e end	oi oil	ur turn	th their	⌊u in upon
ē easy			zh treasure	

doodle—To draw or write without thinking about it, usually while doing something else: *She always* doodled *on scrap paper while she talked on the telephone. Verb.*
—A drawing made without much thought, usually while doing something else. *Noun.*
doo|dle (dū′dəl) *verb,* **doodled, doodling;** *noun, plural* **doodles.**

doom—A bad or unhappy result, frequently death or ruin; horrible fate: *He will soon meet his* doom *if he continues taking such foolish risks. Noun.*
—To be destined to result in a bad end: *Lack of money* doomed *the project from the start. Verb.*
doom (dūm) *noun, plural* **dooms;** *verb,* **doomed, dooming.**

door—A panel made of wood or other hard material that closes an entrance into a place. It opens and closes by moving on hinges and fits into a frame around an opening in a wall.
door (dawr) *noun, plural* **doors.**
■ **next door to:** In the next house or room: *The dining room is* next door to *the kitchen.*
out of doors: Out in the open air; outside: *We play* out of doors *all day when the weather is beautiful.*
show (one) **the door:** To insist that someone leave: *She became angry and* showed *me the* door.

doorbell—A bell, chime, buzzer, or other device inside a house that is attached, usually by electric wires, to a button outside a door. When the button is pushed, it mades a sound to let anyone inside know that someone is at the door.
door|bell (dawr′bel′) *noun, plural* **doorbells.**

doorknob—A round handle that turns to open or close a door. It sometimes has a lock in it.
door|knob (dawr′nob′) *noun, plural* **doorknobs.**

doorstep—A step or a series of steps leading to the ground that appears in front of an outside door.
door|step (dawr′step′) *noun, plural* **doorsteps.**

doorway—A wall opening, usually framed, into which a door fits.
door|way (dawr′wā′) *noun, plural* **doorways.**

dope—**1.** Any mood-changing or habit-forming drug; narcotic. **2.** A tip; news; information: *When I was absent from school, he gave me all the* dope *on our homework.* **3.** A foolish or stupid person. **4.** A varnish or liquid of the type that is used in making model airplanes and other wooden objects.
dope (dōp) *noun, plural* **dopes,** *for* **3.**
■ **dope out:** To study something and come to an understanding: *It took him a while to* dope out *the math problem.*

dormant—Soundly sleeping; not active: *Some animals lie* dormant *during the winter months.*
dor|mant (dawr′mənt) *adjective.*

dormitory—A building with many bedrooms, such as at a college or boarding school, where students live and sleep. It may have a kitchen, dining hall, and lounges.
dor|mi|to|ry (dawr′mə tawr′ē) *noun, plural* **dormitories.**

dormouse—A small brown or gray animal that has a bushy tail and a little face like a squirrel. During the winter it hibernates, or sleeps soundly.
dor|mouse (dawr′mous′) *noun, plural* **dormice.**

dormouse

dory—A popular fishing craft; a kind of rowboat. It has high sides and a flat bottom.
do|ry (dawr′ē) *noun, plural* **dories.**

dory

dose—A certain portion, usually of medicine: *Mother made sure I took the right* dose *of cough syrup when I was sick.*
dose (dōs) *noun, plural* **doses.**

dot—A small, round spot or mark such as a period at the end of a sentence. *Noun.*
—1. To make small marks all over something: *Paint blotches* dotted *the artist's smock.* 2. To appear scattered in a random way: *From the plane we saw houses* dotting *the landscape. Verb.*
dot (dot) *noun, plural* **dots;** *verb,* **dotted, dotting.**
■ **on the dot:** At the exact time expected: *She arrived at the party* on the dot.

double—1. Twice another in size, strength, speed, amount, or value: *a* double *scoop of ice cream.* 2. Having two parts: double *windows.* 3. Meant for two: *a* double *bed. Adjective.*
—Two times; twice the number or amount of: *She earned* double *pay on the holiday. Adverb.*
—1. The result of something doubled: *Because everyone brought a friend, we had* double *the number of people expected.* 2. Something just like another; duplicate. 3. In baseball, a hit that allows a player to reach second base. *Noun.*
—1. To increase by twice as much: *By agreeing to do extra chores, I* doubled *my allowance from three to six dollars.* 2. To fill in for something or someone else; substitute: *Our broom handle* doubles *as a stick bat.* 3. In baseball, to get to second base with a hit. *Verb.*
dou|ble (dub′əl) *adjective; adverb; noun, plural* **doubles;** *verb,* **doubled, doubling.**
■ **double back:** To turn around and go back the same way: *During the game, she* doubled back *to throw the others off her track.*
double over: To bend down; lean forward from the waist: *He* doubled over *with laughter.*
double up: To share something with someone: *We had to* double up *in tents because too many campers showed up.*
on the double: Fast; more quickly than usual; right away: *She told me to get back to work* on the double!

double bass—A musical instrument that looks like a large cello. It has a very low tone. It is also called a bass viol.
dou|ble bass (dub′əl bās) *noun, plural* **double basses.**

double bass

double-cross—To cheat or deceive someone by doing the opposite of, or not doing, what is supposed or expected to be done; betray: *The pirate captain planned to* double-cross *his crew by not sharing the treasure.*
dou|ble-cross (dub′əl kraws) *verb,* **double-crossed, double-crossing.**

double-header—Two games or events that follow each other on the same day or night.
dou|ble-head|er (dub′əl hed′ər) *noun, plural* **double-headers.**

double play—In baseball, putting two runners out during one player's time at bat.
dou|ble play (dub′əl plā) *noun, plural* **double plays.**

doubly—Twice as: *If you go* doubly *quick, you will get to school in half the time.*
doub|ly (dub′lē) *adverb.*

doubt—To not believe; not be sure of: *I* doubt *that I will finish all my work today. Verb.*
—**1.** A feeling of not being sure or not believing: *I had* doubts *about my grades until I saw my report card.* **2.** The condition of not being certain: *The outcome of the election was still in* doubt. *Noun.*
doubt (dout) *verb,* **doubted, doubting;** *noun, plural* **doubts.**

doubtful—Causing or having uncertainty: *Because of the cloudy conditions, they were* doubtful *that the sun would come out.*
doubt|ful (dout′fəl) *adjective.*

doubtless—Certainly; without question: *The honor student will* doubtless *do well on the test.*
doubt|less (dout′lis) *adverb.*

dough—**1.** A mixture of flour, milk or water, and other ingredients that is thick enough to roll or knead. Dough is used to make bread, pie crusts, cookies, and other foods. **2.** Money: *The bank robbers hid the stolen* dough *under the floor.*
dough (dō) *noun, plural* **doughs.**
● A word that sounds the same is **doe.**

doughnut—A small sweet cake that is fried in fat. It is usually round with a hole in the center.
dough|nut (dō′nut′) *noun, plural* **doughnuts.**
● This word is also spelled **donut.**

Douglas fir—A tall evergreen tree that has very strong wood used in construction.

needles

cone   tree

Douglas fir

Doug|las fir (dug′ləs fur) *noun, plural* **Douglas firs.**

dove[1]—A bird with short legs, a small head, and a thick body. Related to the pigeon, it makes a low, cooing sound.
dove (duv) *noun, plural* **doves.**

dove[2]—*See* **dive.**
dove (dōv) *verb.*

down[1]—**1.** From a higher to a lower position: *He jumped* down *from the tree.* **2.** Toward or in a place or condition thought of as lower: *The audience quieted* down *when the movie started. Adverb.*
—**1.** To or toward the lower end or bottom of: *to ski* down *a hill.* **2.** Along: *to walk* down *a street. Preposition.*
—To throw or bring to a lower place: *The military pilot* downed *the enemy plane. Verb.*
—Any of four chances a football team has to move the ball ten or more yards forward. *Noun.*
down (doun) *adverb; preposition; verb,* **downed, downing;** *noun, plural* **downs.**
■ **down and out:** Without money, health, or friends: *The unfortunate man was* down and out, *so he went to the shelter for the night.*
down with: Get rid of; away with: *Down with the evil king!*

down[2]—Soft, fluffy feathers: *My pillows are filled with* down.
down (doun) *noun.*

downcast—**1.** Turned downward: *The girl stared at the floor with* downcast *eyes when they said she had lied.* **2.** Sad; depressed: *The boy was* downcast *when he learned that his grandfather wasn't coming for a visit.*
down|cast (doun′kast) *adjective.*

a at	i if	oo look	ch chalk	⌐a in ago
ā ape	ī idle	ou out	ng sing	e in happen
ah calm	o odd	u ugly	sh ship	ə = ⎸ i in capital
aw all	ō oats	ū rule	th think	o in occur
e end	oi oil	ur turn	th their	⌐u in upon
ē easy			zh treasure	

downfall—Ruin; overthrow: *The wicked ways of the queen led to her* downfall.
down|fall (doun′fawl) *noun, plural* **downfalls.**

downhearted—Sad; depressed; in low spirits: *We were* downhearted *when our team lost.*
down|heart|ed (down hahr′tid) *adjective.*

downpour—A heavy rain: *The sudden* downpour *left us soaked.*
down|pour (doun′pawr) *noun, plural* **downpours.**

downstairs—1. Toward the bottom of the stairs: *Clean up the steps or someone may trip and fall* downstairs. 2. On or to a lower floor: *Go* downstairs *and play in the basement. Adverb.*
—On a lower floor: *The* downstairs *classrooms are much larger than the ones upstairs. Adjective.*
—The lower level or floors of a building. *Noun.*
down|stairs (doun′stārz′) *adverb, adjective, noun.*

downstream—In the direction that a stream flows: *Rowing* downstream *is easy because the current takes the boat along with it.*
down|stream (doun′strēm′) *adverb.*

downtown—Toward or in the business center of a city or town: *the* downtown *area; to shop* downtown.
down|town (doun′toun′) *adjective, adverb.*

downward or **downwards**—From a higher to a lower place or condition: *The hawk swooped* downward *to catch the snake. The* downward *view from the top of the cliff made me dizzy.*
down|ward or down|wards (doun′wərd or doun′wərds) *adjective, adverb.*

doz.—An abbreviation for **dozen** or **dozens.**

doze—To sleep lightly; nap: *After supper, my father often* dozes *on the couch.*
doze (dōz) *verb,* **dozed, dozing.**

dozen—A group of twelve: *a* dozen *doughnuts.*
doz|en (duz′ən) *noun, plural* **dozens,** but **dozen** after a number.
Abbreviation: **doz.** or **dz.**

Dr.—The abbreviation for **doctor.**

drab—Dull; lacking brightness: *The* drab *hospital rooms did little to cheer up the patients.*
drab (drab) *adjective,* **drabber, drabbest.**

drachma—A unit of money in Greece.
drach|ma (drak′mə) *noun, plural* **drachmas.**
Abbreviation: dr.

draft—1. A current of air, usually in an enclosed place: *Grandmother asked for her sweater when she felt the cold* draft *from the window.* 2. A rough outline or sketch: *The reporter wrote four* drafts *of the article before it was printed in the newspaper.* 3. A method of selecting a person or persons for a special purpose: *The army* draft *makes sure there are enough soldiers. Noun.*
—1. To make a rough outline or sketch: *She* drafted *her speech as an outline, then filled in the details.* 2. To select for a special purpose: *The governor was* drafted *to run for president. Verb.*
—Used for pulling heavy loads: *Oxen and horses are used as* draft *animals on farms. Adjective.*
draft (draft) *noun, plural* **drafts;** *verb,* **drafted, drafting;** *adjective.*

drag—1. To pull or move along slowly; haul: *The Christmas tree was so big that it had to be* dragged *into the house.* 2. To pull a net or hook under the water, usually in search of something: *The police* dragged *the bottom of the pond for the burglar's tools. Verb.*
—1. Anything that holds back or delays: *Those that do not try their very best are a* drag *on the team.* 2. Something that is very boring: *He thinks that baseball is a real* drag *because it is a slow game. Noun.*
drag (drag) *verb,* **dragged, dragging;** *noun, plural* **drags.**
■ **drag in:** To bring up something that has nothing to do with the matter under discussion: *No matter what we are talking about, you always* drag in *batting averages.*
drag on or **drag out:** To make something go slowly, or to seem to be too slow; to make something last too long: *The day seemed to* drag on *forever. He* dragged out *the story until I was bored.*
drag (one's) feet: To go slowly: *I* dragged *my feet because I did not want to finish.*

dragnet—1. A net pulled along the ground or along the bottom of a body of water to catch small animals. 2. A well-organized search for criminals: *The police set up a* dragnet *throughout the city when the prisoner escaped.*
drag|net (drag′net′) *noun, plural* **dragnets.**

dragon—An imaginary fire-breathing beast that was said to look like a huge lizard, with wings, scales, and claws.
drag|on (drag′ən) *noun, plural* **dragons.**

dragon

dragonfly

Language Fact

The **dragonfly** has many other names, and the one you use may depend on which part of the country you come from. If you live in the North of the United States, you might call it a ''darning needle.'' If you live in the South, you might call it a ''snake feeder.'' And if you live in the East, you might call it a ''snake doctor.''

dragonfly—A large insect that has four wings on a long, thin body. It lives near water and catches flies, mosquitoes, and other insects for food.
drag|on|fly (drag′ən flī′) *noun, plural* **dragonflies.**
• Other names for this insect are **darning needle, snake doctor,** and **snake feeder.**

drain—1. To remove water or other liquid from something; empty: *to* drain *the sink.* 2. To take away from slowly; exhaust: *The long race* drained *us of our energy. Verb.*
—1. A channel or pipe that carries off water or other liquid: *There is a long* drain *from the gutter to the ground.* 2. Anything that uses up: *Keeping up with all the latest fashions is a real* drain *on her time. Noun.*
drain (drān) *verb,* **drained, draining;** *noun, plural* **drains.**
■ **go down the drain:** To become worthless or forgotten: *Our hopes for a picnic* went down the drain *when the storm began.*

a at	i if	oo look	ch chalk		a in ago
ā ape	ī idle	ou out	ng sing		e in happen
ah calm	o odd	u ugly	sh ship	ə =	i in capital
aw all	ō oats	ū rule	th think		o in occur
e end	oi oil	ur turn	th their		u in upon
ē easy			zh treasure		

drake—A male duck.
drake (drāk) *noun, plural* **drakes.**
• See picture at **mallard.**

drama—1. A story written to be performed on a stage; a play. 2. An exciting event: *the* drama *of the little girl's rescue from the river.*
dra|ma (drah′mə *or* dram′ə) *noun, plural* **dramas.**

dramatic—1. Having to do with acting: *She hopes her* dramatic *lessons will get her a job in the movies.* 2. Exciting; like a play: *An African safari would be a very* dramatic *vacation.*
dra|mat|ic (drə mat′ik) *adjective.*

drank—*See* **drink.**
drank (drangk) *verb.*

drape—1. To cover with a cloth that hangs loosely, often as decoration: *The holiday table was* draped *with a red tablecloth.* 2. To hang loosely: *He* draped *his coat over the chair. Verb.*
—A heavy curtain hung at a window: Drapes *keep the sunlight out. Noun.*
drape (drāp) *verb,* **draped, draping;** *noun, plural* **drapes.**

drastic—Very strong; extreme: *Closing the factory was a* drastic *way to reduce expenses.*
dras|tic (dras′tik) *adjective.*
• Synonyms: **harsh, severe**

draw—1. To pull or move something in a certain direction or to a certain position: *The hay wagon was* drawn *by a team of horses.* 2. To create a picture; sketch: *The children* drew *pictures of pumpkins in art class.* 3. To attract; bring in: *That store always* draws *a large crowd by giving away free samples. Verb.*
—1. The act of pulling or moving something in a certain direction or to a certain position: *The cowboy was quick on the* draw. 2. A tie score at the end of a contest or game: *A basketball game never ends in a* draw *because they play until one team wins. Noun.*
draw (draw) *verb,* **drew, drawn, drawing;** *noun, plural* **draws.**

drawback—Anything that makes something less pleasant or useful; flaw: *The only* drawback *of taking our camping trip next week is that we'll miss the party.*
draw|back (draw′bak′) *noun, plural* **drawbacks.**
• Synonyms: **disadvantage, hindrance**

drawbridge—A type of bridge that can be raised and lowered, or moved to the side, usually to let tall boats pass through. Castles had drawbridges that could be raised to keep enemies out.
draw|bridge (draw′brij′) *noun, plural* **drawbridges.**

drawer—A compartment like a box that slides in and out of a desk, table, or bureau. Drawers hold things such as clothes, books, pens, and tools. **drawer** (drawr) *noun, plural* **drawers.**

drawing—**1.** A sketch, plan, picture, or figure made with a pen, pencil, or other writing instrument.   **2.** The picking of a winning ticket in a lottery or raffle. **draw|ing** (draw′ing) *noun, plural* **drawings.**

drawl—To speak slowly, especially with long vowel sounds. *Verb.*
—A slow way of talking: *Our new neighbor from the South speaks with a* drawl. *Noun.* **drawl** (drawl) *verb,* **drawled, drawling;** *noun, plural* **drawls.**

drawn—*See* **draw.** **drawn** (drawn) *verb.*

dread—To feel extremely fearful: *Some children* dread *going to a new school until they make friends. Verb.*
—Fear, especially of some harm that may happen: *He was filled with* dread *about the boat ride because he cannot swim. Noun.*
—Causing fear: *a* dread *disease. Adjective.* **dread** (dred) *verb,* **dreaded, dreading;** *noun; adjective.*

dreadful—**1.** Frightening: *The* dreadful *earthquake happened without warning.* **2.** Extremely unpleasant: *a* dreadful *smell.* **dread|ful** (dred′fəl) *adjective.*
● Synonyms: **awful, horrible, terrible,** for **1.**

drawbridge

dream—**1.** A series of thoughts, feelings, and pictures that happen during one's sleep.   **2.** A hope for the future; wish: *Flying a jet airplane is the boy's* dream. *Noun.*
—**1.** To think, feel, see, or hear something during one's sleep: *My sister often* dreams *that she is flying.*   **2.** To think that something may happen: *He never* dreamed *the party would be so successful. Verb.* **dream** (drēm) *noun, plural* **dreams;** *verb,* **dreamed** or **dreamt, dreaming.**

dreamt—*See* **dream.** **dreamt** (dremt) *verb.*

dreary—Dull; gloomy: *The children wondered what to do on the* dreary *rainy day.* **drear|y** (drir′ē) *adjective,* **drearier, dreariest.**

dredge—A machine used for deepening a harbor or channel of water. It has a bucket or suction pipe that scoops up mud or sand from the bottom of the water. *Noun.*
—To clean out or dig up using such a machine. *Verb.* **dredge** (drej) *noun, plural* **dredges;** *verb,* **dredged, dredging.**

dredge (noun)

drench—To make something totally wet; soak: *The downpour* drenched *the boys before they could get inside.* **drench** (drench) *verb,* **drenched, drenching.**

dress—**1.** A one-piece article of clothing, with a top and skirt, that is worn by women and girls.   **2.** A certain type of clothing: *Everyone was in* formal dress *for the ball. Noun.*
—**1.** To put clothes on: *The boy* dressed *in warm clothes when he saw the snow outside.*   **2.** To apply a bandage or medicine to a wound. *Verb.* **dress** (dres) *noun, plural* **dresses;** *verb,* **dressed, dressing.**
■ **dress to kill:** To wear very stylish clothes: *With*

her leather coat and satin shoes, the girl was
dressed to kill.

dress up: To put on especially good clothes.
We dressed up *for my cousin's wedding.*

dresser—A chest of drawers for holding clothes
and other things.
dress|er (dres′ər) *noun, plural* **dressers.**

dressing—**1.** A sauce for adding to salads and
other foods: *French or Italian* dressing.   **2.** A
mixture of bread crumbs and seasonings used to
stuff turkey or chicken.   **3.** Medicine or bandages
applied to a wound.
dress|ing (dres′ing) *noun, plural* **dressings.**

drew—*See* **draw.**
drew (drū) *verb.*

dribble—**1.** To flow or fall in small drops: *The
water* dribbled *out of the broken water fountain.*
2. To move a ball by bounces or light kicks:
Basketball players must know how to dribble *the
ball. Verb.*
—**1.** A drip or trickle: *During the summer there
is only a* dribble *of water in the stream.*   **2.** The
act of bouncing or kicking a ball. *She can really*
dribble *a basketball. Noun.*
drib|ble (drib′əl) *verb,* **dribbled, dribbling;**
noun, plural **dribbles.**

dried—*See* **dry.**
dried (drīd) *verb.*

drier—*See* **dry.** *Adjective.*
—A person or thing that dries. *Noun.*
dri|er (drī′ər) *adjective; noun, plural* **driers.**
● This word is also spelled **dryer** when used as a
noun.

dries—*See* **dry.**
dries (drīz) *verb.*

driest—*See* **dry.**
dri|est (drī′ist) *adjective.*

drift—**1.** To float, or to be moved along by a
current of air or water: *Our boat* drifted *out to
sea.*   **2.** To pile or heap up: *The snow* drifted
over our car during the huge storm. Verb.
—Something that has been piled or heaped up: *It
is fun to jump in the* drifts *after it snows. Noun.*
drift (drift) *verb,* **drifted, drifting;** *noun, plural*
drifts.

driftwood—Wood that is carried along by water
or that washes up on the shore.
drift|wood (drift′wood′) *noun.*

drill—**1.** A tool used to make holes in something.
A drill may be electric or turned by hand.
2. Training or practice that is repeated: *a fire
drill. Noun.*
—**1.** To make a hole with a special tool.   **2.** To
train by repeated practice: *to be* drilled *for a
spelling bee. Verb.*
drill (dril) *noun, plural* **drills;** *verb,* **drilled,
drilling.**

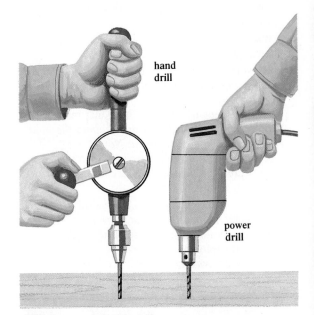

drill (noun, definition 1)

drink—**1.** To swallow a liquid: *I* drink *a glass of
orange juice every morning.*   **2.** To soak up;
absorb: *The towel* drank *up the spilled water.*
3. To swallow an alcoholic beverage. *Verb.*
—**1.** Any liquid for swallowing   **2.** A portion of
such a liquid: *Can I have a* drink *of your soda?*
3. An alcoholic beverage. *Noun.*
drink (dringk) *verb,* **drank, drunk, drinking;**
noun, plural **drinks.**
■ **drink in:** To take in eagerly and happily
through one's senses: *The scenery was so
beautiful that we just* drank *it in as we walked
through the woods.*

drip—To fall or let fall in drops: *The icicles*
dripped *water as they started to melt. She*
dripped *ice cream on the floor. Verb.*
—Fallen drops: *There were* drips *of paint on the
new chair. Noun.*

a at	i if	oo look	ch chalk		a in ago
ā ape	ī idle	ou out	ng sing		e in happen
ah calm	o odd	u ugly	sh ship	ə =	i in capital
aw all	ō oats	ū rule	th think		o in occur
e end	oi oil	ur turn	th their		u in upon
ē easy			zh treasure		

drip (drip) *verb*, **dripped, dripping**; *noun, plural* **drips.**
  • Synonyms: **dribble, trickle**, for *verb*.
    Antonyms: **gush, stream**, for *verb*.
drive—**1.** To operate and steer a vehicle: *to drive a car.* **2.** To cause to feel or go: *My baby brother's crying* drives *me crazy.* **3.** To be carried or go in a vehicle: *Can you* drive *us to school?* **4.** To urge; compel: *Hope for a better life* drove *him to work hard.* **5.** To force, propel, or direct by a hard blow: *to* drive *a nail into wood.* *Verb.*
  —1. A trip in a vehicle; ride: *The fall is a lovely time for a* drive *in the country.* **2.** A short road that leads from a garage or house to the street: *The children left their bicycles in the* drive. **3.** A special effort to do a certain thing: *The school had a* drive *to collect food for the poor.* **4.** A strong, fast hit: *The player's* drive *sent the baseball over the fence.* *Noun.*
  drive (drīv) *verb*, **drove, driven, driving**; *noun, plural* **drives.**
  ■ **drive at:** to mean; intend; suggest: *I was not sure what the speaker was* driving *at.*
  • Synonyms: **force, oblige**, for *verb* **4.**
drive-in—A movie theater, restaurant, bank, or other business that can serve its customers in their cars.
  drive-in (drīv′in′) *noun, plural* **drive-ins.**
driven—*See* **drive.**
  driv|en (driv′ən) *verb.*
driver—A person who operates and steers a vehicle: *a bus* driver; *a taxi* driver.
  driv|er (drī′vər) *noun, plural* **drivers.**
  ■ **in the driver's seat:** In charge; in a position of leadership: *The president of a country is* in the driver's seat.
driveway—A short, private road that leads from a house, garage, or other building to the street.
  drive|way (drīv′wā′) *noun, plural* **driveways.**
drizzle—To rain in light, misty drops: *Even if it is just* drizzling *out, I have to wear a raincoat.* *Verb.*
  —A light, misty rain: *The steady* drizzle *kept people away from the carnival.* *Noun.*
  driz|zle (driz′əl) *verb*, **drizzled, drizzling**; *noun, plural* **drizzles.**
dromedary—A camel with one hump, that is used for riding or carrying loads. Dromedaries are found in India, the Arabian Peninsula, and North Africa.
  drom|e|dar|y (drom′ə der′ē) *noun, plural* **dromedaries.**
  • See picture at **camel.**

Word History

Dromedary comes from a Latin word meaning "runner." This type of camel is known for its speed in walking or running, which is one reason why it is used to move people and things from place to place.

drone¹—A male bee that does not work or sting.
  drone (drōn) *noun, plural* **drones.**

drone¹

drone²—**1.** To make a deep, constant humming sound: *The engine* droned *as it warmed up.* **2.** To speak in a slow, dull way: *The boring man* droned *on endlessly.* *Verb.*
  —A deep, constant humming sound: *We can hear the* drone *of the airplane overhead.* *Noun.*
  drone (drōn) *verb*, **droned, droning**; *noun, plural* **drones.**
drool—To let saliva drip from the mouth: *The baby* drooled *onto the shirt.*
  drool (drül) *verb*, **drooled, drooling.**
droop—To hang or bend down; sag: *The flowers are* drooping *because I forgot to water them.*
  droop (drüp) *verb*, **drooped, drooping.**
drop—**1.** A small amount of liquid that falls in a round shape: *a* drop *of water.* **2.** The act of falling: *The airplane made a sudden* drop *in the storm.* **3.** The distance from which something falls: *There is a* drop *of 50 feet from the roof to the ground.* **4. drops:** liquid medicine given in drops: *eye* drops. *Noun.*
  —1. To fall or cause to fall to a lower position or condition: *to* drop *a mitten; to* drop *a price; to* drop *one's voice to a whisper.* **2.** To stop doing something: *She* dropped *out of the club because she was too old for it.* **3.** To say, give, or do something in a casual way: *to* drop *a hint; to* drop *in for a visit.* **4.** To leave out: *If you* drop *a zero from 100, you get 10.* *Verb.*
  drop (drop) *noun, plural* **drops**; *verb*, **dropped, dropping.**
  ■ **a drop in the bucket:** An extremely small amount: *The money I paid for that toy is just* a

drop in the bucket *compared to what I paid for my bike.*

at the drop of a hat: Right away; immediately upon request: *When I'm in trouble, my girlfriend will help me out* at the drop of a hat.

dropper—A short glass tube with a rubber cap that is squeezed to draw in and release drops of liquid: *The doctor put medicine in the boy's ear with a* dropper.
drop|per (drop′ər) *noun, plural* **droppers.**

drought—A long period of dryness when there is very little or no rain: *The month-long* drought *caused our flowers to die.*
drought (drout) *noun, plural* **droughts.**

drove—*See* **drive.**
drove (drōv) *verb.*

drown—**1.** To die under water from lack of air to breathe: *His brother pulled him from the lake before he* drowned. **2.** To kill by keeping under water or under some other liquid: *Many farm animals were* drowned *in the flood.* **3.** To cover one sound with another, louder sound: *The noise from the lawn mower* drowned *out his voice.*
drown (droun) *verb,* **drowned, drowning.**

drowsy—Sleepy: *She stayed awake all night, so she was* drowsy *the next day.*
drowsy (drou′zē) *adjective,* **drowsier, drowsiest.**

drug—**1.** A nonfood substance that causes a change in the body, usually used to treat or cure a disease; medicine: *The doctor treated the boy's infection with a new* drug. **2.** A harmful substance to which a person can become addicted: *Heroin and cocaine are* drugs *that can kill people. Noun.*
—To give someone or something a substance that causes harm or sleep: *The kidnappers* drugged *the boy to keep him quiet. Verb.*
drug (drug) *noun, plural* **drugs;** *verb,* **drugged, drugging.**

druggist—**1.** A person who owns or runs a store where prescription drugs, cold medicines, cosmetics, and similar items are sold. **2.** A person who has a license to fill prescriptions; pharmacist.
drug|gist (drug′ist) *noun, plural* **druggists.**

a at	i if	oo look	ch chalk		a in ago
ā ape	ī idle	ou out	ng sing		e in happen
ah calm	o odd	u ugly	sh ship	ə =	i in capital
aw all	ō oats	ū rule	th think		o in occur
e end	oi oil	ur turn	th their		u in upon
ē easy			zh treasure		

drugstore—A store where prescription drugs and other medicines are sold. Drugstores also have cosmetics, magazines, greeting cards, and candy.
drug|store (drug′stawr) *noun, plural* **drugstores.**

snare drum   bass drum   oil drum

drum (noun, definitions 1 and 3)

drum—**1.** A hollow musical instrument that makes a deep, loud sound when it is struck. A drum is a rounded container covered on one or both ends with tightly stretched material that is beaten with the hands, sticks, or brushes. **2.** A sound that is like the beating of such an instrument: *He fell asleep to the* drum *of rain hitting the tin roof.* **3.** Anything shaped like such a container: *The truck was loaded with* drums *of oil. Noun.*
—**1.** To play such a musical instrument: *She* drums *in the high school band.* **2.** To make a thumping sound like such an instrument: *I* drummed *my feet on the floor in time with the music.* **3.** To make someone learn something by repeating it over and over: *The army sergeant* drummed *his orders into the soldiers' heads. Verb.*
drum (drum) *noun, plural* **drums;** *verb,* **drummed, drumming.**
■ **drum out of:** To force to leave in disgrace: *The badly behaved child was* drummed out of *the club.*
drum up: To call together, usually by asking again and again: *We tried to* drum up *enough players to have a baseball game.*

drum major—The leader of a marching band.
drum ma|jor (drum mā′jər) *noun, plural* **drum majors.**

drum majorette—A girl or woman who leads a marching band, especially one who twirls a baton.
drum ma|jor|ette (drum mā′jə ret′) *noun, plural* **drum majorettes.**

drummer—A person who plays a drum.
drum|mer (drum′ər) *noun, plural* **drummers.**

drumstick—1. A stick for beating a drum.
2. The cooked lower leg of a chicken, turkey, or other fowl.
drum|stick (drum′stik′) *noun, plural* **drumsticks.**

drunk—Overcome by alcoholic drinks: *They were so* drunk *that they could hardly walk straight. Adjective.*
—A person who drinks too much alcohol: *He played a* drunk *in his latest movie. Noun.*
—*See* **drink.** *Verb.*
drunk (drungk) *adjective,* **drunker, drunkest;** *noun, plural* **drunks;** *verb.*

dry—1. Not moist or wet: *If the soil around the plants is* dry, *then they need to be watered.*
2. Thirsty: *I'm always* dry *after running 40 laps.*
3. Not under or in the water: *After being seasick for ten days, I was glad to be back on* dry *land.*
4. Dull; boring: *Some people think that history is a* dry *subject. Adjective.*
—To make or become free from moisture or wetness: *After our swim, the warm breeze* dried *us. Verb.*
dry (drī) *adjective,* **drier, driest;** *verb,* **dried, drying.**

dry-clean—To clean clothes with a chemical instead of with soap and water.
dry-clean (drī klēn) *verb,* **dry-cleaned, dry-cleaning.**

dryer or **drier**—A machine that uses heat to remove moisture or wetness: *a clothes* dryer.
dry|er or dri|er (drī′ər) *noun, plural* **dryers** or **driers.**

dual—Made up of two; double: *The two girls put forth a* dual *effort.*
du|al (dū′əl) *adjective.*
● A word that sounds the same is **duel.**

duck[1]—1. A wild or tame swimming bird with a broad, flat bill and webbed feet. 2. A female duck. The male is usually called a drake.
duck (duk) *noun, plural* **ducks.**

duck[2]—1. To push someone's head underwater and let it come up quickly: *Children like to* duck *each other when they are playing in a swimming pool.* 2. To lower the head or bend the body quickly to avoid something: *He* ducked *as he walked through the low doorway.*
duck (duk) *verb,* **ducked, ducking.**

duckling—A young duck.
duck|ling (duk′ling) *noun, plural* **ducklings.**

duct—1. A tube or pipe that carries air, liquid, or solid particles: *Fresh cement flowed down the mixer's* duct *to the wheelbarrow.* 2. A channel or tube in the body that carries fluid: *tear* ducts.
duct (dukt) *noun, plural* **ducts.**

due—1. Owed or owing as a debt: *The money for our electric bill is* due *today.* 2. Expected to arrive: *Her flight is* due *in 15 minutes. Adjective.*
—1. A person's right or what is owed to him or her: *We should show our grandparents the respect that is their* due. 2. **dues:** A membership fee: *We belong to the club because we paid our* dues. *Noun.*
—Straight; directly: *The compass pointed* due *east. Adverb.*
due (dū) *adjective; noun, plural* **dues;** *adverb.*
■ **due to:** 1. Caused by: *His headache is* due to *the flu.* 2. Because of: *The house was destroyed* due to *a fire.*
● Words that sound the same are **dew** and **do.**

duel

duel—A formal fight between two people to settle a quarrel. Duels are usually fought with guns or swords in front of witnesses. *Noun.*
—To conduct such a fight: *The knights* dueled *over the fair maiden. Verb.*
du|el (dū′əl) *noun, plural* **duels;** *verb,* **dueled, dueling.**
● A word that sounds the same is **dual.**

duck[1] and **duckling**

duet—1. A piece of music written to be performed by two instruments or two singers. 2. Two players or singers performing together. du|et (dū et′) *noun, plural* **duets.**

dug—*See* **dig.** dug (dug) *verb.*

dull—1. Not having a sharp point; blunt: *The* dull *scissors could not cut the cardboard.* 2. Not clear, definite, or bright: *a* dull *color; a* dull *pain.* 3. Not interesting; boring: *The television program was so* dull *that we turned to another channel.* 4. Slow to learn; stupid: *She had a* dull *mind and was sent back to first grade. Adjective.* —To become or make blunt: *Sawing all the boards for the treehouse* dulled *father's saw. Verb.* dull (dul) *adjective,* **duller, dullest;** *verb,* **dulled, dulling.**

• Synonyms: **dark, dim,** for *adjective* 2. Antonyms: **brilliant, luminous, radiant,** for *adjective* 2.

dumb—1. Lacking the ability to speak: *A rabbit is a* dumb *animal because it does not talk.* 2. Slow to learn or understand: *He felt* dumb *because he could not remember where he left his sneakers.* dumb (dum) *adjective,* **dumber, dumbest.**

dumbbell—A short bar with heavy disks or weights at each end, usually made of metal. Dumbbells are lifted or swung to exercise and strengthen arm muscles. dumb|bell (dum′bel′) *noun, plural* **dumbbells.**

dumbbell

dummy—1. A model of a person that is used to display clothing in a store, to tackle in football practice, to be used by a ventriloquist, and the like. 2. Any copy of something that is real: *That wax apple is a* dummy. dum|my (dum′ē) *noun, plural* **dummies.**

dump—To unload in a heap; let fall or empty out: *We* dumped *the toys on the floor. Verb.* —1. A place for unloading garbage and trash: *the city* dump. 2. A dirty or untidy place: *His old shack is a real* dump. 3. A place for storing military supplies: *an ammunition* dump. *Noun.* dump (dump) *verb,* **dumped, dumping;** *noun, plural* **dumps.**

■ **dump on** (someone): To attack a person with strong words: *The candidate was prepared to* dump on *her opponent if necessary.*

dumpling—1. A small, round mass of dough that is cooked by steaming or boiling. It is usually filled with meat: *chicken* dumplings. 2. A biscuit dough that is baked with a fruit filling and eaten as a dessert. dump|ling (dump′ling) *noun, plural* **dumplings.**

dumps—Sadness; low spirits. dumps (dumps) *plural noun.*

■ **in the dumps:** Sad, gloomy: *He has been* in the dumps *ever since he lost his wallet.*

dumpster—A large bin for trash that can be emptied into or carried by a truck. dump|ster (dump′stər) *noun, plural* **dumpsters.**

dunce—A stupid person or one who is slow to learn. dunce (duns) *noun, plural* **dunces.**

dune—A hill of sand formed by the wind. Dunes are found in the desert or at the beach. dune (dūn *or* dyūn) *noun, plural* **dunes.**

dune buggy—A light vehicle with very large tires, used to drive on beaches and sand dunes. dune bug|gy (dūn bug′ē *or* dyūn bug′ē) *noun, plural* **dune buggies.**

dungarees—Pants, work clothes, or overalls made from a heavy cotton cloth that is called dungaree. dun|ga|rees (dung′gə rēz′ *or* dung′gə rēz) *noun.*

dungeon—A dark underground prison. dun|geon (dun′jən) *noun, plural* **dungeons.**

dunk—1. To dip something into a liquid: *She liked to* dunk *cookies in milk before she ate them.* 2. In basketball, to jump very high and forcefully throw a ball into the basket from above. *Verb.*

—The act of dipping something into a liquid. *Noun.*

dunk (dungk) *verb,* **dunked, dunking,** *noun, plural* **dunks.**

dupe—A person who is easily tricked or deceived. *Noun.*

—To trick or deceive: *The dishonest salesman* duped *many of his customers. Verb.*

dupe (dūp *or* dyūp) *noun, plural* **dupes;** *verb,* **duped, duping.**

duplex—Having two main parts: *a duplex system. Adjective.*

—1. An apartment that has rooms on two floors. 2. A house divided in half for two families to live in. *Noun.*

du|plex (dū′pleks *or* dyū′pleks) *adjective; noun, plural* **duplexes.**

duplicate—Being the same as something else: *He made* duplicate *greeting cards for his two grandmothers. Adjective.*

—Something that is the same as something else: *She returned the gift to the store since it was a* duplicate *of a book she already owned. Noun.*

—To copy something exactly: *She learned the dance by* duplicating *her teacher's steps. Verb.*

du|pli|cate (dū′plə kit *or* dyū′plə kit for *adjective* and *noun;* dū′plə kāt *or* dyū′plə kāt for *verb*) *adjective; noun, plural* **duplicates;** *verb,* **duplicated, duplicating.**

• Synonyms: **copy, replica, reproduction,** for *noun.*

duplication—The act or process of copying or doing something again exactly; duplicating: *If both of us do the same thing, that's useless* duplication *of effort.*

du|pli|ca|tion (dū′plə kā′shən *or* dyū′plə kā′shən) *noun, plural* **duplications.**

durable—Able to be used for a long time without wearing out; lasting: *He bought a* durable *book bag that would last the whole school year.*

du|ra|ble (door′ə bəl *or* dyoor′ə bəl) *adjective.*

duration—The length of time during which something lasts; the entire time: *We enjoyed ourselves for the* duration *of our vacation.*

du|ra|tion (doo rā′shən *or* dyoo rā′shən) *noun, plural* **durations.**

during—1. For the whole time of: *She sat in the front row* during *the movie.* 2. At some time in the course of: *The phone rang* during *supper.*

dur|ing (door′ing *or* dyoor′ing) *preposition.*

dusk—The time of day just after sunset when it begins to grow dark.

dusk (dusk) *noun.*

dusky—1. Dark colored; somewhat dark. 2. Dim; shadowy: *It was hard to see in the* dusky *cellar.*

dusk|y (dus′kē) *adjective,* **duskier, duskiest.**

dust—Tiny particles of dirt, powder, or other material: *We swept* dust *off the floor. Noun.*

—1. To clean away such particles by wiping or brushing: *We* dusted *the furniture with a cloth.* 2. To sprinkle with tiny particles of something: *to* dust *powder on a baby. Verb.*

dust (dust) *noun; verb,* **dusted, dusting.**

■ **bite the dust:** To be killed or wounded: *He heard the shot and saw the soldier* bite the dust.

dust off: To put into use again: *When spring came, he* dusted off *his roller skates and skated down the street.*

gather dust: To be not used or cared for; be ignored: *Her old toys just* gathered dust *after she received new ones for Christmas.*

leave (one) in the dust: To get well ahead of someone or something: *The runner stepped up his pace,* leaving *the others* in the dust.

make the dust fly: To work with great activity and speed: *When she wants to finish a job, she can really* make the dust fly.

dustpan—A flat pan with a handle, used to sweep dust into.

dust|pan (dust′pan) *noun, plural* **dustpans.**

dusty—1. Covered or filled with tiny particles of dirt, powder, or other material: *Father got very* dusty *while cleaning out the basement.* 2. Having the appearance or grayish color of such particles.

dust|y (dus′tē) *adjective,* **dustier, dustiest.**

dutiful—Having or showing a sense of duty; doing what is expected of one; obedient. *He is a* dutiful *boy and does his homework before he watches television.*

du|ti|ful (dū′tə fəl *or* dyú tə fəl) *adjective.*

duty—1. Something that a person should do: *a* duty *to obey the law.* 2. The thing a person does as part of his or her job; responsibility: *A fire fighter's* duties *include putting out fires and saving lives.* 3. A tax paid on goods that are taken out of or brought into a country.

du|ty (dū′tē *or* dyū′tē) *noun, plural* **duties.**

■ **off duty:** Not at one's job or work: *The police officer was* off duty *while he ate his lunch.*

on duty: At one's job or work: *The doctor was* on duty *all night at the emergency room.*

• Synonyms: **chore, task,** for **2.** Antonyms: For **2,** see Synonyms at **amusement.**

dwarf—1. A person, plant, or animal that is much smaller in size than normal.   2. A little person with magical powers who appears in some fairy tales. *Noun.*
—To make something look small as compared with something else: *The elephants* dwarfed *the other animals in the circus.*
dwarf (dwawrf) *noun, plural* **dwarfs** or **dwarves** (dwawrvs); *verb,* **dwarfed, dwarfing.**

Language Fact

Dwarf and **midget** are both used for things and people that are much smaller than others. But when used for people, **dwarf** and **midget** have different meanings. A dwarf is a person with a body of normal size and very short arms and legs. A midget is a person whose body, legs, arms, and head are all much smaller than usual.

---

dwell—To live in; make one's home in: *the animals that* dwell *in the forest.*
dwell (dwel) *verb,* **dwelt** or **dwelled, dwelling.**
■ **dwell on:** To think about for a long time: *Mom told me not to* dwell on *my problem, but to go out and play.*

dwelling—A place to live in; house.
dwell|ing (dwel′ing) *noun, plural* **dwellings.**
● Synonyms: **home, residence**

dwindle—To become smaller; shrink: *When the supply of paper* dwindled, *he bought more.*
dwin|dle (dwin′dəl) *verb,* **dwindled, dwindling.**
● Synonyms: **decrease, diminish, lessen, reduce**

dye—A substance used for coloring or staining something: *a hair* dye; *a fabric* dye. *Noun.*
—To color or stain with such a substance: *We*

dyed *the Easter eggs yellow, blue, and pink. Verb.*
dye (dī) *noun, plural* **dyes;** *verb,* **dyed, dying.**
● A word that sounds the same is **die.**

dyed-in-the-wool—Through and through; complete: *He is a* dyed-in-the-wool *baseball fan.*
dyed-|in-|the-|wool (dīd′in *th*ə wool′) *adjective.*

dying—See **die**[1].
dy|ing (dī′ ing) *verb.*

dynamic—Full of energy, force, or enthusiasm: *The speaker was very* dynamic *and made the audience eager to hear more.*
dy|nam|ic (dī nam′ik) *adjective.*

dynamite—A very strong explosive that is often used for blasting rock. *Noun.*
—To blast or blow up with such an explosive: *The soldiers* dynamited *the enemy's bridge. Verb.*
dy|na|mite (dī′nə mīt) *noun; verb,* **dynamited, dynamiting.**

Word History

Dynamite comes from a Greek word meaning "power." Dynamite is so powerful that it can destroy or shatter some of the largest objects that exist, such as buildings and mountain sides.

---

dynamo—1. A machine that makes electricity; generator.   2. A person who is full of energy and enthusiasm; dynamic: *She is a real* dynamo *when she gets going.*
dy|na|mo (dī′nə mō) *noun, plural,* **dynamos.**

dynasty—A powerful line of rulers from the same family who govern a country, one after another, for a long time: *That* dynasty *was in power for more than 100 years.*
dy|nas|ty (dī′nə stē) *noun, plural* **dynasties.**

dyslexia—A disorder marked by difficulty in reading. A person suffering from dyslexia reverses words and letters, reading *was* for *saw* or *d* for *b* or *p.*
dys|lex|i|a (dis lek′sē ə) *noun.*

dz.—An abbreviation for **dozen** or **dozens.**

a at	i if	oo look	ch chalk		a in ago
ā ape	ī idle	ou out	ng sing		e in happen
ah calm	o odd	u ugly	sh ship	ə =	i in capital
aw all	ō oats	ū rule	th think		o in occur
e end	oi oil	ur turn	th their		u in upon
ē easy			zh treasure		

About 1,900 years ago, the Romans gave the capital E its present form. The small letter e was first used about 1,700 years ago. It reached its present form about 1,500 years ago.

About 5,000 years ago, the ancient Egyptians used a symbol of a person shouting for joy.

About 3,500 years ago, people in the Middle East used a symbol of a person shouting. They called it *he*.

About 3,000 years ago, other people in the Middle East used this form.

About 2,600 years ago, the Greeks gave the letter this form. They called it *epsilon*.

E or **e**—The fifth letter of the alphabet: *There are two* e's *in the word "bee."*
 E, e (ē) *noun, plural* **E's** or **Es, e's** or **es.**

E.—The abbreviation for **east.**

each—Every single one of the group named: *The clown made* each *child smile. Adjective.*
 —Every one, not omitting anyone: Each *of the three men had a beard. Pronoun.*
 —For or to every one: *You may have two cookies* each. *Adverb.*
 each (ēch) *adjective, pronoun, adverb.*
 ▪ **each other:** One another: *The bride and groom danced with* each other *at their wedding.*

eager—Wanting very much; impatient: *I was* eager *to open my birthday presents.*
 ea|ger (ē′gər) *adjective.*
 ▪ **eager beaver:** A very hard-working or enthusiastic person: *We need an* eager beaver *as chairperson of the committee.*

eagle—A large bird that has a hooked beak, powerful wide wings, and very sharp vision. Eagles fly high in the air, and their keen eyesight and strong claws make them good hunters of small animals.
 ea|gle (ē′gəl) *noun, plural* **eagles.**
 ▪ **eagle-eyed:** Having keen eyesight, like an eagle: *The* eagle-eyed *sales clerk saw the thief grab a woman's purse.*

ear¹—**1.** The part of the body with which people and animals hear. **2.** The sense of hearing: *The sound of the dinner bell was music to my* ears.
 ear (ēr) *noun, plural* **ears.**
 ▪ **be all ears:** To listen carefully; pay close

attention: *Tell me the good news, for I* am all ears.
 bend (one's) **ear:** To keep on talking even though no one wants to listen: *He's been* bending *my* ear *all afternoon, and I wish he'd just be quiet.*
 chew (one's) **ear off:** To scold: *The boy* chewed *the dog's* ear off *for barking too much.*
 fall on deaf ears: To be ignored; go unheeded:

eagle

When she tried to borrow money from her friends, her requests *fell on deaf ears*.

go in one ear and out the other: To go through a person's mind without having any effect: *She has told me that story so often that it just* goes in one ear and out the other.

have (one's) **ear to the ground** or **keep** (one's) **ear to the ground:** To pay attention to what is being said in order to act upon it: *Keep your* ear to the ground *at the meeting so you can tell us what was discussed.*

play by ear: To play an instrument without using written music or to do something without preparation: *He played the song on his guitar* by ear *after hearing it only once. Since I have never skated before, I will just have to* play *it* by ear.

up to (one's) **ears:** Deeply involved: *She's* up to *her* ears *in trouble for lying and staying out late.*

wet behind the ears: Lacking experience: *The new boy was* wet behind the ears *and got lost on his newspaper route.*

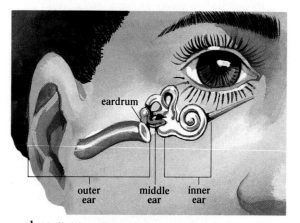
eardrum
outer ear | middle ear | inner ear

ear¹ (definition 1)

ear²—The top part of grain plants, such as wheat or corn, that contains the seeds or kernels.
ear (ēr) *noun, plural* **ears.**
• See picture at **corn.**

earache—A pain in the ear.
ear|ache (ēr′āk′) *noun, plural* **earaches.**

eardrum—A thin layer of tissue inside the ear that receives and sends sound waves.
ear|drum (ēr′drum′) *noun, plural* **eardrums.**
• See picture at **ear.**

early—1. At or near the beginning: *Farmers start to work* early *in the morning.* 2. Before the regular time: *I went to bed* early *last night. Adverb.*
—Before the usual time: *We had an* early *supper so that we could go fishing before it got dark. Adjective.*
ear|ly (ur′lē) *adverb; adjective,* **earlier, earliest.**
■ **early bird:** Someone who does something, arrives, or gets up before others: *My mom calls me an* early bird *because I wake up before the rest of the family.*

earn—1. To receive for work done or services performed; be paid: *I hope to* earn *money by baby-sitting this summer.* 2. To deserve or gain by effort; win: *He* earned *his teacher's praise for his science project.*
earn (urn) *verb,* **earned, earning.**
• A word that sounds the same is **urn.**

earnest—1. Sincere and firm in purpose: *She must be* earnest *about losing weight because she exercises every day.* 2. Without humor; grave: *He is so* earnest, *I think he never smiles.*
ear|nest (ur′nist) *adjective.*
• Synonyms: **serious, solemn,** for 2.
Antonyms: **comical, funny, hilarious,** for 2.

earnings—Money that one has worked for: *My* earnings *from that job were enough to buy a bicycle.*
earn|ings (ur′ningz) *plural noun.*
• Synonyms: **pay, salary, wages**

earring—A piece of jewelry for the ear.
ear|ring (ēr′ring′) *noun, plural* **earrings.**

earth—1. Earth: The planet on which we live. Earth is the third planet from the sun in our solar system. 2. Dry land; the ground: *every creature that walks the* earth. 3. Dirt; soil: *There are many minerals in the* earth.
earth (urth) *noun, plural* **earths.**
■ **down to earth:** Realistic; using common sense: *She's always* down to earth, *and therefore she comes up with practical ideas.*
• See picture at **solar system.**

earthquake—A sudden shaking of the ground, caused by the shifting of a great mass of rock deep below the surface of the earth.
earth|quake (urth′kwāk′) *noun, plural* **earthquakes.**

a at	i if	oo look	ch chalk		a in ago
ā ape	ī idle	ou out	ng sing		e in happen
ah calm	o odd	u ugly	sh ship	ə =	i in capital
aw all	ō oats	ū rule	th think		o in occur
e end	oi oil	ur turn	th their		u in upon
ē easy			zh treasure		

earthworm—A long, thin worm that lives in the soil.
earth|worm (urth′wurm′) *noun, plural* **earthworms.**

ease—1. Comfort; freedom from hard work: *The young princess lived a life of* ease *in the castle.* 2. Freedom from effort or difficulty: *the ease with which a ballerina dances. Noun.*
—1. To free from pain, trouble, or worry; make comfortable: *A hot bath will* ease *your sore muscles.* 2. To move slowly and carefully: *He* eased *the heavy box onto the floor. Verb.*
ease (ēz) *noun; verb,* **eased, easing.**
■ **ease off** or **ease up:** To slow down; lessen: *She ducked into a doorway until the rain* eased off.
ill at ease: Not comfortable: *I was* ill at ease *in my new school at first.*

easel—A frame that stands upright to hold an artist's painting, chalkboard, or the like.
ea|sel (ē′zəl) *noun, plural* **easels.**

easel

Word History

Easel comes from a Latin word for a donkey or other beast of burden. Like a donkey, an easel holds heavy objects that would be a burden for people to hold themselves.

easily—1. Without effort or trouble: *A race horse can* easily *run a mile.* 2. Without any doubt; by far: *You are* easily *the best speller in the class.* 3. Very likely: *We could* easily *get lost in these woods at night.*
eas|i|ly (ē′zə lē) *adverb.*

east—1. The direction in which one faces to see the sun rise; the opposite of west. 2. **East:** The part of any country that is in the east. 3. **the East:** The part of the United States that is along the coast of the Atlantic Ocean: *Maine is in* the East. 4. **the East:** The eastern part of the world, including Asia and its nearby islands: *Japan is in* the East. *Noun.*
—1. Located toward or in the east: *the east side of the house; the east coast.* 2. Coming from the east: *an east wind. Adjective.*
—Toward the east: *Walk two blocks* east. *Adverb.*
east or **East** (ēst) *noun, adjective, adverb.* Abbreviation: **E.**

Easter—A Christian celebration of the day on which Christ rose from the dead. Easter comes on a different Sunday each year between March 22 and April 25.
East|er (ēs′tər) *noun, plural* **Easters.**

eastern—1. Toward the direction in which the sun rises; toward the east: *This window has an* eastern *view.* 2. From or in the east: *an* eastern *way of talking; an* eastern *city.* 3. **Eastern:** Of, in, or from the part of the United States that lies along the Atlantic Ocean. 4. **Eastern:** Of, in, or from the part of the world that includes Asia and its nearby islands.
east|ern or **East|ern** (ēs′tərn) *adjective.*

Eastern Orthodox Churches—A group of churches that follow Christian beliefs but which differs from Roman Catholic and Protestant churches on certain subjects. This group includes the Greek Orthodox Church and the Russian Orthodox Church.
East|ern Or|tho|dox Church|es (ēs′tərn awr′thə doks chur′chəz) *plural noun.*

eastward—Toward the direction in which the sun rises; toward the east: *Lava ran down the* eastward *side of the volcano. Our living room faces* eastward.
east|ward (ēst′wərd) *adjective; adverb.*

easy—1. Not difficult; needing very little work or effort: *Flying a kite is* easy. 2. Free from pain, trouble, or worry: *He had an* easy *recovery from his operation.* 3. Not strict: *an* easy *teacher; an* easy *boss.*
eas|y (ē′zē) *adjective,* **easier, easiest.**
■ **easier said than done:** Seeming to be simple but extremely hard or impossible to do: *Passing the test if you haven't studied is* easier said than done.
easy as pie: Very simple: *Printing my name is as* easy as pie.

easy come, easy go: Something that is easy to get may be just as easy to spend or lose: *I found $1 on the sidewalk and spent it all on candy; oh, well,* easy come, easy go.

easy does it: Be careful: *This icy path is very slippery, so* easy does it.

go easy on: Be gentle with; don't punish: Go easy on *her, for she didn't mean to spill the paint.*

take it easy: To put out very little effort; rest: *It is wise to* take it easy *after an operation.*

eat—1. To take in as food: *Mashed potatoes are easy to eat.* 2. To have a meal: *We eat breakfast in the kitchen.* 3. To wear away; consume: *Rust eats through metal.*
eat (ēt) *verb,* **ate, eaten, eating.**
▪ **eat (one's) heart out:** To feel deep sorrow or longing: *That man is* eating *his* heart out *over the job he lost.*

eat (one's) words: To take back what one has said: *I told everyone that yesterday would be sunny and had to* eat *my* words *when it rained.*

eat out: To eat at a restaurant; to eat away from home: *It's too hot to cook tonight, so let's* eat out.

eat out of (one's) hand: To follow someone else's wishes: *He didn't want to do her work, but now she's got him* eating out of *her* hand.

eat up: 1. To use up completely: *The cost of the movie and a hamburger* ate up *all my allowance.* 2. To enjoy very much: *She* eats up *mystery novels.*

eaves—The part of a roof that hangs out from the walls of a building: *Birds often build nests under the* eaves *of our house.*
eaves (ēvz) *noun, singular* **eave.**

eaves

eaves

a at	i if	oo look	ch chalk		a in ago
ā ape	ī idle	ou out	ng sing		e in happen
ah calm	o odd	u ugly	sh ship	ə =	i in capital
aw all	ō oats	ū rule	th think		o in occur
e end	oi oil	ur turn	th their		u in upon
ē easy			zh treasure		

eavesdrop—To listen to a conversation that one is not supposed to hear: *He learned about their plan by hiding behind a tree and* eavesdropping *on them.*
eaves|drop (ēvz′drop′) *verb,* **eavesdropped, eavesdropping.**

Word History

Eavesdrop comes from an Old English word meaning "the dripping of rain water from eaves." A person who eavesdrops is like someone standing under the eaves, close to a wall, in order to hear what is said inside.

---

ebb—The flowing of the ocean's tide away from the shore: *We dug for clams during the tide's* ebb. *Noun.*
—1. To flow out; go back: *After the water had* ebbed, *the boat sat on dry land.* 2. To grow weaker; lessen: *As daylight* ebbed, *it became hard for us to see. Verb.*
ebb (eb) *noun, plural* **ebbs;** *verb,* **ebbed, ebbing.**
▪ **ebb and flow:** Changing patterns or circumstances: *the* ebb and flow *of a busy day.*

ebony—A hard, black wood that comes from a tropical tree. It is used to make black piano keys and some types of furniture.
eb|on|y (eb′ə nē) *noun, plural* **ebonies.**

eccentric—Odd in behavior or appearance: *That woman is* eccentric *because she has 20 cats.*
ec|cen|tric (ek sen′trik) *adjective.*

echo—A repeating of a sound. An echo is caused by sound waves bouncing off an object and returning to their source: *We heard* echoes *in the cave when we talked. Noun.*
—1. To be heard again: *His voice* echoed *down the hallway.* 2. To repeat; send back a sound: *The canyon* echoed *the horses' hoofbeats. Verb.*
ech|o (ek′ō) *noun, plural* **echoes;** *verb,* **echoed, echoing.**

eclipse—A blocking of light from the sun or the moon. In a solar eclipse, the moon passes between the earth and the sun, blocking all or some light from the sun. In a lunar eclipse, the earth passes between the moon and the sun, blocking all or some of the light the moon usually reflects from the sun.
e|clipse (i klips′) *noun, plural* **eclipses.**

ecology—The study of how plants and animals relate to each other and to their environment. Ecology is part of the science of biology.
e|col|o|gy (ē kol′ə jē) *noun, plural* **ecologies.**

economic—Having to do with the making and use of goods and services: *Making and selling lots of products can lead to* economic *wealth.*
e|co|nom|ic (ē′kə **nom**′ik *or* ek′ə **nom**′ik) *adjective.*

economical—Making the best possible use of something so as not to waste anything; *The* economical *student used both sides of the paper.*
e|co|nom|i|cal (ē′kə **nom**′ə kəl *or* ek′ə **nom**′ə kəl) *adjective.*

economics—The science that deals with how goods, services, and money are made, distributed, and used by people.
e|co|nom|ics (ē′kə **nom**′iks *or* ek′ə **nom**′iks) *plural noun.*

economize—**1.** To use only what is needed so as not to waste anything: *We bought a smaller car in order to* economize *on gasoline.* **2.** To lower one's spending; not waste money: *Unless you* economize, *your allowance will soon be gone.*
e|con|o|mize (i **kon**′ə mīz) *verb,* **economized, economizing.**

economy—**1.** Making the best use of money and goods so as not to waste anything; thrift: *My mother practices* economy *by never buying anything she doesn't need.* **2.** The way in which a country handles the production, delivery, and use of its money and goods: *The United States has a good* economy, *but poor countries do not.*
e|con|o|my (i **kon**′ə mē) *noun, plural* **economies.**

ecosystem—All of the plants and animals as well as nonliving things such as climate, soil, and water, in a particular place. A pond, forest, or ocean can be an ecosystem.
e|co|sys|tem (ek′ō sis′təm *or* ē′kō sis′təm) *noun, plural* **ecosystems.**

ecstasy—A strong feeling of joy; extreme happiness: *We were overcome with* ecstasy *after winning the game in the final second.*
ec|sta|sy (**eks**′tə sē) *noun, plural* **ecstasies.**

-ed—A suffix added to verbs to show that the action took place in the past. *I talk*ed *to her yesterday. We have talk*ed *before. They had talk*ed *to me a month ago.*

Word Power

You can understand the meanings of many words that end with **-ed**, if you add the meaning of the suffix to the meaning of the rest of the word.
washed, have washed, or had washed: made clean
dropped, have dropped, or had dropped: let fall

---

ed.—The abbreviation for **edition** and **editor.**

edge—**1.** The line or place where something ends; border: *She sat on the* edge *of her chair.* **2.** The cutting side of a blade: *razor's* edge. *Noun.*
—**1.** To form a border on: *Ice* edged *the pond.*
2. To move very slowly, bit by bit: *He* edged *his car into the heavy traffic. Verb.*
edge (ej) *noun, plural* **edges;** *verb,* **edged, edging.**
■ **on edge:** Tense; anxious; nervous: *We were all* on edge *waiting for the contest's results.*
take the edge off: To lessen the force or enjoyment of: *Eating a sandwich before dinner* took the edge off *my appetite.*

edible—Safe to eat; able to be eaten: *Are these mushrooms the* edible *kind?*
ed|i|ble (**ed**′ə bəl) *adjective.*

edit—**1.** To prepare written material for publication: *Your story is too long, but the newspaper will* edit *it to the right length.* **2.** To be in charge of a newspaper or magazine and decide what will be printed in it: *I hope to* edit *our class yearbook.* **3.** To put film or tape recordings into final form: *She* edited *two scenes out of the movie.*
ed|it (**ed**′it) *verb,* **edited, editing.**

edition—**1.** The form in which a text is published: *a new* edition *of an encyclopedia.* **2.** One of many copies of the same book, magazine, or newspaper: *I own the first* edition *of that book.*
e|di|tion (i **dish**′ən) *noun, plural* **editions.**
Abbreviation: **ed.**

editor—**1.** A person who runs a newspaper or magazine and decides what will be printed in it: *I sent my article on the baseball game to the* editor *of the newspaper.* **2.** A person in charge of a

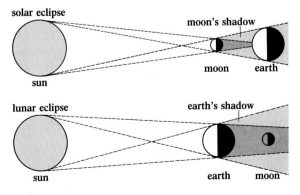

solar eclipse
moon's shadow
sun
moon earth

lunar eclipse
earth's shadow
sun
earth moon

eclipse

department of a newspaper, magazine, or book publisher: *the sports* editor.   **3.** A person who prepares written material for publication.   **4.** A person who puts film or tape recordings into final form.
ed|i|tor (ed′ə tər) *noun, plural* **editors.**
Abbreviation: **ed.**

editorial—**1.** An article in a newspaper or magazine stating the opinion of the editor or publisher on a certain subject.   **2.** A television or radio broadcast stating the opinion of the management of the station. *Noun.*
—Having to do with an editor or an editorial: *Putting the mayor's picture on the front page was an* editorial *decision. Adjective.*
ed|i|to|ri|al (ed′ə tawr′ē əl) *noun, plural* **editorials;** *adjective.*

educate—**1.** To teach: *A police officer came to school to* educate *us about bicycle safety.*   **2.** To provide with schooling: *He was* educated *at the state university.*
ed|u|cate (ej′oo kāt) *verb,* **educated, educating.**

education—**1.** The act of gaining knowledge from study: *She went back to college to finish her* education.   **2.** The knowledge gained from study: *His* education *prepared him to be a lawyer.*
ed|u|ca|tion (ej′oo kā′shən) *noun, plural* **educations.**

educational—**1.** Having to do with the gaining of knowledge through study: *Our town has a fine* educational *system.*   **2.** Providing a way of learning: educational *toys;* educational *television.*
ed|u|ca|tion|al (ej′oo kā′shə nəl) *adjective.*

eel—A snakelike fish that lives in fresh or salt water.
eel (ēl) *noun, plural* **eels.**

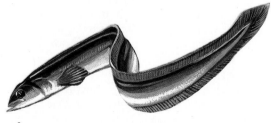

eel

a at	i if	oo look	ch chalk		
ā ape	ī idle	ou out	ng sing		a in ago
ah calm	o odd	u ugly	sh ship	ə =	e in happen
aw all	ō oats	ū rule	th think		i in capital
e end	oi oil	ur turn	th their		o in occur
ē easy			zh treasure		u in upon

eerie—Strange and frightening; weird: *Eerie noises came from the haunted house.*
ee|rie (ēr′ē) *adjective,* **eerier, eeriest.**

effect—**1.** Something that is caused by someone or something; result: *One* effect *of the bus drivers' strike is that more people walk to work.*   **2.** The power to bring something about: *The alarm clock had no* effect *on the sleeper. Noun.*
—To bring about; cause: *The new owner* effected *many changes at the factory. Verb.*
ef|fect (ə fekt′) *noun, plural* **effects;** *verb,* **effected, effecting.**
● Words that sound the same are **affect**[1] and **affect**[2].
● See Language Fact at **affect**[1].
● Synonyms: **consequence, outcome,** for *noun.*

effective—Able to cause something or bring something about: *She is very* effective *in getting what she wants.*
ef|fec|tive (ə fek′tive) *adjective.*

efficiency—The ability to get results without wasting time or energy: *He worked with such* efficiency *that he finished early.*
ef|fi|cien|cy (ə fish′ən sē) *noun, plural* **efficiencies.**

efficient—Able to get something done without wasting time or energy: *An* efficient *worker can do things quickly and well.*
ef|fi|cient (ə fish′ənt) *adjective.*

effort—**1.** Energy or strength: *Shoveling the snow after the blizzard took much* effort.   **2.** A hard try; sincere attempt: *an* effort *to be friendly.*
ef|fort (ef′ərt) *noun, plural* **efforts.**

egg[1]—**1.** A round or oval mass from which young animals hatch. Birds, fish, reptiles, and insects lay eggs to reproduce.   **2.** The contents of such a mass, usually laid by a hen and eaten as food: *I had* eggs *for breakfast.*   **3.** A cell produced by female humans and other mammals to create new life when it joins with a male cell.
egg (eg) *noun, plural* **eggs.**
■ **egg on** (one's) **face:** Shame; embarrassment: *She entered the room with* egg on *her face because everyone knew about her mistake.*

have all (one's) **eggs in one basket** or **put all** (one's) **eggs in one basket:** To risk all that a person has on one chance to do or get something: *She put all her eggs in one basket by quitting her job in case she was elected mayor.*

lay an egg: To fail completely: *The comedian tried to make the audience laugh, but he laid an egg.*

walk on eggs: To be in a situation where one must act very carefully: *We had to walk on eggs to keep him from losing his temper.*

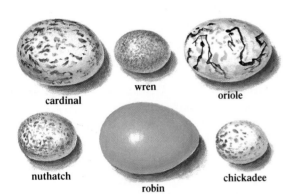

cardinal

wren

oriole

nuthatch

robin

chickadee

egg¹: Birds' eggs come in all sizes and colors.

egg²—To urge; encourage: *I did not think I could finish the race, but the crowd kept egging me on.*
egg (eg) *verb,* **egged, egging.**

eggplant

eggplant—A large, shiny purple vegetable that is shaped somewhat like an egg.
egg|plant (eg′plant′) *noun, plural* **eggplants.**

eight—A number that is one more than seven; 8.
eight (āt) *adjective; noun, plural* **eights.**

■ **behind the eight ball:** In trouble: *My neighbor is* behind the eight ball *for wrecking her father's car.*

● A word that sounds the same is **ate.**

eighteen—A number that is eight more than ten; 18.
eight|een (ā′tēn′) *adjective; noun, plural* **eighteens.**

eighteenth—1. Next after the seventeenth. 2. One of eighteen equal parts.
eight|eenth (ā′tēnth′) *adjective; noun, plural* **eighteenths.**

eighth—1. Next after the seventh. 2. One of eight equal parts.
eighth (ātth) *adjective; noun, plural* **eighths.**

eightieth—1. Next after the seventy-ninth. 2. One of eighty equal parts.
eight|i|eth (ā′tē ith) *adjective; noun, plural* **eightieths.**

eighty—Eight times ten; one more than seventy-nine; 80.
eight|y (ā′tē) *adjective; noun, plural* **eighties.**

either—1. Being the one or the other of two: *Hop on* either *foot.* Either *take it with you, or leave it here.* 2. Each of two: *Bushes grew on* either *side of the path.* Either *of the roads will take you into town. Adjective. Pronoun. Conjunction.*
—Also; too: *If I do not eat carrots, my little brother will not eat them* either. *Adverb.*
ei|ther (ē′th̲ər or i′th̲ər) *adjective, pronoun, conjunction, adverb.*

eject—1. To throw out with great force: *The cannon* ejected *the cannon ball with a loud boom.* 2. To drive out; force out: *The player was* ejected *from the football game for fighting.*
e|ject (i jekt′) *verb,* **ejected, ejecting.**

elaborate—Planned or done with great care or detail: *The wallpaper had an* elaborate *design. Adjective.*
—To add more details; plan or work out with great care: *to* elaborate *on an answer; to* elaborate *a new design. Verb.*

e|lab|o|rate (i **lab′**ər it for *adjective;* i **lab′**ə rāt′ for *verb*) *adjective; verb,* **elaborated, elaborating.**

elapse—To slip or go by; pass: *Ten minutes have* elapsed *since I asked you to do your work.*
e|lapse (i **laps′**) *verb,* **elapsed, elapsing.**

elastic—Can come back to normal shape and size after being stretched, expanded, or pressed together: *When rubber bands are this* elastic, *they have to be new. Adjective.*
—A tape, cord, or fabric that will return to its normal shape after being stretched: *My socks have* elastic *around the tops. Noun.*
e|las|tic (i **las′**tik) *adjective; noun, plural* **elastics.**

elbow—1. The bend of the arm, where the bones of the upper and lower arm come together.
2. Any bend or corner shaped like an arm bent at the joint: *The town is located at the* elbow *of the river. Noun.*
—To push or bump with the point at which one's arm bends: *He* elbowed *his way through the crowd. Verb.*
el|bow (el′bō) *noun, plural* **elbows;** *verb,* **elbowed, elbowing.**

■ **elbow grease:** Hard work: *After four hours and plenty of* elbow grease, *we had all the leaves raked.*
elbowroom: Enough room in which to move or work: *Give me some* elbowroom, *and I will show you how to do a cartwheel.*
rub elbows with: To know well; be friendly with: *The man who was once poor now* rubs elbows with *the city's richest people.*
up to (one's) **elbow:** Having a lot to do; busy: *She's* up to *her* elbows *in community activities.*

elder—Older; more aged: *My* elder *sister is three grades ahead of me in school. Adjective.*
—A person of greater age: *She is always polite to her* elders. *Noun.*
el|der (el′dər) *adjective; noun, plural* **elders.**

elderly—In the later years of one's life; past middle age: *He gave his seat on the bus to an* elderly *woman.*
eld|er|ly (el′dər lē) *adjective.*
● See Language Fact at **old.**

eldest—Oldest child in a family or person in a group: *I am the* eldest *of four brothers.*
eld|est (el′dist) *adjective.*

elect—1. To fill an office by voting: *We* elect *class officers in the fall.*   2. To choose; select; pick: *He* elected *to stay home while the rest of his family went for a walk.*
e|lect (i **lekt′**) *verb,* **elected, electing.**

election—The filling of an office by voting: *The* election *of this city's mayor is next week.*
e|lec|tion (i **lek′**shən) *noun, plural* **elections.**

electric—Relating to or getting power from electricity; electrical: *an* electric *cord; an* electric *guitar.*
e|lec|tric (i **lek′**trik) *adjective.*

electrical—Relating to or getting power from electricity; electric: *an* electrical *storm with thunder and lightning; an* electrical *outlet.*
e|lec|tri|cal (i **lek′**trə kəl) *adjective.*

electrician—A person who installs or fixes electrical equipment.
e|lec|tri|cian (i lek′**trish′**ən *or* ē′lek **trish′**ən) *noun, plural* **electricians.**

electricity—1. A popular form of energy throughout the world. It happens freely in nature, but people now can also produce it in generators. It is used to run motors and provide light and heat for homes, offices, schools, and factories.
2. Electric current: *The* electricity *was turned on after we moved into our new house.*
e|lec|tric|i|ty (i lek′**tris′**ə tē *or* ē′lek **tris′**ə tē) *noun.*

electrocute—To end life by using a powerful electric current.
e|lec|tro|cute (i **lek′**trə kyūt′) *verb,* **electrocuted, electrocuting.**

electromagnet—A piece of iron enclosed in a coil of wire. When an electric current passes through the wire, the iron turns magnetic.
e|lec|tro|mag|net (i lek′trō **mag′**nit) *noun, plural* **electromagnets.**

a at	i if	oo look	ch chalk		a in ago
ā ape	ī idle	ou out	ng sing		e in happen
ah calm	o odd	u ugly	sh ship	ə =	i in capital
aw all	ō oats	ū rule	th think		o in occur
e end	oi oil	ur turn	th their		u in upon
ē easy			zh treasure		

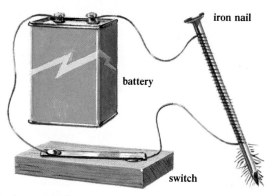

iron nail
battery
switch

electromagnet

electron—A tiny particle that carries a negative electrical charge. Every atom has one or more electrons around its center, or nucleus. The movement of many electrons produces an electric current.
e|lec|tron (i lek′tron) *noun, plural* **electrons.**

electronic—Having to do with electrons or electronics.
e|lec|tron|ic (i lek′tron′ik *or* ē′lek tron′ik) *adjective.*

electronics—The study of electrons in motion and how they work. It is a branch of the science of physics. Work in this field has helped develop many modern inventions such as television and computers.
e|lec|tron|ics (i lek′tron′iks *or* ē′lek tron′iks) *noun.*

elegance—Grace and beauty in a person's behavior and appearance: *Everyone admired her* elegance *as she stepped onto the stage and bowed to the audience.*
el|e|gance (el′ə gəns) *noun.*

elegant—In good taste, luxurious, and of the finest quality: *Everyone admired her* elegant *jewelry.*
el|e|gant (el′ə gənt) *adjective.*

element—1. One of more than 100 materials from which everything in the universe is made. It cannot be divided by chemicals into simpler parts. Gold, iron, oxygen, and hydrogen are examples of elements. 2. One of the basic parts that make up something: *Beautiful scenery and plenty of food are the* elements *of a good picnic.* 3. An environment that suits one's nature; habitat: *The Antarctic is a penguin's* element.
el|e|ment (el′ə mənt) *noun, plural* **elements.**
■ **the elements:** The forces that make up the weather, such as wind, rain, and snow: *My bicycle rusted because I left it outdoors unprotected from* the elements.

elementary—Having to do with the first, most simple steps or beginnings of something; basic: *This is an* elementary *class for someone who's never played tennis.*
el|e|men|ta|ry (el′ə men′tər ē *or* el′ə men′trē) *adjective.*

elephant—A huge mammal; the largest land animal now on earth. It has gray, wrinkled, nearly hairless skin, a long snout called a trunk, and two long, curved, pointed ivory teeth called tusks. Elephants live in Asia and Africa.
el|e|phant (el′ə fənt) *noun, plural* **elephants** *or* **elephant.**

Asian elephant

African elephant

elephant

Word History

Elephant comes from a Greek word that was formed from two other words. One meant "a beast with antlers" and the other word meant "ivory." The elephant's "antlers" are made of ivory, but they are called tusks today.

elevate—To raise up: *He* elevated *the car with a jack in order to change the tire.*
el|e|vate (el′ə vāt) *verb,* **elevated, elevating.**

elevation—1. A place at a higher level than the area around or near it: *We climbed to the top of a steep* elevation *to look at the view.* 2. The height of something above the earth's surface or above sea level: *The crest of these mountains has an* elevation *of more than 5,000 feet (1,525 meters).* 3. The act of moving up or being raised: *The dancer's leaps increased in* elevation *as he moved across the stage.*
el|e|va|tion (el′ə vā′shən) *noun, plural* **elevations.**

elevator—1. A cage or platform in a building that moves people and things from one level or floor to another: *We took the* elevator *to the top of the building.* 2. A building where grain such as corn is kept.
el|e|va|tor (el′ə vā′tər) *noun, plural* **elevators.**

Word History

Eleven comes from an old English word meaning "one left." In early times people with no education counted things on their fingers. When someone had one more thing left after using all ten fingers, this word was used for the total number of things being counted, ten plus "one left" over.

eleven—A number that is one more than ten; 11.
e|lev|en (i lev′ən) *adjective; noun, plural* **elevens.**

eleventh—**1.** Following right after tenth. **2.** One of eleven equal parts.
e|lev|enth (i lev′ənth) *adjective; noun, plural* **elevenths.**

elf—A tiny, mischievous fairy who looks like a human being and is said to have magical powers.
elf (elf) *noun, plural* **elves.**

elf

eligible—Fit or qualified to be chosen for something: *You must pass the test to be* eligible *for a driver's license.*
el|i|gi|ble (el′ə jə bəl) *adjective.*

eliminate—**1.** To do away with; remove: *Her advice may not* eliminate *the problem, but it makes me feel better.* **2.** To not include; omit: *To save time, we will* eliminate *roll call.*

a at	i if	oo look	ch chalk		a in ago
ā ape	ī idle	ou out	ng sing		e in happen
ah calm	o odd	u ugly	sh ship	ə =	i in capital
aw all	ō oats	ū rule	th think		o in occur
e end	oi oil	ur turn	<u>th</u> their		u in upon
ē easy			zh treasure		

e|lim|i|nate (i lim′ə nāt′) *verb,* **eliminated, eliminating.**

elite—The best or most distinguished people: *All of the* elite *in town were at the dance. Noun.*
—Best or most distinguished: *An* elite *group of teachers went to the meeting. Adjective.*
e|lite (i lēt′ *or* ā lēt′) *noun, plural* **elite;** *adjective.*

elk—A large North American deer . It has a reddish color and has long, thin antlers.
elk (elk) *noun, plural* **elks** *or* **elk.**

elk

Word History

Elk is thought to come from old Norwegian and English words and before that from a Greek word meaning "deer." Until about 600 years ago, all game animals were known as deer.

ellipse—A curved shape that looks like a circle that has been flattened; oval.
el|lipse (i lips′) *noun, plural* **ellipses.**

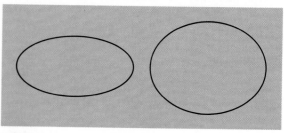

ellipse

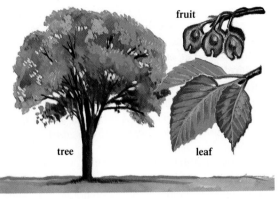

fruit

tree

leaf

elm

elm—A tall shade tree. Its wood is very hard.
elm (elm) *noun, plural* **elms.**

elope—To run away to get married secretly.
e|lope (i lōp′) *verb,* **eloped, eloping.**

eloquent—Having the ability to express oneself
clearly and forcefully: *The president is an
eloquent speaker.*
el|o|quent (el′ə kwənt) *adjective.*

else—**1.** Of another kind; different: *Is there
anything* else *to eat?* **2.** Further; more; in
addition: *Do you have anything* else *to say?*
Adjective.
—Under other circumstances; otherwise: *Be
quiet, or* else *you will wake my father. Adverb.*
else (els) *adjective, adverb.*

elsewhere—In another place: *That store has run
out of batteries, so we had better look* elsewhere.
else|where (els′hwār) *adverb.*

elude—To avoid or slip away from cleverly;
evade: *Cats* elude *dogs by climbing trees.*
e|lude (i lūd′) *verb,* **eluded, eluding.**

elves—*See* **elf.**
elves (elvz) *plural noun.*

em-—A prefix that takes the place of **en-** before
b, p, and sometimes *m.*
● See **en-.**

emancipate—To free from any kind of unfair
control: *President Lincoln* emancipated *black
people from slavery in this country.*
e|man|ci|pate (i man′sə pāt) *verb,*
emancipated, emancipating.

embalm—To use chemicals or spices as a
treatment to reduce decay in a dead body. This
procedure prepares the body for burial.
em|balm (em bahm′ *or* em bahlm′) *verb,*
embalmed, embalming.

embankment—A large bank of earth, stones, or
other material used to hold back water or raise a
road.
em|bank|ment (em bangk′mənt) *noun, plural*
embankments.

embargo—A law preventing ships from entering
or leaving a port for some period of time: *The
president called for an* embargo *of the enemy's
harbors during the war.*
em|bar|go (em bahr′gō) *noun, plural*
embargoes.

embark—**1.** To go on or board a ship or an
airplane as a passenger: *We* embarked *on the
plane just five minutes before it took off.* **2.** To
set off on: *She* embarked *on a new job.*
em|bark (em bahrk′) *verb,* **embarked,
embarking.**

embarrass—To cause another to feel shy, not at
ease, and somewhat ashamed: *My bad grade*
embarrassed *me.*
em|bar|rass (em bar′əs) *verb,* **embarrassed,
embarrassing.**
● Synonyms: **humble, humiliate, shame**
  Antonym: **honor**

embarrassment—The act or condition of
feeling shy, uncomfortable, and ashamed: *The
dog's behavior was an* embarrassment *to the
family.*
em|bar|rass|ment (em bar′əs mənt) *noun,
plural* **embarrassments.**

embassy—The offices and home of an
ambassador in the foreign country to which he or
she has been assigned.
em|bas|sy (em′bə sē) *noun, plural* **embassies.**

embed—**1.** To fix firmly in surrounding material:
My father embedded *the flagpole in concrete.*
2. To fix firmly in the mind: *Every word of the
poem is* embedded *in my mind.*
em|bed (em bed′) *verb,* **embedded, embedding.**

ember—A glowing bit of wood or other material
that remains after a fire has died down: *He stared
into the fireplace long after the fire had turned to*
embers.
em|ber (em′bər) *noun, plural* **embers.**
● Synonyms: **cinder, coal**

embezzle—To take or use for one's own benefit
money belonging to another that has been placed
in one's care: *The banker was sentenced to
prison because she had* embezzled *money.*
em|bez|zle (em bez′əl) *verb,* **embezzled,
embezzling.**

emblem: the emblem of the Olympic Games

emblem—A symbol or picture that stands for something else: *A heart on a Valentine's Day card is an* emblem *of love.*
em|blem (em′bləm) *noun, plural* **emblems.**

embrace—To throw one's arms around; hold to show love or affection; hug: *Dad* embraced *me when I started crying. Verb.*
—A folding of one's arms around another; hug: *A tight* embrace *will frighten the kitten. Noun.*
em|brace (em brās′) *verb,* **embraced, embracing;** *noun, plural* **embraces.**

embroider—1. To sew designs on cloth with a needle and thread: *I embroidered my initials on the sweater.* 2. To make up parts of a story as one tells it; add details that are not true: *She embroidered her report of the game to make it more exciting.*
em|broi|der (em broi′dər) *verb,* **embroidered, embroidering.**

embroidery—1. The act of sewing designs on cloth: *My friend enjoys* embroidery *as a hobby.* 2. A design on cloth that is made with a needle and thread.
em|broi|der|y (em broi′dər ē) *noun, plural* **embroideries.**

embryo—An animal or plant at the beginning of its development before it is born or before it sprouts. A plant inside a seed and a bird in an egg are two examples of embryos.
em|bry|o (em′brē ō) *noun, plural* **embryos.**

emerald—1. A rare and valuable stone that is used in expensive jewelry. Its rich, bright-green color makes this stone distinctive. It is the birthstone of people who are born in the month of May. 2. A rich, bright-green color. *Noun.*
—Having a rich, bright-green color. *Adjective.*
em|er|ald (em′ər əld *or* em′rəld) *noun, plural* **emeralds;** *adjective.*

emerge—To arise or appear; come into sight: *Legend says that the ground hog* emerges *from its hole every February. After I had known him for a while, his true personality began to emerge.*
e|merge (i murj′) *verb,* **emerged, emerging.**

emergency—A serious situation that arises suddenly and demands a fast response: *The police officers came immediately when we said that it was an* emergency. *Noun.*
—Having to do with a serious situation that arises suddenly and demands a fast response: *an* emergency *plan. Adjective.*
e|mer|gen|cy (i mur′jən sē) *noun, plural* **emergencies;** *adjective.*

emigrant—A person who goes away from his or her home in one country to make a new home in another country.
em|i|grant (em′ə grənt) *noun, plural* **emigrants.**

emigrate—To go away from one's home in a certain country to make a new home in another country: *Many families who* emigrated *from Sweden came to the United States.*
em|i|grate (em′ə grāt) *verb,* **emigrated, emigrating.**

Language Fact

Emigrate is a word having a meaning close to the meaning of **immigrate**. But **emigrate** is to move out of a country, and **immigrate** is to move into a country. You would emigrate from the United States or Canada if you moved from your home here to another country. You would immigrate to the United States or Canada if you came here to settle from another country.

---

emit—To give off or throw out: *The lamp* emitted *a soft light.*
e|mit (i mit′) *verb,* **emitted, emitting.**

emotion—Any intense or strong feeling that one has. Love, hate, anger, and sadness are emotions. *He showed his* emotion *when he cried at the funeral.*
e|mo|tion (i mō′shən) *noun, plural* **emotions.**

emotional—1. Having to do with an intense or strong feeling like love or anger: *Some people suffer from* emotional *problems after being in a*

a at	i if	oo look	ch chalk		a in ago
ā ape	ī idle	ou out	ng sing		e in happen
ah calm	o odd	u ugly	sh ship	ə =	i in capital
aw all	ō oats	ū rule	th think		o in occur
e end	oi oil	ur turn	th their		u in upon
ē easy			zh treasure		

war. **2.** Showing a strong feeling: *My sister became quite emotional when her friends gave her a surprise party*. **3.** Directed at one's feelings: *Her emotional answer when accused of lying convinced her father she was telling the truth.*
e|mo|tion|al (i mō′shə nəl) *adjective.*

emperor—A man who is crowned as ruler of an empire.
em|per|or (em′pər ər) *noun, plural* **emperors.**

emphasis—**1.** Extra attention or stress: *My boss puts a lot of emphasis on getting to work on time.* **2.** In speaking, extra stress given to a certain syllable or word; accent: *Mother put emphasis on the word ''now'' when she called us in to supper.*
em|pha|sis (em′fə sis) *noun, plural* **emphases** (em′fə sēz).

emphasize—To stress the importance of something: *The teacher emphasized the need to study.*
em|pha|size (em′fə sīz) *verb,* **emphasized, emphasizing.**

empire—A group of countries or states under the rule of a single leader or government: *The United States was once a part of the British Empire.*
em|pire (em′pīr) *noun, plural* **empires.**

employ—**1.** To use someone's services for pay: *The hospital employs many workers in this town.* **2.** To use something: *The artist employed many types of tools in creating her sculptures.*
em|ploy (em ploi′) *verb,* **employed, employing.**

employee—A person who is paid to work for a business or another person: *He is an employee of the sporting goods store.*
em|ploy|ee (em ploi′ē *or* em′ploi ē′) *noun, plural* **employees.**

employer—A person or business that pays a worker or group of workers for their services: *Her employer gave her a raise after she had been working there a year.*
em|ploy|er (em ploi′ər) *noun, plural* **employers.**

employment—**1.** A person's work or job: *He had little trouble finding employment after college.* **2.** The act of using or hiring workers for pay; the state of being a paid worker: *The factory owner filled the extra orders through the employment of more workers. His employment by the restaurant allowed him to learn a lot about cooking.*
em|ploy|ment (em ploi′mənt) *noun, plural* **employments.**

empress—A woman who rules an empire or who is married to an emperor.
em|press (em′pris) *noun, plural* **empresses.**

empty—Having nothing or no one inside: *an empty refrigerator; an empty park. Adjective.*
—**1.** To remove everything that is inside: *He emptied the wastebasket to search for his keys.* **2.** To have the people or things inside leave or be taken away: *The stadium emptied when the game was over.* **3.** To flow out; drain: *After reaching the valley, the stream empties into a river. Verb.*
emp|ty (emp′tē) *adjective; verb,* **emptied, emptying.**

emu—A tall Australian bird that is like an ostrich but smaller. It has tiny wings and cannot fly, although it runs swiftly.
e|mu (ē′myū) *noun, plural* **emus.**

emu

en-—**1.** A prefix meaning ''to make happen'' or ''to cause to be'': *He en*raged *them with his insults.* **2.** A prefix meaning ''to surround by or place in or on'': *en*circle *a word; en*close *a message; en*throne *a king.*
 See also **em-.**

Word Power

You can understand the meanings of many words that begin with **en-**, if you add a meaning of the prefix to the meaning of the rest of the word.
    enlarge: to make larger
    enrich: to cause to be rich
    enhalo: to surround by a halo
    enfold: to place in a fold
    entrain: to place on a train

-en—1. A suffix meaning "to make happen" or "to cause to be": *She closed the curtains to dark*en *the room.* **2.** A suffix meaning "to come to be": *The cement will hard*en *by the next day.*

Word Power

You can understand the meanings of many words that end with **-en,** if you add a meaning of the suffix to the meaning of the rest of the word.
　　brighten: to make bright
　　sweeten: to cause to be sweet
　　harden: to come to be hard

---

enable—To give help that makes something possible: *My knowledge of Spanish* enabled *me to get the job.*
en|a|ble (en a′bəl) *verb,* **enabled, enabling.**

enact—1. To pass into law by the government: *Congress* enacted *the bill to protect wildlife early this year.* **2.** To perform as an actor or actress in the role of: *It will take special talent to* enact *the main character in this play.*
en|act (en akt′) *verb,* **enacted, enacting.**

enamel—1. A substance that forms a hard, shiny surface on metal, glass, or pottery. **2.** A paint that dries to form a hard, shiny surface. **3.** A hard, white substance that forms a tooth's thin outer layer.
e|nam|el (i nam′əl) *noun, plural* **enamels.**

enchant—1. To use magical powers to place under a spell; bewitch: *The evil witch* enchanted *the dog, turning it into a bear.* **2.** To please a great deal; delight: *The little girl's poem* enchanted *the audience.*
en|chant (en chant′) *verb,* **enchanted, enchanting.**

encircle—1. To draw or make a circle around: *Please* encircle *the correct words in red. The crowd* encircled *the juggler to see the show.* **2.** To move around something or someone: *The earth* encircles *the sun.*
en|cir|cle (en sur′kəl) *verb,* **encircled, encircling.**

enclose—1. To surround; shut in all around: *The rancher* enclosed *the dangerous bull in a wooden pen.* **2.** To place into the same envelope or box as something else: *My aunt* enclosed *a letter when she sent me a book.*
en|close (en klōz′) *verb,* **enclosed, enclosing.**

enclosure—1. A place that is shut in all around; pen: *The pigs escaped from their wooden* enclosure *and raced away in all directions.* **2.** Something placed inside something else: *She sealed the envelope after putting in two articles as* enclosures.
en|clo|sure (en klō′zhər) *noun, plural* **enclosures.**

enclosure (definition 1)

encore—1. An audience demand that a performer who has left the stage come back and continue to entertain: *After three* encores, *she collapsed in her dressing room.* **2.** An extra appearance or song after an audience has demanded it: *The audience whistled and clapped for an* encore *after the singer walked off the stage.*
en|core (ahng′kawr) *noun, plural* **encores.**

encounter—To meet by surprise: *We* encountered *our teacher at the fair. Verb.* —A meeting that happens by surprise: *Their first* encounter *in three years delighted the old friends. Noun.*
en|coun|ter (en koun′tər) *verb,* **encountered, encountering;** *noun, plural* **encounters.**

encourage—1. To cause another to be hopeful, brave, or confident: *The coach's words* encouraged *the tired players.* **2.** To urge to do something: *Grandmother* encouraged *us to stay for a week.* **3.** To aid; promote: *I placed the plant in a sunny window to* encourage *early blooming.*
en|cour|age (en kur′ij) *verb,* **encouraged, encouraging.**

encouragement—Something that makes one hopeful, brave, or confident: *Her parents'*

---

a at	i if	oo look	ch chalk		a in ago
ā ape	ī idle	ou out	ng sing		e in happen
ah calm	o odd	u ugly	sh ship	ə =	i in capital
aw all	ō oats	ū rule	th think		o in occur
e end	oi oil	ur turn	th their		u in upon
ē easy			zh treasure		

encouragement *convinced her she could make the team.*

en|cour|age|ment (en **kur′**ig mənt) *noun.*

encyclopedia—A book or collection of books that is designed to present facts about many different topics. The topics are listed in alphabetical order.

en|cy|clo|pe|di|a (en sī′klə pē′dē ə) *noun, plural* **encyclopedias.**

Word History

Encyclopedia comes from a Latin word and before that from a Greek word meaning "a well-rounded education." The Greek word is formed from a word meaning "circle" and another word meaning "child." An encyclopedia is useful in helping a child learn all sorts of things.

---

end—**1.** The part remaining when most of something is gone or over: *the* end *of a book; the* end *of the party.* **2.** The point that marks where a thing stops; finish: *We walked to the* end *of the block.* **3.** The purpose one has for doing something; goal: *He works hard but to what* end? *Noun.*
—**1.** To stop doing something: *The teacher told the girls to* end *their argument.* **2.** To reach the finish; conclude: *The race* ended *at the park. Verb.*

end (end) *noun, plural* **ends;** *verb,* **ended, ending.**

■ **at loose ends:** In a state of confusion: *After hearing the bad news, I was* at loose ends *all day.*

get the short end of the stick: To receive less than others: *Because he's shy, he always seems to* get the short end of the stick.

go off the deep end: To take action suddenly without thinking or planning: *She always* goes off the deep end *whenever she's in a bad mood.*

keep (*or* **hold**) **up** (one's) **end:** To do everything expected; perform one's share of work: *I* kept up my end, *but others failed to do the jobs they were assigned.*

make (**both**) **ends meet:** Stay within one's budget; not spend more than one can afford: *When she was young and just starting out, she found it hard to* make ends meet. *His salary is so small that he can't* make both ends meet.

on end: **1.** Being upright or on its edge: *Hold the book* on end *so we can see the cover.*
2. One after the other: *My cold seemed to last for days* on end.

endanger—To place in a situation or bring on conditions that could cause harm; risk: *The speeding traffic* endangered *the life of anyone who tried to cross the street.*

en|dan|ger (en **dān′**jər) *verb,* **endangered, endangering.**

endangered—Being at risk of becoming extinct, or dying without any survivors: *The giant panda is an* endangered *animal.*

en|dan|gered (en **dān′**jərd) *adjective.*

endeavor—To do one's best or try hard: *She* endeavors *to do her best in every race. Verb.*
—A serious attempt: *His* endeavor *to become president was finally successful when he won the election. Noun.*

en|deav|or (en **dev′**ər) *verb,* **endeavored, endeavoring;** *noun, plural* **endeavors.**

ending—The part remaining when most of something is gone or over: *Does the movie have a happy* ending?

end|ing (en′ding) *noun, plural* **endings.**

endorse—**1.** To sign the back of a check: *The bank teller asked the man to* endorse *his check.*
2. To show public approval of; support: *He asked the crowd to* endorse *him as a candidate for mayor.*

en|dorse (en **dawrs′**) *verb,* **endorsed, endorsing.**

endurance—The ability to last through pain or hardship: *Marathon runners must have great* endurance *because they run so far.*

en|dur|ance (en **door′**əns *or* en **dyoor′**əns) *noun.*

endure—**1.** To continue to be; to last: *The bride told the groom that their marriage would* endure *forever.* **2.** To take patiently; tolerate: *She* endured *great pain when she broke her leg on the camping trip.*

en|dure (en **door′** *or* en **dyoor′**) *verb,* **endured, enduring.**

● **Synonyms: abide, bear², stand,** for 2.

enemy—**1.** One who is unfriendly with and ready to do harm to another; foe: *The* enemy *of the queen is plotting against her.* **2.** A country that takes military action against another.
3. Anything that causes harm or damage: *An* enemy *of the cotton plant is an insect known as the boll weevil.*

en|e|my (en′ə mē) *noun, plural* **enemies.**

energetic—Having lots of energy; eager and ready to go: *Grandfather is so* energetic *that he walks several miles to work every day.*
en|er|get|ic (en′ər jet′ik) *adjective.*
• Synonyms: **brisk, lively, vigorous**

energy—1. The will or ability to do things: *When you are sick, you feel as if you have no* energy.
2. A force having the power to make things move or work. The sun, gas, and electricity are forms of energy.
en|er|gy (en′ər jē) *noun, plural* **energies.**

enforce—To cause a law to be obeyed: *Police officers* enforce *traffic laws.*
en|force (en fawrs′) *verb,* **enforced, enforcing.**

enforcement—The act of seeing that rules or laws are obeyed: *Strict* enforcement *of the rules will reduce the number of injuries in football.*
en|force|ment (en fawrs′mənt), *noun.*

engage—1. To put to work; employ; hire: *He* engaged *a carpenter to build a new porch.*
2. To involve; occupy: *Playing basketball* engages *most of her weekends.* 3. To make a pledge to marry someone: *My brother is* engaged *to a doctor.*
en|gage (en gāj′) *verb,* **engaged, engaging.**

engagement—1. The state of being involved or occupied: *Her* engagement *with her work keeps her from having fun.* 2. An agreement to marry: *Their* engagement *was announced in the newspaper.* 3. An appointment or promise made to meet with another person: *Don't forget you have an* engagement *at three o'clock today.*
4. The act of hiring: *The new project would call for the* engagement *of ten more workers.*
en|gage|ment (en gāj′mənt) *noun, plural* **engagements.**

engaging—Very pleasing; attractive; charming: *My brother's* engaging *manner has won him many friends.*
en|gag|ing (en gā′jing) *adjective.*

engine—1. A machine that starts other machines working; motor: *a car* engine. 2. A machine that pulls or pushes railroad cars; locomotive.
en|gine (en′jən) *noun, plural* **engines.**

engineer—1. A person who is specially trained to design and build things like roads, bridges,

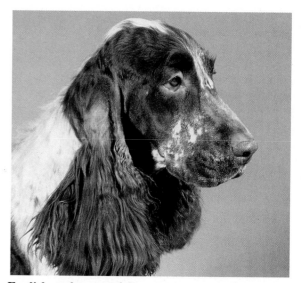
English cocker spaniel

pipelines, or canals. 2. The person who drives a train's engine.
en|gin|eer (en′jə nir′) *noun, plural* **engineers.**

English cocker spaniel—A medium-sized hunting dog that has a wide nose, a flat skull, and a very short tail. Originally bred in England, it is like the cocker spaniel but larger in size.
Eng|lish cock|er span|iel (ing′glish kok′ər span′yəl) *noun, plural* **English cocker spaniels.**

English foxhound—A large dog with short ears and a smooth coat of white, black, and tan hair. This dog was originally bred in England for hunting foxes.
Eng|lish fox|hound (ing′glish foks′hound′) *noun, plural* **English foxhounds.**

a at	i if	oo look	ch chalk		⌈ a in ago
ā ape	ī idle	ou out	ng sing		e in happen
ah calm	o odd	u ugly	sh ship	ə =	i in capital
aw all	ō oats	ū rule	th think		o in occur
e end	oi oil	ur turn	<u>th</u> their		⌊ u in upon
ē easy			zh treasure		

English foxhound

English horn

English horn—A musical instrument that is long and thin like an oboe, but its tube is longer and it makes a lower sound.
Eng|lish horn (ing′glish hawrn) *noun, plural* **English horns.**

English setter—A large, long-haired dog with a flat, silky coat of white, black, and tan. Originally bred in England, it can be trained to hunt for wild birds by pointing its nose at them.
Eng|lish set|ter (ing′glish set′ər) *noun, plural* **English setters.**

English springer spaniel—A large hunting dog with a muscular build and a long, silky coat of white and black or brown.
Eng|lish spring|er span|iel (ing′glish spring′ər span′yəl) *noun, plural* **English springer spaniels.**

English springer spaniel

English toy spaniel—A small dog with a round head, a short, turned-up nose, and long, silky hair. Originally bred in Japan and China, this dog was introduced into England about 300 years ago.
Eng|lish toy span|iel (ing′glish toi span′yəl) *noun, plural* **English toy spaniels.**

engrave—1. To carve a message or design into something: *He must be a very talented artist to*

be able to engrave *jewelry with such lovely patterns.* **2.** To cut a message or design into a wooden, glass, or metal plate for use in printing: *The local printer engraved the invitations.*
en|grave (en grāv′) *verb,* **engraved, engraving.**

engulf—To overwhelm or cover completely: *The tidal wave engulfed the small island.*
en|gulf (en gulf′) *verb,* **engulfed, engulfing.**

enhance—To add to; make greater: *The new room will enhance the value of our house. An apple tree might enhance the look of the yard.*
en|hance (en hans′) *verb,* **enhanced, enhancing.**

enjoy—1. To be pleased with: *We enjoyed our dinner at the restaurant.* **2.** To have as a pleasing quality: *Florida enjoys warm weather nearly all year long.*
en|joy (en joi′) *verb,* **enjoyed, enjoying.**

enjoyable—Providing delight and joy: *A day in the country can be very enjoyable.*
en|joy|able (en joi′ə bəl) *adjective.*

enjoyment—Fun; pleasure; delight: *He gets enjoyment from rowing his boat on the lake.*
en|joy|ment (en joi′mənt) *noun.*

enlarge—To make or become bigger: *Enlarge the photo so that we can use it on the cover.*
en|large (en lahrj′) *verb,* **enlarged, enlarging.**
• Synonyms: **expand, lengthen**
  Antonyms: See Synonyms at **abbreviate.**

enlargement—1. The state of being made bigger: *The enlargement of the factory was going according to plan.* **2.** Something that has been added: *The enlargement to our house takes up the whole backyard.*
en|large|ment (en lahrj′mənt) *noun, plural* **enlargements.**

enlighten—To inform or give knowledge to: *A visit to an art museum could enlighten you about famous painters.*
en|light|en (en lī′tən) *verb,* **enlightened, enlightening.**

enlist—1. To sign up for service in the army or another branch of the armed forces: *They enlisted in the Navy the day after they graduated from high school.* **2.** To get another to help in support of a cause; recruit: *The teachers are enlisting their students in the fight against drugs.*
en|list (en list′) *verb,* **enlisted, enlisting.**

enormous—Huge; unusually big in size: *The enormous castle had 60 rooms and a dungeon.*
e|nor|mous (i nawr′məs) *adjective.*
• Synonyms: See Synonyms at **big.**
  Antonyms: See Antonyms at **small.**

enough—Of a sufficient amount: *Make sure you have* enough *food for the party. Adjective.*
—The amount called for or desired: *There is* enough *to give each child one cup of cider. Noun.*
—Until the amount is sufficient; *Have you learned* enough *to do your report? Adverb.*
e|nough (i nuf′) *adjective; noun; adverb.*
• Synonyms: **abundant, ample, plentiful,** for *adjective.*
Antonyms: **rare, scanty, scarce,** for *adjective.*

enrage—To cause to have enormous anger: *He* enraged *me by insulting my sister.*
en|rage (in rāj′) *verb,* **enraged, enraging.**

enrich—1. To develop or make more valuable; enhance: *Reading* enriches *the mind. Working extra hours* enriches *my bank account.* 2. To improve quality by putting in something more: *Vitamins and minerals* enrich *the milk we drink.*
en|rich (en rich′) *verb,* **enriched, enriching.**

enroll—To sign up to become a member; register; join: *They* enrolled *in a class to learn ballet.*
en|roll (en rōl′) *verb,* **enrolled, enrolling.**

enrollment—1. The process of signing up to become a member: Enrollment *for the volleyball club takes place at the high school gym.* 2. The number of people signed up for something: *The* enrollment *for this class is limited to 15 students.*
en|roll|ment (en rōl′mənt) *noun, plural* **enrollments.**

ensign—1. A flag flown as a country's symbol: *The* ensign *of the United States was raised on the captured island.* 2. The lowest rank of officer in the United States Navy.
en|sign (en′sīn *or* en′sən, for definition 1; en′sən for definition 2) *noun, plural* **ensigns.** Abbreviation: Ens.

ensure—1. To guarantee; take away all doubt of: *Studying will* ensure *a good grade on the test.* 2. To keep safe and secure: *A heavy parka will* ensure *you against the cold of the snowstorm.*
en|sure (en shoor′) *verb,* **ensured, ensuring.**

entangle—To get tangled or caught up in: *The fly* entangled *itself in the spider's web.*
en|tan|gle (en tang′gəl) *verb,* **entangled, entangling.**

enter—1. To pass into; come in: *Guests* enter *our house through the front door.* 2. To sign up or register for; join: *She* entered *the race even though her chances of winning were poor.* 3. To write in a book or other record: *Mother* enters *the amount of each check she writes in her checkbook.*
en|ter (en′tər) *verb,* **entered, entering.**

enterprise—1. Something of difficulty or importance that is to be tried: *Jumping from a plane with a parachute is an exciting* enterprise. 2. The condition of being ready and willing to begin a bold project: *The boys were full of* enterprise *as they began the job of building the model.*
en|ter|prise (en′tər prīz′) *noun, plural* **enterprises.**

entertain—1. To perform in a way to hold the interest of; amuse; divert: *The magician* entertained *the children.* 2. To provide a meal or open one's home to someone as a guest: *My parents are* entertaining *friends this weekend.* 3. To give one's attention to; consider; ponder: *She* entertained *thoughts of becoming a brain surgeon.*
en|ter|tain (en′tər tān′) *verb,* **entertained, entertaining.**

entertainer—One who performs before an audience, such as an actor, singer, or magician.
en|ter|tain|er (en′tər tā′nər) *noun, plural* **entertainers.**

entertainment—1. An activity that gives pleasure; amusement: *The* entertainment *at the party was a live disk jockey.* 2. Pleasure; fun; relaxation: *He told jokes for our* entertainment *while we waited.*
en|ter|tain|ment (en′tər tān′mənt) *noun, plural* **entertainments.**
• Synonyms: **game, pastime, play, recreation, sport,** for **1.**
Antonyms: **chore, duty, task, work,** for **1.**

enthusiasm—A feeling of great interest and eagerness: *The children were full of* enthusiasm *as they set out for their picnic.*
en|thu|si|asm (en thū′zē az əm) *noun, plural* **enthusiasms.**

Word History

Enthusiasm comes from a Latin word and before that a Greek word meaning ''inspired by a god.'' A person with great enthusiasm was thought to be influenced by a divine being.

---

a at	i if	oo look	ch chalk		a in ago
ā ape	ī idle	ou out	ng sing		e in happen
ah calm	o odd	u ugly	sh ship	ə =	i in capital
aw all	ō oats	ū rule	th think		o in occur
e end	oi oil	ur turn	<u>th</u> their		u in upon
ē easy			zh treasure		

enthusiastic—Full of interest and eagerness; keen: *The class was* enthusiastic *about collecting autographs of famous people.*
en|thu|si|as|tic (en thū′zē **as′**tik) *adjective.*

enthusiastic

entire—Having everything that makes up the whole; complete: *The* entire *family was there for Grandma's birthday.*
en|tire (en tīr′) *adjective.*

entitle—1. To give a right to: *Your ticket* entitles *you to one soda and one hot dog.* 2. To give a name to something made or created: *He* entitled *his short story "The Treasure."*
en|ti|tle (en tī′təl) *verb,* **entitled, entitling.**

entrance¹—1. The act of coming in: *The king and queen made a grand* entrance *into the garden.*
2. Place where one comes in; entry: *Come in through the main* entrance *on the ground floor.*
3. The right to come in or be admitted: *Women have gained* entrance *to the space program.*
en|trance (en′trəns) *noun, plural* **entrances.**

entrance²—1. To fill with delight, wonder, or joy: *We were all* entranced *by the performing seals.* 2. To put into a trance: *The hypnotist soon* entranced *his subject.*
en|trance (en trans′) *verb,* **entranced, entrancing.**

entreat—To beg; plead: *He* entreated *his pal not to go without him.*
en|treat (en trēt′) *verb,* **entreated, entreating.**
• Synonym: **appeal**

entry—1. The act of coming in: *Her silent* entry *through the back door fooled us all.* 2. A place

to enter through; entrance: *The* entry *to the zoo is blocked by a chain at night.* 3. A note or other written addition to a book or list: *She makes an* entry *in her diary every day.* 4. A person or thing that is allowed to be part of a contest or race: *There were 300* entries *in the dog show.*
en|try (en′trē) *noun, plural* **entries.**

enunciate—To pronounce words; articulate: *Actors must* enunciate *loudly and clearly when they are on stage.*
e|nun|ci|ate (i nun′sē āt′) *verb,* **enunciated, enunciating.**

envelop—To enclose or surround; cover; wrap: *The movie star was* enveloped *in furs.*
en|vel|op (en vel′əp) *verb,* **enveloped, enveloping.**

envelope—A wrapper made of paper that holds letters and other flat, thin objects, usually for mailing. It often has a flap that can be licked and pressed down to form a seal.
en|ve|lope (en′və lōp′ *or* ahn′və lōp′) *noun, plural* **envelopes.**

Language Fact

Envelope is a word that can be pronounced in two ways. The first syllable can be made to rhyme either with "den" or with "on." The word comes from a French word, and in French the first syllable is close to rhyming with "on." In English, you will hear people say it both ways, and both are correct.

---

envious—Feeling unhappy because of wanting something that belongs to someone else; jealous: *She was* envious *of her sister's artistic ability.*
en|vi|ous (en′vē əs) *adjective.*

environment—1. The state of natural elements such as the air, water, land, and life forms: *Automobile smoke and other types of pollution are spoiling our* environment. 2. All of the surroundings that have an effect on life: *Bright colors and friendly nurses make a cheerful* environment *in a hospital.*
en|vi|ron|ment (en vī′rən mənt) *noun, plural* **evironments.**

environmental—Having to do with the environment: *Acid rain is an* environmental *problem.*
en|vi|ron|men|tal (en vī rən men′təl) *adjective.*

envoy—1. A messenger. 2. A diplomat just below an ambassador in rank.
en|voy (en′voi) *noun, plural* **envoys.**

envy—1. A feeling of unhappiness or dislike caused by wanting what someone else has or gets; jealousy: *The children were filled with* envy *when he showed them his new skateboard.* 2. Someone or something having a quality others find desirable: *Her popularity makes her the* envy *of her classmates. Noun.*
—To feel jealous because of or toward: *He* envied *her batting record this season. I don't* envy *her because I know her life is harder than it seems. Verb.*
en|vy (en′vē) *noun, plural* **envies;** *verb,* **envied, envying.**

enzyme—A substance found in living cells that causes a change in a biological process. Enzymes break down food to aid digestion, help make cheese, and dissolve laundry stains.
en|zyme (en′zīm) *noun, plural* **enzymes.**

eon—A very long period of time; many thousands of years: *The last of the dinosaurs died out* eons *ago.*
e|on (ē′ən *or* ē′on) *noun, plural* **eons.**

epic—1. A long poem that tells a story about a great hero or heroine. 2. A long book, movie, or other work that tells a story about a great hero or heroine. *Noun.*
—1. Like a long poem about a heroic person: *This* epic *film is about the life of Columbus.* 2. Magnificent; great; heroic: *Sudden flooding turned his weekend fishing trip into an* epic *event. Adjective.*
ep|ic (ep′ik) *noun, plural* **epics;** *adjective.*

epidemic—The spread of a disease that happens so fast many people are sick at the same time: *Last winter, a flu* epidemic *kept the schools closed for a week.*
ep|i|dem|ic (ep′ ə dem′ik) *noun, plural* **epidemics.**

epilepsy—A disorder of the nervous system. A person who has epilepsy sometimes trembles or convulses and may lose consciousness.
ep|i|lep|sy (ep′ə lep′sē) *noun.*

Epiphany—The anniversary of the arrival of the Three Wise Men in Bethlehem to honor the birth of Jesus Christ. Epiphany, which falls on January 6, is a holy day for Christians.
E|piph|a|ny (i pif′ə nē) *noun, plural* **Epiphanies.**

Episcopal Church—A Protestant church in the United States. It has about the same beliefs as the Church of England and, like that church, is a member of the Anglican communion.
E|pis|co|pal Church (i pis′kə pəl church) *noun.*

Episcopalian—A Protestant who belongs to the Episcopal Church.
E|pis|co|pa|lian (i pis′kə pāl′yən *or* i pis′kə pā′lē ən) *noun, plural* **Episcopalians.**

episode—1. A happening or period of time viewed as a part of one's life: *Getting his driver's license was an important* episode *in his life.* 2. A scene, event, or series of events that happens in a story or one's life: *Each* episode *in the cowboy's life was exciting.*
ep|i|sode (ep′ə sōd) *noun, plural* **episodes.**
• Synonyms: **event, incident, occurrence,** for **1.**

epoch—A period of time that is marked by some important happening: *Sending people to the moon began a new* epoch *in the study of space.*
e|poch (ep′ək) *noun, plural* **epochs.**

equal—Alike in size, value, number, or other way: *Seven days are* equal *to one week. Adjective.*
—A person or thing like another: *She is his* equal *in height and weight. Noun.*
—To be exactly like another: *He played hard until his score* equaled *mine. Verb.*
e|qual (ē′kwəl) *adjective; noun, plural* **equals;** *verb,* **equaled, equaling.**
■ **equal to:** Able to do; having the qualities needed to perform: *I don't think he is* equal to *the job.*

equality—The state of being the same and being treated in an identical way: *My mother belongs to a group that works for the* equality *of women.*
e|qual|i|ty (i kwol′ə tē) *noun, plural* **equalities.**

equation—A mathematical statement showing that two quantities are equal to each other. There is usually an equal sign between the two sides of an equation. For example, $4 + 4 = 8$.
e|qua|tion (i kwā′zhən) *noun, plural* **equations.**

equator—The imaginary line that circles the middle of the earth. It is located the same distance from both the North Pole and the South Pole.
e|qua|tor (i kwā′tər) *noun, plural* **equators.**
• See picture at **latitude.**

equilateral—Shaped or designed so that all sides are exactly the same: *Let's measure to see whether this is an* equilateral *triangle. The three countries have an* equilateral *agreement that sets up trade laws all must obey.*
e|qui|lat|er|al (ē′kwə lat′ər əl) *adjective.*

a at	i if	oo look	ch chalk		a in ago
ā ape	ī idle	ou out	ng sing		e in happen
ah calm	o odd	u ugly	sh ship	ə =	i in capital
aw all	ō oats	ū rule	th think		o in occur
e end	oi oil	ur turn	th their		u in upon
ē easy			zh treasure		

equinox—A point in time that happens twice each year when the equator lies directly below the sun. It is the only time when night and day are of equal length all over the earth. The spring equinox takes place around March 21, and the fall equinox takes place around September 23.
e|qui|nox (ē′kwə noks) *noun, plural* **equinoxes**.
• *See also* **solstice**.

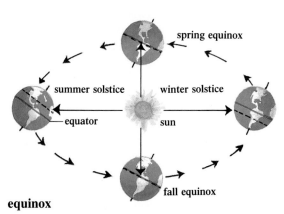

equinox

Word History

Equinox comes from a Latin word. That word was formed from a word meaning ''equal'' and another word meaning ''night.'' People used this word to describe the time of the year when days are the same length as nights, and so days and nights are equal.

equip—To provide with what is required: *The school* equips *the team with uniforms*.
e|quip (i kwip′) *verb,* **equipped, equipping**.
• Synonyms: **furnish, supply**

equipment—1. The supplies needed for a certain activity: *The scuba diver's* equipment *included an air tank, a mask, and flippers*. 2. The act of providing what is required: *The* equipment *of the*

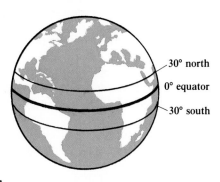

equator

mountain climbers with gear and supplies took weeks of planning.
e|quip|ment (i kwip′mənt) *noun*.

equivalent—The same in the end; equal in an important way: *The price of this is* equivalent *to a year's pay*. *Adjective*.
—Something that is equal in an important way: *Four quarts are the* equivalent *of one gallon*. *Noun*.
e|quiv|a|lent (i kwiv′ə lənt) *adjective; noun, plural* **equivalents**.

-er[1]—1. A suffix added to verbs that means ''a person or thing that does something'': *A horse that jumps is a jump*er. *A person who paints is a paint*er.

Word Power

You can understand the meanings of many words that end with **-er**[1], if you add the meaning of the suffix to the meaning of the rest of the word.
  mourner: a person who mourns
  cleanser: a thing that cleanses

-er[2]—A suffix added to adjectives and adverbs that means ''more.'' This suffix shows comparison: *Our house is bigg*er *than yours*. *Tom runs fast*er *than Jerry*.

Word Power

You can understand the meanings of many words that end with **-er**[2], if you add the meaning of the suffix to the meaning of the rest of the word.
  odder: more odd
  quieter: more quiet

era—1. A period of time that has special importance; a historical age: *The Soviet Union has begun an* era *of ''openness.'' The years when Queen Elizabeth ruled England are called the Elizabethan* era.
e|ra (ir′ə *or* ē′rə) *noun, plural* **eras**.

erase—1. To rub or wipe out: *The teacher asked her to* erase *the chalkboard*. 2. To remove; take away; eliminate: *Time will* erase *the memory of that sad event*.
e|rase (i rās′) *verb,* **erased, erasing**.

eraser—Something used for rubbing or wiping out marks made by a pencil or piece of chalk: *My little brother has an* eraser *shaped like a dinosaur*.
e|ras|er (i rās′ər) *noun, plural* **erasers**.

erect—Straight; stiff; upright: *The cat's hair stood* erect *when the dog entered the room. Adjective.*
—**1.** To put together or up: *The children* erected *a treehouse in the oak tree.* **2.** To set straight up; raise: *They* erected *telephone poles along the side of the road. Verb.*
e|rect (i rekt′) *adjective; verb,* erected, erecting.
• Synonyms: **build, construct,** for *verb* **1.**

ermine—A kind of weasel whose brown fur changes to white in the winter as a way of hiding. It is hunted for its white fur.
er|mine (ur′mən) *noun, plural* ermines *or* ermine.

ermine

erode—To wear away over a period of time: *The heavy snowfall that winter* eroded *the gravel driveway and made large holes.*
e|rode (i rōd′) *verb,* eroded, eroding.

erosion—The act of slowly wearing or being worn away: *Spring rains and flooding caused the* erosion *of the riverbank.*
e|ro|sion (i rō′zhən) *noun.*

errand—A short trip to get or deliver something: *The teacher sent me on an* errand *to the office.*
er|rand (er′ənd) *noun, plural* errands.

error—**1.** Something wrong caused by a person's mistake: *Because of an addition* error, *we were charged too much at the store.* **2.** In baseball, a catching or throwing mistake made by a player in the field that lets a batter get on base or lets a runner advance to the next base rather than being put out.

a at	i if	oo look	ch chalk		⌈ a in ago
ā ape	ī idle	ou out	ng sing		e in happen
ah calm	o odd	u ugly	sh ship	ə =	i in capital
aw all	ō oats	ū rule	th think		o in occur
e end	oi oil	ur turn	th their		⌊ u in upon
ē easy			zh treasure		

er|ror (er′ər) *noun, plural* errors.
• Synonyms: **blunder, slip,** for **1.**

erupt—To break out or burst forth suddenly: *As we were watching, water* erupted *from the fountain.*
e|rupt (i rupt′) *verb,* erupted, erupting.

escalator—A moving stairway used to carry people from one floor of a building to another.
es|ca|la|tor (es′ kə lā′tər) *noun, plural* escalators.

escape—To get away; avoid: *She tried to* escape *from the bee that kept following her around the backyard. Verb.*
—**1.** The act of getting away or getting free: *We could not figure out how the gerbil had made its* escape *from its cage.* **2.** A way of getting away or getting free: *a fire* escape. *Noun.*
es|cape (es kāp′) *verb,* escaped, escaping; *noun, plural* escapes.

escort—A person or group of people who go along with a person or group for protection or as an honor: *A student* escort *led the visitors around the school. Noun.*
—To go along with someone or something for protection or as an honor; accompany: *The guide* escorted *us through the museum. Verb.*
es|cort (es′kawrt for *noun;* es kawrt′ for *verb*) *noun, plural* escorts; *verb,* escorted, escorting.

Eskimo—**1.** A member of a group of people who live in arctic areas, including Alaska and parts of northern Canada. **2.** The language that is spoken by these people. *Noun.*
—Of or having to do with a group of people who live in arctic areas: Eskimo *sled dogs. Adjective.*
Es|ki|mo (es′kə mō) *noun, plural* Eskimos *or* Eskimo; *adjective.*

esophagus—A tube that connects the mouth and stomach, and through which food travels.
e|soph|a|gus (ē sof′ə gəs) *noun, plural* esophagi (ē sof′ə jī).
• See picture at **alimentary canal.**

especially—Particularly; unusually: *The apple pie tasted* especially *good because we picked the apples ourselves.*
es|pe|cial|ly (es pesh′ə lē *or* es pesh′lē) *adverb.* Abbreviation: esp.

espionage—The use of spies to get secret information from another country; spying.
es|pi|o|nage (es′pē ə nahzh *or* es′pē ə nij) *noun.*

essay—A short piece of writing about a topic: *He wrote an* essay *about what his family meant to him.*
es|say (es′ā) *noun, plural* essays.

essence—The important or necessary part of something: *Consideration for others is the* essence *of good manners.*
es|sence (es′əns) *noun, plural* **essences.**

essential—Necessary; very important: *It is* essential *to set the oven at the correct temperature when baking brownies. Adjective.*
—Something that is necessary or very important: *The* essentials *for fishing include bait, a fishing rod, and patience. Noun.*
es|sen|tial (ə sen′shəl) *adjective; noun, plural* **essentials.**
  • Synonyms: **basic, fundamental, primary,** for *adjective.*
    Antonym: **trivial,** for *adjective.*

-est—A suffix that means "most." *The* sweetest *peach is the one that tastes the most sweet.*

Word Power

You can understand the meanings of many words that end with **-est,** if you add the meaning of the suffix to the meaning of the rest of the word.
  highest—most high
  softest—most soft

---

establish—1. To set up; bring about: *The club* established *rules for its members.* 2. To prove; clearly show: *The investigation* established *that he was not near the scene of the crime.*
es|tab|lish (es tab′lish) *verb,* **established, establishing.**
  • Synonyms: **confirm, verify** for **2.**

establishment—1. The act of setting up or bringing about: *The* establishment *of a computer classroom took a lot of time and money.*
2. Something that is set up, such as a household, business, or church.
es|tab|lish|ment (es tab′lish mənt) *noun, plural* **establishments.**

estate—1. A large piece of land, often with a large home. 2. Everything that is owned by someone: *He willed his* estate *to his son.*
es|tate (es tāt′) *noun, plural* **estates.**

esteem—To respect and admire greatly: *The students* esteemed *their principal for her fairness and sense of humor. Verb.*
—Great respect and admiration: *People have great* esteem *for America's astronauts. Noun.*
es|teem (es tēm′) *verb,* **esteemed, esteeming;** *noun.*

estimate—A guess or opinion about something: *His* estimate *was that it would take about six*

hours *to paint the garage. Noun.*
—To make a guess or give an opinion about something: *She* estimated *that she would be done with her homework by the time dinner was ready. Verb.*
es|ti|mate (es′tə mit for *noun;* es′tə māt for *noun* and *verb*) *noun,* plural **estimates;** *verb,* **estimated, estimating.**
  • Synonyms: For *verb,* see Synonyms at **appraise.**

estimation—A guess or opinion: *Our* estimation *is that we will need five packages of hot dogs for the picnic.*
es|ti|ma|tion (es′tə mā′shən) *noun, plural* **estimations.**

etc.—And so forth; and so on: *She had all the things she needed for class, such as books, paper, pencils,* etc.
etc. *abbreviation.*

Word History

Etc. is the abbreviation for the Latin words "et cetera" (et **set′**ər ə), meaning "and other things." The abbreviation is commonly used today. The two full words are not.

---

etch—To cut or carve a design in glass, metal, wood, or other material through the use of acid or heat: *The spilled acid* etched *an unusual pattern in the table.*
etch (ech) *verb,* **etched, etching.**

eternal—1. Timeless; lasting forever. 2. Lasting a long time: *an* eternal *train ride.*
e|ter|nal (i tur′nəl) *adjective.*
  • Synonyms: **everlasting, perpetual,** for **1.**

eternity—1. All of time; time that has no beginning or end. 2. A long time.
e|ter|ni|ty (i tur′nə tē) *noun, plural* **eternities.**

ether—A colorless liquid that has a strong, sweet smell. It was once widely used to put people to sleep during operations.
e|ther (ē′thər) *noun.*

ethnic—Having to do with large groups of people who share the same language and customs: *She has an album of* ethnic *songs from around the world.*
eth|nic (eth′nik) *adjective.*

etiquette—The rules of polite behavior; good manners: *According to* etiquette, *you should keep your elbows off the table during a meal.*
et|i|quette (et′ə ket) *noun, plural* **etiquettes.**

etymology—An explanation of the history of a word. It tells the original meaning of the word and the language from which it first came. It also gives any changes in the spelling or meaning of the word over the years.
et|y|mol|o|gy (et′ə mol′ə jē) *noun, plural* **etymologies.**

eucalyptus—A tall tree that grows mainly in Australia. Its wood is used for building, and its leaves contain an oil used in some medicines.
eu|ca|lyp|tus (yū kə lip′təs) *noun, plural* **eucalyptuses** or **eucalypti** (yū kə lip′tī).

tree

leaf

flower

eucalyptus

evacuate—**1.** To leave a dangerous place: *We are prepared to* evacuate *the moment a tornado is sighted.* **2.** To empty; remove from: *The building was* evacuated *long before the wrecking crew arrived.*
e|vac|u|ate (i vak′yū āte) *verb,* **evacuated, evacuating.**

evade—To avoid by clever thinking; dodge: *The escaped convict* evaded *the police for a few hours before being caught.*
e|vade (i vād′) *verb,* **evaded, evading.**

evaluate—To figure out the worth or importance of: *The art expert* evaluated *the student's painting.*

evaluate (i val′yū āt) *verb,* **evaluated, evaluating.**
• Synonyms: See Synonyms at **appraise.**

evangelist—**1.** A traveling minister who preaches the Gospels of Matthew, Mark, Luke, and John. **2.** Any preacher of the gospels.
e|van|ge|list (i van′jə list) *noun, plural* **evangelists.**

Word History

Evangelist comes from a Greek word meaning "bringing good news." In the early Christian church, the word referred to missionaries who traveled to non-Christian lands, "bringing the good news" of the Gospels with them. The word still refers mainly to traveling preachers of the Gospels.

---

evaporate—**1.** To change from a solid or liquid into a gas: *The morning dew* evaporated *as the sun rose.* **2.** To disappear: *My bad mood* evaporated *when my dog ran to meet me.*
e|vap|o|rate (i vap′ə rāt) *verb,* **evaporated, evaporating.**

eve—The evening or day before a holiday or other special day: *Christmas* Eve.
eve (ēv) *noun, plural* **eves.**

even—**1.** Flat; level: *To make sure the milk would not spill, she kept her lunch tray* even. **2.** At the same level: *He filled the measuring cup with water until it was* even *with the top line.* **3.** Not changing; constant: *an* even *pulse; an* even *pace.* **4.** Equal; alike: *She cut the cake so that the pieces were* even. **5.** Able to be divided by two without leaving a remainder. The numbers 2, 16, and 44 are even numbers. *Adjective.*
—**1.** Actually; indeed: *She was happy,* even *delighted, with her report card.* **2.** Although it is not expected: *Even I knew the answer to that question.* **3.** Still; yet: *His case of poison ivy seemed* even *worse today. Adverb.*
—To make equal; level: *He* evened *the amount of coffee in the two cups. Verb.*
e|ven (ē′vən) *adjective; adverb; verb,* **evened, evening.**

■ **break even:** To finish up no better or worse than at the beginning: *Although the children spent $5.00 on supplies for their lemonade stand, they* broke even *at the end of the day.*
get even: To take revenge: *Father kidded that he would* get even *with me for beating him at basketball.*

a at	**i** if	**oo** look	**ch** chalk		a in ago
ā ape	**ī** idle	**ou** out	**ng** sing		e in happen
ah calm	**o** odd	**u** ugly	**sh** ship	ə =	i in capital
aw all	**ō** oats	**ū** rule	**th** think		o in occur
e end	**oi** oil	**ur** turn	**th** their		u in upon
ē easy			**zh** treasure		

evening—The early part of the night: *The family sat on the porch in the* evening. *Noun.*
—Having to do with the early part of the night: *the* evening *news. Adjective.*
eve|ning (ēv′ning) *noun, plural* **evenings;** *adjective.*

event—1. A happening, especially an important happening: *His first trip on an airplane was an exciting* event.   2. One of the competitions at a sports contest: *His best* event *is the long jump.*
e|vent (i vent′) *noun, plural* **events.**
• Synonyms: **episode, incident, occurrence,** for **1.**

eventual—Happening at last; final: *We could hardly wait for the* eventual *return of spring.*
e|ven|tu|al (i ven′choo əl) *adjective.*

ever—1. At any time: *Does that boy* ever *stop telling jokes?*   2. Always: *She is* ever *trying to get better grades.*   3. In any way: *Let me know if I can* ever *help you.*
ev|er (ev′ər) *adverb.*

evergreen (noun)

evergreen—Having leaves or needles that remain green all year: evergreen *trees. Adjective.*
—A plant or tree having green leaves or needles all year. Pine trees, holly, and some types of ivy are evergreens. *Noun.*
ev|er|green (ev′ər grēn′) *adjective; noun, plural* **evergreens.**

everlasting—1. Never ending: *The bride and groom pledged their* everlasting *love to each other.*   2. Lasting a long time: *the* everlasting

chatter of the squirrels in the tree outside my window.
ev|er|last|ing (ev′ər las′ting) *adjective.*
• Synonyms: **eternal, perpetual,** for **1.**

every—1. Each one of a group: *She put* every *checker back in the box.*   2. All that there is: *He spent* every *cent of his allowance on baseball cards.*
eve|ry (ev′rē) *adjective.*
■ **every now and then:** Once in a while; from time to time: *Every now and then, Grandmother bakes cookies for us.*
every other: Every second one; skipping one: *He has gym class* every other *day.*
every which way: In all directions: *The swirling wind blew the leaves* every which way.

everybody—Everyone; each person: *Everybody enjoyed the day at the beach.*
eve|ry|bod|y (ev′rē bod′ē) *pronoun.*

everyday—1. Daily; happening each day: *Combing your hair is an* everyday *event.*   2. Used on an average day; not special or different: *He changed into his* everyday *clothes before going out to play.*
eve|ry|day (ev′rē dā′) *adjective.*

everyone—Everybody; each person: *Everyone danced at the party.*
eve|ry|one (ev′rē wun *or* ev′rē wən) *pronoun.*

everything—All things: *After they finished painting the room, they put* everything *back in its place.*
eve|ry|thing (ev′rē thing) *pronoun.*

everywhere—In every place; in all places: *He looked* everywhere *for his coat.*
eve|ry|where (ev′rē hwar) *adverb.*

evict—To force someone by law to leave a place, such as a house: *She was* evicted *from her apartment because she did not pay her rent.*
e|vict (i vikt′) *verb,* **evicted, evicting.**

evidence—Something that shows clearly what is true and what is false: *His stained pants were* evidence *that he had sat on the freshly painted chair.*
ev|i|dence (ev′ə dəns) *noun.*

evident—Easy to see or understand: *It is* evident *from her smile that she enjoys hot fudge sundaes.*
ev|i|dent (ev′ə dənt) *adjective.*
• Synonyms: **apparent, clear, obvious, plain**
Antonyms: **hazy, obscure, vague**

evil—Bad; sinful; wicked: *The* evil *wizard cast a spell on the queen. Adjective.*
—Wickedness; something that is bad or does

harm: *The doctor spoke about the* evils *of drugs.* Noun.

e|vil (ē′vəl) *adjective; noun, plural* **evils.**

evolution—1. A slow development or change: *His speech was about the* evolution *of clocks from the Middle Ages to the present.* 2. A scientific theory that says that the simple living things of millions of years ago changed and developed into the more complex living things of today.

ev|o|lu|tion (ev′ə lū′shən) *noun, plural* **evolutions.**

evolve—To change or develop slowly: *The exhibit showed how jet airplanes* evolved *from planes that had propellers.*

e|volve (i **volv**′) *verb,* **evolved, evolving.**

ewe—A female sheep.

ewe (yū) *noun, plural* **ewes.**

• Words that sound the same are **yew** and **you.**

ex-—A prefix that means "former." An ex-president is a former president.

Word Power

You can understand the meaning of many words that begin with **ex-,** if you add the meaning of the prefix to the rest of the word.

ex-convict—former convict

ex-member—former member

ex-principal—former principal

---

exact—Without any mistakes; accurate; precise: *an* exact *measurement; the* exact *time.*

ex|act (eg **zakt**′) *adjective.*

exactly—1. Accurately; without any mistakes: *She described him so* exactly *that we had no trouble finding him in the crowd.* 2. In every way: *His plans worked* exactly *as he had hoped.*

ex|act|ly (eg **zakt**′lē) *adverb.*

• Synonyms: **just, precisely,** for **2.**
 Antonyms: **approximately, nearly, roughly, somewhat,** for **2.**

exaggerate—To go beyond the truth by making something seem to be more or better than it really is: *He* exaggerated *when he said that he had 1,000 baseball cards.*

a at	i if	oo look	ch chalk		a in ago
ā ape	ī idle	ou out	ng sing		e in happen
ah calm	o odd	u ugly	sh ship	ə =	i in capital
aw all	ō oats	ū rule	th think		o in occur
e end	oi oil	ur turn	th their		u in upon
ē easy			zh treasure		

ex|ag|ger|ate (eg **zaj**′ə rāt) *verb,* **exaggerated, exaggerating.**

examination—1. The act of looking at something closely and carefully: *Upon* examination, *we saw that it was a toad and not a frog.* 2. A test; set of questions: *Our English teacher will give the final* examination *on Thursday.*

ex|am|i|na|tion (eg zam′ə **nā**′shən) *noun, plural* **examinations.**

examine—1. To look closely or carefully: *The Boy Scouts* examined *a map before starting their hiking trip.* 2. To test: *The teacher* examined *the students on their history assignment.*

ex|am|ine (eg **zam**′in) *verb,* **examined, examining.**

• Synonyms: **analyze, inspect, investigate, study,** for **1.**

example—1. Something that is used to show what other things in a group are like; sample: *A snake is an* example *of a reptile.* 2. A problem, especially in mathematics: *She had 20 long division* examples *to do for homework.*

ex|am|ple (eg **zam**′pəl) *noun, plural* **examples.**

■ **for example:** For instance; like the following: *There are many kinds of cats—*for example, *Siamese, Persian, and Manx.*
 set an example: To be a model for others to follow or copy: *Mother asked me to* set an example *for my younger brother by keeping my room neat.*

exasperate—To anger; annoy greatly: *The puppy's constant barking* exasperated *its owner.*

ex|as|per|ate (eg **zas**′pə rāt) *verb,* **exasperated, exasperating.**

excavate—1. To dig or scoop out: *The workers* excavated *part of the backyard to put in a swimming pool.* 2. To uncover something by digging: *Scientists* excavated *several dinosaur fossils at this site.*

ex|ca|vate (eks′kə vāt) *verb,* **excavated, excavating.**

exceed—1. To be greater than; be better than: *The money raised at this year's book fair* exceeded *last year's total.* 2. To go beyond a limit: *The police issue tickets to drivers who* exceed *the speed limit.*

ex|ceed (ek **sēd**′) *verb,* **exceeded, exceeding.**

excel—To rank above others; be better than others: *My brother* excels *in wrestling and is the state champion.*

ex|cel (ek **sel**′) *verb,* **excelled, excelling.**

excellence—The state of being of very high quality: *Her* excellence *as a cook brings many requests for her recipes.*
ex|cel|lence (ek′sə ləns) *noun.*

excellent—Very good or fine; superior; superb: *She is an* excellent *musician and has been asked to play a solo number at the concert.*
ex|cel|lent (ek′sə lənt) *adjective.*
• Synonyms: **outstanding, wonderful**

except—Besides; not including: *You may go anywhere in the area* except *the pond. Preposition.*
—But: *I would like to go swimming* except *I forgot to bring my bathing suit. Conjunction.*
ex|cept (ek sept′) *preposition; conjunction.*

exception—1. The condition of being left out: *My brother likes all sports with the* exception *of boxing.* 2. Something that is not usual or like the rest; that which is not included: *The train runs on the same schedule almost every day, but Sunday is an* exception.
ex|cep|tion (ek sep′shən) *noun, plural* **exceptions.**

exceptional—Unusual; beyond the ordinary: *He showed his* exceptional *ability by juggling six objects at the same time.*
ex|cep|tion|al (ek sep′shə nəl) *adjective.*

excess—Too much of something; more than is needed: *We had an* excess *of tomatoes in our garden, so we gave some away. Noun.*
—Extra; more than usual: excess *baggage. Adjective.*
ex|cess (ek ses′ for *noun* and *adjective;* ek′ses for *adjective*) *noun, plural* **excesses;** *adjective.*

excessive—Too much; more than is needed: *There was* excessive *arguing during the game.*
ex|ces|sive (ek ses′iv) *adjective.*

exchange—To give one thing for another: *The two friends* exchanged *birthday presents. Verb.*
—1. The act of trading one thing for another: *I agreed to give him my pie in* exchange *for his cake.* 2. A place where things are traded or bought and sold: *the stock* exchange. *Noun.*
ex|change (eks chānj′) *verb,* **exchanged, exchanging;** *noun, plural* **exchanges.**
• Synonyms: **barter, swap, trade,** for *verb.*

excite—To stir up: *The sound of birds always* excites *our cat.*
ex|cite (ek sīt′) *verb,* **excited, exciting.**

excited—Having strong feelings; stirred up: *The* excited *boy could hardly wait for the parade to start.*
ex|cit|ed (ek sī′tid) *adjective.*

excitement—1. The state of being stirred up: *There was great* excitement *when school closed early because of the snowstorm.* 2. Something that stirs up or thrills: *Her ride on the fire engine was such an* excitement *for her that she could not stop talking about it.*
ex|cite|ment (ek sīt′mənt) *noun.*

exclaim—To cry out or speak suddenly with strong feelings, such as surprise, excitement, joy, or anger: *"This letter says that I won first prize!" she* exclaimed.
ex|claim (ek sklām′) *verb,* **exclaimed, exclaiming.**

exclamation—Something that is said suddenly and with strong feelings.
ex|cla|ma|tion (eks′klə mā′shən) *noun, plural* **exclamations.**

exclamation mark or **exclamation point**—The mark of punctuation that looks like this !. It is used after a word, group of words, or sentence to show strong feelings.
ex|cla|ma|tion mark or ex|cla|ma|tion point (eks′klə mā′shən mahrk or eks′klə mā′shən point) *noun, plural* **exclamation marks** or **exclamation points.**

exclude—To shut out; prevent from entering: *Children are* excluded *from visiting patients at the hospital except on Sunday afternoons.*
ex|clude (ek sklūd′) *verb,* **excluded, excluding.**

excursion—A short trip usually taken with a group: *We went on an* excursion *to the zoo.*
ex|cur|sion (ek skur′zhən or ek skur′shən) *noun, plural* **excursions.**

excuse—1. To explain or be a reason for: *Her age* excuses *her mistake.* 2. To pardon or forgive: *I hope you will* excuse *me for calling you by the wrong name.* 3. To free from doing something: *being* excused *from school. Verb.*
—A reason or explanation for something: *He brought a written* excuse *from his doctor and was allowed to skip football practice. Noun.*
ex|cuse (ek skyūz′ for *verb;* ek skyūs′ for *noun*) *verb,* **excused, excusing;** *noun, plural* **excuses.**

execute—1. To put to death as ordered by law: *The traitor was* executed. 2. To carry out: *The soldier* executed *the general's orders.*
ex|e|cute (ek′sə kyūt) *verb,* **executed, executing.**

execution—1. The act of putting to death as ordered by law: *the* execution *of a criminal.* 2. A putting into effect: *One of the duties of the club's president was the* execution *of the rules.*
ex|e|cu|tion (ek′sə kyū′shən) *noun, plural* **executions.**

executive—**1.** Having to do with managing the affairs of a business or organization: *the* executive *vice-president of a bank.* **2.** Having to do with the branch of government that puts laws into action. *Adjective.*
—**1.** A person who runs a company or directs an organization: *a business* executive. **2.** The branch of government that is responsible for putting laws into action. *Noun.*
ex|ec|u|tive (eg **zek′**yə tiv) *adjective; noun, plural* **executives.**

exercise—**1.** An activity, usually a regular or repeated one, that improves or maintains the condition of the mind or body: *Jumping rope is good* exercise *for your heart and legs.* **2.** Something practiced to develop or improve a skill or ability: *piano* exercises; *subtraction* exercises. **3.** A ceremony or celebration: *Graduation* exercises *are held in the gym. Noun.*
—**1.** To carry out an activity to improve or maintain the condition of the mind or body; train; practice: *She* exercises *three times a week by running around the block.* **2.** To use actively: *Please* exercise *good safety habits when riding a bicycle. Verb.*
ex|er|cise (**ek′**sər sīz) *noun, plural* **exercises;** *verb,* **exercised, exercising.**

Word History

Exercise comes from a Latin word meaning ''to keep busy'' or ''to keep at work.'' It was usually used in connection with keeping farm animals at work in the fields. The French later borrowed the word, and it came to have its present meanings of ''to train'' or ''to drill.''

---

exercycle—An indoor exercise machine. It looks very much like the front half of a bicycle attached to a metal frame. An exercycle stays in one place while a person pedals.
ex|er|cy|cle (**ek′**sər sī′kəl) *noun, plural* **exercycles.**

exert—To use, especially to the fullest extent: *He had to* exert *all his patience to wait in the long line at the theater.*

ex|ert (eg **zurt′**) *verb,* **exerted, exerting.**
- **exert oneself:** To try hard or work hard: *She had to* exert *herself to lift the big box.*

exhale—To breathe out: *He* exhaled *on the cold window so that he could see his breath on it.*
ex|hale (eks **hāl′**) *verb,* **exhaled, exhaling.**

exhaust—**1.** To use up or empty entirely: *She* exhausted *her supply of postage stamps and had to buy more.* **2.** To make very tired: *The heat of the day* exhausted *him. Verb.*
—The used steam or gases given off by an engine: *automobile* exhaust. *Noun.*
ex|haust (eg **zawst′**) *verb,* **exhausted, exhausting;** *noun, plural* **exhausts.**

exhausted—**1.** Completely used up: exhausted *strength.* **2.** Tired out: *the* exhausted *hikers.*
ex|haust|ed (eg **zaws′**tid) *adjective.*

exhaustion—**1.** The condition of being very tired: *She collapsed from* exhaustion *after the race.*
ex|haus|tion (eg **zaws′**chən) *noun.*
- Synonyms: **fatigue, weariness**

exhibit—To display; present for viewing: *The science projects were* exhibited *in the auditorium. Verb.*
—A show or display: *a photography* exhibit. *Noun.*
ex|hib|it (eg **zib′**it) *verb,* **exhibited, exhibiting;** *noun, plural* **exhibits.**

exhibition—**1.** A showing or display: *an* exhibition *of skill.* **2.** A public showing: *a crafts* exhibition *at a fair.*
ex|hi|bi|tion (ek′sə **bish′**ən) *noun, plural* **exhibitions.**

exercycle

a at	i if	oo look	ch chalk		a in ago
ā ape	ī idle	ou out	ng sing		e in happen
ah calm	o odd	u ugly	sh ship	ə =	i in capital
aw all	ō oats	ū rule	th think		o in occur
e end	oi oil	ur turn	th their		u in upon
ē easy			zh treasure		

exile—To punish people by forcing them to leave their home or country: *The spy was exiled for stealing the plans. Verb.*
—A person who is sent away from his or her home or country, often as a punishment for breaking a law. *Noun.*
ex|ile (eg′zīl *or* ek′sīl) *verb,* **exiled, exiling;** *noun, plural* **exiles.**

exist—**1.** To be; to have being: *The United States has existed for more than 200 years.* **2.** To be real: *Do you believe that elves exist?* **3.** To be found: *Kangaroos exist in Australia.*
ex|ist (eg zist′) *verb,* **existed, existing.**

existence—**1.** The fact of being alive; life: *Many birds depend on bird feeders for their existence during the winter.* **2.** The condition of being real: *Some people believe in the existence of beings on other planets.* **3.** A way of living: *Stray dogs have a difficult existence.*
ex|ist|ence (eg zis′təns) *noun, plural* **existences.**

exit—**1.** A way out: *We headed for the exit when the circus was over.* **2.** The act of departing or leaving: *She made a noisy exit by slamming the door behind her. Noun.*
—To go out: *The flight attendant asked the passengers to exit through the rear doors. Verb.*
ex|it (eg′zit *or* ek′zit) *noun, plural* **exits;** *verb,* **exited, exiting.**

Word History

At one time, two separate Latin words were formed from a single Latin word meaning "go out." One of these words, meaning "he or she goes out," gave us **exit** as a verb. The other word, meaning "a going out," gave us **exit** as a noun.

exotic—Foreign; interesting; out of the ordinary: *Many exotic fruits from around the world are sold in our local supermarket.*
ex|ot|ic (eg zot′ik) *adjective.*

expand—**1.** To make or become larger: *He saved the money so that he could expand his bank account.* **2.** To spread out: *The parachute expanded as it filled with air.*
ex|pand (ek spand′) *verb,* **expanded, expanding.**
● Synonyms: **enlarge, lengthen,** for **1.**
Antonyms: For **1,** see Synonyms at **abbreviate.**

expanse—A stretch of open space: *a wide expanse of cloudless sky.*
ex|panse (ek spans′) *noun, plural* **expanses.**

expansion—**1.** The act or condition of becoming or making larger: *The expansion of the library took six months to complete.* **2.** The part that results from an increase in size: *The hospital's new expansion holds 100 beds.*
ex|pan|sion (ek span′shən) *noun, plural* **expansions.**

expect—**1.** To look forward to; believe that (something) is about to happen: *We expect his letter soon.* **2.** To require: *I expect you to be home for dinner at 6 o'clock.* **3.** To guess; suppose: *I expect you know what to do now.*
ex|pect (ek spekt′) *verb,* **expected, expecting.**
● Synonyms: **anticipate, await,** for **1.**

expectation—The act of looking forward to; hope: *the expectation of success.*
ex|pec|ta|tion (eks′pek tā′shən) *noun, plural* **expectations.**

expedition—**1.** A trip, especially one made to carry out scientific research or to explore an unknown area: *We made an expedition to see the ancient ruins.* **2.** The group of people that takes such a trip: *She led an expedition up the river.*
ex|pe|di|tion (eks′pə dish′ən) *noun, plural* **expeditions.**

Word History

Expedition comes from a Latin word meaning "to free one's feet" or "to set right." When you go on an expedition, you "free your feet" from your home to gather information to "set things right."

expel—**1.** To force out: *The student was caught cheating and was expelled from school.*
ex|pel (ek spel′) *verb,* **expelled, expelling.**

expenditure—**1.** The spending or using up of something: *Winning a race requires a great expenditure of effort.* **2.** The amount spent; expense: *He compared his income with his expenditures to see if his business made a profit.*
ex|pen|di|ture (ek spen′də choor *or* ek spen′də chər) *noun, plural* **expenditures.**

expense—**1.** The cost of something; price: *She could not afford the expense of a bus ride, so she walked home.* **2.** The reason for spending money: *The new playground was a large expense in the school budget.*
ex|pense (ek spens′) *noun, plural* **expenses.**
■ **at the expense of:** A giving up of one thing for something else: *I stayed up to watch the movie at the expense of a good night's sleep.*

expensive—Costing a lot of money; high-priced: expensive *jewelry*.
ex|pen|sive (ek spen′siv) *adjective*.

experience—1. A happening in a person's life; anything that one has lived through: *It was quite an* experience *when I took my first airplane ride*. 2. The knowledge and training gained by doing something: *My* experience *as a reporter for the school paper helped me in my English class*. *Noun*.
—To go through; feel: *to* experience *pain*. *Verb*.
ex|pe|ri|ence (ek spēr′ē əns) *noun, plural* experiences; *verb*, **experienced, experiencing.**

experienced—Having knowledge about something by having done it: *He had been in many races and was the most* experienced *runner on our team*.
ex|pe|ri|enced (ek spēr′ē ənst) *adjective*.

experiment—A test to prove or learn something: *She gave her cat a different food each day as an* experiment *to see which one it liked best*.
—To try out: *We* experimented *with several recipes, looking for the perfect chocolate cake*. *Verb*.
ex|per|i|ment (ek sper′ə mənt for *noun*; ek sper′ə ment for *verb*) *noun, plural* experiments; *verb*, **experimented, experimenting.**

experimental—Of or relating to tests to prove or learn something: Experimental *evidence shows that lack of sleep is related to poor scores on examinations*.
ex|per|i|men|tal (ek sper′ə men′təl) *adjective*.

expert—Someone who has a special skill or knowledge about something; specialist: *After years of working with computers, she has become an* expert *with them*. *Noun*.
—Very experienced; showing a special skill: *an* expert *mechanic*. *Adjective*.
ex|pert (eks′pərt for *noun*; ek spurt′ or eks′pərt for *adjective*) *noun, plural* experts; *adjective*.

expire—1. To come to an end; run out: *My magazine did not come in the mail because my subscription has* expired. 2. To die; perish.
ex|pire (ek spīr′) *verb*, **expired, expiring.**

explain—1. To make something able to be understood; make clear: *A police officer* explained *bicycle safety to the children last spring*. 2. To tell why something happened; give a reason for: *The coach asked me to* explain *why I missed practice*.
ex|plain (ek splān′) *verb*, **explained, explaining.**
■ **explain** (oneself): To give a reason for the way one has behaved: *She felt she should* explain *herself after leaving the room so suddenly*.

explanation—1. The act of making something clear and able to be understood: *I need an* explanation *of what the word means*. 2. A reason or an understanding of why something happened: *Mother wanted an* explanation *for the mud on my pants*.
ex|pla|na|tion (eks′plə nā′shən) *noun, plural* **explanations.**

explode—1. To burst violently; blow up: *The top of the erupting volcano* exploded, *sending flames and smoke into the sky*. 2. To burst out loudly because of strong feelings, such as excitement, enthusiasm, disapproval, or anger: *The stadium* exploded *when the home team scored*. 3. To grow or expand rapidly: *His leaf-raking business* exploded *when heavy winds caused the leaves to fall from the trees*.
ex|plode (ek splōd′) *verb*, **exploded, exploding.**

exploit—A brave act; heroic deed: *That book tells the story of the* exploits *of the astronauts*. *Noun*.
—1. To take advantage of (someone or something): *We* exploited *the teacher's offer of help while we were studying for the test*. 2. To take advantage of unfairly: *Some early settlers* exploited *the Indians by tricking them into selling their land too cheaply*. *Verb*.
ex|ploit (eks′ploit or ek sploit′ for *noun*; ek sploit′ for *verb*) *noun, plural* **exploits;** *verb*, **exploited, exploiting.**

exploration—1. The act of traveling over an unknown area and studying it: *the* exploration *of space*. 2. The act of studying or examining something very carefully: *an* exploration *of the facts in the case*.
ex|plo|ra|tion (eks′plə rā shən) *noun, plural* **explorations.**

explore—1. To travel over an unknown area for adventure and discovery: *There were still some parts of the jungle that had not been* explored. 2. To investigate; look into: *We* explored *the differences among bicycles before we bought one*.
ex|plore (ek splawr′) *verb*, **explored, exploring.**

a at	i if	oo look	ch chalk		⎡ a in ago
ā ape	ī idle	ou out	ng sing		e in happen
ah calm	o odd	u ugly	sh ship	ə =	i in capital
aw all	ō oats	ū rule	th think		o in occur
e end	oi oil	ur turn	th their		⎣ u in upon
ē easy			zh treasure		

explorer—One who travels over an unknown area for adventure and discovery.
ex|plor|er (ek **splawr′**ər) *noun, plural* **explorers.**

explosion—1. The act of blowing up or bursting; blast: *the* explosion *of a firecracker.* 2. A sudden outbreak of noise or activity: *an* explosion *of applause.* 3. A large increase over a short period of time: *a population* explosion.
ex|plo|sion (ek **splō′**zhən) *noun, plural* **explosions.**

explosive—1. Having to do with a blast; easily blown up: Explosive *materials should be kept away from heat.* 2. Easily set off or angered: *an* explosive *temper. Adjective.*
—A substance that explodes: *The bomb squad is trained to know how all* explosives *work. Noun.*
ex|plo|sive (ek **splō′**siv *or* ek **splō′**ziv) *adjective; noun, plural* **explosives.**

export—To ship goods grown or made in one country to another country for sale: *We* export *grain to countries that cannot grow their own. Verb.*
—A product that is shipped to another country to be sold: *Bananas are the island's leading* export. *Noun.*
ex|port (ex **spawrt′** *or* eks′pawrt for *verb;* eks′pawrt for *noun*) *verb,* **exported, exporting;** *noun, plural* **exports.**

expose—1. To leave out in the open or unprotected: *He forgot to wear his boots and* exposed *his new shoes to the snow.* 2. To uncover or give information on: *The spy* exposed *the enemy's secret plan.* 3. To permit light to shine on photographic film.
ex|pose (ek **spōz′**) *verb,* **exposed, exposing.**

exposition—A public exhibition or show: *The crafts* exposition *at the fair had many interesting handmade items on display.*
ex|po|si|tion (eks′pə **zish′**ən) *noun, plural* **expositions.**

exposure—1. The act of bringing out into the open: *The* exposure *of all the facts helped us to understand the reason for the new rule.* 2. The condition or state of being unprotected or uncovered: *His skin became burned from too much* exposure *to the sun.* 3. The position of something in relation to a direction or the weather: *His room is bright and sunny in the morning but dark in the afternoon because it has an eastern* exposure. 4. The act of allowing light to touch photographic film.
ex|po|sure (ek **spō′**zhər) *noun, plural* **exposures.**

express—To make something known through words or through a sign, such as a look or a tone of voice: *She wrote to* express *her thanks for the gift. Verb.*
—1. Precise; clear; definite: *The teacher gave* express *instructions about where we should put our tests when we finished them.* 2. Having to do with rapid delivery or transportation methods: *an* express *package service. Adjective.*
—1. A method of rapid delivery: *The letter sent by* express *arrived the next day.* 2. A method of rapid transportation: *My train was an* express *and did not stop between big cities. Noun.*
ex|press (ek **spres′**) *verb,* **expressed, expressing;** *adjective; noun, plural* **expresses.**

expression—1. The act of communicating thoughts or feelings: *an* expression *of love.* 2. A word or phrase that has a special meaning: *"In one ear and out the other" is an* expression *that means one listens but then immediately forgets or ignores what was said.* 3. A way of looking that shows what one is feeling: *He had an* expression *of relief on his face when the test was over.*
ex|pres|sion (ek **spresh′**ən) *noun, plural* **expressions.**

expressive—Full of feeling or meaning: *an* expressive *gesture; an* expressive *voice.*
ex|pres|sive (ek **spres′**iv) *adjective.*

expressway—A highway with two or more lanes on either side of a wall or a dividing strip of land. An expressway has few stops, entrances, or exits, and traffic generally travels at high speeds.
ex|press|way (ek **spres′**wā′) *noun, plural* **expressways.**

exquisite—Beautiful; delicate; finely made: *The lace on her dress was* exquisite.
ex|qui|site (eks′kwi zit *or* ek **skwiz′**it) *adjective.*

extend—1. To stretch out or unbend; lengthen; make larger: *Her brother is so tall that when he* extends *his arms above his head he can touch the ceiling.* 2. To make an offer of something: *He* extended *an invitation to us to join the club.*
ex|tend (ek **stend′**) *verb,* **extended, extending.**

extension—1. The act of stretching out or lengthening something: *The* extension *of the deadline for the book report gave me extra time to finish it.* 2. An enlargement of or an addition to something: *The family room was added as an* extension *of the house.* 3. An additional telephone connected to the main line.
ex|ten|sion (ek **sten′**shən) *noun, plural* **extensions.**

extensive—Large in amount; wide; broad: *He bought an old house and had to make* extensive *repairs.*
ex|ten|sive (ek sten′siv) *adjective.*

extent—The degree, range, or limit of something: *The* extent *of the damage was not as great as we had thought.*
ex|tent (ek stent′) *noun, plural* **extents.**

exterior—The outside surface or outer appearance of someone or something: *A coconut has a soft inside and a hard* exterior. *Noun.*
—On the outside; outer; external: *One of the* exterior *doors of the building leads to the parking lot. Adjective.*
ex|te|ri|or (ek stēr′ē ər) *noun, plural* **exteriors;** *adjective.*

exterminate—To get rid of completely; kill off: *My father* exterminated *the wasps that were building a nest above our front door.*
ex|ter|mi|nate (ek stur′mə nāt) *verb,* **exterminated, exterminating.**

external—Having to do with the outside; outer; exterior: *The skin is the* external *covering of the human body.*
ex|ter|nal (ek stur′nəl) *adjective.*

extinct—1. No longer in existence; dead: *Dinosaurs became* extinct *millions of years ago.* 2. Not active or no longer active: *Volcanoes can remain* extinct *for hundreds of years before they erupt again.*
ex|tinct (ek stingkt′) *adjective.*

extinction—1. The condition of being no longer in existence or wiped out: *The* extinction *of world hunger is a worthy goal.* 2. The act of destroying something or putting something out: *The quick* extinction *of the forest fire saved many valuable trees.*
ex|tinc|tion (ek stingk′shən) *noun, plural* **extinctions.**

extinguish—1. To cause to stop burning: *She* extinguished *all the candles on the cake with one breath.* 2. To put an end to: *The storm* extinguished *all our hopes of going on a picnic.*
ex|tin|guish (ek sting′gwish) *verb,* **extinguished, extinguishing.**

extra—More than what is usual, due, or expected: *There were two* extra *cupcakes after each person had been served. Adjective.*
—1. Something additional: *We have to do* extra *to get a higher mark.* 2. A special edition of a newspaper: *The paper published an* extra *to announce the signing of the peace treaty. Noun.*
—Especially: *He was* extra *careful with the final copy of his report. Adverb.*
ex|tra (eks′trə) *adjective; noun, plural* **extras;** *adverb.*

extra-—A prefix that means "beyond" or "outside." An extraordinary pianist has talent that is beyond what is ordinary for pianists. Extrascientific subjects lay outside the range of science.

Word Power

You can understand the meanings of many words that begin with **extra-,** if you add a meaning of the prefix to the meaning of the rest of the word.
extralunar: beyond the moon
extraliterary: outside the range of literature

---

extract—To remove by pulling: *Before painting, we had to* extract *the nails that were used for hanging pictures. Verb.*
—A substance used as flavoring: *The recipe for the cake called for a teaspoon of lemon* extract. *Noun.*
ex|tract (ek strakt′ for *verb;* eks′trakt for *noun*) *verb,* **extracted, extracting;** *noun, plural* **extracts.**

extraordinary—Very unusual; remarkable; special: *She has an* extraordinary *ability to sense other people's feelings.*
ex|traor|di|nar|y (ek strawr′də ner′ē or eks′trə awr′də ner ē) *adjective.*

extraterrestrial—Not of the earth; from or occurring in outer space: *Scientists use telescopes to see* extraterrestrial *objects more clearly. Adjective.*
—A being that comes from outer space: *The* extraterrestrial *in the movie said that all creatures on its planet have three eyes. Noun.*
ex|tra|ter|res|tri|al (eks′trə tə res′trē əl) *adjective; noun, plural* **extraterrestrials.**

extravagant—1. Spending more money than necessary; wasteful: *The* extravagant *bachelor owned five cars.* 2. More complicated than necessary; going beyond the limits of reason: *The*

a at	i if	oo look	ch chalk		a in ago
ā ape	ī idle	ou out	ng sing		e in happen
ah calm	o odd	u ugly	sh ship	ə =	i in capital
aw all	ō oats	ū rule	th think		o in occur
e end	oi oil	ur turn	th their		u in upon
ē easy			zh treasure		

plans for the party are too extravagant *to be carried out in time.*
ex|trav|a|gant (ek strav′ə gənt) *adjective.*

extreme—**1.** Very great in degree; severe; unusual: *We all went swimming during the* extreme *heat.* **2.** Farthest: *We live on the* extreme *north side of town. Adjective.*
—**1.** Either of two complete opposites: *Our weather is hot during the day and, at the other* extreme, *cold at night. Noun.*
ex|treme (ek strēm′) *adjective,* **extremer, extremest;** *noun, plural* **extremes.**
  ■ **go to extremes:** To go beyond what is necessary or proper in actions or words: *He wants the prize so much that I am afraid he will* go to extremes *to win it.*
  ● Synonyms: **drastic, harsh**

extremely—A great deal more than usual; very: *We have had* extremely *cold weather this winter.*
ex|treme|ly (ek strēm′lē) *adverb.*

extremity—**1.** The very end; the last part or point; the tip: *The lighthouse is at the northern* extremity *of the peninsula.* **2. extremities:** the hands and feet.
ex|trem|i|ty (ek strem′ə tē) *noun, plural* **extremities.**

extricate—To set free; release from a difficult or embarrassing situation: *It was not easy to* extricate *my kite from the tree.*
ex|tri|cate (ek′strə kāt) *verb,* **extricated, extricating.**

extrovert—An outgoing person who makes friends easily: *She is such an* extrovert *you can't help but like her.*
ex|tro|vert (ek′strə vurt) *noun, plural* **extroverts.**
  ● Antonym: **introvert**

exuberance—**1.** High spirits; excitement: *In his* exuberance *at our return, the dog jumped all over us.* **2.** An overflowing with growth: *An* exuberance *of tropical flowers.*
ex|u|ber|ance (eg zū′bər əns) *noun, plural* **exuberances.**

exuberant—**1.** Full of high spirits: *He was very* exuberant *upon hearing he had won the prize.* **2.** Very abundant; overflowing growth: *The* exuberant *jungle vegetation.*
ex|u|ber|ant (eg zū′bər ənt) *adjective.*

exult—To be very happy; rejoice greatly: *The runner* exulted *in his victory.*
ex|ult (eg zult′) *verb,* **exulted, exulting.**

exultant—Showing great joy: *The fans gave an* exultant *shout when they saw the final score.*
ex|ult|ant (eg zul′tənt) *adjective.*

eye—**1.** The organ of the body that makes sight possible. **2.** That part of this organ that is colored; iris: *Her blue blouse matched her* eyes. **3.** The area of the face surrounding and including this organ: *He bumped into the door and gave himself a black* eye. **4.** A look: *He cast a hungry* eye *at the chocolate cake.* **5.** Anything that looks like an eye, such as the hole in a needle or a bud on a potato. *Noun.*
—To look at carefully; watch: *He* eyed *himself in the mirror before having his picture taken. Verb.*
eye (ī) *noun, plural* **eyes;** *verb,* **eyed, eying** or **eyeing.**
  ■ **be all eyes:** To watch carefully; pay close attention: *We were all eyes as she opened the gift.*
  catch (one's) eye: To get someone's attention: *Catch his eye and signal that we are going to leave.*
  in the public eye: Well known; often seen: *The actress has been in the public eye since her successful movie.*
  keep an eye on: To take care of; watch: *She kept an eye on the dog to make sure it did not leave the yard.*
  make eyes at: To flirt with: *She was embarrassed by the way he kept making eyes at her at the dance.*
  see eye to eye: To have the same opinion or feelings; agree completely: *My friend and I see eye to eye on most things.*
  with (one's) eyes open: Being aware of the possible dangers or consequences of an action: *The explorer went into the jungle with his eyes open and knew he might not return.*
  without batting an eye: Without showing any emotion; calmly: *I cried when I heard the sad music, but she listened to it without batting an eye.*
  ● Words that sound the same are **aye** and **I.**

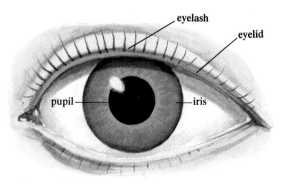

eye (noun, definition 1)

eyeball—The eye itself, without the eyelids or socket. It is shaped like a ball.
eye|ball (ī′bawl′) *noun, plural* **eyeballs.**
• See picture at **eye.**

eyebrow—The hair that grows on the bony ridge at the top of the eye socket.
eye|brow (ī′brou′) *noun, plural* **eyebrows.**

eyedropper—A small glass or plastic tube with a rubber bulb at one end. When the bulb is squeezed and slowly released, liquid is drawn up the tube and held in it. Squeezing the bulb again pushes the liquid from the tube in the form of drops.
eye|drop|per (ī′drop′ər) *noun, plural* **eyedroppers.**

eyeglass—1. A piece of glass that is ground and formed in a certain way to correct eyesight; lens. 2. **eyeglasses:** Two pieces of specially prepared glass that are set in a frame and are worn to improve a person's vision.
eye|glass (ī′glas) *noun, plural* **eyeglasses.**

eyelash—One of the short hairs on an eyelid.
eye|lash (ī′lash′) *noun, plural* **eyelashes.**
■ **by an eyelash:** By a very small amount: *He ran as fast as he could to catch the ball but missed it* by an eyelash.
• See picture at **eye.**

eyelet—A small, round hole for a lace or cord to go through: *He put his shoelace through the eyelet.*
eye|let (ī′lit) *noun, plural* **eyelets.**
• A word that sounds the same is **islet.**

eyelid—One of the movable pieces of skin that cover the eye. The upper eyelid moves up and down to open and close the eye.
eye|lid (ī′lid′) *noun, plural* **eyelids.**
• See picture at **eye.**

eyesight—The power or ability to see: *He has perfect* eyesight *and does not need eyeglasses.*
eye|sight (ī′sīt′) *noun.*

eyesore—Something that is very unpleasant to look at: *That yard with all the junk in it is an eyesore.*
eye|sore (ī′sawr) *noun, plural* **eyesores.**

eyestrain—A condition in which the eyes are tired or weak. It is often caused by reading in poor light.
eye|strain (ī′strān) *noun.*

eyetooth—One of the two pointed teeth on either side of the four center teeth in the upper jaw.
eye|tooth (ī′tūth′) *noun, plural* **eyeteeth** (i′tēth′).
■ **give (one's) eyeteeth:** To give up something of great value; give anything for: *He would give his* eyeteeth *to meet his favorite baseball player.*

eyewitness—A person who is present at the scene of an act or event while it is occurring: *An* eyewitness *helped the police catch the bank robbers by giving a good description of them.*
eye|wit|ness (ī′wit′nis) *noun, plural* **eyewitnesses.**

a at	i if	oo look	ch chalk		⎡ a in ago
ā ape	ī idle	ou out	ng sing		e in happen
ah calm	o odd	u ugly	sh ship	ə =	i in capital
aw all	ō oats	ū rule	th think		o in occur
e end	oi oil	ur turn	th their		⎣ u in upon
ē easy			zh treasure		

About 5,000 years ago, the ancient Egyptians used a symbol of a hook.

People in the Middle East used the same symbol. They called it *waw,* their word for "hook."

About 3,000 years ago, other people in the Middle East used a similar symbol.

About 1,900 years ago, the Romans gave the capital F its present form. The small letter f was first used about 1,500 years ago. It reached its present form about 500 years ago.

About 2,800 years ago, the Greeks gave the letter this form. They called it *digamma* and made it the sixth letter in their alphabet.

F or **f**—**1.** The sixth letter of the English alphabet: *There are three* f's *in "fluff."* **2.** The lowest or failing grade in school: *He got an F on his history test.*
F, f (ef) *noun, plural* **F's** or **Fs, f's** or **fs.**

F.—An abbreviation for the Fahrenheit temperature scale: *The thermometer reads 60 degrees F.*

fable—A short story that teaches a lesson, often with imaginary animals who talk: *a fable about a race between a rabbit and a turtle.*
fa|ble (fā′bəl) *noun, plural* **fables.**

fabric—Material made from natural fibers, such as cotton, or artificial fibers, such as nylon; cloth.
fab|ric (fab′rik) *noun, plural* **fabrics.**

fabulous—Amazing; extraordinary: *The king had a* fabulous *treasure hidden in his castle.*
fab|u|lous (fab′yə ləs) *adjective.*

face—**1.** The front of the head; eyes, nose, mouth, cheeks, and chin. **2.** A look that people make; an expression: *She made an ugly* face *at her brother.* **3.** The front or surface of something: *Our house is wood with a brick* face. *Noun.*
—**1.** To look upon: *My window* faces *the garden.* **2.** To meet bravely: *We must* face *the fact that we are lost. Verb.*
face (fās) *noun, plural* **faces;** *verb,* **faced, facing.**

　lose face: To feel great shame: *He* lost face *when his bad play let the other team win.*

to (one's) face: Openly; directly to someone. *Would you say that* to her face?

facial—Of or for the face: facial *bones; a* facial *tissue.*
fa|cial (fā′shəl) *adjective.*

facility—**1.** Ease in doing something; skill: *She solved even the most complicated puzzles with* facility. **2. facilities**—Something that helps serve a purpose: *Our school has excellent sports* facilities.
fa|cil|i|ty (fə sil′ə tē) *noun, plural* **facilities.**

fact—A thing that happened or that is known to be true: *It is a* fact *that rocks are hard.*
fact (fakt) *noun, plural* **facts.**

factor—**1.** A cause of something: *The sudden rain and the high water level in the river were two* factors *that caused the flood.* **2.** Any of the numbers that when multiplied together form a product: *The numbers 3 and 5 are* factors *of 15.*
fac|tor (fak′tər) *noun, plural* **factors.**

factory—One or more buildings used for making things; a plant: *a clothing* factory.
fac|to|ry (fak′tər ē) *noun, plural* **factories.**

factual—Having to do with things that happened or are known to be true: *The newspaper gave a* factual *report on the town meeting.*
fac|tu|al (fak′choo əl) *adjective.*

faculty—**1.** One of the powers of the body or mind: *Hearing and sight are important* faculties. **2.** A natural ability; talent: *The old man had the*

faculty *of making friends with wild animals.*
3. The teachers of a school.
fac|ul|ty (**fak′**əl tē) *noun, plural* **faculties.**

fad—A practice or interest that is very popular for a short time; craze: *Wearing our shirts backwards was a fad in our school last year.*
fad (fad) *noun, plural* **fads.**

fade—**1.** To decrease in brightness, color, or freshness; dim: *The old photographs faded.*
2. To lessen; disappear slowly: *With all this rain, hope is fading for us to go on a picnic.*
fade (fād) *verb,* **faded, fading.**

Fahrenheit—Having to do with the temperature scale on which water freezes at 32 degrees and boils at 212 degrees.
Fahr|en|heit (**far′**ən hīt) *adjective.*
Abbreviation: **F.**

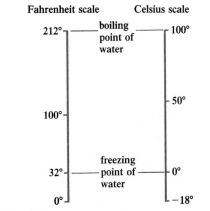

Fahrenheit scale   Celsius scale

Fahrenheit

Word History

Fahrenheit comes from a man's name, Gabriel Daniel Fahrenheit. He was a German scientist who lived from 1686 to 1736 and who invented the mercury thermometer. He used the scale of temperature that is now called after him.

fail—**1.** To not succeed; not pass: *to fail to reach the bus in time for school; to fail an examination.* **2.** To be lacking or not be enough: *We had to use candles when the electricity*

failed. **3.** To become weak; lose strength: *He cheered until his voice* failed. **4.** To be unable to pay one's debts; become bankrupt: *After two summers with little rain, the farm* failed.
fail (fāl) *verb,* **failed, failing.**

failure—**1.** The lack of success: *He blamed his failure to win the race on a cramp in his foot.*
2. The fact of being lacking or not being enough: *a power* failure; *a crop* failure. **3.** A becoming weak or feeble; loss of strength: *With the failure of the battery, the radio stopped playing.* **4.** A person or thing that lacks success: *The dance was a failure because the band never came.*
fail|ure (**fāl′**yər) *noun, plural* **failures.**

faint—**1.** Not clear; weak: *She left* faint *footprints in the wet sand.* **2.** Dizzy and weak: *Standing for an hour in the hot sun made him* faint. *Adjective.*
—The state of being asleep for a short time, caused by great hunger, illness, or shock. *Noun.*
—To become dizzy or weak for a short time: *I nearly* fainted *when they told me I had won first prize. Verb.*
faint (fānt) *adjective,* **fainter, faintest;** *noun, plural* **faints;** *verb,* **fainted, fainting.**

fainthearted—Not having courage; timid: *Being a police officer is not a job for the* fainthearted.
faint|heart|ed (**fānt′**hahr′tid) *adjective.*

fair¹—**1.** Showing favor to no one; just: *a* fair *referee.* **2.** Being within the rules or boundaries; allowed: fair *play;* a fair *ball.* **3.** Neither very good nor very bad; average: *She is a* fair *tennis player.* **4.** Light in color; blond: fair *skin;* fair *hair.* **5.** Not stormy or cloudy; clear: *It should be* fair *and warm tomorrow.* **6.** Pleasing to look at; attractive: *a* fair *maiden. Adjective.*
—Justly; honestly: *A good sport always plays* fair. *Adverb.*
fair (fār) *adjective,* **fairer, fairest;** *adverb.*
● A word that sounds the same is **fare.**

fair²—**1.** A public show where farm or manufactured goods may be bought and sold: *Attendance at the world's* fair *was greater than expected.* **2.** A show and sale of things to raise money for a cause or charity: *I bought this quilt at the church* fair.
fair (fār) *noun, plural* **fairs.**
● A word that sounds the same is **fare.**
■ **fair and square:** Honestly: *She won the photography award* fair and square.

fairly—**1.** In a just way; honestly: *The judges awarded all the prizes* fairly. **2.** Rather; somewhat: *a* fairly *easy job.*
fair|ly (**fār′**lē) *adverb.*

a at	i if	oo look	ch chalk		a in ago
ā ape	ī idle	ou out	ng sing		e in happen
ah calm	o odd	u ugly	sh ship	ə =	i in capital
aw all	ō oats	ū rule	th think		o in occur
e end	oi oil	ur turn	th their		u in upon
ē easy			zh treasure		

fairy

fairy—A small imaginary being with magic powers.
fair|y (fãr′ē) *noun, plural* **fairies.**

fairy tale—1. A story about imaginary beings with magic powers: *"Cinderella" is my favorite fairy tale.* 2. Something said that is not true; a made-up story: *The story of his trip to China was a fairy tale.*
fair|y tale (fãr′ē tāl) *noun, plural* **fairy tales.**

faith—1. Trust; confidence: *I have faith that the airplane will arrive on time.* 2. Religious belief: *the Jewish faith; the Christian faith.*
faith (fāth) *noun, plural* **faiths.**

faithful—1. Worthy of confidence; loyal: *The faithful dog waits for the boy at the schoolhouse door.* 2. True; exact: *The artist painted a faithful picture of the old house.*
faith|ful (fāth′fəl) *adjective.*

fake—1. To make up or change something so it will seem real or true: *She tried to fake the rock star's way of singing.* 2. To pretend something, usually in order to fool people: *He faked a limp so we would feel sorry for him. Verb.*
—A person or thing that is not real; fraud. *Noun.*
fake (fāk) *verb,* **faked, faking;** *noun, plural* **fakes.**

falcon—A bird like a hawk, with long wings, a short tail, a hooked bill, and sharp, hooked claws. The falcon flies very fast and can be trained to hunt small animals and birds.
fal|con (fawl′kən, fal′kən, *or* faw′kən) *noun, plural* **falcons.**

fall—1. To drop from a higher to a lower place: *to fall off the wall.* 2. To hang down: *Her long hair fell to her waist.* 3. To be captured or defeated: *The country fell to the invaders.* 4. To pass into a different state or condition: *to fall ill; to fall in love.* 5. To happen; occur: *My birthday falls on April 19th.* 6. To become lower or less; decrease: *The temperature fell rapidly before the storm. Verb.*
—1. A dropping from a higher to a lower place: *She had a fall from her bicycle.* 2. The amount that comes down: *There was a heavy fall of snow last night.* 3. A defeat; overthrow: *The king's cruelty led to his fall.* 4. A lowering, lessening, or reduction: *a fall in prices; a fall in temperature.* 5. The season of the year between summer and winter; autumn: *Apples ripen in the fall.* 6. **falls**—A waterfall. *Noun.*
—Having to do with autumn season: *fall weather; a fall jacket. Adjective.*
fall (fawl) *verb,* **fell, fallen, falling;** *noun, plural* **falls;** *adjective.*
■ **fall flat:** To have no result or effect; fail: *She tried to make her story funny, but the jokes fell flat.*

fallen—See **fall.**
fall|en (faw′lən) *verb.*

fallout—The radioactive particles that fall to earth after a nuclear explosion.
fall|out (fawl′out′) *noun.*

falcon

Word History

Falcon comes from a Latin word meaning "sickle." A sickle is a curved blade for cutting plants. The hooked claws of a falcon are shaped like sickles.

false—1. Not true; incorrect; wrong: *a false statement.*   2. Used to trick or deceive; misleading: *Saying that this brand of cereal will make people grow faster is false advertising.*   3. Not real or genuine; artificial: *The clown wore a false nose.*
false (fawls) *adjective,* **falser, falsest.**

falter—To hesitate in speaking or moving: *He faltered when he sang the fourth verse of the song.*
fal|ter (fawl′tər) *verb,* **faltered, faltering.**

fame—The condition of being very well known: *The artist gained great fame for her beautiful paintings.*
fame (fām) *noun.*

familiar—1. Often seen or experienced; well-known: *She took the familiar path to her home.*   2. Closely acquainted: *Are you familiar with the rules of this game?*   3. Close; intimate: *Few people are on familiar terms with a famous person like the President.*
fa|mil|iar (fə mil′yər) *adjective.*
• Synonyms: **accustomed, customary, habitual, usual,** for 1.
Antonyms: **odd, strange, unusual,** for 1.

family—1. A father, mother, and their children: *Our family lives in the city.*   2. The children of a father and mother: *She comes from a family of six girls.*   3. All the people living in the same house: *The baby's crying kept the family awake all night.*   4. All of a person's relatives: *The whole family will spend the summer at my grandmother's house.*   5. A group of animals or plants that are related: *Onions are in the lily family.*   6. Any group of related or similar things: *All people belong to the human family.*
fam|i|ly (fam′ə lē) *noun, plural* **families.**

famine—A great shortage of food: *When the grain harvest was poor, the country suffered a terrible famine.*
fam|ine (fam′ən) *noun, plural* **famines.**

famished—Very hungry; starving: *I missed lunch and was famished by dinnertime.*
fam|ished (fam′isht) *adjective.*

famous—Widely known: *The cafe is famous for its bread pudding.*
fa|mous (fā′məs) *adjective.*

fan¹—1. An object often shaped like a half circle that, when held in the hand and moved back and forth, creates an air current to cool the face.   2. An object made of flat or curved blades that move the air in heating and cooling units. The blades are turned by an electric motor. *Noun.*
—To move the air by such a method: *The wind fanned the flames higher and higher. Verb.*
fan (fan) *noun, plural* **fans;** *verb,* **fanned, fanning.**

fan²—1. A devoted follower of some activity, such as a sport or entertainment, or of a person: *Fans crowded around to get the movie star's autograph.*
fan (fan) *noun, plural* **fans.**

fanatic—A person whose beliefs or feelings about something are extremely strong or beyond reason: *a fanatic about exercise. Noun.*
—Much too enthusiastic or devoted: *a fanatic believer. Adjective.*
fa|nat|ic (fə nat′ik) *noun, plural* **fanatics;** *adjective.*

fancy—1. The ability to form pictures in the mind; imagination: *Myths contain many stories created by fancy.*   2. The picture that is imagined: *I sometimes have a fancy that I will become a great star.*   3. A liking or love: *She has a fancy for crazy hats.*   4. A notion; whim: *I have a fancy for some popcorn. Noun.*
—1. To form pictures in the mind; imagine: *Do you ever fancy that you are a great athlete?*   2. To like: *I fancy a cheeseburger right now. Verb.*
—Not plain; elegant: *He sent her a fancy valentine. Adjective.*
fan|cy (fan′sē) *noun, plural* **fancies;** *verb,* **fancied, fancying;** *adjective,* **fancier, fanciest.**

fancy-free—Having no worries or troubles: *With my homework finished and my chores done, I feel fancy-free.*
fan|cy-free (fan′sē frē′) *adjective.*

fang—A long, pointed tooth. Dogs, wolves, and snakes have fangs.
fang (fang) *noun, plural* **fangs.**

fantastic—1. Strange; odd: *The movie was about fantastic creatures from outer space.*   2. Wonderful: *We had a fantastic time on our vacation.*
fan|tas|tic (fan tas′tik) *adjective.*

fantasy—Something that a person imagines; something not real: *Daydreams and fairy tales are fantasies.*
fan|ta|sy (fan′tə sē) *noun, plural* **fantasies.**

a at	i if	oo look	ch chalk		⌐ a in ago
ā ape	ī idle	ou out	ng sing		e in happen
ah calm	o odd	u ugly	sh ship	ə =	i in capital
aw all	ō oats	ū rule	th think		o in occur
e end	oi oil	ur turn	th their		⌐ u in upon
ē easy			zh treasure		

far—Not near; distant: *The ship sailed to a* far *island. Adjective.*
—1. At or to a great distance: far *above;* far *away.*   2. Very much: *You can dance* far *better than I can. Adverb.*
far (fahr) *adjective,* **farther, farthest;** *adverb,* **farther, farthest.**

fare—The price of a ride in a bus, taxi, train, ship, or airplane. *Noun.*
—To get along; do: *How did you* fare *on the final exam? Verb.*
fare (fār) *noun, plural* **fares;** *verb,* **fared, faring.**
● A word that sounds the same is **fair.**

farewell—Good-by. *Interjection.*
—Good wishes that people make when departing; good-by: *We said our* farewells *at the airport. Noun.*
—Parting; last; final: *a* farewell *speech; a* farewell *concert. Adjective.*
fare|well (fār′wel′) *interjection; noun, plural* **farewells;** *adjective.*

farm—An area of land used for raising crops or animals: *a wheat* farm; *a sheep* farm. *Noun.*
—To raise crops or animals on an area of land: *Our family has* farmed *this land for 50 years. Verb.*
farm (fahrm) *noun, plural* **farms;** *verb,* **farmed, farming.**

farmer—A person who raises crops or animals: *a potato* farmer; *a dairy* farmer.
farm|er (fahr′mər) *noun, plural* **farmers.**

far-sighted or **farsighted**—1. Able to see distant objects more clearly than nearby objects: *A* far-sighted *person may need glasses for reading or close work.*   2. Able to see ahead; planning wisely for the future: *My* far-sighted *brother has saved enough money to go to college.*
far-sight|ed or **far|sight|ed** (fahr′si′tid) *adjective.*

farther—*See* **far.**
far|ther (fahr′thər) *adjective, adverb.*

farthest—*See* **far.**
far|thest (fahr′thist) *adjective, adverb.*

fascinate—To attract irresistibly and to hold one's attention as if under a spell: *The department store's charming holiday display* fascinated *the children.*
fas|ci|nate (fas′ə nāt) *verb,* **fascinated, fascinating.**
● Synonyms: **bewitch, enchant**

fashion—1. The way in which something is made or done; manner: *Write your book report in this* fashion.   2. The latest style in dress or conduct:

Short haircuts are in fashion *this year. Noun.*
—To make; construct: *The bird* fashioned *its nest of twigs and grass. Verb.*
fash|ion (fash′ən) *noun, plural* **fashions;** *verb,* **fashioned, fashioning.**
■ **after a fashion** or **in a fashion:** In some way or other, usually not very well: *He sings* after a fashion, *but he doesn't sound good.*

fast[1]—1. Quick; swift: *a* fast *worker.*   2. Before the correct time: *I arrived early because my watch is* fast.   3. Firmly fixed and secure: *a* fast *hold of his hand; hard and* fast *rules.*   4. Constant in loyalty and faith: *old and* fast *friends.*   5. Permanently dyed: *I hope this red sweater was made with* fast *dyes. Adjective.*
—1. Quickly; swiftly: *A rabbit can run* fast.   2. Securely; tightly: *stuck* fast *in the mud.*   3. Very soundly; completely: *The children pretended to be* fast *asleep when their mother came home. Adverb.*
fast (fast) *adjective,* **faster, fastest;** *adverb.*
■ **play fast and loose:** To not keep one's word; be insincere: *The person that sold you this worthless thing must have been* playing fast and loose *with you.*
pull a fast one: To trick someone: *While we waited at the front door, she* pulled a fast one *and went out the back.*

fast[2]—1. To go without eating either all food or certain kinds of foods: *The doctor told the man to* fast *and have only liquids on the night before his physical exam. Verb.*
—A period of not eating: *Some religions observe* fasts *on certain days of the year. Noun.*
fast (fast) *verb,* **fasted, fasting;** *noun, plural* **fasts.**

fasten—To attach firmly by pinning, tying, nailing, or the like: *to* fasten *a poster to the wall; to* fasten *a seat belt.*
fas|ten (fas′ən) *verb,* **fastened, fastening.**

fat—A white or yellowish oily material formed in the bodies of animals and some plants. *Noun.*
—1. Being, having, or containing such material; plump: *a* fat *stomach; a* fat *meaty sausage.*   2. Containing a lot; well filled: *a* fat *raise. Adjective.*
fat (fat) *noun, plural* **fats;** *adjective,* **fatter, fattest.**
■ **chew the fat:** To have a long talk: *My friends and I like to meet and* chew the fat.
fat chance: Not much or almost no chance of happening: *Without having studied, I have a* fat chance *of passing the test.*
live off the fat of the land: To have everything

one wants or needs: *His father made a great deal of money, and now he* lives off the fat of the land.

the fat is in the fire: There is no way to stop something bad from happening: *As soon as my brother sees that I ruined the puzzle he has been putting together,* the fat will be in the fire.

• Synonyms: **plump, stout,** for *adjective* 1. Antonyms: See Synonyms at **lean**[2].

fatal—1. Causing death: *a* fatal *illness.* 2. Causing ruin or harm: *Thinking I could pass this test without studying was a* fatal *mistake.* fa|tal (fā′təl) *adjective.*

fate—A power beyond human control, believed by some to decide and cause everything that happens. *I believe that* fate *was the cause of our meeting and becoming best friends.* fate (fāt) *noun, plural* **fates.**

father—1. A male parent. 2. **Father:** A title of respect that is given to a priest or other clergyman. fa|ther (fah′thər) *noun, plural* **fathers.** Abbreviation for 2: Fr.

father-in-law—The father of one's wife or husband. fa|ther-in-law (fah′thər in law′) *noun, plural* **fathers-in-law.**

Father's Day—A day set apart to honor fathers. Father's Day falls on the third Sunday in June each year. It is celebrated in the United States and Canada. Fa|ther's Day (fah′thərz dā) *noun.*

fathom—A unit of length equal to six feet (1.8 meters). It is used mostly to measure the depth of water: *This lake is six* fathoms *deep.* fath|om (fath′əm) *noun, plural* **fathoms.**

fatigue—Tiredness caused from great use or effort; exhaustion: *After we had walked for three hours,* fatigue *set in. Noun.* —To make tired; exhaust: *We were all* fatigued *after football practice. Verb.* fa|tigue (fə tēg′) *noun; verb,* **fatigued, fatiguing.**

• Synonyms: **exhaustion, weariness,** for *noun.*

faucet—A device for controlling the flow of water or other liquid from a pipe or container. fau|cet (faw′sit) *noun, plural* **faucets.**

Language Fact

Faucet, spigot, and **tap** all mean the device that turns the water off and on at your sink. The name that you use for this device probably depends on where you live. The word **faucet** is the most commonly used term for the device throughout most of the United States, but the word **spigot** is often used in the southern United States. **Tap** is commonly used in England.

---

fault—1. A failing that keeps something from being all it should be; defect: *Carelessness is his worst* fault. 2. A mistake; error: *We got lost due to a* fault *in the map.* 3. The responsibility for something wrong: *It was my* fault *that the door was left open.* fault (fawlt) *noun, plural* **faults.**

■ **to a fault:** More than necessary; too much: *He works so slowly because he is careful* to a fault.

faulty—Not perfect; defective: *The house fire was caused by* faulty *wiring.* fault|y (fawl′tē) *adjective,* **faultier, faultiest.**

favor—1. A kind act: *I loaned her the money as a* favor. 2. Liking; acceptance: *The boy brought his teacher flowers to win her* favor. 3. A small gift given to each guest at a party: *Party hats and noise makers were handed out as* favors. *Noun.* —1. To do a kind act for; show kindness to: *When I picked up the book she dropped, she* favored *me with a smile.* 2. To like; support; accept: *Most of us* favor *the idea of a class party.* 3. To give special treatment to; prefer: *Parents try not to* favor *one of their children over another.* 4. To look like: *Which parent does your sister* favor? *Verb.* fa|vor (fā′vər) *noun, plural* **favors;** *verb,* **favored, favoring.**

favorable—1. Showing approval: *Do you think the vote on the plan will be* favorable? 2. To one's advantage; helpful: *It is a* favorable *time to talk to her, since she is in a good mood.* fa|vor|a|ble (fā′vər ə bəl) *adjective.*

favorite—Liked better than all the others; preferred: *Chocolate is her* favorite *flavor. Adjective.* —A person or thing that is liked better than all the others: *The red jelly beans are my* favorites. *Noun.*

a at	i if	oo look	ch chalk		ə =	a in ago
ā ape	ī idle	ou out	ng sing			e in happen
ah calm	o odd	u ugly	sh ship			i in capital
aw all	ō oats	ū rule	th think			o in occur
e end	oi oil	ur turn	th their			u in upon
ē easy			zh treasure			

fa|vor|ite (fā′vər it) *adjective; noun, plural* **favorites.**

fawn—A deer that is less than a year old.
fawn (fawn) *noun, plural* **fawns.**

fawn

fax—1. A copy of written words or pictures sent by telephone or radio: *This fax just came for you.*   2. A device for sending copies; fax machine: *Turn on the* fax. *Noun.*
—to send by fax. *I'll fax the letter today. Verb.*
fax (faks) *noun, plural* **faxes;** *verb,* **faxes, faxing.**

fear—A strong emotion caused by feeling or knowing that danger is near: *The crew's worst* fear *is a storm at sea. Noun.*
—1. To be afraid of: *Our dog is so big that some people* fear *him.*   2. To feel uneasy about: *I* fear *that we are lost. Verb.*
fear (fēr) *noun, plural* **fears;** *verb,* **feared, fearing.**

fearful—1. Terrible; awful; frightful: *The tree fell with a* fearful *crash.*   2. Afraid: *I have always been* fearful *of storms.*
fear|ful (fēr′fəl) *adjective.*
• See Synonyms and Antonyms at **brave.**

fearless—Unafraid; brave; courageous: *The fire fighter was* fearless *as she battled the flames.*
fear|less (fēr′les) *adjective.*
• See Synonyms and Antonyms at **brave.**

feast—A rich, plentiful meal that is prepared for a special occasion, usually for many guests; banquet: *Our family and friends gathered for the Thanksgiving* feast. *Noun.*
—To enjoy a rich or plentiful meal: *We* feasted *on fresh vegetables from his garden. Verb.*

feast (fēst) *noun, plural* **feasts;** *verb,* **feasted, feasting.**

feat—An act showing great bravery, skill, or strength: *The sky divers performed amazing* feats.
feat (fēt) *noun, plural* **feats.**
• A word that sounds the same is **feet.**
• Synonyms: **accomplishment, achievement, deed**

feather—One of the light, thin out-growths that cover and protect the body of a bird.
feath|er (fe<u>th</u>′ər) *noun, plural* **feathers.**
■ **birds of a feather:** Things or people that are all of the same kind or character: *Birds of a* feather *flock together.*
feather in (one's) **cap:** An honor; something to take pride in: *Winning is a* feather in *her* cap.
feather (one's) **nest:** To take advantage of a situation to provide for oneself or make oneself richer: *He* feathered his nest *while in office.*
ruffle (someone's) **feathers:** To annoy, upset, or irritate slightly: *It was hard to manage the committee without* ruffling *anyone's* feathers.
smooth (someone's) **feathers:** To calm; soothe: *A few kind words* smoothed *his* feathers.

feature—1. The appearance of the face or a part of the face: *Her sparkling eyes and pretty smile are her best* features.   2. A part or quality of something that attracts the most attention: *The trained tigers were the main* feature *at the circus.*   3. A full-length movie. *Noun.*
—To give a major part to: *The book* features *a large, white whale. Verb.*
fea|ture (fē′chər) *noun, plural* **features;** *verb,* **featured, featuring.**
• Synonyms: **characteristic, trait,** for *noun* 2.

Feb.—The abbreviation for **February.**

February—The second month of the year. February has 28 days except in leap years, when it has 29 days.
Feb|ru|ar|y (feb′ro͞o er′ē *or* feb′yo͞o er′ē) *noun.* Abbreviation: **Feb.**

Word History

February comes from the Latin name of an ancient Roman religious holiday that was celebrated on February 15.

fed—*See* **feed.**
fed (fed) *verb.*

federal—1. Containing separate states joined together as one country: *The United States has a* federal *government.*   2. Having to do with the central government rather than the governments of the individual states. Some of the responsibilities of the federal government are providing for the country's defense and taking care of foreign affairs.

fed|er|al (fed′ər əl) *adjective.*

fee—Money charged for a service: *What is the* fee *for parking here?*

fee (fē) *noun, plural* **fees.**

feeble—1. Lacking strength; weak: *I could not read by the candle's* feeble *light.* 2. Not effective, forceful, or adequate: *We need more than a* feeble *protest to get Father to change his mind.*

fee|ble (fē′bəl) *adjective,* **feebler, feeblest.**

• Synonyms: **lame, poor,** for 1.

feed—1. To give food to: *a cat* feeding *her kittens; to* feed *the children their lunch.* 2. To eat; use as food: *Squirrels* feed *on nuts and seeds.* 3. To supply or provide something: *to* feed *a quarter into the parking meter; to* feed *him false hopes. Verb.*
—Food for animals: *This corn is used as chicken* feed. *Noun.*

feed (fēd) *verb,* **fed, feeding;** *noun, plural* **feeds.**

feel—1. To touch: Feel *this silk scarf and see how soft it is.* 2. To search for something with one's fingers; grope: *She* felt *in her purse for a handkerchief.* 3. To find out, test, or examine by touching: *The doctor* felt *her pulse.* 4. To be aware of through one's senses: *I could* feel *the heat from the fire.* 5. To become aware of in one's mind; experience: *to* feel *happy, sad, or sorry.* 6. To think; believe: *She* feels *that you are wrong. Verb.*
—The way a thing seems to the touch: *I like the* feel *of grass under my bare feet. Noun.*

feel (fēl) *verb,* **felt, feeling;** *noun, plural* **feels.**

■ **feel out:** To try cautiously to learn from someone: *I* felt out *my brother about lending me his stereo.*

feeler—The part of an animal's body that it uses for touch. A cat's whiskers, an insect's antennae, and an octopus's tentacles serve as feelers.

feel|er (fē′lər) *noun, plural* **feelers.**

• See picture at **antenna.**

a at	i if	oo look	ch chalk		⌈ a in ago
ā ape	ī idle	ou out	ng sing		e in happen
ah calm	o odd	u ugly	sh ship	ə =	i in capital
aw all	ō oats	ū rule	th think		o in occur
e end	oi oil	ur turn	th their		⌊ u in upon
ē easy			zh treasure		

feeling—1. The sense of touch: Feeling *can tell you if something is hot or cold.* 2. A being aware of something through one's senses; sensation: *a* feeling *of hunger, pain, relaxation, or peace.* 3. An emotion; state of mind: *a happy, sad, angry, or loving* feeling. 4. **feelings:** The sensitive part of a person's makeup: *She hurt my* feelings *when she ignored me at the party.* 5. An opinion; idea: *She had a very strong* feeling *about people who steal.*

feel|ing (fē′ling) *noun, plural* **feelings.**

feet—*See* **foot.**

feet (fēt) *plural noun.*

• A word that sounds the same is **feat.**

fell¹—*See* **fall.**

fell (fel) *verb.*

fell²—To cut, beat, or knock down: *a boxer being* felled *in the third round; to* fell *trees.*

fell (fel) *verb,* **felled, felling.**

fellow—1. A man or a boy. 2. A companion or friend: *Ed and the other* fellows *went to a hockey game. Noun.*
—Being very much alike: *my* fellow *Americans; his* fellow *workers. Adjective.*

fel|low (fel′ō) *noun, plural* **fellows;** *adjective.*

felt¹—*See* **feel.**

felt (felt) *verb.*

felt²—A type of fabric made by pressing together fur, wool, or hair. *Noun.*

felt (felt) *noun, plural* **felts.**

female—1. A woman or girl; a person of the sex that bears young. 2. An animal that lays eggs or bears young: *A cat that has kittens is a* female. *Noun.*
—1. Having to do with women and girls: *a* female *college; a* female *astronaut.* 2. Belonging to the sex that produces young: *A ewe is a* female *sheep. Adjective.*

fe|male (fē′māl) *noun, plural* **females;** *adjective.*

• See picture at **symbol.**

feminine—Having to do with women and girls.

fem|i|nine (fem′ə nin) *adjective.*

fence—1. A barrier put around a garden, field, building, or yard to keep people or animals in or out, or to mark the boundary of the property. 2. A person engaged in the unlawful occupation of buying and selling stolen items: *The* fence *tried to sell the stolen watch. Noun.*
—1. To put a barrier around: *to* fence *my yard.* 2. To take part in the sport of fencing. *Verb.*

fence (fens) *noun, plural* **fences;** *verb,* **fenced, fencing.**

■ **on the fence:** Undecided; not giving support to either side of an issue: *The politician refused to* *make a decision and stayed* on the fence *about building a new road.*

fencing—The sport of fighting with swords.
fenc|ing (fen′sing) *noun.*

fencing

fender—The metal rim over the wheel of a car, bicycle, or the like. The fender protects the wheel and keeps water and mud from splashing.
fend|er (fen′dər) *noun, plural* **fenders.**

fern—A type of plant that has delicate, feathery leaves, but no flowers or seeds. They reproduce from spores that grow on the backs of the leaves.
fern (furn) *noun, plural* **ferns.**

fern

ferocious—Very fierce; mean: *a ferocious beast; a ferocious storm.*
fe|ro|cious (fə rō′shəs) *adjective.*
● Synonyms: **savage, vicious, wild**

ferret—A small animal like a weasel. Ferrets have white or yellowish fur often with a dark, masklike marking around the face. They can be trained to hunt small rodents, such as mice. *Noun.*
—**1.** To hunt with this animal.   **2.** To search for: *He* ferreted *through his tool box for the screwdriver. Verb.*
fer|ret (fer′it) *noun, plural* **ferrets;** *verb,* **ferreted, ferreting.**

Ferris wheel

Word History

The **Ferris wheel** is named after George Ferris, an American engineer who invented it. The first Ferris wheel was made for the Chicago World's Fair in 1893.

Ferris wheel—A very large revolving wheel found at amusement parks, that carries people in seats attached to its rim.
Fer|ris wheel (fer′is hwēl) *noun, plural* **Ferris wheels.**

ferry—To carry people and things across a narrow body of water. *Verb.*
—The boat used to carry people and things across a body of water. *Noun.*
fer|ry (fer′ē) *verb,* **ferried, ferrying;** *noun, plural* **ferries.**
● A word that sounds the same is **fairy.**

ferret (noun)

fertile—1. Capable of producing easily and plentifully, especially crops or young: Fertile *land and animals make for a productive farm.* 2. Able to develop into a new plant or animal: *A chick can grow only from a* fertile *egg.* 3. Able to produce many ideas; creative: *Many artists have* fertile *imaginations.*
fer|tile (fur′təl) *adjective.*

fertilize—1. To make capable of producing: *An egg that has been* fertilized *will usually grow into a baby.* 2. To help soil by applying a natural or chemical substance that enriches it.
fer|ti|lize (fur′tə līz) *verb,* **fertilized, fertilizing.**

fertilizer—A natural or chemical substance that is added to soil to make it richer for growing plants. Fertilizers are used on crops, gardens, lawns, and house plants.
fer|ti|liz|er (fur′tə lī′zər) *noun, plural* **fertilizers.**

festival—1. A special time, especially a holiday, often marked by feasting and rejoicing to celebrate something: *Christmas and Hanukkah are religious* festivals. 2. A celebration often set at a fixed time of year for a special event or entertainment: *a music* festival; *a harvest* festival.
fes|ti|val (fes′tə vəl) *noun, plural* **festivals.**

fetch—To go get something and bring it back; get: *teaching a dog to* fetch *a stick;* fetch *Mother a glass of water.*
fetch (fech) *verb,* **fetched, fetching.**
• See picture at **retrieve.**

feud—A hateful quarrel between two people, families, or groups that lasts for many years and often many generations. *Noun.*
—To participate in a long, hateful quarrel. *Verb.*
feud (fyūd) *noun, plural* **feuds;** *verb,* **feuded, feuding.**

feudalism—The social and political system of Europe during the Middle Ages. Under this system, a lord provided protection for the peasants that worked for him.
feu|dal|ism (fyū′də liz əm) *noun.*

fever—A rise in body temperature above normal. For human beings, a fever brings a temperature above 98.6 degrees Fahrenheit (37 degrees Celsius).
fe|ver (fē′vər) *noun, plural* **fevers.**

few—Not many: *The candidate lost the election by just a* few *votes. Adjective.*
—A small number: *Most of the days were nice, but it rained on a* few. *Noun.*
few (fyū) *adjective,* **fewer, fewest;** *noun.*

fez—A flat-topped hat that is usually red with a long, black tassel. Fezzes are worn by men in Egypt.
fez (fez) *noun, plural* **fezzes.**

fez

fib—A lie: *I told a* fib *about how many records I own. Noun.*
—To tell a lie: *She* fibbed *about finishing all the peas on her plate. Verb.*
fib (fib) *noun, plural* **fibs;** *verb,* **fibbed, fibbing.**

fiber—1. A tiny, threadlike part of something: *cotton* fibers; *muscle* fibers. 2. Any part of a food that cannot be broken down by the body and that aids in digestion.
fi|ber (fī′bər) *noun, plural* **fibers.**

fiction—1. A story about people and events that are not real. 2. Something that has been made up: *The judge decided that the man's excuse was* fiction *and fined him $100.*
fic|tion (fik′shən) *noun.*

a at	i if	oo look	ch chalk		a in ago
ā ape	ī idle	ou out	ng sing		e in happen
ah calm	o odd	u ugly	sh ship	ə =	i in capital
aw all	ō oats	ū rule	th think		o in occur
e end	oi oil	ur turn	th their		u in upon
ē easy			zh treasure		

fiddle—A violin. *Noun.*
—To play a violin. *Verb.*
fid|dle (fid′əl) *noun, plural* **fiddles;** *verb,*
fiddled, fiddling.
■ **fit as a fiddle:** In outstanding physical shape:
Grandfather is fit as a fiddle *because he walks
several miles each morning.*

fidget—To make restless movements: *The
children* fidgeted *in their seats as they waited for
the movie to begin.*
fid|get (fij′it) *verb,* **fidgeted, fidgeting.**
• Synonyms: **squirm, wiggle, wriggle**

field—1. An area of open land: *a* field *of wild
flowers.*   2. An area of land used for a certain
purpose: *a football* field; *a corn*field.   3. A piece
of land that is rich in a natural product: *an oil*
field; *a diamond* field.   4. An area of knowledge
or activity: *My father and uncle both work in the
field of engineering. Noun.*
—To pick up or catch a baseball and throw it
into play: *He* fielded *the ball and threw it back
to the pitcher.*
field (fēld) *noun, plural* **fields;** *verb,* **fielded,
fielding.**

field spaniel—A medium-sized hunting dog
with a long, flat, silky coat and drooping ears.
They were originally bred in England.
field span|iel (fēld span′yəl) *noun, plural*
field spaniels.

field spaniel

field trip—A trip taken away from school so
that students can see things or places they have
studied in class.
field trip (fēld trip) *noun, plural* **field trips.**

fiend—1. A devil; demon.   2. A wicked or cruel
person.
fiend (fēnd) *noun, plural* **fiends.**

fierce—1. Violent; hostile; mean: *a lion's* fierce

roar; *a* fierce *temper.*   2. Very strong; severe:
She has a fierce *cold.*
fierce (fērs) *adjective,* **fiercer, fiercest.**
• Synonyms: **ferocious, savage, vicious, wild,**
for **1.**

fiesta—A festival. In Spanish-speaking countries,
fiestas include ceremonies to honor saints.
fi|es|ta (fē es′tə) *noun, plural* **fiestas.**

fife—A musical instrument that is like a flute but
smaller and makes a higher sound.
fife (fīf) *noun, plural* **fifes.**

fifteen—Five more than ten; one more than
fourteen; 15.
fif|teen (fif′tēn′) *adjective; noun, plural* **fifteens.**

fifteenth—1. Next after the fourteenth.   2. One
of fifteen equal parts.
fif|teenth (fif′tēnth′) *adjective; noun, plural*
fifteenths.

fifth—1. Next after the fourth.   2. One of five
equal parts.
fifth (fifth) *adjective; noun, plural* **fifths.**

fiftieth—1. Following the forty-ninth.   2. One of
fifty equal parts.
fif|ti|eth (fif′tē ith) *adjective; noun, plural*
fiftieths.

fifty—Five times ten; one more than forty-nine; 50.
fif|ty (fif′tē) *adjective; noun, plural* **fifties.**

fifty-fifty—Half and half; in equal parts: *a*
fifty-fifty *chance; split the cost* fifty-fifty.
fif|ty-fif|ty (fif′tē fif′tē) *adjective, adverb.*

fig—A small, soft, pear-shaped fruit that grows on
tropical trees.
fig (fig) *noun, plural* **figs.**

tree   leaves and fruit

fig

fight—**1.** A physical battle or struggle: *a cat* fight; *a* fight *for freedom.* **2.** A verbal quarrel: *My sister and I have a lot of* fights, *but we never stay angry with each other. Noun.*
—**1.** To take part in a battle or struggle: *The soldiers* fought *against the enemy all night.* **2.** To quarrel verbally: *My brothers are always* fighting *over what to watch on television.* **3.** To get, make, or overcome by great effort: *She* fought *to stay alive in the barren desert. Verb.*
fight (fīt) *noun, plural* **fights;** *verb,* **fought, fighting.**
• Synonyms: **combat, conflict,** for *noun* **1.**
Antonym: **peace,** for *noun* **1.**

figure—**1.** A written symbol for a number; numeral: *2, 7, 9, and 16 are* figures. **2. figures:** the use of numbers in arithmetic; calculation: *I can do* figures *in my head.* **3.** An amount that is shown in numbers: *She came up with a* figure *for this year's budget.* **4.** A form or shape: *A square is a four-sided* figure. **5.** A person or character: *Presidents are important* figures *in the history of the United States. Noun.*
—**1.** To use numbers to find an answer: *The waitress* figured *how much we owed her.* **2.** To think or consider: *The hikers* figured *that they would arrive home before dark. Verb.*
fig|**ure** (fig′yər) *noun, plural* **figures;** *verb,* **figured, figuring.**

figure of speech—A word or phrase that is used in a way that differs from its actual meaning. ''She worked her fingers to the bone'' is an example of a figure of speech.
fig|**ure of speech** (fig′yər əv spēch) *noun, plural* **figures of speech.**

Language Fact

Figures of speech make our language more colorful and expressive. When someone says ''I blew my top,'' you get the feeling that this person is really angry. Poets often use figures of speech to add beauty to their writings. Figures of speech include exaggerations, idioms, irony, metaphors, and similes. You can find these figures of speech, with examples of what they are, in this dictionary.

---

a at	i if	oo look	ch chalk		a in ago
ā ape	ī idle	ou out	ng sing		e in happen
ah calm	o odd	u ugly	sh ship	ə =	i in capital
aw all	ō oats	ū rule	th think		o in occur
e end	oi oil	ur turn	th their		u in upon
ē easy			zh treasure		

filament—A very thin thread or threadlike part or object. The wire that gives off light in a light bulb is a filament.
fil|**a**|**ment** (fil′ə mənt) *noun, plural* **filaments.**

file¹—**1.** A folder or cabinet for keeping papers, records, or the like in order. **2.** Information or records that are kept in order: *The doctor keeps a* file *on every patient she sees.* **3.** A collection of data for a computer, kept on a tape or disk. **4.** A line of persons, things, or animals arranged one behind the other: *Soldiers marched in a* file *in the parade. Noun.*
—**1.** To arrange or place records or information in a certain order: *I* filed *the patients' charts in alphabetical order.* **2.** To enter or record legally or officially: *to* file *a lawsuit; to* file *an income tax return.* **3.** To walk or move in a line: *Each class* filed *out of the school for the fire drill. Verb.*
file (fīl) *noun, plural* **files;** *verb,* **filed, filing.**

file²—A steel instrument with a rough surface, used for smoothing, grinding, or shaping. *Noun.*
—To use such an instrument: *to* file *her fingernails. Verb.*
file (fīl) *noun, plural* **files;** *verb,* **filed, filing.**

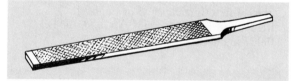

file² (noun)

fill—**1.** To pack or pour something into all the available space: *I* filled *my glass to the top with milk.* **2.** To use all the time or space available: *My day is* filled *with activities, and I cannot fit in anything else.* **3.** To supply; provide: fill *an order.* **4.** To close or plug up: *We* filled *the cracks in the wall before we painted it.* **5.** To occupy and perform the functions of a certain job: *The school board* filled *the teacher's position.*
fill (fil) *verb,* **filled, filling.**

fillet or **filet**—Meat or fish that has had the bones removed. *Noun.*
—To remove the bones from fish or meat. *Verb.*
fil|**let** (fi lā′ *or* fil′ā) *noun, plural* **fillets;** *verb,* **filleted, filleting.**

filling—Anything used to take up an open space: filling *for a pillow; a tooth* filling.
fill|**ing** (fil′ing) *noun, plural* **fillings.**

filly—A female horse under the age of five.
fil|**ly** (fil′ē) *noun, plural* **fillies.**

film—1. A thin coating of something: *A film of dust covered the table.* 2. A thin, chemically treated material that when put in a camera and exposed to light makes pictures. 3. A movie. *Noun.*
—1. To cover or cloud over with a thin layer; coat: *Her eyes* filmed *with tears of joy.* 2. To take pictures or make a movie: *My father* filmed *my birthday party to show to my grandparents. Verb.*
film (film) *noun, plural* **films;** *verb,* **filmed, filming.**

filmstrip—A series of pictures on film, often used as a teaching aid.
film|strip (film′strip′) *noun, plural* **filmstrips.**

filter—1. A device with small holes that traps things that are not wanted in a liquid, a substance, or the air. 2. Anything through which substances pass to be cleaned. Special papers, sand, and charcoal can be filters. *Noun.*
—1. To cleanse, purify, or separate by passing through something: *We* filtered *the pebbles out of the sand with our hands.* 2. To seep through; trickle: *Water* filters *down through rocks and dirt to get to the plant roots. Verb.*
fil|ter (fil′tər) *noun, plural* **filters;** *verb,* **filtered, filtering.**
• Synonyms: **screen, sift, strain,** for *verb* 1.

filth—Dirty, foul matter: *The garbage cans are coated with* filth *and need a good cleaning.*
filth (filth) *noun.*

filthy—Not clean; filled with dirty, foul matter: *Please clean these* filthy *dishes.*
filth|y (fil′thē) *adjective,* **filthier, filthiest.**

fin—1. One of the thin, outside parts of a fish that enables it to swim and to keep its balance. A fin is flat and spread out, somewhat like the wing of a bird. 2. Anything that resembles this part of a fish: *A dart has* fins *to help balance and guide it through the air.*
fin (fin) *noun, plural* **fins.**

final—1. Last; latest; closing: *These are the* final *words of my report, and now I am finished.* 2. Definite; not changeable: *The director will decide what* final *action will be taken. Adjecitve.*
—1. The last test in a school class: *My* final *in science was easy.* 2. A deciding match, game, or event: *I did not make it to the* finals *in wrestling. Noun.*
fi|nal (fī′nəl) *adjective; noun, plural* **finals.**

finale—The end; conclusion; last part: *As a* finale *to the concert, the band played a march as it left the stage.*
fi|na|le (fə nah′lē) *noun, plural* **finales.**

finalist—A person who reaches the end of a contest or other event by being one of the best or making fewer mistakes.
fi|nal|ist (fī′nə list) *noun, plural* **finalists.**

finally—Lastly; in the end: *The prize I had been waiting for* finally *came in the mail.*
fi|nal|ly (fī′nə lē) *adverb.*

finance—1. The handling of money affairs for a person or a company. 2. **finances:** The money or funds available to a person, business, or government: *Our* finances *increased when my father got a raise. Noun.*
—To pay for: *I paid half the price of the bicycle, and my father* financed *the rest. Verb.*
fi|nance (fə nans′ *or* fī′nans) *noun, plural* **finances;** *verb,* **financed, financing.**

financial—Having to do with managing money: *The* financial *affairs of the company are handled by the accountant.*
fi|nan|cial (fə nan′shəl *or* fī nan′shəl) *adjective.*

finch—A small songbird that eats cracked seeds. The most common finches are cardinals, sparrows, and canaries.
finch (finch) *noun, plural* **finches.**

finch

find—1. To discover by chance; stumble upon: *You can* find *many types of shells when you walk along the beach.* 2. To search for and locate: *I* found *the keys in the car.* 3. To learn; uncover: *We* found *an easier way to walk to school.* 4. To obtain or reach by calculating: *Did you* find *the answer to the mathematics problem?* 5. To rule; judge: *The student council* found *the students innocent of breaking the school rule. Verb.*
—Something discovered: *The scientists were rewarded for their important* find. *Noun.*
find (find) *verb,* **found, finding;** *noun, plural* **finds.**

fine¹—1. Superior quality; very good: *Fine restaurants can be very expensive,* 2. Delicate; thin: *The baby's hair was so* fine *that it felt like silk.* 3. Consisting of tiny pieces; not coarse: *The coffee beans were ground into a* fine *powder. Adjective.*
—Wonderfully; well: *I am coming along* fine *on the report, and it is almost finished. Adverb.*
fine (fīn) *adjective,* **finer, finest;** *adverb.*

fine²—Money a person must pay as a penalty when judged guilty of breaking a law or rule: *a* fine *for speeding. Noun.*
—To punish by setting a penalty: *The driver was* fined *for overloading the truck. Verb.*
fine (fīn) *noun, plural* **fines;** *verb,* **fined, fining.**

finger—Any of the five separate divisions at the end of the hand. *Noun.*
—To feel, touch, or handle with the five separate divisions at the end of the hand: *He* fingered *the cards while he was deciding what his next play would be. Verb.*
fin|ger (fing′gər) *noun, plural* **fingers;** *verb,* **fingered, fingering.**

- **cross** (one's) **fingers:** To put one finger over another, as a sign that one hopes for good luck or does not mean something said: *When we saw the clouds, we* crossed *our* fingers *and hoped it would not rain.*
not lift a finger: To not help in even the smallest way: *The lazy boy would* not lift a finger *to help around the house.*
twist around (one's) **finger:** To have control over someone: *Since I am the judge in the competition, I have the contestants* twisted around *my* finger.

fingernail—The hard covering on the top part of the end of a finger.
fin|ger|nail (fing′gər nāl′) *noun, plural* **fingernails.**

fingerprint—A mark made by the pattern of lines on the underside part of a finger. Each finger has a different pattern, and each person has different fingerprints.
fin|ger|print (fing′gər print′) *noun, plural* **fingerprints.**

finicky—Overly picky; particular: *Our neighbor is very* finicky *about the neatness of his yard.*
fin|ick|y (fin′ə kē) *adjective.*

finish—1. To conclude; *We finished the game and stood around talking.* 2. To complete something: *Finish your carrots before starting dessert.* 3. To put a final coat or surface on something: *The workers finished the road with tar. Verb.*
—1. Conclusion; ending: *the finish of the story.* 2. The coating of or condition on the surface of something: *a smooth or shiny finish. Noun.*
fin|ish (fin′ish) *verb,* **finished, finishing;** *noun, plural* **finishes.**

- Synonyms: **end, stop,** for *verb* **1.**
Antonyms: For *verb* **1,** See Synonyms at **begin.**

fiord—A long, narrow inlet of a sea that runs between steep cliffs or slopes.
fiord (fyawrd) *noun, plural* **fiords.**

- This word is also spelled **fjord.**

fiord

fir—An evergreen tree that is part of the family of pine trees.
fir (fur) *noun, plural* **firs.**

- A word that sounds the same is **fur.**

needles

cone

tree

fir

a at	i if	oo look	ch chalk		a in ago
ā ape	ī idle	ou out	ng sing		e in happen
ah calm	o odd	u ugly	sh ship	ə =	i in capital
aw all	ō oats	ū rule	th think		o in occur
e end	oi oil	ur turn	th their		u in upon
ē easy			zh treasure		

fire—1. The flame, light, and heat caused by burning; blaze. **2.** Something that is burning: *The* fire, *caused by the lightning, raged through the forest.* **3.** A powerful feeling or emotion; eagerness; enthusiasm: *the* fire *of faith and courage.* **4.** The shooting of a gun or guns: *The battle's* fire *could be heard in the woods. Noun.* —1. To cause to burn; ignite: *Dad* fired *the grill to cook the steaks.* **2.** To stir up; fill with excitement: *The captain tried to* fire *up the team before the big game.* **3.** To shoot a gun: *She* fired *the gun at the practice target.* **4.** To let someone go from a job: *She was* fired *because she was never on time. Verb.*
fire (fīr) *noun, plural* **fires;** *verb,* **fired, firing.**
■ **add fuel to the fire:** To make a bad situation even worse: *After coming home late, he* added fuel to the fire *by asking to borrow the car.*
catch fire: To gain great support: *The new hair fad* caught fire *and spread across the country.*
play with fire: To become involved with or do something that is unsafe or dangerous: *The boys were* playing with fire *when they skated on the thin ice.*
● Synonyms: **discharge, dismiss,** for *verb* **4.** Antonyms: For *verb* **4,** see Antonyms at **discharge.**

firearm—A shooting weapon. Pistols, revolvers, and rifles are examples of firearms.
fire|arm (fīr'ahrm') *noun, plural* **firearms.**

fireboat—A boat used to fight fires on or near water.
fire|boat (fīr'bōt') *noun, plural* **fireboats.**

fireboat

firecracker—An explosive made with a fuse and gunpowder wrapped in paper. When the fuse is lit, the firecracker explodes loudly.
fire|crack|er (fīr'krak'ər) *noun, plural* **firecrackers.**

fire engine—A truck with special equipment, such as hoses and ladders, for fighting fires.
fire en|gine (fīr en'jən) *noun, plural* **fire engines.**

fire escape—Stairs that are built on the outside of a building for use in escaping from a fire.
fire es|cape (fīr es kāp') *noun, plural* **fire escapes.**

fire extinguisher—A long, narrow container holding chemicals that can be sprayed on a fire to put it out.
fire ex|tin|guish|er (fīr ek sting'gwi shər) *noun, plural* **fire extinguishers.**

fire fighter—A person whose job is to put out fires.
fire fight|er (fīr fī'tər) *noun, plural* **fire fighters.**

Language Fact

Many words in the English language end in -man, such as **fireman, policeman,** and **mailman.** As more and more women enter these and other professions, different words are used to show that both men and women have these jobs. Hence, we now have **fire fighter, police officer,** and **mail carrier,** among others.

firefly—A small, flying beetle that comes out at night and gives off a soft, blinking light.
fire|fly (fīr'flī') *noun, plural* **fireflies.**

firefly

Language Fact

A **firefly** is also called a lightning bug. Although not all adult fireflies give off light, all their young, often called glowworms, do.

firehouse—A building where fire fighters work and where fire engines and other equipment are kept; fire station.
fire|house (fīr'hous') *noun, plural* **firehouses.**

fireman—1. A person who works as a fire fighter.   2. A person who keeps the fire going in a steam engine or furnace.
fire|man (fīr′mən) *noun, plural* **firemen.**
• For **1**, see Language Fact at **fire fighter.**

fireplace—A structure built to hold a fire. It is made of fireproof material, such as stone or brick, and when indoors is connected to a chimney to channel away the smoke.
fire|place (fīr′plās′) *noun, plural* **fireplaces.**

fireproof—Not able to burn: *Brick and stone are* fireproof, *but wood and cloth are not.*
fire|proof (fīr′prūf′) *adjective.*

firewood—Wood that is used to make a fire.
fire|wood (fīr′wood) *noun.*

fireworks—A display of exploding lights and loud noises made by firecrackers and other explosive devices.
fire|works (fīr′wurks′) *plural noun.*

firm[1]—1. Not soft; stiff: *He put air in the basketball until it was* firm *and would bounce high.*   2. Not able to be moved; secure: *Once the cement hardened, the wall was* firm.   3. Constant; definite; fixed: *My father is a* firm *believer in hard work.*   4. Strong and steady: *a* firm *handshake.*
firm (furm) *adjective,* **firmer, firmest.**

firm[2]—An organization for making or selling things.
firm (furm) *noun, plural* **firms.**
• Synonyms: **business, company**

first—Above or before everything or everyone else; leading: *She was the* first *one in the ticket line. Adjective.*
—1. At the beginning; before someone or something else: *We will study* first *and then watch the game on television.*   2. Before all other times; initially: *I* first *saw my friend when we were both seven. Adverb.*
—1. The beginning: *the* first *of April.*   2. Any person or thing that comes before all others: *the* first *in line. Noun.*
first (furst) *adjective; adverb; noun, plural* **firsts.**

first aid—Emergency medical treatment given to an injured or ill person, usually before treatment from a doctor is possible.
first aid (furst ād) *noun.*

first class—1. The best seats or rooms for travelers on airplanes, trains, or ships. In first class, the passenger pays more for a ticket but receives more or better service.   2. One of the fastest ways to send mail: *If you send that letter by* first class, *it will get there in a day.*
first class (furst klas) *noun.*

firsthand—Having to do with the original source: *I am a farmer and have* firsthand *experience with growing vegetables. Adjective.*
—Directly from the original source: *I heard the story* firsthand *from those involved. Adverb.*
first|hand (furst′hand′) *adjective, adverb.*

fish—1. A water animal that has a backbone, fins, and gills for breathing. It is covered with scales.   2. The fleshy part of such an animal that is eaten, usually cooked.
—1. To try to catch fish.   2. To look for: *She* fished *in her pocket for some loose change. Verb.*
fish (fish) *noun, plural* **fish** *or* **fishes;** *verb,* **fished, fishing.**
▪ **a fish out of water:** Someone or something not belonging or not fitting: *The champion bowler was* a fish out of water *on the ski slope.*
have other fish to fry: To have other interests; be occupied with something else: *I am not interested in playing this afternoon because I* have other fish to fry.

Language Fact

The plural of **fish,** and of many words ending in -fish, can be either fish or fishes. When you mean more than one fish, but all of the same kind, the plural is fish. When you mean more than one kind of fish, the plural is fishes. *There are two fish in this bowl, both of them goldfish. Goldfish and guppies are common aquarium fishes.*

---

fisherman—One who catches fish for pleasure or for a living.
fish|er|man (fish′ər mən) *noun, plural* **fishermen.**

fishhook—The curved object on the end of a fishing line that catches and holds a fish. It is where the bait is put.
fish|hook (fish′hook′) *noun, plural* **fishhooks.**

fishy—1. Having the taste, feel, or smell of a fish: *a* fishy *smell.*   2. Questionable; unlikely: *When are you going to stop your* fishy *answers and tell me the real story?*
fish|y (fish′ē) *adjective,* **fishier, fishiest.**

a at	i if	oo look	ch chalk		a in ago
ā ape	ī idle	ou out	ng sing		e in happen
ah calm	o odd	u ugly	sh ship	ə =	i in capital
aw all	ō oats	ū rule	th think		o in occur
e end	oi oil	ur turn	th their		u in upon
ē easy			zh treasure		

fission—The process of dividing or splitting an atom, resulting in the release of great amounts of energy.
fis|sion (fish′ən) *noun.*

fist—A hand with the fingers curled tightly under, touching the palm.
fist (fist) *noun, plural* **fists.**

fistfight—A fight using bare hands.
fist|fight (fist′fīt′) *noun, plural* **fistfights.**

fit¹—1. Proper or appropriate: *Mother thought that the dress was* fit *to wear to the dance.* 2. Well; in good physical condition: *A physical examination showed that I was* fit *to play sports. Adjective.*
—1. To be proper or appropriate for: *Make sure that your style of dress* fits *the occasion.* 2. To be correct in size: *Do your old sneakers still* fit *you?* 3. To make correct, proper, or appropriate: *He could* fit *his music to happy occasions or to sad ones.* 4. To supply the necessary equipment for something: *The football team was* fitted *with uniforms, helmets, and shoulder pads.* 5. To join; put in: *Can you* fit *together the pieces of the chair? Verb.*
—The manner in which something adapts to something else: *Be sure your boots are a good* fit *so you do not get blisters. Noun.*
fit (fit) *adjective,* **fitter, fittest;** *verb,* **fitted, fitting;** *noun, plural* **fits.**
■ **fit to be tied:** Upset; angry: *He was* fit to be tied *when the bus came early and he wasn't ready.*
● Synonyms: **correct, suitable,** for *adjective* 1.

fit²—1. A sudden attack of illness; seizure. 2. A sudden outburst: *a* fit *of sneezing; a crying* fit.
fit (fit) *noun, plural* **fits.**

fitness—The fact of being in good physical condition: *All athletes must prove their* fitness *before they can run the race.*
fit|ness (fit′nis) *noun.*

five—Four more than one; one less than six; 5.
five (fīv) *adjective; noun, plural* **fives.**

fix—1. To adjust or repair: *to* fix *my hair; to* fix *a broken chair leg.* 2. To establish; make definite: *The chairman* fixed *the meeting time so that everyone would be able to attend.* 3. To place or put: *to* fix *the blame on her.* 4. To fasten or attach something so that it cannot be removed: *to* fix *a stamp to an envelope.* 5. To prepare: *Please* fix *the salads for the picnic.* 6. To arrange something so that the results are in one's favor: *Because the election was conducted fairly, he does not think it was* fixed. *Verb.*
—A difficult troublesome situation: *When the car broke down on the highway, we were really in a* fix. *Noun.*
fix (fiks) *verb,* **fixed, fixing;** *noun, plural* **fixes.**

fixture—A permanent part of something, or an attachment to something: *There are three electrical* fixtures *on the wall.*
fix|ture (fiks′chər) *noun, plural* **fixtures.**

fizz—To bubble up, making a hissing sound: *The chemical mixture* fizzed *over the top of the pan during the science experiment. Verb.*
—A hissing or bubbling sound: *the* fizz *of firecrackers; the* fizz *of soda. Noun.*
fizz (fiz) *verb,* **fizzed, fizzing;** *noun.*

fizzle—To die out before getting off to a full start: *Plans for the party* fizzled *when they could not find a place to have it. Verb.*
—A hissing or bubbling sound. *Noun.*
fiz|zle (fiz′əl) *verb,* **fizzled, fizzling;** *noun, plural* **fizzles.**

flabbergast—To shock; astonish: *She was* flabbergasted *when her name was announced as the winner of the grand prize.*
flab|ber|gast (flab′ər gast) *verb,* **flabbergasted, flabbergasting**

flag—1. A cloth banner with pictures and sometimes writing on it. Flags are used as symbols for a country, state, or organization. 2. A cloth banner that is part of a signaling system. *Noun.*
—To signal with a banner or as if with a banner: *The road crew* flagged *the drivers to warn them of the stop ahead. Verb.*
flag (flag) *noun, plural* **flags;** *verb,* **flagged, flagging.**

Flag Day—A holiday that celebrates the anniversary of the day, June 14, 1777, that Congress adopted the flag of the United States.
Flag Day (flag dā) *noun.*

flair—A natural talent or ability: *His* flair *for dramatics brought him the lead in the play.*
flair (flâr) *noun, plural* **flairs.**
● A word that sounds the same is **flare.**

flake—A tiny, flat piece of something: *Flakes of paint fell from the walls of the old building. Noun.*
—To peel or fall off in tiny, flat pieces: *I* flaked *the dried mud off my shirt. Verb.*
flake (flāk) *noun, plural* **flakes;** *verb,* **flaked, flaking.**

flame—1. The yellow-red glowing part of a fire. 2. The fire that comes from a burning gas, such as a lit burner on a gas stove. 3. The condition of being on fire: *The paper burst into* flames *when he lit it. Noun.*
—1. To catch on fire or be on fire: *The torch*

flamed *throughout the sports event.* **2.** To redden; blush: *Her face* flamed *with embarrassment when she dropped her food tray. Verb.*
flame (flām) *noun, plural* **flames;** *verb,* **flamed, flaming.**

flamingo

Word History

Flamingo may come from a Latin word meaning ''flame,'' because of the bird's color. Or it may come from the word ''Flemish'' (**flem′**ish), which refers to a group of people in the area around the border between France and Belgium. These people were once thought to have especially red faces, and the color of the bird was thought to look like the color of their faces.

flamingo—A wading bird with reddish-pink feathers that lives in tropical climates. It has a curved bill, a long graceful neck, and thin legs with webbed feet.
fla|min|go (flə **ming′**gō) *noun, plural* **flamingos** *or* **flamingoes.**

flammable—Likely to catch on fire; easily ignited: *Do not light a match near gasoline*

because gasoline is very flammable *and can also explode.*
flam|ma|ble (**flam′**ə bəl) *adjective.*

flank—The fleshy part of a person's or an animal's body between the hip and the ribs. *Noun.*
—To be at the side of; border: *Tall trees* flanked *the road. Verb.*
flank (flangk) *noun, plural* **flanks;** *verb,* **flanked, flanking.**

flannel—A soft wool or cotton cloth. Flannel is used for warm shirts and trousers, blankets, and babies' clothes.
flan|nel (**flan′**əl) *noun, plural* **flannels.**

flap—**1.** To sway about loosely and noisily in the air: *sails* flapping *in the breeze.* **2.** To move up and down in a beating motion: *The bird* flapped *its wings. Verb.*
—**1.** The sound or motion of something moving back and forth: *I heard the* flap *of the screen door as they went out.* **2.** A piece of something that is broad, thin, and flat and is loosely attached along one side or edge: *a pocket* flap; *an envelope* flap. *Noun.*
flap (flap) *verb,* **flapped, flapping;** *noun, plural* **flaps.**

flare—**1.** To burn or shine with a bright flame or light: *The match* flared *as it lit.* **2.** A sudden outburst: *a* flare *of temper during the argument.* **3.** To open or spread out gradually: *The shape of a trumpet* flares *at one end. Verb.*
—**1.** A bright light or flame that is unsteady or lasts only a short time: *the* flare *of a fireworks display.* **2.** A fire or a device that produces a blaze of light, used for signaling or to light up an area for a short time: *The police set* flares *around the fallen tree. Noun.*
flare (flār) *verb,* **flared, faring;** *noun, plural* **flares.**
● A word that sounds the same is **flair.**

flash—**1.** A sudden, brief burst of light: *a flash of lightning.* **2.** A very short time: *The accident happened in a flash. Noun.*
—**1.** To light up suddenly and briefly: *A comet* flashed *across the sky.* **2.** To appear suddenly: *An idea* flashed *into my mind.* **3.** To come and go rapidly: *the train* flashed *by. Verb.*
flash (flash) *noun, plural* **flashes;** *verb,* **flashed, flashing.**
■ **flash in the pan:** A person or thing that looks promising but that fails to produce steadily good results: *We hoped that she could win another trophy for us, but she proved to be just a* flash in the pan.

a at	i if	oo look	ch chalk		a in ago
ā ape	ī idle	ou out	ng sing		e in happen
ah calm	o odd	u ugly	sh ship	ə =	i in capital
aw all	ō oats	ū rule	th think		o in occur
e end	oi oil	ur turn	<u>th</u> their		u in upon
ē easy			zh treasure		

flashback—A break in a story to show some event that happened in the past: *The movie contains a* flashback *to the old gentleman's childhood.*
flash|back (flash′bak′) *noun, plural* **flashbacks.**

flashbulb—An electric bulb used in photography to give a brief, bright burst of light.
flash|bulb (flash′bulb′) *noun, plural* **flashbulbs.**

flashlight—A battery-operated electric light that can be carried in the hand.
flash|light (flash′līt′) *noun, plural* **flashlights.**

flask—A small bottle, usually narrow at the top, that is used to hold liquids.
flask (flask) *noun, plural* **flasks.**

flat—1. Having a level, smooth, or even surface: *A table has a* flat *top.* 2. Stretched out along a surface: *to lie* flat *on the bed.* 3. Having a broad, smooth surface with little thickness: *a* flat *piece of glass.* 4. With little or no air in it; collapsed: *a* flat *tire.* 5. Not able to be changed; fixed: *The doctor charges a* flat *fee for measles shots.* 6. Lacking in zest, interest, or the like; dull: *the* flat *taste of stale soda. Adjective.*
—1. A level, smooth, or even surface: *She slapped the mosquito with the* flat *of her hand.* 2. A tire containing little or no air. 3. A musical tone or note that is one half step or half note below its natural pitch: *The song is written in the key of E* flat. 4. The sign ♭, which shows such a tone or note. *Noun.*
—1. In or into a level, smooth, or even position: *He fell* flat *on his face.* 2. Below the true pitch in music: *He threw the whole band off key by playing* flat. 3. Exactly: *I can be at your door in three minutes* flat. *Adverb.*
flat (flat) *adjective,* **flatter, flattest;** *noun, plural* **flats;** *adverb.*
■ **flat out:** At top speed: *She ran* flat out *toward the finish line.*

flatcar

flatcar—A railroad freight car that has a floor but no sides or roof.
flat|car (flat′kahr′) *noun, plural* **flatcars.**

flat-coated retriever—A medium-sized hunting dog with a flat wavy coat, drooping ears, and strong legs. Originally bred in England, these dogs hunt by smell and are good swimmers.
flat-coat|ed re|triev|er (flat′kō′tid ri trē′vər) *noun, plural* **flat-coated retrievers.**

flat-coated retriever

flatfish—Any of a group of ocean fishes that have a flat body, with both eyes on the upper side of the body. Halibut and flounder are flatfishes.
flat|fish (flat′fish′) *noun, plural* **flatfishes** or **flatfish.**

flatten—To make or become level or smooth: *Someone ran over my ball and* flattened *it.*
flat|ten (flat′ən) *verb,* **flattened, flattening.**

flatter—1. To praise too much or without meaning it: *Father* flattered *me when he said that the first cake I ever made was delicious.* 2. To show something very favorably: *This dress* flatters *me.*
flat|ter (flat′ər) *verb,* **flattered, flattering.**

flattery—Praise that is false or too much: *I enjoy compliments, but not* flattery.
flat|ter|y (flat′ər ē) *noun, plural* **flatteries.**

flavor—1. The way something tastes: *Do you like the* flavor *of garlic?* 2. A special quality: *The decorations give the room a party* flavor. *Noun.*
—To season; give taste to: Flavor *the stew with pepper. Verb.*
fla|vor (flā′vər) *noun, plural* **flavors;** *verb,* **flavored, flavoring.**

flavoring—Something that is used to add a certain taste to food or drink: *chocolate* flavoring; *peppermint* flavoring.
fla|vor|ing (flā′vər ing) *noun, plural* **flavorings.**

flaw—A crack, break, weakness, or other defect; imperfection: *A flaw in the dam caused it to collapse. There's a flaw in his speech.*
flaw (flaw) *noun, plural* **flaws.**

flax—A plant with blue flowers and whose stems are used to make linen cloth. The stems are separated into fibers, also called flax, that are spun into thread and then woven into linen.
flax (flaks) *noun.*

flea—A tiny, flat, jumping insect that has no wings. Fleas survive by feeding on the blood of humans, cats, dogs, rats, and other animals.
flea (flē) *noun, plural* **fleas.**
■ **flea in** (one's) **ear:** A sharp scolding or warning: *I put a flea in her ear about her constant lateness.*
● A word that sounds the same is **flee.**
● See picture at **insect.**

fled—*See* **flee.**
fled (fled) *verb.*

flee—**1.** To run away, usually from danger or trouble: *He stole my wallet and fled down the road.* **2.** To move away quickly; disappear: *Darkness fled when the sun rose.*
flee (flē) *verb,* **fled, fleeing.**
● A word that sounds the same is **flea.**

fleece—The wool coat on a sheep. *Noun.*
—To remove the wool from a sheep; shear: *We fleece the sheep to sell their wool.*
fleece (flēs) *noun, plural* **fleeces;** *verb,* **fleeced, fleecing.**

fleet[1]—**1.** A group of warships under the command of one officer: *The admiral led his fleet into battle.* **2.** Any group of ships, airplanes, trucks, or automobiles that move or work together: *a fleet of sailboats in a race; a factory's fleet of trucks.*
fleet (flēt) *noun, plural* **fleets.**

fleet[2]—Swift; fast: *a fleet runner; a fleet rabbit.*
fleet (flēt) *adjective,* **fleeter, fleetest.**

fleeting—Moving very quickly; very brief: *The fleeting days of our vacation were over too soon.*
fleet|ing (flē′ting) *adjective.*

flesh—**1.** The soft parts of an animal's body that are covered by the skin, especially the muscles.
2. The soft, edible part of fruits and vegetables; pulp.
flesh (flesh) *noun.*
■ **flesh and blood:** Family; relatives by one's birth: *I am loyal to my brother because he's my own flesh and blood.*
in the flesh: Present; in person: *We saw the President of the United States in the flesh when we were in Washington, D.C.*

flew—*See* **fly**[2].
flew (flū) *verb.*
● Words that sound the same are **flu** and **flue.**

flex—To bend: *to flex the knee; to flex an arm.*
flex (fleks) *verb,* **flexed, flexing.**

flexible—Able to be bent without breaking: *a flexible hose; a flexible wire.*
flex|i|ble (flek′sə bəl) *adjective.*

flick—A sudden, jerky movement; snap: *With a flick of the switch, she turned on the lights. Noun.*
—**1.** To remove with a snap or by brushing quickly and lightly: *She flicked the insect off her sleeve.* **2.** To make a sudden, jerky movement: *The girl flicked her bright scarf to catch his attention. Verb.*
flick (flik) *noun, plural* **flicks;** *verb,* **flicked, flicking.**

flicker[1]—**1.** To burn or shine unsteadily; flutter: *candles flickering in the wind.* **2.** To move quickly back and forth: *The cat's tail flickered as it watched the birds. Verb.*
—**1.** An unsteady flame or light: *The flicker of their torches threw shadows on the wall.* **2.** A quick, unsteady movement: *We knew that she was awake by the flicker of her eyelids. Noun.*
flick|er (flik′ər) *verb,* **flickered, flickering;** *noun, plural* **flickers.**
● Synonyms: **blink, glimmer, twinkle** for *verb* **1.**

flicker[2]—A large woodpecker with a brown back, yellow under its wings and tail, spots on its breast, and a wide black band on its throat. Flickers are common in North America.
flick|er (flick′ər) *noun, plural* **flickers.**

flied—*See* **fly**[2].
flied (flīd) *verb.*

flier—A thing or person that flies, especially the pilot of an aircraft: *The seagull is a strong flier. My brother is a flier with the air force.*
fli|er (flī′ər) *noun, plural* **fliers.**
● This word is also spelled **flyer.**

flies—*See* **fly**[1] and **fly**[2].
flies (flīz) *plural noun; verb.*

a at	i if	oo look	ch chalk	a in ago
ā ape	ī idle	ou out	ng sing	e in happen
ah calm	o odd	u ugly	sh ship	ə = i in capital
aw all	ō oats	ū rule	th think	o in occur
e end	oi oil	ur turn	th their	u in upon
ē easy			zh treasure	

flight¹—**1.** The act of moving through the air or flying: *the* flight *of a bee.*   **2.** The distance covered or path followed by an object as it moves through the air: *the* flight *of a spaceship.* **3.** A group of things moving through the air together: *a* flight *of geese.*   **4.** A trip in or by an aircraft: *We took an overnight* flight *to New York.*   **5.** A series of stairs leading from one floor of a building to another: *Their apartment is three* flights *up.*
flight (flīt) *noun, plural* **flights.**

flight²—The act of fleeing; running away: *With the enemy in* flight, *the soldiers celebrated.*
flight (flīt) *noun, plural* **flights.**

flimsy—**1.** Light and thin; easily broken: *A butterfly's wings are* flimsy.   **2.** Feeble; weak: *We did not accept his* flimsy *excuse for missing the meeting.*
flimsy (flim′zē) *adjective,* **flimsier, flimsiest.**

flinch—To draw back or shrink from something that is difficult, unpleasant, or painful: *He* flinched *as he waded into the icy water.*
flinch (flinch) *verb,* **flinched, flinching.**
● Synonyms: **recoil, wince**

fling—To throw or send something with force: *to* fling *a pillow across the room. Verb.*
—**1.** A sudden throw: *a powerful* fling *of the baseball.*   **2.** A period of time of doing as one wants: *We went to the beach for a last* fling *before school opened. Noun.*
fling (fling) *verb,* **flung, flinging;** *noun, plural* **flings.**
■ **have a fling at** or **take a fling at:** To try: *I decided to* take a fling *at learning to play chess.*
● Synonyms: For *verb,* see Synonyms at **cast.**

flint—A very hard type of stone that makes a spark when it is struck against steel: *Because we*

forgot to bring matches, we used flint to start our campfire.
flint (flint) *noun, plural* **flints.**

flip—To turn by tossing; to move suddenly with a jerk: *to* flip *a coin; to* flip *the pages of a book. Verb.*
—A toss or sudden jerk: *Give the pancakes a* flip *to brown the other side. Noun.*
flip (flip) *verb,* **flipped, flipping;** *noun, plural* **flips.**
■ **flip out:** To become very excited or angry: *My mom* flipped out *when I forgot to call her.*

flipper—**1.** A wide, flat limb of certain animals that is used for swimming. Seals, whales, penguins, dolphins, and turtles have flippers. **2.** Either of a pair of flat, rubber shoes shaped like a goose's foot that are worn to help a person swim easily.
flip|per (flip′ər) *noun, plural* **flippers.**
● See picture at **penguin.**

flirt—To play at being in love without meaning it: *He winked at her, but she knew he was only flirting.*
flirt (flurt) *verb,* **flirted, flirting.**

float—**1.** To rest on the surface of water or some other liquid: *Put this ball into the water to see if it will* float.   **2.** To drift slowly with the flow of water or air: *The balloon* floated *away in the breeze. Verb.*
—**1.** Anything that rests on the surface of water for some purpose: *We built a* float *of logs to use as a raft.*   **2.** A low, flat platform on wheels, used to carry a display in a parade. *Noun.*
float (flōt) *verb,* **floated, floating;** *noun, plural* **floats.**

flock—**1.** A group of animals of one type that feed, live, or travel together: *a* flock *of sheep; a* flock *of crows.*   **2.** A crowd of people: *A* flock *of students waited at the bus stop. Noun.*
—To gather or move in a group: *Tourists* flocked *to the museum.*
flock (flok) *noun, plural* **flocks;** *verb,* **flocked, flocking.**

floe—A large, flat mass of ice floating on the sea or other body of water.
floe (flō) *noun, plural* **floes.**
● A word that sounds the same is **flow.**

flood—**1.** An overflowing of water onto dry land: *The lake got so high that it caused a* flood *on the road.*   **2.** A large amount or flow of anything: *The huge window let in* floods *of sunlight. Noun.*
—**1.** to cover or fill with water: *After the big storm, our basement was* flooded.   **2.** To fill or cover with more than plenty of something: *His*

flicker²

hospital room was flooded *with get-well cards.* Verb.

flood (flud) *noun, plural* **floods;** *verb,* **flooded, flooding.**

floor—**1.** The bottom side of a room, on which one stands: *A red rug covered the* floor. **2.** Any surface at the bottom of something: *the ocean* floor; *the* floor *of a canyon.* **3.** A story of a building: *the first* floor; *the top* floor. *Noun.*
—**1.** To put such a surface on or in: *The cabin was* floored *with logs.* **2.** To knock down: *I ran into the tree branch so hard that it* floored *me.* Verb.

floor (flawr) *noun, plural* **floors;** *verb,* **floored, flooring.**

flop—**1.** To move or flap about loosely or clumsily: *sheets on the clothesline* flopping *in the breeze.* **2.** To throw the body down heavily or clumsily: *The tired dog* flopped *down on the floor.* **3.** To fail: *My science experiment* flopped *when the flame wouldn't light.* Verb.
—**1.** The act or sound of moving or flapping about loosely or clumsily: *The stone landed in the puddle with a* flop. **2.** A failure: *The new TV show was a* flop. *Noun.*

flop (flop) *verb,* **flopped, flopping;** *noun, plural* **flops.**

floppy—Tending to hang loosely or to flop: *Some dogs have* floppy *ears.*

flop|py (flop′ē) *adjective,* **floppier, floppiest.**

floppy disk or **floppy disc**—A small, flexible, plastic disk that is covered with a magnetic material and used to store computer information.

flop|py disk or **flop|py disc** (flop′ē disk) *noun, plural* **floppy disks** or **floppy discs.**

florist—A person whose business is the selling of flowers and plants.

flo|rist (flawr′ist) *noun, plural* **florists.**

floss—**1.** A shiny cotton or silk thread that is used in embroidery. **2.** A strong thread used to clean between the teeth; dental floss.

floss (flos) *noun, plural* **flosses.**

flounder[1]—To toss about or struggle unsteadily; move in a clumsy way: *The child* floundered *in the water because he was just learning how to swim.*

floun|der (floun′dər) *verb,* **floundered, floundering.**

flounder[2]—A flat fish that lives in salt water and is caught for food.

floun|der (floun′dər) *noun, plural* **flounders** or **flounder.**

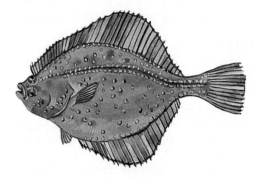

flounder[2]

flour—A fine powder that is made by grinding wheat, corn, or other grains. It is used in making bread and other baked products.

flour (flour) *noun, plural* **flours.**

flourish—**1.** To grow rapidly; be successful: *Trees* flourish *in rich soil. Business at my father's restaurant is* flourishing, *so he has to add on another room.* **2.** To swing or wave something boldly: *The cheerleaders* flourished *their banners.* Verb.
—A bold, attention-getting action: *With a* flourish, *the students walked their teacher to her surprise party.* Noun.

flour|ish (flur′ish) *verb,* **flourished, flourishing;** *noun, plural* **flourishes.**
● Synonyms: **prosper, thrive,** for *verb* 1.

flow—**1.** To go along smoothly and steadily: *water* flowing *from a faucet; crowds* flowing *out of the movie theater.* **2.** To hang freely and gracefully: *Ribbons* flowed *from the girl's hair.* Verb.
—**1.** The act of moving smoothly and steadily: *the* flow *of water.* **2.** Anything that moves in such a manner: *the* flow *of work; the* flow *of traffic.* Noun.

flow (flō) *verb,* **flowed, flowing;** *noun, plural* **flows.**
● A word that sounds the same is **floe.**

flower—**1.** A blossom on a plant. A flower has colored petals and holds the plant's seeds.
2. The best time or part: *The members of the honor guard are the* flower *of the army.* Noun.

a at	i if	oo look	ch chalk		a in ago
ā ape	ī idle	ou out	ng sing		e in happen
ah calm	o odd	u ugly	sh ship	ə =	i in capital
aw all	ō oats	ū rule	th think		o in occur
e end	oi oil	ur turn	th their		u in upon
ē easy			zh treasure		

Word Power

If you are interested in flowers, here are some useful words to know. Each is the name of part of a flower. You can find these words in this dictionary.

anther	nectar	seed
blossom	ovary	sepal
bud	petal	stamen
bulb	pistil	stem
leaf	pollen	thorn

You can also find the names of many kinds of flowers, and pictures of many flowers.

—To bloom: *This plant* flowers *only during the Christmas season. Verb.*
flow|er (flou′ər) *noun, plural* **flowers;** *verb,* **flowered, flowering.**
■ **in full flower:** Being at one's very best: *My cousin is* in full flower *when he is on stage.*

flown—*See* **fly².**
flown (flōn) *verb.*

flu—An illness, like a cold, that is spread from person to person through contact with a virus. Its full name is **influenza.**
flu (flū) *noun, plural* **flus.**
● Words that sound the same are **flew** and **flue.**

Word History

Flu is a short, informal form of the word **influenza.** It comes from a Latin word meaning "influence." Long ago, people who became ill were said to be under the influence of the stars. Today, it is known that people get the flu from other people who carry the virus.

flue—An opening, usually in a pipe or a chimney, that carries smoke to the outside.
flue (flū) *noun, plural* **flues.**
● Words that sound the same are **flew** and **flu.**

fluff—A soft, light, fuzzy material: *My mittens are lined with* fluff. *Noun.*
—To shake or pat into a soft, puffy mass: *Mother* fluffs *the pillows when she makes the bed. Verb.*
fluff (fluf) *noun; verb,* **fluffed, fluffing.**

fluffy—Having, full of, or like a soft, light, fuzzy material: *a fluffy* kitten; *fluffy* clouds.
fluf|fy (fluf′ē) *adjective,* **fluffier, fluffiest.**

fluid—Anything that flows; any liquid or gas: *Water is a* fluid. *Noun.*
—Capable of flowing like a liquid or gas:

Chocolate, when it melts, is fluid. *Adjective.*
flu|id (flū′id) *noun, plural* **fluids;** *adjective.*

flung—*See* **fling.**
flung (flung) *verb.*

flunk—**1.** To fail to achieve a passing grade on: *I am going to study so I do not* flunk *my test.* **2.** To give a failing grade: *That teacher* flunks *students who don't work hard.*
flunk (flungk) *verb,* **flunked, flunking.**

fluorescent lamp—An electric lamp whose light is produced by ultraviolet rays shining through a layer of fluorescent powder. It has a narrow, tube-like bulb and gives off a soft light.
flu|o|res|cent lamp (flū′ə res′ənt lamp) *noun, plural* **fluorescent lamps.**

fluoridation—The act of adding fluoride, which helps to prevent tooth decay, to drinking water.
fluor|i|da|tion (floor′ə dā′shən) *noun.*

flurry—**1.** A brief, sudden wind or snowfall: *The snow* flurries *did not leave much snow on the ground.* **2.** A brief, sudden commotion: *The* flurry *of activity signaled to the crowd that the parade was approaching.*
flur|ry (flur′ē) *noun, plural* **flurries.**

flush—**1.** To have a sudden redness in the face, usually due to a fever or because of embarrassment; blush: *The boy's face* flushed *when he realized he had run the wrong way with the ball.* **2.** To flow through or across suddenly; flood: *Rain* flushed *the roof with water.* **3.** To drain water in order to wash clean or remove something: *to* flush *a toilet. Verb.*
—**1.** A soft, red glow; blush: *The bride's face had a joyful* flush. **2.** A sudden flow or draining of liquid: *The* flush *of water flooded the basement when the pipe broke.* **3.** A sudden emotion: *The* flush *of excitement showed on the children's faces as the circus began. Noun.*
flush (flush) *verb,* **flushed, flushing;** *noun, plural* **flushes.**

flute—A pipe-like musical instrument that produces high notes. Its long, thin, rounded tube is played by blowing through or across a hole on one end and by covering or uncovering other holes with the fingers or by pressing keys.
flute (flūt) *noun, plural* **flutes.**

flute

flutter—To move or flap quickly and lightly: *to flutter one's eyelids; a kite fluttering in the breeze. Verb.*
—**1.** A light, quick, flapping motion: *the flutter of sheets hanging on a clothesline.* **2.** A state of excitement and commotion: *We were in a flutter when we saw our friend on TV. Noun.*
flut|ter (**flut′**ər) *verb*, **fluttered, fluttering;** *noun, plural* **flutters.**

fly¹—A type of small insect with two thin, see-through wings: *A mosquito is a type of* fly.
fly (flī) *noun, plural* **flies.**

fly¹

fly²—**1.** To move through the air with the help of wings: *An airplane* flew *through the clouds.*
2. To flutter and flap in the air: *flags* flying *in a parade.* **3.** To ride in or pilot an aircraft: *Our family* flew *to a warmer climate for a winter vacation.* **4.** To move very quickly: *He* flew *into the house when the lightning flashed nearby.*
5. To hit a baseball high into the air: *The batter* flied *to center field. Verb.*
—**1.** A baseball that is hit high into the air: *The batter hit a* fly *to left field.* **2.** A flap of material, usually on pants and skirts, that covers a zipper, buttons, or the like: *The* fly *on his pants was open. Noun.*
fly (flī) *verb*, **flew, flown, flying** for definitions 1 through 4; **flied** or **flying** for definition 5; *noun, plural* **flies.**
■ **fly in the face of:** To resist openly; defy: *His whistling in class* flew in the face of *the rules.*

a at	i if	oo look	ch chalk	
ā ape	ī idle	ou out	ng sing	
ah calm	o odd	u ugly	sh ship	ə =
aw all	ō oats	ū rule	th think	
e end	oi oil	ur turn	<u>th</u> their	
ē easy			zh treasure	

ə = ⎡ a in ago
e in happen
i in capital
o in occur
⎣ u in upon

Flied is a past tense and past participle of the word **fly.** It is used only to refer to the hitting of a fly ball in baseball. **Flew** is used for the other meanings of **fly:** *The crowd* flew *from its seats when the batter* flied *into the bleachers.*

flycatcher—Any of several types of birds so named because they catch and eat insects while in the air.
fly|catch|er (flī′kach′ər) *noun, plural* **flycatchers.**

flycatcher

flyer—*See* **flier.**
fly|er (flī′ər) *noun, plural* **flyers.**

flying fish—A warm-water ocean fish with side fins spread like wings that enable it to leap out of the water and glide through the air.
fly|ing fish (flī′ing fish′) *noun, plural* **flying fish** or **flying fishes.**

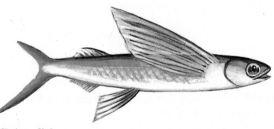

flying fish

flying saucer—Any of the many plate-shaped objects that people have sighted flying in the sky. These flying saucers, thought by some to contain life from other planets, have never been identified and so are called unidentified flying objects, or UFOs.
fly|ing sau|cer (flī′ing saw′sər) *noun, plural* **flying saucers.**

flypaper—A strip of paper covered with a sticky material or poison that is used to catch flies.
fly|pa|per (flī′pā′pər) *noun.*

foal—A baby horse, donkey, or like animal. A male foal is called a colt, and a female foal is called a filly.
foal (fōl) *noun, plural* **foals.**
● See picture at **colt.**

foam—A white airy mass of tiny bubbles formed in or on the surface of a liquid. The bubbles are formed from the force of beating, whipping, or other types of rapid movement. *Noun.*
—To form tiny bubbles; lather or fizz up: *The soap* foamed *as I washed my hands. Verb.*
foam (fōm) *noun; verb,* **foamed, foaming.**

focus—1. The point where rays of light come together after being reflected by a lens, mirror, or other device. 2. The distance between the lens or mirror and the point where the light rays meet: *Near-sighted and far-sighted people have different* focuses *than do people with normal eyesight.* 3. The center of interest or activity: *The office of the mayor is the* focus *of our town's government. Noun.*
—1. To bring to a point where rays of light meet: *The lens of a camera* focuses *light on film to produce a photograph.* 2. To bring or come to a clear image: *The scientist* focused *her telescope on a distant planet.* 3. To direct all attention to one thing: *She couldn't* focus *on reading her book because everyone around her was talking.*
fo|cus (fō′kəs) *noun, plural* **focuses** or **foci** (fō′sī); *verb,* **focused, focusing.**

fodder—Coarse food, such as hay or cornstalks, that is fed to horses, cattle and some other kinds of animals.
fod|der (fod′ər) *noun.*

foe—An enemy: *Cats and dogs are thought to be natural* foes.
foe (fō) *noun, plural* **foes.**

fog—1. A haze or mist close to the ground; low cloud: *My father drove very slowly through the* fog *because he could not see very far ahead.* 2. A confused state; daze: *The girl was in a* fog *and did not hear her mother speak to her. Noun.*
—1. To cover, enclose, or become hidden with a haze or mist: *Planes could not land because the airport was* fogged *in.* 2. To make or become confused: *His mind* fogged *with all the mathematical equations he had to learn. Verb.*
fog (fog *or* fawg) *noun, plural* **fogs;** *verb,* **fogged, fogging.**

foggy—1. Full of or covered with mist or haze: *It was* foggy *in the early morning, so everything looked dim and blurred.* 2. Dim, cloudy, or confused; unclear: *She had only a* foggy *understanding of the lesson until a classmate explained it to her.*
foggy (fog′ē *or* fawg′ē) *adjective,* **foggier, foggiest.**

foghorn—A horn that is sounded as a warning to ships during foggy weather when vision is poor: *The* foghorn *helped our ship avoid crashing into a nearby ship.*
fog|horn (fog′hawrn′ *or* fawg′hawrn′) *noun, plural* **foghorns.**

foil¹—To prevent something from happening; make something impossible to carry out: *Our plans for an outdoor party were* foiled *by a sudden storm.*
foil (foil) *verb,* **foiled, foiling.**
● Synonyms: **dash, frustrate, ruin**

foil²—A very thin, flexible, metal sheet used to wrap things such as food in: *aluminum* foil.
foil (foil) *noun, plural* **foils.**

fold¹—1. To bend something over on itself so that it is less than its original size: *Please* fold *the laundry so that it will fit into the dresser drawers.* 2. To clasp together; bring together and wrap around each other: *"First* fold *your arms together and then bend over," instructed the exercise teacher. Verb.*
—1. An overlap, such as a pleat or a gather, in material: *The skirt pattern calls for* folds *across the front at the waist.* 2. The mark left by bending something; crease: *Tear the paper in half at the* fold. *Noun.*
fold (fōld) *verb,* **folded, folding;** *noun, plural* **folds.**
■ **fold in:** In a recipe, to add an ingredient to a mixture by slowly and gently turning one part over another with a spoon: Fold *the eggs in the cake batter.*

fold²—A pen in which sheep are kept.
fold (fōld) *noun, plural* **folds.**

folder—1. A stiff or heavy outside cover for holding papers: *I put my writing assignment in a blue* folder *and gave it to my teacher.* 2. A

small booklet or pamphlet made of one or many sheets of folded paper: *That store gives out free* folders *about its products.*
fold|er (fōl′dər) *noun, plural* **folders.**

folk—1. Everyone of a particular group; people: *The town's* folk *often shop at the new mall.*
2. folks: One's family; relatives: *His folks are coming for Thanksgiving dinner. Noun.*
folk (fōk) *noun, plural* **folk** or **folks.**

folk dance—1. A traditional dance done by the common people of a country or region, usually handed down through many generations: *The Irish jig is a type of* folk dance. 2. The music that accompanies such a dance.
folk dance (fōk dans) *noun, plural* **folk dances.**

folklore—The fables, myths, beliefs, and traditions coming from the common people of a country or region.
folk|lore (fōk′lawr′) *noun.*

folk music—The traditional music or songs handed down through many generations of the common people from a certain country or region.
folk mu|sic (fōk myū′zik) *noun.*

folk song—A traditional song handed down through many generations of the common people from a certain country or region.
folk song (fōk sawng) *noun, plural* **folk songs.**

folk tale—A traditional story handed down through many generations of common people from a certain country or region. Folk tales contain the legends, myths, beliefs, and customs of the group.
folk tale (fōk tāl) *noun, plural* **folk tales.**

follow—1. To go behind or come after someone or something: *I will* follow *you because you know the way.* 2. To move along: *If you* follow *the nature trail marked in blue, you will see some interesting plants.* 3. To do as instructed; obey: *This meal is easy to prepare if you* follow *the recipe.* 4. To focus on someone or something with the eyes or the mind: *If you* follow *the path of the string, you will see the kite way up high in the sky.* 5. To understand or keep up with: *to* follow *a lesson.*
fol|low (fol′ō) *verb,* **followed, following.**

■ **follow through:** To do or complete something: *He asked me to deliver the message, and I* followed through.
follow up: To hear about or see something and then later act on it: *The store had a big sale, and I* followed up *on it by buying many sale items.*

follower—1. Someone or something that goes behind or comes after someone or something else: *When we played "follow the leader," I was a* follower. 2. Someone who believes in the traditions, ideals, and customs of another person or group; disciple: *The local minister has many* followers.
fol|low|er (fol′ō ər) *noun, plural* **followers.**

following—A group of admirers or disciples: *The music group's* following *traveled to all their concerts. Noun.*
—Coming next or after: *On the morning* following *the dance, we will take down the decorations. Adjective.*
fol|low|ing (fol′ō ing) *noun, plural* **followings;** *adjective.*

fond—Having or showing affection or love for: *My girlfriend is very* fond *of her grandmother and visits her every day.*
fond (fond) *adjective,* **fonder, fondest.**

food—What is eaten or taken in by people, animals, and plants to maintain life; nourishment: *Meat, cheese, fruits, milk, and vegetables are types of* foods.
food (fūd) *noun, plural* **foods.**

■ **food for thought:** Some idea or statement that makes one think or that is worth thinking about: *Her remark about my attitude gave me* food for thought.

food chain—An arrangement of all living things into levels, with higher forms of life eating the forms below them to survive: *Birds are higher in the* food chain *than insects.*
food chain (fūd chān) *noun, plural* **food chains.**

fool—1. Someone who lacks good sense or wise judgment: *She is a* fool *to think that she can read that whole book in one hour.* 2. In medieval times, a person whose job was to entertain a king and his court with silly antics, very much as a clown entertains today. *Noun.*
—1. To joke; tease: *We were just* fooling *when we told our friend that beings from outer space were in our backyard.* 2. To try to make something appear other than it is; trick: *My friend tried to make believe that he had the ball, but I wasn't* fooled. *Verb.*

a at	i if	oo look	ch chalk		a in ago
ā ape	ī idle	ou out	ng sing		e in happen
ah calm	o odd	u ugly	sh ship	ə =	i in capital
aw all	ō oats	ū rule	th think		o in occur
e end	oi oil	ur turn	th their		u in upon
ē easy			zh treasure		

fool (fūl) *noun, plural* **fools;** *verb,* **fooled, fooling.**
- Synonyms: **kid², jest, joke,** for *verb* **1.**

foolish—Not wise; lacking good sense: *It is foolish to wear good clothes when you are painting.*
fool|ish (fū'lish) *adjective.*
- Synonyms: **absurd, ridiculous, silly, senseless**
  Antonyms: **reasonable, sensible**

foot—**1.** A part of the body at the end of the leg, on which to stand or walk.   **2.** The area where the feet would go, or that part opposite the head: *He tucked the blankets in at the* foot *of the bed.* **3.** The lowest part of something: *the* foot *of the stairs; the* foot *of a hill.*   **4.** A length of twelve inches, which is equal to 0.3048 meter. *Noun.*
—To take care of paying for something: *I have to* foot *the bill for the entertainment. Verb.*
foot (foot) *noun, plural* **feet;** *verb,* **footed, footing.** Abbreviation: **ft.**
- **get** (one's) **foot in the door:** To have a chance to get what one wants: *Before you can join a professional team, you have to* get *your* foot in the door *as an amateur.*
  put (one's) **best foot forward:** To make the best effort that one is capable of: *He put his* best foot forward *when he tried out for the school baseball team.*
  put (one's) **foot down:** To stand firmly by one's decision: *The librarian* put *her* foot down *and insisted that the children be quiet.*
  put (one's) **foot in it:** To say the wrong thing; interfere in someone else's business: *I certainly* put *my* foot in it *when I tried to tell the mechanic how to fix a motor.*
  put (one's) **foot in** (one's) **mouth:** To make thoughtless, inconsiderate remarks: *I* put *my* foot in *my* mouth *when I told her I dislike doctors and found out later that she is a doctor.*
- For *noun* **1,** see picture at **instep;** for *noun* **4,** see picture at **yard².**

football—**1.** A game in which two teams of eleven players each try to advance a ball down a rectangular field by throwing, carrying, or kicking it. A score is made by moving the ball over the opponent's goal line or by kicking it through the goal posts.   **2.** The leather, oval ball used in this game.
foot|ball (foot'bawl') *noun, plural* **footballs** for definition 2.

foothold—A place that will support a foot, especially while climbing: *When mountain climbing, always be sure to have a good* foothold.
foot|hold (foot'hōld') *noun, plural* **footholds.**

footlights—Lights that run across the front edge of a stage: *The footlights* shined *on the actors.*
foot|lights (foot'līts') *noun, singular* **footlight.**

footnote—A note of explanation or comment at the bottom of a page. A footnote refers to something being discussed on the same page and often tells the source of an idea or a quote.
foot|note (foot'nōt') *noun, plural* **footnotes.**

Language Fact

People think of many things as having a head and a foot, such as beds, stairs, and pages. A **footnote** gets its name because it is a note at the bottom, or foot, of a page. A footnote gives more information about something on the page. Usually, a number or mark appears on the page and in front of the footnote, to show which part of the page the footnote is connected with. * is a mark often used for footnotes.

---

footprint—The impression or outline of a shoe or foot made in sand, mud, dirt, snow, or the like.
foot|print (foot'print') *noun, plural* **footprints.**

footstep—**1.** A step of someone's foot: *If you follow my* footsteps, *you will learn how to do this dance.*   **2.** The sound of someone walking: *The woman heard every* footstep *in the apartment above her.*
foot|step (foot'step') *noun, plural* **footsteps.**
- **follow in** (someone's) **footsteps:** To do what another person has done: *My friend is studying law and will* follow in *his father's* footsteps *by becoming a lawyer.*

for—**1.** Rather than; as a substitute: *Mother used strawberries* for *the cherries the pie recipe listed.*   **2.** In support or defense of: *This student-council candidate is* for *longer lunch periods.*   **3.** With the purpose of getting or having: *We are going* for *ice cream after the game.*   **4.** Intended to be used by; suited to: *a coat* for *a boy; movies* for *children.*   **5.** In honor of: *The dinner was* for *our new neighbor.*   **6.** As long as: *The family rode in the car* for *two hours.*   **7.** Sent to; directed at: *This letter is* for *you. The phone call is* for *my sister.*   **8.** In the amount of: *He bought a record* for *$10. Preposition.*
—Because: *I need help,* for *I cannot do it myself. Conjunction.*
for (fawr *or* fər) *preposition, conjunction.*
- Words that sound the same are **fore** and **four.**

forbade or **forbad**—*See* **forbid**.
for|bade or for|bad (fər bād′ *or* fər bad′) *verb*.

forbid—To not allow; prohibit: *Riding bicycles on the lawn is* forbidden.
for|bid (fər bid′) *verb*, **forbade** or **forbad**, **forbidden** or **forbid**, **forbidding**.

force—1. Energy; power: *The* force *of the wind blew down three branches from our tree.* 2. The energy, strength, or power used against someone or something: *The boys used* force *to move the heavy bags of sand.* 3. A group of people who do the same work together: *the air* force. 4. The natural cause of a motion or a change in a motion: *the* force *of magnetism. Noun.*
—1. To make someone do something that he or she does not want to do: *The rain* forced *us to stay indoors.* 2. To use strength or power to break something open: *We* forced *a window when we locked ourselves out of the house. Verb.*
force (fawrs) *noun, plural* **forces**; *verb*, **forced**, **forcing**.
• Synonyms: **compel**, **drive**, **oblige**, for *verb* 1.

ford—A place on a river that is shallow enough to wade or drive across. *Noun*.
—To wade or drive across a body of water at a shallow spot: *The pioneers* forded *the river in covered wagons. Verb.*
ford (fawrd) *noun, plural* **fords**; *verb*, **forded**, **fording**.

fore—Front: *The* fore *part of a television set holds the screen.*
fore (fawr) *adjective*.
• Words that sound the same are **for** and **four**.

Word Power

You can understand the meanings of many words that begin with **fore-**, if you add a meaning of the prefix to the meaning of the rest of the word.
forebrain: the front part of the brain
foreknowledge: knowledge or awareness of something before it happens
forename: a person's first name

---

fore-—A prefix that means "at the front" or "before." A foreword is the section in front of and introducing the main part of a book. A weather forecast tells what kind of weather is predicted before it occurs.

forearm—The part of the arm between the wrist and the elbow.
fore|arm (fawr′ahrm′) *noun, plural* **forearms**.

forecast—To figure out what is likely to happen based on facts, past experience, or the like; predict: *to* forecast *the future. Verb.*
—A prediction of what will probably happen in the future: *a weather* forecast. *Noun*.
fore|cast (fawr′kast′) *verb*, **forecasted**, **forecasting**; *noun, plural* **forecasts**.
• Synonyms: **foretell**, **predict**, for *verb*.

forefather—A member of a family that came before; ancestor: *Our* forefathers *came to the United States two hundred years ago.*
fore|fa|ther (fawr′fah′thər) *noun, plural* **forefathers**.

forefinger—The finger next to the thumb; index finger: *Most people point with their* forefinger.
fore|fin|ger (fawr′fing′gər) *noun, plural* **forefingers**.

forefoot—A front foot of an animal that has four feet.
fore|foot (fawr′foot′) *noun, plural* **forefeet**.

foreground—The part of a picture that appears nearest to and right in front of the person looking at it: *The* foreground *of the picture showed a boat that was ready to sail on the lake that was in the background.*
fore|ground (fawr′ground′) *noun, plural* **foregrounds**.
▪ **in the foreground**: At the center of attention: *That movie star is always* in the foreground *at parties.*

forehand—A basic stroke in racket sports in which the racket is held with the palm of the hand facing in the direction in which the hand is moving. The racket, such as a tennis racket, is swung forward to hit the ball. *Noun*.
—Done with the palm of the hand facing in the direction in which the hand is moving: *a* forehand *ping-pong stroke. Adjective.*
fore|hand (fawr′hand′) *noun, plural* **forehands**; *adjective*.

forehead—The front part of the face, above the eyes and nose and below the hair line.
fore|head (fawr′id *or* fawr′hed) *noun, plural* **foreheads**.

foreign—1. Not belonging to one's own country; *My sister is going to school in a* foreign *country.*

a at	i if	oo look	ch chalk		a in ago
ā ape	ī idle	ou out	ng sing		e in happen
ah calm	o odd	u ugly	sh ship	ə =	i in capital
aw all	ō oats	ū rule	th think		o in occur
e end	oi oil	ur turn	th their		u in upon
ē easy			zh treasure		

2. Of or coming from another country: *a foreign car.*   **3.** Having to do with relations with other nations: foreign *policy.*
for|eign (fawr′ən) *adjective.*

foreigner—A person who comes from another country.
for|eign|er (fawr′ə nər) *noun, plural* **foreigners.**

foreleg—A front leg of a four-legged animal.
fore|leg (fawr′leg′) *noun, plural* **forelegs.**

foreman—**1.** A person in charge of a group of workers, especially in a factory.   **2.** A person chosen to be the leader and speaker for a jury: *The jury* foreman *counts the votes of the jury and states their decision.*
fore|man (fawr′mən) *noun, plural* **foremen.**

foresaw—*See* **foresee.**
fore|saw (fawr′saw) *verb.*

foresee—To see or know what is going to happen beforehand: *The boys could* foresee *a tough game ahead of them when they saw the size of the players on the other team.*
fore|see (fawr′sē) *verb,* **foresaw, foreseen, foreseeing.**

foreseen—*See* **foresee.**
fore|seen (fawr′sēn) *verb.*

foresight—Care and planning in preparing for the future; anticipating what might happen: *We are lucky that Mother had the* foresight *to pack warm clothes for our camping trip last summer, because it got quite cold.*
fore|sight (fawr′sīt′) *noun.*

forest—Trees and other plants grouped thickly together in one large area; woods: *The scouts laid out a trail that ran through the middle of the forest.*
for|est (fawr′ist) *noun, plural* **forests.**

forestry—The study, care, and management of forests.
for|est|ry (fawr′ə strē) *noun.*

foretell—To tell of something before it happens: *We could not* foretell *the outcome of the game because the teams were so evenly matched.*
fore|tell (fawr tel′) *verb,* **foretold, foretelling.**
● Synonyms: **forecast, predict**

foretold—*See* **foretell.**
fore|told (fawr tōld′) *verb.*

forever—**1.** For all time; never ending: *She had so much fun at camp that she wanted to stay there* forever.   **2.** Always; continually: *Her parents are* forever *complaining about her messy room.*
for|ev|er (fər ev′ər) *adverb.*

forewarn—To caution beforehand: *The traffic report* forewarned *my father of the traffic jam ahead.*
fore|warn (fawr wawrn′) *verb,* **forewarned, forewarning.**

forfeit—To lose or give up because of fault or error: *When the other team did not show up on time, they* forfeited *the game and we were given the victory. Verb.*
—Something that is lost or given up in such a way. *Noun.*
for|feit (fawr′fit) *verb,* **forfeited, forfeiting;** *noun, plural* **forfeits.**

forgave—*See* **forgive.**
for|gave (fər gāv′) *verb.*

forge¹—A fireplace used for heating metal to a high degree so that it can be bent or hammered into different shapes: *a blacksmith's* forge. *Noun.*
—**1.** To bend or hammer very hot metal into a particular shape: *The artist made a picture out of many nails* forged *into unusual shapes.*   **2.** To shape something; construct: *The pioneers* forged *a road through the wilderness.*   **3.** To copy or imitate for the purpose of cheating or deceiving: *The police called in an expert to tell them whether the signature was* forged *or real.*
forge (fawrj) *noun, plural* **forges;** *verb,* **forged, forging.**

forge²—To move forward at a slow but steady pace: *We* forged *ahead through the snow.*
forge (fawrj) *verb,* **forged, forging.**

forgery—A copy or imitation that is presented as the real thing: *We did not get the money because the signature on the check turned out to be a forgery.*
for|ger|y (fawr′jər ē) *noun, plural* **forgeries.**

forehand (noun)

forget—1. To be unable to remember: *She* forgot *the zip code and had to look it up.* 2. To fail to do something at the proper time: *He forgot to meet her before the game, so they did not sit together.*
for|get (fər get′) *verb,* forgot, forgotten or forgot, forgetting.

forgetful—Not likely to remember: *My brother is very* forgetful, *and always leaves the lights on when he leaves the house.*
for|get|ful (fər get′fəl) *adjective.*

forget-me-not—A small, low plant with white or blue flowers clustered together at the end of each stem. It is the state flower of Alaska.
for|get-me-not (fər get′mē not′) *noun, plural* forget-me-nots.

forget-me-not

forgive—To stop being angry at: *He* forgave *her for the unkind things she said.*
for|give (fər giv′) *verb,* forgave, forgiven, forgiving.
• Synonyms: excuse, pardon

forgiven—*See* forgive.
for|giv|en (fər giv′ən) *verb.*

forgot—*See* forget.
for|got (fər got′) *verb.*

forgotten—*See* forget.
for|got|ten (fər got′ən) *verb.*

fork—1. A long, thin tool with a handle and two or more prongs used to lift or spear something: *a dinner* fork, *a pitch*fork. 2. A place where a

tree, road, or stream divides into two or more branches: *Take the path on the left when you get to the* fork *in the road. Noun.*
—1. To lift or dig with a multi-pronged tool: *to* fork *hay into the barn.* 2. To divide into branches: *The road* forks *up ahead. Verb.*
fork (fawrk) *noun, plural* forks; *verb,* forked, forking.

form—1. The shape or structure of something: *The* form *of a cat could be seen at the window.* 2. A kind; type: *Lightning is a* form *of electricity.* 3. A way or style of doing something, often according to an accepted standard: *The figure skater's performance showed nearly perfect* form. 4. A document with blank spaces where a person may write information: *She filled out a* form *to apply for a library card. Noun.*
—1. To give shape to; make: *He* formed *a snowball with his hands.* 2. To set up; establish: *The parents* formed *a committee to raise money for the school.* 3. To take or be arranged in a particular shape or order: *The soldiers* formed *a line. Verb.*
form (fawrm) *noun, plural* forms; *verb,* formed, forming.
• Synonyms: For *noun* 2, see Synonyms at **class.**

formal—1. Extremely proper; not casual or relaxed: *The gentleman's greeting was so* formal *that the child did not dare smile at him.* 2. Based on a fixed custom or a set of rules: *She received a* formal *invitation to the wedding. Adjective.*
—An event that requires a person to get dressed up: *The dance was a* formal. *Noun.*
for|mal (fawr′məl) *adjective; noun, plural* formals.

formation—1. The act or process of making or shaping something: *the* formation *of islands from volcanic eruptions.* 2. The thing that is made or shaped: *a cloud* formation. 3. The order in which something is arranged: *Eight students got into* formation *before the square dance began.*
for|ma|tion (fawr mā′shən) *noun, plural* formations.

former—1. The first of two people, places, or things that are named: *I like both walking and driving, but only the former gives me a chance to exercise.* 2. Earlier; past: *The* former *president is now writing a book about his experiences.*
for|mer (fawr′mər) *adjective.*

formula—1. A certain way of doing something: *a* formula *for being successful.* 2. A set order of numbers, letters, or symbols that expresses a

a at	i if	oo look	ch chalk	a in ago
ā ape	ī idle	ou out	ng sing	e in happen
ah calm	o odd	u ugly	sh ship	ə = i in capital
aw all	ō oats	ū rule	th think	o in occur
e end	oi oil	ur turn	th their	u in upon
ē easy			zh treasure	

rule, an idea, or the composition of something: CO_2 *is the chemical* formula *for carbon dioxide.*
for|mu|la (**fawr′**myə lə) *noun, plural* **formulas.**

forsake—To give up; abandon: *The bluebirds will* forsake *the birdhouse to fly south for the winter.*
for|sake (fawr **sāk′**) *verb,* **forsook, forsaken, forsaking.**

forsaken—*See* **forsake.**
for|sak|en (fawr **sā′**kən) *verb.*

forsook—*See* **forsake.**
for|sook (fawr **sook′**) *verb.*

forsythia—A small, woody shrub with yellow, bell-shaped flowers that bloom in the early spring.
for|syth|i|a (fawr **sith′**ē ə) *noun, plural* **forsythias.**

forsythia

Word History

Forsythia comes from a man's name. William Forsyth was a Scottish plant scientist who lived in the 1700's.

fort—A building or place that is especially strengthened to protect against attack; fortress.
fort (fawrt) *noun, plural* **forts.**

forth—1. Onward in time: *From that day* forth, *the prince and princess lived happily ever after.* 2. Out where it can be seen: *The lava burst* forth *from the volcano.*
forth (fawrth) *adverb.*
■ **and so forth:** And so on; and like things: *We bought paints, crayons, chalk,* and so forth.
● A word that sounds the same is **fourth.**

fortieth—1. Next after the thirty-ninth. 2. One of forty equal parts.
for|ti|eth (**fawr′**tē ith) *adjective; noun, plural* **fortieths.**

fortification—1. The act of making strong; an adding of strength to: *The* fortification *of the city took many years.* 2. A ditch, wall, fort, or other kind of defense used to make a place strong.
for|ti|fi|ca|tion (fawr′tə fə **kā′** shən) *noun, plural* **fortifications.**

fortify—1. To protect or strengthen: *Before the hurricane struck, the family* fortified *their home by boarding up all the windows.* 2. To add vitamins or minerals so as to enrich: *This orange juice is now* fortified *with calcium.*
for|ti|fy (**fawr′**tə fī) *verb,* **fortified, fortifying.**

fortnight—Two weeks: *He planned to spend a* fortnight *at the lake.*
fort|night (**fawrt′** nīt) *noun, plural* **fortnights.**

fortress—A building or place that is especially strengthened to protect against attack; fort.
for|tress (**fawr′**tris) *noun, plural* **fortresses.**

fortunate—Having good luck: *He felt* fortunate *to have so many good friends.*
for|tu|nate (**fawr′**chə nit) *adjective.*

fortune—1. What will happen to a person in the future; fate. 2. Good or bad luck: *It was her good* fortune *to win a new bicycle in the raffle.* 3. Great wealth: *The rich man had a* fortune *in gold and jewels.*
for|tune (**fawr′**chən) *noun, plural* **fortunes.**

fortuneteller—A person who claims to be able to predict what will happen in the future.
for|tune|tell|er (**fawr′**chən tel′ər) *noun, plural* **fortunetellers.**

forty—Four times ten, one more than thirty-nine; 40.
for|ty (**fawr′**tē) *adjective; noun, plural* **forties.**

forward or **forwards**—1. To or toward the front: *She leaned* forward *to lace her ice skates.* 2. Ahead in time; in the future: *He looks* forward *to the game tomorrow. Adverb.*
—1. Toward or at the front: *He sat down in the* forward *part of the canoe.* 2. Bold or outspoken: *The* forward *girl shouted out the answer before the teacher finished talking. Adjective.*
—To send to a new address: *The post office* forwarded *his mail after he moved to a new town. Verb.*
—A player in hockey, soccer, or basketball whose place is near the front lines. *Noun.*
for|ward or for|wards (**fawr′**wərd *or* **fawr′** wərds) *adverb; adjective; verb,* **forwarded, forwarding;** *noun, plural* **forwards.**

fossil

Word History

Fossil comes from a Latin word meaning "dug up." Because fossils are usually buried in the ground, they must be dug up to be studied.

fossil—The hardened remains of a plant or animal that lived long ago. Fossils are preserved in earth or rock.
fos|sil (fos'əl) *noun, plural* **fossils.**

foster—To help to grow or develop: *He fostered a friendship with the new boy by asking him to play. Verb.*
—Part of the same family, although not related by birth or adoption: *The family welcomed the foster child who came to live with them. Adjective.*
fos|ter (faws'tər) *verb,* **fostered, fostering;** *adjective.*

fought—*See* **fight.**
fought (fawt) *verb.*

foul—**1.** Nasty, filthy, or very unpleasant: *a foul odor.* **2.** Very bad; wicked: *Foul play is suspected in the fire at the old barn.* **3.** Unfair; against the rules: *Hitting the player on the hand was a foul play.* **4.** Outside of the bounds marked on a playing field: *The batter hit a foul ball.* **5.** Cloudy or stormy: *The foul weather upset our plans for a picnic. Adjective.*
—**1.** To make unclean or unpleasant: *Dirt and leaves fouled the water in the swimming pool.* **2.** To break the rules of a game: *The girl caught the basketball but fouled another player when*

she did. **3.** To become tangled: *The kite string fouled in the branches of the tree. Verb.*
—**1.** Something that is done against the rules: *The hockey player committed a* foul *and was sent to the penalty box.* **2.** A baseball hit outside the boundaries of the playing field.
foul (foul) *adjective,* **fouler, foulest;** *verb,* **fouled, fouling;** *noun, plural* **fouls.**
• A word that sounds the same is **fowl.**
• Synonyms: **horrid, offensive,** for *adjective* **1.**

found[1]—*See* **find.**
found (found) *verb.*

found[2]—To start up; begin: *The thirteen colonies* founded *a new nation on July 4, 1776.*
found (found) *verb,* **founded, founding.**

foundation—**1.** A part of something that is used as a base or a support: *the cement* foundation *of a house.* **2.** A starting up; beginning: *After the* foundation *of a Boy Scout troop in our neighborhood, my uncle became a troop leader.*
foun|da|tion (found dā'shən) *noun, plural* **foundations.**

fountain—**1.** A stream of water that is made to rise up into the air. **2.** A person, place, or thing from which something comes or begins; source: *That boy is a real* fountain *of baseball facts.*
foun|tain (foun'tən) *noun, plural* **fountains.**

four—**1.** Three more than one; one less than five; 4.
four (fawr) *adjective; noun, plural* **fours.**
• Words that sound the same are **for** and **fore.**

Four-H club or **4-H club**—An organization for young people that teaches farming and homemaking skills.
Four-H club or 4-H club (fawr'āch' klub) *noun, plural* **Four-H clubs** or **4-H clubs.**

fourteen—Four more than ten; one more than thirteen; 14.
four|teen (fawr'tēn) *adjective; noun, plural* **fourteens.**

fourteenth—**1.** Next after the thirteenth. **2.** One of fourteen equal parts.
four|teenth (fawr'tēnth) *adjective; noun, plural* **fourteenths.**

fourth—**1.** Next after the third. **2.** One of four equal parts.
fourth (fawrth) *adjective; noun, plural* **fourths.**
• A word that sounds the same is **forth.**

Fourth of July—A holiday in the United States that honors the signing of the Declaration of Independence on July 4, 1776, by the thirteen original colonies.
Fourth of Ju|ly (fawrth ov joo lī') *noun.*
• This holiday is also called **Independence Day.**

a at	i if	oo look	ch chalk		a in ago
ā ape	ī idle	ou out	ng sing		e in happen
ah calm	o odd	u ugly	sh ship	ə =	i in capital
aw all	ō oats	ū rule	th think		o in occur
e end	oi oil	ur turn	th their		u in upon
ē easy			zh treasure		

fowl—1. Any kind of bird that is raised for food. Turkeys, chickens, geese, and ducks are types of fowl. 2. Any bird: *She watched the wild* fowl.
fowl (foul) *noun, plural* **fowl** *or* **fowls**.
• A word that sounds the same is **foul**.

fox—An animal that is related to the wolf and dog. It has reddish fur, a pointed nose, sharp ears, and a bushy tail. Foxes hunt small animals and are known for their intelligence.
fox (foks) *noun, plural* **foxes**.

fox

foxhound—*See* **American foxhound; English foxhound**.
fox|hound (foks′hound′) *noun, plural* **foxhounds**.

fox terrier—*See* **smooth fox terrier; wire fox terrier**.
fox ter|ri|er (foks ter′ē′ər), *noun, plural* **fox terriers**.

fraction—1. One or more of the equal parts into which a whole is divided. The following are examples of fractions: 1/3, 2/5, and 11/16. 2. A small part of a whole; segment or portion: *Only a* fraction *of the people in the contest won prizes.*
frac|tion (frak′shən) *noun, plural* **fractions**.

fracture—A breaking or cracking of something, especially a bone. *Noun.*
—To break; crack: *He* fractured *his leg when he fell off the porch. Verb.*
frac|ture (frak′chər) *noun, plural* **fractures;** *verb,* **fractured, fracturing**.
• Synonyms: **shatter, smash,** for *verb.*

fragile—Easily broken or damaged: *a* fragile *piece of glass.*
frag|ile (fraj′əl) *adjective.*
• Synonyms: **delicate, frail**
Antonym: **sturdy**

fragment—A small piece that has broken off something; bit: Fragments *of the robin's egg were scattered on the ground.*
frag|ment (frag′mənt) *noun, plural* **fragments**.

fragrance—A pleasant smell: *the* fragrance *of her mother's perfume.*
fra|grance (frā′grəns) *noun, plural* **fragrances**.
• Synonyms: **aroma, odor, scent**

fragrant—Having a pleasant smell: *The spring air was* fragrant *with the scent of lilacs.*
fra|grant (frā′grənt) *adjective.*

frail—1. Not physically strong; weak: *The* frail *old man used a cane to help him walk.* 2. Easily damaged or broken: *a* frail *spider's web.*
frail (frāl) *adjective,* **frailer, frailest**.
• Synonyms: **delicate, fragile,** for 2.
Antonym: **sturdy,** for 2.

frame—1. The part of a structure that supports the whole; the border: *the* frame *of a house; a picture* frame. 2. The physical makeup of a person's body: *the large* frame *of a weight lifter. Noun.*
—1. To shape or construct: *to* frame *my sentence in the form of a question.* 2. To provide with a border: *to* frame *a window.* 3. To make a person appear to be guilty: *The accused man claimed that he was* framed. *Verb.*
frame (frām) *noun, plural* **frames;** *verb,* **framed, framing**.

framework—The part of a thing that provides its shape or support: *The* framework *of the Ferris wheel was outlined in colored lights.*
frame|work (frām′wurk′) *noun, plural* **frameworks**.

franc—A unit of money in France and some other countries in Europe and Africa.
franc (frangk) *noun, plural* **francs**. Abbreviation: fr.
• A word that sounds the same is **frank**.

frank—Not afraid to tell one's real opinions or feelings; honest; sincere: *She was* frank *in saying that she did not like his new haircut.*
frank (frangk) *adjective,* **franker, frankest**.
• A word that sounds the same is **franc**.
• Synonyms: **open, outspoken, straightforward**

frankfurter—A long, thin sausage made from a finely chopped mixture of beef and pork; a hot dog.
frank|furt|er (frangk′fər tər) *noun, plural* **frankfurters**.

Word History

Frankfurter comes from Frankfurt, a city in what is now West Germany, where this kind of sausage was first made, in the Middle Ages. The sausage is also called a hot dog or a red hot.

frantic—Very upset or excited, usually by fear or worry; wild: *The mother bird was* frantic *when the cat climbed the tree near her nest.*
fran|tic (fran′tik) *adjective.*

fraud—1. A tricking of someone; the act of cheating: *When the coin proved to be worthless, the seller was accused of* fraud.   2. A person who tricks another, usually for money; cheat: *The woman who said that she could get us front row tickets for the championship game was a* fraud.
fraud (frawd) *noun, plural* **frauds.**

fray—To wear away or become ragged: *Daily wear had* frayed *the knees of her favorite blue jeans.*
fray (frā) *verb,* **frayed, fraying.**

freak—Something or someone that is unusual; abnormal: *The pumpkin at the fair weighing 200 pounds (90 kilograms) was a* freak. *Noun.*
—Unusual or abnormal: *A* freak *storm brought snow to the desert. Adjective.*
freak (frēk) *noun, plural* **freaks;** *adjective.*

freckle—A small, light brown mark on the skin, sometimes caused by exposure to the sun.
freck|le (frek′əl) *noun, plural* **freckles.**

free—1. Not restricted or controlled by someone or something; independent: *a* free *country;* free *time.*   2. Able to think, act, or speak as one pleases: *Please feel* free *to tell me what you think.*   3. At no cost: *She received a* free *ticket to the natural history museum. Adjective.*
—1. At no cost: *Children under age six can ride the train* free.   2. Not held back; loose: *The wild animals ran* free *in the safari park. Adverb.*
—To let loose; release: *He* freed *his fishing line from the branch and cast it back into the water. Verb.*
free (frē) *adjective,* **freer, freest;** *adverb; verb,* **freed, freeing.**
● Synonyms: **liberate, release,** for *verb.*
  Antonyms: For *verb,* see Synonyms at **catch.**

freedom—1. The state of being independent; liberty: *The revolution was fought to win* freedom *from the king's rule.*   2. The ability to think, act, or speak as one pleases.
free|dom (frē′dəm) *noun, plural* **freedoms.**

Freedom Day—A United States holiday that is celebrated on February 1. It honors the day in 1865 that President Abraham Lincoln signed a proposal to amend the Constitution to make slavery illegal.
Free|dom Day (frē′dəm dā) *noun.*

freeway—A major highway designed for quick driving without stop signs or tolls.
free|way (frē′wā′) *noun, plural* **freeways.**

freeze—1. To make a liquid into ice by hardening with cold: *The water in the birdbath* froze *overnight.*   2. To become very cold: *She* froze *while waiting at the bus stop.*   3. To be absolutely still, usually from fear: *The boy* froze *when he saw the large spider on his sleeve. Verb.*
—A time when the weather is very cold: *The farmer's crops were damaged by the unexpected* freeze. *Noun.*
freeze (frēz) *verb,* **froze, frozen, freezing;** *noun, plural* **freezes.**

freeze-dry—To dry food by first freezing the water in it and then getting rid of the water with microwaves in a vacuum. Food that is freeze-dried does not need to be refrigerated.
freeze-dry (frēz′ drī′) *verb,* **freeze-dried, freeze-drying.**

freezer—A cabinet or compartment in a refrigerator for storing frozen food.
freez|er (frē′zər) *noun, plural* **freezers.**

freight—1. Things that are carried by trains, trucks, ships, or airplanes; cargo: *The airplane was loaded with* freight *for the next flight.*
2. The carrying of things by such means: *The box of Hawaiian pineapples was sent by air* freight.
freight (frāt) *noun.*

freighter—A ship that is used to carry things: *an oil* freighter.
freight|er (frā′tər) *noun, plural* **freighters.**

French bulldog—A small, heavy dog with a large square head, a flat face, a short tail, and large pointed ears. Originally bred in France, these dogs are usually kept as pets.
French bull|dog (french bul′dawg′) *noun, plural* **French bulldogs.**

French Coach—A strong horse that was bred in France and first used to pull wagons and coaches.
French Coach (french kōch) *noun.*

French horn—A curved, brass musical instrument with a long, coiled tube that widens

a at	i if	oo look	ch chalk		a in ago
ā ape	ī idle	ou out	ng sing		e in happen
ah calm	o odd	u ugly	sh ship	ə =	i in capital
aw all	ō oats	ū rule	th think		o in occur
e end	oi oil	ur turn	th their		u in upon
ē easy			zh treasure		

into a bell shape at the end. The French horn developed from a kind of hunting horn.
French horn (french hawrn) *noun, plural* **French horns.**

French horn

frenzy—Temporary, wild excitement; frantic upset: *The people were in a frenzy when the queen appeared in her golden coach.*
fren|zy (fren′zē) *noun, plural* **frenzies.**

frequency—1. The quantity of times something happens or is repeated: *What was the frequency of school cancellations last winter?* 2. The fact that something happens often or is repeated: *He was amazed at the frequency of trips the mother bird made to feed her babies.*
fre|quen|cy (frē′kwən sē) *noun, plural* **frequencies.**

frequent—Happening or repeated often: *The children made frequent visits to their grandparents because they lived in the same town.*
fre|quent (frē′kwənt) *adjective.*

French bulldog

fresh—1. Newly done, made, picked, or the like; not old or stale: *a fresh coat of paint; a fresh loaf of bread.* 2. Something that is added; different: *a fresh start; fresh news from home.* 3. Not salty: *Trout live in fresh water.* 4. Clean; cool; pleasant: *The fresh spring air smelled wonderful.* 5. Not polite; rude: *She was punished for the fresh answer that she gave to her teacher.*
fresh (fresh) *adjective,* **fresher, freshest.**

freshman—A student who is in the first year of high school or college.
fresh|man (fresh′mən) *noun, plural* **freshmen.**

freshwater—Living in water that is not salty: *a freshwater fish.*
fresh|wa|ter (fresh′wawt′ər) *adjective.*

fret—To worry: *He fretted about the grades he would get on his report card.*
fret (fret) *verb,* **fretted, fretting.**

friar—A man who is a member of a religious order of the Roman Catholic Church.
fri|ar (frī′ər) *noun, plural* **friars.**

friction—1. The rubbing of one thing against another: *The friction of the sandpaper soon made the board smooth.* 2. A force that slows down movement between two things that are touching: *By dragging my feet on the ground, I created enough friction to stop my bike.* 3. Bad feeling; disagreement: *The teacher placed the two girls at opposite sides of the classroom because of the friction between them.*
fric|tion (frik′shən) *noun.*

Friday—The sixth day of the week; the day that follows Thursday.
Fri|day (frī′dē *or* frī′dā) *noun, plural* **Fridays.** Abbreviation: **Fri.**

Word History

Friday comes from the name of a goddess of love. Long ago in Germany, Denmark, Sweden, and Norway, people called the day after her and thought of it as a lucky day. Today, though, many people think of Friday as an unlucky day, if it is also the 13th day of the month.

fried—*See* **fry.**
fried (frīd) *adjective, verb.*

friend—1. A person one likes; comrade. 2. Friend—A member of the religious group called the Society of Friends; Quaker.
friend (frend) *noun, plural* **friends.**

friendly—**1.** Like a comrade; helpful; pleasant: *She gave her neighbor a* friendly *wave.*
2. Getting along well; not fighting: *Six* friendly *countries signed an agreement to stop polluting the environment.*
friend|ly (frend′lē) *adjective.*

friendship—A liking between people.
friend|ship (frend′ship) *noun, plural* **friendships.**

frigate—**1.** A fast, three-masted warship used between 1750 and 1860. **2.** A small escort vessel equipped to fight submarines.
frig|ate (frig′it) *noun, plural* **frigates.**

fright—**1.** Sudden fear; panic: *At the sound of thunder, the cat took* fright *and hid.* **2.** Someone or something whose looks shock: *The troll at the amusement park is a* fright.
fright (frīt) *noun, plural* **frights.**

frighten—**1.** To scare: *The mask really* frightened *me because I thought it was real.* **2.** To force away by making afraid: *The large dog* frightened *the small boy away from the house.*
fright|en (frī′tən) *verb,* **frightened, frightening.**

frigid—**1.** Freezing cold: frigid *temperatures.*
2. Lacking in friendliness; cold: *She gave her brother a* frigid *look when he walked into her room without knocking.*
frig|id (frij′id) *adjective.*

fringe—**1.** A decorative edge consisting of short, hanging threads or strips; a border: *the* fringe *of a scarf or bedspread.* **2.** Anything or anyone on the edge of something: *on the* fringe *of the group; on the* fringe *of town.*
fringe (frinj) *noun, plural* **fringes.**

Frisbee—A round, flat, plastic toy for throwing through the air. The name Frisbee is a trademark for this toy.
Fris|bee (friz′bē) *noun, plural* **Frisbees.**

frisky—Having pep; active: *a* frisky *puppy.*
frisk|y (fris′kē) *adjective,* **friskier, friskiest.**

frog—A small animal with webbed feet for swimming and long, strong hind legs for jumping.
frog (frog *or* frawg) *noun, plural* **frogs.**
  ■ **frog in (one's) throat:** A hoarseness that makes speech sound like the croak of a frog: *I had a* frog in *my throat after yelling so hard at the game.*

frogman—A trained swimmer who has special equipment that permits underwater work.
frog|man (frog′man *or* frawg′man) *noun, plural* **frogmen.**

frolic—A merry time; fun: *Our trip to the amusement park was a* frolic. *Noun.*
—To romp; to have fun: *The puppies* frolicked *around the large beach ball. Verb.*
frol|ic (frol′ik) *noun, plural* **frolics;** *verb,* **frolicked, frolicking.**

from—**1.** Out of: *to come* from *Europe; to escape* from *jail.* **2.** Out of one's control: *His father took the car* from *him for driving too fast.*
3. Starting with: *You have one month* from *tomorrow to finish your book report.* **4.** As a result of: *I know how to swim* from *lessons.*
5. As being different: *Can you tell one twin* from *the other?*
from (from *or* frum) *preposition.*

front—**1.** The first part: *the* front *of the train; the* front *of the building.* **2.** Land facing something: *Our building is on the ocean* front. **3.** The battle line in a war: *Trains carried wounded soldiers home from the* front. **4.** A pretending to be something that one is not: *He put up a brave* front *even though he felt afraid.* **5.** A dividing line for different types of weather: *a warm* front; *a cold* front. *Noun.*
—Having to do with the first part: *the* front *cover of the magazine. Adjective.*
—To face out: *My bedroom* fronts *the street. Verb.*
front (frunt) *noun, plural* **fronts;** *adjective; verb,* **fronted, fronting.**

frontier—**1.** The boundary between settled land and unsettled land: *As the settlers moved west, the* frontier *of the country shrank.* **2.** The boundary between two countries; border: *No walls or fences mark the* frontier *between Canada and*

frog

the United States.   **4.** The point beyond which something has not been discovered or developed: *Many* frontiers *in computer science remain to be explored. Noun.*
—Having to do with a land on the border: frontier *life; a* frontier *town. Adjective.*
fron|tier (frun tir′) *noun, plural* **frontiers;** *adjective.*

frost—**1.** Freezing weather: *the first* frost *of the season.*   **2.** Small ice particles that form when moisture in the air freezes. *Noun.*
—**1.** To spread small ice particles on something: *In the morning cold, the fields were* frosted *in white.*   **2.** To spread with a substance similar to frost; to put icing on: *to* frost *the cupcakes. Verb.*
frost (frawst *or* frost) *noun, plural* **frosts;** *verb,* **frosted, frosting.**

frostbite—An injury to a part of the body, usually the fingers or the toes, caused by freezing temperatures. *Noun.*
—To become injured by freezing temperatures: *The tomato plants were* frostbitten. *Verb.*
frost|bite (frawst′bīt′ *or* frost′bīt′) *noun, plural* **frostbites;** *verb,* **frostbitten, frostbiting.**

frosting—A sweet covering for a cake or other baked goods; icing.
frost|ing (fraws′ting *or* fros′ting) *noun, plural* **frostings.**

frosty—**1.** Having to do with freezing temperatures or objects: *a* frosty *day; a* frosty *glass of juice.*   **2.** Not warm or friendly in manner: *a* frosty *reply.*
frost|y (fraws′tē *or* fros′tē) *adjective,* **frostier, frostiest.**

frown—A creasing of the forehead that people make when deep in thought, displeased, or angry. *Noun.*
—To make such an expression: *Mother* frowned *when she read the latest newspaper report on rising food prices. Verb.*
frown (froun) *noun, plural* **frowns;** *verb,* **frowned, frowning.**

froze—*See* **freeze.**
froze (frōz) *verb.*

frozen—*See* **freeze.**
fro|zen (frō′zən) *verb.*

fruit—**1.** The part of a plant that one can eat. Fruits such as pears, peaches, and apples contain the seeds of a plant.   **2.** A result; outcome: *The* fruit *of my research was a very interesting term paper.*
fruit (frūt) *noun, plural* **fruits.**

frustrate—To make impossible to finish or continue; block; defeat: *The lack of transportation* frustrated *the students' plans to visit the capitol.*
frus|trate (frus′trāt) *verb,* **frustrated, frustrating.**
• Synonyms: **dash, foil[1], ruin**

fry—To cook something in very hot oil, butter, or other fat.
fry (frī) *verb,* **fried, frying.**

ft.—The abbreviation for **foot** or **feet.**

fudge—A soft, creamy candy that usually has a chocolate flavor.
fudge (fuj) *noun, plural* **fudges.**

fuel—A material, such as wood, gas, coal, or oil, that will burn to create heat and energy.
fu|el (fyū′əl) *noun, plural* **fuels.**

fugitive—Someone who escapes or hides from the law; runaway.
fu|gi|tive (fyū′jə tiv) *noun, plural* **fugitives.**

-ful—A suffix that means "full of," "enough to fill," or "likely to." A colorful picture is one that is full of color. A spoonful of sugar is enough to fill a spoon. Something that is harmful is likely to cause harm.

Word Power

You can understand the meaning of many words that end in **-ful,** if you add a meaning of the suffix to the meaning of the rest of the word.
   powerful: full of power
   cupful: enough to fill a cup
   forgetful: likely to forget

---

fulcrum—The support on which a lever turns when it is lifting or moving something.
ful|crum (ful′krəm *or* fool′krəm) *noun, plural* **fulcrums.**

fulcrum

fulcrum

fulfill or **fulfil**—**1.** To carry out: *I promise to* fulfill *my duties as president.* **2.** To meet or satisfy: *He fulfilled all the requirements to receive the first-aid badge.*
ful|fill or ful|fil (fool fil′) *verb,* **fulfilled, fulfilling.**

full—**1.** Filling all the available space; packed; brimming: *Get another box, because this one is* full. **2.** Whole; total: *He drank a* full *bottle of juice after mowing the lawn.* **3.** Having a large number: *The library is* full *of books.* **4.** Having a rounded appearance: *a* full *face. Adjective.*
—Entirely; completely: *Mother knew* full *well where I had been by the stains on my shirt. Adverb.*
full (fool) *adjective,* **fuller, fullest;** *adverb.*

fully—Completely; totally: *The students are* fully *aware that vacation begins tomorrow.*
ful|ly (fool′ē) *adverb.*

fumble—**1.** To look for something in an awkward way: *She* fumbled *around in the dark closet for her shoes.* **2.** To handle in a clumsy way: *He* fumbled *with the keys until he found the one that fit the lock.* **3.** To drop: *The quarterback* fumbled *the football when he was tackled. Verb.*
—The act of dropping something: *His* fumble *of the ball ended his team's chances of winning the game. Noun.*
fum|ble (fum′bəl) *verb,* **fumbled, fumbling;** *noun, plural* **fumbles.**

fume—Smoke or gas that is harmful or has a strong, unpleasant smell: *The* fumes *from the cleaning fluid made him dizzy. Noun.*
—**1.** To give off smoke or gas: *The engine* fumed *when it became too hot.* **2.** To express anger; rage: *My sister* fumed *at me for borrowing her dress without asking her first. Verb.*
fume (fyūm) *noun, plural* **fumes;** *verb,* **fumed, fuming.**

fun—Amusement or enjoyment; playfulness; entertainment: *The family had a lot of* fun *ice skating. Noun.*
—Enjoyable or entertaining: *A* fun *time was had by all at the party. Adjective.*
fun (fun) *noun, adjective.*

function—**1.** The purpose or use; role: *The* function *of the treasurer is to keep track of the*
club's money. **2.** A social gathering with a particular purpose, such as honoring a person or raising funds for charity. *Noun.*
—To work; serve a purpose: *The elevator was* not functioning *so we had to use the stairs. Verb.*
func|tion (fungk′shən) *noun, plural* **functions;** *verb,* **functioned, functioning.**

fund—**1.** A sum of money set aside for a certain purpose: *a* fund *to help poor people; a building* fund *for a school.* **2.** An accumulation of something that can be used; supply: *My older brother has a* fund *of information about old cars.* **3.** Funds: money: *I do not have the* funds *today, but I can pay you tomorrow. Noun.*
—To pay for: *My parents will* fund *my trip, but I will have to pay for any souvenirs I want. Verb.*
fund (fund) *noun, plural* **funds;** *verb,* **funded, funding.**

fundamental—Basic; key: *The coach taught the* fundamental *rules of the game to the beginners. Adjective.*
—The basic part: *The course taught the* fundamentals *of dancing before going on to more complicated steps. Noun.*
fun|da|men|tal (fun′də men′təl) *adjective; noun, plural* **fundamentals.**
• Synonyms: **essential, primary,** for *adjective.*
  Antonym: **trivial,** for *adjective.*

fundamentalist—A person who believes that the words of the Bible are true exactly as they are written and that they are not open to other interpretations.
fun|da|men|tal|ist (fun′də men′tə list) *noun, plural* **fundamentalists.**

funeral—The service held for a dead person before burial.
fu|ner|al (fyū′nər əl) *noun, plural* **funerals.**

fungi—*See* **fungus.**
fun|gi (fun′jī) *noun.*

fungus—Any one of a number of plants that are not green, have no flowers or leaves, and grow on other living things. A mushroom is a fungus.
fun|gus (fung′gəs) *noun, plural* **fungi** or **funguses.**

funnel—A cone-shaped device used to pour liquid or some other substance into a container with a small opening without spilling. A funnel has a wide opening at one end and a narrow opening at the other. *Noun.*
—To pour into or pass through a funnel: *He* funneled *water from the pitcher into the canteen. Verb.*

a at	i if	oo look	ch chalk		a in ago
ā ape	ī idle	ou out	ng sing		e in happen
ah calm	o odd	u ugly	sh ship	ə =	i in capital
aw all	ō oats	ū rule	th think		o in occur
e end	oi oil	ur turn	th their		u in upon
ē easy			zh treasure		

—Having a cone shape: *the funnel cloud of a tornado. Adjective.*
fun|nel (fun′əl) *noun, plural* **funnels;** *verb,* **funneled, funneling;** *adjective.*

funnies—The cartoons in a newspaper; comic strips.
fun|nies (fun′ēz) *noun.*

funny—1. Causing laughter; entertaining; amusing: *a funny clown; a funny story.*
2. Peculiar; curious: *It is funny that she did not come over when she said she would.*
fun|ny (fun′ē) *adjective,* **funnier, funniest.**
● Synonyms: **comical, hilarious, humorous,** for **1.**
Antonyms: **earnest, serious, solemn,** for **1.**

fur—1. The soft hair on the skin of some animals.
2. An article of clothing made from the skins of fur-bearing animals.
fur (fur) *noun, plural* **furs.**
■ **make the fur fly:** To stir things up; cause a quarrel: *Our disagreement over how to arrange our room certainly* made the fur fly.
rub (one's) **fur the wrong way:** To annoy: *My little brother's constant teasing* rubbed *my* fur the wrong way.
● A word that sounds the same is **fir.**

furious—1. Very mad; angry; enraged: *Mother was* furious *with me for missing my appointment with the dentist.* 2. Fierce; stormy; violent: *The* furious *wind blew down many tree branches.*
fu|ri|ous (fyoor′ē əs) *adjective.*

furnace—A container in which a fire burns to produce heat: *The old* furnace *failed to keep the house warm.*
fur|nace (fur′nis) *noun, plural* **furnaces.**

furnish—1. To provide with furniture: *When my family moved into the new house, my parents*

furnished *the dining room with a new table and chairs.* 2. To provide with needed items: *His father's company* furnishes *the paper for the school.*
fur|nish (fur′nish) *verb,* **furnished, furnishing.**
● Synonyms: **equip, supply,** for **2.**

furniture—Movable household goods, such as beds, dressers, tables, chairs, and sofas.
fur|ni|ture (fur′nə chər) *noun.*

furrow—1. A long, narrow trench that is plowed in the ground and in which seeds are planted.
2. Any long, narrow trench; groove; track: *Our bicycle tires made* furrows *in the dirt.*
fur|row (fur′ō) *noun, plural* **furrows.**

furrow (definition 1)

furry—1. Having fur: *a* furry *cat.* 2. Feeling like fur: *a soft,* furry *hat.*
fur|ry (fur′ē) *adjective,* **furrier, furriest.**

further—1. Farther on or away: *Now that the store on the corner has closed, we have to go to the* further *one down the road.* 2. More; additional: *She needs* further *help in science if she wants to pass the test. Adjective.*
—1. At an additional distance; beyond: *The hikers traveled* further *after lunch before they stopped for the night.* 2. Additionally; more: *If you read* further, *you will find the answer to your question. Adverb.*
—To advance; help; promote: *The treaty* furthered *the cause of peace. Verb.*
fur|ther (fur′thər) *adjective; adverb; verb,* **furthered, furthering.**

fungus

furthermore—Also; as well.
fur|ther|more (fur′thər mawr) *adverb*.
• Synonyms: **besides, likewise, moreover, too**

furthest—As far away as possible; most in distance: *Of everyone who was at the party, we came from the* furthest *city. Of all your throws, this one went the* furthest.
fur|thest (fur′thist) *adjective, adverb.*

furtive—**1.** Done so as to avoid being seen or noticed: *He took a* furtive *glance behind him as he left the room.* **2.** Sly; cunning: *The spy had a* furtive *manner.*
fur|tive (fur′tiv) *adjective.*

fury—**1.** Very strong anger: *Father tried to control his* fury *when he found the tire marks on the newly planted lawn.* **2.** Violent force: *the* fury *of a blizzard.*
fur|y (fyoor′ē) *noun, plural* **furies.**
• Synonyms: **rage, wrath,** for 1.
Antonyms: **calm, peace,** for 1.

fuse[1]—An electrical safety device that has a piece of metal that melts when the current becomes too strong. In this way, the circuit is interrupted and the flow of electricity is turned off so that a fire cannot start.
fuse (fyūz) *noun, plural* **fuses.**
■ **blow a fuse:** To get angry: *He blew a fuse when he found out that the dog had chewed his slippers.*

fuse[2]—**1.** To make metals or other hard substances stick together by melting their surfaces, joining them, and letting them cool and harden; weld. **2.** To combine; band together; unite: *The groups forgot their differences and* fused *to fight for their rights.*
fuse (fyūz) *verb,* **fused, fusing.**

fuselage—The body of an airplane or other flying machine.
fu|se|lage (fyū′zə lahzh) *noun, plural* **fuselages.**

fusion—**1.** The act or process of joining by melting. **2.** The act or process of combining or mixing: *Rock 'n' roll resulted from a* fusion *of many different types of music.* **3.** The joining of the nuclei of two atoms to produce a vast amount of energy.
fu|sion (fyū′zhən) *noun, plural* **fusions.**

fuss—A bother or excitement about something that is not worth so much attention; commotion: *Do not make a* fuss *about how your boots look as long as they keep your feet dry. Noun.*
—**1.** To worry about something that is not worth worrying about: *She* fussed *too much with her hair and was late for school.* **2.** To complain; gripe: *He* fussed *about how tight his collar was. Verb.*
fuss (fus) *noun, plural* **fusses;** *verb,* **fussed, fussing.**
• Synonyms: **grumble, whine,** for *verb* 2.

fuss-budget—A person who worries or bothers about things too much.
fuss-budg|et (fus′buj′it) *noun, plural* **fuss-budgets.**

future—**1.** The time after the present: *In the* future, *you will have your own book, but today you have to share.* **2.** The events that are to come; outcome: *I do not know what her* future *will be after she finishes college. Noun.*
—Being yet to come; coming: Future *meetings will be held at her house. Adjective.*
fu|ture (fyū′chər) *noun, plural* **futures;** *adjective.*

fuzz—Short, soft hairs or fibers: *His shirt was covered with* fuzz *from his sweater.*
fuzz (fuz) *noun.*

fuzzy—**1.** Having short, soft hairs or fibers: *a* fuzzy *robe.* **2.** Not clear or distinct; out of focus; confused: *Everything looks* fuzzy *when I take off my glasses.*
fuz|zy (fuz′ē) *adjective,* **fuzzier, fuzziest.**

---

a at	i if	oo look	ch chalk		a in ago
ā ape	ī idle	ou out	ng sing		e in happen
ah calm	o odd	u ugly	sh ship	ə =	i in capital
aw all	ō oats	ū rule	th think		o in occur
e end	oi oil	ur turn	th their		u in upon
ē easy			zh treasure		

Word Power

You can understand the meaning of many words that end in **-fy**, if you add a meaning of the suffix to the meaning of the rest of the word.
  simplify: to make simple
  solidify: to become solid

-fy—A suffix that means "to make" or "to become." To purify water means to make it pure. A substance that starts to acidify is starting to become an acid.

About 5,000 years ago, the ancient Egyptians used a symbol of a boomerang. The letters G and C both came from this symbol.

About 3,000 years ago, people in the Middle East used a symbol that looked more like a hook.

About 2,600 years ago, the Greeks gave the letter this form. They called it *gamma* and made it the third letter in their alphabet.

About 1,900 years ago, the Romans gave the capital **G** its present form. The small letter **g** was first used about 1,700 years ago. It reached its present form about 500 years ago.

G or **g**—The seventh letter of the alphabet: *The word "giggle" has three g's.*
G, g (jē) *noun, plural* **G's** or **Gs, g's** or **gs.**

g—The abbreviation for **gram** or **grams.**

gadget—A small mechanical device or tool used for a specific purpose: *An electric knife is a kitchen gadget.*
gadg|et (gaj′it) *noun, plural* **gadgets.**

gag—**1.** Something put in or over the mouth to keep a person from speaking or yelling. **2.** A joke; trick: *The boys thought it would be a funny gag to put pepper in the salt shaker. Noun.*
—**1.** To put something in or over the mouth to prevent a person from speaking or yelling: *The robbers told the man that if he yelled, they would gag him.* **2.** To choke: *She gags at the thought of eating beets. Verb.*
gag (gag) *noun, plural* **gags;** *verb,* **gagged, gagging.**

gaily—In a happy and cheerful manner: *The girls skipped gaily through the meadow.*
gai|ly (gā′lē) *adverb.*

gain—**1.** To get possession of, earn, or win: *to gain knowledge through experience.* **2.** To get as an advantage; profit: *What does he have to gain by being so mean to people?* **3.** To increase or improve: *our team gaining in the standings; a storm gaining strength; to gain weight. Verb.*
—Something that is obtained or won: *A rapid gain in speed may cause a car to skid. Noun.*
gain (gān) *verb,* **gained, gaining;** *noun, plural* **gains.**

gait—A manner or style of walking or running: *A horse's gallop is a very fast gait.*
gait (gāt) *noun, plural* **gaits.**
• A word that sounds the same is **gate.**

gal.—The abbreviation for **gallon** or **gallons.**

gala—Joyous; festive: *The wedding was a gala event. Adjective.*
—A festive or joyous celebration: *The club held a gala to welcome its new members. Noun.*
ga|la (gāl′ə *or* ga′lə) *adjective; noun, plural* **galas.**

galaxy—One of billions of groups of stars that make up the universe. The earth and sun are in the galaxy known as the Milky Way.
gal|ax|y (gal′ək sē) *noun, plural* **galaxies.**

Word History

Galaxy comes from a Greek word meaning "milk." The Milky Way is the galaxy that includes the earth and sun. It is called the Milky Way because its white light is like milk in the dark sky.

---

gale—**1.** A very powerful wind. **2.** A loud, emotional outburst: *The movie sent us into gales of laughter.*
gale (gāl) *noun, plural* **gales.**

gall—**1.** A yellowish liquid that is important for the body's digestion. It is produced by the liver and stored in the gall bladder. **2.** Rudeness or boldness: *It took a lot of gall for her to go to that party since she was not invited.*
gall (gawl) *noun.*

gallant—Brave and noble: *The gallant soldiers fought to the end of the battle.*
gal|lant (gal′ənt) *adjective.*

galleon

galleon—A fighting ship of long ago that had at least three decks and square sails.
gal|le|on (gal′ē ən) *noun, plural* **galleons.**

gallery—1. A balcony, especially the highest, in a hall, theater, or church. 2. A building or room for displaying or selling works of art.
gal|ler|y (gal′ər ē) *noun, plural* **galleries.**

galley—1. A long, narrow ship of long ago that used both oars and sails. 2. The kitchen of an airplane or a ship.
gal|ley (gal′ē) *noun, plural* **galleys.**

gallon—A unit of measure for liquids. A gallon is equal to 4 quarts (3.7853 liters).
gal|lon (gal′ən) *noun, plural* **gallons.**
Abbreviation: **gal.**
 • See picture at **quart.**

gallop—The fastest pace of a four-footed animal, usually a horse. *Noun.*
—To move at a fast pace: *The wild horses galloped across the open field. Verb.*
gal|lop (gal′əp) *noun, plural* **gallops;** *verb,* **galloped, galloping.**

gallows—A tall, wooden frame used for putting criminals to death by hanging.
gal|lows (gal′ōz) *noun, plural* **gallowses** or **gallows.**

galoshes—Rubber shoes worn over regular shoes to protect them from rain, mud, and snow.
ga|losh|es (gə losh′iz) *plural noun.*

gamble—1. To bet money or valuable items on the results of a game or contest: *She gambled her ring in the card game.* 2. To take a risk: *I*

gambled *that my mother wouldn't care if I borrowed her watch without asking. Verb.*
—A risky act: *We took a gamble that it wouldn't rain and went ahead with our ball game. Noun.*
gam|ble (gam′bəl) *verb,* **gambled, gambling;** *noun, plural* **gambles.**

game—1. A form of play or sport for one's amusement: *party* games; *a game of soccer.*
2. A contest that one person or team tries to win: *a hockey* game. 3. Wild animals that are hunted as a sport or for food: *Pheasants are a kind of* game. *Noun.*
—Brave, daring, and spirited enough to do something: *Are you* game *for a ride on the Ferris wheel? Adjective.*
game (gām) *noun, plural* **games;** *adjective,* **gamer, gamest.**
 ■ **ahead of the game:** To be winning at something or to be ahead of a deadline: *My dad said I was* ahead of the game *in housework because I had the dishes done before he asked me to do them.*
 • Synonyms: **entertainment, pastime, recreation,** for *noun* 1.
Antonyms: **chore, duty, task,** for *noun* 1.

gander—A male goose.
gan|der (gan′dər) *noun, plural* **ganders.**

gang—1. A group of persons who do things together as friends: *The gang and I are going to play basketball tonight.* 2. An organized group of criminals. 3. A group of persons who work together at a certain job.
gang (gang) *noun, plural* **gangs.**
 • Synonyms: For **1,** see Synonyms at **band¹.**

gangplank—A movable platform used as a bridge for boarding and leaving a boat.
gang|plank (gang′plangk′) *noun, plural* **gangplanks.**

gangster—One of a group of criminals.
gang|ster (gang′stər) *noun, plural* **gangsters.**

gangway—A passage into, through, or out of a ship or building. *Noun.*
—A call meaning "Make Way!" *Interjection.*
gang|way (gang′wā′) *noun, plural* **gangways;** *interjection.*

Word History

Gangway comes from two old English words meaning "a way for going." A gangway is a way for people to go into or out of a ship or building. Also, if you hear someone yell "Gangway!" it means "Make way! Going through!"

a at	i if	oo look	ch chalk		
ā ape	ī idle	ou out	ng sing		a in ago
ah calm	o odd	u ugly	sh ship	ə =	e in happen
aw all	ō oats	ū rule	th think		i in capital
e end	oi oil	ur turn	th their		o in occur
ē easy			zh treasure		u in upon

gap—1. An opening or empty part: *Light came through a* gap *between the curtains.* 2. A great difference in opinions: *a generation* gap. 3. A pass through mountains.
gap (gap) *noun, plural* **gaps.**

gape—1. To stare in amazement with one's mouth open: *The children* gaped *at the huge dinosaur skeleton. Verb.*
—A wide opening or space: *We crossed the street when there was a* gape *in the parade. Noun.*
gape (gāp) *verb,* **gaped, gaping;** *noun, plural* **gapes.**

garage—1. A place for parking automobiles and other vehicles. 2. A place for repairing automobiles and other vehicles.
ga|rage (gə **rahzh**′ *or* gə **rahj**′) *noun, plural* **garages.**

garbage—Scraps of food and other trash to be thrown away.
gar|bage (**gahr**′bij) *noun.*
• Synonyms: **refuse², rubbish, waste**

garden—A piece of land where flowers and vegetables are grown. *Noun.*
—To take care of or work in such an area: *Our yard is so beautiful this summer because Dad* gardens *every weekend. Verb.*
gar|den (**gahr**′dən) *noun, plural* **gardens;** *verb,* **gardened, gardening.**

gardenia—A rose-shaped flower that has a sweet smell. Gardenias have white or yellow petals.
gar|de|nia (gahr **dēn**′yə) *noun, plural* **gardenias.**

gardenia

gargle—To rinse the inside of the mouth or throat with a liquid, breathing out to keep it in motion: *Your sore throat will feel better if you* gargle *with warm saltwater.*
—A liquid used to rinse the inside of the mouth or throat: *I use a* gargle *to freshen my breath.*
gar|gle (**gahr**′gəl) *verb,* **gargled, gargling;** *noun, plural* **gargles.**

Word History

Gargle and **gargoyle** both come from the same French word meaning "to bubble." When gargling, a person makes a bubbling sound. The same kind of sound might be heard coming from a gargoyle as water drains from it. A person gargling may also make a face like the face on a gargoyle.

---

gargoyle—A fancy, carved spout on the roof or eaves of a building, shaped in the form of a very ugly human or animal figure. Gargoyles carry rain water away from the edge of a building.
gar|goyle (**gahr**′goil) *noun, plural* **gargoyles.**

gargoyle

garlic—A plant from the onion family. It has a strong smell and flavor and is used in cooking.
gar|lic (**gahr**′lik) *noun.*

garment—An article of clothing: *Mom brought several* garments *to the cleaners.*
gar|ment (**gahr**′mənt) *noun, plural* **garments.**

garnet—A dark-red mineral used for jewelry.
gar|net (**gahr**′nit) *noun, plural* **garnets.**

garnish—Something used to decorate a plate or dish of food. *Noun.*
—To place something on or around food as a decoration: *The chef* garnished *the dish with leaves of parsley. Verb.*

gar|nish (gahr′nish) *noun, plural* **garnishes;** *verb,* **garnished, garnishing.**

garrison—Military troops stationed in a fort or town for protection; military post.
gar|ri|son (gar′ə sən) *noun, plural* **garrisons.**

garter—A band of elastic worn around the leg to hold up a sock or stocking.
gar|ter (gahr′tər) *noun, plural* **garters.**

garter snake—A small snake that is brown or green with three yellow or white stripes running from head to tail on the back. Garter snakes are harmless.
gar|ter snake (gahr′tər snāk) *noun, plural* **garter snakes.**

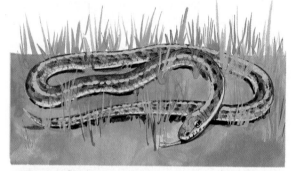

garter snake

gas—1. A substance that is not liquid or solid and has no shape or size of its own. Oxygen and nitrogen are gases in the air we breathe. 2. A substance that is not liquid or solid used for heating and cooking: *Is your house heated by gas, oil, or electricity?* 3. Gasoline. Gas is a shortened form of gasoline: *Stop and get some gas before we get on the highway.*
gas (gas) *noun, plural* **gases.**
■ **step on the gas:** To go faster either in an automobile or on foot: *We had better* step on the gas, *or we will be late for school.*

gaseous—Made or in the form of a substance that is not liquid or solid: *Steam is the* gaseous *form of water.*
gas|e|ous (gas′ē əs) *adjective.*

gash—A deep, long cut; wound. *Noun.*
—To make a deep, long cut: *I gashed my hand on the broken glass. Verb.*
gash (gash) *noun, plural* **gashes;** *verb,* **gashed, gashing.**

gasoline—A colorless liquid that burns easily and is used as a motor fuel.
gas|o|line (gas′ə lēn *or* gas′ə lēn′) *noun.*

gasp—1. A struggle to breathe: *We heard the choking man's* gasps *for air.* 2. A catching of one's breath out of surprise or shock: *We heard* gasps *from the movie audience during the scary scene. Noun.*
—1. To struggle for breath; catch one's breath: *I was* gasping *for air towards the end of the race.* 2. To utter with very little breath: *"Run for your lives,"* the soldier gasped. *Verb.*
gasp (gasp) *noun, plural* **gasps;** *verb,* **gasped, gasping.**

gate—1. A movable barrier in a wall or fence that opens and closes like a door: *Shut the* gate *before the dog gets out.* 2. An opening in a wall or fence: *The elephant was so big that it barely fit through the* gate *to the circus tent.*
gate (gāt) *noun, plural* **gates.**
■ **get the gate:** To be dismissed or fired: *His sister is looking for another job after* getting the gate *from that factory.*
give (one) **the gate:** To dismiss or fire: *My boss hates to* give *any employee* the gate, *but sometimes he has no choice.*
● A word that sounds the same is **gait.**

gateway—1. An opening in a wall or fence where a movable barrier is put: *The* gateway *was blocked off with a rope.* 2. A way to get to something: *A good education can be a* gateway *to success.*
gate|way (gāt′wā′) *noun, plural* **gateways.**

gather—1. To bring or come together in one place; collect: *to* gather *to watch an event; to* gather *flowers for a bouquet.* 2. To gain slowly: *The plane* gathered *speed and finally got off the ground.* 3. To accumulate over time: *to* gather *the courage to dive.* 4. To understand or conclude: *I* gather *from the look on your face that something is wrong.* 5. To bring or stitch fabric into folds: *The clown's pants were* gathered *at the ankles.*
gath|er (ga<u>th</u>′ər) *verb,* **gathered, gathering.**
● Synonyms: **assemble, congregate,** for **1.**
Antonym: **scatter,** for **1.**

gathering—A group of people; meeting; party: *We had a family* gathering *to celebrate grandmother's birthday.*
gath|er|ing (ga<u>th</u>′ər ing) *noun, plural* **gatherings.**

a at	i if	oo look	ch chalk		a in ago
ā ape	ī idle	ou out	ng sing		e in happen
ah calm	o odd	u ugly	sh ship	ə =	i in capital
aw all	ō oats	ū rule	th think		o in occur
e end	oi oil	ur turn	<u>th</u> their		u in upon
ē easy			zh treasure		

gaudy—Too bright, showy, or flashy to be in good taste: *The clown had a big red nose and gaudy orange hair.*
gaud|y (gaw′dē) *adjective,* **gaudier, gaudiest.**

gauge—**1.** One of many standards or systems of measurement. There are gauges to measure capacity, speed, temperature, distance, and pressure.   **2.** An instrument used for measuring: *A thermometer is a gauge for measuring a person's body temperature. Noun.*
—To measure accurately: *She used a stop watch to gauge the time it took to run a mile. Verb.*
gauge (gāj) *noun, plural* **gauges;** *verb,* **gauged, gauging.**

gaunt—A very thin, bony appearance: *The lost dog was gaunt and hungry when we found it.*
gaunt (gawnt) *adjective,* **gaunter, gauntest.**
• Synonyms: **lean², scrawny, skinny, spare**
  Antonyms: **fat, plump, stout**

gauze—A light, thinly woven cloth often used to make bandages.
gauze (gawz) *noun, plural* **gauzes.**

gave—*See* **give.**
gave (gāv) *verb.*

gavel—A wooden hammer that is used to call for quiet and attention in a courtroom or other meeting.
gav|el (gav′əl) *noun, plural* **gavels.**

gay—**1.** Happy; merry: *We had a gay time at the holiday dance!*   **2.** Colorful; bright: *The parrot has a yellow beak and gay blue, green, and red feathers.*
gay (gā) *adjective,* **gayer, gayest.**
• Synonym: **cheerful, for 1.**
  Antonyms: For **1,** see Antonyms at **happy.**

gaze—To keep the eyes in a fixed, long look; stare: *We gazed at the adorable puppy in the pet store window. Verb.*
—A long, fixed stare: *The principal's gaze fell on us as we tried to sneak in late. Noun.*
gaze (gāz) *verb,* **gazed, gazing;** *noun, plural* **gazes.**

gazelle—A small, fast antelope that lives in Africa and Asia. They are known for their beautiful eyes and the graceful way they move.
ga|zelle (gə zel′) *noun, plural* **gazelles.**

gear—**1.** A wheel with notches that fit into the notches of another wheel. When one wheel turns, so does the other wheel.   **2.** Equipment needed for a specific purpose: *The painter loaded his ladder, paint, and other gear into his truck. Noun.*
—To make or adjust something so as to have it fit; adapt: *The polar bear's thick white coat is geared for Arctic living. Verb.*
gear (gēr) *noun, plural* **gears;** *verb,* **geared, gearing.**

gearshift—A part that connects gears to a motor to send power to the rest of a machine. Automobiles and trucks have a gearshift.
gear|shift (gēr′shift′) *noun, plural* **gearshifts.**

geese—*See* **goose.**
geese (gēs) *plural noun.*

Geiger counter—A device used to detect and measure the amount of radioactivity in something. It is named after its inventor, Hans Geiger, a German scientist.
Gei|ger count|er (gī′gər koun′tər) *noun, plural* **Geiger counters.**

gelatin or **gelatine**—A jellylike substance made from the skin, bones, and other parts of an animal. It is used to make desserts, film, and glue.
gel|a|tin or gel|a|tine (jel′ə tən) *noun.*

gem—A precious stone that has been cut and polished for use in jewelry. Diamonds, emeralds, rubies, and sapphires are gems.
gem (jem) *noun, plural* **gems.**

gene—A tiny part of an animal or plant cell that is passed on to the animal or plant's offspring. Genes determine what characteristics the offspring will have.
gene (jēn) *noun, plural* **genes.**
• A word that sounds the same is **jean.**

gazelle

general—1. Of, for, or from all: *There was a* general *assembly of all the grades in our school.* 2. For many or most; widespread: *As our vacation grew near, there was* general *excitement in our house. Adjective.*
—A high-ranking officer in the armed forces who is above a colonel. *Noun.*
gen|er|al (jen′ər əl) *adjective; noun, plural* **generals.** *Abbreviation:* Gen., *for noun.*

generalize—To conclude that something is for the most part true because particular parts of it are true: *If every deer you've ever seen has run fast, you would be* generalizing *when you say that all deer are fast runners.*
gen|er|al|ize (jen′ər ə līz *or* jen′rə līz) *verb,* **generalized, generalizing.**

generally—1. Most of the time; ordinarily: *I* generally *bring my lunch to school.* 2. Without a great deal of explanation: Generally *speaking, I like animals.*
gen|er|al|ly (jen′ər ə lē *or* jen′rə lē) *adverb.*

generate—To cause to exist; make; produce: *Beating a drum* generates *sound.*
gen|er|ate (jen′ə rāt′) *verb,* **generated, generating.**

generation—1. Everyone born close in time to each other: *my mother's* generation; *the younger* generation. 2. The average period between the time someone is born and the time he or she becomes a parent, usually considered to be about thirty years: *My father says music was very different a* generation *ago.*
gen|er|a|tion (jen′ə rā′shən) *noun, plural* **generations.**

generator—A device for producing energy such as electricity, gas, or steam.
gen|er|a|tor (jen′ə rā′tər) *noun, plural* **generators.**

generic—1. Concerning a group or class of people or things that are alike; general, not specific: *"Children" is a* generic *term, but "boy" and "girl" are specific terms.* 2. Not having a brand name: *This* generic *drug is just like the one advertised on television but not as expensive.*
ge|ner|ic (jə ner′ik) *adjective.*

generous—1. Not selfish; happy to share: *She is* generous *with her stereo and lets her brother play his records on it.* 2. Big; ample: *The restaurant served me such a* generous *helping of spaghetti that I could not eat it all.*
gen|er|ous (jen′ər əs *or* jen′rəs) *adjective.*
• Synonym: **unselfish** for **1.**
Antonyms: **selfish, stingy** for **1; scanty, small** for **2.**

genie—A spirit in old Arab stories who can take human form and go to aid the person who calls.
ge|nie (jē′nē) *noun, plural* **genies** *or* **genii** (jē′nē ī).

genius—1. Very great mental ability, especially for creating, inventing, and discovering things; intelligence: *The inventor of the wheel must have been a person of* genius. 2. Someone with such mental ability; intellectual: *Only a* genius *could compose such beautiful music.*
gen|ius (jēn′yəs) *noun, plural* **geniuses.**

gentile *or* **Gentile**—Someone who is not of the Jewish religion.
gen|tile *or* Gen|tile (jen′tīl) *noun, plural* **gentiles** *or* **Gentiles.**

gentle—1. Mild; not rough: *She gave the swing a* gentle *push.* 2. Hushed; low and soothing in sound: *He heard the* gentle *patter of raindrops.* 3. Moderate; gradual; not extreme: *That country enjoys a* gentle *climate all year round.*
gen|tle (jen′təl) *adjective,* **gentler, gentlest.**
• Synonyms: **kind¹, tender,** for **1.**
Antonyms: For **1,** see Synonyms at **brutal.**

gentleman—1. An honorable man who is kind and thoughtful of others. 2. An adult male person: *Who was that* gentleman *I saw you with yesterday?* 3. A man accepted as a member of high society or the aristocracy.
gen|tle|man (jen′təl mən) *noun, plural* **gentlemen.**

gentlewoman—1. An honorable woman who is kind and thoughtful of others; lady. 2. A woman accepted in high society or among the aristocracy.
gen|tle|wom|an (jen′təl woom′ən) *noun, plural* **gentlewomen.**

gently—With a light touch; in a soft, not rough, way: *tiptoeing* gently *past the sleeping baby; tapping* gently *on the door.*
gen|tly (jen′tlē) *adverb.*

genuine—1. Real; true; authentic: *I have a* genuine *gold coin.* 2. Sincere; earnest: *She felt* genuine *sorrow when her goldfish died.*
gen|u|ine (jen′yoo ən) *adjective.*
• Synonyms: **actual, original,** for **1.**
Antonyms: **counterfeit, false,** for **1.**

a at	i if	oo look	ch chalk		a in ago
ā ape	ī idle	ou out	ng sing		e in happen
ah calm	o odd	u ugly	sh ship	ə =	i in capital
aw all	ō oats	ū rule	th think		o in occur
e end	oi oil	ur turn	th their		u in upon
ē easy			zh treasure		

genus—A group of animals or plants having enough similar features to be considered related. A genus is a smaller group than a family but larger than a species. Abbreviation: gen.
ge|nus (jē′nəs) *noun, plural* **genera** (gen′ə rə) *or* **genuses.**

geo-—A prefix that means ''earth'': Geo*graphy is the study of the earth and its life forms.*

Word Power

You can understand the meanings of many words that begin with **geo-,** if you add the meaning of the prefix to the meaning of the rest of the word.
geomagnetism: the magnetism of the earth
geoscience: any science dealing with the earth

---

geographical—Having to do with the study of the earth's surface and its life forms.
ge|o|graph|i|cal (jē′ə graf′ə kəl) *adjective.*

geography—The study of the earth's surface and the life forms on it. It includes the study of land and water, climate, plants and animals, countries, people, and industries.
ge|og|ra|phy (jē og′rə fē) *noun, plural* **geographies.**

geology—The study of the earth's history through its soil and rocks, considering how they have changed and how they are changing.
ge|ol|o|gy (jē ol′ə jē) *noun, plural* **geologies.**

geometric or **geometrical**—Having to do with the branch of mathematics concerned with lines, angles, and plane and solid figures: *A rectangle and a triangle are* geometric *figures.*
ge|o|met|ric *or* ge|o|met|ri|cal (jē′ə met′rik *or* jē′ə met′rə kəl) *adjective.*

geometry—The branch of mathematics that is concerned with measuring and finding relationships among lines, angles, and plane and solid figures.
ge|om|e|try (jē om′ə trē) *noun, plural* **geometries.**

geothermal—Having to do with or produced by the heat inside the earth: Geothermal *energy can be used as a source of power.*
ge|o|ther|mal (jē′ō thur′məl) *adjective.*

geranium—A sweet-smelling plant with red, pink, or white flowers. It is popular for growing in gardens and as a house plant.
ge|ra|ni|um (jə rā′nē əm) *noun, plural* **geraniums.**

gerbil—A small desert rodent that looks like a mouse but with long hind legs for leaping. It is sometimes kept as a pet.
ger|bil (jur′bəl) *noun, plural* **gerbils.**

gerbil

germ—An animal or a plant that is so tiny it cannot be seen except with a microscope. Some germs cause diseases. Bacteria and viruses are germs.
germ (jurm) *noun, plural* **germs.**

German Coach—A large, heavy horse that was once used to pull carriages. Native to Germany, they were popular in North America when horse travel was a major form of transportation.
Ger|man Coach (jur′mən kōch) *noun, plural* **German Coach horses.**

German measles—A disease that is like measles but is less serious for children. It is caused by a virus.
Ger|man mea|sles (jur′mən mē′zəlz) *noun.*

geranium

German shepherd dog

German shepherd dog—A medium-sized
dog with short thick hair, a long body, strong
legs, and pointed ears. Originally bred in
Germany, this dog is often used in the military,
by the police, and as a guide dog for the blind.
Ger|man shep|herd (jur′mən shep′ərd) *noun,*
plural **German shepherd dogs.**

German shorthaired pointer—A medium-
sized hunting dog with a short, smooth coat and
drooping ears. Originally bred in Germany, this
dog hunts by smell and swims well.
Ger|man short|haired point|er (jur′mən
shawrt′hārd′ poin′tər) *noun, plural* **German**
shorthaired pointers.

German wirehaired pointer—A medium-
sized hunting dog with a stiff, wiry outer coat
and a soft, thick coat underneath. Originally bred
in Germany, this dog is known for its ability to
retrieve prey from thick underbrush and from
water.
Ger|man wire|haired point|er (jur′mən
wīr′hārd′ poin′tər) *noun, plural* **German**
wirehaired pointers.

germinate—To start the process of growth;
sprout: Seeds need warmth, moisture, and
oxygen in order to germinate: *If these acorns*
germinate, *they will grow into oak trees.*
ger|mi|nate (jur′mə nāt) *verb,* **germinated,**
germinating.

a at	i if	oo look	ch chalk		a in ago
ā ape	ī idle	ou out	ng sing		e in happen
ah calm	o odd	u ugly	sh ship	ə =	i in capital
aw all	ō oats	ū rule	th think		o in occur
e end	oi oil	ur turn	th their		u in upon
ē easy			zh treasure		

gesture—**1.** A body movement that helps express
one's thoughts or feelings. *She made a* gesture
with her hand to show him where to sit.
2. Something said or done for the impression it
creates: *He offered to help me with my homework*
as a gesture *of friendship. Noun.*
—To make or use body movements to express
thoughts or ideas: *She opened the door and*
gestured *for us to come in. Verb.*
ges|ture (jes′chər) *noun, plural* **gestures;** *verb,*
gestured, gesturing.

German shorthaired pointer

German wirehaired pointer

get—1. To receive or obtain: *to get a puppy for my birthday; to get a part in the school play.*
2. To put together or prepare: *to get supper; getting Dad a glass of milk.* 3. To cause to happen: *He got his sleeve caught on the branch. Can you get the baby to eat her carrots?* 4. To arrive: *When will she get here?* 5. To be or become: *to get sick; to get rich; to get lost.*
get (get) *verb,* **got** or **gotten, getting.**

■ **get along: 1.** To manage or succeed: *I do not know how we will get along without your help.*
2. To agree or be agreeable: *Do you and your brother get along with each other?*
get it: 1. To figure out or understand: *She explained the problem to him, but he still didn't get it.* **2.** To be punished: *He will get it for teasing his sister.*
get off: 1. To avoid being punished: *He thought he might get off, so he was surprised to learn he had to pay a fine.* **2.** To begin: *Our vacation got off to an exciting start.*

geyser—A hot spring from which a combination of water and steam gushes forth regularly. A famous geyser at Yellowstone Park is called "Old Faithful."
gey│ser (gī′zər *or* gī′sər) *noun, plural* **geysers.**

ghastly—Causing horror; frightening: *Last Halloween I dressed up as a ghastly monster.*
ghast│ly (gast′lē) *adjective,* **ghastlier, ghastliest.**

ghetto—A section of a city, usually old and in poor condition, where some people are forced to live because they are poor or because they are the victims of racial or other prejudice.
ghet│to (get′ō) *noun, plural* **ghettos** or **ghettoes.**

ghost—The spirit of someone dead that is sometimes said to appear to living people, usually as a pale shadow.
ghost (gōst) *noun, plural* **ghosts.**

■ **give up the ghost:** To die or come to an end: *Our old television set finally gave up the ghost—the picture just faded away.*

ghostly—Like an eerie, shadowy figure: *The trees looked ghostly in the fog.*
ghost│ly (gōst′lē) *adjective,* **ghostlier, ghostliest.**

giant—1. A creature in fairy tales and other stories that looks like a man but is much larger.
2. A person or thing that stands out for some important reason: *He is a giant among writers because his books have been read by millions. Noun.*
—Of a very large size; enormous: *The elephant is a giant animal. Adjective.*
gi│ant (jī′ənt) *noun, plural* **giants;** *adjective.*

giant schnauzer

giant schnauzer—A large dog with whiskers on the face, bushy eyebrows, and a stiff, wiry coat. This dog was originally bred in Germany to herd cattle.
gi│ant schnau│zer (jī′ənt shnou′zər) *noun, plural* **giant schnauzers.**

gibbon

gibbon—A small ape that lives in the trees of southern Asia and the East Indies.
gib│bon (gib′ən) *noun, plural* **gibbons.**

giblets—The heart, liver, and gizzard of a chicken, turkey, or other kind of fowl.
gib│lets (jib′lits) *noun, singular* **giblet.**

Gila monster

Language Fact

Gila monster is a phrase that comes from the southwestern United States. The Gila River flows through Arizona. This area of the country was settled by the Spanish before it became part of the United States. The word *Gila* uses the Spanish pronunciation with the ''g'' pronounced as ''h.''

giddy—1. Feeling dizzy or as if one's head is spinning; faint: *We were blindfolded and then whirled around until we were* giddy.   2. Silly; frivolous or fickle: *In the school play, she played a* giddy *teenager who takes nothing seriously.*
gid|dy (gid′ē) *adjective,* **giddier, giddiest.**

gift—1. Something given to another as a present.   2. Ability one was born with; natural talent; aptitude: *The librarian has a* gift *for storytelling.*
gift (gift) *noun, plural* **gifts.**

gifted—Being naturally able or talented: *She is a* gifted *artist whose paintings hang in museums.*
gift|ed (gif′tid) *adjective.*

gigantic—As large as a giant; huge; enormous: *One* gigantic *storm cloud filled the whole sky.*
gi|gan|tic (jī gan′tik) *adjective.*
● Synonyms: See Synonyms at **big.**
Antonyms: See Synonyms at **small.**

giggle—To laugh in a silly way, catching one's breath repeatedly: *Father tickled me until I* giggled. *Verb.*
—A silly laugh in which one's breath is caught repeatedly: *Her* giggle *was so loud it caused those near her to start laughing. Noun.*

gig|gle (gig′əl) *verb,* **giggled, giggling;** *noun, plural* **giggles.**
● Synonyms: **chuckle, snicker,** for *verb.*
Antonyms: For *verb,* see Synonyms at **cry,** *verb* **1.**

Gila monster—A large, poisonous, orange-and-black lizard that lives in the southwestern United States.
Gi|la mon|ster (hē′lə mon′stər) *noun, plural* **Gila monsters.**

gill—A part of the body of fish and other water animals that lets the animal breathe underwater. It has a thin wall that lets in oxygen from the water that passes through it.
gill (gil) *noun, plural* **gills.**
■ **to the gills:** To the point of being filled; until there's no room left: *The hotel was packed* to the gills *with tourists.*

gin[1]—An alcoholic drink that has no color, usually made from grain and juniper berries.
gin (jin) *noun, plural* **gins.**

gin[2]—A machine used in processing cotton that removes the seeds and waste material from the fibers.
gin (jin) *noun, plural* **gins.**

ginger—A spice made from the dried and ground root of a tropical plant that is used in food and medicine. It has a strong, sharp smell and a hot taste.
gin|ger (jin′gər) *noun, plural* **gingers.**

ginger ale—A soft drink with tiny bubbles that has ginger as its strongest flavor.
gin|ger ale (jin′jər āl) *noun, plural* **ginger ales.**

gingerbread—A spicy cake or cookie made with ginger, often formed into a special shape and colorfully decorated before serving.
gin|ger|bread (jin′jər bred′) *noun, plural* **gingerbreads.**

gingham—A durable fabric woven of colored cotton threads, usually in checked, plaid, or striped designs.
ging|ham (ging′əm) *noun, plural* **ginghams.**

giraffe—An African animal with an unusually long neck and large, tan spots all over its body. It eats grass and leaves and can run very fast. It is the tallest animal now on earth.
gi|raffe (jə raf′) *noun, plural* **giraffes.**

girder—A long, heavy beam made of steel, wood, or concrete. It is used in construction as a supporting device for floors and as part of the structure of buildings.
gird|er (gur′dər) *noun, plural* **girders.**

a at	i if	oo look	ch chalk		a in ago
ā ape	ī idle	ou out	ng sing		e in happen
ah calm	o odd	u ugly	sh ship	ə =	i in capital
aw all	ō oats	ū rule	th think		o in occur
e end	oi oil	ur turn	th their		u in upon
ē easy			zh treasure		

girl—A female child or teenager up to the age of about 18.
girl (gurl) *noun, plural* **girls.**

Word History

Girl is a word whose complete history is unknown. While no one is sure how or when it was first used, it may come from an old German word meaning "a young person." However it began, it was used in England in the Middle Ages as a word meaning "child." As time went on, people gradually came to mean only a female child when they used this word.

Girl Scouts—An organization for girls formed in 1912 to develop good character, citizenship, and sound health care habits.
Girl Scouts (gurl skouts) *noun, singular* **Girl Scout.**

give—1. To provide something to another, usually without receiving anything in return: *Please* give *me the correct time. She* gave *her little brother her old skates.* 2. To offer or deliver; present: *to* give *a speech;* giving *a concert.* 3. To provide or produce; supply: *to* give *a yell; Does this cow* give *much milk?* 4. To break or fall apart when force or pressure is applied: *The thin ice* gave *under our feet.*
give (giv) *verb,* **gave** *or* **given, giving.**
■ **give it to:** To scold or discipline: *Mom* gave *it to us for forgetting to feed our kitten.*

giraffe

give (one) **a break:** To relax the rules and allow something: *The teacher* gave *me a break on turning in my report on time because I had been sick.*
give up: 1. To surrender: *The robber* gave *himself up after being chased by the police officer.* 2. To quit doing or using something: *to* give up *sweets while on a diet; to* give up *playing children's games when I grow up.*
what gives?: What is going on?: *The boy asked "What gives?" when he realized his friends were trying to fool him.*

given—1. That has been provided earlier; fixed; specific: *Bills are generally due on a* given *date, like the tenth of the month.* 2. Disposed; tending; attracted: *She is* given *to making many gestures as she talks. Adjective.*
—*See* **give.** *Verb.*
giv|en (giv′ən) *adjective; verb.*

gizzard—Part of a bird's digestive system that has strong walls and a rough lining. It takes food that has passed through the stomach and grinds it up.
giz|zard (giz′ərd) *noun, plural* **gizzards.**

glacier—A huge body of ice formed from unmelted snow. It slowly moves down a slope or spreads across flat land until it melts or something causes it to be broken up.
gla|cier (glā′shər) *noun, plural* **glaciers.**

glad—Happy; pleased; delighted: *My grandmother is always* glad *to see us.*
glad (glad) *adjective,* **gladder, gladdest.**
● See Synonyms and Antonyms at **happy.**

Word History

Gladiator and gladiolus (see page 320) have very different meanings, but they both come from the same Latin word meaning "sword." Gladiator was first used in ancient Rome as a name for the warriors who fought in the public shows using swords as their weapons. Gladiolus is the name for a plant with long, spiked leaves that look like swords.

---

gladiator—A man who fought another man until one of them died in a show to entertain the public in ancient Rome.
glad|i|a|tor (glad′ē ā′tər) *noun, plural* **gladiators.**

gladiolus

gladiolus—A plant with stalks of large, brightly colored flowers clustered together and long leaves that grow pointing upward.
glad|i|o|lus (glad′ē ō′ləs) *noun, plural* **gladioli** (glad′ē ō′lī) *or* **gladioluses.**
● See Word History at **gladiator.**

glamor—A romantic, exciting, and often mysterious attraction; magical charm: *The* glamor *of the theater draws many people to New York City.*
glam|or (glam′ər) *noun.*

glamorous—Attractive in an exciting way: *My aunt's new haircut makes her look* glamorous.
glam|or|ous (glam′ər əs) *adjective.*

glance—A fast look; glimpse: *She gave the book only a* glance *but she knew she would not like the story. Noun.*
—**1.** To look for just a moment: *He* glanced *at the man waiting to cross the street before driving on.* **2.** To strike a surface at such an angle as to bounce off in another direction: *The basketball* glanced *off the backboard and flew into the stands. Verb.*
glance (glans) *noun, plural* **glances;** *verb,* **glanced, glancing.**

a at	i if	oo look	ch chalk		a in ago
ā ape	ī idle	ou out	ng sing		e in happen
ah calm	o odd	u ugly	sh ship	ə =	i in capital
aw all	ō oats	ū rule	th think		o in occur
e end	oi oil	ur turn	th their		u in upon
ē easy			zh treasure		

gland—One of several organs of the body that make a certain substance for further use in the body. Sweat glands operate to control the body's temperature. Glands near the eyes produce tears to clean the eyes. Other glands work to control the height, weight, and growth of the body.
gland (gland) *noun, plural* **glands.**

glare—**1.** A harsh, almost blinding light: *The* glare *of the flashlight hurt my eyes.* **2.** A fixed look or stare showing annoyance or anger: *The woman looked with a* glare *at the man who had interrupted her. Noun.*
—**1.** To shine with a harsh light; dazzle: *The sun* glared *down on the tennis court, making it hard to follow the game.* **2.** To look in an angry way: *The customer* glared *at the rude cashier. Verb.*
glare (glâr) *noun, plural* **glares;** *verb,* **glared, glaring.**

glass—**1.** A hard substance produced by melting sand and other materials together. It is often made to be seen through and used in such things as eyeglasses and windows. **2.** A drinking container, generally made of glass: *He handed her a* glass *to fill.* **3.** The amount of liquid an average drinking container holds: *The doctor told her to drink at least six* glasses *of water each day.* **4. glasses:** A pair of lenses worn to improve vision or correct eye problems; eyeglasses. *Noun.*
glass (glas) *noun, plural* **glasses.**

glaze—**1.** To provide the surface of something with a smooth shine that is like glass: *My mother always* glazes *her ham with brown sugar.* **2.** To take on a shiny appearance of glass: *Her eyes* glazed *with tears. The sidewalk* glazed *with ice. Verb.*
—**1.** A shiny coating that reflects light: *There was a* glaze *of ice on every tree after the storm.* **2.** Any substance used to give a shiny coating to such things as china, paintings, or food. *Noun.*
glaze (glāz) *verb,* **glazed, glazing;** *noun, plural* **glazes.**

gleam—A sudden, quick beam of light; glint: *He saw the* gleam *of the cat's eyes in the darkness. Noun.*
—To glow with a bright light; shine; glint: *The stars* gleamed *brilliantly that night. Verb.*
gleam (glēm) *noun, plural* **gleams;** *verb,* **gleamed, gleaming.**
● Synonyms: **glisten, glitter, sparkle,** for *verb.*

glee—Great joy; lively delight: *The children laughed with* glee *as they opened their gifts.*
glee (glē) *noun.*

glen—A valley that is small, narrow, and often sheltered or hidden.
glen (glen) *noun, plural* **glens.**

glide—**1.** To move along smoothly with little or no effort: *Watch that graceful couple* glide *across the dance floor.*   **2.** To pass quickly without being noticed: *The hours just* glide *by when we are having fun!*   **3.** To come or slow down without the use of a motor: *The paper airplane* glided *slowly across the room. As I ran out of gas, my car* glided *to a stop.*
glide (glīd) *verb,* **glided, gliding.**

glider—An airplane that has no motor. It flies by floating on air currents.
glid|er (glī′dər) *noun, plural* **gliders.**

glider

glimmer—**1.** A light that appears weak or wavering, usually because it is far away: *From the top of the hill, the lights of the farmhouse were only a* glimmer.   **2.** A sign or hint that is not clear or strong: *The men would not give up bailing water while there was a* glimmer *of hope they could save their ship. Noun.*
—To glow with a faint light or flicker: *The lights of the city* glimmered *in the distance. Verb.*
glim|mer (glim′ər) *noun, plural* **glimmers;** *verb,* **glimmered, glimmering.**
• Synonyms: **blink, flicker¹, twinkle,** for *verb.*

glimpse—A fast, short look; glance: *She caught only a* glimpse *of her friend before he was lost in the crowd. Noun.*
—To take a fast look; glance: *If you only* glimpsed *at the book, how could you tell you wouldn't like it? Verb.*
glimpse (glimps) *noun, plural* **glimpses;** *verb,* **glimpsed, glimpsing.**

glint—**1.** A sudden, quick light; gleam: *A* glint *in his eyes told me that he had a secret.*
2. Sparkling, brilliant light that is often caused by reflection: *The* glint *of the gold earrings showed off her dark hair beautifully. Noun.*
—To gleam; glisten: *The new car* glinted *in the bright sun. Verb.*
glint (glint) *noun, plural* **glints;** *verb,* **glinted, glinting.**
• Synonyms: **glitter, sparkle,** for *verb.*

glisten—To sparkle with a brilliant light; gleam: *Tears of happiness* glistened *in her eyes when her lost ring was found.*
glis|ten (glis′ən) *verb,* **glistened, glistening.**
• Synonyms: **glint, glitter**

glitter—To sparkle; flash with light: *The minerals in the rock* glittered *as she moved it in her hand. Verb.*
—A brilliant, twinkling light: *the* glitter *of gold and silver. Noun.*
glit|ter (glit′ər) *verb,* **glittered, glittering;** *noun, plural* **glitters.**
• Synonyms: **gleam, glint, glisten,** for *verb.*

gloat—To feel or express too much satisfaction about something one has done: *It is not good sportsmanship for a winning team to* gloat *over its victory.*
gloat (glōt) *verb,* **gloated, gloating.**

global—Of, in, or affecting the whole world: *Preventing sea and air pollution is a* global *problem.*
glob|al (glō′bəl) *adjective.*

globe—**1.** The world; earth.   **2.** Any object that is round like the earth: *a lamp with a white glass* globe.   **3.** A representation of the earth or a map of the world on a large ball.
globe (glōb) *noun, plural* **globes.**
• Synonyms: **ball¹, sphere,** for **2.**

gloom—**1.** A condition of dim light or cloudiness; darkness: *He walked home from school in the gathering* gloom *of a late winter afternoon.*   **2.** A state of sadness or depression: *Nothing could lift the* gloom *in the locker room after the basketball team lost its championship game.*
gloom (glüm) *noun.*

gloomy—**1.** Dark or shadowed; lacking light: *The children all hated to walk past the* gloomy, *old house.*   **2.** Filled with feelings of sadness: *Dark winter days always made her* gloomy.
gloomy (glü′mē) *adjective,* **gloomier, gloomiest.**
• For **2,** see Synonyms and Antonyms at **happy.**

glorify—To respect as deserving of very high honor; praise: *People* glorify *men and women*

who often risk their lives to do things that help others, like astronauts or firefighters.
glo|ri|fy (glawr′ə fī′) *verb*, **glorified, glorifying.**

glorious—Marked by particular excellence, beauty, or brilliance: *The crowd enjoyed a glorious victory parade down our town's main street.*
glo|ri|ous (glawr′ē əs) *adjective.*

glory—1. High praise or regard for someone or something: *He received the glory of scoring the winning touchdown.* 2. Brilliant, radiant splendor; majesty: *the glory of a perfect summer day.*
glo|ry (glawr′ē) *noun, plural* **glories.**
■ **in (one's) glory:** Feeling very joyful and satisfied: *Grandmother was in her glory, having the whole family home for the holidays.*

gloss—A shine with a smooth, gleaming finish: *the gloss of a polished table.*
gloss (glaws *or* glos) *noun, plural* **glosses.**
■ **gloss over:** To deal with something quickly, especially in order to avoid a possible problem: *I boasted that my family has three cars, but I glossed over the fact that two of the cars are not running.*

glossary—A section at the end of a book, that gives an alphabetical list of difficult or technical words and their meanings.
glos|sa|ry (glaws′ər ē *or* glos′ər ē) *noun, plural* **glossaries.**

glove—Something that covers one's hand, generally with parts that enclose separately each finger and the thumb. It is usually part of a pair, with one glove for the left hand and one for the right. Some sports use a single glove, like a baseball mitt with a special design that holds the four fingers together in fewer than four parts. Work gloves keep the hands clean or protected. Other kinds of gloves are made to give warmth or as part of an outfit or a uniform.
glove (gluv) *noun, plural* **gloves.**
■ **fit like a glove:** Giving a tight, snug, or perfect fit: *The coat you outgrew fits me like a glove.*

glow—1. To shine brightly: *The embers from the campfire glowed all night. These decals glow in the dark.* 2. To have a rich, warm, rosy color:

The children's faces glowed when they came in from ice-skating. Verb.
—1. A gleaming light: *the glow from the setting sun; the glow of brass.* 2. A fresh, rosy brightness or color: *She had the glow of a healthy young woman. Noun.*
glow (glō) *verb*, **glowed, glowing;** *noun, plural* **glows.**

glower—To stare crossly or angrily at someone: *The singer glowered at the noisy audience.*
glow|er (glou′ər) *verb*, **glowered, glowering.**

glue—A sticky material used to attach things to each other. *Noun.*
—1. To hold together by using glue: *to glue new photographs in my album.* 2. To fix tightly onto something: *The boy glued his eyes on the race horses as they neared the finish line. Verb.*
glue (glū) *noun, plural* **glues;** *verb*, **glued, gluing.**

glum—Unhappy; filled with gloom: *He always has a glum look on his face.*
glum (glum) *adjective*, **glummer, glummest.**
● See Synonyms and Antonyms at **happy.**

gnarled—Having a rugged, rough, and twisted appearance; not smooth or soft: *the gnarled face of a gnome; the gnarled branches of an old maple tree.*
gnarled (nahrld) *adjective.*

Language Fact

Gnarled is a word that sounds different than it looks. The ''g'' is not pronounced, so the word sounds as if ''n'' is the first letter. Other words beginning with ''gn'' are pronounced the same way. They include **gnash, gnat, gnaw, gnome,** and **gnu.**

---

gnash—To grind the teeth together, usually in anger: *The traffic jam made him so late that he gnashed his teeth.*
gnash (nash) *verb*, **gnashed, gnashing.**

gnat—One of a variety of tiny, two-winged insects that often suck blood from people and animals.
gnat (nat) *noun, plural* **gnats.**

gnaw—To wear away by repeated biting; chew: *Some dogs gnaw on a bone until it breaks.*
gnaw (naw) *verb*, **gnawed** or **gnawn, gnawing.**

gnome—An odd-looking little person or dwarf in fairy tales.
gnome (nōm) *noun, plural* **gnomes.**

a at	i if	oo look	ch chalk		a in ago
ā ape	ī idle	ou out	ng sing		e in happen
ah calm	o odd	u ugly	sh ship	ə =	i in capital
aw all	ō oats	ū rule	th think		o in occur
e end	oi oil	ur turn	th their		u in upon
ē easy			zh treasure		

gnu—An African antelope with a buffalolike head, a flowing mane and tail, curved horns, and high, powerful shoulders. It lives in herds.
gnu (nū *or* nyū) *noun, plural* **gnus** *or* **gnu.**
- Words that sound the same are **knew** and **new.**
- Another name for this animal is **wildebeest.**

gnu

go—1. To move or travel away from one place to another; leave; depart: *When can we go home? He is* going *tonight.* 2. To move or run by working or operating: *That clock goes too fast.* 3. To become or continue to be: *The crowd is going wild with joy.* 4. To stretch out or reach; lead; extend: *This fence goes all the way around our property. That door goes to the cellar.* 5. To be given or sold: *A door prize goes to the person whose name is drawn from the box. That*

gnome

car goes *for a high price.* 6. To have a particular result or conclusion: *Her interview with the reporter did not* go *too well.* 7. To have a proper place; belong: *The salt* goes *on the shelf.* 8. To fit or blend with: *This blue hat does not* go *with the brown coat very well. Verb.*
—1. A try or turn at something: *He had a go at fixing the engine before they took it to a mechanic.* 2. Success: *She wanted to make a go of her job. Noun.*
go (gō) *verb,* **goes, went, gone, going;** *noun, plural* **goes.**
- **go back on:** To not be true to: *He* went back on *his promise when he did not practice the day before the big game.*

goal—1. The place at which a race finishes or in certain games where the ball or puck must land for a team to score: *The basic purpose of soccer is to kick the ball into the* goal. 2. Something that one strongly desires and works for; aim: *Her* goal *is to become a lawyer.*
goal (gōl) *noun, plural* **goals.**

goat—A milk-giving animal with short horns that curve backward, a beardlike growth of hair under its chin, and a smooth coat. This animal is raised for its meat, hair, and skin. It is also valued for its milk, which is used for drinking and for making into cheese.
goat (gōt) *noun, plural* **goats.**
- **get (one's) goat:** Annoy or irritate someone: *He got her goat when he teased her about her singing.*

goat

gobble¹—To eat or swallow quickly large bites of food: *The children* gobbled *their dinners so they could get to the movie on time.*
gob|ble (gob′əl) *verb,* **gobbled, gobbling.**
gobble²—To make the special noisy sound natural to a turkey. *Verb.*

—The special noisy sound that a male turkey makes naturally. *Noun.*
gob|ble (gob′əl) *verb,* **gobbled, gobbling;** *noun, plural* **gobbles.**

goblet—A tall drinking glass with a long stem.
gob|let (gob′lit) *noun, plural* **goblets.**

goblin—An ugly elf in fairy tales that is full of mischief.
gob|lin (gob′lən) *noun, plural* **goblins.**

God—The Supreme Being worshiped by many people as the creator and ruler of all that exists.
God (god) *noun.*

god—1. A supernatural being with great powers whom people worship and call upon for favors: *Ancient myths tell about the* gods *of the earth, sky, and sea.* 2. A supernatural being believed to be male whom people worship.
god (god) *noun, plural* **gods.**

godchild—A child who has a special relationship with an adult who acts as a witness at his or her baptism.
god|child (god′chīld′) *noun, plural* **godchildren.**

goddess—A supernatural being believed to be female whom people worship.
god|dess (god′is) *noun, plural* **goddesses.**

godfather—The man who has a special relationship with a child because of having been a witness when that child was baptized.
god|fa|ther (god′fah′thər) *noun, plural* **godfathers.**

godmother—The woman who has a special relationship with a child because of having been a witness when that child was baptized.
god|mo|ther (god′muth′ər) *noun, plural* **godmothers.**

goes—*See* **go.**
goes (gōz) *verb, noun.*

goggles—A pair of glasses with a frame that completely encircles the eyes and fits snugly against the face. Swimmers and machine operators often use goggles to protect their eyes.
gog|gles (gog′əlz) *noun.*

gold—1. The soft, yellow metal from which coins and jewelry are often made. Gold is a very expensive metal. 2. The bright yellow color of that metal. *Noun.*
—Having the bright yellow color of that metal. *Adjective.*
gold (gōld) *noun; adjective.*

■ **heart of gold:** A natural way of acting that is very kind and generous: *My grandmother has a heart of gold when it comes to stray animals.*
good as gold: Very reliable: *She would never betray a friend, so her promise is as* good as gold.

golden—1. Made of or like the precious metal gold: *his* golden *hair; a* golden *necklace.* 2. Of great value or excellent quality; precious: *Because he had played professional football, his advice to the school team was* golden.
gold|en (gōl′dən) *adjective.*

golden retriever—A medium-sized hunting dog with a thick, light-yellow to dark-gold coat. Originally bred in Scotland, this dog swims well and is often trained to retrieve animals from water.
gold|en re|triev|er (gōl′dən ri trē′vər) *noun, plural* **golden retrievers.**

golden retriever

goldenrod—A plant having long stems and small yellow flowers that bloom in the late summer or early fall. Goldenrod is the state flower of Kentucky and Nebraska.
gold|en|rod (gōl′dən rod′) *noun, plural* **goldenrods.**

goldfinch—An American bird of the sparrow family. It is yellow with black markings and has a lovely song.
gold|finch (gōld′finch′) *noun, plural* **goldfinches.**

a at	i if	oo look	ch chalk		a in ago
ā ape	ī idle	ou out	ng sing		e in happen
ah calm	o odd	u ugly	sh ship	ə =	i in capital
aw all	ō oats	ū rule	th think		o in occur
e end	oi oil	ur turn	th their		u in upon
ē easy			zh treasure		

goldfish—A small, reddish or golden color fish that is popular for keeping in glass bowls or tanks.
gold|fish (gōld′fish′) *noun, plural* **goldfish** or **goldfishes**.

golf—An outdoor game played on a special grassy course with a small, hard ball that is hit with various long, thin clubs. The course is made up of a series of holes into which the player tries to hit the ball, taking as few strokes as possible. *Noun.*
—To play the game of golf: *Sarah likes to golf with her mother on weekends. Verb.*
golf (golf) *noun; verb,* **golfed, golfing.**

gondola (definition 1)

gondola—1. A long, narrow boat with high peaks in the front and back. These specialized boats carry passengers through the canals of Venice, Italy. 2. A passenger and equipment compartment under a dirigible or large balloon filled with hot air. 3. An enclosed compartment that hangs from a cable and carries passengers to a mountain top.
gon|do|la (gon′də lə) *noun, plural* **gondolas.**

gone—*See* **go.**
gone (gawn) *verb.*

gong—A kind of bell that looks like a large, metal plate. A gong makes a loud sound when hit.
gong (gawng *or* gong) *noun, plural* **gongs.**

good—1. Of high quality; excellent: *Only* good *swimmers should apply for the lifeguard's job.* 2. As it is best to do; proper: *Returning the money that was lost was the* good *thing to do.* 3. Polite and well behaved: *a* good *child.* 4. Kind; helpful: *We have* good *neighbors that watch over our house when we are away. Adjective.*
—1. An advantage, benefit, or use: *Of what* good *is an umbrella on a sunny day?* 2. That which is kindly and worthy of one's trust: *He tries to see the* good *in every person he meets.* 3. Nice people or things: *The sun shines on both the* good *and the bad. Noun.*
good (good) *adjective,* **better, best;** *noun, plural* **goods.**
  ■ **for good:** Permanently: *The problem was finally solved* for good.
  ● Synonyms: **moral, right,** for *adjective* **2.** Antonyms: For *adjective* **2,** see Synonyms at **bad.**

good-by—A word used to say farewell. "Good-by!" *he called to us. They said their* good-bys *and left for the trip home.*
good-by (good′bī′) *interjection; noun, plural* **good-bys.**
  ● This word is also spelled **goodby, good-bye,** and **goodbye.**

Good Friday—The Friday before Easter, observed by Christians as the anniversary of the day Jesus Christ died.
Good Fri|day (good frī′dā) *noun.*

good-hearted—Kindly and generous toward others; *The* good-hearted *baker gave a free cookie to the crying child.*
good-heart|ed (good′hahr′tid) *adjective.*

good-natured—Having a kindly and cheerful attitude: *The* good-natured *art teacher just smiled when the students accidentally knocked down his display.*
good-na|tured (good′nā′chərd) *adjective.*

goodness—The state of being naturally kind and thoughtful: *Her* goodness *inspired her to help out with many charities. Noun.*

goldenrod

—An expression of surprise: "Goodness, *you startled me!" Interjection.*
good|ness (good′nis) *noun, interjection.*

goods—1. Things belonging to someone: *When they moved, all of their* goods *fit in one truck.* 2. Things that are for sale: *The store's* goods *consisted mainly of sports equipment.*
goods (goodz) *plural noun.*
■ **deliver the goods:** To do what one is expected or supposed to do: *He promised to help me mow the lawn, but he did not* deliver the goods.

goose—1. A web-footed bird that belongs to the duck family. It has a larger body and a longer neck than a duck. 2. A female goose. The male goose is called a gander.
goose (gūs) *noun, plural* **geese.**
■ **cook (one's) goose:** To damage one's chances: *Her* goose *was* cooked *when she came late for the team tryouts.*

goose (definition 1)

gooseflesh—Bumps on the skin caused by cold or fear; goosebumps.
goose|flesh (gus′flesh) *noun.*

gopher—A small, ratlike rodent of North America having large cheek pouches. Gophers burrow under the ground and build long tunnels.
go|pher (gō′fər) *noun, plural* **gophers.**

a at	i if	oo look	ch chalk		⌈ a in ago
ā ape	ī idle	ou out	ng sing		e in happen
ah calm	o odd	u ugly	sh ship	ə =	i in capital
aw all	ō oats	ū rule	th think		o in occur
e end	oi oil	ur turn	th their		⌊ u in upon
ē easy			zh treasure		

Gordon setter

Gordon setter—A medium-sized hunting dog with tan markings especially above the eyes. These dogs were originally bred in Scotland.
Gor|don set|ter (gawr′dən set′ər) *noun, plural* **Gordon setters.**

gorge—A deep, narrow canyon or valley. *Noun.* —To eat greedily: *He* gorged *himself with six large pieces of pizza. Verb.*
gorge (gawrj) *noun, plural* **gorges;** *verb,* **gorged, gorging.**

gopher

Word History

Gopher comes from a French word meaning "honeycomb." The gopher's underground tunnels must have reminded people of the tunnels inside a wax honeycomb made by bees to store their honey, eggs, and pollen.

gorgeous—Beautiful: *The warm sun and calm sea made it a* gorgeous *day for swimming.*
gor|geous (gawr′jəs) *adjective.*
● Synonyms: **lovely, pretty**
Antonyms: See Synonyms at **ugly.**

gorilla—An African ape related to the chimpanzee. The largest of all apes, the gorilla has a thick, hairy body with long, powerful arms and short, strong legs.
go|ril|la (gə ril′ə) *noun, plural* **gorillas.**
● A word that sounds the same is **guerrilla.**

gorilla

gosling—A young goose.
gos|ling (goz′ling) *noun, plural* **goslings.**

gospel—1. The teachings of Christ and the Apostles as described in the New Testament portion of the Bible. 2. Gospel: The teachings and life of Christ as contained in the first four books of the New Testament (Matthew, Mark, Luke, and John). 3. Anything that is believed to be completely true: *He did not take the older boy's comments as* gospel, *so he went to see for himself.*
gos|pel (gos′pəl) *noun, plural* **gospels.**

gossamer—A very light, thin cloth or other material that is easily seen through: *a* gossamer *dress; the* gossamer *wings of an insect.*
gos|sa|mer (gos′ə mər) *adjective.*

gossip—1. Rumors about people that often prove to be unkind and false: *The school play was poorly attended due to the* gossip *that the actors were bad.* 2. A person who repeats rumors about other people: *Because he was known to be*

a gossip, *no one told him any secrets. Noun.*
—To repeat rumors that one hears or knows about other people: *She* gossips *about her classmates. Verb.*
gos|sip (gos′ip) *noun, plural* **gossips;** *verb,* **gossiped, gossiping.**

got—*See* **get.**
got (got) *verb.*

gotten—*See* **get.**
got|ten (got′ən) *verb.*

gouge—1. A chisel-like tool with a curved blade used for making holes or grooves in wood. 2. A hole or groove: *Some of the library tables had* gouges *made with pencils and pens. Noun.*
—To dig or scoop out: *We shaped animal figures from bars of soap by* gouging *them out with a knife. Verb.*
gouge (gouj) *noun, plural* **gouges;** *verb,* **gouged, gouging.**

gourd—A rounded fruit with a hard rind that grows on vines. Gourds come from the same family as pumpkins and squash. They are sometimes dried and used for decorations.
gourd (gawrd) *noun, plural* **gourds.**

gov.—The abbreviation for **government.**

Gov.—The abbreviation for **governor.**

govern—To rule or control: *The king governed the country wisely.*
gov|ern (guv′ərn) *verb,* **governed, governing.**

government—1. The people ruling a country, state, or other area: *The* government *of the United States is primarily in Washington, D.C.* 2. The style or type of ruling system in a country, state, or area: *Great Britain has a democratic* government.
gov|ern|ment (guv′ərn mənt *or* guv′ər mənt) *noun, plural* **governments.** Abbreviation: **gov.**

Word Power

If you are interested in government, here are some useful words to know. You can find these words in this dictionary.

cabinet	ratify
capitol	repeal
communism	republican
Congress	Republican Party
constitution	Senate
democracy	socialism
Democratic Party	tariff
election	tax
House of Representatives	treaty
legislature	veto

governor—**1.** The elected person serving as the head of a state government of the United States. **2.** The person who rules over a colony, province, or other special area.　**3.** A device that automatically controls the speed of an engine.
gov|er|nor (guv′ər nər) *noun, plural* **governors.**
Abbreviation: **Gov.** for 1 and 2.

gown—**1.** A woman's dress, especially a fancy one for special occasions.　**2.** A long, loose robe as worn by judges, clergy, and students participating in graduation ceremonies.
gown (goun) *noun, plural* **gowns.**

grab—To take hold of quickly; snatch: *The mother grabbed her child away from the busy street. Verb.*
—A snatching movement: *The fans made a grab for the foul ball as it went into the stands. Noun.*
grab (grab) *verb,* **grabbed, grabbing;** *noun, plural* **grabs.**

grace—**1.** Smoothness and beauty of movement: *The swan's grace was a pleasure to watch.*　**2.** Good manners, kindness, and courtesy shown toward others: *She had the grace to arrive on time and not delay the ceremony.*　**3.** A short prayer of thanks said before or after a meal: *Being the youngest grandchild, she always says grace before Thanksgiving dinner. Noun.*
—**1.** To decorate; adorn: *a beautiful, red carpet gracing the stairs to the ballroom.*　**2.** To honor: *The opening-night performance was graced by the attendance of the king and queen. Verb.*
grace (grās) *noun, plural* **graces;** *verb,* **graced, gracing.**
■ **fall from grace:** To lose someone's favor: *After failing to attend meetings for several months, he fell from grace with his scoutmaster.*
in the bad graces of: To be out of favor with someone: *The owner of the constantly barking dog was soon in the bad graces of all the neighbors.*
in the good graces of: To be liked or approved of: *I hope that I am soon back in the good graces of my father.*
with bad grace: Unwillingly and in an unpleasant way: *He apologized for what he said, but with bad grace.*
with good grace: Quite willingly and in a pleasant way: *She lost the tennis match, but took her defeat with good grace.*

graceful—Beautiful in movement or pleasing in manner: *the ballerina's graceful movements; writing a graceful note of apology.*
grace|ful (grās′fəl) *adjective.*

gracious—Having a pleasant and courteous attitude: *It was gracious of the loser to congratulate the winner on running a fine race.*
gra|cious (grā′shəs) *adjective.*

grackle—A kind of blackbird that has shiny, black or dark color feathers. It is in the same family as the oriole.
grack|le (grak′əl) *noun, plural* **grackles.**

grackle

grade—**1.** The year or level of a student's work in elementary or high school: *in the fourth grade.*　**2.** A position or degree in quality; rank: *The grocer took pride in selling only the best grade of fruits and vegetables.*　**3.** A letter or number that indicates the quality of a student's work: *Because he studied often, his grade in mathematics was usually an A.*　**4.** The slope of a road, path, or track: *The old horse could barely pull the cart up the steep mountain grade. Noun.*
—**1.** To sort into groups of the same quality or rank: *The tomatoes were graded by size first and then by ripeness.*　**2.** To mark with a number or letter to show its level of quality: *The science teacher graded the tests.*　**3.** To make more level: *The bulldozer graded the front yard of our new house. Verb.*
grade (grād) *noun, plural* **grades;** *verb,* **graded, grading.**
■ **make the grade:** To measure up; be successful: *After much practice, she made the grade and got on the team.*

gradual—Taking place or changing slowly: *There was a gradual improvement in her health.*
grad|u|al (graj′ū əl) *adjective.*

a at	i if	oo look	ch chalk		a in ago
ā ape	ī idle	ou out	ng sing		e in happen
ah calm	o odd	u ugly	sh ship	ə =	i in capital
aw all	ō oats	ū rule	th think		o in occur
e end	oi oil	ur turn	th their		u in upon
ē easy			zh treasure		

graduate—1. To complete a course of study at a school or college: *My brother received a diploma when he* graduated *from high school.* 2. To divide into equal measurements: *A ruler is* graduated *in inches. Verb.*
—A person who has completed a course of study at a school or college. *Noun.*
grad|u|ate (graj′ū āt for *verb;* graj′ūit for *noun*) *verb,* **graduated, graduating;** *noun, plural* **graduates.**

graduation—1. The act of graduating from a school or college: *He looks forward to getting a job after* graduation *from college.* 2. The ceremony of graduating from a school or college: *Bad weather kept many people from attending this year's* graduation *ceremony.*
grad|u|a|tion (graj′ū ā′shən) *noun, plural* **graduations.**

graffiti—Drawings or writings usually made on surfaces visible to the public: *The walls of the train station were covered with* graffiti.
graf|fi|ti (grə fē′tē) *noun, singular* **graffito.**

graft—1. To place the shoot or bud of one plant into a slit made in the stem of another plant, allowing them to grow together as one plant. 2. To move a section of skin or bone to a new place on the same body, or to a different body, allowing it to grow there permanently: *Fire victims sometimes have skin* grafted *over their burns to help healing and prevent scars. Verb.*
—The bud or shoot of a plant, or a piece of skin or bone, used in grafting. *Noun.*
graft (graft) *verb,* **grafted, grafting;** *noun, plural* **grafts.**

grain—1. The seed of cereal plants such as wheat, corn, or rice; kernel. 2. A small, hard piece of something, especially sugar, sand, salt, or the like: grains *of salt.* 3. Tiny lines or markings that run through wood, marble, and other materials, giving a pattern.
grain (grān) *noun, plural* **grains.**
■ **go against the grain:** To be contrary to what is wanted: *Sharing their toys often* goes against the grain *of young children.*
with a grain of salt: With less than complete belief; not seriously: *Because he had never had a pet, she took his advice about her dog* with a grain of salt.

gram—A metric unit of weight or mass equal to 0.035 ounces.
gram (gram) *noun, plural* **grams.** Abbreviation: **g**

grammar—1. A series of rules according to which words are arranged in sentences to make sense. 2. What is generally accepted as the correct use of words: *using the correct* grammar.
gram|mar (gram′ər) *noun.*

grammatical—According to or having to do with the rules of grammar: *In addition to getting all of my facts correct, I have to make sure there are no* grammatical *errors in my report.*
gram|mat|i|cal (grə mat′ə kəl) *adjective.*

grand—1. Large and magnificent: *The princess rode in a* grand *coach to the ball.* 2. Most important: *a* grand *prize.* 3. Including everything; complete: *a* grand *total of five hundred dollars.* 4. Wonderful; excellent: *She had a* grand *time at the zoo.*
grand (grand) *adjective,* **grander, grandest.**
• Synonyms: **majestic, splendid, stately,** for 1.
Antonym: **humble,** for 1.

grandchild—The child of one's own daughter or son.
grand|child (grand′chīld′) *noun, plural* **grandchildren.**

granddaughter—The daughter of one's own daughter or son.
grand|daugh|ter (gran′daw′tər) *noun, plural* **granddaughters.**

grandeur—The quality or state of being grand; greatness. *She was amazed by the* grandeur *of the mountains.*
gran|deur (gran′jər) *noun.*

grandfather—The father of one's own mother or father.
grand|fa|ther (grand′fah′thər) *noun, plural* **grandfathers.**

grandmother—The mother of one's own mother or father.
grand|moth|er (grand′muth̲′ər) *noun, plural* **grandmothers.**

grandparent—A grandmother or a grandfather.
grand|par|ent (grand′par′ənt) *noun, plural* **grandparents.**

grandson—The son of one's own daughter or son.
grand|son (grand′sun′) *noun, plural* **grandsons.**

grandstand—A seating place from which people view a parade or sports event. The rows of seats or benches are raised behind one another like steps.
grand|stand (grand′stand′) *noun, plural* **grandstands.**

granite—A hard, gray rock that is often used in making monuments and buildings.
gran|ite (gran′it) *noun.*

grant—**1.** To give in to; allow; permit: *The teacher* granted *his request to take the test at a later date.* **2.** To admit as being true: *I'll* grant *that your plan was the best. Verb.*
—An award or gift, usually of money or land: *The government* grant *will help pay for her first year of college. Noun.*
grant (grant) *verb,* granted, granting; *noun,* plural grants.

grape—A small, smooth, juicy fruit that grows in bunches on vines. Grapes may be green, red, or purple in color. They may be eaten raw, dried to make raisins, or processed to make jelly, juice, or wine.
grape (grāp) *noun,* plural grapes.

grapefruit—A round citrus fruit, about the size of a softball, with a tough, yellow skin.
grape|fruit (grāp′frūt′) *noun,* plural grapefruits.

flower · leaf · fruit · split fruit

grapefruit

grapevine—**1.** The long, winding vine on which clusters of grapes grow. **2.** An informal, person-to-person network by which news and rumors are spread.
grape|vine (grāp′vīn′) *noun,* plural grapevines.

graph—A drawing used to show the relationship between two or more things: *The bar* graph *showed how the number of girls compared to the number of boys in the school.*
graph (graf) *noun,* plural graphs.

graphics—Images such as drawings, maps, or graphs that are on a computer monitor screen.
graph|ics (graf′iks) *noun.*

graphite—Carbon in a soft form. Graphite is used as pencil lead.
graph|ite (graf′īt) *noun.*

grasp—**1.** To grab and clutch something; wrap the fingers tightly around: *She* grasped *the dog's leash tightly when the dog tried to run away.* **2.** To figure out; understand: *After much practice, I felt I had* grasped *the art of knitting. Verb.*
—**1.** A tight hold: *Make sure you have a good* grasp *on the lamp when you move it.* **2.** The act of understanding: *He proved he had a* grasp *of the problem by coming up with a solution. Noun.*
grasp (grasp) *verb,* grasped, grasping; *noun,* plural grasps.
• Synonyms: clasp, grip, for *noun* 1.

grass—A common, green plant that grows naturally in pastures, meadows, and fields and is used to cover the grounds around a building.
grass (gras) *noun,* plural grasses.
■ **let the grass grow under** (one's) **feet:** To be lazy and not take advantage of opportunities: *If you start your term paper early and do not let the grass grow under your feet, then it will be done in time.*

grasshopper—An insect with two pairs of wings and very strong back legs that it uses for jumping.
grass|hop|per (gras′hop′ər) *noun,* plural grasshoppers.

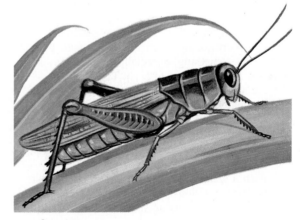

grasshopper

grassland—A large area of grass, with little or no trees, usually used as a feeding place for animals; pasture: *The farm is surrounded by* grassland *where the farmer's cows graze.*
grass|land (gras′land′) *noun,* plural grasslands.

a at	i if	oo look	ch chalk		a in ago
ā ape	ī idle	ou out	ng sing		e in happen
ah calm	o odd	u ugly	sh ship	ə =	i in capital
aw all	ō oats	ū rule	th think		o in occur
e end	oi oil	ur turn	th their		u in upon
ē easy			zh treasure		

grate¹—1. Metal bars shaped to hold burning wood or coal in a fireplace or furnace. 2. A set of metal bars that cross each other put over an opening to prevent entry. Grates are often put over windows and heating and drainage ducts.
grate (grāt) *noun, plural* **grates.**
• A word that sounds the same is **great.**

grate²—1. To annoy; irritate: *Her constant talking began to* grate *on us.* 2. To rub two things together, making a loud, grinding sound; scrape: *The sand on our shoes* grated *against the pavement.* 3. To shred or grind by scraping against a rough surface: *The cook* grates *cheese to sprinkle over pizza.*
grate (grāt) *verb,* **grated, grating.**
• A word that sounds the same is **great.**

grateful—Full of appreciation for something that has been done or said: *She was* grateful *to her friends for helping her find the lost key.*
grate|ful (grāt′fəl) *adjective.*

grating¹—A set of metal bars that cross each other put over an opening to prevent entry.
grat|ing (grā′ting) *noun, plural* **gratings.**

grating²—1. Annoying; displeasing; offensive: *a* grating *personality; a* grating *habit.* 2. Annoying to the ears: *The chalk made a* grating *sound as she wrote on the blackboard.*
grat|ing (grā′ting) *adjective.*

gratitude—Thankfulness for something that has been done or said; appreciation: *The president expressed her* gratitude *to the members of the club for their show of support.*
grat|i|tude (grat′ə tūd *or* grat′ə tyūd) *noun.*

grave¹—The piece of ground where a dead person or animal will be or has been buried.
grave (grāv) *noun, plural* **graves.**
■ **dig (one's) own grave:** To be responsible for one's own failure or ruin: *He is* digging *his* own grave *when he does not study for the test.*

grave²—1. Serious; gloomy: *The* grave *look on our friend's face told us that something was wrong.* 2. Significant; very important: *Finding a place to sleep is a* grave *concern of the homeless.*
grave (grāv) *adjective,* **graver, gravest.**

gravel—Small stones. Gravel is often spread on country roads, driveways, and paths.
grav|el (grav′əl) *noun.*

graveyard—An area of land used for burying the dead; cemetery.
grave|yard (grāv′yahrd′) *noun, plural* **graveyards.**

gravitation—1. The natural force that draws the objects of the universe toward each other.

Gravitation pulls people, objects, and animals to the earth's surface, keeping them from floating into space. 2. A natural attraction toward something.
grav|i|ta|tion (grav′ə tā′shən) *noun.*

gravity—1. A natural force that draws things toward the earth's surface or toward each other. Gravity gives weight to things and causes them to fall to the ground when they are dropped or thrown into the air. 2. Importance; seriousness: *In order to teach him about the* gravity *of his mistake, his parents did not allow him to watch television for a month.*
grav|i|ty (grav′ə tē) *noun, plural* **gravities.**

gravy—A sauce made by thickening the juices and fat produced by meat during cooking.
gra|vy (grā′vē) *noun, plural* **gravies.**

gray—A color made by combining white with black. *Noun.*
—Being such a color: *a* gray *horse;* gray *hair. Adjective.*
gray (grā) *noun, plural* **grays;** *adjective,* **grayer, grayest.**
• This word is also spelled **grey.**

graze¹—To eat grass: *We saw cows* grazing *in the field.*
graze (grāz) *verb,* **grazed, grazing.**

graze²—1. To brush against lightly; touch barely: *Although his foot* grazed *the highjump bar when he went over it, the bar did not fall.* 2. To scratch or scrape the surface: *The rock* grazed *the front fender of my brother's new car.*
graze (grāz) *verb,* **grazed, grazing.**

grease—1. The melted fat of meat. 2. Any substance like melted animal fat. Grease reduces friction between moving parts, such as in a car's engine. *Noun.*
—To apply melted fat or a similar substance: *to* grease *a hinge; to* grease *a baking dish. Verb.*
grease (grēs for *noun;* grēs *or* grēz for *verb*) *noun, plural* **greases;** *verb,* **greased, greasing.**

great—1. Huge; enormous: *a* great *amount of money.* 2. More than expected; extraordinary: great *relief.* 3. Noted; outstanding; important: *The showing of the* great *painting attracted crowds to the museum. Adjective.*
—Excellently; splendidly: *The show is going* great, *and audiences love it. Adverb.*
great (grāt) *adjective,* **greater, greatest;** *adverb.*
• A word that sounds the same is **grate.**
• Synonyms: For *adjective* 1, see Synonyms at **big.**
Antonyms: For *adjective* 1, see Synonyms at **small.**

Great Dane—A large dog with smooth short
hair, a large squared head, short, pointed ears,
and a long tail. Originally bred in Germany,
these dogs are known for their power and
strength.
Great Dane (grāt dān) *noun, plural* **Great
Danes.**

Great Dane

Great Pyrenees—A large dog with long,
thick, white hair and a big head. Originally bred
in France, these dogs guard sheep and are good
watchdogs.
Great Pyr|e|nees (grāt pir′ə nēz) *noun, plural*
Great Pyrenees.

greed—The desire to have more than is necessary
or deserved: *Greed caused him to hide the candy
and not share it with his friends.*
greed (grēd) *noun, plural* **greeds.**

greedy—Wanting more than is necessary or
deserved: *That greedy girl has eaten every cookie
in the package.*
greed|y (grē′dē) *adjective,* **greedier, greediest.**

Greek Orthodox Church—A church that
follows Christian beliefs but which differs from
Roman Catholic and Protestant Churches on
certain subjects. It is part of the group of Eastern
Orthodox Churches.
Greek Or|tho|dox Church (grēk awr′thə doks
church) *noun, plural* **Greek Orthodox
Churches.**

green—1. The color of most growing plants.
Green is made by mixing the colors blue and
yellow. 2. **greens:** The stems and leaves of
certain plants, used as food: *He added lettuce
and other* greens *to the salad.* 3. A grassy
place, usually in the center of a town or village.
4. The area of smooth, short grass surrounding a
hole on a golf course: *It was a long putt from the
edge of the* green *to the hole. Noun.*
—1. Being the color of a growing plant: green
uniforms. 2. Filled with trees, plants, and grass:
a green *landscape.* 3. Not completely grown;
immature: *These* green *tomatoes are not ready to
be picked.* 4. Not trained; inexperienced: *Even
though she was a* green *player, she learned
easily and soon made the team. Adjective.*
green (grēn) *noun, plural* **greens;** *adjective,*
greener, greenest.

■ **green with envy:** Extremely jealous: *My
brother is* green with envy *because I get to go
to the circus and he has to stay home to do
homework.*
green thumb: A natural talent for growing
plants: *Our garden is so beautiful because my
father has a* green thumb.

greenhorn—Someone who is not experienced at
something; newcomer: *I was a greenhorn as a
seamstress, but I made a dress by the end of the
sewing classes.*
green|horn (grēn′hawrn′) *noun, plural*
greenhorns.

Great Pyrenees

a at	i if	oo look	ch chalk		⎡a in ago
ā ape	ī idle	ou out	ng sing		e in happen
ah calm	o odd	u ugly	sh ship	ə =	i in capital
aw all	ō oats	ū rule	th think		o in occur
e end	oi oil	ur turn	<u>th</u> their		⎣u in upon
ē easy			zh treasure		

greenhouse—A heated building in which plants are grown and kept. Greenhouses usually have glass or plastic walls and roofs to let in a lot of sunlight.
green|house (grēn′hous′) *noun, plural* **greenhouses.**

greet—1. To welcome with words or actions: *The teacher* greeted *her students at the classroom door each morning.* 2. To react to: *They* greeted *his idea with enthusiasm.*
greet (grēt) *verb,* **greeted, greeting.**

greeting—1. Words spoken or an action done to welcome someone or something: *The rooster's crow is his* greeting *to the sun.* 2. **greetings:** Good wishes at special times: *birthday* greetings.
greet|ing (grē′ting) *noun, plural* **greetings.**

grenade—A small exploding device that is thrown with the hand.
gre|nade (grə nād′) *noun, plural* **grenades.**

grew—*See* **grow.**
grew (grū) *verb.*

grey—*See* **gray.**
grey (grā) *noun, plural* **greys;** *adjective,* **greyer, greyest.**

greyhound—A large dog with a slender graceful body, short smooth hair, small ears, long legs, and a long tail. Originally bred in ancient Egypt, these dogs are known for their speed and are often raced.
grey|hound (grā′hound′) *noun, plural* **greyhounds.**

greyhound

grid—1. A set of metal bars that cross each other put over an opening to prevent entry; grating: *The heel of her shoe became caught in the* grid *that covered the drain in the street.* 2. A set of equally spaced lines on which information may be charted: *We plotted the information on a* grid *to show how the temperature changes from month to month.*
grid (grid) *noun, plural* **grids.**

griddle—A flat, metal pan or plate for cooking foods, such as pancakes and hamburgers.
grid|dle (grid′əl) *noun, plural* **griddles.**

gridiron—1. A set of metal bars that cross each other, usually with a handle, used to cook meat and other foods over a fire; grill. 2. Something that looks like such a set of metal bars. 3. A football field.
grid|i|ron (grid′ī′rən) *noun, plural* **gridirons.**

grief—A feeling of great unhappiness: *The loss of my sister's favorite doll caused her much* grief.
grief (grēf) *noun, plural* **griefs.**

grieve—1. To feel very sad; feel bad about the loss of someone or something: *The whole class* grieved *over the death of the hamster.* 2. To cause someone to feel very sad: *The unfriendly words of his cousins* grieved *him.*
grieve (grēv) *verb,* **grieved, grieving.**

grill—1. A set of metal bars that cross each other put over an opening to prevent entry. Grills are used as gates or to cover windows. 2. A set of metal bars that cross each other, usually with a handle, used to cook meat and other foods over a fire. *Noun.*
—1. To cook meat and other foods on a set of metal bars that cross each other over a fire: *We* grilled *steaks at the beach.* 2. To ask many questions about a certain subject: *My friends* grilled *me about the movie I saw last night. Verb.*
grill (gril) *noun, plural* **grills;** *verb,* **grilled, grilling.**

grim—1. Harsh; severe; stern: *The weather looked so* grim *that we could not go outside for recess.* 2. Going on despite difficulties; not giving up: *Even though she was in last place, my sister finished the race with* grim *determination.*
grim (grim) *adjective,* **grimmer, grimmest.**

grime—Dirt that has been rubbed into or coats something: *My mother's clothes and tools were covered with* grime *after she cleaned out the fireplace.*
grime (grīm) *noun.*

grin—To smile widely: *She* grinned *at the thought of seeing her old friend again. Verb.*
—A big smile: *a wide* grin *of satisfaction. Noun.*
grin (grin) *verb,* **grinned, grinning;** *noun, plural* **grins.**

grind—1. To reduce to small pieces by crushing: *At the quarry, we watched them* grind *large*

rocks into gravel. **2.** To wear away a surface by rubbing it against something rough: *He ground the blades of the scissors until their edges were sharp again.* **3.** To rub together making a grating sound: *When we heard the two gears grinding against each other we knew it was time to oil the machine.*
grind (grīnd) *verb,* **ground, grinding.**

grindstone—A flat, rounded stone that is turned by a crank. A grindstone is used to sharpen a tool's edge or to smooth and polish a surface.
grind|stone (grīnd′stōn′) *noun, plural* **grindstones.**

■ **keep** (one's) **nose to the grindstone:** To keep working at something: *He* kept *his* nose to the grindstone *until he had learned his lines for the play.*

grindstone

grip—**1.** A tight hold; strong grasp: *She held onto her mother's hand with a firm* grip *when they crossed the street.* **2.** Something that can be grasped and held onto: *My radio has a hand* grip *so I can carry it easily.* **3.** Control; understanding: *She had such a* grip *of the subject that the teacher asked her to explain it to the rest of the class. Noun.*
—To grasp tightly: Grip *each rung tightly when you climb a ladder. Verb.*

a at	**i** if	**oo** look	**ch** chalk		⎡ a in ago
ā ape	**ī** idle	**ou** out	**ng** sing		e in happen
ah calm	**o** odd	**u** ugly	**sh** ship	ə =	i in capital
aw all	**ō** oats	**ū** rule	**th** think		o in occur
e end	**oi** oil	**ur** turn	**th** their		⎣ u in upon
ē easy			**zh** treasure		

grip (grip) *noun, plural* **grips;** *verb,* **gripped, gripping.**

■ **come to grips with:** To try to work out or adjust to; struggle to accept: *She finally* came to grips with *the fact that she did not make the team.*
lose (one's) **grip:** To act crazy; be out of control: *We felt that she was working too hard and would* lose *her* grip *if she did not get some rest.*
● Synonyms: **clasp, clutch,** for *noun* **1.**

gripe—To say something is wrong; express unhappiness: *He* griped *about his tie being too tight. Verb.*
—A complaint: *If you have a* gripe *about your grade, talk to your teacher. Noun.*
gripe (grīp) *verb,* **griped, griping;** *noun, plural* **gripes.**
● Synonyms: **complain, fuss, grumble, whine,** for *verb.*

grit—**1.** Tiny pieces of sand or rock. **2.** Determination; courage: *It took a lot of* grit *for him to get back on his bike after his accident. Noun.*
—To grind together very tightly: *to* grit *one's teeth. Verb.*
grit (grit) *noun; verb,* **gritted, gritting.**
● Synonyms: **heart, pluck, spirit,** for *noun* **2.**

grizzly bear—A very large North American bear. The grizzly's fur can be any color from light tan to almost black.
griz|zly bear (griz′lē bār) *noun, plural* **grizzly bears.**

grizzly bear

groan—A low, sad moan that shows unhappiness, disappointment, or pain: *He let out a groan when his mother said he could not go to the movies.* *Noun.*
—To make a low, sorrowful sound: *She groaned in pain when the nurse washed her scraped knee.* *Verb.*
groan (grōn) *noun, plural* **groans;** *verb,* **groaned, groaning.**
• A word that sounds the same is **grown.**

grocer—A person who sells food and other household items.
gro|cer (grō′sər) *noun, plural* **grocers.**

grocery—1. A store that sells food and other household items.   2. groceries: The food and other products sold in such a store.
gro|cer|y (grō′sər ē) *noun, plural* **groceries.**

groom—1. A newly married man or one who will soon be married.   2. A person whose job is to care for horses. *Noun.*
—1. To wash and brush the coat of an animal, especially a horse or a dog.   2. To put in order; tidy the appearance of: *In her neighborhood, people groom their yards often. Verb.*
groom (grüm) *noun, plural* **grooms;** *verb,* **groomed, grooming.**

groove—A long, thin dip or channel formed naturally in a surface or carved there by some object or tool; depression.
groove (grüv) *noun, plural* **grooves.**

grope—1. To use one's hands to search about for something: *She groped about in the large bag to find a pencil.*   2. To look for uncertainly: *She groped for the correct spelling of the word without success.*   3. To find one's way by feeling; feel one's way: *When the lights went out, we groped our way toward the drawer where we keep our candles.*
grope (grōp) *verb,* **groped, groping.**

gross—1. Being the amount before anything is taken out; whole; entire: *Our gross income from ticket sales was $100, but we had to spend $25 for refreshments.*   2. Both plain to see and clearly wrong: *a gross mistake in reporting an event.*   3. Not proper; not in good taste; crude: *He had such gross manners that he tried to push his way to the front of the line. Adjective.*
—1. The overall total before anything is taken out: *The club's earnings from the bake sale amounted to a gross of $150.*   2. 144 units, or 12 dozen of something. *Noun.*
gross (grōs) *adjective,* **grosser, grossest;** *noun, plural* **grosses.**

grouch—A person who grumbles or complains a lot; bad-tempered person. *Noun.*
—To complain; grumble: *When my uncle does not feel well, he grouches about everything. Verb.*
grouch (grouch) *noun, plural* **grouches;** *verb,* **grouched, grouching.**

ground[1]—1. The solid surface of the earth; land: *We stood on the ground and watched the plane climb in the sky.*   2. grounds: The land around a building: *museum grounds.*   3. grounds: Land set aside for a specific reason: *camping grounds.*   4. grounds: The basis, cause, or reason for something: *The coach's grounds for canceling the game were bad weather and sickness among the players.*   5. grounds: The solid bits of coffee that remain after it has been brewed. *Noun.*
—1. To bring to land; cause to stay on the land: *A sudden gust of wind grounded our new kite.*   2. To base on; establish: *The club was grounded on the desire to learn more about other cultures.*   3. To hit a baseball along the ground: *The batter grounded back to the pitcher.*   4. To stick on the bottom of a body of water or on the shore: *We grounded our boat while we gathered shells on the beach. Verb.*
ground (ground) *noun, plural* **grounds;** *verb,* **grounded, grounding.**
■ **cover ground:** To do a certain amount of work or travel a certain distance: *We hope to cover a lot of ground during the meeting.*
gain ground: To make progress: *The idea for a new school gained ground when the mayor spoke in favor of it.*
hold (one's) ground: To stand firmly: *Although we tried to change her mind, mother held her ground and would not let us get a dog.*
run into the ground: To use something too much; go beyond what is reasonable; overdo: *We laughed at his joke the first time, but he ran it into the ground by telling it over and over.*
stand (one's) ground: To stand firmly for one's beliefs: *It is hard to stand one's ground when everyone else is in favor of something else.*

ground[2]—See grind.
ground (ground) *verb.*

groundhog—See woodchuck.
ground|hog (ground′hog′) *noun, plural* **groundhogs.**

Groundhog Day—February 2. Legend says that the ground hog wakes up on this day and comes out of its burrow to check the weather. If the day is sunny, the ground hog will be frightened back into its hole by its own shadow, and there will be six more weeks of winter weather.

Ground-Hog Day (ground′hog′ dā) *noun.*

group—1. A number of people or things gathered together: *One* group *of people after another arrived to watch the game.* 2. A number of people or things having something in common: *Those singers are her favorite* group. *Noun.*
—1. To gather together: *They had* grouped *all the family pictures on one wall.* 2. To assign to a group: *The dogs were* grouped *according to breed for the dog show. Verb.*
group (grūp) *noun, plural* **groups;** *verb,* **grouped, grouping.**
• Synonyms: **batch, bunch, lot, set**[2], for *noun* **1.**

grouse—A reddish-brown bird that is hunted for sport and for food. It is plump and has strong, feathered legs.
grouse (grous) *noun, plural* **grouse** or **grouses.**

grouse

grove—A bunch of trees.
grove (grōv) *noun, plural* **groves.**

grow—1. To get bigger; increase in size: *His sister has* grown *so much that she is almost as tall as he is.* 2. To exist; be able to live: *It is*

difficult for vegetables to grow *in poor soil.*
3. To develop: *Good eating habits help children* grow *into healthy adults.* 4. To become gradually: *It* grew *darker as the storm approached.* 5. To plant and care for a crop: *My uncle* grows *corn on his farm.*
grow (grō) *verb,* **grew, grown, growing.**
• Synonyms: **cultivate, raise,** for **5.**

growl—1. To make a low, rumbling, angry sound; snarl: *The dog* growled *at the girl when she took the toy away from it.* 2. To grumble; be dissatisfied: *The students* growled *about the shortened lunch period. Verb.*
—A low, rumbling, angry sound. *Noun.*
growl (groul) *verb,* **growled, growling;** *noun, plural* **growls.**

grown—Having achieved full development; mature: *The pet shop had several* grown *cats along with a number of kittens. Adjective.*
—*See* **grow.** *Verb.*
grown (grōn) *adjective, verb.*
• A word that sounds the same is **groan.**

grown-up—Like an adult; not childish; mature: *Mom told us that she expected* grown-up *behavior from us at the restaurant. Adjective.*
—An adult. *Noun.*
grown-up (grōn′up′) *adjective; noun, plural* **grown-ups.**

growth—1. The process of growing: *The town went through a time of rapid* growth *when gold was discovered nearby.* 2. Something that has grown or appeared: *a* growth *of weeds in a garden.*
growth (grōth) *noun, plural* **growths.**

grub—1. The early stage of growth of a beetle or other insect. A grub looks like a worm.
2. Food. *Noun.*
—To seek by digging in the ground: *The bear* grubbed *for ants with its claws. Verb.*
grub (grub) *noun, plural* **grubs;** *verb,* **grubbed, grubbing.**

grudge—A long-time feeling of anger or dislike: *He has held a* grudge *against me since I beat him in the spelling bee. Noun.*
—To be unwilling to give or admit, often because of envy: *She* grudged *me my trophy even though she had won one herself. Verb.*
grudge (gruj) *noun, plural* **grudges;** *verb,* **grudged, grudging.**

gruesome—Filling one with fear or disgust; horrible: *Many campers like to tell* gruesome *stories around a campfire even though they may have trouble sleeping afterward.*
grue|some (grū′səm) *adjective.*

a at	i if	oo look	ch chalk		a in ago
ā ape	ī idle	ou out	ng sing		e in happen
ah calm	o odd	u ugly	sh ship	ə =	i in capital
aw all	ō oats	ū rule	th think		o in occur
e end	oi oil	ur turn	th their		u in upon
ē easy			zh treasure		

gruff—1. Sounding rough, hoarse, or harsh: *The coach shouted instructions in a* gruff *voice.* 2. Rough in one's speech or manner; not friendly: *Was the story about a* gruff *giant or a gentle one?*
gruff (gruf) *adjective,* **gruffer, gruffest.**

grumble—To complain or mutter unhappily, usually to oneself: *The customers* grumbled *when the store announced that it had run out of the popular toy. Verb.*
—1. Unhappy muttering: *Tired of being teased by her brother, she went to her room with a* grumble. 2. A low growl or rumble: *We heard the* grumble *of an animal just beyond our campfire. Noun.*
grum|ble (grum′bəl) *verb,* **grumbled, grumbling;** *noun, plural* **grumbles.**
• Synonyms: **fuss, gripe, whine,** for *verb.*

grumpy—Cranky and bad-tempered; in a bad mood: *After dropping my favorite book in a puddle, I was* grumpy *all day.*
grump|y (grum′pē) *adjective,* **grumpier, grumpiest.**

grunt—1. The deep, harsh sound that a pig makes. 2. Any sound like the one a pig makes: *His big brother did not want to talk to us and answered only with a* grunt *when we asked him questions. Noun.*
—To make a deep, harsh sound: *The man* grunted *as he lifted the heavy box. Verb.*
grunt (grunt) *noun, plural* **grunts;** *verb,* **grunted, grunting.**

guarantee—A promise to do something if another fails to do it; to fix or replace something if anything goes wrong with it in a certain amount of time: *The air conditioner comes with a one-year* guarantee. *Noun.*
—1. To give a promise to repair or replace something: *Does your company* guarantee *its merchandise?* 2. To make certain; assure: *Good food and good music will* guarantee *the success of our party.* 3. To promise: *The teacher* guaranteed *that there would not be a test tomorrow. Verb.*
guar|an|tee (gar′ən tē′) *noun, plural* **guarantees;** *verb,* **guaranteed, guaranteeing.**
• Synonyms: **assurance, pledge, word,** for *noun.*

guard—1. To watch over and keep safe; protect; defend: *The cat* guarded *her kittens.* 2. To watch over so as to keep from escaping: *Several police officers* guarded *the prisoners.* 3. To try to keep another player from scoring: *He scored the winning basket even though he was* guarded *by two players. Verb.*
—1. A person or group of people that protects or defends: *a security* guard. 2. Anything that gives protection: *She wore a hat as a* guard *against the hot sun.* 3. A close watch: *The miser kept a* guard *over his money night and day.* 4. A player at either side of the person playing center in football. 5. Either of the two basketball players whose position is near the center of the court. *Noun.*
guard (gahrd) *verb,* **guarded, guarding;** *noun, plural* **guards.**
• Synonyms: **shelter, shield,** for *verb* 1.

guardian—Someone chosen by a court of law to take care of a person who is young or who cannot take care of himself or herself.
guard|i|an (gahr′dē ən) *noun, plural* **guardians.**

guerrilla—A member of a small military group that usually is not part of a regular army. Guerrillas fight the enemy by such tactics as sudden raids and the theft of the enemy's food and supplies.
guer|ril|la (gə ril′ə) *noun, plural* **guerrillas.**
• A word that sounds the same is **gorilla.**

guess—1. To form an opinion using few or no facts; estimate: *I* guess *there were about 500 people at the parade.* 2. To get right without really knowing for sure: *If you* guess *the exact number of jelly beans in the jar, you win a prize.* 3. To think; believe; suppose: *I* guess *I can give you a ride home. Verb.*
—An opinion formed using few or no facts: *I have not heard a weather report, but my* guess *is that it will rain tomorrow. Noun.*
guess (ges) *verb,* **guessed, guessing;** *noun, plural* **guesses.**

guest—1. A person who is visiting or eating a meal at another's home; visitor: *She invited her best friend as a* guest *for dinner.* 2. A person who is staying at a hotel or motel or who is eating at a restaurant: *The hotel is so large that there are often 1,000* guests *there at one time.*
guest (gest) *noun, plural* **guests.**

guidance—1. The act of leading or directing: *Under her teacher's* guidance, *she learned to play the violin beautifully.* 2. Advice and assistance given to students to help them plan their courses, choose their careers, and work out personal problems. *Noun.*
—Having to do with leading or directing: *a* guidance *counselor. Adjective.*
guid|ance (gī′dəns) *noun, adjective.*

guide—To show a person the correct way; direct: *The park ranger* guided *the people through the cave. Verb.*

—A person or thing that leads the way or directs: *They used a compass as a guide for finding their way back to camp.* Noun.
guide (gīd) *verb,* **guided, guiding;** *noun, plural* **guides.**

guided missile—A flying weapon that is controlled by radio signals from the ground or by an automatic device placed inside it.
guid|ed mis|sile (gī′did mis′əl) *noun, plural* **guided missiles.**

guide word—The word or words appearing at the top of a page in a dictionary or other reference book. Guide words show the first and last entries on the page. The guide words on this page are **guided missile** and **gulf.**
guide word (gīd wurd) *noun, plural* **guide words.**

guild—**1.** An association of people with similar interests or a common goal: *She joined the writers' guild after her first book was published.* **2.** A union of people in the same trade or craft in the Middle Ages.
guild (gild) *noun, plural* **guilds.**

guilder—A unit of money in the Netherlands.
guil|der (gil′dər) *noun, plural* **guilders.**
Abbreviation: Gld.

guillotine—A machine that was used for putting people to death by cutting off their heads. It had a heavy blade that slid down along grooves made in two side posts.
guil|lo|tine (gil′ə tēn) *noun, plural* **guillotines.**

Word History

Guillotine was named after Joseph I. Guillotin, a French doctor. In 1792, he suggested that this machine could be used to execute people quickly and mercifully.

---

guilt—**1.** The fact of having done something wrong: *The criminal admitted his guilt.* **2.** A feeling of having done something wrong: *I felt a lot of guilt about making my sister cry.*
guilt (gilt) *noun.*

guilty—**1.** Having done something wrong; deserving of blame or punishment: *The student was guilty of cheating on the test.* **2.** Feeling

that one has done wrong: *I felt guilty about playing instead of mowing the lawn.*
guilt|y (gil′tē) *adjective,* **guiltier, guiltiest.**

guinea pig—A ratlike animal with a plump body, short ears, and no tail. It is often kept as a pet and is sometimes used in scientific experiments.
guin|ea pig (gin′ē pig) *noun, plural* **guinea pigs.**

guinea pig

guitar—A long-necked, musical instrument with six or more strings. It is played by strumming or plucking the strings with one's fingers or a pick.
gui|tar (gə tahr′) *noun, plural* **guitars.**

guitar

a at	i if	oo look	ch chalk		⌈ a in ago
ā ape	ī idle	ou out	ng sing		e in happen
ah calm	o odd	u ugly	sh ship	ə =	i in capital
aw all	ō oats	ū rule	th think		o in occur
e end	oi oil	ur turn	th their		⌊ u in upon
ē easy			zh treasure		

gulf—**1.** An area of an ocean or sea that is partly enclosed by land. **2.** A wide separation: *There has been a gulf between them since their fight.*
gulf (gulf) *noun, plural* **gulfs.**

gull—A large sea bird. It has long wings, webbed feet, a hooked beak, and, in most cases, gray and white feathers. It makes a loud, harsh call. This bird is often called a **sea gull**.
gull (gul) *noun, plural* **gulls**.

gull

gullible—Willing to believe almost anything; easily tricked or cheated: *He's so gullible he'd believe you if you told him that frogs have wings.*
gul|li|ble (gul′ə bəl) *adjective.*

gully—A trench, especially one made by running water or heavy rains.
gul|ly (gul′ē) *noun, plural* **gullies**.

gulp—1. To swallow quickly or in large portions: *Eager to go out and play, the boy* gulped *his dinner.* 2. To draw in or swallow air as if taking a drink: *She* gulped *when she heard her name called as the winner of the contest. Verb.*
—The act of swallowing quickly or in large portions: *a big* gulp *of milk. Noun.*
gulp (gulp) *verb,* **gulped, gulping;** *noun, plural* **gulps**.

gum[1]—1. The sticky juice of some trees and plants. It hardens when exposed to the air. 2. A sweetened product that is made from such juice and used for chewing. *Noun.*
—To make or cause to become sticky or stuck: *The sap from the pine tree* gummed *up my fingers. Verb.*
gum (gum) *noun, plural* **gums;** *verb,* **gummed, gumming.**

gum[2]—The firm, pink flesh around the teeth.
gum (gum) *noun, plural* **gums**.

gumball—Chewing gum in the form of a brightly colored ball of candy.
gum|ball (gum′bawl) *noun, plural* **gumballs**.

gumbo—A soup usually made of chicken and rice and thickened with okra.
gum|bo (gum′bō) *noun, plural* **gumbos**.

gumdrop—A small piece of candy that is made

from gum or gelatin and coated with sugar.
gum|drop (gum′drop′) *noun, plural* **gumdrops**.

gummy—Sticky, like gum: *The melted chocolate bar felt all* gummy *when she picked it up.*
gum|my (gum′ē) *adjective.*

gun—1. A weapon that has a metal tube for shooting bullets or the like out of one end. Rifles, cannons, and pistols are types of guns. 2. Anything that looks or works like such a weapon: *Dad painted the fence with a spray* gun. *Noun.*
—1. To shoot using a gun: *The farmer* gunned *down the fox that was raiding the chicken coop each night.* 2. To increase speed; accelerate: *The race car driver* gunned *his engine after the turn and sped to the finish line. Verb.*
gun (gun) *noun, plural* **guns;** *verb,* **gunned, gunning.**

- **beat the gun:** To begin before receiving the signal to start: *He was so eager to get a good start that he* beat the gun *and we had to start the race over again.*
  give it the gun: To speed up; go faster: *If you are going to pass that truck,* give it the gun.
  go great guns: To move ahead with much success: *With the bake sale* going great guns, *it looked as if we would raise all the money we needed for the trip.*
  jump the gun: 1. To start doing something too soon; begin before receiving the signal to start: *The teacher told the class to wait for directions and not to* jump the gun. 2. To get a head start on a rival; to do something before someone else: *We* jumped the gun *and got our Christmas lights up before our neighbor.*
  spike (one's) guns: To prevent someone from carrying out a plan: *We found out about the other team's new pass play and were able to* spike their guns.
  stick to (one's) guns: To refuse to give up one's ideas or opinions: *The mayor* stuck to her guns *about the need for a new library in spite of opposition from some groups.*

gundog—A dog such as a pointer, retriever, or setter, trained to work with a hunter.
gun|dog (gun′dawg) *noun, plural* **gundogs**.

gunfire—The shooting of guns: *We heard the sound of* gunfire *as soon as the hunting season began.*
gun|fire (gun′fīr′) *noun.*

gung ho—Eager; keen; enthusiastic: *All the players were* gung ho *to get the game started.*
gung ho (gung hō) *adjective.*

gunpowder—An explosive powder that is used in fireworks, guns, and blasting.
gun|pow|der (gun′pou′dər) *noun, plural* **gunpowders.**

gun-shy—1. Afraid of the sound of a gun.   2. Cautious; watchful; suspicious; distrusting, usually because of an earlier experience: *He has fooled me so many times it is no wonder I'm gunshy around him.*
gun-shy (gun′shī) *adjective.*

gunwhale—The upper edge of the side of a ship or boat.
gun|wale (gun′əl) *noun, plural* **gunwhales.**

guppy—A tiny, tropical fish with a brightly colored, fanned tail. Guppies are popular as pets in aquariums.
gup|py (gup′ē) *noun, plural* **guppies.**

gurgle—1. To flow with a low, bubbling sound: *The water* gurgled *down the drain.*   2. To make a low, bubbling sound: *My stomach* gurgles *when I am hungry. Verb.*
—A bubbling sound. *Noun.*
gur|gle (gur′gəl) *verb,* **gurgled, gurgling;** *noun, plural* **gurgles.**

gush—1. To flow or pour out suddenly and forcefully in large amounts; stream: *Water* gushed *from the hydrant when the hose came off.*   2. To speak with so much feeling that one seems silly: *The actor* gushed *about how he loved everybody for making him famous. Verb.*
—A sudden rush of a liquid: *There was a* gush *of water as the dam broke. Noun.*
gush (gush) *verb,* **gushed, gushing;** *noun, plural* **gushes.**

gust—A sudden, brief rush of wind.
gust (gust) *noun, plural* **gusts.**

gutter—1. A small channel built along the side of a street for carrying off water.   2. A long trough built along the edge of a roof for carrying off rain water.
gut|ter (gut′ər) *noun, plural* **gutters.**

guy—A man or boy: *He is a nice* guy *once you get to know him.*
guy (gī) *noun, plural* **guys.**

gym—A gymnasium.
gym (jim) *noun, plural* **gyms.**

gymkhana—A sports contest or meet: *She plans to ride her horse in the* gymkhana *next week.*
gym|kha|na (jim kah′nə) *noun, plural* **gymkhanas.**

gymnasium—A room or building that has equipment for physical exercise, training, and indoor sports.
gym|na|si|um (jim nā′zē əm) *noun, plural* **gymnasiums.**

Word History

Gymnasium comes from a Greek word meaning ''exercise naked.'' In ancient Greece, gymnasiums were public places set aside for athletic games. Greek boys and young men did not wear clothes when taking part in games, in order to move freely.

---

gymnast—An expert in gymnastics.
gym|nast (jim′nast) *noun, plural* **gymnasts.**

gymnastics—Exercises for developing the muscles and improving health. They are often performed on special equipment.
gym|nas|tics (jim nas′tiks) *noun.*

gyp—To cheat; to swindle: *He tried to* gyp *me out of two dollars.*
gyp (jip) *verb,* **gypped, gypping.**

Gypsy—A member of a group of wandering people whose ancestors left India about A.D. 1000. Gypsies came to Europe from the Middle East in the 1400's and can now be found throughout the world.
Gyp|sy (jip′sē) *noun, plural* **Gypsies.**

Word History

Gypsy is a shortened form of ''Egyptian.'' When the Gypsies first arrived in Europe in the 1400's, they were believed to have come from Egypt.

---

gyrate—To spin around in a circle; whirl: *It makes me dizzy just watching figure skaters when they* gyrate *so fast.*
gy|rate (jī′rāt) *verb,* **gyrated, gyrating.**

gyroscope—A heavy wheel or disk that is mounted so its axis can turn in any direction. When a gyroscope spins quickly, the direction of its axis does not change. Gyroscopes are used in navigating ships, planes, and guided missiles.
gy|ro|scope (jī′rə skōp) *noun, plural* **gyroscopes.**

a at	i if	oo look	ch chalk	⌐ a in ago
ā ape	ī idle	ou out	ng sing	e in happen
ah calm	o odd	u ugly	sh ship	ə = i in capital
aw all	ō oats	ū rule	th think	o in occur
e end	oi oil	ur turn	<u>th</u> their	⌊ u in upon
ē easy			zh treasure	

About 1,900 years ago, the Romans gave the capital **H** its present form. The small letter **h** was first used about 1,700 years ago. It reached its present form about 500 years ago.

About 5,000 years ago, the ancient Egyptians used a symbol that represented a twisted length of rope.

About 3,500 years ago, people in the Middle East made a simpler symbol. They called it *cheth*.

About 3,000 years ago, other people in the Middle East used this form.

About 2,600 years ago, the Greeks gave the letter this form. They called it *eta*.

H or h—The eighth letter of the alphabet: *There are two* h's *in the word "harsh."*
H, h (āch) *noun, plural* **H's** or **Hs, h's** or **hs.**

ha—1. A word that is used to show surprise, happiness, triumph, or similar feelings: *"Ha! I have figured out the puzzle!" she cried.* **2.** A word that is used to show the sound of laughter: *"Ha, ha, ha," laughed the audience when they saw the clown's silly costume.*
ha (hah) *interjection.*

habit—1. An action that a person has done so often and in the same way that he or she does it without thinking: *He has a* habit *of drumming his fingers on the desk during class.* **2.** A special set of clothes, especially those worn by some monks and nuns and those worn for riding.
hab|it (hab′it) *noun, plural* **habits.**

habitat—The place or area where a plant or animal naturally lives and grows: *The arctic region is the* habitat *of polar bears.*
hab|i|tat (hab′ə tat) *noun, plural* **habitats.**

habitual—Done often and in the same way; regular; usual: *Rubbing his chin was a* habitual *action he made when he did not know the answer to a question.*
ha|bit|u|al (hə bich′ū əl) *adjective.*

hacienda—1. A large piece of land, usually in a Spanish-speaking country, that is used for farming or raising cattle. **2.** The main building of such a farm or ranch, in which the owner and the owner's family live.
ha|ci|en|da (hah′sē en′də) *noun, plural* **haciendas.**

hack—1. To cut or chop roughly or unevenly: *The man used an ax to* hack *a hole in the ice for fishing.* **2.** To cough making short, dry sounds. **3.** To try new things on a computer, either by slightly changing existing programs or by writing new ones.
hack (hak) *verb,* **hacked, hacking.**

Hackney—A strong English breed of horse that is known for its high-stepping gait. It is used for riding and for pulling carriages.
Hack|ney (hak′nē) *noun, plural* **Hackneys.**

riding habit

nun's habit

habit (definition 2)

Hackney pony

Hackney pony—An English pony that stands from 48 to 58 inches (120 to 148 centimeters) tall and weighs from 600 to 850 pounds (270 to 385 kilograms).
Hack|ney po|ny (hak′nē pō′nē) *noun, plural* **Hackney ponies.**

had—*See* **have**
had (had) *verb.*

haddock—A fish that lives in the northern Atlantic Ocean. It has a black stripe that runs from its head to its tail.
had|dock (had′ək) *noun, plural* **haddocks.**

haddock

hadn't—The contraction of ''had not.''
had|n't (had′ənt).

haiku—A short poem that is written in three lines of verse that usually have no rhyme. The first line has five syllables, the second line has seven syllables, and the last line has five syllables. Haiku is a very old form of Japanese poetry and is often about things in nature.
hai|ku (hī′kū) *noun, plural* **haiku** or **haikus.**

a at	i if	oo look	ch chalk		a in ago
ā ape	ī idle	ou out	ng sing		e in happen
ah calm	o odd	u ugly	sh ship	ə =	i in capital
aw all	ō oats	ū rule	th think		o in occur
e end	oi oil	ur turn	th their		u in upon
ē easy			zh treasure		

hail¹—1. To call, shout, or wave so as to welcome or cheer someone: *The crowd* hailed *the astronauts who rode in the parade.* 2. To call, shout, or wave so as to get someone's notice: *We* hailed *the friend who was looking for us in the crowd at the game.*
hail (hāl) *verb,* **hailed, hailing.**

Word History

Hail¹ comes from an old English word meaning ''healthy.'' People used to say hello and good-by by saying, ''Be healthy!'' Later they said just, ''Hail!'' So the act of greeting someone came to be known as hailing.

hail²—1. Small lumps of ice that come in a shower from storm clouds; frozen raindrops. 2. Anything that gives the effect of a heavy shower of hail: *a* hail *of bullets. Noun.*
—To rain or pour down in or like a shower of hail: *The leaves* hailed *down on the windy day. Verb.*
hail (hāl) *noun; verb,* **hailed, hailing.**

hailstone—A piece of hail.
hail|stone (hāl′stōn′) *noun, plural* **hailstones.**

hair—1. A thin, threadlike growth on the skin of people and some animals. 2. The mass or covering of such threadlike growths: *The boy had black* hair. 3. A threadlike growth on a plant.
hair (hār) *noun, plural* **hairs.**

■ **get in** (someone's) **hair:** To bother; annoy: *Her little brother was always* getting in *her* hair *when she wanted to be left alone.*
make (one's) **hair stand on end:** To scare or frighten one: *That ghost story will* make *your* hair stand on end!
split hairs: To argue about unimportant things; be too picky: *He* split hairs *about who got a bigger slice of cake.*
● A word that sounds the same is **hare.**

haircut—The act of cutting a person's hair or the style in which it is cut.
hair|cut (hār′kut′) *noun, plural* **haircuts.**

hairy—Covered with a lot of hair; furry: *a hairy dog.*
hair|y (hār′ē) *adjective,* **hairier, hairiest.**

half—1. One of two equal parts into which a thing is or could be divided: *If you give me* half *of the $6 you owe me, I will have the $3 I need to buy the book.* 2. One of two equal periods of playing time in certain games: *Our football team scored a touchdown during the first* half. *Noun.*

—Being one of two equal parts into which a thing is or could be divided: *a half* gallon. *Adjective.*
—1. As far as half the full quantity or total amount: *He filled the dog's bowl* half *full of water.* 2. Partly; not completely: *I was already* half *awake when the alarm clock went off. Adverb.*
half (haf) *noun, plural* **halves;** *adjective; adverb.*

halfhearted—Having little interest, enthusiasm, or courage: *She made a* halfhearted *attempt to study for the test.*
half|heart|ed (haf′hahr′tid) *adjective.*

half-mast—A position halfway down a pole or mast. Flags are flown at half-mast as a sign of mourning for someone who has died or as a signal of distress.
half-mast (half′ mast′) *noun.*

halfway—1. Half of an entire distance: *He ran* halfway *home from school.* 2. Not completely: *I am only* halfway *done with this book. Adverb.*
—1. Half of a whole thing: *They met at the* halfway *point between their two houses.* 2. Incomplete; unfinished; partial: *The city council took only* halfway *steps to solve the parking problem. Adjective.*
half|way (haf′wā′) *adverb, adjective.*

halibut—A large fish with a flat body. It lives in the northern Atlantic and Pacific oceans.
hal|i|but (hal′ə bət *or* hol′ə bət) *noun, plural* **halibuts** *or* **halibut.**

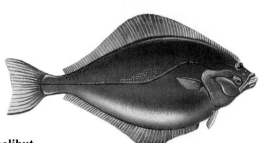

halibut

Word History

Halibut comes from two old English words meaning ''holy flatfish.'' The first four letters in **halibut** are from the word meaning ''holy.'' Halibut is a flatfish, and it used to be eaten especially on holy days.

hall—1. A corridor that connects the rooms of a building; hallway; passageway. 2. A room or long, narrow hallway near the entrance of a building; lobby. 3. A large room or a building used for public gatherings, such as parties, meetings, and dinners: *a dining* hall; *a concert* hall; *city* hall.
hall (hawl) *noun, plural* **halls.**
● A word that sounds the same is **haul.**

hallelujah—A word that means ''Praise the Lord!'' It is used in many religious writings, prayers, and songs.
hal|le|lu|jah (hal′ə lū′yə) *interjection.*

Halloween or **Hallowe'en**—October 31. On this holiday, children dress up in costumes and go from house to house asking for treats.
Hal|low|een or Hal|low|e'en (hal′ō ēn′ *or* hol′ō ēn′) *noun.*

hallway—A corridor in a building; hall.
hall|way (hawl′wā′) *noun, plural* **hallways.**

halo—1. A ring of light that can sometimes be seen shining around the sun, moon, and other objects in the sky. 2. A circle or ring of light that artists put around the heads of saints and angels in paintings and statues.
ha|lo (hā′lō) *noun, plural* **halos** *or* **haloes.**

halt—To stop: *The parade* halted *in front of the town hall. Verb.*
—A stop: *Traffic came to a* halt *while the children got off the bus. Noun.*
halt (hawlt) *verb,* **halted, halting;** *noun, plural* **halts.**
● Synonyms: **cease, quit,** for *verb.*

halter—1. A rope or strap that fits around the head of an animal and is used to lead or tie it. 2. A short blouse for girls and women. It is sleeveless and is tied around the neck and across the back.
hal|ter (hawl′tər) *noun, plural* **halters.**

halve—1. To divide into two parts of the same size: *She* halved *the melon and scooped out the seeds inside.* 2. To lower by half: *He thought the lemonade was too sweet, so he* halved *the amount of sugar in the next pitcher he made.*
halve (hav) *verb,* **halved, halving.**
● A word that sounds the same is **have.**

halves—See **half.**
halves (havz) *plural noun.*

ham—1. Meat from a hog's back leg or shoulder. It is normally salted or smoked. 2. A performer or any person who enjoys showing off. 3. An amateur radio operator.
ham (ham) *noun, plural* **hams.**
■ **ham it up:** To show off: *She would never just smile when she had her pciture taken but would always* ham it up *instead.*
● See Language Fact at **pork.**

Word History

Hamburger comes from the name of a city, Hamburg, in what is now West Germany. The food used to be called "Hamburger steak."

hamburger—1. Ground beef. 2. A flat, round cake of fried or broiled ground beef. It is usually served in a bun or roll.
ham|burg|er (ham′bər gər) *noun, plural* **hamburgers.**

hammer—1. A hand tool that has a heavy metal head set across a long handle. It is used for hitting nails and pounding metal into certain shapes. 2. Anything that is used like or shaped like this tool. *Noun.*
—1. To hit or beat with a hammer: *She* hammered *a nail into the floor of the tree house.* 2. To hit or pound again and again: *The woodpecker* hammered *its beak against the tree. Verb.*
ham|mer (ham′ər) *noun, plural* **hammers;** *verb,* **hammered, hammering.**

hammerhead shark—A medium-sized shark with a flattened head that looks like a hammer.
ham|mer|head shark (ham′ər həd′ shahrk) *noun, plural* **hammerhead sharks.**

hammerhead shark

hammock—A kind of hanging bed that is made of canvas or rope netting. It is strung between two trees or posts.
ham|mock (ham′ək) *noun, plural* **hammocks.**

hamper¹—To hold back by getting in the way of; restrict: *The heavy traffic* hampered *her effort to make her appointment on time.*

ham|per (ham′pər) *verb,* **hampered, hampering.**
• Synonyms: **handicap, hinder**
Antonyms: **aid, help**

hamper²—A large covered basket or container: *a laundry* hamper; *a picnic* hamper.
ham|per (ham′pər) *noun, plural* **hampers.**

hamster—A small, furry animal that looks like a large mouse. It has a short tail and pouches in its cheeks for storing food.
ham|ster (ham′stər) *noun, plural* **hamsters.**

hamster

hand—1. The end of the arm below the wrist. It consists of four fingers, a thumb, and the palm. 2. Something that is like a hand in the way that it looks or is used: *the* hands *of a watch.* 3. A worker, especially one who works with his or her hands: *The farm* hands *all helped harvest the wheat.* 4. One's share or part in doing something; role: *Everyone in the family had a* hand *in decorating the tree.* 5. Applause: *The children gave the performers a big* hand *at the end of their song.* 6. Help; assistance: *She gave her brother a* hand *with washing the dishes.* 7. One round of a card game or the cards that a player is holding after a deal. 8. A promise of marriage. *Noun.*
—To pass or give with one's hand: *Please* hand *me the pencil. Verb.*
—Used for or with the hand: *a* hand *tool; a* hand *towel. Adjective.*
hand (hand) *noun, plural* **hands;** *verb,* **handed, handing;** *adjective.*

■ **all hands:** Everyone, especially sailors on a ship: *When the storm began, the captain shouted, "All* hands *on deck!"*
at first hand: By one's own experience; directly: *She went on a special cruise to see whales* at first hand.

a at	i if	oo look	ch chalk		a in ago
ā ape	ī idle	ou out	ng sing		e in happen
ah calm	o odd	u ugly	sh ship	ə =	i in capital
aw all	ō oats	ū rule	th think		o in occur
e end	oi oil	ur turn	th their		u in upon
ē easy			zh treasure		

force (one's) hand: To make a person act immediately or unwillingly: *The injury to the star player* forced *the coach's* hand, *and he had to use a substitute.*

hand and foot: Sparing no effort; continually: *The queen had servants to wait on her* hand and foot.

hand and glove: Closely associated: *The robbers got into the bank, because they were* hand and glove *with the security guard.*

hand over fist: A good deal; quickly: *His vision improved* hand over fist *when he got glasses.*

hands down: With no trouble; easily: *He won the spelling bee* hands down.

out of hand: Out of control: *The crowd at the game got* out of hand *and started throwing things onto the field.*

throw up (one's) hands: To give up; stop trying: *After spending five minutes trying to thread the needle, she* threw up *her* hands *and asked for help.*

tip (one's) hand: To let information or one's plans be known before the proper time: *My sister tried to get me to* tip *my* hand *about her birthday present.*

handbag—A woman's small bag that is used for carrying such items as keys and a wallet; purse.
hand|bag (hand′bag′) *noun, plural* **handbags.**

handbook—A small book that has information on a certain subject.
hand|book (hand′book′) *noun, plural* **handbooks.**

handcuff—One of a pair of metal fastenings that are locked around the wrists to restrict the use of one's hands. Handcuffs are attached to each other by a short chain. *Noun.*
—To put handcuffs on. *Verb.*
hand|cuff (hand′kuf′) *noun, plural* **handcuffs;** *verb,* **handcuffed, handcuffing.**

handful—**1.** As much or as many as a person's hand can grasp: *He took a* handful *of popcorn from the box.* **2.** Just a few: *Only a* handful *of people stayed at the baseball game when it began to rain.*
hand|ful (hand′fəl) *noun, plural* **handfuls.**

handicap—Anything that makes it harder to do what one wants to do: *Her heavy boots were a* handicap *when she ran to catch the bus. Noun.*
—To make it harder to do what one wants to do: *His shyness* handicapped *him when he had to speak in front of the class. Verb.*
hand|i|cap (han′dē kap) *noun, plural* **handicaps;** *verb,* **handicapped, handicapping.**

● Synonyms: **hamper**[1], **hinder,** for *verb.*
   Antonyms: **aid, help,** for *verb.*

handicraft—**1.** A hobby or job that requires skill with one's hands. Knitting, sewing, and crocheting are handicrafts. **2.** Something that is made by working carefully with the hands.
hand|i|craft (han′dē kraft′) *noun, plural* **handicrafts.**

handkerchief—A piece of soft cloth that is used to wipe the nose or face.
hand|ker|chief (hang′kər chif) *noun, plural* **handkerchiefs.**

handle—The part of something that is designed to be grasped by the hand. A bucket, a shovel, a lunch box, and a paint brush have handles. *Noun.*
—**1.** To touch or grasp with the hands: *Please* handle *the kitten carefully so that you do not hurt it.* **2.** To manage or control; deal with: *She* handles *problems well and never lets them bother her. Verb.*
han|dle (han′dəl) *noun, plural* **handles;** *verb,* **handled, handling.**
■ **fly off the handle:** To become very upset or angry: *Mother* flew off the handle *when she saw the mess in my room.*

handmade—Produced by the hands and not by a machine: *He gave his mother a* handmade *valentine.*
hand|made (hand′mād′) *adjective.*

hand-me-down—Something that is passed along from one person to another, usually within a family: *That sweater is a* hand-me-down *from her older sister. Noun.*
—Being something that is passed along from one person to another; not new. *Adjective.*
hand-me-down (hand′mē doun′) *noun, plural* **hand-me-downs;** *adjective.*

handshake—The act of two people firmly holding right hands and usually moving them up and down slightly. People shake hands when saying hello or good-by, to show friendship, to congratulate someone, and to show that two people have agreed on something.
hand|shake (hand′shāk′) *noun, plural* **handshakes.**

handsome—**1.** Having a pleasing appearance: *a* handsome *man; a* handsome *collie.* **2.** Large: *He paid a* handsome *amount of money for that new car.*
hand|some (han′səm) *adjective,* **handsomer, handsomest.**

handspring—A jump done in gymnastics in which a person leaps onto the hands, brings the feet over the head, and then lands on the feet. A handspring can be done going forward or backward.

hand|spring (hand′spring′) *noun, plural* **handsprings.**

handwriting—Writing that is done by the hand with a pen or pencil.

hand|writ|ing (hand′rī′ting) *noun, plural* **handwritings.**

■ **see the handwriting on the wall** or **read the handwriting on the wall:** To be aware that an old way of life is ending and will bring about unpleasant changes: *Because my friends fought all the time, I saw the handwriting on the wall and knew they would soon be friends no more.*

handy—1. Close by; easy to reach: *She always keeps an eraser* handy *when doing her homework.* 2. Able to use one's hands well: *She is very* handy *at fixing bicycles.* 3. Easy to use or carry; helpful: *This lightweight saw is very* handy. *My notebook has a* handy *pocket for my pens and pencils.*

hand|y (han′dē) *adjective,* **handier, handiest.**

hang—1. To fasten or attach something at the top only, with no support from below: *She* hung *her coat on a hook.* 2. To attach something so that it can swing back and forth: *to* hang *wind chimes by a window.* 3. To kill a person by dangling him or her from a rope tied around the neck: *The cowboy* hanged *the outlaw from a tree. Verb.*
—1. A way of doing or using something: *It took a while for him to get the* hang *of driving a car.* 2. The way that something falls or dangles: *the* hang *of the curtains. Noun.*

hang (hang) *verb,* **hanged** (for definition 3 only) or **hung, hanging;** *noun.*

hangar—A large building in which airplanes are stored and repaired.

hang|ar (hang′ər) *noun, plural* **hangars.**
• A word that sounds the same is **hanger.**

hanger—A frame or hook of wood, wire, or plastic for dangling something: *a coat* hanger; *a plant* hanger.

hang|er (hang′ər) *noun, plural* **hangers.**
• A word that sounds the same is **hangar.**

hangnail—A bit of skin that has partly torn away from the side or base of a fingernail.

hang|nail (hang′nāl′) *noun, plural* **hangnails.**

Hanukkah or **Hanukka**—A Jewish religious holiday that is celebrated in December and lasts eight days. It is also called the Festival of Lights.

Ha|nuk|kah or **Ha|nuk|ka** (hah′noo kah) *noun.*
• This word is also spelled **Chanukah.**

haphazard—Marked by a lack of planning or order; happening by chance: *The pick-up sticks fell in a* haphazard *pile on the table.*

hap|haz|ard (hap′haz′ərd) *adjective.*

happen—1. To take place; come about: *The bicycle race* happened *yesterday.* 2. To take place or come about by chance: *He* happened *to win a radio in the raffle.* 3. To have the chance or opportunity: *She* happened *to meet the new neighbors while taking a walk.* 4. To be done: *Something must have* happened *to this pen because the ink is not coming out.*

hap|pen (hap′ən) *verb,* **happened, happening.**

happening—Something that takes place: *He told her about the* happenings *in school while she was out sick.*

hap|pen|ing (hap′ə ning) *noun, plural* **happenings.**

happiness—The state of being pleased or glad: *A visit to her grandparents brought her* happiness.

hap|pi|ness (hap′ē nis) *noun.*
• **Synonyms: bliss, delight, joy, pleasure**
  Antonyms: misery, sorrow, woe

happy—Glad; pleased: *He was* happy *to see his friends again after summer vacation.*

hap|py (hap′ē) *adjective,* **happier, happiest.**
• **Synonyms: cheerful, gay, merry**
  Antonyms: blue, dejected, gloomy, glum, miserable, sad, unhappy

happy-go-lucky—Free of cares and worries: *She is a* happy-go-lucky *person who enjoys whatever she does.*

hap|py-go-luck|y (hap′ē gō luk′ē) *adjective.*

harass—To keep on bothering or annoying: *The mosquitoes* harassed *him every time he went outside.*

har|ass (hə ras′ *or* har′əs) *verb,* **harassed, harassing.**
• **Synonyms: badger, hound, pester, plague**

Word History

Harass comes from an old French word that was shouted in order to excite dogs to attack. A special type of dog called a **harrier** was used for this purpose, especially to attack hares and rabbits.

a at	i if	oo look	ch chalk		ə =	a in ago
ā ape	ī idle	ou out	ng sing			e in happen
ah calm	o odd	u ugly	sh ship			i in capital
aw all	ō oats	ū rule	th think			o in occur
e end	oi oil	ur turn	th their			u in upon
ē easy			zh treasure			

harbor—A place along a coast that has water deep enough for boats or ships to dock and be given shelter from storms; port: *Noun.*
—**1.** To give safety or shelter: *The hole in the tree* harbored *a squirrel.* **2.** To keep holding a thought or feeling for some time: *Why does she* harbor *the idea that I do not like her? Verb.*
har|bor (hahr′bər) *noun, plural* **harbors;** *verb,* **harbored, harboring.**

hard—**1.** Not soft; firm: *a* hard *lump of coal; water that is frozen* hard. **2.** Needing or using a lot of skill, work, or effort; not easy: *a* hard *task; a* hard *worker; to run* hard. **3.** Having or filled with unpleasantness, harshness, or difficulty: *to hold* hard *feelings toward him; a* hard *winter; to take a loss* hard. **4.** Having much strength or power: *a wind that blows* hard.
hard (hahrd) *adjective,* **harder, hardest;** *adverb.*
▪ **hard and fast:** Strict; not able to be changed or broken: *a* hard and fast *rule.*
hard put: Having a lot of trouble or difficulty: *He was* hard put *to name all the states.*
hard up: Badly in need of something: *She is* hard up *for money.*

hard copy—Information that is written for or printed by a computer on paper.
hard cop|y (hahrd kop′ē) *noun, plural* **hard copies.**

hard disk—A stiff disk coated with a magnetic material that is permanently fixed in a computer. It can store more information than a floppy disk.
hard disk (hahrd′ disk) *noun, plural* **hard disks.**

harden—To become or make solid and firm: *The pan of fudge* hardened *as it cooled.*
hard|en (hahr′dən) *verb,* **hardened, hardening.**

hardly—**1.** Barely; just: *There were* hardly *enough cupcakes to go around.* **2.** Probably not: *They would* hardly *go swimming in this cold weather!*
hard|ly (hahrd′lē) *adverb.*

hardship—Something that is difficult or painful to live with or do: *Homelessness is a* hardship.
hard|ship (hahrd′ship) *noun, plural* **hardships.**

hardware—**1.** Items made of metal that are used to make or fix things: *Hammers, saws, locks, and nails are types of* hardware. **2.** The parts that make up a computer, such as the monitor, disk drive, and keyboard.
hard|ware (hahrd′wār′) *noun.*
● See pictures at **saw**[1] and **screw** for **1.**

hardy—Strong, healthy, and able to resist harsh conditions: hardy *pioneers; a* hardy *plant.*
har|dy (hahr′dē) *adjective,* **hardier, hardiest.**

hare

hare—A furry mammal that has strong front teeth, long ears, strong back legs, and a short tail. Hares are related to but larger than rabbits.
hare (hār) *noun, plural* **hares.**
● A word that sounds the same is **hair.**

harm—**1.** Damage or hurt; injury: *Bees can cause* harm *when they sting.* **2.** Wrong: *He saw no* harm *in staying out late. Noun.*
—To hurt or damage; injure: *A late frost* harmed *the young plants in the garden. Verb.*
harm (hahrm) *noun, plural* **harms;** *verb,* **harmed, harming.**

harmful—Causing damage or hurt: *Smoking cigarettes is* harmful *to your health.*
harm|ful (hahrm′fəl) *adjective.*

harmless—Not able to cause damage or hurt: *That insect looks as if it may bite, but it really is* harmless.
harm|less (hahrm′lis) *adjective.*

harmonica—A small musical instrument that has a rectangular metal case with a row of slots outside and reeds inside. It is held in the hands and played by blowing in and out of the slots to make the reeds vibrate.
har|mon|i|ca (hahr mon′ə kə) *noun, plural* **harmonicas.**

harmonica

harmonious—**1.** Able to get along well together: *Although the boys were from different countries, they were* harmonious.   **2.** Having a pleasing sound: *The church bells made* harmonious *music.* **har|mo|ni|ous** (hahr mō′nē əs) *adjective.*

harmonize—**1.** To play or sing together in a pleasing way: *The school chorus* harmonized *on the national anthem.*   **2.** To go well together; not clash: *Do the colors of my blouse and skirt* harmonize? **har|mo|nize** (hahr′mə nīz) *verb,* **harmonized, harmonizing.**

harmony—**1.** Agreement: *The family was in* harmony *about where to go on summer vacation.* **2.** Two or more musical notes played at the same time, forming a chord. **har|mo|ny** (hahr′mə nē) *noun, plural* **harmonies.**

harness—The leather bands, straps, and metal pieces that are used to attach a horse or other work animal to a plow or a vehicle such as a wagon. *Noun.* —**1.** To put such a leather attachment on: *The farmer* harnessed *his plow horse.*   **2.** To control for a specific use: *The solar panels on the roof* harness *the energy of the sun to heat our house. Verb.* **har|ness** (hahr′nis) *noun, plural* **harnesses;** *verb,* **harnessed, harnessing.** ● See picture at **bridle.**

harp—A large musical instrument with a wooden frame shaped like a triangle, with a set of strings inside the frame. A person plucks the strings with the fingers of both hands to make music. Each string sounds a different note. **harp** (hahrp) *noun, plural* **harps.** ■ **harp on** or **harp upon:** To talk to someone about something for much too long: *Mother is always* harping on *my brother's dirty room.*

harpoon—A large barbed spear with a rope tied to one end that is used to catch and kill whales and other large fish. It can be thrown by hand or shot from a special gun. *Noun.* —To strike or kill with such a spear: *The sea captain* harpooned *the great, white whale. Verb.* **har|poon** (hahr′pūn′) *noun, plural* **harpoons;** *verb,* **harpooned, harpooning.**

harp

harpsichord—A stringed musical instrument that looks and is played like a piano but has a high, thin, clinking sound. It often has more than one keyboard. **harp|si|chord** (hahrp′sə kawrd) *noun, plural* **harpsichords.**

harrier—A medium-sized hound dog that looks like a large beagle and that has drooping ears, a short coat, and a long tail. Originally bred in France, these dogs are popular in England for hunting hares and rabbits. **har|ri|er** (har′ē ər) *noun, plural* **harriers.** ● See Word History at **harass.**

harsh—**1.** Rough and not pleasant to touch, taste, see, or hear: *The sound of fingernails scraping on a blackboard is* harsh *to the ears.* **2.** Having no feelings; cruel: *Punching and bullying is* harsh *treatment for anyone to put up with.* **harsh** (hahrsh) *adjective,* **harsher, harshest.** ● Synonyms: **drastic, extreme, severe,** for **2.**

harvest—**1.** The act of gathering a crop: *When the tomatoes are red, they are ready for* harvest.

a at	i if	oo look	ch chalk		a in ago
ā ape	ī idle	ou out	ng sing		e in happen
ah calm	o odd	u ugly	sh ship	ə =	i in capital
aw all	ō oats	ū rule	th think		o in occur
e end	oi oil	ur turn	th their		u in upon
ē easy			zh treasure		

harpoon

harpsichord

2. The crop that is gathered: *The wheat* harvest *was small this year. Noun.*
—To gather a crop: *The farmer hired extra workers to* harvest *the apples. Verb.*
har|vest (hahr′vist) *noun, plural* **harvests;** *verb,* **harvested, harvesting.**

Word History

Harvest comes from an old English word meaning "autumn." That word was related to a Latin word meaning "gather" or "pluck." Most crops are ready for gathering or plucking in the autumn. See Language Fact at **autumn.**

---

has—*See* **have.**
has (haz) *verb.*

hash—1. A dish made of chopped meat and potatoes cooked together. 2. A mess: *We tried to play a piano duet but made an awful* hash *of it. Noun.*
—To cut into tiny bits: hashed *potatoes. Verb.*
hash (hash) *noun, plural* **hashes;** *verb,* **hashed, hashing.**
■ **hash over:** To talk about; review: *We hashed over what happened at the basketball game.*
● Synonyms: **chop, mince,** for *verb.*

hasn't—The contraction of "has not."
has|n't (haz′ənt).

hassle—An argument; disagreement: *My brother and I had a* hassle *over who was going to take out the trash. Noun.*
—To constantly annoy or bother: *His parents were always* hassling *him about being neat. Verb.*
has|sle (has′əl) *noun, plural* **hassles;** *verb,* **hassled, hassling.**

haste—Quickness; speed: *In my* haste *to finish the work, I made too many errors.*
haste (hāst) *noun.*

hasten—To go quickly or cause to go quickly: *He fertilized the garden to* hasten *its growth.*
has|ten (hā′sən) *verb,* **hastened, hastening.**
● Synonyms: **hurry, rush, speed**
Antonyms: See Synonyms at **dawdle.**

hasty—1. Quick; speedy: *I wrote a* hasty *note to tell mom where I was going.* 2. Done too quickly and carelessly: *A* hasty *decision can lead to mistakes.*
hast|y (hās′tē) *adjective,* **hastier, hastiest.**
● Synonyms: **abrupt, sudden,** for 2.
Antonyms: **gradual, slow,** for 2.

hat—A covering for the head, usually having a brim and crown.
hat (hat) *noun, plural* **hats.**
■ **hold on to your hat:** Get ready for a surprise: *We got our test papers back today, and—hold on to your hat—I got an "A"!*
pass the hat: To take up a collection of money; get contributions: *We passed the hat around class to buy our teacher a present.*
talk through (one's) hat: To speak boldly without knowing what one is really talking about: *I hope he can prove what he says and is not just talking through his hat.*

hatch¹—1. To produce young from an egg: *The duck* hatched *ten baby ducklings.* 2. To come out of an egg: *After the ducklings* hatched, *their mother led them to the pond.*
hatch (hach) *verb,* **hatched, hatching.**

hatch²—1. An opening in a ship's deck, the side of an airplane, or the floor or roof of a building. 2. The cover for such an opening.
hatch (hach) *noun, plural* **hatches.**

hatchet—A small, short-handled ax made for use with one hand. A tomahawk is a kind of hatchet.
hatch|et (hach′it) *noun, plural* **hatchets.**
■ **bury the hatchet:** To stop fighting; make peace: *We both forgot what we had been arguing about, so we* buried the hatchet.

hate—To dislike very much: *I* hate *waiting in long lines.*
hate (hāt) *verb,* **hated, hating.**

Havana Brown

hatred—A very strong dislike: *She felt* hatred *toward the cruel boy.*
ha|tred (hā′trid) *noun, plural* **hatreds.**

haughty—Being too proud of oneself and looking down on others: *Now that he is a basketball star, he is too* haughty *to speak to his old friends.*
haugh|ty (haw′tē) *adjective,* **haughtier, haughtiest.**

haul—1. To pull or drag with much effort: *A team of horses* hauled *the wagon.* 2. To transport with a truck, cart, wagon, or the like: *The farmer* hauled *his load of vegetables to market. Verb.*
—1. The act of pulling or dragging with much effort: *He gave the large dog's leash a* haul *to teach the dog to walk beside him.* 2. The distance over which something is transported: *It's a short* haul *from here to the center of town.*
3. The amount caught or taken at one time: *The fish traps contained a record* haul *of lobsters. Noun.*
haul (hawl) *verb,* **hauled, hauling;** *noun, plural* **hauls.**
• A word that sounds the same is **hall.**

haunt—1. To visit often: *She* haunted *the mailbox, waiting for a letter.* 2. To stay or appear somewhere in the form of a ghost: *They say the old captain's ghost* haunts *the ship.*
haunt (hawnt) *verb,* **haunted, haunting.**

haunted—Visited by ghosts: *Strange lights were seen in the* haunted *house.*
haunt|ed (hawn′tid) *adjective.*

Havana Brown—A short-haired breed of house cat with large ears, dark green eyes, and dark brown fur that is smooth and glossy. This type of cat gets its name from the rich brown tobacco that is used to make Havana cigars.
Ha|van|a Brown (hə van′ə broun) *noun.*

have—1. To hold, possess, or own: *I* have *a surprise in this box. My mother* has *red hair. We* have *a new car.* 2. To take or get: Have *one of my cookies. I need to* have *a vacation.* 3. To experience: *She* has *a headache.* Have *a nice day!* 4. To be forced to do something: *I* have *to walk the dog.* 5. A helping verb that is used to show action that has already taken place: *I* have *read that book. They* have *gone home.*
have (hav) *verb,* **had, having.**
■ **have at:** To attack: *He was ready to* have at *the buzzing insect with a rolled-up newspaper.*
have to do with: To deal with; be connected with: *Arithmetic* has to do with *numbers. I refuse to* have *anything* to do with *such a silly plan.*
• A word that sounds the same is **halve.**

haven—A safe place: *We found a* haven *from the storm in a barn.*
ha|ven (hā′vən) *noun, plural* **havens.**
• Synonyms: **refuge, sanctuary**

haven't—The contraction of "have not."
have|n't (hav′ənt).

hawk—A large bird of prey with a sharp, curved beak, broad wings, powerful claws, and keen eyesight. Hawks hunt in the daytime for small animals and birds.
hawk (hawk) *noun, plural* **hawks.**

hawthorn—A shrub or small tree with sharp thorns, pink or white flowers, and red berries. It is the state flower of Missouri.
haw|thorn (haw′thawrn) *noun, plural* **hawthorns.**

hay—Grass, clover, or other plants that are cut down and partly dried for use as food for cattle and other livestock.
hay (hā) *noun, plural* **hays.**
■ **hit the hay:** To go to bed: *We must* hit the hay *early if we want to see the sunrise.*
make hay or **make hay while the sun shines:** To take full advantage of an opportunity: *In the hot summer weather, the ice cream store really* makes hay.
• A word that sounds the same is **hey.**

a at	i if	oo look	ch chalk		a in ago
ā ape	ī idle	ou out	ng sing		e in happen
ah calm	o odd	u ugly	sh ship	ə =	i in capital
aw all	ō oats	ū rule	th think		o in occur
e end	oi oil	ur turn	th their		u in upon
ē easy			zh treasure		

haystack—A pile of hay.
  hay|stack (hā′stak) *noun, plural* **haystacks.**
hazard—A source of risk or harm: *A fallen electrical wire in the road is a* hazard.
  haz|ard (haz′ərd) *noun, plural* **hazards.**
  • Synonyms: **danger, peril**
    Antonyms: **safety, security**

Word History

Hazard comes from an old French word for a very old game of dice that is no longer played. In this game, a throw of the dice could bring good luck or misfortune to a player. Today, **hazard** is used to mean a risk or danger.

---

haze—Small floating particles of dust, smoke, or water vapor that make it difficult to see clearly: Haze *from the forest fire hid the road from view.*
  haze (hāz) *noun, plural* **hazes.**
hazel—A shrub or small tree of the birch family that has edible, light-brown nuts. *Noun.*
  —A yellowish-brown color like that of hazel nuts: *He has brown hair and* hazel *eyes. Adjective.*
  ha|zel (hā′zəl) *noun, plural* **hazels;** *adjective.*
hazy—**1.** Foggy, misty, or smoky; dim: *Will the weather today be clear or* hazy? **2.** Confused; not clear: *She has only* hazy *memories of her early childhood.*
  ha|zy (hā′zē) *adjective,* **hazier, haziest.**

hawk

  • Synonyms: **obscure, vague,** for **2.**
    Antonyms: For **2,** see Synonyms at **clear.**
H-bomb—A nuclear bomb which produces enormous energy through the forcing together of hydrogen atoms, causing an explosion that is many times more powerful than that of the atom bomb. It is also called a hydrogen bomb.
  H-bomb (āch′bom) *noun, plural* **H-bombs.**
he—**1.** A word used for the man, boy, or male animal that has been named or described earlier in a sentence or statement: *My brother says that* he *is tired. When I call my dog,* he *comes.* **2.** Any person: *He who crosses this line first wins the race. Pronoun.*
  —A man, boy, or male animal: *I think my goldfish is a* he. *Noun.*
  he (hē) *pronoun; noun, plural* **hes.**

leaf

fruit

nut

tree

hazel

head—**1.** The top or upper part of the body containing the brain, eyes, nose, ears, and mouth. **2.** Anything that is round like the top part of the body: *a* head *of lettuce; the* head *of a pin.* **3.** The top, front, or end part of anything: *the* head *of a nail; the* head *of a line; the* head *of a table.* **4.** A person who rules or leads: *My dad is the* head *of that business.* **5.** One person or animal: *Admission to the show is fifty cents a* head. *The barn holds ten* head *of cattle. Noun.*
  —Leading; chief: *The* head *nurse has charge of the other nurses. Adjective.*
  —**1.** To lead or take charge of: *The shortest person will* head *the line. The chairperson* heads *the committee.* **2.** To go in a certain direction: *The birds* headed *south. Verb.*
  head (hed) *noun, plural* **heads;** *adjective; verb,* **headed, heading.**
  ■ **come to a head:** To reach a crisis: *The*

argument came to a head *when neither of us would admit that we were wrong.*

go to (one's) **head** or **turn** (one's) **head:** To make someone think too much of himself or herself: *Her success* went to *her head, and she ignored all her old friends.*

head over heels: Completely: *He is* head over heels *in love with his new car.*

lose (one's) **head:** To get so excited as to lose control: *I was so angry that I* lost *my head and shouted at him.*

make heads or tails of: To understand or figure out: *She speaks so fast that I can't* make heads or tails of *what she's saying.*

over (one's) **head:** Too difficult to understand: *I tried reading that book, but it was* over *my* head.

• Synonyms: **captain, chief, director,** for *noun* **4.**
Antonym: **follower,** for *noun* **4.**

headache—A pain in the head: *The loud music gave me a* headache.
head|ache (hed′āk′) *noun, plural* **headaches.**

headdress—A very fancy covering for the head: *A wedding veil is a type of* headdress.
head|dress (hed′dres′) *noun, plural* **headdresses.**

headfirst—With the head going first: *The rabbit dived* headfirst *into its burrow.*
head|first (hed′furst′) *adverb.*

heading—**1.** Something printed or written at the top of a page or at the beginning of a section of a book, paper, or topic. **2.** The address and date at the beginning of a letter.
head|ing (hed′ing) *noun, plural* **headings.**

headlight—A light mounted on the front of a car or other vehicle: *We saw the* headlight *of the train far down the track.*
head|light (hed′līt′) *noun, plural* **headlights.**

headline—A sentence or phrase that is usually printed in thick or big letters at the top of a newspaper or magazine article, telling what the article is about. *Noun.*
—To be the main performer in a show or movie; to be the main article in a newspaper or magazine: *A famous actor* headlined *the spy*

movie. The robbery headlined *the morning newspaper. Verb.*
head|line (hed′līn′) *noun, plural* **headlines;** *verb,* **headlined, headlining.**

headlong—**1.** With the head going first: *He made a* headlong *plunge into the pool. He caught the ball but ran* headlong *into the fence.* **2.** In a hasty, careless way: *Our* headlong *rush out the door nearly broke the nearby mirror. I rushed* headlong *into buying the wrong-sized clothes.*
head|long (hed′lawng) *adjective, adverb.*

head-on—With the front end or head going first: *a* head-on *crash; walking* head-on *into the wind.*
head-on (hed′on′ *or* hed′awn′) *adjective, adverb.*

headphone—A phone or radio receiver made to fit over the ears by a band worn over the head: *By wearing* headphones, *the pilot had both hands free to fly the airplane.*
head|phone (hed′fōn′) *noun, plural* **headphones.**

headquarters—A center of operations; the main office from which orders are issued: *The officer phoned* headquarters *for further instructions.*
head|quar|ters (hed′kwawr′terz) *noun, singular or plural.*

head start—**1.** An advantage that is given to someone at the beginning of a race or other activity: *If you give me a* head start, *I can beat you to the corner.* **2. Head Start:** An educational program for preschool children who come from poor or disadvantaged families. The program provides basic educational training in a classroom to those children whose familes are unable to provide it at home. It gives these children a chance to do well in school later on.
head start (hed stahrt) *noun, plural* **head starts.**

headstone—A special stone that is placed at the front end of a grave to identify the person who is buried there. It also lists the dates on which the person was born and died.
head|stone (hed′stōn′) *noun, plural* **headstones.**

headwaters—The place at which small streams flow together to form a river.
head|wa|ters (hed′waw′terz *or* hed′wot′ərz) *plural noun.*

headway—Progress; movement forward: *It was hard to make* headway *walking against the wind.*
head|way (hed′wā′) *noun.*

heal—To make or become well or healthy again: *This medicine should* heal *your rash. I have to wear this bandage until my cut* heals.
heal (hēl) *verb,* **healed, healing.**
• Words that sound the same are **heel** and **he'll.**

a at	i if	oo look	ch chalk		a in ago
ā ape	ī idle	ou out	ng sing		e in happen
ah calm	o odd	u ugly	sh ship	ə =	i in capital
aw all	ō oats	ū rule	th think		o in occur
e end	oi oil	ur turn	th their		u in upon
ē easy			zh treasure		

Word History:

Heal comes from an old English word meaning "whole." Wounds that cause breaks in the skin, for example, are said to be healed when the skin comes together again or is made whole. Broken bones also heal when they become whole. A person who has no injury or disease is said to be whole in mind and body, or completely **healthy.**

health—1. Freedom from illness or pain: *We hope you get over your flu and are back in* health *soon.* 2. The condition of one's body or mind: *My grandmother is old but still in good* health. **health** (helth) *noun.*

Word Power

If you are interested in studying health, here are some useful words to know. You can find these words in this dictionary.

AIDS	exercise	medication
alcoholism	fitness	mumps
antibiotic	flu	nutrition
cancer	German	polio
chicken pox	measles	tetanus
diet	immunization	tuberculosis
diphtheria	malaria	vaccine
epidemic	measles	vitamin

healthy—Well, strong, or showing good health: *a* healthy *man; a* healthy *appetite.* **health|y** (hel′thē) *adjective,* **healthier, healthiest.**
• See Word History at **heal.**

heap—A bunch of things thrown or lying in a pile; stack: *a heap of papers; a heap of wood. Noun.*
—1. To pile or stack up: *She heaped the rocks together.* 2. To fill with large amounts of: *He heaped the shopping cart with groceries. Verb.* **heap** (hēp) *noun, plural* **heaps;** *verb,* **heaped, heaping.**
• Synonyms: **mass**[1], **mound,** for *noun.*

hear—1. To receive sounds through the ear: *I hear music. Can you hear me?* 2. To listen to; pay attention to: *He refused to hear my excuse.* 3. To find out about: *I heard the news.* **hear** (hēr) *verb,* **heard** (hurd), **hearing.**
• A word that sounds the same is **here.**

heard—*See* **hear.** **heard** (hurd) *verb.*
• A word that sounds the same is **herd.**

hearing—1. The sense through which sound is received: *My* hearing *is so good that I can hear the clock ticking in the next room.* 2. The act of listening or of finding out about: Hearing *that you are sick makes me sad.* 3. A chance for someone to be listened to closely: *Please give us a* hearing *before you get angry.* **hear|ing** (hēr′ing) *noun, plural* **hearings.**

heart—1. The muscular organ inside the chest that pumps blood through the body. 2. The source of a person's feelings; soul: *I love you with all my* heart. *He has a kind* heart. 3. Courage; determination: *It took a great deal of* heart *to survive the disaster.* 4. The middle part of something; center: *the* heart *of the city; the* heart *of a house.* 5. A figure shaped like this (♡): *He made a valentine card with a big, red* heart *on it.* 6. A playing card that is marked with one or more red figures shaped like this (♡): *the king of* hearts; *the four of* hearts. **heart** (hahrt) *noun, plural* **hearts.**
■ **by heart:** From one's memory: *I do not need to look up your telephone number because I know it* by heart.
cross (one's) heart: To draw an imaginary cross or X over one's heart while swearing that one is telling the truth: *I believed him because he* crossed *his* heart *as he told me.*
take heart: To be encouraged; remain hopeful: Take heart, *we will find our way out of the forest soon!*
take to heart: 1. To be very troubled by: *She* took *our teasing* to heart. 2. To think about long and hard: *He took our offer* to heart.
wear (one's) heart on (one's) sleeve: To show one's feelings freely and openly: *We all know he likes her because he* wears *his* heart *on his* sleeve.
with all (one's) heart: 1. Sincerely: *I promise you* with all *my* heart. 2. With much pleasure; gladly: With all *my* heart *I would like to play with you.*
• Synonyms: **grit, pluck, spirit,** for 3.

heartbroken—Filled with much sadness; overwhelmed by grief: *She was* heartbroken *when her pet died.* **heart|bro|ken** (hahrt′brō′kən) *adjective.*

hearth—The floor of a fireplace, especially the front part. **hearth** (hahrth) *noun, plural* **hearths.**

hearty—1. Friendly or enthusiastic: *a* hearty *welcome; a round of* hearty *applause.* 2. Plentiful; satisfying: *Soup, a sandwich, and dessert make a* hearty *lunch.* **heart|y** (hahr′tē) *adjective,* **heartier, heartiest.**

heat—**1.** The state of being hot; warmth: *the* heat *from the oven; the* heat *of the sun.* **2.** High temperature: *summer's* heat. **3.** Strong feelings; intense anger or excitement: *She lost her temper in the* heat *of the argument. Noun.*
—To make or become warm or hot: *The furnace* heats *the house. The sand* heated *quickly under the sun. Verb.*
heat (hēt) *noun; verb,* **heated, heating.**

heather—An evergreen plant having tiny pink or purple flowers shaped like bells.
heath|er (he<u>th</u>′ər) *noun, plural* **heathers.**

heave—**1.** To lift with much effort; hoist: *The fishermen* heaved *their full nets into the boat.* **2.** To throw: *to* heave *a snowball.* **3.** To breathe in and out with force or effort: *to* heave *a sigh of relief.* **4.** To rise and fall: *The stormy sea* heaved *under the small boat.*
heave (hēv) *verb,* **heaved** or **hove, heaving.**
• Synonyms: **cast, hurl, toss,** for **2.**

heaven—**1.** In some religions, the place where God and angels live and where good people go when they die. **2. heavens:** The sky: *The* heavens *grew dark with storm clouds.*
heav|en (hev′ən) *noun, plural* **heavens.**

heavenly—**1.** Of or from God; divine: *The family asked for a* heavenly *blessing on their Thanksgiving feast.* **2.** Of or in the sky: *The sun and moon are* heavenly *bodies.* **3.** Wonderful; delightful: *What a* heavenly *day!*
heav|en|ly (hev′ən lē) *adjective,* **heavenlier, heavenliest.**
• Synonyms: **marvelous, sensational, terrific,** for **3.**

heavy—**1.** Having much weight; hard to lift, move, or carry: *These rocks make a* heavy *load.* **2.** Greater than average for its kind: *a* heavy *snowfall; a* heavy *eater;* heavy *breathing.* **3.** Thick: *a* heavy *coat; a* heavy *beard.*
heav|y (hev′ē) *adjective,* **heavier, heaviest.**

Hebrew—**1.** A member of one of the ancient tribes of Israel; Jew. **2.** The ancient language of the Jews. A modern form of Hebrew is spoken today in Israel. *Noun.*
—Jewish: *the* Hebrew *nation. Adjective.*
He|brew (hē′brū) *noun, plural* **Hebrews;** *adjective.*

a at	i if	oo look	ch chalk		a in ago
ā ape	ī idle	ou out	ng sing		e in happen
ah calm	o odd	u ugly	sh ship	ə =	i in capital
aw all	ō oats	ū rule	th think		o in occur
e end	oi oil	ur turn	<u>th</u> their		u in upon
ē easy			zh treasure		

heckle—To annoy or bother a public speaker or performer by making loud remarks or asking rude questions: *The audience* heckled *the bad actor.*
heck|le (hek′əl) *verb,* **heckled, heckling.**

hectic—Full of excitement or confusion; very busy: *Our day was very* hectic *because we rushed from one place to another.*
hec|tic (hek′tik) *adjective.*

he'd—The contraction of "he had" or "he would."
he'd (hēd).
• A word that sounds the same is **heed.**

hedge—A fence or boundary formed by a thick row of bushes or low trees. *Noun.*
—**1.** To line or surround with such a boundary: *The path was* hedged *with rose bushes.* **2.** To avoid giving a direct answer: *She did not want to go to the dance with him so she* hedged *her answer and said she would think about it. Verb.*
hedge (hej) *noun, plural* **hedges;** *verb,* **hedged, hedging.**

hedgehog—A small animal that looks somewhat like a porcupine. It has sharp spines on its back, a long, pointed snout, and small beadlike eyes that can see in the dark. Hedgehogs eat insects, roam around at night, and defend themselves from attack by rolling up into a ball.
hedge|hog (hej′hog′ or hej′hawg′) *noun, plural* **hedgehogs.**

hedgehog

heed—To pay attention to: *He failed to* heed *the warning thunder and got caught in the rain.*
heed (hēd) *verb,* **heeded, heeding.**
• A word that sounds the same is **he'd.**

heel—**1.** The back of the human foot, below the ankle and behind the arch. **2.** Anything that looks or is used like this part of the foot: *The rounded ends of bread loaves are called* heels. *I tore the* heel *of my stocking. Noun.*

helicopter

—To follow closely behind someone: *Her dog heels at her command. Verb.*
heel (hēl) *noun, plural* **heels;** *verb,* **heeled, heeling.**

■ **kick up** (one's) **heels:** To enjoy oneself: celebrate: *I work hard all week, but I kick up my* heels *on the weekends.*
take to (one's) **heels:** To flee; run away: *Surprised by the cat, the mouse* took to *its* heels.
● Words that sound the same are **heal** and **he'll.**

hefty—1. Very heavy or large: *That's a* hefty *suitcase. The workers want a* hefty *pay raise.* 2. Powerful; strong: *a* hefty *boxer.*
heft|y (hef′tē) *adjective,* **heftier, heftiest.**

heifer—A young cow, especially one that has not given birth to a calf.
heif|er (hef′ər) *noun, plural* **heifers.**

height—1. The distance from the bottom to the top of someone or something: *The boy's* height *is increasing as he gets older.* 2. A point or place far above the ground: *I am afraid of* heights. 3. The very top; peak: *the* height *of the summer season; the* height *of a career.*
height (hīt) *noun, plural* **heights.**

heir—A person who receives the money or belongings of someone who has died: *He made his grandson* heir *to his stamp collection.*
heir (ār) *noun, plural* **heirs.**
● A word that sounds the same is **air.**

heiress—A woman or girl who receives the money or belongings of someone who has died: *My aunt is the* heiress *of a great fortune.*
heir|ess (ār′is) *noun, plural* **heiresses.**

heirloom—Something of special value that is handed down from one generation to the next: *The antique locket she wore on her wedding day is a family* heirloom.
heir|loom (ār′lūm′) *noun, plural* **heirlooms.**

held—*See* **hold.**
held (held) *verb.*

helicopter—An aircraft that flies or stays in the air by means of the blades that rotate above it.
hel|i|cop|ter (hel′ə kop′tər) *noun, plural* **helicopters.**

helium—A very light gas that has no color or smell and will not burn. It is often used to inflate dirigibles and balloons. Helium is a chemical element.
he|li|um (hē′lē əm) *noun.*

hell—In some religions, the place where Satan or the Devil lives and where evil people are punished after they die.
hell (hel) *noun.*

he'll—The contraction of "he will" or "he shall."
he'll (hēl).
● Words that sound the same are **heal** and **heel.**

hello—A word of greeting: *"Hello, Mom," said the girl as her mother entered the room. We shout* hellos *to people we know.*
hel|lo (he lō′ *or* hə lō′) *interjection; noun, plural* **hellos.**

helm—The steering device on a ship, usually a lever or wheel that controls the rudder.
helm (helm) *noun, plural* **helms.**

helmet—A covering for the head that is made of a hard material such as metal or heavy plastic. Helmets are worn for protection: *We put on our* helmets *before going on our bicycle trip.*
hel|met (hel′mit) *noun, plural* **helmets.**

football helmet

astronaut's helmet

motorcycle helmet

combat helmet

helmet

help—**1.** To give or do something that is useful or needed; assist; aid: *We collected money to* help *the homeless. Please* help *me fasten my skates.* **2.** To stop; keep from: *Will an aspirin* help *your headache? The room was so dusty that I couldn't* help *sneezing. Verb.*
—**1.** Something useful or needed that is given or done: *Her directions were a big* help *to us in finding her house.* **2.** The act of giving or doing something that is useful or needed: *I could use some* help *with cleaning my room.* **3.** Someone or something that gives or does something that is useful or needed: *The store hired extra* help *during the busy season. The dictionary is a* help *in spelling difficult words. Noun.*
help (help) *verb,* **helped, helping;** *noun, plural* **helps.**
■ **help** (oneself): **1.** To use control: *I try not to lose my temper, but sometimes I can't* help *myself.* **2.** To take what one wants or needs: *We have plenty of extra copies, so please* help *yourself to some.*

helpful—Useful: *A flashlight would be* helpful *in this dark room.*
help|ful (help′fəl) *adjective.*

helping—A portion of food; serving: *She put a big* helping *of carrots on her plate.*
help|ing (hel′ping) *noun, plural* **helpings.**

helpless—Unable to protect or take care of oneself: *A fish is* helpless *out of water.*
help|less (help′lis) *adjective.*

hem—The border of a piece of cloth or clothing made by folding back the edge of the cloth and sewing it down: *The* hem *of her skirt touched the floor. Noun.*
—To provide with such a border: *The curtain was* hemmed *by hand. Verb.*
hem (hem) *noun, plural* **hems;** *verb,* **hemmed, hemming.**

hemisphere—One of two halves of the earth. The equator circles the middle of the earth and divides it into Northern and Southern hemispheres. A meridian or line passing vertically through the North and South poles divides the earth into Western and Eastern hemispheres.
hem|i|sphere (hem′ə sfēr) *noun, plural* **hemispheres.**
● See pictures at **equator** and **meridian.**

hemlock (definition 1)

hemlock—**1.** An evergreen tree that has short, flat needles, small cones, and reddish bark. It is very tall and found mostly on the West Coast of North America, where it is used for lumber. **2.** A poisonous plant that has thin, featherlike leaves and bunches of tiny white flowers.
hem|lock (hem′lok) *noun, plural* **hemlocks.**

hemp—The strong, tough fibers that are taken from the bark of a tall plant that grows in Asia. Hemp is used to make rope, string, and a rough type of cloth.
hemp (hemp) *noun, plural* **hemps.**

hen—**1.** An adult female chicken: *The* hen *laid an egg.* **2.** The female of other birds: *a turkey* hen.
hen (hen) *noun, plural* **hens.**

hence—**1.** So; as a result: *She spoke softly;* hence *I listened very carefully.* **2.** From now: *I will meet you an hour* hence.
hence (hens) *adverb.*
● Synonyms: **consequently, therefore, thus,** for **1.**

her—A word used for the girl, woman, or female animal that has been named or described earlier in a sentence or statement: *I like my girlfriend so much that I see* her *every day. Pronoun.*
—Belonging to or done by such a person or animal: *The girl lost* her *coat. Adjective.*
her (hur) *pronoun, adjective.*

herb—**1.** A plant whose roots, stems, leaves, or seeds are used in food, medicine, or perfume: *Parsley and mustard seeds are cooking* herbs. **2.** A flowering plant whose soft stems live for only one growing season. It usually grows back each year: *Roses are* herbs.
herb (urb *or* hurb) *noun, plural* **herbs.**

a at	**i** if	**oo** look	**ch** chalk		**a** in ago
ā ape	**ī** idle	**ou** out	**ng** sing		**e** in happen
ah calm	**o** odd	**u** ugly	**sh** ship	**ə** =	**i** in capital
aw all	**ō** oats	**ū** rule	**th** think		**o** in occur
e end	**oi** oil	**ur** turn	**th** their		**u** in upon
ē easy			**zh** treasure		

herbicide—A chemical used to kill plants, especially weeds.
her|bi|cide (hur′bə sīd *or* ur′bə sīd) *noun, plural* **herbicides.**

herbivore—An animal that eats only plants and grasses. Cattle, deer, and horses are herbivores.
her|bi|vore (hur′bə vawr) *noun, plural* **herbivores.**
● Antonym: **carnivore**

herbivorous—Eating grass or other plants. Deer are herbivorous animals.
her|biv|o|rous (hur biv′ər əs) *adjective.*
● Antonym: **carnivorous**

herd—A group of animals of one kind kept or living together: *a* herd *of elephants; a* herd *of cattle. Noun.*
—To come together or move as a group: *The children* herded *around their mother. The farmer* herded *the sheep into the pasture. Verb.*
herd (hurd) *noun, plural* **herds;** *verb,* **herded, herding.**
● A word that sounds the same is **heard.**

here—In, to, or at this place: *Come* here *and let me brush your hair. Adverb.*
—This place: *Drop the quarter in* here. *Noun.*
—1. A word that is used to call out one's location or presence in a roll call: *"Here!" said each student as his or her name was called.*
2. A word that is used to get someone's attention or to order someone or something to come: *"Here!" yelled the boy to his dog. Interjection.*
here (hēr) *adverb, noun, interjection.*
■ **neither here nor there:** Of no importance: *Which of the two toys you buy is* neither here nor there.
up to here: To one's limit of patience: *"I have had it* up to here *with your dog's barking!" shouted the woman.*
● A word that sounds the same is **hear.**

hereditary—Given or able to be given to a plant or living creature by its parents: *The chance of having twins is* hereditary.
he|red|i|tar|y (hə red′ə ter′ē) *adjective.*

heredity—The passing of characteristics that a person, an animal, or a plant has from one generation to another: *The color of my eyes is determined by* heredity.
he|red|i|ty (hə red′ə tē) *noun, plural* **heredities.**

here's—A contraction of "here is": *Here's the game you asked for.*
here's (hērz) *verb.*

heritage—Traditions, customs, values, or property that is handed down from one generation to another: *The right to live where one wants to is part of the American* heritage.
her|it|age (her′ə tij) *noun, plural* **heritages.**

Word History

Heritage comes from a Latin word meaning "to inherit." Countries and people inherit beliefs, ideas, practices, and the like from other countries and people, usually from ancestors. Thus they are said to have a **heritage** or a form of inheritance.

---

hermit—A person who lives alone and away from other people, especially for religious reasons.
her|mit (hur′mit) *noun, plural* **hermits.**

hermit crab—A crab with a soft body, that attaches itself to the empty shells of other sea animals such as snails for protection.
her|mit crab (hur′mit krab) *noun, plural* **hermit crabs.**

hero—1. A man or boy who is well thought of for his brave actions or noble character: *That man became our* hero *when he rescued our cat.*
2. The most important male person in a movie, play, story, or poem. 3. A small, long, hard roll of bread that is filled with sandwich meats, cheese, lettuce, and the like; a type of sandwich.
he|ro (hēr′ō) *noun, plural* **heroes.**

heroic—Brave or noble: *We read in the newspaper about the woman's* heroic *rescue of her drowning child.*
he|ro|ic (hē rō′ik) *adjective.*

heroin—A very dangerous drug made from morphine. Heroin is a narcotic that causes addiction.
her|o|in (her′ō in) *noun.*
● A word that sounds the same is **heroine.**

heroine—1. A woman or girl who is well thought of for her brave actions or noble character: *She became a* heroine *after she saved two people from a burning building.* 2. The most important female person in a movie, play, story, or poem.
her|o|ine (her′ō in) *noun, plural* **heroines.**
● A word that sounds the same is **heroin.**

heroism—An act or set of actions that is marked by bravery or courage, often done at risk to one's own life: *His* heroism *in battle won him a medal.*
her|o|ism (her′ō iz əm) *noun.*

heron—A wading bird with a long, pointed bill, a long neck, and long legs.
her|on (her′ən) *noun, plural* **herons.**

heron

herring—A small, bony fish with a narrow body. Herring live in salt water and are eaten as food.
her|ring (her′ing) *noun, plural* **herring** or **herrings.**

herring

hers—A word used to describe something that belongs to the woman, girl, or female animal that has been named or described earlier: *Do you see that girl? That glove is* hers.
hers (hurz) *pronoun.*

herself—**1.** A word used to identify or emphasize a woman or girl who does something to or by her own self: *She hurt* herself. *She* herself *cooked the meal.* **2.** A woman or girl's true nature: *After*

being sick, my aunt felt like herself *again.*
her|self (hur self′) *pronoun.*

he's—The contraction of ''he is'' or ''he has.''
he's (hēz).

hesitant—Not decided or certain; doubtful: *He is* hesitant *about taking music lessons.*
hes|i|tant (hez′ət ənt) *adjective.*

hesitate—**1.** To be slow to do or decide something because of doubt: *I* hesitated *to believe the story until I heard proof.* **2.** To pause before continuing to speak or act: *The boy* hesitated *for a moment, and then continued walking.*
hes|i|tate (hez′ə tāt′) *verb,* **hesitated, hesitating.**

hew—**1.** To chop down or cut with an ax or sword: *We* hewed *our way through the thick brush.* **2.** To cut and form into shape with a tool: *The workmen* hewed *the rough stones until they were smooth.*
hew (hyū) *verb,* **hewed, hewn** or **hewed, hewing.**
• A word that sounds the same is **hue.**

hewn—*See* **hew.**
hewn (hyūn) *verb.*

hexagon—A figure with six angles and six sides.
hex|a|gon (hek′sə gon) *noun, plural* **hexagons.**

hey—A word that is used to get someone's attention, to show surprise, or to begin a question: *She yelled, ''Hey! You are stepping on my foot!''*
hey (hā) *interjection.*
• A word that sounds the same is **hay.**

hi—A word of greeting; the short form of ''hello.''
hi (hī) *interjection.*
• A word that sounds the same is **high.**

hibernate—To live in a deep sleep during the winter: *Some bears and insects* hibernate.
hi|ber|nate (hī′bər nāt′) *verb,* **hibernated, hibernating.**

hibiscus—A tropical flowering plant, shrub, or tree that has large, bell-shaped blossoms in red, pink, or white. It is the state flower of Hawaii.
hi|bis|cus (hə bis′kəs *or* hī bis′kəs) *noun, plural* **hibiscus** or **hibiscuses.**

hiccup—**1.** A sudden, uncontrolled breathing movement caused by a muscle contraction that forces the lungs to pull in a rush of air for an instant, making a short, shrill noise. **2.** hiccups: The condition of having a series of such contractions: *I get the* hiccups *when I laugh too long and hard. Noun.*

a at	i if	oo look	ch chalk		a in ago
ā ape	ī idle	ou out	ng sing		e in happen
ah calm	o odd	u ugly	sh ship	ə =	i in capital
aw all	ō oats	ū rule	th think		o in occur
e end	oi oil	ur turn	th their		u in upon
ē easy			zh treasure		

—To have one or more such contractions: *I was bothered by his* hiccuping. *Verb.*

hic|cup (hik′up *or* hik′əp) *noun, plural* hiccups; *verb,* hiccuped, hiccuping.

hickory—A tall North American tree of the walnut family, that has hard, tough wood. The hickory produces edible nuts.

hick|o|ry (hik′ər ē) *noun, plural* hickories.

husk

nut

tree

leaf

hickory

hid—*See* hide.

hid (hid) *verb.*

hidden—Not able to be seen: *a hidden treasure. Adjective.*

—*See* hide. *Verb.*

hid|den (hid′ən) *adjective, verb.*

hide¹—1. To put something out of sight or to keep oneself out of sight: *She will* hide *the kitten in the box. I will* hide *behind the door.* 2. To keep secret: *The man* hid *his anger and kept on smiling.*

hide (hīd) *verb,* hid, hidden *or* hid, hiding.

hide²—An animal skin: *Indians' tepees are made from the* hides *of cattle.*

hide (hīd) *noun, plural* hides.

■ **neither hide nor hair:** Not even the smallest sign or clue: *He must have moved away because we have seen* neither hide nor hair *of him for three months.*

hideous—Extremely ugly, shocking, or terrible: *The puppet was made to look* hideous *to scare the children.*

hid|e|ous (hid′ē əs) *adjective.*

● Synonyms: See Synonyms at **ugly.**

Antonyms: **gorgeous, lovely, pretty**

hideout—A safe place used for hiding: *We used the abandoned cabin in the woods as a* hideout.

hide|out (hīd′out′) *noun, plural* hideouts.

hieroglyphic—A picture or written symbol used in ancient Egypt to represent a sound, a word, or an idea. Hieroglyphics were used because the Egyptians had no alphabet.

hi|er|o|glyph|ic (hī′ər ə glif′ik) *noun, plural* hieroglyphics.

hieroglyphic

hibiscus

high—1. Very tall: *That tree is* high. 2. Far above the ground: *Airplanes fly very* high. 3. Greater or more important than others in some way: *a* high *wind; a* high *court of law.* 4. Not low or deep; shrill: *a* high *voice; a* high *musical note. Adjective.*

—At the topmost position or to the greatest degree: *Hang the picture as* high *as you can. The price of food rose very* high. *Adverb.*

—1. A top level or figure: *Her score set a new*

high. *The temperature reached a* high *today of 92°*. **2.** The setting on a machine or vehicle that gives the most power or greatest speed: *The air conditioner ran on* high *that hot day*. *Noun*.
high (hī) *adjective*, **higher, highest;** *adverb; noun, plural* **highs.**

■ **high and dry:** Alone with no help or support: *Someone stole my bicycle and left me* high and dry *in the middle of the woods*.
high and low: Everywhere: *I searched* high and low *for my lost necklace*.

● A word that sounds the same is **hi.**

highland—Land that has many mountains or hills.
high|land (hī′lənd) *noun, plural* **highlands.**

highlight—The best or most important part: *The magician's performance was the* highlight *of the show*.
high|light (hī′līt′) *noun, plural* **highlights.**

Highness—A title used in speaking of or to a member of a royal family: *Always address the princess as ''Your* Highness.*''*
High|ness (hī′nis) *noun, plural* **Highnesses.**

high-rise—A very tall building with many stories: *a* high-rise *apartment building*.
high-rise (hī′rīz′) *noun, plural* **high-rises.**

high school—A school attended by children who have completed elementary school or junior high school. It contains grades 9 or 10 through 12.
high school (hī skūl) *noun, plural* **high schools.**

high seas—The open ocean far from any one country and therefore freely used by all; international waters.
high seas (hī sēz) *plural noun*.

highway—A public road that handles much traffic. Speeds are often faster or higher on highways than on streets.
high|way (hī′wā) *noun, plural* **highways.**

hijack—To take control of goods or a vehicle by force: *to* hijack *an airplane*.
hi|jack (hī′jak′) *verb*, **hijacked, hijacking.**

● This word is also spelled **highjack.**

hike—To walk a long way, especially through woods or in other difficult country: *We* hiked *along the mountain trail to the cave*.

—A long, pleasurable walk: *Let's go for a* hike *on the beach*. *Noun*.
hike (hīk) *verb*, **hiked, hiking;** *noun, plural* **hikes.**

hilarious—Extremely funny: *Her joke was so* hilarious *that I laughed uncontrollably*.
hi|lar|i|ous (hi lār′ē əs) *adjective*.

● Synonyms: **comical, humorous**
Antonyms: **earnest, serious, solemn**

hill—**1.** A portion of land that is higher than the rest of the earth's surface but smaller than a mountain. It is usually rounded and gently sloping. **2.** Any small pile or mound: *an ant hill*.
hill (hil) *noun, plural* **hills.**

hillside—The slope of a hill, between the top and the bottom: *to ski down the* hillside.
hill|side (hil′sīd′) *noun, plural* **hillsides.**

hilly—Having several hills in an area; uneven: *The ground was* hilly *and hard to walk on*.
hill|y (hil′ē) *adjective*, **hillier, hilliest.**

hilt—The handle of a dagger or sword.
hilt (hilt) *noun, plural* **hilts.**

him—A word used for the boy, man, or male animal that has been named or described earlier in a sentence or statement: *My uncle wants us to make* him *some popcorn*.
him (him *or* im) *pronoun*.

● A word that sounds the same is **hymn.**

Himalayan—A long-haired breed of house cat with a short neck hidden in fur, stubby legs, a short, puffy tail, and a long, thick coat that stands out all over the body like a powder puff. Himalayans are related to Siamese cats and have similar dark patches of color on their ears, face, and paws.
Him|a|lay|an (him′ə lā′ən) *noun, plural* **Himalayans.**

a at	i if	oo look	ch chalk		a in ago
ā ape	ī idle	ou out	ng sing		e in happen
ah calm	o odd	u ugly	sh ship	ə =	i in capital
aw all	ō oats	ū rule	th think		o in occur
e end	oi oil	ur turn	<u>th</u> their		u in upon
ē easy			zh treasure		

Himalayan

himself—1. A word used to identify or emphasize a man or boy who does something to or by his own self: *He drove* himself *home. He* himself *built the house.* 2. A man or boy's true nature: *He felt more like* himself *in jeans rather than in a suit.*
him|self (him self' *or* im self') *pronoun.*

hind—At the rear or back: *When the bear stood up on its* hind *feet, it was taller than a man.*
hind (hīnd) *adjective*, **hinder, hindmost** or **hindermost.**

hinder—To block or hold back the progress of; obstruct: *The snow from the avalanche* hindered *the rescuers.*
hin|der (hin'dər) *verb*, **hindered, hindering.**
• Synonyms: **hamper**[1], **handicap**
Antonym: **help**

Word History

Hinder comes from an old English word meaning "behind." People who are hindered are forced to go so slowly that they are far behind in reaching the place or thing they are headed toward.

hindrance—A person or thing that prevents or slows action or progress; obstacle: *The loud music was a* hindrance *to the students' concentration.*
hin|drance (hin'drəns) *noun, plural* **hindrances.**
• Synonyms: **disadvantage, drawback**

Hindu—1. A native of India. 2. A person whose religion is Hinduism.
Hin|du (hin'dū) *noun, plural* **Hindus.**

Hinduism—The major religion of India. The worship of many gods and goddesses, and a social system with many levels of classes are basic beliefs of this religion.
Hin|du|ism (hin'dū iz əm) *noun.*

hinge—A connecting part between two surfaces that lets one part turn or swing on the other: *a door* hinge. *Noun.*
—1. To attach by or provide with such a connecting part: *Father* hinged *my toy box lid so I could open and close it more easily.* 2. To depend on completely: *Our travel plans* hinged *upon good weather. Verb.*
hinge (hinj) *noun, plural* **hinges;** *verb*, **hinged, hinging.**

hint—A slight suggestion; clue: *The teacher gave us a* hint *to help us solve the math problem. Noun.*
—To give a slight suggestion: *He admired my radio so much that I thought he was* hinting *to borrow it. Verb.*
hint (hint) *noun, plural* **hints;** *verb*, **hinted, hinting.**

hip—The area of the body between the waist and the leg, where the upper part of the leg joins the body.
hip (hip) *noun, plural* **hips.**
■ **shoot from the hip:** To act or speak without thought; behave recklessly: *She* shot from the hip *and said the first thing that crossed her mind.*

hippopotamus—A large, plant-eating animal that lives in and near the rivers and lakes of Africa. It has a wide mouth, short legs, and thick, almost hairless skin.
hip|po|pot|a|mus (hip'ə pot'ə məs) *noun, plural* **hippopotamuses.**

Word History

Hippopotamus comes from two Greek words meaning "river horse." The fact that the large four-legged hippopotamus spends much of its time in the water probably led to its name.

hire—To pay or use the services of someone or something; employ: *to* hire *a babysitter; to* hire *a taxi. Verb.*
—The act of offering employment or other services for pay: *The farmer had his horse for* hire. *Noun.*
hire (hīr) *verb*, **hired, hiring;** *noun.*

his—Belonging to or done by the man, boy, or other male referred to before: *He lost* his *coat.*
his (hiz) *adjective; pronoun.*

Hispanic—A native of Spain or of a Spanish-speaking country or a person living in the United States who is descended from a Spanish-speaking family. *Noun.*
—Of or relating to the people, speech, or culture of these groups. *The guitar and the drum are important in* Hispanic *music. Adjective.*
His|pan|ic (his pan'ik) *noun, plural* **Hispanics;** *adjective.*

hiss—1. To make a long, sharp "ssss" sound: *When the kettle* hissed, *we knew the water was boiling.* 2. To make such a sound to show one's dislike: *Those behind us* hissed *at the performer's jokes. Verb.*
—A long, sharp, "ssss" sound: *the* hiss *of a snake.*

hiss (his) *verb,* **hissed, hissing;** *noun, plural* **hisses.**

historian—A person who studies or writes about important past events.
his|to|ri|an (his **tawr′**ē ən) *noun, plural* **historians.**

historic—An event important enough to be noted in history; history-making: *When the astronauts went to the moon, it was an* historic *occasion.*
his|tor|ic (his **tawr′**ik) *adjective.*

history—A record or study of important past events, often with an explanation of their causes: *the* history *of England.*
his|to|ry (**his′**tər ē) *noun, plural* **histories.**

hit—**1.** To strike someone or something with force: *He* hit *the soccer ball with his foot.* **2.** To reach and come against; collide with: *The snowball* hit *the barn.* **3.** To arrive at; reach: *Turn left when you* hit *the next stop sign.* **4.** To have a strong impact on: *Their cruel comments* hit *him hard. Verb.*
—**1.** A stroke; blow: *the* hit *on the arm.* **2.** A great success: *Did you get tickets for the new theater* hit? **3.** A batting of the baseball that allows the player to safely reach base. *Noun.*
hit (hit) *verb,* **hit, hitting;** *noun, plural* **hits.**
■ **hit it off:** To agree and be friendly with; get along easily with: *The teacher and the pupils* hit if off *right away.*
● Synonyms: **slug**², **smack, whack,** for *noun* **1.**

hitch—**1.** To attach or tie by a rope or hook: *She* hitched *a rope from her bicycle to her little brother's wagon.* **2.** To tug or pull up in a quick, jerky way: *He bent to* hitch *up his socks. Verb.*
—**1.** A hook or catch that fastens: *a trailer* hitch. **2.** A rough or jerky movement: *The lame pony walked with a* hitch *in its step.* **3.** An unexpected problem: *Lack of drinking water became the* hitch *in our plans to camp on the island. Noun.*
hitch (hich) *verb,* **hitched, hitching;** *noun, plural* **hitches.**

hive—**1.** The box or house that bees live in. **2.** All the bees living in the same box or house.
hive (hīv) *noun, plural* **hives.**
● See picture at **beehive.**

hives—An allergic skin condition that is marked by an itchy rash.
hives (hīvz) *noun.*

hoard—To save or hide away for future use: *In autumn, squirrels* hoard *nuts for the winter. Verb.*
—That which is stored away for future use: *The squirrel's* hoard *of nuts will provide him with food all winter. Noun.*
hoard (hawrd) *verb,* **hoarded, hoarding;** *noun, plural* **hoards.**
● Synonyms: **collect, keep, store,** for *verb.*

hoarse—**1.** Having a rough or harsh sound: *the beagle's* hoarse *bark.* **2.** Having a rough or harsh voice: *The cheerleaders' voices were* hoarse *from all their yelling.*
hoarse (hawrs) *adjective,* **hoarser, hoarsest.**
● A word that sounds the same is **horse.**

hoax—An act meant to trick someone, especially a false story presented as being true: *When I found out that the scary voices in the old house were really my brother's* hoax, *I was angry.*
hoax (hōks) *noun, plural* **hoaxes.**

hobble—**1.** To walk in an unsteady way; limp: *Her bruised ankle caused her to* hobble *for several days.* **2.** To cause to walk unsteadily: *The cowboy tied a rope around his horse's front legs to* hobble *it. Verb.*
—Any device, such as a rope, used to make a horse or other animal walk unsteadily. *Noun.*
hob|ble (**hob′**əl) *verb,* **hobbled, hobbling;** *noun, plural* **hobbles.**

hobby—An activity that a person enjoys doing in his or her spare time: *Her favorite* hobby *is building model cars.*
hob|by (**hob′**ē) *noun, plural* **hobbies.**

hockey—A game played on ice or a field by two teams of players, six each in ice hockey and eleven each in field hockey. Using curved sticks, the players try to hit a rubber disk or a ball into their opponent's goal.
hock|ey (**hok′**ē) *noun.*

hoe—A tool used to break up the soil or cut weeds. It has a long handle with a thin, flat blade at the end. *Noun.*
—To work using such a tool: *He* hoes *the garden often to get rid of weeds. Verb.*
hoe (hō) *noun, plural* **hoes;** *verb,* **hoed, hoeing.**

hog—**1.** A full-grown pig. **2.** A selfish or unclean person. *Noun.*
—To take more of something than is one's fair share: *She* hogged *all the cake, and we got none. Verb.*
hog (hog *or* hawg) *noun, plural* **hogs;** *verb,* **hogged, hogging.**

a at	i if	oo look	ch chalk		⎡ a in ago
ā ape	ī idle	ou out	ng sing		e in happen
ah calm	o odd	u ugly	sh ship	ə =	i in capital
aw all	ō oats	ū rule	th think		o in occur
e end	oi oil	ur turn	<u>th</u> their		⎣ u in upon
ē easy			zh treasure		

hog (noun, definition 1)

■ **go the whole hog:** To do something to the limit: *He decided to* go the whole hog *and buy a shirt and tie to go with his new suit.*
high on the hog: In a lavish or luxurious way: *With her inheritance, she bought a new car and lived* high on the hog.

hoist—To lift; raise: *The ship's crew* hoisted *the sails and set out to sea. Verb.*
—**1.** The act of lifting or raising: *The trainer gave her a* hoist *onto the horse's back.* **2.** A device used to raise something: *The workers used a* hoist *to lift the bricks to the top of the building. Noun.*
hoist (hoist) *verb,* **hoisted, hoisting;** *noun, plural* **hoists.**

hold[1]—**1.** To grasp and keep in one's hands or arms: *Please* hold *my glasses while I take a quick swim.* **2.** To maintain in a certain place or position: *to* hold *the ladder steady.* **3.** To contain: *Her car will* hold *five passengers.* **4.** To carry on; conduct: *They usually* hold *their meetings in the town hall.* **5.** To have and keep: *to* hold *an office; to* hold *him to his promise.* **6.** To believe or think to be: *I* hold *that all people are created equal. Verb.*
—**1.** The act of grasping: *He did not let go of the dock until she had a firm* hold *on the oars.* **2.** Something that can be grasped: *The tree had enough* holds *to make climbing it easy. Noun.*
hold (hōld) *verb,* **held, holding;** *noun, plural* **holds.**

■ **no holds barred:** Without anything to limit or restrain: *After their formal soccer match, the teams played a wild game,* no holds barred, *just for fun.*

hold[2]—The storage place for cargo on a ship or airplane.
hold (hōld) *noun, plural* **holds.**

holdup—**1.** An armed robbery.   **2.** A delay or interruption: *The fire drill caused a* holdup *in serving lunch.*
hold|up (hōld′up′) *noun, plural* **holdups.**

hole—**1.** An open or hollow place in something; gap: *The squirrel stored nuts in the* hole *in the tree.* **2.** An opening through something: *the* hole *in my pants.* **3.** The small opening in the green of a golf course into which the golf ball is hit.
hole (hōl) *noun, plural* **holes.**
● A word that sounds the same is **whole.**

holiday—A day or days when people honor or celebrate a certain event: *In the United States, Thanksgiving is a* holiday.
hol|i|day (hol′ə dā′) *noun, plural* **holidays.**

hollow—**1.** Having only empty space within: *A drinking straw is* hollow.   **2.** Having an inward-curving shape, like a bowl or cup; sunken. **3.** Sounding deep and dull, as an echo: *He could hear the* hollow *sound of the distant drum. Adjective.*
—**1.** An empty place; hole: *Rain water collected in the* hollows *of the road.* **2.** A low area between hills; valley: *The best mushrooms grew in the* hollow *between the two steep hills. Noun.*
—To dig out an empty space: *After raking, the boy* hollowed *out a cozy place to sit in the pile of leaves. Verb.*
hol|low (hol′ō) *adjective,* **hollower, hollowest;** *noun, plural* **hollows;** *verb,* **hollowed, hollowing.**

holly—An evergreen tree whose pointed leaves and red berries are often used as decorations at Christmas.
hol|ly (hol′ē) *noun, plural* **hollies.**

fruit

leaf

tree

holly

hollyhock—A tall garden plant with clusters of brightly colored flowers.
hol|ly|hock (hol′ē hok) *noun, plural* **hollyhocks.**

holocaust—1. Complete destruction by fire, especially of living things.   2. the Holocaust: The mass murder of the Jews and other Europeans by the German Nazis during World War II.
hol|o|caust (hol′ə kawst) *noun, plural* **holocausts.**

hologram—A kind of photograph made by using lasers. Shining light through it makes a picture appear in three dimensions, like a real object.
hol|o|gram (hol′ə gram) *noun, plural* **holograms.**

holster—A case for carrying a pistol, often made of leather and worn on a belt.
hol|ster (hōl′stər) *noun, plural* **holsters.**

Word History

Holster may come from a word related to an old English word meaning "concealment." When a pistol is placed in a holster, the holster conceals it from view.

holy—1. Belonging to or coming from God; sacred: *Both Christians and Jews believe that the Old Testament is a* holy *book.*   2. Very religious: *A saint is a* holy *man or woman.*
ho|ly (hō′lē) *adjective,* **holier, holiest.**
• A word that sounds the same is **wholly.**
• Synonyms: **devout, pious,** for **2.**

home—1. The place where a person lives: *Her* home *is the brown house on the corner.*   2. A group of people living together; family: *She comes from a large* home.   3. The place that a person comes from or was born: *His* home *is Ohio.*   4. In baseball and certain other sports, the goal or place where one is safe.   5. A place or institution providing care for people who are unable to take care of themselves: *a nursing* home. *Noun.*
—1. At or toward the place one lives: *They came* home *last week.*   2. To the point or place aimed at: *The blow struck* home. *Adverb.*
home (hōm) *noun, plural* **homes;** *adverb.*

a at	i if	oo look	ch chalk		a in ago
ā ape	ī idle	ou out	ng sing		e in happen
ah calm	o odd	u ugly	sh ship	ə =	i in capital
aw all	ō oats	ū rule	th think		o in occur
e end	oi oil	ur turn	th their		u in upon
ē easy			zh treasure		

■ **home free:** Sure of success: *When she saw her high score, she knew she was* home free.
• Synonyms: **dwelling, residence,** for *noun* **1.**

homeland—A person's country of birth or where one has lived for a long time: *Although he lived in France, England was his* homeland.
home|land (hōm′land′) *noun, plural* **homelands.**

homely—1. Plain in appearance; lacking beauty: *The troll in the fairy tale was* homely.   2. Being simple, plain, or basic; not fancy: homely *food.*
home|ly (hōm′lē) *adjective,* **homelier, homeliest.**

homemade—Made in one's home or by one's hands: *Mother's* homemade *cookies.*
home|made (hōm′mād′) *adjective.*

homemaker—A person who takes care of a household.
home|mak|er (hōm′mā′kər) *noun, plural* **homemakers.**

homeroom—The room where pupils of the same class meet at the beginning of the school day to take attendance and hear announcements.
home|room (hōm′rūm′ *or* hōm′room′) *noun, plural* **homerooms.**

homesick—To feel sad or ill because of being away from one's home or family: *After he stopped feeling* homesick, *he had fun.*
home|sick (hōm′sik′) *adjective.*

homespun—Cloth that has been made at home instead of in a factory.
home|spun (hōm′spun′) *noun.*

homeward—Moving toward one's home: *At dusk, they turned* homeward.
home|ward (hōm′wərd) *adverb.*

homework—School lessons that are assigned to a student to be done at home.
home|work (hom′wurk′) *noun.*

homicide—The killing of one person by another, either accidentally or on purpose: *In mystery stories, there is usually at least one* homicide.
hom|i|cide (hom′ə sīd) *noun, plural* **homicides.**

hominy—A food made from dried kernels of white corn whose outer coverings have been removed, ground up, and boiled.
hom|i|ny (hom′ə nē) *noun.*

homogenized milk—Milk in which the fat is spread equally throughout, not separated in the form of cream.
ho|mog|en|ized milk (hō moj′ə nīzd milk), *noun.*

homograph—A word that has the same spelling as another word but a different meaning. "Lead" (to show the way) and "lead" (a soft, gray metal) are homographs.

hom|o|graph (hom′ə graf) *noun, plural* **homographs.**

homonym—A word that has the same sound and spelling as another word but a different meaning. "Duck" (a bird with webbed feet) and "duck" (to bend down quickly) are homonyms.
hom|o|nym (hom′ə nim) *noun, plural* **homonyms.**

Language Fact

Some people use **homonym** to mean words that are pronounced the same but spelled differently. Some people use **homonym** to mean words that are spelled the same but pronounced differently. But there are other names for such words: **homophone** and **homograph.** So the most precise meaning for homonyms is words that are spelled the same, and pronounced the same, but that mean different things, like the bark of a dog and the bark of a tree.

---

homophone—A word that has the same sound as another word but a different meaning. "Sew" and "so" are homophones.
hom|o|phone (hom′ə fon) *noun, plural* **homophones.**

honest—Truthful; fair; not given to cheating or stealing: *an* honest *answer; an* honest *man.*
hon|est (on′ist) *adjective.*

honesty—The quality of being truthful and fair: Honesty *is the best policy.*
hon|es|ty (on′ə stē) *noun.*

honey—1. A sweet, golden liquid that bees make from the nectar of flowers and then store in their honeycomb. 2. Someone or something that is very sweet; sweetheart; dear; darling.
hon|ey (hun′ē) *noun, plural* **honeys.**

honey bee—Any of various bees that make and store honey.
hon|ey bee (hun′ē bē) *noun, plural* **honey bees.**

honeycomb—1. A wax structure with six-sided parts that bees make to store honey. 2. Anything that has many parts like a bee's honeycomb: *There was a* honeycomb *of hallways in the basement of the library. Noun.*
—To form with many parts like a bee's honeycomb: *Hidden tunnels* honeycombed *the old fort. Verb.*
hon|ey|comb (hun′ē kōm′) *noun, plural* **honeycombs;** *verb,* **honeycombed, honeycombing.**

honeydew—A kind of melon with a smooth green skin and green flesh.
hon|ey|dew (hun′ē dū *or* hun′ē dyū) *noun, plural* **honeydews.**
• See picture at **melon.**

honeymoon—A vacation that a newly married couple spends together. *Noun.*
—To take or go on a honeymoon: *The couple* honeymooned *on the island for a week. Verb.*
hon|ey|moon (hun′ē mūn′) *noun, plural* **honeymoons;** *verb,* **honeymooned, honeymooning.**

honeysuckle—A shrub or climbing plant with fragrant, trumpet-shaped flowers.
hon|ey|suck|le (hun′ē suk′əl) *noun, plural* **honeysuckles.**

honeysuckle

honk—1. The sound made by a goose. 2. A sound like that of a goose made by a motor vehicle: *the* honk *of the car's horn. Noun.*
—To make the sound of or like a goose: *The geese* honked *as they flew over the pond. Verb.*
honk (hongk) *noun, plural* **honks;** *verb,* **honked, honking.**

honor—1. An understanding of what is fair and honest: *As a person of* honor, *she treated all of us fairly.* 2. A good reputation: *His* honor *was at stake because he had lied.* 3. A source of respect or pride: *It was an* honor *to be elected.* 4. **honors:** A special award for excellent work: *The twins graduated with* honors. *Noun.*
—To show admiration; respect: *The retiring principal was* honored *with a gold watch. Verb.*
hon|or (on′ər) *noun, plural* **honors;** *verb,* **honored, honoring.**
■ **do the honors:** To perform the duties of a host or hostess: *Dad did the honors at the party.*
in honor of: As a mark of respect. *We had a party* in honor of *our story contest winners.*

hood—1. A covering for the head and neck, sometimes attached to a coat or jacket. 2. A metal engine cover, especially on an automobile. 3. Anything that is used to cover or shield; veil: *The* hood *over the buggy protects the baby from sun and rain.*
hood (hood) *noun, plural* **hoods.**

-hood—A suffix that means "the condition" or "a group." Childhood is the condition of being a child. A neighborhood is a group of neighbors.

Word Power

You can understand the meanings of many words that end in **-hood,** if you add a meaning of the suffix to the meaning of the rest of the word.
motherhood: the condition of being a mother
knighthood: a group of knights

---

hoodlum—A tough, often brutal, person who causes trouble and breaks laws; gangster.
hood|lum (hūd′ləm) *noun, plural* **hoodlums.**

hoof—The tough, hard covering on the feet of horses, cattle, pigs, and some other animals.
hoof (hoof *or* hūf) *noun, plural* **hoofs** or **hooves.**

hook—1. A curved piece of metal, wood, or other hard substance used for holding, fastening, pulling, or catching something: *a clothes* hook; *a dress* hook; *a boat* hook; *a fish* hook. 2. In some sports, a curving throw or hit of the ball: *The bowler knocked down nine pins with his* hook. *Noun.*
—1. To fasten with a hook: *Mother hooked the apron around her waist.* 2. To catch; to hold in a curve: *to* hook *a fish; square dancers hooking arms.* 3. To throw or hit a ball so that it curves sharply. *Verb.*
hook (hook) *noun, plural* **hooks;** *verb,* **hooked, hooking.**

■ **hook, line, and sinker:** Completely; totally: *Her story sounded strange, but he bought it* hook, line, and sinker.
off the hook: Freed of responsibility; no longer in trouble: *She is* off the hook *because her sister admitted breaking the vase.*

hoop—A circular band made of stiff material such as metal or plastic. Hoops may be used as children's toys or to hold objects together, such as barrels.
hoop (hoop *or* hūp) *noun, plural* **hoops.**

hoot—1. The cry of an owl. 2. A shout of disapproval: *The mean wrestler left the ring amid the* hoots *of the crowd.* 3. A small amount; not worth considering: *That advice is not worth a* hoot. *Noun.*
—1. To make the sound of an owl. 2. To call out loudly in disapproval: *The audience* hooted *when it was announced that the band would not perform. Verb.*
hoot (hūt) *noun, plural* **hoots;** *verb,* **hooted, hooting.**

hooves—*See* **hoof.**
hooves (hoovz *or* hūvz) *noun, plural.*

hop—1. To jump on one foot: *Can you* hop *ten times on your right foot?* 2. To move in short leaps with both or all feet at the same time: *Rabbits and kangaroos* hop. *Verb.*
—1. A short, brisk jump: *The frog reached the lily pad in one* hop. 2. A dance. *Noun.*
hop (hop) *verb,* **hopped, hopping;** *noun, plural* **hops.**

hope—1. A feeling that something one wishes for will happen; a chance; possibility: *There is* hope *that the sun will come out in time for the picnic.* 2. Something that is wished for: *World peace is the* hope *of many people. Noun.*
—To look forward to something, expecting it to happen: *I* hope *to go to the beach often this summer. Verb.*
hope (hōp) *noun, plural* **hopes;** *verb,* **hoped, hoping.**

hopeful—Feeling, showing, or giving hope: *The doctors are* hopeful *that the disease will be cured soon.*
hope|ful (hōp′fəl) *adjective.*

hopeless—Feeling or having no hope: *It is* hopeless *to try to find your friend in this crowd.*
hope|less (hōp′lis) *adjective.*

hopscotch—A child's game that is played on numbered squares drawn on the ground. Players toss a stone or other object into one of the squares and then hop from one square to another to regain the object.
hop|scotch (hop′skoch′) *noun.*

horizon—1. The line marking where the sky seems to meet the earth or sea: *the sun setting on the* horizon. 2. The farthest reach of one's thinking, knowledge, and experience: *Going to college can broaden one's* horizons.
ho|ri|zon (hə rī′zən) *noun, plural* **horizons.**

a at	i if	oo look	ch chalk		a in ago
ā ape	ī idle	ou out	ng sing		e in happen
ah calm	o odd	u ugly	sh ship	ə =	i in capital
aw all	ō oats	ū rule	th think		o in occur
e end	oi oil	ur turn	th their		u in upon
ē easy			zh treasure		

horizontal—Parallel to the ground; level: *The top of a table is* horizontal.
hor|i|zon|tal (hawr′ə **zon**′təl or hor′ə **zon**′təl) *adjective.*

horn—1. One of the two hard, pointed, and often curved growths on the heads of animals such as sheep, cattle, and goats. 2. Any of the various brass musical instruments that are played by blowing into the narrow end. 3. A device on a vehicle that makes a warning sound. 4. Something that is shaped like a horn: *a shoe horn; the horn of a saddle.*
horn (hawrn) *noun, plural* **horns.**
■ **blow** (one's) **own horn:** To boast; brag: *That player has not stopped* blowing *his* own horn *since he scored the winning basket in the championship game.*
lock horns: To fight; quarrel: *The two candidates for mayor* locked horns *over the issue of the school budget.*

horned lizard—A harmless reptile with a broad, flat body, a short tail, and many spines that is found in the southwestern United States. This animal is also called a **horned toad.**
horned lizard (hawrnd **liz**′ərd) *noun, plural* **horned lizards.**

horned lizard

hornet—A large wasp that gives a painful sting.
hor|net (hawr′nit) *noun, plural* **hornets.**

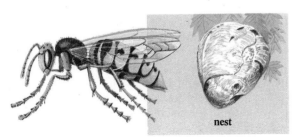
nest

hornet

horrible—1. Filling one with fear: *The horrible fire destroyed the farm.* 2. Very unpleasant: *Our camping trip was canceled because of the horrible weather.*
hor|ri|ble (hawr′ə bəl) *adjective.*
● Synonyms: **awful, dreadful, terrible,** for **2.**

horrid—1. Causing shock or disgust; frightful: *a horrid crime; a horrid disease.* 2. Very unpleasant: *Our meal at the new restaurant was horrid.*
hor|rid (hawr′id) *adjective.*
● Synonyms: **foul, offensive,** for **2.**

horrify—1. To cause to feel horror or fear: *He was horrified by the sight of blood.* 2. To cause a strong feeling of shock: *I knew that my messy room would horrify my mother.*
hor|ri|fy (hawr′ə fī) *verb,* **horrified, horrifying.**

horror—1. A strong feeling of surprise and fear; terror; dread: *The townspeople ran in horror when the volcano erupted.* 2. A very strong feeling of shock or disgust: *The lady looked at her ruined carpet with horror.* 3. Someone or something that is terrible or disgusting: *Everyone says that my room is a horror. Noun.*
—Causing fear or terror: *a horror movie. Adjective.*
hor|ror (hawr′ər) *noun, plural* **horrors;** *adjective.*

horse—1. A large, hoofed animal that has four legs, a tail, and mane. People ride horses and use them for pulling loads. 2. A piece of gymnastic equipment with a heavy, padded body used to swing on or jump over. 3. A simple frame with two sets of V-shaped legs, used as a work table or to support something: *a saw horse.*
horse (hawrs) *noun, plural* **horses.**
■ **from the horse's mouth:** From the person most informed or in charge: *The reporter said she got the story about the governor's election right from the horse's mouth.*
hold (one's) **horses:** To slow down; be patient: *The waitress told the eager children to hold their horses.*
horse around: To fool around; play roughly: *The students liked to horse around instead of studying at home after school.*
● A word that sounds the same is **hoarse.**

horseback—On the back of a horse: *The child rode horseback while his father walked. Adverb.*
horse|back (hawrs′bak′) *adverb.*

horseplay—Fun that is rough and noisy: *A lot of horseplay takes place in the locker room after a winning game.*
horse|play (hawrs′plā′) *noun.*

Word History

Horsepower is a unit of measurement first used in Scotland in the 1700's. Before steam engines were invented, heavy work was done by horses. When people wanted to know how strong the new steam engines were, they had to compare the work done by an engine to the amount of work that could be done by an average horse.

horsepower—A measuring unit for rating the power of an engine. One unit is equal to the power it takes to lift 550 pounds (250 kilograms) a distance of one foot (0.3 meter) in one second. **horse|pow|er** (hawrs′pou′ər) *noun.* Abbreviation: h.p.

horseshoe—1. A flat, U-shaped protective metal plate that is nailed to a horse's hoof. 2. **horseshoes**—A game in which players toss U-shaped objects at a fixed post in the ground. **horse|shoe** (hawrs′shū *or* hawrsh′shū) *noun, plural* **horseshoes.**

horseshoe crab—A sea animal with a large horseshoe-shaped shell and a long, spiny tail; king crab. **horse|shoe crab** (hawrs′shū krab) *noun, plural* **horseshoe crabs.**

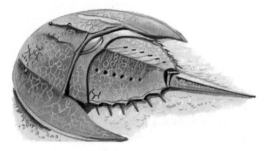

horseshoe crab

hose—1. A long, flexible tube usually made of rubber, plastic, or canvas, used to carry liquids or air. 2. Socks and stockings. *Noun.*
—To water or wash with a long, flexible tube: Hose *off the car before you apply polish. Verb.* **hose** (hōz) *noun, plural* **hoses;** *verb,* **hosed, hosing.**

a at	i if	oo look	ch chalk		⎡ a in ago
ā ape	ī idle	ou out	ng sing		e in happen
ah calm	o odd	u ugly	sh ship	ə =	i in capital
aw all	ō oats	ū rule	th think		o in occur
e end	oi oil	ur turn	th their		⎣ u in upon
ē easy			zh treasure		

hospitable—Welcoming guests or strangers with kindness; friendly: *The motel manager was very* hospitable. **hos|pi|ta|ble** (hos′pi tə bəl *or* hos **pit′**ə bəl) *adjective.*

hospital—A place where sick or injured people can be cared for by doctors and nurses. **hos|pi|tal** (hos′pi təl) *noun, plural* **hospitals.**

Word History

Hospital comes from a Latin word meaning "guest." The first hospitals provided rooms not just for sick people, but for travelers and the poor as well. Later, hospitals came to be places especially for sick people. The same Latin word also turned into our word **hotel.**

hospitality—A welcoming treatment of guests or strangers; friendliness: *We thanked the hostess for her* hospitality *when we left the party.* **hos|pi|tal|i|ty** (hos′pə **tal′**ə tē) *noun, plural* **hospitalities.**

hospitalize—To place someone in a hospital for medical care: *The doctor thought it best to* hospitalize *the sick child.* **hos|pi|tal|ize** (hos′pi tə līz) *verb,* **hospitalized, hospitalizing.**

host[1]—1. A man who entertains guests: *He was a very polite* host *at his birthday party.* **2.** A plant or animal that has a parasite: *Dogs and cats are* hosts *for fleas.* **host** (hōst) *noun, plural* **hosts.**

host[2]—A great number: *A* host *of tiny fish swam around our feet in the water.* **host** (hōst) *noun, plural* **hosts.**

Host[3]—The bread or wafer used during the ceremony of Holy Communion in certain Christian churches. **Host** (hōst) *noun, plural* **Hosts.**

hostage—A person who is held captive until certain demands are met: *The* hostage *was set free when the ransom money was paid.* **hos|tage** (hos′tij) *noun, plural* **hostages.**

hostel—A place of lodging for young people on biking or hiking trips; inn. **hos|tel** (hos′təl) *noun, plural* **hostels.**
• A word that sounds the same is **hostile.**

hostess—1. A woman who welcomes and entertains guests. 2. A woman who welcomes customers to a restaurant or other establishment: *The* hostess *led us to our table.* **host|ess** (hōs′tis) *noun, plural* **hostesses.**

hostile—Not friendly; not favorable: *a hostile nation; a hostile remark.*
hos|tile (hos′təl) *adjective.*
- A word that sounds the same is **hostel.**

hostility—1. The fact or condition of being unfriendly: *His hostility makes me uncomfortable.* **2. hostilities:** fighting; battle.
hos|til|i|ty (ho stil′ə tē) *noun, plural* **hostilities.**

hot—1. Having much heat; very warm: *a hot oven; the hottest day of summer.* **2.** Burning taste; spicy: Hot *foods such as chili or tacos make you thirsty.* **3.** Filled with rage; angry: *a hot temper.* **4.** New; fresh: *a news item hot off the press; a hot tip.* **5.** Very close: *a hot chase.*
hot (hot) *adjective,* **hotter, hottest.**

hot dog—A long, thin sausage usually served on a bun; frankfurter.
hot dog (hot dawg) *noun, plural* **hot dogs.**

hotel—A building that provides rooms for sleeping and usually food and other services to paying guests.
ho|tel (hō tel′) *noun, plural* **hotels.**
- See Word History at **hospital.**

hothouse—A heated, glass-enclosed building that is used for raising plants; greenhouse.
hot|house (hot′hous′) *noun, plural* **hothouses.**

hound—Any of several kinds of dogs that are bred for hunting. Hounds were often named for the animal they were first trained to hunt, such as the wolfhound and foxhound. *Noun.*
—To ask or pursue constantly: *The fan hounded the movie star for her autograph. Verb.*
hound (hound) *noun, plural* **hounds;** *verb,* **hounded, hounding.**
- Synonyms: **badger, harass, pester, plague,** for *verb.*

hour—1. A unit of time that contains 60 minutes: *A day has 24 hours.* **2.** A certain time of day: *At what hour are they expecting us?* **3.** A specific time for something: *Working hours are nine to five.*
hour (our) *noun, plural* **hours.** Abbreviation: **hr.**
- A word that sounds the same is **our.**

hourglass—An instrument that measures one hour of time. It takes one hour for sand to pass from one clear glass bulb in the hourglass through a narrow neck to another bulb.
hour|glass (our′glas′) *noun, plural* **hourglasses.**

hourly—1. Occurring every hour: *an hourly news bulletin.* **2.** By the hour: *My job pays an hourly wage. Adjective.*
—Each hour: *The nurse took my temperature hourly. Adverb.*
hour|ly (our′lē) *adjective, adverb.*

house—1. A building that people live in; home. **2.** All the people in a house; family; household: *The whole house was sick with the flu.* **3.** A building used for a special function: *an opera house; a house of worship.* **4. House:** A group of people whose job is to make laws; legislature: *The House of Representatives and the Senate make up the Congress of the United States.* **5.** The audience in a theater: *The house was sold out for opening night. Noun.*
—To provide a place for living or storage: *The animal shelter houses many homeless dogs and cats. Verb.*
house (hous for *noun;* houz for *verb*) *noun, plural* **houses;** *verb,* **housed, housing.**
- **bring down the house:** To receive loud and enthusiastic applause: *Night after night, the new play brought down the house.*
on the house: Given by the owner of a business; free: *That restaurant is always crowded because it offers dessert on the house.*

houseboat—A boat that has a small house built on the deck. A houseboat can be used during vacations or as a year-round home.
house|boat (house′bōt′) *noun, plural* **houseboats.**

household—All of the people who share a living space, such as a house or apartment. *Noun.*
—Of or having to do with a house and the people who share it: household *expenses. Adjective.*
house|hold (hous′hōld) *noun, plural* **households;** *adjective.*

housekeeper—A person who is paid to perform household duties, such as cleaning and cooking.
house|keep|er (hous′kē′pər) *noun, plural* **housekeepers.**

hourglass

House of Representatives—One of the two lawmaking bodies of the United States Congress. **House of Rep|re|sent|a|tives** (hous ov rep′ri zen′tə tivz) *noun.*

housewife—A woman whose job is to take care of her home and family. A housewife often does tasks such as cleaning, washing, and cooking. **house|wife** (hous′wīf′) *noun, plural* **housewives.**

hover—**1.** To hang in the air, staying near one place: *The helicopter* hovered *overhead.* **2.** To stay close to a person or thing; wait close by: *The mother hen* hovered *around her chicks.* **hov|er** (huv′ər *or* hov′ər) *verb,* **hovered, hovering.**

how—**1.** In what manner or way: How *do you spell "Mississippi"?* **2.** To what amount or degree: How *did you like the party?* **3.** In what condition: How *is your mother today?* **4.** For what reason; why: How *did he fail the test?* **how** (hou) *adverb.*

however—But; nevertheless: *She did not win;* however, *she finished second. Conjunction.*
—**1.** In whatever manner or way: However *did you find the lost mitten?* **2.** To whatever amount or degree: However *bad the weather, he delivers the newspapers every day. Adverb.* **how|ev|er** (hou ev′ər) *conjunction, adverb.*

howl—To make a long, loud, and very sad sound: *Our dog* howls *when we leave him alone. Verb.*
—Such a long, loud, sad sound: *The* howls *of the wolves were heard through the forest. Noun.* **howl** (houl) *verb,* **howled, howling;** *noun, plural* **howls.**

hr.—The abbreviation for **hour.**

hub—**1.** The center part of a wheel. **2.** A central point of activity or interest. **hub** (hub) *noun, plural* **hubs.**

hubcap—A round metal piece that covers the hub of an automobile wheel. **hub|cap** (hub′kap′) *noun, plural* **hubcaps.**

huckleberry—A small, dark-blue berry that looks and tastes very much like a blueberry. It grows on small bushes. **huck|le|ber|ry** (huk′əl ber′ē) *noun, plural* **huckleberries.**

huddle—To crowd closely together: *We* huddled *under the umbrella during the rainstorm. Verb.*
—A crowd of people or animals pressed closely together: *a huddle of sheep. Noun.* **hud|dle** (hud′əl) *verb,* **huddled, huddling;** *noun, plural* **huddles.**

hue[1]—A color or shade of a color: *The rose had a bright red hue.* **hue** (hyū) *noun, plural* **hues.**
● A word that sounds the same is **hew.**

hue[2]—A loud outcry: *There was a great* hue *when the batter hit a home run.* **hue** (hyū) *noun, plural* **hues.**
● A word that sounds the same is **hew.**

huff—An angry mood: *When the boy lost the game of checkers, he left in a* huff. *Noun.*
—To breathe heavily; puff: *She was* huffing *after she ran up three flights of stairs. Verb.* **huff** (huf) *noun, plural* **huffs;** *verb,* **huffed, huffing.**

hug—**1.** To place one's arms tightly around a person or thing to comfort or to show love or affection: *He* hugged *his sister when she came home from her vacation.* **2.** To stay close to; hold close to: *She* hugged *the shoreline when the water farther out got too cold. Verb.*
—A close embrace with the arms: *His father gave him a* hug. *Noun.* **hug** (hug) *verb,* **hugged, hugging;** *noun, plural* **hugs.**

huge—Enormous; very large: *a huge skyscraper.* **huge** (hyūj) *adjective,* **huger, hugest.**
● Synonyms: See Synonyms at **big.**
Antonyms: See Synonyms at **small.**

hull[1]—**1.** The outer covering of a seed or nut. The shell of a nut is its hull. **2.** The small, green leaves at the stem of some fruits, such as the strawberry. *Noun.*
—To remove the outer covering from a seed, nut, or piece of fruit: *Please help me* hull *these berries for Mother's pie. Verb.* **hull** (hul) *noun, plural* **hulls;** *verb,* **hulled, hulling.**

huckleberry

a at	i if	oo look	ch chalk		a in ago
ā ape	ī idle	ou out	ng sing		e in happen
ah calm	o odd	u ugly	sh ship	ə =	i in capital
aw all	ō oats	ū rule	th think		o in occur
e end	oi oil	ur turn	<u>th</u> their		u in upon
ē easy			zh treasure		

hull²—The bottom and sides of a boat or ship.
hull (hul) *noun, plural* **hulls.**

hum—**1.** To make a soft, continuous sound like
that made when saying the letter ''m'' with your
lips together: *The engine of the car* hummed *as
we drove along.* **2.** To sing with the lips closed:
She hummed *along with the music.* **3.** To be
busy; full of activity: *The gymnasium was*
humming *with preparations as everyone worked
to decorate for the party. Verb.*
—A soft, continuous sound like that of the letter
''m'': *the* hum *of a hair dryer. Noun.*
hum (hum) *verb,* **hummed, humming;** *noun,
plural* **hums.**

human—Of or having to do with people: *The*
human *brain can imagine many wonderful things.
Adjective.*
—A person: *It may be possible for* humans *to
live in outer space someday. Noun.*
hu|man (hyū′mən) *adjective; noun, plural*
humans.

humane—Full of compassion; kind: *It was*
humane *of you to feed the stray cat.*
hu|mane (hyū mān′) *adjective.*

humanity—**1.** All people everywhere: *Humanity
may someday live in a world without hunger.*
2. Compassion; kindness: *Her* humanity *made her
glad to help out at the nursing home.*
hu|man|i|ty (hyū man′ə tē) *noun.*

humble—**1.** Of low or unimportant status: *He had
a* humble *little apartment.* **2.** Not overly proud;
modest: *Even after she was elected class president,
she remained a* humble *person. Adjective.*
—To make a person feel low or unimportant: *He
was* humbled *by his poor performance on the test.
Verb.*
hum|ble (hum′bəl) *adjective,* **humbler,
humblest;** *verb,* **humbled, humbling.**
● Synonyms: **embarrass, humiliate, shame,** for
verb.
Antonym: **honor,** for *verb.*

Word History

Humble comes from a Latin word meaning
''low.'' That word came from another Latin
word meaning ''earth.'' A humble building stays
near the earth because even its top is low. A
humble person does not feel above others. To be
humbled is to be lowered in pride.

---

humid—Moist; damp: *a* humid *climate.*
hu|mid (hyū′mid) *adjective.*

humidity—Moisture in the air: *The* humidity
made it feel damp outside.
hu|mid|i|ty (hyū mid′ə tē) *noun.*

humiliate—To cause someone to feel disgraced:
He felt humiliated *when his team lost the game
because of his error.*
hu|mil|i|ate (hyū mil′ē āt) *verb,* **humiliated,
humiliating.**
● Synonyms: **embarrass, humble, shame**
Antonym: **honor**

hummingbird—A tiny, brightly colored bird
with a long, narrow bill. Its name comes from
the sound its wings make as they beat rapidly
back and forth.
hum|ming|bird (hum′ing burd′) *noun, plural*
hummingbirds.

hummingbird

humor—**1.** Something funny that makes a person
laugh or smile: *Some people do not see any*
humor *in elephant jokes.* **2.** The ability to see
things in a funny way: *a good sense of* humor.
3. The way a person feels; mood: *in a fine*
humor. *Noun.*
—To allow another person to have what he or
she wants: *The parents* humored *the little girl
and checked under the bed for monsters. Verb.*
hu|mor (hyū′mər) *noun, plural* **humors;** *verb,*
humored, humoring.
● Synonyms: For *verb,* see Synonyms at **coddle.**

humorous—Amusing; funny: *She laughed at the*
humorous *comic strip.*
hu|mor|ous (hyū′mər əs) *adjective.*
● Synonyms: **comical, hilarious**
Antonyms: **earnest, serious, solemn**

hump—A rounded lump; bulge: *The African
camel has one* hump.
hump (hump) *noun, plural* **humps.**

humus—The dark part of the soil that is formed by the decay of rotted leaves and other dead plants. Humus contains many important foods that help new plants grow.
hu|mus (hyū′məs) *noun.*

hunch—A guess or unexplained feeling about something: *She had a* hunch *that the teacher would give a surprise quiz. Noun.*
—To pull up one's shoulders and bend over as in a hump: *He was* hunched *over his desk working on math homework. Verb.*
hunch (hunch) *noun, plural* **hunches;** *verb,* **hunched, hunching.**

hunchback—Someone with a badly curved back.
hunch|back (hunch′ bak′) *noun, plural* **hunchbacks.**

hundred—Ten times ten; one more than 99; 100.
hun|dred (hun′drəd) *adjective; noun, plural* **hundreds.**

hundredth—1. Next after the ninety-ninth. 2. One of one hundred equal parts.
hun|dredth (hun′drədth) *adjective; noun, plural* **hundredths.**

hung—*See* **hang.**
hung (hung) *verb.*

hunger—1. A strong desire for food: *Because of his* hunger, *he ate very quickly.* 2. A lack of food: *Many children in the world suffer from* hunger. 3. A strong desire for something; longing: *The boy had a* hunger *to learn everything he could about dinosaurs. Noun.*
—To have a strong desire for something; yearn: *She* hungered *for the shiny new bicycle. Verb.*
hun|ger (hun′gər) *noun, plural* **hungers;** *verb,* **hungered, hungering.**

hungry—1. Needing or wanting food: *He was so* hungry *when he came home from school that he ate two sandwiches.* 2. Feeling a strong need for something: *The lonely puppy was* hungry *for affection.*
hun|gry (hung′grē) *adjective,* **hungrier, hungriest.**

hunt—1. To chase for the purpose of capturing or killing: *to* hunt *a bear.* 2. To search for; look hard for: *She* hunted *for her fishing pole. Verb.*

—1. A chase for the purpose of capturing or killing: *a fox* hunt. 2. A search for something: *an Easter egg* hunt. *Noun.*
hunt (hunt) *verb,* **hunted, hunting;** *noun, plural* **hunts.**

hurdle—1. A barrier, such as a fence, that people or horses jump over during a race. 2. **hurdles:** A race in which runners have to leap over low fences while running toward the finish line. 3. A difficult task or problem: *Finding a job was the first* hurdle *of the summer. Noun.*
—To leap or jump over: *The horse* hurdled *the stone wall. Verb.*
hur|dle (hur′dəl) *noun, plural* **hurdles;** *verb,* **hurdled, hurdling.**

hurl—To throw; heave: *We* hurled *snowballs at the side of the barn.*
hurl (hurl) *verb,* **hurled, hurling.**
• Synonyms: **cast, toss**

hurrah or **hurray**—A shout showing happiness or approval: *The crowd shouted, ''Hurrah!'' as the fireworks exploded.*
hur|rah or hur|ray (hə rah′ *or* hə rā′) *interjection; noun, plural* **hurrahs** or **hurrays.**

hurricane—A powerful storm with very high winds and a lot of rain. Hurricanes occur along both coasts of the United States and in the Gulf of Mexico.
hur|ri|cane (hur′ə kān) *noun, plural* **hurricanes.**

hurried—Quick; hasty: *We ate a* hurried *breakfast so we could get to school on time.*
hur|ried (hur′ēd) *adjective.*

hurry—To move quickly; rush: *She had to* hurry *to catch up with her friends. Verb.*
—1. A movement or action done quickly: *He dropped his books in his* hurry *to catch the school bus.* 2. The desire to move or act quickly: *We were in a* hurry *to finish our work before the movie started. Noun.*
hur|ry (hur′ē) *verb,* **hurried, hurrying;** *noun, plural* **hurries.**
• Synonyms: **hasten, speed,** for *verb.*
Antonyms: For *verb,* see Synonyms at **dawdle.**

hurt—1. To feel pain; *Does your broken hand still* hurt? 2. To cause pain; injure: *He* hurt *his ankle while roller-skating.* 3. To do damage or harm: *Luckily, the frost did not* hurt *the vegetables in the garden. Verb.*
—A pain or injury: *She had a* hurt *on her elbow. Noun.*
hurt (hurt) *verb,* **hurt, hurting;** *noun, plural* **hurts.**

a at	i if	oo look	ch chalk		a in ago
ā ape	ī idle	ou out	ng sing		e in happen
ah calm	o odd	u ugly	sh ship	ə =	i in capital
aw all	ō oats	ū rule	th think		o in occur
e end	oi oil	ur turn	<u>th</u> their		u in upon
ē easy			zh treasure		

hurtle—To move or drive with great force; rush: *The car hurtled along at 60 miles per hour.*
hur|tle (her′təl) *verb*, **hurtled, hurtling.**

husband—A married man.
hus|band (huz′bənd) *noun, plural* **husbands.**

hush—A silence; quiet: *A hush fell over the audience when the announcer came on stage. Noun.*
—To make or become quiet: *A glance from their mother hushed the children. The students in the cafeteria hushed when the principal made an announcement. Verb.*
—Be silent: *"Hush!" said Dad. "Do not talk in church!" Interjection.*
hush (hush) *noun, plural* **hushes;** *verb,* **hushed, hushing;** *interjection.*

husk—The dry, leafy, outer covering of some fruits and vegetables. The green leaves that cover an ear of corn are its husk. *Noun.*
—To remove the outer covering of something: *to husk an ear of corn. Verb.*
husk (husk) *noun, plural* **husks;** *verb,* **husked, husking.**

husky[1]—1. Hoarse and dry in sound: *Her voice was husky from cheering during the whole football game.* **2.** Big and powerful: *The furniture movers were husky men.*
husk|y (hus′kē) *adjective,* **huskier, huskiest.**

husky[2]—A strong, medium-sized dog with a thick outer coat. Originally bred in Alaska, these dogs are used by the Eskimos to pull sleds.
hus|ky (hus′kē) *noun, plural* **huskies.**

hustle—To hurry; be in a rush: *He had to hustle to finish mowing the lawn before it got dark.*
hus|tle (hus′əl) *verb,* **hustled, hustling.**

hut—A small, roughly built shelter; shack: *The survivors of the shipwreck built a hut with the scraps of wood that washed up on the island.*
hut (hut) *noun, plural* **huts.**

hyacinth—A sweet-smelling spring flower that has bunches of bell-shaped flowers around a thick green stem.
hy|a|cinth (hī′ə sinth) *noun, plural* **hyacinths.**

hybrid—A plant or animal that is a mix between two different species or groups. A mule is a hybrid because it is a mix between a female horse and a male donkey. *Noun.*
—Produced or made from a mix between two different kinds of things: hybrid *corn. Adjective.*
hy|brid (hī′brid) *noun, plural* **hybrids;** *adjective.*

hydrant—A covered pipe that sticks out of the ground along the curb and is connected to an underground water supply. Fire fighters can attach a hose to the hydrant to get water to put out fires.
hy|drant (hī′drənt) *noun, plural* **hydrants.**
• A hydrant is also called a **fire hydrant** or a **fire plug.**

hydro-—A prefix meaning "of or having to do with water." Hydrogen is a gas that combines with oxygen to form water.

Word Power

You can understand the meanings of many words that begin in **hydro-,** if you add the meaning of the prefix to the meaning of the rest of the word.
   hydroairplane: an airplane that can take off or land on water
   hydroelectricity: electricity made from water power

---

hydrogen—A very light, easily burnable gas with no color or taste. Hydrogen combines with oxygen to produce water.
hy|dro|gen (hī′drə jən) *noun.*

hyena—An animal of Africa and Asia that is closely related to dogs and wolves. Hyenas have a loud bark or howl that sounds almost like laughter.
hy|e|na (hī ē′nə) *noun, plural* **hyenas.**

hyena

hygiene—The things done in order to keep the body clean and healthy: *It is good hygiene to wash your hands before eating.*
hy|giene (hī′jēn) *noun.*

hymn—A song of praise, especially one sung to honor God: *We sang a hymn in church.*
hymn (him) *noun, plural* **hymns.**
• A word that sounds the same is **him.**

hymnal—A book of hymns; hymnbook.
hym|nal (him′nəl) *noun, plural* **hymnals.**

hymnbook—A book containing a collection of hymns for use in religious services; hymnal.
hymn|book (him′book′) *noun, plural* **hymnbooks**

hyper—A prefix meaning ''over; overly; above; more than normal; excessive; excessively.'' A person who is hyperactive is more active than is normal.

Word Power

You can understand the meanings of many words that begin with **hyper-,** if you add a meaning of the prefix to the meaning of the rest of the word.

hypercritical: too critical.

hypersensitive: overly sensitive.

hypersuspicious: excessively suspicious.

---

hyphen—A mark that looks like this -, used to join together two or more words or two or more parts of a word. Jack-in-the-box has three hyphens.
hy|phen (hī′fən) *noun, plural* **hyphens.**

hyphenate—To place a hyphen or hyphens in a word or between two words.
hy|phen|ate (hī′fə nāt′) *verb,* **hyphenated, hyphenating.**

hypnotism—The act of putting a person into a sleeplike state in which he or she can still see and hear.
hyp|no|tism (hip′nə tiz əm) *noun.*

hypnotist—A person who hypnotizes.
hyp|no|tist (hip′nə tist) *noun, plural* **hypnotists.**

hypnotize—To put a person in a sleeplike condition. A person who is hypnotized is very likely to do what he or she is told to do.
hyp|no|tize (hip′nə tīz) *verb,* **hypnotized, hypnotizing.**

hypochondriac—A person who imagines that he or she is sick when he or she is not.
hy|po|chon|dri|ac (hī′pə kon′drē ak) *noun, plural* **hypochondriacs.**

hypocrisy—The act of pretending to be what one is not, especially if one claims to be very good or religious but does not act that way: *To say that you believe something when you really don't is hypocrisy.*
hy|poc|ri|sy (hi pok′rə sē) *noun, plural* **hypocrisies.**

hypocrite—A person who pretends to be something that he or she is not; one who is insincere: *He felt like a hypocrite when he told his aunt he really liked the ugly, orange sweater she had given him.*
hyp|o|crite (hip′ə krit) *noun, plural* **hypocrites.**

hypodermic—Injected or used to inject under the skin: *a hypodermic needle.*
hy|po|der|mic (hī′pə dur′mik) *adjective.*

hypodermic needle—A hollow needle used to inject medicine under the skin.
hy|po|der|mic nee|dle (hī′pə der′mik ne′dəl) *noun, plural* **hypodermic needles.**

hypodermic syringe—A small syringe fitted with a hollow needle. It is used to inject medicine under the skin.
hy|po|der|mic sy|ringe (hī pə der′mik sə rinj′) *noun, plural* **hypodermic syringes.**

hypotenuse—The longest side of a triangle that has a 90-degree angle.
hy|pot|e|nuse (hī pot′ə nūs) *noun, plural* **hypotenuses.**

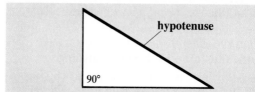

hypotenuse

hysteria—A wild outburst of uncontrollable panic, fear, or other strong emotion: *mob* hysteria.
hys|te|ri|a (his ter′ē ə) *noun.*

hysterical—1. Showing an extreme lack of control; unable to stop laughing or crying or showing some other strong emotion: *The* hysterical *child would not stop crying.* **2.** Very funny: *I thought the movie was* hysterical.
hys|ter|i|cal (his ter′ə kəl) *adjective.*

hysterics—A fit of uncontrolled crying or laughing or, often, both at the same time.
hys|ter|ics (his ter′iks) *plural noun.*

a at	i if	oo look	ch chalk		a in ago
ā ape	ī idle	ou out	ng sing		e in happen
ah calm	o odd	u ugly	sh ship	ə =	i in capital
aw all	ō oats	ū rule	th think		o in occur
e end	oi oil	ur turn	th their		u in upon
ē easy			zh treasure		

About 1,900 years ago, the Romans gave the capital **I** its present form. The small letter **i** was first used about 1,700 years ago. It reached its present form about 500 years ago.

About 5,000 years ago, the ancient Egyptians used a symbol of a hand. The letters I and J both came from this symbol.

About 3,500 years ago, people in the Middle East made a simpler symbol.

About 3,000 years ago, other people in the Middle East used this form. They called it *yod*, their word for "hand."

About 2,600 years ago, the Greeks gave the letter this form. They called it *iota*.

I or **i**—**1.** The ninth letter of the alphabet: *There are two i's in "imagine."* **2.** The Roman numeral for 1.
I, i (ī) *noun, plural* **I's** *or* **Is, i's** *or* **is**.

I—A word used for the person who is speaking or writing: *I am a good artist.*
I (ī) *pronoun.*
● Words that sound the same are **aye** and **eye**.

ibex—A wild goat that lives in the mountains of Europe, Asia, and Africa. The male ibex has very large horns that curve backward.
i|bex (ī′beks) *noun, plural* **ibexes** (i′bek sez) *or* **ibex**.

Ibizan hound—A medium-sized hunting dog that looks a lot like a greyhound. Originally bred on an island near Spain, these dogs hunt by sight and smell.
I|bi|zan hound (ē bē′zən hound) *noun, plural* **Ibizan hounds**.

-ible—A suffix that means "able to": If something is edible, then it is able to be eaten.

Word Power

You can understand the meanings of many words that end in **-ible**, if you add a meaning of the suffix to the meaning of the rest of the word.
divisible: able to be divided
permissible: able to be permitted

---

ice—**1.** Water that has been made solid by freezing. **2.** A frozen dessert made of crushed ice flavored with fruit juice or syrup. *Noun.*
—**1.** To make or keep cold with ice; chill: *We should* ice *the soda now so it will be cold later when we drink it.* **2.** To cover or turn into ice; freeze: *The rain-covered streets* iced *over when the temperature dropped.* **3.** To decorate with

Ibizan hound

frosting: *The cake was* iced *with pink frosting for my birthday. Verb.*
ice (īs) *noun, plural* **ices;** *verb,* **iced, icing.**
■ **break the ice:** To get through the awkward time of first getting to know a person or a group: *His joke* broke the ice *at the party and then everyone began to talk with one another.*

iceberg—A large mass of ice floating in the ocean. Icebergs are pieces of glacier that have broken off. The largest part of an iceberg is below the water's surface.
ice|berg (īs′burg′) *noun, plural* **icebergs.**
■ **the tip of the iceberg:** A very small part of something that is very large: *Her teacher thought that her problems at school were just* the tip of the iceberg *and that she had a lot of problems at home, too.*

icebox—1. A refrigerator. 2. A container filled with ice, used to keep food and drinks stored in it cold.
ice|box (īs′boks′) *noun, plural* **iceboxes.**

ice cream—A smooth, frozen food made of milk or cream, sweeteners, and flavorings such as fruit.
ice cream (īs krēm) *noun, plural* **ice creams.**

ice skate—A boot or shoe with a metal blade fixed on its sole for skating on ice.
ice skate (īs skāt) *noun, plural* **ice skates.**

ice-skate—To skate on ice.
ice-skate (īs′skāt′) *verb,* **ice-skated, ice-skating.**

icicle—A thin, pointed, hanging piece of ice. Icicles are formed from water that freezes as it drips: *The icicles hanging from the roof glistened in the sun.*
i|ci|cle (ī′si kəl) *noun, plural* **icicles.**

icing—A mixture of sugar, eggs, and butter used to cover cakes, cookies, or the like; frosting.
ic|ing (ī′sing) *noun, plural* **icings.**

icon—1. A picture of a religious figure painted on a small, wooden panel and considered sacred in the Eastern Orthodox Church 2. A picture, figure, or statue that is considered sacred.
i|con (ī′kon) *noun, plural* **icons.**
● This word is also spelled **ikon.**

icy—1. Feeling very cold like ice: icy *fingers.*
2. Covered with or chilled by ice: *an* icy *road;*

an icy *glass of lemonade.* 3. Cold and hostile: *Her* icy *greeting made us feel very uncomfortable.*
i|cy (ī′sē) *adjective,* **icier, iciest.**

I'd—The contraction of "I had," or "I would," or "I should."
I'd (īd).

idea—1. A thought, plan, or belief formed in one's mind: *She had an* idea *of just how she wanted the dress to look.* 2. A central meaning; purpose: *To play a new game, you have to understand the* idea *of the game first.*
i|de|a (ī dē′ə) *noun, plural* **ideas.**

ideal—A person or thing that is seen as perfect and therefore set as an example to be followed: *That beautiful actress is my sister's* ideal. *Noun.* —Perfect; the best that is possible: *Since it was warm and sunny, it was an* ideal *day for the parade. Adjective.*
i|de|al (ī dē′əl) *noun, plural* **ideals;** *adjective.*
● Synonyms: **model, pattern, standard,** for *noun.*

identical—Being exactly the same: *My brother and I are* identical *twins, and no one can tell us apart.*
i|den|ti|cal (ī den′tə kəl) *adjective.*

identification—1. The act or process of recognizing someone or something: *The* identification *of the robber was difficult because he wore a mask.* 2. Proof that a person is who he or she says: *The bank clerk asked the young man for a driver's license or other* identification.
i|den|ti|fi|ca|tion (ī den′tə fə kā′shən) *noun, plural* **identifications.**

a at	i if	oo look	ch chalk		a in ago
ā ape	ī idle	ou out	ng sing		e in happen
ah calm	o odd	u ugly	sh ship	ə =	i in capital
aw all	ō oats	ū rule	th think		o in occur
e end	oi oil	ur turn	th their		u in upon
ē easy			zh treasure		

icon

identify—1. To know or say what a particular person or thing is: *Can you* identify *any of the constellations?* 2. To think of as the same or connected in some way: *Some people* identify *happiness as having a healthy family.*
i|den|ti|fy (ī den′tə fī) *verb,* **identified, identifying.**
• Synonyms: **distinguish, recognize,** for 1.

identity—1. Who a person is or what a thing is: *The spy wore a disguise to hide his* identity. 2. The condition of being exactly or almost exactly the same: *The* identity *of the two paintings made me think that they were done by the same artist.*
i|den|ti|ty (ī den′tə tē) *noun, plural* **identities.**

idiom—An expression that has a meaning different from the regular meaning of each word contained in it, and that cannot be understood from those regular meanings. For example, "bats in the belfry" means craziness or mental problems, not animals in a bell tower.
id|i|om (id′ē əm) *noun, plural* **idioms.**

idiot—A very stupid or foolish person.
id|i|ot (id′ē ət) *noun, plural* **idiots.**

idle—1. Not active, busy, or working; doing nothing: *The lifeguards were* idle *on the cool, rainy days when no one came to the beach.* 2. Being lazy; avoiding work: *The teacher asked the* idle *students to leave the ballet class until they were willing to work harder.* 3. Not valuable or useful: idle *chatter; to do* idle *worrying. Adjective.*
—1. To spend one's time doing nothing of value or use: *She* idled *away her afternoon by daydreaming when she should have been studying for tomorrow's test.* 2. To run a motor slowly or out of gear so that its power is not used: *It is good to let the car engine* idle *a while in cold weather so it warms up. Verb.*
i|dle (ī′dəl) *adjective,* **idler, idlest;** *verb,* **idled, idling.**
• A word that sounds the same is **idol.**

idol—1. A picture, statue, or other object that is worshiped as sacred or as a god. 2. A person or thing that is loved and admired very much: *Famous actors are* idols *of many people.*
i|dol (ī′dəl) *noun, plural* **idols.**
• A word that sounds the same is **idle.**

if—1. On the condition that; in the event that: *Buy the shirt* if *you like it. If I am not able to meet you at the movies, I will call you.* 2. Whether: *Grandma went to the mailbox to see* if *a letter had come.*
if (if) *conjunction.*

igloo—An Eskimo hut that is made from blocks of ice and hard snow. Igloos are usually made in the shape of a dome.
ig|loo (ig′lū) *noun, plural* **igloos.**

igloo

ignite—To catch or set on fire; begin to burn: *The bonfire was* ignited *by the burning torch.*
ig|nite (ig nīt′) *verb,* **ignited, igniting.**
• Synonyms: **kindle, light**[1]

ignorant—Having little or no knowledge or education: *When we visited the desert, we realized how* ignorant *we were about the animals that lived there.*
ig|no|rant (ig′nər ənt) *adjective.*

ignore—To refuse to pay attention to or take notice of: *The girls* ignored *the freezing temperature and played happily in the snow for hours.*
ig|nore (ig nawr′) *verb,* **ignored, ignoring.**
• Synonyms: **disregard, neglect, overlook**

iguana—A large, tree-climbing lizard that lives in the hot areas of North and South America. Iguanas have a ridge of spines along the back and are brownish-green in color.
i|gua|na (i gwah′nə) *noun, plural* **iguanas.**

iguana

ikon—*See* icon.
i|kon (ī′kon) *noun, plural* **ikons.**

il-—A prefix that means "not": Something that is illegal is not legal. Something that is illogical is not logical.

Word Power

You can understand the meanings of many words that begin with **il-,** if you add the meaning of the prefix to the meaning of the rest of the word.
illiterate: not literate
illimitable: not able to be limited

---

ill—**1.** Not in good health; sick: *My* ill *sister has the chicken pox.* **2.** Not good or helpful: *The* ill *effects of this medicine are that you may feel dizzy or sleepy. Adjective.*
—**1.** A disease: *Someday there will be a cure for nearly every* ill. **2.** Something that causes harm or trouble: *The early pioneers faced many* ills *as they tried to settle in a new land. Noun.*
—In a bad, unkind, or unfavorable way: *She speaks* ill *of her neighbors. Adverb.*
ill (il) *adjective,* **worse, worst;** *noun, plural* **ills;** *adverb.*
■ **ill at ease:** Nervous; not comfortable: *He was* ill at ease *when he had to talk in front of a large group.*

I'll—The contraction of "I will" or "I shall."
I'll (īl).
● Words that sound the same are **aisle** and **isle.**

illegal—Going against the law or the rules: *In some states, it is* illegal *not to wear your seatbelt.*
il|le|gal (i lē′gəl) *adjective.*

illiterate—Unable to read and write: *The children grew up* illiterate *because there were no schools near their mountain home. Adjective.*
il|lit|er|ate (i lit′ər it) *adjective.*

illness—An unhealthy condition of the body or mind; sickness: *The common cold is an* illness *that most people suffer at some time in their lives.*
ill|ness (il′nis) *noun, plural* **illnesses.**
● Synonyms: **ailment, disease**
Antonym: **health**

illogical—Not reasonable; not showing good sense: *It is* illogical *to expect snow when the sun is shining and the temperature is warm.*
il|log|i|cal (i loj′ə kəl) *adjective.*

illuminate—**1.** To brighten with light; make shining: *The stadium lights* illuminated *the field for the night game.* **2.** To make something clear; help someone understand: *His lecture was so* illuminating, *it made me feel I really understood the subject.*
il|lu|mi|nate (i lü′mə nāt) *verb,* **illuminated, illuminating.**

illusion—**1.** A misleading image that is falsely believed to be true: *The magician created the* illusion *of sawing his assistant in half.* **2.** A false or mistaken idea: *When I woke up, I had the* illusion *that it was Saturday until I saw a school bus.*
il|lu|sion (i lü′zhən) *noun, plural* **illusions.**

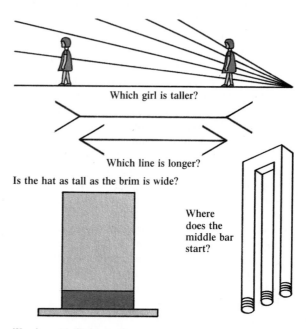

Which girl is taller?

Which line is longer?

Is the hat as tall as the brim is wide?

Where does the middle bar start?

illusion (definition 1)

illustrate—**1.** To explain something by using pictures, stories, or examples: *The scientist* illustrated *her experiment with photographs of the many types of germs.* **2.** To add pictures or diagrams to explain or decorate a book or other written work: *The reporter* illustrated *his story with pictures of the building before and after the fire.*
il|lus|trate (il′ə strāt *or* i lus′trāt) *verb,* **illustrated, illustrating.**

a at	i if	oo look	ch chalk		⌐a in ago
ā ape	ī idle	ou out	ng sing		e in happen
ah calm	o odd	u ugly	sh ship	ə =	i in capital
aw all	ō oats	ū rule	th think		o in occur
e end	oi oil	ur turn	th their		⌐u in upon
ē easy			zh treasure		

illustration—1. A picture, diagram, or the like that explains or decorates a book or other written work.   2. Something used as an example or explanation: *Our teacher showed us a sample book report for us to use as an illustration of how to do our own.*
il|lus|tra|tion (il'ə strā′shən) *noun, plural* **illustrations.**

im-—A prefix that means "not" or "the opposite of." The prefix "in-" becomes "im-" before the letters *b, m,* and *p:* Something that is imbalanced is not balanced. A person who is immature is the opposite of mature.

Word Power

You can understand the meanings of many words that begin with **im-,** if you add a meaning of the prefix to the meaning of the rest of the word.
  impractical: not practical
  impossible: not possible

I'm—The contraction of "I am."
  I'm (īm).

image—1. Something very much like another in appearance; likeness; imitation: *That boy is the image of his grandfather.*   2. A copy of a person or thing that is made, carved, or painted on a surface: *The statue is an image of a famous American Indian.*   3. A picture of something in one's mind: *Before their birthdays, many children have images of what they will receive as presents.*   4. A picture formed through a lens or by reflected light: *The baby noticed her own image in the mirror for the first time.*
im|age (im′ij) *noun, plural* **images.**
  • See picture at **reflection.**

imaginary—Being real only in one's mind: *Flying elephants are imaginary.*
i|mag|i|nar|y (i maj′ə ner′ē) *adjective.*

imagination—1. The mental picturing of something: *In his imagination he traveled to many distant lands.*   2. The creative ability to form new ideas or images: *The wonderful pictures she drew revealed her active imagination.*
i|mag|i|na|tion (i maj′ə nā′shən) *noun, plural* **imaginations.**

imagine—1. To form a mental picture of a person or thing: *In my daydreams, I imagine that I am a famous ballerina.*   2. To make a guess: *Because the trains are running behind schedule, I imagine that she will be late.*

i|mag|ine (i maj′ən) *verb,* **imagined, imagining.**

imitate—1. To try to copy the actions or behavior of someone or something; mimic: *The little boy imitates his older brother.*   2. To have the same look as something else: *The plastic box was painted to imitate real wood.*
im|i|tate (im′ə tāt) *verb,* **imitated, imitating.**

immature—Not full-grown: *I think it is immature for a college student to play with dolls.*
im|ma|ture (im′ə choor′ *or* im′ə tyoor′) *adjective.*
  • Synonyms: **childish, juvenile**
    Antonyms: **adult, grown-up, mature**

immediate—1. Taking place right away; with no delay: *His cut needed the nurse's immediate attention.*   2. Nearby in time or space: *I hope there is good luck for me in the immediate future. I wish there was an ice-cream parlor in our immediate neighborhood.*
im|me|di|ate (i mē′dē it) *adjective.*

immediately—Right now; without delay: *I returned his phone call immediately and caught him before he left his house.*
im|me|di|ate|ly (i mē′dē it lē) *adverb.*
  • Synonyms: **directly, instantly, presently**

immigrant—A person who comes from the country of his or her birth to live in a foreign land: *My grandmother was an immigrant to the United States from her native Sweden.*
im|mi|grant (im′ə grənt) *noun, plural* **immigrants.**

immigrate—To come from the country of one's birth to live in a foreign land: *My parents immigrated to the United States from Mexico.*
im|mi|grate (im′ə grāt) *verb,* **immigrated, immigrating.**
  • See Language Fact at **emigrate.**

immoral—Not behaving in a good or fair manner; bad: *Stealing is an immoral thing to do.*
im|mor|al (i mawr′əl) *adjective.*

immortal—Living or lasting forever: *Many religions believe that a person's soul is immortal.*
im|mor|tal (i mawr′təl) *adjective.*

immune—Able to resist and not be affected by a disease: *The vaccination made her immune to polio.*
im|mune (i myūn′) *adjective.*

immunization—Protection against a disease: *Before entering kindergarten, each student must have an immunization against measles.*
im|mu|ni|za|tion (im′yū nī zā′shən) *noun, plural* **immunizations.**

imp—A naughty child: *The teacher was annoyed because one of his students was behaving like an imp.*
im·p (imp) *noun, plural* **imps.**

impact—The colliding of two things, or the effect of such a collision: *The impact of the baseball on the player's bat broke the bat in two.*
im|pact (im′pakt) *noun, plural* **impacts.**

impala—An African antelope with a slender, brownish-gold body and long, thin horns. It runs very fast and makes long, graceful leaps.
im|pa|la (im pah′lə) *noun, plural* **impalas.**

impala

impeach—To accuse a public official of doing something wrong, often leading to his or her removal from office if the charge is proven to be true.
im|peach (im pēch′) *verb,* **impeached, impeaching.**

impersonate—To pretend to be another person in look, voice, or behavior; mimic: *To amuse us, he impersonated a movie star at the family gathering.*
im|per|son|ate (im pur′sə nāt) *verb,* **impersonated, impersonating.**

implement—A piece of equipment used to do a certain task; tool. Hammers, pliers, chisels, and screwdrivers are examples of implements.
im|ple|ment (im′plə mənt) *noun, plural* **implements.**

imply—To express or indicate by hinting or suggesting: *His quick acceptance of my offer to help implied that he needed it.*
im|ply (im plī′) *verb,* **implied, implying.**
• See Language Fact at **infer.**

import—To bring merchandise into a country from another country: *This country imports certain spices, coffee, and tea from other countries. Verb.*
—Merchandise brought into a country from another country: *Rice is one of the imports to this country from the Far East. Noun.*
im|port (im pawrt′ *for verb;* im′pawrt *for noun*) *verb,* **imported, importing;** *noun, plural* **imports.**

importance—The state of being valuable or meaning much: *He understood the importance of daily practice in learning to play the piano.*
im|por|tance (im pawr′təns) *noun.*

important—Generally considered to be valuable or have great meaning: *Regular watering is important to the growth of house plants.*
im|por|tant (im pawr′tənt) *adjective.*
• Synonyms: **momentous, significant**
Antonym: **petty**

impose—To set an assignment, chore, tax, fine, or prison sentence: *The teacher imposed a severe penalty for late assignments.*
im|pose (im pōz′) *verb,* **imposed, imposing.**

impossible—1. Not capable of being, happening, or being done; hopeless: *It is impossible to count the grains of sand in a desert.* 2. Not able to be tolerated: *She is an impossible person to study with because of her silliness.*
im|pos′|si|ble (im pos′ə bəl) *adjective.*

imposter—Someone who intends to deceive others by dressing or acting like someone else; fraud: *They knew he was an imposter because his costume was not right.*
im|pos|ter (im pos′tər) *noun, plural* **imposters.**

impractical—Not sensible or useful: *Having more clothes than you need is impractical.*
im|prac|ti|cal (im prak′tə kəl) *adjective.*

impress—1. To affect, usually in one's own favor, another person's thoughts or feelings: *He impressed them as being trustworthy.* 2. To set firmly in one's mind: *The police officer*

a at	i if	oo look	ch chalk		a in ago
ā ape	ī idle	ou out	ng sing		e in happen
ah calm	o odd	u ugly	sh ship	ə =	i in capital
aw all	ō oats	ū rule	th think		o in occur
e end	oi oil	ur turn	<u>th</u> their		u in upon
ē easy			zh treasure		

impressed *upon the children the importance of crossing streets carefully.*
im|press (im pres´) *verb,* **impressed, impressing.**

impression—**1.** An influence or effect produced on one's attitudes, feelings, or thoughts: *The fire fighter's warning about being careless with matches made an* impression *on her.* **2.** A general or vague idea, notion, belief, or feeling: *I have an* impression *that we have met before.* **3.** A mark or imprint made by pressure: *The truck's tires left* impressions *in the muddy road.* **4.** A copy; imitation: *Her* impression *of an opera singer made us all laugh.*
im|pres|sion (im presh´ən) *noun, plural* **impressions.**

impressive—Able to create a strong effect on one's attitudes, thoughts, or feelings: *Our team has an* impressive *list of victories, winning nearly every game of the season.*
im|pres|sive (im pres´iv) *adjective.*
● Synonyms: **notable, remarkable**

imprint—**1.** Something marked onto a surface by force or pressure; impression: *The children made* imprints *of their hands in clay.* **2.** An obvious effect: *Time and neglect had left their* imprint *on the old house. Noun.*
—To print; mark by pressure: *I was given a diary with my name* imprinted *on the cover. Verb.*
im|print (im´print for *noun;* im print´ for *verb*) *noun, plural* **imprints;** *verb,* **imprinted, imprinting.**

imprison—To place or hold in prison; put in jail: *They* imprisoned *him for committing a crime.*
im|pris|on (im priz´ən) *verb,* **imprisoned, imprisoning.**

improve—To make or become better in value, quality, or health; enhance: *He improved his appearance by getting a haircut.*
im|prove (im prūv´) *verb,* **improved, improving.**

impudent—Not respectful of or regarding others; extremely rude or impolite: *She was sent to her room for making an* impudent *remark to her mother.*
im|pu|dent (im´pyə dənt) *adjective.*

impulse—**1.** A feeling that stirs one to act; urge: *He was so happy that he felt an* impulse *to sing.* **2.** A force or thrust that starts something moving; push: *A strong gust of wind provided the* impulse *that caused the tree to fall.*
im|pulse (im´puls) *noun, plural* **impulses.**

impure—Not pure, clean, or clear: *Thick smoke from the factory made the air* impure.
im|pure (im pyoor´) *adjective.*

in—**1.** On the inside of; within: in *the closet;* in *the shade;* in *the middle.* **2.** Into; among: *Put some salt* in *the soup.* **3.** In the midst of: *a ski trail* in *the mountains; a friend* in *the crowd.* **4.** Wearing: *The soldiers are* in *uniform. Preposition.*
—**1.** Within or to a place, general location, or state of being: *They ran* in *the house from the cold.* **2.** Present; at home: *Is your mother* in? *Adverb.*
in (in) *preposition, adverb.*
■ **ins and outs:** Details: *The coach knows all the* ins and outs *of managing a baseball team.*
● A word that sounds the same is **inn.**

in-—A prefix that means "not" or "the opposite of." An *in*formal party is not formal. The *in*direct route is not the direct way to get there.

Word Power

You can understand the meanings of many words that begin with **in-,** if you add a meaning of the prefix to the meaning of the rest of the word.
    insincere: not sincere
    injustice: the opposite of justice

---

in.—The abbreviation for **inch** or **inches.**

inaugurate—**1.** To have a special ceremony that brings a person into an elected office; install: *The city will* inaugurate *its new mayor tomorrow.* **2.** To have a formal ceremony to open or begin something: *The orchestra gave a concert to* inaugurate *the new auditorium.*
in|au|gu|rate (in aw´gyə rāt) *verb,* **inaugurated, inaugurating.**

inauguration—**1.** A ceremony to place a person in office: *The club president's* inauguration *began with her taking the oath of office.* **2.** The formal opening or introduction of something: *Children and parents came to the* inauguration *of the new playground.*
in|au|gu|ra|tion (in aw´gyə rā´shən) *noun, plural* **inaugurations.**

Inca—A member of a group of highly civilized South American Indians who lived in what is now Peru. The empire of the Incas was destroyed by Spanish conquerors searching for gold in the 1500's.
In|ca (ing´kə) *noun, plural* **Incas** or **Inca.**

incense—A material that produces a sweet or spicy smell when burned. It can be one or a combination of sweet-smelling tree gums or spices.
in|cense (in′sens) *noun, plural* incenses.

inch—A measure of length that is the same as 1/12 of a foot or 1/36 of a yard. It is equal to 2.54 centimeters. *Noun.*
—To go along at a slow pace; crawl: *We had to* inch *along the icy path. Verb.*
inch (inch) *noun, plural* inches; *verb,* inched, inching. Abbreviation for *noun:* in.

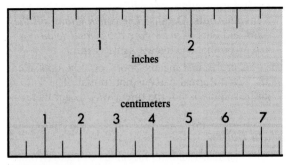

inch (noun)

incident—Something that takes place; happening: *After two* incidents *of theft, we learned to keep the door locked.*
in|ci|dent (in′sə dənt) *noun, plural* incidents.
• Synonyms: **episode, event, occurrence**

incidentally—While on the subject; by the way: *I enjoyed your party, and,* incidentally, *so did she.*
in|ci|den|tal|ly (in′sə den′tə lē *or* in′sə dent′lē) *adverb.*

incinerator—A furnace for burning or melting down waste materials.
in|cin|er|a|tor (in sin′ə rā′tər) *noun, plural* incinerators.

incline—To lie at an angle; slope; slant: *The path* inclined *steeply up the mountainside. Verb.*
—Something that lies at an angle; slope; slant: *She pulled her sled up the* incline *and coasted down. Noun.*
in|cline (in klīn′ for *verb;* in′klīn *or* in klīn′ for *noun) verb,* inclined, inclining; *noun, plural* inclines.

include—**1.** To take in; contain: *The park* includes *two playing fields.* **2.** To make a part of a whole, total, or group: *The lunch* includes *dessert.*
in|clude (in klūd′) *verb,* included, including.

income—Money received from work or investments; receipts: *My newspaper route gives me an* income *of nine dollars a week.*
in|come (in′kum) *noun, plural* incomes.

incompetent—Not able or fit to do something; unqualified: *A small child is* incompetent *to drive an automobile.*
in|com|pe|tent (in kom′pə tənt) *adjective.*

increase—To make or grow larger in size or number: *His bank account* increased *when he deposited his allowance. Verb.*
—A growth or gain: *The corn crop is larger than last year because of the* increase *in rainfall. Noun.*
in|crease (in krēs′ for *verb;* in′krēs for *noun) verb,* increased, increasing; *noun, plural* increases.

incredible—Too unlikely or extraordinary to be possible; unbelievable: *Your story that the depth of this lake is so great it has never been measured is* incredible.
in|cred|i|ble (in kred′ə bəl) *adjective.*

incubator—A box or container equipped to provide warmth or oxygen. Eggs are hatched in incubators. Another kind of incubator keeps very tiny babies warm and helps them breathe.
in|cu|ba|tor (in′kyə bā′tər) *noun, plural* incubators.

incline (noun)

a at	i if	oo look	ch chalk		a in ago
ā ape	ī idle	ou out	ng sing		e in happen
ah calm	o odd	u ugly	sh ship	ə =	i in capital
aw all	ō oats	ū rule	th think		o in occur
e end	oi oil	ur turn	th their		u in upon
ē easy			zh treasure		

indeed—Without any question; with certainty: *I am* indeed *sorry that you are sick.*
in|deed (in dēd′) *adverb.*

indefinite—1. Without being exact or precise; vague: *His eyes are an* indefinite *color between blue and gray.* 2. Not decided or limited in advance; uncertain: *We don't know when he will go home because he is visiting for an* indefinite *period.*
in|def|i|nite (in def′ə nit) *adjective.*

indefinite article—Either of the words **a** or **an,** used to refer to any person, place, or thing, not a particular one.
in|def|i|nite ar|ti|cle (in def′ə nit ahr′tə kəl) *noun, plural* indefinite articles.

indent—To move the point at which a written line begins farther to the right than the other lines: *It is common to* indent *the first line in a paragraph.*
in|dent (in dent′) *verb,* indented, indenting.

independence—The right or ability to operate or be on one's own; freedom from control; liberty: *The city fought to gain its* independence *from the cruel king.*
in|de|pend|ence (in′di pen′dəns) *noun.*

Independence Day—Another name for the Fourth of July, a national holiday in the United States. The day celebrates the adoption of the Declaration of Independence.
In|de|pend|ence Day (in′di pen′dəns dā) *noun.*

independent—Free from the control or influence of others: *He refused to listen to them because he wanted to make an* independent *decision.*
in|de|pend|ent (in′di pen′dənt) *adjective.*

index—A list at the end of a book showing on what page each important name, place, subject, or other information in the book can be found. The index is arranged in alphabetical order. *Noun.*
—To prepare such a list or place in such a list: *The author* indexed *the geography book so it is easy to find the page for each country. Verb.*
in|dex (in′deks) *noun, plural* indexes *or* indices (in′də sēz); *verb,* indexed, indexing.

index finger—The finger next to the thumb, usually used for pointing; forefinger.
in|dex fin|ger (in′deks fing′gər) *noun, plural* index fingers.

Indian—1. One of the native American people who occupied the continents of North and South America before the arrival of the Europeans. 2. A person born or living in the country of India. *Noun.*
—1. Concerning the American Indians: *an* Indian *reservation.* 2. Concerning the country or people of India: *an* Indian *elephant. Adjective.*
In|di|an (in′dē ən) *noun, plural* Indians; *adjective.*

indicate—1. To point out; designate; show: *The arrow* indicated *that we must turn right.* 2. To act as a signal or sign of: *A baby's crying often* indicates *hunger.*
in|di|cate (in′də kāt) *verb,* indicated, indicating.

indifferent—Not feeling or showing interest or concern; not caring how something is or will turn out: *He hates broccoli, and she loves it; but I am* indifferent *toward it.*
in|dif|fer|ent (in dif′ər ənt *or* in dif′rənt) *adjective.*

indigestion—Inability to digest food properly or completely: *Your stomachache after eating three cheeseburgers is probably caused by* indigestion.
in|di|ges|tion (in′də jes′chən *or* in′dī jes′chən) *noun.*

indigo—1. A deep blue dye made from certain plants or chemicals. 2. A plant from which this dye can be made. 3. A deep purplish-blue color. *Noun.*
—Deep purplish-blue: *Stars shone in an* indigo *sky. Adjective.*
in|di|go (in′də gō) *noun, plural* indigos *or* indigoes; *adjective.*

indirect—1. Not following a straight line to reach something: *You'll get there faster on the highway even though it's an* indirect *way to go.* 2. Going around a subject rather than approaching it in a straightforward way: *His* indirect *answer was a sign he wasn't ready to make a decision yet.* 3. Related in only a secondary way: *I admit I was careless, but an* indirect *cause of the accident was her placing the glass so close to the edge of the table.*
in|di|rect (in′də rect′ *or* in′dī rect′) *adjective.*

indirect object—A person or thing for which the action of a verb is done. The indirect object often comes before the direct object: *I brought her a gift.* The indirect object is "her," and "gift" is the direct object. The indirect object can follow the direct object: *I brought a gift for her.*
in|di|rect ob|ject (in′də rekt′ *or* in′dī rekt′ ob′jikt *or* ob′jekt) *noun, plural* indirect objects.

individual—1. Single, distinct, or separate; singular: *Each* individual *slice of cheese is wrapped in plastic.* 2. Setting off a person or thing from others: *an* individual *taste in clothes. Adjective.*

—A human being; person: *She is an important* individual. *Noun.*

in|di|vid|u|al (in′də **vij′**ū əl) *adjective; noun,* *plural* **individuals.**

- Synonyms: **particular, special, specific, unique,** for *adjective* 2.
  Antonym: **general,** for *adjective* 2.

individuality—The unique set of qualities that sets off one person or thing and makes it distinct from another: *The identical twins showed their* individuality *by dressing differently.*

in|di|vid|u|al|i|ty (in′də vij′ū **al′**ə tē) *noun,* *plural* **individualities.**

indivisible—Not able to be separated into equal whole numbers or amounts: *The number 6 can be divided by 3, but 5 is* indivisible *by 3.*

in|di|vis|i|ble (in′də **viz′**ə bəl) *adjective.*

indoor—Designed to be used or performed inside rather than outdoors: *Pajamas are* indoor *clothing.*

in|door (**in′**dawr′) *adjective.*

indoors—Inside or into a building: *Please do not wear your boots* indoors.

in|doors (**in′**dawrs′) *adverb.*

indulge—**1.** To permit oneself to enjoy a special treat or luxury: *On Sunday mornings, we* indulge *in a big breakfast.* **2.** To allow someone to have or do what he or she wants; humor: *We* indulge *her because she is the youngest.*

in|dulge (in **dulj′**) *verb,* **indulged, indulging.**

- Synonyms: **coddle, pamper, spoil,** for 2.

industrial—**1.** Of, about, or resulting from any business, manufacture, craft, or trade: *Factories turn raw materials into* industrial *products.* **2.** Having a large number of businesses or factories: *Our city is an* industrial *center.*

in|dus|tri|al (in **dus′**trē əl) *adjective.*

industrious—Hard-working; busy; diligent: Industrious *bees gather honey all day.*

in|dus|tri|ous (in **dus′**trē əs) *adjective.*

industry—**1.** All factories, businesses, and trades considered as one: *The nation's* industry *is the source of its wealth.* **2.** A group of businesses involved in the same general area of manufacture or trade: *Farms produce crops used by the*

food-packing industry.   **3.** Work; labor; effort: *A neat report was the result of her* industry.

in|dus|try (**in′**də strē) *noun, plural* **industries.**

inequality—The state of being unequal or different: *There is great* inequality *in playing ability between the two teams.*

in|e|qual|i|ty (in′i **kwol′**ə tē) *noun, plural* **inequalities.**

inevitable—Sure to come about; certain to take place: *It was* inevitable *that someone would fall on the slippery sidewalk.*

in|ev|i|ta|ble (in **ev′**ə tə bəl) *adjective.*

infant—A baby; a child in his or her first year of life.

in|fant (**in′**fənt) *noun, plural* **infants.**

- Synonyms: **babe, newborn**

infantry—Members of an army who have been trained and armed to fight on foot.

in|fan|try (**in′**fən trē) *noun, plural* **infantries.**

infect—To cause to become sick by spreading germs that carry disease: *He stayed home while he had the chicken pox so he would not* infect *the other children.*

in|fect (in **fekt′**) *verb,* **infected, infecting.**

infection—A germ-caused sickness or disease: *If not kept clean, even a small scratch can lead to a painful* infection.

in|fec|tion (in **fek′**shən) *noun, plural* **infections.**

infer—To figure out or gather after careful thought: *He* inferred *that his sister was upset when she slammed the door.*

in|fer (in **fur′**) *verb,* **inferred, inferring.**

Language Fact

Infer means to get an idea, while **imply** means to suggest an idea. *I* inferred *from his remark about the heat that he wanted to go outdoors. She* implied *that she was hungry by asking when dinner would be.* People who use language carefully use these words only with these meanings. But many people use **infer** as though it had the same meaning as **imply.**

---

inferior—**1.** Of little value; cheap: *Any radio that stops working less than a week after it is bought is* inferior. **2.** Of less value or importance; worse than: *As a beginning swimmer, she felt* inferior *to the members of the swim team.*

in|fe|ri|or (in **fir′**ē ər) *adjective.*

a at	**i** if	**oo** look	**ch** chalk		**a** in ago
ã ape	**ī** idle	**ou** out	**ng** sing		**e** in happen
ah calm	**o** odd	**u** ugly	**sh** ship	ə =	**i** in capital
aw all	**ō** oats	**ū** rule	**th** think		**o** in occur
e end	**oi** oil	**ur** turn	**th** their		**u** in upon
ē easy			**zh** treasure		

infield—1. That portion of a baseball field that is completely enclosed by bases and the paths between them. It is also called a diamond. 2. Those players on a baseball team who fill the positions of shortstop and first, second, and third base.
in|field (in′fēld′) *noun, plural* **infields.**

infinite—1. Endless; having no limits or boundaries: *an* infinite *number of stars.* 2. Enormous; very much: *With* infinite *care, she picked up the baby bird.*
in|fi|nite (in′fə nit) *adjective.*

infinitive—The form of a verb that has the word "to" in front of it: *The dog likes to chase cats.* The infinitive is "to chase."
in|fin|i|tive (in fin′ə tiv) *noun, plural* **infinitives.**

infinity—The condition of having no end or limits: *the* infinity *of the universe.*
in|fin|i|ty (in fin′ə tē) *noun, plural* **infinities.**

inflame—1. To anger or excite; stir up strong feelings: *The umpire's call* inflamed *the crowd.* 2. To cause to swell, ache, or become red as a result of sickness or injury: *Sunburn* inflamed *his skin.*
in|flame (in flām′) *verb,* **inflamed, inflaming.**

inflammable—Capable of catching on fire easily: *A match is* inflammable.
in|flam|ma|ble (in flam′ə bəl) *adjective.*

inflammation—Redness, swelling, and pain in a body part: *The speck of dirt in her eye caused an* inflammation.
in|flam|ma|tion (in′flə mā′shən) *noun, plural* **inflammations.**

inflate—1. To fill something with air or gas in order to make it bigger and more solid: *to inflate a beach ball.* 2. To rise or cause to rise; become higher; increase: *Higher housing prices have* inflated *the cost of living.*
in|flate (in flāt′) *verb,* **inflated, inflating.**

inflation—1. The act of getting bigger and more solid by being filled with air or gas: *the inflation of a bicycle tire.* 2. A sudden rise in the price of things: Inflation *has made it more expensive to buy new cars.*
in|fla|tion (in flā′shən) *noun, plural* **inflations.**

influence—1. The ability to cause a change in someone or something without using physical strength: *Good teachers use their* influence *to help students do their best.* 2. A person or thing capable of changing something about another: *She is a strong* influence *on her younger brother because he looks up to her. Noun.*
—To have power over or cause to change:

Mom's opinion influenced *him to play soccer instead of baseball. Verb.*
in|flu|ence (in′floo əns) *noun, plural* **influences;** *verb,* **influenced, influencing.**

influential—Having the ability to cause a change in someone or something: *The rainy weather was* influential *in our decision to cancel the picnic.*
in|flu|en|tial (in′floo en′shəl) *adjective.*

inform—1. To provide the facts about something; give out the news: *When we asked her, the librarian* informed *us that the book could be checked out for only a week.* 2. To tell something bad or secret about someone: *The students* informed *on those who had broken windows in the school.*
in|form (in fawrm′) *verb,* **informed, informing.**
• Synonyms: **answer, respond, reply, tell,** for **1.**
Antonyms: **ask, inquire, question,** for **1.**

informal—Not fancy; relaxed; casual: *We wore* informal *clothes to the class picnic.*
in|for|mal (in fawr′məl) *adjective.*

information—Knowledge about someone or something; facts; data: *The book gave* information *about whales and dolphins.*
in|for|ma|tion (in′fər mā′shən) *noun.*

infuriate—To cause to become very upset or angry: *His rude behavior* infuriated *her.*
in|fu|ri|ate (in fyoor′ē āt) *verb,* **infuriated, infuriating.**

ing—A suffix that means "continues" or "continued," "the act of" or "the result of," or "able to" or "used for." A walking dog continues to walk. Writing is the act or result of one who writes. A sewing machine is able to sew or used for sewing.

Word Power

You can understand the meanings of many words that end with **-ing,** if you add a meaning of the suffix to the meaning of the rest of the word.
acting: continues to act; continued to act
cutting: the act of one who cuts; the result of one who cuts
cooking: able to cook; used to cook

---

ingredient—A thing that is mixed with others to make a whole: *Chocolate chips were one of the* ingredients *needed to make this cake batter.*
in|gre|di|ent (in grē′dē ənt) *noun, plural* **ingredients.**

inhabit—To make one's home in; live in; occupy: *Bats* inhabit *that cave.*
in|hab|it (in hab'it) *verb,* **inhabited, inhabiting.**

inhabitant—One who lives in a certain place: *The* inhabitants *of the island were fishermen.*
in|hab|it|ant (in hab'ə tənt) *noun, plural* **inhabitants.**

inhale—To breathe air into the lungs: *He* inhaled *the delicious smell of an apple pie baking in the oven.*
in|hale (in hāl') *verb,* **inhaled, inhaling.**

inherit—1. To receive a person's money or belongings after he or she dies: *She* inherited *her grandmother's ring.* 2. To be born with a feature, quality, or trait like that of a parent or earlier family member: *He* inherited *his mother's brown eyes.*
in|her|it (in her'it) *verb,* **inherited, inheriting.**

inheritance—Money or belongings passed on to someone else after a person dies: *A collection of old coins was his* inheritance *from his uncle.*
in|her|it|ance (in her'ə təns) *noun, plural* **inheritances.**

inhuman—Cruel; mean; having no heart: *The way the boys tease her is* inhuman.
in|hu|man (in hyū'mən) *adjective.*

initial—First; placed at the beginning: *When he saw the snake, his* initial *feeling was fear. Adjective.*
—The first letter of a word in a person's name: *George Washington's* initials *were G. W. Noun.*
—To write one or more first letters of words in one's name on: *Her father* initialed *her report card to show that he had seen it. Verb.*
i|ni|tial (i nish'əl) *adjective; noun, plural* **initials;** *verb,* **initialed, initialing.**

initiate—1. To get something started; be the first person to try something: *Once someone* initiated *a game of kick ball, everyone joined in.* 2. To follow a formal procedure to accept someone as a member of a club or group: *The Boy Scouts* initiated *new members at a special meeting.*
i|ni|ti|ate (i nish'ē āt) *verb,* **initiated, initiating.**
• Synonyms: **begin, commence,** for 1.
Antonyms: **end, finish, stop,** for 1.

initiation—1. Beginning; start: *At the* initiation *of space exploration, many people did not believe that a trip to the moon was possible.* 2. A special meeting of a group or club during which new people become members.
i|ni|ti|a|tion (i nish'ē ā'shən) *noun, plural* **initiations.**

inject—To put liquid medicine into the body by forcing it out of a needle through the skin: *The veterinarian* injected *the puppy with a rabies vaccine.*
in|ject (in jekt') *verb,* **injected, injecting.**

injure—To cause pain; damage: *She* injured *her ankle when she slipped on the stairs.*
in|jure (in'jər) *verb,* **injured, injuring.**

injury—A hurt; harm; damage; loss: *His knee* injury *took six months to heal.*
in|ju|ry (in'jər ē) *noun, plural* **injuries.**

injustice—1. Unfairness; an absence of equal or reasonable treatment: *He thought it was an* injustice *to lose recess when another student had misbehaved.* 2. An unfair act or deed: *To dislike people because of the clothes they wear is to do them an* injustice.
in|jus|tice (in jus'tis) *noun, plural* **injustices.**

ink—A colored fluid used with a pen or in a printing press to draw or print letters and images.
ink (ingk) *noun, plural* **inks.**

inland—Set in the inner part of a country; away from an ocean: *The* inland *states fly in fresh seafood from the coast. Adjective.*
—Within or in the direction of the inner part of an area: *People drove* inland *when a bad storm was predicted for the coast. Adverb.*
in|land (in'lənd for *adjective;* in'lənd *or* in'land' for *adverb) adjective, adverb.*

in-law—A person who belongs to a family through marriage: *Her husband's father brought the rest of her* in-laws *to the family reunion.*
in-|law (in'law') *noun, plural* **in-laws.**

inlet—A narrow water passage that stretches between islands or through peninsulas into a bay.
in|let (in'let) *noun, plural* **inlets.**

inn—A place, often small in size, where people who are traveling can eat and sleep; hotel.
inn (in) *noun, plural* **inns.**
• A word that sounds the same is **in.**

inner—1. Placed deep within; near the center; internal: *The hikers explored the* inner *rooms of the cave.* 2. More personal or secret: *He wrote his* inner *thoughts and feelings in his diary.*
in|ner (in'ər) *adjective.*

a at	i if	oo look	ch chalk		a in ago
ā ape	ī idle	ou out	ng sing		e in happen
ah calm	o odd	u ugly	sh ship	ə =	i in capital
aw all	ō oats	ū rule	th think		o in occur
e end	oi oil	ur turn	<u>th</u> their		u in upon
ē easy			zh treasure		

inning—One of the divisions of a baseball game in which both teams get to bat. It is over when each team has made three outs. There are usually nine innings in a baseball game.
in|ning (in′ing) *noun, plural* **innings.**

innocence—1. Freedom from blame or guilt: *The captured thief insisted on his* innocence.
2. Simple trust and belief: *the* innocence *of a young child.*
in|no|cence (in′ə səns) *noun.*

innocent—1. Free from blame; not guilty: *An* innocent *woman was accused of the crime by mistake.* 2. Causing no harm to anyone or anything: *The class played an* innocent *prank on their teacher on April Fool's Day.*
in|no|cent (in′ə sənt) *adjective.*

innumerable—More than can be counted; very many: innumerable *grains of sand on the beach.*
in|nu|mer|a|ble (i nū′mər ə bəl *or* i nyū′mər ə bəl) *adjective.*

input—1. Something, especially ideas, that is placed or brought in: *The teacher asked the students for their* input *on planning the class play.* 2. Information that is entered into a computer. *Noun.*
—To enter information into a computer: *She* input *the spelling game she had written. Verb.*
in|put (in′poot′) *noun; verb,* **input, inputting.**

inquire—To question; ask: *The waitress* inquired *about my choice of drink.*
in|quire (in kwīr′) *verb,* **inquired, inquiring.**

inquiry—1. A search for an answer to a question: *The librarian made* inquiries *into the whereabouts of the lost encyclopedia.*
2. Something asked: *The teacher answered the students'* inquiries *about the field trip.*
in|quir|y (in kwīr′rē *or* in′kwər ē) *noun, plural* **inquiries.**

inquisitive—Curious; eager to learn: *The* inquisitive *little boy was always asking, "Why?"*
in|quis|i|tive (in kwiz′ə tiv) *adjective.*

insane—1. Having an illness of the mind; crazy; mad: *an* insane *individual.* 2. Having to do with mentally ill people: *an* insane *asylum.* 3. Not carefully thought out or sensible; foolish: *Running away from home was an* insane *thought.*
in|sane (in sān′) *adjective.*

inscribe—To mark or imprint letters or symbols onto a surface by writing, cutting, or carving: *The builder* inscribed *the town hall with the date it was completed.*
in|scribe (in skrīb′) *verb,* **inscribed, inscribing.**

inscription—Something that is written, imprinted, or carved on an object: *The* inscription *on his watch read, "To my grandson."*
in|scrip|tion (in skrip′shən) *noun, plural* **inscriptions.**

insect—1. One of a large group of small animals, each having three pairs of jointed legs, no backbone, and a body with three main parts. Insects normally have two pairs of wings. Flies, grasshoppers, bees, and butterflies are examples of this kind of animal. 2. An animal that is like a member of this group in some ways but whose body parts or number of legs or wings vary. Centipedes and spiders are often called insects.
in|sect (in′sekt) *noun, plural* **insects.**

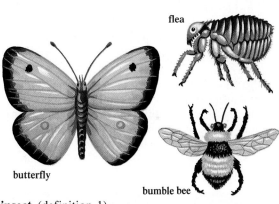

flea

butterfly

bumble bee

insect (definition 1)

Word History

Insect comes from a Latin word meaning "divided." All insects have bodies with three parts: head, thorax, and abdomen. Some insects, such as ants, bees, and flies, have body parts that are very clearly divided from each other. So these, and all other insects, were known in Latin as "divided animals."

insecticide—One of many kinds of chemical poisons that are used to kill insects that are considered harmful.
in|sec|ti|cide (in sek′tə sīd′) *noun, plural* **insecticides.**

insert—To put or place in something: *She* inserted *a quarter into the candy machine. Verb.*
—Something that is put or placed in something else: *The school newspaper had a special* insert *telling about graduation ceremonies. Noun.*
in|sert (in surt′ for *verb;* in′surt for *noun*) *verb,* **inserted, inserting;** *noun, plural* **inserts.**

inside—The surface within; inner part or side; interior: *The* inside *of her coat was lined. Noun.*
—**1.** At or in the inner part or side: *There were no seats left on the aisle, so we had to take the* inside *seats.* **2.** Not known by many people; secret or private: *He had an* inside *tip on who would get the job. Adjective.*
—**1.** To or in the inner part or side: *The dog walked to the doghouse and lay down* inside.
2. Indoors: *We moved the lawn chairs* inside *before the storm. Adverb.*
—In or into the inner part or side of: *What is that* inside *your coat pocket? Preposition.*
in|side (in′sīd′ *or* in′sīd′ for *noun and adjective;* in′sīd′ for *adverb and preposition) noun, plural* **insides;** *adjective; adverb; preposition.*
■ **inside out: 1.** So that the inside is on the outside: *He had his sweater on* inside out.
2. Perfectly or completely: *After she studied for the quiz, she knew her spelling words* inside out.

insignia—A special mark or sign, often imprinted on a badge or medal, that shows a person's job, rank, or honors. An insignia may also stand for a club, group, or organization: *The* insignia *of the Red Cross is a red cross on a white background.*
in|sig|ni|a (in sig′nē ə) *noun, plural* **insignia** *or* **insignias.**

insignia: In the United States Army, crossed rifles is the insignia of the infantry.

insist—To hold in a firm way to what one wants; demand: *He* insists *on always having things his way.*
in|sist (in sist′) *verb,* **insisted, insisting.**

inspect—To view or examine with care: *The fire chief* inspected *the school to be sure everyone could leave safely in case of a fire.*
in|spect (in spekt′) *verb,* **inspected, inspecting.**
● Synonyms: **analyze, investigate, study**

inspiration—**1.** The cause of something worthwhile; stimulus: *The book on volcanoes was the* inspiration *for her science project.* **2.** A good idea that comes unexpectedly: *He had an* inspiration *to make his mother a bookshelf for Mother's Day.*
in|spi|ra|tion (in′spə rā′shən) *noun, plural* **inspirations.**

inspire—**1.** To arouse another's emotions for a good or high purpose: *The sermon this Sunday* inspired *me to try harder to obey my parents.*
2. To encourage or cause something worthwhile: *The beautiful spring weather* inspired *him to go for a long walk.*
in|spire (in spīr′) *verb,* **inspired, inspiring.**

install—**1.** To set in place so that it can be used: *to* install *a telephone.* **2.** To hold a ceremony or special meeting for a person who is taking a new job or position: *The student council* installed *her as its new president.*
in|stall (in stawl′) *verb,* **installed, installing.**

installment—**1.** A fixed portion of the full amount of money owed, that must be paid at certain times: *She plans to pay for her new television set in six monthly* installments *of $100.*
2. One of a thing's sections, released to the public or shown as part of a series: *The television coverage of the Olympics was shown in nightly* installments *for two weeks.*
in|stall|ment (in stawl′mənt) *noun, plural* **installments.**

instance—Someone or something used to explain or illustrate: *Television and automobiles are* instances *of inventions that changed the world.*
in|stance (in′stəns) *noun, plural* **instances.**

instant—**1.** A certain moment in time: *Come here this* instant! **2.** A very short time; moment; flash: *The shooting star disappeared in an* instant. *Noun.*
—**1.** Immediate: *A calculator gives us an* instant *answer to difficult math problems.* **2.** Very important; urgent: *There is an* instant *need to leave the ship because it is sinking.* **3.** Able to be served quickly: instant *pudding;* instant *coffee. Adjective.*
in|stant (in′stənt) *noun, plural* **instants;** *adjective.*

a at	i if	oo look	ch chalk		a in ago
ā ape	ī idle	ou out	ng sing		e in happen
ah calm	o odd	u ugly	sh ship	ə =	i in capital
aw all	ō oats	ū rule	th think		o in occur
e end	oi oil	ur turn	th their		u in upon
ē easy			zh treasure		

instantly—Right away; at once: *She* instantly *put her hands out to catch the falling vase.*
in|stant|ly (in′stənt lē) *adverb.*
• Synonyms: **directly, immediately, presently**

instead—In place of (something or someone else): *There was no more cake for dessert, so she served fruit* instead.
in|stead (in sted′) *adverb.*
■ **instead of:** As an alternative to; as a substitute for; rather than: *He walked* instead of *taking the bus to school.*

instep—The arched, upper part of a person's foot between the ankle and the toes.
in|step (in′step) *noun, plural* **insteps.**

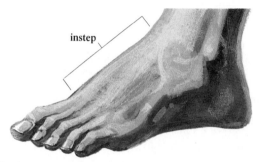

instep

instep

instinct—A way a person or animal does or knows something from birth without having to learn it; natural behavior or response: *Birds fly south for the winter by* instinct.
in|stinct (in′stingkt) *noun, plural* **instincts.**

institution—1. Any organization that is set up for a special reason: *A hospital is an* institution *whose purpose is to treat sick people.*
2. Something that is done or believed for a long time; custom: *A ham dinner is an* institution *at our house on Christmas Day.*
in|sti|tu|tion (in′stə tū′shən *or* in′stə tyū′shən) *noun, plural* **institutions.** *Abbreviation:* Inst.

instruct—1. To teach; show how: *The swimming coach* instructed *us in diving.* 2. To order: *The sergeant* instructed *the company to run ten miles.*
in|struct (in strukt′) *verb,* **instructed, instructing.**
• Synonyms: **command, direct,** for 2.
Antonyms: **follow, obey,** for 2.

instructor—One who teaches or shows how to do something: *a dance* instructor.
in|struc|tor (in struk′tər) *noun, plural* **instructors.**

instrument—1. A device that is made for a certain job: *A thermometer is an* instrument *for telling temperature.* 2. A device made to create musical sounds: *A trumpet is a brass* instrument.
in|stru|ment (in′strə mənt) *noun, plural* **instruments.**

insulate—To hold electricity, sound, or heat in or out by covering with a material: *Her winter coat* insulated *her against the cold.*
in|su|late (in′sə lāt) *verb,* **insulated, insulating.**

insult—To say or do something that upsets someone; to hurt: *He* insulted *me when he said that I had played a poor game. Verb.*
—Something that is said or done that upsets someone: *Compliments win friends,* insults *do not. Noun.*
in|sult (in sult′ for *verb;* in′sult for *noun*) *verb,* **insulted, insulting;** *noun, plural* **insults.**
■ **add insult to injury:** To make things worse: *The painter* added insult to injury *by criticizing our curtains when he was wiping up spilled paint.*
• Synonyms: **offend, outrage,** for *verb.*
Antonym: **honor,** for *verb.*

insurance—A contract that guarantees a person or business against loss or damage to life or property. In return, a person or business agrees to pay a regular, fixed amount of money. Fire, health, life, theft, and accident insurance are some of the many kinds of insurance.
in|sur|ance (in shoor′əns) *noun, plural* **insurances.**

insure—To protect against loss or damage by paying money to an insurance company: *to* insure *a car.*
in|sure (in shoor′) *verb,* **insured, insuring.**

intake—1. The act of drawing in: *Too fast an* intake *of ice water may cause stomach cramps.* 2. The place where liquids or gases enter some kind of opening: *The swimming pool filter's* intake *was filled with leaves.*
in|take (in′tāk′) *noun, plural* **intakes.**

integrate—1. To open facilities equally to people of all races: *to* integrate *state universities.* 2. To combine parts to make a whole: *After the opinion poll, the man* integrated *everyone's choices onto a single chart.*
in|te|grate (in′tə grāt) *verb,* **integrated, integrating.**

integration—1. The act of opening facilities equally to people of all races: *the* integration *of public housing.* 2. The act of combining all the parts of something to make it whole: *The*

integration *of all the voices in the chorus makes for a lovely sound.*
in|te|gra|tion (in′tə **grā′**shən) *noun, plural* **integrations.**

integrity—Honesty; truthfulness; principle: *The governor was known as a man of* integrity.
in|teg|ri|ty (in **teg′**rə tē) *noun.*

intellect—Ability to think and understand; intelligence: *The author was honored as a person of great* intellect.
in|tel|lect (**in′**tə lekt) *noun, plural* **intellects.**

intellectual—1. Needing or using the ability to think and understand: *Chess is an* intellectual *game.* 2. Having the ability to think and understand: *an* intellectual *student. Adjective.*
—A person with a great ability to think and understand: *The college professor was an* intellectual. *Noun.*
in|tel|lec|tu|al (in′tə lek′choo əl) *adjective; noun, plural* **intellectuals.**

intelligence—1. The ability to learn and understand; intellect. 2. News or information, often secret: *What* intelligence *did he gather while spying on the enemy?*
in|tel|li|gence (in **tel′**ə jəns) *noun.*

intelligent—Having the ability to think and understand; quick to learn: *Dolphins are* intelligent *animals and master new tasks rapidly.*
in|tel|li|gent (in **tel′**ə jənt) *adjective.*

intend—1. To have a goal; to plan: *He* intends *to be a musician when he grows up.* 2. To mean for a certain purpose: *Those cookies are* intended *for tonight's party.*
in|tend (in **tend′**) *verb,* **intended, intending.**

intense—Extremely strong; great; deeply felt: intense *heat of the summer sun.*
in|tense (in **tens′**) *adjective.*

intensity—1. Strength; power: *the* intensity *of a jet engine's roar.* 2. The quantity of power given off by electricity, heat, light, or sound per unit of area or volume; degree: *The* intensity *of this light bulb is 100 watts.*
in|ten|si|ty (in **ten′**sə tē) *noun, plural* **intensities.**

intent[1]—A goal; purpose; aim: *Her* intent *was to finish her homework by 7 P.M.*
in|tent (in **tent′**) *noun, plural* **intents.**

intent[2]—Giving full attention to; concentrating on: *He was* intent *on building the model airplane and did not hear the phone ringing.*
in|tent (in **tent′**) *adjective.*

intention—A plan; purpose; goal: *His* intention *was to camp out for a week.*
in|ten|tion (in **ten′**shən) *noun, plural* **intentions.**

inter-—A prefix that means "between or among." An international agreement is an agreement between nations.

Word Power

You can understand the meanings of many words that begin with **inter-**, if you add the meaning of the prefix to the meaning of the rest of the word.
   interconnect: to connect between or among
     things
   interplanetary: between or among planets

---

intercept—To stop a person or thing on its course; to take away: *He tried to* intercept *the quarterback's pass before it reached the receiver.*
in|ter|cept (in′tər **sept′**) *verb,* **intercepted, intercepting.**

intercom—A radio or telephone machine that allows people in different areas of a house, office, ship, or airplane to talk with one another.
in|ter|com (**in′**tər kom′) *noun, plural* **intercoms.**

interest—1. A feeling of wanting to know about or take part in something: *Even at an early age, the child showed much* interest *in building things.* 2. The ability of something to cause this feeling: *This television show is of great* interest *to me.* 3. A right or legal share in something, usually land or a business: *His mother owns a half* interest *in a shoe store.* 4. Something that helps a person or thing; benefit: *His parents were helpful because they cared about his* interests. 5. An amount of money that is paid for the use of money. People or companies who borrow money from another person, a bank, or other lending service pay interest for the money borrowed: *The bank charged my father 11 percent* interest *on his car loan. Noun.*
—To arouse in someone a feeling of wanting to know about or to take part in something: *Can I* interest *you in a game of checkers? Verb.*
in|ter|est (**in′**tər ist *or* **in′**trist) *noun, plural* **interests;** *verb,* **interested, interesting.**

---

a at	i if	oo look	ch chalk		a in ago
ā ape	ī idle	ou out	ng sing		e in happen
ah calm	o odd	u ugly	sh ship	ə =	i in capital
aw all	ō oats	ū rule	th think		o in occur
e end	oi oil	ur turn	<u>th</u> their		u in upon
ē easy			zh treasure		

interesting—Gaining or holding a person's attention: *He watched an* interesting *television show about grizzly bears.*
in|ter|est|ing (in′tər ə sting, in′trə sting, *or* in′tə res′ting) *adjective.*

interfere—1. To get in the way of; clash; oppose: *The warm weather softened the ice and* interfered *with our plans to go ice-skating.* 2. To enter unasked into the affairs of others; meddle: *Her little brother* interfered *every time her friends came over to play.*
in|ter|fere (in′tər **fir′**) *verb,* **interfered, interfering.**

interior—1. The inside of something: *The* interior *of the library is used for storing books.* 2. The part of a country or area that is not on or near the coast or boundary: *The* interior *of the country is very mountainous. Noun.*
—1. Being on the inside of something: *The* interior *of the pyramid held a great treasure.* 2. Being away from the coast or boundary; inland: *The Great Lakes are located in the* interior *part of North America. Adjective.*
in|te|ri|or (in ter′ē ər) *noun, plural* **interiors;** *adjective.*

interjection—A word or group of words that shows strong feeling; exclamation. **Alas, hurrah,** and **ouch** are interjections.
in|ter|jec|tion (in′tər **jek′**shən) *noun, plural* **interjections.**

intermediate—In the middle; between: *A junior high school is an* intermediate *school between grammar school and high school.*
in|ter|me|di|ate (in′tər **mē′**dē it) *adjective.*

intermission—A short break or pause, as in a long movie, play, or concert.
in|ter|mis|sion (in′tər **mish′**ən) *noun, plural* **intermissions.**

internal—1. Inside; on the inner surface: *A person's heart and lungs are* internal *organs.* 2. Concerning affairs within a country; domestic: *The ambassador was told not to meddle in* internal *politics.*
in|ter|nal (in **tur′**nəl) *adjective.*

international—Between or among countries: *The Olympic Games are an* international *event with athletes from most countries in the world participating.*
in|ter|na|tion|al (in′tər **nash′**ə nəl) *adjective.*

International Date Line—An imaginary line on the earth that runs north and south through the middle of the Pacific Ocean. Each new day begins at the International Date Line. For example, when it is Thursday to the east of the

International Date Line, it is Friday to the west of it.
In|ter|na|tion|al Date Line (in′tər **nash′**ə nəl dāt līn) *noun.*

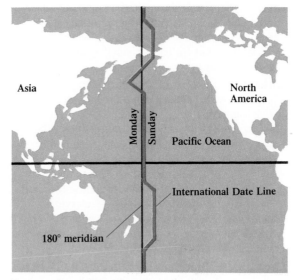

International Date Line

interpret—1. To explain; make clear: *The museum guide* interpreted *what the artist was trying to show in her painting.* 2. To understand in a certain way: *When my dog sees me put my coat on, he* interprets *it as a sign that we are going for a walk.* 3. To translate from one language into another: *My friend* interpreted *into English what his grandmother said to us in Spanish.*
in|ter|pret (in **tur′**prit) *verb,* **interpreted, interpreting.**

interrogate—To ask questions of: *When we got home late, my father* interrogated *us about where we had been.*
in|ter|ro|gate (in **ter′**ə gāt) *verb,* **interrogated, interrogating.**

interrogative—Used in asking questions. ''Who'' is an interrogative pronoun. *Adjective.*
—A word used in asking questions: *Who goes there?* The word ''who'' is an interrogative. *Noun.*
in|ter|rog|a|tive (in′tə **rog′**ə tiv) *adjective; noun, plural* **interrogatives.**

interrupt—To break in upon an action or upon a person speaking; stop: *A fallen tree across the path* interrupted *our progress.*
in|ter|rupt (in′tə **rupt′**) *verb,* **interrupted, interrupting.**

intersect—To divide; cross: *There is a signal light where the highway and the railroad* intersect.
in|ter|sect (in′tər sekt′) *verb,* **intersected, intersecting.**

intersection—A place where things cross each other: *There is a stop sign at the* intersection *of Broad Street and Maple Avenue.*
in|ter|sec|tion (in′tər sek′shən) *noun, plural* **intersections.**

interval—The time or space between; a break; gap: *Afternoon classes begin after a half-hour lunch* interval.
in|ter|val (in′tər vəl) *noun, plural* **intervals.**

interview—A meeting to discuss a particular subject: *A sports writer's* interview *with that hockey star was in today's newspaper. Noun.*
—To ask someone questions to gain information on a particular subject: *Reporters* interviewed *the candidates about their plans for the city. Verb.*
in|ter|view (in′tər vyū) *noun, plural* **interviews;** *verb,* **interviewed, interviewing.**

intestine—The very long, tube-shaped part of the digestive system that continues below the stomach. The small and large intestines absorb nutrients and eliminate waste materials.
in|tes|tine (in tes′tən) *noun, plural* **intestines.**
• See picture at **alimentary canal** and at **appendix.**

into—Toward the inner part of; to the inside of; to take the form of: into *a room; trees sawed* into *logs; a cold that turned* into *pneumonia.*
in|to (in′tū) *preposition.*

Word Power

You can understand the meanings of many words that begin with **intra-,** if you add the meaning of the prefix to the meaning of the rest of the word.
intrafamily: within a family
intramuscular: within a muscle

---

intra-—A prefix meaning "within." Intramural games are games within a school.

intramural—Having to do with sports or other activities carried on by members of the same school or college: *The sixth-graders played the fifth-graders in* intramural *basketball.*
in|tra|mu|ral (in′trə myoor′əl) *adjective.*

intricate—Difficult to do or solve; complex: *an* intricate *code for sending secret messages; an* intricate *spider's web.*
in|tri|cate (in′trə kit) *adjective.*

intrigue—To arouse the interest and curiosity of; fascinate: *The locked closet* intrigued *me—what could be inside?*
in|trigue (in trēg′) *verb,* **intrigued, intriguing.**

introduce—1. To cause to be acquainted: *She* introduced *her teacher to her mother.* 2. To bring into use, knowledge, or fashion: *The ice-cream store* introduced *a new flavor.* 3. To begin; start with: *He* introduced *his book report with a few words about the author.*
in|tro|duce (in′trə dūs′ *or* in′trə dyūs′) *verb,* **introduced, introducing.**

introduction—1. The act of being made acquainted with someone or something: *Soon after our* introduction *to each other, we became friends.* 2. The beginning; something before the main part: *In the* introduction *to his lecture, the speaker said he planned to show slides.*
in|tro|duc|tion (in′trə duk′shən) *noun, plural* **introductions.**

introvert—A person more interested in himself or herself than in others or in what is going on: *He is such an* introvert *he has few friends.*
in|tro|vert (in′trə vurt) *noun, plural* **introverts.**
• Antonym: **extrovert**

intrude—To enter without being asked or wanted: *We closed the door so no one could* intrude *on our meeting.*
in|trude (in trūd′) *verb,* **intruded, intruding.**

invade—1. To enter with plans to seize; attack: *The army* invaded *the neighboring country to seize its rich farmland.* 2. To intrude on; trespass: *My brother and I* invaded *the neighbor's orchard to get apples.*
in|vade (in vād′) *verb,* **invaded, invading.**

invalid¹—A person who is too sick or weak to care for himself or herself or who is not able to get around: *She will be an* invalid *for a while because of her broken ankle.*
in|va|lid (in′və lid) *noun, plural* **invalids.**

invalid²—Not true or based on fact; having no force, value, or effect: *This bus ticket is* invalid *on Sundays and holidays.*
in|val|id (in val′id) *adjective.*

invasion—An invading; attack; trespass: *The science-fiction book was about the* invasion *of the earth by creatures from another planet.*
in|va|sion (in vā′zhən) *noun, plural* **invasions.**

a at	i if	oo look	ch chalk		a in ago
ā ape	ī idle	ou out	ng sing		e in happen
ah calm	o odd	u ugly	sh ship	ə =	i in capital
aw all	ō oats	ū rule	th think		o in occur
e end	oi oil	ur turn	th their		u in upon
ē easy			zh treasure		

invent—1. To think up or create something for the first time: *Do you know how people lit their homes before the electric light bulb was invented?* 2. To make or think up as an excuse, story, or lie: *She invented a sore throat to keep from having to give her speech.*
in|vent (in vent′) *verb,* invented, inventing.
• Synonyms: design, devise, for 1.

invention—1. The act of making something new: *The invention of the car made travel easier.* 2. A thing that is invented: *The wheel was an early invention.* 3. A made-up or imagined story: *Her tale of seeing a flying saucer was just an invention.*
in|ven|tion (in ven′shən) *noun, plural* inventions.

inventor—Someone who invents.
in|ven|tor (in ven′tər) *noun, plural* inventors.

invert—1. To turn upside down or inside out: *A gust of wind inverted my umbrella.* 2. To change the order, position, or direction; reverse: *If you invert the words in the question "Do I?" you have an answer, "I do."*
in|vert (in vurt′) *verb,* inverted, inverting.

invertebrate—Being without a backbone: *A jellyfish is an invertebrate animal. Adjective.* —An animal without a backbone: *A worm is an invertebrate. Noun.*
in|ver|te|brate (in vur′tə brit *or* in vur′tə brāt) *adjective; noun, plural* invertebrates.
• See pictures at **jellyfish, octopus, squid,** and **starfish**

invest—1. To use one's money to purchase something that pays interest or that may increase in value and thereby make more money: *to invest in the stock market.* 2. To put one's time or effort into something for future benefit or advantage: *He invested all his spare time in building his own boat.*
in|vest (in vest′) *verb,* invested, investing.

investigate—To explore or examine carefully in order to find out the facts: *We could hardly wait to investigate the contents of the mysterious box.*
in|ves|ti|gate (in ves′tə gāt) *verb,* investigated, investigating.
• Synonyms: analyze, inspect, study .

investment—1. The act of putting one's money, time, or effort into something for future benefit or advantage: *My investment in studying paid off when I took the test.* 2. An amount of money that is invested: *Her many investments added up to more than $50,000.* 3. Something bought that is expected to pay interest or increase in value: *He did not like the painting by the famous artist and bought it only as an* investment.
in|vest|ment (in vest′mənt) *noun, plural* investments.

invisible—Not able to be seen: *The path was invisible in the darkness.*
in|vis|i|ble (in viz′ə bəl) *adjective.*

invitation—A polite written or spoken request to do something or go somewhere: *Did you receive an invitation to her party?*
in|vi|ta|tion (in′və tā′shən) *noun, plural* invitations.

invite—1. To ask someone politely to do something or go somewhere: *She invited me to join the group that was going to the movie.* 2. To request; ask for politely: *The speaker invited questions from the audience.* 3. To attract, tempt, or encourage: *The cool, clear water of the lake invited swimmers.*
in|vite (in vīt′) *verb,* invited, inviting.

involve—1. To have as part of itself; include: *Being a ballet dancer involves talent and a lot of hard work.* 2. To cause to be included in something, especially trouble or a difficulty: *The fight that began between the two players soon involved the rest of both teams.* 3. To interest very much; absorb: *He was so involved in the book that he forgot to eat lunch.*
in|volve (in volv′) *verb,* involved, involving.

involved—Complicated: *We found the involved instructions very difficult to follow.*
in|volved (in volvd′) *adjective.*

inward—Toward the inside, center, or the interior: *The road leads inward from the edge to the center of the city.*
in|ward (in′wərd) *adverb.*

iodine—1. A chemical element in the form of grayish-black crystals. It is used in medicine, photography, and dye-making. 2. A brown liquid made with this chemical. It is put on wounds to prevent infection.
i|o|dine (ī′ə dīn; ī′ə dēn for 1 only) *noun.*

-ion—A suffix that means "act of" or "state of being." An investigation is an act of investigating. Separation is the state of being separated.

Word Power

You can understand the meanings of many words that end in **-ion,** if you add a meaning of the suffix to the meaning of the rest of the word.
  agitation: state of being agitated
  rebellion: act of rebelling

iota—A very small part; bit: *There isn't an* iota *of truth in his tall tales.*
i|o|ta (ī ō′tə) *Noun.*

irate—Angry; enraged. *My father was really* irate *when I told him I had broken his tennis racket.*
i|rate (ī′rāt *or* ī rāt′) *adjective.*

ire—Anger. *I tried very hard not to show my* ire.
ire (īr) *noun.*

iris—**1.** Any one of a number of garden flowers that grow on plants that have long, sword-shaped leaves. Most irises are purple, blue, or white. The iris is the state flower of Tennessee. **2.** The colored part of the eye. It surrounds the pupil and controls the amount of light entering the eye.
i|ris (ī′ris) *noun, plural* **irises.**
• For **2**, see picture at **eye.**

Irish setter—A medium-sized hunting dog with a thick, red coat. Originally bred in Ireland, these dogs are used for bird hunting.
I|rish set|ter (ī′rish set′ər) *noun, plural* **Irish setters.**

Irish terrier

Irish setter

Irish terrier—A small hunting dog with small, drooping ears and a coarse, wiry, red coat.

Originally bred in Ireland, these dogs are retrievers and make excellent watchdogs.
I|rish ter|ri|er (ī′rish ter′ē ər) *noun, plural* **Irish terriers.**

Irish water spaniel—A medium-sized hunting dog with a curly, oily coat. Originally bred in Ireland, these dogs are good swimmers and retrievers.
I|rish wa|ter span|iel (ī′rish wawt′ər span′yəl) *noun, plural* **Irish water spaniels.**

a at	i if	oo look	ch chalk		⌈ a in ago
ā ape	ī idle	ou out	ng sing		e in happen
ah calm	o odd	u ugly	sh ship	ə =	i in capital
aw all	ō oats	ū rule	th think		o in occur
e end	oi oil	ur turn	th their		⌊ u in upon
ē easy			zh treasure		

Irish water spaniel

Irish wolfhound—A large hunting dog with a coarse, wiry coat. Originally bred in Ireland, these dogs run very fast and were used to hunt wolves and large game, such as deer.
I|rish wolf|hound (ī′rish woolf′hound′) *noun, plural* **Irish wolfhounds.**

Irish wolfhound

iron—1. A chemical element in the form of a hard, grayish-white metal. It is one of the most important metals and is used to make steel. 2. A utensil made from iron: *a tire* iron. 3. A handheld electrical appliance that has a flat surface and is used to smooth or press clothes and other items made of fabric. *Noun.*
—To press or smooth with such an appliance. *Verb.*
—Hard or strong: iron *muscles; an* iron *will. Adjective.*
iron (ī′ərn) *noun, plural* **irons;** *verb,* **ironed, ironing;** *adjective.*
  ■ **have too many irons in the fire:** To try to do too many things at the same time: *She said she could not join our club because she already* had too many irons in the fire.
  iron out: To smooth out, settle, or overcome: *They had a big argument but soon* ironed out *their differences and became friends again.*
  pump iron: To exercise by lifting weights: Pumping iron *has made him very strong.*
  strike while the iron is hot: To act quickly when conditions are right or a chance presents itself: *Your sister is in a good mood, so let's* strike while the iron is hot *and ask her for a ride.*

irony—A way of using words to express the exact opposite of what one really means. To say "What a beautiful day!" while standing in the rain is an example of irony.
i|ron|y (ī′rə nē) *noun, plural* **ironies.**

irregular—1. Not in the normal way; unusual: irregular *behavior.* 2. Not smooth, even, or straight: *The dirt road had an* irregular *surface.*
ir|reg|u|lar (i reg′yə lər) *adjective.*

irresistible—Impossible to be resisted; too strong or great to be opposed: *I tried to stay indoors and study, but the urge to play outside was* irresistible.
ir|re|sist|i|ble (ēr′i zist′ə bəl) *adjective.*

irresponsible—Having no sense of one's duties or obligations; not reliable: *It was very* irresponsible *of him to forget to call his mother to tell her that he would be late.*
ir|re|spon|si|ble (ēr′i spon′sə bəl) *adjective.*

irrigate—To supply land with water by means of canals, pipes, or sprinklers.
ir|ri|gate (ēr′ə gāt) *verb,* **irrigated, irrigating.**

irritable—Easily annoyed or made angry: *My brother is very* irritable *when he does not get enough sleep.*
ir|ri|ta|ble (ēr′ə tə bəl) *adjective.*

irritate—1. To annoy or make angry; bother: *The barking dog* irritated *her.* 2. To make a part of the body especially sensitive: *The sand in his shoe* irritated *his foot.*
ir|ri|tate (ēr′ə tāt) *verb,* **irritated, irritating.**

is—*See* **be.**
is (iz) *verb.*

-ish—A suffix that means "somewhat" or "like a." Reddish hair is somewhat red. Clownish behavior is behavior like that of a clown.

Word Power

You can understand the meanings of many words that end in **-ish,** if you add a meaning of the suffix to the meaning of the rest of the word.
  childish: like a child
  oldish: somewhat old

Islam—The religion preached by the prophet and teacher Muhammad. Members of this religion are called Muslims. Its holy book is the Koran.
Is|lam (is′ləm, iz′ləm, is lahm′, *or* iz lahm′) *noun.*

island—1. A piece of land that is completely surrounded by water and too small to be called a continent. 2. Something that resembles a piece

of land surrounded by water: *A traffic* island *separates the two lanes of the road.*
is|land (ī′lənd) *noun, plural* **islands.**
Abbreviation: **is.** or **isl.**

isle—An island, especially a small one.
isle (īl) *noun, plural* **isles.**
● Words that sound the same are **aisle** and **I'll.**

islet—A very small island.
is|let (ī′lit) *noun, plural* **islets.**
● A word that sounds the same is **eyelet.**

-ism—A suffix that means "act or practice of" or "condition of being." Criticism is the act or practice of criticizing. Patriotism is the condition of being a patriot.

Word Power

You can understand the meanings of many words that end in **-ism,** if you add a meaning of the suffix to the meaning of the rest of the word.
baptism: act of baptizing
heroism: condition of being a hero

isn't—The contraction of "is not."
is|n't (iz′ənt).

isolate—To set or place apart; separate from others: *I will* isolate *myself in my room until I finish my homework.*
i|so|late (ī′sə lāt) *verb,* **isolated, isolating.**

isosceles triangle—A triangle that has two sides of the same length.
i|sos|ce|les tri|an|gle (ī sos′ə lēz trī′ang gəl) *noun, plural* **isosceles triangles.**

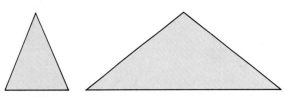

isosceles triangle

issue—1. To put forth or pass out officially: *A uniform was* issued *to each team member.* 2. To publish or print: *We will* issue *our next school paper in a month. Verb.*

—1. Something that has been officially printed or sent out: *the June* issue *of a magazine.*
2. The act of sending out, putting forth, or passing out: *The office controls the* issue *of supplies for each classroom.* 3. An unsettled matter that needs to be considered or decided; problem: *The student council will discuss the* issue *of a new school dress code. Noun.*
is|sue (ish′ū) *verb,* **issued, issuing;** *noun, plural* **issues.**
■ **take issue:** To dispute or disagree with: *We like the old motto for the club and* take issue *with the president's plan for a new one.*
● Synonyms: **dispense, distribute,** for *verb* **1.**

-ist—A suffix that means "a person who is an expert in something" or "a person who does something." A biologist is an expert in biology. An organist is a person who plays the organ.

Word Power

You can understand the meanings of many words that end in **-ist,** if you add a meaning of the suffix to the meaning of the rest of the word.
botanist: expert in botany
novelist: person who writes novels

isthmus—A narrow strip of land that connects two larger land areas and that has water on both sides.
isth|mus (is′məs) *noun, plural* **isthmuses** or **isthmi** (is′mī).

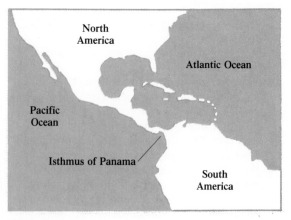

isthmus

it—1. The animal or object spoken about; that one: *If my hat fits you, you may wear* it. 2. An unspecific subject: *It is raining today.*
it (it) *pronoun.*

a at	i if	oo look	ch chalk		a in ago
ā ape	ī idle	ou out	ng sing		e in happen
ah calm	o odd	u ugly	sh ship	ə =	i in capital
aw all	ō oats	ū rule	th think		o in occur
e end	oi oil	ur turn	<u>th</u> their		u in upon
ē easy			zh treasure		

Italian greyhound—A very small dog with a slender body, slender legs, and a smooth coat with white markings. Originally bred in Italy, these dogs make good pets.
I|tal|ian grey|hound (i tal′yən grā′hound′) *noun, plural* **Italian greyhounds.**

Italian greyhound

italic—Of or in a style of type having letters that slant upward to the right: *This entire sentence is printed in italic type. Adjective.*
—**italics:** Italic type. *Noun.*
i|tal|ic (i tal′ik *or* ī tal′ik) *adjective; plural noun.* Abbreviation: **ital.**

itch—**1.** A prickling or tickling feeling in the skin causing an urge to scratch. **2.** A restless desire to do or get something: *Every winter I get an itch to go skiing. Noun.*
—**1.** To feel a prickling or tickling in the skin: *When I had chicken pox, I* itched *all over.* **2.** To have a restless desire to do or get something: *She* itched *to try out her new bicycle. Verb.*
itch (ich) *noun, plural* **itches;** *verb,* **itched, itching.**

item—**1.** A separate article in a group, series, or list: *Pizza is the most popular* item *on the menu.* **2.** A piece of news or information: *I saw an* item *in the newspaper about your sister's softball game.*
i|tem (ī′təm) *noun, plural* **items.**

itemize—To list each item in a group: *My father asked me to* itemize *what I had bought, showing the price of each item.*
i |tem|ize (ī′tə mīz) *verb,* **itemized, itemizing.**

it'll—The contraction of "it will" or "it shall."
it|'ll (it′əl).

its—Of or belonging to it: *The tree lost* its *leaves.*
its (its) *adjective.*
• A word that sounds the same is **it's.**

it's—The contraction of "it is" or "it has."
it's (its).
• A word that sounds the same is **its.**

itself—**1.** The form of "it" used for stress: *I saw the nest, but the bird* itself *had flown away.*
2. The form of "it" used to refer to someone or something already mentioned: *The monkey scratched* itself.
it|self (it self′) *pronoun.*

-ity—A suffix that means "state or condition of being." Superiority is the state of being superior.

Word Power

You can understand the meanings of many words that end in **-ity**, if you add a meaning of the suffix to the meaning of the rest of the word.
   equality: state or condition of being equal
   rapidity: state or condition of being rapid

I've—The contraction of "I have."
I've (īv).

ivory—**1.** A hard, creamy-white substance that forms the tusks of elephants and the teeth of some whales. **2.** A yellowish-white color like cream. *Noun.*
—Having a yellowish-white color. *Adjective.*
i|vo|ry (ī′vər ē) *noun, adjective.*

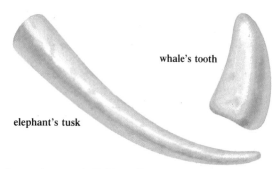

whale's tooth

elephant's tusk

ivory (noun, definition 1)

ivy—An evergreen vine with smooth, shiny leaves. It can cling to walls or trail along the ground.
i|vy (ī′vē) *noun, plural* **ivies.**

About 5,000 years ago, the ancient Egyptians used a symbol of a hand. The letters I and J both came from this symbol.

About 3,500 years ago, people in the Middle East made a simpler symbol.

About 3,000 years ago, other people in the Middle East used this form. They called it *yod*, their word for "hand."

About 2,600 years ago, the Greeks gave the letter this form. They called it *iota*.

The letter **J** was the last letter to be added to our alphabet. During the Middle Ages (the period between about A.D. 500 and 1450), writers would sometimes add a tail to the capital **I**. The present form of the capital **J** came from this practice. The small letter **j** came from the small letter **i**. It was first used about 800 years ago.

J or **j**—The tenth letter of the alphabet: *There is one j in the word "jump."*
J, j (jā) *noun, plural* **J's** or **Js, j's** or **js.**

jab—To hit suddenly or quickly with something that is pointed; poke: *My friend* jabbed *me with her elbow when I started to laugh. Verb.*
—A hit with something pointed. *Noun.*
jab (jab) *verb,* **jabbed, jabbing;** *noun, plural* **jabs.**

jack—1. A device for raising a heavy object a short distance off the ground: *He could not change the flat tire because he had no* jack *to lift the car.* **2.** A playing card with a picture of a young man on it. **3. jacks:** A game played with a ball and several small, six-pointed, metal pieces also called jacks. In this game, a player picks up a certain number of jacks while bouncing and catching the ball. *Noun.*
—To raise with a jack: *The crew quickly* jacked *up the racing car and changed the tires. Verb.*
jack (jak) *noun, plural* **jacks;** *verb,* **jacked, jacking.**
■ **jack up:** To increase: *The movie theater recently* jacked up *the price of admission by $2.*

jackal—A wild dog of Africa, Asia, and eastern Europe. It is about the size of a fox. It feeds on smaller animals, eggs, and the remains of animals that are already dead.
jack|al (jak′awl *or* jak′əl) *noun, plural* **jackals.**

jackal

jacket—1. A short coat for the upper body, usually reaching to the hips. **2.** An outer casing or covering: *a book* jacket; *a record* jacket.
jack|et (jak′it) *noun, plural* **jackets.**

jack-in-the-box—A toy consisting of a figure, usually a clown, that pops out of a small, decorated box when the top is opened.
jack-in-the-box (jak′in <u>th</u>ə boks′) *noun, plural* **jack-in-the-boxes.**

a at	i if	oo look	ch chalk		a in ago
ā ape	ī idle	ou out	ng sing		e in happen
ah calm	o odd	u ugly	sh ship	ə =	i in capital
aw all	ō oats	ū rule	th think		o in occur
e end	oi oil	ur turn	<u>th</u> their		u in upon
ē easy			zh treasure		

jack-in-the-pulpit—A North American plant that flowers in the spring. Its tiny greenish-yellow flowers grow in a club-shaped spike on top of a slender stalk. A purplish-green section like a leaf arches over the spike.
jack-in-the-pulpit (jak′in t͟hə **pool**′pit) *noun, plural* **jack-in-the-pulpits.**

jack-in-the-pulpit

jackknife—1. A pocketknife with blades that fold into the handle.   2. A swimming dive in which the person bends at the waist and, extending the hands, touches the feet before straightening out to enter the water.
jack|knife (jak′nīf′) *noun, plural* **jackknives.**

jack-o'-lantern—A hollowed-out pumpkin that has a face carved on it. A candle is usually placed inside it. Jack-o'-lanterns are made to celebrate Halloween.
jack-o'-lan|tern (jak′ə lan′tərn) *noun, plural* **jack-o'-lanterns.**

jackpot—The best prize or largest amount of money that can be won in a contest or game.
jack|pot (jak′pot′) *noun, plural* **jackpots.**

jack rabbit—A hare found in western North America. It has very long ears and strong back legs that allow it to run very fast and jump far.
jack rab|bit (jak **rab**′it) *noun, plural* **jack rabbits.**

Jacuzzi—A special bathtub that has a device for making the water churn and swirl.
Ja|cuz|zi (jə kū′zē) *noun, plural* **Jacuzzis.**

jade—A hard, green or white stone that takes a high polish and is used for jewelry and carvings.
jade (jād) *noun.*

jagged—Sharply pointed; not evenly cut or torn; ragged: *the* jagged *edge of ripped paper; a* jagged *cliff.*
jag|ged (jag′id) *adjective.*

jaguar—A large, black-spotted member of the cat family. Found in tropical America, the jaguar looks like a leopard but has a thicker body.
jag|uar (jag′wahr) *noun, plural* **jaguars.**

jaguar

jail—A prison. It is usually one where people are kept who are waiting for a trial or being punished for a crime that is not very serious. *Noun.*
—To confine in such a prison: *The police* jailed *the man arrested for stealing. Verb.*
jail (jāl) *noun, plural* **jails;** *verb,* **jailed, jailing.**

jam[1]—1. To squeeze or force into a tight position: *Six of us* jammed *into one small car to go to the movies.*   2. To injure by squeezing; crush or bruise: *He* jammed *his fingers while trying to close the window.*   3. To become stuck or caught so as not to work: *My camera* jammed, *and I could not take any more pictures.*   4. To push or shove with great force: *The basketball player* jammed *the ball into the basket. Verb.*
—1. A large crowd of people or things: *a traffic* jam.   2. A difficult or tricky situation: *She was in a real* jam *when she discovered that she had locked herself out of the house. Noun.*
jam (jam) *verb,* **jammed, jamming;** *noun, plural* **jams.**

jam[2]—A food that is a mixture of fruit and sugar boiled until it is thick enough to spread: *strawberry* jam.
jam (jam) *noun, plural* **jams.**

jamboree—1. A large party or celebration.   2. A large group of Boy Scouts gathered together for a rally, especially an international one.
jam|bo|ree (jam′bə rē′) *noun, plural* **jamborees.**

Jan.—The abbreviation for **January.**

janitor—A person whose job is the care and cleaning of a building; custodian.
jan|i|tor (jan′ə tər) *noun, plural* **janitors.**

January—The first month of the year. January has 31 days.
Jan|u|ar|y (jan′yoo er′ē) *noun.* Abbreviation: **Jan.**

Word History

January got its name from the Roman god Janus. He was the god of beginnings and endings and was shown with two faces that looked in opposite directions. January, the first month of the year, can be thought to look back over the past year and forward to the new year.

Japanese beetle—A small, green and brown beetle that was accidentally brought to the United States from Japan. It causes much damage by feeding on flowers, leaves, and fruits.
Jap|a|nese bee|tle (jap′ə nēz′ bē′təl) *noun, plural* **Japanese beetles.**

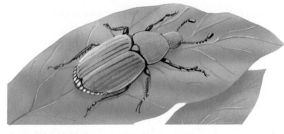

Japanese beetle

Japanese bobtail—A short-haired cat with a very short tail and back legs that are longer than the front legs. Originally bred in Japan, these cats were considered to bring good luck.
Jap|a|nese bob|tail (jap′ə nēz′ bob′tāl′) *noun, plural* **Japanese bobtails.**

Japanese chin—A very small dog with a short nose, large eyes, and a broad, rounded head. It has long, thick, silky hair. Originally bred in ancient China, these dogs were brought to Japan. They used to be called Japanese spaniels.
Jap|a|nese chin (jap′ə nēz′ chin) *noun, plural* **Japanese chins.**

jar¹—A deep container with a wide mouth, usually made of glass or pottery: *a jar of pickles.*
jar (jahr) *noun, plural* **jars.**

jar²—**1.** To bump; rattle; shake: *The pencil fell to the floor when he* jarred *the desk.* **2.** To have an unpleasant effect on: *The sudden burst of loud music* jarred *my ears. Verb.*
—**1.** A violent shaking; very sudden movement: *The building received quite a* jar *during the earthquake. Noun.*
jar (jahr) *verb,* **jarred, jarring;** *noun, plural* **jars.**
• Synonyms: For *verb* **1,** see Synonyms at **bump.**

javelin—**1.** A light spear thrown as a weapon or for hunting. **2.** A wooden or metal spear that is thrown for distance in track-and-field contests.
jave|lin (jav′ə lin) *noun, plural* **javelins.**

jaw—**1.** The lower part of one's face. **2.** Either of the two sets of bones that form the structure of the mouth and hold the teeth in place. The upper jaw is fixed in place, but the lower jaw can move. **3.** Either of two parts of a device, such as a vice, that can be opened and closed. *Noun.*
—**1.** To talk for a long time: *The two friends* jawed *on the telephone all evening. Verb.*
jaw (jaw) *noun, plural* **jaws;** *verb,* **jawed, jawing.**

jaywalk—To walk across a street without paying attention to the traffic laws.
jay|walk (jā′wawk′) *verb,* **jaywalked, jaywalking.**

jazz—A kind of music that originated in the United States. It has a strong and sometimes unusual rhythm. Musicians often add to the music as they play it. *Noun.*
—Of or like such music: jazz *musicians;* a jazz *record album. Adjective.*
jazz (jaz) *noun, adjective.*

jealous—**1.** Afraid that a person one loves or is fond of may be fond of someone else or love someone else more: *At first I was* jealous *when my best friend met new people at camp, but now we all play together.* **2.** Resenting what another has or can do: *She is* jealous *of his good grades.*

Japanese bobtail

a at	i if	oo look	ch chalk		a in ago
ā ape	ī idle	ou out	ng sing		e in happen
ah calm	o odd	u ugly	sh ship	ə =	i in capital
aw all	ō oats	ū rule	th think		o in occur
e end	oi oil	ur turn	th their		u in upon
ē easy			zh treasure		

3. Careful; watchful: *The dog keeps a* jealous *eye on its owner's house.*
jeal|ous (jel′əs) *adjective.*

jealousy—A feeling of envy; condition of being jealous: *There is no reason for* jealousy *because he has a new coat and you do not.*
jeal|ous|y (jel′ə sē) *noun, plural* **jealousies.**

jean—**1.** A heavy, cotton cloth used to make work and informal clothes.   **2. jeans:** Pants made of this cloth.
jean (jēn) *noun, plural* **jeans.**
• A word that sounds the same is **gene.**

jeepers—An exclamation of surprise: Jeepers! *That dinosaur skeleton is huge!*
jee|pers (jē′pərz) *interjection.*

jeer—To speak to, shout at, or treat in a rude and unkind way; mock; ridicule: *The audience* jeered *at the villain in the play. Verb.*
—A mocking remark: *The umpires were greeted with* jeers *when they came onto the field. Noun.*
jeer (jēr) *verb,* **jeered, jeering;** *noun, plural* **jeers.**

Jefferson Davis's Birthday—June 3 or the first Monday in June. Seven Southern states honor the president of the Confederacy on this day. Davis was born on June 3, 1808.
Jef|fer|son Da|vis's Birth|day (jef′ər sən dā′vis iz burth′dā) *noun.*

Jehovah—A name for God in the Old Testament of the Bible.
Je|ho|vah (ji hō′və) *noun.*

Jehovah's Witness—A member of a religious group that believes the end of the world is near. The group was founded in the 1870's in Pennsylvania.
Je|ho|vah's Wit|ness (ji hō′vəz wit′nis) *noun, plural* **Jehovah's Witnesses.**

jelly—**1.** A soft food made by boiling sugar and fruit juice together. A substance such as gelatin may be added to make the liquid harden when it cools.   **2.** Any substance like this food. *Noun.*
—To turn into or make jelly: *We* jellied *blueberries at summer camp so we would have something to put on our morning toast. Verb.*
jel|ly (jel′ē) *noun, plural* **jellies;** *verb,* **jellied, jellying.**

jellybean—A bean-shaped candy made from jellied sugar.
jel|ly|bean (jel′ē bēn′) *noun, plural* **jellybeans.**

jellyfish—A sea animal that has no backbone and feels like jelly. It has a rounded, bell-shaped body with dangling tentacles. Small hairs on the tentacles can cause a painful sting to people.
jel|ly|fish (jel′ē fish′) *noun, plural* **jellyfishes** or **jellyfish.**

jeopardize—To put in danger: *Her fall* jeopardizes *her chances of winning the ice-skating competition.*
jeop|ard|ize (jep′ər dīz) *verb,* **jeopardized, jeopardizing.**

jerk—A sudden, sharp motion: *The train started with a* jerk *but then moved smoothly. Noun.*
—**1.** To give something a sudden pull or twist: *She* jerked *the handle, and the door popped open.*   **2.** To move with or make a sudden motion: *The old car* jerked *and chugged down the street. Verb.*
jerk (jurk) *noun, plural* **jerks;** *verb,* **jerked, jerking.**

jersey—**1.** A soft, knitted cloth made from wool or other material.   **2.** A shirt or sweater made of this cloth and pulled on over the head.
jer|sey (jur′zē) *noun, plural* **jerseys.**

jest—A joke or amusing trick; prank: *They put a rubber snake in his sleeping bag as a* jest. *Noun.*
—To say or do something as a joke: *I was* jesting *when I told her I won a million dollars in the lottery. Verb.*
jest (jest) *noun, plural* **jests;** *verb,* **jested, jesting.**
• Synonyms: **fool, kid²,** for *verb.*

Jesus—In the Christian religion, the Son of God. His teachings are the basis of Christianity. He is thought to have been born between 8 B.C. and 1 B.C. and to have died about A.D. 29. He is also known as Jesus Christ.
Je|sus (jē′zəs) *noun.*

jet—**1.** A fast stream of liquid, steam, or gas sent through a small opening by strong pressure: *The fire fighters aimed the* jet *of water at the burning*

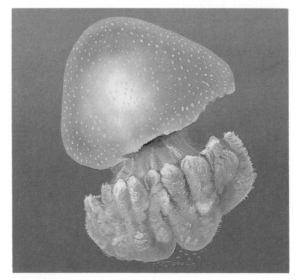

jellyfish

building. **2.** An engine powered by forcing a stream of gas through a small opening, or an aircraft powered by such engines. *Noun.*
—To spurt; gush out: *Oil* jetted *from the well. Verb.*
jet (jet) *noun, plural* **jets;** *verb,* **jetted, jetting.**

jet engine—An engine that is powered by forcing a stream of gas through a small opening.
jet en|gine (jet en′jin) *noun, plural* **jet engines.**

jet stream—A fast-moving current of air that occurs at high altitudes. It is very important in predicting weather and in piloting aircraft.
jet stream (jet strēm) *noun.*

Jew—**1.** A person who is descended from the ancient Hebrews. **2.** A follower of Judaism.
Jew (jū) *noun, plural* **Jews.**

jewel—**1.** A gem; valuable stone: *The bracelet had several rubies and other* jewels. **2.** A valuable ornament that contains one or more gems: *The necklace on display at the museum is a rare* jewel. **3.** Someone or something that is valuable: *My grandmother is a* jewel. *Noun.*
—To decorate or set with gems: *The crown was* jeweled *with four diamonds. Verb.*
jew|el (ju′əl) *noun, plural* **jewels;** *verb,* **jeweled, jeweling.**

jeweler—A person whose job is to make, repair, or sell jewelry and related articles.
jew|el|er (jū′ə lər) *noun, plural* **jewelers.**

jewelry—Ornaments people wear. Rings, necklaces, bracelets, and pins are all jewelry.
jew|el|ry (jū′əl rē) *noun.*

Jewish—Having to do with Jews or their religion: *a* Jewish *holiday.*
Jew|ish (jū′ish) *adjective.*

jib—A sail shaped like a triangle that hangs in front of a boat's or ship's front mast.
jib (jib) *noun, plural* **jibs.**

jiffy—An instant; very short time: *The cat, chased by a barking dog, climbed the tree in a* jiffy.
jif|fy (jif′ē) *noun, plural* **jiffies.**

jig—**1.** A fast and lively dance. **2.** Music for such a dance: *He played a* jig *on his fiddle. Noun.*
—To do such a dance *Verb.*
jig (jig) *noun, plural* **jigs;** *verb,* **jigged, jigging.**

jiggle—To rock or shake lightly: *The baby* jiggled *the playpen as he tried to stand up in it. Verb.*
—A slight shaking movement: *There was only a* jiggle *of the tightrope as the circus performer balanced on one foot. Noun.*
jig|gle (jig′əl) *verb,* **jiggled, jiggling;** *noun, plural* **jiggles.**

jigsaw—A saw that has a narrow blade and is set in a frame. It is used to cut curved lines.
jig|saw (jig′saw′) *noun, plural* **jigsaws.**

jigsaw puzzle—A picture that has been cut up into many different pieces that can be fitted together to remake the picture.
jig|saw puz|zle (jig′saw′ puz′əl) *noun, plural* **jigsaw puzzles.**

jingle—**1.** A tinkling sound: *the* jingle *of sleigh bells.* **2.** A short song that rhymes or has repeated sounds. Jingles are used in radio and television commercials. *Noun.*
—To make a tinkling sound: *He always* jingles *the coins in his pocket when he is nervous. Verb.*
jin|gle (jing′gəl) *noun, plural* **jingles;** *verb,* **jingled, jingling.**

jinx—Someone or something that causes bad luck: *Many people think that walking under ladders is a* jinx. *Noun.*
—To bring bad luck: *She felt that she could not do anything right after she was* jinxed *by a black cat crossing her path. Verb.*
jinx (jingks) *noun, plural* **jinxes;** *verb,* **jinxed, jinxing.**

jitters—An uncomfortable, nervous feeling: *The boy had the* jitters *before he took the math test.*
jit|ters (jit′ərz) *plural noun.*

jittery—Uncomfortable and nervous: *He was* jittery *before the championship game.*
jit|ter|y (jit′ər ē) *adjective.*

job—**1.** Employment; paid work: *She has a* job *as a police officer.* **2.** A task; chore: *Her* job *is to clean up after dinner.*
job (job) *noun, plural* **jobs.**

jockey—Someone who rides horses in races.
jock|ey (jok′ē) *noun, plural* **jockeys.**

jodhpurs—Pants worn for horseback riding that are loosely fitted above the knees and tightly fitted below the knees.
jodh|purs (jod′pərz) *plural noun.*

jog—To run slowly at a steady pace: *I* jog *around the block every evening. Verb.*
—A slow, steady run: *My neighbors took a* jog *around the park. Noun.*
jog (jog) *verb,* **jogged, jogging;** *noun, plural* **jogs.**

a at	i if	oo look	ch chalk		a in ago
ā ape	ī idle	ou out	ng sing		e in happen
ah calm	o odd	u ugly	sh ship	ə =	i in capital
aw all	ō oats	ū rule	th think		o in occur
e end	oi oil	ur turn	th their		u in upon
ē easy			zh treasure		

join—1. To fasten or bring together; connect: *to join hands; to join the ends of a chain.*   2. To come together; meet up with each other: *The two roads join at the intersection.*   3. To become a member of: *My sister joined the Girl Scouts.* 4. To enter into company with: *We will join you for lunch after class.*
join (join) *verb,* **joined, joining.**

joint—1. The place where two or more things come together: *My uncle tightened the joint connecting the table leg to the table top.*   2. The point at which two bones are connected together. The joint allows one or both parts to move or bend freely: *The knuckles on your fingers are joints. Noun.*
—Shared; done with someone else: *My parents have a joint bank account. Adjective.*
joint (joint) *noun, plural* **joints;** *adjective.*
■ **out of joint:** In a bad way: *I am feeling out of joint today, so I want to stay in bed.*

joke—Something said or done in order to make someone laugh: *My sister is good at telling funny jokes. Noun.*
—To say or do something funny in order to make someone laugh: *He was only joking when he pretended not to know me. Verb.*
joke (jōk) *noun, plural* **jokes;** *verb,* **joked, joking.**
● Synonyms: **fool, jest, kid²,** for *verb.*

jolly—Very cheerful; full of fun: *a jolly old elf; having a jolly time at the fair.*
jol|ly (jol′ē) *adjective,* **jollier, jolliest.**

jolt—1. To move or shake with a jerk: *We were jolted forward when Dad suddenly stopped the car.*   2. To surprise; alarm: *News of the robbery jolted everyone in town. Verb.*
—1. A sudden jerk: *The Ferris wheel stopped with a jolt.*   2. A shock or surprise: *What a jolt it was to hear about your mother's sudden operation. Noun.*
jolt (jōlt) *verb,* **jolted, jolting;** *noun, plural* **jolts.**
● Synonyms: For *verb* **1,** see Synonyms at **bump.**

jonquil—A garden plant similar to a daffodil, with long, thin leaves and yellow or white flowers having cup-shaped centers surrounded by six petals.
jon|quil (jong′kwəl) *noun, plural* **jonquils.**

journal—1. A brief record or account of daily events; diary: *My grandfather keeps a journal of his thoughts.*   2. A newspaper or magazine: *The professor writes for several scientific journals.*
jour|nal (jur′nəl) *noun, plural* **journals.**

journalism—1. The business of writing for, editing, or publishing magazines and newspapers. 2. The writing itself that is done for magazines and newspapers: *That article about the mayor is an example of good journalism.*
jour|nal|ism (jur′nə liz əm) *noun.*

journalist—Someone who writes for or edits a magazine or newspaper for a living.
jour|nal|ist (jur′nə list) *noun, plural* **journalists.**

journey—The act of traveling to some place; trip: *My parents will take a journey through Europe next summer. Noun.*
—To travel; go on a long trip: *My brother wants to be an astronaut and journey into space. Verb.*
jour|ney (jur′nē) *noun, plural* **journeys;** *verb,* **journeyed, journeying.**

joust—A fight with lances between two knights in armor who are on horseback. *Noun.*
—To fight on horseback with lances: *The two knights jousted in the tournament while the king watched. Verb.*
joust (joust) *noun, plural* **jousts;** *verb,* **jousted, jousting.**

jovial—Jolly; full of fun: *I like to visit my uncle because he is so jovial and makes us feel so welcome.*
jo|vi|al (jō′vē əl) *adjective.*

joy—1. A happy feeling; delight: *My sister was full of joy as she opened her birthday presents.* 2. Someone or something that brings much happiness: *The new baby is a joy to my family.*
joy (joi) *noun, plural* **joys.**
● Synonyms: **bliss, pleasure,** for **1.**
Antonyms: **misery, sorrow, woe,** for **1.**

jodhpurs

joy stick—A control lever, especially for a computer: *By using the joy stick, I can move the figures around on the computer screen.*
joy stick (joi stik) *noun, plural* **joy sticks.**

Jr.—The abbreviation for **junior.** It is placed after the name of a man or boy who has the same name as his father.

jubilant—Full of joy; very happy: *The basketball players were* jubilant *after their team won the state tournament.*
ju|bi|lant (jū′bə lənt) *adjective.*

Judaism—The Jewish religion, based on the teachings of Moses and the prophets in the Old Testament of the Bible.
Ju|da|ism (jū′dē iz əm) *noun.*

judge—1. Someone who is elected or appointed to hear cases and make decisions on them in a court of law: *The* judge *sentenced the burglar to five years in prison.* 2. Someone who decides the winner in a contest or race: *The judges voted him the winner of the dance competition.* 3. Someone who knows a lot about something and can give an opinion on it: *A veterinarian is a good* judge *of cats. Noun.*
—1. To hear cases and make decisions on them in a court of law: *The traffic court will* judge *who caused the accident.* 2. To decide the winner in a contest or race: *Our teacher* judged *the projects the class made for the science fair.* 3. To form an opinion about someone or something: *You* judge *your brother too harshly. Verb.*
judge (juj) *noun, plural* **judges;** *verb,* **judged, judging.**

judgment—1. Good sense; wisdom: *My girlfriend always looks nice because she uses* judgment *when selecting clothes.* 2. An opinion; belief: *Mother is a good cook, in my* judgment. 3. A decision made by a judge or a law court: *The* judgment *of the court allowed the man to go free.*
judg|ment (juj′mənt) *noun, plural* **judgments.**

judo—A sport of self-defense that uses no weapons.
ju|do (jū′dō) *noun.*

jug—A glass or pottery container for liquids that has a small opening at the top and a handle. It looks like a very wide bottle.
jug (jug) *noun, plural* **jugs.**

juggle—To keep several objects in motion through the air by alternately tossing them up and catching them: *My cousin's favorite trick is* juggling *four tennis balls at once.*
jug|gle (jug′əl) *verb,* **juggled, juggling.**

juggler—Someone who juggles objects to amuse people: *The* juggler *in the circus was a clown.*
jug|gler (jug′lər) *noun, plural* **jugglers.**

juice—The liquid that comes from fruits, vegetables, and meats: *tomato* juice; *carrot* juice; *beef* juice.
juice (jūs) *noun, plural* **juices.**

Jul.—The abbreviation for **July.**

July—The seventh month of the year. This month has 31 days.
Ju|ly (joo lī′) *noun.* Abbreviation: **Jul.**

Word History

July is named after a famous ruler of ancient Rome, Julius Caesar, who was born in this month.

jumble—To mix up in a confusing way: *The puzzle pieces are* jumbled *in the box. Verb.*
—A mess; confused condition: *The clothes in my dresser drawer are in such a* jumble *that I cannot find two matching socks. Noun.*
jum|ble (jum′bəl) *verb,* **jumbled, jumbling;** *noun, plural* **jumbles.**

jumbo—Very large; huge: *I couldn't finish eating the* jumbo *hot dog.*
jum|bo (jum′bō) *adjective.*

Word History

Jumbo was the name of a very large elephant that appeared in a circus in the 1800's. The elephant became so famous that anything very large was called after him. Today the jumbo size still means the biggest.

jump—1. To leap; spring: *The boy* jumped *up and down with joy.* 2. To move suddenly in surprise: *I* jumped *when the door slammed.* 3. To leap or skip over: *to* jump *a fence; to* jump *rope.* 4. To increase quickly and unexpectedly: *The price of the radio* jumped *ten dollars after the sale. Verb.*

a at	i if	oo look	ch chalk	
ā ape	ī idle	ou out	ng sing	a in ago
ah calm	o odd	u ugly	sh ship	e in happen
aw all	ō oats	ū rule	th think	ə = i in capital
e end	oi oil	ur turn	th their	o in occur
ē easy			zh treasure	u in upon

—**1.** An act of springing or leaping: *The cat made a* jump *to a tree limb to escape the dog.* **2.** A sudden movement caused by surprise: *The girl gave a* jump *when her friend tickled her.* **3.** A quick and unexpected increase: *a* jump *in prices. Noun.*
jump (jump) *verb,* **jumped, jumping;** *noun, plural* **jumps.**

  ■ **get the jump on** or **have the jump on:** To have an advantage over: *She read ahead in her history book to* get the jump on *her classmates.*
  jump from the frying pan into the fire: To go from a bad situation to a worse one: *He* jumped from the frying pan into the fire *when he left a difficult job for an even harder one.*
  jump on: To scold; blame: *Please do not* jump on *me for breaking the dish.*

jumper—A one-piece, sleeveless dress, usually worn over a blouse or sweater.
jump|er (jum′pər) *noun, plural* **jumpers.**

Jun.—The abbreviation for **June.**

junco—A small, gray, North American bird related to the sparrow.
jun|co (jung′kō) *noun, plural* **juncos.**

junction—A point or place where things meet or cross: *the* junction *of the two main roads; the* junction *of railroad lines.*
junc|tion (jungk′shən) *noun, plural* **junctions.**

June—The sixth month of the year. June has 30 days.
June (jūn) *noun.* Abbreviation: **Jun.**

Word History

June comes from Junius, the name of a powerful family in ancient Rome. That name may have come from Juno, the queen of the gods and goddesses in Roman mythology.

---

jungle—A hot and humid area in tropical climates, thickly covered with trees, bushes, and tangled vines: *The heat, wild animals, and overgrown plants make it difficult to travel through the* jungle.
jun|gle (jung′gəl) *noun, plural* **jungles.**

jungle gym—An open structure of metal bars for children to climb and swing on. A jungle gym is often found at a playground.
jun|gle gym (jung′gəl jim) *noun, plural* **jungle gyms.**

junior—**1.** The younger. The word ''junior'' is added to the name of a son who has the same name as his father: *John Smith, Junior, is named*

after his father, John Smith. **2.** Having a lower rank or shorter time of service: *A* junior *secretary is not as experienced or as important as a senior secretary.* **3.** For or of the third-year class in high school or college: *the* junior *prom. Adjective.*
—**1.** A person who is younger or in a lower position than another: *My cousin is two years his sister's* junior. **2.** A student in the third year of high school or college. *Noun.*
jun|ior (jūn′yər) *adjective; noun, plural* **juniors.** Abbreviation: **Jr.**

juniper—A kind of evergreen shrub or tree having prickly leaves and brown or purple cones that look like berries.
ju|ni|per (jū′nə pər) *noun, plural* **junipers.**

junk¹—Old things, such as pieces of wood, metal, or rags, that are not wanted: *We removed lots of* junk *from our basement and threw it in the garbage cans.*
junk (jungk) *noun.*

junk²—A Chinese ship with a flat bottom and bamboo sails.
junk (jungk) *noun, plural* **junks.**

junk²

Jupiter—The biggest planet in our solar system. It is the fifth planet in distance from the sun.
Ju|pi|ter (jū′pə tər) *noun.*
  ● See picture at **solar system.**

juror—A person who is part of a jury and who helps decide the verdict in a legal case.
ju|ror (joor′ər) *noun, plural* **jurors.**

jury—**1.** A group of people who decide a case in a court of law. The jury decides whether an accused person is guilty or not guilty after hearing the facts of the case and understanding the law. **2.** A group of people selected to judge

a contest: The jury *chose my girlfriend the winner in the ice skating competition.*
ju|ry (joor′ē) *noun, plural* **juries.**

just—**1.** Only; merely: *My dog has not learned any tricks yet because he is* just *a puppy.* **2.** Barely; by only a little: *The fielder* just *missed the ball as it went over the fence.* **3.** Truly: *Your new dress is* just *lovely.* **4.** Exactly; precisely: *This is* just *the color that I've been looking for.* **5.** A short time ago: *Mother* just *went out, but she will be back soon. Adverb.*
—Right; fair: *I agreed that it was* just *to pay for the window that I had broken. Adjective.*
just (just) *adverb, adjective.*

a at	**i** if	**oo** look	**ch** chalk		**a** in ago
ā ape	**ī** idle	**ou** out	**ng** sing		**e** in happen
ah calm	**o** odd	**u** ugly	**sh** ship	ə =	**i** in capital
aw all	**ō** oats	**ū** rule	**th** think		**o** in occur
e end	**oi** oil	**ur** turn	**th** their		**u** in upon
ē easy			**zh** treasure		

justice—**1.** The quality of being right; fairness: *There is* justice *in giving everyone the same chance to succeed.* **2.** One of the nine judges of the United States Supreme Court.
jus|tice (jus′tis) *noun, plural* **justices.**

justify—**1.** To show or prove to be right or reasonable: *My friend* justified *my trust in her because she kept my secret.* **2.** To prove to be without blame or guilt: *My mother* justified *my absence from class.*
jus|ti|fy (jus′tə fī) *verb,* **justified, justifying.**

juvenile—**1.** Of or for children: juvenile *books;* juvenile *furniture.* **2.** Like a child's; young: *Making mud pies is a* juvenile *activity. Adjective.*
—A young person: *The theater has entertaining shows for* juveniles *as well as for adults. Noun.*
ju|ve|nile (jū′və nəl *or* jū′və nīl′) *adjective; noun, plural* **juveniles.**
● Synonyms: **childish, immature,** for *adjective* **2.**
  Antonyms: **adult, grown-up, mature,** for *adjective* **2.**

About 5,000 years ago, the ancient Egyptians used a symbol of a slightly cupped hand.

About 3,500 years ago, people in the Middle East made a simpler symbol. They called it *kaph*, their word for "palm of the hand."

About 3,000 years ago, other people in the Middle East used a symbol with three prongs.

About 2,600 years ago, the Greeks gave the letter this form. They called it *kappa*.

About 2,600 years ago, the Greeks gave the capital **K** its present form. The Romans adopted it about 1,900 years ago. The small letter **k** was first used about 1,200 years ago. It reached its present form about 500 years ago.

K¹ or k—The 11th letter of the alphabet: *There are two* k's *in the word "kick."*
K, k (kā) *noun, plural* **K's** *or* **Ks, k's** *or* **ks.**

K²—A unit of memory in a computer equal to 1,024 bits.
K (kā) *noun.*

kaleidoscope—A tube with bits of colored glass at one end. When you look through the other end and turn the tube, mirrors inside reflect colorful patterns.
ka|lei|do|scope (kə lī′də skōp′) *noun, plural* **kaleidoscopes.**

Word History

Kaleidoscope comes from two Greek words meaning "beautiful" and "shape." This seemingly simple device forms shapes that are so beautiful and complex that they fascinate viewers with their endless variety.

Kamehameha Day—A holiday in Hawaii celebrated on June 11. It honors the birthday of the first king of the Hawaiian Islands, Kamehameha I.
Ka|me|ha|me|ha Day (kah mā′hah mā′hah dā) *noun.*

kangaroo—An animal of Australia that has small front legs, large, powerful hind legs that are used for leaping, and a long, heavy tail that provides balance. The female kangaroo has a front pouch in which she carries her babies.
kan|ga|roo (kang′gə rū′) *noun, plural* **kangaroos.**

karate—A Japanese way of defending oneself by using short, quick kicks and strikes against an opponent with the hands and feet.
ka|ra|te (kə rah′tē) *noun.*

katydid—A large, green insect that is related to grasshoppers and crickets. It gets its name from the shrill noise the male katydid makes when it rubs its wings together, which sounds like "katydid."
ka|ty|did (kā′tē did′) *noun, plural* **katydids.**

kayak—1. An Eskimo canoe made of animal skins stretched over a wooden or bone frame. The rider sits in a small opening in the center and propels the kayak with a double-bladed paddle.
2. A similar canoe, made of lightweight

kangaroo

materials, that is used for recreation and sport. It can hold one or two people.

kay|ak (kī′ak) *noun, plural* **kayaks.**

keel—A piece of wood or steel that runs along the center part of the bottom of a ship or boat. The structure of the rest of the ship is built up from the keel. *Noun.*
—To fall; collapse: *a boat that* keels *over in a storm; a plant that* keels *over in the heat. Verb.*
keel (kēl) *noun, plural* **keels;** *verb,* **keeled, keeling.**

■ **on an even keel:** Steady; not easily upset: *My mother stays* on an even keel *no matter how trying things become.*

keen—1. Sharp-edged for cutting or slicing: *a* keen *knife.* **2.** Quick or sharp in thinking or sensing: *a* keen *mind; a* keen *sense of hearing; a hawk's* keen *vision.* **3.** Eager: *We are* keen *to play your new game.*
keen (kēn) *adjective,* **keener, keenest.**

keep—1. To have for a long time or forever: *I* keep *the letter she sent in my desk.* **2.** To save or hold for future use: *During the winter, we* keep *our summer clothes in the attic.* **3.** To hold back; stop; prevent: *The dam* keeps *the water from flooding the fields.* **4.** To take care of; maintain in good condition: *to* keep *house; to* keep *one's clothes neat.* **5.** To cause to continue in a certain place, condition, or position: *a fence that* keeps *our dog in the yard; to* keep *warm with a sweater; to* keep *the motor running.* **6.** To stay faithful to; fulfill: *He* kept *his promise to fix his brother's wagon. Verb.*
—**1.** The necessities of life, such as food and shelter: *When my uncle got a job, he was able to earn his* keep. **2.** The strongest part or main tower of a castle. *Noun.*
keep (kēp) *verb,* **kept, keeping;** *noun, plural* **keeps.**

■ **for keeps:** For always and ever: *We will be friends* for keeps.
keep in the dark: To not tell about something: *Let's* keep *her* in the dark *about her surprise party.*
keep (one's) end up: To do one's share: *You can* keep *your* end up *by washing the dishes.*

keep (one's) head: To stay calm: *I* keep *my head even when I'm angry.*
● Synonyms: **collect, hoard, store,** for *verb* 2.

keeper—1. A person or thing that takes care of something: *a lighthouse* keeper. **2.** A watcher or guard: *the jail* keeper. **3.** A person who owns or manages a business or other establishment: *a shop* keeper; *an inn* keeper.
keep|er (kē′pər) *noun, plural* **keepers.**

keeping—1. Care; custody: *We left our cats in our friend's* keeping *for the weekend.* **2.** Agreement: *The bright decorations were in* keeping *with the cheerful mood of the holiday.*
keep|ing (kē′ping) *noun.*

keepsake—Something that is saved in memory of the person who gave it or in memory of a special place or time: *My grandmother gave me this ring as a* keepsake.
keep|sake (kēp′sāk′) *noun, plural* **keepsakes.**
● Synonyms: **memento, reminder, souvenir, token**

keeshond—A medium-sized dog with a thick rough grayish-black coat, small pointed ears, and a curled tail. Originally bred in Holland, this dog was used as a guard on canal barges.
kees|hond (kās′hond *or* kēs′hond) *noun, plural* **keeshonden** *or* **keeshonds.**

keeshond

keg—A small barrel used for containing liquids: *a* keg *of water.*
keg (keg) *noun, plural* **kegs.**

kennel—1. A structure to house one or more dogs: *We have a* kennel *for our dog in our back yard.* **2.** A place where dogs are bred and trained, or where a dog can be boarded: *We left our dog in a* kennel *while we were on vacation.*
ken|nel (ken′əl) *noun, plural* **kennels.**

kept—*See* **keep.**
kept (kept) *verb.*

kerchief—A square scarf that is worn over the head or around the neck.
ker|chief (kur′chif) *noun, plural* **kerchiefs.**

kernel—**1.** The soft part inside the hard shell of a nut, inside the pit of a fruit, or inside the coating of a seed. **2.** A seed or grain like that of corn or rye: *To make popcorn, heat some* kernels *and oil in a covered pot.*
ker|nel (kur′nəl) *noun, plural* **kernels.**
● A word that sounds the same is **colonel.**

kerosene—A thin, clear oil that is made from petroleum. It is used as a fuel for lighting some lamps, heating stoves, and powering engines in machines such as tractors.
ker|o|sene (ker′ə sēn′) *noun.*

Kerry blue terrier—A medium-sized hunting dog with a thick, soft, wavy, blue-gray coat. These dogs are the national dog of Ireland, where they were first bred.
Ker|ry blue ter|ri|er (ker′ē blū ter′ē ər) *noun, plural* **Kerry blue terriers.**

ketch—A small sailing boat with two masts. The mast at the front of this boat is much larger than the one in the back.
ketch (kech) *noun, plural* **ketches.**

ketchup—A thick, spicy tomato sauce that is used to add flavor to hot dogs, hamburgers, and other foods.
ketch|up (kech′əp) *noun.*
● This word is also spelled **catsup.**

Word History

Ketchup can be traced back to a Chinese word meaning ''pickled fish sauce.'' The Chinese did not make the sauce from tomatoes, as it is made today. The people of Malaysia, a country in Southeast Asia, used a word for this sauce that is very close in sound to **ketchup.** It is from them that we get our word.

---

kettle—A metal pot in which foods are cooked and liquids are boiled: *a kettle of stew.*
ket|tle (ket′əl) *noun, plural* **kettles.**

kettledrum—A large copper or brass drum shaped like a kettle. Parchment stretched across the top of the drum produces sounds when beaten with a drumstick.
ket|tle|drum (ket′əl drum′) *noun, plural* **kettledrums.**

key[1]—**1.** A metal device shaped so it will fit into a special hole to lock or unlock a door, a safe, a drawer, or the like, or to start a vehicle. **2.** Any similar device for winding a clock or tightening a spring: *the wind-up* key *on a toy.* **3.** The solution or answer to something, such as a puzzle: *If they can find the* key *to the code, they will know the secret message.* **4.** That which is most important to getting the final result: *The* key *to a fluffy cake is the length of time you beat the batter.* **5.** The finger-operated part of a piano, typewriter, computer, or a similar device that is pushed to produce a certain sound, symbol, or other result: *To type an ''m,'' I press the ''m''* key *on my typewriter.* **6.** In music, a group of related notes that are based on a particular note: *The tune was played in the* key *of A. Noun.*
—Basic; main: *The* key *ingredients of bread are flour, eggs, and milk. Adjective.*
—To adjust a musical instrument so that it produces the correct degree of high and low notes: *I* keyed *my guitar to the sound of my friend's piano. Verb.*
key (kē) *noun, plural* **keys;** *adjective; verb,* **keyed, keying.**
■ **key up: 1.** To increase one's courage in order to do something difficult: *The boy* keyed *himself* up *to give a speech to his class.* **2.** To be very nervous and tense: *My mother is* keyed up *because her boss is coming over for dinner.*
● A word that sounds the same is **quay.**

key[2]—A small, flat island; reef: *the Florida* keys.
key (kē) *noun, plural* **keys.**
● A word that sounds the same is **quay.**

keyboard—A row or system of keys set up for a specific purpose: *a piano* keyboard; *a computer* keyboard.
key|board (kē′bawrd′) *noun, plural* **keyboards.**

kettledrum

keyhole—The hole of a lock into which a key fits to lock or open something.
key|hole (kē′hōl′) *noun, plural* **keyholes.**

keynote—The main idea or theme: *The keynote of her speech was the need to raise money to help the poor.*
key|note (kē′nōt′) *noun, plural* **keynotes.**

keystone—The middle stone at the top of an arch that holds all the other stones in place.
key|stone (kē′stōn′) *noun, plural* **keystones.**

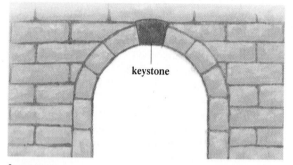

keystone

keystone

kg—The abbreviation for **kilogram** or **kilograms.**

khaki—1. A light yellowish-brown color. 2. A strong cotton cloth of this color, used mostly for military uniforms, work clothes, and other articles requiring a tough material. *Noun.*
—Having a light, yellowish-brown color: khaki *paint. Adjective.*
khak|i (kak′ē) *noun, plural* **khakis;** *adjective.*

Word History

Khaki comes from a word used in northern India that meant ''dusty.'' People, such as soldiers, who are likely to be in dusty places often wear khaki. The dust blends in with the khaki so that the clothes don't look too dirty.

---

kick—1. To swing the foot with force: *This exercise has us* kick *as high as we can.* 2. To strike something by swinging the foot: *She* kicked *the ball halfway down the field.* 3. To spring back with force, after being fired: *The*

rifle kicked *her shoulder hard after firing. Verb.*
—1. A strike or thrust with the foot: *I gave the stone a* kick *that sent it rolling.* 2. A forceful backward spring: *The* kick *from a shotgun can leave a bruise on the shoulder.* 3. Great pleasure or excitement: *She got a* kick *out of singing in the play. Noun.*
kick (kik) *verb,* **kicked, kicking;** *noun, plural* **kicks.**

■ **kick around: 1.** To do nothing important or special: *We are just going to* kick around *our friend's house until it is time to go to the game.* **2.** To look at all sides of an idea to see if it will work: *They* kicked around *the thought of going swimming, but they decided it might be too cold out.*
kick up (one's) **heels:** To enjoy oneself: *I* kicked up *my heels at my friend's party.*

kickball—A game similar to baseball, in which a large, lightweight ball is kicked rather than batted.
kick|ball (kik′bawl′) *noun.*

kickoff—1. The kick of the ball that begins each half of a football game and that resumes play after each score. 2. A beginning; start: *The* kickoff *of the winter carnival was a snow-sculpture contest.*
kick|off (kik′awf′) *noun, plural* **kickoffs.**

kickstand—The metal bar on the frame of a bicycle or motorcycle that is kicked down for support so that the vehicle can remain upright when not being used.
kick|stand (kik′stand′) *noun, plural* **kickstands.**

kid¹—1. A young goat. 2. A soft leather made from the hide of a young goat: kid *gloves.* 3. A young person; child. *Noun.*
—Younger: *My* kid *sister has not started school yet. Adjective.*
kid (kid) *noun, plural* **kids;** *adjective.*

kid²—To joke; make fun: *Mother was only* kidding *when she said that she saw a green dog.*
kid (kid) *verb,* **kidded, kidding.**
• Synonyms: **fool, jest**

kidnap—To carry off someone by force and hold him or her until a sum of money is paid or other demand is met: *The beautiful princess was* kidnapped, *but the prince rescued her.*
kid|nap (kid′nap) *verb,* **kidnapped, kidnapping.**

kidney—A body organ that keeps blood clean. Humans have two kidneys, one on either side of the spine near the waist. The kidneys clean the blood by separating out waste products that then go on to the bladder to be passed from the body as urine.
kid|ney (kid′nē) *noun, plural* **kidneys.**

a at	i if	oo look	ch chalk		a in ago
ā ape	ī idle	ou out	ng sing		e in happen
ah calm	o odd	u ugly	sh ship	ə =	i in capital
aw all	ō oats	ū rule	th think		o in occur
e end	oi oil	ur turn	th their		u in upon
ē easy			zh treasure		

kill—1. To end the life of someone or something: *The early frost* killed *the late summer flowers.* 2. To stop; bring to an end: *When we lost the last game, we* killed *our chances of being in the finals.* 3. To fill time with no active purpose; waste time: *She* killed *an hour watching television while waiting for her sister. Verb.* —1. The act of ending a life: *The lion caught the sheep and made a quick* kill. 2. The person or thing whose life has been ended: *The lion fed on his* kill *for two days. Noun.*
kill (kil) *verb,* **killed, killing;** *noun, plural* **kills.**

killdeer—A small, brown North American bird with two black bands across its breast. It lives near water and in fields, and makes a sharp cry that sounds like its name.
kill|deer (kil′dēr′) *noun, plural* **killdeers** or **killdeer.**

killdeer

killjoy—Someone who ruins the fun of others: *My sister is a* killjoy *at parties because she always looks glum.*
kill|joy (kil′joi′) *noun, plural* **killjoys.**

kilo-—A prefix that means "one thousand." A kilometer is one thousand meters.

Word Power

You can understand the meanings of many words that begin with **kilo-**, if you add the meaning of the prefix to the meaning of the rest of the word.
   kiloliter: a measure equal to 1,000 liters
   kilowatt: a measure equal to 1,000 watts

kilogram—A unit of weight and mass in the metric system. One kilogram equals 1,000 grams, about 2.2 pounds.
kil|o|gram (kil′ə gram) *noun, plural* **kilograms.** Abbreviation: **kg**

kilometer—A unit of length in the metric system. One kilometer equals 1,000 meters, about five-eighths of a mile.
kil|o|me|ter (kə lom′ə tər *or* kil′ə mē′tər) *noun, plural* **kilometers.** Abbreviation: **km**

kilt—A knee-length skirt made of a wool plaid and having pleats. Kilts traditionally are worn by men in parts of Scotland.
kilt (kilt) *noun, plural* **kilts.**

kimono—A long, loose robe that usually is made of silk, has wide sleeves, and is tied with a wide sash around the waist. Kimonos are worn by men and women in Japan.
ki|mo|no (kə mō′nə *or* kə mō′nō) *noun, plural* **kimonos.**

kin—The entire family of a person; relatives: *Most of his* kin *work on the family farm.*
kin (kin) *noun.*

kind[1]—Being of good nature; good-hearted; considerate: *It was* kind *of you to shop for me.*
kind (kīnd) *adjective,* **kinder, kindest.**
 • Synonyms: **gentle, tender**
   Antonyms: **bloodthirsty, brutal, cruel, violent**

kind[2]—A certain type: *My bicycle is the* kind *that is used for racing.*
kind (kīnd) *noun, plural* **kinds.**
 ■ **kind of:** Sort of; almost: *Your blue coat is* kind *of, but not quite, the same color as my dress.*
 • Synonyms: See Synonyms at **class.**

kindergarten—A school or class for children between the ages of four and six, that comes right before first grade.
kin|der|gar|ten (kin′dər gahr′tən) *noun, plural* **kindergartens.**

Word History

Kindergarten comes from two German words meaning "children" and "garden." This type of class is meant to be a "garden" of delight for young children.

kindle—1. To cause to start burning; set on fire: *We had better* kindle *the charcoal in the grill now so we can cook the hamburgers.* 2. To awaken; stir up: *The movie about foreign lands* kindled *my desire to travel.*
kin|dle (kin′dəl) *verb,* **kindled, kindling.**
 • Synonyms: **ignite, light**[1], for 1.

kindling—Scraps of wood, twigs, or other easily ignited material used to start a fire and keep it going.
kin|dling (kin′dling) *noun.*

kindly—Warm-hearted and considerate: *Our kindly neighbors shoveled the snow from our driveway after the storm. Adjective.*
  —**1.** In a gentle, friendly way: *The boy spoke kindly to the frightened dog.* **2.** Please: *Kindly open the door for me.* **3.** Out of consideration or friendliness: *My friend kindly sewed my hem for me. Adverb.*
  kind|ly (kīnd′lē) *adjective,* **kindlier, kindliest;** *adverb.*

kindness—**1.** A warm-hearted, considerate quality or nature: *Kindness is shown by helping a friend in need.* **2.** The act of being warm-hearted or considerate: *We do many kindnesses for our neighbors.*
  kind|ness (kīnd′nis) *noun, plural* **kindnesses.**

king—**1.** The male ruler of a country. A king is not elected but comes to his position through being a member of a royal family. **2.** A person or thing that is the best or most important of its type or place: *the king of rock and roll; the king of the jungle.* **3.** A playing piece in chess or checkers. **4.** A high-ranking playing card. It has a picture of a king on one side.
  king (king) *noun, plural* **kings.**

kingdom—**1.** A country and its people that are ruled by a king or queen. **2.** One of the divisions in nature into which all natural or living things are classed: *the animal kingdom, the plant kingdom, the kingdom of fungi.*
  king|dom (king′dəm) *noun, plural* **kingdoms.**

king-size—Larger than usual: *a king-size bed; a king-size bag of potato chips.*
  king-size (king′sīz′) *adjective.*

kink—**1.** A sharp, tight bend or knot in a rope, wire, cable, or strand of hair: *The kink in the garden hose stopped the water from flowing.* **2.** A sharp muscle pain; cramp: *He dropped out of the race because of a kink in his leg. Noun.*
  —To form a tight bend or knot; twist: *The kite's string kinked in the wind. Verb.*
  kink (kingk) *noun, plural* **kinks;** *verb,* **kinked, kinking.**

kinship—**1.** The fact of being related by family: *The two boys' kinship was discovered through old family records.* **2.** A special relationship; similarity: *I feel a kinship with handicapped people and want to work with them someday.*
  kin|ship (kin′ship) *noun.*

kiss—To show affection by touching one's lips to another person: *The girl kissed her mother good night. Verb.*
  —**1.** A sign of affection shown by touching one's lips to another person: *I gave him a kiss on the cheek to thank him.* **2.** A small piece of chocolate candy usually shaped like a teardrop with a flat bottom. It is usually covered with a small piece of foil. *Noun.*
  kiss (kis) *verb,* **kissed, kissing;** *noun, plural* **kisses.**

kit—**1.** All the parts needed to build or put together something: *a model car kit; a candle-making kit.* **2.** All the necessary materials or tools for some purpose, together in one container: *a sewing kit; a first-aid kit.*
  kit (kit) *noun, plural* **kits.**

kitchen—The room in a house or other building where food is kept, prepared, and cooked.
  kitch|en (kich′ən) *noun, plural* **kitchens.**

kitchenette—A very small kitchen, usually with no room for a table and chairs.
  kitch|en|ette (kich′ə net′) *noun, plural* **kitchenettes.**

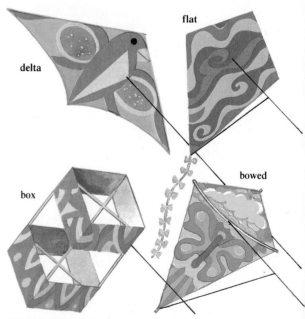

kite (definition 1)

kite—**1.** A flying toy made of paper or other light material stretched over a frame. A kite is attached to a long string and is flown in a gentle wind. **2.** A type of hawk having long, narrow

a at	i if	oo look	ch chalk		a in ago
ā ape	ī idle	ou out	ng sing		e in happen
ah calm	o odd	u ugly	sh ship	ə =	i in capital
aw all	ō oats	ū rule	th think		o in occur
e end	oi oil	ur turn	th their		u in upon
ē easy			zh treasure		

wings and a tail with two points. Most kites feed on insects.

kite (kīt) *noun, plural* **kites.**

■ **fly a kite:** A command to get out or go away: *My sister told me to go* fly a kite *because I interrupted her.*

kitten—A young cat.

kit|ten (kit′ən) *noun, plural* **kittens.**

■ **have kittens:** To become very angry and upset: *The girl's parents* had kittens *when they found out she had taken the car without telling them.*

kitty-corner—See **cater-corner.**

kit|ty-cor|ner (kit′ē kawr′nər) *adjective, adverb.*

km—The abbreviation for **kilometer** or **kilometers.**

knack—An ability to do something easily and well: *She has a* knack *for arranging flowers.*

knack (nak) *noun, plural* **knacks.**

knapsack—A bag of leather, canvas, or other material that has shoulder straps. It is used to carry belongings on one's back, allowing free use of one's hands and arms: *We carried our camping equipment in* knapsacks.

knap|sack (nap′sak′) *noun, plural* **knapsacks.**

knee—A joint in the leg that allows the leg to bend. The knee is located in the middle of the leg between the thigh and the lower leg.

knee (nē) *noun, plural* **knees.**

kneecap—A flat, protective bone covering the front of the knee. It moves as the knee moves.

knee|cap (nē′kap′) *noun, plural* **kneecaps.**

kneel—To lower oneself to the ground by bending the knees: *We* kneeled *in prayer.*

kneel (nēl) *verb,* **knelt** or **kneeled, kneeling.**

knelt—See **kneel.**

knelt (nelt) *verb.*

knew—See **know.**

knew (nū *or* nyū) *verb.*

● Words that sound the same are **gnu** and **new.**

knickknack—A small object that is used for decoration: *My job is to dust the statues and other* knickknacks *on the shelves.*

knick|knack (nik′nak′) *noun, plural* **knickknacks.**

knife—**1.** A cutting instrument made of a thin piece of metal sharpened along one or both edges. It is attached to a handle made of wood, metal, or plastic: *a kitchen* knife. **2.** The cutting edge of a machine or tool; blade. *Noun.*

—To cut or stab with a cutting instrument: *The butcher* knifed *the meat into steaks. Verb.*

knife (nīf) *noun, plural* **knives;** *verb,* **knifed, knifing.**

knight—**1.** A mounted soldier in the Middle Ages. A knight was able to own land in return for his loyalty to a king or lord. **2.** A title given in Great Britain to a man who has done something outstanding. He is then called ''Sir.'' **3.** A chess piece, usually shaped like a horse's head. *Noun.*

—To give someone this special rank or title: *The soldier was* knighted *for his brave deeds. Verb.*

knight (nīt) *noun, plural* **knights;** *verb,* **knighted, knighting.** Abbreviation: **Kt.** or **kt.**

● A word that sounds the same is **night.**

● See picture at **armor.**

knit—**1.** To create a garment, blanket, or the like from a strand of yarn, by looping stitches together by hand on large needles or by using a machine: *I* knitted *my father a scarf.* **2.** To connect or grow together very closely: *Her broken arm is* knitting *quickly.*

knit (nit) *verb,* **knitted** or **knit, knitting.**

■ **knit (one's) brows:** To frown: *He* knit *his brows and glared at the naughty child.*

knives—See **knife.**

knives (nīvz) *plural noun.*

knob—**1.** A round handle that can be grasped to push, pull, or adjust something: *a door* knob; *a* knob *on a cabinet; a stove* knob; *a television* knob. **2.** A small, round mass; lump: *After he hit his head, there was a* knob *on it for days.*

knob (nob) *noun, plural* **knobs.**

knock—**1.** To hit with a hard blow: *I* knocked *my arm as I was getting into the car.* **2.** To hit something so that it comes apart or falls: *When the boys* knocked *against the snowman, it toppled over.* **3.** To make a loud, rattling noise: *The pipes in the old house sometimes* knock *when you first turn the water on. Verb.*

—**1.** A sharp blow: *a* knock *on the head.* **2.** A sound made by hitting or rattling: *The wind made the tree branches* knock *on the window. Noun.*

knock (nok) *verb,* **knocked, knocking;** *noun, plural* **knocks.**

■ **knock about** or **knock around:** To go about aimlessly doing little or nothing: *We spent the day* knocking about *the mall.*

knock off: To finish for a time; quit. *If we* knock off *work early, we can go to a movie.*

knock out: To defeat or force out of a game: *Our star pitcher was* knocked out *in the third inning.*

knocker—A metal device on or by a door that, when pulled back and let go, signals that someone is at the door.

knock|er (nok′ər) *noun, plural* **knockers.**

knockout—A hit that causes unconsciousness: *The* knockout *made the boxer fall down. Noun.* —Causing unconsciousness: *a knockout punch.* **knock|out** (nok′out′) *noun, plural* **knockouts;** *adjective.*

knoll—A small rise of land; little hill: *That knoll over there is a good place to learn how to ski.* **knoll** (nōl) *noun, plural* **knolls.**

knot—**1.** A secure fastening resulting from tying together strands of rope, string, yarn, ribbon, or the like: *I tied the scarf around my neck with a knot.* **2.** A twist in thread, rope, or other material that forms a bump: *I could not thread the needle because of the* knot *in the thread.* **3.** A close gathering of people or things: *a knot of trees.* **4.** A place on a tree out of which a limb grows. When wood is cut from trees, knots appear as darker marks. **5.** A unit used to measure speed on water and in the air. One knot is about 6,076 feet (1.852 meters) per hour. *Noun.* —To fasten by tying: *We* knotted *the rope securely around the dog's collar. Verb.* **knot** (not) *noun, plural* **knots;** *verb,* **knotted, knotting.**
 • A word that sounds the same is **not.**

knothole—A hole in a piece of wood, made by a knot that has become loose and fallen out. **knot|hole** (not′hōl′) *noun, plural* **knotholes.**

knotty—**1.** Having many knots or bumps: *The* knotty *piece of wood made an interesting table top.* **2.** Difficult; puzzling: *This* knotty *problem will take us hours to solve.* **knot|ty** (not′ē) *adjective,* **knottier, knottiest.**

know—**1.** To have information about something; understand the truth or nature of something: *I* know *who took her wagon.* **2.** To be experienced or skilled in: *She* knows *how to knit well.* **3.** To be familiar with: *My cousin* knows *that city.* **know** (nō) *verb,* **knew, known, knowing.**
 ■ **in the know:** Having all the facts; having special information that few others have: *Ask that girl because she is* in the know *and can tell you what really happened.*
 • A word that sounds the same is **no.**

know-how—The necessary skill to do something well: *I have the* know-how *to build a birdhouse.* **know-how** (nō′hou′) *noun.*

know-it-all—A person who thinks he or she knows everything and who tends to brag about it: *That* know-it-all *thinks she can tell me what to do.* **know-it-all** (nō′it awl′) *noun, plural* **know-it-alls.**

knowledge—**1.** All the information and learning that one has; wisdom: *My dad has lots of* knowledge *about life.* **2.** Specific information about something: *The* knowledge *that deep water can be dangerous makes me wear a life jacket.* **knowl|edge** (nol′ij) *noun.*

known—*See* **know.** **known** (nōn) *verb.*

knuckle—One of the three joints of a finger, or one of the two joints of the thumb. Knuckles make it possible for fingers to bend, make a fist, and perform other functions. **knuck|le** (nuk′əl) *noun, plural* **knuckles.**
 ■ **knuckle down:** To forget about what is not important and work hard at what has to be done: *She wanted to play but realized she should* knuckle down *and do her homework first.*
 knuckle under: To give in to pressure: *At first she refused to clean her room, but when they stopped her allowance, she* knuckled under.

koala—A small, gray, furry animal that has round, fluffy ears but no tail, and that looks like a very small bear. Koalas live in Australia and eat the bark and leaves of certain trees that grow there. Females have a pouch like kangaroos, where they carry their babies. **ko|a|la** (kō ah′lə) *noun, plural* **koalas.**

a at	i if	oo look	ch chalk		a in ago
ā ape	ī idle	ou out	ng sing		e in happen
ah calm	o odd	u ugly	sh ship	ə =	i in capital
aw all	ō oats	ū rule	th think		o in occur
e end	oi oil	ur turn	th their		u in upon
ē easy			zh treasure		

koala

komondor

komondor—A large herding dog with a thick, shaggy white coat and long ears. Originally bred in Hungary, these dogs were used as sheepdogs and are frequently used as police and guard dogs.
ko|mon|dor (kō′mon dawr) *noun, plural* **komondors** or **komondorok** (kō′mon daw′rək).

Koran—The sacred book of the Islamic religion. It contains the teachings that Muslims believe Allah, or God, gave to the prophet Muhammed.
Ko|ran (kaw rahn′ *or* kaw ran′) *noun.*

Word History

Koran comes from an Arabic word meaning ''recitation.'' Many Muslims know the Koran so well they can recite much or all of it from memory.

Korat—A short-haired breed of house cat with silver-blue fur, large golden-green eyes, a heart-shaped face, and large rounded ears. This type of cat originally came from Thailand.
Ko|rat (kō raht′) *noun, plural* **Korats.**

kosher—Following or prepared according to the law of the Jewish religion: *a kosher* restaurant; kosher *food.*
ko|sher (kō′shər) *adjective.*

kowtow—1. To show blind obedience; act in a way that shows too much respect. 2. To kneel and touch the ground with one's forehead to show great respect and obedience.
kow|tow (kou tou) *verb,* **kowtowed, kowtowing.**

Kt. or **kt.**—The abbreviation for **knight.**

kukui—An oil-producing tree that has long branches and small white flowers.
ku|ku|i (kū kī′ē) *noun.*

kumquat—A round, orange fruit, about the size of a plum, that grows on trees. Its juice tastes sour, but its skin is sweet.
kum|quat (kum′kwot) *noun, plural* **kumquats.**

kung-fu or **kung fu**—A Chinese way of defending oneself by using one's hands. The hands are used in forceful, flowing movements that can bring down even a larger opponent.
kung-fu or kung fu (kung′fū′) *noun.*

kuvasz—A large herding dog with a heavy white coat and a long head and tail. Originally bred in Tibet and further developed in Hungary, these dogs are also used for hunting and guarding.
ku|vasz (kū′vaws) *noun, plural* **kuvaszok** (kū′vaw sōk).

kuvasz

Word History

Kuvasz comes from a Turkish word meaning ''armed guard of the nobility.'' This beautiful, strong dog was used in Hungary to guard members of that country's royal family and the nobility. They also used the kuvasz for hunting. At one time, part of Hungary was under Turkish rule, and many Turkish words, such as kuvasz, entered the Hungarian language.

Kwanza or **Kwanzaa**—A festival held every year for seven days by black people in the United States in celebration of their cultural heritage. It lasts from December 26 to January 1.
Kwan|za or Kwan|zaa (kwahn′zə) *noun.*

About 5,000 years ago, the ancient Egyptians used a symbol of a crooked staff.

About 3,500 years ago, people in the Middle East used a similar symbol. They called it *lamed,* their word for "staff."

About 3,000 years ago, other people in the Middle East used a symbol of an upside-down staff.

About 2,600 years ago, the Greeks gave the letter this form. They called it *lambda.*

About 1,900 years ago, the Romans gave the capital **L** its present form. The small letter **l** was first used about 1,500 years ago. It reached its present form about 1,200 years ago.

L or **l**—**1.** The 12th letter of the alphabet: *There are two* l's *in "little."* **2.** The Roman numeral for 50.
L, l (el) *noun, plural* **L's** or **Ls, l's,** or **ls.**

l—The abbreviation for **liter** or **liters.**

label—A strip of paper or other material attached to something to identify what it is or what it contains: *a designer* label *on a dress; a shipping* label *on a package. Noun.*
—**1.** To put on or mark with such a piece of material: *to* label *a bottle of medicine with its name and correct dose.* **2.** To call or describe: *The boy was* labeled *a hero for finding the lost child in the woods. Verb.*
la|bel (lā′bəl) *noun, plural* **labels;** *verb,* **labeled, labeling.**
• Synonyms: **tab, tag[1]**, for *noun.*

labor—**1.** Hard work; toil: *It took three weeks of* labor *to finish paving the street.* **2.** Workers as a group: *The candidate was popular with* labor. *Noun.*
—**1.** To work hard: *Workers* labored *in the field under a hot sun.* **2.** To move with great difficulty; struggle: *The exhausted runner* labored *up the final hill of the race. Verb.*
la|bor (lā′bər) *noun, plural* **labors;** *verb,* **labored, laboring.**

a at	i if	oo look	ch chalk		a in ago
ā ape	ī idle	ou out	ng sing		e in happen
ah calm	o odd	u ugly	sh ship	ə =	i in capital
aw all	ō oats	ū rule	th think		o in occur
e end	oi oil	ur turn	th their		u in upon
ē easy			zh treasure		

laboratory—A place with equipment for doing scientific experiments: *a physics* laboratory.
lab|o|ra|to|ry (lab′rə tawr′ē) *noun, plural* **laboratories.**

Labor Day—A legal holiday in the United States and Canada that honors workers. It is celebrated on the first Monday in September.
La|bor Day (lā′bər dā) *noun.*

Labrador retriever—A medium-sized hunting dog with a thick black, yellow, or brown coat. Originally bred to help fishermen in Canada, these dogs are good swimmers.
Lab|ra|dor re|triev|er (lab′rə dawr ri trē′ vər) *noun, plural* **Labrador retrievers.**

Labrador retriever

lace—**1.** A thread or string that is pulled through holes to fasten together the sides of some material: *shoe* laces. **2.** A piece of cloth made of fine threads woven in an open pattern. *Noun.*

—To pull together or fasten with thread or string: *He laced his sneakers. Verb.*
lace (lās) *noun, plural* **laces;** *verb,* **laced, lacing.**
■ **lace into:** To criticize harshly: *The foreman laced into his workers for being careless.*

lack—To be without; not have: *The downtown shopping area* lacks *adequate parking. Verb.*
—**1.** The state of not having: *A* lack *of customers forced the store to close.*   **2.** A thing that is not had: *Time is our* lack, *so we must hurry. Noun.*
lack (lak) *verb,* **lacked, lacking;** *noun, plural* **lacks.**

lackadaisical—**1.** Lacking interest; indifferent: *The student was* lackadaisical *about doing his homework, so he did poorly in school.*
lack|a|dai|si|cal (lak′ə dā′zə kəl) *adjective.*

lacquer—A clear liquid that is put on wood, paper, or metal and hardens to protect it.
lac|quer (lak′ər) *noun, plural* **lacquers.**

lacrosse—A ball game played by two teams, each with 10 men or 12 women. Players throw, catch, or carry the ball with a stick that has a net at one end.
la|crosse (lə kraws′) *noun.*

lad—A boy or young man.
lad(lad) *noun, plural* **lads.**

ladder—A device used for climbing. It is made of two long, parallel pieces connected by shorter pieces that are used as steps.
lad|der (lad′ər) *noun, plural* **ladders.**
● See picture at **rung.**

laden—Being weighed down; loaded: *A hiker,* laden *with a heavy backpack, stumbled down the trail.*
lad|en (lā′dən) *adjective.*

ladies—*See* **lady.**
la|dies (lā′dēz) *noun.*

ladle—A deep spoon with a long handle, used for serving liquids: *a soup* ladle.
la|dle (lā′dəl) *noun, plural* **ladles.**

lady—**1.** A woman: *The* lady *talked to our principal.*   **2.** A woman respected for her wealth or high social position.   **3.** A woman or girl who has good manners.   **4. Lady:** A title for a woman of noble rank in Great Britain.
la|dy (lā′dē) *noun, plural* **ladies.**
● See Word History at **lord.**

ladybug—A small, round beetle with black spots on a red or orange back. Ladybugs feed on insects that are harmful to plants.
la|dy|bug (lā′dē bug′) *noun, plural* **ladybugs.**

lady's-slipper

lady's-slipper—A plant with pink, white, or yellow flowers that look like slippers. The pink and white lady's-slipper is the state flower of Minnesota.
la|dy's-slip|per (lā′dēz slip′ər) *noun, plural* **lady's-slippers.**

lag—To fail to keep up; fall behind: *One duckling* lagged *behind the others. Verb.*
—The state of having fallen behind: *a* lag *in the payment of the bills. Noun.*
lag (lag) *verb,* **lagged, lagging;** *noun, plural* **lags.**

lagoon—A shallow lake or pond connected to a larger body of water.
la|goon (lə gūn′) *noun, plural* **lagoons.**

laid—*See* **lay**[1].
laid (lād) *verb.*

lain—*See* **lie**[2].
lain (lān) *verb.*

lair—The living place of a wild animal; den: *the lion's* lair.
lair (lār) *noun, plural* **lairs.**

lake—A body of water completely surrounded by land.
lake (lāk) *noun, plural* **lakes.**

lakeland terrier—A small dog with a narrow body and a long head, with a beard around its chin. Originally bred in the Lake District of

ladybug

lakeland terrier

northern England, these dogs were first raised to hunt foxes and to protect sheep.
lake|land ter|ri|er (lāk′lənd ter′ē ər) *noun, plural* **lakeland terriers.**

lamb—1. A young sheep. 2. The meat from a young sheep, used as food.
lamb (lam) *noun, plural* **lambs.**

lamb (definition 1)

lame—1. Not able to walk easily or normally; limping: *He was* lame *for a month after hurting his foot.* 2. Stiff and sore: *Her back was* lame *from bending over so often.* 3. Not very good; unsatisfactory: *"I thought the report was due tomorrow"* is a lame *excuse. Adjective.*
—To cause not to walk normally: *The horse was* lamed *by a stone caught in its hoof. Verb.*
lame (lām) *adjective,* **lamer, lamest;** *verb,* **lamed, laming.**
• Synonyms: **feeble, poor, weak,** for *adjective* 3.

lamp—A device that gives off light: *a reading* lamp.
lamp (lamp) *noun, plural* **lamps.**

lance—A long spear with a sharp point. *Noun.*
—To cut open with a sharp knife: *The doctor* lanced *the blister. Verb.*
lance (lans) *noun, plural* **lances;** *verb,* **lanced, lancing.**

land—1. The portion of the earth's surface that is above the water; dry ground. 2. A particular country or region: *Would you like to learn about people from another* land? *Noun.*
—1. To arrive or touch down on solid ground: *The spacecraft* landed *on the moon.* 2. To come on shore from a boat: *The sailors* landed *after being at sea for three months.* 3. To cause to end up in a certain way or place: *Stealing cars* landed *him in prison. Verb.*
land (land) *noun, plural* **lands;** *verb,* **landed, landing.**

landing—1. The act of coming down on a surface: *The airplane's* landing *was smooth.* 2. A place where people or cargo are unloaded: *They got off the boat at the* landing. 3. A level area between flights of stairs: *She stopped for a rest on the third* landing.
land|ing (lan′ding) *noun, plural* **landings.**

landlady—1. A woman who owns property and rents it to others. 2. A woman who runs an inn or rents rooms to others.
land|la|dy (land′lā′dē) *noun, plural* **landladies.**

landlord—1. A man who owns property and rents it to others. 2. A man who runs an inn or rents rooms to others.
land|lord (land′lawrd′) *noun, plural* **landlords.**

landlubber—Any person with little experience at sea; one who feels awkward when on a ship.
land|lub|ber (land′lub′ər) *noun, plural* **landlubbers.**

landmark—1. A thing used as a guide because it is easy to see or is familiar: *The mountain was a* landmark *for the hikers.* 2. An important event or discovery: *The first human heart transplant was a* landmark *for medicine.*
land|mark (land′mahrk′) *noun, plural* **landmarks.**

a at	i if	oo look	ch chalk		⌈ a in ago
ā ape	ī idle	ou out	ng sing		e in happen
ah calm	o odd	u ugly	sh ship	ə =	i in capital
aw all	ō oats	ū rule	th think		o in occur
e end	oi oil	ur turn	<u>th</u> their		⌊ u in upon
ē easy			zh treasure		

landscape—1. Any portion of land observed as scenery: *Autumn brought a magnificent change to the* landscape *along the highway.* 2. Any picture or painting that shows scenery: *His water-color* landscapes *were beautiful. Noun.*
—To improve the natural beauty of land by planting flowers, bushes, or trees: *They* landscaped *their yard. Verb.*
land|scape (land′skāp) *noun, plural* **landscapes;** *verb,* **landscaped, landscaping.**

landslide—1. A slipping down of earth and rocks along a slope: *The earthquake started a* landslide. 2. An easy or great victory, especially in an election, in which one person or group wins by a large margin.
land|slide (land′slīd′) *noun, plural* **landslides.**

lane—1. A narrow path or road: *She rode her bicycle along the* lane. 2. A portion of a road marked for one line of traffic.
lane (lān) *noun, plural* **lanes.**
• A word that sounds the same is **lain.**

language—1. The written and spoken words of humans: *We express ourselves by using* language. 2. The speech of one group or nation: *the English* language. 3. A way to express one's ideas or feelings without using words: *sign* language.
lan|guage (lang′gwij) *noun, plural* **languages.**

lantern—A portable case that encloses a light and protects it from wind and rain. A lantern has sides of glass or other material through which the light can shine.
lan|tern (lan′tərn) *noun, plural* **lanterns.**

lap[1]—The front part of the body of a seated person, from the waist to the knees. *He held his daughter on his* lap.
lap (lap) *noun, plural* **laps.**

lap[2]—To lay things together so that one thing partially covers the other: *Her scarf was tied so that the ends would* lap *over each other. Verb.*
—The entire length of something: *to swim a* lap *in a pool. Noun.*
lap (lap) *verb,* **lapped, lapping;** *noun, plural* **lap.**

lap[3]—1. To drink liquid by using the tongue to scoop it up: *The dog* lapped *the water.* 2. To beat or rock gently against: *Waves* lapped *against the sailboat.*
lap (lap) *verb,* **lapped, lapping.**

lapel—Either of the two front flaps on a jacket or coat that are folded back.
la|pel (lə pel′) *noun, plural* **lapels.**

larch—A type of pine tree with small cones and needles that fall off every year.
larch (lahrch) *noun, plural* **larches.**

lard—A soft, white cooking fat. It is made from pig fat that is melted down.
lard (lahrd) *noun, plural* **lards.**

large—Bigger than the normal amount or size: *The child wanted a* large *ice cream cone.*
large (lahrj) *adjective,* **larger, largest.** Abbreviation: lg.
■ **at large:** Free; not caught or shut up: *The escaped prisoner is still* at large.
• Synonyms: See Synonyms at **big.**
Antonyms: See Synonyms at **small.**

large intestine—The lower part of the intestines, including the appendix, colon, and rectum. The large intestine removes water from the waste material that the small intestine has not digested.
large in|tes|tine (lahrj in tes′tən) *noun, plural* **large intestines.**
• See picture at **alimentary canal** and at **appendix.**

lariat—A rope with a loop at one end; lasso. It is used to catch or tie down animals.
lar|i|at (lar′ē ət) *noun, plural* **lariats.**
• See Word History at **lasso.**

lark[1]—A small singing bird with brown feathers and a long nail on each back toe.
lark (lahrk) *noun, plural* **larks.**

lark[2]—A thing done just for fun; prank: *As a* lark, *the girls took off their shoes and splashed in the puddle.*
lark (lahrk) *noun, plural* **larks.**

lark[1]

larkspur—A tall plant with bunches of blue, pink, white, or reddish-purple flowers.
lark|spur (lahrk′spur′) *noun, plural* **larkspurs.**

larva—The stage early in an insect's life when it looks like a worm. A caterpillar is a larva of a butterfly or a moth.
lar|va (lahr′və) *noun, plural* **larvae** (lahr′vē).
• See picture at **metamorphosis**.

larynx—The upper portion of the windpipe that contains the vocal cords; voice box.
lar|ynx (lar′ingks) *noun, plural* **larynxes**.

laser—A device that makes light travel in a very narrow, bright, powerful beam. Lasers are used in medicine and industry.
la|ser (lā′zər) *noun, plural* **lasers**.

lash[1]—1. A blow from a whip: *The jockey gave his horse a* lash *as they neared the finish line.*
2. Any of the small hairs that grow along the eyelid; eyelash. *Noun.*
—1. To beat with a whip: *The angry man* lashed *his donkey, but the animal would not move.*
2. To hit against or strike: *Large waves* lashed *the beach.* 3. To move forcefully back and forth: *The cat* lashed *its tail. Verb.*
lash (lash) *noun, plural* **lashes**; *verb,* **lashed, lashing.**

lash[2]—To bind with a rope or other thick material; tie: *The boys* lashed *logs together to make a raft.*
lash (lash) *verb,* **lashed, lashing.**

lass—A girl or young woman.
lass (las) *noun, plural* **lasses**.

Word History

Lasso comes from a Latin word meaning "noose." **Lariat** comes from two Spanish words, *la reata* (lah rā ah′tə), meaning "the rope." When the name came into English, the two Spanish words were combined into one word, and the spelling changed. Now the word for the rope and the word for the noose on the end are both used to mean the rope and the noose together.

---

lasso—A long rope with a loop at the end, used especially to catch cattle or horses; lariat. *Noun.*
—To catch with a rope; loop: *The rancher* lassoed *the wild stallion. Verb.*
las|so (las′ō *or* la sū′) *noun, plural* **lassos** or **lassoes**; *verb,* **lassoed, lassoing.**

a at	i if	oo look	ch chalk		a in ago
ā ape	ī idle	ou out	ng sing		e in happen
ah calm	o odd	u ugly	sh ship	ə =	i in capital
aw all	ō oats	ū rule	th think		o in occur
e end	oi oil	ur turn	th their		u in upon
ē easy			zh treasure		

last[1]—1. Coming after everything; final: *The* last *class of the year is tomorrow.* 2. Most recent: last *night;* last *summer.* 3. Being the only one that remains: *the* last *show; my* last *dollar.*
4. Least likely: *Winning the contest was the* last *thing I expected to happen. Adjective.*
—1. After everything or everyone: *She arrived* last. 2. Most recently: *When did you* last *call about our newspaper delivery? Adverb.*
—The person or thing that comes after everyone or everything else: *He was the* last *to finish. Noun.*
last (last) *adjective, adverb, noun.*
■ **at last** or **at long last:** After a long wait; finally: At long last, *my package arrived.*

last[2]—1. To go on; continue: *His speech was so long that it seemed to* last *forever.* 2. To continue in good condition: *If you take care of your new car, it will* last *a long time.*
last (last) *verb,* **lasted, lasting.**

latch—A device made of wood or metal to fasten a door, window, or gate. *Noun.*
—To shut with such a device: *It is useless to* latch *the barn door after the horse is out.*
latch (lach) *noun, plural* **latches**; *verb,* **latched, latching.**

late—1. Taking place after the usual time: *a* late *breakfast.* 2. Happening toward the end: *She asked the hairdresser for a* late *appointment because she was working until dinner time.*
3. Not long ago; recent: *the* latest *fashions; a* late *news bulletin.* 4. Having died recently: *the* late *bank president. Adjective.*
—1. After the usual time: *She woke up* late *and missed the school bus.* 2. Toward the end: *They should get here* late *in the morning. Adverb.*
late (lāt) *adjective,* **later, latest;** *adverb.*

lately—Happening not long ago; recently: *Have you been to the shopping mall* lately?
late|ly (lāt′lē) *adverb.*

lather—1. Foam made from a mix of soap and water; suds. 2. Foam caused by much sweating, particularly on a horse. *Noun.*
—1. To create foam or suds: *He* lathered *the soap in his hands before rinsing.* 2. To cover with foam or suds: *We held our dog,* lathered *him, and then scrubbed and rinsed him. Verb.*
lath|er (la<u>th</u>′ər) *noun, plural* **lathers**; *verb,* **lathered, lathering.**

Latin—1. The language of ancient Rome. 2. Any person who speaks a language developed from that language, such as French, Italian, or Spanish. *Noun.*
—Having to do with the ancient Roman

language or people: *a Latin class;* Latin *literature. Adjective.*
La|**tin** (lat′ən) *noun, plural* **Latins;** *adjective.*

latitude—A distance north or south of the equator on the earth. Latitude, measured in degrees, is shown on a map or globe by parallel lines running east and west.
lat|**i**|**tude** (lat′ə tūd *or* lat′ə tyūd) *noun, plural* **latitudes.**

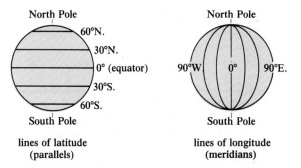

lines of latitude   lines of longitude
(parallels)   (meridians)

latitude

latter—**1.** The second of two things: *Of a yard and a meter, the* latter *is longer.* **2.** Close to the end: *I have difficulty playing the* latter *part of my piano piece.*
lat|**ter** (lat′ər) *adjective.*

laugh—To make sounds that show a person is happy or amused: *We* laughed *at his joke. Verb.*
—The sound made by a person who is happy or amused: *She has a very unusual* laugh. *Noun.*
laugh (laf) *verb,* **laughed, laughing;** *noun, plural* **laughs.**
■ **have the last laugh:** To get the better of someone after seeming to lose: *The governor seemed to be losing the election, but he* had the last laugh *when the votes were counted again.*
● Synonyms: **chuckle, giggle, snicker** for *verb.* Antonyms: For *verb,* see Synonyms at **cry,** *verb* **1.**

laughter—The sounds made by a person who is happy or amused.
laugh|**ter** (laf′tər) *noun.*

launch[1]—**1.** To send off; put in motion: *The scientists* launched *a small weather balloon.* **2.** To lower or slide into water; set afloat: *The new submarine was* launched *at noon.* **3.** To begin; start: *Her acting career was* launched *by a television appearance. Verb.*
—The act of sending off or putting into motion: *The* launch *of the missile could be seen for miles. Noun.*
launch (lawnch) *verb,* **launched, launching;** *noun, plural* **launches.**

launch[2]—A small, open motorboat, often used to carry passengers between a larger ship and the shore.
launch (lawnch) *noun, plural* **launches.**

launching pad—The platform or structure used for sending off rockets and missiles.
launch|**ing pad** (lawn′ching pad) *noun, plural* **launching pads.**

laundromat—A place where people may wash and dry clothing and other items using coin-operated machines.
laun|**dro**|**mat** (lawn′drə mat) *noun, plural* **laundromats.**

laundry—**1.** A place where clothes and other items are washed. **2.** Clothes or other items that have been or are to be washed: *Please put the clean* laundry *away.*
laun|**dry** (lawn′drē) *noun, plural* **laundries.**

laurel—An evergreen shrub or tree with stiff, shiny leaves and purple berries. Heroes in ancient Greece and Rome were crowned with wreaths of laurel.
lau|**rel** (lor′əl) *noun, plural* **laurels.**
■ **look to (one's) laurels:** To protect one's good name or fame: *The coach said that we must* look to *our* laurels *and keep practicing, or we will lose first place.*
rest on (one's) laurels: To be satisfied with the awards and honors that one has already gained: *Instead of trying to do better, he would rather* rest on *his* laurels.

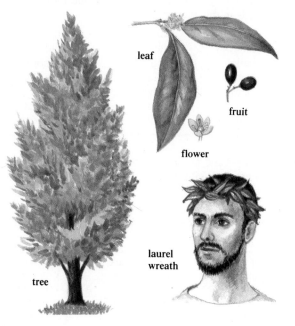

leaf

fruit

flower

laurel
wreath

tree

laurel

lava—1. The hot, melted rock that flows from an erupting volcano. 2. The rock that cools and hardens after such an eruption.
la|va (**lah′**və *or* **lav′**ə) *noun.*

lavender—Having a pale purple color: *a* lavender *dress. Adjective.*
—1. A pale purple color. 2. A small plant with fragrant, pale purple flowers. *Noun.*
lav|en|der (**lav′**ən dər) *adjective; noun, plural* **lavenders.**

lavish—1. Giving or costing very great amounts; extravagant: *He likes to buy* lavish *gifts.* 2. More than one needs or can use: *The restaurant gave me such a* lavish *helping of food that I could not finish it. Adjective.*
—To give or spend in large amounts: *The man* lavished *affection on his grandchildren. Verb.*
lav|ish (**lav′**ish) *adjective; verb,* **lavished, lavishing.**

law—1. A rule or set of rules that a government makes for its people to follow: *Driving a car through a red light is against the* law. 2. The study of such a system of rules; the profession of a lawyer: *She is going to college to study* law. 3. Any kind of rule: *the* laws *of science, nature, or mathematics.*
law (law) *noun, plural* **laws.**

Word Power

If you are interested in law, here are some useful words for you to know. You can find these words in this dictionary.

arrest	court	parole
attorney	custody	plead
bail	defendant	probation
bench	defense	prosecution
charge	judge	sentence
crime	lawyer	summons
criminal	liable	verdict

---

lawn—Land around a house or other building that is covered with grass and requires regular mowing.
lawn (lawn) *noun, plural* **lawns.**

lawyer—Any person whose job is to understand the laws of a country and give advice to people and represent them in court; attorney.
law|yer (**law′**yər) *noun, plural* **lawyers.**

lax—1. Not strict, tight, or exact; careless: *He is very* lax *about doing his chores.*
lax (laks) *adjective.*

lay¹—1. To put; place: Lay *the book down.* 2. To put in position; to fasten: *to* lay *new tiles on the kitchen floor.* 3. To produce eggs: *My chickens* lay *dozens of eggs.*
lay (lā) *verb,* **laid, laying.**
■ **lay about:** To strike or hit on all sides: *While exploring the jungle, he* laid about *him with a branch to keep flies away.*
● A word that sounds the same is **lei.**

Language Fact

Lay¹ means to set down: *Lay your coat on that chair.* **Lay²** means to have been resting on something: *I* lay *in bed last night.* **Lay²** is used when the resting happened a while ago. When the resting is happening now, the word to use is **lie²**: *I need to* lie *down.* People confuse these words and sometimes use **lay¹** when they should use **lie².** Careful speakers and writers do not say, for instance, "The ball is laying on the table" or "The dog lays on the floor."

---

lay²—*See* **lie.**
lay (lā) *verb.*
● A word that sounds the same is **lei.**

layer—A single thickness, coat, or fold: *the top* layer *of clothing; a* layer *of paint.*
lay|er (**lā′**ər) *noun, plural* **layers.**

lazy—1. Not liking or willing to work; idle: *a* lazy *child; a* lazy *mood.* 2. Slow moving; sluggish: *a* lazy *stream.*
la|zy (**lā′**zē) *adjective.*

lb.—The abbreviation for **pound¹.** *Plural,* **lb** or **lbs.**

Word History

Lb. is the abbreviation for **pound¹** because the Latin word for a pound was *libra* (**lī′**brə). You can see why **lb.** would be the abbreviation for *libra.* **Pound²** comes from a Latin word meaning "in weight." The abbreviation **lb.** and the word **pound¹** both come from a two-word Latin phrase meaning "a pound in weight." But the abbreviation comes from the first Latin word, and the word the abbreviation stands for comes from the second Latin word.

---

a at	i if	oo look	ch chalk		⌈a in ago
ā ape	ī idle	ou out	ng sing		e in happen
ah calm	o odd	u ugly	sh ship	ə =	i in capital
aw all	ō oats	ū rule	th think		o in occur
e end	oi oil	ur turn	<u>th</u> their		⌊u in upon
ē easy			zh treasure		

lead¹—**1.** To guide; direct: *Markers on the trees will lead you along the trail.* **2.** To go at the head of; be first: *She leads the class with her excellent grades.* **3.** To be the way to some place; bring: *That road will lead you to the center of town.* **4.** To be in charge of; command; head: *The conductor leads the orchestra.* **5.** To live; spend time: *Grandpa leads a busy life. Verb.*
—**1.** An example: *If you want to do as well as he does, follow his lead.* **2.** The chief part: *He has the lead in the play.* **3.** Anything that points the way; clue: *The police checked all leads before arresting a suspect in the robbery. Noun.*
lead (lēd) *verb,* **led, leading;** *noun, plural* **leads.**
■ **lead on:** To convince someone to believe or do something that may be untrue or unwise: *The salesman was leading on customers by telling them the new cars would arrive right away.*

lead²—**1.** A heavy, blue-gray metal that melts and bends easily. Lead is used to make pipes and machines. Lead is a chemical element. **2.** A marking substance used in a pencil.
lead (led) *noun, plural* **leads.**
● A word that sounds the same is **led.**

leader—The one that leads, directs, or heads: *The prime minister is the leader of his political party.*
lead|er (lē′dər) *noun, plural* **leaders.**
● Synonyms: **captain, chief, director, head**
Antonym: **follower**

leadership—The ability to direct others: *Wise leadership made him a popular president.*
lead|er|ship (lē′dər ship) *noun, plural* **leaderships.**

leaf—**1.** The thin, flat, green part of a plant that grows on a stem or from roots. **2.** A sheet or piece of paper; page: *to tear out a leaf from a notebook. Noun.*
—**1.** To bear or grow these plant parts: *The cold spring weather caused the trees to leaf later in the year.* **2.** To turn pages quickly in a book or magazine: *He leafed through the science book before reading the assigned pages. Verb.*
leaf (lēf) *noun, plural* **leaves;** *verb,* **leafed, leafing.**
■ **turn over a new leaf:** To begin again; try to do better: *She decided to turn over a new leaf and practice her piano more often.*

leaflet—A sheet of printed paper, sometimes folded; pamphlet: *The candidate sent leaflets to all the voters in her district.*
leaf|let (lēf′lit) *noun, plural* **leaflets.**

league¹—A group of people or countries that join together for a certain purpose: *a softball league.*
league (lēg) *noun, plural* **leagues.**

league²—A former measure of distance, equal to about three miles (4.8 kilometers).
league (lēg) *noun, plural* **leagues.**

leak—An opening such as a hole or crack that lets something in or out accidentally: *The leak in the water faucet dripped all night. Noun.*
—**1.** To have a hole or crack that lets something in or out accidentally: *Because that thermos leaks, my lunch was soaked.* **2.** To tell a secret: *He leaked the news of the surprise party. Verb.*
leak (lēk) *noun, plural* **leaks;** *verb,* **leaked, leaking.**
● A word that sounds the same is **leek.**

lean¹—**1.** To bend; be not upright; slant: *He leaned over to pet the dog.* **2.** To put against something at an angle: *She leaned the sled against the tree.* **3.** To depend on; look to for help; rely: *He leaned on his father for help with his math homework.*
lean (lēn) *verb,* **leaned, leaning.**

lean²—**1.** Having very little fat: *a lean hamburger.* **2.** Very thin: *a lean young man.* **3.** Unproductive; poor: *Very slow sales made it a lean year for the automobile dealer.*
lean (lēn) *adjective,* **leaner, leanest.**
● Synonyms: **gaunt, scrawny, skinny, spare,** for **2.**
Antonyms: **fat, plump, stout,** for **2.**

leap—A jump: *The squirrel made a leap from one tree to another. Noun.*
—To jump: *The girl leaped into the pile of leaves. Verb.*
leap (lēp) *noun, plural* **leaps;** *verb,* **leaped** or **leapt, leaping.**
■ **by leaps and bounds:** Very fast; very much. *Our puppy grew by leaps and bounds.*

leapfrog—A children's game in which players jump over the backs of other players who are bending over.
leap|frog (lēp′frog′ or lēp′frawg′) *noun.*

leap year—A year with one extra day, February 29, that occurs every four years.
leap year (lēp yēr) *noun, plural* **leap years.**

learn—**1.** To get knowledge or a skill in something; study: *to learn Spanish; to learn to ski.* **2.** To memorize: *to learn the words of the song.* **3.** To find out about; discover: *He learned that her birthday was September 19.*
learn (lurn) *verb,* **learned, learning.**

learned—Educated; showing knowledge: *The scientist was learned in astronomy.*
learn|ed (lur′nid) *adjective.*

learning—The gaining of knowledge or skill; knowledge or skill that is gained; education: *Learning takes place not only in school but also at home.*
learn|ing (lur′ning) *noun, plural* **learnings.**

lease—A written agreement that states how much money must be paid, for how long, for a person to rent a house, apartment, or land. *Noun.*
—To have such a written agreement for renting a house, apartment, or land: *We are leasing this house until we can afford to buy our own. Verb.*
lease (lēs) *noun, plural* **leases;** *verb,* **leased, leasing.**
  ■ **a new lease on life:** A second chance to do, be, or have something better: *A fresh coat of paint and new tires gave the old bicycle a new lease on life.*

leash—A strap or chain used to hold or tie an animal: *a dog leash. Noun.*
—To hold or tie an animal with a strap or chain: *He leashed his dog before he took it to the veterinarian. Verb.*
leash (lēsh) *noun, plural* **leashes;** *verb,* **leashed, leashing.**
  ■ **strain at the leash:** To be very restless; be unable to concentrate: *The children strained at the leash to get outside for recess.*

least—Less than any other; smallest: *She could not do her homework if there was the least amount of noise in the house. Adjective.*
—The smallest thing or amount: *Sending a card was the least he could do for his sick friend. Noun.*
—In the smallest amount or degree: *She liked cherry sundaes least of all. Adverb.*
least (lēst) *adjective, noun, adverb.*
  ■ **at least:** In spite of that; at any rate: *He may have finished the race last, but at least he tried.*

leather—A material made from treated animal skins and used for clothing, shoes, and many kinds of cases.
leath|er (leth′ər) *noun, plural* **leathers.**

leave¹—1. To go away: *We must leave the party at four o'clock.* 2. To allow something or someone to remain behind: *The letter carrier left a package on our front steps.* 3. To let something remain in a certain way: *to leave the water running.* 4. To let alone; not touch: *She washed the lower windows and left the higher ones for her father.* 5. To give to another after a person dies: *His grandfather left him a valuable coin collection.* 6. To have remaining: *Eight minus two leaves six.*
leave (lēv) *verb,* **left, leaving.**

leave²—1. Permission; the act of allowing: *The teacher gave the class leave to go to lunch.* 2. Permission to be away from duty or usual routine: *The soldier asked for leave so she could visit her family.*
leave (lēv) *noun, plural* **leaves.**

leaves—*See* **leaf.**
leaves (lēvz) *plural noun.*

lecture—1. A talk on a certain subject that is presented to a group: *The scientist gave a lecture on polar bears to the fifth graders, who were studying the Arctic.* 2. Angry talk; scolding: *Dad gave me a lecture because I left my bicycle out in the rain. Noun.*
—1. To give a talk on a certain subject to a group: *The fire fighter lectured the class on fire safety.* 2. To scold; talk to angrily: *Mother lectured us for tracking dirt into the kitchen. Verb.*
lec|ture (lek′chər) *noun, plural* **lectures;** *verb,* **lectured, lecturing.**

led—*See* **lead¹.**
led (led) *verb.*
  • A word that sounds the same is **lead².**

ledge—A shelf, usually a narrow one: *a window ledge; a rocky ledge on a mountain.*
ledge (lej) *noun, plural* **ledges.**

leech—A worm that gets food by attaching itself to the skin of animals and sucking their blood. This worm usually lives in ponds and rivers.
leech (lēch) *noun, plural* **leeches.**

leech

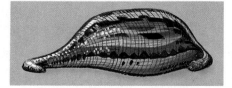

leek—A vegetable that looks like a large, green onion. Its flavor is similar to an onion's, but milder.
leek (lēk) *noun, plural* **leeks.**
  • A word that sounds the same is **leak.**

a at	i if	oo look	ch chalk		a in ago
ā ape	ī idle	ou out	ng sing		e in happen
ah calm	o odd	u ugly	sh ship	ə =	i in capital
aw all	ō oats	ū rule	th think		o in occur
e end	oi oil	ur turn	th their		u in upon
ē easy			zh treasure		

left¹—On the opposite of the right side: *He wrote his name on the upper* left *side of the paper. Adjective.*

—On, to, or toward the opposite of the right side: *To get to my house, go* left *at the corner. Adverb.*

—The opposite of the right side: *Walking to school, I see my grandma's house on my right, and across the street on the* left *is my aunt's home. Noun.*

left (left) *adjective, adverb, noun.*

left²—*See* **leave¹**.

left (left) *verb.*

leftover—Something that remains, usually scraps of food: *Mother used* leftovers *from dinner to make soup. Noun.*

—That is remaining: *We used* leftover *lumber from our new porch to build a tree house. Adjective.*

left|o|ver (left′ō′vər) *noun, plural* **leftovers;** *adjective.*

leg—1. One of the body parts that a person or animal stands or walks on.   2. The part of a piece of clothing that covers the leg: *a pants* leg.   3. Something that looks like or is used like a leg: *a chair* leg; *a table* leg.   4. A part or section of something, such as a course or trip: *He ran the last* leg *of the relay race.*

leg (leg) *noun, plural* **legs.**

  ◼ **on** (one's) **last legs:** About to collapse: *After shopping, she came home* on *her* last legs.

  pull (one's) **leg:** To fool or trick someone: *She was* pulling *your* leg *when she said that you had a spider on your shoulder.*

  shake a leg: Hurry up: *You had better* shake a leg *or you'll be late for school!*

legal—1. Of or having to do with the law: *A judge is a* legal *expert.*   2. Lawful; permitted by law: *It is not* legal *to park in front of a fire hydrant.*

le|gal (lē′gəl) *adjective.*

legend—1. A very old story that has been told and believed by many people over the years. Some or all of the story may not be true.   2. Words written near a picture, map, chart, or diagram that explain something about it: *The map* legend *shows that a star is used to mark the state capital.*

leg|end (lej′ənd) *noun, plural* **legends.**

legendary—Of or like a legend: *a* legendary *hero.*

leg|end|ar|y (lej′ən dār′ē) *adjective.*

legible—Able to be read easily; clear: *The address on the letter was not* legible.

leg|i|ble (lej′ə bəl) *adjective.*

legion—1. A section of the ancient Roman army.   2. Any army: *Legions* marched into battle.

le|gion (lē′jən) *noun, plural* **legions.**

legislation—1. The process of making laws: *The job of Congress is* legislation.   2. The laws that are made: *The town council passed* legislation *that set aside money for a new park.*

leg|is|la|tion (lej′is lā′shən) *noun.*

legislative—Of or having the power to make laws: *The student council has some* legislative *responsibilities for our school.*

leg|is|la|tive (lej′is lā′tiv) *adjective.*

legislature—A group of people whose job is to make laws: *Congress is the national* legislature *of the United States.*

leg|is|la|ture (lej′is lā′chər) *noun, plural* **legislatures.**

legitimate—1. Allowed; correct; acceptable: *She had a* legitimate *reason for not doing her homework: the storm had caused a power failure.*

le|git|i|mate (lə jit′ə mit) *adjective.*

lei—A necklace made of flowers. *Leis are popular in Hawaii.*

lei (lā) *noun, plural* **leis.**

  • A word that sounds the same is **lay.**

leisure—Free time when you may do enjoyable things: *During summer vacation, he had the* leisure *to swim and play baseball every day. Noun.*

—Not busy doing required jobs; free: *She likes to do crossword puzzles in her* leisure *time. Adjective.*

lei|sure (lē′zhər *or* lezh′ər) *noun, adjective.*

lemon—1. A sour-tasting, yellow citrus fruit that is grown in warm climates.   2. A worthless item: *Our new car turned out to be a* lemon.   3. A bright yellow color. *Noun.*

—Having a bright yellow color. *Adjective.*

lem|on (lem′ən) *noun, plural* **lemons;** *adjective.*

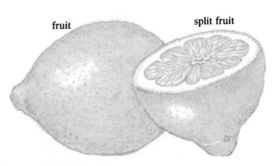

fruit   split fruit

lemon (definition 1)

lemonade—A drink that is made from lemon juice, water, and sugar.
lem|on|ade (lem′ə nād′) *noun, plural* **lemonades.**

lend—**1.** To let a person have or use something for a short time: *Please* lend *me a pencil so I can take the spelling test.* **2.** To give a person or business money that must be paid back in certain amounts by a certain time: *Mother will* lend *me the money to buy a new bicycle, but I must pay her back at five dollars a week for the next five months.* **3.** To give; add: *The blanket of snow* lends *beauty to the field.*
lend (lend) *verb,* **lent, lending.**

length—**1.** How long something is: *The* length *of the yard is twice its width.* **2.** How long something lasts or takes to happen: *The movie was two hours in* length. **3.** A piece of something: *Dad bought a* length *of chicken wire to make a cage for my rabbit.*
length (lengkth *or* length) *noun, plural* **lengths.**
■ **go to any length:** To do all that one can do: *I would* go to any length *to keep my dog.*
● For **1**, see picture at **dimension.**

lengthen—To become or make longer: *The man had to* lengthen *the seat belt so that it would fit around him.*
length|en (lengk′thən *or* leng′thən) *verb,* **lengthened, lengthening.**
● Synonyms: **enlarge, expand**
Antonyms: see Synonyms at **abbreviate.**

lengthwise—In or along the direction of the length: *She made a* lengthwise *cut in the cloth in order to get two narrow strips for curtains. He folded the paper* lengthwise *to make a paper airplane.*
length|wise (lengkth′wīz′ *or* length′wīz′) *adjective, adverb.*

lens—**1.** A curved piece of glass, or other material like glass, that brings light rays closer together or farther apart so that things are shown to be clearer, larger, or closer. Lenses are used in eyeglasses, microscopes, telescopes, and cameras. **2.** The clear, curved part at the front of the eye that brings together light rays entering the eye so that they shine clearly on the retina.
lens (lenz) *noun, plural* **lenses.**

a at	i if	oo look	ch chalk		a in ago
ā ape	ī idle	ou out	ng sing		e in happen
ah calm	o odd	u ugly	sh ship	ə =	i in capital
aw all	ō oats	ū rule	th think		o in occur
e end	oi oil	ur turn	th their		u in upon
ē easy			zh treasure		

lent—*See* **lend.**
lent (lent) *verb.*

Lent—In the Christian religion, the forty days before Easter.
Lent (lent) *noun.*

leopard—A large member of the cat family that lives in Africa and Asia. A leopard's fur is usually dark yellow with black spots.
leop|ard (lep′ərd) *noun, plural* **leopards.**

leopard

leotard—A piece of clothing worn for dancing and gymnastics. It covers the body and may or may not include sleeves or legs. A leotard fits very close to the body but stretches to permit movement.
le|o|tard (lē′ə tahrd) *noun, plural* **leotards.**

leotard

less—**1.** Of reduced size or degree; smaller: *The new bed takes up* less *space in my room, and now I have room for a table.* **2.** In a more limited quantity; not so much: *There was* less *snow than the weather service had predicted. Adjective.*
—A smaller portion or amount: *The box of paints costs* less *than three dollars. Noun.*
—Not so; not as: *The social studies test was* less *difficult than he had expected it to be. Adverb.*
—Minus; with something taken away: *Nine* less *four is five. Preposition.*
less (les) *adjective, noun, adverb, preposition.*
■ **none the less:** Anyway; nevertheless: *The soccer players knew they would lose the match, but they gave their best* none the less.

-less—A suffix that means "without." A restless night is a night without rest.

Word Power

You can understand the meanings of many words that end in **-less,** if you add the meaning of the suffix to the meaning of the rest of the word.
  careless: without care
  homeless: without a home

lessen—To become less; decrease: *The heavy rain* lessened *around noon, and a rainbow appeared.*
less|en (les′ən) *verb,* **lessened, lessening.**
● A word that sounds the same is **lesson.**
● Synonyms: **diminish, dwindle, reduce**

lesson—**1.** An assignment to be taught or learned: *Our* lesson *today will be on volcanoes.* **2.** A unit of study; class: *a singing* lesson *lasting an hour.*
les|son (les′ən) *noun, plural* **lessons.**
● A word that sounds the same is **lessen.**

lest—For fear that: *He put his homework near the front door* lest *he forget it in the morning.*
lest (lest) *conjunction.*

let—**1.** To allow; not stop from doing: *Mother* let *me sleep over at a friend's house.* **2.** To permit to enter, pass, or leave: *Please* let *me in the house.* **3.** To cause to; make: *I'll* let *you know when supper is ready.* **4.** To rent: *This large house has extra rooms to* let.
let (let) *verb,* **let, letting.**
■ **let down:** To disappoint: *She felt that she had* let down *her parents when she brought home a bad report card.*
let off: Allow to go free without punishment: *My father was* let off *with only a warning ticket from the police officer.*

let on: To show that one knows something: *Do not* let on *that you know about the surprise party.*
let up: To stop or lessen: *The barking of our neighbor's dog did not* let up *all night.*

-let—A suffix that means "small." A booklet is a small book.

Word Power

You can understand the meanings of many words that end in **-let,** if you add the meaning of the suffix to the meaning of the rest of the word.
  piglet: a small pig
  streamlet: a small stream

let's—The contraction of "let us."
let's (lets).

letter—**1.** A symbol that stands for a spoken sound. There are 26 letters in the English alphabet. **2.** A written message, usually sent through the mail: *She wrote a* letter *to her parents telling them about summer camp. Noun.*
—To write letters on: *The children* lettered *a sign that read: "Lemonade for sale." Verb.*
let|ter (let′ər) *noun, plural* **letters;** *verb,* **lettered, lettering.**
■ **to the letter:** Exactly; to the smallest detail: *He followed the instructions for building the model airplane* to the letter, *and it came out perfectly.*

letter-perfect—Exactly right; without any mistakes: *She worked at memorizing the poem until she had it* letter-perfect.
let|ter-per|fect (let′ər pur′fikt) *adjective.*

lettuce—A green plant whose large leaves are eaten mainly in salads.
let|tuce (let′is) *noun, plural* **lettuces.**

leukemia—A disease in which a person's body makes too many white blood cells. Leukemia is a form of cancer.
leu|ke|mi|a (lü kē′mē ə) *noun.*

level—**1.** Smooth; flat: *The children used a* level *field for playing baseball.* **2.** Equal in height: *The snow was so deep that it was* level *with the bottom of the kitchen window. Adjective.*
—**1.** A flat surface; floor: *The toy store was on the upper* level *of the shopping mall.* **2.** A tool used to check whether a surface is even or not. **3.** Height: *The tree I planted has grown to the* level *of my knee. Noun.*
—To make even or flat: *He* leveled *the flour in the cup to see how much was there. Verb.*

lev|el (lev′əl) *adjective; noun, plural* **levels;** *verb,* **leveled, leveling.**
- **level with:** To tell the truth to; be honest with: *I want you to* level with *me, and not to tell me what you think I want to hear.*
  on the level: Honest; fair: *Are you* on the level, *or are you trying to fool me?*

lever—1. A pole or bar used to lift a weight at one end of the bar by pushing down on the other end. A seesaw is an example of a lever. **2.** A bar or handle that is attached to a machine: *He pushed the* lever *down on the toaster.*
lev|er (lev′ər *or* lē′vər) *noun, plural* **levers.**

lever (definition 1)

Lhasa apso—A small dog with long, wiry hair thickly covering its whole body and hanging over its eyes. It has long, drooping ears, and its tail curves over its back. Originally bred in Tibet, these dogs were used as guard dogs and pets.
Lha|sa ap|so (lah′sə ap′sō) *noun, plural* **Lhasa apsos.**

liable—1. Likely: *You are* liable *to drop those books if you carry too many at once.*
2. Responsible for by law: *She was* liable *for her neighbor's broken window since she had hit the baseball that broke it.*
li|a|ble (lī′ə bəl) *adjective.*

liar—A person who says things that are not true; one who tells lies.
li|ar (lī′ər) *noun, plural* **liars.**

liberal—1. Generous: *Our neighbor is very* liberal *when he gives out Halloween candy.* **2.** Large; abundant: *She put a* liberal *amount of whipped cream on her hot fudge sundae.* **3.** Eager to hear or try new ideas: *a* liberal *thinker. Adjective.*

—A person eager for new ideas. *Noun.*
lib|er|al (lib′ər əl) *adjective; noun, plural* **liberals.**

liberate—To set loose: *After watching them for a while, the girl* liberated *the fireflies that she had caught.*
lib|er|ate (lib′ə rāt) *verb,* **liberated, liberating.**
• Synonyms: **free, release**
  Antonyms: See Synonyms at **catch.**

liberty—1. Freedom from control by another: *The prisoners gained their* liberty *by digging a tunnel out of the jail.* **2.** The right to think, say, or do as one pleases: *A person has the* liberty *to shout and cheer at a baseball game.*
lib|er|ty (lib′ər tē) *noun, plural* **liberties.**

librarian—A person trained to work in or manage a library.
li|brar|i|an (lī brār′ē ən) *noun, plural* **librarians.**

library—1. A book collection, along with other written materials. **2.** A place where a book collection is housed. Some homes have a special room in which books are kept. Cities, towns, and schools usually have libraries where books can be borrowed for a certain period of time.
li|brar|y (lī′brār ē) *noun, plural* **libraries.**

lice—*See* **louse.**
lice (līs) *plural noun.*

license—A paper, card, tag, or other object that shows that a person is allowed by law to do or have something: *a driver's* license; *a dog* license; *a fishing* license. *Noun.*

—To give a person legal permission to do or have something; permit: *She is* licensed *to be a nurse. Verb.*
li|cense (lī′səns) *noun, plural* **licenses;** *verb,* **licensed, licensing.**

a at	i if	oo look	ch chalk		⎡ a in ago
ã ape	ī idle	ou out	ng sing		e in happen
ah calm	o odd	u ugly	sh ship	ə =	i in capital
aw all	ō oats	ū rule	th think		o in occur
e end	oi oil	ur turn	th their		⎣ u in upon
ē easy			zh treasure		

Lhasa apso

lichen

lichen—A living thing that is a combination of a plant and a fungus. It clings to rocks, trees, and soil. Lichens have no roots, stems, leaves, or flowers. They may be gray, yellow, brown, black, or green.
li|chen (lī′kən) *noun, plural* **lichens.**

lick—1. To move the tongue over something: *The puppy* licked *my face.* **2.** To take into the mouth with the tongue; lap up: *to lick an ice-cream cone.* **3.** To beat; win over: *Our class* licked *the other classes in the spelling bee. Verb.*
—**1.** A wipe of the tongue over something: *She gave the candy cane a big* lick. **2.** A hit; blow: *He gave the dead tree a few* licks *with an ax, and it fell over.* **3.** Not very much; a small amount: *The coach does not have even a* lick *of patience for players who do not come to practice. Noun.*
lick (lik) *verb,* **licked, licking;** *noun, plural* **licks.**
■ **a lick and a promise:** Something done quickly and not very well: *She was late for school and had time only to give her hair* a lick and a promise *before leaving the house.*

licorice—1. A plant whose roots provide a sweet-tasting juice that is used to flavor candy, soft drinks, and medicine. **2.** Candy flavored with this juice.
lic|o|rice (lik′ər is *or* lik′ər ish) *noun.*

lid—1. A top or cover that can be removed: *She took the* lid *off the cookie jar.* **2.** A movable piece of skin that opens and closes over the eye; eyelid.
lid (lid) *noun, plural* **lids.**

lie[1]—Something that is not true and is said to fool another person; false statement: *He could not tell a* lie *and confessed that he broke the window. Noun.*
—To say something false or misleading: *She* lied *about having a sore throat so she would not have to read her report to the class. Verb.*
lie (lī) *noun, plural* **lies;** *verb,* **lied, lying.**
● A word that sounds the same is **lye.**

lie[2]—1. To place oneself flat on a surface: *to lie in bed; to lie on the beach.* **2.** To be in a flat position on something: *The letters* lie *on the desk.* **3.** To remain a certain way: *The dog has been* lying *asleep in front of the fire all day.* **4.** To be positioned or placed: *A bicycle path* lies *along the river.* **5.** To exist; belong: *Her success as a cook* lies *in her ability to follow recipes exactly.*
lie (lī) *verb,* **lay, lain, lying.**
● A word that sounds the same is **lye.**
● See Language Fact at **lay[1].**

lieutenant—An officer in the army, air force, or marine corps, or in a police or fire department, who ranks just below a captain. In the navy, a lieutenant ranks just below a lieutenant commander.
lieu|ten|ant (lū ten′ənt) *noun, plural* **lieutenants.** Abbreviation: **Lt.**

life—1. The quality or condition that separates people, animals, plants, and fungi from all other things. It makes growth and reproduction possible. **2.** The time from birth until death: *She spent her whole* life *on a farm.* **3.** How long a thing is useful or works: *The* life *of his alarm clock was shortened when he dropped it on the floor.* **4.** A living person: *Seat belts have saved many* lives. **5.** A way of living: *The circus performer had an exciting* life. **6.** A person's story; biography: *She read the* life *of the famous explorer.* **7.** Energy; excitement: *The cheerleaders were full of* life.
life (līf) *noun, plural* **lives.**
■ **as big as life: 1.** True to the last detail: *The model of the dinosaur stood in the middle of the museum* as big as life. **2.** Really there; in person: *She opened the door, and there stood her cousin* as big as life.
for dear life: Desperately; because one's life depends on it: *The mouse ran* for dear life *as the cat chased it.*

lifeboat—A small, sturdy boat that is designed to save lives in an emergency at sea. It is often carried on a large ship.
life|boat (līf′bōt′) *noun, plural* **lifeboats.**

lifeguard—A person trained to rescue swimmers in need of help. A lifeguard works at a beach or swimming pool.
life|guard (līf′gahrd) *noun, plural* **lifeguards.**

lifelong—Continuing throughout a life: *Stamp collecting was her* lifelong *hobby.*
life|long (līf′lawng′) *adjective.*

lifetime—1. The length of time during which someone is alive: *She hopes to travel all over the world in her* lifetime. **2.** How long a thing lasts

or can be used: *The lifetime of the watch was about five years.*
life|time (līf′tīm′) *noun, plural* **lifetimes.**

lift—1. To raise; pick up: *He lifted the bag of groceries out of the cart.* 2. To rise up and disappear: *When the dust from his slide lifted, he was standing safely on second base. Verb.*
—1. A good feeling: *A wink from his father gave him a lift.* 2. The act of raising or picking up: *A lift of the lid showed that the cookie jar was empty.* 3. A free ride: *Her brother gave her a lift to the movies. Noun.*
lift (lift) *verb,* **lifted, lifting;** *noun, plural* **lifts.**

lift-off—The launching of a rocket or spacecraft.
lift|off (lift′awf′) *noun, plural* **lift-offs.**

ligament—A strip of strong tissue that holds two bones or other body parts together.
lig|a|ment (lig′ə mənt) *noun, plural* **ligaments.**

light[1]—1. The type of energy that allows us to see. 2. Something that gives off this energy, such as a lamp. 3. Something, such as a match, that can cause something else to burn: *She needed a light for the birthday candles.* 4. Information; knowledge: *I am confused and need more light on how to multiply fractions. Noun.*
—1. Bright; having the energy by which we see: *His bedroom was light in the morning but shaded in the afternoon.* 2. Pale: *light brown hair. Adjective.*
—1. To cause to give off the energy by which we see: *Please light the lamp.* 2. To give such energy to: *The fireworks lighted the night sky.* 3. To make or become bright or happy: *Her face lighted up when she saw her new bicycle.* 4. To show with a lamp or something similar: *The farmer lighted his way to the barn with a lantern.* 5. To set on fire: *He lit the bonfire. Verb.*
light (līt) *noun, plural* **lights;** *adjective,* **lighter, lightest;** *verb,* **lighted** or **lit, lighting.**
■ **bring to light:** To uncover; make known: *The scientist brought to light the cause of the disease.*
come to light: To be shown; be made known: *The facts of the case, kept secret for so many years, have only recently come to light.*

a at	**i** if	**oo** look	**ch** chalk		**a** in ago
ā ape	**ī** idle	**ou** out	**ng** sing		**e** in happen
ah calm	**o** odd	**u** ugly	**sh** ship	ə =	**i** in capital
aw all	**ō** oats	**ū** rule	**th** think		**o** in occur
e end	**oi** oil	**ur** turn	**th** their		**u** in upon
ē easy			**zh** treasure		

● See picture at **prism.**
● Synonyms: **ignite, kindle,** for *verb* **5.**

light[2]—1. Having little weight; not heavy: *We bought only a few groceries, so the bag was light.* 2. Easily done; not hard: *He has to clean his room and do a few other light chores to earn his allowance.* 3. Graceful; moving well: *The dancer is light on her feet.* 4. Meant to amuse or entertain: *The movie was a light comedy that kept everyone laughing.* 5. Small in amount: *She ate a light breakfast, because she was not very hungry.*
light (līt) *adjective,* **lighter, lightest.**
■ **make light of:** To give something very little importance: *She made light of winning the championship, because she had already won it two other times.*

lighten[1]—To make or become brighter or lighter: *The fresh coat of yellow paint lightened the room.*
light|en (lī′tən) *verb,* **lightened, lightening.**

lighten[2]—1. To make less heavy: *They lightened the car's load by removing some of the luggage.* 2. To make or become more cheerful or happier: *Her mood lightened when she heard that her grandparents were coming to visit.*
light|en (lī′tən) *verb,* **lightened, lightening.**

light-hearted—Happy; having no worries or cares: *He is the most light-hearted person I know, and he always lifts my spirits.*
light-heart|ed (līt′hahr′tid) *adjective.*

lighthouse—A tall structure with a bright, flashing light. It is usually located near a rocky or shallow place in the water that is dangerous for ships. A lighthouse warns ships to steer away from these places.
light|house (līt′hous′) *noun, plural* **lighthouses.**

lightning—A sudden flash of light in the sky. It is caused by electricity, often as it passes between clouds or between a cloud and the surface of the earth.
light|ning (līt′ning) *noun.*

light-year—In astronomy, a unit of distance equal to the distance that light travels in one year. This distance is about 5.88 trillion miles (9.46 trillion kilometers).
light-year (līt′yēr′) *noun, plural* **light-years.**

like[1]—1. Having or showing the same or similar qualities or abilities as someone or something else; similar to: *a toy like hers; to run like a deer.* 2. In the right mood, frame of mind, or conditions for: *I feel like having pizza.* 3. Such as: *It is good to eat vegetables like carrots, peas, and squash. Preposition.*

—Being similar or the same as: *The band wore* like *outfits. Adjective.*
—That which is the same or similar: *I doubt we will ever see his* like *as a painter again. Noun.*
like (līk) *preposition; adjective; noun, plural* **likes.**

■ **and the like:** And more of the same kind of thing: *He had always been interested in science, math,* and the like.

Language Fact

Many people feel that **like¹** should not be used with verbs. So careful speakers and writers do not say, for instance, "I did it like you told me to," or "She sings like her mother does." They say, "I did it as you told me to," or "She sings as her mother does." With verbs it is correct to use **as,** or sometimes "as if": *They look as if they know how to do the work.* **Like¹** is correct with nouns and pronouns: *a talent like hers; to bark like a dog.*

like²—**1.** To find pleasing or enjoyable; be fond of: *I* like *going to the beach in the summer.*
2. To have a desire for; want or choose: *I would* like *to travel around the world someday. Verb.*
—**likes:** Things that a person is fond of; preferences: *She says that sunny days are among her* likes *and cloudy ones among her dislikes. Noun.*
like (līk) *verb,* **liked, liking;** *noun, plural* **likes.**
-like—A suffix that means "similar to" or "resembling." A trumpetlike sound is similar to the sound of a trumpet. A catlike movement resembles a movement a cat would make.

Word Power

You can understand the meanings of many words that end in **-like,** if you add a meaning of the suffix to the meaning of the rest of the word.
cottonlike: resembling cotton
springlike: similar to spring

likelihood—The chance or probability that something will occur: *The weather bureau said there is a* likelihood *of snow for the weekend.*
like|li|hood (līk'lē hood) *noun.*
likely—**1.** Possible, probable, or expected: *Forest fires are more* likely *in dry weather.*
2. Appropriate or fitting for the purpose: *She*

figured out the most likely *place for viewing the parade. Adjective.*
—In all probability: *He will* likely *go to the dance. Adverb.*
like|ly (līk'lē) *adjective,* **likelier, likeliest;** *adverb.*
likeness—**1.** A similarity or resemblance: *The mother and daughter had a strong* likeness *to each other.* **2.** A picture or portrait: *The book had a* likeness *of the author on the back.*
like|ness (līk'nis) *noun, plural* **likenesses.**
likewise—**1.** In a similar way: *Watch how he swings at the baseball, and then you try to do* likewise. **2.** Also; besides: *She was chosen for the team, and then her friend was* likewise.
like|wise (līk'wīz') *adverb.*
● Synonyms: **furthermore, moreover, too,** for **2.**
liking—A good feeling or fondness for something; preference: *He has a* liking *for big dogs instead of small ones.*
lik|ing (lī'king) *noun, plural* **likings.**
lilac—**1.** A shrub that has large clusters of fragrant purple or white flowers. **2.** A pale, medium-purple color. *Noun.*
—Having a pale, medium-purple color: *a* lilac *dress. Adjective.*
li|lac (lī'lək) *noun, plural* **lilacs;** *adjective.*

lilac (definition 1)

lily—**1.** A trumpet-shaped flower. It is usually white, and it grows on a tall plant that has long narrow leaves. **2.** Any of various plants related to this one: *a tiger* lily; *a water* lily.
lil|y (lil'ē) *noun, plural* **lilies.**

lily of the valley

lily of the valley—A small plant with tiny, white bell-shaped flowers. The flowers have a delicate, sweet scent.
lil|y of the val|ley (lil′ē əv thə val′ē) *noun, plural* **lilies of the valley.**

Lima bean—A flat, pale-green or white bean that is eaten as a vegetable.
Li|ma bean (lī′mə bēn) *noun, plural* **Lima beans.**

limb—**1.** A leg, arm, wing, or flipper. **2.** A large branch of a tree; bough.
limb (lim) *noun, plural* **limbs.**

lime¹—A white, powdery substance that is made up of calcium and oxygen. It is used as a fertilizer and in the making of cement and glass.
lime (līm) *noun.*·

lime²—**1.** A small, juicy, yellowish-green citrus fruit with a sour taste. It grows in the tropics. **2.** The tree on which the fruit grows. *Noun.*
—Having a yellowish-green color. *Adjective.*
lime (līm) *noun, plural* **limes;** *adjective.*

limerick—A humorous poem that is five lines long. Usually the first, second, and fifth lines rhyme with one another, and the third and fourth lines rhyme with each other.
lim|er|ick (lim′ər ik) *noun, plural* **limericks.**

limestone—A light-colored rock used for building and as a source of lime. Marble is a type of limestone.
lime|stone (līm′stōn′) *noun.*

limit—**1.** A boundary; border: *city* limits. **2.** The greatest amount allowed: *the speed* limit. *Noun.*

—To restrict: *He* limited *his eating because he was trying to lose weight. Verb.*
lim|it (lim′it) *noun, plural* **limits;** *verb,* **limited, limiting.**

limp¹—A lame movement or way of walking: *The dog walked with a* limp *because it had once been hit by a car. Noun.*
—To move or walk in a lame way: *She* limped *home after she twisted her ankle. Verb.*
limp (limp) *noun, plural* **limps;** *verb,* **limped, limping.**

limp²—Not stiff, strong, or rigid: *The baseball glove became* limp *after so much use.*
limp (limp) *adjective,* **limper, limpest.**

Lincoln's Birthday—February 12. It is the day that Abraham Lincoln, the sixteenth president of the United States, was born. It is a legal holiday in some states.
Lin|coln's Birth|day (ling′kənz burth′dā) *noun.*
• See also **Presidents' Day.**

linden—A shade tree having large heart-shaped leaves and clusters of small, yellow flowers.
lin|den (lin′dən) *noun, plural* **lindens.**

line¹—**1.** A long, narrow mark, usually made by a pencil, pen, or chalk: *She drew three* lines *to form a triangle.* **2.** Anything that looks like such a mark: *the* lines *on a face; the* line *of the equator; the finish* line. **3.** A rope, wire, string, cord, or thread: *bathing suits hanging on the* line *to dry; a busy telephone* line; *a fishing* line. **4.** A border; boundary: *At this rate, we should reach the state* line *by noon.* **5.** A row of people or things: *When the bell rang, the children formed* lines *and walked to their school buses.* **6.** A row of words on a page: *a poem of twenty* lines. **7.** A short, written note: *I dropped my aunt a* line *to thank her for a present.* **8. lines:** The words spoken in a play: *How did you manage to learn all the* lines *for that part?* **9.** A course of conduct, action, or thought: *I have trouble understanding that* line *of thinking.* **10.** A type or supply of goods: *The clothing*

a at	i if	oo look	ch chalk	a in ago
ā ape	ī idle	ou out	ng sing	e in happen
ah calm	o odd	u ugly	sh ship	ə = i in capital
aw all	ō oats	ū rule	th think	o in occur
e end	oi oil	ur turn	<u>th</u> their	u in upon
ē easy			zh treasure	

store has a new line *of winter coats.*   **11.** A transportation system: *He called the bus* line *to find out the schedule. Noun.*
—**1.** To make one or more long, narrow marks: *We* lined *the banner before we wrote on it so that we could keep our letters straight.*   **2.** To put or arrange so as to form a row: *They* lined *the driveway with bushes. Verb.*
line (līn) *noun, plural* lines; *verb,* lined, lining.

■ **lay on the line:** To speak in a serious way: *The librarian laid it on the line when he told her she would have to pay a fine on the overdue books or lose her card.*
out of line: Behaving badly: *He was out of line to say such a rude thing.*
toe the line: To obey a rule and behave as expected: *She is toeing the line by making sure that she is always home on time.*

line²—To add a layer of fabric to the inside of a piece of clothing: *She* lined *her wool pants so they would not feel scratchy.*
line (līn) *verb,* lined, lining.

linen—**1.** A strong fabric made from flax fibers. **2. linens:** Tablecloths, napkins, towels, shirts, and other household or clothing articles that are made of linen or a similar fabric.
lin|en (lin′ ən) *noun, plural* linens.

-ling—A suffix that means "young" or "one who is." A duckling is a young duck. A hireling is one who is hired.

Word Power

You can understand the meanings of many words that end in **-ling,** if you add a meaning of the suffix to the meaning of the rest of the word.
    princeling: a young prince
    underling: one who is under someone else in rank

linger—To delay leaving; move slowly as if wanting to stay: *He* lingered *by the stage door, hoping to get the singer's autograph.*
lin|ger (ling′ gər) *verb,* lingered, lingering.

lining—The inside layer of something: *Mother's jewelry box has a velvet* lining.
lin|ing (lī′ning) *noun, plural* linings.

link—**1.** A ring that is part of a chain. **2.** Anything that joins or connects: *The bridge is a* link *between the two cities. Noun.*
—To connect; join together: *The sisters* linked *arms as they crossed the street. Verb.*

link (lingk) *noun, plural* **links;** *verb,* **linked, linking.**

linoleum—A hard, washable floor covering. It is made of ground cork or wood that is coated with oil and padded with a canvas backing.
li|no|le|um (lə nō′ lē əm) *noun, plural* **linoleums.**

lion—A large, powerful animal of the cat family, found in Africa and southwest Asia. It has a yellowish-brown, short-haired coat and a long tail with a clump of black hair at the end. Male lions have shaggy manes covering their heads and necks.
li|on (lī′ ən) *noun, plural* **lions.**

■ **throw to the lions:** To destroy by abandoning: *The political party took away its support of the candidate and* threw *him to the lions.*

lion and **lioness**

lioness—An adult female lion.
li|on|ess (lī′ ə nis) *noun, plural* **lionesses.**

lion-hearted—Very brave; full of courage: *a* lion-hearted *knight; a* lion-hearted *police officer.*
li|on-heart|ed (lī′ ən hahr′ tid) *adjective.*

lip—**1.** Either of the two fleshy parts of the mouth.   **2.** The rim or edge of an opening: *There is a crack in the* lip *of the cup.*
lip (lip) *noun, plural* **lips.**

■ **curl (one's) lip:** To lift the upper lip to show strong dislike: *He* curled *his lip when he saw the bully picking on the smaller boy.*
give (one) lip: To speak rudely and boldly: *Do as I tell you, and don't* give *me any* lip.
keep a stiff upper lip: To be brave; be not discouraged: *He* kept a stiff upper lip *during the tornado and did not panic.*

Lipizzaner

Lipizzaner—A European show horse. It is born with a dark coat that turns white after several years.
Lip|iz|za|ner (lip'ə zah′nər) *noun, plural* **Lipizzaners.**

lipstick—A small stick of colored wax set in a tube and used to color the lips.
lip|stick (lip′stik′) *noun, plural* **lipsticks.**

liquid—A substance that flows freely. Milk, water, gravy, and gasoline are all liquids. *Noun.*
—Flowing; in the form of a fluid: *Does she use a powdered or a* liquid *detergent to wash her clothes? Adjective.*
liq|uid (lik′wid) *noun, plural* **liquids;** *adjective.*

liquor—An alcoholic drink, such as whiskey, rum, or vodka.
liq|uor (lik′ər) *noun, plural* **liquors.**

lira—A unit of money in Italy, Malta, and Turkey.
li|ra (lēr′ə) *noun, plural* **lira.** Abbreviation: **l.**

lisp—To say the sounds of "*s*" and "*z*" as though they have the sounds of "*th*" in *thick* and *the. Verb.*
—The act of talking in this way. *Noun.*

a at	i if	oo look	ch chalk		⌈a in ago
ā ape	ī idle	ou out	ng sing		e in happen
ah calm	o odd	u ugly	sh ship	ə =	i in capital
aw all	ō oats	ū rule	th think		o in occur
e end	oi oil	ur turn	th their		⌊u in upon
ē easy			zh treasure		

lisp (lisp) *verb,* **lisped, lisping;** *noun, plural* **lisps.**

list—A series of words, names, or numbers: *She made a* list *of the words she misspelled. Noun.*
—To put into such a series: *He* listed *the items he needed to buy at the grocery store. Verb.*
list (list) *noun, plural* **lists;** *verb,* **listed, listing.**

listen—To pay attention so as to hear: *The children* listened *as their teacher read them a story.*
lis|ten (lis′ən) *verb,* **listened, listening.**

listless—Having no interest in anything; lacking energy: *The hot day seemed to make everyone* listless.
list|less (list′lis) *adjective.*

lit—*See* **light[1].**
lit (lit) *verb.*

liter—A basic unit of measuring liquids in the metric system. It is equal to about 1.06 quarts.
li|ter (lē′tər) *noun, plural* **liters.** Abbreviation: **l**
• See picture at **quart.**

literacy—The condition of being able to read and write: *Where there are few schools, the rate of* literacy *is low.*
lit|er|a|cy (lit′ər ə sē) *noun.*

literally—**1.** Word for word: *to translate a novel* literally. **2.** In fact; in plain truth: *He* literally *shook with laughter at the joke.*
lit|er|al|ly (lit′ər ə lē) *adverb.*

literary—Of or relating to literature: *a* literary *magazine;* literary *interests.*
lit|er|ar|y (lit′ə rār′ē) *adjective.*

literate—Having the ability to read and write: *The country introduced several programs designed to make more of its people* literate.
lit|er|ate (lit′ər it) *adjective.*

literature—**1.** Writings that have a lasting value because of their beauty, style, or contribution to learning. Literature includes essays, novels, plays, poems, and short stories. **2.** Any printed material: *We read the* literature *on various types of computers before deciding on which one we wanted.*
lit|er|a|ture (lit′ər ə choor *or* lit′ər ə chər) *noun.*

litmus paper—A paper treated with a dye and used to test if a chemical is an acid or a base.
lit|mus pa|per (lit′məs pā′pər) *noun.*

litter—**1.** Scraps of paper, trash, or other material that are scattered about: *The beach was covered with* litter *after the storm.* **2.** Animals born at one time and to the same mother: *My dog had a* litter *of four puppies.* **3.** A stretcher for carrying

people who are sick or wounded. *Noun.*
—To scatter about scraps of paper or other material; make messy: *People can be arrested if they* litter *the highways. Verb.*
lit|ter (lit′ər) *noun, plural* **litters;** *verb,* **littered, littering.**

little—1. Small in size or quantity: *a little mouse; a little luck; a little child.* 2. Not much in time or distance; brief: *The line was not very long, so it took only a* little *while to get some popcorn.* 3. Unimportant: *When I am tired, every* little *thing seems to bother me. Adjective.*
—Not much: *They* little *remembered that they had already met and so acted like strangers toward each other. Adverb.*
—1. A small amount: *Take only a* little *because there is not much left.* 2. Not much in time or distance: *She opened the window a* little *to get some fresh air. Noun.*
lit|tle (lit′əl) *adjective,* **less** or **lesser** or **littler, least** or **littlest;** *adverb,* **less, least;** *noun.*
• Synonyms: For *adjective* 1, see Synonyms at **small.**
Antonyms: For *adjective* 1, see Synonyms at **big.**

live¹—1. To be alive: *Her favorite poet* lived *two hundred years ago.* 2. To keep being alive; survive: *His grandfather* lived *for ninety years.* 3. To support oneself: *She* lives *on the money she makes as a nurse.* 4. To eat: *She* lived *on soup when she was sick.* 5. To dwell; reside: *His older sister* lives *in an apartment.*
live (liv) *verb,* **lived, living.**
▪ **live down:** To live long enough to be forgiven for a past error: *She did not think she would ever* live down *dropping her baton while marching at the head of the parade.*
live it up: To get all the enjoyment that is possible: *We are going to* live it up *on this trip and do everything there is to do.*

live²—1. Alive; full of life: *I saw a* live *tiger at the circus.* 2. Glowing; still burning: live *coals in a fireplace.* 3. Not exploded: *a* live *bomb.* 4. Carrying an electric current: live *wires.* 5. Broadcast at the time it is happening: *Is this show* live, *or is it taped?*
live (līv) *adjective.*

livelihood—The way one makes a living or supports oneself: *He earns his* livelihood *by working as a carpenter.*
live|li|hood (līv′lē hood) *noun, plural* **livelihoods.**

lively—1. Spirited or active; full of energy: *The puppies had a* lively *romp on the grass.* 2. Happy or bright: *a* lively *melody; a* lively *color. Adjective.*
—In a spirited or energetic way: *The dancers stepped* lively *around the room. Adverb.*
live|ly (līv′lē) *adjective,* **livelier, liveliest;** *adverb.*
• Synonyms: **brisk, energetic, vigorous,** for *adjective* 1.

liver—1. A large, reddish-brown organ in people and animals. It helps the body absorb food. 2. This organ of some animals, used as food: *beef* liver; *chicken* livers.
liv|er (liv′ər) *noun, plural* **livers.**

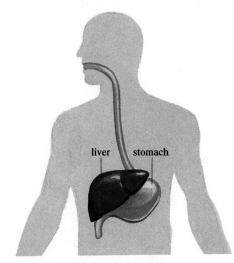

liver (definition 1)

lives—*See* **life.**
lives (līvz) *plural noun.*

livestock—Animals, such as horses, cows, pigs, sheep, and goats, that are raised on a farm or ranch.
live|stock (līv′stok′) *noun.*

living—1. Alive and not dead: *a* living *tree.* 2. Still being in use; existing: *a* living *language.* 3. Having to do with supporting life; of life: Living *conditions in his apartment improved after he had the plumbing repaired. Adjective.*
—1. The state of being alive or of staying somewhere: *We like* living *in the country.* 2. A way of staying alive; livelihood: *She earns her* living *by selling insurance.* 3. A style of life: *My cousin enjoys the fast-paced* living *of a large city. Noun.*
liv|ing (liv′ing) *adjective; noun, plural* **livings.**

living room—The room in a house that is used by the whole family for general activities.
liv|ing room (liv′ing rūm *or* liv′ing room) *noun, plural* **living rooms.**

lizard—A four-legged reptile with scaly skin and a long, tapering tail. Lizards are related to alligators, crocodiles, and snakes, and come in many sizes. They live in warm climates.
liz|ard (liz′ərd) *noun, plural* **lizards.**
• See picture at **reptile.**

llama—A South American animal with a soft, woolly coat. Llamas are related to camels, but they are smaller and have no humps. They are used to carry heavy loads and are also raised for their wool.
lla|ma (lah′mə) *noun, plural* **llamas.**

llama

load—1. Something that is carried: *He brought in a* load *of wood for the fireplace.* 2. Something that bothers one's mind: *After she paid back the money she owed, she felt that a* load *had been lifted from her.* 3. The amount of work a person is expected to do: *He had a* load *of chores to finish before he could go out and play. Noun.*
—1. To put on or in something for carrying: *The men* loaded *furniture into the moving van.* 2. To fill a device with something needed: *to* load *a camera with film; to* load *a rifle with bullets.* 3. To fill: *He* loaded *the washing machine with dirty clothes. Verb.*
load (lōd) *noun, plural* **loads;** *verb,* **loaded, loading.**

loaf¹—1. A shaped or molded mass of bread baked as one piece. 2. Any food or other thing shaped like a loaf of bread: *a meat* loaf.
loaf (lōf) *noun, plural* **loaves.**

loaf²—To spend time doing nothing important; lounge; relax: *We ran errands in the morning and* loafed *in the afternoon.*
loaf (lōf) *verb,* **loafed, loafing.**

loan—1. The act of lending: *She asked for the* loan *of his eraser.* 2. Something that is lent: *My money for tonight's movie is a* loan *from my brother. Noun.*
—To lend: *The museum* loaned *the painting to the traveling exhibit. Verb.*
loan (lōn) *noun, plural* **loans;** *verb,* **loaned, loaning.**
• A word that sounds the same is **lone.**

loaves—*See* **loaf¹.**
loaves (lōvz) *plural noun.*

lobby—1. An entrance hall that serves as a passageway to a room or between rooms: *a hotel* lobby; *the* lobby *of the office building.* 2. One or more persons who try to get public officials to vote a certain way. *Noun.*
—To try to get public officials to vote a certain way: *A group of parents* lobbied *the city council to have a playground built in their neighborhood. Verb.*
lob|by (lob′ē) *noun, plural* **lobbies;** *verb,* **lobbied, lobbying.**

lobster—1. An ocean animal with five pairs of legs. Four of the pairs are thin. The fifth pair extends in front of the head and ends in large claws. The lobster's soft body parts are covered by a hard shell. 2. The meat of a lobster, eaten as food.
lob|ster (lob′stər) *noun, plural* **lobsters.**
• See picture at **crustacean.**

local—1. Having to do with a certain place: *the* local *news report; the* local *drugstore.* 2. Making all the stops on a route: *a* local *train; a* local *bus. Adjective.*
—A train, subway, or bus that stops at all stations. *Noun.*
lo|cal (lō′kəl) *adjective; noun, plural* **locals.**

locate—1. To find or show the position or place of something: *The map of the museum helped us* locate *the dinosaur room.* 2. To settle in a

a at	i if	oo look	ch chalk		⌐ a in ago
ā ape	ī idle	ou out	ng sing		e in happen
ah calm	o odd	u ugly	sh ship	ə =	i in capital
aw all	ō oats	ū rule	th think		o in occur
e end	oi oil	ur turn	th their		⌐ u in upon
ē easy			zh treasure		

certain place: *They* located *their lemonade stand on a busy corner.*
lo|cate (lō′kāt *or* lō kāt′) *verb,* **located, locating.**

location—1. A place; position: *A good* location *for camping is near a stream.* 2. The act or process of finding or showing something.
lo|ca|tion (lō kā′shən) *noun, plural* **locations.**
• Synonyms: **site, situation, spot,** for 1.

lock¹—1. A device for fastening a door, window, box, or the like. A key of a special shape is needed to open a lock. 2. A part of a canal, dock, or other waterway in which the water level can be changed. It is used to raise or lower a ship from one level of water to another. *Noun.*
—1. To secure or fasten with a special device: *He* locked *the tool shed after he put the lawn mower away.* 2. To shut something in or out of a place: *She* locked *her diary in the desk drawer.* 3. To hold or join securely: *We* locked *our arms together so we would not be separated in the crowd. Verb.*
lock (lok) *noun, plural* **locks;** *verb,* **locked, locking.**
■ **lock, stock, and barrel:** Leaving out nothing; including everything: *He packed up* lock, stock, and barrel *and moved out of his apartment.*
under lock and key: Kept locked up: *The art treasures were placed* under lock and key *while the museum was being painted.*

lock²—A curl of hair.
lock (lok) *noun, plural* **locks.**

locker—A small chest, cabinet, or closet that can be locked: *a gym* locker.
lock|er (lok′ər) *noun, plural* **lockers.**

locket—A small, thin, metal case for holding a keepsake, such as a picture of someone or a lock of hair. It usually has a round, oval, or heart shape and is worn on a chain around the neck.
lock|et (lok′it) *noun, plural* **lockets.**

lockjaw—A disease in which the jaws become firmly closed. It is caused by germs that enter the body through a cut or other type of wound. This disease is also called **tetanus.**
lock|jaw (lok′jaw′) *noun.*

locksmith—A person whose job is making or fixing locks and keys.
lock|smith (lok′smith′) *noun, plural* **locksmiths.**

locomotive—An engine that is used to pull or push a railroad train.
lo|co|mo|tive (lō′kə mō′tiv) *noun, plural* **locomotives.**

locust—1. A kind of grasshopper that often migrates in great swarms and destroys crops.

2. A tree with small, rounded leaves, hard wood, and clusters of white or pink flowers.
lo|cust (lō′kəst) *noun, plural* **locusts.**

lodge—1. A house, cabin, or inn. Often it is rented for temporary use: *We stayed at a* lodge *on the lake last summer.* 2. A club or secret organization or a meeting place for its members. *Noun.*
—1. To settle in a place for a while: *The scouts* lodged *in tents on their hike.* 2. To supply with a temporary place to live; provide rented rooms to: *The inn* lodges *many skiers during the winter.* 3. To get caught or stuck in a place: *The penny* lodged *in a crack in the sidewalk.* 4. To bring to an authority: *The citizens* lodged *a complaint with the city council about the holes in the streets. Verb.*
lodge (loj) *noun, plural* **lodges;** *verb,* **lodged, lodging.**

lodging—1. A dwelling place to use for a short while. 2. **lodgings:** A rented room or rooms in another person's house.
lodg|ing (loj′ing) *noun, plural* **lodgings.**

loft—1. The top floor, room, or open space just below the roof in a building, cabin, or barn. It is usually used as a storage area. 2. A balcony or top floor in a church or hall. 3. A room or floor in a warehouse or other business building: *a* loft *converted to an apartment.*
loft (lawft) *noun, plural* **lofts.**

lofty—1. Extremely tall or high: *the* lofty *peaks of a mountain range.* 2. Very high-minded, noble, or grand: *a* lofty *idea;* lofty *goals.*
loft|y (lawf′tē) *adjective,* **loftier, loftiest.**

log—1. A bulky piece of timber with its bark still on: *to gather* logs *to burn in the fireplace; a fort*

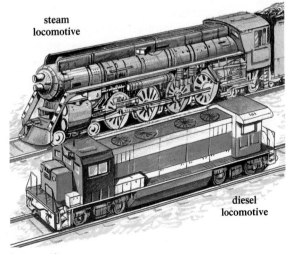

steam locomotive

diesel locomotive

locomotive

made of logs. **2.** The record of a trip on a ship or airplane: *The captain described the storm in the ship's log. Noun.*
—**1.** To cut trees for lumber. **2.** To write entries in the record of a ship or airplane. *Verb.*
log (log *or* lawg) *noun, plural* **logs;** *verb,* **logged, logging.**
- **like a bump on a log:** Without doing anything; without activity: *Don't sit there* like a bump on a log *when everyone else is working.*
  log off: To stop using a computer.
  log on: To enter a computer program by using a command.
  sleep like a log: To sleep deeply and soundly: *After playing all day in the snow, she slept like a log.*

loganberry—The purplish-red fruit of a thorny shrub. It is a cross between a blackberry and a red raspberry.
lo|gan|ber|ry (lō′gən ber′ē) *noun, plural* **loganberries.**

loganberry

logger—A person whose job is to cut trees for lumber; lumberjack.
log|ger (log′ər *or* lawg′ər) *noun, plural* **loggers.**

logic—Sound thinking or reasoning that provides a convincing argument or proof: *The club decided to follow her plan at once, because the* logic *of it was so clear.*
log|ic (loj′ik) *noun.*

logical—**1.** Using or according to sound thinking: *An open window was the* logical *explanation for the draft in the room.* **2.** Expected as a natural

outcome: *Wet feet are the* logical *result of walking in puddles.*
log|i|cal (loj′ə kəl) *adjective.*

LOGO—A computer language designed to help people learn how to work with computers. It is often used in schools.
LO|GO (lō′gō′) *noun.*

loin—**1. loins**—The part of the body on either side of the backbone between the lower ribs and the hips. **2.** A cut of meat taken from this part of an animal's body.
loin (loin) *noun, plural* **loins.**

loiter—**1.** To stand around wasting time; linger: *He* loitered *in the hallway because he had nothing to do.* **2.** To move slowly; dawdle: *If you* loiter *on the way to the station, you will miss the train.*
loi|ter (loi′tər) *verb,* **loitered, loitering.**
- Synonyms: **delay, dilly-dally,** for **2.**
  Antonyms: For **2,** see Synonyms at **rush.**

lollipop or **lollypop**—A lump of hard candy on the end of a small stick.
lol|li|pop or **lol|ly|pop** (lol′ē pop) *noun, plural* **lollipops** or **lollypops.**

lone—**1.** Without others; single: *The room was lit by a* lone *candle.* **2.** Apart from others; isolated: *a* lone *cabin on the mountain.*
lone (lōn) *adjective.*
- A word that sounds the same is **loan.**

lonely—**1.** Feeling sad from being left by oneself; lonesome: *She felt* lonely *after all her friends went home.* **2.** Not often visited; deserted: *The swimming pool is a* lonely *place in the winter.* **3.** Without others nearby; alone: *One* lonely *mountain rose above the flat plains.*
lone|ly (lōn′lē) *adjective,* **lonelier, loneliest.**

lonesome—**1.** Feeling sad from being left by oneself; lonely: *She was* lonesome *at first in the new city.* **2.** Not often visited; deserted: *The path through the woods is a* lonesome *route to town.*
lone|some (lōn′səm) *adjective,* **lonesomer, lonesomest.**

long[1]—**1.** Measuring much in distance or time: *a* long *rope; a* long *trip.* **2.** Having a certain length: *The yardstick is three feet* long. **3.** Being a sound that takes more time to pronounce than a short one: *Adding an "e" to "not" changes the short "o" to a* long *one. Adjective.*
—**1.** For or during a great amount of time: *Study as* long *as you want.* **2.** At a point of time in the distant past: *She learned the alphabet* long *before she went to school.* **3.** For the entire time: *We worked all day* long. *Adverb.*

a at	i if	oo look	ch chalk		a in ago
ā ape	ī idle	ou out	ng sing		e in happen
ah calm	o odd	u ugly	sh ship	ə =	i in capital
aw all	ō oats	ū rule	th think		o in occur
e end	oi oil	ur turn	th their		u in upon
ē easy			zh treasure		

—A large amount of time: *Will it take* long *to color the pictures? Noun.*
long (lawng) *adjective,* **longer, longest;** *adverb; noun.*

■ **the long and the short of it:** The total or basic idea of something: *After all our discussion,* the long and the short of it *was that he did not like my idea.*

long²—To feel a strong desire for: *She* longed *to have a chance to learn to play the guitar.*
long (lawng) *verb,* **longed, longing.**
● Synonyms: **crave, yearn**

longhand—Ordinary handwriting, not done in shorthand or by machine: *She wrote her story in* longhand *first and typed it later.*
long|hand (**lawng′**hand′) *noun.*

longhorn—Any of a kind of cattle with very long horns.
long|horn (**lawng′**hawrn′) *noun, plural* **longhorns.**

longhorn

longing—A strong wish: *She felt a* longing *to share her secret with someone. Noun.*
—Having a strong desire: *His* longing *eyes were fixed on the radio in the store window. Adjective.*
long|ing (**lawng′**ing) *noun, plural* **longings;** *adjective.*

longitude—A distance on the earth east or west of an imaginary line that passes through England. Maps and globes show longitude, measured in degrees, by parallel lines pointing north and south.
lon|gi|tude (**lon′**jə tūd *or* **lon′**jə tyūd) *noun, plural* **longitudes.**
● See picture at **latitude.**

look—1. To direct the eyes so as to see: *She* looked *up quickly when the door opened.* 2. To seek or search for: *He* looked *in the closet for his airplane model.* 3. To seem; appear: *The room*

looks *different in the dark.* 4. To face in a particular direction: *Her window* looks *out over the forest. Verb.*
—1. A glance or gaze: *With one* look, *she spotted her friend in the crowd.* 2. Expression or appearance: *The children at the party had an excited* look. *Noun.*
look (look) *verb,* **looked, looking;** *noun, plural* **looks.**

lookout—1. A close watch for someone or something: *Keep a* lookout *for the markers along the trail.* 2. A place from which one keeps a close watch: *From the* lookout *on the hill, the captain could see the enemy army.* 3. A person whose job is to keep a close watch: *The* lookout *in the church tower signaled that the enemy ships were coming.*
look|out (**look′**out′) *noun, plural* **lookouts.**

loom¹—A frame or machine used to weave thread into cloth.
loom (lūm) *noun, plural* **looms.**

loom²—To look or seem large and dangerous: *The mountain* loomed *against the dark sky.*
loom (lūm) *verb,* **loomed, looming.**

loon—A large fish-eating bird with webbed feet. It has a loud, laughing cry.
loon (lūn) *noun, plural* **loons.**

loon

loop—1. The curved shape formed by folding a piece of string, rope, or similar material back on itself. 2. Anything that is shaped in such a way: *the* loops *of the letters "P" and "D." Noun.*
—To make or form such a curved shape: *We* looped *the ribbon to make a bow. Verb.*
loop (lūp) *noun, plural* **loops;** *verb,* **looped, looping.**

■ **knock for a loop:** To strongly impress; overwhelm: *Seeing the movie star* knocked *the boy* for a loop.

loophole—A small opening in a wall that can be used to look through, to let in light and air, or to shoot through when an enemy is outside.
loop|hole (**lūp′**hōl′) *noun, plural* **loopholes.**

loose—1. Not tightly fastened: *a loose leg on a chair.* 2. Not bound or joined together: *He put the* loose *pages back into his folder.* 3. Not shut up or confined; free: *In some zoos, the tame animals are* loose *to walk around.* 4. Not in a box or other container: *She found some* loose *marbles on the floor.* 5. Not fitting tightly: *a* loose *shirt.* 6. Not packed tightly together: *We covered the seeds with* loose *soil. Adjective.* —1. To release; allow to go free: *She* loosed *the paper kite, and the wind carried it up.* 2. To make less tight: *He* loosed *the collar from around the dog's neck. Verb.*
loose (lūs) *adjective,* **looser, loosest;** *verb,* **loosed, loosing.**

loose-leaf—Made so that sheets or pages can be taken out or put back in: *a* loose-leaf *notebook.*
loose-leaf (lūs′lēf′) *adjective.*

loosen—To become or make less tight: *When I* loosened *my grip on the leash, the dog was able to run away.*
loos|en (lū′sən) *verb,* **loosened, loosening.**

loot—Stolen items: *The burglars hid their* loot *in an abandoned building. Noun.* —To rob of valuable items: *The pirates* looted *the ship. Verb.*
loot (lūt) *noun; verb,* **looted, looting.**
• A word that sounds the same is **lute.**

lope—To run with long, easy steps: *The horses* loped *around the track. Verb.* —A long, easy running step: *He ran down the road at a* lope. *Noun.*
lope (lōp) *verb,* **loped, loping;** *noun, plural* **lopes.**

lopsided—Bigger or heavier on one side than on the other; unevenly balanced: *The* lopsided *pile tilted and began to fall.*
lop|sid|ed (lop′sī′did) *adjective.*

lord—1. One having great authority and power over others: *Kings and owners of estates are sometimes called* lords. 2. **Lord:** A title for a man of noble rank in Great Britain. 3. **Lord: a.** God. **b.** Jesus Christ.
lord (lawrd) *noun, plural* **lords.**

Word History

Lord comes from two old English words meaning "keeper of the loaf of bread." **Lady** comes from two old English words meaning "one who makes a loaf of bread." Long ago, the lord or man of the house was considered the protector for the household, while the lady or woman of the house had the job of making the bread and other types of food for the household.

lose—1. To not have any longer; be without: *to* lose *a glove.* 2. To be unable to keep: *to* lose *my place in a book.* 3. To fail to win: *He was sad because he* lost *the tennis match.* 4. To not take advantage of; waste: *We will* lose *time if we have to wait for her.*
lose (lūz) *verb,* **lost, losing.**

loss—1. The act of losing something: *She was unhappy over the* loss *of her bracelet.* 2. Someone or something that is gone: *I am sorry she is quitting the team, because she will be a great* loss.
loss (laws) *noun, plural* **losses.**

lost—*See* **lose.** *Verb.* —1. Misplaced or missing: *Mother looked for her* lost *gloves.* 2. Not used; wasted: *a* lost *opportunity.* 3. Ruined or destroyed: *homes* lost *in the flood.* 4. Not won: *a* lost *game. Adjective.*
lost (lawst) *verb, adjective.*

lot—1. A large amount: *A* lot *of children like candy.* 2. A group of people or things of the same type: *This kitten is the biggest of the* lot. 3. A piece of land: *a parking* lot. 4. A small piece of paper or wood, or a similar object, used in deciding something by chance: *The players drew* lots *to decide who would go first.* 5. This method of deciding something: *The team selected its captain by* lot. 6. One's fate or destiny: *Perhaps it was her* lot *in life to become famous. Noun.* —Very much; a great deal: *She is a* lot *taller than he is. Adverb.*
lot (lot) *noun, plural* **lots;** *adverb.*
• Synonyms: **batch, bunch, set²,** for *noun 2.*

lotion—A creamy liquid used to soften, clean, or heal the skin: *She uses hand* lotion *in cold weather to keep her hands from chapping.*
lo|tion (lō′shən) *noun, plural* **lotions.**

lottery—A contest in which winners are decided by chance.
lot|ter|y (lot′ər ē) *noun, plural* **lotteries.**

lotus

lotus—A water plant with floating leaves and large, colorful flowers.
lo|tus (lō′təs) *noun, plural* **lotuses.**

loud—Making much sound; noisy: loud *music. Adjective.*
—In a noisy way: *Playing your radio so* loud *will hurt your ears. Adverb.*
loud (loud) *adjective,* **louder, loudest;** *adverb.*

loudspeaker—A device that increases sound: *The mayor used a* loudspeaker *to talk to the large crowd.*
loud|speak|er (loud′spē′kər) *noun, plural* **loudspeakers.**

lounge—To sit or lie in a lazy, relaxed way: *He* lounged *in the comfortable chair. Verb.*
—A place where someone relaxes in such a way: *We sat in the hotel* lounge *and watched television. Noun.*
lounge (lounj) *verb,* **lounged, lounging;** *noun, plural* **lounges.**

louse—A tiny insect with no wings. It lives on the bodies of animals and humans and sucks blood.
louse (lous) *noun, plural* **lice.**

louse

love—1. A very strong, tender feeling for someone.
2. Deep liking or fondness: *She has a* love *for animals. Noun.*
—1. To have a very strong, tender feeling for:

She loves *her little brother.* **2.** To have a deep liking or fondness for: *He* loves *to play the drums. Verb.*
love (luv) *noun, plural* **loves;** *verb,* **loved, loving.**

lovely—1. Having a pleasing appearance: *My aunt is a* lovely *woman.* **2.** Causing pleasure; enjoyable: *We had a* lovely *time at the concert.*
love|ly (luv′lē) *adjective,* **lovelier, loveliest.**
• Synonyms: **beautiful, gorgeous, pretty,** for **1.**
Antonyms: For **1,** see Synonyms at **ugly.**

low—1. Not high or tall: *a* low *fence.* **2.** Less than the normal level: *The river is* low. **3.** Not loud; soft: *The librarian spoke in a* low *voice.*
4. Less than the normal amount: *Our food supplies were* low *after we had camped for a week.* **5.** Not good or favorable: *The boys have a* low *opinion of bullies.* **6.** Having a deep pitch: *He can sing* low *tones.* **7.** Not happy; sad: *I feel* low *today because it is raining. Adjective.*
—At or to a level or position that is not high: *The geese flew* low *over the pond. Adverb.*
—1. A level, position, or point that is not high: *The temperature dropped to a new* low *yesterday.*
2. The gear that gives the greatest power and least speed: *My father shifted his car into* low *to drive it up the steep hill. Noun.*
low (lō) *adjective,* **lower, lowest;** *adverb; noun, plural* **lows.**

lower—1. To move someone or something downward: *We* lowered *the window shades to block out the sun.* **2.** To lessen or reduce in value or amount: *The store* lowers *its prices on bathing suits in the fall.*
low|er (lō′ər) *verb,* **lowered, lowering.**

loyal—Faithful to someone or something: *He is a* loyal *friend of mine.*
loy|al (loi′əl) *adjective.*

loyalty—Faithful behavior: *As a sign of* loyalty *to the team, he goes to all of his school's football games.*
loy|al|ty (loi′əl tē) *noun, plural* **loyalties.**

lubricate—To place grease or oil on the parts of a machine so they will move easily: *He* lubricated *the lawn mower so it would work well when he cut the grass.*
lu|bri|cate (lū′brə kāt′) *verb,* **lubricated, lubricating.**

luck—1. Something good or bad that happens by chance: *She said it was* luck *that she met her friend in the crowd.* **2.** Good fortune: *He hopes he has* luck *finding a job.*
luck (luk) *noun.*

luckily—By good fortune; by chance: *Luckily, the dish did not break when I dropped it.*
luck|i|ly (luk′ə lē) *adverb.*

lucky—**1.** Having good things happen to one; fortunate: *We were lucky to catch the last train home.* **2.** Causing good things to happen: *a* lucky *charm; my* lucky *day.*
luck|y (luk′ē) *adjective,* **luckier, luckiest.**

lug—To carry or pull with great effort: *He* lugged *six books home from the library.*
lug (lug) *verb,* **lugged, lugging.**

luggage—The suitcases and bags taken on a trip by someone; baggage: *Can you fit all the* luggage *into the car?*
lug|gage (lug′ij) *noun.*

lukewarm—Between hot and cold; mildly warm: *The campfire went out, so we ate* lukewarm *stew.*
luke|warm (lūk′wawrm′) *adjective.*

lull—To make quiet and relaxed: *Mother sang softly to* lull *the baby. Verb.*
—A brief pause in noise or activity: *There was a* lull *in the conversation. Noun.*
lull (lul) *verb,* **lulled, lulling;** *noun, plural* **lulls.**
• Synonyms: **calm, soothe,** for *verb.*
  Antonyms: For *verb,* see Synonyms at **annoy.**

lullaby—A soft song that is sung to help a baby go to sleep.
lul|la|by (lul′ə bī) *noun, plural* **lullabies.**

lumber—Wood that has been cut into boards: *Have we enough* lumber *to build a dog house?*
lum|ber (lum′bər) *noun.*

lumberjack—A person whose job is cutting down trees for lumber.
lum|ber|jack (lum′bər jak′) *noun, plural* **lumberjacks.**

lumberyard—A place where cut wood is stored and sold.
lum|ber|yard (lum′bər yahrd′) *noun, plural* **lumberyards.**

luminous—Giving off light; shining: *Luminous stars twinkled in the night.*
lu|mi|nous (lū′mə nəs) *adjective.*
• Synonyms: **bright, brilliant, radiant**
  Antonyms: **dark, dim, dull**

lump—**1.** A solid piece of something, having no special shape: *The mashed potatoes are full of* lumps. **2.** A bump or swelling: *A book fell on my foot and left a big* lump. *Noun.*
—**1.** To form a shapeless piece of something: *Stir the gravy or it will* lump. **2.** To bring or put together in a pile or group: *Books, games, and papers were all* lumped *on the shelf. Verb.*
lump (lump) *noun, plural* **lumps;** *verb,* **lumped, lumping.**

lunar—Of, on, or like the moon: *The spacecraft made a* lunar *landing so the astronauts could study the moon's surface.*
lu|nar (lū′nər) *adjective.*

lunatic—A person who is or acts crazy: *Only a* lunatic *would leave the warm house to go out in this storm.*
lu|na|tic (lū′nə tik) *noun, plural* **lunatics.**

lunch—A meal eaten in the middle of the day. *Noun.*
—To eat such a meal: *We* lunched *in the cafeteria. Verb.*
lunch (lunch) *noun, plural* **lunches;** *verb,* **lunched, lunching.**

luncheon—A midday meal, usually eaten with other people: *The school served a* luncheon *to visiting parents.*
lunch|eon (lun′chən) *noun, plural* **luncheons.**

lung—One of the pair of organs for breathing found in the chest of humans and other air-breathing animals. The lungs take in oxygen from the air and remove carbon dioxide from the blood.
lung (lung) *noun, plural* **lungs.**
■ **at the top of** (one's) **lungs:** In one's loudest voice: *He shouted* at the top of *his* lungs *so I could hear him across the large room.*
• See picture at **respiratory system.**

lunge—A sudden forward movement: *She made a* lunge *for the door when the bell rang. Noun.*
—To move suddenly forward: *The frightened horse* lunged, *throwing the rider off. Verb.*
lunge (lunj) *noun, plural* **lunges;** *verb,* **lunged, lunging.**

lure—**1.** Anything that attracts or tempts: *Hot cocoa was the* lure *that brought us indoors from playing in the snow.* **2.** An artificial bait used in fishing: *The trout snapped at the* lure. *Noun.*
—To attract; tempt: *We put up a feeder to* lure *birds to our yard. Verb.*
lure (loor) *noun, plural* **lures;** *verb,* **lured, luring.**

lurk—To wait or move about secretly, keeping out of sight; hide: *The cat* lurked *in the bushes waiting to pounce on the mouse.*
lurk (lurk) *verb,* **lurked, lurking.**

a at	i if	oo look	ch chalk		a in ago
ā ape	ī idle	ou out	ng sing		e in happen
ah calm	o odd	u ugly	sh ship	ə =	i in capital
aw all	ō oats	ū rule	th think		o in occur
e end	oi oil	ur turn	th their		u in upon
ē easy			zh treasure		

luscious—Very good to taste; delicious: *A* luscious *cake was served for dessert.*
lus│cious (lush′əs) *adjective.*

luster—A bright shine on the surface of something: *The new car has a beautiful* luster.
lus│ter (lus′tər) *noun, plural* **lusters.**

lute—A stringed musical instrument with a long neck and a pear-shaped body.
lute (lūt) *noun, plural* **lutes.**
● A word that sounds the same is **loot.**

Lutheran—A member of the world's largest Protestant church, founded in Germany in the 1500's. *Noun.*
—Having to do with this church. *Adjective.*
Lu│ther│an (lū′thər ən *or* lūth′rən) *noun, plural* **Lutherans;** *adjective.*

luxurious—1. Fond of fine things: *a* luxurious *taste for food.* 2. Very beautiful and comfortable: *A soft,* luxurious *carpet covered the floor.*
lux│u│ri│ous (lug zhoor′ē əs *or* luk shoor′ē əs) *adjective.*

luxury—1. Something that provides great comfort and enjoyment but is not really needed: *The movie star bought jewels, fur coats, and other* luxuries. 2. The use of things that provide great comfort and enjoyment but are not really needed: *Kings and queens are used to* luxury.
lux│u│ry (lug′zhər ē *or* luk′shər ē) *noun, plural* **luxuries.**

-ly[1]—A suffix that means "in a certain manner or way." To walk quietly is to walk in a quiet manner.

-ly[2]—A suffix that means "Like a" or "happening during a certain period of time." To act in a friendly way is to act like a friend. A weekly magazine is published once a week.

Word Power

You can understand the meanings of many words that end in **-ly,** if you add a meaning of one of the suffixes to the meaning of the rest of the word.
   cheerfully: in a cheerful way
   brotherly: like a brother
   monthly: happening once a month

lye—A strong solution made by soaking wood ashes in water. It is used in making soap and other cleaning substances.
lye (lī) *noun.*
● A word that sounds the same is **lie.**

lying—*See* **lie[1]** and **lie[2].**
ly│ing (lī′ing) *verb.*

lynch—To kill an accused person without a legal trial, usually by hanging: *The angry mob* lynched *the man they thought was the thief.*
lynch (linch) *verb,* **lynched, lynching.**

lynx—A wild cat with a spotted coat, long legs, a short tail, and bunches of fur on its ears.
lynx (lingks) *noun, plural* **lynxes.**

lynx

lyre—A stringed musical instrument something like a small harp. It was used in ancient times to accompany singing and reciting.
lyre (līr) *noun, plural* **lyres.**

lyre

lyric—1. A short poem expressing one's feelings. 2. **lyrics:** The words for a song: *I wrote the music for a school song, and she wrote the* lyrics. *Noun.*
—Having to do with poetry that expresses one's feelings. *Adjective.*
lyr│ic (lēr′ik) *noun, plural* **lyrics;** *adjective.*

lyrical—Like a short poem or song.
lyr│i│cal (lēr′ə kəl) *adjective.*

About 1,900 years ago, the Romans gave the capital **M** its present form. The small letter **m** was first used about 1,700 years ago. It reached its present form about 500 years ago.

About 5,000 years ago, the ancient Egyptians used a symbol that represented waves of water.

About 3,500 years ago, people in the Middle East made a simpler symbol. They called it *mem*, their word for "water."

About 3,000 years ago, other people in the Middle East used this form.

About 2,600 years ago, the Greeks gave the letter this form. They called it *mu*.

M or **m**—1. The thirteenth letter of the alphabet: *There are two* m's *in the word "moment."*
2. The Roman numeral for 1,000.
M, m (em) *noun, plural* **M's** or **Ms, m's** or **ms.**

m—The abbreviation for **meter.**

ma'am—Madam: *"Excuse me, ma'am," said the polite boy.*
ma|am (mam) *noun, plural* **ma'ams.**

macaroni—A food made from a paste of flour and water, formed into short, hollow tubes and dried.
mac|a|ro|ni (mak′ə rō′nē) *noun.*

machine—1. A mechanical device in which each part works together with the other parts to perform some function: *a washing* machine; *a sewing* machine; *vending* machines. **2.** A simple device that can do work by passing along or changing the direction of some force: *A lever, a pulley, and a wheel and axle are simple* machines.
ma|chine (mə shēn′) *noun, plural* **machines.**

machinery—1. A group of mechanical devices; machines: *The factory was full of* machinery.
2. A group of people or things that keeps something going or gets something done: *Teachers, students, and schools are parts of the* machinery *of education.*
ma|chin|er|y (mə shē′nər ē) *noun.*

machinist—A person who has special training and ability to use machine-operated tools, especially those that cut, grind, or shape materials.
ma|chin|ist (mə shē′nist) *noun, plural* **machinists.**

mackerel—A saltwater fish that is silver and has dark, wavy bands on its back. It is used for food.
mack|er|el (mak′ər əl) *noun, plural* **mackerel** or **mackerels.**

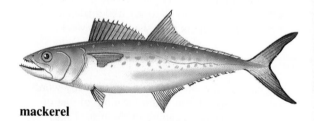

mackerel

macron—A short horizontal line placed over a vowel to show that it has a long sound. For examples see the Pronunciation Key.
ma|cron (mā′kron) *noun, plural* **macrons.**

mad—1. Very angry; furious: *My brother is* mad *at me for losing his basketball.* **2.** Crazy: *Only a* mad *person would jump out of an airplane without a parachute.* **3.** Wildly excited; frantic: *When the last bell rang, there was a* mad *rush*

a at	i if	oo look	ch chalk		a in ago
ā ape	ī idle	ou out	ng sing		e in happen
ah calm	o odd	u ugly	sh ship	ə =	i in capital
aw all	ō oats	ū rule	th think		o in occur
e end	oi oil	ur turn	<u>th</u> their		u in upon
ē easy			zh treasure		

for the door. **4.** Very unwise; reckless: *She had a* mad *desire to dye her hair blue.* **5.** Carried away by enthusiasm: *She is so* mad *about baseball that she thinks of nothing else.* **6.** Having rabies: *A* mad *animal will often bite.*
mad (mad) *adjective,* **madder, maddest.**
■ **like mad:** Very fast or enthusiastically: *They cheered* like mad *for their hero.*

madam—A polite way to address a woman: *May I help you,* madam?
mad|am (mad′əm) *noun, plural* **madams.**

madame—The French word for **Mrs.**
ma|dame (mə dam′) *noun, plural* **mesdames** (mā dam′). Abbreviation: **Mme.**

made—*See* **make.**
made (mād) *verb.*
● A word that sounds the same is **maid.**

made-up—Not true; invented: *A novel is a* made-up *story.*
made-up (mād′up′) *adjective.*

magazine—**1.** A publication containing articles, stories, and pictures written or produced by different people. Most magazines are printed weekly or monthly: *We subscribe to a sports* magazine. **2.** The part of a rifle or gun that holds the cartridges.
mag|a|zine (mag′ə zēn′ *or* mag′ə zēn) *noun, plural* **magazines.**

Word History

Magazine comes from an old French word meaning "storehouse." The magazines that people read store information in the form of articles and stories. Magazines in pistols and rifles store ammunition. And a room or building where guns and explosives are stored is called a magazine.

maggot—A fly just hatched from its egg, that looks like a worm. It has a soft, fat body and no legs.
mag|got (mag′ət) *noun, plural* **maggots.**

magic—**1.** A make-believe ability to do impossible things by using charms and spells: *The wizard said his* magic *could turn any metal into gold.* **2.** The skill of performing tricks that fool the eye: *The magician used her* magic *to pull a rabbit from a hat. Noun.*
—Having to do with charms or the use of special tricks: *a* magic *spell; a* magic *trick. Adjective.*
mag|ic (maj′ik) *noun, adjective.*
■ **like magic:** Very fast: *The hamburgers we ordered appeared* like magic.

magical—Caused or working by magic or as if by magic: *The fairy tale told of a* magical *flying boat.*
mag|i|cal (maj′ə kəl) *adjective.*

magician—**1.** A person who is skilled in magic: *The magician in the fairy tale made the girl's wishes come true.* **2.** A person who entertains people with magic tricks: *The magician made flowers appear from nowhere.*
ma|gi|cian (mə jish′ən) *noun, plural* **magicians.**

magnesium—A light, silvery metal. It burns with a brilliant white light and so is often used in fireworks and signal flares. It is a chemical element.
mag|ne|si|um (mag nē′zē əm *or* mag nē′zhəm) *noun.*
● See Word History at **magnet.**

magnet—A piece of stone, iron, or steel that attracts bits of iron and steel: *The sewing pins stick to my* magnet.
mag|net (mag′nit) *noun, plural* **magnets.**

Word History

Magnet comes from the name of a part of Greece, Magnesia. Some stones from this region act as natural magnets. The ancient Greeks discovered that these stones would attract iron. You might guess that **magnesium** also comes from Magnesia, and that is true—but no one is sure how it got its name.

magnetic—Having the ability to attract bits of iron and steel: *The pins are held to the metal by* magnetic *force.*
mag|net|ic (mag net′ik) *adjective.*

magnetic pole—**1.** One of the two points on a magnet that has a strong force. **2.** One of the two polar areas of the earth where the earth's magnetic force is strongest. The magnetic poles are near the North and South poles. A compass needle points toward one of the magnetic poles.
mag|net|ic pole (mag net′ik pōl) *noun, plural* **magnetic poles.**
● See picture at **North Pole.**

magnetism—The ability to attract iron and steel. Magnets and electric currents have this ability.
mag|net|ism (mag′nə tiz′əm) *noun.*

magnificent—Very fine and beautiful; splendid: *The museum contains many* magnificent *paintings.*
mag|nif|i|cent (mag nif′ə sənt) *adjective.*
● Synonyms: **grand, majestic, stately**
  Antonym: **humble**

magnify—**1.** To make something look bigger than its true size: *Scientists use microscopes to* magnify *very tiny things so they can be easily seen.* **2.** To make too much of something; exaggerate: *She* magnified *her importance until it sounded as if she had won the baseball game alone.* **mag|ni|fy** (**mag′**nə fī′) *verb,* **magnified, magnifying.**

magnifying glass—A combination of lenses or one lens alone that makes things look larger than their true size: *He examined the fly with a* magnifying glass. **mag|ni|fy|ing glass** (**mag′**nə fī′ing glas) *noun, plural* **magnifying glasses.**

magnitude—**1.** Great size: *The* magnitude *of the ocean makes it a thrilling sight.* **2.** Meaning, value, or importance: *The Constitution of the United States is a document of great* magnitude. **mag|ni|tude** (**mag′**nə tūd′ *or* **mag′**nə tyūd′) *noun.*

magnolia—An evergreen tree with long, shiny, oval leaves and large flowers that are white, pink, yellow, or purple. The magnolia is the state flower of both Louisiana and Mississippi. **mag|no|lia** (mag nōl′yə) *noun, plural* **magnolias.**

magpie—A black and white bird that has a thick bill, short wings, and a long tail. Magpies are very noisy and mischievous birds. **mag|pie** (**mag′**pī) *noun, plural* **magpies.**

magpie

mahogany—**1.** A large, tropical evergreen tree that has hard, reddish-brown wood. This wood is often used to make furniture. **2.** A dark reddish-brown color. *Noun.*
—Having a dark reddish-brown color: mahogany *eyes. Adjective.*
ma|hog|a|ny (mə **hog′**ə nē *or* mə **hawg′**ə nē) *noun, plural* **mahoganies;** *adjective.*

maid—**1.** A girl or young, unmarried woman; maiden: *All the* maids *and young men danced in the moonlight.* **2.** A female servant: *Our* maid *helps mom clean the house twice a month.* **maid** (mād) *noun, plural* **maids.**
• A word that sounds the same is **made.**

maiden—A girl or young, unmarried woman; maid: *The princess in the fairy tale is a* maiden *of twelve. Noun.*
—First: *a brand-new spaceship's* maiden *voyage. Adjective.*
maid|en (**mād′**ən) *noun, plural* **maidens;** *adjective.*

maiden name—A woman's last name before she marries. Some women choose to keep their maiden names after marriage also. **maid|en name** (**mād′**ən nām) *noun, plural* **maiden names.**

maid of honor—The main, unmarried female attendant of a bride at her wedding. **maid of hon|or** (mād əv **on′**ər) *noun, plural* **maids of honor.**

mail—**1.** Letters, cards, papers, and packages received and sent through the post office: *I received your letter in today's* mail. **2.** The system, usually run by the government, through which letters, packages, and other materials are delivered: *The* mail *took three days to deliver our card. Noun.*
—To send through such a delivery system: *Will you* mail *this letter for me? Verb.*
mail (māl) *noun, plural* **mails;** *verb,* **mailed, mailing.**
• A word that sounds the same is **male.**

mailbox—**1.** A public box from which everybody's mail is picked up and delivered by the post office: *I put the letter in the* mailbox *at the corner of Elm and Main.* **2.** A person's own box to which his or her mail is delivered: *My mother put a note in our neighbor's* mailbox. **mail|box** (**māl′**boks′) *noun, plural* **mailboxes.**

mail carrier—A person whose job is to carry and deliver letters, packages, and other materials from the post office to homes and businesses. **mail car|ri|er** (māl **kar′**ē ər) *noun, plural* **mail carriers.**

mailman—A man who carries or delivers mail; a mail carrier.
mail|man (māl′man′) *noun, plural* **mailmen**.
● See Language Fact at **fire fighter**.

main—Most important; biggest: *The bank is on the town's* main *street. Our group's* main *purpose is to study nature. Adjective.*
—A large pipe, cable, or channel that carries electricity, water, gas, and the like. *Noun.*
main (mān) *adjective; noun, plural* **mains**.
■ **in the main**: Mostly: *Our town is a good place to live,* in the main.
● A word that sounds the same is **mane**.
● Synonyms: **central, chief, major, principal,** for *adjective.*
Antonym: **minor,** for *adjective.*

Maine Coon—A large, long-haired breed of house cat that has wide paws, a striped coat that lies close to its body, and a tail that looks like that of a raccoon. Maine Coons were originally bred in New England in the United States.
Maine Coon (mān kūn) *noun, plural* **Maine Coons**.

Maine Coon

mainland—A country's or a continent's major area of land: *The island's food and supplies come by boat from the* mainland.
main|land (mān′land′ *or* mān′lənd) *noun, plural* **mainlands**.

mainly—Mostly; chiefly: *Their diet consists* mainly *of vegetables.*
main|ly (mān′lē) *adverb.*

mainsail—The largest or chief sail on a ship. It is found on the tallest mast.
main|sail (mān′sāl′) *noun, plural* **mainsails**.

maintain—1. To keep or continue: *He and I have* maintained *our friendship for many years.*
2. To provide for; take care of: *Our neighbors* maintain *a family of four. She* maintains *her bicycle in perfect condition.*   3. To state something firmly and definitely: *I thought I saw him at the mall, but he* maintains *that he was not there.*
main|tain (mān tān′) *verb,* **maintained, maintaining**.
● Synonyms: **conserve, preserve,** for **1**.
Antonyms: **alter, change, modify, vary,** for **1**.

maintenance—1. The act of taking care of something: *daily* maintenance *of good health; an airplane that needs constant* maintenance.   2. The means of providing what is necessary for life, such as food and clothing: *Our parents provide our* maintenance, *but we must work if we want extras.*
main|te|nance (mān′tə nəns) *noun.*

majestic—Very grand; stately; dignified: *The parade was led by a* majestic *elephant.*
ma|jes|tic (mə jes′tik) *adjective.*
● Synonyms: **magnificent, splendid**
Antonym: **humble**

majesty—1. Greatness and dignity: *On the lawn stood an oak tree of great size and* majesty.
2. Majesty: A title used in talking to or about a king, queen, or other noble ruler: *"Welcome, Your* Majesty," *said the peasant to the king.*
maj|es|ty (maj′ə stē) *noun, plural* **majesties**.

major—Larger or more important: *Saving money for new roller skates was her* major *reason for taking the job delivering newspapers. Adjective.*
—An army, air force, or marine officer ranking below a lieutenant colonel and above a captain. *Noun.*
ma|jor (mā′jər) *adjective; noun, plural* **majors**.
Abbreviation: Maj. for *noun.*
● Synonyms: **central, chief, main, principal,** for *·adjective.*
Antonym: **minor,** for *adjective.*

majority—1. The larger part or number; more than half of a group: *The* majority *of the audience liked the movie.*   2. The number representing the difference between a larger number and a smaller one: *Because my sister had fifteen votes and I had twelve, my sister won by a* majority *of three votes.*
ma|jor|i|ty (mə jawr′ə tē) *noun, plural* **majorities**.

make—1. To cause to be or happen: *She will* make *a picture with crayons.*   2. To get or earn: *He* makes *fifty cents for walking his neighbor's dog.*   3. To add up to; equal: *Two fours* make *eight.*   4. To go to; arrive at: *She had to run to* make *her meeting on time.*   5. To succeed in getting a position on: *He* made *the hockey team. Verb.*

—The type or brand of something: *That* make *of car is very popular this year. Noun.*
make (māk) *verb,* **made, making;** *noun, plural* **makes.**

■ **make believe:** To pretend: *My friend and I like to* make believe *that we're airplane pilots.*
make do: To get along or manage with something that is less than adequate: *The art teacher had to* make do *with only three colors of paper.*
make up: 1. To invent something in the mind: *The children like to* make up *interesting stories.* **2.** To settle an argument and be friends again: *Their disagreement was silly, so they decided to* make up. **3.** To apply cosmetics to the face: *My mother* makes up *before going out to dinner with my father.*

make-believe—An act of pretending: *Many television shows are only* make-believe. *Noun.*
—Not real; pretended: *The pile of rocks was their* make-believe *fort. Adjective.*
make-be|lieve (māk′bi lēv′) *noun, adjective.*

makeup or **make-up**—**1.** The way in which something is put together: *That table holds a lot because of its strong* makeup. **2.** A person's nature or disposition: *It is not in his honest* makeup *to tell a lie.* **3.** Cosmetics that are applied to the face to change its appearance. Makeup *includes rouge, cream, lipstick, and the like.*
make|up or make-up (māk′up′) *noun, plural* **makeups** or **make-ups.**

mal-—A prefix meaning "bad." Malnutrition is bad nutrition.

Word Power

You can understand the meanings of many words that begin with **mal-,** if you add the meaning of the prefix to the meaning of the rest of the word.
maladjustment: a bad adjustment
malodorous: having a bad smell

---

malamute—*See* **Alaskan malamute.**
ma|la|mute (mah′lə myūt′) *noun, plural* **malamutes.**

malaria—A disease carried by certain kinds of

mosquitoes that causes fever, chills, and sweating in humans bitten by such a mosquito.
ma|lar|i|a (mə lãr′ē ə) *noun.*

male—A man, boy, or animal having the sex that men and boys have: *My brother and father are* males. *The* male *deer is called a buck. Noun.*
—**1.** Of or relating to men or boys: Male *students don't wear dresses.* **2.** Of or relating to the sex that men and boys have: *The* male *chicken is a rooster. Adjective.*
male (māl) *noun, plural* **males;** *adjective.*
● A word that sounds the same is **mail.**

mall—**1.** A shady public walk. **2.** A shopping center or group of connected shops.
mall (mawl) *noun, plural* **malls.**
● A word that sounds the same is **maul.**

mallard—A common type of wild North American duck. The male has a rust-colored chest, gray back, green head, and white ring around the neck.
mal|lard (mal′ərd) *noun, plural* **mallards** or **mallard.**

mallard

mallet—A short-handled hammer with a wooden or rubber head, used as a tool. Longer-handled mallets are used to hit balls in the games of croquet and polo.
mal|let (mal′it) *noun, plural* **mallets.**
● See pictures at **croquet** and **polo.**

malnutrition—The condition of being poorly nourished that can be brought on by lack of food or by eating the wrong foods.
mal|nu|tri|tion (mal′nū trish′ən *or* mal′nyū trish′ən) *noun.*

malt—A grain, such as barley, that is soaked in water until it sprouts and then is dried. Malt is used in brewing beer and ale, and as a flavoring.
malt (mawlt) *noun.*

a at	i if	oo look	ch chalk		a in ago
ā ape	ī idle	ou out	ng sing		e in happen
ah calm	o odd	u ugly	sh ship	ə =	i in capital
aw all	ō oats	ū rule	th think		o in occur
e end	oi oil	ur turn	<u>th</u> their		u in upon
ē easy			zh treasure		

Maltese—A very small dog with long, silky, white hair that touches the ground. These dogs were first bred long ago in Malta. They are popular as pets.
Mal|tese (mol tēz′ *or* mol tēs′) *noun, plural* **Maltese.**

Maltese

mama or **mamma**—Mother: *Little children often call their mothers* Mama
ma|ma or mam|ma (mah′mə) *noun, plural* **mamas** or **mammas.**

mammal—A warm-blooded animal that has a backbone, usually has fur or hair, and can feed its offspring with milk from the mother's breast. Mammals include human beings, dogs, cats, apes, and whales.
mam|mal (mam′əl) *noun, plural* **mammals.**

mammoth—A very large type of elephant with long tusks and shaggy, brown hair, that lived more than 10,000 years ago. Mammoths no longer exist. *Noun.*
—Extremely large; huge: *The campers brought a* mammoth *tent so they could all sleep under it. Adjective.*
mam|moth (mam′əth) *noun, plural* **mammoths;** *adjective.*

man—1. An adult male human being: *My brother is a* man *now with a job and a home of his own.* 2. One person; a human being: *Unlike other animals, a* man *can talk.* 3. All people; all human beings: *Many books describe the scientific accomplishments of* man. 4. A movable piece used in playing checkers, chess, or other board games. *Noun.*
—To provide with people to do a certain job: *The fifth-grade class* manned *the refreshment booth at the school fair. Verb.*
man (man) *noun, plural* **men;** *verb,* **manned, manning.**

manage—1. To guide or control: *The professional trainer* managed *the boy's dog with ease.* 2. To be able to do something: *He* managed *to mow the whole yard by dinner time.*
man|age (man′ij) *verb,* **managed, managing.**

manager—Someone who guides or controls something: *The* manager *of the store makes sure everthing runs smoothly.*
man|ag|er (man′i jər) *noun, plural* **managers.** Abbreviation: mgr.

Manchester terrier—A small hunting dog having a short, glossy, black coat with tan markings throughout its fur. These dogs were originally bred in Manchester, England, to hunt rats.
Man|ches|ter ter|ri|er (man′chə stər ter′ē ər) *noun, plural* **Manchester terriers.**

Manchester terrier

mammoth (noun)

mandolin—A pear-shaped musical instrument with metal strings that is played like a guitar. man|do|lin (man′də lin′ *or* man′de lin′) *noun, plural* **mandolins.**

mane—The long, thick hair on the heads or along the necks of such animals as horses and lions. mane (mān) *noun, plural* **manes.**
* A word that sounds the same is **main.**
* See picture at **lion.**

maneuver—1. An organized military movement involving troops or ships: *The army's* maneuver *was designed to capture the town.* 2. A clever plan: *Through various* maneuvers, *like promising him bedtime stories, Mother finally got my little brother to go to bed.* ma|neu|ver (mə nū′vər) *noun, plural* **maneuvers.**

manger—A box or trough from which horses or cattle eat. man|ger (mān′jər) *noun, plural* **mangers.**

mangle—1. To tear or cut skin unevenly: *Our dog came back from the fight with its ear* mangled. 2. Ruin; wreck: *The car rolled over the bike and* mangled *its frame.* man|gle (mang′gəl) *verb,* **mangled, mangling.**

mango—An oval, yellow-orange fruit that tastes sweet and spicy. Mangoes grow on evergreen trees in warm climates. man|go (mang′gō) *noun, plural* **mangoes** *or* **mangos.**

manhole—A hole, usually in the street, which has a removable cover. Workers can get through it to water pipes, sewer lines, or wires to inspect or repair them. man|hole (man′hōl′) *noun, plural* **manholes.**

manicure—A cleaning and trimming of the fingernails, sometimes including a polishing. *Noun.*
—To perform such a cleaning and trimming: *The woman who* manicured *my nails did a very good job.* man|i|cure (man′ə kyoor) *noun, plural* **manicures;** *verb,* **manicured, manicuring.**

mankind—All human beings: *This new medicine will help* mankind. man|kind (man′kīnd′) *noun.*

man-made—Made by human beings; not natural: *Glass and steel are* man-made, *but trees and rocks are not.* man-made (man′mād′) *adjective.*

manner—1. A way or style of doing something: *The girl excused herself from the room in a polite* manner. 2. A way or style of acting: *Despite his gruff* manner, *the policeman was very helpful.* 3. **manners:** A way of doing things: *His bad* manners *keep him from gaining friends.* man|ner (man′ər) *noun, plural* **manners.**
■ **to the manner born:** Naturally suited or used to something: *Although he had never been on a stage, he took to acting as if* to the manner born.
* A word that sounds the same is **manor.**
* Synonyms: **behavior, conduct,** for **3.**

manor—1. A large estate owned by a lord in the Middle Ages. Peasants lived on part of this land in return for goods, services, or rent. 2. A large home; mansion. man|or (man′ər) *noun, plural* **manors.**
* A word that sounds the same is **manner.**

mansion—A large and stately home: *The* mansion *had twenty-three rooms and a huge lawn.* man|sion (man′shən) *noun, plural* **mansions.**

manslaughter—The accidental, unlawful killing of one person by another. man|slaugh|ter (man′slaw′tər) *noun, plural* **manslaughters.**

mantel—The shelf that sticks out from the frame above a fireplace. man|tel (man′təl) *noun, plural* **mantels.**

mantis—A large insect that sometimes holds its front legs up in a position like a person praying, which is why it is also called a **praying mantis.** man|tis (man′tis) *noun, plural* **mantises.**

manual—Done by the hands: *Picking apples is* manual *work. Adjective.*
—A handbook that provides information or instructions: *She followed the directions in the* manual *to learn how to build a model plane. Noun.* man|u|al (man′yoo əl) *adjective; noun, plural* **manuals.**

manufacture—1. To make into a finished product by hand or machine: *That company* manufactures *furniture.* 2. To make up: *She began to* manufacture *excuses for her frequent lateness. Verb.*
—The making of products by hand or machine, especially in large numbers: *Cloth is important to the* manufacture *of furniture. Noun.*

a at	i if	oo look	ch chalk	⎡ a in ago
ā ape	ī idle	ou out	ng sing	e in happen
ah calm	o odd	u ugly	sh ship	ə = i in capital
aw all	ō oats	ū rule	th think	o in occur
e end	oi oil	ur turn	th their	⎣ u in upon
ē easy			zh treasure	

man|u|fac|ture (man′yə **fak**′chər) *verb,* **manufactured, manufacturing;** *noun.*

manuscript—A page or pages written on a typewriter or by hand.
man|u|script (**man**′yə skript′) *noun, plural* **manuscripts.**

Manx—A small, short-haired breed of house cat that has thick, soft fur, back legs that are longer than its front legs, an arched back, and usually no tail. These cats were first bred on the Isle of Man, near England.
Manx (mangks) *noun, plural* **Manx.**

Manx

many—A great number of; a lot of: *There are* many *kinds of fishes in the ocean. Adjective.*
—A large number; a lot: Many *of the students were absent because of illness. Noun.*

—A great number of people or things: Many *went to the concert. Pronoun.*
man|y (**men**′ē) *adjective,* **more, most;** *noun; pronoun.*

map—A drawing of all or part of the earth's surface, including countries, cities, mountains, oceans, rivers, and so forth: *We found the United States on the* map. *Noun.*
—**1.** To make such a drawing of something: *The Boy Scouts* mapped *the nature trails as a project.* **2.** To plan in detail: *She* mapped *out a schedule of the things she is going to do this week. Verb.*
map (map) *noun, plural* **maps;** *verb,* **mapped, mapping.**

Word History

Map comes from a Latin word meaning ''napkin'' or ''cloth.'' Long ago, maps were drawn on cloth.

---

maple—A shade tree with pairs of seeds that look like two wings and leaves with deep notches. Maple wood is used in making furniture and flooring. Maple sap is made into maple syrup or maple sugar.
ma|ple (**mā**′pəl) *noun, plural* **maples.**

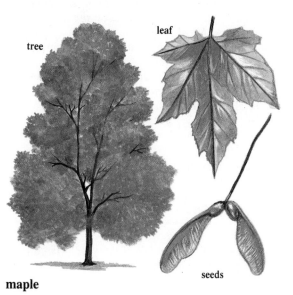

tree leaf seeds

maple

mar—To damage or ruin: *His leather boots* marred *the shiny surface of the floor.*
mar (mahr) *verb,* **marred, marring.**

Mar.—The abbreviation for **March.**

mantis

marathon—**1.** A long-distance race in which runners travel 26 miles and 385 yards (42.2 kilometers).   **2.** Any test of endurance: *They won the dance* marathon *by dancing the longest.*
mar|a|thon (**mar'**ə thon') *noun, plural* **marathons.**

Word History

Marathon is named after a plain in ancient Greece called Marathon. In 490 B.C., a messenger ran a long distance from this plain to let the Greeks know that they had won a great victory at Marathon.

---

marble—**1.** A hard, smooth stone that is either white or streaked with colors and can be highly polished. It is used in buildings and for statues.   **2.** A small glass ball that is used in certain games.
mar|ble (**mahr'**bəl) *noun, plural* **marbles.**

march—**1.** To walk like soldiers, with measured steps and at a steady rate: *The town's police* marched *in the parade.*   **2.** To move steadily: *The water from the flood* marched *through the town. Verb.*
—**1.** The act of walking like soldiers: *The Scouts started their long* march *at dawn.*   **2.** Music with a strong beat to which people can walk in measured steps at the same, steady rate: *That* march *is often played at parades and public gatherings. Noun.*
march (mahrch) *verb,* **marched, marching;** *noun, plural* **marches.**
■ **steal a march:** To gain an advantage secretly: *Some contestants started the puzzle early to* steal a march *on their competitors.*

Word History

March comes from a Latin word meaning "of Mars." Mars was the Roman god of war. The ancient Romans named this month after him. The planet **Mars** is also named after him.

March—The third month of the year. March has 31 days. Abbreviation: **Mar.**
March (mahrch) *noun.*

a at	i if	oo look	ch chalk		a in ago
ā ape	ī idle	ou out	ng sing		e in happen
ah calm	o odd	u ugly	sh ship	ə =	i in capital
aw all	ō oats	ū rule	th think		o in occur
e end	oi oil	ur turn	<u>th</u> their		u in upon
ē easy			zh treasure		

Mardi Gras—A celebration held on the day before the Christian season of Lent begins. The city of New Orleans, Louisiana, is especially known for the parades and other festivities held there on this day.
Mar|di Gras (**mahr'**dē grah) *noun.*

mare—A female horse, zebra, or other similar animal.
mare (mār) *noun, plural* **mares.**

margarine—A food that looks and tastes similar to butter and is used as a substitute for butter. It is made from vegetable or animal oils.
mar|ga|rine (**mahr'**jə rin) *noun, plural* **margarines.**

margin—**1.** A rim; edge: *the* margin *of the woods.*   **2.** The space at the top, bottom, and sides of a page, where there is no writing or printing.   **3.** An amount that is slightly more than what is needed: *The candidate won by a small* margin *of 300 votes.*
mar|gin (**mahr'**jən) *noun, plural* **margins.**

marigold—A garden plant that produces round red, orange, or yellow flowers and that has slender, spiked leaves.
mar|i|gold (**mar'**ə gōld') *noun, plural* **marigolds.**

marigold

marijuana or **marihuana**—The dried leaves and flowers of a plant that are smoked in a pipe or cigarette as a drug.
mar|i|jua|na or **mar|i|hua|na** (mar'ə **wah'**nə) *noun.*

marine—1. Having to do with or living in the sea: marine *currents;* marine *fish.* 2. Having to do with ships or sailors: *The* marine *weather report warned small boats not to go out during the storm. Adjective.*
—**Marine:** A person who is in the Marine Corps. *Noun.*
ma|rine (mə rēn′) *adjective; noun, plural* **Marines.**

Marine Corps—A branch of the armed forces of the United States that is specially trained for amphibious assaults.
Ma|rine Corps (mə rēn′ cawr) *noun.*

marionette—A wooden puppet that has wires or strings attached to its arms, legs, and head so that the person holding it can make it move.
mar|i|o|nette (mar′ē ə net′) *noun, plural* **marionettes.**

mark¹—1. A spot, scratch, line, or the like, that one thing makes on another thing: *There was a* mark *on his arm where the bee had stung him.* 2. A line, object, or sign that shows the position of something: *The water rose above yesterday's* mark *on the measuring stick.* 3. A sign of something; means of identification: *A robin on the lawn is a sure* mark *of spring.* 4. A letter or number that is used to rate someone's work or performance: *Report cards contain* marks *in several subjects.* 5. A target; thing that is aimed at: *The arrow missed its* mark. *Noun.*
—1. To write, scratch, or leave a spot or line on something: *Our car is* marked *with dents and scratches.* 2. To show plainly: *The tears on her face* marked *her sadness.* 3. To be a sign of something: *Fall is* marked *by cool weather and leaves turning bright colors.* 4. To give grades or ratings to: *The judges* marked *the entries in the contest.*
mark (mahrk) *noun, plural* **marks;** *verb,* **marked, marking.**
■ **make (one's) mark:** To win success and fame: *The astronaut made his* mark *as the first human to walk on the moon.*
toe the mark: To behave in a way that is expected and considered proper: *She did not like to study, but she decided to* toe the mark *after her parents complained about her work.*

mark²—A unit of money in Germany.
mark (mahrk) *noun, plural* **marks.**
Abbreviation: m.

market—1. A store or open area in which food or goods are offered for sale: *We bought fruits and vegetables at the corner* market. 2. The willingness of people to buy something; demand: *During the winter, there is a big* market *for boots and mittens. Noun.*
—1. To sell or take to a place that sells food or goods: *After the harvest, we will* market *the apples.* 2. To buy products in such a place: *Before food was kept in refrigerators, people had to* market *almost every day. Verb.*
mar|ket (mahr′kit) *noun, plural* **markets;** *verb,* **marketed, marketing.**

marmalade—A kind of jam made by boiling a fruit, especially oranges, with sugar and part of the fruit's peel.
mar|ma|lade (mahr′mə lād′) *noun, plural* **marmalades.**

maroon¹—Having a dark brownish-red color. *Adjective.*
—A dark brownish-red color. *Noun.*
ma|roon (mə rūn′) *adjective; noun, plural* **maroons.**

maroon²—To leave helpless on a deserted beach, shore, or island, without one's ship or boat: *The sailors were* marooned *when their boat crashed onto a rocky shore.*
ma|roon (mə rūn′) *verb,* **marooned, marooning.**

marriage—1. The condition of living together as husband and wife: *My aunt and uncle's* marriage *has lasted for many years.* 2. The act of becoming husband and wife; wedding: *The* marriage *took place in a church.*
mar|riage (mar′ij) *noun, plural* **marriages.**

marry—1. To perform a ceremony that joins two people as husband and wife: *A captain can* marry *people aboard his ship.* 2. To take someone as one's husband or wife: *The man will* marry *his lawyer in the spring.*
mar|ry (mar′ē) *verb,* **married, marrying.**

Mars—The fourth planet from the sun. Mars is known for its red color.
Mars (mahrz) *noun.*
● See Word History at **March.**
● See picture at **solar system.**

marsh—Land that is low and often covered by water. Reeds and grasses grow in marshes.
marsh (mahrsh) *noun, plural* **marshes.**

marshal—1. A federal law officer who does the same kind of work as a police officer or a sheriff. 2. The head of a police or fire department. 3. A public official who is in charge of public ceremonies and other special events: *The town's* marshal *organized and led the Fourth of July parade. Noun.*
—To put into the right order: *The teacher*

marshaled *the children into line according to height. Verb.*
mar|shal (mahr′shəl) *noun, plural* **marshals;** *verb,* **marshaled, marshaling.**

• A word that sounds the same is **martial.**

marshmallow—A soft, white candy made mostly of sugar and gelatin and coated with powdered sugar. It is popular for roasting over a campfire.
marsh|mal|low (mahrsh′mal′ō *or* mahrsh′mel′ō) *noun, plural* **marshmallows.**

marshy—Wet and soft like a marsh.
marsh|y (mahr′shē) *adjective,* **marshier, marshiest.**

marsupial—A mammal, such as a kangaroo or opossum, that carries its young in an outside pouch near the mother's stomach.
mar|su|pi|al (mahr sū′pē əl) *noun, plural* **marsupials.**

• See picture at **kangaroo.**

mart—A trade center; market. *Our city is a major mart for grain.*
mart (mahrt) *noun, plural* **marts.**

martial—Having to do with war: *The soldiers marched to the* martial *beat of the drums.*
mar|tial (mahr′shəl) *adjective.*

• A word that sounds the same is **marshal.**

martin—A type of bird related to swallows, found world-wide, and having a forked tail and long, pointed wings. The purple martin of North America has a bluish-black color.
mar|tin (mahr′tən) *noun, plural* **martins.**

Martin Luther King Day—A holiday observed on the third Monday in January to celebrate the birthday of this civil-rights leader and winner of the 1964 Nobel Peace Prize. His birthday actually falls on January 15.
Mar|tin Lu|ther King Day (mahr′tən lū′thər king dā) *noun.*

martyr—A person who suffers or dies for the sake of religious or other beliefs.
mar|tyr (mahr′tər) *noun, plural* **martyrs.**

marvel—Something wonderful and amazing: *The pyramids of Egypt are* marvels *of ancient building. Noun.*
—To be amazed and full of wonder: *The boy marveled at how well his sister could sing. Verb.*
mar|vel (mahr′vəl) *noun, plural* **marvels;** *verb,* **marveled, marveling.**

marvelous—1. Causing amazement and wonder: *The* marvelous *beanstalk in the fairy tale grew taller than the house overnight.* 2. Fine; excellent: *It was a* marvelous *day for a picnic.*
mar|vel|ous (mahr′və ləs) *adjective.*

• Synonyms: **delightful, heavenly, sensational, terrific,** for 2.

mascot—An animal, person, or thing that is thought to bring good luck to its friends or owners: *The basketball team has a bear as its mascot.*
mas|cot (mas′kot) *noun, plural* **mascots.**

Word History

Mascot comes from an old French word meaning "witch." Just as some witches were believed to cast spells bringing fortune and good luck, so too are mascots believed to bring luck. Schools and athletic teams often have mascots.

---

masculine—Having to do with or having qualities of men or boys: *Broad shoulders are considered a* masculine *trait.*
mas|cu|line (mas′kyə lin) *adjective.*

mash—A soft mixture, especially one of grains and water used as food for farm animals. *Noun.*
—To beat or grind something into a soft mass: *Mother* mashed *the bananas and pears for the baby. Verb.*
mash (mash) *noun, plural* **mashes;** *verb,* **mashed, mashing.**

• Synonyms: **crush, squash,** for *verb.*

mask—1. A covering worn over all or part of the face as a protection or disguise or to aid breathing: *a catcher's* mask; *an oxygen* mask; *a dog* mask *for the play.* 2. Anything that is used to cover up or hide something: *She hid her anger under a* mask *of smiles. Noun.*
—1. To put on such a facial covering: *We* masked *our faces for the party.* 2. To cover up or hide: *Dark clouds* masked *the sun. Verb.*
mask (mask) *noun, plural* **masks;** *verb,* **masked, masking.**

masking tape—A sticky tape used to protect surfaces when painting.
mask|ing tape (mask′ing tāp) *noun.*

mason—A skilled worker who builds things with bricks, stones, or the like: *A mason* helped build that brick house.
ma|son (mā′sən) *noun, plural* **masons.**

a at	i if	oo look	ch chalk		a in ago
ā ape	ī idle	ou out	ng sing		e in happen
ah calm	o odd	u ugly	sh ship	ə =	i in capital
aw all	ō oats	ū rule	th think		o in occur
e end	oi oil	ur turn	<u>th</u> their		u in upon
ē easy			zh treasure		

masquerade—To dress in a disguise: *The soldiers* masqueraded *as farmers so they could get past the enemy guards. Verb.*
—A party or dance at which people wear costumes and masks. *Noun.*
mas|quer|ade (mas′kə rād′) *verb,* **masqueraded, masquerading;** *noun, plural* **masquerades.**

mass[1]—**1.** A lump or amount of something that has no set shape or size: *a mass of garbage; a mass of ice; a mass of wet clay.* **2.** A large amount; a great number: *The letter carrier's bag held a mass of letters.* **3.** The larger part; majority: *The mass of people at the baseball game were cheering for the home team.* **4.** Large size or great weight: *The huge mass of the mountain seemed to weigh down the earth.* **5.** The amount of matter that is contained in an object. *Noun.*
—To gather or collect in a lump: *He massed all his clothes onto his bed. Verb.*
mass (mas) *noun, plural* **masses;** *verb,* **massed, massing.**
• Synonyms: **heap, mound, stack** for *noun* **2.**

Mass[2]—The main religious service in the Roman Catholic Church. Mass is also celebrated in some other faiths.
Mass (mas) *noun, plural* **Masses.**

massacre—A cruel and bloody killing of large numbers of people or animals. *Noun.*
—To kill many people or animals in a way that is cruel or unnecessary: *The army* massacred *the people in the enemy village. Verb.*
mas|sa|cre (mas′ə kər) *noun, plural* **massacres;** *verb,* **massacred, massacring.**

massage—A method of relaxing the muscles and improving blood flow by rubbing the muscles and joints of the body: *My mother gave my sore shoulders a massage. Noun.*
—To rub and knead someone's muscles and joints in a relaxing way: *He* massaged *his sore leg until the pain went away. Verb.*
mas|sage (mə sahzh′) *noun, plural* **massages;** *verb,* **massaged, massaging.**

massive—Very big and heavy; solid and great in size: *The statue was carved from a* massive *block of stone.*
mas|sive (mas′iv) *adjective.*
• Synonyms: See Synonyms at **big.**
  Antonyms: See Synonyms at **small.**

mast—A tall, straight pole of wood or metal that supports the sails and rigging on a ship or boat.
mast (mast) *noun, plural* **masts.**

master—**1.** A person in a position of power and authority; one who heads, directs, or controls others in a certain setting: *a school* master; *the* master *of a ship; a dog and its* master. **2.** A person having great skill or knowledge in a certain field of work or art: *a master of glassmaking.* **3.** A male teacher, especially in a private school: *a school* master. **4. Master:** A word used before the name of a boy to show respect. *Noun.*
—**1.** Highly skilled in some field of work or art: *a master craftsman; a master builder; a master chef.* **2.** Main; most important: *A master key can open all the different locks in the house. Adjective.*
—**1.** To become very skilled in or expert at: *With a little practice, she* mastered *the new dance steps.* **2.** To get control over: *The rider finally* mastered *the runaway horse. Verb.*
mas|ter (mas′tər) *noun, plural* **masters;** *adjective; verb,* **mastered, mastering.**

masterpiece—A thing done with a high level of skill; a great work of art: *The museum of art contains* masterpieces *of painting and sculpture.*
mas|ter|piece (mas′tər pēs′) *noun, plural* **masterpieces.**

mastiff—A very large working dog with a short, smooth, light brown coat, a squared head, a short muzzle, and a broad chest. Originally bred in Asian and Middle Eastern countries, these dogs make good guard dogs.
mas|tiff (mas′tif) *noun, plural* **mastiffs.**

mastiff

mat—**1.** A piece of material, usually made of strong woven fibers or of rubber, that is used as a small rug on a floor or for wiping the soles of the shoes before entering a house. **2.** A small piece of material that is used to protect or decorate a piece of furniture: *Put the vase on a* mat *so that it doesn't leave a ring on the table.* **3.** A big, thick pad that is used as a cushion on a

floor where wrestling, boxing, gymnastics, or other athletics take place.   **4.** A mass of something that is thickly tangled: *A mat of grass and leaves clogged the pool's drain. Noun.*
—To become a thick, tangled mass: *The shaggy carpet was matted with mud from everyone's boots. Verb.*
mat (mat) *noun, plural* **mats;** *verb,* **matted, matting.**

matador—The person who must fight and kill the bull with his sword in a bullfight. The matador usually performs with a brightly colored cape.
mat|a|dor (mat′ə dawr) *noun, plural* **matadors.**

match¹—A small, thin stick of wood or cardboard whose tip is coated at one end with a chemical substance. The tip of a match flames easily when it is rubbed sharply against a rough surface.
match (mach) *noun, plural* **matches.**

match²—**1.** A person or thing that is very much the same as or in many ways equal to another: *My dog is a* match *for any greyhound when it comes to running.*   **2.** A person or thing that goes well with another: *That light blue blouse is a good* match *for that dark blue skirt.*   **3.** A contest or game: *a wrestling* match; *a spelling* match. *Noun.*
—**1.** To be equal to or the same as: *These shoes* match.   **2.** To be very similar or go well together: *I hope that my new shoes will* match *my green dress.*   **3.** To put two similar or equal things together in pairs: *My father* matches *up his socks after he does the laundry.*   **4.** To be equal to someone or something in competition: *He* matched *his brother's speed in the race. Verb.*
match (mach) *noun, plural* **matches;** *verb,* **matched, matching.**
• Synonyms: **coincide, correspond,** for *verb* **1.**
Antonym: **differ,** for *verb* **1.**

mate—**1.** One of two items that form a pair: *The lamps on either side of the sofa are* mates.   **2.** A husband or wife.   **3.** The male or female of a pair of animals: *The mother eagle sat on the nest while her* mate *hunted for food.*   **4.** One of the officers on a ship. *Noun.*
—To join as a couple in order to breed: *After the*

pair of foxes mated, *they prepared a den in which to raise their young. Verb.*
mate (māt) *noun, plural* **mates;** *verb,* **mated, mating.**

material—A substance; that from which or with which a thing is made: *Paper, pencils, paints, and brushes are art* materials.
ma|te|ri|al (mə tēr′ē əl) *noun, plural* **materials.**

maternal—**1.** Having to do with or being like a mother: *She looks after her sick kitten with* maternal *care.*   **2.** Related through one's mother's side of the family: *Your mother's sister is your* maternal *aunt.*
ma|ter|nal (mə tur′nəl) *adjective.*

math—A shortened form of **mathematics.**
math (math) *noun.*

mathematician—A person who has special skill and training in mathematics.
math|e|ma|ti|cian (math′ə mə tish′ən) *noun, plural* **mathematicians.**

mathematics—The study of numbers, measurements, quantities, and shapes, and of the relationships among them. Some of the branches of mathematics are arithmetic, algebra, and geometry.
math|e|mat|ics (math′ə mat′iks) *noun.* Abbreviation: math.

matinee—A performance of a play, movie, concert, or other entertainment in the afternoon.
mat|i|nee (mat′ə nē′) *noun, plural* **matinees.**

matter—**1.** Anything that has substance. Matter takes up space and has weight. It can be liquid, solid, or gas.   **2.** Any subject of interest: *They talked about business* matters *after the party.*   **3.** An amount: *Summer vacation will be over in a* matter *of days.*   **4.** A problem; difficulty: *I wonder what's the* matter *with her leg.*   **5.** Written or printed things: *newspaper* matter; *reading* matter. *Noun.*
—To be of value or importance: *Does it* matter *to you if I stay or go? Verb.*
mat|ter (mat′ər) *noun, plural* **matters;** *verb,* **mattered, mattering.**

mattress—A heavy cloth case filled with cotton, straw, foam rubber, or other soft material. Some mattresses are made of heavy plastic and filled with water. A mattress is used as a bed or as padding on a bed.
mat|tress (mat′ris) *noun, plural* **mattresses.**

mature—Fully developed: *a* mature *man; tall,* mature *trees. Adjective.*
—To reach full growth or development: *The melons are* maturing *so fast that they'll be ready to eat soon. Verb.*

a at	i if	oo look	ch chalk		a in ago
ā ape	ī idle	ou out	ng sing		e in happen
ah calm	o odd	u ugly	sh ship	ə =	i in capital
aw all	ō oats	ū rule	th think		o in occur
e end	oi oil	ur turn	th their		u in upon
ē easy			zh treasure		

ma|ture (mə **toor´**, mə **tyoor´**, or mə **choor´**)
adjective; verb, **matured, maturing.**
* Synonyms: **adult, grown-up,** for *adjective.*
Antonyms: **childish, immature, juvenile,** for
adjective.

matzo—A thin bread similar to a cracker, made
without yeast or other ingredients that would
make it rise. It is eaten especially during
Passover, a Jewish holiday.
mat|zo (**maht´**sō) *noun, plural* **matzoth**
(**maht´**sōth) or **matzos.**

maul—A large, heavy hammer that is used to
drive stakes and posts into the ground. *Noun.*
—To strike so as to damage: *The boy who
bagged our groceries* mauled *the bananas. Verb.*
maul (mawl) *noun, plural* **mauls;** *verb,* **mauled,
mauling.**
* A word that sounds the same is **mall.**
* Synonyms: **batter**[1]**, beat, pelt**[1]**, thrash, whip,**
for *verb.*

maximum—The highest or greatest possible
number, amount, or degree: *I can swim
underwater for a* maximum *of one minute. Noun.*
—The greatest, highest, or largest possible: *The*
maximum *number of students allowed in the
photography class is 30. Adjective.*
max|i|mum (**mak´**sə məm) *noun, plural*
maximums; *adjective.*

may—**1.** To have permission: *Mother,* may *I go
now?* **2.** To happen, possibly: *It* may *rain today.*
3. A word showing hope for something to
happen: May *you always be happy.*
may (mā) *verb,* **might.**
* See Language Fact at **can.**

May—The fifth month of the year. May has 31
days.
May (mā) *noun.*

Word History

May probably comes from the name of a Roman
goddess. The ancient Romans held ceremonies in
her honor on the first day of the month that they
named for her. Her name seems to be related to
a Latin word meaning ''growth'' or ''increase,''
and she was a goddess of the spring, when
everything is growing.

---

maybe—Possibly; perhaps: Maybe *you can come
to the movies with us tonight.*
may|be (**mā´**bē) *adverb.*

mayonnaise—A thick, white sauce made from
egg yolks, oil, seasonings, and lemon juice or
vinegar. It is used to add flavor to salads,
sandwiches, and other foods.
may|on|naise (mā´ə **nāz´** or **mā´**ə nāz´) *noun.*

mayor—The head of a town or city government.
may|or (**mā´**ər) *noun, plural* **mayors.**

maze—A very complicated series of passages or
paths through which it is hard to find one's way:
Her house is so big that the hallways are like a
maze.
maze (māz) *noun, plural* **mazes.**

me—The person speaking, when something is
done to or for that person: *They told* me *to leave
the room. Give* me *the book.*
me (mē) *pronoun.*

meadow—An area of grassy land: *The cows
grazed in the wide* meadow.
mead|ow (**med´**ō) *noun, plural* **meadows.**

meadowlark or **meadow lark**—A North
American songbird that has a yellow breast with
a V-shaped black mark on it. Meadowlarks are
about the size of robins.
mead|ow|lark or mead|ow lark
(**med´**ō lahrk´) *noun, plural* **meadowlarks** or
meadow larks.

meadowlark

meal[1]—The food eaten in one sitting: *My favorite*
meal *is turkey, potatoes, beans, and pie.*
meal (mēl) *noun, plural* **meals.**

meal[2]—Grain that has been ground into tiny
pieces.
meal (mēl) *noun, plural* **meals.**

mean[1]—**1.** To stand for; have as its definition: *Do
you know what that word* means? **2.** To want to
say or do: *I* mean *to do my chores, but I forget
sometimes.* **3.** To be used for a certain purpose:
The chair is not meant *for standing on.*
mean (mēn) *verb,* **meant, meaning.**

mean²—1. Unkind; cruel: *It's mean to lie about someone.*   2. Hard to handle; troublesome: *That dog is mean.*   3. Poor in quality or low in rank: *The poor widow lives in a mean apartment.*
mean (mēn) *adjective,* **meaner, meanest.**

mean³—In the middle of two extremes; average: *a mean temperature. Adjective.*
—Something that is in the middle of two extremes: *Walking is the mean between crawling and running. Noun.*
mean (mēn) *adjective; noun, plural* **means.**

meander—To move along a winding path: *The river meanders lazily through the countryside.*
me|an|der (mē an′dər) *verb,* **meandered, meandering.**

meander

meaning—The way in which something can be understood; significance: *the meaning of a word; the meaning of a story.*
meaning (mē′ning) *noun, plural* **meanings.**

means—1. The way in which something is done; method: *Will bicycle, train, or car be your means of travel?*   2. Money; wealth: *They are a family of means, so they live in a large house with a swimming pool in back.*
means (mēnz) *plural noun.*
▪ **by all means:** Certainly; of course: *By all means, your friends are welcome.*

meant—*See* **mean¹.**
meant (ment) *verb.*

a at	i if	oo look	ch chalk		a in ago
ā ape	ī idle	ou out	ng sing		e in happen
ah calm	o odd	u ugly	sh ship	ə =	i in capital
aw all	ō oats	ū rule	th think		o in occur
e end	oi oil	ur turn	<u>th</u> their		u in upon
ē easy			zh treasure		

meantime—The time between two events: *We will go out for pizza later; in the meantime, finish your homework.*
mean|time (mēn′tīm′) *noun.*

meanwhile—1. During the time between two events: *Dinner is in five minutes; meanwhile wash your hands and set the table.*   2. At the same time: *Dad washed the dishes; meanwhile I dried them.*
mean|while (mēn′hwīl′) *adverb.*

measles—A disease that has some of the symptoms of a bad cold along with fever and small, red spots all over the body. Measles are easily spread from one person to another by a virus.
mea|sles (mē′zəlz) *noun.*

measure—1. To find the size, weight, volume, or amount of something: *to measure a line with a ruler; to measure the distance between two towns; to measure a person's height.*   2. To take out or mark off a certain amount: *to measure out a cup of water to add to the recipe.*   3. To estimate by comparing with another person or thing: *The boys measured their strength by arm wrestling.*   4. To have as size, weight, volume, or amount: *The box measures two square feet.*
5. To be a unit of size, weight, volume, or amount: *Grams measure weight and liters measure volume. Verb.*
—1. The size, weight, volume, or amount of something: *What is the measure of the boards we need for the tree house?*   2. Something that is used to find the size, weight, volume, or amount of something else: *The butcher used the scale as a measure to find the weight of the meat.*   3. A unit or system for finding size, weight, and the like: *Quarts and liters are liquid measures.*
4. An amount or degree: *His new puppy is in large measure responsible for the smile on the boy's face.*   5. The written notes between two bar lines of music: *The piano teacher told her students to begin at the third measure.*   6. An action taken for a certain purpose: *We must take new measures to get people to come to our meetings.*   7. A bill that may become law: *The state legislature passed two measures dealing with highway safety. Noun.*
meas|ure (mezh′ər) *verb,* **measured, measuring;** *noun, plural* **measures.**
▪ **for good measure:** More than what is needed; something extra: *Grandmother put more sugar in the cookie mix for good measure.*

measurement—1. The act of finding the size, weight, volume, or amount of something: *The*

measurement *of the window had to be taken very carefully to make sure that the new pane of glass would fit.* **2.** An amount found in such a manner: *The carpenter told her assistant the measurements of the door.* **3.** A system for finding the size, weight, volume, or amount of something: *Scientists use metric* measurement *to do their experiments.*
meas|ure|ment (mezh′ər mənt) *noun, plural* **measurements.**

meat—**1.** The flesh of animals that is eaten as food: *Beef, pork, chicken, turkey, and lamb are types of* meat. **2.** The part of fruits and nuts that can be eaten: *The baker cracked the walnuts and used their* meats *to decorate the cake.* **3.** The main part or idea: *The first section is the* meat *of a newspaper.*
meat (mēt) *noun, plural* **meats.**
● A word that sounds the same is **meet.**

mechanic—A person whose job is fixing machines or engines: *an automobile* mechanic; *a washing machine* mechanic.
me|chan|ic (mə kan′ik) *noun, plural* **mechanics.**

mechanical—**1.** Having to do with machines: mechanical *equipment; a* mechanical *job.* **2.** Done in a routine way, with little thought or feeling: *The girl said the speech so poorly and quickly that she sounded* mechanical.
me|chan|i|cal (mə kan′ə kəl) *adjective.*

mechanism—The parts of a machine that make it work: *The* mechanism *of my typewriter is broken, so it will not print when I press the keys.*
mech|a|nism (mek′ə niz′əm) *noun, plural* **mechanisms.**

medal—A flat piece of metal with a design or writing on it. Medals are awarded to honor a special achievement. They may also be worn to honor a religious figure, such as a saint.
med|al (med′əl) *noun, plural* **medals.**
● A word that sounds the same is **meddle.**

meddle—To interfere in other people's business: *She is so nosy that she never stops* meddling.
med|dle (med′əl) *verb,* **meddled, meddling.**
● A word that sounds the same is **medal.**

median—In the middle; halfway between highest and lowest: *The test was fairly easy, and the* median *grade for the class was B.*
me|di|an (mē′dē ən) *adjective.*

Medicaid—A program in the United States that provides medical care for many people who cannot afford it. It is run by the federal

government and state governments working together.
Med|i|caid (med′ə kād′) *noun.*

medical—Having to do with the science of medicine or with the treatment of disease: *a* medical *school; to receive* medical *attention.*
med|i|cal (med′ə kəl) *adjective.* Abbreviation: med.

Medicare—A United States government program that provides medical care for those who are 65 and older.
Med|i|care (med′ə kār′) *noun.*

medicine—**1.** A substance, such as a drug, used to prevent or treat a disease or to relieve pain. **2.** The science of the prevention and treatment of disease: *She plans to study* medicine *and become a doctor.*
med|i|cine (med′ə sən) *noun, plural* **medicines.** Abbreviation: med.
■ **take (one's) medicine:** To do what one must, especially something unpleasant: *If you want her to forgive you, you'll have to take your* medicine *and apologize for what you did.*

medieval—Of, like, or from the Middle Ages, the period of time in Europe from about A.D. 500 to A.D. 1450: *a* medieval *castle.*
me|di|e|val (mē′dē ē′vəl, med′ē ē′vəl, *or* mid ē′vəl) *adjective.*

medium—Having a position in the middle; midway between two extremes: *The blouse comes in small,* medium, *and large sizes. Adjective.* —**1.** Something having a position in the middle of two extremes: *Autumn and spring are the two* mediums *between winter and summer.* **2.** A substance or thing in which something is carried or is done: *The newspaper is the main* medium *of communication she uses to find out the news.*
me|di|um (mē′dē əm) *adjective; noun, plural* **mediums** or, for **2, media** (mē′dē ə). Abbreviation: m. or med. for *adjective.*

meek—Not likely to argue or fight; mild; yielding: *She is very* meek *compared to her loud and rough sister.*
meek (mēk) *adjective,* **meeker, meekest.**

meet—**1.** To come upon; come face to face with someone or something: *The scouts* met *a deer in a clearing in the forest.* **2.** To be introduced: *I* met *her at a science fair last year, and we have been friends ever since.* **3.** To join; connect: *The roads* meet *near the church.* **4.** To come together by appointment: *They* met *their friends for lunch at noon.* **5.** To be at a place for the arrival of someone or something: *to* meet *a plane; to* meet *the winning team.* **6.** To pay or

pay for: *My parents helped me* meet *the expenses of a new bicycle.* Verb.
—A gathering of people, usually for a sports contest: *a track and field* meet. *Noun.*
meet (mēt) *verb,* **met, meeting;** *noun, plural* **meets.**

• A word that sounds the same is **meat.**

meeting—1. An assembly or gathering of people for a specific purpose: *a business* meeting; *a club* meeting. **2.** A coming together: *We had a* surprise *meeting with our neighbors on vacation.* **3.** A place where things join: *The city was built at the* meeting *of the two rivers.*
meet|ing (mē′ting) *noun, plural* **meetings.**

mega-—A prefix meaning ''large'' or ''one million.'' A megajet is a large jet airplane. A megaton equals one million tons.

Word Power

You can understand the meanings of many words that begin with **mega-,** if you add a meaning of the prefix to the meaning of the rest of the word.
  megastructure: a large building
  megawatt: one million watts

---

megaphone—A funnel-shaped device used to make a voice sound louder.
meg|a|phone (meg′ə fōn) *noun, plural* **megaphones.**

mellow—1. Soft, sweet, and ripe: mellow *fruit.* **2.** Pleasant and soothing: *the* mellow *tones of a violin.* **3.** Grown wiser and gentler with age: *He had a bad temper when he was younger, but now he is* mellow.
mel|low (mel′ō) *adjective,* **mellower, mellowest.**

melody—A pleasing arrangement of musical notes; tune: *She hummed the* melody *of her favorite song while she did her chores.*
mel|o|dy (mel′ə dē) *noun, plural* **melodies.**

melon—A large, round fruit that has a hard skin and sweet, juicy flesh. Melons grow on vines. Watermelons, cantaloupes, and honeydews are melons.
mel|on (mel′ən) *noun, plural* **melons.**

melt—1. To change from a solid to a liquid by means of heat: *We melted* some butter for our popcorn. **2.** To dissolve: *This chocolate cake just* melts *in your mouth.* **3.** To disappear or change gradually: *His fear of the dark* melted *away as he got older.* **4.** To make gentler: *The sight of the playful kittens* melted *her heart.*
melt (melt) *verb,* **melted, melting.**

member—1. A person, thing, or animal belonging to a group: *a* member *of the reptile family; a* member *of a club.* **2.** A part of a plant or animal. Branches, wings, arms, and legs are members.
mem|ber (mem′bər) *noun, plural* **members.**

membrane—1. A thin layer of soft tissue that covers and separates cells and organs in a person's or animal's body. **2.** A similar layer of tissue in a plant.
mem|brane (mem′brān) *noun, plural* **membranes.**

memento—Something that serves as a reminder; souvenir: *My scrapbook is full of* mementos *of my summer vacations.*
me|men|to (mə men′tō) *noun, plural* **mementos** or **mementoes.**

• Synonyms: **keepsake, token**

memo—A short note written as a reminder. **Memo** is a shortened form of the word ''memorandum.''
mem|o (mem′ō) *noun, plural* **memos.**

memorandum—A short note written as a reminder: *The club sent a* memorandum *about the new uniforms to all its members.*

honeydew

cantaloupe

watermelon

melon

a at	i if	oo look	ch chalk		┌ a in ago
ā ape	ī idle	ou out	ng sing		e in happen
ah calm	o odd	u ugly	sh ship	ə =	i in capital
aw all	ō oats	ū rule	th think		o in occur
e end	oi oil	ur turn	th their		└ u in upon
ē easy			zh treasure		

mem|o|ran|dum (mem'ə ran'dəm) *noun, plural* **memorandums** or **memoranda** (mem'ə ran'də).

memorial—Anything built, written, or done as a reminder of a person or event; tribute: *a war memorial. Noun.*
—Serving as a reminder or as an honor to a person or event: *The town held a memorial service for the mayor after he died. Adjective.*
me|mo|ri|al (mə mawr'ē əl) *noun, plural* **memorials;** *adjective.*

Memorial Day—A legal holiday in the United States to honor all who died while serving in the nation's armed forces. Most states celebrate Memorial Day on the last Monday of May.
Me|mo|ri|al Day (mə mawr'ē əl dā) *noun.*
• This holiday is also called **Decoration Day.**

memorize—To learn something so well as to know it by heart: *She had to memorize the poem and recite it to the class.*
mem|o|rize (mem'ə rīz) *verb,* **memorized, memorizing.**

memory—**1.** The ability to remember: *She has such a good memory that she can name all the presidents.* **2.** Someone or something that one remembers: *fond memories; memories of camp.* **3.** Everything a person can remember: *If memory serves, I was sick that winter.* **4.** A device in a computer that stores information.
mem|o|ry (mem'ər ē) *noun, plural* **memories.**

men—*See* **man.**
men (men) *plural noun.*

menace—Something or someone that is a threat; danger: *The smoke from the factory is a menace to the health of the community. Noun.*
—To threaten with harm or danger: *The flood menaced the town. Verb.*
men|ace (men'is) *noun, plural* **menaces;** *verb,* **menaced, menacing.**

mend—To fix or put back into good condition; repair: *I mended the hole in my sweater. Verb.*
—A repaired place: *You can hardly see the mend where I ripped my pants. Noun.*
mend (mend) *verb,* **mended, mending;** *noun, plural* **mends.**
■ **on the mend:** Getting better: *She is finally on the mend after being sick for so long.*

Mennonite—A member of a Protestant group that believes the Bible forbids baptizing infants, performing military service, and taking oaths.
Men|non|ite (men'ə nīt) *noun, plural* **Mennonites.**

menorah—A candlestick with places for eight candles, used in the celebration of the Jewish holiday of Hanukkah. One candle is lit on each night of the holiday. Many menorahs have a place for a ninth candle, which is used to light the others.
me|nor|ah (mə nawr'ə) *noun, plural* **menorahs.**

menorah

-ment—A suffix that means "the act or process of," "the condition of," or "the result of." Enjoyment is the act of enjoying. Amazement is the condition of being amazed. An improvement is the result of improving something.

Word Power

You can understand the meanings of many words that end in **-ment,** if you add a meaning of the suffix to the meaning of the rest of the word.
government: the act of governing
amusement: the condition of being amused
arrangement: the result of arranging

---

mental—**1.** Of or done by the mind: *Her great mental abilities were obvious in math class.* **2.** Having to do with a disease of the mind or the treatment of such a disease: *a mental patient; a mental hospital.*
men|tal (men'təl) *adjective.*

mention—To speak or write about briefly: *The teacher mentioned that there would be a quiz tomorrow. Verb.*
—A short note or remark: *There was mention of the garage sale in the newspaper. Noun.*
men|tion (men'shən) *verb,* **mentioned, mentioning;** *noun.*

menu—**1.** A list of the food and drinks served by a restaurant or similar business. **2.** A list shown on a computer screen that gives the user a choice

of operations the computer can perform.
men|u (men′yū) *noun, plural* menus.

meow—The sound made by a cat. *Noun.*
—To make this sound: *The cat* meowed *loudly when it saw the bird. Verb.*
me|ow (mē ou′) *noun, plural* meows; *verb,*
meowed, meowing.

merchandise—Goods that can be bought and sold: *Department stores offer a wide variety of* merchandise.
mer|chan|dise (mur′chən dīz *or* mur′chən dīs) *noun.* Abbreviation: mdse.

merchant—1. A person who buys and sells things as a business: *The merchant bought rugs in one country and then sold them in another.* 2. A person who runs a store: *The village* merchants *are having a sidewalk sale this week. Noun.*
—Having to do with business or trade: *The merchant ships unloaded their goods at the dock. Adjective.*
mer|chant (mur′chənt) *noun, plural* merchants; *adjective.*

merciful—Showing or having mercy: *The judge was* merciful *and gave the prisoner a light sentence.*
mer|ci|ful (mur′si fəl) *adjective.*

Mercury—The planet that is closest to the sun.
Mer|cu|ry (mur′kyər ē) *noun.*

mercury—A heavy, silver-colored metal that is a liquid at room temperature. It is a chemical element. It is used in thermometers.
mer|cu|ry (mur′kyər ē) *noun.*

mercy—1. More kindness than is deserved: *The librarian showed* mercy *and did not charge me a fine for my overdue book.* 2. Something for which to be thankful; blessing: *It is a* mercy *that the cat was not hurt when it fell from the tree.*
mer|cy (mur′sē) *noun, plural* mercies.

mere—Being no more than; only: *The* mere *thought of going to the game makes me excited.*
mere (mēr) *adjective,* merest.

merely—Only; simply: *Are you reading that book or* merely *looking at the pictures in it?*
mere|ly (mēr′lē) *adverb.*

merge—To join together into one; unite: *The two clubs* merged *to form a new organization.*
merge (murj) *verb,* merged, merging.
• Synonyms: blend, combine, compound, mix
Antonyms: divide, part, separate

meridian—1. An imaginary line circling the earth and passing through the North and South poles. 2. A line of longitude. 3. The highest point in the path of the sun or a star through the sky. The sun reaches its meridian about noon.
mer|id|i|an (mə rid′ē ən) *noun, plural* meridians.
• See picture at latitude.

merit—Value or goodness: *The school board thought that the plan to get new computers for the school had great* merit. *Noun.*
—To earn; deserve: *He* merited *the praise he got for his excellent report card. Verb.*
mer|it (mer′it) *noun, plural* merits; *verb,* merited, meriting.

mermaid—An imaginary sea creature with the head and upper body of a woman but the tail of a fish instead of legs.
mer|maid (mur′mād′) *noun, plural* mermaids.

merry—Cheerful and jolly: *My uncle is a* merry *man who always makes me smile and feel happy.*
mer|ry (mer′ē) *adjectives,* merrier, merriest.
• See Synonyms and Antonyms at happy.

merry-go-round—A round, decorated platform that is turned by a motor while music plays. It has animal figures or benches for people to ride on.
mer|ry-go-round (mer′ē gō round′) *noun, plural* merry-go-rounds.

mesa—An isolated hill that has a flat top and steep, rocky sides. Mesas are found in dry, desert areas in the western and southwestern United States.
me|sa (mā′sə) *noun, plural* mesas.

mesh—A web of threads or wires, such as a net or window screen.
mesh (mesh) *noun, plural* meshes.

mess—1. A dirty or untidy condition: *After baking the cake, they cleaned up the* mess *in the kitchen.* 2. A confused, troublesome, or unpleasant condition: *The heavy rains made a* mess *of the parade.* 3. A group of people, especially in the military, who regularly eat together. *Noun.*
—1. To cause to be dirty or untidy: *He* messed *up his room as he threw clothes and papers everywhere looking for his lost homework.* 2. To confuse or ruin: *The airline strike* messed *up our vacation plans. Verb.*

a at	i if	oo look	ch chalk		a in ago
ā ape	ī idle	ou out	ng sing		e in happen
ah calm	o odd	u ugly	sh ship	ə =	i in capital
aw all	ō oats	ū rule	th think		o in occur
e end	oi oil	ur turn	th their		u in upon
ē easy			zh treasure		

mess (mes) *noun, plural* **messes;** *verb,* **messed, messing.**

message—A communication in words, such as a letter, note, telegram, or broadcast announcement: *Mother left a* message *on the refrigerator to remind me of my dentist appointment.*
mes|sage (mes′ij) *noun, plural* **messages.**

messenger—Someone who delivers messages or does other errands: *Our teacher sent one of us as a* messenger *to the principal to tell her we were ready for the assembly.*
mes|sen|ger (mes′ən jər) *noun, plural* **messengers.**

met—*See* **meet.**
met (met) *verb.*

metal—A substance that, in most cases, has a shiny surface, can be melted, and conducts electricity and heat. Bronze, copper, gold, iron, lead, and silver are metals.
met|al (met′əl) *noun, plural* **metals.**

metallic—Made from, containing, or like a metal: *a metallic case for a radio; a metallic color.*
me|tal|lic (mə tal′ik) *adjective.*

metamorphosis—The series of stages in the development of some animals from their immature form into adulthood. Caterpillars change into butterflies through metamorphosis.
met|a|mor|pho|sis (met′ə mawr′fə sis) *noun, plural* **metamorphoses** (met′ə mawr′fə sēz).

1. egg

2. caterpillar

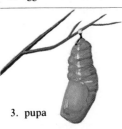
3. pupa

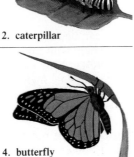
4. butterfly

metamorphosis

metaphor—A figure of speech in which one thing is compared to another to show that they are similar in some way. For example, the sentence, "She is an angel," means that the person is good and considerate.
met|a|phor (met′ə fawr′) *noun, plural* **metaphors.**

meteor—A metal or stone mass that burns as it travels from space through the earth's atmosphere at very high speed. Because it burns with a bright light as it falls to earth, it is sometimes called a falling star or a shooting star.
me|te|or (mē′tē ər) *noun, plural* **meteors.**

meteorite—A mass of metal or stone that has fallen from space and reached the surface of the earth.
me|te|or|ite (mē′tē ə rīt) *noun, plural* **meteorites.**

meteorology—The science that involves the study of the earth's atmosphere and weather.
me|te|or|ol|o|gy (mē′tē ə rol′ə jē) *noun.*

meter[1]—The basic unit of length in the metric system. It equals 39.37 inches.
me|ter (mē′tər) *noun, plural* **meters.** Abbreviation: **m**
• See picuture at **yard**[2].

meter[2]—A measuring or recording device, such as those that measure the speed of a car or the amount of electricity being used in a building.
me|ter (mē′tər) *noun, plural* **meters.**

meter[3]—1. A regular, rhythmic pattern of accented words in poetry. 2. A regular, rhythmic pattern of beats or accented notes in music.
me|ter (me′tər) *noun, plural* **meters.**

-meter—A suffix that means "a device for measuring." A car's speedometer is a device for measuring its speed.

Word Power

You can understand the meanings of many words that end in **-meter**, if you add the meaning of the suffix to the meaning of the rest of the word.
voltmeter: instrument for measuring volts

---

method—1. A manner or way of accomplishing something: *He chose the easiest* method *of doing the project and finished early.* 2. An order or system: *There was no apparent* method *to the arrangement of the files, so it was hard to find what we wanted.*
meth|od (meth′əd) *noun, plural* **methods.**

Methodist—A member of a Protestant church founded in England in the 1700's. *Noun.*
—Of this church or its members. *Adjective.*

Meth|od|ist (meth′ə dist) *noun, plural* **Methodists;** *adjective.*

metric—Of or concerning the metric system: *a metric scale; a metric ruler.*
met|ric (met′rik) *adjective.*

metric system—A group of units based on measuring by tens. The basic unit of length is the meter. The basic unit of weight is the kilogram. The basic unit of volume is the liter.
met|ric sys|tem (met′rik sis′təm) *noun.*

metropolis—A large city.
me|trop|o|lis (mə trop′ə lis) *noun, plural* **metropolises.**

metropolitan—Of or having to do with a large city: *a metropolitan skyline; a metropolitan area.*
met|ro|pol|i|tan (met′rə pol′ə tən) *adjective.*

mi.—The abbreviation for mile or miles.

mice—*See* **mouse.**
mice (mīs) *plural noun.*

micro-—A prefix that means "very small." A microbus is a very small bus.

Word Power

You can understand the meanings of many words that begin with **micro-**, if you add the meaning of the prefix to the meaning of the rest of the word.
> microcassette: a very small cassette
> microfilm: very small film

microbe—A very small living thing; germ. Some microbes cause disease.
mi|crobe (mī′krōb) *noun, plural* **microbes.**

microcomputer—A computer with a very small central working part.
mi|cro|com|put|er (mī′krō kəm pyū′tər) *noun, plural* **microcomputers.**

microorganism—A very small living thing; germ. Bacteria are a kind of microorganism.
mi|cro|or|gan|ism (mī′krō awr′gə niz əm) *noun, plural* **microorganisms.**

microphone—A device used to send or magnify sound by changing the sound waves to electrical signals.

mi|cro|phone (mī′krə fōn) *noun, plural* **microphones.**

microscope—A device with a lens or lenses that make things look larger. These lenses are so powerful that they allow the viewer to see things too tiny to be seen by the eye alone.
mi|cro|scope (mī′krə skōp) *noun, plural* **microscopes.**

microscope

microwave oven—An electronic device that heats and cooks food by means of microwaves, a form of energy also used in radio and radar.
mi|cro|wave ov|en (mī′krō wāv′ uv′ən) *noun, plural* **microwave ovens.**

mid-—A prefix that means "the middle point or portion of." Midnight is the middle of the night.

Word Power

You can understand the meanings of many words that begin with **mid-,** if you add the meaning of the prefix to the meaning of the rest of the word.
> midday: the middle of the day
> midstream: the middle of a stream

middle—The point halfway between two things; center: *the middle of a room; the middle of a forest; the middle of the afternoon. Noun.*
—Central; halfway between two things: *a middle seat; a middle aisle. Adjective.*
mid|dle (mid′əl) *noun, plural* **middles;** *adjective.*

a at	i if	oo look	ch chalk		a in ago
ā ape	ī idle	ou out	ng sing		e in happen
ah calm	o odd	u ugly	sh ship	ə =	i in capital
aw all	ō oats	ū rule	th think		o in occur
e end	oi oil	ur turn	<u>th</u> their		u in upon
ē easy			zh treasure		

middle-aged—Having to do with the years of life between about 40 and 65; neither young nor old.
mid|dle-aged (mid′əl ājd′) *adjective.*

Middle Ages—The period of European history from about A.D. 500 to about A.D. 1450.
Mid|dle A|ges (mid′əl ā′jəz) *noun.*

midget—A very small person. A midget's body has the same proportions as that of a normal adult but is smaller.
midg|et (mij′it) *noun, plural* **midgets.**
• See Language Fact at **dwarf.**

midnight—Twelve o'clock at night.
mid|night (mid′nīt) *noun.*

midst—The middle part; center: *They were so hungry that they stopped in the* midst *of their game for a snack.*
midst (midst) *noun.*

midway—Half the whole way: *It started to rain as he reached the* midway *point between his home and school. Adjective.*
—In the center or middle part: *The equator runs* midway *between the North and South poles. Adverb.*
—The location of the games and rides at a carnival, fair, or amusement park. *Noun.*
mid|way (mid′wā′) *adjective; adverb; noun, plural* **midways.**

might¹—*See* **may.**
might (mīt) *verb.*
• A word that sounds the same is **mite.**

might²—Force, power, or strength: *She tried with all her* might *to lift the heavy box.*
might (mīt) *noun.*
■ **with might and main:** Using all of one's power and strength: *The two boys struggled with might and main to move the huge rock.*
• A word that sounds the same is **mite.**

mighty—Very powerful, strong, or great: *a* mighty *river; a* mighty *ship; a* mighty *mountain.*
might|y (mī′tē) *adjective,* **mightier, mightiest.**

migrant—Moving from place to place; wandering: migrant *workers. Adjective.*
—A person or animal that moves from one place to another. *Noun.*
mi|grant (mī′grənt) *adjective; noun, plural* **migrants.**

migrate—To leave one place and go to another: *The geese* migrated *to the south for the winter.*
mi|grate (mī′grāt) *verb,* **migrated, migrating.**

mild—1. Kind or gentle: *a* mild *nature; a* mild *voice.* 2. Not harsh or extreme: *a* mild *soap; a*

mild *winter.* 3. Not strong, sharp, or bitter in taste: *a* mild *cheese.*
mild (mīld) *adjective,* **milder, mildest.**

mildew—A fungus that forms a whitish coating on plants, paper, and clothing in damp weather.
mil|dew (mil′dū) *noun.*

mile—A unit of distance that equals 5,280 feet (1.609 kilometers).
mile (mīl) *noun, plural* **miles.** Abbreviation: **mi.**

Word History

Mile comes from the Latin word for "thousand." The Romans were the first people to use the mile as a measurement of distance. The Roman mile contained 1,000 paces, each 5 feet (1.5 meters) in length. About the year 1500, the mile was changed to the length it has today.

mileage—Distance traveled in terms of miles: *The* mileage *on the used car he bought is low.*
mile|age (mī′lij) *noun.*

milestone—1. A stone set alongside a road to serve as a marker for a certain distance in miles. 2. An important event or an important point in development: *Winning the award was a* milestone *in the baseball player's career.*
mile|stone (mīl′stōn′) *noun, plural* **milestones.**

military—The armed forces: *When my brother grows up, he wants to join the* military. *Noun.*
—Having to do with soldiers, arms, or war: *a* military *base,* military *uniforms. Adjective.*
mil|i|tar|y (mil′ə ter′ē) *noun, plural* **militaries** *or* **military;** *adjective.*

militia—A group of citizens trained to fight and keep order in emergencies.
mi|li|tia (mə lish′ə) *noun, plural* **militias.**

milk—1. A white liquid produced by the glands of female mammals to feed their young. Many people drink cow's milk as food. 2. A white liquid produced by certain plants and fruits: *coconut* milk. *Noun.*
—To take this liquid from a cow or other animal: *While visiting my uncle's farm, I learned how to* milk *cows. Verb.*
milk (milk) *noun; verb,* **milked, milking.**

Milky Way—1. The galaxy that includes the earth, the sun, and the rest of our solar system. 2. A part of this galaxy that can be seen across the sky at night as a broad band of light.
Milk|y Way (mil′kē wā) *noun.*

mill—1. A building with machines for grinding grain into flour or meal. 2. A machine used to

grind or crush substances into tiny pieces: *a coffee* mill; *a pepper* mill.   **3.** A building with machines for making certain things: *a paper* mill; *a steel* mill. *Noun.*
—**1.** To crush or grind: *He* milled *the corn into meal after the harvest.*   **2.** To move around in a confused or aimless way: *People* milled *around the lobby of the theater during intermission. Verb.*
mill (mil) *noun, plural* **mills;** *verb,* **milled, milling.**

milliliter—A metric unit of volume that is equal to 1/1000 liter.
mi|li|li|ter (mil′ə lē′tər) *noun, plural* **milliliters.** Abbreviation: **ml**

millimeter—A metric unit of length that is equal to 1/1000 meter.
mil|li|me|ter (mil′ə mē′tər) *noun, plural* **millimeters.** Abbreviation: **mm**

million—A number that is equal to one thousand times one thousand; 1,000,000. *Noun.*
—**1.** Being equal to one thousand times one thousand.   **2.** Very many: *He has a* million *reasons for not doing his homework. Adjective.*
mil|lion (mil′yən) *noun, plural* **millions;** *adjective.*

millionaire—A person having a million dollars or more.
mil|lion|aire (mil′yə nâr′) *noun, plural* **millionaires.**

mime—**1.** A person who is trained in the art of pantomime, using actions and gestures instead of speaking to act out a part. Mimes often wear white paint on their faces.   **2.** A comic play using actions and gestures instead of words. *Noun.*
—To act out something without speaking; mimic: *He* mimed *the way a person would look walking against a strong wind. Verb.*
mime (mīm) *noun, plural* **mimes;** *verb,* **mimed, miming.**

mimeograph—A machine for making one or more copies of a written, printed, or ink-drawn page of paper. *Noun.*
—To copy with a mimeograph: *He* mimeographed *the directions to his house so that everyone invited to his party would have a copy. Verb.*
mim|e|o|graph (mim′ē ə graf) *noun, plural* **mimeographs;** *verb,* **mimeographed, mimeographing.**

mimic—**1.** To copy or imitate in order to make fun of; mock: *He teased his sister by* mimicking *the way she talked.*   **2.** To imitate closely: *She can* mimic *the sounds of birds. Verb.*
—Someone or something that imitates or copies another. *Noun.*
mim|ic (mim′ik) *verb,* **mimicked, mimicking;** *noun, plural* **mimics.**

min.—An abbreviation for **minute** or **minutes.**

minaret—A slender tower that is attached to a mosque, which is a Muslim house of worship. A minaret has one or more balconies, from which a crier calls people to prayer several times a day.
min|a|ret (min′ə ret′ *or* min′ə ret) *noun, plural* **minarets.**
• See picture at **mosque.**

mince—To cut or chop into tiny pieces; hash: *Mother* minced *onions and garlic for the spaghetti sauce.*
mince (mins) *verb,* **minced, mincing.**

mincemeat—A pie filling. Mincemeat is a cooked mixture of finely chopped apples, raisins, spices, and, in many cases, meat.
mince|meat (mins′mēt′) *noun.*

mind—**1.** The part of a person that thinks, reasons, feels, learns, understands, remembers, imagines, and dreams. The mind is in the brain, or is produced by the brain.   **2.** Intelligence; ability to understand: *He learns his schoolwork quickly because he has a good* mind.   **3.** An opinion; way of thinking: *She changed her* mind *about going to the movies when she heard that her friend could not go. Noun.*
—**1.** To pay careful attention in one's thoughts or actions: *to* mind *your manners; to* mind *the stairs so you do not fall.*   **2.** To take care or charge of someone or something: *The assistant* minded *the store while the owner was on vacation.*   **3.** To obey; do as someone says: *Our parents told us to* mind *our aunt while she was taking care of us.*   **4.** To worry about, object to, or dislike something: *He does not* mind *doing the dishes. Verb.*
mind (mīnd) *noun, plural* **minds;** *verb,* **minded, minding.**
■ **be of one mind:** To agree with or have the same opinion as another or others: *My parents are of one mind* when it comes to setting my bedtime.

a at	**i** if	**oo** look	**ch** chalk		a in ago
ā ape	**ī** idle	**ou** out	**ng** sing		e in happen
ah calm	**o** odd	**u** ugly	**sh** ship	ə =	i in capital
aw all	**ō** oats	**ū** rule	**th** think		o in occur
e end	**oi** oil	**ur** turn	**th** their		u in upon
ē easy			**zh** treasure		

have half a mind to: To have almost enough reason or desire to; have serious thoughts about: *I had half a mind to* go to the party even though my best friend would not be there.
make up (one's) **mind:** To make a decision: *She* made up *her* mind *to be friends with him.*
out of (one's) **mind:** Crazy: *They thought I was* out of *my* mind *for wanting to walk home in the rain when I could have ridden the bus.*

mine¹—Belonging to the person speaking: *That magazine is* mine.
mine (mīn) *pronoun.*

mine²—**1.** A large hole or tunnel dug under the ground, from which metals, minerals, or valuable stones are taken: *a gold* mine. **2.** A good source of something: *A veterinarian is a* mine *of information about pets.* **3.** An underground or underwater bomb that explodes when something comes near or touches it. *Noun.*
—**1.** To take metals, minerals, or valuable stones out of the ground by digging holes or tunnels: *to* mine *coal.* **2.** To place bombs in or under: *The soldiers walked carefully through the jungle because the enemy had* mined *the paths. Verb.*
mine (mīn) *noun, plural* **mines;** *verb,* **mined, mining.**

mineral—A solid, natural substance that is not a plant or animal and which was never alive. Quartz and salt are types of minerals. *Noun.*
—Of, like, or having such a substance or substances: mineral *springs;* mineral *water. Adjective.*
min|er|al (min′ər əl) *noun, plural* **minerals;** *adjective.*

mingle—**1.** To mix or become mixed together: *The shouts of the children on the playground* mingled *with their laughter.* **2.** To come in contact; associate in company: *They* mingled *with friends at the party.*
min|gle (ming′gəl) *verb,* **mingled, mingling.**

mini—A prefix that means ''very small'' or ''very short.'' A minisub is a small submarine. A miniskirt is a short skirt.

miniature—A small model or copy of something: *He collects* miniatures *of racing cars. Noun.*
—Much smaller than usual; very small: *a* miniature *poodle; a* miniature *train. Adjective.*
min|i|a|ture (min′ē ə chər) *noun, plural* **miniatures;** *adjective.*
• Synonyms: For *adjective,* see Synonyms at **small.**
  Antonyms: For *adjective,* see Synonyms at **big.**

miniature pinscher—A small dog with a short, shiny, brown-red or black-red coat and a sleek, thin body. Originally bred in Germany, these dogs make good watchdogs.
min|i|a|ture pin|scher (min′ē ə chər pin′shər) *noun, plural* **miniature pinschers.**

miniature pinscher

miniature schnauzer—A small dog with a shaggy beard and bushy eyebrows. The color of its coat may be salt and pepper, black and silver, black and tan, or all black. Originally bred in Germany, these dogs make good watchdogs.
min|i|a|ture schnau|zer (min′ē ə chər shnou′zər) *noun, plural* **miniature schnauzers.**

miniature schnauzer

minimum—The lowest amount; least quantity: *The* minimum *it will take to do the job is five*

hours, but it will probably take longer. Noun.
—Lowest or smallest: *The* minimum *age for entering the contest is 10. Adjective.*
min|i|mum (**min′**ə məm) *noun, plural* **minimums;** *adjective.*

minister—**1.** A person trained and authorized to lead religious services, especially in a Protestant church. **2.** Someone who is in charge of a department of the government: *the defense* minister; *the* minister *of transportation. Noun.*
—To care for; comfort or give aid: *The social worker* ministered *to poor people. Verb.*
min|is|ter (**min′**ə stər) *noun, plural* **ministers;** *verb,* **ministered, ministering.**

mink—A small, slender mammal having thick, soft fur. Minks live in parts of North America, northern and central Asia, and northern Europe. Their fur is used to make coats.
mink (mingk) *noun, plural* **minks** or **mink.**

mink

minnow—A tiny fish that lives in fresh water. Minnows are used as bait to catch larger fish.
min|now (**min′**ō) *noun, plural* **minnows.**

minor—Not very important; small in size or amount: *He was lucky that he got only a* minor *cut when he fell off his bicycle. Adjective.*
—Someone who is not of legal adult age or old enough to take complete care of himself or herself. *Noun.*
mi|nor (**mī′**nər) *adjective; noun, plural* **minors.**

minority—**1.** Less than half of a group or whole. **2.** A group that is different from most of the people in a country or a community in race, religion, or nationality.
mi|nor|i|ty (mə **nawr′**ə tē *or* mī **nawr′**ə tē) *noun, plural* **minorities.**

mint¹—**1.** A plant whose leaves are used for flavoring. Spearmint and peppermint are types of mint. **2.** A mint-flavored piece of candy.
mint (mint) *noun, plural* **mints.**

mint²—**1.** A place where the government makes coins. **2.** A great amount of money: *The diamond necklace on the movie star must have cost a* mint. *Noun.*
—To manufacture coins: *The government* mints *millions of quarters each year. Verb.*
mint (mint) *noun, plural* **mints;** *verb,* **minted, minting.**

minus—Less; reduced by: *Six* minus *four equals two. Preposition.*
—**1.** Under zero: *The temperature was* minus *five degrees yesterday.* **2.** Less than: *She got a grade of A* minus *on the science test, but she had hoped for an A.* **3.** Showing that something is to be or has been subtracted: *a* minus *sign. Adjective.*
—The sign that looks like this −. It shows that something is to be or has been subtracted. It also means below zero. *Noun.*
mi|nus (**mī′**nəs) *preposition; adjective; noun, plural* **minuses.**

minute¹—**1.** A unit of time made up of 60 seconds. **2.** A short amount of time: *Please wait for me because I will be ready to go in a* minute. **3.** An exact moment in time: *Clean up your room this* minute. **4. minutes:** The official, written record of what happened at a meeting: *The secretary took the* minutes *at the club meeting.*
min|ute (**min′**it) *noun, plural* **minutes.**

minute²—**1.** Extremely small: *Fleas are* minute *insects.* **2.** Exact; very careful or detailed: *Because she gave the police a* minute *description of the burglar, they caught him quickly.*
mi|nute (mī **nūt′** *or* mī **nyūt′**) *adjective.*
• Synonyms: For **1,** see Synonyms at **small.**
Antonyms: For **1,** see Synonyms at **big.**

miracle—**1.** An amazing event that cannot be explained by the laws of nature: *It would be a* miracle *if people could fly without the help of machines.* **2.** An amazing and marvelous thing: *It was a* miracle *that no one was hurt in the car crash.*
mir|a|cle (**mēr′**ə kəl) *noun, plural* **miracles.**

a at	i if	oo look	ch chalk		a in ago
ā ape	ī idle	ou out	ng sing		e in happen
ah calm	o odd	u ugly	sh ship	ə =	i in capital
aw all	ō oats	ū rule	th think		o in occur
e end	oi oil	ur turn	th their		u in upon
ē easy			zh treasure		

miraculous—1. Unable to be explained by the laws of nature: *She made a* miraculous *recovery from a fatal illness.*   2. Able to work wonders; extraordinary: *a* miraculous *drug.*
mi|rac|u|lous (mə **rak′**yə ləs) *adjective.*

mirage—An optical illusion that is sometimes seen at sea, in deserts, or above hot pavement. It gives the appearance of something that is not really there.
mi|rage (mə **rahzh′**) *noun, plural* **mirages.**

mirror—A smooth surface that reflects the images of objects placed in front of it. A mirror is usually a piece of glass that is backed with silver or aluminum, which gives it the ability to reflect light. *Noun.*
—To reflect an image of something: *When she looked into the clear pond, it* mirrored *her face. Verb.*
mir|ror (**mēr′**ər) *noun, plural* **mirrors;** *verb,* **mirrored, mirroring.**

mis-—A prefix that means "wrong" or "bad." To misspell a word is to spell it the wrong way. To misbehave is to behave badly.

Word Power

You can understand the meanings of many words that begin with **mis-**, if you add a meaning of the prefix to the meaning of the rest of the word.
  misunderstand: to understand in a wrong way
  misfortune: bad luck

---

misbehave—To behave badly or improperly: *He* misbehaved *at school when he ran in the halls.*
mis|be|have (mis′bi **hāv′**) *verb,* **misbehaved, misbehaving.**

miscellaneous—Mixed; of different kinds: *A library has a* miscellaneous *collection of books.*
mis|cel|la|ne|ous (mis′ə **lā′**nē əs) *adjective.* Abbreviation: **misc.**
• Synonyms: **assorted, diverse, various** Antonym: **uniform**

mischief—Playful actions that often cause trouble or damage without meaning to: *The boys got into* mischief *on Halloween.*
mis|chief (**mis′**chif) *noun.*

mischievous—Behaving in a playful way that often annoys or causes trouble: *The* mischievous *kitten knocked over the vase and broke it.*
mis|chie|vous (**mis′**chə vəs) *adjective.*

miser—A person who is stingy with his or her money; someone with an excessive desire to save money rather than spend it.
mi|ser (**mī′**zər) *noun, plural* **misers.**

miserable—1. Very unfortunate or unhappy: *He felt* miserable *about breaking his little brother's toy by mistake.*   2. Causing one to suffer: *a* miserable *cold;* miserable *weather.*   3. Very poor; inferior: *The actors gave a* miserable *performance, and few people enjoyed the play.*
mis|er|a|ble (**miz′**ər ə bəl) *adjective.*
• Synonyms: **blue, gloomy, glum, sad,** for 1. Antonyms: For 1, see Synonyms at **happy.**

misery—1. Great suffering or unhappiness: *The bad weather destroyed the crops and caused* misery *for the farmers.*   2. Poverty; very bad conditions: *A large number of people in our country live in* misery.
mis|er|y (**miz′**ər ē) *noun, plural* **miseries.**
• Synonyms: **sorrow, woe,** for 1. Antonyms: For 1, see Synonyms at **bliss.**

misfortune—1. Bad luck: *She had the* misfortune *to lose her purse.*   2. An unfortunate event: *The flood was a great* misfortune *because many families lost their homes.*
mis|for|tune (mis **fawr′**chən) *noun, plural* **misfortunes.**

mishap—An unfortunate accident: *He injured his knee in a skiing* mishap.
mis|hap (**mis′**hap) *noun, plural* **mishaps.**

mislead—1. To lead in the wrong direction: *I hope you know the way to her house and will not* mislead *us.*   2. To give the wrong information to: *The bank robbers lied to* mislead *the police.*
mis|lead (mis **lēd′**) *verb,* **misled, misleading.**
• Synonyms: **bluff², deceive, trick,** for 2.

misplace—1. To lose; forget where something is: *My father* misplaced *his glasses.*   2. To put in a wrong place: *The book was* misplaced *on the shelf, so the librarian could not find it.*
mis|place (mis **plās′**) *verb,* **misplaced, misplacing.**

mispronounce—To say a word incorrectly: *He does not speak French well because he* mispronounces *many words.*

mis|pro|nounce (mis′prə nouns′) *verb,*
mispronounced, mispronouncing.

miss¹—**1.** To fail to hit, reach, or contact: *an
arrow* missing *its target; to* miss *the school bus.*
2. To fail to be present at: *She* missed *her dance
lesson because she was sick.* **3.** To let go by: *He*
missed *a chance to take a trip to the carnival.*
4. To feel sad because someone or something is
absent: *She* missed *her brother when he went
away to college. Verb.*
—A failure to hit, meet, or reach something: *She
hit every ball without a* miss. *Noun.*
miss (mis) *verb,* **missed, missing;** *noun, plural*
misses.

■ **A miss is as good as a mile:** To miss
something by a little is the same as missing
something by a lot: *He almost broke the
window with his ball, but* a miss is as good as
a mile.

miss²—**1.** A girl; woman who is not married.
2. Miss: A title used to address a woman who is
not married: *The librarian is* Miss *Lopez.*
miss (mis) *noun, plural* **misses.**

missile—Any object, such as a rocket, bullet,
arrow, rock, or the like, that is shot or thrown
through the air: *a guided* missile.
mis|sile (mis′əl) *noun, plural* **missiles.**

missing—**1.** Lacking; not present: *There are a
few cards* missing *from this deck.* **2.** Lost or
absent: *My wallet is* missing.
miss|ing (mis′ing) *adjective.*

mission—**1.** A special task: *The fire fighter's*
mission *was to rescue the child from the burning
house.* **2.** A group of people sent to a place to
do a special job: *The government sent a* mission
to Africa to feed people who were starving. **3.** A
place where missionaries work.
mis|sion (mish′ən) *noun, plural* **missions.**

missionary—Someone sent by a religious group
to teach religion or to help set up schools and
hospitals.
mis|sion|ar|y (mish′ə när′ē) *noun, plural*
missionaries.

misspell—To spell a word in a wrong way: *She*
misspelled *two words on her test.*
mis|spell (mis spel′) *verb,* **misspelled** or
misspelt, misspelling.

mist—A cloud made up of tiny drops of water in
the air; fog: *The* mist *made it hard to see our
house from the road. Noun.*
—**1.** To rain in tiny drops: *It* misted *as we drove
home last night.* **2.** To become covered, dim, or
clouded; fog: *Her glasses* misted *as she poured
the boiling water out of the pot. Verb.*
mist (mist) *noun, plural* **mists;** *verb,* **misted,
misting.**

mistake—A wrong action or statement; error:
The secretary corrected her typing mistakes.
Noun.
—**1.** To understand in a wrong way: *She* mistook
the meaning of his joke and got angry. **2.** To
take in a wrong way: *The man* mistook *her for
her twin sister. Verb.*
mis|take (mis tāk′) *noun, plural* **mistakes;** *verb,*
mistook, mistaken, mistaking.
• Synonyms: **blunder, slip,** for *noun.*

mistaken—*See* **mistake.** *Verb.*
—Wrong or misunderstood; having made an
error: *She had a* mistaken *idea about how long
the cookies should bake, and they burned.
Adjective.*
mis|tak|en (mis tā′kən) *verb, adjective.*

mister—**1.** A title used without a name when
speaking to a man; sir: *May I see your driver's
license,* mister? **2. Mister:** A title used before a
man's last name. It is usually abbreviated: Mr.
Chin.
mis|ter (mis′tər) *noun, plural* **misters.**
Abbreviation: **Mr.**

mistletoe—A plant with white berries, yellow
flowers, and light-green leaves. Mistletoe is often
hung as a Christmas decoration; it is the state
flower of Oklahoma.
mis|tle|toe (mis′əl tō) *noun.*

a at	i if	oo look	ch chalk		⌈ a in ago
ā ape	ī idle	ou out	ng sing		e in happen
ah calm	o odd	u ugly	sh ship	ə =	i in capital
aw all	ō oats	ū rule	th think		o in occur
e end	oi oil	ur turn	th their		⌊ u in upon
ē easy			zh treasure		

mistletoe

mistook—*See* **mistake.**
mis|took (mis took′) *verb.*

mistreat—To treat in a bad, wrong, or cruel way; abuse: *The boy* mistreated *his dog when he left him without water all day.*
mis|treat (mis trēt′) *verb,* **mistreated, mistreating.**

mistress—A woman who owns something or has power or authority over something: *the* mistress *of the house; the dog's* mistress.
mis|tress (mis′tris) *noun, plural* **mistresses.**

misty—1. Covered with mist: *The lake is* misty *in the morning.* 2. Dim; not distinct: *My grandparents have only* misty *memories of their childhood.*
mist|y (mis′tē) *adjective,* **mistier, mistiest.**

misunderstand—To understand in a wrong way: *When I* misunderstand *the directions, I make mistakes on tests.*
mis|un|der|stand (mis′un dər stand′) *verb,* **misunderstood, misunderstanding.**

misunderstanding—1. A failure to understand correctly: *Ask her again, because I think you have a* misunderstanding *of the rules.* 2. An argument: *The girls were no longer friends after their* misunderstanding.
mis|un|der|stand|ing (mis′un dər stan′ding) *noun, plural* **misunderstandings.**

misunderstood—*See* **misunderstand.**
mis|un|der|stood (mis′un dər stood′) *verb.*

mite—A very tiny animal that belongs to the spider family. Some mites live on land and some in water. They are found in foods, on plants, or on other animals.
mite (mīt) *noun, plural* **mites.**
• A word that sounds the same is **might.**

mitt—A thick, padded leather glove that is used in baseball: *a catcher's* mitt.
mitt (mit) *noun, plural* **mitts.**

mitten—A knitted or leather covering to keep the hand warm. A mitten has a large space for the four fingers and a separate, smaller space for the thumb.
mit|ten (mit′ən) *noun, plural* **mittens.**

mix—1. To put or be put together; blend: *to* mix *pancake batter.* 2. To join together; do at the same time: *She* mixed *learning with vacationing by visiting two museums on her trip.* 3. To get along in a friendly manner with others: *He* mixes *well with the other children in his class. Verb.*
—Something that is made by putting together or blending: *cake* mix; *pudding* mix. *Noun.*

mix (miks) *verb,* **mixed, mixing;** *noun, plural* **mixes.**
■ **mix up:** 1. To confuse or place out of order: *She always gets* mixed up *when giving people directions to her house.* 2. To involve oneself in: *If they can prove that the man was* mixed up *in the robbery, he will be arrested.*
• Synonyms: **combine, compound, merge,** for *verb* 1.
Antonyms: **divide, part, separate,** for *verb* 1.

mixed number—A number that is made up of a whole number and a fraction. For example, 7⅔ is a mixed number.
mixed num|ber (mikst num′bər) *noun, plural* **mixed numbers.**

mixture—Things that have been put together: *The* mixture *of raisins, nuts, and cereal was delicious.*
mix|ture (miks′chər) *noun, plural* **mixtures.**

ml—The abbreviation for **milliliter** or **milliliters.**

mm—The abbreviation for **millimeter** or **millimeters.**

moan—A long, low, sad sound that usually shows sorrow or pain: *She gave a* moan *when the doctor touched her sprained ankle. Noun.*
—To make a sound as if suffering from sorrow or pain: *The old stairs creaked and* moaned *when anyone climbed them. Verb.*
moan (mōn) *noun, plural* **moans;** *verb,* **moaned, moaning.**
• A word that sounds the same is **mown.**

moat—A deep, wide trench filled with water. Long ago, a moat was dug around a castle or town to keep enemies out. A bridge could be lowered across the moat so that people could come and go across it.
moat (mōt) *noun, plural* **moats.**

mob—A crowd, especially one that is excited or upset: *A* mob *of fans waited to get into the concert. Noun.*
—To crowd around, in excitement or anger: *Children* mobbed *the ice cream truck when it stopped at the playground. Verb.*
mob (mob) *noun, plural* **mobs;** *verb,* **mobbed, mobbing.**

moccasin—A soft leather shoe without a heel.
moc|ca|sin (mok′ə sən) *noun, plural* **moccasins.**

mock—1. To make fun of in a rude or unfriendly way: *The girl* mocked *the way her little brother cried when he fell down.* 2. To mimic in a rude or unfriendly way: *The cartoon* mocked *the movie star by making his ears and nose bigger than they really were. Verb.*

—Not real; fake: *They may look real, but those are* mock *diamonds in that necklace. Adjective.*
mock (mok) *verb,* **mocked, mocking;** *adjective.*

mockingbird—A bird noted for its ability to copy the songs of other birds. Mockingbirds have gray and white feathers. They live in North and South America.
mock|ing|bird (mok′ing burd′) *noun, plural* **mockingbirds.**

mockingbird

model—1. A copy of something, especially a small copy: *The young girl played with the* model *of a farm.* 2. A type or style of something: *Our computer is the newest* model. 3. A person or thing that sets a good example of something: *She is a* model *of a good athlete.* 4. A person whose job is posing to have his or her picture painted or photograph taken. Clothing stores or designers often hire models to show customers new clothing styles. *Noun.*
—1. To construct; shape: *The boys* modeled *race cars from blocks of wood.* 2. To imitate the good things about a person: *The boy tried to* model *his swing after that of his favorite baseball player.* 3. To pose for an artist or photographer, or to wear something so as to show it as an example: *He* modeled *a new ski jacket. Verb.*
—1. Perfect, especially in behavior: *a* model

student. 2. Serving as a small copy of something: *a* model *train. Adjective.*
mod|el (mod′əl) *noun, plural* **models;** *verb,* **modeled, modeling;** *adjective.*
 • Synonyms: **ideal, pattern, standard,** for *noun* 3.

modem—A device connected to a computer, for sending or receiving information through a telephone line.
mo|dem (mō′dəm *or* mod′əm) *noun, plural* **modems.**

moderate—Average; being neither too much nor too little: *a* moderate *climate; a* moderate *tone of voice. Adjective.*
—To become less strong or severe; lessen: *The temperature in the room* moderated *when I turned the thermostat down. Verb.*
mod|er|ate (mod′ər it for *adjective;* mod′ə rāt for *verb*) *adjective; verb,* **moderated, moderating.**

modern—1. Having to do with the present or the immediate past: *The computer is everywhere in* modern *life.* 2. New in fashion; not old or outdated: *The new manager had some* modern *ideas about how to make the store more efficient.*
mod|ern (mod′ərn) *adjective.*

modest—1. Not proud; humble: *She was very* modest *about winning the gold medal.* 2. Average; not too much: *He made only a* modest *amount of money this week from his lemonade stand because the weather was cool.*
mod|est (mod′ist) *adjective.*

modify—1. To change a little; adjust: *She* modified *the plans for the tree house to include a bench.* 2. To limit the meaning of a word: *The dog had a red ball.* The word ''red'' modifies the word ''ball.''
mod|i|fy (mod′ə fī) *verb,* **modified, modifying.**
 • Synonyms: **alter, vary,** for 1.
 Antonyms: **conserve, maintain, preserve,** for 1.

Mohammed—*See* **Muhammad.**
Mo|ham|med (mō ham′əd) *noun.*

moist—Damp; slightly wet: *The grass was* moist *from the heavy dew.*
moist (moist) *adjective,* **moister, moistest.**

moisten—To dampen; make slightly wet: *He* moistened *the sponge before he wiped the kitchen counter.*
moist|en (moi′sən) *verb,* **moistened, moistening.**

moisture—Tiny drops of water, or some other liquid, that are in the air or on a surface;

a at	i if	oo look	ch chalk		⌐a in ago
ā ape	ī idle	ou out	ng sing		e in happen
ah calm	o odd	u ugly	sh ship	ə =	i in capital
aw all	ō oats	ū rule	th think		o in occur
e end	oi oil	ur turn	th their		⌐u in upon
ē easy			zh treasure		

dampness: *There is a lot of* moisture *in the air on a humid summer day.*
mois|ture (mois′chər) *noun.*

molar—A tooth with a wide, flat surface that is used to grind food. An adult human being has up to 12 molars in the back of the mouth.
mo|lar (mō′lər) *noun, plural* **molars.**

molasses—A thick, sweet, brown syrup that is made from sugar cane. It is used in cooking and baking.
mo|las|ses (mə las′iz) *noun.*

mold¹—A container designed to be filled with a soft substance or liquid that can be hardened. The solid thing that results is shaped like the container: *He poured the chocolate into a* mold *shaped like a star. Noun.*
—1. To use the hands or special equipment to form something into a certain shape: *We* molded *the dough into pretzels.* 2. To help a person develop by providing education, encouragement, and a good example: *Our teacher helps to* mold *us into good students. Verb.*
mold (mōld) *noun, plural* **molds;** *verb,* **molded, molding.**

mold²—A fungus that grows on things that are rotting or damp. It is furry-looking and usually green or white in color.
mold (mōld) *noun, plural* **molds.**

molding—A thin, decorative piece of wood or other material that is fastened along the edges of a ceiling, wall, window, or door.
mold|ing (mōl′ding) *noun, plural* **moldings.**

mole¹—A dark spot on a person's skin.
mole (mōl) *noun, plural* **moles.**

mole²—A small mammal that lives mostly underground. It has soft fur, small eyes, and strong forefeet.
mole (mōl) *noun, plural* **moles.**

molehill—1. A small mound or ridge of dirt made by moles digging under the ground. 2. A

mole²

thing of no importance: *Crying about losing a penny is making a mountain out of a* molehill.
mole|hill (mōl′hil) *noun, plural* **molehills.**

molecule—The smallest unit remaining when a substance has been divided as much as possible without having undergone a chemical change.
mol|e|cule (mol′ə kyūl) *noun, plural* **molecules.**

mollusk—Any of many animals with a soft body that has no backbone. They generally live in salt water. A hard outer shell protects most mollusks, such as snails, clams, and oysters. Others, such as octopuses, do not have such a covering.
mol|lusk (mol′əsk) *noun, plural* **mollusks.**

molt—To shed the feathers, hair, horns, shell, or outer skin at certain times. The parts lost are replaced by new growth: *A snake* molts *its skin.*
molt (mōlt) *verb,* **molted, molting.**

mom—Female parent; mother.
mom (mom) *noun, plural* **moms.**

moment—1. A brief or fleeting instant: *It only takes a* moment *to blink your eyes.* 2. A certain exact time: *We all shouted, "Surprise!" the* moment *he came through the door.*
mo|ment (mō′mənt) *noun, plural* **moments.**

momentary—Continuing for only a brief time; temporary: *There was a* momentary *pause as I thought about how to answer the question.*
mo|men|tar|y (mō′mən tār′ē) *adjective.*

momentous—Very serious; mattering a lot: *Where to go to college is a* momentous *decision.*
mo|men|tous (mō men′təs) *adjective.*
• Synonyms: **important, significant**
 Antonym: **petty**

momentum—The speed or force that a moving object has because of its weight and motion: *The sled gained* momentum *as it slid down the hill.*
mo|men|tum (mō men′təm) *noun, plural* **momentums.**

Mon.—The abbreviation for **Monday.**

monarch—1. A person who governs or leads a country, such as a king, queen, or emperor; sovereign. 2. A large North American butterfly with colorful black and orange markings.
mon|arch (mon′ərk) *noun, plural* **monarchs.**

monarchy—1. A government that is headed by a king, queen, emperor, or the like. 2. A nation or state that is led by a king, queen, or emperor.
mon|arch|y (mon′ər kē) *noun, plural* **monarchies.**

monastery—A house in which monks make their home and work and pray together.
mon|as|ter|y (mon′ə stār′ē) *noun, plural* **monasteries.**

Monday—The second day of the week; day that is between Sunday and Tuesday.
Mon|day (mun′dē *or* mun′dā) *noun, plural* **Mondays.** Abbreviation: **Mon.**

Word History

Monday comes from two old English words meaning "moon" and "day." The people of ancient times thought the moon had great power. So the day after Sunday came to be called the day of the moon as a way of showing respect to this power.

---

money—The specially marked coins and pieces of paper that are used to buy things and to pay people for their work; currency; cash. Most countries of the world have their own forms of money. The United States uses coins, such as pennies, nickels, and dimes, and paper bills in various fixed values.
mon|ey (mun′ē) *noun, plural* **moneys** or **monies.**

mongoose—A slim, furry animal that lives in Africa and Asia. It has a pointed face, a slender, agile body, and a long tail. It is a ferocious fighter that can kill rats and poisonous snakes.
mon|goose (mong′gūs) *noun, plural* **mongooses.**

mongoose

mongrel—An animal, especially a dog, whose parents were of different breeds: *Our dog is a* mongrel *that looks partly like a beagle and partly like a collie.*
mon|grel (mung′grəl *or* mong′grəl) *noun, plural* **mongrels.**

a at	i if	oo look	ch chalk		a in ago
ā ape	ī idle	ou out	ng sing		e in happen
ah calm	o odd	u ugly	sh ship	ə =	i in capital
aw all	ō oats	ū rule	th think		o in occur
e end	oi oil	ur turn	th their		u in upon
ē easy			zh treasure		

monitor—1. A student assigned by the teacher to perform a special job, such as taking attendance or giving out books or paper. 2. A person or thing that reminds or warns: *A smoke alarm is a* monitor *that will warn of fire.* 3. In computers, a display like a television screen that shows what information is being put into a computer, how the computer is processing and storing that information, and any answers or information the computer is told to produce. *Noun.*
—To watch over or listen in to; check up on, often for a period of time: *The boy* monitored *the temperature in the new fish tank. Verb.*
mon|i|tor (mon′ə tər) *noun, plural* **monitors;** *verb,* **monitored, monitoring.**

monk—A man who belongs to a religious order that lives in a monastery; friar.
monk (mungk) *noun, plural* **monks.**

monkey—A furry mammal that is very intelligent and is closely related to apes, gorillas, and chimpanzees. It has a long tail and hands and feet that are good for climbing. *Noun.*
—To tamper with something in a playful way; toy: *Do not* monkey *with the lawnmower. Verb.*
mon|key (mung′kē) *noun, plural* **monkeys;** *verb,* **monkeyed, monkeying.**

- **make a monkey out of:** To cause a person to appear silly or foolish: *She* made a monkey out of *her brother when she beat him at his favorite game, checkers.*
  monkey business: Mischief; behavior intended to deceive: *His first prank should have let us know he was up to* monkey business.

mono-—A prefix that means "having one" or "a single." *A* monotonous *voice has one tone. A* monopoly *is control by a single person or business.*

Word Power

You can understand the meanings of many words that begin with **mono-,** if you add a meaning of the prefix to the meaning of the rest of the word.
monosyllable: A word having one syllable
monorail: A railway track having only a single rail

---

monopoly—A power over the selling of a product or service, held by just one person or business: *Because only one store in our town sells ice skates, it has a* monopoly *on that business.*
mo|nop|o|ly (mə nop′ə lē) *noun, plural* **monopolies.**

monotonous—Boring because it is always the same; dull; tedious: *Weeding the garden is a* monotonous *chore.*
mo|not|o|nous (mə not′ə nəs) *adjective.*

monsoon—A powerful wind of southern Asia that changes direction with the seasons. It blows from the sea to the land in the summer and brings heavy rains. In the winter, it blows from the land to the sea.
mon|soon (mon sūn′) *noun, plural* **monsoons.**

monster—1. A big, ugly creature who scares others in a story; ogre. It is not real. 2. A wicked, cruel person: *Only a* monster *could have committed a crime this horrible.* 3. A living thing with physical qualities that are not common or normal: *A dog with two tails would be considered a* monster.
mon|ster (mon′stər) *noun, plural* **monsters.**

monstrous—1. Ugly and scary: *The giant was a* monstrous *creature.* 2. Of a great size; huge: *Each child raked a small pile of leaves to the center of the yard, making one* monstrous *pile.* 3. Wicked; evil: *Setting fire to the building was a* monstrous *crime.*
mon|strous (mon′strəs) *adjective.*

month—One of the twelve parts into which the year is divided.
month (munth) *noun, plural* **months.**
- **month of Sundays:** A very long time: *It had been a* month of Sundays *since we had seen her last.*

monument—A stone, statue, or other structure that is set up in a public place to show respect for an important person or happening; memorial: *In the center of our town, there is a* monument *to honor all the soldiers who lived there.*
mon|u|ment (mon′yə mənt) *noun, plural* **monuments.**

moo—The sound that is made by a cow. *Noun.*
—To make a sound like that of a cow. *Verb.*
moo (mū) *noun, plural* **moos;** *verb,* **mooed, mooing.**

mood—One's general attitude; the way one is feeling: *He was in a good* mood *because it was his birthday.*
mood (mūd) *noun, plural* **moods.**

moody—Capable of frequently changing one's feelings or general state of mind: *Because she is so* moody, *you never know if she will smile at you or not.*
mood|y (mū′dē) *adjective,* **moodier, moodiest.**

moon—1. A natural satellite that makes one complete trip around the earth every 29 1/2 days. Its light is actually light from the sun that reflects

off its surface. 2. Any natural satellite revolving around a planet: *Saturn has many* moons.
moon (mūn) *noun, plural* **moons.**
- **once in a blue moon:** Hardly ever; on rare occasions: *She's been so busy that I now get to see her only* once in a blue moon.

moonbeam—A ray or stream of light from the moon: *A* moonbeam *shone through her bedroom window.*
moon|beam (mūn′bēm) *noun, plural* **moonbeams.**

moonlight—The light of the moon.
moon|light (mūn′līt′) *noun.*

moose—A four-legged animal that looks somewhat like a large deer. It lives in Canada and the northern United States. A male moose has antlers that are broad and jagged.
moose (mūs) *noun, plural* **moose.**

moose

mop—A device used to dust or to wash and dry floors, made of a sponge or bundle of yarn attached to a pole. *Noun.*
—To wash, clean, or dust with a cloth, a sponge, or any device used to wash and dry floors or other surfaces: *to* mop *the kitchen floor. Verb.*
mop (mop) *noun, plural* **mops;** *verb,* **mopped, mopping.**

mope—To have sad and gloomy feelings: *She* moped *because it rained on the day of the picnic.*
mope (mōp) *verb,* **moped, moping.**

moral—1. Honest; just: *a* moral *deed.*
2. Concerning right and wrong: *It is a* moral *choice whether or not to lie. Adjective.*
—1. What one learns about right and wrong from a story or a real-life happening: *The* moral *of the story was "Be kind to others."*

2. morals: One's attitudes about right and wrong: *His* morals *did not allow him to steal.* Noun.
mor|al (mawr′əl) *adjective; noun, plural* **morals.**
• Synonyms: **good, right,** for *adjective* 1. Antonyms: **bad, naughty, wicked, wrong,** for *adjective* 1.

morale—The general mood or attitude of a person or group of people about what is happening; spirit: *The* morale *of my class was high when it won the school field day.*
mo|rale (mə ral′) *noun.*

more—1. Larger or greater in amount, size, or some other way: *He has* more *baseball cards than I do.* **2.** Extra; added: *Would you like* more *chocolate cake? Adjective.*
—An additional amount or number: *We invited ten people, but somehow* more *are coming. Noun.*
—**1.** To a larger extent: *She likes dogs* more *than cats.* **2.** Again: *Try once* more. *Adverb.*
more (mawr) *adjective, noun, adverb.*
■ **more or less: 1.** A little bit; somewhat: *The weather was* more or less *rainy.* **2.** In general terms; approximately: *We are going at two o'clock,* more or less.

moreover—In addition; besides; also: *I enjoy playing tennis, and* moreover *it is good exercise.*
more|o|ver (mawr ō′vər) *adverb.*
• Synonyms: **furthermore, likewise, too**

Morgan—An American breed of horse that is strong and light in weight. It is used for working and riding.
Mor|gan (mawr′gən) *noun, plural* **Morgans.**

Mormon—A person who belongs to the Church of Jesus Christ of Latter-day Saints, a religion started in the United States in 1830. *Noun.*
—Having to do with this church or its members. *Adjective.*
Mor|mon (mawr′mən) *noun, plural* **Mormons;** *adjective.*

morning—1. The beginning hours of daylight, from sunrise until noon. **2.** The time from midnight until noon. *Noun.*
—Of or in the beginning hours of daylight: *In the summer, he likes to take a* morning *swim. Adjective.*

morn|ing (mawr′ning) *noun, plural* **mornings;** *adjective.*
• A word that sounds the same is **mourning.**

morning-glory—A vine with leaves that are shaped like hearts. It has trumpet-shaped flowers that open in the early morning but close for the rest of the day.
morn|ing-glo|ry (mawr′ning glawr′ē) *noun, plural* **morning-glories.**

morning-glory

morsel—A little bit or piece, especially of food: *He was so full that he could not eat another* morsel.
mor|sel (mawr′səl) *noun, plural* **morsels.**

mortal—1. Not going to live forever; bound to die at some time: mortal *man.* **2.** Causing one to die; fatal; deadly: *Smallpox can be a* mortal *illness. Adjective.*
—A person: *All* mortals *have a reason to care about each other. Noun.*

a at	i if	oo look	ch chalk		a in ago
ā ape	ī idle	ou out	ng sing		e in happen
ah calm	o odd	u ugly	sh ship	ə =	i in capital
aw all	ō oats	ū rule	th think		o in occur
e end	oi oil	ur turn	th their		u in upon
ē easy			zh treasure		

Morgan

mor|tal (mawr′təl) *adjective; noun, plural* **mortals.**

mortar—A blend of sand, water, lime, and often cement, used in construction to hold bricks or stones together.
mor|tar (mawr′tər) *noun, plural* **mortars.**

mosaic—A piece of art created by arranging small bits of stone, glass, wood, or tile of different colors on a surface. They are then cemented into place.
mo|sa|ic (mō zā′ik) *noun, plural* **mosaics.**

Moslem—*See* **Muslim.**
Mos|lem (moz′ləm *or* mos′ləm) *noun, plural* **Moslems.**

mosque—A building set up as a public place for Muslims to pray.
mosque (mosk) *noun, plural* **mosques.**

mosque

mosquito—A small, slim insect with two wings. The female mosquito gives an itchy bite to people and animals and may carry diseases.
mos|qui|to (mə skē′tō) *noun, plural* **mosquitoes** or **mosquitos.**

moss—A very small, green or brown plant with a short stem and many soft, narrow leaves. It grows in tight clusters in damp and shady locations, covering like a rug the ground, rocks, and trees over which it spreads.
moss (maws) *noun, plural* **mosses.**

most—1. Largest in amount, greatest in number, or highest in degree: *He found the* most *eggs at the Easter egg hunt.* 2. Practically all; the majority of: Most *birds can fly. Adjective.*
—The largest amount, greatest number, or highest degree: *She shoveled* most *of the snow from the sidewalk. Noun.*
—Of the largest amount, in the greatest number, or of the highest degree: *It was the* most *beautiful sunset he had ever seen. Adverb.*
most (mōst) *adjective, noun, adverb.*

mostly—Nearly all; chiefly: *The horse was* mostly *black, with a white face and feet.*
most|ly (mōst′lē) *adverb.*

motel—A hotel where people traveling by car may stay overnight. Motels are often built near busy roads.
mo|tel (mō tel′) *noun, plural* **motels.**

moth—A flying insect that is similar to a butterfly except that its wings are not as brightly colored and it is not generally seen during the daytime.
moth (mawth) *noun, plural* **moths.**

mother—A female person or animal who is a parent.
moth|er (mu<u>th</u>′ər) *noun, plural* **mothers.**

mother-in-law—The mother of a person's husband or wife.
moth|er-in-law (mu<u>th</u>′ər in law′) *noun, plural* **mothers-in-law.**

Mother's Day—A holiday when mothers receive special recognition. It is celebrated in the United States on the second Sunday in May.
Moth|er's Day (mu<u>th</u>′ərz dā) *noun.*

motion—1. Movement; action: *the* motion *of a swing.* 2. A suggestion requiring a vote that is made at a meeting of a club or other group: *She made a* motion *to end this meeting of the student council. Noun.*
—To gesture; make a movement of the hand or head that tells something: *Dad* motioned *to us to be quiet. Verb.*
mo|tion (mō′shən) *noun, plural* **motions;** *verb,* **motioned, motioning.**
■ **go through the motions:** To do something only because you must or should, not as well as you could: *She went through the motions of cleaning her room, but it still looked messy.*

motive—A cause or reason for a person's behavior: *His* motive *for being a paperboy was to earn money for a new bicycle.*
mo|tive (mō′tiv) *noun, plural* **motives.**

motor—A machine that uses energy from gasoline, electricity, water, wind, or some other source to make itself or another thing move;

engine: *an automobile* motor; *a lawnmower* motor. *Noun.*
—**1.** Run by or having to do with a motor: *a* motor *car.* **2.** Of the nerves in the body that control muscle movement: *A knee jerk is a* motor *response when a doctor taps your knee. Adjective.*
mo|tor (mō′tər) *noun, plural* **motors;** *adjective.*

motorboat—A boat powered by a motor that is attached to the outside of the boat at the back, or inside at the bottom of the boat.
mo|tor|boat (mō′tər bōt′) *noun, plural* **motorboats.**

motorcycle—A vehicle powered by a motor. It has two wheels, can carry one or two people, and looks like a large, heavy bicycle.
mo|tor|cy|cle (mō′tər sī′kəl) *noun, plural* **motorcycles.**

motto—An expression that briefly states an important belief held by a person or group; slogan: *The Boy Scout* motto *is "Be prepared."*
mot|to (mot′ō) *noun, plural* **mottoes** or **mottos.**

mound—**1.** A pile of things heaped together: *a* mound *of leaves; a* mound *of sand.* **2.** A small hill. **3.** A raised dirt area on which a baseball or softball pitcher stands when throwing the ball. *Noun.*
—To pile or heap on: *She* mounded *whipped cream on top of her hot-fudge sundae. Verb.*
mound (mound) *noun, plural* **mounds;** *verb,* **mounded, mounding.**
• Synonyms: **mass, stack,** for *noun* 1.

mount[1]—**1.** To rise up; climb; ascend: *He* mounted *the ladder to reach the top shelf.* **2.** To climb onto; get up on: *to* mount *a bicycle.* **3.** To place; put: *She* mounted *the photographs in the scrapbook.* **4.** To become larger or higher; rise: *The temperature* mounted *inside the oven. Verb.*
—Something that a person can ride, especially a horse: *Her* mount *was a pony. Noun.*
mount (mount) *verb,* **mounted, mounting;** *noun, plural* **mounts.**

mount[2]—A mountain or large hill: Mount *Everest.* Abbreviation: **Mt.**
mount (mount) *noun, plural* **mounts.**

mountain—**1.** A piece of land that is much higher than the rest of the land around it, often

rising steeply to a peak. **2.** A tall stack or heap of things: *The snowplow created a* mountain *of snow in the parking lot.* Abbreviation: **mt.** or **mtn.** or **Mtn.**
moun|tain (moun′tən) *noun, plural* **mountains.**
■ **make a mountain out of a molehill:** To think that something is much more important than it really is: *He is* making a mountain out of a molehill *by being so upset about losing his pencil.*

mountain goat—A kind of white antelope that lives in the Rocky Mountains of the western United States. It is a very good climber. The male has large, black horns that curl over the sides of his head.
moun|tain goat (moun′tən gōt) *noun, plural* **mountain goats.**

mountain goat

mountain laurel—An evergreen bush that grows wild in the eastern United States. Its flower is pink or white, blooms in June, and has been named the state flower of Connecticut and Pennsylvania.
moun|tain laur|el (moun′tən lawr′əl) *noun.*

mountain lion—A large, wild cat that lives in North America and looks like a female lion.
moun|tain li|on (moun′tən lī′ən) *noun, plural* **mountain lions.**
• Other names for this animal are **cougar, panther,** and **puma.**

mountainous—**1.** Having a surface filled with mountains: *The* mountainous *area was difficult for the hikers to cross.* **2.** Big and high; very large: *There were* mountainous *sand dunes at the edge of the beach.*
moun|tain|ous (moun′tə nəs) *adjective.*

a at	i if	oo look	ch chalk		a in ago
ā ape	ī idle	ou out	ng sing		e in happen
ah calm	o odd	u ugly	sh ship	ə =	i in capital
aw all	ō oats	ū rule	th think		o in occur
e end	oi oil	ur turn	<u>th</u> their		u in upon
ē easy			zh treasure		

mourn—To grieve; show or feel great sadness: *The whole country* mourned *the death of its president.*
mourn (mawrn) *verb,* **mourned, mourning.**

mourning dove—A wild dove found throughout the United States. It gets its name from its mournful call.
mourn|ing dove (mawr′ning duv) *noun, plural* **mourning doves.**

mourning dove

mouse—**1.** A small, fast-moving animal with soft brown, gray, or white fur. It has a pointed nose, small ears, and a thin tail with almost no hair. There are many kinds of mice, among them the common house mouse and the field mouse.   **2.** A mechanism for use with a computer. It is moved across a flat surface to control the image on the screen.
mouse (mous) *noun, plural* **mice.**

mouse (definition 1)

moustache—*See* **mustache.**
mous|tache (mus′tash *or* mə stash′) *noun, plural* **moustaches.**

mouth—**1.** The section of the body containing the tongue and teeth, which opens to allow food to pass through.   **2.** An opening through which something passes: *the* mouth *of a bottle; the* mouth *of a river.*
mouth (mouth) *noun, plural* **mouths.**

■ **down in the mouth:** Sad; low in spirits; less than enthusiastic: *The team was very* down in the mouth *after losing the big game.*
make (one's) **mouth water:** To excite the appetite; cause pleasure of expecting: *The thought of his birthday presents* made *his* mouth water.

● See picture at **alimentary canal.**

mouthpiece—That part of a musical instrument or other object that is placed against or inside the mouth.
mouth|piece (mouth′pēs′) *noun, plural* **mouthpieces.**

move—**1.** To go or cause to go from one place to another: *to* move *the chair closer to the window; to* move *to another city.*   **2.** To go on; make progress: *Our plans to start a business are finally* moving.   **3.** To affect one in an emotional way: *The sad music* moved *her to tears.*   **4.** To begin or maintain the action of: *An electric engine*

mountain lion

moves *that mixer*. **5.** To inspire or cause an action: *Her good example* moved *me to try harder*. **6.** To make a proposal at a meeting: *The vice-president* moved *that the dues of the club be increased*. *Verb*.
—**1.** Action; motion: *Every* move *of her hands signaled a different command to the dog she was training*. **2.** One's turn in certain kinds of games: *Everyone else had to wait, because it was now his* move. *Noun*.
move (mūv) *verb*, **moved, moving;** *noun, plural* **moves.**

movement—**1.** Motion; going: *a* movement *of the head; a car in* movement. **2.** A mechanism with many moving parts: *The clock's* movement *was so old that we could not get replacement parts*. **3.** A group of people interested in achieving a particular goal, or the actions of this group: *He joined a* movement *to improve the city parks*.
move|ment (mūv′mənt) *noun, plural* **movements.**

mover—A person or business whose work is taking people's belongings from one place to another: *He hired a* mover *when he took his office to another building*.
mov|er (mū′vər) *noun, plural* **movers.**

movie—**1.** A strip of film that is projected onto a screen and viewed as a moving picture. **2.** The place where a moving picture is shown or viewed.
mov|ie (mū′vē) *noun, plural* **movies.**

mow—**1.** To use a machine with a sharp blade to cut down grass, grain, or hay: *My weekly chore in the summer is to* mow *the lawn*. **2.** To cause the destruction of large numbers: *The strong wind* mowed *down all the flowers in our garden*.
mow (mō) *verb,* **mowed, mowed** or **mown, mowing.**

mown—*See* **mow.**
mown (mōn) *verb.*

Mr.—The abbreviation for **mister.**

Mrs.—A title used in front of a woman's name to show that she is married.
Mrs. (mis′iz) *noun.*

Ms.—A title used before a woman's name.
Ms. (miz) *noun.*

mt.—An abbreviation for **mountain.**

Mt.—An abbreviation for **mount.**

mtn. or **Mtn.**—An abbreviation for **mountain.**

much—In a large amount or quantity, or to a great degree: much *help;* much *food; too* much *snow*. *Adjective*.
—**1.** A large amount, quantity, or degree: *Because* much *of the weekend was sunny, I played outdoors a lot*. **2.** Anything of value or significance: *He did not start with* much, *but he eventually became very rich*. *Noun*.
—**1.** To a very large degree: *He could swim* much *farther than I could*. **2.** Almost; nearly; about: *Her watch is* much *like the one I just bought*. *Adverb*.
much (much) *adjective,* **more, most;** *noun; adverb,* **more, most.**

mud—Dirt mixed with water.
mud (mud) *noun, plural* **muds.**

muddy—**1.** Having a surface cover of wet dirt: *their* muddy *boots;* muddy *floors*. **2.** Murky; not clear: *The sound coming from the speakers seemed* muddy, *so I moved to the front of the auditorium*.
mud|dy (mud′ē) *adjective,* **muddier, muddiest.**

muff—An article of clothing, shaped like a tube and open at each end, into which the hands can be inserted for warmth. It is usually covered with fur on the outside and is most often used by women and girls.
muff (muf) *noun, plural* **muffs.**

muffin—A form of bread, baked in a tin, that comes in small, individual servings.
muf|fin (muf′ən) *noun, plural* **muffins.**

muffle—To deaden or dull the sound of something, often by padding or wrapping with heavy cloth: *The heavy draperies* muffled *the sound of the stereo coming from the other room*.
muf|fle (muf′əl) *verb,* **muffled, muffling.**

muffler—**1.** A device used to dull or deaden noise: *All cars are required to have a* muffler *as part of the exhaust system*. **2.** A scarf wrapped about the neck for protection and comfort in cold weather.
muf|fler (muf′lər) *noun, plural* **mufflers.**

mug—**1.** A tall cup with a handle, usually made of pottery or metal, that is used for drinking: *a coffee* mug. **2.** A hoodlum; thug: *He prepared to defend himself when the* mug *began to threaten him*. *Noun*.
—To begin a fight with or attack someone in order to steal something he or she has; assault: *Because the bank messenger was carrying a lot*

a at	i if	oo look	ch chalk		a in ago
ā ape	ī idle	ou out	ng sing		e in happen
ah calm	o odd	u ugly	sh ship	ə =	i in capital
aw all	ō oats	ū rule	th think		o in occur
e end	oi oil	ur turn	th their		u in upon
ē easy			zh treasure		

of money, he was afraid of being mugged. *Verb.*
mug (mug) *noun, plural* **mugs;** *verb,* **mugged, mugging.**

muggy—Warm and damp: *The day was so muggy that we felt tired even in the shade.*
mug|gy (mug′ē) *adjective,* **muggier, muggiest.**

Muhammad or **Muhammed**—An Arab prophet who founded the Muslim religion, Islam. He was born about A.D. 570 and died in A.D. 632. His teachings are in the Koran, the sacred book of Islam. They say that Allah is the one God, Muhammad is His prophet, and one must treat others fairly.
Mu|ham|mad or **Mu|ham|med** (mū ham′əd) *noun.*
• This word is also spelled **Mohammed.**

mulberry—A tree that has small, dark berries with a sweet flavor. A certain kind of mulberry has leaves that silkworms feed on.
mul|ber|ry (mul′ber′ē) *noun, plural* **mulberries.**

mule—An animal that has a horse as its mother and a donkey as its father. It looks a great deal like a horse, except that it has the long ears, hoofs, and tail of a donkey. It is very strong and is generally used to haul and carry heavy loads.
mule (myūl) *noun, plural* **mules.**

mule

multi-—A prefix meaning "many." A multivitamin pill contains many vitamins.

Word Power

You can understand the meanings of many words that begin with **multi-,** if you add the meaning of the prefix to the meaning of the rest of the word.
  multiengine: having many engines
  multivolume: having many volumes

multiple—More than one; several; many: multiple *births;* multiple-*choice test;* multiple *stops along a bus route. Adjective.*
  —A number containing a smaller number more than one time without anything left over. Eight is a multiple of 4 because 8 contains 4 exactly twice. Ten is not a multiple of 4. Although 10 contains 4 twice, there is a remainder of 2. *Noun.*
mul|ti|ple (mul′tə pəl) *adjective; noun, plural* **multiples.**

multiplication—In mathematics, a process of adding a number a certain amount of times; the act of multiplying. The multiplication of 3 times 4 is the act of adding 3 four times, to equal 12.
mul|ti|pli|ca|tion (mul′tə plə kā′shən) *noun.*

multiply—1. To add a number a certain amount of times: *When one multiplies 3 by 4, 3 is added 4 times, with 12 as a result.* 2. To get bigger in number or quantity: *As the crowd watching the parade multiplied, everyone grew noisier and more excited.*
mul|ti|ply (mul′tə plī) *verb,* **multiplied, multiplying.**

multitude—A group of people or things that is very large in size: *A multitude of ideas flooded his mind.*
mul|ti|tude (mul′tə tūd *or* mul′tə tyūd) *noun, plural* **multitudes.**
• Synonyms: **crowd, crush, throng**

mumble—To speak softly without pronouncing the words carefully: *It is hard to understand you when you mumble.*
mum|ble (mum′bəl) *verb,* **mumbled, mumbling.**
• Synonyms: **mutter, whisper**
  Antonyms: See synonyms at **cry,** *verb* **2.**

mummy—A dead body, wrapped in strips of cloth and kept from decay. The ancient Egyptians produced mummies that have remained preserved for thousands of years.
mum|my (mum′ē) *noun, plural* **mummies.**

mumps—A disease that is easily spread from person to person and results in a painful swelling of glands in the neck, jaw, and cheeks.
mumps (mumps) *noun.*

munch—To chew at a steady pace, making a crunching sound: *She* munched *on celery sticks and crackers.*
munch (munch) *verb,* **munched, munching.**

municipal—Having to do with town or city activities, management, and government: *The* municipal *offices are located in the town hall.*
mu|ni|ci|pal (myū nis′ə pəl) *adjective.*
• Synonyms: **civic, urban**

mural—A large picture painted on a wall, usually covering all or much of the wall.
mu|ral (**myoor′**əl) *noun, plural* **murals.**

murder—The killing of one person by another in violation of the law and on purpose. *Noun.*
—To kill a person in violation of the law and on purpose. *Verb.*
mur|der (**mur′**dər) *noun, plural* **murders;** *verb,* **murdered, murdering.**
- **get away with murder:** To do something wrong without being punished: *He always acts so innocent after he's misbehaved that he* gets away with murder.

murderer—One who kills another; assassin.
mur|der|er (**mur′**dər ər) *noun, plural* **murderers.**

murmur—A gentle sound that wavers and continues: *It was so quiet in the forest that we could hear the* murmur *of wind in the trees. Noun.*
—To make sounds softly and unclearly: *While studying his spelling, he* murmured *the letters to himself so he would remember them. Verb.*
mur|mur (**mur′**mər) *noun, plural* **murmurs;** *verb,* **murmured, murmuring.**

muscle—**1.** A tissue within the body that tightens and relaxes in order to cause a part of the body to move. It can be developed by exercise, so that it grows larger and gains strength. **2.** Bodily power; strength; might: *It takes* muscle *to dig a ditch.*
mus|cle (**mus′**əl) *noun, plural* **muscles.**
● A word that sounds the same is **mussel.**

Word History

Muscle comes from a Latin word meaning "a little mouse." Some muscles, when they move, look as though a little mouse were moving under a cloth.

---

muscular—Having big, powerful muscles; strong: *The* muscular *fellow lifted the heavy box with ease.*
mus|cu|lar (**mus′**kyə lər) *adjective.*
● Synonyms: **brawny, robust**

a at	i if	oo look	ch chalk		a in ago
ā ape	ī idle	ou out	ng sing		e in happen
ah calm	o odd	u ugly	sh ship	ə =	i in capital
aw all	ō oats	ū rule	th think		o in occur
e end	oi oil	ur turn	th their		u in upon
ē easy			zh treasure		

museum—A building or place where important objects of art, history, science, or some other field of interest are collected and set up for viewing by the people who visit.
mu|se|um (myū zē′əm) *noun, plural* **museums.**

mushroom—A small, fast-growing fungus often shaped like an umbrella. Some of the different kinds of mushrooms can be eaten, while other kinds cannot because they are poisonous. *Noun.*
—To spring up or develop very fast: *The gathering* mushroomed *into a crowd. Verb.*
mush|room (**mush′**rūm) *noun, plural* **mushrooms;** *verb,* **mushroomed, mushrooming.**

music—**1.** A form of art in which one creates an arrangement of sounds that is pleasant or interesting to hear: *She studies* music *with a famous violinist.* **2.** A particular arrangement of sounds for a voice to sing or for musical instruments to play: *He played a piece of* music *on the guitar.* **3.** Written notes, or musical signs, that show the sounds to be sung or played in a musical composition: *The piano teacher gave the students a new sheet of* music *to practice.*
mu|sic (**myū′**zik) *noun.*
- **face the music:** To accept going into a difficult situation: *When you forget to do your homework, you have to* face the music *in class.*
  music to (one's) **ears:** A sound or something said that is welcome or pleasant to hear: *Her compliments were* music to *my* ears.

Word Power

If you are interested in music, here are some useful words for you to know. You can find these words in this dictionary.

alto	duet	signature
bar	key	solo
bass	measure	soprano
beat	melody	staff
brass	note	string
chord	octave	tenor
chorus	percussion	tempo
clef	rhythm	woodwind

---

musical—Having to do with music: *a* musical *instrument;* musical *notes. Adjective.*
—A show or play in which the performers sing and dance. *Noun.*
mu|si|cal (myū′zə kəl) *adjective; noun, plural* **musicals.**

musician—Someone who is good at singing, playing a musical instrument, or writing musical compositions.
mu|si|cian (myū zish′ən) *noun, plural* **musicians.**

musket—A heavy gun with a long barrel that soldiers carried before the rifle was developed.
mus|ket (mus′kit) *noun, plural* **muskets.**

muskmelon—A sweet, juicy fruit with a hard skin, such as the cantaloupe and honeydew.
musk|mel|on (musk′mel′ən) *noun, plural* **muskmelons.**

musk ox—A large mammal like a cow, with long, shaggy hair and curved horns. It lives in very cold regions of North America.
musk ox (musk oks) *noun, plural* **musk oxen.**

musk ox

muskrat—A North American water animal that is similar to a rat but is larger and has webbed hind feet and a flat tail.
musk|rat (musk′rat′) *noun, plural* **muskrats** or **muskrat.**

muskrat

Muslim—A person who is a believer in the religion of Islam, founded by Muhammad.
Mus|lim (muz′ləm) *noun, plural* **Muslims.**
• This word is also spelled **Moslem.**

mussel—A soft-bodied animal that has a hard outer shell and is related to the clam. Mussels live in both salt and fresh water, and some can be eaten.
mus|sel (mus′əl) *noun, plural* **mussels.**

must—1. To have to do something out of necessity: *A robin* must *build a nest in which to lay its eggs.* 2. Ought to: *I* must *remember to thank my aunt for her gift.* 3. To be sure to: *The store* must *be closed by this time.*
must (must) *verb.*

mustache—Hair that grows on the upper lip of a man.
mus|tache (mus′tash *or* mə stash′) *noun, plural* **mustaches.**
• This word is also spelled **moustache.**

mustang—A small, wild horse that lives on the western plains of North America.
mus|tang (mus′tang) *noun, plural* **mustangs.**

mustard—A yellow spread or powder made from the seeds of a plant. It is used to give a sharp taste to food.
mus|tard (mus′tərd) *noun, plural* **mustards.**

muster—1. To gather or call together: *The children were* mustered *for the parade in the schoolyard.* 2. To bring or call up from within: *The boy had to* muster *up all his courage to jump down from the tree.*
mus|ter (mus′tər) *verb,* **mustered, mustering.**

mustn't—The contraction of "must not."
must|n't (mus′ənt).

mute—1. Not able to speak: *She had such a bad sore throat that she was* mute *for two days.* 2. Not speaking or making noise; silent: *We watched the magic tricks in* mute *amazement.* 3. Not pronounced: *The "k" in "knife" is* mute. *Adjective.*
—1. A person who cannot speak because of deafness, illness, or damage to the speech organs. 2. An object that is made to fit into a musical instrument, such as a trumpet or trombone, to soften the sound. *Noun.*
mute (myūt) *adjective; noun, plural* **mutes.**

mutiny—An act of rebellion against authority, especially by a group of sailors or soldiers against their leaders. *Noun.*
—To take part in a rebellion against authority: *The sailors* mutinied *against the cruel captain. Verb.*
mu|ti|ny (myū′tə nē) *noun, plural* **mutinies;** *verb,* **mutinied, mutinying.**

mutt—A dog of mixed breeds; mongrel.
mutt (mut) *noun, plural* **mutts.**

mutter—**1.** To speak unclearly in a low voice, with the lips barely open: *I could hear people muttering in the hall but could not understand what they were saying.* **2.** To complain: *The young man muttered about having to wear a tie and jacket on such a hot day. Verb.*
—Words spoken softly and unclearly; grumble: *A mutter was heard among the passengers when the train did not arrive on time. Noun.*
mut|ter (mut′ər) *verb,* **muttered, muttering;** *noun.*
  • Synonyms: **mumble, whisper,** for *verb* **1.** Antonyms: For *verb* **1,** see synonyms at **cry,** *verb* **2.**

mutton—The meat of a full-grown sheep.
mut|ton (mut′ən) *noun.*
  • See Language Fact at **pork.**

mutual—**1.** Done or felt by two or more persons toward each other: mutual *affection.*
2. Belonging to each one equally; shared: *We have a mutual interest in stamp collecting.*
mu|tu|al (myū′chū əl) *adjective.*

muzzle—**1.** The nose, mouth, and jaws of an animal, such as a dog, bear, or horse. **2.** An arrangement of straps fitted over an animal's mouth to keep it from biting. **3.** The opening of a gun through which the bullet is fired. *Noun.*
—To place an arrangement of straps over an animal's mouth: *Our dog had to be muzzled when we took him on the train. Verb.*
muz|zle (muz′əl) *noun, plural* **muzzles;** *verb,* **muzzled, muzzling.**

my—Belonging to the person speaking: *I painted my room blue. Adjective.*
—An expression showing surprise: My! *How wonderful you look! Interjection.*
my (mī) *adjective, interjection.*

myrtle—**1.** An evergreen vine with shiny leaves and blue flowers that is grown to cover an area of land. **2.** An evergreen shrub with glossy leaves, white flowers, and black berries.
myr|tle (mur′təl) *noun, plural* **myrtles.**

myself—**1.** A word that is used to refer to the person speaking or writing: *I bought* myself *a new notebook.* **2.** One's true or usual self: *I do not feel like* myself *in these funny clothes.*
my|self (mī self′) *pronoun, plural* **ourselves.**

mysterious—Difficult to understand or explain: *We were puzzled by the* mysterious *shadow on the wall.*
mys|te|ri|ous (mis tēr′ē əs) *adjective.*

mystery—**1.** Some hidden or secret thing that is beyond explanation or cannot be understood: *How the dog found its way home from so far away is a* mystery. **2.** A story, play, or movie about a suspenseful crime. It usually ends with a solution to the crime.
mys|ter|y (mis′tər ē) *noun, plural* **mysteries.**

myth—**1.** A story or tale that tries to explain something that has happened in the past or that occurs in nature. Myths often include gods, goddesses, and heroes. **2.** Any made-up person, thing, or idea: *The idea that a cat has nine lives is a popular* myth.
myth (mith) *noun, plural* **myths.**

mythical—Having to do with stories that try to explain the past or something in nature; existing only in the imagination: *One* mythical *beast was supposed to have been half man and half horse.*
myth|i|cal (mith′ə kəl) *adjective.*

mythology—**1.** A collection of old stories from one culture, region, or country: *Greek* mythology *includes many tales of gods, giants, and heroes.* **2.** The study of such stories.
my|thol|o|gy (mi thol′ə jē) *noun, plural* **mythologies.**

a at	i if	oo look	ch chalk		a in ago
ā ape	ī idle	ou out	ng sing		e in happen
ah calm	o odd	u ugly	sh ship	ə =	i in capital
aw all	ō oats	ū rule	th think		o in occur
e end	oi oil	ur turn	th their		u in upon
ē easy			zh treasure		

myrtle (definition 2)

About 1,900 years ago, the Romans gave the capital N its present form. The small letter n was first used about 1,500 years ago. It reached its present form about 500 years ago.

About 5,000 years ago, the ancient Egyptians used a symbol of a snake.

About 3,500 years ago, people in the Middle East made a similar symbol.

About 3,000 years ago, other people in the Middle East made the symbol much more simple.

About 2,600 years ago, the Greeks gave the letter this form. They called it *nu.*

N or n—The fourteenth letter of the alphabet: *There are two* n's *in "none."*
N, n (en) *noun, plural* **N's** or **Ns, n's** or **ns.**
N. or **N**—The abbreviation for **north.**
nag—To annoy by always finding fault: *My parents keep* nagging *me about the way I keep my room.*
nag (nag) *verb,* **nagged, nagging.**
nail—**1.** A small, thin piece of metal with a point at one end and a flattened cap at the other, used to fasten things together. Nails are pounded into wood by hitting the flat head of the nail with a hammer. **2.** The hard layer on the end of a finger or toe. *Noun.*
—To hold or fasten together with a nail or nails: *The store owner* nailed *the sign to the door. Verb.*
nail (nāl) *noun, plural* **nails;** *verb,* **nailed, nailing.**
■ **hit the nail on the head:** To be exactly right in saying, doing, or figuring out something: *He* hit the nail on the head *when he guessed that the clue was hidden inside the suitcase.*

common nail

finishing nail

nail (noun, definition 1)

naked—**1.** Without clothes; not covered: *After working in the hot sun with no shirt on, he found his* naked *back had become red and sore.*
2. Plain and simple; with nothing added: *The* naked *truth was that she did not know how to solve the problem.*
na|ked (nā′kid) *adjective.*
name—**1.** The word or phrase used to speak of or to address a particular person, animal, thing, or place: *My brother's* name *is John.* **2.** A mean or unkind word or phrase: *I felt insulted when the woman who bumped into me called me a* name. **3.** Reputation; fame: *My sister's kindness gave her a good* name *in the neighborhood. Noun.*
—**1.** To assign a word or phrase to identify someone or something: *We* named *our black cat "Coal."* **2.** To call or mention by using the word or phrase that identifies someone or something: *She* named *the six friends she would invite to her party.* **3.** To choose; appoint: *He was* named *the outstanding student in the school. Verb.*
name (nām) *noun, plural* **names;** *verb,* **named, naming.**
■ **in name only:** Appearing to be a certain thing, but not so in fact: *Our neighbor proved to be a friend* in name only, *for he did not help us when we needed him.*
● Synonyms: **designate, select,** for *verb* **3.** Antonyms: **discharge, dismiss, fire,** for *verb* **3.**
namely—That is to say; by name: *There are three types of flowers in the garden,* namely *roses, tulips, and irises.*
name|ly (nām′lē) *adverb.*

nap¹—A short sleep, usually taken in the daytime: *I was so tired from the morning's work that I took a* nap *after lunch. Noun.*
—To sleep for a little time; doze: *My cat likes to* nap *on a soft pillow. Verb.*
nap (nap) *noun, plural* **naps;** *verb,* **napped, napping.**

nap²—The short threads that give a soft, fuzzy texture to cloth: *the towel's* nap.
nap (nap) *noun.*

napkin—A piece of cloth or paper that is used during a meal to protect clothing or to wipe one's mouth and hands.
nap|kin (nap′kin) *noun, plural* **napkins.**

narcissus—A plant, such as the daffodil, having yellow or white flowers and long, thin leaves. It grows from a bulb and blooms in the spring.
nar|cis|sus (nahr sis′əs) *noun, plural* **narcissuses.**
• See picture at **daffodil.**

narcotic—A type of drug that encourages sleep and reduces pain. Narcotics taken in large amounts are very harmful and can cause death.
nar|cot|ic (nahr kot′ik) *noun, plural* **narcotics.**

narrate—To tell a story; describe: *His cousin* narrated *the events of his camping adventure.*
nar|rate (na rāt′ *or* nar′āt) *verb,* **narrated, narrating.**
• Synonyms: **recite, relate**

narrow—**1.** Small in width; slender: *The hallway was too* narrow *for two people to walk side by side.* **2.** Limited in size or range: *His knowledge of trees was so* narrow *that he could not tell a pine from a maple.* **3.** Barely successful; very close: *Our team had a* narrow *victory, winning by only one point. Adjective.*
—To make or become smaller in width or range: *She* narrowed *her choices down to the blue or red hat. Verb.*
—narrows: A part of a river or other body of water that is especially small in width. *Noun.*
nar|row (nar′ō) *adjective,* **narrower, narrowest;** *verb,* **narrowed, narrowing;** *noun.*

narwhal—A whale that lives in arctic waters. The male narwhal has a long tusk like a horn.

narwhal: The male narwhal has a spiral ivory tusk jutting out of the left side of its head.

nar|whal (nahr′hwəl *or* nahr′wəl) *noun, plural* **narwhals.**

nasal—Of or relating to the nose: *The boxer's nose was crooked because his* nasal *bone had been broken.*
na|sal (nā′zəl) *adjective.*

nasturtium—A plant with bright yellow, orange, or red flowers. Its large, sharp-tasting seeds can be used to flavor food.
na|stur|tium (nə stur′shəm) *noun, plural* **nasturtiums.**

Word History

Nasturtium may come from two Latin words meaning "nose twist." The leaves and seeds of this plant have a very strong taste and smell. Probably, some people reacted to the taste and smell by making a face.

---

nasty—**1.** Unkind; spiteful; mean: *In a* nasty *fit of temper, the girl broke her brother's toy.* **2.** Disgusting; filthy; offensive: *the* nasty *smell.* **3.** Very unpleasant: *It is my responsibility to give her the bad news, and it is a* nasty *job.* **4.** Harmful or serious: *a* nasty *cut on the leg.*
nas|ty (nas′tē) *adjective,* **nastier, nastiest.**

nation—A country in which a group of people live together under one government, sharing a common language or languages: *Athletes from many* nations *competed at these games.*
na|tion (nā′shən) *noun, plural* **nations.**

national—Of or having to do with an entire nation: *The Fourth of July is a* national *holiday.*
na|tion|al (nash′ə nəl) *adjective.*

nationalism—A strong feeling of loyalty to one's own country; patriotism.
na|tion|al|ism (nash′ə nə liz′əm) *noun.*

a at	i if	oo look	ch chalk		a in ago
ā ape	ī idle	ou out	ng sing		e in happen
ah calm	o odd	u ugly	sh ship	ə =	i in capital
aw all	ō oats	ū rule	th think		o in occur
e end	oi oil	ur turn	th their		u in upon
ē easy			zh treasure		

nationality—1. The condition of being a member of a certain nation: *Her parents have different* nationalities. 2. A group of people who live together under one government, sharing a common language or languages: *In social studies class, we learned about many different* nationalities.
na|tion|al|i|ty (nash'ə **nal'**ə tē) *noun, plural* **nationalities.**

nationwide—Extending throughout all parts of a country: *The drop in rainfall across the United States has hurt farmers* nationwide.
na|tion|wide (nā'shən wīd') *adjective.*

native—1. One who was born in a particular place or country: *She is a* native *of the mountains.* 2. A person, animal, or plant that lives or grows naturally in a particular place: *The giraffe is a* native *of Africa. Noun.*
—1. Born in a particular place or country: *He is a* native *Canadian.* 2. Belonging to a person by nature of place of birth: *French is her* native *language.* 3. Naturally born or raised in a particular region or place: *The tiger is* native *to Asia. Adjective.*
na|tive (nā'tiv) *noun, plural* **natives;** *adjective.*

Native American—An American Indian. Many people prefer **Native American** to American Indian.
Na|tive A|mer|i|can (nā'tiv ə mer'ə kən) *noun, plural* **Native Americans.**

NATO—An organization that provides for the common defense of the United States, Canada, and many of the countries in Western Europe. The name of the organization was formed from the first letters of North Atlantic Treaty Organization.
NA|TO (nā'tō) *noun.*

natural—1. As found in nature; not produced by humans: *The* natural *course of the river was quickly changed by the new dam.* 2. Of or having to do with nature: *Tornadoes are a dangerous* natural *event.* 3. From birth: *She has a* natural *musical talent.* 4. Coming at an appropriate time in a life or a series of events: *death by* natural *causes.* 5. Having a close likeness to nature; lifelike: *The color of the artificial flower was really very* natural. *Adjective.*
—Someone who is able to do something easily without being taught: *She is a* natural *at gymnastics. Noun.*
nat|u|ral (nach'ər əl) *adjective; noun, plural* **naturals.**

naturalist—A person who studies animals and plants.
nat|u|ral|ist (nach'ər ə list) *noun, plural* **naturalists.**

naturally—1. According to what one might expect; of course: Naturally, *it got colder when the sun went down.* 2. Without help or training; by nature: *having* naturally *curly hair.* 3. In a normal way: *The officer was distrustful because the suspect did not answer the questions* naturally.
nat|u|ral|ly (nach'ər ə lē) *adverb.*

nature—1. The physical world; all things not made by humans: *To me, a sunset is one of the most beautiful things in* nature. 2. The basic qualities of a person or thing: *It is in the* nature *of cats to climb trees.* 3. A particular variety or type: *He enjoys art, music, and things of that* nature.
na|ture (nā'chər) *noun, plural* **natures.**
• Synonyms: **character, disposition,** for 2.

naughty—Behaving in a disobedient way; bad: *He was caught with his hand in the cookie jar and was scolded for being* naughty.
naugh|ty (naw'tē) *adjective,* **naughtier, naughtiest.**
• Synonyms: **wicked, wrong**
Antonyms: **good, moral, right**

nausea—A feeling of sickness in the stomach, with a need to vomit.
nau|sea (naw'shə *or* naw'zē ə) *noun.*

nautical—Of or about ships, sailors, or sailing: *Her blouse was printed with anchors and other* nautical *designs.*
nau|ti|cal (naw'tə kəl) *adjective.*

Word Power

If you are interested in boats and ships, here are some useful nautical words to know. Each is a thing or term that has to do with boats and ships. You can find these words in this dictionary.

aft	gangplank	rig
anchor	helm	rigging
boom	hull	rudder
bow[3]	jib	sail
buoy	keel	starboard
cabin	line	stern
cockpit	mainsail	tiller
crow's nest	mast	transom
deck	oar	wheel
dock	port[2]	winch
galley	prow	windlass

• See also Word Power at **boat.**

nautilus

nautilus—One of two small, soft-bodied animals with spiral shells that live in tropical seas.
nau|ti|lus (naw′tə ləs) *noun, plural* **nautiluses.**

naval—Of or about the navy or ships: *After a great* naval *battle, the young sea captain claimed his first victory.*
na|val (nā′vəl) *adjective.*
• A word that sounds the same is **navel.**

navel—The small, hollow area in the center of the belly. This mark shows where a cord attached the baby to the mother before birth.
na|vel (nā′vəl) *noun, plural* **navels.**
• A word that sounds the same is **naval.**

navigate—**1.** To sail or steer an airplane or ship: *The sailor* navigated *his boat through the narrow channel.* **2.** To travel on or across: *The ferry* navigates *the harbor every day.*
nav|i|gate (nav′ə gāt) *verb,* **navigated, navigating.**

navigator—**1.** A person whose job it is to direct or steer a ship or airplane. **2.** A person who sails over the seas, often to explore unknown areas: *Christopher Columbus was a famous* navigator.
nav|i|ga|tor (nav′ə gā′tər) *noun, plural* **navigators.**

navy—**1.** A nation's warships. **2.** The people, equipment, and supplies that make up a nation's sea force. **3.** A very dark shade of blue. *Noun.*
—Being very dark blue in color. *Adjective.*
na|vy (nā′vē) *noun, plural* **navies;** *adjective.*

nay—A way of saying "no" that is not often used now. *Adverb.*
—A negative response or vote: *There were so many* nays *that the new highway plan was defeated. Noun.*
nay (nā) *adverb; noun, plural* **nays.**
• A word that sounds the same is **neigh.**

NE—The abbreviation for **northeast.**

near—Not far away in distance or time: *His birthday draws* near. *Adverb.*
—**1.** Not far off; close by: *Keep walking a little farther; the house is* near. **2.** Closely related; very familiar: *a* near *relative.* **3.** Almost happening; barely avoided: *He had a* near *miss but did not hit the window with the ball. Adjective.*
—Close to: *She lives* near *her grandmother's home. Preposition.*
—To come close: *We hurried to finish the decorations as the day of the party* neared. *Verb.*
near (nēr) *adverb; adjective,* **nearer, nearest;** *preposition; verb,* **neared, nearing.**

nearby—Close by; not far away: *They ice-skate on a* nearby *pond. She jogs* nearby.
near|by (nēr′bī′) *adjective, adverb.*

nearly—Just about; almost but not quite: *It is* nearly *time to go home.*
near|ly (nēr′lē) *adverb.*
• Synonyms: **approximately, roughly**
Antonyms: **exactly, just, precisely**

near-sighted or **nearsighted**—Able to see close objects more clearly than far away ones: *Although he is* near-sighted, *his new glasses allow him to see the blackboard clearly from the back row.*
near-sight|ed or **near|sight|ed (nēr′sī′tid)** *adjective.*

neat—**1.** Clean and orderly; tidy: *Because she takes great care with it, her homework is usually* neat *as well as correct.* **2.** Showing skill or clever thinking: *The math teacher taught them a* neat *solution to the problem.* **3.** Very good; terrific: *They had a* neat *time sledding.*
neat (nēt) *adjective,* **neater, neatest.**

necessarily—As a result: *Having a lot of money does not* necessarily *mean you will be happy.*
nec|es|sar|i|ly (nes′ə sār′ə lē) *adverb.*

necessary—**1.** Required; needed: *Gasoline is* necessary *for the operation of an automobile.* **2.** Bound to happen; not to be otherwise: *Poor crops were a* necessary *outcome of the dry growing season.*
nec|es|sar|y (nes′ə sār′ē) *adjective.*

necessity—**1.** The condition of being required or needed: *The* necessity *of eating proper foods in order to remain healthy is sometimes forgotten.*

a at	i if	oo look	ch chalk		a in ago
ā ape	ī idle	ou out	ng sing		e in happen
ah calm	o odd	u ugly	sh ship	ə =	i in capital
aw all	ō oats	ū rule	th think		o in occur
e end	oi oil	ur turn	th their		u in upon
ē easy			zh treasure		

2. Something that is required or needed: *Warm clothes were a* necessity *for the winter camping trip.*

ne|ces|si|ty (nəs ses′ə tē) *noun, plural* **necessities.**

neck—**1.** The part of the body that joins the head with the shoulders. **2.** The portion of a piece of clothing that covers or fits around this body part: *Her blouse had lace around the* neck. **3.** A narrow part of something: *The cork became stuck in the* neck *of the bottle. Noun.*

neck (nek) *noun, plural* **necks.**

■ **neck and neck:** Running very close or evenly: *The boys ran* neck and neck, *and the race ended in a tie.*

neckerchief—A scarf or piece of cloth that is worn around the neck.

neck|er|chief (nek′ər chif) *noun, plural* **neckerchiefs.**

necklace—A piece of jewelry worn around the neck, such as a gold chain or a string of beads.

neck|lace (nek′lis) *noun, plural* **necklaces.**

necktie—A narrow piece of cloth placed under a shirt collar and knotted in front. A necktie is most often worn by men or boys, especially with a sport coat or suit.

neck|tie (nek′tī′) *noun, plural* **neckties.**

nectar—A sweet liquid found in many flowers. It is the substance from which bees make honey.

nec|tar (nek′tər) *noun, plural* **nectars.**

nectarine—A kind of firm peach with a smooth outer skin.

nec|tar|ine (nek′tə rēn′) *noun, plural* **nectarines.**

need—**1.** The lack of something required or wanted: *The tired girl has a* need *for sleep.* **2.** Something necessary: *Food is a basic* need. **3.** Necessity; obligation: *There is no* need *for you to help.* **4.** A period of bad luck or difficulty: *The charity provides warm clothes to persons in* need. *Noun.*
—**1.** To require; have to have: *The sun is bright, and she will* need *sunglasses to drive.* **2.** To have to do; have to be; must: *I* need *to be home for dinner. Verb.*

need (nēd), *noun, plural* **needs;** *verb,* **needed, needing.**

needle—**1.** A short, thin tool used in sewing. It has a point at one end and a hole in the other. **2.** A metal or plastic rod used to make stitches in knitting. **3.** A thin pointer on a compass or dial. **4.** A slender, hollow tube used to inject fluids into the body or withdraw fluids from the body: *The nurse used a* needle *to remove some of his*

blood *for testing.* **5.** A slender, pointed leaf of a fir or pine tree. **6.** Anything thin and sharp like a needle.

nee|dle (nē′dəl) *noun, plural* **needles.**

■ **a needle in a haystack:** Something that is very hard or impossible to find: *The little girl looked for her lost button, but with all the pebbles on the path, it was like looking for* a needle in a haystack.

needless—Of no use; unnecessary: *a* needless *expense.*

need|less (nēd′lis) *adjective.*

needlework—Work done with a needle, such as sewing or knitting.

nee|dle|work (nē′dəl wurk′) *noun.*

needn't—A contraction for "need not."

need|n't (nē′dənt) *verb.*

needy—Without enough money, food, or clothing to live on; very poor: *The school collected cans of food for the* needy *families in town.*

need|y (nē′dē) *adjective,* **needier, neediest.**

negative—**1.** Saying "no"; expressing a refusal: *a* negative *reply.* **2.** Not helpful; disagreeable: *a* negative *attitude.* **3.** A number or amount less than zero: −4 *is a* negative *number.* **4.** A type of electrical charge. **5.** Showing that a certain condition or disease is not in the body: *He was relieved that the results of his medical tests were all* negative. *Adjective.*
—**1.** A word or phrase that expresses a refusal: *The answer "No" is a* negative. **2.** A photographic image in which the dark and light areas of the original subject are reversed: *They had extra prints of the photograph made from its* negative. *Noun.*

neg|a|tive (neg′ə tiv) *adjective; noun, plural* **negatives.**

neglect—**1.** To not give proper care or attention: *The hungry kitten had been* neglected *by its mother.* **2.** To not do something: *He* neglected *to brush his teeth before going to bed. Verb.*
—**1.** The act of not giving proper care or attention: *Her* neglect *of the garden allowed many weeds to grow.* **2.** The condition of not getting proper care or attention: *The unused shed in the woods has fallen into* neglect. *Noun.*

neg|lect (ni glekt′) *verb,* **neglected, neglecting;** *noun.*

● Synonyms: **disregard, ignore, overlook,** for *verb* **1.**

negligence—A failure to give proper care or attention; carelessness: *The bowl lay shattered on the floor because of his* negligence *in carrying it.*

neg|li|gence (neg′lə jəns) *noun.*

negligent—Showing lack of care or attention: *Because he was* negligent *about cleaning his room, it became very dirty.*
neg|li|gent (neg′lə gənt) *adjective.*

negotiate—**1.** To discuss together so as to decide the conditions of: *The teachers met with the school board to* negotiate *a contract for the next year.* **2.** To talk things over in order to come to an agreement: *After years of arguing, the two neighbors were ready to* negotiate.
ne|go|ti|ate (ni gō′shē āt) *verb,* **negotiated, negotiating.**

Negro—A member of the black race; a person who is, or whose ancestors were, native to central and southern Africa. *Noun.*
—Of or relating to this race or a member of this race. *Adjective.*
Ne|gro (nē′grō) *noun, plural* **Negroes;** *adjective.*

Language Fact

The term "black" is now considered preferable to **Negro** when referring to this race or to a member of this race.

---

neigh—The sound made by a horse. *Noun.*
—To make such a sound. *Verb.*
neigh (nā) *noun, plural* **neighs;** *verb,* **neighed, neighing.**
• A word that sounds the same is **nay.**

neighbor—**1.** Someone who lives next to or near another: *The two children play together often because they are* neighbors. **2.** Someone or something that is next to or close to another: *The school is a* neighbor *of the park.*
neigh|bor (nā′bər) *noun, plural* **neighbors.**

neighborhood—**1.** A small area where people live within a town or city: *Our* neighborhood *has many playgrounds.* **2.** Those who live near one another in such an area: *The entire* neighborhood *attends an annual July picnic.*
neigh|bor|hood (nā′bər hood) *noun, plural* **neighborhoods.**

neither—Not the one or the other; not either: *Neither apple is ripe yet. Neither he nor she won. Neither of the hats fits him.*

neither (ne′thər *or* nī′thər) *adjective, conjunction, pronoun.*

nene—A rare Hawaiian goose that is grayish-brown with a black face and bill. It is Hawaii's state bird.
nene (nā′nā′) *noun, plural* **nenes.**

nene

neon—A gas without color or smell, found in very small amounts in the air. Glass tubes containing neon are sometimes used in colored electric signs. It is a chemical element.
ne|on (nē′on) *noun.*

nephew—**1.** The son of one's brother or sister. **2.** The son of one's brother-in-law or sister-in-law.
neph|ew (nef′yū) *noun, plural* **nephews.**

Neptune—The eighth planet from the sun.
Nep|tune (nep′tūn *or* nep′tyūn) *noun.*
• See picture at **solar system.**

nerve—**1.** One of the threadlike fibers that carry messages to and from the brain or spinal cord and other parts of the body. Nerves control movement and make sensation possible. **2.** Courage; daring: *He did not have the* nerve *to try the highest ski jump.*
nerve (nurv) *noun, plural* **nerves.**

nervous—**1.** Easily made excited or worried: *a* nervous *driver.* **2.** Worried; fearful: *Traveling on airplanes makes her* nervous.
nerv|ous (nur′vəs) *adjective.*
• Synonyms: **tense², upset,** for **1.**
  Antonyms: **placid, tranquil,** for **1.**

-ness—A suffix that means "quality" or "state of being." *Darkness* means the quality or state of being dark.

a at	i if	oo look	ch chalk		⌈ a in ago
ā ape	ī idle	ou out	ng sing		e in happen
ah calm	o odd	u ugly	sh ship	ə =	i in capital
aw all	ō oats	ū rule	th think		o in occur
e end	oi oil	ur turn	th their		⌊ u in upon
ē easy			zh treasure		

nest—1. A shelter made by a bird to lay its eggs and raise its young. 2. Such a shelter made and used by other animals for laying eggs and raising young. 3. A group of birds or other animals living in such a shelter: *a nest of sparrows.* 4. A comfortable place to sleep or take shelter: *The kitten made a nest in the basket of clothes. Noun.*
—To make or live in such a shelter: *Sea gulls nest among the rocks along the shore. Verb.*
nest (nest) *noun, plural* **nests;** *verb,* **nested, nesting.**

nestle—1. To lie comfortably and securely: *The boy felt safe nestled in his father's arms.* 2. To press close so as to feel sheltered: *The puppy nestled up to its mother.*
nes|tle (nes′əl) *verb,* **nestled, nestling.**
● Synonyms: **cuddle, snuggle,** for **1.**

net[1]—A piece of material with a regular pattern of evenly spaced holes: *She hit the volleyball high over the* net. *Noun.*
—To catch with such a piece of material: *The fisherman* netted *six fish. Verb.*
net (net) *noun, plural* **nets;** *verb,* **netted, netting.**

net[2]—The amount remaining after all costs and other subtractions have been made: *He made ten dollars selling cookies, but after his costs his* net *profit was four dollars. Adjective.*
—To bring as a profit: *The cookie sale* netted *him four dollars. Verb.*
net (net) *adjective; verb,* **netted, netting.**

network—1. A system of lines or other objects that cross: *a network of streets.* 2. A group of radio or television stations that use many of the same programs.
net|work (net′wurk′) *noun, plural* **networks.**

neutral—1. Not taking any side in a disagreement: *He was* neutral *on the issue of whether the town should build a new road.*
2. Having little or no color: *Gray is considered a* neutral *color.* 3. In chemistry, a substance that is neither acid nor base. *Adjective.*
—In a vehicle, the gear position that does not send power from the engine: *When a car is in* neutral, *it cannot move. Noun.*
neu|tral (nū′trəl *or* nyū′trəl) *adjective, noun.*

neutron—A small particle with no electrical charge that is found in the nucleus of an atom.
neu|tron (nū′tron *or* nyū′tron) *noun, plural* **neutrons.**

never—1. Not at any time: *She has* never *skied.*
2. In no way: *He will* never *know the difference.*
nev|er (nev′ər) *adverb.*

nevertheless—In spite of that; still: *Although it was raining, she* nevertheless *walked to the library.*
nev|er|the|less (nev′ər thə les′) *adverb.*

new—1. Having just been made: *He was anxious to buy the* new *record album.* 2. Having just been discovered, learned, or found: *The doctor was pleased with the* new *medicine for the disease.*
3. Never before experienced; not familiar: *He could not type quickly because the skill was* new *to him.* 4. Starting again: *the* new *year.*
new (nū *or* nyū) *adjective,* **newer, newest.**
● Words that sound the same are **gnu** and **knew.**

newborn—Just now or very recently born: *The* newborn *baby was a joy to her parents.*
new|born (nū′bawrn′ *or* nyū′bawrn′) *adjective.*

newcomer—Someone who has arrived recently: *Being a* newcomer *to the school, he had difficulty finding his classroom.*
new|com|er (nū′kum′ər) *or* nyū′kum′ər) *noun, plural* **newcomers.**

newfangled—New and unusual: *newfangled clothes.*
new|fan|gled (nū′fang′gəld *or* nyū′fang′gəld) *adjective.*

Newfoundland—A large working dog with a long, black coat, a large head, a long bushy tail, and webbed feet. Originally bred in Newfoundland, Canada, these dogs are good

Newfoundland

swimmers and are often used in water rescues.
New|found|land (nū′ fən lənd *or*
nū found′lənd) *noun, plural* **Newfoundlands.**

newly—Recently: *Are the* newly *painted walls dry yet?*
new|ly (nū′lē *or* nyū′lē) *adverb.*

news—Information about something that has recently happened: *Her letter contained much* news *about the family.*
news (nūz *or* nyūz) *noun.*
■ **break the news:** To tell someone something new: *The boy was anxious to* break the news *to his friends that he just got a dog.*

newscast—A radio or television show that broadcasts the news.
news|cast (nūz′kast′ *or* nyūz′kast′) *noun, plural* **newscasts.**

newspaper—Sheets of paper that are printed daily or weekly, presenting news, opinions, and advertisements.
news|pa|per (nūz′pā′pər *or* nyūz′pā′pər) *noun, plural* **newspapers.**

newt—A small salamander that lives in or near water.
newt (nūt *or* nyūt) *noun, plural* **newts.**

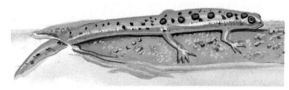

newt

New Testament—The part of the Bible presenting the life and teachings of Jesus and his disciples.
New Tes|ta|ment (nū tes′tə mənt *or* nyū tes′tə mənt) *noun.* Abbreviation: NT

New Year's Day—The first day of the year, January 1. It is a legal holiday in the United States, Canada, and many other countries.
New Year's Day (nū yērz dā *or* nyū yērz dā) *noun.*

next—Nearest in time or place: *He lives in the* next *house. Adjective.*
—Immediately following in time, place, or order: *Who goes* next? *Adverb.*
next (nekst) *adjective, adverb.*

next-door—In or at the nearest house, apartment, or building: *Our* next-door *neighbor takes in our mail when we go on vacation.*
next-door (nekst′dawr′) *adjective.*

next door—Located in or at the nearest house, apartment, or building: *Her best friend lives* next door.
next door (nekst′dawr′) *adverb.*

nibble—To eat with small, quick bites: *The rabbits* nibbled *on the lettuce. Verb.*
—A small, quick bite: *The fish took a* nibble *at the bait. Noun.*
nib|ble (nib′əl) *verb,* **nibbled, nibbling;** *noun, plural* **nibbles.**

nice—**1.** Pleasant; delightful: *a* nice *time at the beach.* **2.** Kind; considerate: *It was* nice *of you to come with me.* **3.** Showing skill: *The bookcase is a* nice *piece of work.*
nice (nīs) *adjective,* **nicer, nicest.**

nick—A small cut or chip in a surface: *The knife made a* nick *in the table. Noun.*
—To make such a mark in a surface: *Dad* nicked *his chin when he shaved. Verb.*
nick (nik) *noun, plural* **nicks;** *verb,* **nicked, nicking.**
■ **in the nick of time:** At the last moment: *When we saw that the gates were about to close, we knew we had arrived* in the nick of time.

nickel—**1.** A silvery metal that is hard and strong. It is a chemical element. **2.** A coin of the United States or Canada worth five cents.
nick|el (nik′əl) *noun, plural* **nickels.**

Word History

Nickel comes from a German word meaning ''copper devil.'' Stone containing this metal looks as if it has copper in it. People used to value copper much more than nickel. When they found stone with nickel but no copper, they blamed their bad luck on a devil.

---

nickname—A name or form of a name used instead of or along with one's given name: *Because he is smiling all the time, his* nickname *is ''Happy.'' Noun.*
—To call by a name other than one's given name: *He* nicknamed *his sister ''Sis.'' Verb.*
nick|name (nik′nām′) *noun, plural* **nicknames;** *verb,* **nicknamed, nicknaming.**

a at	i if	oo look	ch chalk		a in ago
ā ape	ī idle	ou out	ng sing		e in happen
ah calm	o odd	u ugly	sh ship	ə =	i in capital
aw all	ō oats	ū rule	th think		o in occur
e end	oi oil	ur turn	th their		u in upon
ē easy			zh treasure		

nicotine—A harmful substance found in tobacco plants. Cigars and cigarettes contain nicotine.
nic|o|tine (nik′ə tēn) *noun.*

niece—1. A daughter of one's brother or sister. 2. A daughter of one's brother-in-law or sister-in-law.
niece (nēs) *noun, plural* **nieces.**

night—1. The time between the setting and the rising of the sun, especially the hours of darkness. 2. The darkness that occurs at night.
night (nīt) *noun, plural* **nights.**
● A word that sounds the same is **knight.**

nightfall—The coming of darkness in the evening: *The park closes at* nightfall.
night|fall (nīt′fawl′) *noun.*

nightgown—A loose garment worn to sleep in.
night|gown (nīt′goun′) *noun, plural* **nightgowns.**

nightingale—A small, reddish-brown bird that is native to Europe. The male has a beautiful song.
night|in|gale (nī′tən gāl *or* nī′ting gāl) *noun, plural* **nightingales.**

nightingale

Word History

Nightingale comes from an old English word meaning ''night singer.'' The male nightingale sings its beautiful song both during the day and at night. At night, however, few other birds are singing, so the nightingale can be heard very clearly.

nightly—Happening every night: *I have to take our dog for a* nightly *walk. Adjective.*
—Every night: *We eat dinner* nightly *at six o'clock. Adverb.*
night|ly (nīt′lē) *adjective, adverb.*

nightmare—1. A frightening dream: *My uncle had a* nightmare *about falling out of a plane.* 2. An experience so terrible that it feels like a bad dream: *The fierce blizzard turned our trip into a* nightmare.
night|mare (nīt′mār′) *noun, plural* **nightmares.**

nighttime—The hours between sunset and sunrise; night: *I can often hear owls hooting in the* nighttime. *Noun.*
—Of the nighttime; taking place during the night: nighttime *TV. Adjective.*
night|time (nīt′tīm′) *noun, adjective.*

nimble—Able to move quickly and easily: *The* nimble *goats darted up the steep hill.*
nim|ble (nim′bəl) *adjective,* **nimbler, nimblest.**

nine—One more than eight; 9.
nine (nīn) *adjective; noun, plural* **nines.**

nineteen—One more than eighteen; 19.
nine|teen (nīn′tēn′) *adjective; noun, plural* **nineteens.**

nineteenth—1. Next after the eighteenth. 2. One of nineteen equal parts.
nine|teenth (nīn′tēnth′) *adjective; noun, plural* **nineteenths.**

ninetieth—1. Next after the eighty-ninth. 2. One of ninety equal parts.
nine|ti|eth (nīn′tē ith) *adjective; noun, plural* **ninetieths.**

ninety—Nine times ten; ten more than eighty; 90.
nine|ty (nīn′tē) *adjective; noun, plural* **nineties.**

ninth—1. Next after the eighth. 2. One of nine equal parts.
ninth (nīnth) *adjective; noun, plural* **ninths.**

nip—1. To bite or pinch sharply and suddenly: *The playful puppy* nipped *at her hand.* 2. To remove by pinching, biting, or cutting: *Mother* nips *the dead leaves off the plants in the garden.* 3. To sting; hurt in a biting way: *The cold air* nipped *the faces of the skaters. Verb.*
—1. A small but sharp pinch or bite: *My hamster gave my sister a* nip *on her finger.* 2. Biting coldness: *a* nip *in the air. Noun.*
nip (nip) *verb,* **nipped, nipping;** *noun, plural* **nips.**

nipple—1. The small tip on a breast or udder through which an infant or newborn animal gets milk from its mother. 2. The rubber piece on a baby bottle through which a baby drinks liquids.
nip|ple (nip′əl) *noun, plural* **nipples.**

nippy—Harsh; sharp: *autumn's* nippy *weather; a* nippy *flavor.*
nip|py (nip′ē) *adjective,* **nippier, nippiest.**

nitrogen—A colorless, odorless gas that makes up most of the atmosphere. It is a necessary part of all plant and animal life. It is a chemical element.
ni|tro|gen (nī′trə jən) *noun.*

no—1. A word used to indicate that one refuses something or that something is wrong: No, *I do not want any.* 2. Not at all: *He is* no *better at singing than you are. Adverb.*
—Not any: *There is* no *food in the house. Adjective.*
—A negative answer or vote: *Raise your hand if your vote is a* "no." *Noun.*
no (nō) *adverb; adjective; noun, plural* **noes.**
● A word that sounds the same is **know.**

no.—The abbreviation for **number.**

nobility—1. People of a high rank, usually with great wealth and power. 2. Great and good character: *She was a woman of* nobility, *always willing to help those in need.*
no|bil|i|ty (nō **bil**′ə tē) *noun, plural* **nobilities.**

noble—1. High in rank or class: *a* noble *family.* 2. Having or showing good qualities: *a* noble *deed.* 3. Magnificent and impressive: *The old church is a* noble *building. Adjective.*
—A person of high rank: *The carriage brought the* nobles *to the palace. Noun.*
no|ble (nō′bəl) *adjective,* **nobler, noblest;** *noun, plural* **nobles.**

nobody—No one: *If the door is locked, then* nobody *is home. Pronoun.*
—A person of no great importance: *He was a* nobody *when he began his campaign for governor. Noun.*
no|bod|y (nō′bod ē *or* nō′bə dē) *pronoun; noun, plural* **nobodies.**

nod—1. To move the head up and down in a rapid motion as a way to say yes, indicate a greeting, or express recognition: *The children* nodded *when they were asked if they had behaved themselves.* 2. To show by moving the head in this way: *We passed in the hall and* nodded *hello to each other.* 3. To let the head fall forward with drowsiness: *We* nodded *in our chairs after the big dinner and were all soon fast asleep. Verb.*
—An up-and-down motion of the head. *Noun.*
nod (nod) *verb,* **nodded, nodding;** *noun, plural* **nods.**

Word History

Noel is the French name for Christmas. **Noel** comes from a Latin word meaning "birthday." Noel, or Christmas, is the birthday of Jesus.

Noel—Christmas.
No|el (nō el′) *noun, plural* **Noels.**

noise—1. A loud or harsh sound: *the* noise *of carpenters pounding with their hammers; the* noise *of a jet airplane taking off.* 2. Any sound: *The old house made all kinds of* noises *at night.*
noise (noiz) *noun, plural* **noises.**

noisy—1. Making a lot of noise: *The* noisy *crowd cheered for the home team.* 2. Filled with noise: *Workers in* noisy *factories wear plugs in their ears.*
nois|y (noi′zē) *adjective,* **noisier, noisiest.**

nomad—1. A member of a wandering group of people who move from place to place to find food for themselves and their animals. 2. Anyone who wanders with no certain purpose.
no|mad (nō′mad) *noun, plural* **nomads.**

nomadic—1. Having to do with nomads or their life. 2. Wandering: *The band leads a* nomadic *life, going from city to city for concerts.*
no|mad|ic (nō **mad**′ik) *adjective.*

nominate—1. To choose as a candidate; put up for election: *Each political party* nominates *one person to run for president.* 2. To appoint to a position or name for an honor: *The top students were* nominated *to the honor society.*
nom|i|nate (nom′ə nāt) *verb,* **nominated, nominating.**

nominee—Someone who is nominated for an office or an honor; candidate.
nom|i|nee (nom′ə nē′) *noun, plural* **nominees.**

Word Power

You can understand the meanings of many words that begin with **non-,** if you add a meaning of the prefix to the meaning of the rest of the word.
nonathletic: not athletic
nonviolent: opposite of violent
nonexistence: lack of existence

non-—A prefix that means "not," "opposite of," or "lack of." Nonsense is not sense. Nonfiction is the opposite of fiction. A nonstop flight is one that lacks stops.

none—1. Not any: *I wanted to have an apple, but there are* none *left.* 2. No person; no one: *Many*

a at	**i** if	**oo** look	**ch** chalk	⌈	**a** in ago
ā ape	**ī** idle	**ou** out	**ng** sing		**e** in happen
ah calm	**o** odd	**u** ugly	**sh** ship	ə =	**i** in capital
aw all	**ō** oats	**ū** rule	**th** think		**o** in occur
e end	**oi** oil	**ur** turn	<u>**th**</u> their	⌊	**u** in upon
ē easy			**zh** treasure		

people were expected at the ceremony but none *showed up because of the bad weather. Pronoun.*
—Not at all: *She was* none *too happy about receiving a low grade on her essay. Adverb.*
none (nun) *pronoun, adverb.*
• A word that sounds the same is **nun.**

Language Fact

None and **no one** can often be used in place of each other. **None** may take a singular or plural verb, but **no one** is always singular. "None of my friends is going to the play" and "None of my friends are going to the play" are both correct. But "No one of my friends are going to the play" is wrong. It should be, "No one of my friends is going to the play." Some people feel that **none** should be used only with a singular verb, but this rule is followed less and less.

---

nonfiction—A type of writing that deals with real people and true events. Biographies, science books, histories, and newspaper articles are nonfiction.
non|fic|tion (non fik′shən) *noun.*

nonsense—Foolish talk or behavior: *Her story about meeting creatures from another planet is* nonsense. *Noun.*
—Having no meaning: *A baby speaks* nonsense *words. Adjective.*
non|sense (non′sens) *noun, adjective.*

nonstop—Without making stops: *We took a* nonstop *flight from the east coast to the west coast. The trip seems short because the train goes* nonstop *between the two cities.*
non|stop (non′stop′) *adjective, adverb.*

noodle—A flat strip of dough made of eggs, flour, and water.
noo|dle (nū′dəl) *noun, plural* **noodles.**

nook—1. A cozy corner: *a breakfast* nook. 2. A hidden or private spot: *We had our picnic in a* nook *in the woods.*
nook (nook) *noun, plural* **nooks.**

noon—Twelve o'clock in the daytime; middle of the day.
noon (nūn) *noun.*

no one—Nobody: *No one is allowed to leave the room until the bell rings.*
no one (nō′wun′ *or* no′wən) *pronoun.*
• See Language Fact at **none.**

noose—A loop of rope with a special knot that allows the loop to be tightened by pulling the end

of the rope. A lasso has a loop of this kind.
noose (nūs) *noun, plural* **nooses.**

nor—And not; or not; neither; not either: *The vase was neither pretty* nor *valuable.*
nor (nawr) *conjunction.*

Norfolk terrier—A small hunting dog with a short, wiry coat and ears that droop toward the front. Originally bred in England, these dogs were used to hunt small animals.
Nor|folk ter|ri|er (nawr′fek ter′ē ər) *noun, plural* **Norfolk terriers.**

Norfolk terrier

normal—Regular and expected; typical; usual: *My* normal *bedtime is nine o'clock. Adjective.*
—The usual; average: *The weather was colder than* normal *this summer. Noun.*
nor|mal (nawr′məl) *adjective; noun, plural* **normals.**

north—1. The direction opposite south and to the left when you face east. It is the direction toward which the needle of a compass points. 2. **North:** A region or territory that lies in this direction. *Noun.*
—Facing or in the north: *the* north *side of a house. Adjective.*
—Northward: *My parents go* north *in the winter to ski. Adverb.*
north (nawrth) *noun, adjective, adverb.*
Abbreviation: **N.**

northeast—The direction that lies between north and east. *Noun.*
—1. In the direction between north and east.
2. Coming out of the direction between north and east: *a* northeast *wind. Adjective.*
north|east (nawrth′ēst′) *noun, adjective.*
Abbreviation: **NE.**

northern—**1.** To the north: *a northern route*.
2. From the north: *a northern storm bringing snow*. **3.** Having to do with the north: *a northern climate; the northern landscape*.
north|ern (nawr′<u>th</u>ərn) *adjective*.

northern lights—*See* **aurora borealis**.

north magnetic pole—*See* **magnetic pole**.

North Pole—The most northern point on the earth, where one end of the earth's axis is located.
North Pole (nawrth pōl) *noun*.

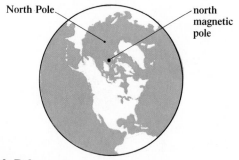

North Pole

North Star—The bright star almost directly over the North Pole; Polaris; polestar. Sailors used to use it as a guide.
North Star (nawrth stahr) *noun*.

northward—Toward the north: *Geese fly northward in the spring*. *Adverb*.
—In a northern direction: *a northward route*. *Adjective*.
north|ward (nawrth′wərd) *adverb, adjective*.

northwest—The direction that lies between north and west. *Noun*.
—**1.** In the direction between north and west. **2.** Coming from the direction between north and west. *Adjective*.
north|west (nawrth′west′) *noun, adjective*. Abbreviation: **NW**.

Norwegian elkhound—A medium-sized hunting and herding dog with a thick, gray-black coat, a thick tail that bends over its back, and straight ears. Originally bred in Norway, these dogs hunt large game, especially elk and moose. They are also used as guard dogs.

a at	i if	oo look	ch chalk		a in ago
ā ape	ī idle	ou out	ng sing		e in happen
ah calm	o odd	u ugly	sh ship	ə =	i in capital
aw all	ō oats	ū rule	th think		o in occur
e end	oi oil	ur turn	<u>th</u> their		u in upon
ē easy			zh treasure		

Nor|we|gian elk|hound (nawr wē′jən elk′hound′) *noun, plural* **Norwegian elkhounds**.

Norwich terrier—A small hunting dog with a wiry, reddish-brown coat, a broad head, and short, straight ears. Originally bred in England, these dogs are used to hunt small game.
Nor|wich ter|ri|er (nawr′ij ter′ē ər *or* nawr′ich ter′ē ər) *noun, plural* **Norwich terriers**.

nose—**1.** A body part on the face just below the eyes, through which air passes and through which one smells. The nose has two passageways, or nostrils. **2.** The sense of smell: *a fragrance that is pleasing to the nose; a dog with a good nose*. **3.** The front part of something, especially a part that sticks out: *the nose of an airplane; the nose of a car*. *Noun*.
—**1.** To seek out by smelling: *The hound nosed out the fox for the hunt*. **2.** To move along in a cautious way: *He nosed through the dark room until he found the light switch*. **3.** To push, touch, or rub with the nose: *The cat nosed the screen loose and climbed onto the window ledge*. **4.** To be nosy; interfere in other people's business: *She told her brother not to nose through her record collection*. *Verb*.
nose (nōz) *noun, plural* **noses**; *verb*, **nosed, nosing**.

■ **on the nose:** Exactly; correctly; precisely: *He hit it right on the nose when he said that it would snow in the morning*.
put (one's) nose out of joint: To upset; disturb: *It put his nose out of joint when he did not make the team*.
turn up (one's) nose at: To act as if one cannot be bothered with someone or something; snub: *He turned up his nose at the idea of extra help with science until he saw his low grade*.
● See picture at **respiratory system**.

Norwegian elkhound

nose cone—The cone-shaped front piece of a rocket. It usually separates from the rocket and flies on its own through space.
nose cone (nōz kōn) *noun, plural* **nose cones.**

nostril—One of two passageways in the nose through which air moves in and out of the body.
nos|tril (nos′trəl) *noun, plural* **nostrils.**

nosy—Looking closely into other people's business; overly curious: *Our neighbor is very nosy and often watches us from her window.*
nos|y (nō′zē) *adjective,* **nosier, nosiest.**

not—A word used to make a word or group of words negative: *We do* not *go to school on Saturday.*
not (not) *adverb.*
● A word that sounds the same is **knot.**

notable—Deserving notice; having importance; outstanding: *The pianist gave a* notable *performance of the difficult piece of music. Adjective.*
—A person who is well known and important: *There will be many* notables *at the dinner to raise money for charity. Noun.*
no|ta|ble (nō′tə bəl) *adjective; noun, plural* **notables.**
● Synonyms: **impressive, remarkable,** for *adjective.*

notch—V-shaped cut or nick in wood or other material. *Noun.*
—To make a V-shaped nick or cut in something: *He* notched *the fence post to show how high the snow was. Verb.*
notch (noch) *noun, plural* **notches;** *verb,* **notched, notching.**

note—1. A brief, written reminder to help one recall something: *She took* notes *during geography class.* 2. A careful look in order to remember; detailed observation: *He took* note *of how to work the camera so he could take pictures on his vacation.* 3. A short letter: *to write a* note *on a postcard.* 4. A brief comment added to a book, to explain a word or group of words in the main text. Notes are put at the bottom of a page or at the back of the book. 5. A certain tone in music. 6. A key on a piano. 7. A suggestion or indication of a certain quality: *a* note *of sadness in a poem.* 8. A high rank; important or highly regarded position: *The principal was a man of* note *in the community. Noun.*
—1. To write down a brief reminder of something; jot down: *Do you have a pencil and paper to* note *the time and place of the next meeting?* 2. To watch carefully; observe: *Be sure to* note *the way the puzzle is put together so you can do it at home later. Verb.*
note (nōt) *noun, plural* **notes;** *verb,* **noted, noting.**

notebook—A book of blank or lined paper in which to write notes for future reference.
note|book (nōt′book′) *noun, plural* **notebooks.**

nothing—1. Not anything; no thing: *We were disappointed when we opened the box and found that there was* nothing *in it.* 2. Someone or something of no worth: *A glass imitation is* nothing *compared to a real diamond.* 3. Zero: *We won by a score of three to* nothing. *Noun.*
—Not at all: *Our new house is* nothing *like our old one. Adverb.*
noth|ing (nuth′ing) *noun, adverb.*
■ **in nothing flat:** Very rapidly; in hardly any time at all: *She crossed the field* in nothing flat *and caught the ball before it hit the ground.*
nothing doing: Certainly not: *His mother said, ''Nothing doing!'' when he asked if he could stay out late.*

notice—1. Observation or attention: *He wore a brightly colored shirt that was sure to attract* notice. 2. A warning that something will happen: *The store manager gave* notice *that the store would close in fifteen minutes.* 3. An announcement: *Each student was handed a* notice *about the fair next week. Noun.*
—To catch sight of; happen to observe: *She* noticed *that the new girl was alone and went over to talk to her. Verb.*
no|tice (nō′tis) *noun, plural* **notices;** *verb,* **noticed, noticing.**

notify—To tell someone about something important; give information to: *The council president* notified *the members that the meeting was canceled because of bad weather.*
no|ti|fy (nō′tə fī) *verb,* **notified, notifying.**

notion—1. Concept, idea, or understanding about something: *My* notion *of space travel comes from what I have seen in movies.* 2. A whim; fancy; wish: *I have a* notion *to travel around the world*

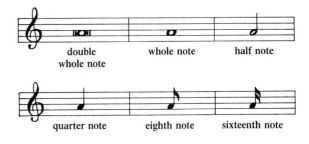

note (noun, definition 5)

someday. **3. notions:** Small, useful items, such as clips, pins, thread, and tacks.

no|tion (nō'shən) *noun, plural* **notions.**

notorious—Having fame as a result of bad and usually criminal activities; of a bad reputation: *In class, we studied about a* notorious *pirate.*

no|to|ri|ous (nō **tawr'**ē əs) *adjective.*

noun—A word that is used to name a person, place, or thing: *The house is by the side of the road.* The words "house," "side," and "road" are nouns.

noun (noun) *noun, plural* **nouns.**

nourish—To feed or provide with something so that growth occurs or health is maintained: *Sunlight, minerals, and water* nourish *plants and make them grow.*

nour|ish (nur'ish) *verb,* **nourished, nourishing.**

nourishment—That which is needed for something to stay alive and grow; food, water, and other things taken in as part of life: *A baby needs good* nourishment *so it can become large and strong.*

nour|ish|ment (nur'ish mənt) *noun, plural* **nourishments.**

Nov.—The abbreviation for **November.**

novel[1]—A book that tells a made-up story.

nov|el (nov'əl) *noun, plural* **novels.**

novel[2]—New; original: *When it was first introduced, the automobile was a* novel *way to travel.*

nov|el (nov'əl) *adjective.*

novelist—One who writes made-up stories.

nov|el|ist (nov'ə list) *noun, plural* **novelists.**

novelty—**1.** A thing or happening that is new and interesting or amusing: *The* novelty *of having her own camera lasted about a year, and then she did not take as many pictures.* **2. novelties:** Small items, such as souvenirs and inexpensive toys: *While on vacation, we bought* novelties *at a gift shop for friends back home.*

nov|el|ty (nov'əl tē) *noun, plural* **novelties.**

November—The eleventh month of the year. November has 30 days.

No|vem|ber (nō vem'bər) *noun.* Abbreviation: **Nov.**

Word History

November comes from the Latin word meaning "nine." It was the ninth month in the old Roman calendar.

novice—**1.** Someone who is just beginning at something; learner: *Although he was a* novice *at computers, he learned quickly and soon moved to a more advanced class.* **2.** A person who is studying and training to be a full member of a religious community.

nov|ice (nov'is) *noun, plural* **novices.**

now—**1.** At this very moment in time; at present; immediately: *We are* now *going to go over the history homework, so open your notebooks.* **2.** By this moment in time: *She must have my letter* now *and knows I will not be able to visit.* **3.** Because of things that have happened: Now *we can go, since my mother will drive us.* Adverb. —This present time: *We should have reached home by* now. *Noun.* —Because of; due to the fact that: Now that *you have pointed out the scratch in the table, I can see it.* Conjunction.

now (nou) *adverb, noun, conjunction.*

■ **now and again:** Every once in a while; not very often: Now and again, *Mother gets a letter from an old high school friend.*

now and then: Every once in a while; not very often: *My sister plays basketball* now and then, *but she does not want to join a team.*

nowadays—During this time; at present: Nowadays, *people use computers more and more.*

now|a|days (nou'ə dāz') *adverb.*

nowhere—Not anywhere; no place: *We ended up going* nowhere, *because we got lost. Adverb.*

no|where (nō'hwār) *adverb.*

nozzle—A device on the end of a hose or a pipe that, when turned, controls the flow of liquid.

noz|zle (noz'əl) *noun, plural* **nozzles.**

nuclear—**1.** Having to do with the energy released by atoms: *Some of our electricity is produced by* nuclear *energy plants.* **2.** Having to do with the nucleus of a cell.

nu|cle|ar (nū'klē ər *or* nyū'klē ər) *adjective.*

nucleus—**1.** The central part or core on which everything revolves or is based: *Lawn mowing was the* nucleus *of his landscaping business.* **2.** The middle part of an atom. It contains neutrons and protons and can produce energy.

a at	i if	oo look	ch chalk		a in ago
ā ape	ī idle	ou out	ng sing		e in happen
ah calm	o odd	u ugly	sh ship	ə =	i in capital
aw all	ō oats	ū rule	th think		o in occur
e end	oi oil	ur turn	th their		u in upon
ē easy			zh treasure		

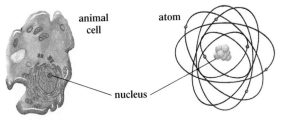

animal cell

atom

nucleus

nucleus (definitions 2 and 3)

3. The center of a cell in living things. It controls growth and heredity.
nu|cle|us (nū′klē əs *or* nyū′klē əs) *noun, plural* **nuclei** (nū′klē ī *or* nyū′klē ī) *or* **nucleuses.**

nude—Having no clothes on; stripped bare; undressed: *The room looked* nude *when the painters finished, because it had no furniture.*
nude (nūd *or* nyūd) *adjective.*

nudge—To push lightly against someone or something; poke gently: *When I* nudge *you with my arm, it is time to say your lines. Verb.*
—A gentle poke; light push: *Give me a* nudge *when it is my turn to go. Noun.*
nudge (nuj) *verb,* **nudged, nudging;** *noun, plural* **nudges.**

nugget—Something in the form of a lump: *a* nugget *of gold ore.*
nug|get (nug′it) *noun, plural* **nuggets.**

nuisance—Someone or something that is a bother or irritation; annoyance: *It is a* nuisance *when the puppy barks all night.*
nui|sance (nū′səns *or* nyū′səns) *noun, plural* **nuisances.**

numb—Having no feeling: *My foot was* numb, *and I could not move it. Adjective.*
—To cause to have no feeling: *The dentist gave me a shot that* numbed *my tooth. Verb.*
numb (num) *adjective,* **number, numbest;** *verb,* **numbed, numbing.**

number—1. The sum of everything counted up; total count; quantity: *The* number *of months in the year is 12.* 2. A word or symbol used in counting: *Twelve, or 12, is the* number *that tells how many are in a dozen.* 3. A large quantity; more than several: *A* number *of fans turned out for the football game, and the stands were full.* 4. A specific set of figures: *My house* number *is 2216. Noun.*
—1. To put a numeral or set of numerals on: *In school the lockers are* numbered *so that each one is easy to locate.* 2. To have as a total; add up to: *The student body at the high school* numbers *about 1,000.* 3. To include in: *If you want to be* numbered *among those who go on the trip, you must come to this meeting. Verb.*
num|ber (num′bər) *noun, plural* **numbers;** *verb,* **numbered, numbering.**
Abbreviation: **No.**

numberless—Too many to count: *The pieces of confetti on the street were* numberless.
num|ber|less (num′bər ləs) *adjective.*

numeral—A figure that stands for a number. Roman numerals are letters.
nu|mer|al (nū′mər əl *or* nyū′mər əl) *noun, plural* **numerals.**

numerator—The top number in a fraction, which shows how many parts of the bottom number are meant. In 5/11, 2/7, and 32/35, the numerators are 5, 2, and 32.
nu|mer|a|tor (nū′mə rā′tər *or* nyū′mə rā′tər) *noun, plural* **numerators.**

numerical—Of numbers; shown by numbers: *Every customer at the bakery takes a number, and the baker serves people in* numerical *order.*
nu|mer|i|cal (nū mer′ə kəl *or* nyū mer′ə kəl) *adjective.*

numerous—1. Forming a great amount; many: Numerous *students came to the auditorium for the band concert.* 2. Containing a great amount; abundant: *A* numerous *crowd filled the hall.*
nu|mer|ous (nū′mər əs *or* nyū′mər əs) *adjective.*

nun—A woman who enters a religious order and devotes her life to prayer and helping others.
nun (nun) *noun, plural* **nuns.**
• A word that sounds the same is **none.**

nurse—1. Someone employed to take care of sick and disabled people. 2. A person, usually a woman, who takes care of another person's children. *Noun.*
—1. To give care to one who is sick, injured, or disabled: *My parents* nursed *my brother back to health.* 2. To encourage by protecting so that growth and development take place: *He* nursed *the support for a new library until the town government agreed to build one.* 3. To feed a baby with milk from the mother's breast: *Mother* nursed *my baby sister for about one year. Verb.*
nurse (nurs) *noun, plural* **nurses;** *verb,* **nursed, nursing.**

nursery—1. A room specially equipped to care for a baby. 2. Land set aside for growing plants and trees.
nurs|er|y (nurs′ər ē) *noun, plural* **nurseries.**

nut—1. The dry seed or fruit of a tree or other plant that is good to eat. Nuts have a hard, outer

shell that must be cracked open.   **3.** A piece of metal or plastic with a round hole in the center into which a bolt or screw can be tightened.
nut (nut) *noun, plural* **nuts.**

■ **a hard nut to crack:** Any difficult person, activity, or problem: *He found mathematics* a hard nut to crack *and didn't get a very good grade in it.*

nutcracker—**1.** A V-shaped, hinged metal device that, when squeezed around a nut, cracks its shell.   **2.** A crowlike bird that eats nuts and seeds.
nut|crack|er (nut′krak′ər) *noun, plural* **nutcrackers.**

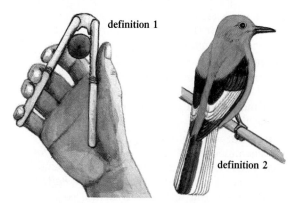

definition 1

definition 2

nutcracker

nuthatch—A small, sharp-beaked bird that climbs on tree trunks in search of nuts, seeds, and insects to eat.
nut|hatch (nut′hach′) *noun, plural* **nuthatches.**

nutmeg—A spice used as a flavoring in cooking. Nutmeg is ground from a seed that grows in tropical climates.
nut|meg (nut′meg) *noun, plural* **nutmegs.**

nutrient—Any substance, such as food, that is nourishing and that promotes growth and good health: *A baby's formula should contain all the* nutrients *needed for an infant to grow.*

nu|tri|ent (nū′trē ənt *or* nyū′trē ənt) *noun, plural* **nutrients.**

nutrition—**1.** The way that food is taken into a body and used there: *During their study of animal* nutrition, *the class visited a farm at feeding time.*   **2.** Food that is needed for growth and health: *When she goes on a diet, my sister makes sure she still gets proper* nutrition.
nu|tri|tion (nū trish′ən *or* nyū trish′ən) *noun.*

nutritious—Having the foods that are needed; helping growth and health: *The school cafeteria serves* nutritious *meals.*
nu|tri|tious (nū trish′əs *or* nyū trish′əs) *adjective.*

nutty—**1.** Full of nuts: *a* nutty *candy bar;* nutty *ice cream.*   **2.** Crazy; silly: *The* nutty *movie we saw kept us laughing for days.*
nut|ty (nut′ē) *adjective,* **nuttier, nuttiest.**

nuzzle—**1.** To push or rub one's nose against something: *The horse* nuzzled *his hand, hoping to get the sugar cube.*   **2.** To get closer and closer to; cuddle up to: *The baby* nuzzled *up to her father and fell asleep in his arms.*
nuz|zle (nuz′əl) *verb,* **nuzzled, nuzzling.**

nuzzle (definition 1)

NW—The abbreviation for **northwest.**

nylon—A very strong, artificial material used in cloth and thread. *Noun.*
ny|lon (nī′lon) *noun, plural* **nylons.**

nymph—**1.** A forest or water goddess in ancient legends.   **2.** A growing insect that has left its egg but has not yet become an adult.
nymph (nimf) *noun, plural* **nymphs.**

a at	i if	oo look	ch chalk		a in ago
ā ape	ī idle	ou out	ng sing		e in happen
ah calm	o odd	u ugly	sh ship	ə =	i in capital
aw all	ō oats	ū rule	th think		o in occur
e end	oi oil	ur turn	th their		u in upon
ē easy			zh treasure		

O o

About 1,900 years ago, the Romans gave the capital O its present form. The small letter o was first used about 1,700 years ago. Its shape has not changed much since then.

About 5,000 years ago, the ancient Egyptians used a symbol of an eye.

About 3,500 years ago, people in the Middle East made a simpler symbol. They called it 'ayin, their word for "eye."

About 3,000 years ago, other people in the Middle East made the symbol much more simple.

About 2,600 years ago, the Greeks gave the letter this form. They called it omicron.

O or **o**—The fifteenth letter of the alphabet: *The word "motor" has two o's.*
O, o (ō) *noun, plural* **O's** or **Os, o's** or **os.**

oak—Any of several trees and bushes that bear rounded, thin-shelled nuts called acorns. Oak wood is used for furniture and floors. *Noun.*
oak (ōk) *noun, plural* **oaks.**
● See picture at **acorn.**

oar—1. A long, slender pole used for rowing or steering a boat. It has a thin, flat blade at one end and is usually made of wood. **2.** Someone who rows a boat.
oar (awr) *noun, plural* **oars.**
● Words that sound the same are **or** and **ore.**
● See picture at **rowboat.**

oasis—A green, fertile area in a desert, where a supply of water allows trees and plants to grow.
o|a|sis (ō ā′sis) *noun, plural* **oases** (ō ā′sēz).

oath—A pledge to tell the truth: *She took an* oath *to tell the truth about the crime.*
oath (ōth) *noun, plural* **oaths.**

oatmeal—1. Oats that have been ground into a flaky substance. **2.** A cooked cereal made from this substance.
oat|meal (ōt′mēl′) *noun, plural* **oatmeals.**

oats—The seeds of a type of grass that are used as food for people and as feed for horses, cows, and other livestock.
oats (ōts) *noun, singular* **oat.**

obedience—The act of doing what one is asked or ordered to do: *We were rewarded for our* obedience *in the library with a candy bar.*
o|be|di|ence (ō bē′dē əns) *noun.*

obedient—Doing what one is asked or ordered to do: *The* obedient *soldiers saluted the general.*
o|be|di|ent (ō bē′dē ənt) *adjective.*

obelisk—A tall stone pillar with four sides that taper toward the top and end in a point.
ob|e|lisk (ob′ə lisk) *noun, plural* **obelisks.**

obelisk: The Washington Monument is an obelisk.

obey—1. To follow the instructions or orders of: *The children* obeyed *the teacher and sat quietly during the movie.* **2.** To follow or carry out: *People who drive cars should* obey *all traffic laws.*
o|bey (ō bā′) *verb,* **obeyed, obeying.**

object—1. Something that can be seen or touched: *He has many* objects *on his desk.* **2.** Someone or something toward which attention is focused: *Her*

sick kitten was the object *of her concern.* **3.** A goal; aim: *The* object *of the trip to the museum was to learn about dinosaurs.* **4.** Someone or something to which the action of a verb is directed or to which a preposition is related: *He blew the whistle.* The object of the verb "blew" is "whistle." *The ball went over the net.* The object of the preposition "over" is "net." *Noun.*
—To disapprove of; oppose: *The neighbors* objected *to the loud noise coming from the party. Verb.*
ob|ject (ob′jikt for *noun;* əb jekt′ for *verb*) *noun, plural* **objects;** *verb,* **objected, objecting.**

objection—Something written or said as a reason for being against or not liking something; protest: *The team's* objection *to the rule was that they felt it was not fair.*
ob|jec|tion (əb jek′shən) *noun, plural* **objections.**

objective—A goal or purpose: *His* objective *is to go to college. Noun.*
—Dealing with facts without allowing personal beliefs or feelings to have an influence: *Members of a jury try to be* objective *in coming to a decision in a trial. Adjective.*
ob|jec|tive (əb jek′tiv) *noun, plural* **objectives;** *adjective.*

obligation—Something such as a promise or a contract that binds a person to a course of action; responsibility: *A doctor has an* obligation *to care for patients.*
ob|li|ga|tion (ob′lə gā′shən) *noun, plural* **obligations.**

oblige—**1.** To be required by a rule, promise, contract, or the like to do something or behave in a certain way: *A person who borrows a book from a library is* obliged *to return it.* **2.** To do a favor for someone; make someone feel grateful: *I am* obliged *to you for helping me solve the problem.*
o|blige (ə blīj′) *verb,* **obliged, obliging.**
• Synonyms: **compel, drive, force,** for **1.**

oblique—Having a slanting position; not being straight up and down or straight across: *an* oblique *line.*
ob|lique (ə blēk′) *adjective.*

oblong—Having greater length than width: *an* oblong *swimming pool; an* oblong *table.*
ob|long (ob′lawng) *adjective.*

obnoxious—Very unpleasant; disagreeable: *While eating dinner, he interrupted everyone, spilled his food, and displayed other* obnoxious *behavior.*
ob|nox|ious (əb nok′shəs) *adjective.*

oboe—A musical instrument shaped like a slender tube with holes and keys along one side. It makes a high-pitched sound that is produced by blowing into its mouthpiece.
o|boe (ō′bō) *noun, plural* **oboes.**

oboe

obscure—**1.** Difficult to understand: *The instructions for baking the cake were* obscure *for me, so I needed my mother's help.* **2.** Hard to see, feel, or hear: *They were puzzled by the* obscure *sounds coming from the vacant building.* **3.** Not well known: *There are many* obscure *islands in the Pacific Ocean. Adjective.*
—**1.** To hide or be concealed from view: *A heavy fog* obscured *the ship on the ocean.* **2.** To make difficult to understand: *His poor pronunciation of words* obscures *his speech. Verb.*
ob|scure (əb skyoor′) *adjective; verb,* **obscured, obscuring.**
• Synonyms: **hazy, vague,** for *adjective* **1.**
Antonyms: **apparent, clear, evident, obvious, plain,** for *adjective* **1.**

observation—**1.** The act of noticing or watching: *She knows a lot about birds from her* observation *of them.* **2.** The fact of being noticed or

a at	i if	oo look	ch chalk		a in ago
ā ape	ī idle	ou out	ng sing		e in happen
ah calm	o odd	u ugly	sh ship	ə =	i in capital
aw all	ō oats	ū rule	th think		o in occur
e end	oi oil	ur turn	th their		u in upon
ē easy			zh treasure		

watched: *The children escaped* observation *by hiding behind the bushes.* **3.** A remark, comment, or statement: *He made an* observation *about his friend's new clothes.*
ob|ser|va|tion (ob'zər vā'shən) *noun, plural* **observations.**

observatory—A place or building with telescopes for observing and studying the stars and planets.
ob|serv|a|to|ry (əb zur'və tawr'ē) *noun, plural* **observatories.**

observe—**1.** To see or sense through careful attention; watch: *She observed the puppies as they played in the yard.* **2.** To follow a rule, law, or custom; obey: *He always observes the rules when he swims in the pool.* **3.** To honor by celebrating: *My parents observe their wedding anniversary on April 28th.*
ob|serve (əb zurv') *verb,* **observed, observing.**

obsolete—No longer needed, used, or useful: *Cars made horses and carriages* obsolete.
ob|so|lete (ob'sə lēt) *adjective.*

obstacle—A person or thing that stands in the way or interferes: *Having an injured knee is an* obstacle *to playing football.*
ob|sta|cle (ob'stə kəl) *noun, plural* **obstacles.**

obstinate—**1.** Not willing to give in; stubborn: *The* obstinate *boy would not eat his vegetables.* **2.** Hard to treat or cure: *an* obstinate *disease.*
ob|sti|nate (ob'stə nit) *adjective.*

obstruct—**1.** To stand in the way; block: *A mud slide* obstructed *the road.* **2.** To shut off from one's sight: *Clouds* obstructed *his view of the moon.*
ob|struct (əb strukt') *verb,* **obstructed, obstructing.**

obtain—To gain, acquire, or earn, usually by planning or making an effort: *To* obtain *the soccer title, the team had to win the most games in the league.*
ob|tain (əb tān') *verb,* **obtained, obtaining.**

obtuse angle—An angle that is larger than a right angle.
ob|tuse an|gle (əb tūs' ang'gəl *or* əb tyūs' ang'gəl) *noun, plural* **obtuse angles.**

obtuse angle   right angle   acute angle

obtuse angle

obvious—Easy to see, discover, or understand; clear: *It is* obvious *that she cares about her little brother because she worries about him a lot.*
ob|vi|ous (ob'vē əs) *adjective.*
● Synonyms: **apparent, evident, plain**
Antonyms: **hazy, obscure, vague**

occasion—**1.** The exact time when something occurs: *They visited us on several* occasions. **2.** A special time or event: *The* occasion *for the party was her birthday.* **3.** A favorable opportunity or chance: *We had an* occasion *to talk during the long bus trip.*
oc|ca|sion (ə kā'zhən) *noun, plural* **occasions.**
■ **on occasion:** Sometimes; every so often: *She visits her grandmother* on occasion.

occasional—Happening once in a while; not regular: *In the winter, I get an* occasional *cold.*
oc|ca|sion|al (ə kā'zhə nəl) *adjective.*

Occident—The part of the world that is west of Asia. The Occident includes Europe, Africa, North America, and South America.
Oc|ci|dent (ok'sə dənt) *noun.*
● See Word History at **Orient.**

occupant—One who lives in a certain place or fills a certain position: *An elderly couple are the* occupants *of that apartment.*
oc|cu|pant (ok'yə pənt) *noun, plural* **occupants.**

occupation—**1.** The activity or work that someone does to earn a living; job: *For her* occupation, *she wants to be a lawyer.* **2.** The act of taking possession and control of something: *the* occupation *of the conquered country by enemy soldiers.*
oc|cu|pa|tion (ok'yə pā'shən) *noun, plural* **occupations.**
● Synonyms: **business, career, profession, trade, vocation** for **1.**

occupy—**1.** To fill up an amount of space or time: *Knitting* occupies *most of my mother's spare time.* **2.** To live in: *We* occupy *the house next to the river.* **3.** To engage one's attention or energy: *The girls* occupied *themselves with a puzzle.* **4.** To capture and take control of: *The invading army* occupied *the country until the end of the war.* **5.** To have or hold; possess: *He* occupies *the position of principal at the high school.*
oc|cu|py (ok'yə pī) *verb,* **occupied, occupying.**

occur—**1.** To happen; come about: *The argument between the sisters* occurred *when they were both tired.* **2.** To be found; live, appear, or grow: *Snow* occurs *in the mountains in winter.* **3.** To

present itself; enter one's mind: *It did not occur to her to bring an umbrella.*
oc|cur (ə **kur′**) *verb*, **occurred, occurring.**

occurrence—**1.** The act of taking place; happening: *a frequent* occurrence *of forest fires that summer.* **2.** Something that takes place; event: *Newscasts report the daily* occurrences *in the world.*
oc|cur|rence (ə **kur′**əns) *noun, plural* **occurrences.**
• Synonyms: **episode, incident,** for **2.**

ocean—**1.** The entire body of salt water that covers about three-fourths of the surface of the earth. **2.** Any of the main sections of this large body of salt water.
o|cean (**ō′**shən) *noun, plural* **oceans.**

oceanography—The science having to do with the study of the ocean and the things that live there.
o|cean|og|ra|phy (ō′shə **nog′**rə fē) *noun.*

ocelot—A medium-sized wild cat that has a yellowish or gray coat somewhat like a leopard's, marked with spots.
o|ce|lot (**o′**sə lot *or* **ōs′**ə lot) *noun, plural* **ocelots.**

o'clock—By or according to the clock: *We are leaving for the circus at seven o'clock.*
o'clock (ə **klok′**) *adverb.*

Oct.—The abbreviation for **October.**

octagon—A closed figure with eight sides and eight angles.
oc|ta|gon (**ok′**tə gon) *noun, plural* **octagons.**

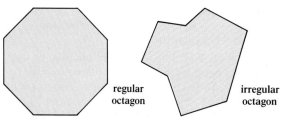

regular octagon

irregular octagon

octagon

octave—**1.** The interval between a musical tone and the next tone of the same name, which is

eight degrees higher or lower. **2.** The group of eight tones within this interval.
oc|tave (**ok′**tiv) *noun, plural* **octaves.**

October—The tenth month of the year, between September and November. October has 31 days.
Oc|to|ber (ok tō′bər) *noun.* Abbreviation: **Oct.**

Word History

October comes from a Latin word meaning "eight." According to early Roman calendars, October was the eighth month of the year. Today, October is the tenth month. **Octopus** comes from two Greek words meaning "eight-footed." Anytime you see the letters "oct" in a word, the word probably has something to do with the number eight.

---

octopus—A saltwater animal with a soft, bulb-shaped body and eight long arms covered with rows of suckers. The suckers enable the octopus to cling to things and to grab and hold its food.
oc|to|pus (**ok′**tə pəs) *noun, plural* **octopuses** or **octopi** (**ok′**tə pī).

octopus

odd—**1.** Uncommon; unusual: *Sleeping all day is* odd *behavior for healthy kittens.* **2.** Extra; remaining: *The four girls bought five candy bars and saved the* odd *one for a friend.* **3.** Being the only one of a pair or set: *She had an* odd *earring.* **4.** Happening now and then; in addition to what

a at	i if	oo look	ch chalk		a in ago
ā ape	ī idle	ou out	ng sing		e in happen
ah calm	o odd	u ugly	sh ship	ə =	i in capital
aw all	ō oats	ū rule	th think		o in occur
e end	oi oil	ur turn	<u>th</u> their		u in upon
ē easy			zh treasure		

is usual: *He does* odd *jobs at his uncle's store.*
5. Not even; not divisible by two without leaving a remainder: *The numbers 9, 15, and 27 are* odd *numbers.*
odd (od) *adjective,* **odder, oddest.**
• Synonyms: **abnormal, different,** for **1.**
Antonyms: **common, regular, typical,** for **1.**

oddity—**1.** The quality or state of being uncommon or unusual: *the* oddity *of snow on a warm summer's day.* **2.** A person or thing that is uncommon or unusual: *The short boy was an* oddity *on the basketball team.*
odd|i|ty (od′ə tē) *noun, plural* **oddities.**

odds—**1.** The difference by which one side or thing is favored over another: *The* odds *are 2 to 1 in favor of their team winning the hockey title.* **2.** The likely chance of something happening: *The* odds *are that the boys will go camping next weekend instead of tomorrow.*
odds (odz) *plural noun.*
■ **odds and ends:** Things that have been left over: *Her knitting basket was filled with* odds and ends *of yarn.*

odor—A pleasant or unpleasant smell: *the* odor *of gasoline; the* odor *of perfume.*
o|dor (ō′dər) *noun, plural* **odors.**
• Synonyms: **aroma, fragrance, scent**

of—**1.** Belonging to or connected with: *the dog of our neighbors; a window* of *the house; friends* of *mine.* **2.** Made with: *a purse* of *black leather.* **3.** Containing: *a box* of *candy.* **4.** Called or named: *the state* of *Kentucky.* **5.** From: *west of this road.* **6.** Concerning; about: *a tale* of *the sea.* **7.** Used for a certain purpose: *a day* of *rest; a house* of *worship.* **8.** Owing to: *He died* of *old age.* **9.** Among: *the best* of *its kind.* **10.** Before the hour: *five minutes* of *eight.*
of (ov, uv, *or* əv) *preposition.*

off—**1.** So as to be no longer on or attached: *to take* off *our shoes.* **2.** Away from the present place or time: *Summer is only two weeks* off. **3.** So as to not work or operate: *Please turn* off *the lights when you leave the room.* **4.** Away from regular work: *She is taking the day* off *to go shopping. Adverb.*
—**1.** Away from the surface: *The coat fell* off *the hook.* **2.** Less than: *one dollar* off *the regular price.* **3.** Below standard in: *The champion ice skater is* off *his performance.* **4.** To seaward of: *to sail* off *the Florida coast.* **5.** Out from or aside: *He turned* off *the highway onto a dirt road. Preposition.*
—**1.** Not in use or operating; stopped: *The radio is* off. **2.** Not taking place; canceled: *The party*

is off. **3.** Away from work: *He was* off *Friday and went to the zoo.* **4.** Provided for: *Those rich people are well* off. **5.** Not good; inferior: *The team is having an* off *season.* **6.** Not correct: *Because his addition was* off, *he got the wrong answer. Adjective.*
off (awf) *adverb, preposition, adjective.*
■ **off and on:** Every so often; occasionally: *The bushes around our house need trimming* off and on.

offend—To cause anger, dislike, or bad feelings: *She was* offended *by the rude joke.*
of|fend (ə fend′) *verb,* **offended, offending.**
• Synonyms: **insult, outrage**
Antonym: **honor**

offense—**1.** A breaking of a law or rule; crime: *They are going to jail for their* offense. **2.** Something that causes anger, dislike, or bad feelings: *Her nasty remark was an* offense *to the other girls in the room.* **3.** An attack, or the members of an attacking force or team: *our football team's* offense.
of|fense (ə fens′) *noun, plural* **offenses.**

offensive—**1.** Causing anger, dislike, or bad feelings: *She was upset by his* offensive *manner.* **2.** Not appealing, especially to one's senses; distasteful: *an* offensive *odor.* **3.** Of or having to do with making an attack: *an* offensive *play in football;* offensive *weapons in war. Adjective.*
—Attack: *The soldiers took the* offensive *and surrounded the enemy's camp. Noun.*
of|fen|sive (ə fen′siv) *adjective; noun, plural* **offensives.**
• Synonyms: **foul, horrid,** for *adjective* **2.**

offer—**1.** To present something for another's acceptance or as a payment: *He* offered *me his advice.* **2.** To state one's willingness: *They* offered *to help the victims of the flood.* **3.** To put up: *The bank robbers* offered *little resistance when they were captured by the police. Verb.*
—**1.** The act of putting something forward for another's acceptance: *She accepted the* offer *of his help.* **2.** Something that is presented: *The musicians hoped for an* offer *to play at the jazz festival. Noun.*
of|fer (awf′ər) *verb,* **offered, offering;** *noun, plural* **offers.**

office—**1.** A place where the work of a business is handled or where a service is supplied: *My father works in an* office *downtown.* **2.** A special duty or position, especially one of authority in government: *He was elected to the* office *of governor.* **3.** All the people who work

in a place of business: *The* office *sent flowers to the boss after her operation.*
of|**fice** (awf′is) *noun, plural* **offices.**

officer—1. Someone who is given the authority to command people in the armed forces.
2. Someone who holds a position of authority or trust: *The president of a company is one of its* officers. 3. A member of the police force: *The* officer *stopped the speeding car.*
of|**fi**|**cer** (awf′ə sər) *noun, plural* **officers.**

official—Someone who holds a public office; officer: *The mayor is a city* official. *Noun.*
—1. Having to do with a special duty or position of authority: *to wear* official *uniforms.*
2. Having the formal or legal power to do something; authorized: *the* official *referee at the game. Adjective.*
of|**fi**|**cial** (ə fish′əl) *noun, plural* **officials;** *adjective.*

offshoot—1. A branch of a main stem of a plant.
2. Something that grows out of something else: *Her interest in sewing is an* offshoot *of her doll collection.*
off|**shoot** (awf′shūt′) *noun, plural* **offshoots.**

offspring—The young produced by any living thing: *His parents had four* offspring.
off|**spring** (awf′spring′) *noun, plural* **offspring** or **offsprings.**

often—Many times; frequently: *We* often *listen to music on the radio.*
of|**ten** (awf′ən *or* awf′tən) *adverb.*

ogre—1. A monster in fairy tales that was supposed to feed on human beings. 2. A cruel or nasty person.
o|**gre** (ō′gər) *noun, plural* **ogres.**

oh—A word used to show surprise, happiness, sadness, anger, or other emotion: Oh! *You frightened me!*
oh (ō) *interjection.*
● A word that sounds the same is **owe.**

oil—1. Any one of a number of thick, greasy substances obtained from plants, animals, or minerals. Oils are used for fuel, food, lighting, medicine, and manufacturing: *corn* oil; *heating* oil; *cod-liver* oil. 2. Petroleum: *Gasoline is made out of crude* oil. 3. Artist's colors made

with a greasy substance, or a painting done with such colors. *Noun.*
—To put a greasy substance on or in something: *He* oiled *the machine to keep it from getting rusty. Verb.*
oil (oil) *noun, plural* **oils;** *verb,* **oiled, oiling.**

oily—Covered with or containing a greasy substance: *an* oily *rag.*
oil|**y** (oi′lē) *adjective,* **oilier, oiliest.**

ointment—An oily, thick substance that usually contains a medicine and that is used to heal or protect the skin.
oint|**ment** (oint′mənt) *noun, plural* **ointments.**

OK or **O.K.**—Fine; all right: *He was* OK *after he fell. Adjective.*
—Well; fine: *She slept* OK *during the storm. Adverb.*
—All right: OK, *you may borrow my book. Interjection.*
OK or **O.K.** (ō′kā′) *adjective, adverb, interjection.*
● This word is also spelled **okay.**

okapi—An African mammal related to the giraffe but having a smaller body and shorter neck. It has a deep brown coat with black and white stripes on its legs.
o|**ka**|**pi** (ō kah′pē) *noun, plural* **okapis** or **okapi.**

okapi

okay—*See* OK.

okra—A tall plant that has sticky, green seed pods. The pods are cooked and eaten separately as a vegetable or put in soups and stews.
o|**kra** (ō′krə) *noun.*

old—1. Having lived or existed for a long time; not young, recent, or new: *an* old *horse; an* old *city;* old *books.* 2. Of a certain age: *My cousin*

a at	i if	oo look	ch chalk		a in ago
ā ape	ī idle	ou out	ng sing		e in happen
ah calm	o odd	u ugly	sh ship	ə =	i in capital
aw all	ō oats	ū rule	th think		o in occur
e end	oi oil	ur turn	<u>th</u> their		u in upon
ē easy			zh treasure		

is six years old.   **3.** Belonging to a much earlier time or a past era: old *customs*.   **4.** Showing the effects of age or use: *She wore* old *shoes when she worked in the soggy garden*.   **5.** Former: *She visited her* old *school*.   **6.** Known for a long time: *The boys are* old *friends. Adjective.*
—Earlier times; past days: *There are many legends about the heroes of* old. *Noun.*
old (ōld) *adjective,* **older** or **elder,** **oldest** or **eldest;** *noun.*

Language Fact

Many words mean old, but various words are used in different ways. **Ancient** and **antique** are used mainly for things, but **ancient** is also used for places. **Ancient** normally means older than **antique** does. **Aged, elderly,** and **senior** are used for people. **Senior** means a person who is older than many others, or who has been doing something longer than others. **Elderly** means a person who is older than most other people, while **aged** means a person who is very old.

Old English sheepdog—A large herding dog with a long, shaggy coat, hair over its eyes, and a short tail. Originally bred in England, these dogs were used to herd cattle and sheep.
Old Eng|lish sheep|dog (ōld **in′**glish shēp′dawg′) *noun, plural* **Old English sheepdogs.**

Old English sheepdog

old-fashioned—**1.** No longer in fashion; not up-to-date: *She dressed up in old-fashioned clothes for the costume party*.   **2.** Holding to old ideas or customs: *an* old-fashioned *wedding*.
old-fash|ioned (ōld′fash′ənd) *adjective.*

Old Testament—The writings that make up the Jewish Bible and the first part of the Christian Bible.
Old Tes|ta|ment (ōld **tes′**tə mənt) *noun.* Abbreviation: O.T.

olive—**1.** An evergreen tree that has gray-green leaves. It is grown for its fruit and wood.   **2.** The fruit of the olive tree. An olive is small and firm and has a hard pit in its center.   **3.** A dull yellow-green color. *Noun.*
—Having a dull yellow-green color: *He wore* olive *pants. Adjective.*
ol|ive (ol′iv) *noun, plural* **olives;** *adjective.*

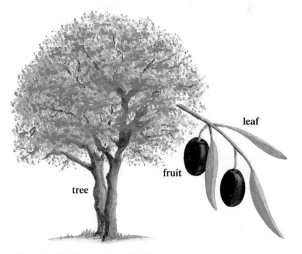

leaf

fruit

tree

olive (definitions 1 and 2)

olive oil—An oil that is squeezed from olives. It is used for salads and cooking.
ol|ive oil (ol′iv oil) *noun.*

Olympic Games—**1.** In ancient Greece, contests held every four years in athletics, music, and poetry.   **2.** In the present time, contests in summer and winter sports that are held every four years for athletes from around the world.
O|lym|pic Games (ō lim′pik gāmz) *noun.*

omelet or **omelette**—A mixture of beaten eggs and milk or water that is cooked in a frying pan and folded over. An omelet may also contain such foods as onions, cheese, and tomatoes.
om|e|let or **om|e|lette** (om′ə lit *or* om′lit) *noun, plural* **omelets** or **omelettes.**

omen—Something that is thought to mean that good or bad luck will happen: *My cousin said that having a black cat cross your path is a bad* omen.
o|men (ō′mən) *noun, plural* **omens.**

omission—Something that is left out: *Her poem was the only* omission *from the ones printed in the school newspaper.*
o|mis|sion (ō mish′ən) *noun, plural* **omissions.**

omit—To leave out; not include: *He omitted his address from the coupon and never got his prize.*
o|mit (ō mit′) *verb,* **omitted, omitting.**

on—1. Atop; supported by: *to sit on a chair; a glass on a table.* 2. Upon: *a mirror on a wall; a ring on a finger.* 3. Near or along: *a cottage on the river.* 4. At the time of; during: *The concert is on Saturday.* 5. In the state or process of: *on sale; on loan.* 6. About: *a book on baseball.* 7. By means of: *to cross town on a bus. Preposition.*
—1. Upon someone or something: *He put on his new shirt.* 2. In or into a condition; into a state: *Turn the heat on. Adverb.*
—Happening or in operation: *The race already was on when we arrived. Adjective.*
on (on) *preposition, adverb, adjective.*

once—1. A single time; not done again: *I went there only once.* 2. In the past: *This busy street was once a farm. Adverb.*
—Only one time: *May I leave early just this once? Noun.*
—Whenever; as soon as: *You may go out and play once you have finished washing the dishes. Conjunction.*
once (wuns) *adverb, noun, conjunction.*

oncoming—Approaching: *The fog made it hard to see the lights of oncoming cars.*
on|com|ing (on′kum′ing) *adjective.*

one—1. The first and lowest number; 1. 2. A single person or thing: *All of your sweaters are pretty, but I like the red one best. Noun.*
—1. Being a single person or thing: *in one year.* 2. Some: *She hopes that one day she will be a fire fighter. Adjective.*
—1. Some particular person or thing of a group: *Will one of you go to the store for me?* 2. Any person at all; people in general: *One does not like to be told a lie. Pronoun.*
one (wun) *noun, plural* **ones;** *adjective; pronoun.*
■ **one by one:** One following another: *The players were introduced one by one.*

oneself—A person's own self: *One might be embarrassed if one is overheard talking to oneself.*
one|self (wun self′ *or* wunz self′) *pronoun.*
■ **by oneself:** Alone: *Sometimes it is nice to spend the day by oneself instead of with others.*

one-sided—1. Seeing or showing only one side; unfair: *The newspaper's story about the candidate was very one-sided.* 2. Not equal or even: *We hoped the score would be close, but the game turned out to be one-sided.*
one-sid|ed (wun′sī′did) *adjective.*

one-way—Permitting movement in only one direction: *a one-way street.*
one-way (wun′wā′) *adjective.*

onion—The bulb of a plant, used for eating and cooking. It has a strong smell and sharp taste.
on|ion (un′yən) *noun, plural* **onions.**

onlooker—A person who watches an activity without joining in.
on|look|er (on′look′ər) *noun, plural* **onlookers.**

only—1. One and no more; one alone: *an only child; the only ticket left.* 2. The best: *That cat is the only one for me. Adjective.*
—And nothing more; and no one else: *He ran home only because he was hungry and not because he was late. Adverb.*
—But: *He would have gone swimming, only it was too cold. Conjunction.*
on|ly (ōn′lē) *adjective, adverb, conjunction.*

onset—Beginning: *Her sneezes warned of the onset of a cold.*
on|set (on′set′) *noun.*

onto—On or upon: *The papers blew onto the floor.*
on|to (on′tū) *preposition.*

onward or **onwards**—Forward; ahead: *We drove onward after checking our location on the map. Adverb.*
—Forward; farther on: *the onward rush of the water. Adjective.*
on|ward *or* on|wards (on′wərd *or* on′wərdz) *adverb, adjective.*

ooze[1]—To leak or pass through slowly: *Pudding oozed through the crack in the bowl.*
ooze (ūz) *verb,* **oozed, oozing.**

ooze[2]—Soft mud.
ooze (ūz) *noun, plural* **oozes.**

opal—A mineral that is used as a gem for jewelry. Opals come in different shades of red, black, and white. Some reflect light in a rainbow pattern.
o|pal (ō′pəl) *noun, plural* **opals.**

a	at	i	if	oo	look	ch	chalk		a	in ago
ā	ape	ī	idle	ou	out	ng	sing		e	in happen
ah	calm	o	odd	u	ugly	sh	ship	ə =	i	in capital
aw	all	ō	oats	ū	rule	th	think		o	in occur
e	end	oi	oil	ur	turn	th	their		u	in upon
ē	easy					zh	treasure			

opaque—Not clear; not letting light shine through: *Dirt made the water* opaque, *and we could not see the bottom of the river.*
o|paque (ō pāk′) *adjective.*

open—**1.** Not shut; allowing movement in and out: *The cat entered through the* open *door.* **2.** Not having its lid, top, or other cover closed: *an* open *jar of jelly; an* open *book.* **3.** Not closed in or covered: *the* open *air.* **4.** Available; able to be used: *an* open *seat.* **5.** Willing to take suggestions or take in new facts or ideas: *She has an* open *mind and never gives her opinion of a book until she has finished reading it.* **6.** Honest; frank: *They were* open *with each other about the reasons for their quarrel. Adjective.*
—An area that is not closed in: *We had the picnic out in the* open. *Noun.*
—**1.** To change something from a closed condition: *Please* open *the window so we can get some fresh air.* **2.** To spread out: *to* open *a magazine.* **3.** To establish or become available: *to* open *a new store; a museum* opening *in the spring.* **4.** To start: *She* opened *her essay with a question. Verb.*
o|pen (ō′pən) *adjective; noun; verb,* **opened, opening.**
• Synonyms: **outspoken, straightforward,** for *adjective* **6.**

opener—**1.** Someone or something that opens: *Use the* opener *to get the cap off the bottle.* **2.** The first thing or part, especially of a series: *The pianist played my favorite song as the* opener *of her performance.*
o|pen|er (ō′pə nər) *noun, plural* **openers.**

opening—**1.** A way to enter; space: *The mouse came in through the small* opening *in the wall.* **2.** The beginning: *the* opening *of the school day.* **3.** A job that is available: *an* opening *for a cook at the restaurant.*
o|pen|ing (ō′pə ning *or* ōp′ning) *noun, plural* **openings.**

openly—Honestly; frankly: *We talked* openly *about our problems and felt better.*
o|pen|ly (ō′pən lē) *adverb.*

opera—A type of play in which all or most of the words are sung instead of spoken.
op|er|a (op′ə rə) *noun, plural* **operas.**

operate—**1.** To function; work; run: *Do you know how this machine* operates? **2.** To make work: *The teacher* operated *the film projector so we could watch the movie.* **3.** To perform surgery on a sick or injured person: *The doctors* operated *on the accident victim.*
op|er|ate (op′ə rāt) *verb,* **operated, operating.**

operation—**1.** The act or process of working or continuing to work: *The* operation *of the company required many people.* **2.** The way something works: *The book explained the* operation *of a computer.* **3.** Surgery: *a knee* operation.
op|er|a|tion (op′ə rā′shən) *noun, plural* **operations.**

operator—**1.** Someone who runs a business, a machine, or another thing: *a crane* operator.
op|er|a|tor (op′ə rā′tər) *noun, plural* **operators.**

operetta—A short, humorous opera.
op|er|et|ta (op′ə ret′ə) *noun, plural* **operettas.**

opinion—**1.** What someone thinks about something; belief: *I thought that movie was great, but my sister had a different* opinion *about it.* **2.** A judgment by an expert: *a doctor's* opinion.
o|pin|ion (ə pin′yən) *noun, plural* **opinions.**

opossum—A small, furry mammal that feeds at night and lives mainly in trees. The mother opossum carries her newborn in a pouch. After about two months, she carries them on her back. One kind of opossum falls down as though dead if it is frightened. The opossum is found in North and South America.
o|pos|sum (ə pos′əm) *noun, plural* **opossums.**
• Another name for this animal is **possum.**

opossum

opponent—A person who is on the opposite side in an argument, a game, an election, or a fight.
op|po|nent (ə pō′nənt) *noun, plural* **opponents.**

opportunity—A good or lucky chance; favorable time or occasion: *The snowy day gave me an* opportunity *to try my new sled.*
op|por|tu|ni|ty (op′ər tū′nə tē) *noun, plural* **opportunities.**

oppose—**1.** To be against; try to keep something from happening: *We like that open field and* oppose *paving over it for a parking lot.* **2.** To

set as the opposite: *Happiness is* opposed *to sadness.*
op|pose (ə pōz′) *verb,* **opposed, opposing.**

opposite—**1.** Directly across from someone or something else: *We sat* opposite *each other in class.* **2.** Completely different: *I felt like studying, but she was in the* opposite *mood. Adjective.*
—Someone or something that is completely different from another: *Tall is the* opposite *of short. Noun.*
op|po|site (op′ə zit) *adjective; noun, plural* **opposites.**

opposition—**1.** Action or feeling against: *Mother ended her* opposition *to our game when we promised to pick up afterward.* **2.** A political party against the party in power.
op|po|si|tion (op′ə zish′ən) *noun, plural* **oppositions.**

optical—**1.** Having to do with the eye or sense of sight: *We thought we saw a giant fish in the desert, but it was an* optical *illusion.* **2.** Helping the eye or sense of sight: *A telescope is an* optical *device to make things far away appear closer.*
op|ti|cal (op′tə kəl) *adjective.*

optician—Someone who is trained to make or sell eyeglasses.
op|ti|cian (op tish′ən) *noun, plural* **opticians.**

optimist—A person who looks at the bright side of things and believes things will turn out well.
op|ti|mist (op′tə mist) *noun, plural* **optimists.**

optimistic—Believing things will turn out well; hopeful: *Even though it was raining, he was still* optimistic *that the sun would shine for our picnic.*
op|ti|mis|tic (op′tə mis′tik) *adjective.*

option—A choice; thing that can be chosen: *The music program offers the* option *of learning to play the flute, trumpet, violin, or drums.*
op|tion (op′shən) *noun, plural* **options.**

optional—Able to be chosen; not required: *Art classes are* optional, *but you must take math and reading.*
op|tion|al (op′shə nəl) *adjective.*

optometrist—Someone who is trained to examine the eyes and prescribe eyeglasses.
op|tom|e|trist (op tom′ə trist) *noun, plural* **optometrists.**

-or—A suffix meaning ''a person or thing that.'' The director of a play is the person who directs it.

Word Power

You can understand the meanings of many words that end with **-or,** if you add the meaning of the suffix to the meaning of the rest of the word.
actor: person who acts
refrigerator: thing that refrigerates

---

or—**1.** A word used to show a difference; a word used to show a choice: *You may order this sweater in red* or *blue.* **2.** And if not; otherwise: *I had better start my homework now,* or *I will never get it finished.*
or (awr) *conjunction.*
• Words that sound the same are **oar** and **ore.**

oral—**1.** Spoken; said aloud: *an* oral *report.* **2.** Of the mouth: *The dentist gave us special toothbrushes to help with our* oral *hygiene.*
o|ral (awr′əl) *adjective.*

orange—**1.** A round fruit with a firm, reddish yellow skin and a juice that is usually sweet. It grows in warm climates. **2.** A reddish yellow color. *Noun.*
—Having a reddish yellow color: *an* orange *pumpkin. Adjective.*
or|ange (awr′inj) *noun, plural* **oranges;** *adjective.*

orangeade—A drink made by combining orange juice, sugar, and water.
or|ange|ade (awr′inj ād′) *noun, plural* **orangeades.**

orangutan—A large ape with very long arms and reddish brown hair. It lives in trees and is found in Asia.
o|rang|u|tan (ō rang′oo tan′) *noun, plural* **orangutans.**

orbit—**1.** The path that one planet or heavenly body follows as it circles another: *the moon's* orbit *around the earth.* **2.** One complete trip around a heavenly body by a spacecraft or satellite: *The spacecraft made three* orbits *of the earth before it landed. Noun.*
—To circle a heavenly body: *The earth* orbits *the sun. Verb.*

---

a at	i if	oo look	ch chalk	
ã ape	ī idle	ou out	ng sing	a in ago
ah calm	o odd	u ugly	sh ship	e in happen
aw all	ō oats	ū rule	th think	ə = i in capital
e end	oi oil	ur turn	<u>th</u> their	o in occur
ē easy			zh treasure	u in upon

or|bit (awr′bit) *noun, plural* **orbits;** *verb,*
orbited, orbiting.

orchard—A section of land where fruit trees are
grown.
or|chard (awr′chərd) *noun, plural* **orchards.**

orchestra—1. A group of musicians performing
together on a variety of instruments. **2.** The
violins, flutes, horns, and other instruments
played by a group of musicians. **3.** The main
floor of a theater. **4.** The section in front of the
stage of a theater, where the musicians are
sometimes seated.
or|ches|tra (awr′kə strə) *noun, plural*
orchestras.

orchid—1. Any one of a number of plants with
flowers that come in various shapes and colors,
often very bright and showy. **2.** A light purple
color. *Noun.*
—Having a light purple color. *Adjective.*
or|chid (awr′kid) *noun, plural* **orchids;**
adjective.

ordain—1. To appoint or order by law or some
other authority: *The law* ordains *that thieves shall
be punished.* **2.** To admit someone officially to
the ministry or other religious position: *to be*
ordained *a priest.*
or|dain (awr dān′) *verb,* **ordained, ordaining.**

ordeal—An experience that is unpleasant or
difficult, or that tests one's courage or patience:

orchid (definition 1)

Getting his first haircut was quite an ordeal *for
the small boy.*
or|deal (awr dēl′) *noun, plural* **ordeals.**

order—1. The arrangement of things or events;
sequence: *The cards were put in numerical*
order. **2.** A clean or tidy situation; proper
condition: *His tools were in perfect* order.
3. The condition in which rules are obeyed: *The
teacher restored* order *in the noisy auditorium.*
4. A strict instruction or command: *The soldiers
were given* orders *to guard the fort.* **5.** A request
for goods or supplies: *She sent an* order *for the
book through the mail.* **6.** The goods or supplies
obtained by such a request: *Would you like an*
order *of bacon to go with your eggs?* **7.** A group
of persons belonging to the same organization or
living together under the same rules or with the
same beliefs: *an* order *of nuns. Noun.*
—1. To arrange according to some plan; tidy or
straighten: *He* ordered *the material in the file
drawers so that information could be easily
located.* **2.** To give a strict instruction;
command: *The coach* ordered *the team to come
back for extra practice before the big game.*
3. To ask for something, or to instruct that
something be made or delivered: *She* ordered *a
hamburger at the restaurant. Verb.*
or|der (awr′dər) *noun, plural* **orders;** *verb,*
ordered, ordering.
■ **out of order:** Not working properly: *They all
had cereal for breakfast because their toaster
was* out of order.

orderly—1. Well organized: *The supply
cupboards in the art room were very* orderly, *and
we found what we needed quickly.* **2.** Not
troublesome; well behaved: *The scout leader
complimented the members of his troop on their*
orderly *behavior.*
or|der|ly (awr′dər lē) *adjective.*

orangutan

ordinal number—A number showing position in a sequence. First, second, third, fourth, and fifth are ordinal numbers.
or|di|nal num|ber (awr′də nəl num′bər) *noun, plural* **ordinal numbers.**

ordinary—1. Usual; customary; routine: *Her* ordinary *arrival time is noon.* 2. Not special or different; plain: *He said the new movie was very* ordinary *and we should not make a special effort to see it.*
or|di|nar|y (awr′də ner′ē) *adjective.*

ore—A mineral or rock that contains a valuable metal or metals and that is mined from the ground: *copper* ore; *iron* ore.
ore (awr) *noun, plural* **ores.**
● Words that sound the same are **oar** and **or.**

organ—1. A musical instrument that makes sounds as air is blown from a bellows through pipes of different lengths. It has one or more keyboards. 2. A similar musical instrument that makes sounds by electronic devices. 3. A specialized part of a living thing that does a particular job. The heart and lungs are organs.
or|gan (awr′gən) *noun, plural* **organs.**

organic—1. Of or coming from living things: *an* organic *process, such as breathing;* organic *matter, such as vegetable scraps.* 2. Grown or produced without the use of artificial fertilizers and insecticides: *I subscribe to a magazine about* organic *vegetable gardening.*
or|gan|ic (awr gan′ik) *adjective.*

organism—A living thing.
or|gan|ism (awr′gə niz əm) *noun, plural* **organisms.**

organization—1. People united for a special purpose: *He joined the* organization *so that he could meet other people who were interested in stamp collecting.* 2. The act or process of putting something in order: *The committee worked hard on the* organization *of this year's fair.* 3. The order by which things are arranged: *In the encyclopedia, the* organization *of articles is alphabetical.*
or|gan|i|za|tion (awr′gə nə zā′shən) *noun, plural* **organizations.**

organize—1. To arrange, compose, or set up in a particular way: *She* organized *the project so that*
each person had a different job. 2. To bring together in a group, such as a labor union, theater group, or choir.
or|gan|ize (awr′gə nīz) *verb,* **organized, organizing.**

Orient—The countries of Asia, especially eastern and southeastern Asia.
O|ri|ent (awr′ē ənt) *noun.*

Word History

Orient comes from a Latin word meaning "to rise." **Occident** comes from a Latin word meaning "to set." The countries of the Orient lie to the east of Europe, in the direction of the rising sun. The countries of the Occident lie to the west, the direction where the sun sets.

Oriental—Having to do with the countries of Asia, especially eastern and southeastern Asia. *Adjective.*
—A person from Asia. *Noun.*
O|ri|en|tal (awr′ē en′təl) *adjective; noun, plural* **Orientals.**

origami—An art form in which paper is folded to form flowers, birds, or other shapes used as decorations. It originated in Japan.
or|i|ga|mi (awr′ə gah′mē) *noun.*

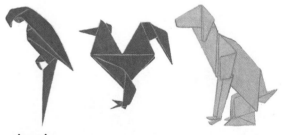

origami

origin—1. The point at which something begins or causes something else to begin: *The* origin *of the stream lies far to the north.* 2. Ancestry, birth, or history: *The stray dog in our neighborhood is of unknown* origin.
or|i|gin (awr′ə jin) *noun, plural* **origins.**

original—1. Having to do with the first one or the beginning of something: *That champion dog has had many trainers, but my neighbor was the* original *one.* 2. That has not been done, thought, or produced before; not copied; authentic: *an* original *idea; an* original *statue; the* original *version from which copies were made.*

a at	i if	oo look	ch chalk		a in ago
ā ape	ī idle	ou out	ng sing		e in happen
ah calm	o odd	u ugly	sh ship	ə =	i in capital
aw all	ō oats	ū rule	th think		o in occur
e end	oi oil	ur turn	th their		u in upon
ē easy			zh treasure		

3. Inventive; creative: *She won a prize for the most* original *costume. Adjective.*

—Something new or first: *We had copies of the photograph made for other members of the family, but we kept the* original. *Noun.*
o|rig|i|nal (ə rij′ə nəl) *adjective; noun, plural* **originals.**

- Synonyms: **actual, genuine, real, true,** for *adjective* **2.**
  Antonyms: **counterfeit, false,** for *adjective* **2.**

originally—At or from the beginning; at the start: *I* originally *thought I would go to the dance, but now I have changed my mind.*
o|rig|i|nal|ly (ə rij′ə nə lē) *adverb.*

originate—To bring or come into being: *He* originated *the idea of an annual skating party several years ago.*
o|rig|i|nate (ə rij′ə nāt) *verb,* **originated, originating.**

oriole—Any of a group of songbirds that are found in nearly all parts of the world. Most male orioles are orange or yellow with black markings on the head, tail, and wings.
o|ri|ole (awr′ē ōl) *noun, plural* **orioles.**

oriole

ornament—Something pretty; decoration: *The family hung* ornaments *on the Christmas tree. Noun.*

—To decorate with pretty things: *Several tiny bows* ornamented *the little girl's hair. Verb.*
or|na|ment (awr′nə mənt for *noun;* awr′nə ment for *verb*) *noun, plural* **ornaments;** *verb,* **ornamented, ornamenting.**

- Synonyms: **adorn, trim,** for *verb.*

orphan—A child whose parents are no longer living. *Noun.*

—To cause to be without parents: *He and his sisters were* orphaned *by the tornado and were raised by an aunt. Verb.*
or|phan (awr′fən) *noun, plural* **orphans;** *verb,* **orphaned, orphaning.**

orphanage—A home for orphans.
or|phan|age (awr′fə nij) *noun, plural* **orphanages.**

orthodontist—A dentist who specializes in straightening teeth.
or|tho|don|tist (awr′thə don′tist) *noun, plural* **orthodontists.**

orthodox—**1.** Generally approved of or believed to be true: *an* orthodox *style of dress; an* orthodox *idea.* **2.** Sharing views widely held to be true: *He was* orthodox *in his political opinions.*
or|tho|dox (awr′thə doks) *adjective.*

osprey—A large hawk with a white underside and a dark brown back and wings. It lives near water and feeds on fish.
os|prey (os′prē) *noun, plural* **ospreys.**

ostrich—The largest of all living birds. It has a small head atop a long neck and two toes at the base of each of its long, strong legs. It cannot fly but is a fast runner. It lives in Africa.
os|trich (aws′trich *or* os′trich) *noun, plural* **ostriches.**

ostrich

other—**1.** Remaining: *There are no* other *cookies in the jar.* **2.** Additional: *Is that your only pencil, or do you have* other *ones?* **3.** Different: *Any* other *time would be better. Adjective.*

—**1.** A different one: *I do not like this bicycle as much as I like the* other. **2.** Another one;

additional person or thing: *He tries to help* others. *Pronoun.*

—Differently; otherwise: *He could not do other than try again. Adverb.*

oth|er (u<u>th</u>′ər) *adjective, pronoun, adverb.*

otherwise—**1.** In a different manner: *Having learned to tie his shoes one way, he could not do otherwise.* **2.** In every way but one: *It rained in the early morning but was a beautiful day otherwise. Adverb.*

—Different: *They wished it could have been otherwise. Adjective.*

—Or else; if not: *You had better write your book report now; otherwise you will not get it done in time. Conjunction.*

oth|er|wise (u<u>th</u>′ər wīz′) *adverb, adjective, conjunction.*

otter—A water animal with webbed feet, a long tail, and thick, brown fur.

ot|ter (ot′ər) *noun, plural* **otters** or **otter.**

otter

otter hound—A large hunting dog with a thick, rough outer coat, slightly webbed feet, and drooping ears. Originally bred in England to hunt otters, these dogs are good swimmers.

ot|ter hound (ot′ər hound) *noun, plural* **otter hounds.**

ouch—A cry of sudden pain: Ouch! *I pinched my finger!*

ouch (ouch) *interjection.*

ought—**1.** Must; should: *We ought to help them.* **2.** To be probable or very likely: *He ought to be here soon.*

ought (awt) *verb.*

a at	i if	oo look	ch chalk		⌈ a in ago
ā ape	ī idle	ou out	ng sing		e in happen
ah calm	o odd	u ugly	sh ship	ə =	i in capital
aw all	ō oats	ū rule	th think		o in occur
e end	oi oil	ur turn	<u>th</u> their		⌊ u in upon
ē easy			zh treasure		

ounce—**1.** A unit of weight equaling 1/16 pound (28.3 grams). **2.** A unit of liquid measure equaling 1/16 pint (.03 liter). **3.** A very small amount: *The jury did not have an* ounce *of sympathy for the criminal.*

ounce (ouns) *noun, plural* **ounces.** *Abbreviation:* **oz.**

our—Belonging or referring to us: our *car;* our *best wishes.*

our (our) *adjective.*

• A word that sounds the same is **hour.**

ours—Something belonging to us: *The cat is* ours.

ours (ourz) *pronoun.*

ourselves—**1.** A form of **we** or **us** used for emphasis: *We* ourselves *will solve the mystery.* **2.** Our own selves: *We can take care of* ourselves. **3.** Our normal or true selves: *We were not* ourselves *when we behaved badly.*

our|selves (our selvz′) *pronoun.*

-ous—A suffix that means "possessing the quality of" or "full of." A courageous person possesses the quality of courage. A humorous story is full of humor.

Word Power

You can understand the meanings of many words that end with **-ous,** if you add a meaning of the suffix to the meaning of the rest of the word.

poisonous: possessing the quality of poison
joyous: full of joy

---

oust—To force out; cause to leave: *The leader of the country was* ousted *from office.*

oust (oust) *verb,* **ousted, ousting.**

out—**1.** Away from the inside or center: *The candy tumbled* out *of the bag.* **2.** Away from one's home, office, or work: *I called just after you went* out. **3.** So as to be no longer working or in action: *The storm caused the lights to go* out. *Adverb.*

—**1.** Not used, working, or in action: *The fire was* out *by the time we went to bed.* **2.** Not allowed to continue to bat or run in baseball: *He was* out *on a close play. Adjective.*

—Through or coming forward from: *He stepped* out *the door. Preposition.*

out (out) *adverb, adjective, preposition.*

out-—A prefix that means "outward," or "at a distance," or "better than." An outflung arm is one flung outward. The outfield is at a distance

Word Power

You can understand the meanings of many words that begin with **out-**, if you add a meaning of the prefix to the meaning of the rest of the word.
   outbound: outward bound
   outlying: lying at a distance
   outswim: swim better than

from the infield. A racer who outruns the other racers runs better than they do.

outbreak—A sudden appearance or increase of something: *There was an outbreak of the flu in the school.*
out|break (out′brāk′) *noun, plural* **outbreaks.**

outburst—A sudden display or expression; a bursting forth: *an outburst of applause; an angry outburst.*
out|burst (out′burst) *noun, plural* **outbursts.**

outcast—A person rejected by friends and family: *He became an outcast after he was caught stealing from the church. Noun.*
   —Abandoned; having no friends: *We took the outcast puppy home. Adjective.*
out|cast (out′kast′) *noun, plural* **outcasts;** *adjective.*

outcome—The result: *She was anxious to learn the outcome of the championship game.*
out|come (out′kum′) *noun, plural* **outcomes.**
• Synonyms: **consequence, effect**

outcry—A sudden or loud noise or shout: *There was a joyous outcry from the crowd when the president was introduced.*
out|cry (out′krī′) *noun, plural* **outcries.**

outdistance—To go faster and farther, leaving one's competition behind; outdo: *She easily outdistanced the other runners in the race.*
out|dis|tance (out dis′təns) *verb,* **outdistanced, outdistancing.**

outdo—To do better than: *She outdid all the others in the craft fair with her wonderful needlework.*
out|do (out dū′) *verb,* **outdid, outdone, outdoing.**

outdoor—Done or happening in the open air: *The rain ruined the outdoor events.*
out|door (out′dawr′) *adjective.*

outdoors—Out in the open: *They slept outdoors under the starry sky. Adverb.*
   —The area outside of buildings: *He liked his office job, but he always said that nothing beats the great outdoors. Noun.*
out|doors (out dawrz′) *adverb, noun.*

outer—Being situated on the outside; exterior: *an outer layer of fur.*
out|er (ou′tər) *adjective.*

outer space—The region lying outside the earth's atmosphere: *the stars and planets of outer space.*
out|er space (ou′tər spās′) *noun.*

outfield—1. In baseball, that part of the playing field lying beyond the infield and between the foul lines.   2. The three players positioned in the outfield.
out|field (out′fēld′) *noun, plural* **outfields.**

outfit—1. All the tools, equipment, or clothes required for some purpose or activity: *a hiking outfit.*   2. A set of clothes: *He bought a new outfit for graduation.*   3. A group of people who work together: *An outfit from the television station arrived to film our school assembly. Noun.*
   —To provide with the articles necessary for some purpose; equip: *They were outfitted for skiing. Verb.*
out|fit (out′fit) *noun, plural* **outfits;** *verb,* **outfitted, outfitting.**

outgoing—1. Leaving; departing: *The outgoing president thanked the club members for their help during her term in office.*   2. Talkative and friendly: *His outgoing personality made him a friend to all.*
out|go|ing (out′gō′ing) *adjective.*

outgrow—1. To become too large to fit into something: *She outgrew her party dress in six months.*   2. To lose interest in or leave behind as time passes: *He outgrew his habit of biting his nails.*
out|grow (out grō′) *verb,* **outgrew, outgrown, outgrowing.**

outing—A short walk or drive for pleasure: *a Sunday outing.*
out|ing (ou′ting) *noun, plural* **outings.**

outlast—To last or live longer than: *Her sneakers have outlasted mine, which are full of holes.*
out|last (out last′) *verb,* **outlasted, outlasting.**

outlaw—A person who does not obey laws; criminal. *Noun.*
   —To make illegal: *The city outlawed parking on the main streets when it was snowing. Verb.*
out|law (out′law′) *noun, plural* **outlaws;** *verb,* **outlawed, outlawing.**
• Synonyms: **ban, prohibit,** for *verb.*
   Antonyms: **license, permit,** for *verb.*

outlet—1. The opening where something is let out: *The holes near the top of the tub provide an outlet in case the water level gets too high.*   2. A

way of expressing or letting out something: *Jogging provided an excellent* outlet *for all her energy.* **3.** The place for plugging appliances and other devices into an electrical system: *She plugged the radio into an* outlet *by the door.*
out|let (out′let) *noun, plural* **outlets.**

outline—**1.** The shape formed by marking along the outside edge of something: *The children drew* outlines *of their own hands on paper.* **2.** A plan, summary, or short report of something, especially a piece of writing: *Before she started writing her essay, she prepared an* outline *of the topics she wanted it to cover. Noun.*
—To make a plan or give a summary: *He* outlined *the story of the book for the other members of the class. Verb.*
out|line (out′līn′) *noun, plural* **outlines;** *verb,* **outlined, outlining.**

outlook—**1.** A chance; likelihood: *The* outlook *for success is good.* **2.** A way of thinking; attitude: *His cheerful* outlook *helped him through difficult times.*
out|look (out′look′) *noun, plural* **outlooks.**

outnumber—To be more or larger in number than: *The girls in our class* outnumber *the boys.*
out|num|ber (out num′bər) *verb,* **outnumbered, outnumbering.**

out-of-date—No longer used or in style; old-fashioned: *Our typewriter is so* out-of-date *that nobody knows how to fix it.*
out-of-date (out′əv dāt′) *adjective.*

outpost—A military station set up away from the main camp to guard against surprise attacks or to control a frontier.
out|post (out′pōst′) *noun, plural* **outposts.**

output—**1.** The amount of something made or done: *The* output *of new cars increased as sales grew.* **2.** Information produced from the storage unit of a computer: *Here is the* output *of expenses for last month.*
out|put (out′poot′) *noun.*

outrage—**1.** An act of severe violence: *Outrages by the enemy included burning several towns.* **2.** Great anger, especially anger brought on by a shocking offense: *The people felt* outrage *when they learned the mayor had lied. Noun.*
—To cause extreme anger or resentment: *His*

rude behavior at the dance outraged *her. Verb.*
out|rage (out′rāj) *noun, plural* **outrages;** *verb,* **outraged, outraging.**
• Synonyms: **insult, offend,** for *verb.*

outrageous—Insulting or disgraceful; shocking: *His* outrageous *behavior during the match caused the crowd to boo him.*
out|ra|geous (out rā′jəs) *adjective.*

outrigger—A floating frame attached to a canoe or similar boat that helps keep the boat from turning over.
out|rig|ger (out′rig′ər) *noun, plural* **outriggers.**

outrigger

outright—**1.** All at once; entirely: *He sold the boat and its equipment* outright. **2.** In an open, honest way: *The children could not hide their amazement and stared* outright. *Adverb.*
—Absolute; complete: *Juggling 12 apples was an* outright *wonder. Adjective.*
out|right (out′rīt′) *adverb, adjective.*

outside—The side or surface that is the outer part; exterior: *The cabinet looks good on the* outside, *but I need to open the doors to see if it has enough shelves. Noun.*
—**1.** Outer: *The main door was open, but the* outside *screen door was locked.* **2.** Not very possible or likely: *Although the forecast is for sunny skies, there is an* outside *chance that it will rain. Adjective.*
—Outdoors: *Because the weather is so nice, we should eat our lunches* outside. *Adverb.*
—Beyond or out of: *They buy their eggs at a small farm just* outside *town. Preposition.*

a at	i if	oo look	ch chalk		⌐a in ago
ā ape	ī idle	ou out	ng sing		e in happen
ah calm	o odd	u ugly	sh ship	ə =	i in capital
aw all	ō oats	ū rule	th think		o in occur
e end	oi oil	ur turn	<u>th</u> their		⌊u in upon
ē easy			zh treasure		

out|side (out′sīd′ *or* out′sīd′) *noun, plural* **outsides;** *adjective; adverb; preposition.*

outskirts—The areas far from the center and near the edge of a town or city.
out|skirts (out′skurts′) *noun.*

outsmart—To outdo in skill, knowledge, or cleverness: *She* outsmarted *her dad and won the chess game.*
out|smart (out smahrt′) *verb,* **outsmarted, outsmarting.**

outspoken—Boldly honest: *His* outspoken *criticism of the club's rules offended some of the other members.*
out|spo|ken (out′spō′kən) *adjective.*
• Synonyms: **frank, open, straightforward**

outstanding—**1.** Excellent; better than others: *The painting that won first prize in the art show was* outstanding. **2.** Not paid yet: *an* outstanding *debt.*
out|stand|ing (out stan′ding) *adjective.*
• Synonyms: **superb, wonderful,** for **1.**

outward—Going or facing toward the outside; on the outside: *an* outward *glance to see if it is raining;* outward *appearance. Adjective.*
—Heading away from something or someplace; toward the outside: *Six streets run* outward *from the center of the park. Adverb.*
out|ward (out′wərd) *adjective, adverb.*

outwit—To get the better of someone or something by being cleverer: *She won every chess game by* outwitting *the other players.*
out|wit (out wit′) *verb,* **outwitted, outwitting.**

oval—**1.** Having a shape like an egg. **2.** Having a shape like an ellipse. *Adjective.*
—Something shaped like an egg or an ellipse. *Noun.*
o|val (ō′vəl) *adjective; noun, plural* **ovals.**

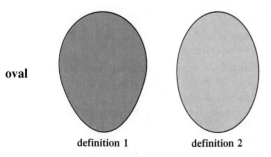

oval

definition 1   definition 2

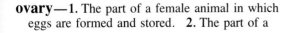

ovary—**1.** The part of a female animal in which eggs are formed and stored. **2.** The part of a flowering plant that makes and holds the seeds.
o|va|ry (ō′vər ē) *noun, plural* **ovaries.**

oven—**1.** An enclosed space, usually part of a stove or fireplace, in which food is heated or cooked. **2.** An enclosed structure in which things made of clay are baked.
ov|en (uv′ən) *noun, plural* **ovens.**

over—**1.** Above: *Pictures of the family are arranged* over *the sofa.* **2.** From one side to the other; across and above: *to sail* over *the ocean; to throw a ball* over *a net.* **3.** Down from the edge of: *The river flows* over *the cliff in a waterfall.* **4.** On; on top of: *The boy wore a jacket* over *his sweater.* **5.** Through all or some parts of: *She looked all* over *the gym for her lost sneaker.* **6.** During: *We went to the beach* over *the summer.* **7.** More than: *My grandfather is* over *60 years old.* **8.** About: *He laughed* over *his silly mistake. Preposition.*
—**1.** From one person, place, or thing to another: *When you come, bring your baseball cards* over.
2. Down: *The old tree fell* over *in the strong wind.* **3.** At some distance: *Stack the books* over *by the desk.* **4.** All through: *I thought the question* over *before answering.* **5.** Upside down; reversed: *He turned the record* over *to play the other side.* **6.** Again: *After she spilled juice on her report, she decided to copy it* over. *Adverb.*
—Ended; finished: *We were tired when the long day was* over. *Adjective.*
o|ver (ō′vər) *preposition, adverb, adjective.*
■ **over and over:** Again and again; many times: *He studied the spelling words* over and over *before the test.*

over-—A prefix that means "above," or "too much," or "too." An overhead light is one that is above one's head. If a dinner is overcooked, it is cooked too much. An overthrifty person is too thrifty.

Word Power

You can understand the meanings of many words that begin with **over-,** if you add a meaning of the prefix to the meaning of the rest of the word.
  overhang: hang above
  overworry: worry too much
  overbashful: too bashful

---

overall—With everything included: *Your* overall *grade will be based on homework, class work, and tests. Adjective.*
—For the most part; generally: *Although it is a*

bit small, the room is very pleasant overall.
Adverb.
o|ver|all (ō′vər awl′) *adjective, adverb.*

overalls—Loose trousers, usually having a part
that covers the chest. They are often worn over
other clothes to protect those clothes from dirt.
o|ver|alls (ō′vər awlz′) *noun.*

overboard—Into the water from a ship or boat:
to fall overboard.
o|ver|board (ō′vər bawrd′) *adverb.*

overcame—*See* overcome.
o|ver|came (ō′vər **kām**′) *verb.*

overcast—Cloudy; darkened by clouds: *The day
became* overcast *as the storm approached.*
o|ver|cast (ō′vər kast′) *adjective.*

overcoat—A heavy coat worn for warmth over
other clothing.
o|ver|coat (ō′vər kōt′) *noun, plural* **overcoats.**

overcome—1. To get the better of; defeat;
conquer: *The wrestler was strong enough to*
overcome *anyone who challenged him.* 2. To
make helpless, weak, or tired: *to be* overcome *by
fits of laughter; to be* overcome *by smoke.*
o|ver|come (ō′vər **kum**′) *verb,* **overcame,
overcome, overcoming.**

overdue—Supposed to have been done or paid or
to have arrived some time ago: overdue *books
that need to be returned to the library; a report
that is a week* overdue.
o|ver|due (ō′vər **dū**′) *adjective.*

overflow—1. To flow over or beyond the normal
boundaries: *The heavy rains caused the pond to*
overflow. 2. To be full beyond the brim so that
the contents spill over: *I left the water running,
and the sink* overflowed. 3. To flow over so as
to cover or flood: *When the drain clogged, soapy
water* overflowed *the bathroom floor.* 4. To
flow over the top rim of: *She was not paying
attention as she poured the milk, and she caused
it to* overflow *the bowl. Verb.*
—That which runs or flows over; something that
is too much to be contained: *The jar was too
small for all the honey I poured in, and the*
overflow *dripped down its sides. Noun.*
o|ver|flow (ō′vər **flō**′ for *verb;* ō′vər flō′ for
noun) verb, **overflowed, overflown,
overflowing;** *noun, plural* **overflows.**

overhand—With the hand lifted higher than the
shoulder and the arm making a downward
motion: *She served the ball with an* overhand
*swing of her tennis racket. Can you throw a
baseball* overhand?
o|ver|hand (ō′vər hand′) *adjective, adverb.*

overhand

overhang—To hang or stick out over: *There is a
nice view from the balcony that* overhangs *the
garden. Verb.*
—Something that hangs or sticks out over
something else: *The hikers huddled under an*
overhang *of rock until the rain stopped. Noun.*
o|ver|hang (ō′vər **hang**′ for *verb;* ō′vər hang′
for *noun) verb,* **overhung, overhanging;** *noun,
plural* **overhangs.**

overhaul—1. To look over carefully and then
make what repairs or changes are needed: *The
appliance store* overhauled *our old washing
machine.* 2. To catch up with and then pass:
The galloping horses soon overhauled *the
slow-moving wagon. Verb.*
—The act of looking over and then fixing
completely: *Our car is in the repair shop for an*
overhaul *of its engine. Noun.*
o|ver|haul (ō′vər **hawl**′ for *verb;* ō′vər hawl′
for *noun) verb,* **overhauled, overhauling;** *noun,
plural* **overhauls.**

overhead—Over the head; high above: *We
looked up to watch the airplane that was flying*
overhead. *Adverb.*
—Located above the head: *an* overhead *branch;*
overhead *lights. Adjective.*
—The general expenses of running a business,
such as the costs of rent, taxes, and telephone.
Noun.
o|ver|head (ō′vər **hed**′ for *adverb;* ō′vər hed′
for *adjective* and *noun) adverb, adjective, noun.*

a at	i if	oo look	ch chalk		a in ago
ā ape	ī idle	ou out	ng sing		e in happen
ah calm	o odd	u ugly	sh ship	ə =	i in capital
aw all	ō oats	ū rule	th think		o in occur
e end	oi oil	ur turn	th their		u in upon
ē easy			zh treasure		

overhear—To hear what is not intended for one to hear: *He* overheard *what she whispered to me.* o|ver|hear (ō′vər hēr′) *verb,* **overheard, overhearing.**

overload—To weigh down too much: *The roof was* overloaded *with snow and collapsed.* o|ver|load (ō′vər lōd′) *verb,* **overloaded, overloading.**

overlook—**1.** To fail to see or think of: *She* overlooked *two items on her shopping list and had to go back to the store.*   **2.** To give no importance to; excuse: *The coach* overlooked *my absence from practice, because I had a doctor's appointment.*   **3.** To have a view of someone or something from higher up: *The tower* overlooks *the castle and the fields all around it. Verb.*
—A place that gives a view from high up: *While driving through the mountains, we stopped at a scenic* overlook *to enjoy the view. Noun.* o|ver|look (ō′vər look′ for *verb;* ō′vər look′ for *noun*) *verb,* **overlooked, overlooking;** *noun, plural* **overlooks.**
• Synonyms: **disregard, ignore, neglect,** for *verb* **2.**

overnight—**1.** Through or during the night: *It rained* overnight, *so the streets were wet in the morning.*   **2.** Suddenly; quickly; all at once: *She did not learn to play the piano* overnight *but practiced at it for years. Adverb.*
—**1.** Happening during or all through the night: *The* overnight *storm covered the town with deep snow.*   **2.** For the night: *an* overnight *guest; an* overnight *trip. Adjective.* o|ver|night (ō′vər nīt′ for *adverb;* ō′vər nīt′ for *adjective*) *adverb, adjective.*

overpass—A bridge or road crossing over another road or route. o|ver|pass (ō′vər pas′) *noun, plural* **overpasses.**

overpower—**1.** To use one's greater force to get the better of or conquer: *The police* overpowered *the robber and took him to jail.*   **2.** To be much stronger than; make weaker or less powerful: *Nervousness so* overpowered *her that for a moment she could not move or speak.* o|ver|pow|er (ō′vər pou′ər) *verb,* **overpowered, overpowering.**

overrule—To put aside what someone has said; decide against: *My mother* overruled *my request for another piece of cake.* o|ver|rule (ō′vər rūl′) *verb,* **overruled, overruling.**

overseas—On the other side of the sea or ocean; abroad: *The soldiers are stationed* overseas. *Adverb.*
—**1.** Placed, in use, or in service across the ocean: *an* overseas *telephone call; an* overseas *flight.*   **2.** Having to do with nations across the ocean: *an* overseas *trading partner. Adjective.* o|ver|seas (ō′vər sēz′ for *adverb;* ō′vər sēz′ for *adjective*) *adverb, adjective.*

overshoe—A shoe or boot that is usually made of rubber and is waterproof. It is worn over another shoe to keep the foot from getting wet and cold. o|ver|shoe (ō′vər shū′) *noun, plural* **overshoes.**

oversight—A mistake caused by a lack of attention: *Not putting a stamp on the letter was an* oversight. o|ver|sight (ō′vər sīt′) *noun, plural* **oversights.**

oversleep—To sleep longer than one meant to sleep: *I* overslept *this morning and was late for school.* o|ver|sleep (ō′vər slēp′) *verb,* **overslept, oversleeping.**

overtake—to catch up to; pass: *I walked so fast that I* overtook *the people who started before me.* o|ver|take (ō′vər tāk′) *verb,* **overtook, overtaken, overtaking.**

overthrow—**1.** To throw a ball or other object past its mark: *The shortstop* overthrew *the first baseman, and the runner was safe.*   **2.** To remove from power; defeat: *After the harsh ruler was* overthrown, *the people voted for a new leader.* o|ver|throw (ō′vər thrō′) *verb,* **overthrew, overthrown, overthrowing.**

overtime—Extra time added to the usual amount set for work or for a game or sporting event: *Our team broke the tie score to win the game in* overtime. *Noun.*
—Beyond usual working hours: *She will have to work* overtime *if she plans to finish the project by next week. Adverb.*
—Having to do with extra time: overtime *pay. Adjective.* o|ver|time (ō′vər tīm′) *noun, plural* **overtimes;** *adverb; adjective.*

overture—**1.** A musical piece played by an orchestra as the opening part of a longer work, such as an opera or ballet.   **2.** A suggestion or offer: *He accepted the* overtures *to join the team.* o|ver|ture (ō′vər chər) *noun, plural* **overtures.**

overturn—**1.** To turn something over or upside down: *The baby* overturned *his bowl of cereal.*   **2.** To fall over: *The bucket* overturned *when the horse kicked it.* o|ver|turn (ō′vər turn′) *verb,* **overturned, overturning.**

overweight—Having more weight than is usual, healthy, or allowed: *He started a diet because he was* overweight.
o|ver|weight (ō′vər wāt′) *adjective.*

overwhelm—To be too much for; defeat or weaken: *The excitement of the carnival* overwhelmed *the children.*
o|ver|whelm (ō′vər hwelm′) *verb,*
overwhelmed, overwhelming.

overwork—Too much or too strong an effort: *He was so tired from* overwork *that he fell asleep in his chair. Noun.*
—To use too much or too hard: *He* overworked *the new toy and broke it. Verb.*
o|ver|work (ō′vər wurk′ for *noun;* ō′vər **wurk′** for *verb*) *noun; verb,* **overworked, overworking.**

owe—1. To have to pay; have a debt: *I* owe *a fine to the library.* 2. To be or feel obliged to someone: *I* owe *my friend a letter, because I received one from her last week.*
owe (ō) *verb,* **owed, owing.**
● A word that sounds the same is **oh.**

owl

owl—A bird with a large head, big eyes, and a short, curved beak. Owls usually hunt at night, feeding on mice, insects, and other small creatures.
owl (oul) *noun, plural* **owls.**

owlet—A young owl.
owl|et (ou′lit) *noun, plural* **owlets.**

own—To have as one's possession: *The people in that house* own *a dog and a cat. Verb.*
—Of or belonging to oneself: *I have my* own *room. Adjective.*
—Something belonging to one: *He wanted to have a bicycle of his* own, *so he would not have to keep borrowing his brother's. Noun.*
own (ōn) *verb,* **owned, owning;** *adjective; noun.*
■ **on** (one's) **own:** By oneself; not in the care of someone else: *No one wanted to go to the library with her, so she went* on *her* own.

owner—One who possesses something: *The* owner *of such a beautiful car must be rich.*
own|er (ō′nər) *noun, plural* **owners.**

ox—1. The strong, full-grown male of domestic cattle. It is used as a work animal or for meat. 2. Any of the animals related to domestic cattle, such as water buffalo and bison.
ox (oks) *noun, plural* **oxen.**

oxcart—A cart pulled by an ox or a team of oxen.
ox|cart (oks′kahrt′) *noun, plural* **oxcarts.**

ox (definition 1) and oxcart

oxen—*See* **ox.**
ox|en (ok′sən) *plural noun.*

oxygen—A gas having no color, smell, or taste. It is a chemical element and makes up about one-fifth of the air. Animals and plants need oxygen to live.
ox|y|gen (ok′sə jən) *noun.*

oyster—A sea animal with a soft body covered by a hard, two-piece shell. Oysters are eaten as food and also raised for the pearls some kinds produce.
oys|ter (ois′tər) *noun, plural* **oysters.**

oz.—The abbreviation for **ounce** or **ounces.**

ozone—A form of oxygen that is produced by lightning or other electricity in the air. It has a very sharp smell.
o|zone (ō′zōn) *noun.*

ozone layer—A layer of concentrated ozone in the upper atmosphere. It protects the earth from harmful radiation from the sun.
o|zone lay|er (ō′zōn lā′ər) *noun.*

a at	i if	oo look	ch chalk		a in ago
ā ape	ī idle	ou out	ng sing		e in happen
ah calm	o odd	u ugly	sh ship	ə =	i in capital
aw all	ō oats	ū rule	th think		o in occur
e end	oi oil	ur turn	th their		u in upon
ē easy			zh treasure		

About 1,900 years ago, the Romans gave the capital **P** its present form. The small letter **p** was first used about 1,400 years ago. It reached its present form about 500 years ago.

About 5,000 years ago, the ancient Egyptians used a symbol of a mouth.

About 3,500 years ago, people in the Middle East used a similar symbol. They called it *pe*, their word for "mouth."

About 3,000 years ago, other people in the Middle East used a rounded hook-shaped letter.

About 2,600 years ago, the Greeks gave the letter this form. They called it *pi*.

P or **p**—The sixteenth letter of the alphabet: *The word "paper" has two p's.*
P, p (pē) *noun, plural* **P's** or **Ps, p's** or **ps.**

p.—The abbreviation for **page** or **part.**

pace—**1.** A step: *She took five* paces *across the floor.* **2.** The length of a step: *I saw my friend about ten* paces *ahead of me.* **3.** A certain manner of stepping: *The* paces *of a horse include the canter and gallop.* **4.** The rate of speed of doing something: *The car moved through traffic at a fast* pace. *Noun.*
—**1.** To walk back and forth with slow, even steps: *His lawyer, deep in thought,* paced *the floor.* **2.** To measure by counting steps: *We* paced *off a small area where we would plant a garden. Verb.*
pace (pās) *noun, plural* **paces;** *verb,* **paced, pacing.**
■ **go through** (one's) **paces:** To show one's skill or knowledge: *The piano teacher had the children* go through *their* paces *when their parents visited the class.*
keep pace with: Stay even with; go as quickly as: *The girl struggled to* keep pace with *her older sister as they hurried to the bus stop.*
put through (one's) **paces:** To test what someone or something can do: *The judges at the talent show* put *the performers* through *their* paces.

pack—**1.** Several things wrapped or held together in a bundle for easy carrying: *My brother* fastened the pack *of books on his back.* **2.** A group of things, animals, or people that are the same: *a* pack *of coyotes. Noun.*
—**1.** To put into a box or other container: *The workers* packed *the oranges in crates for shipping.* **2.** To fill something by putting things into it: *We* packed *a picnic basket to take to the park.* **3.** To press together: *The gardener* packed *the earth around the flowers he had planted.*
4. To fill up completely by putting in as much as will fit: *He* packed *the refrigerator with food for the party. Verb.*
pack (pak) *noun, plural* **packs;** *verb,* **packed, packing.**
■ **pack it in:** To quit; give up on: *After two hours of pulling weeds in the hot sun, I decided to* pack it in.
● Synonyms: **cram, stuff,** for *verb* **4.**

package—**1.** A number of things tied or packed together: *We sent a* package *of food and clothes to the needy family.* **2.** A box, bag, or other container in which something is packed. *Noun.*
—To place in a box, bag, or other container: *We* packaged *our homemade fudge. Verb.*
pack|age (pak'ij) *noun, plural* **packages;** *verb,* **packaged, packaging.**

pact—An agreement between people or nations to act in a certain way: *The two countries signed a* pact *to defend one another.*
pact (pakt) *noun, plural* **pacts.**

pad—**1.** A piece of soft material used for protection or comfort; cushion: *We put a* pad *on*

the hard chair seat to make it easier to sit on.
2. Sheets of paper joined together along one side:
The reporter carried a pad *for his notes.* **3.** The
thick piece of skin on the bottom of the feet of
certain animals, such as dogs and cats. **4.** A
piece of cloth soaked with ink for use with a
rubber stamp. *Noun.*
—To fill or cover with soft material: *We* padded
*the inside of the trunk before packing the dishes
in it. Verb.*
pad (pad) *noun, plural* **pads;** *verb,* **padded,
padding.**

paddle¹—**1.** A short oar that is used to move a
small boat, such as a canoe. **2.** A wooden tool
with a flat blade used for stirring or mixing.
3. A small, flat, wooden racket used to hit the
ball in table tennis and other games. *Noun.*
—**1.** To move a canoe or small boat with a short
oar: *We* paddled *around the island.* **2.** To strike
with a flat blade or with the open hand; spank:
The boy knew he would be paddled *for breaking
the lamp. Verb.*
pad|dle (pad′əl) *noun, plural* **paddles;** *verb,*
paddled, paddling.

paddle²—To splash and kick about in shallow
water: *The baby* paddled *happily at the edge of
the pool.*
pad|dle (pad′əl) *verb,* **paddled, paddling.**

paddy—A field in which rice is grown.
pad|dy (pad′ē) *noun, plural* **paddies.**

padlock—A removable lock that has a curved bar
that can be snapped shut. *Noun.*
—To fasten with such a lock: *We wanted to
open the old trunk, but it was* padlocked.
Verb.
pad|lock (pad′lok′) *noun, plural* **padlocks;**
verb, **padlocked, padlocking.**

pagan—A person who is not a Christian, Jew, or
Muslim. A pagan may worship many gods or
may not believe in any god.
pa|gan (pa′gən) *noun, plural* **pagans.**

page¹—**1.** One side of a sheet of written material,
such as in a magazine or book: *We found an
article about the bus trip on the back* page *of the
newspaper.* **2.** An important event or period of

time: *The discovery of penicillin was a major*
page *in medical history.*
page (pāj) *noun, plural* **pages.** Abbreviation: **p.**

page²—**1.** A person who runs errands, makes
deliveries, and carries messages for someone, as
for a member of Congress. **2.** A boy or young
man in the Middle Ages who served a royal or
noble family. *Noun.*
—To try and locate someone in a public area by
calling by name, usually over a loudspeaker:
*When the woman arrived at the restaurant, she
asked the clerk to* page *her friends. Verb.*
page (pāj) *noun, plural* **pages;** *verb,* **paged,
paging.**

pageant—**1.** A show, ceremony, or parade to
celebrate something important: *Everyone looked
forward to the announcement of the winner at the
end of the beauty* pageant. **2.** A play showing
scenes or events from history: *I played the part
of a pilgrim in last year's Thanksgiving* pageant.
pag|eant (paj′ənt) *noun, plural* **pageants.**

pagoda—A temple or tower that has several
levels. Each level has its own roof, which curves
upward at the edges. Pagodas are found in Asia.
pa|go|da (pə gō′də) *noun, plural* **pagodas.**

pagoda

paid—*See* **pay.**
paid (pād) *verb.*

pail—A round, flat-bottomed container with a
handle, used for carrying things such as sand or
water; bucket.
pail (pāl) *noun, plural* **pails.**
• A word that sounds the same is **pale.**

pain—1. Physical suffering caused by being hurt or ill: *My elbow was in* pain *all day after I fell on the icy sidewalk.* **2.** Emotional suffering; grief: *The child's mother hugged her to ease the* pain *of losing her favorite doll.* **3. pains:** Special care or effort: *The teacher took* pains *to explain the work he had missed while he was absent. Noun.*
—To hurt or cause suffering to: *Her injured leg* pained *her. Verb.*
pain (pān) *noun, plural* **pains;** *verb,* **pained, paining.**
• A word that sounds the same is **pane.**

paint—A substance made by mixing solid coloring matter with oil or water. A thin layer of this mixture can be spread on a surface to decorate or protect it. *Noun.*
—**1.** To cover with such a substance: *He painted the bird house blue.* **2.** To use such a substance to make a picture: *In art class today, I painted a bowl of fruit.* **3.** To use words to describe something: *The newspaper article painted a detailed picture of life in the small town. Verb.*
paint (pānt) *noun, plural* **paints;** *verb,* **painted, painting.**

painter—1. Someone who paints pictures; artist: *Portraits by many famous* painters *hang in the museum.* **2.** Someone whose job is to cover walls or other surfaces with paint: *The* painters *are at work changing the color of our classroom from red to green.*
paint|er (pān′tər) *noun, plural* **painters.**

painting—1. A picture made with paint: *A painting of my grandfather hangs in the hall.* **2.** The act or art of using paint: *Always clean your brushes after painting.*
paint|ing (pān′ting) *noun, plural* **paintings.**

pair—1. Two things that are alike or go together: *a* pair *of candlesticks.* **2.** A thing made up of two parts: *a* pair *of scissors.* **3.** Two people or two animals that are alike or often go together: *A* pair *of robins built a nest in that tree. Noun.*
—To form or arrange into twos. Verb.
pair (pār) *noun, plural* **pairs** or **pair;** *verb,* **paired, pairing.**
• Words that sound the same are **pare** and **pear.**

pajamas—A loose shirt and pants usually worn for sleeping.
pa|ja|mas (pə jah′məz *or* pə jam′əz) *plural noun.*

Word History

Pajamas comes from two Persian words meaning "leg clothing." At first, pajamas were loose pants worn by people who lived in and around what is now Iran. Later, Europeans started sleeping in these comfortable clothes.

pal—A good friend; buddy: *My sister is my best* pal.
pal (pal) *noun, plural* **pals.**
• Synonyms: **chum, comrade**
  Antonyms: **enemy, foe**

palace—A large, very grand house where a king, queen, or other head of state lives: *The emperor's* palace *had 100 rooms.*
pal|ace (pal′is) *noun, plural* **palaces.**

pale—1. Lacking color; whitish: *The girl's face was* pale *because she had been sick.* **2.** Lacking brightness; dim: *The old jeans have faded to a* pale *blue. Adjective.*
—To turn a whitish color: *He* paled *in fright at the horrible sound. Verb.*
pale (pāl) *adjective,* **paler, palest;** *verb,* **paled, paling.**
• A word that sounds the same is **pail.**

palette—A thin board with a hole for the thumb at one end, used by an artist to hold and mix paints.
pal|ette (pal′it) *noun, plural* **palettes.**

palm¹—The flat, inner part of the hand, between the fingers and wrist. *Noun.*
—To hide something in that part of the hand: *She* palmed *the candy so we would think it was all gone. Verb.*
palm (pahm) *noun, plural* **palms;** *verb,* **palmed, palming.**
■ **grease the palm of:** To offer someone money so that he or she will do something wrong; bribe: *If we have to* grease his palm *to get good seats, I won't go.*
in the palm of (one's) **hand:** Under total control: *The storyteller had the children* in the palm of *his hand.*
palm off: To get rid of something by tricking or cheating: *The store tried to* palm off *the old bread as fresh.*

palm²—Any of a family of trees that grow in warm regions. Their large, feathery or fan-shaped leaves usually grow directly from the top of the trunk.
palm (pahm) *noun, plural* **palms.**
• See picture at **date²** and at **palmetto.**

palm² (left) and **palmetto**

palmetto—A low palm tree with fan-shaped leaves. Palmettos are found in some parts of the southern United States.
pal|met|to (pal met′ō) *noun, plural* **palmettos** or **palmettoes**.

Palm Sunday—In the Christian religion, the Sunday before Easter. It celebrates Christ's arrival in Jerusalem, where people welcomed Him by spreading palm branches along His path.
Palm Sun|day (pahm sun′dē *or* pahm sun′dā) *noun, plural* **Palm Sundays**.

palomino—A light tan horse with a white or creamy white mane and tail.
pal|o|mi|no (pal′ə mē′nō) *noun, plural* **palominos**.

pamper—To yield to the desires of; spoil: *The father* pampered *his sick daughter*.
pam|per (pam′pər) *verb*, **pampered**, **pampering**.
• Synonyms: **coddle, indulge**

pamphlet—A small book with a paper cover: *We chose our vacation place after looking at* pamphlets *describing several resorts*.
pam|phlet (pam′flit) *noun, plural* **pamphlets**.

pan—1. A cooking dish, usually with low sides and no cover: *I cooked the eggs in a frying* pan. 2. Any dish or container that looks like a pan. Gold and some other metals are sometimes shaken in pans with water to separate them from the gravel in which they are found. *Noun.*
—To wash sand and gravel from gold in a flat container: *to* pan *for gold. Verb.*
pan (pan) *noun, plural* **pans**; *verb,* **panned**, **panning**.
  ▪ **pan out:** To work out or turn out well; succeed: *We hope our plans for a big party will* pan out.

pancake—A flat cake made of batter and cooked in a pan or on a griddle.
pan|cake (pan′kāk′) *noun, plural* **pancakes**.

panda—1. A large animal found in China that looks like a bear and is thought to be related to bears. It is mostly white with black legs, shoulders, and ears, and black rings around its eyes. 2. A reddish brown animal related to the raccoon and found in and around China. It has a long, bushy tail with light-colored rings.
pan|da (pan′də) *noun, plural* **pandas**.

panda (definition 1)

pane—A piece of glass in a window or door: *The baseball hit the window and broke a* pane *of glass*.
pane (pān) *noun, plural* **panes**.
• A word that sounds the same is **pain**.

panel—1. A part of a surface that is different from the rest of the surface. It may be higher or lower than the surface, have a different color, or have a border around it. 2. A surface on which the instruments used to control something are placed: *The director watched the control* panel *in the television studio*. 3. A group of people

a at	i if	oo look	ch chalk		⌈ a in ago
ā ape	ī idle	ou out	ng sing		e in happen
ah calm	o odd	u ugly	sh ship	ə =	i in capital
aw all	ō oats	ū rule	th think		o in occur
e end	oi oil	ur turn	th their		⌊ u in upon
ē easy			zh treasure		

gathered to discuss or decide something: *a panel of doctors speaking on a radio show. Noun.*
—To cover or arrange with sections of something: *Carpenters* paneled *the room with boards. Verb.*
pan|el (pan′əl) *noun, plural* **panels;** *verb,* **paneled, paneling.**

pang—A sudden, sharp pain or feeling: *hunger* pangs.
pang (pang) *noun, plural* **pangs.**

panic—A feeling of great fear: *The earthquake caused* panic *in the city as tall buildings trembled. Noun.*
—To be greatly frightened: *I* panicked *when I thought I saw a bear circling our camp. Verb.*
pan|ic (pan′ik) *noun, plural* **panics;** *verb,* **panicked, panicking.**

pansy—A garden plant with soft, colorful flowers that look like large violets.
pan|sy (pan′zē) *noun, plural* **pansies.**

pant—1. To breathe hard and quickly as when out of breath; gasp: *The runner was* panting *when he crossed the finish line.* 2. To speak between short gasps for air: *"Fire! Fire!" he* panted *as he ran from the burning building.*
pant (pant) *verb,* **panted, panting.**

panther—1. A large, all-black leopard. 2. A mountain lion.
pan|ther (pan′thər) *noun, plural* **panthers** or **panther.**
• *See also* picture at **mountain lion.**

panther (definition 1)

pantomime—1. A play in which the story is acted out but in which the actors do not speak. 2. The acting out of a story or message using face and body movements only: *Noun.*
—To show by silently acting out: *She made us laugh by* pantomiming *the words to the song. Verb.*
pan|to|mime (pan′tə mīm) *noun, plural* **pantomimes;** *verb,* **pantomimed, pantomiming.**

pantry—A small room with shelves and cupboards for keeping food, dishes, and pots and pans.
pan|try (pan′trē) *noun, plural* **pantries.**

pants—A piece of clothing for the lower body that covers each leg individually; trousers.
pants (pants) *plural noun.*
■ **beat the pants off:** To defeat soundly or completely: *We played so badly that the visiting team* beat the pants off *us.*
catch with (one's) pants down: To challenge someone who is not prepared or ready: *That surprise quiz* caught *me with my* pants down.
scare the pants off: To frighten badly: *My mask* scared the pants off *my little brother.*

paper—1. A material made by processing wood, straw, or other vegetable fiber in a special way and cutting it into very thin sheets. It is used for writing, drawing, and printing. It is also used to cover or wrap things, such as a wall or a package. 2. A sheet of this material: *There is a* paper *lying on the floor.* 3. A piece of this material on which something has been written or printed in a formal way; written proof: *We had to show our identification* papers *before crossing the border.* 4. A newspaper: *He read the comics in the* paper. 5. An article, report, or essay on a particular subject: *My science* paper *is about electricity. Noun.*
—To cover or decorate with this material: *The kitchen walls are* papered *in a striped design. Verb.*
pa|per (pā′pər) *noun, plural* **papers;** *verb,* **papered, papering.**
■ **paper over:** To hide; make seem less obvious or unpleasant: *She wants to* paper over *their differences rather than try to work out their problems.*

paperback—A book with a paper cover.
pa|per|back (pā′pər bak′) *noun, plural* **paperbacks.**

paper clip—A fastener made of bent wire for holding papers together.
pa|per clip (pā′pər klip) *noun, plural* **paper clips.**

papier-mâché—A material made of wet paper or paper pulp mixed with glue. It can be molded into shapes while damp, and as it dries, it

becomes hard. Decorative objects, puppets, and objects used on the stage are often made of it.
pa|pier-mâ|ché (pā′pər mə shā′) *noun.*

papillon—A small dog with large ears that stand erect, like wings, from each side of the head. It has long, straight hair, a pointed muzzle, and a long tail curved above its back. Originally bred in Spain, this dog makes a good pet.
pap|il|lon (pap′ə lon) *noun, plural* **papillons.**

papillon

Word History

Papillon comes from an old French word meaning ''butterfly.'' This breed of dog has large ears that are somewhat like the wings of a butterfly. They stand straight up and have curved edges.

paprika—A seasoning for food made by grinding dried, mild red peppers into a powder.
pap|ri|ka (pa prē′kə *or* pap′rə kə) *noun.*

papyrus—1. A tall, slender water plant. 2. A material made from the stems of this plant, used for writing on by some ancient peoples.
pa|py|rus (pə pī′rəs) *noun, plural* **papyri**
(pə pī′rī).

par—1. A common or shared level; equal standing: *Her athletic ability is on a* par *with yours.* 2. A standard considered average or

a at	i if	oo look	ch chalk		a in ago
ā ape	ī idle	ou out	ng sing		e in happen
ah calm	o odd	u ugly	sh ship	ə =	i in capital
aw all	ō oats	ū rule	th think		o in occur
e end	oi oil	ur turn	th their		u in upon
ē easy			zh treasure		

normal: *The orchestra's performance was above* par *this evening.*
par (pahr) *noun.*
- **par for the course:** What is normal or expected: *Her behavior surprised some people, but I've known her long enough to know it was* par for the course.

par.—The abbreviation for paragraph.

parachute—An umbrella-shaped device made of nylon or other thin fabric, used to slow the speed of a person or an object diving or falling from an airplane in flight or other high place. *Noun.*
—To go down or drop while using this device: *At the air show, I saw a team of divers* parachute *one after another. Verb.*
par|a|chute (par′ə shūt) *noun, plural* **parachutes;** *verb,* **parachuted, parachuting.**

parade—A type of celebration or procession in which spectators watch as decorated vehicles and people in costumes or uniforms travel along a set route: *a circus* parade; *a Veterans Day* parade. *Noun.*
—1. To march or participate in such a procession: *The returning astronauts* paraded *through the city.* 2. To display something to others in a grand way; show off: *She* paraded *her new dress in front of her friends. Verb.*
pa|rade (pə rād′) *noun, plural* **parades;** *verb,* **paraded, parading.**

paradise—1. The home of God; heaven. 2. A place or condition of complete happiness and delight: *After our long journey, home seemed like a* paradise.
par|a|dise (par′ə dīs) *noun.*

paraffin—A waxy, white substance made chiefly from petroleum and used to produce candles, cosmetics, and wax paper and for sealing jars of jam and jelly.
par|af|fin (par′ə fin) *noun.*

paragraph—Several sentences that together make a particular point or express a single idea. Each paragraph begins on a new line, usually indented. An essay or a chapter of a book contains several or many paragraphs.
par|a|graph (par′ə graf) *noun, plural* **paragraphs.** Abbreviation: **par.**

parakeet—A small parrot having bright, colorful feathers and a long, pointed tail. It can be taught to imitate sounds and is often kept as a pet.
par|a|keet (par′ə kēt) *noun, plural* **parakeets.**

parallel—1. Extending in the same direction, always the same distance apart, and never meeting. Railroad tracks and printed lines on a sheet of paper are parallel. 2. Nearly the same;

like; comparable: *The two boys go to different schools but get a* parallel *education. Adjective.*
—**1.** A line, surface, or curve that extends in the same direction as another and maintains the same distance from another. **2.** One of the imaginary lines around the earth that at any point is the same distance from the equator. They are used to indicate degrees of latitude. **3.** A likeness; similarity: *Study the two stories and list their* parallels. *Noun.*
—**1.** To extend in the same direction and remain the same distance apart: *A path* parallels *the road for several miles.* **2.** To be nearly the same as or comparable: *The plot of the film* parallels *that of the book. Verb.*
par|al|lel (par′ə lel) *adjective; noun, plural* **parallels;** *verb,* **paralleled, paralleling.**
• See picture at **latitude** for *noun* **2.**

paralysis—A condition that involves the loss of movement or feeling in some part of the body.
pa|ral|y|sis (pə ral′ə sis) *noun, plural* **paralyses** (pə ral′ə sēz).

paralyze—**1.** To cause a loss of movement or feeling in some part of the body: *My grandmother's accident* paralyzed *her left arm and leg for a week.* **2.** To make powerless or unable to speak or move. *Terror* paralyzed *the kitten when it saw the dog approaching.*
par|a|lyze (par′ə līz) *verb,* **paralyzed, paralyzing.**

paramecium—An animal that lives in fresh water and consists of just one cell. As seen through a microscope, it is shaped something like the sole of a shoe.
par|a|me|ci|um (par′ə mē′shē əm) *noun, plural* **paramecia** (par′ə mē′shē ə).

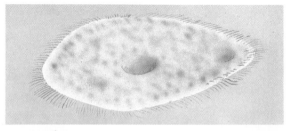

paramecium

parasite—A living thing that attaches itself to another living thing for food and survival. Fleas and ticks are common parasites on animals. Mistletoe is a parasite on plants.
par|a′|site (par′ə sīt) *noun, plural* **parasites.**

parasol—An umbrella used to provide shade from the sun: *Some of us wore hats to shade our faces, while others carried* parasols.
par|a|sol (par′ə sawl) *noun, plural* **parasols.**
• See Word History at **umbrella.**

paratrooper—A soldier trained to parachute from an aircraft.
par|a|troop|er (par′ə trū′pər) *noun, plural* **paratroopers.**

parcel—**1.** Things bundled together; a wrapped package: *We carried our* parcels *home from the shopping mall.* **2.** A piece of land; plot: *The barn stands on a large* parcel *of land owned by my grandfather. Noun.*
—To divide into or give out in portions: *The zoo keeper* parceled *out hay to all the elephants. Verb.*
par|cel (pahr′səl) *noun, plural* **parcels;** *verb,* **parceled, parceling.**

parch—**1.** To cause to become dry through heating: *The long drought* parched *the farmer's corn crop.* **2.** To cause to be in great need of water: *A week in the desert sun* parched *even the camels.*
parch (pahrch) *verb,* **parched, parching.**

parchment—The hide of a sheep, goat, or other animal that has been dried and prepared as a writing surface, or paper treated to look like this material. It is used for diplomas and other formal documents.
parch|ment (pahrch′mənt) *noun, plural* **parchments.**

pardon—**1.** The excusing of a guilty person from punishment or blame: *I asked his* pardon *for my bad behavior.* **2.** The releasing of a person judged guilty from having to perform the penalty set by the law: *The prisoner requested a* pardon *from the governor. Noun.*
—**1.** To excuse from punishment or blame; forgive: *I hope you will* pardon *me for losing your book.* **2.** To release from punishment by the law; set free: *The new mayor* pardoned *all parking violators. Verb.*
par|don (pahr′dən) *noun, plural* **pardons;** *verb,* **pardoned, pardoning.**

pare—**1.** To cut away something's outer part, skin, or rind; peel; trim: *Please* pare *six potatoes.* **2.** To make smaller gradually, as if by peeling: *Our goal is to make monthly payments and* pare *away what we owe.*
pare (pār) *verb,* **pared, paring.**
• Words that sound the same are **pair** and **pear.**

parent—**1.** A father or mother.   **2.** Any living thing that produces offspring.
par|ent (pār′ənt) *noun, plural* **parents.**

parenthesis—One of a pair of upright curved lines that look like this ( ) and are used to set off part of a sentence from the rest.
pa|ren|the|sis (pə ren′thə sis) *noun, plural* **parentheses** (pə ren′thə sēz).

parish—**1.** The area served by a church and its clergy.   **2.** The residents of the area who belong to this church.
par|ish (par′ish) *noun, plural* **parishes.**

park—**1.** A piece of land set aside by a government for public enjoyment and recreation.   **2.** A large land area kept in its wild state by a government to preserve its natural beauty and wildlife. *Noun.*
—To stop a vehicle and leave it in a place temporarily: *Visitors′ automobiles are allowed to* park *beside the building. Verb.*
park (pahrk) *noun, plural* **parks;** *verb,* **parked, parking.**

parka—A warm jacket with a hood: *The hood of her* parka *is trimmed with fur.*
par|ka (pahr′kə) *noun, plural* **parkas.**

parliament—**1.** A national law-making council. **2. Parliament:** The national law-making council of Great Britain or of Canada. The British Parliament consists of the House of Lords and the House of Commons. The Canadian Parliament consists of the Senate and the House of Commons.
par|lia|ment (pahr′lə mənt) *noun, plural* **parliaments.**

Word History

Parliament and **parlor** both come from an old French word meaning "to speak." A parliament is a meeting of certain people in public so that they can speak about questions of law and government. A parlor is a room where people can meet privately to talk together about whatever they choose.

---

parlor—**1.** A room in one's home used for spending time with or entertaining guests; living room: *The adults talked in the* parlor *while the children played outdoors.*   **2.** A certain kind of shop or place of business: *a beauty* parlor; *an ice cream* parlor.
par|lor (pahr′lər) *noun, plural* **parlors.**

parochial—Having to do with a parish: *The priest performed his* parochial *duties by visiting sick members of his church.*
pa|ro|chi|al (pə rō′kē əl) *adjective.*

parole—A prisoner's early release from jail, before he or she has spent the amount of time called for by the sentence. A person released on parole must promise good behavior and report to an official assigned to check on his or her conduct. *Noun.*
—To release a prisoner from jail earlier than called for by his or her sentence: *They paroled her because of her good record in prison. Verb.*
pa|role (pə rōl′) *noun, plural* **paroles;** *verb,* **paroled, paroling.**

parrot—A large tropical bird with a thick, hooked beak and glossy, colorful feathers. It often can be taught to imitate sounds and repeat words. *Noun.*
—To repeat someone else's words without understanding their meaning: *Babies* parrot *the words spoken by their parents as part of learning to talk. Verb.*
par|rot (par′ət) *noun, plural* **parrots;** *verb,* **parroted, parroting.**

parrot (noun)

parsley—A garden herb with fragrant, curly, deep green leaves, often used to season or decorate food.
pars|ley (pahrs′lē) *noun, plural* **parsleys.**

a at	i if	oo look	ch chalk		a in ago
ā ape	ī idle	ou out	ng sing		e in happen
ah calm	o odd	u ugly	sh ship	ə =	i in capital
aw all	ō oats	ū rule	th think		o in occur
e end	oi oil	ur turn	th their		u in upon
ē easy			zh treasure		

parsnip—A vegetable with a white, pointed root that is peeled and cooked before eating.
pars|nip (pahrs′nip) *noun, plural* **parsnips.**

parson—A member of the clergy; minister; preacher.
par|son (pahr′sən) *noun, plural* **parsons.**

part—1. A portion of the whole; less than all: *I read* part *of the book, but I don't care to finish it.* 2. A necessary piece of a whole: *Some* parts *of my puzzle are missing.* 3. One's share of a duty or performance: *Each member of the class had a* part *in the program.* 4. One of the sides opposing each other in a quarrel or dispute: *We all thought she was wrong, so no one took her* part. 5. A character in a play or other performance; role: *Who played the* part *of the wizard in that television show?* 6. The line made by the scalp showing through after one's hair has been divided with a comb: *She wears her hair with a center* part. *Noun.*
—1. To cause to come apart; divide or come between; separate: *a referee* parting *the two men who were fighting; the diver* parting *the water with her body.* 2. To comb one's hair so that it creates a line with the scalp showing through where the hair has been divided: *He* parts *his hair on the left side.* 3. To go away from each other; separate: *When school closed in June, we* parted *for the summer. Verb.*
—Not whole; less than complete: *She is* part *owner of a drugstore. Adjective.*
—To some extent; in an incomplete way: *The dog is* part *black and* part *white. Adverb.*
part (pahrt) *noun, plural* **parts;** *verb,* **parted, parting;** *adjective; adverb. Abbreviation:* **p.**
■ **part and parcel:** A very important or necessary part: *Well-informed voters are* part and parcel *of good government.*
part with: To give up something: *This shirt is worn out, but I hate to* part with *it.*
take part: To participate: *If you want a pet, you must* take part *in its care.*

partial—1. Less than full or whole; incomplete: *Only one lamp was lit, so the room was in* partial *darkness.* 2. Tending to unfairly treat one more favorably than another: *The critic was* partial *to one actor and ignored the others.* 3. Particularly fond of; having a special liking for: *I am* partial *to jelly doughnuts.*
par|tial (pahr′shəl) *adjective.*

participate—To be a part of an activity with others; take part: *All the music students* participated *in the recital.*
par|tic|i|pate (pahr tis′ə pāt) *verb,* **participated, participating.**

participle—A verb form that can act as an adjective or noun. It also can act as a verb when it is used with another verb: *a* singing *bird; the* broken *glass. The man, when he had* walked *a mile, found a* resting *place.* The words ''singing,'' ''broken,'' ''walked,'' and ''resting'' are participles.
par|ti|ci|ple (pahr′tə sip′əl) *noun, plural* **participles.**

Language Fact

There are two main kinds of **participle.** One kind includes participles that end in **-ing:** *singing, flying, skiing.* These are called present participles, even if they describe an action in the past: *She was* going *up the road.* The other kind are past participles. They often end in **-ed** or **-en,** but they can have other endings: *decided, eaten, said.* They describe actions that are finished: *I have* told *you all I know.*

---

particle—A tiny piece or bit: *Particles of colored sugar decorated the cake.*
par|ti|cle (pahr′tə kəl) *noun, plural* **particles.**

particular—1. Separate from others; single; individual: *This* particular *book was always my favorite.* 2. Concerning one individual, group, or thing; specific: *Our team's* particular *strong point is its defense.* 3. Not like others of the same kind; unique; special: *The storm struck with* particular *force.* 4. Very concerned with details; difficult to satisfy: *My father is* particular *about keeping his new automobile clean. Adjective.*
—A single thing or part; item; detail: *Please tell me every* particular *about your trip. Noun.*
par|tic|u|lar (pər tik′yə lər) *adjective; noun, plural* **particulars.**

partition—A thin or low wall: *A* partition *separates the bank tellers from the customers. Noun.*
—1. To separate into portions or sections: *The owners* partitioned *the large, old house into small apartments.* 2. To divide with a wall: *The farmer* partitioned *off several stalls for the cows in his barn. Verb.*
par|ti|tion (pahr tish′ən) *noun, plural* **partitions;** *verb,* **partitioned, partitioning.**

partly—Somewhat; not totally or completely: *an argument* partly *my fault and* partly *his.*
part|ly (pahrt′lē) *adverb.*

partner—1. A person who is in business with another or others and who shares in the money

the firm makes or loses: *My doctor and her partner share a waiting room.* **2.** Either of two people who dance together: *Will you be my partner for the square dance?* **3.** A person who plays on the same team or side in certain games: *a tennis* partner.
part|ner (**pahrt′**nər) *noun, plural* **partners.**

part of speech—One of the groups into which words are classified, based on how they are used. In the English language, the parts of speech are noun, verb, adjective, adverb, pronoun, preposition, conjunction, and interjection.
part of speech (pahrt əv spēch) *noun, plural* **parts of speech.**

partridge—A medium-sized bird with a small head and a short tail. It is able to make only short flights, and it builds its nest on the ground. It is often hunted as game and considered a food delicacy.
par|tridge (**pahr′**trij) *noun, plural* **partridges** or **partridge.**

partridge

part-time—Present, working, or active less than the usual or total amount of time: *All part-time students at the college are to register this week. Adjective.*
—For less than the usual or total amount of time: *working part-time to earn some money. Adverb.*
part-time (**pahrt′tīm′**) *adjective, adverb.*

party—**1.** A group of people gathered to have fun together: *The class had a* party *during graduation week.* **2.** A group of people gathered for some purpose: *a rescue* party; *a search* party. **3.** A group of people who want the same kind of government and are organized to support their political views: *the Democratic* Party; *the Republican* Party; *the Communist* Party. **4.** A person who joins in doing or planning something: *Our teacher was a* party *to our plan to organize a class trip. Noun.*
—To give or attend a gathering for amusement: *We* partied *until ten o'clock. Verb.*
par|ty (**pahr′**tē) *noun, plural* **parties;** *verb,* **partied, partying.**
● Synonyms: For *noun* 1, see synonyms at **band**[1].

pass—**1.** To move past someone or something: *The bus* passed *this corner an hour ago.* **2.** To transfer or give over from one person to another: passing *the peas;* passing *along a secret.* **3.** To get or go through, across, or over: *to* pass *the time until dinner; the highway* passing *the railroad track.* **4.** To complete successfully: *to* pass *a test; to* pass *the sixth grade.* **5.** To make into law: *The state legislature* passed *the highway bill. Verb.*
—**1.** A permit or other document that enables one to do something: *We had to show the guard our* passes *at the gate.* **2.** A ticket that allows one to enter without paying admission: *He has two* passes *to the rock concert.* **3.** A throwing, handing, or moving of a ball or puck to a teammate: *She caught the* pass *and made a basket.* **4.** A road or way through difficult country, especially through mountains: *We will head off the bandits at the* pass. *Noun.*
pass (pas) *verb,* **passed, passing;** *noun, plural* **passes.**
■ **bring to pass:** To make happen; accomplish: *She was able to* bring to pass *all that she had promised.*
pass (oneself) **off as:** To take on the identity of; pretend to be: *He* passed *himself* off as *a great athlete, but some of us knew he was just average.*
pass out: To faint: *I nearly* passed out *from shock when I won first prize.*

passage—**1.** A way through from one place to another; hall, road, route, channel, or path: *A narrow* passage *led between the buildings.* **2.** The act of moving forward: *The hands of the clock showed the* passage *of time.* **3.** A short selection taken from a written or musical work: *quoting a* passage *from the mayor's speech; practicing a difficult* passage *on her violin.* **4.** The act of going from one place to another; voyage: *The explorers had a difficult* passage

a at	i if	oo look	ch chalk		a in ago
ā ape	ī idle	ou out	ng sing		e in happen
ah calm	o odd	u ugly	sh ship	ə =	i in capital
aw all	ō oats	ū rule	th think		o in occur
e end	oi oil	ur turn	<u>th</u> their		u in upon
ē easy			zh treasure		

through unknown territory. **5.** The act of making into law: *The President expects quick* passage *of his tax bill.*

pas|sage (pas′ij) *noun, plural* **passages.**

passenger—One who travels in but does not operate an automobile, train, aircraft, or other vehicle: *The helicopter has room for the pilot and two* passengers.

pas|sen|ger (pas′ən jər) *noun, plural* **passengers.**

passion—**1.** Any feeling one has that is strong and deep: *The passion of the colonists for liberty led them to found an independent nation.* **2.** A keen interest or enthusiasm: *He has a passion for chocolate.*

pas|sion (pash′ən) *noun, plural* **passions.**

passive—**1.** Not involved in an active way; being the object of an action without doing anything in return: *The mother cat remained* passive *and kept on napping while her kittens climbed all over her.* **2.** Having to do with a form of verbs showing that something is done to the subject: *The kittens* were washed *by their mother.* The verb phrase ''were washed'' is passive.

pas|sive (pas′iv) *adjective.*

Passover—A Jewish holiday held over an eight-day period every year. It is celebrated in memory of the Jewish people's escape from slavery in Egypt during the time of Moses.

Pass|o|ver (pas′ō′vər) *noun.*

passport—An official paper showing that a person is a citizen of a certain country. It permits one to travel outside the country and to come back into the country.

pass|port (pas′pawrt′) *noun, plural* **passports.**

password—A secret word that a person must use to be allowed to pass a guarded place.

pass|word (pas′wurd′) *noun, plural* **passwords.**

past—**1.** Gone by; at an end: *My childhood is past.* **2.** Having happened not long ago; just ended: *We had little snow this* past *winter.* **3.** Of a former time: *She is a* past *president of the club. Adjective.*
—The time gone by: *He has helped me on many occasions in the* past. *Noun.*
—Beyond, in location, time, number, age, or amount: *the house* past *the corner;* past *30 years of age; counting* past *100. Preposition.*
—Alongside; by: *He saluted as the flag went* past. *Adverb.*

past (past) *adjective; noun, plural* **pasts;** *preposition; adverb.*

pasta—A food made from a paste of flour and water that has been formed into shapes and dried.

Spaghetti, macaroni, and noodles are kinds of **pasta.**

pas|ta (pahs′tə) *noun.*

paste—**1.** A soft mixture, often made with flour and water, that hardens in the air and is used to stick paper to paper or another kind of surface. **2.** Any thick, soft mixture: *tomato* paste. *Noun.*
—**1.** To fasten with a sticky mixture: *The children* pasted *together strips of paper to make chains.* **2.** To cover with things fastened by a sticky mixture: *He* pasted *white paper with red hearts to make his valentines. Verb.*

paste (pāst) *noun, plural* **pastes;** *verb,* **pasted, pasting.**

pastel—**1.** A kind of crayon that is like chalk. **2.** A picture made with such crayons: *A pastel of her two children hung on her wall.* **3.** Any soft, pale color: *The flowers come in pink, lavender, and other* pastels.

pas|tel (pas tel′) *noun, plural* **pastels.**

pasteurize—To kill harmful germs in liquids by heating at a very high temperature. Most milk is pasteurized.

pas|teur|ize (pas′chə rīz) *verb,* **pasteurized, pasteurizing.**

pastime—An activity that makes one's spare time pass pleasantly, such as a hobby or sport: *The bus driver says walking is her favorite* pastime.

pas|time (pas′tīm′) *noun, plural* **pastimes**
● Synonyms: See synonyms at **amusement.**
Antonyms: **chore, duty, task**

pastor—A minister responsible for a particular church or group.

pas|tor (pas′tər) *noun, plural* **pastors.**

Word History

Pastor comes from a Latin word meaning ''shepherd,'' which comes from a Latin word meaning ''feed.'' A pastor has a connection with the people who attend a church that is somewhat like that of a shepherd with a flock of sheep. Like a shepherd who provides food for a flock, a pastor gives the people spiritual nourishment.

---

pastry—**1.** Sweetened baked goods, such as pies and cakes. **2.** A baked crust made of flour, water, and fat, used to hold a fruit or meat filling.

pas|try (pās′trē) *noun, plural* **pastries.**

pasture—**1.** A field with grass and plants that provide food for the cows, sheep, or other

animals grazing there.   **2.** The grass and other plants eaten by grazing animals: *That hillside furnishes enough* pasture *for the sheep. Noun.*
—To let out or put animals to graze in a grassy field: *He* pastured *his cows on the other side of the stream. Verb.*
pas|ture (pas′chər) *noun, plural* **pastures;** *verb,* **pastured, pasturing.**

pat—**1.** To tap gently with one's hand open, to show love or sympathy: *He* patted *his daughter's shoulder while she cried.*   **2.** To mold or make flat by tapping: *She* patted *the wrinkles from her dress. Verb.*
—**1.** A soft tap with an open hand or other flat object: *He gave one last* pat *to his clay sculpture to smooth the top.*   **2.** A small amount of something, especially butter. *Noun.*
pat (pat) *verb,* **patted, patting;** *noun, plural* **pats.**

patch—**1.** A small piece of cloth or other material used to repair a weak spot or hole in something: *His old jacket had* patches *at the elbows.*   **2.** A small piece of material used as a bandage for an injured eye or a wound: *The nurse taped a gauze* patch *over the girl's scraped knee.*   **3.** A small piece of cloth attached as a badge or decoration: *The young scout had several* patches *on her shirt to show her achievements.*   **4.** A small spot unlike the area surrounding it: *The red* patch *on his arm was caused by poison ivy.*   **5.** A small garden: *The dog ran through the berry* patch. *Noun.*
—**1.** To repair something with a bit of material: *He* patched *his torn jeans with a small piece of denim.*   **2.** To make something by connecting pieces together: *to* patch *a quilt.*   **3.** To fix something quickly or carelessly: *They tried to* patch *the wading pool with tape before all the water ran out. Verb.*
patch (pach) *noun, plural* **patches;** *verb,* **patched, patching.**

patchwork—Small pieces of cloth of many colors cut into different shapes and sewn together: *His pillow was made of* patchwork *like his quilt.*
patchwork (pach′wurk′) *noun.*

patent—A legal right given by the government to a person or company, protecting a new invention from being copied by others. Only those having such a right may make, use, or sell a new invention: *She applied for a* patent *on the new bird feeder she had invented. Noun.*
—To earn such a legal right over a new invention: *He* patented *his electric brush before offering it for sale. Verb.*
pat|ent (pat′ənt) *noun, plural* **patents;** *verb,* **patented, patenting.**

paternal—**1.** Similar to a father: *Although he was not the boy's real father, he felt very* paternal *toward him.*   **2.** Related to or inherited from the father's side of the family: *Having no resemblance to her mother's side at all, she looks a lot like her* paternal *grandmother.*
pa|ter|nal (pə tur′nəl) *adjective.*

path—**1.** A trail or track walked by people or animals: *They followed the mowed* path *through the tall weeds.*   **2.** The course or route traveled by a person or thing: *Luckily, the ball rolled out of the* path *of the oncoming car.*
path (path) *noun, plural* **paths.**

pathetic—Producing feelings of pity or sadness: *The little boy and his broken airplane were a* pathetic *pair.*
pa|thet|ic (pə thet′ik) *adjective.*

patience—The calm acceptance of bad luck, waiting, pain, or disappointment without feeling anger: *Her* patience *was tested when the airplane took off an hour late.*
pa|tience (pā′shəns) *noun.*

patient—Able to accept bad luck, pain, delays, or disappointments calmly: *The teacher's* patient *manner put his students at ease. Adjective.*
—A person who is receiving treatment from a doctor. *Noun.*
pa|tient (pā′shənt) *adjective; noun, plural* **patients.**

patio—**1.** A space or yard without a roof that is within a house; inner courtyard: *Homes in hot countries are often built around a* patio.   **2.** A paved area, usually next to a house, used for outdoor eating and recreation: *The neighbors had a picnic on their* patio.
pat|i|o (pat′ē ō) *noun, plural* **patios.**

patriot—A person loyal to his or her country: *The brave soldier was a* patriot.
pa|tri|ot (pā′trē ət) *noun, plural* **patriots.**

patriotic—Loyal to one's country: *She felt it was her* patriotic *duty to vote on election day.*
pa|tri|ot|ic (pa′trē ot′ik) *adjective.*

a at	i if	oo look	ch chalk		a in ago
ā ape	ī idle	ou out	ng sing		e in happen
ah calm	o odd	u ugly	sh ship	ə =	i in capital
aw all	ō oats	ū rule	th think		o in occur
e end	oi oil	ur turn	th their		u in upon
ē easy			zh treasure		

patriotism—Loyalty to one's country.
pa|tri|ot|ism (pā′trē ə tiz′əm) *noun.*

Patriots' Day—April 19. It celebrates the anniversary of the opening battles of the Revolutionary War in 1775. Observed on the third Monday in April, it is a legal holiday in Maine and Massachusetts.
Pa|tri|ots' Day (pā′trē əts dā) *noun.*

patrol—To move about an area to guard it: *Since the recent robbery, the police* patrol *this area more often. Verb.*
—**1.** The act of going through an area to guard it: *The hall monitor has to make a* patrol *of the school halls to be sure all students are in class.*
2. One or more people who move about an area to guard it: *She was a proud new member of the police* patrol. **3.** One or more soldiers, ships, or airplanes sent to learn about the enemy: *an army* patrol. *Noun.*
pa|trol (pə trōl′) *verb,* **patrolled, patrolling;** *noun, plural* **patrols.**

pattern—**1.** Shapes, colors, or lines arranged in a certain way; design: *Her new shirt had a* pattern *of wide pink and white stripes.* **2.** An example or guide to be followed: *To make her kite, she followed the* pattern *in the book.* **3.** Behavior that is repeated: *Scientists study the migration* patterns *of birds. Noun.*
—To do or make by following an example or guide: *They tried to* pattern *their dance steps after those of the instructor. Verb.*
pat|tern (pat′ərn) *noun, plural* **patterns;** *verb,* **patterned, patterning.**
• Synonyms: **ideal, model, standard,** for *noun* 2.

pause—To stop or wait for a short while: *The athletes* paused *for a moment before beginning the next race. Verb.*
—A short rest or stop: *They worked without* pause *all afternoon. Noun.*
pause (pawz) *verb,* **paused, pausing;** *noun, plural* **pauses.**

pave—To cover a road or area with a smooth, hard material that can be traveled upon: *They* paved *their driveway with concrete.*
pave (pāv) *verb,* **paved, paving.**

pavement—A hard, durable material, such as concrete or asphalt, used to cover a road, sidewalk, or similar area: *In the summer, the* pavement *is too hot to walk on without shoes.*
pave|ment (pāv′mənt) *noun, plural* **pavements.**

paw—An animal's foot having nails or claws. Bears, monkeys, lions, rats, and dogs have paws. *Noun.*
—**1.** To scrape with the nails or claws: *The dog* pawed *a hole in the ground to bury his bone.*
2. To handle or touch in a rough or careless way: *The baby* pawed *through the toy box. Verb.*
paw (paw) *noun, plural* **paws;** *verb,* **pawed, pawing.**

pawn[1]—To allow a money lender to hold something of value that one owns, as a promise to repay a loan. When the loan is paid back, the valuable item is returned.
pawn (pawn) *verb,* **pawned, pawning.**

pawn[2]—**1.** In the game of chess, one of the eight pieces of lowest value that each player has.
2. Someone or something used by another for his or her own selfish benefit: *For the general, ordinary soldiers were only* pawns *who would help him win medals.*
pawn (pawn) *noun, plural* **pawns.**

pay—**1.** To give money to another for work done or things bought: *to* pay *the grocer for the fruit.*
2. To give a certain amount of money: *I* paid *two dollars for this book.* **3.** To make, give, or offer: *The principal* paid *a visit to our classroom.*
4. To be important or worthwhile to someone: *If you like to watch TV in the evening, it* pays *to do your homework early.* **5.** To give or get rewards or punishments: *He* paid *for his lateness by missing the show. Verb.*
—Money given for work done or things bought: *She quit her job because of the low* pay. *Noun.*
pay (pā) *verb,* **paid, paying;** *noun.*
• Synonyms: **earnings, salary, wages,** for *noun.*

payment—**1.** The act of giving money to someone for work done or things bought: *She asked that* payment *for her services be made by next week.* **2.** That which is given to someone for work done or things bought: *A new train set was his* payment *for taking care of his little brother all month.*
pay|ment (pā′mənt) *noun, plural* **payments.**

payroll—**1.** A list of the people who are to receive payment, and the amount that each person is to receive: *Her name was removed from the* payroll *after she quit working there.* **2.** The total sum of money paid to employees at a given time: *The bank delivered the* payroll *to the factory each Friday.*
pay|roll (pā′rōl′) *noun, plural* **payrolls.**

PC—The abbreviation for **personal computer.**

pea—A small, round, green vegetable that is one of the seeds in the pods of certain plants.
pea (pē) *noun, plural* **peas.**
■ **like two peas in a pod:** Very similar or exactly alike: *She and her sister are* like two peas in a

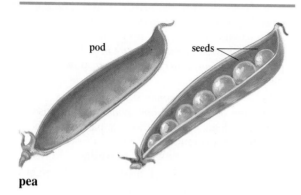

pea

peacock

Word History

Pea comes from an old English word, *pease*. You may know that word from a nursery rhyme that begins "Pease porridge hot, pease porridge cold." A pease was the old name for one pea. But to some people, *pease* sounded as though it were a word meaning more than one of something, and they thought that this something, when there was only one, must be called a **pea**. So now, instead of one pease and two peases, we have one pea and two peas.

pod, *always together and always dressed the same.*

peace—**1.** The absence of fighting or argument: *He kept* peace *among the children by giving each a toy.* **2.** A calm, still atmosphere; silence: *She enjoyed the* peace *and quiet of the library's reading room.*
peace (pēs) *noun.*
■ **keep** (one's) **peace:** To hold back from speaking; stay silent: *Instead of arguing, he* kept *his* peace *and quietly walked away.*
● A word that sounds the same is **piece.**

peach—**1.** An almost round, juicy fruit that grows on a tree and has fuzzy, yellow-red or yellow skin. **2.** A yellowish-pink color. *Noun.*
—Having a yellowish-pink color. *Adjective.*
peach (pēch) *noun, plural* **peaches;** *adjective.*

peacock—A large bird known for its beautiful blue body feathers and long, bright green and gold tail feathers. The male's tail feathers have spots on them that resemble eyes, and can be raised and spread out like a fan.
pea|cock (pē′kok′) *noun, plural* **peacocks.**

peak—**1.** A pointed top of a mountain or hill: *Climbers could be seen near the* peak. **2.** A tapering or pointed end or top: *the* peak *of the roof.* **3.** The point of greatest importance or strength: *She wrote that music at the* peak *of her career.* **4.** The part of a baseball or similar cap that sticks out over one's forehead; brim.
peak (pēk) *noun, plural* **peaks.**
● A word that sounds the same is **peek.**

peal—A loud, long sound: peals *of thunder; a* peal *of laughter. Noun.*
—To ring out: *All the bells in town* pealed. *Verb.*
peal (pēl) *noun, plural* **peals;** *verb,* **pealed, pealing.**
● A word that sounds the same is **peel.**

peanut—**1.** A nutlike seed that grows underground on a plant related to the pea plant. It is roasted and eaten, used to make peanut butter, and pressed for its oil. **2. peanuts:** A little bit of money or something worth very little: *He paid only* peanuts *for his bicycle.*
pea|nut (pē′nut′) *noun, plural* **peanuts.**

peanut butter—A food made from ground, roasted peanuts. It is spread on crackers and bread and is used in cookies and candies.
pea|nut but|ter (pē′nut′ but′ər) *noun.*

pear—A bell-shaped fruit that grows on a tree and has a thin, smooth, yellow or brown skin.
pear (pār) *noun, plural* **pears.**
● Words that sound the same are **pair** and **pare.**

pearl—**1.** A white or almost-white gem formed inside the shells of certain kinds of oysters.

a at	i if	oo look	ch chalk		a in ago
ā ape	ī idle	ou out	ng sing		e in happen
ah calm	o odd	u ugly	sh ship	ə =	i in capital
aw all	ō oats	ū rule	th think		o in occur
e end	oi oil	ur turn	th their		u in upon
ē easy			zh treasure		

Pearls look like tiny, hard balls and have a soft shine.   **2.** Something that is small, round, and white or shiny like this gem: *A large* pearl *of dew sparkled on the flower petal.*
pearl (purl) *noun, plural* **pearls.**

peasant—An owner of a small farm or someone who works on a small farm.
peas|ant (pez′ənt) *noun, plural* **peasants.**

pebble—A little piece of rock that has become smooth all around because of the effects of water or of a glacier.
peb|ble (peb′əl) *noun, plural* **pebbles.**

pecan—A sweet-tasting nut that grows on a tree and has a thin, olive-shaped shell.
pe|can (pi **kahn′** *or* pi **kan′**) *noun, plural* **pecans.**

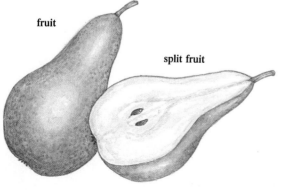

tree

nut

kernel

pecan

peck[1]—**1.** To pick up something by tapping at it with the beak: *The bird* pecked *for bugs under the tree bark.*   **2.** To tap at something rapidly

fruit

split fruit

pear

with the beak: *The robin* pecked *at his reflection in the window. Verb.*
—**1.** A fast tap using the beak: *The parrot gave the man's hand a* peck.   **2.** A light kiss, often given with little affection: *The little boy gave his aunt a* peck *on the cheek. Noun.*
peck (pek) *verb,* **pecked, pecking;** *noun, plural* **pecks.**

peck[2]—**1.** A unit used to measure fruits, vegetables, and other dry things. It is equal to 8 quarts (8.8 liters). There are 4 pecks in 1 bushel.   **2.** A great amount; heap: *The boy got into a* peck *of trouble for letting his dog run loose.*
peck (pek) *noun, plural* **pecks.**
● See picture at **bushel.**

peculiar—**1.** Not ordinary; different in an unusual way: *It was* peculiar *that the cat did not chase the mouse.*   **2.** Belonging to or having to do with a particular person, group, location, or thing; special: *Football players wear uniforms* peculiar *to the sport.*
pe|cul|iar (pi **kyūl′**yər) *adjective.*
● Synonyms: For **1,** see synonyms at **curious.**

peculiarity—**1.** The state of being odd, unusual, or unique; strangeness: *The* peculiarity *of the man's behavior made him a suspect when a crime occurred.*   **2.** A unique quality or feature that clearly marks a person or thing as different from another: *One of her* peculiarities *was that she never used an umbrella, even in heavy rain.*
pe|cu|li|ar|i|ty (pi kyū′lē ar′ə tē) *noun, plural* **peculiarities.**

pedal—A lever that is worked by one foot or both feet to make something operate: *a sewing machine* pedal; *the brake and gas* pedals *of a car. Noun.*
—To move something by using such a lever: *He quickly learned to* pedal *his tricycle. Verb.*
ped|al (ped′əl) *noun, plural* **pedals;** *verb,* **pedaled, pedaling.**
● A word that sounds the same is **peddle.**

peddle—To sell something by going from place to place and approaching many different people: *He* peddled *programs at the football games to earn extra money. Verb.*
ped|dle (ped′əl) *verb,* **peddled, peddling.**
● A word that sounds the same is **pedal.**

pedestrian—Someone who travels about by walking: *The bridge had a walkway for* pedestrians.
pe|des|tri|an (pə des′trē ən) *noun, plural* **pedestrians.**

pediatrician—A doctor whose practice is the care of babies and children.
pe|di|a|tri|cian (pē′dē ə **trish′**ən) *noun, plural* **pediatricians.**

pedigree—The record of a line of ancestors for a person or animal.
ped|i|gree (ped′ə grē) *noun, plural* **pedigrees.**

peek—To take a quick, shy, or sly look; peep: *She* peeked *through the stage curtain to see the audience. Verb.*
—A quick, sly, or shy look: *The mother often took a peek at her sleeping baby. Noun.*
peek (pēk) *verb,* **peeked, peeking;** *noun, plural* **peeks.**
• A word that sounds the same is **peak.**

peel—The thick skin or rind of a fruit that is usually not eaten: *a banana* peel. *Noun.*
—**1.** To fall away or come off, usually in small pieces or thin layers: *Old wallpaper* peeled *from the walls.* **2.** To detach or strip off: *to* peel *off a label; to* peel *off my wet socks.* **3.** To remove the outer skin or rind of a fruit, vegetable, or plant: *to* peel *a potato. Verb.*
peel (pēl) *noun, plural* **peels;** *verb,* **peeled, peeling.**
• A word that sounds the same is **peal.**

peep¹—**1.** To look briefly or in secret through a small opening or from a hidden place; peek: *He* peeped *through the curtains to see who was at the door.* **2.** To begin to come into sight: *Tiny flowers* peeped *through the snow. Verb.*
—A brief or secret look, especially through a tiny opening; quick glance: *She said it was her turn to take a* peep *through the telescope. Noun.*
peep (pēp) *verb,* **peeped, peeping;** *noun, plural* **peeps.**

peep²—The short, sharp, chirping sound made by young birds and some other animals: *the* peep *of a baby bird; the* peep *of frogs in the spring. Noun.*
—To make this sound: *Birds were* peeping *in the branches above. Verb.*
peep (pēp) *noun, plural* **peeps;** *verb,* **peeped, peeping.**

peer¹—**1.** One who is equal to or like another: *Many teen-agers prefer the opinions of their* peers *to those of their parents.* **2.** Someone who by birth is of high rank or nobility; noble: *A* peer *usually has a title of "Lord" or "Lady."*
peer (pēr) *noun, plural* **peers.**

peer²—**1.** To stare intently: *A man* peered *at the menu posted on the restaurant window.* **2.** To appear briefly or slightly: *The groundhog* peered *out of his burrow and then disappeared.*
peer (pēr) *verb,* **peered, peering.**

peg—A small, pointed, wooden or metal object used to hold things together, or to pin, mark, or hang things, or to fit into a hole. *Noun.*
—**1.** To fasten or hold together with such an object: *The builder* pegged *the floors of that old house instead of nailing them.* **2.** To identify; mark: *The teacher* pegged *him immediately as a good speller. Verb.*
peg (peg) *noun, plural* **pegs;** *verb,* **pegged, pegging.**
■ **take down a peg:** To make another feel less proud: *Her brother says she needs to be* taken down a peg *because she thinks she is better than anyone else.*

pegboard—A board with holes for pegs. Pegboards are hung on walls and used to store things that hang on hooks placed in the holes.
peg|board (peg′bawrd′) *noun, plural* **pegboards.**

Pekingese—A very small dog with a long, thick coat, a flat face, short legs, and a long-haired tail that curves over its back. Originally bred in China, this dog was once a popular pet among the royalty.
Pe|king|ese (pē′kə nēz′ *or* pē′king ēz′) *noun, plural* **Pekingese.**

pelican—A large water bird with webbed feet. It has a pouch under its very big bill that is used for scooping fish out of the water.
pel|i|can (pel′ə kən) *noun, plural* **pelicans.**

pelican

pellet—A substance in the form of a little ball. Things such as animal food and medicine are often shaped into this form.
pel|let (pel′it) *noun, plural* **pellets.**

pelt[1]—**1.** To hit or attack quickly, again and again, with one's hands, thrown objects, or words: *to pelt someone with snowballs; to pelt with questions at a press conference.* **2.** To beat on heavily and repeatedly: *The rain pelted down on the corn, damaging many plants.*
pelt (pelt) *verb,* **pelted, pelting.**
- Synonyms: **batter**[1], **maul, thrash, whip,** for **1.**

pelt[2]—A skin, especially of an animal having fur. Pelts are sometimes used to make clothing and rugs.
pelt (pelt) *noun, plural* **pelts.**

Pembroke Welsh corgi—A small herding dog with a medium-length coat, erect ears, a pointed muzzle, a long body, and very short legs. Originally bred in Wales, this dog is often trained to work with cattle.
Pem|broke Welsh cor|gi (pem′brook welsh kawr′gē) *noun, plural* **Pembroke Welsh corgis.**
- See also **Cardigan Welsh corgi.**

Pembroke Welsh corgi

pen[1]—A device that has a point which is dipped in ink or through which ink flows, allowing one to write or make other marks on a surface. A fountain pen and a ballpoint pen contain an inner tube of ink. *Noun.*
—To write: *He had penned more than thirty mystery novels. Verb.*
pen (pen) *noun, plural* **pens;** *verb,* **penned, penning.**

pen[2]—**1.** A small, closed-off area to hold or protect animals. **2.** Any area closed off in order to hold or protect. *Noun.*
—To confine closely by shutting into a closed-off area: *The police told them to pen up their dog and not let it run free. Verb.*
pen (pen) *noun, plural* **pens;** *verb,* **penned, penning.**

penalize—To set the penalty a person must pay for breaking a rule or law: *The teacher penalized them ten points for each wrong answer.*
pe|nal|ize (pē′nə līz *or* pen′ə līz) *verb,* **penalized, penalizing.**

penalty—**1.** A punishment for a crime or an offense: *The penalty for littering is $25.* **2.** A disadvantage or loss a person suffers as the result of improper action or failure to do something: *a penalty during a football game; a penalty of five points for a mistake on a test.*
pen|al|ty (pen′əl tē) *noun, plural* **penalties.**

penance—**1.** A punishment accepted to show sorrow for a sin, to make up for having done a wrong, and to be forgiven. **2.** A sacrament in the Roman Catholic, Greek Orthodox, and other churches.
pen|ance (pen′əns) *noun.*

pencil—A writing or drawing tool consisting of a thin graphite rod within a cylinder made of wood, metal, or plastic. *Noun.*
—To draw or write with such a tool: *The mayor penciled the time of the meeting on her calendar. Verb.*
pen|cil (pen′səl) *noun, plural* **pencils;** *verb,* **penciled, penciling.**

pendulum—Something hung so that it can swing freely from one side to another. Pendulums are sometimes used to operate clocks.
pen|du|lum (pen′jə ləm) *noun, plural* **pendulums.**

penetrate—**1.** To enter or pass through something; pierce: *The light of the lantern penetrated the darkness.* **2.** To understand the meaning of: *The science of psychology helps us to penetrate the reasons for human behavior.*
pen|e|trate (pen′ə trāt) *verb,* **penetrated, penetrating.**

penguin—A sea bird of Antarctica and nearby areas that has webbed feet and flippers for

---

Word History

Pen[1] comes from a Latin word meaning "feather." Before modern pens were invented, people wrote by sharpening the point of a feather, dipping it in ink, and then using it to make marks on paper.

penguin

swimming, and that cannot fly. Penguins have black and white feathers.
pen|guin (pen′gwin *or* peng′gwin) *noun, plural* **penguins.**

penicillin—A strong drug that kills germs. It is made from a type of fungus and helps fight many infections.
pen|i|cil|lin (pen′ə sil′in) *noun.*

peninsula—A strip of land that is surrounded by water except at the point where it connects to a larger piece of land.
pen|in|su|la (pə nin′sə lə *or* pə nin′syə lə) *noun, plural* **peninsulas.**

penitentiary—A prison for those who have committed serious crimes.
pen|i|ten|tia|ry (pen′ə ten′shər ē) *noun, plural* **penitentiaries.**

penknife—A small knife whose blades fold into its handle. It is carried in a pocket.
pen|knife (pen′nīf′) *noun, plural* **penknives.**

penmanship—The art or style of handwriting: *The second graders are proud of their neat* penmanship.
pen|man|ship (pen′mən ship) *noun.*

pen name—A name used by an author in place of his or her actual name.
pen name (pen nām) *noun, plural* **pen names.**

pennant—A long, triangle-shaped flag used for signaling on ships or decorated with a name or emblem to show support for a school or sports team.
pen|nant (pen′ənt) *noun, plural* **pennants.**

penny—1. A copper coin worth one cent or 1/100 of a dollar in the United States and Canada.
2. A British coin worth 1/100 of a pound.
pen|ny (pen′ē) *noun, plural* **pennies** (for **1**), **pence** (for **2**).
■ **a penny for** (one's) **thoughts:** An expression used when asking someone what he or she is thinking.
a pretty penny: A great deal of money: *We're all trying to save for our vacation because it will cost* a pretty penny.

pen pal—A person one regularly writes to and receives letters from. Pen pals often live in different countries or different parts of the same country.
pen pal (pen pal) *noun, plural* **pen pals.**

pension—A payment of money made on a regular basis to a person who is retired or disabled.
pen|sion (pen′shən) *noun, plural* **pensions.**

pentagon—A figure having five sides.
pen|ta|gon (pen′tə gon) *noun, plural* **pentagons.**

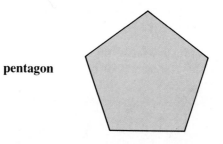

pentagon

Pentecost—1. The Christian festival that celebrates the descent of the Holy Spirit upon the Apostles. It occurs on the seventh Sunday after Easter. **2.** Shabuot.
Pen|te|cost (pen′tə kawst) *noun.*

Pentecostal church—One of a group of Protestant churches which believe that the Holy Spirit descends upon their members, allowing them to speak in other languages than their own and to see visions. They also believe that the Holy Spirit can heal people.
Pen|te|cost|al church (pen′tə kawst′əl church) *noun, plural* **Pentecostal churches.**

penthouse—An apartment or house on the top of a tall building.
pent|house (pent′hous′) *noun, plural* **penthouses.**

peony—A garden plant that has large pink, red, or white flowers. It is the state flower of Indiana.
pe|o|ny (pē′ə nē) *noun, plural* **peonies.**

a at	i if	oo look	ch chalk		⌜a in ago
ā ape	ī idle	ou out	ng sing		e in happen
ah calm	o odd	u ugly	sh ship	ə =	i in capital
aw all	ō oats	ū rule	th think		o in occur
e end	oi oil	ur turn	th their		⌊u in upon
ē easy			zh treasure		

people—1. Human beings: *One day, we hope, all the* people *of the world will live in peace.* 2. A group of persons of the same race, culture, or country: *the Jewish* people. 3. The general public: *The* people *want better schools.* 4. Members of a family; ancestors: *Our* people *have always been farmers. Noun.*
—To supply or fill with human beings: *The new nation* peopled *its land with refugees from many countries. Verb.*
peo|ple (pē′pəl) *noun, plural* **people** *or* **peoples;** *verb,* **peopled, peopling.**

pep—Energy; high spirits: *My cousin is fun to be with because she is always full of* pep.
pep (pep) *noun.*

pepper—1. A seasoning that is hot to the taste and is used to flavor foods during cooking and at the table. It is made by grinding the dried berries or seeds of a tropical shrub. 2. A hollow red, green, or yellow fruit with many seeds that grows on a low, bushy plant. It can taste either sweet or hot, and it may be eaten cooked or raw, or be dried and ground for a seasoning. *Noun.*
—1. To flavor or sprinkle with one of these seasonings: *The waiter asked if he should* pepper *our salads.* 2. To sprinkle or hit with small things: *The boys* peppered *each other with snowballs. Verb.*
pep|per (pep′ər) *noun, plural* **peppers;** *verb,* **peppered, peppering.**

peppermint—1. A plant, related to mint, grown for its strongly flavored and scented oil. The oil is used to give flavor to some medicines and candy. 2. A candy flavored with this oil.
pep|per|mint (pep′ər mint) *noun, plural* **peppermints.**

per—1. For each: *one* per *person; one dollar* per *pound.* 2. By means of: *Send the letter* per

peony

special delivery. 3. As directed by: *We prepared the cake* per *the recipe.*
per (pər *or* pur) *preposition.*

percent or **per cent**—The number of parts in each one hundred. Ten percent means ten in each one hundred. The symbol for percent is %. *Noun.*
per|cent *or* **per cent** (pər sent′) *noun, plural* **percents** *or* **per cents.** Abbreviation: pct.

percentage—1. A portion of a whole, considered as a fraction of 100; number per hundred: *What* percentage *of students made the honor roll last semester?* 2. A part of something: *A large* percentage *of the people in the United States are more than 60 years old.*
per|cent|age (pər sen′tij) *noun, plural* **percentages.**

perch[1]—1. A branch, peg, or other place on which a bird roosts or sits: *The bird feeder had six* perches. 2. Any place higher than its surroundings on which one can rest, often to observe what is happening below: *The girls looked down from their* perch *in the tree. Noun.*
—1. To land and roost or sit: *The sparrows* perched *on a branch high above the cat.* 2. To put at a high point: *She* perched *herself on the top row of the stadium to watch the race. Verb.*
perch (purch) *noun, plural* **perches;** *verb,* **perched, perching.**

perch[2]—A small freshwater food fish with a sharp, stiff fin.
perch (purch) *noun, plural* **perches.**

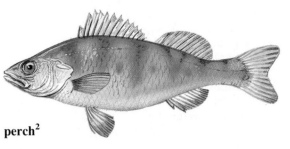

perch[2]

Percheron—A large and powerful workhorse that was first bred in the Perche district in France.
Per|che|ron (pur′chə ron *or* pur′shə ron) *noun, plural* **Percherons.**

percussion instrument—A musical instrument that produces a sound when it is struck or shaken. Drums, gongs, tambourines, and pianos are percussion instruments.
per|cus|sion in|stru|ment (pər kush′ən in′strə mənt) *noun, plural* **percussion instruments.**

perfect—1. Having no defect; containing no flaws or mistakes: *My brother did* perfect *work and got a score of 100 on his math test.* 2. Complete; lacking nothing: *Now that my best friend is back in town, my life is* perfect. 3. Exact; precise: *a* perfect *match. Adjective.*
—To remove all flaws or problems from: *The automobile manufacturer* perfected *its popular new car. Verb.*
per|fect (pur′fikt for *adjective;* pər **fekt′** for *verb*) *adjective; verb,* **perfected, perfecting.**

perform—1. To entertain an audience by displaying a talent or skill: *The student orchestra* performed *for the senior citizens.* 2. To behave; function: *The car* performed *so badly that we took it to the mechanic.* 3. To begin something and carry it through to the end: *to* perform *an experiment; to* perform *a job.*
per|form (pər **fawrm′**) *verb,* **performed, performing.**

performance—1. The act of doing or accomplishing something: *The coach grades our* performance *after every game.* 2. The presenting of a play, concert, or other entertainment: *All* performances *by the popular singer are sold out.* 3. The way in which something behaves or functions: *My father likes the* performance *of his new lawn mower.*
per|form|ance (pər **fawr′**məns) *noun, plural* **performances.**

perfume—1. A sweet-smelling liquid that is used to give someone or something a pleasing odor: *This new* perfume *smells like roses.* 2. Any pleasant odor: *The meadow's* perfume *arrived with the breeze. Noun.*
—To add a sweet odor to; put sweet-smelling liquid on someone or something: *Mother uses a shampoo that* perfumes *her hair. Verb.*
per|fume (pur′fyūm *or* pər **fyūm′** for *noun;* pər **fyūm′** for *verb*) *noun, plural* **perfumes;** *verb,* **perfumed, perfuming.**

perhaps—Possibly; maybe: Perhaps *you left your doll on the train.*
per|haps (pər **haps′**) *adverb.*

peril—1. The risk of being hurt, destroyed, or lost; danger: *Their lives were in* peril *when the sailboat turned over in the storm.* 2. A source or cause of danger; hazard: *The snarling dog is a* peril *to the neighborhood children.*
per|il (per′əl) *noun, plural* **perils.**

perimeter—The distance measured around the edge of a figure or area: *The* perimeter *of the triangle is equal to the total of the lengths of the three sides.*
pe|rim|e|ter (pə **rim′**ə tər) *noun, plural* **perimeters.**

period—1. A certain amount of time: *The basketball player scored four baskets in the third* period. 2. A punctuation mark that looks like this . and is used at the end of a statement or after most abbreviations.
pe|ri|od (per′ē əd) *noun, plural* **periods.**

periodic—Happening repeatedly or at regular times: *Our new car requires* periodic *visits to the dealer for service.*
per|ri|od|ic (pēr′ē od′ik) *adjective.*

periodical—A magazine that is published regularly, such as once a month or once a week.
pe|ri|od|i|cal (pēr′ē od′ə kəl) *noun, plural* **periodicals.**

periscope—A kind of tube containing several lenses and mirrors with which it is possible to see from the bottom of the tube whatever can be seen at the top. Periscopes are used on submarines.
per|i|scope (per′ə skōp′) *noun, plural* **periscopes.**

perish—To die; be destroyed or ruined: *One hundred people* perished *in the earthquake.*
per|ish (per′ish) *verb,* **perished, perishing.**

periscope

perishable—Likely to spoil or become rotten: *Because meat is* perishable *it should be refrigerated.*
per|ish|a|ble (per′i shə bəl) *adjective.*

permanent—Lasting or meant to last a long time: *The dogs in the animal shelter need* permanent *homes.*
per|ma|nent (pur′mə nənt) *adjective.*

permission—Approval given by someone in authority to do something; consent: *He asked his mother for* permission *to set up his tent in the yard.*
per|mis|sion (pər mish′ən) *noun.*

permit—To allow: *Radios are not* permitted *in the classroom. Verb.*
—A written order allowing someone to do something: *a driving* permit; *a gun* permit. *Noun.*
per|mit (pər mit′ *for verb;* pur′mit *or* pər mit′ *for* noun) *verb,* **permitted, permitting;** *noun, plural* **permits.**

perpendicular—1. Standing very straight; upright: *Our fence was* perpendicular *until the wind blew it crooked.* 2. At a right angle to another line or surface: *The sides of a box are* perpendicular *to each other. Adjective.*
—A line or surface that is at right angles to another line or surface. *Noun.*
per|pen|dic|u|lar (pur′pən dik′yə lər) *adjective; noun, plural* **perpendiculars.**

perpetual—1. Permanent; never ending: *The two girls promised each other* perpetual *friendship.* 2. Constant; never stopping: *He is a* perpetual *talker.*
per|pet|u|al (pər pech′ū əl) *adjective.*
• Synonyms: **eternal, everlasting,** for **1.**

perplex—To fill with confusion: *He was* perplexed *by the directions to our house and called to get new ones.*
per|plex (per pleks′) *verb,* **perplexed, perplexing.**
• Synonyms: **baffle, puzzle**
  Antonyms: **enlighten, illuminate**

persecute—To treat cruelly or torment, especially because of religion or beliefs: *That gang of bullies* persecutes *him by hiding his things and dirtying his clothes.*
per|se|cute (pur′sə kyūt) *verb,* **persecuted, persecuting.**

Persian—A long-haired breed of house cat with small ears, a short nose, a broad forehead, and shiny, soft fur that stands out all over its body. Persians originally were bred in the Middle East, especially in ancient Persia, which today is known as Iran.
Per|sian (pur′zhən) *noun, plural* **Persians.**

Persian

persist—To stubbornly keep on doing or saying something over and over again: *If he* persists *in misbehaving, his mother will punish him.*
per|sist (pər sist′) *verb,* **persisted, persisting.**

persistent—1. Stubbornly refusing to stop or give up in spite of difficulties: *The* persistent *cat finally caught the mouse.* 2. Continuing for a long time: *a* persistent *cough; a* persistent *ache.*
per|sist|ent (pər sis′tənt) *adjective.*

person—1. A human being; man, woman, or child: *Every* person *needs a ticket to see the movie.* 2. The living body of a human being: *She carried no money on her* person.
per|son (pur′sən) *noun, plural* **persons.**
■ **in person:** Physically present; through one's own actions: *We saw the President* in person.

Word History

Person comes from a Latin word meaning "mask." Hundreds of years ago, the actors in plays wore masks. These masks made it easier to tell one character from another. They also showed what kind of person the actor was playing—good, bad, beautiful, ugly, and so on.

---

personal—1. Of, relating to, or affecting one person; private: *She wouldn't let anyone read the* personal *letter she received from her friend.* 2. Done directly by a certain person: *The mayor made a* personal *visit to the neighboring town.* 3. Having to do with someone's body: personal *beauty;* personal *cleanliness.*
per|son|al (pur′sə nəl) *adjective.*

personal computer—A small computer that is used by one person at a time and that can carry out only one function at a time.
per|son|al com|put|er (pur′sə nəl kəm pyū′tər) *noun, plural* **personal computers.**

personality—**1.** All the habits, behavior, abilities, and traits of a person that make that person different from other people: *She has a lot of friends because she has such a pleasant* personality. **2.** A famous person: *Since he became a television* personality, *he is often asked for his autograph.*
per|son|al|i|ty (pur′sə nal′ə tē) *noun, plural* **personalities.**

personally—**1.** By oneself; without help from anyone else: *My mother spoke with the teacher* personally *after school.* **2.** As far as oneself is concerned: Personally, *I like spinach.* **3.** As a person: *I like the way she sings, but I don't like her* personally.
per|son|al|ly (pur′sə nə lē) *adverb.*

personnel—All the people who work for a business, company, or similar organization: *Only the* personnel *of that store may park there.*
per|son|nel (pur′sə nel′) *plural, noun.*

perspective—**1.** The way objects are drawn or painted on a flat surface so that the picture seems to have depth and appears lifelike. **2.** A way of looking at something; point of view: *They cannot get a clear* perspective *on the problem if they remain angry about it.*
per|spec|tive (pər spek′tiv) *noun, plural* **perspectives.**

perspiration—**1.** The salty moisture that comes through the pores of the skin; sweat: *The jogger's shirt was soaked with* perspiration. **2.** The act of sweating: *Our bodies cool off through* perspiration.
per|spi|ra|tion (pur′spə rā′shən) *noun.*

perspire—To give off moisture through the body's pores, usually because of heat, fever, or exercise; sweat: *to* perspire *on a hot day.*
per|spire (pər spīr′) *verb,* **perspired, perspiring.**

persuade—To get someone to do or believe something by arguing, pleading, or reasoning:
The children persuaded *their mother to let them get a kitten.*
per|suade (pər swād′) *verb,* **persuaded, persuading.**

pertain—To have to do with; be connected with: *The teacher said that she would answer only those questions that* pertain *to the topic we were discussing.*
per|tain (pər tān′) *verb,* **pertained, pertaining.**

peso—A unit of money in Mexico, Latin America, and the Philippines.
pe|so (pā′sō) *noun, plural* **pesos.** *Abbreviation:* p.

pessimistic—Having a usually bad or gloomy view: *She is* pessimistic *about her chances of winning the talent contest.*
pes|si|mis|tic (pes′ə mis′tik) *adjective.*

pest—Someone or something that annoys; bother: *Mosquitoes are* pests *at outdoor parties.*
pest (pest) *noun, plural* **pests.**

pester—To annoy, usually in order to get something; bother: *He* pestered *his father for a cookie.*
pes|ter (pes′tər) *verb,* **pestered, pestering.**
● Synonyms: **badger, harass, hound, plague**

pet—**1.** An animal that someone keeps and takes care of for pleasure rather than for use in work. Dogs, cats, and birds are common pets. **2.** Someone or something that is favored above others: *a teacher's* pet. *Noun.*
—Favorite or special: *a* pet *name; a* pet *chair. Adjective.*
—To pat or stroke gently to show love or affection: *The kittens sat in his lap while he* petted *them. Verb.*
pet (pet) *noun, plural* **pets;** *adjective; verb,* **petted, petting.**

petal—One of the often colorful parts of a flower that surround its center: *Many roses have bright pink or red* petals.
pet|al (pet′əl) *noun, plural* **petals.**

petition—A formal request that is written to ask someone in authority for something: *Many people signed a* petition *asking the city to build a bigger library. Noun.*
—To ask, usually by making a formal, written request: *The people in our neighborhood* petitioned *for better street lights. Verb.*
pe|ti|tion (pə tish′ən) *noun, plural* **petitions;** *verb,* **petitioned, petitioning.**

petrify—**1.** To turn wood or another living material into stone: *a* petrified *forest.* **2.** To make someone unable to move because of fear:

a at	i if	oo look	ch chalk		a in ago
ā ape	ī idle	ou out	ng sing		e in happen
ah calm	o odd	u ugly	sh ship	ə =	i in capital
aw all	ō oats	ū rule	th think		o in occur
e end	oi oil	ur turn	th their		u in upon
ē easy			zh treasure		

The campers were petrified *by the strange noises coming from outside their tent at night.*
pet|ri|fy (pet′rə fī′) *verb,* **petrified, petrifying.**

petroleum—A yellowish black, thick, flammable oil that is found in places below the ground. It is used to make such substances as gasoline and kerosene.
pe|tro|le|um (pə trō′lē əm) *noun.*

petticoat—A garment that is worn under a skirt or dress; slip.
pet|ti|coat (pet′ē kōt′) *noun, plural* **petticoats.**

petty—Not important or valuable; minor; small: petty *cash;* petty *gossip.*
pet|ty (pet′ē) *adjective,* **pettier, pettiest.**

petulant—Given to small fits of bad temper; irritable; showing impatience over trifling annoyances: *The director of the play was unusually* petulant *just before opening night.*
pet|u|lant (pech′ə lənt) *adjective.*

petunia—A garden plant having bright purple, pink, or white flowers that are shaped like funnels.
pe|tu|ni|a (pə tū′nyə *or* pə tyū′nyə) *noun, plural* **petunias.**

petunia

pew—A long wooden bench with a back, which people sit on in rows in a church.
pew (pyū) *noun, plural* **pews.**

pewter—A silver-gray metal made by combining tin with other metals, such as copper and, in former times, lead. Pewter is used for making plates, mugs, jewelry, and candlesticks.
pew|ter (pyū′tər) *noun.*

phantom—Someone or something that seems to exist but does not; ghost.
phan|tom (fan′təm) *noun, plural* **phantoms.**

Pharaoh or **pharaoh**—The title of the kings who ruled ancient Egypt.
Phar|aoh or **phar|aoh** (fār′ō *or* fer′ō) *noun, plural* **Pharaohs** or **pharaohs.**

Pharaoh hound—A medium-sized hunting dog having a short, smooth, tan coat with white markings on the chest, tail, and sometimes the face. The Pharaoh hound's ears and nose turn a deep red when it becomes excited. These dogs were originally bred in ancient Egypt.
Phar|aoh hound (fār′ō hound *or* fer′ō hound) *noun, plural* **Pharaoh hounds.**

Pharaoh hound

pharmacist—A person who is trained to prepare medicines and drugs. Many pharmacists also operate drugstores.
phar|ma|cist (fahr′mə sist) *noun, plural* **pharmacists.**

pharmacy—A store where medicines and drugs are prepared and sold; drugstore.
phar|ma|cy (fahr′mə sē) *noun, plural* **pharmacies.**

phase—**1.** A certain stage in the development of someone or something: *The construction workers have finished the first* phase *of building the bridge.* **2.** A part or side; aspect: *A committee will study all* phases *of the problem and then decide on a solution to it.* **3.** A particular shape that the moon or a planet appears to have at a certain point in its orbit.
phase (fāz) *noun, plural* **phases.**
■ **phase out:** To stop using slowly and in stages: *That clothing store is going to* phase out *the sale of bathing suits.*

pheasant

pheasant—A large bird with brightly colored feathers and a long, pointed tail. Pheasants are used for food and hunted for sport.
phea|sant (fez′ənt) *noun, plural* **pheasants** or **pheasant**.

philodendron—A climbing plant with smooth, shiny leaves shaped like hearts. It is very popular as a house plant.
phil|o|den|dron (fil′ə den′drən) *noun, plural* **philodendrons**.

philosopher—A person who studies philosophy and seeks wisdom, especially to understand the meaning of life and to understand human nature.
phi|los|o|pher (fə los′ə fər) *noun, plural* **philosophers**.

philosophy—1. The study of basic questions about the universe, such as the purpose of life and the causes of human nature. 2. Someone's own beliefs and opinions about life and the world: *His* philosophy *is that hard work is the way to achieve one's goals.*
phi|los|o|phy (fə los′ə fē) *noun, plural* **philosophies**.

phobia—An extreme fear that is not normal or reasonable and that cannot be easily controlled: *He always travels by train, because he has a* phobia *of flying.*
pho|bi|a (fō′bē ə) *noun, plural* **phobias**.

phone—A shortened form of **telephone**.
phone (fōn) *noun, plural* **phones**; *verb*, **phoned**, **phoning**.

phonetic—Having to do with sounds of speech. Phonetic symbols are used to show how to pronounce words. In this book the phonetic symbol ə shows how to pronounce vowels in certain words.
pho|net|ic (fə net′ik) *adjective*.

phonics—A method of teaching people how to read words by using the sounds that certain letters stand for.
phon|ics (fon′iks) *plural noun*.

phonograph—A machine that plays records. As a record turns, the needle in the arm of the phonograph follows each groove, vibrating according to each sound on the record. The sound then comes out of loudspeakers.
pho|no|graph (fō′nə graf′) *noun, plural* **phonographs**.

phony—Fake; false: *a phony name; a phony dollar bill. Adjective.*
—A fake; someone or something that is not genuine: *That picture is a* phony, *not painted by a famous artist. Noun.*
pho|ny (fō′nē) *adjective*, **phonier, phoniest;** *noun, plural* **phonies**.

phosphorus—A poisonous chemical element that is like yellow or white wax, glows in the dark, and is flammable. Phosphorus is used in making matches, fireworks, fertilizers, and detergents.
phos|pho|rus (fos′fər əs) *noun*.

photo—A shortened form of **photograph**.
pho|to (fō′tō) *noun, plural* **photos**.

photo-—A prefix that means ''light.'' A photograph is an image made by the action of light.

Word Power

You can understand the meanings of many words that begin with **photo-,** if you add the meaning of the prefix to the meaning of the rest of the word.

photocopy: a copy made by the use of light
photometer: a device to measure light

---

photograph—A picture that is made on special film by a camera and printed on paper by means of a chemical process. *Noun.*
—To take a picture with a camera: *to* photograph *a wedding. Verb.*
pho|to|graph (fō′tə graf′) *noun, plural* **photographs;** *verb*, **photographed, photographing**.

photographer—A person who takes pictures with a camera, either as a job or as a hobby.
pho|tog|ra|pher (fə tog′rə fər) *noun, plural* **photographers**.

a at	i if	oo look	ch chalk	⎡ a in ago
ā ape	ī idle	ou out	ng sing	e in happen
ah calm	o odd	u ugly	sh ship	ə = i in capital
aw all	ō oats	ū rule	th think	o in occur
e end	oi oil	ur turn	th their	⎣ u in upon
ē easy			zh treasure	

photography—The profession, art, or process of making pictures with a camera.
pho|tog|ra|phy (fə **tog′**rə fē) *noun.*

photosynthesis—The way in which green plants make their own food from carbon dioxide and water with the aid of sunlight and a chemical called chlorophyll.
pho|to|syn|the|sis (fō′tə **sin′**thə sis) *noun.*

phrase—1. Two or more words that together have meaning but do not make a complete sentence. For example, ''down the street'' and ''the blue coat'' are phrases.   2. A short, clear way of saying something: *''The more, the merrier''* is one of Dad's favorite phrases. *Noun.*
—To say in a certain way: *She* phrased *her question in simple terms. Verb.*
phrase (frāz) *noun, plural* **phrases;** *verb,* **phrased, phrasing.**

physical—1. Of or having to do with the body: *Many popular actresses have* physical *beauty.*
2. Of or having to do with material things that can be seen, especially in nature: *Trees and mountains are* physical *parts of our environment.*
3. Of or having to do with energy and matter: *the* physical *force of gravity. Adjective.*
—A medical examination: *I have to get a* physical *before I go to camp. Noun.*
phys|i|cal (**fiz′**ə kəl) *adjective; noun, plural* **physicals.**

physician—A medical doctor who is trained to recognize and treat illness and injury.
phy|si|cian (fə **zish′**ən) *noun, plural* **physicians.**
• See Language Fact at **surgeon.**

physicist—A scientist who studies the nonliving things in nature to figure out how things work and move in the world.
phys|i|cist (**fiz′**ə sist) *noun, plural* **physicists.**

physics—The science of how the nonliving things in nature work and move in the world. Physics includes the study of electricity, heat, force, sound, magnets, and atoms.
phys|ics (**fiz′**iks) *noun.*

pianist—A person who plays the piano.
pi|an|ist (pē **an′**ist *or* **pē′**ə nist) *noun, plural* **pianists.**

piano—A large musical instrument with a keyboard that is played by pressing one or more of its 88 keys with the fingers. Pressing a piano key causes a small hammer to hit a metal string inside the piano, which makes a musical sound.
pi|an|o (pē **an′**ō) *noun, plural* **pianos.**

piccolo—A small flute that has a higher and shriller sound than that of a regular flute.
pic|co|lo (**pik′**ə lō′) *noun, plural* **piccolos.**

pick¹—1. To choose; select: *The teacher* picked *him to take a note to the principal.*   2. To pull away; gather with the fingers: *to* pick *a daisy; to* pick *strawberries.*   3. To remove with a pointed device or with the fingers: *to* pick *walnuts from their shells.*   4. To open with something sharp or pointed instead of a key: *to* pick *a lock.*   5. To steal from: *Someone* picked *my brother's pocket and took all of his money.*   6. To pluck; pull at with the fingers: *to* pick *the strings of a banjo.*
7. To start on purpose: *She* picked *an argument with her brother. Verb.*
—1. The act of choosing or selecting: *She got the first* pick *at the grab bag.*   2. The best part: *That kitten is the* pick *of the litter because of its long, white fur.*   3. A small, thin piece of plastic that is used to pluck the strings of a guitar or banjo. *Noun.*
pick (pik) *verb,* **picked, picking;** *noun, plural* **picks.**
■ **pick at:** To eat slowly and with small bites: *He was not hungry and just* picked at *his dinner.*
pick on: To tease; bother or nag at: *She* picked on *her little sister.*

pick²—1. A tool made of a heavy metal bar that is pointed at both ends and attached to a long wooden handle. A pick is swung to break up dirt or rocks.   2. A small tool with a sharp point on one end: *an ice* pick; *a dental* pick.
pick (pik) *noun, plural* **picks.**

pickerel—A freshwater fish that has a thin body and a long, pointed head. Pickerels look like small pike and are used for food.
pick|er|el (**pik′**ər əl) *noun, plural* **pickerels** or **pickerel.**

pickerel

picket—1. A stick or narrow piece of wood with a sharp point on one end; stake. Pickets are often hammered into the ground to make a fence.
2. A person who joins others in a public show of opinion: *Several* pickets *marched in front of town hall to show their objection to more taxes. Noun.*
—To stand or walk, often in a line with others, as a public show of opinion: *A group of people* picketed *the factory that pollutes the river. Verb.*
pick|et (**pik′**it) *noun, plural* **pickets;** *verb,* **picketed, picketing.**

pickle—A cucumber that has been soaked in salt water or vinegar. *Noun.*
—To soak a food in salt water or vinegar to preserve it or to add flavor: *to* pickle *herring; to* pickle *vegetables. Verb.*
pick|le (pik′əl) *noun, plural* **pickles**; *verb,* **pickled, pickling.**

picnic—A casual party or trip outdoors where food is served: *We had a* picnic *in the meadow last weekend. Noun.*
—To be at a casual outdoor party or trip where food is served: *to* picnic *at the beach. Verb.*
pic|nic (pik′nik′) *noun, plural* **picnics**; *verb,* **picknicked, picnicking.**

picture—1. A drawing, painting, or photograph: *She drew a* picture *of a rainbow.* 2. A thing or person that looks just like another: *She is the* picture *of her mother.* 3. A good example: *He is the* picture *of health.* 4. An idea or image formed in the mind: *Do you get the* picture? 5. A very clear description in words: *My grandfather's stories gave me a* picture *of what life was like 50 years ago.* 6. What can be seen on a movie screen or television screen: *He adjusted the* picture *because it was too dark.* 7. A movie: *Last night we saw a* picture *at the theater about a space adventure. Noun.*
—1. To make a painting or drawing: *She* pictured *a house with a red front door.* 2. To imagine: *Can you* picture *yourself as an astronaut?* 3. To describe something very clearly: *The speaker* pictured *her adventures in the jungle. Verb.*
pic|ture (pik′chər) *noun, plural* **pictures**; *verb,* **pictured, picturing.**

pie—A thin crust of dough filled with meat, fruit, pudding, or vegetables, and baked in the oven in a flat dish or pan. It can be eaten as the main part of a meal or for dessert: *chicken pot* pie; *peach* pie.
pie (pī) *noun, plural,* **pies.**

piece—1. A part or bit that has been separated from a larger whole: *a* piece *of cheese.* 2. One part of a set or group of things: *a chess* piece; *a* piece *of the puzzle.* 3. A work of art, music, or writing: *She is learning a new* piece *on the guitar.* 4. A coin: *A penny is a one-cent* piece.

5. An example: *Winning the contest was a* piece *of hard work. Noun.*
—To join the parts of a thing together: *to* piece *a model airplane together; to* piece *the links of the chain. Verb.*
piece (pēs) *noun, plural* **pieces**; *verb,* **pieced, piecing.**
■ **go to pieces:** To become very upset: *He* went *to* pieces *when his dog was lost for two days.*
piece of (one's) **mind:** Exactly what one thinks; scolding: *Dad gave us a* piece *of his* mind *when he saw that we had not done our chores.*
speak (one's) **piece:** To give an opinion; say what one thinks: *Each person had a chance to* speak *his or her* piece *before we voted.*
● A word that sounds the same is **peace.**
● Synonyms: **portion, section,** for *noun* 1.

pier—1. A platform built on large, thick columns, which extends over the water as a place for boats to dock. 2. A thick structure, such as a pillar, that is used to support or hold up a bridge.
pier (pēr) *noun, plural* **piers.**
● A word that sounds the same is **peer.**

pierce—To make a hole in; go through: *The arrow* pierced *the center of the target.*
pierce (pērs) *verb,* **pierced, piercing.**
● Synonyms: **stab, stick**

pig—A four-footed animal that has short legs, hoofs, a heavy body, large ears, and a wide, flat nose called a snout. Bacon, ham, and pork come from pigs.
pig (pig) *noun, plural* **pigs.**

pig

pigeon—A bird with a plump body, short legs, and thick, often blue-gray feathers. Pigeons make soft cooing sounds and are a common sight in city parks.
pi|geon (pij′ən) *noun, plural* **pigeons.**

a at	i if	oo look	ch chalk	a in ago
ā ape	ī idle	ou out	ng sing	e in happen
ah calm	o odd	u ugly	sh ship	ə = i in capital
aw all	ō oats	ū rule	th think	o in occur
e end	oi oil	ur turn	th their	u in upon
ē easy			zh treasure	

piggyback—On the shoulders or back: *My brother gave me a* piggyback *ride. Her father carried the girl* piggyback *so she could see the parade.*
pig|gy|back (pig′ē bak′) *adjective, adverb.*

pigment—A substance that is used to dye something or to give something a certain color: *Mixing red and blue* pigments *will make the paint a purple color.*
pig|ment (pig′mənt) *noun, plural* **pigments.**

pigpen—1. A fenced-in area on a farm, where pigs are kept.   2. A messy, dirty place: *"Your room is a* pigpen," *Mother said.*
pig|pen (pig′pen′) *noun, plural* **pigpens.**

pigtail—Hair that is braided and hangs from the back of the head.
pig|tail (pig′tāl′) *noun, plural* **pigtails.**

pike—A freshwater fish that has a large, narrow body and a long, pointed head with many sharp teeth. Pike are used for food.
pike (pīk) *noun, plural* **pikes** or **pike.**

pike

pile[1]—1. A heap of things lying on top of each other: *a pile of leaves; a pile of blocks.*   2. A lot; many: *Our family got* piles *of holiday cards in the mail. Noun.*
—1. To heap; put things on top of each other: *We* pile *old newspapers in the corner of our garage.*   2. To cover with a lot of something: *She* piled *the strawberries with whipped cream. Verb.*
pile (pīl) *noun, plural* **piles;** *verb,* **piled, piling.**
• Synonyms: **mound, stack,** for *noun* 1.

pile[2]—A thick, strong piece of wood, steel, or concrete that is put into the ground to form the foundation of a bridge or pier.
pile (pīl) *noun, plural* **piles.**

pilgrim—1. A person who travels to an important holy place, such as a special church, for a religious purpose.   2. Pilgrim: One of the English settlers who started the first colony in Massachusetts in 1620.
pil|grim (pil′grəm) *noun, plural* **pilgrims.**

pill—A small tablet or ball of medicine that one swallows or chews.
pill (pil) *noun, plural* **pills.**

pillar—A thick wood, steel, or concrete post that is sometimes used to hold up a roof or other part of a building. Some pillars are used as monuments and stand alone.
pil|lar (pil′ər) *noun, plural* **pillars.**

pillow—A bag of cloth or other soft material that is filled with feathers or the like to support a person's head during rest or sleep.
pil|low (pil′ō) *noun, plural* **pillows.**

pilot—A person who controls the motion of a boat, airplane, or spacecraft. *Noun.*
—To steer a boat, airplane, or spacecraft: *The astronaut* piloted *the spacecraft to a safe landing on the moon. Verb.*
pi|lot (pī′lət) *noun, plural* **pilots;** *verb,* **piloted, piloting.**

pimento or **pimiento**—A mild, sweet red pepper that is commonly used to stuff green olives. It is also eaten as a vegetable or in a relish.
pi|men|to or pi|mien|to (pə men′tō *or* pi myen′tō) *noun, plural* **pimentos** or **pimientos.**

pimple—A small, red or white swelling on the skin. Pimples are usually filled with pus and can be painful.
pim|ple (pim′pəl) *noun, plural* **pimples.**

pin—1. A thin, short, stiff piece of wire that has one sharp end and one flat, thicker end. Pins are used to fasten things together: *I put* pins *in my skirt hem before I sewed it.*   2. Anything that is used to hold or fasten things together: *a hair* pin; *a clothes* pin.   3. A piece of jewelry or a badge that has a sharp wire attached to it so that it may be fastened to a person's clothing: *She had a Girl Scout* pin *on her blouse.*   4. In bowling, one of the ten carved and painted pieces of wood that a person tries to knock down with a bowling ball. *Noun.*
—1. To hold or fasten together with a sharp wire: *Mother* pinned *the pieces of the quilt together before she sewed them.*   2. To hold firmly in one position: *I had to* pin *my arms to my sides so I could squeeze through the hole in the fence. Verb.*
pin (pin) *noun, plural* **pins;** *verb,* **pinned, pinning.**
■ **on pins and needles:** Very anxious or nervous: *She was* on pins and needles *waiting for the teacher to give out the report cards.*

piñata—A hollow toy animal or person made of papier-mache or clay. It can be filled with candy, fruit, or small toys. The piñata is hung up high at a party in Spanish-speaking countries. A blindfolded person tries to hit the piñata with a

piñata

fruit   split fruit

pineapple

stick and break it open so that the gifts inside spill out for everyone to share.

pi|ña|ta (pē **nyah′**tah) *noun, plural* **piñatas.**

pinch—To squeeze between the finger and thumb or between two edges: *He* pinched *the tube to get the last of the toothpaste out. Verb.*

—**1.** A squeeze, especially between the finger and thumb: *The baby smiled when Mother gave her a gentle* pinch *on the cheek.* **2.** A little bit: *Dad added a* pinch *of garlic to the stew.* **3.** Trouble; need: *My friend asked to borrow lunch money because she was in a* pinch. *Noun.*

pinch (pinch) *verb,* **pinched, pinching;** *noun, plural* **pinches.**

■ **pinch pennies:** To be very careful about one's spending; be thrifty: *I am* pinching pennies *so I can save up for a new bicycle.*

pine—A tall evergreen tree that has cones and long, thin leaves called needles. The wood from this tree is used for lumber.

pine (pīn) *noun, plural* **pines.**

pineapple—A large, juicy fruit with a prickly skin and stiff leaves growing from the top. The inside is yellow, sweet, and good to eat.

pine|ap|ple (pī′nap′əl) *noun, plural* **pineapples.**

Word History

Pineapple comes from an old English word meaning "pine cone." The fruit was given this name because a pineapple looks like a very large pine cone. Pineapples are not related to either pines or apples.

ping-pong—A game, much like tennis, that is played on a large table with wooden paddles and a small, hollow ball that is hit back and forth across a net; table tennis.

ping-pong (ping′pong′ *or* ping′pawng′) *noun.*

pink—**1.** A light red color that is made by mixing white and red. **2.** A garden plant that has spicy-smelling flowers of red, pink, or white.

—Having a light red color: *a* pink *ribbon; a* pink *sky at dawn. Adjective.*

pink (pingk) *noun, plural* **pinks;** *adjective,* **pinker, pinkest.**

■ **in the pink:** In very good health: *My uncle was very ill, but now he's* in the pink.

piñon—A kind of pine tree that grows in the southwestern United States. Its large, nutlike seeds are good to eat.

pi|ñon (pin′yən *or* pēn′yōn′) *noun, plural* **piñons.**

pinpoint—To note or find exactly: *He used the binoculars to* pinpoint *the location of the hawk's nest.*

pin|point (pin′point′) *verb,* **pinpointed, pinpointing.**

a at	i if	oo look	ch chalk		a in ago
ā ape	ī idle	ou out	ng sing		e in happen
ah calm	o odd	u ugly	sh ship	ə =	i in capital
aw all	ō oats	ū rule	th think		o in occur
e end	oi oil	ur turn	<u>th</u> their		u in upon
ē easy			zh treasure		

pint—A unit of liquid measure that is equal to half a quart (0.473 liters).
pint (pīnt) *noun, plural* **pints.**
Abbreviation: **pt.**

pinto—A pony or horse that has spots of two or more colors on its coat.
pin|to (pin′to) *noun, plural* **pintos.**

pinto

pioneer—1. A person who is the first to settle a region: *The* pioneers *faced many dangers in settling the mountains.* 2. A person who is the first to come up with new ideas or findings in science or other fields of investigation: *The person who discovers a cure for cancer will be a true* pioneer. *Noun.*
—To be the first person to do or try something: *Who* pioneered *the use of satellites in space exploration? Verb.*
pi|o|neer (pī′ə nēr′) *noun, plural* **pioneers;** *verb,* **pioneered, pioneering.**

pious—Very religious: *My neighbor is* pious *and goes to church every day.*
pi|ous (pī′əs) *adjective.*
• Synonyms: **devout, holy**

pipe—1. A hollow tube through which a liquid or gas can flow: *a water* pipe; *a fuel* pipe. 2. A wooden, clay, or plastic tube with a small dish or bowl at one end, that is used for smoking tobacco or blowing soap bubbles. 3. Any musical instrument that is shaped like a tube, through which a player blows to make musical sounds: *A flute is one type of* pipe. *Noun.*
—1. To travel or send through a hollow tube: *The United States* pipes *oil from wells in the far north.* 2. To play on a musical instrument that uses a hollow tube or tubes to make sounds: *to* pipe *a tune. Verb.*
pipe (pīp) *noun, plural* **pipes;** *verb,* **piped, piping.**

pipeline—A long series of hollow tubes that are connected together to carry water, oil, gas, or other substances over great distances.
pipe|line (pīp′līn′) *noun, plural* **pipelines.**

pirate—A person who attacks and robs ships at sea.
pi|rate (pī′rit) *noun, plural* **pirates.**

pistil—The part of a flower where seeds grow.
pis|til (pis′təl) *noun, plural* **pistils.**
• A word that sounds the same is **pistol.**

pistol—A small gun that is held and fired with one hand.
pis|tol (pis′təl) *noun, plural* **pistols.**
• A word that sounds the same is **pistil.**

piston—A solid cylinder that fits inside a hollow tube and moves back and forth. Pistons are run by fuel or steam to make an engine or pump work.
pis|ton (pis′tən) *noun, plural* **pistons.**

pit¹—1. A hole in the ground: *We threw the leaves that we raked into a* pit *in the corner of the yard.* 2. A hole or dent in the surface of something: *Stones from the road flew and made* pits *in the paint on my bike. Noun.*
—1. To make a hole or dent in the surface of something: *Rust* pitted *the paint on the car.* 2. To try to win a contest or competition against someone else; match: *The two sisters were* pitted *against each other in a game of tennis. Verb.*
pit (pit) *noun, plural* **pits;** *verb,* **pitted, pitting.**

pit²—A hard seed at the center of a cherry, plum, peach, or other fruit.
pit (pit) *noun, plural* **pits.**
• See picture at **peach.**

pitch¹—1. To throw; toss: *to* pitch *horseshoes; to* pitch *a curve ball.* 2. To put up; set up: *to* pitch *a tent.* 3. To fall forward: *He tripped over a rock and* pitched *forward. Verb.*
—1. A throw or toss: *The batter missed the* pitch *and struck out.* 2. In music, the highness or lowness of a sound: *The notes played by a flute have a high* pitch. 3. The degree of how steep something is; slope: *The steep* pitch *of the hill made walking difficult. Noun.*
pitch (pich) *verb,* **pitched, pitching;** *noun, plural* **pitches.**
■ **pitch in:** To work hard, often in a combined effort: *The whole family* pitched in *to clean the house on Saturday morning.*
• Synonyms: **plunge, topple, tumble,** for *verb* 2.

pitch²—A sticky, black liquid that is made from tar. It is used to seal roofs against leaks from moisture and to pave streets.
pitch (pich) *noun.*

pitcher¹—A container that has a handle on one side and a lip or spout on the other side, from which a liquid may be poured: *a milk* pitcher; *a* pitcher *of lemonade.*
pitch|er (pich′ər) *noun, plural* **pitchers.**

pitcher²—The player in baseball or softball who throws the ball to the batter.
pitch|er (pich′ər) *noun, plural* **pitchers.**

pitchfork—A metal tool with a wooden handle that has several prongs attached. It looks like a large fork and is used for lifting and throwing hay or the like.
pitch|fork (pich′fawrk′) *noun, plural* **pitchforks.**

pith—1. The spongy, soft center of the stems and branches of some plants. 2. The most important part of something; core: *the* pith *of an argument.*
pith (pith) *noun.*

pitiful—Deserving or able to stir up a feeling of sadness for one's troubles and problems: *The lost kitten looked* pitiful, *so we found it a home.*
pit|i|ful (pit′i fəl) *adjective.*

pity—1. A feeling of sadness for the troubles and problems of others: *I feel* pity *for people who are homeless.* 2. Something to be sorry or sad about: *What a* pity *that it rained on the day of the picnic. Noun.*
—To feel sadness for the troubles and problems of others: *He* pitied *those children who did not have enough to eat. Verb.*
pit|y (pit′ē) *noun, plural* **pities;** *verb,* **pitied, pitying.**

pivot—A central pin or point on which something turns: *The windshield wiper on a car turns on a* pivot. *Noun.*
—To turn around on a central point: *The ice skater* pivoted *and skated toward the other end of the pond. Verb.*
piv|ot (piv′ət) *noun, plural* **pivots;** *verb,* **pivoted, pivoting.**

pixel—A single, tiny dot on a television or computer screen. A television picture or computer display is made up of thousands of pixels.
pix|el (pik′səl) *noun, plural* **pixels.**

pizza—A layer of dough that can be topped or stuffed with tomato sauce, cheese, sausage, vegetables, and the like. It is baked in an oven and eaten while hot.
piz|za (pēt′sə) *noun, plural* **pizzas.**

place—1. A certain space or area: *There are many* places *to visit in the city.* 2. A house or other dwelling: *Our family rented a* place *at the beach last summer.* 3. A page or part of a book, magazine, or story: *She marked her* place *with a strip of paper.* 4. A space for one person: *I lost my* place *in line.* 5. A duty; responsibility: *It is not my* place *to tell you that secret.* 6. Standing or rank: *We won first* place *in the contest. Noun.*
—1. To put in a certain spot: Place *your hand over your heart.* 2. To remember: *I cannot* place *where I heard that song before. Verb.*
place (plās) *noun, plural* **places;** *verb,* **placed, placing.**
■ **go places:** To become successful: *If she works hard, she could really* go places.
know (one's) **place:** To know what is right or proper to do: *The dog knew his* place *and did not jump up on the furniture.*
take place: To happen: *When did the robbery* take place?
● Synonyms: **location, position, site, situation, spot,** for *noun* 1.

plague—1. A very serious disease that can cause many people to die. 2. Something or someone that causes trouble: *A* plague *of insects chewed up our rose bushes. Noun.*
—To cause trouble; bother: *Mosquitoes* plagued *us at the picnic. Verb.*
plague (plāg) *noun, plural* **plagues;** *verb,* **plagued, plaguing.**
● Synonyms: **badger, harass, hound, pester,** for *verb.*

plaid—Cloth that has a pattern of stripes that cross each other. The stripes can be of different colors and sizes: *a* plaid *shirt.*
plaid (plad) *noun, plural* **plaids.**

plain—1. Simple; not fancy: *The package is wrapped in* plain *brown paper.* 2. Without seasonings or spices: *I would like a* plain *hot dog.* 3. Common; ordinary: *He was a* plain *man who stayed modest even when he succeeded in life.* 4. Not pretty or handsome: *a* plain *boy.* 5. Easily seen, heard, or understood: *She could not find her pencil, although it was in* plain *sight on the table.* 6. Direct; honest: *To be* plain *with you, I do not like your new haircut. Adjective.*
—Flat and usually treeless land: *You can see for miles in all directions on the* plains. *Noun.*

a at	i if	oo look	ch chalk		a in ago
ā ape	ī idle	ou out	ng sing		e in happen
ah calm	o odd	u ugly	sh ship	ə =	i in capital
aw all	ō oats	ū rule	th think		o in occur
e end	oi oil	ur turn	th their		u in upon
ē easy			zh treasure		

plain (plān) *adjective,* **plainer, plainest;** *noun, plural* **plains.**
* A word that sounds the same is **plane.**
* Synonyms: **apparent, clear, evident, obvious,** for *adjective* 5.
  Antonyms: **hazy, obscure, vague,** for *adjective* 5.

plan—1. A way of doing or making something that a person has thought carefully about before he or she begins: *She had* plans *to make the best use of her time during school vacation.*   2. A drawing that shows how the parts of a thing are or will be put together: *Here are the* plans *for the treehouse we are building. Noun.*
—1. To think carefully about how something is to be made or done: *He* planned *to have ten people at his birthday party.*   2. To make a drawing that shows how the parts of a thing are or will be put together: *The town engineer had to* plan *the new water system so people could see what it would cost. Verb.*
plan (plan) *noun, plural* **plans;** *verb,* **planned, planning.**

plane[1]—1. An airplane.   2. A certain level: *The professor's speech was at such a high* plane *that I couldn't understand it. Noun.*
—Flat; level: *The top of a desk is a* plane *surface. Adjective.*
plane (plān) *noun, plural* **planes;** *adjective.*
* A word that sounds the same is **plain.**

plane[2]—A tool that has a handle on the top and a sharp blade on the bottom for making wood flat and smooth. *Noun.*
—To use such a tool to shape a piece of wood so that it is flat and smooth: *Dad* planed *the door so that it would close properly. Verb.*

plaid

plane (plān) *noun, plural* **planes;** *verb,* **planed, planing.**
* A word that sounds the same is **plain.**

planet—Any of the nine large heavenly bodies that move around the sun. They are Mercury, Venus, Earth, Mars, Jupiter, Saturn, Uranus, Neptune, and Pluto.
plan|et (plan′it) *noun, plural* **planets.**

planetarium—A building with a curved ceiling on which lights are flashed to show the movements of objects in the universe, such as the sun, moon, planets, and stars.
plan|e|tar|i|um (plan′ə tār′ē əm) *noun, plural* **planetariums.**

plank—A long, flat piece of wood.
plank (plangk) *noun, plural* **planks.**

plankton—Tiny animals and plants that float near the surface of a body of water. They are an important source of food for water animals.
plank|ton (plangk′tən) *noun.*

plant—1. Any living thing that is not an animal or a fungus. Trees, flowers, and grass are plants.   2. A living thing with roots, stems, and leaves: *a holly* plant; *a pumpkin* plant.   3. The buildings, machines, and tools used to make something; factory: *We took a tour of a* plant *that makes chocolate candy. Noun.*
—1. To put something into the ground so that it will grow: *to* plant *flowers; to* plant *corn.*   2. To put or set firmly: *She* planted *her feet on her skis and fastened the bindings. Verb.*
plant (plant) *noun, plural* **plants;** *verb,* **planted, planting.**

plantation—A large farm in a warm area. Usually, only one kind of crop is grown. The workers usually live on the plantation.
plan|ta|tion (plan tā′shən) *noun, plural* **plantations.**

plaque—1. A small, flat piece of wood, metal, or stone with writing on it. A plaque is often given to a person as an honor or award, or it may be hung somewhere to explain something important or interesting that happened there.   2. A sticky substance that forms on the teeth and can cause tooth decay. It is made of bacteria and tiny pieces of food.
plaque (plak) *noun, plural* **plaques.**

plasma—The clear, liquid part of blood in which the blood cells float.
plas|ma (plaz′mə) *noun, plural* **plasmas.**

plaster—A soft, sticky mixture of lime, sand, and water that becomes hard as it dries. It is used to cover walls and ceilings. *Noun.*

—**1.** To cover with this substance: *Dad* plastered *the crack in the bedroom wall.* **2.** To spread on in a thick layer: *She* plastered *the slice of bread with peanut butter. Verb.*
plas|ter (**plas′**tər) *noun, plural* **plasters;** *verb,* **plastered, plastering.**

plastic—An artificial substance that can be molded into many shapes when hot. Products such as toys, dishes, furniture, brushes, and bags can be made with plastic. *Noun.*
—**1.** Made of such a substance: *a plastic bag; a plastic cup.* **2.** Capable of being molded or shaped: *Clay and wax are* plastic *materials. Adjective.*
plas|tic (**plas′**tik) *noun, plural* **plastics;** *adjective.*

plate—**1.** A thin, flat dish: *a dinner* plate; *a pie* plate. **2.** Something served on a thin, flat dish: *a* plate *of spaghetti.* **3.** A flat piece of metal: *Steel* plates *covered the armored car carrying the bank's money.* **4.** A thin, flat piece of metal with letters or a picture carved or engraved on it: *a car's license* plate. **5.** Home base on a baseball field: *A batter stands next to home* plate *when the pitcher throws the ball. Noun.*
—To cover with a thin layer of metal, such as gold or silver: *to* plate *a teapot. Verb.*
plate (plāt) *noun, plural* **plates;** *verb,* **plated, plating.**

plateau—A high, flat area that is above the land around it.
pla|teau (pla tō′) *noun, plural* **plateaus.**

platform—**1.** A flat, raised place: *The band played on a* platform *in the park.* **2.** The ideas that a person or group believes in: *The boy ran for student council on a* platform *of better school lunches.*
plat|form (**plat′**fawrm) *noun, plural* **platforms.**

platinum—A precious metal that looks like silver. It is used in manufacturing and jewelry and by dentists. It is a chemical element.
plat|i|num (**plat′**ə nəm) *noun.*

platter—A large dish that is used to hold and serve food: *a* platter *of vegetables; a fish* platter.
plat|ter (**plat′**ər) *noun, plural* **platters.**

platypus—An Australian mammal that has webbed feet and a ducklike bill and lays eggs.
plat|y|pus (**plat′**ə pəs) *noun, plural* **platypuses** or **platypi** (**plat′**ə pī).

platypus

Word History

Platypus comes from a Greek word meaning "flat-footed." A platypus has broad webbed feet that it uses to dig and swim. It also has a ducklike bill, so it is sometimes called a **duckbilled platypus** or **duckbill.**

play—**1.** Something done for fun or enjoyment; amusement: *The children at* play *are lively.* **2.** A move or a person's turn in a game: *She made the winning* play *in the ball game.* **3.** A story that is acted out on a stage: *At the end of the* play, *everyone clapped for the actors.* **4.** A certain way of acting or treating others: *Sharing with someone who has shared with you is fair* play. *Noun.*
—**1.** To take part in a game or sport: *Mother and I* played *checkers.* **2.** To participate in something for fun or enjoyment: *The baby* played *with her pail and shovel in the sand.* **3.** To toy with something: *"Don't* play *with your food,"* Mother scolded. **4.** To act a part in a story on a stage or for fun: *The children* played *pirates in the yard.* **5.** To make music: *The band* played *a lively tune with drums and horns. Verb.*
play (plā) *noun, plural* **plays;** *verb,* **played, playing.**
• Synonyms: **entertainment, game, pastime, sport, recreation,** for *noun* 1.
Antonyms: **chore, duty, task,** for *noun* 1.

player—**1.** A person who can or does take part in a sport or game: *a hockey* player; *a chess* player. **2.** Someone who acts a part in a story on a stage. **3.** One who plays a musical instrument: *a tuba*

a at	i if	oo look	ch chalk		⌈ a in ago
ā ape	ī idle	ou out	ng sing		e in happen
ah calm	o odd	u ugly	sh ship	ə =	i in capital
aw all	ō oats	ū rule	th think		o in occur
e end	oi oil	ur turn	th their		⌊ u in upon
ē easy			zh treasure		

player.   **5.** A thing or machine that plays music: *a tape player.*

play|er (plā′ər) *noun, plural* **players.**

playing card—A card that is part of a set used in various games. A set is usually made up of 52 cards, each with a number, design, or picture.

play|ing card (plā′ing kahrd) *noun, plural* **playing cards.**

playmate—Someone who does something for fun or enjoyment with someone else.

play|mate (plā′māt′) *noun, plural* **playmates.**

playpen—A small enclosure with bars or netting on the sides that makes a safe area for a small child to stay in and play.

play|pen (plā′pen′) *noun, plural* **playpens.**

playwright—One who writes stories meant for a stage.

play|wright (plā′rit′) *noun, plural* **playwrights.**

plaza—An area open to the public in a city or town.

pla|za (plah′zə *or* plaz′ə) *noun, plural* **plazas.**

plea—**1.** A request made with deep feeling; appeal: *The animal shelter made a* plea *for people to adopt homeless animals.*   **2.** The answer made by an accused person to a charge in a court of law: *A* plea *of not guilty was given by the man charged with robbery.*

plea (plē) *noun, plural* **pleas.**

plead—**1.** To ask with deep feeling: *She* pleaded *with her mother to allow her to wear the new dress.*   **2.** To make an answer to a charge in a court of law: *The driver of the car* pleaded *guilty to speeding.*

plead (plēd) *verb,* **pleaded** *or* **pled, pleading.**
• Synonyms: **appeal, beg, entreat,** for **1.**

pleasant—**1.** Pleasing; enjoyable; delightful: *the* pleasant *sound of water trickling over rocks.* **2.** Behaving in a friendly and agreeable way: *The new boy in class was so* pleasant *that he soon had many friends.*

pleas|ant (plez′ənt) *adjective,* **pleasanter, pleasantest.**

please—**1.** To be enjoyable or satisfying: *The student's good report card* pleased *his parents.* **2.** To find agreeable; prefer: *The party is casual, so you may wear whatever you* please.   **3.** To be so kind as to: *Please* turn on the light.

please (plēz) *verb,* **pleased, pleasing.**

pleasure—**1.** A feeling of joy and satisfaction: *Her* pleasure *in watching the kittens play was shown in her smile.*   **2.** Something that causes a

feeling of joy and satisfaction: *It was a* pleasure *to listen to the beautiful music.*

pleas|ure (plezh′ər) *noun, plural* **pleasures.**
• For **1,** see Synonyms and Antonyms at **bliss.**

pleat—A flat fold in cloth made by turning it back on itself and sewing it into place. *Noun.*
—To turn cloth back on itself and sew it into folds: *She* pleated *the material she would use to make curtains. Verb.*

pleat (plēt) *noun, plural* **pleats;** *verb,* **pleated, pleating.**

pled—*See* **plead.**

pled (pled) *verb.*

pledge—**1.** A sincere promise: *She made a* pledge *that she would stay my friend even after she moved away.*   **2.** Something that is given to make sure a loan is paid back; security: *If you let me borrow your bicycle, I will give you my radio as a* pledge *that I will return it. Noun.*
—**1.** To promise sincerely: *The two boys* pledged *their friendship for each other.*   **2.** To give something as a sign that a loan will be paid back: *My father* pledged *his car for the loan. Verb.*

pledge (plej) *noun, plural* **pledges;** *verb,* **pledged, pledging.**
• Synonyms: **assurance, guarantee, word,** for *noun* **1.**

plentiful—More than enough; in great quantity: *The art teacher has a* plentiful *supply of paper and crayons.*

plen|ti|ful (plen′ti fəl) *adjective.*
• Synonyms: **abundant, ample**
  Antonyms: **rare, scanty, scarce**

plenty—All that is needed; a large enough amount: *We packed* plenty *of food for the picnic.*

plen|ty (plen′tē) *noun.*

pliers—A hand tool that opens and closes like scissors and is used to hold, bend, or cut something.

pli|ers (plī′ərz) *plural noun.*

plod—**1.** To walk in a heavy or slow way: *The tired hikers* plodded *along the muddy trail.*   **2.** To work slowly and with steady effort: *She* plodded *through the thick book to find facts for her report.*

plod (plod) *verb,* **plodded, plodding.**

plot—**1.** A secret plan, usually for wrongdoing: *The evil men had a* plot *to kidnap the baby.* **2.** The plan of events in a story: *The* plot *of the mystery was full of surprises.*   **3.** A small area of land: *We put a fence around our garden* plot. *Noun.*
—**1.** To plan in secret: *The prisoners* plotted *their escape.*   **2.** To make a map or chart of: *The*

pirates plotted *the location of the buried treasure. Verb.*

plot (plot) *noun, plural* **plots;** *verb,* **plotted, plotting.**

● Synonyms: **conspire, scheme,** for *verb* **1.**

plover—A small bird with long, pointed wings, a short bill, and a short tail. It lives along the shore.

plo|ver (pluv′ər) *or* plō′vər) *noun, plural* **plovers** or **plover.**

plover

plow—**1.** A large farm tool or machine used for breaking and turning soil so that seeds may be planted in it. **2.** A machine or tool to break, turn, and push something aside, such as a snowplow for pushing snow aside. *Noun.*

—**1.** To turn up or over with a tool: *We plowed our vegetable garden so we could plant seeds.* **2.** To move with slow, steady force: *The elephant plowed through the thick grass. Verb.*

plow (plou) *noun, plural* **plows;** *verb,* **plowed, plowing.**

pluck—**1.** To pull off or out: *The bird plucked a caterpillar from a leaf and ate it.* **2.** To pick at or pull on with force; yank: *The baby plucked at his grandfather's beard.* **3.** To pull the hair or feathers from: *The goose was plucked to prepare it for cooking. Verb.*

—**1.** A quick or sudden pull: *Father took the splinter out of her finger with a pluck of the tweezers.* **2.** Courage; bravery: *The dog showed pluck in jumping into the icy water to save its master. Noun.*

pluck (pluk) *verb,* **plucked, plucking;** *noun, plural* **plucks.**

● Synonyms: **grit, heart, spirit,** for *noun* **2.**

plug—**1.** Something used to fill up a hole; stopper: *The leaky barrel needs a plug.* **2.** A pronged device on the end of a wire, used to connect a light or an electrical appliance to a source of electricity: *The toaster did not work because its plug would not stay in the outlet. Noun.*

—**1.** To keep from leaking or draining by stopping up with something: *The bottle was plugged with a cork.* **2.** To connect to an electrical outlet: *The heater began to warm up soon after it was plugged in.* **3.** To work with slow, steady effort; plod: *The girl plugged away at practicing the piano for hours. Verb.*

plug (plug) *noun, plural* **plugs;** *verb,* **plugged, plugging.**

plum—**1.** A round, juicy fruit with smooth skin that is red, purple, green, or yellow and has a pit. Plums are often dried and eaten as prunes. **2.** The tree on which this fruit grows. **3.** A dark, reddish purple. *Noun.*

—Having a dark, reddish purple color: *a plum dress. Adjective.*

plum (plum) *noun, plural* **plums;** *adjective.*

● A word that sounds the same is **plumb.**

tree　split fruit　fruit

plum (noun, definitions 1 and 2)

plumage—A bird's feathers: *The plumage of some birds is more colorful in the spring than in the fall.*

plum|age (plū′mij) *noun.*

plumb—A lead weight. It is hung at the end of a line used to find out how deep water is or if

something stands straight up and down. Noun.
—To measure or test using such a weight on a line: *The carpenter* plumbed *the wall to make sure it was straight. Verb.*
plumb (plum) *noun, plural* **plumbs;** *verb,* **plumbed, plumbing.**
• A word that sounds the same is **plum.**

plumber—A person whose job is to install and fix water pipes and the fixtures connected to them, such as sinks, toilets, and showers.
plumb|er (plum′ər) *noun, plural* **plumbers.**

plumbing—1. The work of a plumber. 2. The pipes that carry water in and out of a building and the fixtures connected to those pipes: *We had a washing machine hooked up to the* plumbing *in the basement.*
plumb|ing (plum′ing) *noun.*

plume—1. A long feather: *The peacock spread the beautiful* plumes *of its tail.* 2. A feather or bunch of feathers used to decorate a hat or helmet.
plume (plūm) *noun, plural* **plumes.**

plump—Fully rounded; fat in a pleasant way; stout: *Mother chose a* plump *turkey for the family dinner.*
plump (plump) *adjective,* **plumper, plumpest.**

plunder—To rob; steal valuable things: *The army* plundered *the palace. Verb.*
—Valuables that have been stolen: *The thieves fought over their night's* plunder. *Noun.*
plun|der (plun′dər) *verb,* **plundered, plundering;** *noun.*

plunge—1. To throw or put forcefully: *The dog* plunged *its nose into the deep grass where the rabbit was hiding.* 2. To fall quickly or leap suddenly: *The flower pot fell from the window and* plunged *to the ground. Verb.*
—A dive, fall, or sudden leap: *On my vacation, I took a* plunge *in the ocean every day. Noun.*
plunge (plunj) *verb,* **plunged, plunging;** *noun, plural* **plunges.**

plural—Showing more than one: *a* plural *noun. Adjective.*
—A form of a word used when more than one is meant: *The* plural *of "desk" is "desks." Noun.*
plu|ral (ploor′əl) *adjective; noun, plural* **plurals.**

plus—1. In addition to; made more by: *Six* plus *four equals ten.* 2. And also; as well as: *His cold,* plus *the rainy weather, kept him in bed on Friday. Preposition.*
—More or higher than: *a mark of C* plus *on the test. Adjective.*

—A sign that looks like this +. It shows that what follows is to be added. *Noun.*
plus (plus) *preposition; adjective; noun, plural* **pluses** or **plusses.**

Pluto—The smallest planet, and the most distant from the sun.
Plu|to (plū′tō) *noun.*

plutonium—A radioactive metal that is made artificially and is similar to uranium. It is a chemical element used in splitting atoms to produce atomic energy.
plu|to|ni|um (plū tō′nē əm) *noun.*

plywood—Thin layers of wood glued together to form a strong board used for building.
ply|wood (plī′wood′) *noun.*

p.m. or **P.M.**—Between noon and midnight: *We had supper at 6 p.m.*

Language Fact

The abbreviation p.m. (or P.M.) stands for the Latin words **post meridiem** (pōst mə rid′ē əm), which mean "after midday." 12 p.m. is noon. For more information, see **a.m.**

---

pneumonia—A disease in which one or both of the lungs become inflamed, usually due to an infection.
pneu|mo|nia (nū mōn′yə) *noun.*

P.O.—The abbreviation for **post office.**

poach—To cook a food for a short time in boiling water: *The chef* poached *the eggs and served them on toast.*
poach (pōch) *verb,* **poached, poaching.**

pocket—1. A small pouch sewn on or into clothing and used to carry things: *She put her gloves into her coat* pocket. 2. A place in the earth that contains gold or other valuable metals: *The miner's digging uncovered a* pocket *of copper ore. Noun.*
—To place something in a small pouch: *The student* pocketed *his lunch money. Verb.*
—Of a size that fits into a small pouch: *a* pocket *comb. Adjective.*
pock|et (pok′it) *noun, plural* **pockets;** *verb,* **pocketed, pocketing;** *adjective.*
■ **in** (one's) **hip pocket:** In one's power; under one's control: *After two years of working together, the trainer had the horse* in *his* hip pocket.

pocketbook—A bag for carrying money, lipstick, and other personal items; handbag.

pock|et|book (pok′it book′) *noun, plural* **pocketbooks.**

pocketknife—A small knife having a blade or blades that fold into the handle.
pock|et|knife (pok′it nīf′) *noun, plural* **pocketknives.**

pod—The shell or chamber that holds the seeds of some plants, such as beans and peas.
pod (pod) *noun, plural* **pods.**

poem—A form of writing, often in rhyme, in which the words express a strongly felt idea or emotion.
po|em (pō′əm) *noun, plural* **poems.**

poet—A man or woman who writes poems.
po|et (pō′it) *noun, plural* **poets.**

poetic—Having to do with or like poetry: *He wrote a* poetic *description of the birds at the beach.*
po|et|ic (pō et′ik) *adjective.*

poetry—1. Poems or verses: *We read some* poetry *about the settlement of our country.*
2. The art of writing poems or verses: *Poetry requires a feeling for the sounds and meanings of words.*
po|et|ry (pō′ə trē) *noun.*

poinsettia—A plant with large, colorful leaves surrounding a small yellowish flower. Poinsettias are often used for decoration during Christmas.
poin|set|ti|a (poin set′ē ə *or* poin set′ə) *noun, plural* **poinsettias.**

point—1. A sharp, narrow end: *The cook stuck the* points *of the fork into the hot dog.* 2. A very small mark; dot: *The* point *at the end of a sentence is called a period.* 3. A certain place, position, or time: *The hikers rested at the halfway* point *along the trail.* 4. A certain way of acting or being; trait: *Kindness to animals is one of my brother's good* points. 5. The main idea or purpose: *The* point *of the story was that friends help each other.* 6. A piece of land that sticks out into a body of water: *We walked onto the* point *to go fishing.* 7. One of the 32 marks placed on a compass to show direction. 8. A unit used for keeping score in a game: *Our team scored the first* points *in the basketball game. Noun.*

—1. To show the position of something or call attention to something with the finger: *The boy* pointed *to the prize he wanted.*
2. To aim; direct at: *The scientist* pointed *the telescope toward the moon. Verb.*
point (point) *noun, plural* **points;** *verb,* **pointed, pointing.**

pointer—1. Something, such as a stick, that points or is used to point. 2. A useful piece of advice: *She gave me some* pointers *on building the treehouse.* 3. A large hunting dog with a short coat, a long, thin tail, and drooping ears. These dogs help in hunting by pointing their body in the direction that animals are hidden.
point|er (poin′tər) *noun, plural* **pointers.**
• See also **German shorthaired pointer, German wirehaired pointer,** and **wirehaired pointing griffon.**

pointer (definition 3)

poinsettia

a at	i if	oo look	ch chalk		⌈ a in ago
ā ape	ī idle	ou out	ng sing		e in happen
ah calm	o odd	u ugly	sh ship	ə =	i in capital
aw all	ō oats	ū rule	th think		o in occur
e end	oi oil	ur turn	th their		⌊ u in upon
ē easy			zh treasure		

poise—1. A calm and confident manner: *It was hard for him to keep his* poise *when everyone else seemed nervous and unsure.* 2. Balance; steadiness: *The* poise *of mountain goats helps them to climb steep, rocky places without falling. Noun.*
—To be balanced: *The ice skater,* poised *on one skate, moved smoothly across the ice. Verb.*
poise (poiz) *noun; verb,* **poised, poising.**

poison—A drug or other substance that kills or harms a living thing when taken in. *Noun.*
—1. To kill or harm by giving this kind of substance: *Father* poisoned *the weeds in our garden.* 2. To put a dangerous substance on or into: *The smoke from the factory* poisoned *the air.* 3. To harm or ruin: *The man's outbursts of bad temper* poisoned *his neighbors' opinion of him. Verb.*
poi|son (poi′zən) *noun, plural* **poisons;** *verb,* **poisoned, poisoning.**

poison ivy—A plant with shiny, green leaves made up of three leaflets each. It can cause a painful, itchy rash on a person who touches it.
poi|son i|vy (poi′zən ī′vē) *noun.*

poison ivy

poke—1. To push into or against with force; jab: *The woman* poked *the bread with her finger.* 2. To push forward: *The dog* poked *its nose between the rails of the fence.* 3. To move in a slow or lazy way: *The turtle* poked *along at the edge of the pond. Verb.*
—A forceful push; jab: *He gave his friend a* poke *in the arm to get her attention. Noun.*
poke (pōk) *verb,* **poked, poking;** *noun, plural* **pokes.**

poker¹—A metal stick used to stir a fire.
pok|er (pō′kər) *noun, plural* **pokers.**

poker²—A game of cards in which the players bet on the value of the cards they hold.
pok|er (pō′kər) *noun, plural* **pokers.**

polar—Having to do with or being near the North Pole or the South Pole: *the* polar *iceberg.*
po|lar (pō′lər) *adjective.*

polar bear—A large white bear that lives in very far northern regions.
po|lar bear (pō′lər bār) *noun, plural* **polar bears.**

polar bear

Polaris—The North Star; polestar.
Po|lar|is (pō lār′is) *noun.*

pole¹—A long, narrow piece of wood or metal.
pole (pōl) *noun, plural* **poles.**
• A word that sounds the same is **poll.**

pole²—1. Either of the two ends of the earth's axis; North Pole or South Pole. 2. Either end of a magnet or battery.
pole (pōl) *noun, plural* **poles.**
• A word that sounds the same is **poll.**

polecat—The North American skunk.
pole|cat (pōl′kat′) *noun, plural* **polecats.**

polestar—The North Star; Polaris.
pole|star (pōl′stahr′) *noun.*

pole vault—An athletic event in which a long pole is used to jump over a very high bar.
pole vault (pōl vawlt) *noun.*

police—A group of people who keep order and deal with those who break the law. *Noun.*
—To guard or to watch so as to keep under control: *the officers* policing *the prison. Verb.*
po|lice (pə lēs′) *plural noun; verb,* **policed, policing.**

policeman—A man who does police work.
po|lice|man (pə lēs′mən) *noun, plural* **policemen.**

police officer—A person who does police work. po|lice of|fi|cer (pə lēs′ awf′ə sər) *noun, plural* **police officers.**

policewoman—A woman who does police work. po|lice|wom|an (pə lēs′woom′ən) *noun, plural* **policewomen.**

policy¹—An idea or set of ideas that guides the way something is to be done: *Our family's policy is to finish the chores before watching television.* pol|i|cy (pol′ə sē) *noun, plural* **policies.**

policy²—A written agreement between an insurance company and the person or persons being insured. pol|i|cy (pol′ə sē) *noun, plural* **policies.**

polio—A shortened form of **poliomyelitis.** po|li|o (pō′lē ō) *noun.*

poliomyelitis—A disease that injures the nerve cells of the spinal cord and can result in the loss of the ability to move the muscles. po|li|o|my|e|li|tis (pō′lē ō mī′ə lī′tis) *noun.*

polish—To make something shine, usually by rubbing or by covering with a special substance: *to* polish *the furniture. Verb.*
—**1.** A substance applied to make something shiny: *car* polish. **2.** The shine or brightness of something: *the* polish *of the waxed floor. Noun.* pol|ish (pol′ish) *verb,* **polished, polishing;** *noun, plural* **polishes.**

polite—Showing good manners; courteous: *It is* polite *to thank a person for a gift.* po|lite (pə līt′) *adjective,* **politer, politest.**

political—Of or having to do with the workings of the government: *The Senate and the House of Representatives are both part of the* political *system in the United States.* po|lit|i|cal (pə lit′ə kəl) *adjective.*

politician—A person involved in government, especially one who holds or runs for office. pol|i|ti|cian (pol′ə tish′ən) *noun, plural* **politicians.**

politics—**1.** The activities related to the running of a government: *The mayor has been in local* politics *for 30 years.* **2.** A person's beliefs about the workings of a government: *My* politics *are for me to decide.* pol|i|tics (pol′ə tiks) *noun, plural* **politics.**

polka—A lively dance, usually done with a pattern of three steps and then a hop. pol|ka (pōl′kə) *noun, plural* **polkas.**

polka dot—A round spot or dot that is made over and over again to form a pattern on cloth or other material. pol|ka dot (pō′kə dot) *noun, plural* **polka dots.**

poll—**1.** A series of questions meant to find out how people feel or how they might act in a certain situation, such as in an election. **2.** The casting and recording of votes: *The school board had a* poll *to select the best place for the new school.* **3. polls:** The places where votes are cast and counted: *Many citizens volunteer to work at the* polls *during elections. Noun.*
—**1.** To question people so as to find out how they feel or how they might act: *I was* polled *on which television programs I like to watch.* **2.** To receive votes: *The popular mayor* polled *a large vote in winning the election. Verb.* poll (pōl) *noun, plural* **polls;** *verb,* **polled, polling.**

pollen—The yellow dust made in plants and found in a part of the flower. This dust is made up of male cells. It is carried by the wind, insects, or birds and fertilizes the female parts of flowers so as to form seeds. pol|len (pōl′ən) *noun.*

pollinate—To carry pollen and drop it on a flower: *bees* pollinating *a field of flowers.* pol|li|nate (pol′ə nāt) *verb,* **pollinated, pollinating.**

polliwog—*See* **tadpole.** pol|li|wog (pol′ē wog) *noun, plural* **polliwogs.**

pollute—To make unclean or impure: *an oil spill* polluting *a river.* pol|lute (pə lūt′) *verb,* **polluted, polluting.**
• Synonyms: **contaminate, foul**

pollution—The act of making something unclean or the condition of being unclean: *The dirty water was a sign of* pollution. pol|lu|tion (pə lū′shən) *noun.*

polo—A game played on horseback in which each player uses a mallet with a long handle to try and hit a ball into the other team's goal. po|lo (pō′lō) *noun.*

polygon—A shape with three or more straight sides. Triangles and squares are polygons. pol|y|gon (pol′ē gon) *noun, plural* **polygons.**

Pomeranian—A very small dog with pointed ears, a short body, and a full tail. Its coat is of medium length and is thicker around its neck and down its chest.

a at	i if	oo look	ch chalk		
ā ape	ī idle	ou out	ng sing		a in ago
ah calm	o odd	u ugly	sh ship	ə =	e in happen
aw all	ō oats	ū rule	th think		i in capital
e end	oi oil	ur turn	th their		o in occur
ē easy			zh treasure		u in upon

Pom|er|a|ni|an (pom′ə rā′nē ən) *noun, plural* **Pomeranians.**

poncho—1. A piece of clothing that looks like a blanket. It has a center opening for the head and hangs over the shoulders to cover the body. Ponchos are often worn in South America. **2.** A waterproof garment that looks like this and is used as a raincoat.
pon|cho (pon′chō) *noun, plural* **ponchos.**

pond—A body of water that is smaller than a lake and surrounded by land.
pond (pond) *noun, plural* **ponds.**

ponder—To think over carefully: *The chess player* pondered *his choices before making his next move.*
pon|der (pon′dər) *verb,* **pondered, pondering.**
• Synonyms: **consider, contemplate**

pontiff—The Pope.
pon|tiff (pon′tif) *noun, plural* **pontiffs.**

pontoon—A low, floating structure that is used to support a temporary bridge or dock or to float a boat or an airplane.
pon|toon (pon tūn′) *noun, plural* **pontoons.**

pony—A small horse.
po|ny (pō′nē) *noun, plural* **ponies.**

pony express—The method of delivering mail on horseback in the western United States during 1860 and 1861. Relays of men would carry mail between stations on fast horses.
po|ny ex|press (pō′nē ek spres′) *noun.*

ponytail—A hair style in which the hair is pulled to the back of the head and tied with a band, allowing the ends of the hair to hang free.
po|ny|tail (pō′nē tāl′) *noun, plural* **ponytails.**

poodle—A dog with thick, curly hair. Although it was once used for hunting and retrieving, the poodle is now a popular house pet. It can be very small or up to medium size. Poodles were originally bred in Germany as hunting dogs.
poo|dle (pū′dəl) *noun, plural* **poodles.**

poodle

Word History

Poodle comes from a German word meaning ''to splash water.'' The poodle was originally taught to go in and out of the water to retrieve birds and other animals shot by hunters.

pool[1]—1. A tank of water large enough to swim in. **2.** Any small body of water: *a wading* pool. **3.** A small amount of liquid; puddle: *A pool of oil formed underneath the car.*
pool (pūl) *noun, plural* **pools.**

pool[2]—1. A game played on a table with six holes. Balls are hit into these holes with a cue stick. **2.** Money or things that a group of people put together or share: *He joined a car* pool *to get to work, so he could share the driving with others. Noun.*
—To put things or money together in order to share: *The students* pooled *their talents to perform a variety show. Verb.*
pool (pūl) *noun, plural* **pools;** *verb,* **pooled, pooling.**

poor—1. Having few things or little money: *He was too* poor *to buy a winter coat.* **2.** Less than

polo

the amount or quality needed; bad: *The teacher told him that forgetting his paper at home was a* poor *excuse.* **3.** In need of pity; unfortunate: *We found the owners of the poor, lost puppy.*
poor (poor) *adjective,* **poorer, poorest.**
• Synonyms: **feeble, lame, weak,** for 2.

pop—**1.** To make a quick, sharp sound: *The balloon* popped *and startled the baby.* **2.** To appear suddenly, especially without warning: *The lawyer* popped *into school to visit her former teacher. Verb.*
—**1.** A quick, sharp sound: *The light bulb fell and broke with a loud* pop. **2.** A soda; soft drink: *Would you like an orange* pop? *Noun.*
pop (pop) *verb,* **popped, popping;** *noun, plural* **pops.**
• See Language Fact at **soda.**

popcorn—A type of corn with hard kernels that when heated explode with a pop into fluffy, white balls.
pop|corn (pop′kawrn′) *noun.*

Pope or **pope**—The leader of the Roman Catholic Church.
Pope or **pope** (pōp) *noun, plural* **Popes** or **popes.**

poplar—A tree, related to the willow, which grows quickly and has light, soft wood.
pop|lar (pop′lər) *noun, plural* **poplars.**

poppy—A plant that has red, yellow, or white flowers and capsules that contain many tiny seeds. The seeds are used as a flavoring. They are sprinkled on bread and rolls and are used as a filling in cakes.
pop|py (pop′ē) *noun, plural* **poppies.**

popular—**1.** Preferred by many people: *Dogs are* popular *pets.* **2.** Liked by many people; having many friends: *He is the most* popular *boy in the class.* **3.** Of or by the people: *A democracy is a* popular *government.* **4.** Common among most people; widespread: *It is a* popular *superstition that 13 is an unlucky number.*
pop|u|lar (pop′yə lər) *adjective.*

population—**1.** The people who live in a place: *The flood forced most of the* population *of the county to move to higher ground.* **2.** The number of people who live in a certain place:

Our town has a population *of more than 15,000.*
pop|u|la|tion (pop′yə lā′shən) *noun; plural* **populations.** Abbreviation: pop.

porcelain—A type of fine pottery; china. It is white, very hard, and thin enough to let light shine through.
por|ce|lain (pawr′sə lin) *noun.*

porch—Any covered addition or entrance to a building.
porch (pawrch) *noun, plural* **porches.**

porcupine—An animal that has sharp quills growing all over its body. It is a type of rodent.
por|cu|pine (pawr′kyə pīn) *noun, plural* **porcupines** or **porcupine.**

porcupine

pore—A tiny opening in the skin, a leaf, or other surface. Perspiration passes through the pores in human skin.
pore (pawr) *noun, plural* **pores.**
• A word that sounds the same is **pour.**

Language Fact

Many kinds of meat have the same names as the animals that the meat comes from: **chicken, turkey, lamb.** Other kinds of meat have names that are different from the names of the animals. **Mutton** is the meat of a grown sheep. **Beef** comes from grown cattle, while **veal** is the meat of a calf. The meat of pigs has many names: **pork,** or **ham,** or **bacon.**

---

pork—The meat that comes from a pig and is eaten as food.
pork (pawrk) *noun.*

a at	i if	oo look	ch chalk		a in ago
ā ape	ī idle	ou out	ng sing		e in happen
ah calm	o odd	u ugly	sh ship	ə =	i in capital
aw all	ō oats	ū rule	th think		o in occur
e end	oi oil	ur turn	th their		u in upon
ē easy			zh treasure		

porous—Having many small holes or pores: *A sponge is* porous *and soaks up water.*
po|rous (pawr′əs) *adjective.*

porpoise—A sea mammal that resembles a small whale. A porpoise has a blunt snout and a dark body with a lighter belly.
por|poise (pawr′pəs) *noun, plural* **porpoises** or **porpoise.**

porpoise

porridge—A food made by boiling grain in milk or water until the mixture thickens.
por|ridge (pawr′ij) *noun, plural* **porridges.**

port[1]—1. A place where boats or ships are secured and protected from storms; harbor. 2. A city or town that has a harbor.
port (pawrt) *noun, plural* **ports.**

port[2]—The left side of a boat or ship. *Noun.*
—On the left side of a boat or ship. *Adjective.*
port (pawrt) *noun, adjective.*

portable—Easily moved or carried: *a* portable *television; a* portable *crib.*
port|a|ble (pawr′tə bəl) *adjective.*

porter—1. A person whose job is to carry baggage: *a* porter *at a hotel.* 2. A person whose job is to take care of passengers on a train.
por|ter (pawr′tər) *noun, plural* **porters.**

porthole—A small, round window in the side of a boat or ship.
port|hole (pawrt′hōl′) *noun, plural* **portholes.**

portion—A part, share, or serving of something: *The girl asked for a small* portion *of ice cream. Noun.*
—To divide something up into parts, shares, or servings: *The rescue workers* portioned *out the food and clothing to the flood victims. Verb.*
por|tion (pawr′shən) *noun, plural* **portions;** *verb,* **portioned, portioning.**

portrait—A picture of a person. It may be a drawing, painting, or photograph.
por|trait (pawr′trit *or* pawr′trāt) *noun, plural* **portraits.**

portray—1. To make a picture of someone or something: *In his most famous painting, the artist* portrayed *his childhood home as it looked on a*
winter's afternoon. 2. To describe or picture with words: *The story* portrays *life on a farm.*
por|tray (pawr trā′) *verb,* **portrayed, portraying.**

Portuguese water dog—A medium-sized dog that is an excellent swimmer. It has thick hair on the top of its head and a curved tail. It can have a short, curly coat or one that is long and wavy. Originally bred in Portugal, these dogs work with fishing crews.
Por|tu|guese wa|ter dog (pawr′chə gēz′ wawt′ər dawg) *noun, plural* **Portuguese water dogs.**

Portuguese water dog

pose—1. A way of positioning the body; posture: *He always had the same slouching* pose *whenever he was bored.* 2. A pretended attitude: *She looked very confident, but it was just a* pose. *Noun.*
—1. To position one's body and stay still, usually for a picture: *The president* posed *for his official portrait.* 2. To pretend to be someone or something else: *The girl* posed *as a reporter in order to meet the movie star. Verb.*
pose (pōz) *noun, plural* **poses;** *verb,* **posed, posing.**

position—1. The place occupied by something or someone: *He changed the* position *of the light so he could read more easily.* 2. The manner of being placed or arranged: *I must have slept in an awkward* position *last night, because my neck hurts today.* 3. A standing or status; rank: *The principal has an important* position *in the community.* 4. A point of view; attitude; opinion: *a candidate's* position *on taxes.* 5. A job: *She was hired for the* position *of vice president of the new bank.*

po|si|tion (pə **zish′**ən) *noun, plural* **positions.**
● Synonyms: **location, site, situation, spot,** for **1.**

positive—**1.** Absolutely sure; confident; definite: *I have my parents' permission, so now I am* positive *I can go to the dance on Saturday.* **2.** Helpful; useful: *After last week's game, the coach gave the players* positive *criticism that helped them win this week.* **3.** Being greater than zero: *a* positive *number.* **4.** Having a certain kind of electrical charge: *the* positive *end of a battery.*
pos|i|tive (**poz′**ə tiv) *adjective.*

posse—A group that is formed to help a sheriff carry out official duties.
pos|se (**pos′**ē) *noun, plural* **posses.**

possess—**1.** To have as one's property; have as a quality; own: *to* possess *a great sense of humor; to* possess *many valuable paintings.* **2.** To control by great influence: *Greed* possessed *him, and he would do anything to get more money.*
pos|sess (pə **zes′**) *verb,* **possessed, possessing.**

possession—**1.** The act of owning or holding something: *The two hockey players fought for* possession *of the puck.* **2.** The thing that is owned or held: *The bicycle is her favorite* possession. **3.** Any territory that is ruled by another country: *overseas* possessions *including small islands in the ocean.*
pos|ses|sion (pə **zesh′**ən) *noun, plural* **possessions.**

possessive—**1.** Showing that something is owned by or belongs to someone. **My, your, his, her,** and **our** are possessive words. **2.** Showing a desire to keep something, often in a selfish way: *She is* possessive *about her clothes and will not lend them to her sister. Adjective.*
—A word, such as **mine** and **yours,** that is used to show to whom something belongs. *Noun.*
pos|ses|sive (pə **zes′**iv) *adjective; noun, plural* **possessives.**

possibility—**1.** The fact that a thing may happen or be done: *There is a good* possibility *that we will go on a field trip next week.* **2.** A thing that may happen or be done: *Losing electricity is a* possibility *during a storm.*
pos|si|bil|i|ty (pos′ə **bil′**ə tē) *noun, plural* **possibilities.**

possible—**1.** Capable of happening or being done: *It is* possible *that I will finish reading this book by the weekend.* **2.** Able to be reasonably chosen or considered: *"The Purple Zebras" is a* possible *name for our new club.*
pos|si|ble (**pos′**ə bəl) *adjective.*

possum—*See* **opossum.**
pos|sum (**pos′**əm) *noun, plural* **possums.**

post¹—A strong piece of solid material, such as wood or metal, that stands upright to hold or support something firmly: *a fence* post; *a goal* post. *Noun.*
—To display a thing so that it can be easily seen and read: *We looked on the bulletin board to see if the coach had* posted *the names of the people who made the team. Verb.*
post (pōst) *noun, plural* **posts;** *verb,* **posted, posting.**

post²—**1.** The place of duty for such people as nurses, fire fighters, soldiers, and police officers: *The guards took their* posts *at the front gate.* **2.** A military station where soldiers live, work, and get training. **3.** A position; job: *the* post *of ambassador. Noun.*
—To be placed in a certain location for a certain job: *Crossing guards were* posted *at the busy intersection. Verb.*
post (pōst) *noun, plural* **posts;** *verb,* **posted, posting.**

post³—**1.** A method of delivering letters or packages; mail: *We sent our grandfather's birthday gift by* post. **2.** A delivery of mail: *the day's* post. *Noun.*
—**1.** To mail: *Will you please* post *these letters for me?* **2.** To inform: *The nurses kept the family* posted *about the boy's condition after he had his tonsils out. Verb.*
post (pōst) *noun, plural* **posts;** *verb,* **posted, posting.**

post-—A prefix that means "after." A postgame interview is one that takes place after a game.

Word Power

You can understand the meanings of many words that begin with **post-,** if you add the meaning of the prefix to the meaning of the rest of the word.
postoperative: after an operation
postwar: after a war

---

postage—The amount of money needed to send a package or letter by mail.
post|age (**pōs′**tij) *noun.*

a at	i if	oo look	ch chalk		a in ago
ā ape	ī idle	ou out	ng sing		e in happen
ah calm	o odd	u ugly	sh ship	ə =	i in capital
aw all	ō oats	ū rule	th think		o in occur
e end	oi oil	ur turn	th their		u in upon
ē easy			zh treasure		

postal—Having to do with mail service or post offices: *a postal worker; postal delivery.*
post|al (pōs′təl) *adjective.*

post card or **postcard**—A card on which a message can be written and that can be mailed without an envelope.
post card or post|card (pōst′kahrd′) *noun, plural* **post cards** or **postcards.**

poster—A large sheet of paper or cardboard, printed with a message, a picture, or both, that is hung up as an advertisement or notice for people to see; sign.
post|er (pōs′tər) *noun, plural* **posters.**

postmark—An official mark stamped on mail. It shows that the postage stamp has been used and records the place and date of mailing. *Noun.*
—To put such an official mark on a piece of mail: *When I received your letter, I could see that it had been* postmarked *just two days before. Verb.*
post|mark (pōst′mahrk) *noun, plural* **postmarks;** *verb,* **postmarked, postmarking.**

postmaster—A person who heads a post office.
post|mas|ter (pōst′mas′tər) *noun, plural* **postmasters.**

post office—A place in the postal system where mail is received, sorted, and sent out, and where postage stamps are sold.
post of|fice (pōst awf′is) *noun, plural* **post offices.** Abbreviation: **P.O.**

postpone—To put off or aside until later; delay: *The game was* postponed *because of the storm.*
post|pone (pōst pōn′) *verb,* **postponed, postponing.**

postscript—Any writing that is included after the end of a letter, book, or article: *After I signed the note, I added a* postscript *to remind her of my birthday party.*
post|script (pōst′skript) *noun, plural* **postscripts.** Abbreviation: **P.S.**

posture—The way the body is held while at rest or in motion.
pos|ture (pos′chər) *noun, plural* **postures.**

pot—A round container used for cooking or holding things. It can be made of almost any hard material, such as metal or baked clay. *Noun.*
—To put into such a container: *Make sure you use plenty of damp soil when you* pot *those plants. Verb.*
pot (pot) *noun, plural* **pots;** *verb,* **potted, potting.**

potassium—A soft, silver-colored metal that is used in making soaps and fertilizers. It is a chemical element.
po|tas|si|um (pə tas′ē əm) *noun.*

potato—A vegetable that grows as a firm, rounded section on an underground stem of a leafy plant.
po|ta|to (pə tā′tō) *noun, plural* **potatoes.**

potential—Able to become or take place; possible: *The fireman spoke to the class about the* potential *danger of playing with matches.*
po|ten|tial (pə ten′shəl) *adjective.*

pothole—A hole in the surface of a road or street.
pot|hole (pot′hōl′) *noun, plural* **potholes.**

potter—A person who uses clay to make pots, bowls, dishes, or other items.
pot|ter (pot′ər) *noun, plural* **potters.**

pottery—Pots, bowls, dishes, or other items shaped from soft clay and baked into a hardened form.
pot|ter|y (pot′ər ē) *noun.*

pouch—1. A sack or bag. 2. A pocket of skin on certain animals that can be used as a bag: *The kangaroo carries its young in its* pouch.
pouch (pouch) *noun, plural* **pouches.**

poultry—Birds that are raised for their meat or eggs. The most common poultry are chickens, turkeys, geese, and ducks.
poul|try (pōl′trē) *noun.*

pounce—To jump upon suddenly and grab: *The puppy* pounced *on the rubber ball. Verb.*
—The act of jumping upon and grabbing. *Noun.*
pounce (pouns) *verb,* **pounced, pouncing;** *noun, plural* **pounces.**

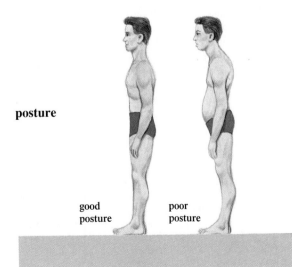

posture

good posture   poor posture

pound¹—1. A unit of weight equal to 16 ounces (453.6 grams). 2. A unit of money used in several countries, including Great Britain and Ireland. Its symbol is £.
pound (pound) *noun, plural* **pounds** or **pound.** Abbreviation: **lb.**; *plural,* **lb.** or **lbs.**
• See Word History at **lb.**

pound²—1. To hit hard with repeated blows: *The carpenter* pounded *the nail into the floor.* 2. To beat fast and hard: *She was nervous, and her heart was* pounding.
pound (pound) *verb,* **pounded, pounding.**

pound³—A place for keeping stray animals, such as dogs and cats.
pound (pound) *noun, plural* **pounds.**

pour—1. To flow or send flowing in a steady stream: *She* poured *maple syrup over her pancakes.* 2. To rain heavily: *The baseball game was canceled because it* poured.
pour (pawr) *verb,* **poured, pouring.**
• A word that sounds the same is **pore.**

pout—To push or thrust out the lips, as when one is showing displeasure: *She* pouted *because her friend did not want to play.*
pout (pout) *verb,* **pouted, pouting.**

poverty—1. The condition of needing money, food, clothing, or shelter; being poor. 2. The condition of being less than good; poor quality: *Because of the* poverty *of the soil, we didn't plant a garden.*
pov|er|ty (pov′ər tē) *noun.*

powder—1. The small particles created by crumbling, crushing, or grinding something. 2. A substance made up of small particles: *baking* powder. 3. A form of fine dust that is explosive: *gun*powder. *Noun.*
—1. To make into small particles: *The soil was so dry that the farmer could* powder *it in his hands.* 2. To cover or sprinkle with small particles: *She* powdered *the muffins with cinnamon and sugar. Verb.*
pow|der (pou′dər) *noun, plural* **powders**; *verb,* **powdered, powdering.**

power—1. Force; strength: *It takes great* power *to launch that large rocket.* 2. The ability, right, or authority to act or to do something: *The police*
have the power *to enforce the laws.* 3. A person or group that has great influence: *That rich man is a* power *in the city.* 4. Any kind of energy or force that can be used to do work: *water* power. *Noun.*
—To supply with energy: *Most autombiles are* powered *by gasoline engines. Verb.*
pow|er (pou′ər) *noun, plural* **powers**; *verb,* **powered, powering.**

powerful—Having great force or influence: *a* powerful *storm.*
pow|er|ful (pou′ər fəl) *adjective.*

practical—1. Having to do with real-life experience instead of study and discussion: *We gained* practical *knowledge about nursing from volunteering in the local hospital.* 2. Useful; helpful: *The director of the play gave* practical *advice to the young actor.* 3. Having common sense: *A* practical *person does not waste time.*
prac|ti|cal (prak′tə kəl) *adjective.*

practical joke—Any trick or prank played on another person in fun.
prac|ti|cal joke (prak′tə kəl jōk) *noun, plural* **practical jokes.**

practically—1. Almost; not quite: *The baseball season is* practically *over.* 2. In a true way; really: *The store still has to be sold, but otherwise the business is* practically *closed.*
prac|ti|cal|ly (prak′tə klē) *adjective.*

practice—1. A repeating something over and over so one can improve in skill: *It takes* practice *to play a musical instrument well.* 2. Custom; habit: *In our house, it is the* practice *to have Sunday dinner late.* 3. Career; profession: *She hopes to take up the* practice *of law. Noun.*
—1. To do a thing over and over again to improve: *After every basketball game, he* practices *his shooting for one hour.* 2. To make a habit of: *You should* practice *good manners at home.* 3. To work at an occupation: *They* practice *nursing at the clinic.*
prac|tice (prak′tis) *noun, plural* **practices**; *verb,* **practiced, practicing.**

prairie—Any large area of flat or rolling land covered with grass and having few trees.
prai|rie (prâr′ē) *noun, plural* **prairies.**

prairie dog—A small animal, related to and resembling the squirrel, that lives in large, underground colonies in prairies.
prai|rie dog (prâr′ē dawg) *noun, plural* **prairie dogs.**

praise—Words that express respect or approval: *The principal had nothing but* praise *for the performance of the school orchestra. Noun.*

a at	i if	oo look	ch chalk		a in ago
ā ape	ī idle	ou out	ng sing		e in happen
ah calm	o odd	u ugly	sh ship	ə =	i in capital
aw all	ō oats	ū rule	th think		o in occur
e end	oi oil	ur turn	th their		u in upon
ē easy			zh treasure		

—To express respect or approval for: *Mother praised my drawing and hung it on the wall.* Verb.
praise (prāz) *noun, plural* **praises**; *verb,* **praised, praising.**

prance—**1.** To move with a high, quick step or leap about: *Twenty horses, leading the parade, pranced proudly.* **2.** To walk or otherwise move about in a proud way; strut: *He pranced in front of his friends after he won the award.*
prance (prans) *verb,* **pranced, prancing.**

prank—A harmless trick or joke: *On my birthday, my sisters played a prank and hid my present in a closet.*
prank (prangk) *noun, plural* **pranks.**

pray—**1.** To express praise or otherwise address God; worship. **2.** To appeal earnestly to God: *She prayed that her grandmother would soon leave the hospital.* **3.** To be so helpful as to; please: Pray, *come with me.*
pray (prā) *verb,* **prayed, praying.**
• A word that sounds the same is **prey.**

prayer—**1.** An act of worship: *Before the meal, we all bowed our heads in* prayer. **2.** The words used in praying: *She was asked to say a* prayer *before the meeting at the church began.* **3.** What is asked or prayed for: *Our prayers for the safety of the travelers were answered when they returned safely.*
prayer (prār) *noun, plural* **prayers.**

praying mantis—A long, thin insect whose front legs bend to grasp food. When they are held in a bent position, the mantis looks as if it is praying.
pray|ing man|tis (prā′ing man′tis) *noun, plural* **praying mantises.**

pre-—A prefix that means ''before.'' Preschool means before school.

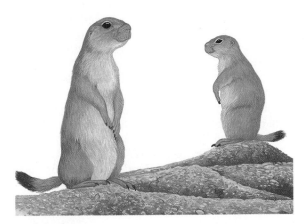

prairie dog

Word Power
You can understand the meanings of many words that begin with **pre-,** if you add the meaning of the prefix to the meaning of the rest of the word.
   prelaunch: before the launch
   prewar: before the war

preach—**1.** To give a speech on a religious or moral subject: *Last Sunday, the minister* preached *on the evils of stealing.* **2.** To give advice, usually in a strong manner: *Her father is always preaching to her about the importance of keeping her room clean.*
preach (prēch) *verb,* **preached, preaching.**

preacher—One who delivers a sermon.
preach|er (prē′chər) *noun, plural* **preachers.**

precaution—An action taken before an event to prevent an injury or other possible danger: *As a precaution, the coach made every player wear knee pads.*
pre|cau|tion (pri kaw′shən) *noun, plural* **precautions.**

precede—To come before or go in front of: *The color guard* preceded *the parade.*
pre|cede (prē sēd′) *verb,* **preceded, preceding.**

precinct—Any one of several sections into which a city or town is officially divided: *The candidate for mayor visited every* precinct *in the city during the campaign.*
pre|cinct (prē′singkt) *noun, plural* **precincts.**

precious—**1.** Being of great value: *Diamonds are* precious *jewels.* **2.** Beloved; treasured: *The little girl's whole family searched for her* precious *doll.*
pre|cious (presh′əs) *adjective.*

precipitate—**1.** To cause something to happen: *The surprise attack on the ships* precipitated *a war.* **2.** To fall as rain, snow, hail, or sleet.
pre|cip|i|tate (pri sip′ə tāt) *verb,* **precipitated, precipitating.**

precipitation—Water that falls as rain, snow, hail, or sleet: *Heavy* precipitation *caused the stream to overflow its banks.*
pre|cip|i|ta|tion (pri sip′ə tā′shən) *noun.*

precise—**1.** Exact; accurate: *The carpenter knew the measurements had to be* precise, *or the door would not close properly.* **2.** Done according to a strict standard; careful: precise *handwriting.*
pre|cise (pri sīs′) *adjective.*

precisely—Exactly; just: *On Tuesday afternoon the boy came to my house,* precisely *as planned.*
pre|cise|ly (pre sīs′lē) *adverb.*

precision—The fact of being accurate; exactness: *The painter did the window edges with such* precision *that almost no paint got on the glass.* pre|ci|sion (pri sizh′ən) *noun.*

predator—An animal that kills other animals and eats them for food: *Tigers and sharks are* predators. pred|a|tor (pred′ə tər) *noun, plural* **predators.**

predecessor—One who held a position now held by another: *Before he became principal of the school, his* predecessor *had been principal for 20 years.* pred|e|ces|sor (pred′ə ses′ər) *noun, plural* **predecessors.**

predicament—A situation that is unpleasant or difficult: *Having accepted two baby-sitting jobs on the same night was certainly a* predicament! pre|dic|a|ment (pri dik′ə mənt) *noun, plural* **predicaments.**

predicate—The part of a sentence that tells about the subject: *He goes to school.* The predicate is "goes to school," because it tells what "he," the subject of the sentence, does. pred|i|cate (pred′ə kit) *noun, plural* **predicates.**

predict—To say beforehand that something will happen: *The coach* predicts *that we will win most of our games next year.* pre|dict (pri dikt′) *verb,* **predicted, predicting.**
• Synonyms: **forecast, foretell**

preface—1. The words that introduce a book or a speech. pref|ace (pref′is) *noun, plural* **prefaces.**

prefer—To choose one thing rather than another: *My grandmother* prefers *warm weather to cold weather.* pre|fer (pri fur′) *verb,* **preferred, preferring.**

preference—Something chosen instead of another: *Dad's* preference *for dinner was steak, not chicken.* pref|er|ence (pref′ər əns) *noun, plural* **preferences.**

prefix—One or more syllables put at the beginning of a word to give that word a different meaning. "Recopy" puts the prefix **re-** before the word **copy.** pre|fix (prē′fiks) *noun, plural* **prefixes.**

pregnant—Having one or more offspring developing within the body: *The* pregnant *dog will have her puppies in less than two weeks.* preg|nant (preg′nənt) *adjective.*

prehistoric—Relating to the time before people began to write down or record events. pre|his|tor|ic (prē′his tawr′ik) *adjective.*

prejudice—An opinion or judgment that is unfair and not based on fact; bias: *a* prejudice *against children. Noun.*
—To cause to have such an unfair opinion or judgment. *Verb.* prej|u|dice (prej′ə dis) *noun, plural* **prejudices;** *verb,* **prejudiced, prejudicing.**

preliminary—Before the main part; acting as an introduction: *As a* preliminary *step to writing a report, the teacher showed the students how to take notes.* pre|lim|i|nar|y (pri lim′ə när′ē) *adjective.*

premature—Coming before the usual time: *The* premature *baby was born two months early.* pre|ma|ture (prē′mə choor′ or prē′mə tyoor′) *adjective.*

premier—A prime minister of a government. pre|mier (pri mēr′) *noun, plural* **premiers.**

premium—1. A bonus or reward for accomplishing a certain goal: *Those who sold more than 10 tickets got a free ticket as a* premium. 2. A high value, sometimes so high that it is unreasonable: *Her friend put such a* premium *on sewing that she had no time for sports.* 3. The payment for an insurance policy. pre|mi|um (prē′mē əm) *noun, plural* **premiums.**

prepare—To get ready: *She* prepared *for her speech by saying it over and over again in front of a mirror.* pre|pare (pri pār′) *verb,* **prepared, preparing.**

preposition—A word that shows how a noun or pronoun is related to some other word in a sentence: *the store in the mall.* The preposition is "in" because it shows the store's relationship to the mall. prep|o|si|tion (prep′ə zish′ən) *noun, plural* **prepositions.**

Presbyterian—One who belongs to a Protestant church that is governed equally by elected members and by their ministers. Pres|by|te|ri|an (prez′bə tēr′ē ən or pres′bə tēr′ē ən) *noun, plural* **Presbyterians.**

a at	i if	oo look	ch chalk		a in ago
ā ape	ī idle	ou out	ng sing		e in happen
ah calm	o odd	u ugly	sh ship	ə =	i in capital
aw all	ō oats	ū rule	th think		o in occur
e end	oi oil	ur turn	th their		u in upon
ē easy			zh treasure		

Presbyterian comes from a Greek word meaning ''elder.'' Elders are members of the church congregation who join their ministers to govern the workings of the Presbyterian church. They are called elders because older people, and people who have long been members of the church, have often been chosen to help govern it. So the church is named after the way it works.

preschool—Of the time or age before going to school: *The recreation department offers* preschool *activities for children under the age of five.*
pre|school (prē′skūl′) *adjective.*

prescription—1. A written order for preparing and taking a medicine, made by a doctor: *The doctor gave me a* prescription *to cure my rash.* 2. A particular medicine ordered by a doctor.
pre|scrip|tion (pri skrip′shən) *noun, plural* **prescriptions.**

presence—1. The act of being somewhere; attendance: *The child's* presence *at dinner was required every night.* 2. Where one is; nearest surroundings: *He felt excited to be in the* presence *of so many great works of art at the museum.*
pres|ence (prez′əns) *noun.*

present[1]—1. In attendance; at hand: *The whole family was* present *for the grandparents' anniversary party.* 2. Happening at the current time: *At the* present *hour, only a little snow has fallen, but much more is expected before the storm ends. Adjective.*
—The current time: *She is not feeling well at* present, *but she should be better tomorrow. Noun.*
pres|ent (prez′ənt) *adjective, noun.*

present[2]—1. To supply with; hand out; give: *The coach* presented *a trophy to the best player.* 2. To introduce: *He* presented *the new student to the class.* 3. To bring into the presence of another person or other people: *The class president* presented *herself at the principal's office.* 4. To show: *She* presented *her project at the science fair. Verb.*
—Something that is given; donation; gift: *a birthday* present. *Noun.*
pre|sent (pri zent′ for *verb;* prez′ənt for *noun*) *verb,* **presented, presenting;** *noun, plural* **presents.**

presentation—1. The act of giving or presenting something: *the* presentation *of the awards.* 2. The act of introducing one person to another or a group: *the* presentation *of the new members to the club.*
pres|en|ta|tion (prez′ən tā′shən *or* prē′zən tā′shən) *noun, plural* **presentations.**

presently—1. In a short time; shortly; soon: *He will be coming through the door* presently, *and then the meeting will start.* 2. Right now; currently: *In gym class, we are* presently *learning to play tennis.*
pres|ent|ly (prez′ənt lē) *adverb.*
• Synonyms: **directly, immediately, instantly,** for **1.**

preservative—A substance that keeps something from rotting or decaying: *Coating wood with a* preservative *will protect it during wet weather.*
pre|serv|a|tive (pri zur′və tiv) *noun, plural* **preservatives.**

preserve—1. To keep something in its present state; protect: *We put the family photograph in a frame to* preserve *it.* 2. To prevent food from rotting: *Keeping apples in a cool, dry place will* preserve *them through the winter. Verb.*
—1. An area set aside to protect plant and animal life: *a wildlife* preserve. 2. **preserves:** Fruit cooked in sugar and then stored in glass jars: *blackberry* preserves. *Noun.*
pre|serve (pri zurv′) *verb,* **preserved, preserving;** *noun, plural* **preserves.**
• Synonyms: **conserve, maintain,** for *verb* **1.**
Antonyms: **alter, change, modify, vary,** for *verb* **1.**

president—1. One who is the head of a country, company, club, or other organization. A president is usually elected but can be appointed. 2. **President:** The chief officer of the government of the United States, who is elected every four years.
pres|i|dent (prez′ə dənt) *noun, plural* **presidents.** Abbreviation: **pres.** or **Pres.**

Presidents' Day—A holiday celebrated in some states to honor George Washington, Abraham Lincoln, and other Presidents of the United States. It is held on the third Monday in February.
Pres|i|dents' Day (prez′ə dəntz dā) *noun, plural* **Presidents' Days.**

press—1. To push on or against something: *We* pressed *our noses against the window as we watched the rabbits in our yard.* 2. To push together hard; squeeze: *He* pressed *all the toothpaste from the tube so none would be*

wasted.   **3.** To get rid of wrinkles; iron: *She pressed her new dress after she took it out of the box.*   **4.** To hold closely in one's arms; embrace: *The small child pressed his stuffed bear to his side when he went to bed.*   **5.** To make steady progress; push forward: *The tired runner pressed on until she finished the race. Verb.*
—**1.** The act of pushing on or against: *All it takes to turn on the radio is a press of the top button.*   **2.** A machine that pushes on or against: *After the laundry workers wash the clothes, they put them through a hot press to remove the wrinkles.*   **3.** A machine that produces printed material; *printing* press.   **4.** Newspapers and other daily, weekly, or monthly publications, as well as the people who work to produce such publications: *the foreign* press; *freedom of the* press. *Noun.*
press (pres) *verb,* **pressed, pressing;** *noun, plural* **presses.**

pressure—**1.** The force caused by pushing on or against something: *The pressure of his weight against the door caused it to fly open.*   **2.** A load that seems to be too heavy to bear; burden: *She really felt the pressure of studying for two tests on the same day.*   **3.** A strong influence or demand: *She gave in to the pressure of her friends and went to the movie even though she had already seen it. Noun.*
—To insist urgently that someone do something: *He pressured his sister into giving him a ride to the game. Verb.*
pres|sure (presh′ər) *noun, plural* **pressures;** *verb,* **pressured, pressuring.**

presume—To suppose something to be true; accept without question; assume: *I presume you are going too, because everyone else is.*
pre|sume (pri **zoom**′) *verb,* **presumed, presuming.**

pretend—**1.** To put on a false front; fake: *She pretended to like the gift, because she did not want to hurt her friend's feelings.*   **2.** To say that one is, has, does, or knows; claim: *He pretended to know everything about the sport, but he could not tell how to score the game.*   **3.** To play a role; imagine; suppose: *Pretend you were born in pioneer times and describe life then.*

pre|tend (pri **tend**′) *verb,* **pretended, pretending.**

pretty—Pleasing to the eye; beautiful: *a pretty garden; a* pretty *picture. Adjective.*
—Somewhat; fairly; quite: *It is getting* pretty *dark, so we should turn on the lights. Adverb.*
pret|ty (prit′ē) *adjective,* **prettier, prettiest;** *adverb.*
■ **sitting pretty:** In a good position; well off: *If I win the big jackpot, I will be* sitting pretty *for the next few months.*
● Synonyms: **gorgeous, lovely,** for *adjective.* Antonyms: For *adjective,* see Synonyms at **ugly.**

pretzel—A snack food made from dough that is rolled into a straight or knotted shape, baked, and coated with glaze and salt.
pret|zel (pret′səl) *noun, plural* **pretzels.**

prevail—**1.** To be the most common or usual: *A feeling of relief* prevailed *in the classroom when the test was finished.*   **2.** To win; succeed: *In spite of some close calls, our team* prevailed *and became the champions of the tournament.*
pre|vail (pri **vāl**′) *verb,* **prevailed, prevailing.**

prevalent—Very common; widespread: *Computers are fast becoming* prevalent *in schools, and many students know how to use them.*
prev|a|lent (prev′ə lent) *adjective.*

prevent—**1.** To keep from happening: *She wrapped herself in a blanket to* prevent *a chill.*
2. To keep or stop from doing something: *The blizzard* prevented *school from opening that day.*
pre|vent (pri **vent**′) *verb,* **prevented, preventing.**

prevention—Something that keeps something else from happening: *The dentist explained that brushing the teeth is the greatest* prevention *against tooth decay.*
pre|ven|tion (pri **ven**′shən) *noun, plural* **preventions.**

preview—A look at something in advance: preview *of a new movie. Noun.*
—To see something in advance: *The students* previewed *the new library before it was opened to the public. Verb.*
pre|view (prē′vyū′) *noun, plural* **previews;** *verb,* **previewed, previewing.**

previous—Coming before; earlier; former: *Her new skates are white, but her* previous *pair was black.*
pre|vi|ous (prē′vē əs) *adjective.*

prey—**1.** An animal that is caught and eaten by another animal.   **2.** A way of life that depends on

a at	i if	oo look	ch chalk		ə =	a in ago
ā ape	ī idle	ou out	ng sing			e in happen
ah calm	o odd	u ugly	sh ship			i in capital
aw all	ō oats	ū rule	th think			o in occur
e end	oi oil	ur turn	th their			u in upon
ē easy			zh treasure			

catching and eating other animals: *The lion is an animal of* prey. **3.** A person or thing that is a victim; target: *She was* prey *to the jokers, because she took herself too seriously. Noun.*
—**1.** To catch and feed upon: *The fox* preyed *upon the chickens.* **2.** To burden; trouble: *Her worries about playing well in the championship game* preyed *upon her constantly. Verb.*
prey (prā) *noun, plural* **preys;** *verb,* **preyed, preying.**
● A word that sounds the same is **pray.**

price—**1.** The cost of something: *The* price *of the dress has been reduced for the sale.* **2.** What is lost or sacrificed to achieve something: *He became a championship skier at the* price *of a normal social life. Noun.*
—**1.** To set the value of something in terms of money: *The autographed baseball was* priced *too high for me to afford it.* **2.** To find out the cost of something: *He* priced *several bicycles before deciding which one to buy. Verb.*
price (prīs) *noun, plural* **prices;** *verb,* **priced, pricing.**

priceless—**1.** Too valuable or treasured to put a price on: *a* priceless *heirloom.* **2.** Delightfully amusing: *She thought his baby pictures were* priceless.
price|less (prīs′lis) *adjective.*

prick—To make a tiny hole with something sharp: *He* pricked *his toe when he stepped on the tack. Verb.*
—A tiny hole made by something sharp: *The pin made a* prick *in the material. Noun.*
prick (prik) *verb,* **pricked, pricking;** *noun, plural* **pricks.**

prickly—**1.** Full of sharp points: *an evergreen tree with* prickly *branches.* **2.** Feeling as though touched by sharp points: *His elbow felt* prickly *after he bumped it against the door.*
prick|ly (prik′lē) *adjective,* **pricklier, prickliest.**

prickly pear—A type of cactus that bears a fruit shaped like a pear. The plant itself is covered with spines and may have red, yellow, or green flowers.
prick|ly pear (prik′lē pār) *noun, plural* **prickly pears.**

pride—**1.** Confidence in oneself; self-respect: *Even though he hit several wrong notes, he continued with his performance out of a sense of* pride. **2.** Pleasure or satisfaction in something one does: *He takes* pride *in always looking clean and neat.* **3.** A feeling that one is very important and above others; too high an opinion of oneself:

Her pride *would not let her admit she was wrong.*
pride (prīd) *noun.*
■ **pride** (oneself) **on:** To be proud of: *She* prided *herself* on *never being late.*
● A word that sounds the same is **pried.**

pried—*See* **pry**[1] *and* **pry**[2].
pried (prīd) *verb.*
● A word that sounds the same is **pride.**

priest—A member of the clergy in certain Christian churches, especially the Roman Catholic Church and the Greek Orthodox Church. A priest has the authority to administer the ceremonies and rites of the church.
priest (prēst) *noun, plural* **priests.**

primary—**1.** Being first in time or in a series; coming before everything else: *The* primary *grades in school include the first, second, and third grades.* **2.** Most important; chief: *The* primary *purpose of exercise is to maintain a healthy body.* **3.** Basic; essential; fundamental: *the* primary *stitches in knitting. Adjective.*
—An election in which members of the same political party run against one another. Its purpose is to help choose a candidate to run against those from other political parties in a future election. *Noun.*
pri|ma|ry (prī′mār′ē *or* prī′mər ē) *adjective; noun, plural* **primaries.**

primary color—One of the basic colors from which all other colors can be made. The primary colors are red, yellow, and blue.
pri|ma|ry col|or (prī′mār′ē kul′ər *or* prī′mər ə kul′ər) *noun, plural* **primary colors.**

primate—A member of the highest group of mammals. Primates include human beings, apes, and monkeys.
pri|mate (prī′māt) *noun, plural* **primates.**

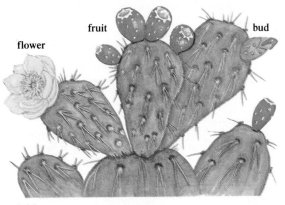

flower fruit bud

prickly pear

prime—1. Most important; primary; first: *The committee's* prime *goal is to choose a slogan for the class float in the parade.* 2. Being the best; superior: *She puts only* prime *ingredients into her cakes. Adjective.*
—The ideal time or part; peak; best: *the* prime *of life; the* prime *of the year. Noun.*
prime (prīm) *adjective; noun, plural* **primes.**

prime minister—The head of the government in Canada, Great Britain, and many other countries.
prime min|is|ter (prīm min′ə stər) *noun, plural* **prime ministers.**

primitive—1. Having to do with early times: primitive *art on cave walls;* primitive *people.* 2. Being early in development: *a* primitive *form of life.* 3. Simple or crude: *In Boy Scouts, he learned how to make a* primitive *shelter out of twigs, leaves, and branches.*
prim|i|tive (prim′ə tiv) *adjective.*

primrose—A small flower that grows in clusters on a garden plant.
prim|rose (prim′rōz) *noun, plural* **primroses.**

primrose

prince—1. A son or grandson of a king or a queen. 2. A noble man of high rank.
prince (prins) *noun, plural* **princes.**

princess—1. The daughter or granddaughter of a king or queen. 2. A noble woman of high rank. 3. The wife of a prince.
prin|cess (prin′ses *or* prin′sis) *noun, plural* **princesses.**

principal—Chief; primary; main: *The* principal *cause of the war was land, but there were many lesser causes. Adjective.*
—1. The most important person; leader; star: *the* principal *of a group of actors.* 2. The head of a school. Noun.
prin|ci|pal (prin′sə pəl) *adjective; noun, plural* **principals.**
• A word that sounds the same is **principle.**
• Synonyms: **central, major,** for *adjective.* Antonym: **minor,** for *adjective.*

Language Fact

Principal and **principle** have completely different meanings. However, many people confuse the two words when writing. **Principal** is both an adjective and a noun. As an adjective, it means "main." As a noun, it means "the top person or head." **Principle,** on the other hand, is only a noun. It means "a rule, truth, or belief."

---

principle—1. A basic truth, rule, law, or belief: *Our system of justice is founded on the* principle *that everyone is equal before the law.* 2. A rule of behavior that one follows through life: *The store owner made it a* principle *to return a customer's money for a faulty product.*
prin|ci|ple (prin′sə pəl) *noun, plural* **principles.**
• A word that sounds the same is **principal.**

print—1. To stamp or press a mark or letter on paper or other material with inked type: *The typewriter* prints *the letters shown on the keyboard as they are pushed.* 2. To publish something: *The school newspaper* printed *my article on photography.* 3. To write in letters that are not joined to each other: *We learned to* print *the alphabet in kindergarten. Verb.*
—1. Letters made by inked type on paper: *The book has large* print *that makes it easy to read.* 2. Fabric that has a design on it: *She preferred the* print *to the dress that was just one color.* 3. A mark made by pressure: *His sunglasses left their* print *on his nose.* 4. A paper copy of a photograph: *I am having another set of* prints *made of our vacation photographs. Noun.*
print (print) *verb,* **printed, printing;** *noun, plural* **prints.**

a at	i if	oo look	ch chalk		⌈ a in ago
ā ape	ī idle	ou out	ng sing		e in happen
ah calm	o odd	u ugly	sh ship	ə =	i in capital
aw all	ō oats	ū rule	th think		o in occur
e end	oi oil	ur turn	<u>th</u> their		⌊ u in upon
ē easy			zh treasure		

■ **out of print:** No longer available from a publisher: *That book was popular several years ago, but it is now* out of print.

printer—1. A person whose job is to produce copies of a newspaper, book, or other reading material. 2. A printing machine, especially a device that produces a computer printout.
print|er (prin′tər) *noun, plural* **printers.**

printing—1. The production of books, newspapers, or other printed matter on a printing press. 2. Letters shaped and separated like those in this book.
print|ing (prin′ting) *noun.*

printing press—A machine that makes copies of written material and photographs by pressing paper against inked type or plates.
print|ing press (prin′ting pres) *noun, plural* **printing presses.**

printout—A piece of paper that contains printed information from a computer.
print|out (print′out′) *noun, plural* **printouts.**

prior—Coming before in time or position; earlier: *She was unable to baby-sit for us because she had accepted a* prior *job.*
pri|or (prī′ər) *adjective.*

priority—The condition of coming before in time, position, or importance: *Studying for the test has* priority *over going to see the game.*
pri|or|i|ty (prī awr′ə tē) *noun, plural* **priorities.**

prism—A solid, clear object that separates light passing through it into the colors of the rainbow. It is a triangular block.
prism (priz′əm) *noun, plural* **prisms.**
● See picture at **spectrum.**

prison—A state or federal building where a convicted criminal is kept to serve out his or her sentence.
pris|on (priz′ən) *noun, plural* **prisons.**

prisoner—1. A person who is kept in a prison or in jail. 2. Any person who is captured or kept somewhere against his or her will: *The soldiers who surrendered were kept as* prisoners *by the enemy.*
pris|on|er (priz′ə nər) *noun, plural* **prisoners.**

privacy—The state of being by oneself; being away from everyone else: *Her room was where she went for* privacy.
pri|va|cy (prī′və sē) *noun, plural* **privacies.**

private—1. Having to do with or belonging to a particular person or group of people: *a* private *club;* private *property; a* private *beach.* 2. Not to be made public; secret: *The name of the award winner was kept* private *until it was announced at the ceremony.* 3. Not in public office: *When he lost the election, the mayor became a* private *citizen again. Adjective.*
—A soldier in the army or marines who holds the lowest rank. *Noun.*
pri|vate (prī′vit) *adjective; noun, plural* **privates.** Abbreviation (for *noun*): Pvt.
■ **in private:** 1. Not in public: *They met* in private *to discuss their problem.* 2. In secret: *The rebel leaders met* in private *to go over the plan of attack.*

privateer—An armed ship with a civilian crew that has a government commission to attack and capture enemy ships.
pri|va|teer (prī′və tir) *noun, plural* **privateers.**

privilege—A right or freedom not enjoyed by everyone; special favor: *He had the* privilege *of meeting the author of his favorite book.*
priv|i|lege (priv′ə lij) *noun, plural* **privileges.**

privileged—Having some right or freedom that others do not have: *Only a few* privileged *guests were invited to have dinner with the governor.*
priv|i|leged (priv′ə lijd) *adjective.*

prize¹—An award for winning a game, contest, or competition: *The team's* prize *for winning the tournament was a huge trophy. Noun.*
—Worthy of an award or having won an award; outstanding: *a* prize *essay; a* prize *speech; a* prize *dog. Adjective.*
prize (prīz) *noun, plural* **prizes;** *adjective.*

prize²—To place a high value on; treasure: *The museum* prizes *its collection of modern sculpture and keeps it guarded.*
prize (prīz) *verb,* **prized, prizing.**

pro—A shortened form of **professional:**
pro (prō) *noun, plural* **pros.**

pro-—A prefix that means "in favor of" or "on the side of." Someone who was proabolition was in favor of the abolition of slavery. Progovernment forces in a civil war are forces that are on the side of the government.

Word Power

You can understand the meanings of many words that begin with **pro-**, if you add a meaning of the prefix to the meaning of the rest of the word.
prodemocracy: in favor of democracy
prolabor: on the side of labor

---

probability—1. The state of being very likely to happen or being very possible: *The* probability *that he will speak out in the meeting is small,*

because he is very shy. **2.** Something that can be expected to happen: *Fallen trees are a* probability *during a hurricane.*
prob|a|bil|i|ty (prob′ə bil′ə tē) *noun, plural* **probabilities.**

■ **in all probability:** Probably: *In all probability, I will be able to go to the library with you on Saturday.*

probable—Having a good chance of taking place or being true; likely: *You had better take your umbrella with you, because rain is* probable *today.*
prob|a|ble (prob′ə bəl) *adjective.*

probably—Without much doubt; most likely: *It will* probably *take about four hours to drive to our destination.*
prob|a|bly (prob′ə blē) *adverb.*

probation—A test period during which a person's ability to do a certain job or behave properly is looked at closely: *The shoplifter committed another crime while on* probation *and was sent to prison.*
pro|ba|tion (prō bā′shən) *noun, plural* **probations.**

probe—**1.** A complete search, study, or exploration: *The town conducted a* probe *to determine if the factory was guilty of polluting the stream.* **2.** A device used to explore or to conduct tests: *a dentist using a* probe *to check for cavities; a space* probe. *Noun.*
—**1.** To research thoroughly; study; examine closely: *In his history paper, he* probed *the causes of the war.* **2.** To use a device to test, search for, or examine something: *When the lights went out, we* probed *the darkness with a flashlight to find some candles. Verb.*
probe (prōb) *noun, plural* **probes;** *verb,* **probed, probing.**

problem—A difficult situation or a hard question; something difficult to solve: *arithmetic* problems; *the* problem *of hunger in the world.*
prob|lem (prob′ləm) *noun, plural* **problems.**

procedure—The steps to follow when doing something: *The children had several fire drills at school so they would know the* procedure *for leaving the building in an emergency.*

pro|ce|dure (prə sē′jər) *noun, plural* **procedures.**

proceed—**1.** To more forward after having stopped; continue: *After picking us up at our stop, the bus* proceeded *to the next stop.* **2.** To begin and carry on an activity: *The scouts* proceeded *to set up their tents as soon as they reached the camp.*
pro|ceed (prō sēd′) *verb,* **proceeded, proceeding.**

proceeds—**1.** Money raised for a certain purpose through a sale or special performance: *The* proceeds *from the car wash will help pay for the band's new uniforms.* **2.** The amount of money that is left after a financial dealing has been completed; profit: *the* proceeds *from selling a house.*
pro|ceeds (prō′sēdz) *noun.*

process—A series of steps that takes place when doing or making something: *the* process *of baking a cake; the* process *of manufacturing an automobile; the* process *of writing a letter. Noun.*
—To do or make something by following a certain series of steps: *The company said it will take about six weeks to* process *my order for a cup with my name on it. Verb.*
proc|ess (pros′es) *noun, plural* **processes;** *verb,* **processed, processing.**

procession—**1.** A group of people moving forward in an organized manner: *The graduation* procession *walked past the proud parents.* **2.** A continuous and orderly forward movement: *The police cars moved in* procession *as they escorted the President's limousine.*
pro|ces|sion (prə sesh′ən) *noun, plural* **processions.**

proclaim—To declare publicly; announce officially; report: *The club president* proclaimed *that all new members were expected to pay their dues by the end of the week.*
pro|claim (prō klām′) *verb,* **proclaimed, proclaiming.**

proclamation—An official notice or announcement: *The leader issued a* proclamation *granting more freedom to the people.*
proc|la|ma|tion (prok′lə mā′shən) *noun, plural* **proclamations.**

prod—**1.** To nudge or poke with something pointed, such as a stick: *She* prodded *her sleeping brother with a finger to wake him up.* **2.** To urge into action: *The closing of the park* prodded *me to write to the mayor. Verb.*
—**1.** A jab or poke: *The boy gave the frog a* prod *to see if it would jump.* **2.** Something used

a at	i if	oo look	ch chalk		⌈ a in ago
ā ape	ī idle	ou out	ng sing		e in happen
ah calm	o odd	u ugly	sh ship	ə =	i in capital
aw all	ō oats	ū rule	th think		o in occur
e end	oi oil	ur turn	th their		⌊ u in upon
ē easy			zh treasure		

to poke or urge on someone or something: *The promise of pizza was just the* prod *we needed to finish our chores quickly.* Noun.
prod (prod) *verb,* **prodded, prodding;** *noun, plural* **prods.**

produce—1. To make or build something; manufacture: *Her company* produces *pens and pencils.* 2. To give birth to; bring forth: *a mare that has* produced *a fine colt; a field that* produces *wheat.* 3. To supply: *The waterfall* produces *electricity for the entire county.* 4. To bring forward or exhibit: *The magician* produced *a rabbit from his hat.* Verb.
—Farm products, especially fresh fruits and vegetables. *Noun.*
pro|duce (prə dūs′ for *verb;* **prod′**ūs *or* **prō′**dūs for *noun*) *verb,* **produced, producing;** *noun.*

product—1. Something that is made or manufactured: *The doctor told her not to have any dairy* products *for a few days.* 2. A number arrived at by multiplying two or more numbers together: *When 2 is multiplied by 5, the* product *is 10.*
prod|uct (prod′ukt) *noun, plural* **products.**

production—1. The act or process of making, building, or raising something: *the* production *of automobiles; the* production *of corn.* 2. Something that is made, built, or raised: *That painting was the final* production *of the famous artist.*
pro|duc|tion (prə duk′shən) *noun, plural* **productions.**

productive—Able to make or do a great deal of something: *I usually am more* productive *if it is quiet while I am doing my homework.*
pro|duc|tive (prə duk′tiv) *adjective.*

profession—1. A line of work that requires years of special study, such as law, medicine, or teaching. 2. What one does to earn a living: *a singer by* profession. 3. A declaration of feelings, belief, or opinion: *a* profession *of innocence; a* profession *of love.*
pro|fes|sion (prə fesh′ən) *noun, plural* **professions.**
● Synonyms: **business, career, occupation, trade, vocation,** for 2.

professional—1. Having to do with a line of work that requires years of special study: *As a* professional *pilot, he has flown many types of airplanes.* 2. Making money and working at something most people enjoy as a hobby or sport: *a* professional *golfer; a* professional *dancer.* Adjective.
—1. One who makes a living doing something

others enjoy as a hobby or sport: *The* professionals *teamed up with the amateurs in the tennis tournament.* 2. A person, such as a doctor or lawyer, who is involved in a line of work that requires years of special study. *Noun.*
pro|fes|sion|al (prə fesh′ə nəl) *adjective; noun, plural* **professionals.**

professor—A person who teaches in a college or university.
pro|fes|sor (prə fes′ər) *noun, plural* **professors.** Abbreviation: Prof.

profile—1. A view of the side of something, especially a person's head: *The brothers do not look much alike if you look straight at them, but they are very similar in* profile. 2. An outline or brief description of a person or thing: *The reporter for the magazine wrote a* profile *of each candidate for governor.*
pro|file (prō′fīl) *noun, plural* **profiles.**

profit—1. The amount of money a business makes after its costs have been subtracted from the total amount of money received. 2. A gain or benefit: *You will get no* profit *from complaining all the time.* Noun.
—To benefit or gain an advantage: *to* profit *from reading a good book.* Verb.
prof|it (prof′it) *noun, plural* **profits;** *verb,* **profited, profiting.**
● A word that sounds the same is **prophet.**

profitable—Making money; showing a profit: *a* profitable *business.*
prof|it|a|ble (prof′ə tə bəl) *adjective.*

program—1. A list of the events and the people performing or taking part in them, as for a ceremony, concert, or meeting. 2. A concert or other performance that includes several items or pieces: *The* program *includes a symphony and a violin concerto.* 3. A television or radio broadcast: *Grandfather told us stories about the* programs *he used to listen to on the radio when he was our age.* 4. A plan for reaching a particular goal: *the town improvement* program; *a fitness* program. 5. A group of instructions that controls a computer as it performs a specific task. *Noun.*
—To prepare a set of instructions for a computer. *Verb.*
pro|gram (prō′gram) *noun, plural* **programs;** *verb,* **programmed, programming,** *or* **programed, programing.**

programmer *or* **programer**—A person who prepares instructions to control the work of a computer.

pro|gram|mer or **pro|gram|er** (prō′gram ər) *noun, plural* **programmers** or **programers**.

progress—1. An improvement: *His health has shown steady* progress *since his operation.* **2.** A forward movement: *The car's* progress *was slowed by the bumps in the road. Noun.*
—1. To improve; get better: *The new quarterback's play* progressed *as the football season went on.* 2. To move forward: *The use of computers has* progressed *greatly over the past several years. Verb.*
prog|ress (**prog′**res for *noun;* prə **gres′** for *verb*) *noun; verb,* **progressed, progressing.**

progressive—1. Wanting changes for the better; interested in new ideas or advances: *a* progressive *approach in solving problems; a* progressive *attitude toward education.* 2. Developing; moving ahead: *The dentist explained the* progressive *stages of tooth decay to the class. Adjective.*
—A person who works for improvements in government, education, and other areas. *Noun.*
pro|gres|sive (prə **gres′**iv) *adjective; noun, plural* **progressives.**

prohibit—To not allow by law; forbid: *Glass containers are* prohibited *on the beach.*
pro|hib|it (prō **hib′**it) *verb,* **prohibited, prohibiting.**
● Synonyms: **ban, outlaw**
  Antonyms: **license, permit**

project—1. A definite plan: *a* project *for arranging books on a shelf.* 2. A special task, assignment, or activity: *an art* project; *a science* project. 3. A group of houses or apartments that forms a unit. *Noun.*
—1. To throw light or an image onto a surface: *The film was* projected *onto the giant screen.* 2. To throw or cast forward: *The actor* projected *his voice so that everyone in the theater could hear what he said.* 3. To forecast or predict: *We can try to* project *the winner of Saturday's game by looking at the records of the two teams. Verb.*
proj|ect (**proj′**ekt for *noun;* prə **jekt′** for *verb*) *noun, plural* **projects;** *verb,* **projected, projecting.**

projector—A machine that displays a movie or slides on a screen, wall, or other surface.
pro|jec|tor (prə **jek′**tər) *noun, plural* **projectors.**

prolong—To draw out; lengthen; continue: *We know you are in a hurry, so we will not* prolong *our stay.*
pro|long (prə **lawng′**) *verb,* **prolonged, prolonging.**

prom—A formal dance sponsored by one high school or college class: *the junior* prom.
prom (prom) *noun, plural* **proms.**

promenade—1. A walk that is taken for pleasure or to be seen: *We went on a* promenade *along the boulevard, stopping now and then to look in the shop windows.* 2. A place for taking such a walk: *The path through the park forms a cool and pleasant* promenade. *Noun.*
—To take a walk for pleasure or to be seen: *The horses* promenaded *around the track after the show. Verb.*
prom|e|nade (prom′ə **nād′** or prom′ə **nod′**) *noun, plural* **promenades;** *verb,* **promenaded, promenading.**

prominent—1. Widely known or important; distinguished: *a* prominent *business leader; a* prominent *sports figure.* 2. Easily noticed or seen; eye-catching: *The trophy holds a* prominent *place on the shelf.* 3. Sticking out: *a* prominent *chin; a* prominent *nose.*
prom|i|nent (**prom′**ə nənt) *adjective.*

promise—1. A declaration in which a person pledges to do or not to do something: *Give me your* promise *that you will not tell anyone.* 2. A sign that gives hope for success in the future: *He shows* promise *as a tennis player. Noun.*
—To give one's word; declare that one will or will not do something: *The bride and groom* promised *to love each other. Verb.*
prom|ise (**prom′**is) *noun, plural* **promises;** *verb,* **promised, promising.**
● Synonyms: **assurance, guarantee, word,** for *noun* 1.

promontory—A high point of land jutting into a sea or lake.
pro|mon|to|ry (**prom′**ən tawr′ē) *noun, plural* **promontories.**

a at	i if	oo look	ch chalk		a in ago
ā ape	ī idle	ou out	ng sing		e in happen
ah calm	o odd	u ugly	sh ship	ə =	i in capital
aw all	ō oats	ū rule	th think		o in occur
e end	oi oil	ur turn	th their		u in upon
ē easy			zh treasure		

promontory

promote—1. To raise to a higher rank: *to be promoted from fourth to fifth grade; to be promoted from vice president of the bank to president.*   2. To help the growth or development of: *The leaders of the two countries met to promote peace.*
pro|mote (prə mōt′) *verb,* **promoted, promoting.**

promotion—1. A raising in rank or importance: *The private received a promotion to corporal.*
2. The act of helping or encouraging the development or growth of something: *the promotion of good health; the promotion of good will.*
pro|mo|tion (prə mō′shən) *noun, plural* **promotions.**

prompt—1. On time: *He was always prompt for dinner.*   2. Made or done right away; without delay: *The cut on her knee needed prompt attention to keep it from getting infected. Adjective.*
—1. To cause someone to act: *The note on the desk prompted her to call her friend.*   2. To remind a speaker or actor of what to say or do next: *The actor had trouble remembering his lines and had to be prompted throughout the play. Verb.*
prompt (prompt) *adjective; verb,* **prompted, prompting.**

prone—1. Lying flat with the face downward: *a prone position.*   2. Likely to feel or act a certain way: *He is prone to telling wild stories to get attention.*
prone (prōn) *adjective.*

prong—A sharp, pointed end, like one on a fork, tool, or antler.
prong (prawng) *noun, plural* **prongs.**

pronghorn—An animal like an antelope that lives in western North America. It has hooves and two branchlike horns.
prong|horn (prawng′hawrn′) *noun, plural* **pronghorns** or **pronghorn.**

pronoun—A word used in place of a noun. **I, he, her, it, we, they,** and **which** are pronouns. *My mother likes horses because she thinks they are beautiful.* The pronoun "she" is used in place of "mother," and "they" is used in place of "horses."
pro|noun (prō′noun) *noun, plural* **pronouns.** Abbreviation: pron.

pronounce—1. To speak a word or make the sounds that letters represent. *There were many difficult words in the poem she read to the class, but she pronounced them all correctly.*   2. To declare something to be so; state officially and formally: *The President pronounced this a day of national celebration.*
pro|nounce (prə nouns′) *verb,* **pronounced, pronouncing.**

pronounced—Noticeable; clearly marked: *He has a pronounced twitch in his left eye when he gets nervous.*
pro|nounced (prə nounst′) *adjective.*

pronto—Right away; immediately: *Make sure the boss gets this message pronto.*
pron|to (pron′tō) *adverb.*

pronunciation—The act or way of saying a letter, word, or words: *A dictionary gives the pronunciation of words.*
pro|nun|ci|a|tion (prə nun′sē ā′shən) *noun, plural* **pronunciations.**

proof—A fact that shows the truth of something; evidence: *The mountain climbers put a flag at the top of the mountain as proof that they had been there.*
proof (prūf) *noun, plural* **proofs.**

proofread—To read through printed or written work to find and correct errors: *As she proofread her paper, she found several careless spelling errors she had made.*
proof|read (prūf′rēd′) *verb,* **proofread** (prūf′red′), **proofreading.**

prop—To place a support under or against something to hold it up: *He propped up the desk by putting an old telephone book under its broken leg. Verb.*
—A thing used to keep something in place: *She used a brick as a prop to make the window stay open. Noun.*

pronghorn

prop (prop) *verb,* **propped, propping;** *noun, plural* **props.**

propaganda—Information and ideas spread by a group of people to try to change the way other people think about something. Propaganda often presents only one side of an issue and is usually unfair or not completely true.
prop|a|gan|da (prop'ə gan'də) *noun.*

propel—To drive forward: *The spacecraft was propelled by rockets.*
pro|pel (prə pel') *verb,* **propelled, propelling.**

propeller—A device that is found on a ship or aircraft and that has blades attached to a center shaft. The blades spin through the air or water and produce the force that moves the ship or aircraft.
pro|pel|ler (prə pel'ər) *noun, plural* **propellers.**
• See pictures at **helicopter** and **seaplane.**

proper—1. Suitable for an occasion; fitting or correct: *A suit and tie is* proper *dress for a wedding.* 2. In the strict or most correct sense of a word: *The mayor's office and the police station are in the town* proper.
prop|er (prop'ər) *adjective.*
• Synonyms: **correct, fit**[1], for **1.**

properly—1. In a correct way or fitting manner: *to do an assignment* properly; *to behave* properly *in the library.* 2. In a strict sense: Properly *speaking, a tomato is a fruit.*
prop|er|ly (prop'ər lē) *adverb.*

proper noun—A noun that names a particular person, place, or thing. Proper nouns begin with a capital letter. ''Carolyn,'' ''New York,'' and ''Mississippi River'' are proper nouns.
prop|er noun (prop'ər noun) *noun, plural* **proper nouns.**

property—1. Anything that someone owns; possession: *That wagon is my* property, *but you may borrow it if you wish.* 2. An area of land that is owned by someone: *My family has* property *on the beach.* 3. A quality of something: *Diamonds have the* property *of being able to cut very hard materials.*
prop|er|ty (prop'ər tē) *noun, plural* **properties.**

prophecy—A statement about what will happen in the future; prediction: *Her* prophecy *about the grade I would get on the test came true.*
proph|e|cy (prof'ə sē) *noun, plural* **prophecies.**

prophet—1. A person who tells what will happen in the future: *The* prophet *claimed that there would be a war in a few years.* 2. A religious person who tells others about messages believed to be given by God.
proph|et (prof'it) *noun, plural* **prophets.**
• A word that sounds the same is **profit.**

proportion—1. The relation of one thing or part to another or to the whole, based on size, shape, amount, number, or degree: *The* proportion *of dogs to cats in our neighborhood is four to five.* 2. The proper balance between parts: *The artist erased his first sketch of the boy, because the arms and legs were out of* proportion *to the body.* 3. **proportions:** The size or extent of something: *the* proportions *of a room; a football player of large* proportions. *Noun.*
pro|por|tion (prə pawr'shən) *noun, plural* **proportions.**

proposal—1. A plan, scheme, or idea put forward for someone to consider: *At the town meeting, he made a* proposal *to reduce the town's budget.* 2. An offer of marriage, usually made by a man to a woman.
pro|pos|al (prə pō'zəl) *noun, plural* **proposals.**

propose—1. To suggest an idea or plan for others to consider or discuss; offer: *to* propose *an amendment to the town charter; to* propose *a vacation trip by car.* 2. To nominate someone for an office or as a new member: *I* propose *him for vice president of the class.* 3. To have as a goal or plan; intend: *I* propose *to lose several pounds this month on my diet.* 4. To offer marriage to someone.
pro|pose (prə pōz') *verb,* **proposed, proposing.**

proposition—Something offered for others to consider: *His brother made a* proposition *to me to buy my old bicycle.*
prop|o|si|tion (prop'ə zish'ən) *noun, plural* **propositions.**

proprietor—The person who owns a store, business, or property.
pro|pri|e|tor (prə prī'ə tər) *noun, plural* **proprietors.**

prose—The ordinary, normal writing or speech that people use, as opposed to poetry.
prose (prōz) *noun.*

prosecute—To bring a person before a court of law to be tried for a crime; start legal action against: *to* prosecute *a suspected thief.*
pros|e|cute (pros'ə kyūt) *verb,* **prosecuted, prosecuting.**

a at	i if	oo look	ch chalk		a in ago
ā ape	ī idle	ou out	ng sing		e in happen
ah calm	o odd	u ugly	sh ship	ə =	i in capital
aw all	ō oats	ū rule	th think		o in occur
e end	oi oil	ur turn	th their		u in upon
ē easy			zh treasure		

prosecution—1. The action of bringing someone to trial before a court of law: *The lawyer was unable to continue his* prosecution *of the case because his only witness disappeared.* 2. The side that brings legal action against someone in a court of law and tries to prove his or her guilt. pros|e|cu|tion (pros′ə kyū′shən) *noun, plural* **prosecutions.**

prospect—1. Something that is eagerly awaited or expected; possibility: *The* prospect *of snow excited the children.* 2. A possible customer or candidate: *to have several* prospects *for buying my old baseball glove; the list of* prospects *running for president. Noun.*
—To search an area for valuable minerals and ores, such as gold, silver, or oil. *Verb.* pros|pect (pros′pekt) *noun, plural* **prospects;** *verb,* **prospected, prospecting.**

prospector—A person who searches an area to discover valuable minerals and ores. pros|pec|tor (pros′pek tər) *noun, plural* **prospectors.**

prosper—To do very well, especially in gaining wealth; be successful: *The children's lemonade stand* prospered *during the heat wave.* pros|per (pros′pər) *verb,* **prospered, prospering.**
• Synonyms: **flourish, thrive.**

prosperity—Steady good fortune or success: *She enjoyed* prosperity *when she sold more computers than anyone else in the company.* pros|per|i|ty (pros per′ə tē) *noun, plural* **prosperities.**

prosperous—Enjoying good fortune, wealth, or success: *He owned several businesses and was the most* prosperous *merchant in town.* pros|per|ous (pros′pər əs) *adjective.*

protect—To keep safe from danger or harm; guard; defend: *Some people keep a guard dog to* protect *their property.* pro|tect (prə tekt′) *verb,* **protected, protecting.**
• Synonyms: **shelter, shield**

protection—1. The act of keeping someone or something safe from danger or harm: *The military services are devoted to our* protection. 2. Anything that keeps someone or something safe from danger or harm: *She wore a heavy coat as* protection *against the cold.* pro|tec|tion (prə tek′shən) *noun, plural* **protections.**

protective—Providing protection against harm, injury, wear, or the like: protective *glasses; a* protective *helmet.* pro|tec|tive (prə tek′tiv) *adjective.*

protein—A substance that is necessary for the cells of living things to live and grow. It contains carbon, hydrogen, nitrogen, and oxygen. Cheese, eggs, fish, meat, and milk are good sources of protein. pro|tein (prō′tēn) *noun, plural* **proteins.**

protest—The act of stating or showing that one denies, opposes, or objects strongly: *people marching in* protest *of the new law; a child's noisy* protests *when told to go to bed. Noun.*
—To state or show that one opposes, denies, or objects strongly: *The girl* protested *about having to come home early from the school dance. Verb.* pro|test (prō′test for *noun;* prə′test′ for *verb*) *noun, plural* **protests;** *verb,* **protested, protesting.**

Protestant—A member of a large group of Christian churches that are not ruled by the Roman Catholic Church, the Greek Orthodox Church, or other Orthodox Churches. Prot|es|tant (prot′ə stənt) *noun, plural* **Protestants.**

proton—A very small particle in the nucleus of an atom. It carries a positive electric charge. pro|ton (prō′ton) *noun, plural* **protons.**

protoplasm—The substance that is the living matter of all cells. It is colorless and jellylike. It is made up of proteins, fats, and other substances mixed in water. pro|to|plasm (prō′tə plaz′əm) *noun.*

protractor—A measuring instrument in the form of a half circle. It is used for drawing and measuring angles. pro|trac|tor (prō trak′tər) *noun, plural* **protractors.**

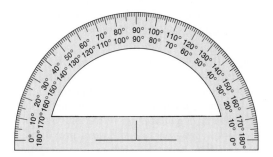
protractor

protrude—To stick out: *The sign* protruded *from the front of the building.* pro|trude (prō trūd′) *verb,* **protruded, protruding.**

proud—1. Having self-respect: *She was willing to ask for help when she needed it, but she was too*

proud *to beg for it.* **2.** Valuing one's achievements: *The boys were* proud *of the tree house they had built by themselves.* **3.** Having too high an opinion of oneself; arrogant: *He became so* proud *after winning the trophy that nobody could stand to talk to him.* **4.** Feeling highly pleased or satisfied: *We are* proud *to be citizens of our country.*
proud (proud) *adjective,* **prouder, proudest.**
■ **do (someone) proud:** To make proud: *She did her parents* proud *when she won the spelling bee.*

prove—To show that something is true or genuine: *She* proved *that she can run faster than I can by beating me in a race.*
prove (prūv) *verb,* **proved, proved** or **proven, proving.**

proven—Shown to be a fact; true or certain: *Because of his* proven *skill at drawing, he was asked to make the posters for the play. Adjective.*
—*See* **prove.**
prov|en (prū′vən) *adjective, verb.*

proverb—A short, simple saying that is known and accepted by many people as stating a simple truth. ''A penny saved is a penny earned'' is a popular proverb.
prov|erb (prov′ərb) *noun, plural* **proverbs.**

provide—**1.** To supply what is needed; make available for use: *Farms* provide *people with food.* **2.** To set down rules, conditions, or instructions in advance: *The club's constitution* provides *for meetings to be held at least once a month.* **3.** To prepare or equip in advance so as to be ready: *He* provided *for the costs of the trip by saving money.*
pro|vide (prə vīd′) *verb,* **provided, providing.**

provided—On the condition or understanding that something happens; if: *Father said I may go skating,* provided *I finish my chores first.*
pro|vid|ed (prə vī′did) *conjunction.*

province—**1.** A large section of a country, similar to a state. Canada has 10 provinces. **2.** An area of authority or responsibility: *Doing experiments is within a scientist's* province.
prov|ince (prov′əns) *noun, plural* **provinces.** Abbreviation: prov.

provision—**1.** A requirement, rule, or condition: *A* provision *for joining the club is the ability to speak a foreign language.* **2.** The act of supplying: *She is in charge of the* provision *of cake for the party.* **3.** The act of providing for a future need; preparing beforehand: *The store asked for our second choice as a* provision *in case the model we wanted was not available.* **4. provisions:** A stock of needed supplies, such as food: *The family took a week's* provisions *on the camping trip.*
pro|vi|sion (prə vizh′ən) *noun, plural* **provisions.**

provoke—**1.** To anger or irritate; annoy: *The little boy's naughty behavior* provoked *his mother, and she scolded him.* **2.** To stir up: *The cheers of the crowd* provoked *the players to do their best.* **3.** To bring on or cause: *Her joke* provoked *a great deal of laughter.*
pro|voke (prə vōk′) *verb,* **provoked, provoking.**
● Synonyms: **aggravate, bother,** for **1.**
Antonyms: **calm, lull, soothe,** for **1.**

prow—The front of a boat or ship; bow.
prow (prou) *noun, plural* **prows.**

prowl—To move about quietly or secretly, often in search of something: *The burglar* prowled *the neighborhood.*
prowl (proul) *verb,* **prowled, prowling.**

prudence—Good sense or judgment; wise caution: *He shows* prudence *when driving a car and never goes too fast.*
pru|dence (prū′dəns) *noun.*

prune¹—A dried plum. It has a dark, wrinkled skin and a sweet taste.
prune (prūn) *noun, plural* **prunes.**

prune²—To cut off or remove dead or unwanted parts; trim: *She* pruned *the bushes to keep them from drooping over the fence.*
prune (prūn) *verb,* **pruned, pruning.**

pry¹—To question or look curiously at or into something; snoop: *Our neighbor is very nosy and is always* prying *into other people's business.*
pry (prī) *verb,* **pried, prying.**

pry²—**1.** To raise, move, or pull apart by using force: *She used a knife to try and* pry *open the locked drawer.* **2.** To find out or get after a lot of effort: *After several hours, the police finally* pried *the details of the theft out of the bank robber.*
pry (prī) *verb,* **pried, prying.**

P.S.—The abbreviation for **postscript.**

psalm—A sacred song or poem, especially one from the Old Testament of the Bible.
psalm (sahm *or* sahlm) *noun, plural* **psalms.**

a at	i if	oo look	ch chalk		⌈ a in ago
ā ape	ī idle	ou out	ng sing		e in happen
ah calm	o odd	u ugly	sh ship	ə =	i in capital
aw all	ō oats	ū rule	th think		o in occur
e end	oi oil	ur turn	th their		u in upon
ē easy			zh treasure		⌊

psychiatrist—A doctor trained to treat mental illness.
psy|chi|a|trist (sī kī′ə trist) *noun, plural* **psychiatrists.**

psychiatry—The branch of medicine that studies and treats mental illness.
psy|chi|a|try (sī kī′ə trē) *noun.*

psychologist—A person who is an expert in psychology.
psy|chol|o|gist (sī kol′ə jist) *noun, plural* **psychologists.**

psychology—The scientific study of the mind and human behavior.
psy|chol|o|gy (sī kol′ə jē) *noun, plural* **psychologies.**

pt.—The abbreviation for **pint** or **pints.**

ptarmigan—A bird that lives in cold and mountainous areas. Its feathers are white in winter and brown in summer. Unlike other birds, it has feathers on its feet.
ptar|mi|gan (tahr′mə gən) *noun, plural* **ptarmigans.**

ptarmigan

pterodactyl—A flying reptile that lived millions of years ago. It had long, batlike wings without feathers on them. The pterodactyl was the largest known flying animal.
pter|o|dac|tyl (ter′ə dak′təl) *noun, plural* **pterodactyls.**

public—1. Having to do with or belonging to the people as a whole: *a* public *building; a* public *beach;* public *schools.* 2. Serving the people: *Many* public *officials, including the mayor and the governor, attended the dinner.* 3. Well known; not private or secret: *The facts of the case were made* public *only after the trial was over. Adjective.*

—All people; everybody: *Many parks are open to the* public. *Noun.*
pub|lic (pub′lik) *adjective, noun.*

publication—1. Something that is printed, such as a newspaper, book, or magazine. 2. The act of printing something, such as a newspaper, book, or magazine: *What is the year of that book's* publication?
pub|li|ca|tion (pub′lə kā′shən) *noun, plural* **publications.**

publicity—1. Notice or attention by a great many people: *The famous author's visit to the library received much* publicity. 2. Information that is given out to the public to gain attention or support: *A group of artists provided the newspaper with* publicity *on the art show.*
pub|lic|i|ty (pub lis′ə tē) *noun.*

publish—To produce and sell books, newspapers, magazines, and other printed material.
pub|lish (pub′lish) *verb,* **published, publishing.**

publisher—A person or company whose business is producing and selling books, newspapers, magazines, and other printed material.
pub|lish|er (pub′li shər) *noun, plural* **publishers.**

puck—A small, hard, black disk that is used to play ice hockey. It is usually made of rubber.
puck (puk) *noun, plural* **pucks.**

pudding—A creamy, cooked dessert that is soft and tastes sweet: *chocolate* pudding; *rice* pudding.
pud|ding (pood′ing) *noun, plural* **puddings.**

puddle—A very small, shallow pool of liquid, usually muddy or dirty water: *a* puddle *on the sidewalk; a* puddle *of spilled milk.*
pud|dle (pud′əl) *noun, plural* **puddles.**

pterodactyl

pudgy—Plump, and short or small; chubby: *a pudgy puppy; a baby's pudgy legs.*
pudg|y (**puj′ē**) *adjective,* **pudgier, pudgiest.**

pueblo—A village of square-shaped stone and adobe buildings where some American Indians of the Southwest live. The buildings are right next to or on top of each other and can be up to five stories high.
pueb|lo (**pweb′lō**) *noun, plural* **pueblos.**

Word History

Pueblo comes from a Spanish word meaning "people" or "town." When Spanish explorers first saw American Indian pueblos, the explorers thought that the pueblos looked like towns in Spain. One group of American Indians is known as Pueblos, because they live in such villages.

---

puff—**1.** To blow, breathe, or give out in short, quick gusts; pant: *hikers* puffing *as they climb the steep hill; a train* puffing *smoke.* **2.** To swell; inflate: *an ankle becoming* puffed *up after being twisted; to* puff *up a balloon or tires with air. Verb.*
—**1.** A quick burst of breath, air, steam, smoke, or the like: *A* puff *of steam came from the hot iron.* **2.** A light and fluffy mass of something: *a powder* puff; *a* puff *of fur; a cream* puff. *Noun.*
puff (**puf**) *verb,* **puffed, puffing;** *noun, plural* **puffs.**

puffin—An arctic sea bird that has a thick body, black and white feathers, a short neck, and a thick, colorful, red-tipped beak.
puf|fin (**puf′ən**) *noun, plural* **puffins.**
• See picture at **auk.**

pug—A small, square-shaped dog with a short, smooth, tan coat, a wrinkled face with big, round eyes, and a curled tail. Originally bred in China, these dogs are pets.
pug (**pug**) *noun, plural* **pugs.**

Pulaski Day—October 11, a day set aside in the United States to honor Casimir Pulaski, a Polish general who served with the American army during the Revolutionary War.
Pu|las|ki Day (**poo las′kē dā**) *noun.*

puli—A small or medium-sized herding dog with a long, thick, shaggy coat. Pulis have round, small heads with short noses, drooping ears, and curled tails. Originally bred in Hungary, these dogs were used to herd cattle and other livestock.
pu|li (**pū′lē**) *noun, plural* **pulik** (**pū′lēk**) or **pulis.**

puli

pull—**1.** To tug forward or toward oneself: *My brother* pulled *the red wagon.* **2.** To move: *Father* pulled *his truck off the road to let the ambulance go by.* **3.** To grab onto someone or something and tug; yank or draw out: *to* pull *weeds out of the ground; to* pull *a tooth. Verb.*
—**1.** A moving of something by tugging at it: *After many* pulls, *she was able to open the stuck door.* **2.** Effort or force that attracts, draws, or moves something: *the* pull *of a swift current; the* pull *of gravity. Noun.*
pull (**pool**) *verb,* **pulled, pulling;** *noun, plural* **pulls.**
■ **pull** (oneself) **together:** To regain control of oneself so as to continue: *Although the skater fell, she quickly* pulled *herself* together *and finished her performance.*

pulley—A strong wheel with a grooved rim in which a rope, belt, or chain moves when pulled. Pulleys are used to lift or lower heavy objects.
pul|ley (**pool′ē**) *noun, plural* **pulleys.**

pulp—**1.** The part of a fruit or vegetable that is soft and juicy and can be eaten. **2.** Any soft, wet mass, especially the moist, ground-up wood that is used to make paper.
pulp (**pulp**) *noun, plural* **pulps.**

pulpit—A raised platform in a church, from which a member of the clergy gives sermons and conducts worship services.
pul|pit (**pool′pit**) *noun, plural* **pulpits.**

a at	i if	oo look	ch chalk		a in ago
ā ape	ī idle	ou out	ng sing		e in happen
ah calm	o odd	u ugly	sh ship	ə =	i in capital
aw all	ō oats	ū rule	th think		o in occur
e end	oi oil	ur turn	th their		u in upon
ē easy			zh treasure		

pulse—1. The rhythmic throbbing of the arteries that is caused by the flow of blood through the body as the heart beats. 2. Any beat that is regular: *the steady* pulse *of the clock; the* pulse *of the car's motor.*
pulse (puls) *noun, plural* **pulses.**

pulverize—To crush or grind to a powder or dust: *The blender* pulverized *the chocolate.*
pul|ver|ize (pul′və rīz′) *verb,* **pulverized, pulverizing.**

puma—A large, brownish yellow, wild member of the cat family that is found in parts of North and South America; mountain lion.
pu|ma (pyū′mə) *noun, plural* **pumas** or **puma.**
• See picture at **mountain lion.**

pump—A device that pushes a liquid or gas through tubes or pipes: *a water* pump. *Noun.*
—1. To use such a device to move a liquid or gas: *to* pump *gasoline into a car.* 2. To fill with a liquid or gas: *I* pumped *up my bicycle tire.*
3. To question closely: *The news reporters* pumped *the scientist for information about her discovery. Verb.*
pump (pump) *noun, plural* **pumps;** *verb,* **pumped, pumping.**

pumpkin—A plant with a large, round fruit with many seeds and a thick, yellowish orange outer covering. Pumpkins grow on vines. They are often eaten as vegetables, and their pulp is often used for making pies.
pump|kin (pump′kin *or* pung′kin) *noun, plural* **pumpkins.**

pun—A funny or playful use of a word or phrase that has two different meanings, or of two words that sound alike but have different meanings. "Saving your money makes a lot of cents" is a pun on the words "cents" and "sense."
pun (pun) *noun, plural* **puns.**

punch[1]—1. To strike someone or something with the fist: *The bully* punched *my brother.* 2. To herd cattle. *Verb.*
—A sharp blow with the fist: *The boxer gave a hard* punch *to his opponent's chin. Noun.*
punch (punch) *verb,* **punched, punching;** *noun, plural* **punches.**

punch[2]—A tool for making holes or for stamping a design on a surface: *A leather* punch *makes holes in belts. Noun.*
—To use such a tool to make holes or stamp a design on a surface: *The bus driver* punched *my transfer. Verb.*
punch (punch) *noun, plural* **punches;** *verb* **punched, punching.**

punch[3]—A sweet drink made of a mixture of fruit juices, sodas, or other liquids.
punch (punch) *noun, plural* **punches.**

punctual—Exactly on time; prompt: *They could rely on his being there for the start of the race because he was always* punctual.
punc|tu|al (pungk′chū əl) *adjective.*

punctuate—To use commas, periods, and other such marks in written or printed material to help make the meaning clear.
punc|tu|ate (pungk′chū āt′) *verb,* **punctuated, punctuating.**

punctuation—The use of commas, periods, and other such marks in written or printed material to help make the meaning clear: *The sentence is difficult to understand because it lacks proper* punctuation.
punc|tu|a|tion (pungk′chū ā′shən) *noun.*

punctuation mark—Any of the marks used in written or printed material to help make the meaning clear. Some punctuation marks are: periods, commas, question marks, and quotation marks.
punc|tu|a|tion mark (pungk′chū ā′shən mahrk) *noun, plural* **punctuation marks.**

puncture—A hole made by something sharp: *She placed a patch over the* puncture *in the bike's tire. Noun.*
—To make a hole in something with a sharp object; pierce: *The bike's tire was* punctured *by a sharp piece of glass on the road. Verb.*
punc|ture (pungk′chər) *noun, plural* **punctures;** *verb,* **punctured, puncturing.**

punish—To make someone suffer because he or she did something wrong; give a penalty: *The father* punished *the boy for his rudeness by making him miss his favorite TV program.*
pun|ish (pun′ish) *verb,* **punished, punishing.**

punishment—1. The act of making someone suffer because he or she did something wrong.
2. The penalty for misbehavior or crime: *A stern scolding was the only* punishment *our puppy needed to make him behave.*
pun|ish|ment (pun′ish mənt) *noun, plural* **punishments.**

punk—1. A spongy material, usually made from fungus, that burns slowly and is sometimes used to light firecrackers. 2. A nasty young person who causes trouble: *He behaved like a* punk *and was well known to the local police.*
punk (pungk) *noun, plural* **punks.**

punt—To kick a football after it drops from the hands but before it hits the ground. *Verb.*
—The kick made to a football after it drops from the player's hands and before it hits the ground. *Noun.*
punt (punt) *verb,* **punted, punting;** *noun, plural* **punts.**

punt

puny—Small and not very strong: *The last puppy in the litter was* puny.
pu|ny (pyū′nē) *adjective,* **punier, puniest.**

pup—1. A newborn or young dog; puppy. 2. A newborn or young animal of certain kinds, such as a fox or seal.
pup (pup) *noun, plural* **pups.**

pupa—A motionless stage of change just before adulthood in the life cycle of certain insects, such as a butterfly in its cocoon.
pu|pa (pyū′pə) *noun, plural* **pupae** (pyū′pē′) or **pupas.**
● See picture at **metamorphosis.**

pupil[1]—A person receiving instruction from a teacher; student.
pu|pil (pyū′pəl) *noun, plural* **pupils.**

pupil[2]—The black dot in the center of an eye's colored part. This dot is actually an opening that controls how much light can get into the eye by widening in darkness and shrinking in bright light.
pu|pil (pyū′pəl) *noun, plural* **pupils.**
● See picture at **eye.**

puppet—A toy figure of a person or animal that is made to move and perform. Hand puppets are worn over the hands and moved by fingers and wrists. Marionettes hang from wires or strings that are pulled from above.
pup|pet (pup′it) *noun, plural* **puppets.**

puppet

puppy—A young dog.
pup|py (pup′ē) *noun, plural* **puppies.**

purchase—To buy something, giving money in exchange for goods or services: *We purchased our lunches in the coffee shop. Verb.*
—Something that is bought: *She carried her food* purchases *in a large shopping bag. Noun.*
pur|chase (pur′chəs) *verb,* **purchased, purchasing;** *noun, plural* **purchases.**

pure—1. Not combined with anything else; free of other ingredients: *a* pure *wool sweater;* pure *silver.* 2. Complete; nothing other than: *The friends met by* pure *chance.*
pure (pyoor) *adjective,* **purer, purest.**

purify—To cleanse; make pure: *I need a new filter to* purify *the water in the fish tank.*
pu|ri|fy (pyoor′ə fī′) *verb,* **purified, purifying.**

Purim—An annual Jewish holiday that celebrates the story of a beautiful Jewish woman named Esther who became a queen and saved her people. Purim is celebrated in late February or early March.
Pu|rim (poor′im) *noun.*

a at	i if	oo look	ch chalk		a in ago
ā ape	ī idle	ou out	ng sing		e in happen
ah calm	o odd	u ugly	sh ship	ə =	i in capital
aw all	ō oats	ū rule	th think		o in occur
e end	oi oil	ur turn	th their		u in upon
ē easy			zh treasure		

Puritan—A member of a Protestant group in England, during the 1500's and 1600's, that desired simpler religious ceremonies and stricter moral rules than those of other Protestants. Many left England and settled in New England.
pu|ri|tan (pyoor′ə tən) *noun, plural* **Puritans.**

purity—The condition of being perfectly clean and pure: *The* purity *of the new, white sheets was ruined when the dog jumped on the bed with muddy paws.*
pu|ri|ty (pyoor′ə tē) *noun.*

purple—The color that is made when red and blue are combined. *Noun.*
—Having this color: *a pair of* purple *socks. Adjective.*
pur|ple (pur′pəl) *noun, plural* **purples;** *adjective.*

purpose—A reason for making or doing something: *The* purpose *of my trip to the store is to buy milk.*
pur|pose (pur′pəs) *noun, plural* **purposes.**

purposely—Intentionally; deliberately: *He* purposely *left the light on because his sister would be coming home late.*
pur|pose|ly (pur′pəs lē) *adverb.*

purr—A soft, fluttering sound, such as that made by a happy or contented cat: *The mysterious* purr *in the kitchen turned out to be the motor of the refrigerator. Noun.*
—To make such a soft sound: *The mechanic promised that the car's engine would* purr *like a kitten when it was properly tuned. Verb.*
purr (pur) *noun, plural* **purrs;** *verb,* **purred, purring.**

purse—1. A small pouch used to carry money, usually coins. 2. A woman's pocketbook: *Her* purse *has a long strap that she wears across her shoulder. Noun.*
—To gather into folds; pucker: *to* purse *one's lips. Verb.*
purse (purs) *noun, plural* **purses;** *verb,* **pursed, pursing.**

pursue —1. To chase with the intention of capturing: *They* pursued *their runaway dog.*
2. To follow; engage in: *She* pursued *a business career after college.*
pur|sue (pər sū′) *verb,* **pursued, pursuing.**

pursuit—1. The act of following in order to catch: *The girl ran with a net in* pursuit *of the butterfly.* 2. An activity that one engages in as an occupation or for pleasure: *Boating is an enjoyable weekend* pursuit.
pur|suit (pər sūt′) *noun, plural* **pursuits.**

pus—A thick, yellowish white fluid found in infected body tissue such as a sore or pimple.
pus (pus) *noun.*

push—1. To press against something in order to make it move: *He* pushed *the baby carriage up the hill.* 2. To progress or move in some direction with force: *He* pushed *through the bushes to look for the lost ball.* 3. To use much effort to accomplish or sell something: *The employees* pushed *for higher salaries. Verb.*
—A strong effort or shove: *The charity made a big* push *this year and collected lots of contributions. Noun.*
push (poosh) *verb,* **pushed, pushing;** *noun, plural* **pushes.**

pushup or **push-up** —An exercise done by lying face-down and raising one's straightened body by pushing up with the arms.
push|up or push-up (poosh′up′) *noun, plural* **pushups** or **push-ups.**

pussy willow—A North American bush with small, furry, grayish white blossoms.
puss|y wil|low (poos′ē wil′ō) *noun, plural* **pussy willows.**

pussy willow

put—1. To place or cause to be in a specific location, condition, or position; set: *Please* put *the milk in the refrigerator.* 2. To say: *He was asked to* put *his feelings into words.*
put (poot) *verb,* **put, putting.**
■ **put one over:** To trick; to deceive: *He wasn't really a prince, but he* put one over *on the guests.*
put out: To make something stop burning: *Don't forget to* put out *the candles.*
put up with: To tolerate; be patient with: *He* puts up with *his brother's silly jokes.*

putt—In golf, to use a gentle stroke with a club in order to hit a ball into a nearby hole: *I putted to the left of the hole. Verb.*
—The golf stroke made in such a way: *It was her best* putt *of the day. Noun.*
putt (put) *verb,* **putted, putting;** *noun, plural* **putts.**

putter¹—A golf club used for putting the ball into a hole.
put|ter (put′ ər) *noun, plural* **putters.**

putter²—To keep busy without really trying to accomplish something: *It was raining, so I* puttered *with my coin collection.*
put|ter (put′ ər) *verb,* **puttered, puttering.**

putty—A patching material similar to soft clay, used to seal cracks in wood and to hold panes of glass.
put|ty (put′ē) *noun, plural* **putties.**

puzzle—A situation, task, or game that is hard to figure out: *a crossword* puzzle; *the* puzzle *of how the missing puppy ended up in the attic. Noun.*
—1. To confuse; bewilder: *The machine's instructions* puzzled *the new employee.* **2.** To try very hard to understand something that is confusing: *The tourist* puzzled *over the foreign signs. Verb.*

a at	i if	oo look	ch chalk		⎡a in ago
ā ape	ī idle	ou out	ng sing		e in happen
ah calm	o odd	u ugly	sh ship	ə =	i in capital
aw all	ō oats	ū rule	th think		o in occur
e end	oi oil	ur turn	th their		u in upon
ē easy			zh treasure		⎣

puz|zle (puz′əl) *noun, plural* **puzzles;** *verb,* **puzzled, puzzling.**
• Synonyms: **baffle, perplex,** for *verb* **1.**
Antonyms: **enlighten, illuminate,** for *verb* **1.**

pygmy—1. A tiny person, animal, or thing. **2. Pygmy:** A member of an African tribe of people who are usually less than 5 feet (1.5 meters) tall.
pyg|my (pig′mē) *noun, plural* **pygmies.**

pyramid—1. A solid object having a flat base and three or more triangular sides that slope and meet at a point at the top. **2.** A tomb shaped like such an object and built by the ancient Egyptians for their kings and queens.
pyr|a|mid (pēr′ ə mid) *noun, plural* **pyramids.**

pyramid (definition 2)

python—A very large and powerful snake that wraps around and crushes its prey before eating it.
py|thon (pī′thon) *noun, plural* **pythons.**

About 5,000 years ago, the ancient Egyptians used a symbol of a monkey. People in the Middle East used the same symbol. They called it *qoph,* their word for "ape" or "monkey."

About 3,500 years ago, other people in the Middle East used a symbol of a knotted cord.

About 1,900 years ago, the Romans gave the capital **Q** its present form. The small letter **q** was first used about 1,500 years ago. It reached its present form about 500 years ago.

About 2,800 years ago, the Greeks gave the letter this form. They called it *koppa.*

Q or q—The 17th letter of the alphabet: *There is one q in "question."*
Q, q (kyū) *noun, plural* Q's *or* Qs, q's *or* qs.
• Other words that sound the same are **cue** and **queue.**

qt.—The abbreviation for **quart.** *Plural,* **qt.** *or* qts.

quack—The sound made by a duck. *Noun.*
—To make such a sound. *Verb.*
quack (kwak) *noun, plural* **quacks;** *verb,* **quacked, quacking.**

quadrilateral—A shape with four sides and four angles, such as a square or diamond.
quad|ri|lat|er|al (kwahd′rə **lat′**ər əl) *noun, plural* **quadrilaterals.**

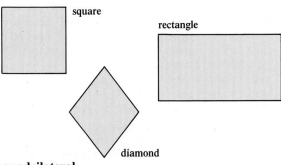

square
rectangle
diamond
quadrilateral

quadruped—An animal having four feet. Horses, rabbits, and bears are quadrupeds.
quad|ru|ped (**kwahd′**rə ped) *noun, plural* **quadrupeds.**

quadruplet—One of four children born to the same mother at the same time.
quad|ru|plet (**kwahd′**rə plit *or* kwahd **rū′**plit) *noun, plural* **quadruplets.**

quail—A bird with brown or gray feathers usually spotted with white. It is a member of the chicken family.
quail (kwāl) *noun, plural* **quails** *or* **quail.**

quail

quaint—Odd in appearance or old-fashioned in a pleasant or amusing way: *The clothes my great-grandmother wore seem so* quaint *to me.*
quaint (kwānt) *adjective,* **quainter, quaintest.**

quake—To shudder or tremble: *She* quaked *with excitement as she boarded the airplane for the first time. Verb.*
—A shuddering or trembling. *Noun.*
quake (kwāk) *verb,* **quaked, quaking;** *noun, plural* **quakes.**

Quaker—A person who belongs to the Christian church officially called the Society of Friends. Quakers are against war and follow plain and simple ways in both their daily lives and their religious services.
Quak|er (kwā′kər) *noun, plural* **Quakers.**

qualification—1. Something that makes someone or something able to do a certain job or other undertaking: *Patience and wisdom are two* qualifications *for a teacher.* 2. Something that limits; a restriction: *I recommend her without any doubts or* qualifications.
qual|i|fi|ca|tion (kwahl′ə fə kā′shən) *noun, plural* **qualifications.**

qualify—1. To make capable or fit for something: *His skill with his hands and knowledge of machines* qualified *him to be a mechanic.* 2. To change slightly; limit: *My enjoyment of the music was* qualified *by the fact that it was played too loudly.*
qual|i|fy (kwahl′ə fī′) *verb,* **qualified, qualifying.**

quality—1. A feature or characteristic that makes a person or thing what it is: *her* qualities *of honesty and kindness make her a good friend.* 2. Level of excellence: *The high* quality *of his school work was rewarded with good grades.*
qual|i|ty (kwahl′ə tē) *noun, plural* **qualities.**

qualm—1. A sudden feeling of fear or uneasiness: *The boy had* qualms *about jumping into the deep, cold water.* 2. A feeling that something is not right, or that one is doing something bad or wrong: *He had* qualms *about picking the apples, though his friend said that they did not belong to anyone.*
qualm (kwahm) *noun, plural* **qualms.**

quantity—1. An amount or number of something: *We put a small* quantity *of pebbles and shells at the bottom of the fish bowl.* 2. A large amount or number of something: *There was such a* quantity *of toys on the floor that there was barely space to walk.*
quan|ti|ty (kwahn′tə tē) *noun, plural* **quantities.**

quarantine—To keep a person or thing apart from others so as to prevent a disease from spreading: *No one could go into or out of the house after the family was* quarantined *for measles. Verb.*
—The keeping of a person or thing in such a manner. *Noun.*
quar|an|tine (kwawr′ən tēn) *verb,* **quarantined, quarantining;** *noun, plural* **quarantines.**

Word History

Quarantine comes from the Latin word for "forty." Long ago, ships sometimes had to wait at sea for forty days before landing because of the fear that some of the passengers might be carrying a disease that would spread to those on shore. The word is still used to refer to any period of isolation that prevents the spread of an illness.

---

quarrel—An angry argument: *The boys had a* quarrel *about who would be the first to bat. Noun.*
—1. To have such an angry argument: *She* quarreled *with her friend over who would use the telephone.* 2. To disagree; find fault: *You may* quarrel *with the rules, but you will still have to live by them. Verb.*
quar|rel (kwawr′əl) *noun, plural* **quarrels;** *verb,* **quarreled, quarreling.**
• Synonyms: **argue, bicker, dispute,** for *verb* 1. Antonym: **agree,** for *verb* 1.

quarrelsome—Fond of arguing; eager to quarrel: *The children were so* quarrelsome *today that the house was filled with noise.*
quar|rel|some (kwawr′əl səm) *adjective.*

quarry—An open place from which stone is taken in order to be used for building.
quar|ry (kwawr′ē) *noun, plural* **quarries.**

quart—1. A unit of measure for liquids, equal to two pints (0.95 liter). Four quarts make a gallon. 2. A unit of measure for dry things, equal to 1/32 of a bushel (1.1 liter).
quart (kwawrt) *noun, plural* **quarts.**
Abbreviation: **qt.**
• See also picture at **bushel.**

quarter—1. One of four equal parts into which something can be divided: *A* quarter *of a year is three months.* 2. A coin of the United States and Canada worth 25 cents. 3. One of four equal time periods of play, in such games as basketball and football. 4. One of the four equal divisions of the time it takes for the moon to travel around the earth, each lasting about seven days. 5. A

a at	i if	oo look	ch chalk		a in ago
ā ape	ī idle	ou out	ng sing		e in happen
ah calm	o odd	u ugly	sh ship	ə =	i in capital
aw all	ō oats	ū rule	th think		o in occur
e end	oi oil	ur turn	th their		u in upon
ē easy			zh treasure		

section or district of a city or town. **6. quarters:** A room or larger area in which to live or stay: *We had very pleasant* quarters *in the hotel. Noun.*
—To cut or divide into four equal parts: *We* quartered *the big sandwich so that my three friends and I could share it. Verb.*
quar|ter (kwawr′tər) *noun, plural* **quarters;** *verb,* **quartered, quartering.**

quarterback—A football player who runs the offense and usually either hands or throws the ball to another player.
quar|ter|back (kwawr′tər bak′) *noun, plural* **quarterbacks.**

quarter horse—A strong horse used by cattle ranchers, polo players, and horseback riders. It is especially good at running very fast for short distances.
quar|ter horse (kwawr′tər hawrs) *noun, plural* **quarter horses.**

quarterly—Done or occurring every three months. *Adjective.*
—Every three months: *We pay the dentist* quarterly. *Adverb.*
quar|ter|ly (kwawr′tər lē) *adjective; adverb.*

quartet—1. A group of four people, often singers or musicians, who perform together. 2. A piece of music written for four singers or musicians.
quar|tet (kwawr tet′) *noun, plural* **quartets.**

quartz—A hard mineral found in sand and many kinds of rocks. It is often clear and colorless but can also be very colorful.
quartz (kwawrts) *noun.*

quasar—A heavenly body, very far away in outer space, that is like a star but much larger and brighter.
qua|sar (kwā′sahr *or* kwā′zahr) *noun, plural* **quasars.**

quay—A place for ships to land and to load or unload, usually made of stone.
quay (kē) *noun, plural* **quays.**
● A word that sounds the same is **key.**

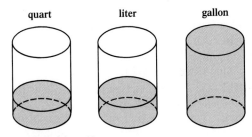

quart (definition 1)

queen—1. A woman who rules a country. 2. The wife of a king. 3. A woman or thing that is especially attractive or important: *That sparkling new plane is* queen *of the sky.* 4. An egg-laying female ant, bee, wasp, or termite. 5. A chess piece.
queen (kwēn) *noun, plural* **queens.**

queer—Different from what is expected; odd: *The* queerest *thing I ever saw was a pair of ice skates on the beach.*
queer (kwēr) *adjective,* **queerer, queerest.**
● Synonyms: **peculiar, strange, weird**

quench—1. To put an end to; satisfy: *She* quenched *her thirst with a quart of milk.* 2. To put out a fire.
quench (kwench) *verb,* **quenched, quenching.**

query—A question: *The lawyer put the same* query *to each of the three witnesses. Noun.*
—1. To ask questions of: *We* queried *the store owner about the price of the skateboard.* 2. To voice doubt about: *Mother* queried *my explanation of how the cookies disappeared. Verb.*
que|ry (kwēr′ē) *noun, plural* **queries;** *verb,* **queried, querying.**

quest—A search to find something: *The campers went in* quest *of firewood.*
quest (kwest) *noun, plural* **quests.**

question—1. Something that is asked in order to learn something: *The store owner answered my* questions *about the fish.* 2. A subject to be discussed: *the* question *of where to go during vacation.* 3. Doubt: *There is some* question *as to whether it will be warm enough to go swimming tomorrow.*
—To ask something of; inquire: *I* questioned *my friend about our homework. Verb.*
ques|tion (kwes′chən) *noun, plural* **questions;** *verb,* **questioned, questioning.**
■ **beside the question:** Not having to do with the subject: *His answer was* beside the question.
out of the question: Not to be thought of as possible: *Sailing our boat was* out of the question *on such a stormy day.*
without question: Without any doubt: *He is* without question *the best player on the team.*

question mark—The punctuation mark that looks like this ? and is put at the end of a question.
ques|tion mark (kwes′chən mahrk) *noun, plural* **question marks.**

questionnaire—A set of questions used to find out how certain people feel: *The customers were*

given questionnaires *that asked how they liked the new store.*
ques|tion|naire (kwes′chə **nār′**) *noun, plural* **questionnaires.**

quetzal—A bird with green and red feathers found in Central and South America.
quet|zal (ket **sahl′**) *noun, plural* **quetzals.**

quetzal

queue—A line, usually of people, waiting their turn: *We stood in the* queue *in the lunch room.*
queue (kyū) *noun, plural* **queues.**
● Other words that sound the same are **cue** and **Q.**

quibble—To get away from the main point of an issue by playing with the meaning of words or arguing over unimportant details: *They* quibbled *over where they should park the car instead of deciding who would drive.*
quib|ble (kwib′əl) *verb,* **quibbled, quibbling.**

quick—**1.** Very fast; swift: *The child's* quick *movements frightened the birds away.*
2. Learning or reacting rapidly and with ease: *a* quick *student in mathematics.*
quick (kwik) *adjective,* **quicker, quickest.**
● Synonyms: **abrupt, hasty, sudden,** for **1.**
Antonyms: **gradual, slow,** for **1.**

a at	i if	oo look	ch chalk		a in ago
ā ape	ī idle	ou out	ng sing		e in happen
ah calm	o odd	u ugly	sh ship	ə =	i in capital
aw all	ō oats	ū rule	th think		o in occur
e end	oi oil	ur turn	th̲ their		u in upon
ē easy			zh treasure		

quicken—To speed up; make quicker: *The dancers* quickened *their movements along with the music.*
quick|en (kwik′ən) *verb,* **quickened, quickening.**

quicksand—Wet, soft sand that is loose enough to cause heavy objects that rest on it to sink.
quick|sand (kwik′sand′) *noun.*

quick-witted—Having a clever and alert mind: *The* quick-witted *boy was the first to guess the answer to the riddle.*
quick-wit|ted (kwik′wit′id) *adjective.*

quiet—**1.** Making little or no noise; silent: *It is so* quiet *in my house at night that only a ticking clock can be heard.* **2.** Making or having little movement; calm: *I spent a* quiet *afternoon listening to music. Adjective.*
—To make or become silent or calm: *The teacher* quieted *the class. Verb.*
—The state or quality of silence or calm: *The actor waited for* quiet. *Noun.*
qui|et (kwī′ət) *adjective,* **quieter, quietest;** *verb,* **quieted, quieting;** *noun.*

quill—**1.** A long, stiff feather. **2.** The hollow stem of a feather, used as a pen. **3.** A sharp, stiff spine of an animal, such as that of a porcupine.
quill (kwil) *noun, plural* **quills.**

quilt—A cover for a bed made by sewing together two pieces of cloth with a layer of feathers or other soft material between them.
—To make a bedcover or other article of cloth in such a manner. *Verb.*
quilt (kwilt) *noun, plural* **quilts;** *verb,* **quilted, quilting.**

quince—A hard, yellowish, sharp-tasting fruit shaped like a pear. It is used to make jam and jelly.
quince (kwins) *noun, plural* **quinces.**

quinine—A bitter-tasting medicine used in treating malaria and other sicknesses.
qui|nine (kwī′nīn) *noun.*

quintet—**1.** A group of five people, often singers or musicians, who perform together. **2.** A piece of music written for five singers or musicians.
quin|tet (kwin **tet′**) *noun, plural* **quintets.**

quintuplet—One of five people who were born at the same time to the same mother.
quin|tu|plet (kwin tu′plit *or* kwin tū′plit) *noun, plural* **quintuplets.**

quip—A funny or clever remark: *The comedian's* quips *kept the audience laughing. Noun.*
—To say something clever or funny. *Verb.*
quip (kwip) *noun, plural* **quips;** *verb,* **quipped, quipping.**

quirt—A short-handled riding whip with a twisted leather end, used to make a horse run faster.
quirt (kwurt) *noun, plural* **quirts.**

quit—1. To stop; give up: *When the skater fell, she did not* quit, *but went on to finish her performance.*   2. To depart; get away from: *Her uncle is* quitting *his job and starting his own business.*
quit (kwit) *verb,* **quit** *or* **quitted, quitting.**
• Synonyms: **cease, halt,** for 1.

quite—1. Completely; fully: *It has not been* quite *one hour yet, so we will wait here for five more minutes.*   2. Really; surely: *There's been* quite *a change in your behavior.*
quite (kwīt) *adverb.*

quiver[1]—To shiver quickly but quietly; tremble: *The kitten* quivered *in my arms.*
quiv|er (kwiv′ər) *verb,* **quivered, quivering.**

quiver[2]—A carrying case for arrows.
quiv|er (kwiv′ər) *noun, plural* **quivers.**

quiz—A brief spoken or written test. *Noun.*
—1. To give a brief test: *She was glad she had read the chapter because the teacher* quizzed *them on it.*   2. To ask questions in order to gather information: *He* quizzed *the children about the broken window. Verb.*
quiz (kwiz) *noun, plural* **quizzes;** *verb,* **quizzed, quizzing.**

quota—An amount of something that is assigned to each person or thing in a group; share: *Each child's* quota *was two cookies.*
quo|ta (kwō′tə) *noun, plural* **quotas.**

quotation—Words that are repeated exactly as they were first said or written: *He started his speech with a* quotation *from his favorite book.*
quo|ta|tion (kwō tā′shən) *noun, plural* **quotations.**

quotation mark—A punctuation mark that looks like this ''or this'' and is used to show where a quotation begins and where it ends: *The principal said, ''Today we will have a fire drill.''*
quo|ta|tion mark (kwō tā′shən mahrk) *noun, plural* **quotation marks.**

quote—To repeat words exactly as they were said or written; *I* quoted *my favorite author. Verb.*
—A repeating of words exactly as they were said or written, quotation. *Noun.*
quote (kwōt) *verb,* **quoted, quoting;** *noun, plural* **quotes.**

quotient—The result when one number is divided by another number: *Eighteen divided by three gives the* quotient *of six.*
quo|tient (kwō′shənt) *noun, plural* **quotients.**

quiver[2]

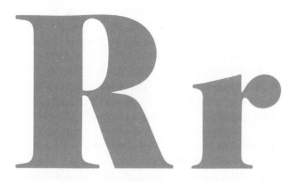

About 1,900 years ago, the Romans gave the capital **R** its present form. The small letter **r** was first used about 1,800 years ago. It reached its present form about 500 years ago.

About 5,000 years ago, the ancient Egyptians used a symbol of a human head.

About 3,500 years ago, people in the Middle East made a simpler symbol. They called it *resh* , their word for "head."

About 3,000 years ago, other people in the Middle East used a symbol of a triangle with a tail.

About 2,600 years ago, the Greeks gave the letter this form. They called it *rho*.

R or **r**—The eighteenth letter of the alphabet: *There are two* r's *in the word "roar."*
R, r (ahr) *noun, plural* **R's** or **Rs**, **r's** or **rs**.

rabbi—A Jewish religious leader. A rabbi usually has a congregation and conducts religious services in a synagogue.
rab|bi (rab′ī) *noun, plural* **rabbis** or **rabbies**.

rabbit—A small, long-eared, fluffy-tailed, furry animal that lives in a burrow underground. Because they have long, strong back legs, rabbits can run fast and leap far.
rab|bit (rab′it) *noun, plural* **rabbits**.

rabies—A deadly disease caused by a virus that can attack warm-blooded animals, including people. If an animal, such as a dog or a squirrel, has rabies and bites a human being, the human can get the disease and die if not treated.
ra|bies (rā′bēz) *noun*.

raccoon—A small, grayish brown animal with a long, furry, black-ringed tail, a pointed face, and black face markings that make the raccoon look as if it is wearing a mask.
rac|coon (ra′kūn′) *noun, plural* **raccoons**.

race¹—A contest in which the winner is the fastest: *a dog* race; *an automobile* race. *Noun.* —**1.** To compete in a contest in which the winner is the fastest: *At the swimming meet, our team* raced *against five other teams.* **2.** To run or move fast; rush: *She* raced *to catch the school bus. Verb.*
race (rās) *noun, plural* **races;** *verb,* **raced, racing**.

race²—A very large group of people who share the same ancestors and physical characteristics and who differ physically from other groups of people: *the American Indian* race; *the black* race.
race (rās) *noun, plural* **races**.

racial—Of or relating to a race of people: *to strive for* racial *equality;* racial *integration.*
ra|cial (rā′shəl) *adjective*.

a at	i if	oo look	ch chalk		a in ago
ā ape	ī idle	ou out	ng sing		e in happen
ah calm	o odd	u ugly	sh ship	ə =	i in capital
aw all	ō oats	ū rule	th think		o in occur
e end	oi oil	ur turn	th their		u in upon
ē easy			zh treasure		

rabbit

rack—1. A frame, usually made of connected bars, that is used to show, hold, or hang things: *a clothing display* rack; *a hat* rack; *a key* rack. 2. A body-stretching device that was once used to torture people. *Noun.*
—To hurt a lot: *a racking cough. Verb.*
rack (rak) *noun, plural* **racks;** *verb,* **racked, racking.**

racket[1]—1. A lot of confusing noise: *The carpenters were making such a racket that my mother didn't hear the phone ring.* 2. A way of making money by cheating others; unlawful scheme: *a racket of demanding money by threats.*
rack|et (rak′it) *noun, plural* **rackets.**
  ● Synonyms: **clamor, commotion, din, uproar,** for **1.**
  Antonyms: **quiet, silence, still,** for **1.**

racket[2]—A rounded, wood or metal frame with a handle and crossed strings tightly laced across the frame's open center. It is used to hit a ball or similar object in tennis, badminton, and other racket sports.
rack|et (rak′it) *noun, plural* **rackets.**

Word History

Racket[2] may come from an Arabic word meaning "palm of the hand." When people first played tennis, they hit the ball back and forth using the palms of their hands. Later they started using rackets instead. So a racket may be named for what it replaced.

---

radar—A machine that measures reflected radio waves to tell the distance, direction, and speed of distant objects: *The police officer used* radar *to track down the speeding car.*
ra|dar (rā′dahr) *noun.*

raccoon

Word History

Radar is made up of the first one or two letters of four words. It stands for "radio detection and ranging." In modern times, many words have been created from the first letters of other words. This is especially common in science and government.
  ● See also Word Histories at **BASIC, scuba,** and **UNICEF.**

---

radiant—1. Glowing; shining: *a radiant moon; a* radiant *gold bracelet.* 2. Giving off a lot of light or heat in rays: *a radiant heater; a radiant lamp.*
ra|di|ant (rā′dē ənt) *adjective.*
  ● Synonyms: **bright, brilliant, luminous,** for **1.**
  Antonyms: **dark, dim, dull,** for **1.**

radiate—1. To spread rays, as of light or heat: *Everyone was comfortable once the heater began to* radiate *warmth.* 2. To be spread out in rays: *Light* radiates *from a lamp.* 3. To branch out in all directions from a central spot: *spokes* radiating *from the middle of an umbrella.*
ra|di|ate (rā′dē āt′) *verb,* **radiated, radiating.**

radiation—1. The giving off of energy as rays of light, electricity, or heat: *The sun warms the earth by* radiation. 2. The rays sent out from a substance that creates energy by breaking up atoms: Radiation *is used to treat some sick people, such as cancer patients.* 3. The act of spreading in all directions from a central point: *the* radiation *of petals on a daisy.*
ra|di|a|tion (rā′dē ā′shən) *noun.*

radiator—1. Several pipes set together through which steam or hot water passes, heating the pipes, which warm the air. 2. A similar device that cools moving water by quickly releasing its heat. Cars have radiators to keep the engine from overheating.
ra|di|a|tor (rā′dē ā′tər) *noun, plural* **radiators.**

radical—1. Extreme; complete: *It was a radical change in the weather when our warm spring day turned to snow.* 2. Favoring a rapid and complete change of basic rules and laws: *The* radical *political candidate will not win many votes because most people like things the way they are. Adjective.*
—Someone who holds extreme ideas and favors a rapid and complete change from the way things are: *Many people think the mayor is a* radical *because of the changes he wants to make. Noun.*
rad|i|cal (rad′ə kəl) *adjective; noun, plural* **radicals.**

radio—1. The sending of sound electronically through the air to a receiver without using connecting wires: *The message was sent to the ship by* radio. 2. A device used for receiving or sending sound in this way: *They turned on the* radio *and heard some of their favorite music. Noun.*
—To send sound electronically through the air without using connecting wires: *The engineer* radioed *ahead that the train was running an hour late. Verb.*
ra|di|o (rā′dē ō′) *noun, plural* **radios;** *verb,* **radioed, radioing.**

radioactive—Having energy that is created by atoms breaking up: Radioactive *materials are making it easier for doctors to cure diseases.*
ra|di|o|ac|tive (rā′dē ō ak′tiv) *adjective.*

radish—The small, round root of a plant, which has a red skin with a white center. It is eaten raw and has a sharp taste that almost stings.
rad|ish (rad′ish) *noun, plural* **radishes.**

radish

radium—A highly radioactive metal. It is a chemical element.
ra|di|um (rā′dē əm) *noun.*

a at	i if	oo look	ch chalk		⌈ a in ago
ā ape	ī idle	ou out	ng sing		e in happen
ah calm	o odd	u ugly	sh ship	ə =	i in capital
aw all	ō oats	ū rule	th think		o in occur
e end	oi oil	ur turn	th their		⌊ u in upon
ē easy			zh treasure		

radius—1. A straight line that goes from the center of a circle or sphere to any point on the outside. 2. The area within a circle of a certain size: *His paper route covers a* radius *of one mile around his house.*
ra|di|us (rā′dē əs) *noun, plural* **radii** (rā′dē ī′) or **radiuses.**
• For 1, see picture at **circle.**

raffle—A game of chance in which a prize is won by someone whose number or name is selected at random from all those who have bought tickets. A raffle is usually conducted to raise money for a worthy cause. *Noun.*
—To give a prize by selecting a name or number at random from all those who bought tickets: *The club* raffled *off a television set to raise money for new equipment. Verb.*
raf|fle (raf′əl) *noun, plural* **raffles;** *verb,* **raffled, raffling.**

raft—1. A floating platform, often made of logs. 2. An inflated craft made of nylon and coated with synthetic rubber.
raft (raft) *noun, plural* **rafts.**

raft (definition 2)

rag—1. An old, worn-out piece of material that is often used to clean or polish furniture and the like: *I cleaned up the spill with a* rag.
2. Anything made of cloth that is worn out and no longer useful in its present form: *dressed in* rags.
rag (rag) *noun, plural* **rags.**

rage—Extreme anger; violent temper: *Her face became red with* rage *when she found her favorite dish broken. Noun.*
—To be or act violently angry: *Mad that he could not get out, the lion* raged *about the cage. Verb.*
rage (rāj) *noun, plural* **rages;** *verb,* **raged, raging.**
• Synonyms: **fury, wrath,** for *noun.*
  Antonyms: **calm, peace,** for *noun.*

ragged—1. Worn out; shabby; torn: *The baby's blanket was* ragged *from being dragged along the floor.*   2. Dressed in worn, torn clothing: *The* ragged *children were given a bath and some clean clothes.*   3. Not smooth or even: *the* ragged *edge of the bread knife.*
rag|ged (rag′id) *adjective.*

ragweed—A common weed whose pollen, carried through the air by wind, can cause hay fever.
rag|weed (rag′wēd′) *noun, plural* **ragweeds.**

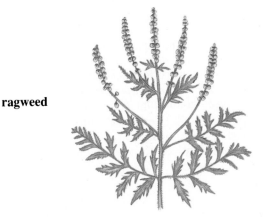

ragweed

raid—A surprise attack: *The police made a* raid *on the smugglers' camp. Noun.*
—To make a surprise attack: *The fort was* raided *by the enemy. Verb.*
raid (rād) *noun, plural* **raids;** *verb,* **raided, raiding.**

rail—1. A strong bar of wood or metal that is used as part of a barrier, such as a fence, or for holding on to, as along a staircase.   2. One of the tracks along which a train travels.   3. The method of traveling by train: *going by* rail.
rail (rāl) *noun, plural* **rails.**

railing—A structure made of a set of rails that forms a fence or other protective support: *The strong* railing *at the edge of the cliff protected people from danger.*
rail|ing (rā′ling) *noun, plural* **railings.**

railroad—1. A track of rails on which a train travels.   2. Everything and everybody in the business of running trains, including engines, cars, tracks, stations, engineers, and other workers; the entire system of train travel: *The conductor for the* railroad *took our tickets.*
rail|road (rāl′rōd′) *noun, plural* **railroads.**
Abbreviation: **R.R.**

rain—1. Drops of water that fall to the ground, formed from moisture in clouds: Rain *from the storm filled the bucket.*   2. The weather created by these drops of water: *The* rain *forced them to cancel their sail on the lake.*   3. Anything that falls quickly in a large amount: *a* rain *of confetti; a* rain *of angry words. Noun.*
—1. To fall from the clouds to the ground in drops of water: *It* rained *so hard that the river overflowed its banks.*   2. To pour or fall in great amounts: *The autumn leaves* rained *down from the trees. Verb.*
rain (rān) *noun, plural* **rains;** *verb,* **rained, raining.**
• Words that sound the same are **reign** and **rein.**

rainbow—A curved band of colors, made by the sun shining through drops of rain.
rain|bow (rān′bō′) *noun, plural* **rainbows.**

raincoat—A coat that sheds water, made to wear in the rain so that a person stays dry.
rain|coat (rān′kōt′) *noun, plural* **raincoats.**

raindrop—A single drop of water from rain.
rain|drop (rān′drop′) *noun, plural* **raindrops.**

rainfall—1. The falling of drops of water from moisture in clouds: *The* rainfall *should help our flowers grow.*   2. The total amount of water in the form of rain, snow, or the like that falls in a certain area over a certain time period: *The* rainfall *for this month has been more than usual and has caused the rivers and lakes to rise.*
rain|fall (rān′fawl′) *noun, plural* **rainfalls.**

rainy—Having or bringing rain; wet from rain: *a* rainy *afternoon; a* rainy *sidewalk.*
rain|y (rā′nē) *adjective,* **rainier, rainiest.**

raise—1. To lift up to a higher level: *She* raised *the window to let in some air.*   2. To build; put up; set up: *to* raise *a tent; to* raise *a house.*   3. To make rise: *The sunburn* raised *blisters on his skin.*   4. To move up: *Because she did so well in history, she was* raised *to the next class level.*   5. To make higher; increase: *The club dues were* raised *from one dollar to two dollars.*   6. To collect; bring in: *The cake sale* raised *money to buy new uniforms.*   7. To help to develop: *to* raise *vegetables.*   8. To ask or bring up: *to* raise *a question. Verb.*
—An increase in pay, amount, or the cost of something: *The* raise *in his allowance made it possible for him to save enough money to buy skates. Noun.*
raise (rāz) *verb,* **raised, raising;** *noun, plural* **raises.**
• Synonyms: **cultivate, grow,** for *verb* 7.

raisin—A sweet grape that has been dried.
rai|sin (rā′zən) *noun, plural* **raisins.**

rake—A lawn or garden tool with a long handle attached to a bar that has many long teeth or prongs. It is used to collect cut grass, fallen leaves, and other light, loose objects from the ground, or to smooth the ground's surface. *Noun.*
—To use such a tool for gathering leaves and the like from the ground or for smoothing the dirt: *He raked the garden carefully. Verb.*
rake (rāk) *noun, plural* **rakes;** *verb,* **raked, raking.**

rally—1. To gather together for a special reason: *The coach rallied the team players in the locker room to talk about the game.* 2. To gather together to help or support someone or something: *The community rallied to find food and clothing for the poor family.* 3. To begin to get well; improve one's health or strength: *Our grandfather seemed to rally when we visited him in the hospital. Verb.*
—A gathering together for a special reason, usually to create enthusiasm or support for someone or something: *The pep rally before the big game fired up the football players. Noun.*
ral|ly (ral′ē) *verb,* **rallied, rallying;** *noun, plural* **rallies.**

ram—1. A male sheep. 2. A machine part that hits with great force, or a device used to hit and knock down something: *The soldiers used a battering ram to break down the gate. Noun.*
—1. To hit with great force: *At the amusement park, we rode little cars that ram each other.* 2. To force by hitting, pushing, or driving down: *He rammed the peg into the hole. Verb.*
ram (ram) *noun, plural* **rams;** *verb,* **rammed, ramming.**

RAM—The abbreviation for **random-access memory.** This is the part of a computer memory that can be used in any way the operator chooses. All information there is equally available.

Ramadan—A holy time in the religion of Islam, during which Muslims fast from dawn until sunset. It lasts through the month of Ramadan in the Muslim year.
Ram|a|dan (ram ə dahn′) *noun.*

ramble—1. To roam around with no particular destination; wander: *The visitors rambled about the city, looking at all the famous sights.* 2. To talk or write about things in a confusing way, without any clear connection between one idea and another: *I couldn't figure out how to put up the tent because the instructions rambled.*
ram|ble (ram′bəl) *verb,* **rambled, rambling.**

ramp—A slanted way that joins one level to another: *We pushed the wheelchair up the ramp.*
ramp (ramp) *noun, plural* **ramps.**

rampage—An outbreak of destructive behavior: *The outlaws went on a rampage and shot anyone in sight. Noun.*
—To act in a wild rage: *a herd of buffalo rampaging across the plains. Verb.*
ram|page (ram′pāj for *noun;* ram **pāj′** or rām′pāj for *verb) noun, plural* **rampages;** *verb,* **rampaged, rampaging.**

rampart—A hill of earth that surrounds and defends a place, such as a fort.
ram|part (ram′pahrt′) *noun, plural* **ramparts.**

ran—*See* run.
ran (ran) *verb.*

ranch—A large farm where livestock, such as sheep, cattle, and horses, are raised. *Noun.*
—To work on such a large farm. *Verb.*
ranch (ranch) *noun, plural* **ranches;** *verb,* **ranched, ranching.**

rand—A unit of money in South Africa.
rand (rand), *noun, plural* **rand.** Abbreviation: **R.**

a at	i if	oo look	ch chalk		a in ago
ā ape	ī idle	ou out	ng sing		e in happen
ah calm	o odd	u ugly	sh ship	ə =	i in capital
aw all	ō oats	ū rule	th think		o in occur
e end	oi oil	ur turn	th their		u in upon
ē easy			zh treasure		

ram (noun, definition 1)

random—Occurring or made without a pattern, plan, or aim; happening by chance: *The store clerk waited on people at* random, *not by who came first.*
ran|dom (ran′dəm) *adjective.*

random-access memory—*See* **RAM.**
ran|dom-ac|cess mem|o|ry (ran′dəm ak′ses mem′ər ē) *noun, plural* **random-access memories.** *Abbreviation:* **RAM**

rang—*See* **ring².**
rang (rang) *verb.*

range—1. Variety; amount within limits: *This ice-cream store has a wide* range *of flavors.* 2. The longest distance something can travel or work: *The sound from that whistle has a* range *of about two blocks.* 3. A place for shooting at targets: *He goes to a rifle* range *to practice shooting his gun.* 4. Land where cattle and other livestock graze. 5. A row of mountains. 6. A stove with an oven and burners. *Noun.*
—1. To be within certain limits: *The test scores* range *from 75 to 100.* 2. To travel through a region; roam about: *Their goats sometimes* range *up the mountain. Verb.*
range (rānj) *noun, plural* **ranges;** *verb,* **ranged, ranging.**

ranger—1. Someone whose job is to protect a forest or national park from harm. 2. A member of a police group that patrols a certain area where few people live and keeps order there.
rang|er (rān′jər) *noun, plural* **rangers.**

rank—1. An official or social position within a group of people or things: *He has the* rank *of admiral in the United States Navy.* 2. A high position: *The president of a large company is someone of* rank. 3. **ranks:** The members of an army; soldiers. *Noun.*
—1. To line up in a row or rows: *The members of the orchestra sit* ranked *on stage.* 2. To have a specific or general standing, as compared to others: *Our dog* ranked *fifth at the pet show. Verb.*
rank (rangk) *noun, plural* **ranks;** *verb,* **ranked, ranking.**
● Synonyms: **standing, station, status,** for *noun* 1.

ransom—A price to set free someone or something that has been captured: *The woman's husband paid a* ransom *to the kidnappers. Noun.*
—To get a captured person or thing set free by paying a price: *The family* ransomed *their stolen jewels for a large sum of money. Verb.*

ran|som (ran′səm) *noun, plural* **ransoms;** *verb,* **ransomed, ransoming.**

rap—A sharp, rapid knock: *He gave a* rap *on the door before entering the room. Noun.*
—To hit or knock a surface sharply and rapidly: *The baby* rapped *the spoon on the table. Verb.*
rap (rap) *noun, plural* **raps;** *verb,* **rapped, rapping.**
● A word that sounds the same is **wrap.**

rapid—Speedy; very fast or quick: *a* rapid *increase in the prices of houses; a* rapid *bicycle ride around the block. Adjective.*
—**rapids:** An area in a river where the water moves very quickly: *Only people with years of experience were allowed to take their canoes through the* rapids. *Noun.*
rap|id (rap′id) *adjective, plural noun.*

rapture—Intense pleasure; bliss: *A look of* rapture *was on her face when she opened her birthday presents.*
rap|ture (rap′chər) *noun, plural* **raptures.**

rare¹—1. Not found, happening, or seen very often; uncommon: *Accidents are* rare *on this highway.* 2. Very valuable; unusually special: *old,* rare *books.*
rare (râr) *adjective,* **rarer, rarest.**
● Synonyms: **scanty, scarce,** for 1.
   Antonyms: **abundant, ample, enough, plentiful,** for 1.

rare²—Not completely cooked: *She likes* rare *roast beef.*
rare (râr) *adjective,* **rarer, rarest.**

rascal—Someone or some animal who is playful and mischievous: *My kitten is a little* rascal *and is always getting into trouble.*
ras|cal (ras′kəl) *noun, plural* **rascals.**

rash¹—Careless; acting too quickly: *He made a* rash *statement when he was angry and now regrets it.*
rash (rash) *adjective,* **rasher, rashest.**

rash²—An outbreak of little red spots or bumps on the skin, often accompanied by an itch: *I have an allergy to strawberries and get a* rash *if I eat them.*
rash (rash) *noun, plural* **rashes.**

rasp—To make a rough, grating noise: *The runners of my sled* rasped *against the gravel under the snow. Verb.*
—A rough, grating noise: *He talked so long that he began to speak with a* rasp. *Noun.*
rasp (rasp) *verb,* **rasped, rasping;** *noun, plural* **rasps.**

raspberry—A small, juicy fruit that is usually red or black and that grows on a prickly bush.
rasp|ber|ry (raz′ber′ē) *noun, plural* **raspberries.**

raspberry

rat—A rodent that is similar to a mouse but that has a bigger body and a much longer tail.
rat (rat) *noun, plural* **rats.**

■ **smell a rat:** To think a trick was played: *She smelled a rat when her friend did not return her bicycle.*

rate—1. An amount compared to another amount: *paid at a* rate *of $500 a week.* 2. The cost of something: *Newspaper* rates *may go up soon.* 3. A level or quality; class: *His effort on the job was only second* rate. *Noun.*
—1. To give a value or rank to: *The judges* rated *my dog as the best in the show.* 2. To consider; think of: *I* rate *you to be my best friend. Verb.*
rate (rāt) *noun, plural* **rates;** *verb,* **rated, rating.**

■ **at any rate:** No matter what happens; in any case: *We may not be able to be at the game, but* at any rate, *we'll be cheering for you.*

● Synonyms: **appraise, assess, estimate, evaluate, judge,** for *verb* 1.

rather—1. More willingly; preferably: *We would* rather *go camping than stay home.* 2. Instead of; not: *You,* rather *than your friends, should decide which sports to play.* 3. More exactly: *He is nearly twelve years old, or* rather, *eleven years and ten months old.* 4. Somewhat; more than just a little: *The hill is* rather *steep.*
rath|er (ra<u>th</u>′ər *or* ra<u>th</u><u>th</u>′ər) *adverb.*

a at	i if	oo look	ch chalk		a in ago
ā ape	ī idle	ou out	ng sing		e in happen
ah calm	o odd	u ugly	sh ship	ə =	i in capital
aw all	ō oats	ū rule	th think		o in occur
e end	oi oil	ur turn	<u>th</u> their		u in upon
ē easy			zh treasure		

ratify—To approve and make official: *The state senate* ratified *the bill to fight water pollution.*
rat|i|fy (rat′ə fī′) *verb,* **ratified, ratifying.**

ratio—The relation between the number or quantity of two different things: *If it rained only once during the week, the* ratio *of sunny days to rainy days is six to one.*
ra|ti|o (rā′shē ō′) *noun, plural* **ratios.**

ration—A set amount of something, usually food: *The cat's daily* ration *of food is one can. Noun.*
—1. To limit the amount each person can get or use: *Water was* rationed *during the driest part of summer.* 2. To give a set amount to each person or thing: *I* ration *my homework time according to the size of the assignments. Verb.*
ra|tion (rash′ən *or* rā′shən) *noun, plural* **rations;** *verb,* **rationed, rationing.**

rational—1. Using good sense; sensible; reasonable: *Please be* rational *and do not go out into the blizzard.* 2. Able to think carefully and clearly; able to use reason: *The baby-sitter is* rational *and dependable.*
ra|tion|al (rash′ə nəl) *adjective.*

rattle—1. To make or cause a rapid series of hard, short, sharp sounds: *The passing train* rattled *the windows of the house.* 2. To speak rapidly without stopping; chatter: *He* rattled *off the names of all the states.* 3. To be confused and upset: *The speaker was* rattled *by the banging noises from outside and began to stutter. Verb.*
—1. A rapid series of hard, short, sharp sounds: *the* rattle *of keys in the lock.* 2. A baby's toy that makes such a series of sounds when shaken. *Noun.*
rat|tle (rat′əl) *verb,* **rattled, rattling;** *noun, plural* **rattles.**

rattlesnake—A poisonous snake with a band of stiff rings at the end of its tail that makes a rattling sound when shaken.
rat|tle|snake (rat′əl snāk′) *noun, plural* **rattlesnakes.**

ravage—To destroy; greatly damage: *The woods were* ravaged *by the forest fire.*
rav|age (rav′ij) *verb,* **ravaged, ravaging.**

rave—1. To speak or yell wildly, making no sense: *The man* raved *about his kingdom in the sky.* 2. To talk about someone or something with great pleasure and excitement: *They* raved *about the new movie. Verb.*
—Very enthusiastic praise: *The writer's new novel got* raves *from everyone who read it. Noun.*

rave (rāv) *verb,* **raved, raving;** *noun, plural*
raves.

raven—A black bird that is similar to but larger
than a crow and that has a hoarse cry. *Noun.*
ra|ven (rā′vən) *noun, plural* **ravens.**

raven

ravenous—Extremely hungry: *The runners were*
ravenous *after a day of constant exercise.*
rav|en|ous (rav′ə nəs) *adjective.*

ravine—A narrow, deep valley carved out by
water that has flowed through an area for a long
time.
ra|vine (rə vēn′) *noun, plural* **ravines.**

raw—**1.** Uncooked: *fresh,* raw *vegetables;* raw
meat. **2.** In a natural, unchanged condition; not
processed: *The* raw *sugar was sent to the factory.*
3. Not experienced or trained: *The* raw *bus driver
needed some practice to get used to her route.*
4. Sore from having some skin scraped off: *Her
elbow was* raw *from her fall from her bicycle.*
5. Damp and chilly: *The wet snow and strong wind*

rattlesnake

made the weather too raw *for us to go walking.*
raw (raw) *adjective,* **rawer, rawest.**

rawhide—The skin of animals, usually cattle,
that has not been made into leather: *a jacket
made of* rawhide.
raw|hide (raw′hīd′) *noun, plural* **rawhides.**

ray[1]—**1.** A beam of light, heat, or other energy:
the rays *from the moon; X* rays. **2.** A line, petal,
or similar part extending from a center: *the* rays
of a daisy; rays *of frost on a window.* **3.** A
small amount, just enough to mention: *a* ray *of
brightness; a* ray *of happiness.*
ray (rā) *noun, plural* **rays.**

ray[2]—A type of fish with a flat body, large,
broad fins, and a thin tail.
ray (rā) *noun, plural* **rays.**

ray[2]

rayon—Cloth or fiber that is chemically made
from a substance found in plants and that is used
as a substitute for cotton, silk, and other fabrics.
ray|on (rā′on) *noun.*

razor—An instrument with a sharp blade that is
used to shave and cut hair.
ra|zor (rā′zər) *noun, plural* **razors.**

rd.—The abbreviation for **road, rod,** or **rods.**

Rd.—The abbreviation for **Road,** as used in a
person's address.

R.D.—The abbreviation for **Rural Delivery.**

re-—A prefix that means "again." A refilled
glass is one that is filled again.

Word Power

You can understand the meanings of many words
that begin with **re-,** if you add the meaning of
the prefix to the meaning of the rest of the word.
rebuild: to build again
reoccur: to occur again

reach—1. To come to; go as far as: *to* reach *the end of our vacation; to* reach *the end of the road.* 2. To stretch out: *The ocean* reaches *as far as the eye can see.* 3. To get to: *The newspaper* reaches *thousands of people each day.* 4. To make contact with: *Sending a letter is the best way to* reach *me.* 5. To make an effort to touch or get something: *to* reach *for the window shade; to* reach *into the drawer for a pair of socks. Verb.*
—1. An effort to touch or get something: *With a good* reach, *I can unlock the window.* 2. The distance to which someone or something can stretch: *The basketball player had a long* reach. 3. The limit of a person's ability to understand or do something: *The meaning of that word is beyond my* reach. *Noun.*
reach (rēch) *verb,* **reached, reaching;** *noun, plural* **reaches.**

react—To do something because of something else that has happened; respond: *We* reacted *with shouting and jumping when our team won.*
re|act (rē akt′) *verb,* **reacted, reacting.**

reaction—An action that occurs because of something else that has happened; response: *What was his* reaction *when you yelled "Surprise!"?*
re|ac|tion (rē ak′shən) *noun, plural* **reactions.**

reactor—A large machine that is used to produce energy by splitting atoms in a controlled manner: *a nuclear* reactor.
re|ac|tor (rē ak′tər) *noun, plural* **reactors.**

read—1. To see what is written and understand it: *Do you like to* read *the newspaper?* 2. To learn from something that is written: *We* read *about the history of our country.* 3. To say out loud the words of something that is written: *On Sundays, I* read *the comics to my sister.* 4. To show by numbers or letters: *The clock* reads *10 A.M.* 5. To understand a hidden or unspoken meaning: *Although she smiled, I could* read *the sadness in her eyes.*
read (rēd) *verb,* **read** (red), **reading.**
• A word that sounds the same is **reed.**

reader—1. Someone who reads. 2. A book that teaches reading skills, usually through stories and practice exercises.
read|er (rē′dər) *noun, plural* **readers.**

readily—1. With no problem; easily: *The girls took* readily *to dancing.* 2. Without being forced; quickly and willingly: *The dog followed* readily *after his master.*
read|i|ly (red′ə lē) *adverb.*

reading—1. The act of seeing what is written and understanding it: *I like* reading *stories of adventure.* 2. The saying out loud of words that are written: *a prayer* reading. 3. Books and other written material: *That library has a lot of* reading *for children.*
read|ing (rē′ding) *noun, plural* **readings.**

read-only memory—See ROM.
read-on|ly mem|o|ry (rēd′ōn′lē mem′ər ē) *noun, plural* **read-only memories.** Abbreviation: **ROM**

ready—1. Prepared or available for action or use: *Is the cake* ready *to eat yet?* 2. Willing: *He is always* ready *to help a friend.* 3. About to or likely to do something: *a tired worker who is* ready *to collapse; to be* ready *to apologize.* 4. Within easy reach; close at hand: *We have candles* ready *in case the power goes out.*
—To make available for action or use; prepare: *Father* readied *the room for our party.*
read|y (red′ē) *adjective,* **readier, readiest;** *verb,* **readied, readying.**

real—1. True; not imaginary: *Her being rescued by a helicopter is* real; *I read about it in the newspaper.* 2. Not fake or artificial: *Is that a* real *pearl?*
re|al (rēl *or* re′əl) *adjective.*
• A word that sounds the same is **reel.**
• Synonyms: **actual, authentic, genuine, original,** for **2.**
Antonyms: **counterfeit, false,** for **2.**

real estate—Land and all that is on it, including buildings, trees, and roads.
re|al es|tate (rēl es tāt′ *or* rē′əl es tāt′) *noun.*

realistic—1. True to life; very similar to the real thing: *The flowers are so* realistic *that at first I didn't know they are plastic.* 2. Based on fact; practical; reasonable: *It was not* realistic *of me to think I could mow the whole lawn in 15 minutes.*
re|al|is|tic (rē′ə lis′tik) *adjective.*

reality—1. A fact or condition of life; truth: *That birds return in the spring is a* reality *of nature.* 2. An actual thing; fact: *I did not believe I could win first prize until it became a* reality.
re|al|i|ty (rē al′ə tē) *noun, plural* **realities.**

a at	i if	oo look	ch chalk		a in ago
ā ape	ī idle	ou out	ng sing		e in happen
ah calm	o odd	u ugly	sh ship	ə =	i in capital
aw all	ō oats	ū rule	th think		o in occur
e end	oi oil	ur turn	th their		u in upon
ē easy			zh treasure		

realize—1. To achieve; make come true: *She realized her dream of becoming a champion skater.* 2. To become completely aware of; understand fully: *The student realized his mistake after he handed in the test.*
re|al|ize (rē′ə līz′) *verb*, **realized, realizing.**

really—1. Actually; in truth: *She seems proud, but she is really shy.* 2. Truly; without a doubt: *I really have had enough of this argument.*
re|al|ly (rē′ə lē or rē′lē) *adverb*.

realm—1. A royal land; kingdom: *Everyone in the realm rejoiced at the prince's marriage.* 2. A field of activity or interest: *the realm of sports; the realm of computers.*
realm (relm) *noun, plural* **realms.**

reap—1. To cut down crops. 2. To gather the crops that have been cut down: *After the farmers reap the fields, they store the harvest for winter.* 3. To get as the result of some action or as a reward; earn: *to reap interest on a savings account; to reap the joys of friendship.*
reap (rēp) *verb*, **reaped, reaping.**

reaper—A person or machine that cuts down or gathers crops.
reap|er (rē′pər) *noun, plural* **reapers.**

reaper

rear[1]—The back or hind part: *the rear of a theater; the rear of the line. Noun.*
—Located at or in the back of something: *the rear window. Adjective.*
rear (rēr) *noun, plural* **rears;** *adjective*.

rear[2]—1. To bring up; take care of during the early years of growth: *My aunt reared three children.* 2. To rise up on the hind legs: *The zebra reared at the sound of thunder.*
rear (rēr) *verb*, **reared, rearing.**

rear admiral—An officer in the navy whose rank is higher than captain and lower than vice-admiral.

rear ad|mir|al (rēr ad′mər əl) *noun, plural* **rear admirals.**

reason—1. A cause or an explanation for something: *What is his reason for not liking the movie?* 2. The ability to think, understand, and make decisions: *If you use your reason, you will solve your problems sooner than by getting upset about them.* 3. Good sense: *Mother expects us to listen to reason and stay inside to play when it rains. Noun.*
—1. To think in a way that is clear and makes sense: *A scientist must be able to reason.* 2. To convince someone by using facts and good sense: *I reasoned with my mother and she let me take tennis lessons. Verb.*
rea|son (rē′zən) *noun, plural* **reasons;** *verb*, **reasoned, reasoning.**

reasonable—1. Using or showing good judgment: *Because he is so angry, he is not being reasonable.* 2. Fair; not too much: *Her request for a new notebook is reasonable.* 3. Not costing too much money: *a reasonable pair of shoes; a reasonable watch.*
rea|son|a|ble (rē′zə nə bəl) *adjective*.
• Synonyms: **rational, sensible,** for **1.**
  Antonyms: For **1,** see Synonyms at **absurd.**

reasoning—1. The process of making decisions and judgments by thinking clearly and logically: *It took a lot of reasoning to do well on the test.* 2. The arguments and evidence used to make a point: *Her reasoning doesn't convince me to vote for that candidate.*
rea|son|ing (rē′zə ning) *noun*.

rebel—A person who chooses to go against authority instead of obeying it: *The rebels were not afraid to fight for their freedom. Noun.*
—1. To go against authority, especially of one's government: *The people rebelled when the mayor wanted to turn the park into a shopping center.* 2. To show or feel strong dislike or unwillingness; turn away or refuse stubbornly: *The horse rebelled when we tried to get him into the barn. Verb.*
reb|el (reb′əl for *noun;* ri bel′ for *verb*) *noun, plural* **rebels;** *verb*, **rebelled, rebelling.**

rebellion—1. An armed battle against a person's own government: *Many countries face rebellions from citizens who don't have the rights they feel they deserve.* 2. A strong fight against or resistance to any power or authority with which a person does not agree: *The angry teen-ager shouted in rebellion against his parents and refused to mow the lawn.*
re|bel|lion (ri bel′yən) *noun, plural* **rebellions.**

rebound—**1.** To bounce back; spring back: *The ball* rebounded *from the wall.* **2.** To come back; recover: *Our vegetable garden* rebounded *well from the heat when we watered it. Verb.*
—**1.** The act of bouncing or springing back: *She threw the ball against the steps and caught it on the* rebound. **2.** A basketball that bounces off the backboard or rim of the basket after a player has missed a shot at the basket: *The player grabbed the* rebound *and passed the ball to his teammate. Noun.*
re|bound (ri bound′ for *verb;* rē′bound′ for *noun*) *verb,* **rebounded, rebounding;** *noun,* plural **rebounds.**

rebus—A combination of letters, numbers, and pictures used in place of words to write something. "U 2" is a rebus for "you too."
re|bus (rē′bəs) *noun,* plural **rebuses.**

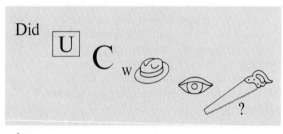

Did

rebus

recall—**1.** To think back; remember: *I cannot* recall *where I left my gloves.* **2.** To take back; ask to return: *The toy company* recalled *the model trains because they had dangerously sharp edges. Verb.*
—The act of taking back or asking to return: *There was a* recall *of all toasters made by the company that year because the wiring was bad. Noun.*
re|call (ri kawl′ for *verb;* rē′kawl′ for *noun*) *verb,* **recalled, recalling;** *noun,* plural **recalls.**

recede—To go back from a certain point; move away: *The water* recedes *from the shore at low tide.*
re|cede (ri sēd′) *verb,* **receded, receding.**

receipt—**1.** A written statement that a person has bought and paid for something or has been given a package or letter: *The sales clerk gave her a* receipt *for the bracelet she bought.* **2. receipts:** All the money that has been taken in or received: *The theater had $1,000 in* receipts *that day.*
re|ceipt (ri sēt′) *noun,* plural **receipts.**

receive—**1.** To get or take: *to* receive *a phone call; to* receive *a gift.* **2.** To welcome; meet: *He* received *the visitors in the garden.*
re|ceive (ri sēv′) *verb,* **received, receiving.**

receiver—**1.** A person or thing that gets or takes something that is sent or given: *the* receiver *of an award.* **2.** A device used for communicating that takes in electrical signals and changes them into sounds or pictures: *a telephone* receiver; *a television* receiver.
re|ceiv|er (ri sē′vər) *noun,* plural **receivers.**

recent—Made, done, or happening a short while ago: *We are just back from our* recent *vacation.*
re|cent (rē′sənt) *adjective.*

receptacle—A container into which things can be put: *Please put your empty plates into that* receptacle *so they can be washed.*
re|cep|ta|cle (ri sep′tə kəl) *noun,* plural **receptacles.**

reception—**1.** The act of greeting or taking in: *The students gave the astronauts an enthusiastic* reception *whey they visited the school.* **2.** A party or other special occasion at which guests are welcomed: *a wedding* reception. **3.** The quality of the sound or picture on a radio or television: *The* reception *on his radio was poor because it needed new batteries.*
re|cep|tion (ri sep′shən) *noun,* plural **receptions.**

recess—**1.** A short time taken as a rest from some activity: *The class went out for* recess *at 11 A.M.* **2.** A part of a wall that is deeper than the rest of the wall: *Dad built bookcases in the* recess *next to the fireplace. Noun.*
—To take a short time for rest from some activity: *The student council* recessed *for lunch. Verb.*
re|cess (rē′səs for *noun,* definition 1 and 2; ri ses′ for *noun,* definition 2, and *verb*) *noun,* plural **recesses;** *verb,* **recessed, recessing.**

recession—**1.** The action of going or moving backward: *The* recession *of the high tide left small pools of water near the rocks.* **2.** A slow-down in the buying and selling of goods and services for a time: *The* recession *made the store lose money last year.*
re|ces|sion (ri sesh′ən) *noun,* plural **recessions.**

a at	i if	oo look	ch chalk		⌈ a in ago
ā ape	ī idle	ou out	ng sing		e in happen
ah calm	o odd	u ugly	sh ship	ə =	i in capital
aw all	ō oats	ū rule	th think		o in occur
e end	oi oil	ur turn	th their		⌊ u in upon
ē easy			zh treasure		

recipe—Instructions for preparing something to eat or drink: *a recipe for cake.*
rec|i|pe (res′ə pē) *noun, plural* **recipes.**

recital—**1.** A spoken telling of facts or of a story: *The scientist gave a* recital *of what is known about African gorillas.*   **2.** A musical or dance performance: *The ballet students gave a* recital *for their parents.*
re|cit|al (ri sīt′əl) *noun, plural* **recitals.**

recitation—A spoken telling of facts or of a story, often as part of a lesson or public performance: *the* recitation *of a poem.*
rec|i|ta|tion (res′ə tā′shən) *noun, plural* **recitations.**

recite—**1.** To say from memory: *to* recite *the multiplication tables.*   **2.** To tell about: *She* recited *her experiences as a mountain climber.*
re|cite (ri sīt′) *verb,* **recited, reciting.**
• Synonyms: **narrate, relate,** for **2.**

reckless—Not avoiding trouble or danger; careless: *It is* reckless *not to wear a seat belt while riding in a car.*
reck|less (rek′lis) *adjective.*

reckon—**1.** To count up; figure: *She* reckoned *that there were five dollars in her jar of coins.*   **2.** To feel or suppose: *I* reckon *that it is time to go home now.*
reck|on (rek′ən) *verb,* **reckoned, reckoning.**

recline—To lie down or lean back: *He* reclined *on the grass to watch the clouds go by.*
re|cline (ri klīn′) *verb,* **reclined, reclining.**

recognition—**1.** The act of realizing that someone or something is already known: *The child smiled in* recognition *when he heard his grandmother's voice on the phone.*   **2.** Praise; attention: *The artist gained* recognition *for her paintings of jungle animals.*   **3.** An acceptance of the truth or value of something: *She finally came to a* recognition *that she had lost her chance.*
rec|og|ni|tion (rek′əg nish′ən) *noun.*

recognize—**1.** To realize that something or someone is already known: *He* recognized *his uncle in the crowd.*   **2.** To notice and appreciate: *Her math teacher* recognized *the girl's ability to write computer programs.*   **3.** To accept the truth or value of something: *The sales clerk* recognized *the justice of the customer's complaint about the tear in the dress.*
rec|og|nize (rek′əg nīz′) *verb,* **recognized, recognizing.**
• Synonyms: **distinguish, identify,** for **1.**

recoil—**1.** To move back quickly out of fear: *to* recoil *from a large spider.*   **2.** To spring or jerk back: *The rifle* recoiled *when it was fired.*

recoil (ri koil′) *verb,* **recoiled, recoiling.**
• Synonyms: **flinch, wince,** for **1.**

recollect—To remember: *He couldn't* recollect *where he had seen the book.*
rec|ol|lect (rek′ə lekt′) *verb,* **recollected, recollecting.**

recommend—**1.** To suggest favorably; speak or write in praise of: *Mother* recommended *that we all go swimming to cool off.*   **2.** To advise a person: *Our dentist* recommends *that I get braces next year.*
rec|om|mend (rek′ə mend′) *verb,* **recommended, recommending.**

record—**1.** To put down in writing: *Please* record *the names of the students who are absent today.*   **2.** To show; indicate: *A clock* records *the time.*   **3.** To put music, words, pictures, or sounds on a disk or tape that is especially made for that purpose: *Dad* recorded *the whole family singing Christmas carols. Verb.*
—1. Anything that is put down in writing: *A calendar is a* record *of the days of the year.*
2. A special disk that is used to copy and save music, words, or other sounds for listening to later: *He bought a* record *of marching songs.*
3. A collection of facts about someone or something: *a* record *of this winter's snowfall; a* record *of the child's marks in social studies.*
4. The best or most that has ever been seen, done, or made: *Our class holds the school* record *for collecting the most contributions. Noun.*
re|cord (ri kawrd′ for *verb;* rek′ərd for *noun*) *verb,* **recorded, recording;** *noun, plural* **records.**

recorder—**1.** A machine that copies and saves music, words, pictures, or sounds: *a tape* recorder; *a video* recorder.   **2.** A musical instrument that looks like a flute. It is played by blowing through a mouthpiece that looks like a whistle and covering or uncovering finger holes.
re|cord|er (ri kawr′dər) *noun, plural* **recorders.**

recorder (definition 2)

recording—A disk or tape on which sounds, usually music or talking, or pictures have been mechanically stored for future playing: *The music teacher made a* recording *of the school chorus.*
re|cord|ing (ri kawr′ding) *noun, plural* **recordings.**

recover—1. To get something back again: *to recover a lost dog.* 2. To make up for: *She woke up late and had to ride her bicycle to school instead of walking to recover lost time.* 3. To get well; feel better: *He is recovering from a bad case of poison ivy.*
re|cov|er (ri kuv′ər) *verb,* **recovered, recovering.**

recreation—Something that a person does for enjoyment: *I fly my kite for recreation.*
rec|re|a|tion (rek′rē ā′shən) *noun, plural* **recreations.**
• Synonyms: **entertainment, game, pastime, play, sport**
Antonyms: **chore, duty, task, work**

recreational vehicle—A van, truck, or other vehicle equipped and used for camping or other leisure-time activities.
rec|re|a|tion|al ve|hi|cle (rek′rē ā′shə nəl ve′ə kəl) *noun, plural* **recreational vehicles.** Abbreviation: **RV.**

recruit—A new member of a group, especially the armed forces: *The sergeant made the army recruits work hard during training.*
—To find new members for a group or activity: *Dad recruited us to shovel snow. Verb.*
re|cruit (ri krūt′) *noun, plural* **recruits;** *verb,* **recruited, recruiting.**

rectangle—A four-sided shape that has four right angles. If all four sides are of equal length, the rectangle is usually called a square.
rec|tan|gle (rek′tang′gəl) *noun, plural* **rectangles.**

rectangle

rectum—The end of the alimentary canal, from which wastes pass out of the body.
rec|tum (rek′təm) *noun, plural* **rectums.**
• See picture at **alimentary canal.**

a at	i if	oo look	ch chalk		a in ago
ā ape	ī idle	ou out	ng sing		e in happen
ah calm	o odd	u ugly	sh ship	ə =	i in capital
aw all	ō oats	ū rule	th think		o in occur
e end	oi oil	ur turn	<u>th</u> their		u in upon
ē easy			zh treasure		

recuperate—To get back one's health or strength; recover: *My sister recuperated from her cold in time to go to the party.*
re|cu|per|ate (ri kyū′pə rāt′ *or* ri kū′pə rāt′) *verb,* **recuperated, recuperating.**

recur—To happen again: *The Olympic Games recur every four years.*
re|cur (ri kur′) *verb,* **recurred, recurring.**

recycle—To change or treat waste material so that it can be used again: *We take our old newspapers to a plant to be recycled.*
re|cy|cle (rē sī′kəl) *verb,* **recycled, recycling.**

red—1. The color of blood or of a male cardinal. 2. A thing having this color: *The red of the sunset is beautiful. Noun.*
—Having this color: *red lips; red hair. Adjective.*
red (red) *noun, plural* **reds;** *adjective,* **redder, reddest.**
■ **in the red:** Owing money; losing money: *The children's lemonade stand was in the red because they had spent more to make the lemonade than they got from selling it.*
see red: To get very angry: *I see red when people are cruel to animals.*

redbud—A tree or bush that has many small, pink flowers in the early spring that bloom before the leaves appear.
red|bud (red′bud′) *noun, plural* **redbuds.**

redcoat—A British soldier in the 1700's.
red|coat (red′kōt′) *noun, plural* **redcoats.**

red-handed—In the act of doing something wrong: *Mother caught me red-handed eating the cookies just before supper.*
red|hand|ed (red′han′did) *adverb.*

red-headed—Having red hair, fur, or feathers on the head: *a red-headed boy; a red-headed woodpecker.*
red|head|ed (red′hed′id) *adjective.*

reduce—To become or make less or smaller: *Dad reduced my allowance for a week to pay for the window I broke.*
re|duce (ri dūs′ *or* ri dyūs′) *verb,* **reduced, reducing.**
• Synonyms: **decrease, diminish, dwindle**

reduction—1. The act or process of making something less or smaller: *The reduction in temperature caused the pond to freeze.* 2. The amount by which a thing is made less or smaller: *During the sale, there was a price reduction of $30 on all bicycles.*
re|duc|tion (ri duk′shən) *noun, plural* **reductions.**
• Synonyms: **deduction, discount,** for **2.**

red-winged blackbird—A North American black bird. Males have a red spot near the shoulder on each wing.
red|winged black|bird (red′wingd′ blak′burd′) *noun, plural* **red-winged blackbirds.**

red-winged blackbird

redwood—A very tall evergreen tree that grows along the northwest coast of the United States and that has reddish brown wood. Redwoods are among the world's tallest and oldest trees, living sometimes for thousands of years.
red|wood (red′wood′) *noun, plural* **redwoods.**
• This tree is also called a **sequoia.**

reed—1. A type of tall grass with straight, hollow stems made up of sections that are joined together. Reeds grow in wet places such as swamps and marshes.   2. A thin, flexible piece of wood, plastic, metal, or the like that vibrates and makes sound in the mouthpiece of a musical instrument when air passes over it.   3. A musical instrument with this type of mouthpiece, such as a clarinet.
reed (rēd) *noun, plural* **reeds.**
• A word that sounds the same is **read.**

reef—A narrow strip of rock, sand, or coral that rises to or near the surface of the ocean.
reef (rēf) *noun, plural* **reefs.**

reel[1]—Something shaped like a spool or a wheel, around which rope, film, wire, fishing line, or the like can be wound and unwound. *Noun.*
—1. To wind on such a spool or wheel: *to reel a garden hose.*   2. To pull in or toward oneself by winding a line on such a spool or wheel: *to reel in a fish.*
reel (rēl) *noun, plural* **reels.**
• A word that sounds the same is **real.**

reel[2]—1. To move slowly back and forth while standing or walking; lose one's balance: *He reeled after he ran into the tree branch.*   2. To seem to turn around and around; whirl: *The*

amusement park reeled *past her as she rode the roller coaster.*
reel (rēl) *verb,* **reeled, reeling.**
• A word that sounds the same is **real.**
• Synonyms: **stagger, sway, teeter, waver,** for **1.**

refer—1. To call attention to: *The teacher* referred *to the map when he taught geography.*   2. To apply to: *The word "ewe"* refers *to a female sheep.*   3. To turn to for information or help; consult: *She* referred *to the table of contents to find the chapter on dolphins.*   4. To show a way to get help or information: *The lady* referred *us to the police officer for directions to the amusement park.*
re|fer (ri fur′) *verb,* **referred, referring.**

referee—A person responsible for watching a game or sport while it is being played to make sure that the players are following the rules: *the* referee *of the hockey game. Noun.*
—To watch a game or sport carefully to make sure that the players are following the rules: *Dad* refereed *our soccer game. Verb.*
ref|er|ee (ref′ə rē′) *noun, plural* **referees;** *verb,* **refereed, refereeing.**

reference—1. A calling of attention; mention: *In her talk about the human body, the doctor made a* reference *to a chart of the skeleton.*   2. A person or thing that one looks to for facts or advice: *He used a biography of the President as a* reference *for his social studies report.*   3. A statement about a person's behavior or work habits written by someone who knows that person well: *The store owner asked for two* references *when the boy applied for a job.*
ref|er|ence (ref′ər əns) *noun, plural* **references.**

refill—To make full again: *He* refilled *his water pistol from the hose. Verb.*
—Something to make a container full again: *She finished her milk shake and asked for a* refill. *Noun.*
re|fill (rē fil′ for *verb;* rē′fil′ for *noun*) *verb,* **refilled, refilling;** *noun, plural* **refills.**

refine—To remove matter that is not wanted or needed; purify: *A special process is used to* refine *sugar, causing it to become white.*
re|fine (ri fīn′) *verb,* **refined, refining.**

refinery—A place where foods or other substances in their natural state, such as sugar or petroleum, are made pure or processed for use.
re|fin|er|y (ri fī′nər ē) *noun, plural* **refineries.**

reflect—1. To send back from a surface: *The moon* reflects *the light of the sun.*   2. To give back a picture or likeness: *The pond reflected the*

clouds that floated overhead.　**3.** To think carefully: *She* reflected *on what she would like to be when she grew up.*　**4.** To show as a cause; be the result of: *His good grades* reflect *his hard work.*
re|flect (ri **flekt′**) *verb,* **reflected, reflecting.**

reflection—**1.** Something that is turned back from a surface: *the* reflection *of the sunlight on the ocean.*　**2.** A picture or likeness: *the* reflection *of her face in the mirror.*　**3.** Careful thought: *On* reflection, *she decided that she would prefer to be a science editor and changed her job.*　**4.** Something that is a result of something else: *His skill in swimming is the* reflection *of long hours of practice.*
re|flec|tion (ri **flek′**shən) *noun, plural* **reflections.**

reflection (definition 2)

reflector—A piece of metal, glass, or plastic designed to send back light in a certain direction: *The plastic* reflectors *placed on bicycles help make sure that the bikes can be seen at night.*
re|flec|tor (ri **flek′**tər) *noun, plural* **reflectors.**

reflex—An automatic reaction of the body that a person cannot control. Sneezing, shivering, and hiccuping are some kinds of reflexes.
re|flex (**rē′**fleks) *noun, plural* **reflexes.**

reform—To change for the better; improve: *After receiving a poor report card, the girl promised to* reform *her study habits.*
re|form (ri **fawrm′**) *verb,* **reformed, reforming.**

reformatory—A special prison for young people who have broken the law.

re|form|a|tor|y (ri **fawr′**mə tawr′ē) *noun, plural* **reformatories.**

refrain¹—To hold back; keep from doing: *Please* refrain *from whistling in the library.*
re|frain (ri **frān′**) *verb,* **refrained, refraining.**

refrain²—A part that is repeated again and again throughout a song or poem.
re|frain (ri **frān′**) *noun, plural* **refrains.**

refresh—**1.** To help to feel better again: *A swim in the lake* refreshed *the hot children.*　**2.** To buy, get, or make a new supply of: *The hikers* refreshed *their supply of water at the stream.*
re|fresh (ri **fresh′**) *verb,* **refreshed, refreshing.**

refreshment—Something to eat or drink: *The* refreshments *at the picnic were hot dogs, potato chips, and lemonade.*
re|fresh|ment (ri **fresh′**mənt) *noun, plural* **refreshments.**

refrigerate—To make or keep cold or cool: *It is necessary to* refrigerate *ice cream so it will not melt.*
re|frig|er|ate (ri **frij′**ə rāt) *verb,* **refrigerated, refrigerating.**

refrigerator—A space that is enclosed within walls or a cabinet and that contains special machinery for keeping its contents, such as food or medicine, cold.
re|frig|er|a|tor (ri **frij′**ə rā′tər) *noun, plural* **refrigerators.**

refuge—A place of safety or shelter: *We found* refuge *from the storm in a cave.*
ref|uge (**ref′**yūj) *noun, plural* **refuges.**
● Synonyms: **haven, sanctuary**

refugee—A person who needs a place of safety or shelter from some danger or trouble: *War* refugees *from many lands have come to our country for a better life.*
ref|u|gee (ref′yə **jē′**) *noun, plural* **refugees.**

refund—To give back money that has been paid: *The clerk at the grocery store* refunded *the money for the sour milk. Verb.*
—Money that has been returned: *He received a* refund *when he brought the toy back. Noun.*
re|fund (ri **fund′** for *verb;* **rē′**fund for *noun*) *verb,* **refunded, refunding;** *noun, plural* **refunds.**

refuse¹—To be unwilling to do or take; decline: *She* refused *a second piece of cake.*
re|fuse (ri **fyūz′**) *verb,* **refused, refusing.**

refuse²—Trash; rubbish: *After the party, we put the* refuse *out for the garbage collector.*
ref|use (**ref′**yūs) *noun.*
● See Synonyms at **garbage.**

a at	i if	oo look	ch chalk		⎡ a in ago
ā ape	ī idle	ou out	ng sing		e in happen
ah calm	o odd	u ugly	sh ship	ə =	i in capital
aw all	ō oats	ū rule	th think		o in occur
e end	oi oil	ur turn	<u>th</u> their		⎣ u in upon
ē easy			zh treasure		

regain—To receive or get back something that had been gone for a time; recover: *With exercise, he regained strength in the leg that had been broken.*
re|gain (ri gān´) *verb,* **regained, regaining.**

regal—Like or suitable for a king or queen; royal: *We had a regal meal on Thanksgiving.*
re|gal (rē´gəl) *adjective.*

regard—1. To think of; consider: *He regarded me as a friend.* 2. To look at closely; watch: *The cat regarded the fish in the bowl. Verb.*
—1. Thoughtfulness; careful consideration: *He is a kind person who always has regard for other people's feelings.* 2. Good opinion; respect: *A good teacher has high regard for students.* 3. regards: Greetings; best wishes: *I hope you gave my regards to your family. Noun.*
re|gard (ri gahrd´) *verb,* **regarded, regarding;** *noun, plural* **regards.**

regardless—No matter what; in spite of: *The parade will be held on Saturday, regardless of the weather.*
re|gard|less (ri gahrd´lis) *adjective.*

Language Fact

Regardless has been turned by some people into "irregardless." The change does not show any difference in meaning. Careful writers and speakers do not use "irregardless."

regiment—An army unit led by a colonel. It is smaller than a brigade and larger than a battalion.
reg|i|ment (rej´ə mənt) *noun, plural* **regiments.**

region—A large geographic area: *the arctic region; a mountainous region.*
re|gion (rē´jən) *noun, plural* **regions.**

register—1. To enter information into a list or record: *New students have to register their names at the office.* 2. To show automatically; indicate: *a postal scale that registers the weight of letters; her face registering surprise when the jack-in-the-box popped up. Verb.*
—1. A list or record of names or other information: *Visitors to the school fair signed a register before they entered.* 2. A machine that makes a printed list or record: *a cash register. Noun.*
reg|is|ter (rej´ə stər) *verb,* **registered, registering;** *noun, plural* **registers.**

regret—To be sorry or sad: *She regretted that summer vacation was almost over. Verb.*
—The disappointment or sadness one feels about a past matter or loss of someone or something: *His one regret in high school was that he had not played in the band. Noun.*
re|gret (ri gret´) *verb,* **regretted, regretting;** *noun, plural* **regrets.**

regular—1. Following a pattern set by rule or by the way something has been done in the past; normal: *Our regular classes will not be held on the day of the field trip.* 2. Done over and over at the same time: *He has a regular morning paper route.* 3. Performed frequently as a habit; steady: *She believes in regular exercise.*
reg|u|lar (reg´yə lər) *adjective.*
• Synonyms: **common, typical**
Antonyms: **abnormal, different, odd, uncommon, unusual**

regulate—1. To control, manage, or run according to a set of rules: *Stop lights regulate the flow of traffic.* 2. To adjust automatically: *This little machine will regulate the water temperature in the aquarium.*
reg|u|late (reg´yə lāt) *verb,* **regulated, regulating.**

regulation—A rule or law: *She followed the safety regulations when riding her bicycle.*
reg|u|la|tion (reg´yə lā´shən) *noun, plural* **regulations.**

rehearsal—A time for practicing a play, concert, or other production before it is performed in front of an audience: *He was worried that he might forget his lines because he missed the last two rehearsals.*
re|hears|al (ri hur´səl) *noun, plural* **rehearsals.**

rehearse—To practice a play, concert, or other production before it is performed in front of an audience: *The school orchestra rehearsed the music for next week's concert.*
re|hearse (ri hurs´) *verb,* **rehearsed, rehearsing.**

Word History

Rehearse comes from an old French word meaning "to rake again." Long ago, farmers had to prepare for planting by hand. One of the things they would do was to rake the soil again and again to make it smooth and to remove rocks, stones, and other objects that might prevent growth. In time, **rehearse** came to mean going over something again and again as a way of preparing.

reign—**1.** The time that a king, queen, empress, or emperor governs a country: *The emperor began his* reign *when he was a young man of twenty-one.* **2.** The act of governing a country: *The* reign *of the queen brought peace to her country. Noun.*
—**1.** To have the power of a king, queen, empress, or emperor: *The emperor* reigned *in a wise manner over his country.* **2.** To be everywhere; be all around: *Silence* reigned *while the class worked on the science test. Verb.*
reign (rān) *noun, plural* **reigns;** *verb,* **reigned, reigning.**
● Words that sound the same are **rain** and **rein.**

rein—**1.** One of the long, narrow straps that are attached to each side of a horse's bridle. A person controls and directs a horse by the reins. **2.** A way of controlling or directing: *The* reins *of government were said to be in the hands of the president's wife. Noun.*
—To control or be guided: *She* reined *in her laughter when people began staring at her. Verb.*
rein (rān) *noun, plural* **reins;** *verb,* **reined, reining.**
● Words that sound the same are **rain** and **reign.**

reindeer—A kind of large deer that lives in cold northern regions. It has large branching antlers.
rein|deer (rān′dēr′) *noun, plural* **reindeer.**

reinforce—To make stronger; strengthen: *She* reinforced *her knowledge of the multiplication tables by saying them aloud every day.*
re|in|force (rē′in fawrs′) *verb,* **reinforced, reinforcing.**

reject—To refuse to accept; say no to: *Mother and Dad* rejected *my request for a higher allowance.*
re|ject (ri jekt′) *verb,* **rejected, rejecting.**

rejoice—To be joyful; show great happiness: *The neighborhood children* rejoiced *when the new playground opened.*
re|joice (ri jois′) *verb,* **rejoiced, rejoicing.**

relapse—To move back or return to a previous state or condition, as into illness: *After several days of feeling better, my friend* relapsed *into a fever again. Verb.*
—A moving back or return to a previous state or condition, as into illness: *He thought he had recovered from the chicken pox, but then he had a* relapse *and began to itch again. Noun.*
re|lapse (ri laps′ *for verb;* rē′laps *for noun*) *verb,* **relapsed, relapsing;** *noun, plural* **relapses.**

relate—**1.** To tell: *Everyone listened to her* relate *her story.* **2.** To join or associate an idea or meaning with another: *The scientist* related *the disappearance of the dinosaurs to a change in the climate.*
re|late (ri lāt′) *verb,* **related, relating.**
● Synonyms: **narrate, recite,** for 1.

related—**1.** Connected in thought or meaning: *A person's mood is often* related *to the weather.* **2.** Belonging to the same family: *Sisters and brothers are* related.
re|lat|ed (ri lā′tid) *adjective.*

relation—**1.** A connection: *the* relation *between father and son; the* relation *between history and geography.* **2.** A family member: *Many of our* relations *came to our home for Thanksgiving dinner.*
re|la|tion (ri lā′shən) *noun, plural* **relations.**

relationship—**1.** A connection: *The teacher explained the* relationship *between addition and multiplication.* **2.** How people or groups get along with each other: *The boy and his grandfather enjoyed a close* relationship.
re|la|tion|ship (ri lā′shən ship) *noun, plural* **relationships.**

a at	i if	oo look	ch chalk	⌐ a in ago
ā ape	ī idle	ou out	ng sing	e in happen
ah calm	o odd	u ugly	sh ship	ə = i in capital
aw all	ō oats	ū rule	th think	o in occur
e end	oi oil	ur turn	th their	⌐ u in upon
ē easy			zh treasure	

reindeer

relative—Someone who is a part of the same family as another: *All of our* relatives *came to my sister's wedding.* Noun.
—Having meaning only when compared to another thing: *"Up" and "down" are* relative *words because their meanings depend on where you start from.* Adjective.
rel|a|tive (rel′ə tiv) *noun, plural* **relatives;** *adjective.*

relax—1. To make or become less tight or tense; calm down: *to* relax *my grip on the bat; to* relax *by listening to soft music.* 2. To change something so as to make it less demanding or harsh: *Mother* relaxed *the rules about bedtime so we could have a longer visit with our aunt.*
re|lax (ri laks′) *verb,* **relaxed; relaxing.**

relay—A person or group that takes the place of another that has been in use: *The messenger had to ride two hours before he could pass the secret orders for the next* relay *to carry.* Noun.
—To receive and cause to go or be sent to another place: *Telegraphs* relay *messages from one railroad station to the next.* Verb.
re|lay (rē′lā for *noun;* rē′lā or ri lā′ for *verb*) *noun, plural* **relays;** *verb,* **relayed, relaying.**

Word History

Relay comes from an old French word meaning "to replace tired animals," such as a team of horses or a pack of hunting dogs. When these had run for a time, new animals were put to work, so the tired ones could rest. Later the word **relay** came to be used for anyone or anything that is part of a system of taking turns in order to keep up speed.

---

relay race—A race in which each member of a team travels over a part of the course and then is replaced by another member of the team.
re|lay race (rē′lā rās) *noun, plural* **relay races.**

release—To let go; set loose: *The rabbit hopped away as soon as I* released *it from the cage.* Verb.
—The act of letting loose; freeing or unfastening: *The parade started with the* release *of hundreds of balloons.* Noun.
re|lease (ri lēs′) *verb,* **released, releasing;** *noun, plural* **releases.**
• Synonyms: **free, liberate,** for *verb.*
Antonyms: For *verb,* see Synonyms at **catch.**

relent—To take a softer attitude; be less harsh: *My dad finally* relented *and let me go on the camping trip.*
re|lent (ri lent′) *verb,* **relented, relenting.**

relentless—Without pity; harsh: not giving up: *The detective pursued the wanted criminal with* relentless *determination.*
re|lent|less (ri lent′lis) *adjective.*

reliable—Capable of being trusted; dependable: *My friend is* reliable *about returning the things she borrows.*
re|li|a|ble (ri lī′ə bəl) *adjective.*

relic—A thing left over from past times: *The statues, pottery, and other* relics *in the museum are hundreds of years old.*
rel|ic (rel′ik) *noun, plural* **relics.**

relief—1. An easing or freeing from pain, worry, or other difficulty; aid or comfort: *It was a* relief *to sit down and rest after the long hike.* 2. Time off from a job or duty, usually by having another person take one's place for a while: *The soldier guarding the gate got* relief *after four hours on duty.* 3. A sculpture that stands out from a flat background.
re|lief (ri lēf′) *noun, plural* **reliefs.**

relieve—1. To ease or take away pain, worry, or other trouble: *a hot bath to* relieve *her aches and pains.* 2. To give someone time away from a job or duty by taking his or her place: *New waiters will* relieve *the waiters who have served lunch and snacks all afternoon.*
re|lieve (ri lēv′) *verb,* **relieved, relieving.**

relay race

religion—1. Belief in or worship of God or gods. 2. A certain system of belief and worship: *The Christian and Muslim* religions *are followed in many countries of the world.*
re|li|gion (ri **lij′**ən) *noun, plural* **religions.**

religious—1. Of or having to do with religion: *Many people came to this country to enjoy* religious *freedom.* 2. Having worship of God or gods be very important in one's life: *The* religious *man prayed each day.*
re|li|gious (ri **lij′**əs) *adjective.*

relish—Certain chopped vegetables, such as pickles or olives, mixed with seasonings and used to flavor food. *Noun.*
—To enjoy or be pleased with: *to* relish *a hot bowl of soup on a cold day. Verb.*
rel|ish (**rel′**ish) *noun, plural* **relishes;** *verb,* **relished, relishing.**

reluctant—Unwilling; not eager: *The shy boy was* reluctant *to speak in front of the class.*
re|luc|tant (ri **luk′**tənt) *adjective.*

rely—To depend on; count on: *The woman knew she could* rely *on the baby-sitter to take good care of her child.*
re|ly (ri **lī′**) *verb,* **relied, relying.**

remain—1. To stay in a place: *We* remained *at the table talking after we finished dinner.* 2. To keep on being: *The children* remained *very quiet while the story was being read to them.* 3. To be left over after the rest of something is gone: *Only one slice of birthday cake* remained.
re|main (ri **mān′**) *verb,* **remained, remaining.**

remainder—1. The part that is left over: *The girl put some of her books on the shelf and the* remainder *on her desk.* 2. The number that is left when one number is substracted from another: *When 5 is subtracted from 8, the* remainder *is 3.* 3. The number that is left over when one number cannot be divided evenly by another: *When 14 is divided by 4, the answer is 3 with a* remainder *of 2.*
re|main|der (ri **mān′**dər) *noun, plural* **remainders.**

remains—1. What is left after something has been eaten, used, or destroyed, or after time has passed: *The pyramids are the* remains *of an old civilization.* 2. The dead body of a person or animal.
re|mains (ri **mānz′**) *plural noun.*

remark—To say in few words; mention; comment: *The teacher* remarked *that vacation was near. Verb.*
—A short statement about something one has noticed: *The visitor made a polite* remark *about the beauty of our town. Noun.*
re|mark (ri **mahrk′**) *verb,* **remarked, remarking;** *noun, plural* **remarks.**
• Synonyms: **comment, observation,** for *noun.*

remarkable—Worthy of being noticed or spoken about; unusual: *The young child had a* remarkable *talent in music.*
re|mark|a|ble (ri **mahr′**kə bəl) *adjective.*
• Synonyms: **impressive, notable**

remedy—A way of taking away a bad condition or of making it better; cure: *He drank some tea with honey as a* remedy *for his sore throat. Noun.*
—To take away or improve a bad condition: *Making the street wider may* remedy *the traffic problem. Verb.*
rem|e|dy (**rem′**ə dē) *noun, plural* **remedies;** *verb,* **remedied, remedying.**

remember—1. To bring or call back to mind: *Mother can* remember *many songs.* 2. To keep in one's mind; make sure not to forget: *Please* remember *to take your umbrella.* 3. To honor someone with an award or a gift: *The family* remembered *grandmother on her birthday with flowers and a present.*
re|mem|ber (ri **mem′**bər) *verb,* **remembered, remembering.**

Remembrance Day—The anniversary of the end of World War I, November 11, 1918. On this day each year, the soldiers killed in World War I and World War II are honored in Canada and Great Britain.
Re|mem|brance Day (ri **mem′**brəns dā) *noun.*

a at	i if	oo look	ch chalk		a in ago
ā ape	ī idle	ou out	ng sing		e in happen
ah calm	o odd	u ugly	sh ship	ə =	i in capital
aw all	ō oats	ū rule	th think		o in occur
e end	oi oil	ur turn	th their		u in upon
ē easy			zh treasure		

remind—To put a thought in someone's mind again; cause to recall: *a cat that* reminds *me of a pet I once had; the teacher* reminding *the students to take the notices home to their parents.*
re|mind (ri mīnd′) *verb,* **reminded, reminding.**

reminder—A thing or things that help a person remember: *to keep some seashells as a reminder of my summer at the beach.*
re|mind|er (ri mīn′dər) *noun, plural* **reminders.**
• Synonyms: **keepsake, memento, souvenir, token**

remnant—A small part of something that is left over: *Only a remnant of the colored paper was left after the students completed their art projects.*
rem|nant (rem′nənt) *noun, plural* **remnants.**

remodel—To change; make different: *When my father remodeled our house, he changed the back porch into a bedroom.*
re|mod|el (rē mod′əl) *verb,* **remodeled, remodeling.**

remorse—A strong feeling of sorrow and regret one has about his or her behavior in the past: *He felt such* remorse *for having stolen from his friend that he could not sleep that night.*
re|morse (ri mawrs′) *noun.*

remote—1. Distant; not close: *From the top of the mountain, you can see the* remote *villages beyond the river.* 2. Not easy to get to: *The park in the forest was so* remote *that few people ever camped there.* 3. Weak; little: *The old man had only a* remote *memory of his first day at school.*
re|mote (ri mōt′) *adjective,* **remoter, remotest.**

remote control—The operation of a machine from a distance, without touching it: *The boy used a radio device to steer his model car by* remote control.
re|mote con|trol (ri mōt′ kən trōl′) *noun.*

remove—1. To move from one place to another; take away or off: *The farmer cleared the field by* removing *the stones and tree stumps.* 2. To be rid of; end: *The teacher's explanation* removed *our confusion about the new dress code.* 3. To dismiss a person from a job or position: *The coach* removed *her from the team for refusing to follow his rules.*
re|move (ri mūv′) *verb,* **removed, removing.**

renaissance—A period when important changes occur that improve life; time when some part of a society becomes better: *The* renaissance *in music led to the composing of many great symphonies.*
ren|ais|sance (ren′ə sahns) *noun, plural* **renaissances.**

render—1. To make or cause to be a certain way: *The hard day of work* rendered *him unable to stay awake after supper.* 2. To turn over something to another; offer or pay: *to* render *help to his brother; to* render *thanks for the favor done.* 3. To perform a musical or dramatic piece: *He* rendered *a folk song on the guitar.*
ren|der (ren′dər) *verb,* **rendered, rendering.**

rendezvous—1. An arrangement to get together at a certain time and place; appointment: *We set up a* rendezvous *with our friends at the park after school.* 2. A particular place to meet or gather: *Our* rendezvous *was at the statue in the park.*
ren|dez|vous (rahn′də vū) *noun, plural* **rendezvous** (rahn′də vūz).

Word History

Rendezvous comes from two French words meaning "to present yourself." When people arrange a rendezvous, they intend to meet in person. They plan to present themselves at the place and time they have named.

renew—1. To cause to become new or like new again: *A coat of wax* renewed *the shine on the car.* 2. To return to something; start doing again: *to* renew *a friendship;* renewing *one's efforts.* 3. To replace that which has been used up or worn out: *The hikers* renewed *their supply of water when they reached the stream.* 4. To cause to go on for an added period of time: *She* renewed *her library card for the next year.*
re|new (ri nū′) *verb,* **renewed, renewing.**

rent¹—A payment made at set times for the use of some thing or property: *The* rent *on our house is paid each month. Noun.*
—1. To make payments for the use of something: *We* rented *a cottage for our summer vacation.* 2. To receive set payments in return for allowing the use of something: *My neighbor* rents *his truck to people who need to carry heavy loads.* 3. To be offered for use in return for payment: *The car* rents *for fifty dollars a week. Verb.*
rent (rent) *noun, plural* **rents;** *verb,* **rented, renting.**

rent²—A tear or rip; split: *A nail sticking out of the fence caused a* rent *in his jacket.*
rent (rent) *noun, plural* **rents.**

repair—To put back into good condition; restore; mend; fix: *We used glue to* repair *the broken dish. Verb.*

—**1.** The act or work of mending or fixing: *The carpenter cut some wood for the* repair *of the porch steps.*   **2.** The condition that a thing is in: *The mechanic keeps his tools in good* repair. *Noun.*
re|pair (ri pār') *verb,* **repaired, repairing;** *noun, plural* **repairs.**

repeal—To get rid of; take back in a formal or official way: *The group wants the town council to* repeal *the new law because they believe it is not fair. Verb.*
—The act of doing away with: *The* repeal *of the old law gave greater freedom to the people of the country. Noun.*
re|peal (ri pēl') *verb,* **repealed, repealing;** *noun, plural* **repeals.**

repeat—To perform an action again: *to* repeat *the dance steps until he had learned them.*
re|peat (ri pēt') *verb,* **repeated, repeating.**

repel—**1.** To force back; drive away: *We used a spray to* repel *mosquitoes from our porch.*   **2.** To protect against; keep off: *The couch is covered with a cloth that* repels *stains.*   **3.** To cause a feeling of disgust; be unpleasant to: *The terrible smell that came from the cellar* repelled *him.*
re|pel (ri pel') *verb,* **repelled, repelling.**

repellent—Unpleasant or disgusting: *The loud, harsh sounds that came from the factory were* repellent *to her ears. Adjective.*
—A thing that keeps a substance off or drives something away, such as animal or insect: *a tent coated with a water* repellent; *an insect* repellent. *Noun.*
re|pel|lent (ri pel'ənt) *adjective; noun, plural* **repellents.**

repent—To feel regret or sorrow for a past act and have a wish to be forgiven: *She angrily broke her sister's radio and later* repented.
re|pent (ri pent') *verb,* **repented, repenting.**

repetition—The act of repeating; doing, making, or saying two or more times: *After many* repetitions *of the same notes, he learned to play the music by heart.*
rep|e|ti|tion (rep'ə tish'ən) *noun, plural* **repetitions.**

replace—**1.** To take another's position or place: *Gray clouds* replaced *the sun as the storm moved in.*   **2.** To cause something to take another's

place: *We* replaced *the burned-out light bulb with a new one.*   **3.** To return something to a position or place: *When the child finished playing with the toys, he* replaced *them on the shelf.*
re|place (ri plās') *verb,* **replaced, replacing.**

replenish—To fill with a new supply: *When his glass of milk was empty, he* replenished *it from the pitcher.*
re|plen|ish (ri plen'ish) *verb,* **replenished, replenishing.**

replica—A copy of something, such as a work of art or other object: *The* replica *of the statue was so well done that I could not tell it apart from the original.*
rep|li|ca (rep'lə kə) *noun, plural* **replicas.**
• Synonyms: **duplicate, reproduction**

reply—To answer by spoken or written words or by action: *I asked my friend to come, and she* replied *that she would. Verb.*
—An answer made in words or actions: *I wrote him a letter and received a* reply *in the mail. Noun.*
re|ply (ri plī') *verb,* **replied, replying;** *noun, plural* **replies.**
• Synonyms: **inform, respond, tell,** for *verb.*
Antonyms: **ask, inquire, question,** for *verb.*

report—A written or spoken description of something seen, done, or learned about, usually presented to other people: *I wrote a* report *about the planets for science class. Noun.*
—**1.** To tell about; describe: *The radio announcer* reported *the baseball scores.*   **2.** To present oneself, as for duty: *The soldier was ordered to* report *to his captain. Verb.*
re|port (ri pawrt') *noun, plural* **reports;** *verb,* **reported, reporting.**
• Synonyms: **announce, declare, proclaim,** for *verb* 1.
Antonyms: **conceal, hide, suppress,** for *verb* 1.

report card—A school's written report of a student's grades and behavior, issued on a regular basis to parents or guardians.
re|port card (ri pawrt' kahrd) *noun, plural* **report cards.**

reporter—A person whose work is gathering and telling news for a newspaper, magazine, or radio or television program.
re|port|er (ri pawr'tər) *noun, plural* **reporters.**

represent—**1.** To stand for; be a sign of; symbolize: *The dots and dashes in Morse code* represent *letters of the alphabet.*   **2.** To act or speak for: *She* represents *our class in the student government.*
rep|re|sent (rep're zent') *verb,* **represented, representing.**

a at	i if	oo look	ch chalk		a in ago
ā ape	ī idle	ou out	ng sing		e in happen
ah calm	o odd	u ugly	sh ship	ə =	i in capital
aw all	ō oats	ū rule	th think		o in occur
e end	oi oil	ur turn	th their		u in upon
ē easy			zh treasure		

representative—Someone chosen by a person in authority or by voters to act or speak for others: *The* representatives *from many countries met to talk about world problems. Noun.*
—**1.** Having persons who are chosen to act or speak for others: *All the citizens of the country have a voice in a* representative *government.*
2. So like others of its kind as to serve as an example of the entire group; typical: *Baseball, football, and basketball are* representative *team sports. Adjective.*
rep|re|sent|a|tive (rep′ri zen′tə tiv) *noun, plural* **representatives;** *adjective.*

reproduce—**1.** To make or cause to exist again: *The movie* reproduced *the way that people lived long ago.* **2.** To bear young; create offspring: *Chickens* reproduce *by laying eggs.*
re|pro|duce (rē′prə dūs′ *or* rē′prə dyūs′) *verb,* **reproduced, reproducing.**

reproduction—**1.** Something that is reproduced; copy: *This new teapot is a* reproduction *of one made long ago.* **2.** The process by which living things bear young: reproduction *of an oak tree is by means of an acorn.*
re|pro|duc|tion (rē′prə duk′shən) *noun, plural* **reproductions.**
• Synonyms: **duplicate, replica,** for 1.

reptile—An animal covered with scales or bony plates that moves on short legs, such as an alligator, or on no legs, such as a snake. Reptiles are cold-blooded, breathe through lungs, have a backbone, and mostly reproduce by laying eggs.
rep|tile (rep′tīl) *noun, plural* **reptiles.**

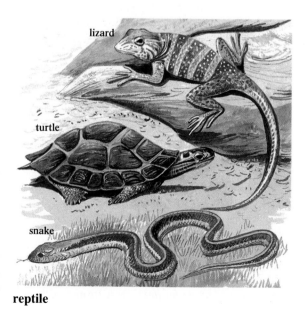

lizard
turtle
snake
reptile

republic—**1.** A country in which citizens vote for the people who manage the government. It usually has a president, not a king or queen.
2. The form of government of a country in which citizens vote for their leaders.
re|pub|lic (ri pub′lik) *noun, plural* **republics.**

republican—Of or favoring a form of government by which citizens vote for their leaders: *The United States has a* republican *form of government. Adjective.*
—**1.** A person who favors a system of government in which citizens vote for their leaders: *The* republicans *plotted the overthrow of the queen.* **2. Republican:** A member of the Republican Party. *Noun.*
re|pub|li|can (ri pub′lə kən) *adjective; noun, plural* **republicans.**

Republican Party—One of the two major political parties in the United States.
Re|pub|li|can Par|ty (ri pub′lə kən par′tē) *noun.*

reputation—The opinion that most people have of someone or something: *That builder has a* reputation *for building beautiful houses.*
rep|u|ta|tion (rep′yə tā′shən) *noun, plural* **reputations.**

request—**1.** To ask for; tell someone what is wanted: *The librarian* requested *quiet.* **2.** To ask: *She* requested *us to sit down. Verb.*
—**1.** The act of telling someone what is wanted: *No one heard his* request *for help.*
2. Something asked for: *Her one* request *is riding lessons. Noun.*
re|quest (ri kwest′) *verb,* **requested, requesting;** *noun, plural* **requests.**

require—**1.** To need or want: *How large a box do you* require? **2.** To demand; bind by something such as a law, order, or favor: *Fire laws* require *that the exits be marked.*
re|quire (ri kwīr′) *verb,* **required, requiring.**

requirement—Something needed or demanded; necessity: *Oxygen is a* requirement *for all living things.*
re|quire|ment (ri kwīr′mənt) *noun, plural* **requirements.**

rescue—To save or set free: *A passing ship* rescued *the survivors of the shipwreck. Verb.*
—The act of saving or setting free: *Helicopters helped in the* rescue *of the flood victims. Noun.*
res|cue (res′kyū) *verb,* **rescued, rescuing;** *noun, plural* **rescues.**

research—A thorough examination or study of a topic to discover facts or solve problems: *to do* research *for a book on space travel; medical*

research *to find a cure for a disease. Noun.*
—To study carefully or examine: *Scientists are researching new uses for plastics. Verb.*
re|search (ri **surch**′ *or* rē′**surch**) *noun, plural*
researches; *verb,* **researched, researching.**

resemblance—The fact of looking like someone or something; similarity: *There is a* resemblance *between my bicycle and yours, but yours is larger.*
re|sem|blance (ri **zem**′bləns) *noun, plural*
resemblances.

resemble—To appear similar to; look like: *Your brother* resembles *your mother.*
re|sem|ble (ri **zem**′bəl) *verb,* **resembled, resembling.**

resent—To feel offended or insulted by: *Our old cat* resented *the new kitten until she got to know him.*
re|sent (ri **zent**′) *verb,* **resented, resenting.**

resentment—The anger one feels when offended or insulted: *He felt* resentment *at being wrongly accused of cheating.*
re|sent|ment (ri **zent**′mənt) *noun, plural*
resentments.

reservation—**1.** A doubt or objection: *She had* reservations *about lending her new baseball glove to her cousin because he was careless with things.* **2.** Land that the government has ruled must be used only in a certain way, such as a home for an Indian tribe or a protected area for wildlife. **3.** An agreement made in advance to hold aside something for a person, such as an airplane seat or a restaurant table.
res|er|va|tion (rez′ər **vā**′shən) *noun, plural*
reservations.

reserve—**1.** To hold back; keep to oneself: *I will* reserve *my opinion of her until I know her better.* **2.** To hold aside or have another hold aside something for a certain reason or for the use of a certain person: *Please* reserve *next Friday night for my birthday party.* **3.** To hold or set aside for later use: *He* reserved *half his glass of milk to drink with dessert. Verb.*
—**1.** Something held back for future use: *We have a* reserve *of light bulbs in case one burns out.* **2.** A way of acting that keeps a distance between oneself and others; keeping quiet about

one's thoughts and doings. *He lost his* reserve *when he realized we really wanted to hear his story.* **3. reserves:** The part of a country's military force not on active duty but waiting and ready to serve if necessary. *Noun.*
re|serve (ri **zurv**′) *verb,* **reserved, reserving;**
noun, plural **reserves.**

reservoir—A place, created by nature or by artificial methods, in which a supply of water is collected and stored.
res|er|voir (rez′ər vwahr) *noun, plural*
reservoirs.

reside—To make one's home; live; dwell: *The two families* reside *on the same street.*
re|side (ri **zīd**′) *verb,* **resided, residing.**

residence—**1.** The place where one lives; home; dwelling: *Our family's* residence *is across the street from the home of my uncle.* **2.** A time during which one lives in a place: *After a* residence *of two years in that country, she speaks the language very well.*
res|i|dence (rez′ə dəns) *noun, plural* **residences.**

resident—A person who lives in a place: *A* resident *of the city should be able to direct us to the post office.*
res|i|dent (rez′ə dənt) *noun, plural* **residents.**

residential—Having to do with, suitable for, or used as a home or homes: *The* residential *section of town, where we live, is far from businesses and factories.*
res|i|den|tial (rez′ə den′shəl) *adjective.*

resign—To quit or withdraw from a job, office, or position: *When the manager* resigned, *the assistant manager took his place.*
re|sign (ri **zīn**′) *verb,* **resigned, resigning.**

resist—**1.** To struggle against; be against: *He* resisted *all our efforts to cheer him up.* **2.** To avoid; keep from: *The doughnuts looked so good I could not* resist *eating one.* **3.** To hold out against the effect or force of: *The little willow tree* resisted *the strong wind.*
re|sist (ri **zist**′) *verb,* **resisted, resisting.**

resistance—**1.** Action against; opposition: *Bus riders have put up some* resistance *to the idea of a fare increase.* **2.** The power or ability to fight off something: *Someone who already has a cold has less* resistance *to other infections.* **3.** A force that slows down or opposes another force: *Wind* resistance *slowed down the airplane..*
re|sist|ance (ri **zis**′təns) *noun.*

resolution—**1.** A decision; firm promise to oneself: *After he failed the test, he made a* resolution *to study harder.* **2.** A formal decision made by an organized group: *The school board*

a at	i if	oo look	ch chalk		⌈ a in ago
ā ape	ī idle	ou out	ng sing		e in happen
ah calm	o odd	u ugly	sh ship	ə =	i in capital
aw all	ō oats	ū rule	th think		o in occur
e end	oi oil	ur turn	<u>th</u> their		⌊ u in upon
ē easy			zh treasure		

passed a resolution *barring skateboards near the school.* **3.** The ability to hold to a decision: *Her resolution helped her to become an expert skater.*
res|o|lu|tion (rez′ə lū′shən) *noun, plural* **resolutions.**
  • Synonyms: **determination, resolve,** for **3.**

resolve—**1.** To make a firm decision: *She resolved to become a scientist.* **2.** To make understandable or clear; give or provide an answer to something: *The addition of two new rooms should* resolve *the problem of overcrowding. Verb.*
  —The ability to keep to a purpose or decision: *a weak, uncertain man of little* resolve. *Noun.*
re|solve (ri **zolv**′) *verb,* **resolved, resolving;** *noun.*
  • Synonyms: **determination, resolution,** for *noun.*

resort—To turn to for aid; seek help from: *I had to* resort *to the dictionary to find the meaning of the word. Verb.*
  —**1.** A place where people go to relax and enjoy themselves; vacation spot: *We got a great tan last weekend at a* resort *at the lake.* **2.** Someone or something that one turns to or seeks help from; resource: *I have looked all over town for a gift for Dad, and this store is my last* resort. *Noun.*
re|sort (ri **zawrt**′) *verb,* **resorted, resorting;** *noun, plural* **resorts.**

resound—**1.** To make a loud sound or echo: *The neighs of the horses* resounded *through the valley.* **2.** To become filled with a loud sound or noise: *The auditorium* resounded *with applause.*
re|sound (ri **zound**′) *verb,* **resounded, resounding.**

resource—**1.** A source of help, advice, supplies, or whatever else is needed: *The library is a vast* resource *of information.* **2.** A means of dealing with an emergency or of handling a problem: *When you are lost in the woods, a compass is your best* resource. **3.** The ability to handle bad situations: *It took all my* resource *to stop them from fighting.* **4. resources:** A region's wealth or sources of wealth: *Iron ore, timber, and salt are natural* resources.
re|source (ri **sawrs**′ *or* rē′sawrs) *noun, plural* **resources.**

respect—**1.** A feeling of admiration or high regard for someone or something: *As a sign of* respect, *the children stood when the mayor entered the room.* **2.** Consideration; special care: *It is an old and valuable book that should be handled with* respect. **3.** A detail; particular

point or feature: *Your plan is excellent in every* respect. **4.** Reference; regard: *I have some suggestions with* respect *to next week's program. Noun.*
  —**1.** To show special consideration for; think highly of: *We* respect *the judge for his knowledge and wisdom. Verb.*
re|spect (ri **spekt**′) *noun, plural* **respects;** *verb,* **respected, respecting.**

respectful—Showing high regard for; considerate: *A good citizen is* respectful *of the rights of others.*
re|spect|ful (ri **spekt**′fəl) *adjective.*

respiration—**1.** The act of breathing. **2.** The process by which a living thing takes in oxygen and gives off carbon dioxide.
res|pi|ra|tion (res′pə **rā**′shən) *noun.*

respiratory system—The organs and passages in the body involved in inhaling and exhaling air. In humans, the respiratory system consists of the nose, throat, windpipe, and lungs.
res|pi|ra|to|ry sys|tem (res′pər ə **tawr**′ē **sis**′təm) *noun, plural* **respiratory systems.**

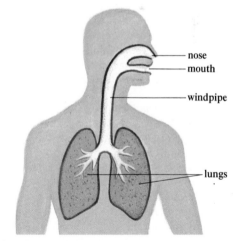

nose
mouth
windpipe
lungs

respiratory system

respond—**1.** To answer; say something in return: *When I asked if she had my pencil, she* responded *that she did.* **2.** To do something in reply; react: *The children* responded *to the dinner bell by racing to the table.*
re|spond (ri **spond**′) *verb,* **responded, responding.**
  • Synonyms: **inform, reply, tell,** for **1.**
    Antonyms: **ask, inquire, question,** for **1.**

response—A reply or action serving as an answer; reaction: *The lifeguard's quick*

response *to her cry for help saved her from drowning.*
re|sponse (ri spons´) *noun, plural* **responses.**

responsibility—**1.** The fact or state of having a duty to perform: *He felt that being in charge of the whole group was too much* responsibility. **2.** Something that one is relied upon to do: *Feeding and walking the dog is my* responsibility.
re|spon|si|bil|i|ty (ri spon´sə bil´ə tē) *noun, plural* **responsibilities.**

responsible—**1.** Required to perform as one's job: *My brother is* responsible *for doing the dishes.* **2.** Being to blame or deserving the credit for something: *A loose screw was* responsible *for the machine's breaking down.* **3.** Reliable; dependable: *The general chose the most* responsible *soldier for the secret mission.* **4.** Involving important tasks: *The chairman has the most* responsible *job on the committee.*
re|spon|si|ble (ri spon´sə bəl) *adjective.*

rest¹—**1.** Sleep: *His* rest *was disturbed by a crowing rooster.* **2.** A break from work or activity: *Leaning on his rake, the gardener took a short* rest. **3.** Freedom from trouble or pain: *His aching muscles gave him no* rest. **4.** A stop in motion or activity: *The ball came to* rest *a foot from the goal.* **5.** Something used as a support: *Our new car has an arm* rest *between the two front seats.* **6.** A pause between two notes of music. *Noun.*
—**1.** To sleep: *The baby* rested *in the crib while the adults talked.* **2.** To be free from hard work, worry, or pain: *On Saturday I* rested *all day.* **3.** To lean on as a support: *a fallen tree* resting *against the house; the letter* resting *on the table.* **4.** To take a break from work or activity; allow a time to be quiet and not active: *Please sit down and* rest *a moment.* **5.** To place or fix upon: *She* rested *her gaze on the sunset. Verb.*
rest (rest) *noun, plural* **rests;** *verb,* **rested, resting.**

rest²—Those things or people that remain after others have left or been taken: *to put the* rest *of the salad in the refrigerator. Noun.*
—To keep on being; remain: *You may* rest

assured *that we will not stop until we catch the thief. Verb.*
rest (rest) *noun; verb,* **rested, resting.**

restaurant—A public eating place.
res|tau|rant (res´tər ənt) *noun, plural* **restaurants.**

Word History

Restaurant comes from a French word meaning "to restore." One goes to a restaurant to eat and drink. By satisfying one's hunger and thirst, a restaurant restores energy and strength to the body.

---

restless—**1.** Unable to sit or lie still; eager for the end of some activity: *It was a long trip, and the children grew* restless. **2.** Giving no rest; uneasy: *We spent a* restless *night waiting for news of our lost pet.*
rest|less (rest´lis) *adjective.*

restore—**1.** To bring back into existence, power, or use; set up again: *to fix a wire and* restore *electricity.* **2.** To return something to its normal, former, or original condition; renew: *She hoped a vacation would* restore *her health.* **3.** To give back or return something: *I will try to* restore *the wallet to its owner.*
re|store (ri stawr´) *verb,* **restored, restoring.**

restrain—To keep under control; keep back or down: *As our trip began, it was hard to* restrain *our excitement.*
re|strain (ri strān´) *verb,* **restrained, restraining.**
• Synonyms: **bridle, check, curb**
　Antonyms: **release, vent**

a at	i if	oo look	ch chalk		⌈ a in ago
ā ape	ī idle	ou out	ng sing		e in happen
ah calm	o odd	u ugly	sh ship	ə =	i in capital
aw all	ō oats	ū rule	th think		o in occur
e end	oi oil	ur turn	th their		⌊ u in upon
ē easy			zh treasure		

restrain

restrict—To set limits; confine: *Please* restrict *your entries in the essay contest to 500 words or less.*
re|strict (ri strikt´) *verb,* **restricted, restricting.**

restriction—1. Something that limits or confines; rule or law: *She thinks she is too old to have her parents place so many* restrictions *on her behavior.* 2. The act of setting limits or confining, or the condition of being limited or confined: *The prison was built for the* restriction *of dangerous criminals.*
re|stric|tion (ri strik´shən) *noun, plural* **restrictions.**

result—Something that happens because of something else; consequence: *His success is the* result *of hard work. Noun.*
—1. To be caused by something else: *Considerable damage* resulted *from the storm.* 2. To have as an end or consequence: *The soldiers' lack of ammunition* resulted *in their defeat. Verb.*
re|sult (ri zult´) *noun, plural* **results;** *verb,* **resulted, resulting.**

resume—1. To go on or continue after a pause: *When the commercial ends, the program will* resume. 2. To take or occupy again: *After the intermission, we* resumed *our seats in the theater.*
re|sume (ri zūm´) *verb,* **resumed, resuming.**

resurrection—1. A return to life after being dead. 2. Resurrection: The rising of Jesus Christ from the dead after crucifixion and burial.
res|ur|rec|tion (rez´ə rek´shən) *noun, plural* **resurrections.**

retail—The direct sale of goods in small quantities to those who will use them: *The beauty shop on the corner now sells hair-care products at* retail. *Noun.*
—Concerning the direct sale of goods in small quantities to those who will use them: *The* retail *price of the shoes is $30. Adjective.*
re|tail (rē´tāl) *noun, adjective.*

retain—1. To keep possession of; hold on to: *to give her one of my apples but to* retain *the other; a sponge* retaining *moisture.* 2. To keep in one's memory: *I* retain *the words on the spelling list by reviewing them every day.* 3. To hire someone's services for a fee: *He* retained *an accountant to help with his taxes.*
re|tain (ri tān´) *verb,* **retained, retaining.**

retarded—Not able to learn at a normal pace; having a mental handicap: *Companies who hire* retarded *people are often surprised at how well these employees are able to work.*
re|tard|ed (ri tar´did) *adjective.*

retina—The membrane lining the back wall of the eyeball. It receives the images of things seen through the eye and sends them along a nerve to the brain.
ret|i|na (ret´ə nə) *noun, plural* **retinas.**

retire—1. To end one's working career; leave one's job, profession, or business forever: *When the shop's owner* retired, *her son took over the business.* 2. To withdraw to one's bed: *As soon as my homework is finished, I shall* retire.
re|tire (ri tīr´) *verb,* **retired, retiring.**

retirement—The end of one's working career, or the time after one has stopped working: *After her* retirement, *she had more time for travel.*
re|tire|ment (ri tīr´mənt) *noun, plural* **retirements.**

retreat—To fall back to an earlier position; withdraw from something that is unpleasant or dangerous: *The mouse snatched the cheese and* retreated *into its hole. Verb.*
—1. The act of moving back; withdrawing: *The army was surrounded, and* retreat *was impossible.* 2. A bugle call or other military signal announcing a withdrawing of troops or the lowering of a flag in a special ceremony: *Each evening at sunset, a bugler blew* retreat. 3. A place to go for peace and quiet: *He owned a small* retreat *in the country. Noun.*
re|treat (ri trēt´) *verb,* **retreated, retreating;** *noun, plural* **retreats.**

retrieve—1. To get and bring back: *The police* retrieved *the stolen money soon after they captured the thieves.* 2. To find and fetch game that a hunter has shot: *The dog swam out and* retrieved *the dead bird.*
re|trieve (ri trēv´) *verb,* **retrieved, retrieving.**

retrieve

retriever—Any one of various breeds of large dogs trained to hunt. Retrievers are often used to run or swim after birds that have been shot and to bring them back to the hunter.
re|triev|er (ri **trēv′**ər) *noun, plural* **retrievers.**
• See also **Chesapeake Bay retriever, curly-coated retriever, flat-coated retriever, golden retriever, Labrador retriever.**

return—1. To go or come back after leaving: *He returned to his home.* 2. To take, bring, send, put, or pay back: *to return a favor.* 3. To report in an official way: *The jury should* return *its verdict soon. Verb.*
—1. The act of going or coming back after leaving: *We look forward to the* return *of summer.* 2. An amount received as a profit; yield: *We expect a good* return *from our garage sale. Noun.*
re|turn (ri **turn′**) *verb,* **returned, returning;** *noun, plural* **returns.**

reunion—A gathering of family, friends, or classmates after a separation: *I will see all my cousins at our family* reunion.
re|un|ion (rē **yūn′**yən) *noun, plural* **reunions.**

Rev.—The abbreviation for **Reverend.**

reveal—1. To make public; tell to others: *The pirates agreed never to* reveal *where they hid the treasure.* 2. To show to others; display: *She took off her hat,* revealing *her red hair.*
re|veal (ri **vēl′**) *verb,* **revealed, revealing.**

reveille—A military bugle call played to wake up the troops.
rev|eil|le (**rev′**ə lē) *noun.*

Word History

Reveille comes from a French word meaning "Wake up!" That is what this bugle call tells the soldiers, so that is the name that was given to the call.

---

revenge—An injury or insult given to pay back for one that has been received: *The rancher swore* revenge *on the thieves who stole his cattle. Noun.*
—To pay back for an injury or insult received; get even for something: *He vowed to* revenge *the damage done to his property. Verb.*
re|venge (ri **venj′**) *noun; verb,* **revenged, revenging.**

revenue—1. Money received from an investment; income: *She bought a chicken farm as a source of* revenue. 2. A government's income from taxes and other sources.
rev|e|nue (**rev′**ə nū *or* **rev′**ə nyū) *noun, plural* **revenues.**

reverence—Honor and great respect, combined with awe and love; adoration; worship: *The people approached the king with* reverence.
rev|er|ence (**rev′**ər əns) *noun.*

Reverend—A title of respect for a member of the clergy. It is usually used with the person's full name: *the* Reverend *Ellen White.*
Rev|er|end (**rev′**ər ənd) *noun.* Abbreviation: **Rev.**

reverent—Feeling or showing deep adoration, honor, and love; very respectful: *They stood in* reverent *silence as the flag was raised.*
rev|er|ent (**rev′**ər ənt) *adjective.*

reverse—1. The opposite of another thing; something completely contrary: *She often does the* reverse *of what she says.* 2. The back part of something: *A description is written on the* reverse *of the photograph.* 3. The arrangement of gears that makes a machine move backward: *He put the truck into* reverse *to back into the parking space.* 4. A change for the worse; defeat; failure: *His recovery from the illness met with several* reverses, *forcing him to stay in bed longer. Noun.*
—1. To move something so its position is the opposite of what it had been or inside out: *When you have filled the page,* reverse *it and write on the other side.* 2. To make entirely different or contrary: *My parents* reversed *their decision not to let me go to the party. Verb.*
re|verse (ri **vurs′**) *noun, plural* **reverses;** *verb,* **reversed, reversing.**

reversible—1. Able to be turned over, upside down, around, or inside out: *Her* reversible *coat is waterproof on one side.*
re|vers|i|ble (ri **vur′**sə bəl) *adjective.*

review—1. To discuss or think about again; take another look at: *We will* review *the chapter the day before the quiz.* 2. To examine in a careful way: *The doctor* reviewed *the patient's medical history.* 3. To think about a series of actions that occurred in the past: *As he* reviewed *his stay at camp, he wished he had made more friends.* 4. To conduct an official inspection or evaluation:

a at	**i** if	**oo** look	**ch** chalk		a in ago
ā ape	**ī** idle	**ou** out	**ng** sing		e in happen
ah calm	**o** odd	**u** ugly	**sh** ship	ə =	i in capital
aw all	**ō** oats	**ū** rule	**th** think		o in occur
e end	**oi** oil	**ur** turn	**th** their		u in upon
ē easy			**zh** treasure		

The manager reviewed *each employee's performance every six months.*   **5.** To praise or criticize a movie, book, concert, art exhibit, or other work, for publication or broadcast: *The newspaper's television critic* reviewed *the new programs being shown this season. Verb.*
—**1.** The act of going over or looking over again: *Just before going on the stage, he made a quick* review *of his part.*   **2.** A survey of past events; a looking back: *A review of her youth made the old woman smile.*   **3.** An official inspection: *The sailors wore their dress uniforms for the admiral's review.*   **4.** A critical report on a play, movie, book, concert, or art exhibit: *That movie got terrible* reviews, *but I liked it. Noun.*
re|view (ri vyū′) *verb,* reviewed, reviewing; *noun, plural* reviews.

revise—**1.** To look something over and make corrections or improvements: *The writers* revised *the movie script to make it funnier.*   **2.** To change something: *We will have to* revise *the dinner menu because our guest does not like fish.*
re|vise (ri vīz′) *verb,* revised, revising.

revival—**1.** A renewed interest in or attention to something: *Big hats are enjoying a fashion* revival.   **2.** A new presentation of something old: *The play has had a* revival *as a television show.*
re|viv|al (ri vī′vəl) *noun, plural* revivals.

revive—**1.** To restore to life or consciousness: *He had almost stopped breathing, but the doctor* revived *him.*   **2.** To strengthen or refresh: *A short nap should* revive *you.*   **3.** To come or bring back into use: *My dance instructor is trying to* revive *ballroom dancing in our town.*
re|vive (ri vīv′) *verb,* revived, reviving.

revoke—To set aside as not good any more; do away with; cancel: *The governor asked the legislature to* revoke *the unpopular law.*
re|voke (ri vōk′) *verb,* revoked, revoking.

revolt—A rebellion against the authority of a government or other power; uprising: *The dictator's wicked deeds caused the* revolt. *Noun.*
—**1.** To rebel against the authority of a government or other power: *The slaves* revolted *against their cruel master.*   **2.** To make one feel disgusted or sick: *The sight of the mess* revolted *him. Verb.*
re|volt (ri vōlt′) *noun, plural* revolts; *verb,* revolted, revolting.

revolution—**1.** A change in the leadership of a country that happens as a result of a group's taking over the government, often using violent means: *The recent* revolution *gave that country a new leader.*   **2.** A major change, sometimes

occurring over a short period of time: *Computers have caused a* revolution *in the way people work.*   **3.** One complete movement around a central point; orbit: *the* revolution *of the planets around the sun.*   **4.** A spinning around an axis; rotation: *a motor's* revolutions *per minute; a complete* revolution *of the earth every 24 hours.*
rev|o|lu|tion (rev′ə lū′shən) *noun, plural* revolutions.

revolutionary—**1.** Having to do with an overthrow of government: *A secret* revolutionary *movement started a war against the emperor.*   **2.** Bringing about sudden or radical change: *The automobile and the computer were* revolutionary *inventions.*
rev|o|lu|tion|ar|y (rev′ə lū′shə när′ē) *adjective.*

revolve—**1.** To move in a circular path around a central point; orbit: *A number of moons* revolve *around the planet Jupiter.*   **2.** To spin on an axis; rotate: *The merry-go-round continued to* revolve *slowly after the motor was shut down.*   **3.** To have as a central point; center on: *The evening's entertainment* revolved *around a movie.*
re|volve (ri volv′) *verb,* revolved, revolving.

revolver—A pistol with a central section that revolves in which bullets are held. It can be fired as many times as it has bullets before it needs to be loaded again.
re|volv|er (ri volv′ər) *noun, plural* revolvers.

reward—**1.** Something given or received because of something one has done: *The children's* reward *for good behavior was being allowed to watch an extra hour of television.*   **2.** Money offered or received for helping to capture a criminal or for returning lost or stolen property: *The police will pay a* reward *for information leading to the arrest of the thieves. Noun.*
—To give something in return for something done; repay: *The old man* rewarded *her kindness with a smile. Verb.*
re|ward (ri wawrd′) *noun, plural* rewards; *verb,* rewarded, rewarding.

Rex—A short-haired, small cat with tight curly hair, large ears, a small head, and a thin body and legs. This cat was originally bred in England.
Rex (reks) *noun, plural* Rex cats.

R.F.D.—The abbreviation for "rural free delivery," the delivery of mail to people living in the country, outside regular delivery routes.

rheumatism—A disease that causes pain, swelling, and a stiff feeling in the joints.
rheu|ma|tism (rū′mə tiz′əm) *noun.*

rhinoceros

Word History

Rhinoceros comes from two Greek words meaning "nose" and "horn." This animal has a horn or horns on its face between the eyes and the mouth. These make it look different from any other animal, and so they gave it its name.

rhinoceros—A very large, thick-skinned animal with one or two upright horns on its snout.
rhi|noc|er|os (rī nos′ər əs) *noun, plural* **rhinoceroses** or **rhinoceros**.

Rhodesian ridgeback—A large hound with a distinctive ridge of hair on its back that grows in the direction opposite to its other short hair. Originally bred in Africa, this dog is used to hunt large game and as a guard dog.
Rho|de|sian ridge|back (rō dē′zhən rij′bak′) *noun, plural* **Rhodesian ridgebacks**.

rhododendron—A large shrub with leatherlike oval leaves that stay green all year around and clusters of white, pink, or purple flowers. It is the state flower of West Virginia.
rho|do|den|dron (rō′də den′drən) *noun, plural* **rhododendrons**.

rhubarb—A plant with large leaves, grown for its thick, bright pink, or red, sour-tasting stalks. The stalks are used in sauces and pies.
rhu|barb (rū′bahrb) *noun*.

rhyme—To have a sound similar to another word's, especially at the end. "Red," "head," and "said" are words that rhyme. *Verb.*
—1. A word or a line that ends with the same sound as another. "Bee" and "see" are rhymes. "I saw a man" and "He had a plan" are rhymes. 2. Verse or poetry having some lines that end with the same sound. *Noun.*
rhyme (rīm) *verb*, **rhymed, rhyming;** *noun, plural* **rhymes**.
■ **without rhyme or reason:** Senseless; without meaning: *She is usually a sensible person, but this week her actions have been* without rhyme or reason.

rhythm—The repeating of a beat or sounds in some kind of order. To dance, tap one's toes, or clap hands to music is to move to the rhythm of the sounds.
rhythm (rith′əm) *noun, plural* **rhythms**.

rib—1. One of the narrow bones that curves around the body from the spine in back to the breastbone in front. The ribs support the walls of the chest cavity and protect the organs inside.
2. Something like one of these bones in shape or purpose, such as part of the framework of an umbrella or an airplane wing.
rib (rib) *noun, plural* **ribs**.
■ **tickle the ribs:** To cause laughter: *A good joke* tickles the ribs.

ribbon—1. A strip of fabric or paper used as trim or to tie things up: *a hat with a striped* ribbon *around it; long braids tied with red* ribbons.
2. A strip of anything: *a typewriter* ribbon; *a flag torn to* ribbons.
rib|bon (rib′ən) *noun, plural* **ribbons**.

a at	i if	oo look	ch chalk		a in ago
ā ape	ī idle	ou out	ng sing		e in happen
ah calm	o odd	u ugly	sh ship	ə =	i in capital
aw all	ō oats	ū rule	th think		o in occur
e end	oi oil	ur turn	<u>th</u> their		u in upon
ē easy			zh treasure		

Rhodesian ridgeback

rice

rice—A kind of grass that grows in warm climates. Its seeds are used as an important food in most of the world, especially in Asia.
rice (rīs) *noun.*

rich—1. Having a great deal of money or other valuable possessions; wealthy: *The discovery of gold on her land made her* rich. 2. Having plenty of something: *The oceans are* rich *in fish.* 3. Very productive; fertile: *Vegetables grow well in this* rich *soil.* 4. Expensive; elegant: *a robe of* rich *velvet.* 5. Having ingredients that are high in quality, hard to digest, or strong in flavor, such as butter, chocolate, cream, or sugar: *He felt very full after eating all that* rich *food.* 6. Deep and mellow; *a* rich *blue carpet; the* rich *sound of a cello.*
rich (rich) *adjective,* **richer, richest.**

riches—A great deal of money or many valuable possessions: *In the museum were gold coins, fine paintings, gems, and other* riches.
rich|es (rich′iz) *plural noun.*

rid—To do away with or relieve of something that is not pleasant: *A bath should* rid *the dog of its fleas.*
rid (rid) *verb,* **rid** or **ridded, ridding.**

ridden—See **ride.**
rid|den (rid′ən) *verb.*

riddle[1]—A puzzle or problem that is given in the form of a question: *When is a door not a door? When it is ajar.*
rid|dle (rid′əl) *noun, plural* **riddles.**

riddle[2]—To fill with holes: *Moths had* riddled *the old coat.*
rid|dle (rid′əl) *verb,* **riddled, riddling.**

ride—1. To sit on the back of an animal or on a device, such as a bicycle, and make it move: *to* ride *a pony; to* ride *a motorcycle.* 2. To be carried in or on a vehicle: *to* ride *in a bus; to* ride *on a train.* 3. To be carried in or on anything: *the butterfly* rode *on the breeze. Verb.*
—A trip on the back of an animal, in or on a vehicle, or on anything that moves: *The* ride *on the elevator made him dizzy. Noun.*
ride (rīd) *verb,* **rode** or **ridden, riding;** *noun, plural* **rides.**

ridge—1. A thin raised area that appears across or along something: *a* ridge *of hair on a dog's back.* 2. A thin strip of hilly land or mountains. 3. Any long, thin raised area: *A frown made* ridges *in her forehead.*
ridge (rij) *noun, plural* **ridges.**

ridicule—To tease or laugh at a person or a thing in a cruel way: *His friends* ridiculed *him because his socks did not match. Verb.*
—The act of making fun of someone or something in a cruel way: *He was the object of much* ridicule *when he dropped the fly ball. Noun.*
rid|i|cule (rid′ə kyūl) *verb,* **ridiculed, ridiculing;** *noun.*

ridiculous—Deserving to be laughed at; silly: *The clown had a* ridiculous *big red nose.*
ri|dic|u|lous (ri dik′yə ləs) *adjective.*
• Synonyms: **absurd, foolish, senseless**
Antonyms: **reasonable, sensible**

rifle—A kind of gun that has grooves cut into the inside of its long barrel. The grooves cause a bullet to spin when it is shot from a rifle, and this spin makes the bullet more likely to go where it is aimed.
ri|fle (rī′fəl) *noun, plural* **rifles.**

rig[1]—1. To put ropes, sails, and masts on a boat. 2. To prepare by attaching or adding equipment: *We* rigged *up our wagon with new wheels for the big race.* 3. To dress, often in special or unusual clothes: *She* rigged *herself out in a clown costume to entertain the children.* 4. To fix for temporary use; put together using materials at hand: *The girls* rigged *a door by hanging a sheet over the opening. Verb.*
—1. Equipment necessary on a boat, including ropes, sails, and masts. 2. An outfit of clothing. 3. The tools, clothing, and any other gear needed for a particular purpose: *The children gathered together their rods, reels, and other* rig *for their*

fishing trip. **4.** Another name for a vehicle, usually a truck: *His* rig *is too small to carry that large load in just one trip.* Noun.

rig (rig) *verb,* **rigged, rigging;** *noun, plural* **rigs.**

rig²—To be set up in an unfair way; be arranged to favor one over the other: *She felt that the pet contest was* rigged *because the winner belonged to the judge's daughter.*

rig (rig) *verb,* **rigged, rigging.**

rigging —**1.** The ropes and other lines used on a boat with the sails and the mast; ship's rig. **2.** Any special equipment: *That* rigging *was set up for the tightrope performers.*

rig|ging (rig′ing) *noun, plural* **riggings.**

right—**1.** Proper; ethical: *He knew that he should do the* right *thing and tell the truth.* **2.** Exact; accurate; correct: *He couldn't remember the* right *answer to the question.* **3.** Appropriate; suitable: *The clerk showed her the* right *gloves to use for skiing.* **4.** Across from one's left. If one faces north, the side toward the east is the right side: *his* right *foot; my* right *ear.* Adjective.

—**1.** In a proper manner; in a good or just way: *He is behaving* right *by not judging the situation until he has all the facts.* **2.** In an exact, accurate, or correct way: *The dancer did the step* right *on the second try.* **3.** In a way that is satisfactory or satisfying: *Her science experiment turned out* right, *even though she made several mistakes in the beginning.* **4.** Toward the opposite of one's left: *The sailboat tilted* right *as the sailors came around the buoy.* **5.** Now; at this moment: *We're leaving* right *away.* Adverb.

—**1.** The proper thing; that which is fair or honest: *The children knew they were doing* right *when they picked up all their litter after the picnic.* **2.** A claim; strong reason for owning: *He had a* right *to the money because he had worked hard for it.* **3.** A fair, just, or legal claim: *The Bill of* Rights *is part of the Constitution of the United States. Her speech was about civil* rights. **4.** That which is opposite to one's left: *After you turn down the street, her house is the second one on the* right. Noun.

—**1.** To make up for; fix; correct: *The judge* righted *the injustice done to the innocent woman.* **2.** To straighten up; return to proper position: *She* righted *her paper cup after the wind had blown it over.* Verb.

right (rīt) *adjective; adverb; noun, plural* **rights;** *verb,* **righted, righting.**

- **in (one's) own right:** Simply on the basis of what someone or something is, regardless of other matters: *The judges rated each painting in* its *own right and did not look at the names of the artists.*
- Words that sound the same are **rite** and **write**.
- Synonyms: **good, moral,** for *adjective* **1.** Antonyms: **bad, naughty, wicked, wrong,** for *adjective* **1.**

right angle—Any angle like the angles in the corners of a square; angle of 90 degrees, formed by perpendicular lines.

right an|gle (rīt ang′gəl) *noun, plural* **right angles.**

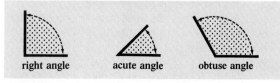

right angle   acute angle   obtuse angle

right angle

righteous—Good; proper; fair: *My mother expects us to be* righteous *enough to admit to our neighbor that we broke his window.*

right|eous (rī′chəs) *adjective.*

right triangle—A triangle that has a right angle.

right tri|an|gle (rīt trī′ang′gəl) *noun, plural* **right triangles.**

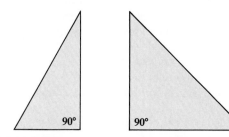

right triangle

rigid—**1.** Firm; hard; not able to bend or be bent: *Water becomes* rigid *when it freezes.* **2.** Set; fixed; not to be changed: *She follows a* rigid *schedule so as to have time for skating practice every day.*

rig|id (rij′id) *adjective.*

a at	i if	oo look	ch chalk		a in ago
ā ape	ī idle	ou out	ng sing		e in happen
ah calm	o odd	u ugly	sh ship	ə =	i in capital
aw all	ō oats	ū rule	th think		o in occur
e end	oi oil	ur turn	th their		u in upon
ē easy			zh treasure		

rile—1. To anger; upset: *Her father was* riled *when he saw the broken chair.*
rile (rīl) *verb,* **riled, riling.**

rim—An outer edge; border: *the* rims *of my new eyeglasses; the* rim *around the plate. Noun.*
—To go around the edge of; border: *A band of ribbon* rimmed *the hem of her skirt. Verb.*
rim (rim) *noun, plural* **rims;** *verb,* **rimmed, rimming.**

rind—The thick skin of certain fruits and cheeses. Lemons, oranges, and melons are fruits that have a rind.
rind (rīnd) *noun, plural* **rinds.**

ring[1]—1. A circular line or formation: *Dad planted flowers in a* ring *around the large stone in the yard.* 2. A piece of thin metal or other material that is curved around into a circle: *a gold* ring; *a chain made of* rings. 3. A closed area, circular, oval, or square, where sporting events, circuses, and other activities take place: *The wrestlers stepped into the* ring *to begin their match.* 4. A group involved in unlawful activities; gang: *The police caught a* ring *of burglars in our town. Noun.*
—To surround; go around something: *The moat that once* ringed *the castle dried up long ago. Verb.*
ring (ring) *noun, plural* **rings;** *verb,* **ringed, ringing.**
■ **run rings around:** To do something much better and more easily than others: *As a hitter, she* runs rings around *everyone else on the team.*

ring[2]—1. To fill the air with a sound like a sharp jingle or chime: *When the bell* rings, *please see who is at the door.* 2. To cause something to make such a sound: *to* ring *a bell.* 3. To echo with sound, usually loudly: *The gymnasium* rang *with the cheering of the fans.* 4. To make a continuing sound like a jingle or hum: *His ears were* ringing *long after the loud music had stopped. Verb.*
—1. A sound of a bell or like a bell: *The* ring *of the alarm woke her up.* 2. A call on the telephone: *Give me a* ring *tomorrow, and we will make plans to go shopping. Noun.*
ring (ring) *verb,* **rang, rung, ringing;** *noun, plural* **rings.**
■ **ring true:** To appear correct; seem right: *His story* rang true *because it explained all the facts.*
■ **ring up:** To enter a charge for something onto

a cash register: *Don't* ring up *my purchases until I've finished shopping.*
● A word that sounds the same is **wring.**

ringleader—One who leads a group in its criminal activities or its protest against rules and regulations: *The* ringleader *of the gang was arrested by the police.*
ring|lead|er (ring′lē′dər) *noun, plural* **ringleaders.**

ringmaster—Someone who announces circus acts.
ring|mas|ter (ring′mas′tər) *noun, plural* **ringmasters.**

rink—1. An enclosed area of ice or other smooth material where people come to skate. 2. The building that encloses this area.
rink (ringk) *noun, plural* **rinks.**

rinse—1. To wash away substances by using water: *Use the hose to* rinse *the mud from your boots.* 2. To wash with clear water for a brief time: *Please* rinse *and dry the bowl before filling it with popcorn. Verb.*
—The act of washing with clear water to remove substances: *She gave the pail a quick* rinse *after she poured out the dirty water. Noun.*
rinse (rins) *verb,* **rinsed, rinsing;** *noun, plural* **rinses.**

riot—1. An uproar by a large number of people that causes a great deal of confusion and often violence; disturbance that is out of control: *Extra police were called out to control the* riot. 2. A funny person or thing: *He was such a* riot *when he came in dressed as a chicken. Noun.*
—To cause an uproar marked by violence and confusion: *The announcement that the show was canceled almost caused the people with tickets to* riot. *Verb.*
ri|ot (rī′ət) *noun, plural* **riots;** *verb,* **rioted, rioting.**

rip—1. To make a quick, rough cut or tear: *He* ripped *the old shirt to use for a rag.* 2. To walk or run very fast: *The dog* ripped *around the room, knocking down everything in its path. Verb.*
—A rough tear: *The* rip *in the curtain was caused by the cat's claws. Noun.*
rip (rip) *verb,* **ripped, ripping;** *noun, plural* **rips.**
■ **let her rip:** To let something go on its natural course no matter what the results are: *He jumped on his sled and* let her rip, *hoping he would not fall off.*

ripe—1. Completely developed; at the peak of growth; ready to eat: *The grapefruits were* ripe

and ready to be picked from the tree. **2.** Ready for; ideal; due: *She is at a ripe age for tennis.*
ripe (rīp) *adjective,* **riper, ripest.**

ripple—**1.** A small movement on the surface of water; tiny wave: *When the frog swam away, it left a trail of* ripples. **2.** Something that looks like a tiny wave: *The wallpaper had a* ripple *in it where it had not been properly pasted.* **3.** A soft or rhythmic noise like that of tiny waves: *A* ripple *of unhappiness sounded through the classroom when the teacher announced that our trip would be delayed. Noun.*
—To sound or move like tiny waves: *The flag* rippled *in the breeze. Verb.*
rip|ple (rip′ əl) *noun, plural* **ripples;** *verb,* **rippled, rippling.**

rise—**1.** To get up to a standing position after sitting, kneeling, or lying down: *They* rose *from their seats to line up for the bus.* **2.** To get out of bed: *She* rises *early to get to school on time.* **3.** To move in an upward direction; go up: *I can see by the lights that the elevator is* rising *to the top floor.* **4.** To reach or extend in an upward direction: *Mountains* rise *on all sides of the lake.* **5.** To increase in price or value: *The price of meat* rose *five cents last week.* **6.** To go up in importance or position: *She* rose *to the highest position* in the *company.* **7.** To come from; begin: *That stream* rises *in the hills.* **8.** To oppose someone or something actively; revolt: *The people* rose *against the evil king. Verb.*
—**1.** An upward movement: *When the skiers saw the* rise *of smoke from the chimney, they knew a warm fire was waiting.* **2.** Something that extends or reaches upward: *the* rise *of the mountains. Noun.*
rise (rīz) *verb,* **rose, risen, rising,** *noun, plural* **rises.**
• Synonyms: **ascend, climb, soar,** for *verb* **3.**
Antonyms: **descend, sink,** for *verb* **3.**

risen—*See* **rise.**
ris|en (riz′ ən) *verb.*

risk—The chance that something bad or harmful could happen: *He took a* risk *when he climbed up in the tree. Noun.*
—**1.** To put in the position of possible harm or danger: *She* risked *her neck when she did not wear her seat belt.* **2.** To take a chance of: *My*

brother risked *losing his bicycle when he left it unlocked. Verb.*
risk (risk) *noun, plural* **risks;** *verb,* **risked, risking.**

rite—An important ceremony, such as a baptism or marriage.
rite (rīt) *noun.*
• Words that sound the same are **right** and **write.**

ritual—A form or system of ceremonies: *The* ritual *of marriage is different in different religions.*
rit|u|al (rich′ ū əl) *noun, plural* **rituals.**

rival—One who competes for the same thing as another; opponent: *Even though we are* rivals *for the starring role in the play, we are still best friends. Noun.*
—Being in competition with another for the same thing: *The* rival *teams both wanted to win the championship. Adjective.*
—**1.** To work to do better than; compete with: *The two girls always* rivaled *each other for the highest mark in math.* **2.** To be the equal of; match: *Nobody can* rival *my mother when it comes to giving parties. Verb.*
ri|val (rī′ vəl) *noun, plural* **rivals;** *adjective; verb,* **rivaled, rivaling.**

Word History

Rival comes from a Latin word meaning "one who uses the same stream as another." People who lived along the same stream often competed for the right to use the stream for fishing and other purposes. The word now means people who compete for any reason.

---

river—**1.** A large stream of water that flows into a lake, ocean, or other body of water. **2.** Any stream of liquid that looks like a river: *a* river *of hot fudge over ice cream.*
riv|er (riv′ ər) *noun, plural* **rivers.**

riverbank—The land along the edge of a river.
riv|er|bank (riv′ ər bangk′) *noun, plural* **riverbanks.**

riverbed—The natural groove in which a river flows.
riv|er|bed (riv′ ər bed′) *noun, plural* **riverbeds.**

riverside—The land on each side of a river.
riv|er|side (riv′ ər sīd′) *noun, plural* **riversides.**

rivet—A strong, metal fastener with a head at one end that is used to connect two or more pieces of metal. *Noun.*
—**1.** To put together with such a metal fastener.

a at	i if	oo look	ch chalk		⌈ a in ago
ã ape	ī idle	ou out	ng sing		e in happen
ah calm	o odd	u ugly	sh ship	ə =	i in capital
aw all	ō oats	ū rule	th think		o in occur
e end	oi oil	ur turn	th their		⌊ u in upon
ē easy			zh treasure		

2. To set; fix; fasten: *She* riveted *her attention on the teacher so that she would not miss a word of the lesson. Verb.*
riv|et (riv′it) *noun, plural* **rivets;** *verb,* **riveted, riveting.**

roach—A shortened form of cockroach.
roach (rōch) *noun, plural* **roaches.**

road—A path along which vehicles and people travel from place to place. A road is often made of pavement but can also be made of dirt or other material.
road (rōd) *noun, plural* **roads.**
• A word that sounds the same is **rode.**

roadblock—Something placed on the road to prevent travel: *The police set up a* roadblock *to catch the bank robbers.*
road|block (rōd′blok′) *noun, plural* **roadblocks.**
• Synonyms: **barricade, barrier**

roadrunner—A bird that can run very fast. Found in the southwestern part of the United States, it has brown, black, and white feathers and a long tail.
road|run|ner (rōd′run′ər) *noun, plural* **roadrunners.**

roadrunner

roadside—The land along either side of a road: *The scouts spent an afternoon picking up litter on the* roadside. *Noun.*
—Being near a road: *The* roadside *motel was easy for travelers to get to. Adjective.*
road|side (rōd′sīd′) *noun, plural* **roadsides;** *adjective.*

roam—To travel around with no special place to go; ramble; wander: *They had a free afternoon and* roamed *the countryside.*
roam (rōm) *verb,* **roamed, roaming.**

roan—A horse with a yellowish-brown or reddish-brown coat sprinkled with gray or white hairs.
roan (rōn) *noun, plural* **roans.**

roar—**1.** To make a loud, deep sound or cry: *The tiger* roared.   **2.** To laugh very loudly: *She could not help but* roar *when she saw the funny movie. Verb.*
—A loud, deep cry or sound: *the* roar *of a passing truck. Noun.*
roar (rawr) *verb,* **roared, roaring;** *noun, plural* **roars.**
• Synonyms: For *verb* **1,** see Synonyms at **cry,** *verb* **2.**
Antonyms: **mumble, mutter, whisper,** for *verb* **1.**

roast—**1.** To cook in an oven or over a fire. **2.** To dry by the use of heat: roasted *peanuts.* **3.** To make or be very hot: *She was* roasting *in the sun and went for a swim to cool off. Verb.*
—Any piece of meat that is already cooked in an oven or over a fire, or that is ready to be cooked in such a way. *Noun.*
roast (rōst) *verb,* **roasted, roasting;** *noun, plural* **roasts.**

rob—To take money or other valuables by force: *The criminals* robbed *the bank.*
rob (rob) *verb,* **robbed, robbing.**

robber—Someone who takes money or other valuables by force.
rob|ber (rob′ər) *noun, plural* **robbers.**

robbery—The act of taking valuables by force: *Priceless paintings were taken during the* robbery *at the museum.*
rob|ber|y (rob′ər ē) *noun, plural* **robberies.**

robe—**1.** A long, loose piece of clothing worn as a covering or wrap: *After her bath, she wore her* robe *until bedtime.* **2.** Such a piece of clothing worn to show one's position or job: *the judge's* robe. *Noun.*
—To put on or get dressed in a robe: *The teachers made sure that the graduates were* robed *before they marched into the auditorium. Verb.*
robe (rōb) *noun, plural* **robes;** *verb,* **robed, robing.**

Robert E. Lee's Birthday—January 19. Most Southern states celebrate this day as a legal holiday in honor of the man who was general in chief of all the Confederate armies.
Rob|ert E. Lee's Birth|day (rob′ərt ē lēz burth′dā) *noun.*

robin

robin—A North American bird with an orange chest and black head and tail.
rob|in (rob′ən) *noun, plural* **robins.**

robot—A machine that acts in some ways like a human. Robots are often made to look like humans as well.
ro|bot (rō′bət) *noun, plural* **robots.**

Word History

Robot comes from a Czech word meaning "work." **Robot** was made up by a writer and was first used in a play in which mechanical people did the work of humans.

---

robust—Very strong and healthy: *a robust wrestler.*
ro|bust (rō bust′ *or* rō′bust) *adjective.*
● Synonyms: **brawny, muscular**

rock[1]—1. A large mass of stone.   2. A small piece of stone; pebble: *His driveway is covered with crushed rocks.*   3. A layer of the outer covering of the earth.   4. Anything that gives great support: *She considered her father her rock, someone she could lean on whenever she needed help.*
rock (rok) *noun, plural* **rocks.**
■ **on the rocks:** In a state of or heading toward disaster; in trouble: *His relationship with his friend was* on the rocks, *and they did not even talk when they passed in the hall.*

rock[2]—1. To move from one side to the other or from back to front: *The boat* rocked *gently when the waves rolled in.*   2. To make something shake: *The earthquake* rocked *the building. Verb.*
—The action of moving from one side to the other or from back to front: *The table had a* rock *to it because it had one short leg. Noun.*
rock (rok) *verb,* **rocked, rocking;** *noun, plural* **rocks.**

rocker—1. Either of the curved pieces on which a cradle, rocking chair, or rocking horse moves back and forth.   2. A rocking chair.
rock|er (rok′ər) *noun, plural* **rockers.**
■ **off (one's) rocker:** Crazy; out of one's mind: *People will think you are* off *your* rocker *if you wear that silly hat to school.*

rocket—A device that flies through the air, powered by burning gases that push out through an opening at one end. Large rockets are used as weapons or as spacecraft. *Noun.*
—To move or rise with great speed: *The race car* rocketed *across the finish line. Verb.*
rock|et (rok′it) *noun, plural* **rockets;** *verb,* **rocketed, rocketing.**

rock'n'roll—A type of popular music with a strong, steady beat.
rock'n'roll (rok′ən rōl′) *noun.*

rod—1. A thin, straight bar or piece of metal, wood, or other material: *a curtain* rod.   2. A pole used for catching fish.   3. A stick used to punish by whipping.   4. A unit used for measuring, equal to 16½ feet (5 meters).
rod (rod) *noun, plural* **rods.**

rode—*See* **ride.**
rode (rōd) *verb.*

rodent—Any of the animals that have two large and very strong front teeth for biting through wood and other things. Mice, rats, squirrels, and beavers are rodents.
ro|dent (rō′dənt) *noun, plural* **rodents.**
● See pictures at **beaver, mouse,** and **squirrel.**

rodeo—A show in which people ride horses and bulls, rope cattle, and exhibit other such skills.
ro|de|o (rō′dē ō *or* rō dā′ō) *noun, plural* **rodeos.**

Word History

Rodeo comes from a Spanish word meaning "to go around." The word was first used to describe a roundup of cattle and later came to mean a contest where cowboys and cowgirls not only rounded up cattle but demonstrated their other skills as well.

---

a at	i if	oo look	ch chalk	
ā ape	ī idle	ou out	ng sing	
ah calm	o odd	u ugly	sh ship	ə =
aw all	ō oats	ū rule	th think	
e end	oi oil	ur turn	th their	
ē easy			zh treasure	

ə = ⎡ a in ago
e in happen
i in capital
o in occur
u in upon ⎦

roe¹—The eggs laid by a fish.
  roe (rō) *noun.*
   • Words that sound the same are **row¹** and **row²**.

roe²—A small deer that lives in Europe and Asia.
  roe (rō) *noun, plural* **roes** or **roe.**
   • Words that sound the same are **row¹** and **row²**.

rogue—1. A dishonest person; cheat. 2. A mischievous or playful person: *Give me back my hat, you* rogue!
  rogue (rōg) *noun, plural* **rogues.**

role—1. A part that an actor or actress plays: *She had the* role *of the queen in the school play.*
  2. A person's job or part in real life: *Dad takes the* role *of judge and quickly settles any family quarrels.*
  role (rōl) *noun, plural* **roles.**
   • A word that sounds the same is **roll.**

roll—1. To move along by turning over and over: *to* roll *a marble.* 2. To move or be moved on wheels or rollers: *The boy* rolled *the skateboard down the ramp.* 3. To wrap around and around: *to* roll *up a sleeping bag.* 4. To turn over: *The cat* rolled *on its back.* 5. To move in a constant manner: *The fog* rolled *in.* 6. To move from side to side; sway: *The ship* rolled *in the high waves.* 7. To make loud, deep sounds; rumble: *The thunder* rolled. 8. To make flat or smooth by the use of a roller. 9. To pronounce by using a long vibrating sound: *to* roll *your r's. Verb.*
  —1. Something that is wrapped around itself or something else: *a* roll *of tape.* 2. An up-and-down or side-to-side movement: *the* roll *of a ship at sea.* 3. A loud, deep sound: *a* roll *of drums.* 4. A list of names: *to call the* roll *of the students in English class.* 5. A small, baked piece of dough: *a hamburger* roll. *Noun.*
  roll (rōl) *verb,* **rolled, rolling;** *noun, plural* **rolls.**
   • A word that sounds the same is **role.**

roller—1. A long tube around which something is wrapped: *a* roller *for a window shade.* 2. A tube that is used as a tool to smooth, crush, or spread along a surface: *Dad painted the bedroom with a* roller *instead of a brush.* 3. A small wheel, such as on a roller skate. 4. A long, huge wave that breaks when it comes to the shoreline.
  roll|er (rōl′lər) *noun, plural* **rollers.**

roller coaster—A small train of open cars in an amusement park that takes people up and down steep slopes and around sharp curves.
  roll|er coast|er (rōl′ər kōs′tər) *noun, plural* **roller coasters.**

roller skate—A skate with four small wheels on the bottom. Roller skates are used to glide along flat surfaces, such as a road, floor, or sidewalk.
  roll|er skate (rōl′lər skāt) *noun, plural* **roller skates.**

roller-skate—To move about on roller skates: *After lunch, we all went* roller-skating.
  roll|er-skate (rō′lər skāt) *verb,* **roller-skated, roller-skating.**

rolling pin—A tubelike kitchen tool with a handle on each end. It is used to smooth and flatten dough.
  roll|ing pin (rō′ling pin) *noun, plural* **rolling pins.**

ROM—An abbreviation for "read-only memory." It is a part of a computer for storing information that can be read by the computer or its operator but not changed.

Roman Catholic—Having to do with the Christian church whose leader is the Pope; Catholic. *Adjective.*
  —A member of this church. *Noun.*
  Ro|man Cath|o|lic (rō′mən kath′ə lik) *adjective; noun, plural* **Roman Catholics.**

Roman Catholic Church—The Christian church whose leader is the Pope.
  Ro|man Cath|o|lic Church (rō′mən kath′ə lik church) *noun.*

romance—1. A story or poem that tells about the exciting adventures of heroes and heroines: *Our class read a* romance *about a servant girl who married a prince.* 2. A sense of love, excitement, adventure, or mystery: *The starry summer night seemed filled with* romance.
  ro|mance (rō mans′ *or* rō′mans) *noun, plural* **romances.**

Roman numeral—Any of a group of letters used long ago by the people of Rome that can stand for certain numbers. The Roman numeral for 1 is I. For 10, it is X. For 1,000, it is M.
  Ro|man nu|mer|al (rō′mən nu′mər əl) *noun, plural* **Roman numerals.**

romantic—1. Having ideas or feelings of love or adventure: *He had* romantic *thoughts of joining the circus when he grew up.* 2. Suitable for love or adventure: *The field full of daisies was a* romantic *place.*
  ro|man|tic (rō man′tik) *adjective.*

romp—To play in a lively way: *The puppies* romped *on the grass. Verb.*
  —Lively play: *After a long morning of school work, the children had a* romp *on the playground. Noun.*
  romp (romp) *verb,* **romped, romping;** *noun, plural* **romps.**

Roof may be pronounced in two different ways. How you pronounce the word may depend on where you live. Some people in the northern central part of the United States pronounce **roof** using the same vowel sound as in **good**. Many people in other parts of the country pronounce **roof** using the same vowel sound as in **tooth**. Both pronunciations are correct.

roof—**1.** The top covering of a building: *the roof of a house.* **2.** Anything like the top of a building: *the roof of a car. Noun.*
—To put on a top covering. *Verb.*
roof (rūf *or* roof) *noun, plural* **roofs;** *verb,* **roofed, roofing.**

rook[1]—A bird that looks somewhat like a crow and is common in Europe.
rook (rook) *noun, plural* **rooks.**

rook[2]—A chess piece that looks like a castle tower.
rook (rook) *noun, plural* **rooks.**

rookie—**1.** A person with no experience; beginner: *She is a rookie at riding a skateboard and falls off often.* **2.** A player in his or her first season of a major league sport.
rook|ie (rook′ē) *noun, plural* **rookies.**

room—**1.** A section of a house or other building that is separated from the rest by walls: *a living room.* **2.** Any open area; space: *There was no room in the suitcase for more shoes.* **3.** A chance; possibility: *There is room for improvement in his spelling. Noun.*
—To live in a place: *Six girls roomed together at college. Verb.*
room (rūm *or* room) *noun, plural* **rooms;** *verb,* **roomed, rooming.**

roommate—A person who shares a place to live with someone else: *The two boys were roommates at camp,*
room|mate (rūm′māt′ *or* room′māt′) *noun, plural* **roommates.**

roost—A horizontal pole or other place for birds to rest or sleep: *The chickens settled into their roost at sundown. Noun.*
—To find a place to rest or sleep: *We roosted on a bench in the park. Verb.*
roost (rūst) *noun, plural* **roosts;** *verb,* **roosted, roosting.**

rooster—A male chicken.
roost|er (rūs′tər) *noun, plural* **roosters.**

root[1]—**1.** The part of a plant that grows down into the ground. **2.** Something that looks or works like that part of a plant: *the root of a hair.* **3.** A cause or beginning of something: *The root of his problem in math is that he does not know the multiplication tables.* **4.** A word to which a prefix or suffix may be added; base word: *"Appear" is the root of "disappear." Noun.*
—**1.** To begin to grow down into the soil: *The rose bushes rooted when we planted them in the garden.* **2.** To keep in one spot: *The cat was rooted at the window as it watched the birds outside.* **3.** To get rid of; pull up or out: *I rooted the weeds out of the yard. Verb.*
root (rūt *or* root) *noun, plural* **roots;** *verb,* **rooted, rooting.**
● A word that sounds the same is **route.**

root[2]—**1.** To dig with the nose, as a pig looking for food. **2.** To search for: *She rooted through the attic looking for her ice skates.*
root (rūt *or* root) *verb,* **rooted, rooting.**
● A word that sounds the same is **route.**

root[3]—To cheer for or support: *We rooted for our brother in the chess match.*
root (rūt *or* root) *verb,* **rooted, rooting.**
● A word that sounds the same is **route.**

root beer—A bubbly soft drink that is flavored with the juice from the roots of certain plants.

rooster

a at	i if	oo look	ch chalk		⌐a in ago
ā ape	ī idle	ou out	ng sing		e in happen
ah calm	o odd	u ugly	sh ship	ə =	i in capital
aw all	ō oats	ū rule	th think		o in occur
e end	oi oil	ur turn	th their		∟u in upon
ē easy			zh treasure		

root beer (rūt bēr *or* root bēr) *noun, plural* **root beers.**

rope—A strong, thick cord that is made by twisting or weaving together thinner strings of fiber or other material: *a jump* rope. *Noun.*
—**1.** To tie or fasten with a strong, thick cord: *Dad* roped *the tree to the roof of our car.* **2.** To separate or mark off with a strong, thick cord: *The old plane in the museum was* roped *off.* **3.** To catch an animal with a strong, thick cord: *The cowboy* roped *the bull. Verb.*
rope (rōp) *noun, plural* **ropes;** *verb,* **roped, roping.**
- **know the ropes** or **learn the ropes:** To know or find out how to do something: *She is still learning the ropes in her new job.*
  on the ropes: In trouble: *He is on the ropes at school because of poor grades.*
  rope in: To lead on or trick someone: *I was roped in by the false advertisement.*

rosary—A string of beads that is used to count and keep track of the prayers that a person has said. It often has a small cross at one end.
ro|sa|ry (rō′zə rē) *noun, plural* **rosaries.**

rosary

rose[1]—**1.** A red, pink, white, or yellow flower that has a sweet, pleasant smell. It grows on a bush or vine that has thorny stems. The rose is the state flower of New York. **2.** A pinkish-red color. *Noun.*
—Having a pinkish red color: *a* rose *sunset. Adjective.*
rose (rōz) *noun, plural* **roses;** *adjective.*
- **come up roses:** To have a good result; turn out well: *We thought our dog was lost for good, but everything* came up roses *when the police found him.*

rose[2]—*See* **rise.**
rose (rōz) *verb.*

rosemary—A sweet-smelling, evergreen bush. Its leaves are used in cooking and in making perfume.
rose|mar|y (rōz′mãr′ē) *noun, plural* **rosemaries.**

Rosh Hashanah or **Rosh Hashana**—A Jewish holiday that celebrates the new year on the Hebrew calendar. It usually takes place in September.
Rosh Ha|sha|nah or Rosh Ha|sha|na (rosh hə shah′nə *or* rōsh hə shah′nə) *noun.*

rosy—**1.** Having a pinkish red color: rosy *cheeks.* **2.** Hopeful; bright: *She has a* rosy *future ahead of her as an artist.*
ros|y (rō′zē) *adjective,* **rosier, rosiest.**

rot—To decay; spoil: *The fruit on the ground underneath the tree has* rotted. *Verb.*
—A decayed part: *The brown* rot *on the apple showed that it was not good to eat. Noun.*
rot (rot) *verb,* **rotted, rotting;** *noun.*

rotary—Having a part or parts that turn: *A wheel moves with a* rotary *motion.*
ro|tar|y (rō′tər ē) *adjective.*

rotate—**1.** To turn or cause to turn around a center point: *The wheels of a bicycle* rotate *when you ride it.* **2.** To take turns at: *My sister and I* rotate *the jobs of mowing the lawn and drying the dishes.*
ro|tate (rō′tāt) *verb,* **rotated, rotating.**

rotten—**1.** Decayed; spoiled: *a* rotten *banana.* **2.** Not strong; likely to break: *The old ladder in the barn was* rotten. **3.** Terrible; awful: *That was a* rotten *thing to say to him.*
rot|ten (rot′ən) *adjective,* **rottener, rottenest.**

rose (noun, definition 1)

rottweiler—A large dog with a short smooth coat, small hanging ears, and a thick, stocky body. Originally bred in Germany to herd cattle, these dogs make excellent guard dogs.
rott|wei|ler (rot′wī′lər) *noun, plural* **rottweilers.**

rottweiler

rotunda—A round building or room. *Many government buildings have a* rotunda *in the front.*
ro|tun|da (rō tun′də) *noun, plural* **rotundas.**

rouge—Makeup used to redden the lips or cheeks.
rouge (rūzh) *noun, plural* **rouges.**

rough—1. Not smooth or even: *Sandpaper is* rough. **2.** Violent; stormy: *The boat swayed and rocked on the* rough *sea.* **3.** Forceful; not gentle: *We played a* rough *game of soccer.* **4.** Not polite; rude: *I do not like to play with those* rough *children.* **5.** Quickly and simply done: *He drew a* rough *map of the trail through the woods.* **6.** Difficult; hard: *She is having a* rough *time learning a new language. Adjective.*
—**1.** To treat badly or rudely: *Our game of football* roughed *up my new sneakers.* **2.** To make a simple, quick drawing of: *He* roughed *out an idea for the poster he wanted to enter in the fire-safety contest. Verb.*
rough (ruf) *adjective,* **rougher, roughest;** *verb,* **roughed, roughing.**

■ **rough it:** To live without the comforts one usually has at home, such as electricity and running water: *Our family* roughed it *when we went camping for a week in the woods.*
● A word that sounds the same is **ruff.**

roughly—About; almost; close to: *I am* roughly *five feet tall.*
rough|ly (ruf′lē) *adverb.*
● Synonyms: **approximately, nearly, somewhat**
Antonyms: **exactly, just, precisely**

round—Having a curved or circular shape: *a* round *marble; a* round *nickel. Adjective.*
—**1.** Anything that has a curved or circular shape: *The students cut the orange paper into* rounds *to make pumpkin decorations.* **2.** A regular path or route that is taken at a certain time or in a certain way: *The letter carrier made his daily* rounds *of the neighborhoods.* **3.** Things that happen one after the other; series: *Because they were so thirsty, the children had several* rounds *of lemonades after playing.* **4.** Part of or all of a game or sport: *the tenth* round *in a boxing match; a* round *of golf.* **5.** One or several shots from a gun, rocket, or the like: *The last* round *of fireworks filled the sky with color.* **6.** An action that a group of people does at the same time: *Good news brought a* round *of cheers from the crowd.* **7.** A short song that can be sung by three or more people, each of whom starts to sing the beginning of the song at a different time. *Noun.*
—**1.** To make or become curved or circular: *Her eyes* rounded *when she saw her birthday cake.* **2.** To go over or about a curve: *The horse* rounded *the last turn on the track and won the race. Verb.*
—In a circular or rotating motion; around: *The dancer spun* round. *Adverb.*
—All about in a circle: *We sat* round *the teacher and listened to a story. Preposition.*
round (round) *adjective,* **rounder, roundest;** *noun, plural* **rounds;** *verb,* **rounded, rounding;** *adverb; preposition.*

roundhouse—A circular building with a turntable in the center where railroad engines are parked and fixed.
round|house (round′hous′) *noun, plural* **roundhouses.**

round number—A number that is given to the nearest whole number or the nearest ten, hundred, thousand, or the like: *A* round number *for 9½ is 10.*
round num|ber (round num′bər) *noun, plural* **round numbers.**

a at	i if	oo look	ch chalk		
ā ape	ī idle	ou out	ng sing		a in ago
ah calm	o odd	u ugly	sh ship	ə =	e in happen
aw all	ō oats	ū rule	th think		i in capital
e end	oi oil	ur turn	th their		o in occur
ē easy			zh treasure		u in upon

round trip—The act of traveling to a place and returning to where one started: *The trip to her grandmother's house takes one hour, so the round trip takes two hours.*
round trip (round trip) *noun, plural* **round trips.**

roundup—The act of bringing many cattle in from the open fields to be counted or sold.
round|up (round′up′) *noun, plural* **roundups.**

rouse—1. To wake from sleep or rest: *The ringing alarm clock roused me.* 2. To cause excitement in; stir up: *The announcement that school would close early because of the storm roused the students.*
rouse (rouz) *verb,* **roused, rousing.**

Word History

Rouse was used long ago as a word for the way that a hawk shakes its feathers when it is getting ready to move or fly. Later the word was used for anyone or anything that starts to move after being still or asleep. Then it came to mean making someone wake up or become excited.

---

rout[1]—A serious loss or defeat: *Today's softball game was a real rout, 18 to 2.* *Noun.*
—To defeat; cause to lose: *The home team routed their opponents and won the game.* *Verb.*
rout (rout) *noun, plural* **routs;** *verb,* **routed, routing.**
• A word that sounds the same is **route.**

rout[2]—1. To search out; dig out: *She routed out a pencil from her book bag.* 2. To force to leave: *We finally routed the enemy from the fort.*
rout (rout) *verb,* **routed, routing.**
• A word that sounds the same is **route.**

route—1. A path or road for travel: *Which route would be faster?* 2. A regular path that is taken at a certain time or in a certain way: *a bus route. Noun.*
—1. To arrange a way to go: *Dad routed our vacation through the mountains.* 2. To send by a certain road or way: *Because of heavy fog, the airplane was routed to a different airport. Verb.*
route (rūt *or* rout) *noun, plural* **routes;** *verb,* **routed, routing.** Abbreviation: **rte.**
• Words that sound the same are **root** and **rout.**

routine—1. A usual, regular way of doing things: *Part of his daily routine is to feed the cat and set the table for dinner.* 2. A set of instructions that tells a computer to carry out a series of activities; program. *Noun.*
—Usual; regular: *a routine day at school. Adjective.*
rou|tine (rū tēn′) *noun, plural* **routines;** *adjective.*

row[1]—A line of people or things with one next to, or in front of, the other: *a row of desks.*
row (rō) *noun, plural* **rows.**
• A word that sounds the same is **roe.**

row[2]—1. To make a boat move by using oars: *The sailor rowed to shore.* 2. To travel or carry in a boat that is moved by using oars: *Please row them to the island.*
row (rō) *verb,* **rowed, rowing.**
• A word that sounds the same is **roe.**

row[3]—A loud argument or fight: *The children had a row about who would get the last piece of cake.*
row (rou) *noun, plural* **rows.**

rowboat—A small boat that is moved by using oars.
row|boat (rō′bōt′) *noun, plural* **rowboats.**

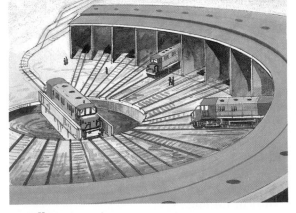

roundhouse

rowboat

royal—**1.** Of or belonging to a king or queen: *the* royal *family*. **2.** Wonderful; magnificent: *The winning baseball team was given a royal welcome when they returned to their home town.* **3.** Bright and rich in color: *a royal blue*.
roy|al (roi′əl) *adjective*.

royalty—**1.** A king or queen, or a member of his or her family, or more than one such persons. **2.** The job or power of a king or queen.
roy|al|ty (roi′əl tē) *noun, plural* **royalties.**

R.R.—The abbreviation for **railroad.**

rte.—The abbreviation for **route.**

rub—**1.** To move back and forth against something: *The boy* rubbed *two sticks together to make a fire.* **2.** To push or press on: *She* rubbed *her hands over her eyes when she woke up.* **3.** To spread or put on: *I* rubbed *oil on the pan. Verb.*
—The act of pushing or pressing on: *After the hike, he gave his sore feet a good* rub. *Noun.*
rub (rub) *verb,* **rubbed, rubbing;** *noun, plural* **rubs.**
▪ **rub the wrong way:** To bother or annoy: *It really* rubbed *the boy* the wrong way *when his friend said something nasty to him.*

rubber—**1.** An elastic substance made from the milky juice of certain tropical plants or by a chemical process. It is strong, airtight, and waterproof. **2.** Something made of an elastic, waterproof substance, such as a pencil eraser or overshoe.
rub|ber (rub′ər) *noun, plural* **rubbers.**

rubber band—A thin loop that is made of rubber and stretches to hold things together; elastic band.
rub|ber band (rub′ər band) *noun, plural* **rubber bands.**

rubber stamp—A stamp made of rubber that has writing or a design on it. It is used with ink to print names, dates, addresses, and the like on a surface.
rub|ber stamp (rub′ər stamp) *noun, plural* **rubber stamps.**

rubbish—**1.** Worthless material; trash; garbage: *Put all the* rubbish *on the curb so that the garbage truck can haul it away tomorrow.* **2.** Nonsense; silly talk: *Her stories are usually*

true, but that one sounds like rubbish *to me.*
rub|bish (rub′ish) *noun.*
• Synonyms: See Synonyms at **garbage,** for **1.**

rubble—Broken pieces of something solid, such as stone or brick: *The tornado destroyed several buildings and turned them into piles of* rubble.
rub|ble (rub′əl) *noun.*

ruble—A unit of money in the Union of Soviet Socialist Republics.
ru|ble (rū′bəl) *noun, plural* **rubles.**
Abbreviation: **r.**

ruby—**1.** A red, precious stone. **2.** The deep red color of this stone. *Noun.*
—Having a deep red color: *a ruby dress. Adjective.*
ru|by (rū′bē) *noun, plural* **rubies;** *adjective.*

ruckus—Noisy activity that disturbs or disrupts others; rumpus: *The people in line raised a* ruckus *when they were told there were no tickets left for the concert.*
ruck|us (ruk′əs) *noun, plural* **ruckuses.**

rudder—**1.** A wooden or metal blade attached to the rear of a boat or ship. It is used for steering. **2.** A similar device on an airplane.
rud|der (rud′ər) *noun, plural* **rudders.**
• For **1,** see picture at **tiller.**

ruddy—Having a healthy pink or red color: *She had a* ruddy *face after being outdoors all day.*
rud|dy (rud′ē) *adjective,* **ruddier, ruddiest.**

rude—**1.** Showing poor manners; not polite: *It was* rude *of him to interrupt me while I was talking.* **2.** Roughly built; primitive: *a rude shelter of branches and rope.*
rude (rūd) *adjective,* **ruder, rudest.**

ruff—**1.** A stiff, pleated collar worn by men and women long ago. **2.** A collar of feathers or hair growing around the neck of a bird or other animal.
ruff (ruf) *noun, plural* **ruffs.**
• A word that sounds the same is **rough.**

ruffian—A tough, mean person; bully.
ruf|fi|an (ruf′ē ən) *noun, plural* **ruffians.**

ruffle—A strip of cloth, lace, or ribbon with folds sewn along one edge. It is used as trimming on such items as pillows and pillow cases, dresses, and tablecloths. *Noun.*
—**1.** To bother; annoy; disturb the calmness of: *He has such a bad temper that even the smallest problem* ruffles *him.* **2.** To make uneven or wrinkled: *He* ruffled *his good clothes by taking a nap in them. Verb.*
ruf|fle (ruf′əl) *noun, plural* **ruffles;** *verb,* **ruffled, ruffling.**

a at	i if	oo look	ch chalk		a in ago
ā ape	ī idle	ou out	ng sing		e in happen
ah calm	o odd	u ugly	sh ship	ə =	i in capital
aw all	ō oats	ū rule	th think		o in occur
e end	oi oil	ur turn	th their		u in upon
ē easy			zh treasure		

rug—A heavy, thick fabric used to cover all or part of a floor.
rug (rug) *noun, plural* **rugs.**

rugged—1. Having a rough and uneven surface: *a* rugged *country road; a* rugged *mountain range.* 2. Strong and tough; sturdy: *The hikers wore* rugged *boots.* 3. Harsh; difficult to put up with or do: *Winters in the north can be very* rugged.
rug|ged (rug′id) *adjective.*

ruin—1. Severe damage or destruction; collapse; complete loss: *The flood caused the* ruin *of many valuable books in the library.* 2. Something that causes severe damage, destruction, or collapse: *Gambling will be her* ruin. 3. **ruins**: That which is left after something has been severely damaged or destroyed: *the* ruins *of an ancient city. Noun.*
—1. To damage or destroy; harm; make useless: *The rain* ruined *our plan for a picnic.* 2. To lose or cause to lose money, a good name, a social position, or the like: *They were* ruined *when their store went bankrupt. Verb.*
ru|in (rū′ən) *noun, plural* **ruins;** *verb,* **ruined, ruining.**
• Synonyms: **dash, foil**[1]**, frustrate,** for *verb* **1.**

rule—1. An order that states what can or cannot be done: *the* rules *of a game;* rules *of good behavior.* 2. Government or authority: *a queen's* rule; *the* rule *of law.* 3. Something that normally happens or is usually done: *Dinner at six o'clock has been the* rule *in my family for years. Noun.*
—1. To make an official decision: *The referee* ruled *that the ball was out of bounds.* 2. To control; govern: *The emperor* ruled *for seven years. Verb.*
rule (rūl) *noun, plural* **rules;** *verb,* **ruled, ruling.**
■ **as a rule:** Usually: As a rule, *they go to the movies every Saturday night.*

ruler—1. A person who governs: *The empress was a powerful* ruler *whose army conquered many countries.* 2. A strip of wood, metal, or plastic with a straight edge. Rulers are marked off into inches or centimeters and are used to draw lines or to measure distance.
ru|ler (rū′lər) *noun, plural* **rulers.**

rum—An alcoholic beverage made from sugar cane or molasses.
rum (rum) *noun, plural* **rums.**

rumble—To make a long, low, heavy sound: *The volcano* rumbled *for several days before it erupted. Verb.*
—A long, low, heavy sound: *the* rumble *of thunder. Noun.*
rum|ble (rum′bəl) *verb,* **rumbled, rumbling;** *noun, plural* **rumbles.**

rummage—To search by moving things around, often quickly and carelessly: *He* rummaged *through his desk for the missing paper. Verb.*
—A search done by moving things around: *We made a* rummage *of the attic to try to find the old picture. Noun.*
rum|mage (rum′ij) *verb,* **rummaged, rummaging;** *noun, plural* **rummages.**

rumor—1. A story or statement that is given to people as fact even though there is no proof that it is true: *A* rumor *that there would be no school tomorrow spread through the class.* 2. What people are generally saying, not necessarily based on any known fact: Rumor *has it that my favorite singer is coming to town. Noun.*
—To spread a story without having any proof of its truth: *It is* rumored *that the band is going to get new uniforms. Verb.*
ru|mor (rū′mər) *noun, plural* **rumors;** *verb,* **rumored, rumoring.**

rump—1. The hind part of an animal that joins the legs to the back. 2. The meat from this part of cattle.
rump (rump) *noun, plural* **rumps.**

rumpus—Noisy activity that disturbs others; ruckus: *The brothers were making a* rumpus *in their room, and their parents had to tell them to be quiet.*
rum|pus (rum′pəs) *noun, plural* **rumpuses.**

run—1. To move with quick steps; go faster than a walk: *She wanted to get home before it started raining, so she* ran *all the way.* 2. To go with haste; rush: *I have to* run *because it is getting late.* 3. To make a short, fast trip, usually as an errand: *Please* run *to the store for me.* 4. To go on a regular basis or schedule: *The train* runs *twice a day.* 5. To go past or through: *a speeding car that* runs *a stop sign; a ship that* runs *an enemy blockade.* 6. To flow: *The brook* runs *through the field.* 7. To spread color: *When she washed her blue skirt, it* ran *and turned the rest of the laundry blue.* 8. To proceed or continue to be in effect: *The show will* run *for two weeks.* 9. To take part in a race or contest: *Two of their horses are* running *today.* 10. To be a political candidate: *Would you ever* run *for the office of mayor?* 11. To operate or cause to operate: *a car engine that* runs *smoothly; to* run *a sewing machine.* 12. To manage a business: *Her family* runs *a clothing store.* 13. To go about freely: *They did not keep their dog on a leash but let it* run *about the neighborhood.* 14. To have stitches in a material come undone: *Her stockings* ran *when the cat scratched her leg. Verb.*

—**1.** The act of moving quickly by foot: *We went for a* run *along the beach to get ready for the race.* **2.** A trip, often a quick one: *They took a* run *into town for groceries.* **3.** A period of time during which something keeps happening: *a* run *of good fortune.* **4.** Freedom to use or move about as desired: *The children had the* run *of the yard.* **5.** A place where stitches have come apart: *a* run *in a stocking.* **6.** A point scored in baseball, when a player has touched all the bases and reaches home plate. *Noun.*
run (run) *verb,* **ran, run, running;** *noun, plural* **runs.**
- **run into:** To meet by chance. *I* ran into *my cousin at the supermarket yesterday.*
  run up: To let something collect or add up. *We* ran up *a big bill at the restaurant.*

runaway—A person or animal that runs away or escapes: *The police searched for the monkey that was a* runaway *from the zoo. Noun.*
—**1.** Running away or escaping: *The* runaway *horse was finally captured.* **2.** Moving or running out of control: *The* runaway *basketball rolled into the street. Adjective.*
run|a|way (run′ə wā) *noun, plural* **runaways;** *adjective.*

run-down—**1.** Tired and not feeling well: *Staying up late has left him very* run-down. **2.** Almost ruined; in a state of neglect: *People said the* run-down *house was haunted.*
run-down (run′doun′) *adjective.*

rung¹—**1.** A step of a ladder. **2.** A piece placed between the legs of a chair or forming the back of a chair.
rung (rung) *noun, plural* **rungs.**
- A word that sounds the same is **wrung.**

rung²—*See* **ring.**
rung (rung) *verb.*
- A word that sounds the same is **wrung.**

runner—**1.** Someone or something that runs: *a fast* runner. **2.** One of the long, thin blades on which a sled or an ice skate moves. **3.** A long, narrow rug, usually for a hall or staircase. **4.** A thin stem of certain plants that grows along the ground and starts more plants by setting new roots into the soil.
run|ner (run′ər) *noun, plural* **runners.**

rung¹ (definitions 1 and 2)

runner-up—A person or team that finishes a contest in second place.
run|ner-up (run′ər up′) *noun, plural* **runners-up.**

runt—An animal, plant, or person smaller than normal size.
runt (runt) *noun, plural* **runts.**

runway—A long, smooth surface on which aircraft land and take off. It is usually paved.
run|way (run′wā′) *noun, plural* **runways.**

rupee—A unit of money of India.
ru|pee (rū pē′) *noun, plural* **rupees.**
Abbreviation: R.

rural—In, belonging to, having to do with, or similar to the country: *Fields of corn ran along both sides of the* rural *highway.*
ru|ral (roor′əl) *adjective.*

rush¹—**1.** To move quickly; hurry: *They* rushed *to get home on time.* **2.** To do too fast: *This is an important decision and I should not* rush *it. Verb.*
—**1.** The act of moving quickly: *The* rush *of the wind rattled the windows.* **2.** A state of haste; hurry: *He waited until the last day to do his project, and then he was in a* rush *to finish it.* **3.** The movement of many people to go somewhere or to get something: *There was a* rush *of shoppers to the store when the sale was announced. Noun.*
—Done fast; requiring quickness: *a* rush *job; a* rush *order. Adjective.*
rush (rush) *verb,* **rushed, rushing;** *noun, plural* **rushes;** *adjective.*
- Synonyms: **hasten, speed,** for *verb* **1.**
  Antonyms: For *verb* **1,** see Synonyms at **dawdle.**

a at	i if	oo look	ch chalk	
ā ape	ī idle	ou out	ng sing	
ah calm	o odd	u ugly	sh ship	ə =
aw all	ō oats	ū rule	th think	
e end	oi oil	ur turn	th their	
ē easy			zh treasure	

a in ago
e in happen
i in capital
o in occur
u in upon

rush²—A grasslike marsh plant. Rushes have hollow stems that are used to weave chair seats, baskets, and mats.
rush (rush) *noun, plural* **rushes.**

Russian Blue—A short-haired cat with a thick, silver-blue coat and green eyes. It has a long, thin body and large, pointed ears. These cats were originally bred in Russia.
Rus|sian Blue (rush′ən blū) *noun, plural* **Russian Blues.**

Russian Blue

Russian Orthodox Church—The national church of Russia until 1918. It is a Christian church, similar to the Greek Orthodox Church.
Rus|sian Or|tho|dox Church (rush′ən awr′thə doks church) *noun.*

Russian wolfhound—*See* **borzoi.**
Rus|sian wolf|hound (rush′ən woolf′hound′) *noun, plural* **Russian wolfhounds.**

rust—**1.** The reddish brown or orange coating that forms on iron or steel when these are exposed to moist air. **2.** A plant disease that causes red or brown spots on leaves and stems. **3.** A reddish brown or orange color. *Noun.*
—To develop a reddish brown or orange coating on metal: *His bicycle* rusted *because he left it outside in the rain. Verb.*
—Having a reddish brown or orange color: *a* rust *sweater. Adjective.*
rust (rust) *noun, plural* **rusts;** *verb,* **rusted, rusting;** *adjective.*

rustle—A light, fluttering sound: *The only sound in the library was the* rustle *of turning pages. Noun.*
—**1.** To make or cause to make a light, fluttering sound: *The breeze* rustled *the tall grass.* **2.** To steal cattle, horses, or other livestock. *Verb.*
rus|tle (rus′əl) *noun, plural* **rustles;** *verb,* **rustled, rustling.**

rustler—A person who steals cattle, horses, or other livestock.
rus|tler (rus′lər) *noun, plural* **rustlers.**

rusty—**1.** Coated with rust: *The lock on the gate is* rusty *and will not open.* **2.** Not as good as something used to be because of lack of use or practice: *I have not played tennis for two years, so my game is a little* rusty.
rus|ty (rus′tē) *adjective,* **rustier, rustiest.**

rut—**1.** A track made by wheels in soft ground. **2.** A routine, dull way of living or being: *She felt she was in a* rut *and needed to do something different, so she signed up for dance lessons. Noun.*
—To make a groove or grooves in: *The tractor* rutted *the meadow. Verb.*
rut (rut) *noun, plural* **ruts;** *verb,* **rutted, rutting.**

ruthless—Having no pity or compassion; cruel: *The king was a* ruthless *person who put all his enemies in prison.*
ruth|less (rūth′lis) *adjective.*

RV—The abbreviation for **recreational vehicle.**

rye—A grass grown for its seeds and grain, which are used as animal feed and for making flour and whiskey. *Noun.*
rye (rī) *noun, plural* **ryes.**

About 5,000 years ago, the ancient Egyptians used a symbol of a tusk.

About 3,500 years ago, people in the Middle East used this form. They called it *shin*, their word for "tooth."

About 3,000 years ago, other people in the Middle East gave the letter this form.

About 2,600 years ago, the Greeks turned the letter on its side. They called it *sigma*.

About 1,900 years ago, the Romans gave the capital S its present form. The small letter s was first used about 1,500 years ago. It reached its present form about 500 years ago.

S or **s**—The nineteenth letter of the alphabet: *There are three s's in the word success.*
S, s (es) *noun, plural* S's *or* Ss, s's *or* ss.

S.—The abbreviation for **south.**

Sabbath—The day of the week on which Jews and Christians rest from work and gather for worship. Jews have their Sabbath on Saturday, and most Christians have theirs on Sunday.
Sab|bath (sab′əth) *noun, plural* Sabbaths.

saber—A sword with a long, curved blade that has one sharp edge.
sa|ber (sā′bər) *noun, plural* sabers.

saber-toothed tiger—A large extinct animal of the cat family. It lived millions of years ago and had long, curved upper teeth.
sa|ber-toothed ti|ger (sā′bər tūtht′ tī′gər) *noun, plural* saber-toothed tigers.

sabotage—1. Deliberate interference with a plan or activity to keep it from being carried out: *The successful* sabotage *of the enemy's plan to attack the village saved many lives.* 2. Deliberate damage to such things as machinery, a factory, or equipment by agents during wartime or by angry workers: Sabotage *of the bridge caused it to collapse as enemy troops were passing over it.* Noun.
—To damage or interfere deliberately: *The angry worker* sabotaged *the machines inside the factory so that they kept breaking down.* Verb.
sab|o|tage (sab′ə tahzh) *noun; verb,* sabotaged, sabotaging.

sack—1. A large bag made of strong, heavy cloth and used to hold such things as mail, grain, and potatoes. 2. Any bag: *I brought a paper* sack *filled with shells home from the beach.*
sack (sak) *noun, plural* sacks.
■ **hit the sack:** To go to sleep: *It was late, so he decided to* hit the sack.
● See Language Fact at **bag.**

sacrament—A sacred Christian ceremony. Baptism is one sacrament.
sac|ra|ment (sak′rə mənt) *noun, plural* sacraments.

sacred—Devoted to or having to do with God or a god; holy: *a* sacred *book; a* sacred *building;* sacred *music.*
sa|cred (sā′krid) *adjective.*

a at	i if	oo look	ch chalk	a in ago
ā ape	ī idle	ou out	ng sing	e in happen
ah calm	o odd	u ugly	sh ship	ə = i in capital
aw all	ō oats	ū rule	th think	o in occur
e end	oi oil	ur turn	th their	u in upon
ē easy			zh treasure	

saber-toothed tiger

sacrifice—1. The act of offering something to God or to a god as a form of worship: *The sacrifice of the sheep was performed on the sacred altar.* 2. The act of giving up something that one wants for the sake of something else: *She made a sacrifice of her time to help out at the bake sale. Noun.*
—1. To make an offering to God or to a god. 2. To give up something for the sake of something else: *We sacrificed our vacation savings to help the flood victims. Verb.*
sac|ri|fice (sak′rə fīs) *noun, plural* **sacrifices;** *verb,* **sacrificed, sacrificing.**

sad—1. Filled with sorrow; unhappy: *The little girl was sad when she broke her favorite doll.* 2. Producing sorrow or unhappiness: *We cried at the end of the sad movie.*
sad (sad) *adjective,* **sadder, saddest.**
• Synonyms: **blue, gloomy, glum, miserable,** for 1.
Antonyms: For 1, see Synonyms at **happy.**

saddle—1. A seat that is strapped to the back of a horse, mule, camel or other animal that is to be ridden by someone. 2. A bicycle seat. *Noun.*
—To put a seat on an animal: *to saddle a horse. Verb.*
sad|dle (sad′əl) *noun, plural* **saddles;** *verb,* **saddled, saddling.**

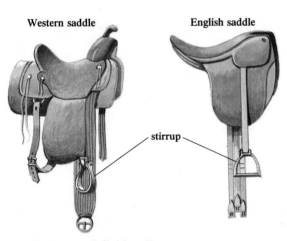

Western saddle

English saddle

stirrup

saddle (noun, definition 1)

safari—A journey or hunting trip, especially in Africa.
sa|fa|ri (sə fahr′ē) *noun, plural* **safaris.**

safe—1. Free from danger, harm, or risk: *The radio announcement said to go to a safe place, such as a basement, during the storm.* 2. Not likely to cause injury or damage: *Make sure you give the baby a safe toy.* 3. Careful; cautious: *a safe driver.* 4. Having little chance of error or failure: *It is safe to say that we will never watch that terrible movie again.* 5. Reaching any of the bases in a baseball or softball game without being called out: *She avoided the tag and was safe on third base. Adjective.*
—A sturdy metal container used for protecting valuable items from theft or damage. *Noun.*
safe (sāf) *adjective,* **safer, safest;** *noun, plural* **safes.**

safety—The state of being free from injury or danger; security: *Our boat sprung a leak while we were on the lake, but we were able to make it back to safety. Noun.*
—Capable of reducing injury or danger: safety belts; a safety pin. *Adjective.*
safe|ty (sāf′tē) *noun, adjective.*

sag—1. To curve or sink downward from weight or pressure: *The old wooden floor sagged when we walked on it.* 2. To droop or hang down: *Her hat was so big that it sagged over her eyes.*
sag (sag) *verb,* **sagged, sagging.**

sagebrush—A bushy plant with gray-green leaves and tiny yellow or white flowers. It grows in dry areas of western North America. It is Nevada's state flower.
sage|brush (sāj′brush′) *noun.*

saguaro—A giant cactus that grows in the southwestern United States. It has white flowers, and its fruit can be eaten. It is the state flower of Arizona.
sa|gua|ro (sə gwah′rō *or* sə wah′rō) *noun, plural* **saguaros.**

saguaro

said—See **say**.
    said (sed) *verb*.

sail—**1.** A piece of strong cloth that is attached to the mast of a boat. A sail catches the wind to make the boat move on the water.   **2.** The blade of a windmill or anything else that catches the wind.   **3.** A trip on a wind-powered boat: *He went for a* sail *across the bay*. *Noun*.
    —**1.** To travel in a wind-powered boat: *to* sail *around the lake*.   **2.** To travel on or across water: *The ship* sailed *around the world in record time*.   **3.** To glide; move easily and smoothly: *The bird* sailed *through the air*.   **4.** To operate a wind-powered boat: *She learned how to* sail *last summer*.   **5.** To start a trip over water: *My parents* sail *for the island tomorrow*. *Verb*.
    sail (sāl) *noun, plural* **sails**; *verb,* **sailed, sailing**.
    • A word that sounds the same is **sale**.

sailboard—A small, light, flat boat that looks like a surfboard but has a single mast with a triangular sail. It can carry only one or two people.
    sail|board (sāl′bawrd′) *noun, plural* **sailboards**.

sailboat—A boat that uses one or more sails in order to move through water.
    sail|boat (sāl′bōt) *noun, plural* **sailboats**.

sailfish—A large ocean fish related to the swordfish. It has a large fin on its back that looks like a sail.
    sail|fish (sāl′fish′) *noun, plural* **sailfish** or **sailfishes**.

sailor—A person who belongs to the crew of a boat or ship and who makes a living by sailing.
    sail|or (sāl′lər) *noun, plural* **sailors**.

saint—**1.** A very holy person.   **2.** A very kind person: *The youth director was so nice to the town's children that the parents all thought she was a* saint.
    saint (sānt) *noun, plural* **saints**. Abbreviation: **St.**

Saint Bernard—A very large working dog that has a large head and reddish brown and white fur. Originally bred in Switzerland, these dogs are good guides and watchdogs.
    Saint Ber|nard (sānt bər nahrd′) *noun, plural* **Saint Bernards**.

Saint Bernard

Word History

Saint Bernard comes from the monastery of Saint Bernard, in the Alps in Switzerland. A group of monks there first bred the dogs in the 1600's to rescue lost or injured people in the mountains.

Saint Patrick's Day—March 17, a holiday that honors Saint Patrick, the special saint of Ireland.
    Saint Pat|rick's Day (sānt **pat′**riks dā) *noun*.

Saint Valentine's Day—See **Valentine's Day**.
    Saint Val|en|tine's Day (sānt **val′**ən tīnz dā) *noun*.

sake—**1.** Reason; purpose: *He studied hard for the* sake *of improving his grades*.   **2.** Advantage; benefit: *I will repeat the names of the winners for the* sake *of everyone who arrived late*.
    sake (sāk) *noun, plural* **sakes**.

salad—A cold food made of lettuce and other vegetables that is usually served with a dressing. Sometimes fruit, meat, fish, or other foods are part of a salad.
    sal|ad (sal′əd) *noun, plural* **salads**.

salad bar—A counter in a restaurant where you make your own salad by helping yourself to the vegetables and dressings.
    sal|ad bar (sal′əd bahr′) *noun, plural* **salad bars**.

salamander—An animal that looks like a small lizard but is related to frogs and toads. It lives in ponds and streams or in cool, dark, moist places, such as caves.
    sal|a|man|der (sal′ə man′dər) *noun, plural* **salamanders**.

salary—A fixed amount of money that a person gets for doing a job on a regular schedule.
    sal|a|ry (sal′ə rē) *noun, plural* **salaries**.
    • Synonyms: **earnings, pay, wages**

a at	i if	oo look	ch chalk	a in ago
ā ape	ī idle	ou out	ng sing	e in happen
ah calm	o odd	u ugly	sh ship	ə = i in capital
aw all	ō oats	ū rule	th think	o in occur
e end	-oi oil	ur turn	th their	u in upon
ē easy			zh treasure	

Word History

Salary, sauce, and **sausage** all come from a Latin word meaning "salt." In ancient Rome, a salary was an amount of money paid to soldiers so that they could buy salt, which was very valuable. Sauces and sausages were both salted foods. Sauces were salted liquids that helped make other food taste better. Sausages were salted meats.

sale—**1.** A giving of something in return for money: *He planned to save half the money from the* sale *of his old bicycle and to spend the other half.* **2.** The selling of something for a lower price than it usually costs: *The store was having a* sale, *and I was able to buy two shirts for the price of one.*
sale (sāl) *noun, plural* **sales.**

• A word that sounds the same is **sail.**

salesperson—Someone whose job it is to sell.
sales|per|son (sālz′pur′sən) *noun, plural* **salespersons.**

saliva—A clear liquid made in the mouth by certain glands. It keeps the mouth wet and helps with chewing, swallowing, and digesting food.
sa|li|va (sə lī′və) *noun.*

salmon—**1.** A large food fish. Its meat is pink. **2.** A yellowish pink color. *Noun.*
—Having a yellowish pink color: *a* salmon *sweater. Adjective.*
salm|on (sam′ən) *noun, plural* **salmon** or **salmons;** *adjective.*

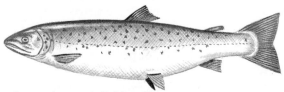

salmon (noun, definition 1)

salt—**1.** A white mineral found in the ground and in sea water. It is used for seasoning and preserving food. **2.** A chemical compound formed by the reaction of an acid with a base. *Noun.*
—Containing this white mineral: salt *water. Adjective.*
—To season or preserve with this white mineral: *He* salted *his potatoes. Verb.*
salt (sawlt) *noun, plural* **salts;** *adjective; verb,* **salted, salting.**

■ **with a grain of salt:** With some doubt or suspicion: *He tends to exaggerate, so we take his stories* with a grain of salt.
worth (one's) **salt:** Deserving of one's salary: *The carpenter did such a nice job that he was certainly* worth his salt.

• See Word History at **salary.**

saltwater—Having to do with or living in the sea: saltwater *fishing.*
salt|wa|ter (sawlt′wawt′ər *or* sawlt′wot′ər) *adjective.*

salty—Having or tasting of salt: salty *food.*
salt|y (sawl′tē) *adjective,* **saltier, saltiest.**

saluki—A medium-sized, slender hunting dog that has a short coat with fringe on the legs, tail, and ears. Originally bred in the Middle East in ancient times, these dogs hunt by sight.
sa|lu|ki (sə lū′kē) *noun, plural* **salukis.**

salutation—**1.** An expression of greeting: *I nodded as a* salutation *to my friend when he walked into the room.* **2.** A form of greeting at the beginning of a letter or speech, such as "Dear Sir or Madam" or "Ladies and Gentlemen."
sal|u|ta|tion (sal′yə tā′shən) *noun, plural* **salutations.**

salute—**1.** To raise the open right hand to the right side of the forehead as a gesture of honor and respect: *The soldiers* saluted *the officer.* **2.** To show such honor and respect by firing guns or cannons. **3.** To greet politely and with respect: *The crowd* saluted *the President by standing and applauding as he entered the auditorium. Verb.*
—An act of greeting or respect: *We put our hands over our hearts as a* salute *to the flag. Noun.*
sa|lute (sə lūt′) *verb,* **saluted, saluting;** *noun, plural* **salutes.**

salvage—The act of saving or rescuing something from a shipwreck, flood, fire, or other disaster: *The divers completed the* salvage *of the ship's sunken cargo. Noun.*
—To save or rescue something from a shipwreck, flood, fire, or other disaster: *We were not able to* salvage *the rugs from the flooded house. Verb.*
sal|vage (sal′vij) *noun; verb* **salvaged, salvaging.**

salvation—**1.** The act of saving from danger or evil: *The fire fighter's* salvation *of the people from the burning building was a mixture of courage, skill, and luck.* **2.** Someone or something that rescues or saves: *Lifeboats were*

the passenger's salvation *when the ship sank.*
sal|va|tion (sal vā′shən) *noun.*

salve—A soothing ointment used on wounded or sore skin.
salve (sav) *noun, plural* **salves.**

same—**1.** Being the exact one that was before; not a different one: *I think I will wear the* same *dress to the prom that I wore to my brother's wedding.* **2.** Exactly like something else: *She has the* same *way of walking as her friend.* **3.** Not altered or made different in any way; unchanged: *He is the* same *funny person he has always been. Adjective.*
—Someone or something that is exactly alike: *He ate cereal in the morning and more of the* same *later. Pronoun.*
same (sām) *adjective, pronoun.*

Samoyed—A medium-sized working dog with a long white coat, a thick tail that curves over the back, and small, pointed ears. Originally bred in northern Russia, these dogs are used to pull sleds and to guard herds of reindeer.
Sam|o|yed (sam′ə yed′) *noun, plural* **Samoyeds.**

Samoyed

sample—A part of something that shows what the rest is like: *a sample of an artist's work; a carpet sample. Noun.*
—To take a part of something to test, taste, or look at: *We sampled the new flavors of ice cream and chose the one we liked best. Verb.*
sam|ple (sam′pəl) *noun, plural* **samples;** *verb,* **sampled, sampling.**

sanctuary—**1.** An area where one or more kinds of animals are protected: *a wildlife* sanctuary. **2.** Protection, shelter; safety: *The wounded soldier found* sanctuary *from the battle behind a wall.*
sanc|tu|ar|y (sangk′chū ār′ē) *noun, plural* **sanctuaries.**
● Synonyms: **haven, refuge,** for **2.**

sand—Tiny grains of worn or crushed rock, found mainly on seashores and in deserts. *Noun.*
—**1.** To sprinkle or cover with these grains: *to* sand *an icy driveway.* **2.** To rub with these grains or with sandpaper in order to clean, smooth, or polish: *He* sanded *the rust off the old metal gate before painting it. Verb.*
sand (sand) *noun, plural* **sands;** *verb,* **sanded, sanding.**

sandal—A kind of shoe that is made up of a sole with straps to hold it to the foot.
san|dal (san′dəl) *noun, plural* **sandals.**

sandbag—A bag filled with sand. Sandbags are piled on one another as protection for soldiers in battle or as a barrier against flood waters.
sand|bag (sand′bag′) *noun, plural* **sandbags.**

sandbar—A hump of sand formed by tides or currents in a river or near a shore.
sand|bar (sand′bahr′) *noun, plural* **sandbars.**

sandbox—A low box filled with sand in which children can play.
sand|box (sand′boks′) *noun, plural* **sandboxes.**

sandpaper—A strong paper coated on one side with sand or a similar rough material. It is rubbed against surfaces such as wood or metal in order to clean, smooth, or polish them. *Noun.*
—To clean, smooth, or polish by rubbing with such paper. *Verb.*
sand|pa|per (sand′pā′pər) *noun; verb,* **sandpapered, sandpapering.**

sandpiper—A small brown or gray bird with a long, thin bill. It lives on sandy beaches.
sand|pi|per (sand′pī′pər) *noun, plural* **sandpipers.**

sandstone—A kind of rock that is made up of many grains of sand stuck together.
sand|stone (sand′stōn′) *noun.*

sandwich—Two or more slices of bread with a filling, such as meat or jam, between them. *Noun.*
—To fit or squeeze between things: *The chairs*

a at	i if	oo look	ch chalk		⌈a in ago
ā ape	ī idle	ou out	ng sing		e in happen
ah calm	o odd	u ugly	sh ship	ə =	i in capital
aw all	ō oats	ū rule	th think		o in occur
e end	oi oil	ur turn	th their		⌊u in upon
ē easy			zh treasure		

in the small room were sandwiched *between the wall and the table. Verb.*
sand|wich (**sand′**wich) *noun, plural* **sandwiches;** *verb,* **sandwiched, sandwiching.**

Word History

Sandwich comes from a man's name. The Earl of Sandwich, an English noble of the 1700's, was playing cards and grew hungry. He ordered a servant to bring him two slices of bread with a piece of roast meat between them.

---

sandy—**1.** Containing, made of, or covered with sand: *When the children came home from the beach, their clothes were* sandy. **2.** Having yellowish red color: *a cat with* sandy *fur.*
sand|y (**san′**dē) *adjective,* **sandier, sandiest.**

sane—**1.** Being healthy of mind; not crazy. **2.** Having or showing good judgment; reasonable: *It is* sane *to keep yourself healthy.*
sane (sān) *adjective,* **saner, sanest.**

sang—*See* **sing.**
sang (sang) *verb.*

sanitary—**1.** Having to do with health: *She explained how disease spread quickly in ancient cities, because of their poor* sanitary *conditions.* **2.** Free from dirt and germs; very clean: *The nurse put* sanitary *bandages on the man's wound.*
san|i|tar|y (**san′**ə tār′ē) *adjective.*

sanitation—The act or process of putting or keeping a thing or place in a clean condition in order to protect people's health. Getting rid of garbage and keeping food and water clean are part of sanitation.
san|i|ta|tion (san′ə tā′shən) *noun.*

sandpiper

sanity—Good health of mind.
san|i|ty (**san′**ə tē) *noun.*

sank—*See* **sink.**
sank (sangk) *verb.*

sap—A liquid made up of water and food that flows through a plant.
sap (sap) *noun, plural* **saps.**

sapling—A young tree.
sap|ling (**sap′**ling) *noun, plural* **saplings.**

sapphire—A bright blue precious stone that is very hard and valued as a gem.
sap|phire (**saf′**īr) *noun, plural* **sapphires.**

sarcasm—**1.** The act of making fun of someone by means of mocking, cutting remarks that say the opposite of what is really meant: *Her* sarcasm *in calling the bully "a big hero" made the other children laugh.* **2.** A mocking, cutting remark: *He never said a kind word about anyone but instead made one* sarcasm *after another.*
sar|casm (**sahr′**kaz əm) *noun, plural* **sarcasms.**

sarcastic—Using bitter, hurtful remarks that say the opposite of what one means in order to make fun of someone; taunting: *"My, you are up early!" was my brother's* sarcastic *greeting when I slept late.*
sar|cas|tic (sahr kas′tik) *adjective.*

sardine—A small saltwater fish that is used for food. Sardines are often sold in cans in which they are packed closely together in oil.
sar|dine (sahr dēn′) *noun, plural* **sardines** or **sardine.**

sash[1]—A long, wide strip of cloth worn around the waist like a belt or over one shoulder as a decoration, badge, or sign of rank.
sash (sash) *noun, plural* **sashes.**

sash[2]—The frame holding the pane or panes of glass in a window or door.
sash (sash) *noun, plural* **sashes.**

sassafras—A North American tree with sweet-smelling, yellow flowers. The bark of its roots is used to make a flavoring for soft drinks, tea, and candy.
sas|sa|fras (**sas′**ə fras) *noun, plural* **sassafrases.**

sat—*See* **sit.**
sat (sat) *verb.*

Sat.—The abbreviation for **Saturday.**

Satan—The evil one; the Devil. Satan is the greatest enemy of God and of people, in Jewish and Christian beliefs.
Sa|tan (**sā′**tən) *noun.*

satellite—**1.** A natural object in space that orbits a planet; moon. **2.** An artificially made object that is launched from the earth and orbits the

earth, the moon, or another body in space: *a weather* satellite; *a communications* satellite. **3.** A country that depends on and is controlled by another country that is more powerful.
sat|el|lite (sat′ə līt) *noun, plural* **satellites.**

satin—A cloth that is very smooth and shiny on one side. It is made of such fabrics as silk, cotton, nylon, and rayon.
sat|in (sat′ən) *noun, plural* **satins.**

satisfaction—**1.** The act or way of meeting a need or wish: *Having his story published in the school newspaper was the* satisfaction *of his dream.* **2.** The state of being contented or pleased: *We felt* satisfaction *at seeing our paintings hung up on the bulletin board.*
sat|is|fac|tion (sat′is fak′shən) *noun.*

satisfy—**1.** To meet or fill a need or wish: *The drink of cool water* satisfied *his thirst.* **2.** To please: *She was very* satisfied *with her new bicycle.* **3.** To convince: *The dog's gentleness soon* satisfied *the boy that it would not bite.*
sat|is|fy (sat′is fī) *verb,* **satisfied, satisfying.**

saturate—To soak all through; fill completely: *The towel was* saturated *with water when it fell into the bathtub.*
sat|u|rate (sach′ə rāt) *verb,* **saturated, saturating.**

Saturday—The seventh and last day of the week.
Sat|ur|day (sat′ər dē *or* sat′ər dā′) *noun, plural* **Saturdays.** Abbreviation: **Sat.**

Word History

Saturday is named for the Roman god of planting and harvest, Saturn. It is the only day named for a Roman god.

Saturn—The second largest planet and the sixth farthest from the sun. Saturn has many large rings around it, which are made up of pieces of ice.
Sat|urn (sat′ərn) *noun.*
 • See Word History at **Saturday.**

sauce—A liquid, which may be thin or thick, that is served with a certain food because the two

flavors taste good together: *a cheese* sauce *on vegetables; ice cream with chocolate* sauce.
sauce (saws) *noun, plural* **sauces.**
 • See Word History at **salary.**

saucer—A small, shallow dish on which a cup is placed.
sau|cer (saw′sər) *noun, plural* **saucers.**

sauna—**1.** A steam bath, usually in a small room. The steam is made by putting water on hot rocks. **2.** The room for such a bath.
sau|na (saw′nah *or* sou′nah) *noun, plural* **saunas.**

sausage—Ground meat mixed with spices. It is usually stuffed into a thin, tube-shaped skin. Hot dogs are a kind of sausage.
sau|sage (saw′sij) *noun, plural* **sausages.**
 • See Word History at **salary.**

savage—**1.** Fierce; cruel: *a* savage *attack.* **2.** Wild; untamed: *the* savage *beasts of the jungle. Adjective.*
—**1.** A person belonging to a society that is not highly developed or civilized. **2.** A person who is cruel and brutal. *Noun.*
sav|age (sav′ij) *adjective; noun, plural* **savages.**
 • Synonyms: **ferocious, vicious,** for *adjective* 1.

save—**1.** To keep someone or something from harm, danger, or loss; make safe; rescue: *The soft grass* saved *the boy from being hurt when he fell.* **2.** To put aside something to be used later: *He* saved *his money until he had enough to buy the book he wanted.* **3.** To keep from spending or wasting something; preserve: *The runner rested in the morning to* save *her energy for the race in the afternoon.* **4.** To prevent having expense or waste: *Turning off lights when no one is using them helps our family to* save *on our electric bill.*
save (sāv) *verb,* **saved, saving.**

savior—Someone who keeps someone or something from harm or who rescues: *That police officer received a medal as the* savior *of the girl who had fallen into the river.*
sav|ior (sāv′yər) *noun, plural* **saviors.**

saw¹—A tool or machine with a thin, metal blade that has sharp teeth on one edge. A saw is used for cutting hard materials, such as wood or metal. *Noun.*
—To cut or be cut with such a tool or machine: *to* saw *through a pipe; wood that will* saw *easily. Verb.*
saw (saw) *noun, plural* **saws;** *verb,* **sawed, sawed** or **sawn, sawing.**

saw²—*See* **see.**
saw (saw) *verb.*

a at	**i** if	**oo** look	**ch** chalk		a in ago
ā ape	**ī** idle	**ou** out	**ng** sing		e in happen
ah calm	**o** odd	**u** ugly	**sh** ship	ə =	i in capital
aw all	**ō** oats	**ū** rule	**th** think		o in occur
e end	**oi** oil	**ur** turn	**th** their		u in upon
ē easy			**zh** treasure		

sawdust—Tiny specks of wood that result when a piece of wood is sawed.
saw|dust (saw′dust′) *noun.*

sawhorse—A framework on which a board is held so that it can be sawed.
saw|horse (saw′hawrs′) *noun, plural* **sawhorses.**

sawmill—A place where logs are cut into lumber by machines.
saw|mill (saw′mill′) *noun, plural* **sawmills.**

saxophone—A musical instrument made of brass, with a curved shape and a wide opening. It has a reed in its mouthpiece.
sax|o|phone (sak′sə fōn) *noun, plural* **saxophones.**

saxophone

say—1. To speak; utter words: *He was so surprised that he could not* say *a thing.* 2. To make a statement in words; express; declare: *The radio announcer* said *that it would rain today. Verb.*
—1. A chance to speak: *You can have your* say *when I have finished talking.* 2. The right or power to help decide something: *The children had a* say *in where their class picnic would be held. Noun.*
say (sā) *verb,* **said, saying;** *noun.*

saying—A well-known statement that people value for its truth or wisdom; proverb. "One good turn deserves another" is a saying.
say|ing (sā′ing) *noun, plural* **sayings.**

scab—The crust that forms on the skin where a sore or cut is healing.
scab (skab) *noun, plural* **scabs.**

scaffold—A temporary platform built to hold workers and equipment during the repair or construction of a building.
scaf|fold (skaf′əld) *noun, plural* **scaffolds.**

scald—1. To burn with very hot liquid or steam: *The cook* scalded *his hand when he spilled hot*

gravy on it. 2. To heat almost to boiling: *The recipe says to* scald *the milk.*
scald (skawld) *verb,* **scalded, scalding.**

scale¹—One of the hard, thin plates that cover the bodies of fish, snakes, and lizards. *Noun.*
—To remove these hard, thin plates: *This knife has an edge made for* scaling *fish. Verb.*
scale (skāl) *noun, plural* **scales;** *verb,* **scaled, scaling.**

scale²—An instrument for finding the weight of something.
scale (skāl) *noun, plural* **scales.**
• See picture at **balance.**

scale³—1. A series of degrees or steps: *a* scale *of 1 to 10; the Celsius* scale *for measuring temperature; a pay* scale. 2. A series of marks placed at equal distances along a line to indicate measurement: *My wooden ruler has two different* scales, *one in inches and the other in centimeters.* 3. The size of a likeness compared with the size of the original; proportion: *The* scale *of the map to the land is 1 to 100,000.* 4. The relative size or extent of something: *The show was done on a large* scale *and had many singers and dancers.* 5. A series of musical tones that go up or down in order of pitch: *to play a* scale *on a piano. Noun.*
—1. To increase or decrease by a certain amount: *The school had to* scale *down its spending on gym equipment by 10 percent.* 2. To climb over or to the top of something: *I* scaled *five flights of stairs, because I got tired of waiting for the elevator. Verb.*
scale (skāl) *noun, plural* **scales;** *verb,* **scaled, scaling.**
• For *noun* 2, see picture at **inch.**

scallop—1. A shellfish somewhat like a clam. It has a fan-shaped shell and a soft body that is good to eat. 2. One of a series of curves, like those of a scallop shell, along an edge: *The dress has* scallops *on the cuffs. Noun.*
—To shape with a series of curves: *The hem of her skirt was* scalloped. *Verb.*
scal|lop (skol′əp *or* skal′əp) *noun, plural* **scallops;** *verb.* **scalloped, scalloping.**

scalp—The skin on top of the head. It is usually covered with hair. *Noun.*
—To cut the hair and skin from the top of the head. *Verb.*
scalp (skalp) *noun, plural* **scalps;** *verb,* **scalped, scalping.**

scan—1. To examine carefully: *He* scanned *the living room to try to find the key he dropped.* 2. To read hastily; look with just a glance: *I think*

I know how to play this game even though I only scanned *the instructions.*
scan (skan) *verb,* **scanned, scanning.**

scandal—**1.** A disgraceful situation that brings shame on those involved, while shocking or offending others: *There was a* scandal *in the school about pupils stealing the answers to tests.* **2.** Talk or gossip that hurts a reputation: *The* scandal *about her turned out to be a mean lie and she was put back on the team.*
scan|dal (skan′dəl) *noun, plural* **scandals.**

scanty—Barely enough; small in size or quantity; scarce: *Her* scanty *lunch left her hungry.*
scant|y (skan′tē) *adjective,* **scantier, scantiest.**

scar—**1.** The mark that remains on the skin after an injury has healed: *The burn left a* scar *on her leg.* **2.** Any mark left by damage: *The wooden floor was covered with* scars *from people walking on it. Noun.*
—To make or cause a damaging mark: *She* scarred *the table when she dropped a box on it. Verb.*
scar (skahr) *noun, plural* **scars;** *verb,* **scarred, scarring.**

scarce—**1.** Not enough to meet a need; scanty: *Water was* scarce *during the drought.* **2.** Hard to find or get; rare: *Those stamps are valuable, because they are so* scarce.
scarce (skārs) *adjective.*

■ **scarce as hen's teeth:** Extremely rare; next to impossible to find: *The parts I need to fix the old radio are as* scarce as hen's teeth.

scarcely—**1.** Almost not at all; barely: *There is so little salt on this popcorn that I can* scarcely *taste it.* **2.** Surely not; very probably not: *One can* scarcely *say that she deserved to lose after she tried so hard.*
scarce|ly (skārs′lē) *adverb.*

scare—**1.** To frighten or be frightened: *a movie that* scares *you; a timid person who* scares *easily.* **2.** To drive away by startling: *The loud alarm* scared *the burglar off. Verb.*
—**1.** A sudden fright: *The noise from that bag popping gave me a* scare. **2.** A condition of fear or panic: *The town had a* scare *that the dam would burst during the heavy rains. Noun.*
scare (skār) *verb,* **scared, scaring;** *noun, plural* **scares.**

■ **scare up:** To get or find, often with some effort: *The campers* scared up *some wood for their fire.*

scarecrow—A figure that looks like a person and is dressed in old clothes. A scarecrow is put out in a field to scare crows and other birds away from crops.
scare|crow (skār′krō′) *noun, plural* **scarecrows.**

scarecrow

scarf—A long piece of material made to be wrapped about the head or neck, for warmth or as decoration.
scarf (skahrf) *noun, plural* **scarfs** or **scarves.**

scarlet—A very bright red color. *Noun.*
—Having a bright red color: *a* scarlet *notebook. Adjective.*
scar|let (skahr′lit) *noun, adjective.*

scarlet tanager—A bird of the eastern part of North America. The male has a scarlet body and black wings and tail.
scar|let tan|a|ger (skahr′lit tan′ə jər) *noun, plural* **scarlet tanagers.**

a at	i if	oo look	ch chalk	⌈ a in ago
ā ape	ī idle	ou out	ng sing	e in happen
ah calm	o odd	u ugly	sh ship	ə = i in capital
aw all	ō oats	ū rule	th think	o in occur
e end	oi oil	ur turn	th their	⌊ u in upon
ē easy			zh treasure	

scarlet tanager

scatter—1. To throw here and there: *The man scattered seed on the ground for the birds and squirrels.*   2. To go in various directions: *The horses scattered all over the farm when the gate blew open.*
scat|ter (skat′ər) *verb*, **scattered, scattering.**

scene—1. The time and place of a story: *The scene is a city 100 years ago.*   2. The place where something happens: *the scene of the crime; the scene of their first meeting.*   3. A part of a play or movie: *If we hurry, we might not miss any of the first scene.*   4. A view; sight: *The picture showed a scene of the mountains.*   5. A show of bad temper in view of other people: *The customer started to shout and cause a scene, because he was angry at having to wait in line.*
scene (sēn) *noun, plural* **scenes.**
■ **behind the scenes:** Out of view of the public; privately: *Many discussions west on behind the scenes before the leaders of the two countries were ready to sign the treaty.*
● A word that sounds the same is **seen.**

scenery—1. The overall appearance of a place; landscape of an area outdoors: *The scenery along the lake is spectacular!*   2. All the furnishings and structures that are used for a staged or filmed performance and that show the settings of the story: *The scenery for the school play was so well done that it was easy to believe the action was taking place in a forest.*
scen|er|y (sē′nər ē) *noun, plural* **sceneries.**

scenic—Having or having to do with beautiful natural scenery: *a scenic view; scenic countryside.*
sce|nic (sē′nik) *adjective*.

scent—1. A smell, especially a distinct, pleasing one: *the scent of flowers; the scent of perfume.*   2. The sense of smell: *Dogs have a much keener scent than people do.*   3. The tracks or trail by which something can be found: *The cat acts as if it is on the scent of that mouse.*
scent (sent) *noun, plural* **scents.**
● Words that sound the same are **cent** and **sent.**
● Synonyms: **aroma, fragrance, odor,** for **1.**

schedule—1. A list of times for events or appointments: *According to the schedule, the relay race will begin at one o'clock.*   2. The time that has been set for something to occur: *Even though the traffic was heavy, we made it to the beginning of the football game right on schedule. Noun.*
—To plan for a certain day or time: *We*

scheduled *the talent show for next weekend. Verb.*
sched|ule (skej′ool) *noun, plural* **schedules;** *verb,* **scheduled, scheduling.**

scheme—1. A plan of action: *She has a scheme for starting her own newspaper.*   2. A system or arrangement of related things; design: *The office was done in a brown and yellow color scheme. Noun.*
—To plan slyly: *He schemed to make it look as if his brother broke the vase. Verb.*
scheme (skēm) *noun, plural* **schemes;** *verb,* **schemed, scheming.**
● Synonyms: **conspire, plot,** for *verb.*

schipperke—A small dog with a thick black coat and small pointed ears. Originally bred in Belgium, these dogs make good watchdogs.
schip|per|ke (skip′ər kē) *noun, plural* **schipperkes.**

schipperke

scholar—1. A person with a great deal of knowledge, especially in a certain subject: *Our teacher invited an astronomy scholar to talk to our class about the stars.*   2. A pupil; student.
schol|ar (skol′ər) *noun, plural* **scholars.**

Word History

Scholar comes from a Greek word meaning ''leisure.'' To be a true scholar, a person must have time free from other work, in which to study. The Greek word was later used to mean ''discussion.'' Talking with others about what one has studied is an important part of learning. **School**[1] comes from this same Greek word.

scholarship—1. Money given to help a student continue his or her schooling: *I was given a scholarship to go to a special class on computers.*   2. Knowledge obtained through

study; learning: *This research paper shows the writer's fine* scholarship.
schol|ar|ship (skol′ər ship) *noun, plural* **scholarships.**

school¹—**1.** A place where students learn from teachers. **2.** Learning in such a place; instruction: *He thinks* school *is hard this year.* **3.** The period of time spent in such a place: *My sister and I feed the animals every morning before* school. **4.** A department within a college or university for learning and teaching a certain subject: *law* school. *Noun.*
—To educate: *The teacher* schooled *the students in watercolor painting. Verb.*
school (skūl) *noun, plural* **schools;** *verb,* **schooled, schooling.**
● See Word History at **scholar.**

school²—A large number of fish or other water animals swimming together: *a* school *of tuna.*
school (skūl) *noun, plural* **schools.**

schooner—A ship with at least two masts and sails that are set lengthwise.
schoon|er (skū′nər) *noun, plural* **schooners.**

schooner

schwa—The symbol that looks like this ə and is used to stand for a vowel sound such as *a* in "ago," *e* in "happen," or *u* in "upon."
schwa (shwah) *noun, plural* **schwas.**

science—**1.** Knowledge or studies based on facts learned by careful testing, observing, and experimenting. **2.** A particular kind of such knowledge or studies, such as biology or chemistry.
sci|ence (sī′əns) *noun, plural* **sciences.**

science fiction—A type of story that combines scientific facts with ideas that are clearly made up: science fiction *about rockets to the stars.*
sci|ence fic|tion (sī′əns fik′shən) *noun.*

scientific—Based on or done according to the facts or methods of science: *a scientific experiment.*
sci|en|tif|ic (sī′ən tif′ik) *adjective.*

scientist—A person who is an expert in one kind of science.
sci|en|tist (sī′ən tist) *noun, plural* **scientists.**

scissors—A cutting tool with two sharp blades that close against each other.
scis|sors (siz′ərz) *plural noun.*

scold—To tell someone angrily what he or she has done wrong: *The guard* scolded *the boy for trying to bring his dog into the museum.*
scold (skōld) *verb,* **scolded, scolding.**

scoop—**1.** A tool that looks like a small shovel and is used to dip into and pick up substances: *The man used a* scoop *to get the ice cream out of its box.* **2.** The amount taken up by a dipping tool: *I put three* scoops *of gravel in the fish tank.* **3.** The part of a steam shovel that lifts out sand, coal, dirt, and similar substances. *Noun.*
—**1.** To lift up and take out with or as if with a dipping tool: *Please* scoop *the flour out of the bag.* **2.** To dig out a space; excavate: *The steam shovel* scooped *a hole in the ground. Verb.*
scoop (skūp) *noun, plural* **scoops;** *verb,* **scooped, scooping.**

scooter—A small vehicle made of a narrow two-wheeled board and a long handle bar. The rider stands on the board, steers with the handle bar, and moves by pushing one foot against the ground.
scoot|er (skū′tər) *noun, plural* **scooters.**

scope—The range of one's understanding or ability: *That difficult book was beyond my* scope.
scope (skōp) *noun.*

scorch—**1.** To burn the surface of; singe: *He* scorched *the kitchen counter by putting a hot pan on it.* **2.** To dry up because of heat: *The sun has* scorched *all the flowers in our yard. Verb.*
—A slight burn: *The fallen candle left a* scorch *on the table. Noun.*
scorch (skawrch) *verb,* **scorched, scorching;** *noun, plural* **scorches.**

a at	i if	oo look	ch chalk		a in ago
ā ape	ī idle	ou out	ng sing		e in happen
ah calm	o odd	u ugly	sh ship	ə =	i in capital
aw all	ō oats	ū rule	th think		o in occur
e end	oi oil	ur turn	th their		u in upon
ē easy			zh treasure		

score—1. The number of points made in a game, contest, or test: *The* score *stood four to two, with just one inning left to play.* 2. A group of twenty: *four* score *and seven years.* 3. A written piece of music that shows all the parts for the different instruments or voices. 4. A debt or grudge: *The criminal felt he had a* score *to settle with the policeman who caught him. Noun.*
—1. To gain points in a game, contest, or test: *He* scored *80 points on the spelling test.* 2. To keep track of or write down these points: *Our spelling tests were* scored *before we went home.* 3. To win; achieve: *The team* scored *a victory. Verb.*
score (skawr) *noun, plural* **scores;** *verb,* **scored, scoring.**

scorn—To consider or treat as low and worthless: *We* scorned *their idea of leaving the trash in the woods. Verb.*
—A feeling that someone or something is low and worthless: *He felt* scorn *for the team that cheated. Noun.*
scorn (skawrn) *verb,* **scorned, scorning;** *noun.*

scorpion—An eight-legged animal that is related to the spider and has a poisonous stinger at the end of its long tail.
scor|pi|on (skawr′pē ən) *noun, plural* **scorpions.**

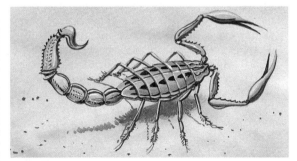

scorpion

Scottish deerhound—A large hunting dog with a long body and narrow legs. Originally bred in Scotland, these dogs run very fast.
Scot|tish deer|hound (skot′ish dēr′hound′) *noun, plural* **Scottish deerhounds.**

Scottish terrier—A small dog with a long, thick coat, small pointed ears, and short legs. Its bushy eyebrows and beard make it look as though it has a long, square face. Originally bred in Scotland, these dogs were used for hunting.
Scot|tish ter|ri|er (skot′ish ter′ē ər) *noun, plural* **Scottish terriers.**

scout—1. Someone sent out to get and bring back information: *an army* scout. 2. A person belonging to the Boy Scouts or Girl Scouts. *Noun.*
—To look at in order to bring back information: *The airplane pilot* scouted *the ocean for enemy ships. Verb.*
scout (skout) *noun, plural* **scouts;** *verb,* **scouted, scouting.**

scoutmaster—The adult leader of a group of Boy Scouts.
scout|mas|ter (skout′mas′tər) *noun, plural* **scoutmasters.**

scowl—To frown angrily: *Our father* scowled *when he saw the mess we left in the kitchen. Verb.*
—An angry frown: *The bus driver wore a* scowl *after he got a speeding ticket. Noun.*
scowl (skoul) *verb,* **scowled, scowling;** *noun, plural* **scowls.**

scramble—1. To climb or move along quickly: *The boys* scrambled *over the fence when the large dog appeared.* 2. To struggle or compete for something: *The puppies* scrambled *for the bone.* 3. To jumble or mix together in a confused manner: *to* scramble *pieces of a puzzle.* 4. To cook eggs with the yolks and whites mixed together. *Verb.*
—1. A quick and difficult climb: *Her team won the* scramble *up the hill.* 2. A struggle for something: *There was a* scramble *for the seat next to the window. Noun.*
scram|ble (skram′bəl) *verb,* **scrambled, scrambling;** *noun, plural* **scrambles.**

scrap—1. A little piece of something: *She used a* scrap *of paper as a bookmark.* 2. Old, worn metal or other material that has been thrown away but is collected to be reused: *Mother used the old dresses as* scrap *for a blanket.* 3. **scraps:**

Scottish terrier

Leftover pieces of food or other matter. *Noun.*
—**1.** To toss aside something as useless: *They had to* scrap *their plans to go to the concert because the car would not start.* **2.** To break into small pieces or fragments: *The junk dealer* scrapped *old cars and sold the metal. Verb.*
scrap (skrap) *noun, plural* **scraps;** *verb,* **scrapped, scrapping.**

scrapbook—A book with empty pages on which to put pictures and clippings.
scrap|book (skrap′book′) *noun, plural* **scrapbooks.**

scrape—**1.** To rub a surface with something in order to clean or smooth it: *to* scrape *the paint off the house.* **2.** To injure or damage by rubbing against something rough or sharp: *She* scraped *her hand as she climbed over the rocks.* **3.** To rub or drag with a harsh noise: *The boy* scraped *the chalk across the blackboard.* **4.** To gather in small amounts and with great difficulty: *It took him a year to* scrape *up enough money to buy a bicycle. Verb.*
—**1.** A scratch: *The cat put some* scrapes *on the chair with its claws.* **2.** A harsh noise: *the* scrape *of metal over gravel.* **3.** A difficult position: *The girls were in a* scrape *when they missed the last bus. Noun.*
scrape (skrāp) *verb,* **scraped, scraping;** *noun, plural* **scrapes.**

scrappy—Liking or eager to fight or argue: *He gets* scrappy *when someone teases him.*
scrap|py (skrap′ē) *adjective,* **scrappier, scrappiest.**

scratch—**1.** To make a mark or cut with something sharp: *He* scratched *his initials on a tree.* **2.** To rub in order to stop an itch: *to* scratch *an insect bite.* **3.** To scrape or damage with the nails or claws: *The kitten* scratched *my hand.* **4.** To cross out or cancel: *The astronauts* scratched *today's launch and will try again tomorrow. Verb.*
—**1.** A mark or injury made by something sharp: *He got* scratches *on his arm from the thorns.* **2.** A scraping noise: *We heard the* scratch *of the puppy at the door. Noun.*
scratch (skrach) *verb,* **scratched, scratching;** *noun, plural* **scratches.**

■ **from scratch:** From the beginning: *The piano teacher told me to start* from scratch *and play the whole song again.*

scrawny—Very thin; skinny: *The* scrawny *dog looked as though it hadn't eaten in a week.*
scraw|ny (skraw′nē) *adjective,* **scrawnier, scrawniest.**
• Synonyms: **gaunt, lean², spare**
Antonyms: **fat, plump, stout**

scream—To make a loud, sharp cry or sound: *He* screamed *when his sister jumped out from behind the bushes. Verb.*
—A loud, sharp cry or sound: *The fans let out a* scream *when they saw the singer. Noun.*
scream (skrēm) *verb,* **screamed, screaming;** *noun, plural* **screams.**
• Synonyms: For *verb,* see Synonyms at **cry,** *verb* **2.**
Antonyms: **mumble, mutter, whisper,** for *verb.*

screech—To make a high-pitched, harsh cry or sound: *the train* screeching *to a stop. Verb.*
—A high-pitched, harsh cry or sound: *the* screech *of a truck's brakes. Noun.*
screech (skrēch) *verb,* **screeched, screeching;** *noun, plural* **screeches.**

screen—**1.** A covered, movable frame that protects, separates or hides: *The nurse put a* screen *between the two beds.* **2.** Something that separates or hides: *You cannot see the lake from the road because of a* screen *of trees.* **3.** Wire netting enclosed in a frame: *a window* screen. **4.** A flat surface on which to show movies or slides. **5.** A flat surface on which a television picture or computer information appears. *Noun.*
—**1.** To cover or hide with or as if with a screen: *She* screened *her eyes from the light with her hand.* **2.** To filter with or as if with a screen: *He* screened *the muddy water to get out some of the big pieces of dirt. Verb.*
screen (skrēn) *noun, plural* **screens;** *verb,* **screened, screening.**
• Synonyms: **sift, strain,** for *verb* **2.**

screw—A long, thin piece of metal with ridges and grooves that go around it. When it is turned, it goes into things and fastens them together. *Noun.*
—**1.** To fasten with such a metal piece: *The carpenter* screwed *the shelf into the wall.* **2.** To twist into place: *She* screwed *the cap on the tube of toothpaste. Verb.*
screw (skrū) *noun, plural* **screws;** *verb,* **screwed, screwing.**

a at	i if	oo look	ch chalk		ə =	a in ago
ā ape	ī idle	ou out	ng sing			e in happen
ah calm	o odd	u ugly	sh ship			i in capital
aw all	ō oats	ū rule	th think			o in occur
e end	oi oil	ur turn	th their			u in upon
ē easy			zh treasure			

screw (noun)

machine screw

wood screw

screwdriver—A tool used to turn a screw.
screw|driv|er (skrū′drī′vər) *noun, plural*
screwdrivers.

scribble—To write or draw carelessly, as when in great haste: *to scribble the answer to the question as the bell rings. Verb.*
—Careless or hasty writing or drawing: *I cannot read his scribbles. Noun.*
scrib|ble (skrib′əl) *verb,* **scribbled, scribbling;**
noun, plural **scribbles.**

scrimmage—1. In football, all the action that takes place between the two teams after each snap of the ball. 2. A practice game between two teams. *Noun.*
—To take part in a practice game. *Verb.*
scrim|mage (skrim′ij) *noun, plural* **scrimmages;**
verb, **scrimmaged, scrimmaging.**

script—1. The style of handwriting in which all the letters are joined together and not printed individually. 2. A written copy of the words spoken in a movie, play, or television or radio show: *The director gave the actors a week to memorize the* script.
script (skript) *noun, plural* **scripts.**

Scripture—The Bible or particular words from it: *to quote* Scripture.
Scrip|ture (skrip′chər) *noun, plural* **Scriptures.**

scroll—1. A roll of paper or parchment with writing on it. 2. A design that looks like a loosely rolled sheet of paper.
scroll (skrōl) *noun, plural* **scrolls.**

scroll (definition 1)

scrub—To clean by rubbing or brushing hard: *Father* scrubs *vegetables before he cooks them. Verb.*
—The act of rubbing or brushing hard: *to give the floors a* scrub. *Noun.*
scrub (skrub) *verb,* **scrubbed, scrubbing;** *noun,*
plural **scrubs.**

scruff—The skin on the back of the neck: *A mother cat carries its kittens by the* scruff *of their necks.*
scruff (skruf) *noun, plural* **scruffs.**

scuba—Equipment worn by divers for breathing while swimming underwater.
scu|ba (skū′bə) *noun.*
● See picture at **aqualung.**

Word History

Scuba comes from the first letters of several words that describe this equipment: self-contained underwater breathing apparatus. It is self-contained because the diver carries a breathing tank and is not linked to any other source of air.

---

scuffle—To fight in a confused, disorderly way: *The guard* scuffled *with the man who tried to push past the gate. Verb.*
—A confused and disorderly fight: *The boys got into a* scuffle *over who won the game. Noun.*
scuf|fle (skuf′əl) *verb,* **scuffled, scuffling;**
noun, plural **scuffles.**

sculptor—An artist who carves or molds figures out of stone, wood, clay, or other material.
sculp|tor (skulp′tər) *noun, plural* **sculptors.**

sculpture—1. The art of carving or molding figures out of stone, wood, clay, or other material. 2. A figure made in this way: *Three of her* sculptures *are in the art gallery. Noun.*
—To carve or mold figures: *to* sculpture *a figure out of snow. Verb.*
sculp|ture (skulp′chər) *noun, plural* **sculptures;**
verb, **sculptured, sculpturing.**

scurry—To hurry; move quickly: *We had to* scurry *to catch the train.*
scur|ry (skur′ē) *verb,* **scurried, scurrying.**

scurvy—A disease caused by too little of a substance called vitamin C in the body. Its symptoms are spongy, bleeding gums and a lack of strength or energy.
scur|vy (skur′vē) *noun.*

scythe—A cutting tool with a long, curved blade

attached to a long handle. It is used for cutting
tall grass and reaping grain.

scythe (sīth) *noun, plural* **scythes.**

• See picture at **sickle.**

S.E.—The abbreviation for southeast.

sea—**1.** The large body of salt water that covers
most of the earth; ocean: *a ship at* sea. **2.** Any
large body of salt water that has some land
around it: *the Red* Sea; *the Black* Sea. **3.** A
large ocean wave and its movement: *The seas
rocked our small ship.*

sea (sē) *noun, plural* **seas.**

• Words that sound the same are **c** and **see.**

seafood—Fish and shellfish from the sea that are
used as food.

sea|food (sē′fūd′) *noun, plural* **seafoods.**

sea gull—A large bird living near the sea, with
gray and white feathers, long wings, a hooked
beak, and webbed feet.

sea gull (sē gul) *noun, plural* **sea gulls.**

• See picture at **gull.**

seahorse—A small sea fish with a head similar
to that of a horse and a long, curving tail that is
used to grasp and hold onto underwater plants.

seahorse (sē′hawrs′) *noun, plural* **seahorses.**

seahorse

seal¹—**1.** A raised design of initials or the like
that is stamped on wax, paper, or other soft
material to show authority or genuineness: *When
the governor put his* seal *on the document, it
became law.* **2.** Something that closes another
thing firmly: *the* seal *on a bottle.* **3.** A special

paper sticker for decorating an envelope or
package: *Easter* seals. *Noun.*
—**1.** To place a mark to authorize or show the
genuineness of something: *The jewelry dealer
signed and* sealed *the certificate proving the
value of the jewel.* **2.** To close something firmly:
My lips are sealed *on that matter.* **3.** To make a
sign showing that something has been decided or
guaranteed: *We* sealed *our agreement by shaking
hands. Verb.*

seal (sēl) *noun, plural* **seals;** *verb,* **sealed,
sealing.**

seal²—A large sea animal with thick fur and
whiskers on its face. Instead of arms and legs, it
has flippers, which make it a fast swimmer. It
lives mainly in cold climates.

seal (sēl) *noun, plural* **seals** or **seal.**

seal²

sea level—The level of the surface of the ocean,
especially midway between high tide and low
tide. This level is used to measure the height of
things on land and under water.

sea lev|el (sē lev′əl) *noun.*

sea lion—A large type of seal with small ears
that lives in the Pacific Ocean.

sea li|on (sē lī′ən) *noun, plural* **sea lions.**

Sealyham terrier—A small dog with a thick,
wiry, white coat, drooping ears, bushy eyebrows,
and a short beard. Originally bred in Wales,
these dogs were used for hunting small animals.

Sea|ly|ham ter|ri|er (sē′lē ham′ ter′ē ər)
noun, plural **Sealyham terriers.**

seam—**1.** A line or fold that is made by joining
two pieces of cloth together near or at their
edges, as by sewing: *The* seams *of his blue jeans
are pulling apart.* **2.** Any line that is made by
joining things: *the* seam *where two pipes
connect. Noun.*
—To make a line or fold by joining things: *They*

a at	i if	oo look	ch chalk		a in ago
ā ape	ī idle	ou out	ng sing		e in happen
ah calm	o odd	u ugly	sh ship	ə =	i in capital
aw all	ō oats	ū rule	th think		o in occur
e end	oi oil	ur turn	th their		u in upon
ē easy			zh treasure		

seamed *three sets of curtains for the living room. Verb.*

seam (sēm) *noun, plural* **seams;** *verb,* **seamed, seaming.**

• A word that sounds the same is **seem.**

seaman—1. A person who sails a ship or is a member of a ship's crew. 2. A sailor of the lowest rank in the United States Navy.
sea|man (sē′mən) *noun, plural* **seamen.**

seamstress—A woman who earns a living by sewing.
seam|stress (sēm′stris) *noun, plural* **seamstresses.**

seaplane—An airplane that is especially made to land on and take off from water.
sea|plane (sē′plān′) *noun, plural* **seaplanes.**

seaplane

seaport—1. A harbor used by ships. 2. A town or city with a harbor.
sea|port (sē′pawrt′) *noun, plural* **seaports.**

search—To seek, go over, or look through carefully: *The children* searched *through the magazines for pictures of wild animals. Verb.*
—An act of seeking, going over, or looking through carefully: *the* search *for gold. Noun.*
search (surch) *noun, plural* **searches.**

■ **search me:** I cannot answer you; I do not

Sealyham terrier

know: *When I asked the man where the library was, he said, "Search me, I don't live here."*

searchlight—A device for giving off a very powerful, bright beam of light: *At night, the runway of the airport is lit by* searchlights.
search|light (surch′līt′) *noun, plural* **searchlights.**

seashell—The shell from a sea animal, such as a clam or oyster.
sea|shell (sē′shel′) *noun, plural* **seashells.**

seashore—The edge of a piece of land next to a sea; coast.
sea|shore (sē′shawr′) *noun, plural* **seashores.**

seasick—Feeling dizzy and sick from the rolling movements of a ship on water.
sea|sick (sē′sik′) *adjective.*

season—1. One of the four parts into which the year is divided: spring, summer, fall, or winter. 2. A certain part of the year that has some special meaning or event: *the Christmas* season; *the baseball* season. *Noun.*
—To add spices or flavoring to food so that it will taste better: *The chef* seasoned *the stew with pepper. Verb.*
sea|son (sē′zən) *noun, plural* **seasons;** *verb,* **seasoned, seasoning.**

Word History

Season comes from a Latin word meaning "to plant." Each season, crops are planted. The type of crop that is planted depends on the season and the weather it brings.

---

seasonal—Happening in or depending on a certain time of year: *Skiing is a* seasonal *sport.*
sea|son|al (sē′zə nəl) *adjective.*

seasoning—Spices or flavoring that can be added to food so that it tastes better.
sea|son|ing (sē′zə ning) *noun, plural* **seasonings.**

seat[1]—1. Something on which to sit, such as a chair or bench. 2. A place to sit: *Please take your* seat *because class is going to start.* 3. The part of clothing or of the body on which a person sits: *She tore the* seat *of her pants when she climbed over the fence.* 4. A position: *a* seat *in the state legislature. Noun.*
—1. To put someone on or lead someone to something on which to sit: *The music teacher* seated *her new student on the piano bench.*
2. To have places to sit for a certain number of

people: *This school bus* seats *48 children. Verb.*
seat (sēt) *noun, plural* seats; *verb,* seated,
seating.

seat²—A place or center: *The capital is the* seat *of
government.*
seat (sēt) *noun, plural* seats.

seat belt—A safety strap that is fastened across
a person's lap to hold him or her in a seat if
there is a bump or sudden stop, as in a car or
airplane.
seat belt (sēt belt) *noun, plural* seat belts.

seaweed—Any of the many kinds of plants and
fungi that grow in the ocean.
sea|weed (sē′wēd′) *noun, plural* seaweeds.

sec.—The abbreviation for **second²** or **seconds.**

secede—To choose to stop being a member of a
group or organization: *Six members* seceded *from
our club and started a club of their own.*
se|cede (si sēd′) *verb,* seceded, seceding.

second¹—**1.** Next after the first: *He sat in the*
second *row.* **2.** Ranking next to the best; lower
in rank than the first: second *prize;* second
lieutenant; second *class.* **3.** Another: *Please take
a* second *piece of cake. Adjective.*
—After the first person, thing, or group: *He
batted* second *during the inning. Adverb.*
—**1.** Someone or something that is next after the
first: *Who would like to be the* second *to try the
trampoline?* **2.** Something for sale that is flawed
or is of poor quality: *These dresses are* seconds
because the patterns on them are crooked.
3. Someone who aids or supports another person:
The boxer's second *helped him cool down. Noun.*
—To support; approve: *She* seconded *the idea
that the class should have a picnic on the last
day of school. Verb.*
sec|ond (sek′ənd) *adjective; adverb; noun,
plural* seconds; *verb,* seconded, seconding.

second²—**1.** One of the 60 equal parts into which
a minute is divided: *He had 30* seconds *to
answer the question.* **2.** A very little while;
moment: *I will be ready to go in a* second.
sec|ond (sek′ənd) *noun, plural* seconds.

secondary—Less important: *Winning the game
should be* secondary *to enjoying yourself.*
sec|ond|ar|y (sek′ən dār′ē) *adjective.*

secondhand—Used or worn; owned previously
by someone else: *a* secondhand *sled; a
secondhand dress.*
sec|ond|hand (sek′ənd hand′) *adjective.*

secrecy—The condition of being hidden or kept
from most people: *We made the plans for the
surprise birthday party in* secrecy.
se|cre|cy (sē′krə sē) *noun, plural* secrecies.

secret—**1.** Not in view or not known by most
people; hidden: *There is a* secret *drawer in the
old desk.* **2.** Acting or working in a way that is
hidden from most people: *a* secret *agent.
Adjective.*
—**1.** Something that is hidden from others: *I
know that you'd like to see what's inside that
box, but it's a* secret. **2.** A hidden cause,
reason, or way of doing something: *He tried to
learn the* secret *of pitching a curve ball. Noun.*
se|cret (sē′krit) *noun, plural* secrets.

secretary—**1.** A person whose job is writing
letters, answering the telephone, typing, and
keeping records for another person, company, or
organization: *The school* secretary *typed a letter
to be sent home to the parents.* **2.** A person who
is the head of a government department: *the
Secretary of the Navy; the Secretary of
Agriculture.* **3.** A desk with drawers, a bookcase
on top, and sometimes other compartments.
sec|re|tar|y (sek′rə tār′ē) *noun, plural*
secretaries. *Abbreviation:* Sec. *for* 2.

section—A separate part of something: *a section
of a grapefruit; a section of the Sunday
newspaper; the dairy section of a grocery store.
Noun.*
—To separate or divide into parts: *The teacher*
sectioned *the class into four groups for the relay
race. Verb.*
sec|tion (sek′shən) *noun, plural* sections.

secular—Of or relating to the world; not of God
or religious matters: *Thanksgiving and the Fourth
of July are* secular *holidays.*
sec|u|lar (sek′yə lər) *adjective.*

secure—**1.** Safe; protected: *She put her eyeglasses
in a* secure *place before she went into the
swimming pool.* **2.** Strong and steady: *The new
gym set is a* secure *place for us to climb and
play.* **3.** Without fear or doubt: *I feel* secure *that
I did well on that test. Adjective.*
—**1.** To guard; make safe: *The man* secured *his
money in a locked metal box.* **2.** To tie or fasten
tightly: *Dad* secured *our suitcases to the roof of
the car.* **3.** To get possession of; acquire: *She*
secured *the library book that she needed for her
science report. Verb.*

a at	i if	oo look	ch chalk		a in ago
ā ape	ī idle	ou out	ng sing		e in happen
ah calm	o odd	u ugly	sh ship	ə =	i in capital
aw all	ō oats	ū rule	th think		o in occur
e end	oi oil	ur turn	th their		u in upon
ē easy			zh treasure		

se|cure (si **kyoor′**) *adjective*, **securer, securest;** *verb*, **secured, securing.**

security—1. Safety; protection: *When the enemy attacked, the settlers ran to the* security *of their fort.* **2.** Something that makes safe or protects: *A smoke alarm is* security *against a fire.* **3.** A state of having no fear or doubts: *The support of his family gave him the* security *to do his best.*
se|cu|ri|ty (si **kyoor′**ə tē) *noun, plural* **securities.**
- Synonyms: **assurance, confidence,** for **3.** Antonyms: **danger, hazard, peril,** for **1.**

Seder—The special meal and religious service that are celebrated on the first night or first two nights of the Jewish holiday of Passover.
Se|der (**sā′**dər) *noun, plural* **Seders** or **Sedarim** (se **dahr′**im).

sediment—Small pieces of things that drift to the bottom of a liquid: *The hot chocolate left a brown* sediment *in the bottom of the cup.*
sed|i|ment (**sed′**ə mənt) *noun, plural* **sediments.**

see—1. To watch with the eyes; look at: *Can you* see *that kite in the sky?* **2.** To understand the meaning or ideas of: *I do not* see *how to do this division problem.* **3.** To find out; discover: *Please* see *who left a scarf here.* **4.** Be sure; make certain: *Please* see *that your pets have been fed.* **5.** To have happen; experience: *That old bicycle has* seen *miles of riding.* **6.** To talk to or meet with: *The principal wants to* see *her.*
see (sē) *verb*, **saw** or **seen, seeing.**
- Words that sound the same are **c** and **sea.**
- Synonyms: **glimpse, observe, spot, spy, view,** for **1.**

seed—The hard part of a plant, usually found at the center, from which another plant like the first can grow: *a tomato* seed. *Noun.*
—**1.** To plant with that part; sow: *Dad* seeded *the flower garden.* **2.** To remove that part from: *He* seeded *the cherries. Verb.*
seed (sēd) *noun, plural* **seeds;** *verb,* **seeded, seeding.**

seedling—A very small or young plant that has been grown from a seed; *a tomato* seedling.
seed|ling (**sēd′**ling) *noun, plural* **seedlings.**

seedy—No longer fresh or new; shabby; run down. *My old coat looks very* seedy. *This is a really* seedy *hotel.*
seed|y (**sē′**dē) *adjective*, **seedier, seediest.**

seek—1. To search for; try to find: *Our club is* seeking *ways to raise money.* **2.** To try to obtain; ask for; request: *She* sought *the teacher's help with the difficult problem.* **3.** To make an attempt; try: *The team is* seeking *to attract new players.*
seek (sēk) *verb*, **sought, seeking.**

seem—To appear to be; look as if: *The moon* seems *closer to the earth than it really is.*
seem (sēm) *verb*, **seemed, seeming.**
- A word that sounds the same is **seam.**

seeming—That appears to be true; apparent: *Our team has a* seeming *advantage because of weight.*
seem|ing (**sē′**ming) *adjective.*

seen—*See* see.
seen (sēn) *verb.*
- A word that sounds the same is **scene.**

seep—To flow slowly through small holes; ooze: *We had so much fun playing in the rain that we didn't mind the mud* seeping *through our clothes.*
seep (sēp) *verb*, **seeped, seeping.**

seesaw—A piece of children's play equipment that is a long board balanced on a support; teeter-totter. A child sitting at one end of the board goes up when the child on the other end goes down. *Noun.*
—To ride up and down on such a balanced board. *Verb.*
see|saw (**sē′**saw′) *noun, plural* **seesaws;** *verb,* **seesawed, seesawing.**
- See picture at **fulcrum.**

segment—A piece or section of a whole: *The wood cutter chopped the log into* segments.
seg|ment (**seg′**mənt) *noun, plural* **segments.**

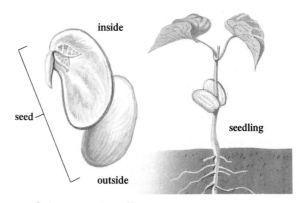

inside

seed

outside

seedling

seed (noun) and **seedling**

sego lily—A flowering plant that has an edible root and white, bell-shaped blossoms. It is the state flower of Utah.
se|go lil|y (sē′gō lil′ē) *noun, plural* **sego lilies.**

sego lily

segregate—1. To separate from the rest; isolate: *The farmer* segregated *the rooster from the hens*. 2. To separate people because of their race: *Black people and white people used to be* segregated.
seg|re|gate (seg′rə gāt′) *verb,* **segregated, segregating.**

segregation—1. The act of separating from the rest: *the* segregation *of rams from sheep on a farm*. 2. The act of separating people because of their race, especially in public places, such as schools, buses, or restaurants.
seg|re|ga|tion (seg′rə gā′shən) *noun.*

seismograph—An instrument that measures and records earthquakes.
seis|mo|graph (sīz′mə graf′ or sīs′mə graf′) *noun, plural* **seismographs.**

seize—1. To grab or grasp suddenly: *The bear skillfully* seized *the fish from the shallow river*. 2. To take forcefully; capture: *The rebels* seized *the capital*.
seize (sēz) *verb,* **seized, seizing.**

seizure—1. The act of taking by force; capture: *Police reported the* seizure *of the criminals*. 2. A sudden attack of certain diseases.
sei|zure (sē′zhər) *noun, plural* **seizures.**

seldom—Not often; hardly ever: *This train is* seldom *late*.
sel|dom (sel′dəm) *adverb.*

select—1. To take by choice; pick out: *She* selected *the reddest apples*. 2. To pick as the best person for some job or position: *She was* selected *to head the committee*.
se|lect (si lekt′) *verb,* **selected, selecting.**
• Synonyms: **appoint, choose, designate, name,** for 2.
Antonyms: **discharge, dismiss, fire,** for 2.

selection—1. The act of picking out; choosing: *The whole family took part in the* selection *of a new automobile*. 2. Something that is chosen: *Her* selection *from the menu was a cheese sandwich*.
se|lec|tion (si lek′shən) *noun, plural* **selections.**

self—One's own person: *He is being his lazy* self *again and refusing to do any work*.
self (self) *noun, plural* **selves.**

self-—A prefix that means "of, to, by, or for oneself or itself." A selfconscious person is someone who is uncomfortably aware of himself or herself because he or she is fearful of being disliked or disapproved of.

Word Power

You can understand the meanings of many words that begin with **self-,** if you add the meaning of the prefix to the meaning of the rest of the word.
self-addressed; addressed to oneself
self-defense: defense of oneself

---

self-conscious—Uncomfortable because of the fear of what others may think about what one is, says, or does; shy: *He is* self-conscious *about playing his trumpet solo in the concert*.
self-con|scious (self′kon′shəs) *adjective.*

selfish—Caring only for oneself and not thinking of the needs of others: *It was very* selfish *of you to give your friend the smaller piece of cake*.
self|ish (sel′fish) *adjective.*

self-respect—Proper regard for oneself; respect for one's own character and behavior: *She had enough* self-respect *not to mind when others laughed at her*.
self-re|spect (self′ri spekt′) *noun.*

sell—1. To trade something for money: *The children* sold *lemonade for five cents a glass*. 2. To offer for someone to buy: *My mother* sells *real estate*. 3. To be available to buy: *This magazine* sells *for a dollar*.
sell (sel) *verb,* **sold, selling.**
• A word that sounds the same is **cell.**

a at	i if	oo look	ch chalk		a in ago
ā ape	ī idle	ou out	ng sing		e in happen
ah calm	o odd	u ugly	sh ship	ə =	i in capital
aw all	ō oats	ū rule	th think		o in occur
e end	oi oil	ur turn	th their		u in upon
ē easy			zh treasure		

selves—*See* **self.**
  selves (selvz) *plural noun.*
semaphore—**1.** An upright post with movable, striped arms and sometimes colored lights or flags, used to signal railroad trains.   **2.** A system for sending messages by holding signal flags in different positions. *Noun.*
  sem|a|phore (sem′ə fawr′) *noun, plural* **semaphores.**

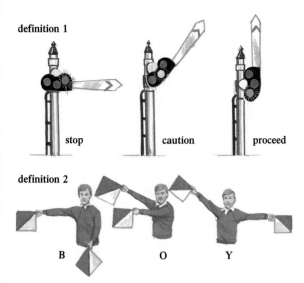

definition 1

stop   caution   proceed

definition 2

B   O   Y

semaphore

semester—One half of a school year: *We will study music during fall* semester *and painting during spring* semester.
  se|mes|ter (sə mes′tər) *noun, plural* **semesters.**
semi-—A prefix that means "half" or "partly." A semicircle is half a circle. A semisweet grapefruit is partly sweet.

Word Power

  You can understand the meanings of many words that begin with **semi,** if you add a meaning of the prefix to the meaning of the rest of the word.
    semimonthly: every half month
    semiconscious: partly conscious

---

semicircle—Half a circle: *He broke the doughnut into two* semicircles *and gave us each one.*
  sem|i|cir|cle (sem′ē sur′kəl) *noun, plural* **semicircles.**
semicolon—The punctuation mark that looks like this ; and is used to show a greater separation between parts of a sentence than a comma, but not so complete a break as a period: *These shoes*

should last for years; they are very well made.
  sem|i|co|lon (sem′ē kō′lən) *noun, plural* **semicolons.**
semiconductor—One of certain minerals that can conduct electricity, but not so well as most metals do. These substances are used in computers, radios, and the like.
  sem|i|con|duc|tor (sem′ē kən duk′tər) *noun, plural* **semiconductors.**
semifinal—A match or game that comes just before the last one and that decides who will compete in the final match or game.
  sem|i|fi|nal (sem′ē fi′nəl) *noun, plural* **semifinals.**
seminary—A school in which students are trained to be ministers, priests, or rabbis.
  sem|i|nar|y (sem′ə när′ē) *noun, plural* **seminaries.**
senate—The smaller part of a group of people that makes laws. The Senate is part of the United States Congress.
  sen|ate (sen′it) *noun, plural* **senates.**
senator—A person who is a member of a senate.
  sen|a|tor (sen′ə tər) *noun, plural* **senators.** Abbreviation: Sen.
send—**1.** To cause to move or go from one location to another: *The teacher sent the girl to the office for some pencils.*   **2.** To cause to happen or to be in a certain condition: *The funny story sent the children into a fit of laughter.*
  send (send) *verb,* **sent, sending.**
  ■ **send in:** To mail to a certain place: *Send in one dollar for this special offer.*
  send out: To order something delivered: *We sent out for a pizza.*

semicircle

senior—1. The older of two males who have the same name, the younger being his son: *John Smith, Junior, is named after his father, John Smith,* Senior. **2.** Older, more experienced, or higher in rank: *My grandfather is a* senior *citizen.* **3.** Of or concerning the last year of high school or college: *The* senior *class will graduate in June. Adjective.*
—1. Someone who is older, more experienced, or higher in rank than another: *My uncle is three years my father's* senior. **2.** A student who is in the last year of high school or college. *Noun.*
sen|ior (sēn′yər) *adjective; noun, plural* **seniors.** Abbreviation: Sr. for **1.**
• For *adjective* 2, see Language Fact at **old.**

sensation—1. The ability to see, hear, feel, taste, or smell: *He lost* sensation *when his arm went numb.* **2.** An awareness; feeling: *She had a* sensation *of hunger when she smelled the pie baking.* **3.** A very strong feeling, especially of excitement, or something that causes such a feeling: *The star of the show was a* sensation.
sen|sa|tion (sen sā′shən) *noun, plural* **sensations.**

sensational—1. Causing very strong or excited feelings; thrilling: *We heard the* sensational *news about the discovery of the pirate treasure.* **2.** Wonderful; so good as to be very exciting: *We had a* sensational *time at the dance.*
sen|sa|tion|al (sen sā′shə nəl) *adjective.*
• Synonyms: **delightful, heavenly, marvelous, terrific,** for **2.**

sense—1. The ability of a person or animal to be aware of events and changes outside of and within the body. The five senses are sight, hearing, touch, smell, and taste. **2.** A feeling; emotion: *He had a* sense *of accomplishment when he finished building the model.* **3.** The ability to understand and to keep in mind: *His* sense *of fairness made him cut equal slices of the pie for himself and his two sisters.* **4.** The ability to judge or reason: *He has enough* sense *not to touch the hot stove.* **5.** A use; purpose: *There's no* sense *in taking an umbrella now that it's stopped raining.* **6.** A meaning; content: *The* sense *of the message wasn't clear. Noun.*
—To be aware of; feel: *She* sensed *that her friend was angry about something. Verb.*
sense (sens) *noun, plural* **senses;** *verb,* **sensed, sensing.**

senseless—Without meaning or without good judgment; silly: *It is* senseless *to look for flowers in winter.*
sense|less (sens′lis) *adjective.*
• Synonyms: See Synonyms at **absurd.**
Antonyms: **reasonable, sensible.**

sensible—Having or showing good judgment; wise: *It is* sensible *to wear long pants and sturdy shoes when hiking in the woods.*
sen|si|ble (sen′sə bəl) *adjective.*
• Synonyms: **rational, reasonable**
Antonyms: See Synonyms at **absurd.**

sensitive—1. Easily affected; reacting readily: *The leaves of the plant are* sensitive *to sunlight.* **2.** Sharply aware; having keen feelings or perceptions: *His paintings show that he is very* sensitive.
sen|si|tive (sen′sə tiv) *adjective.*

sent—*See* **send.**
sent (sent) *verb.*
• Words that sound the same are **cent** and **scent.**

sentence—1. A group of words that expresses a complete thought in the form of a statement, question, command, request, or exclamation. "My friend is singing" is a sentence. **2.** The punishment of a criminal that is decided by a judge or court: *The robber was given a* sentence *of five years in jail. Noun.*
—To decide on the punishment of: *The court* sentenced *the spy to 30 years in prison. Verb.*
sen|tence (sen′təns) *noun, plural* **sentences;** *verb,* **sentenced, sentencing.**

sentiment—A feeling or emotion that is based on one's thoughts and attitude: *The birthday card expressed* sentiments *of humor and love.*
sen|ti|ment (sen′tə mənt) *noun, plural* **sentiments.**

sentimental—Having or expressing tender feelings, such as love or compassion: *We read a* sentimental *story about a dog's loyalty to its owner.*
sen|ti|men|tal (sen′tə men′təl) *adjective.*

sentry—A soldier or other person who keeps watch and looks out for danger at a certain post; guard.
sen|try (sen′trē) *noun, plural* **sentries.**

sepal—One of the plant parts that looks like a green petal underneath a flower or surrounding a bud. Some flowers, such as tulips, have sepals

a at	i if	oo look	ch chalk		a in ago
ā ape	ī idle	ou out	ng sing		e in happen
ah calm	o odd	u ugly	sh ship	ə =	i in capital
aw all	ō oats	ū rule	th think		o in occur
e end	oi oil	ur turn	th their		u in upon
ē easy			zh treasure		

that match the color of their petals.
se|pal (sē′pəl) *noun, plural* **sepals.**

separate—**1.** To keep apart; be between: *A hallway* separates *my room from my sister's.* **2.** To take from a group and put into different sets: *I need to* separate *the apples, oranges, and pears into three bowls.* **3.** To move or come apart: *The ships sailed down the river together and* separated *when they reached the sea. Verb.*
—Placed or kept apart; not connected: *Our garage is* separate *from our house. Adjective.*
sep|a|rate (sep′ə rāt′ for *verb;* sep′ər it for *adjective*) *verb,* **separated, separating;** *adjective.*
• Synonyms: **divide, part,** for *verb* **1.**
  Antonyms: For *verb* **1,** see Synonyms at **combine.**

Sept.—The abbreviation for **September.**

September—The ninth month of the year. It has thirty days.
Sep|tem|ber (sep tem′bər) *noun.* Abbreviation: **Sept.**

Word History

September comes from a Latin word meaning "seven." During ancient times, the Romans used a calendar that began with the month of March. The seventh month after March was September.

---

sequence—**1.** A certain order, one after another: *The magazines were placed on the shelf in* sequence *from the oldest to the newest.* **2.** A series of things that are connected to or follow one another: *The story told the* sequence *of events that led to the solving of the mystery.*
se|quence (sē′kwəns) *noun, plural* **sequences.**

sequoia—A giant evergreen tree with reddish-brown bark, which grows in certain coastal regions of California and Oregon; redwood.
se|quoi|a (si kwoi′ə) *noun, plural* **sequoias.**

serenade—Music that is sung or played in honor of someone, especially romantic music performed by a man for a woman he loves. *Noun.*
—To sing or play such a song to someone: *The young man stood beneath the window and* serenaded *the girl he hoped to marry. Verb.*
ser|e|nade (ser′ə nād′) *noun, plural* **serenades;** *verb,* **serenaded, serenading.**

serf—In the Middle Ages, a person who was like a slave. A serf was forced to work on the land in the service of the lord who owned it. If the land was sold, the serf was part of the sale.
serf (serf) *noun, plural* **serfs.**
• A word that sounds the same is **surf.**

sergeant—A rank of an enlisted member of the armed forces or of a police force. In the United States Army, a sergeant is above a corporal and below a lieutenant.
ser|geant (sahr′jənt) *noun, plural* **sergeants.** Abbreviation: Sgt.

serial—A story that appears one part at a time in a newspaper or magazine or on radio or television.
se|ri|al (sēr′ē əl) *noun, plural* **serials.**
• A word that sounds the same is **cereal.**

series—A number of things or events that are alike and that come one after another: *The team made a* series *of mistakes that caused them to lose the game.*
se|ries (sēr′ēz) *noun, plural* **series.**

serious—**1.** Deeply thoughtful; grave: *The teacher looked* serious *as she talked about the importance of the fire drill.* **2.** Sincere; not fooling: *The girl couldn't believe that her father was* serious *when he promised to buy her a horse.* **3.** Worth thinking about; important: *He had to make a* serious *decision.* **4.** Giving good reason for being fearful or anxious; dangerous: *It can be a* serious *mistake to cross the street without looking.*
se|ri|ous (sēr′ē əs) *adjective.*
• Synonyms: **earnest, solemn,** for **1.**
  Antonyms: **comical, funny, hilarious, humorous,** for **1.**

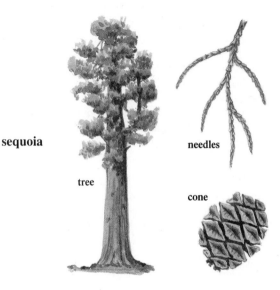

sequoia

needles

tree

cone

sermon—**1.** A talk about religion or morality, given by a minister, priest, or rabbi to a group of people in a church or temple.   **2.** Any long, serious talk about morality or behavior: *The children's father gave them a* sermon *about the importance of telling the truth.*
ser|mon (sur′mən) *noun, plural* **sermons.**

serpent—Any big snake.
ser|pent (sur′pənt) *noun, plural* **serpents.**

serum—**1.** The clear, yellowish liquid part of blood that separates from it when a clot forms.   **2.** A liquid that is used to cure or prevent a disease. Serum is taken from the blood of an animal that has become immune to the disease.
se|rum (sēr′əm) *noun, plural* **serums** or **sera** (sēr′ə).

servant—**1.** A person whose job is to work for others in a household, such as a cook, housekeeper, or gardener.   **2.** A person employed by a local or national government to work for the good of the public, such as a teacher, police officer, or fire fighter: *a public* servant.
serv|ant (sur′vənt) *noun, plural* **servants.**

serve—**1.** To carry out duties for: *She* served *her community as a nurse.*   **2.** To bring food or drink to someone or put something to eat or drink on a table: *Dessert was* served *after dinner.*   **3.** To be of use: *A basket* served *as a bed for the dog.*   **4.** To supply; provide: *This box of cereal* serves *twelve people.*   **5.** To hit a ball in order to start play in certain games: *The volleyball player* served *to the other team.*   **6.** To present, usually in an official manner: *He was* served *with an order to be a witness in court. Verb.*
—In certain games, the hitting of a ball to begin play: *The tennis player's* serve *hit the net. Noun.*
serve (surv) *verb,* **served, serving;** *noun, plural* **serves.**

service—**1.** Action or actions that are useful or helpful to others: *The mayor thanked the volunteer for her* service *to the town.*   **2.** A method of supplying something useful or needed: *The hotel provides a laundry* service *for its guests.*   **3.** Work for others in a household: *He is in* service *to the family as a butler.*   **4.** The armed forces: *The lieutenant has been in the* service *for several years.*   **5.** A ceremony of worship or for another religious purpose: *The church* service *is held on Sunday morning.*   **6.** A set of things to be used in serving or eating food: *Our silver* service *includes knives, forks, and spoons. Noun.*
—To keep in working order; fix: *Our television was* serviced *in the repair shop. Verb.*
serv|ice (sur′vis) *noun, plural* **services;** *verb,* **serviced, servicing.**

session—**1.** An official meeting held for the purpose of having discussions and making decisions: *The case will be decided during a* session *of the court.*   **2.** A series of such meetings: *This* session *of the city council will go on for another week.*   **3.** Any meeting of people assembled for a purpose: *an exercise* session.   **4.** A part of a school day or school year, during which classes are held: *His art class meets during the afternoon* session.
ses|sion (sesh′ən) *noun, plural* **sessions.**

set[1]—**1.** To put; place: *He* set *his boots by the door.*   **2.** To put in the right place or order; arrange; adjust: *I* set *the table for dinner.*   **3.** To put in a certain condition: *I* set *the butterfly free.*   **4.** To determine, fix, or provide: *They* set *the time of the meeting for two o'clock.*   **5.** To start: *My father* set *to work on building a table.*   **6.** To go down; sink: *The sun* set *behind the hills. Verb.*
—**1.** Already decided; fixed: *School begins and ends at a* set *time every day.*   **2.** Completely prepared; ready: *He got* set *to begin work.*   **3.** Fixed in a certain way; not easily changed: *She has* set *ideas and will not listen to our suggestions. Adjective.*
set (set) *verb,* **set, setting;** *adjective.*
• See Language Fact at **sit.**

set[2]—**1.** A collection of related things or persons: *a* set *of friends; a chess* set.   **2.** The scenery used for a play, movie, or other performance.   **3.** A piece of equipment for sending or receiving by television or radio: *We turned on the television* set *and waited a moment for the picture to appear.*   **4.** A group of games in tennis that make up part of a match.
set (set) *noun, plural* **sets.**
• Synonyms: **batch, bunch, group, lot,** for **1.**

setter—Any of a group of medium-sized hunting dogs with a long, smooth coat and drooping ears. These dogs help the hunter by standing still and pointing with the nose toward the prey.
set|ter (set′ər) *noun, plural* **setters.**
• *See also* **English setter, Gordon setter,** and **Irish setter.**

a at	i if	oo look	ch chalk		a in ago
ā ape	ī idle	ou out	ng sing		e in happen
ah calm	o odd	u ugly	sh ship	ə =	i in capital
aw all	ō oats	ū rule	th think		o in occur
e end	oi oil	ur turn	th their		u in upon
ē easy			zh treasure		

settle—**1.** To decide or agree upon: *We asked the teacher to* settle *the question of whose turn was next.* **2.** To establish a home in a new place: *The family moved from the coast and* settled *in the mountains.* **3.** To come to rest or become comfortable: *The children* settled *on the soft rug and read their books.* **4.** To make calm; quiet: *The mother* settled *the restless children by telling them a story.* **5.** To go down slowly; sink: *The heavy wagon* settled *in the mud.*
set|tle (set′əl) *verb,* **settled, settling.**

settlement—**1.** The act or condition of agreeing upon something: *The* settlement *of the argument saved their friendship.* **2.** The act of establishing a home in a new place: *the pioneers'* settlement *of the western lands.* **3.** A colonial establishment: *The colonists left their country and started a* settlement *in a new land.* **4.** A group of houses that form a village: *A wall of logs was built around the frontier* settlement *to protect it from attack.*
set|tle|ment (set′əl mənt) *noun, plural* **settlements.**

settler—A person who goes to live in a new land: *As soon as they arrived, the* settlers *cleared the land to make farms and build homes.*
set|tler (set′lər) *noun, plural* **settlers.**

seven—One more than six; one less than eight; 7: *There are* seven *goldfish in the pond.* Seven *of the students are boys.*
sev|en (sev′ən) *adjective; noun, plural* **sevens.**

seventeen—Seven more than ten; one more than sixteen; 17: *to be* seventeen *years old.*
sev|en|teen (sev′ən tēn′) *adjective; noun, plural* **seventeens.**

seventeenth—**1.** Next after the sixteenth. **2.** One of seventeen equal parts.
sev|en|teenth (sev′ən tēnth′) *adjective; noun, plural* **seventeenths.**

seventh—**1.** Next after the sixth. **2.** One of seven equal parts.
sev|enth (sev′ənth) *adjective; noun, plural* **sevenths.**

Seventh-day Adventist—A member of a branch of the Protestant religion which believes that Christ will physically return to Earth. Seventh-day Adventists take Saturday, the seventh day of the week, as their day of rest and worship.
Sev|enth-day Ad|vent|ist (sev′ənth dā ad′vən tist) *noun, plural* **Seventh-day Adventists.**

seventieth—**1.** Next after the sixty-ninth. **2.** One of seventy equal parts. *Noun.*

sev|en|ti|eth (sev′ən tē ith) *adjective; noun, plural* **seventieths.**

seventy—Seven times ten; one more than sixty-nine; 70.
sev|en|ty (sev′ən tē) *adjective; noun, plural* **seventies.**

several—More than two but not many; some: *The seeds began to sprout* several *days after they were planted. Yesterday, all my classmates were in school, but* several *are absent today.*
sev|er|al (sev′ər əl) *adjective; noun.*

severe—**1.** Stern; strict: *That boy doesn't deserve such a* severe *punishment.* **2.** Dangerous or sharp; causing much pain; serious: *a* severe *illness; a* severe *headache.* **3.** Violent or intense: severe *flooding.*
se|vere (sə vēr′) *adjective,* **severer, severest.**
● Synonyms: **drastic, extreme, harsh,** for **1.**

sew—To fasten by stitches, using a needle and thread: *Mother* sewed *curtains for my bedroom on her new* sewing *machine.*
sew (sō) *verb,* **sewed, sewed** or **sewn, sewing.**
● Words that sound the same are **so** and **sow**[1].

sewage—Liquid waste materials that are carried away from houses, factories, and the like by means of drains and sewers.
sew|age (sū′ij) *noun.*

sewer—An underground drain or pipe that carries away liquid waste materials.
sew|er (sū′ər) *noun, plural* **sewers.**

sewn—*See* **sew.**
sewn (sōn) *verb.*

sex—**1.** Either of the two groups into which people, animals, and some plants are divided: *the male* sex; *the female* sex. **2.** The condition of being female or male: *Everyone will like this movie, regardless of age or* sex.
sex (seks) *noun, plural* **sexes.**

sexism—An unfair action or judgment based on a person's sex; prejudice in business or politics, usually against women: *That company was accused of practicing* sexism *against women when it hired so few of them.*
sex|ism (sek′siz əm) *noun.*

sexist—A person who acts or judges unfairly on the basis of someone's sex: *That man is a* sexist *because he thinks all women are less intelligent than men. Noun.*
—Having to do with this type of prejudice: *a* sexist *remark. Adjective.*
sex|ist (sek′sist) *noun, plural* **sexists;** *adjective.*

shabby—In bad condition from much wear: *She bought a new dress because her old one was shabby.*
shab|by (shab′ē) *adjective,* **shabbier, shabbiest.**

Shabuot or **Shabuoth**—A Jewish holiday that celebrates Moses' receiving the Law of God on Mount Sinai and the wheat harvest in ancient times. Also called "Feast of Weeks," this holiday occurs several weeks after Passover, usually in May.
Sha|bu|ot or Sha|bu|oth (shah vū′ōt *or* shah vū′ōth) *noun.*

shack—A small cabin that is roughly built or in poor condition; hut.
shack (shak) *noun, plural* **shacks.**

shade—1. A dim place that is sheltered from direct, bright sunlight: *We sat in the shade of a beach umbrella.* 2. Something that softens light or keeps light out: *a lamp shade; window shades.* 3. The degree of the darkness of a color: *The sky was a light shade of blue.* 4. A little amount; slight degree: *This piece of wood is a shade too short. Noun.*
—1. To keep or shelter from light: *She shaded her eyes against the bright sun.* 2. To make dark: *She shaded her light brown hair with streaks of dark brown. Verb.*
shade (shād) *noun, plural* **shades;** *verb,* **shaded, shading.**

shadow—1. An area of darkness made when light is blocked by a person or thing: *The trees cast a long shadow in the late afternoon sun.* 2. A little bit: *The shadow of a suspicion crossed her mind. Noun.*
—To follow someone closely or in secret: *The police shadowed the suspected robber in an unmarked car. Verb.*
shadow (shad′ō) *noun, plural* **shadows;** *verb,* **shadowed, shadowing.**

shady—1. In a dim place that is sheltered from direct, bright sunlight; dark or creating darkness: *The porch is shady at this time of day.* 2. Not completely honest; questionable: *That shabby store looks like a shady business.*
shad|y (shā′dē) *adjective,* **shadier, shadiest.**

shaft—1. A bar or rod in a machine that supports a rotating piece or that, by turning, moves other parts. 2. A long, tunnellike passageway that leads downward or upward: *a mine shaft; an elevator shaft.* 3. The long, straight part of an arrow, spear, golf club, tool, or the like. 4. A beam or ray of light: *A few shafts of sunlight broke through the dark cloud.*
shaft (shaft) *noun, plural* **shafts.**

shaggy—1. Thickly covered with a rough mass of long hair, wool, or fiber: *a shaggy buffalo; a shaggy rug.* 2. Long, thick, and messy: *I need to cut this shaggy hair.*
shag|gy (shag′ē) *adjective,* **shaggier, shaggiest.**

shake—1. To move quickly up and down or back and forth: *to shake a tambourine; to shake one's fist.* 2. To tremble or make tremble: *The puppy shook with fear.* 3. To disturb or upset: *The bank robbery had shaken the employees.* 4. To make less firm; weaken: *Nothing can shake my trust in you! Verb.*
—The act of moving quickly up and down or back and forth: *With a shake of his head, he showed that he didn't want to go. Noun.*
shake (shāk) *verb,* **shook, shaken, shaking;** *noun, plural* **shakes.**

■ **no great shakes:** Not special or important: *The movie wasn't bad, but it was no great shakes.*

shall—A verb that is used to express a command or promise, or what is to happen in the future: *You shall not be home late. Shall we call you every day?*
shall (shal) *verb,* **should.**

Language Fact

Shall is used, in formal speech and writing, with **I** and **we** to show what is to happen in the future: *I shall go tomorrow.* **Shall** is used with **you, he, she, it,** and **they** to show a command or promise: *It shall be done, whatever happens.* **Will** is used, in formal speech and writing, in the opposite pattern. With **I** and **we,** it shows a command or promise. With **you, he, she, it,** and **they,** it shows what is to happen: *I swear I will return. Will you call me later?* These rules are often not followed in everyday use.

---

shallow—Not deep: *Children waded in the shallow pond.*
shal|low (shal′ō) *adjective,* **shallower, shallowest.**

shame—1. A painful sense of having done something wrong or embarrassing: *She felt great shame for having tricked her parents.* 2. A loss of one's good reputation; disgrace: *The criminal*

a at	i if	oo look	ch chalk		a in ago
ā ape	ī idle	ou out	ng sing		e in happen
ah calm	o odd	u ugly	sh ship	ə =	i in capital
aw all	ō oats	ū rule	th think		o in occur
e end	oi oil	ur turn	th their		u in upon
ē easy			zh treasure		

brought shame *to his family.* **3.** Something to feel sorry about: *It's a* shame *that you twisted your ankle the day of the race. Noun.*
—To cause another to feel wrong or embarrassed: *My cousin's rudeness toward you* shamed *me. Verb.*
shame (shām) *noun; verb,* **shamed, shaming.**
● Synonyms: **humble, humiliate,** for *verb.*
Antonym: **honor,** for *verb.*

shampoo—To wash the hair, a rug, or the like with soap and water or with a special cleaning substance. *Verb.*
—A special soap or cleaning substance that is used for washing hair, a rug, or the like. *Noun.*
sham|poo (sham pū′) *verb,* **shampooed, shampooing;** *noun, plural* **shampoos.**

Word History

Shampoo comes from an Indian word meaning "to press." When a person shampoos something, he or she presses a cleaning substance into it to work out the dirt.

---

shamrock—A green leaf having three parts and found on plants such as clover. It is the symbol of Ireland.
sham|rock (sham′rok′) *noun, plural* **shamrocks.**

shamrock

shape—**1.** The outline of a person or thing; form: *A marble has a round* shape. **2.** Physical or mental condition: *Swimming keeps us in good* shape. **3.** Proper order: *I am going to put our messy garage in* shape *this weekend. Noun.*
—**1.** To form: *He* shaped *the clay into animal figures.* **2.** To develop; give or get proper order: *My English paper is* shaping *up nicely.*
shape (shāp) *noun, plural* **shapes;** *verb,* **shaped, shaping.**

shaped—Having a certain shape: *a U-*shaped *tube; a bell-*shaped *curve.*
shaped (shāpt) *adjective.*

share—**1.** One part or portion: *Do you want to eat my* share *of pie?* **2.** A part of a business or the like that is owned with others: *My parents own a* share *in that company. Noun.*
—**1.** To use or do together with someone else: *We can* share *this desk.* **2.** To divide into parts for each to use: *My brother and I* shared *the money we earned from our lemonade stand.* **3.** To take part: *We all* shared *in the joy of the holiday. Verb.*
share (shār) *noun, plural* **shares;** *verb,* **shared, sharing.**

shark—A large, saltwater fish with rough, gray skin, a triangle-shaped fin on its back, and a long snout with a large mouth underneath having many sharp teeth. Sharks eat other fish, and some are known to attack humans.
shark (shahrk) *noun, plural* **sharks.**

shark

sharp—**1.** Having a fine point or thin edge: Sharp *scissors; a* sharp *pencil.* **2.** Not smooth or rounded: *The roof top has a* sharp *angle.* **3.** Sudden; not smooth and gradual: *Take a* sharp *right turn after you pass the bridge.* **4.** Harsh to any of the senses; intense: *a* sharp *wind; a* sharp *taste.* **5.** Clear; easy to see: *There is a* sharp *difference between right and wrong.* **6.** Alert; keen: *My senses are at their* sharpest *in the morning. Adjective.*
—Exactly; on time: *The class starts at eight o'clock* sharp. *Adverb.*
—**1.** A musical tone or note that is a half note above the natural pitch: *C* sharp; *F* sharp. **2.** This sign (#), which shows such a tone or note. *Noun.*
sharp (shahrp) *adjective,* **sharper, sharpest;** *adverb; noun, plural* **sharps.**

sharpen—To make or become sharp or sharper: *You need to* sharpen *the knife before you cut the meat.*
sharp|en (shahr′pən) *verb,* **sharpened, sharpening.**

shatter—To break apart into bits: *The mirror* shattered *when it was dropped.*
shat|ter (shat′ər) *verb,* **shattered, shattering.**
• Synonyms: **crack, fracture, smash**

shave—**1.** To cut off hair using a razor: *The barber* shaved *the back of the man's neck.* **2.** To slice in thin pieces: *to* shave *strips from a hunk of cheese. Verb.*
—**1.** The act of cutting hair, especially from the face, with a razor: *He went to the barber for a* shave. **2.** A near miss; narrow escape: *It was a close* shave *when I nearly fell into the mud. Noun.*
shave (shāv) *verb,* **shaved, shaving;** *noun, plural* **shaves.**

shawl—A large piece of cloth used as a loose covering around the shoulders or over the head.
shawl (shawl) *noun, plural* **shawls.**

she—A word used for the girl, woman, or female animal that has been named or described earlier: *Is* she *the girl you were telling me about? Pronoun.*
—A female: *Is your new puppy a* she *or a he? Noun.*
she (shē) *pronoun; noun, plural* **shes.**

shear—**1.** To cut hair, wool, or the like with clippers or scissors; trim: *to* shear *wool from the sheep.* **2.** To cut or break sharply: *The tornado* sheared *the roof from the building.*
shear (shēr) *verb,* **sheared, sheared** or **shorn, shearing.**
• A word that sounds the same is **sheer.**

shears—Large scissors or something that cuts like scissors, usually used with both hands.
shears (shērz) *plural noun.*

shed[1]—A small building used for storing things.
shed (shed) *noun, plural* **sheds.**

shed[2]—**1.** To cause to flow out and let fall: *a child* shedding *tears over a sad story; to* shed *blood.* **2.** To let drop; throw off: *a snake* shedding *its skin; to* shed *worries on a beautiful*

day. **3.** To send forth; give out: *The stars* shed *their glow in the night sky.*
shed (shed) *verb,* **shed, shedding.**

she'd—The contraction of "she had" or "she would."
she'd (shēd).

sheep—An animal with a thick wool coat, related to goats. People raise sheep for their wool, meat, and hide.
sheep (shēp) *noun, plural* **sheep.**
▪ **separate the sheep from the goats:** To separate or tell apart the good from the bad: *At the library, there are so many books that it's difficult to* separate the sheep from the goats.

sheep

sheer—**1.** Very thin and easy to see through: *The* sheer *curtains let in the light of the sun.* **2.** Pure; total: *That idea is a stroke of* sheer *genius.* **3.** Very steep: *That* sheer *cliff drops straight down to the sea.*
sheer (shēr) *adjective,* **sheerer, sheerest.**
• A word that sounds the same is **shear.**

sheet—**1.** A large, usually rectangular piece of thin cloth that is put on a bed. **2.** A thin, broad, flat surface or piece: *a* sheet *of ice; a* sheet *of metal; a* sheet *of glass.* **3.** A piece of paper.
sheet (shēt) *noun, plural* **sheets.**

sheik—An Arab chief or leader.
sheik (shēk) *noun, plural* **sheiks.**

shekel—A unit of money in Israel.
shek|el (shek′əl) *noun, plural* **shekels.**
Abbreviation: IS

shelf—**1.** A thin, flat piece of wood, metal, or other material that is fastened to a wall or frame and is used to hold books and other things. **2.** Something having this shape: *There's a huge* shelf *of rock just below the surface in this lake.*
shelf (shelf) *noun, plural* **shelves.**

a at	i if	oo look	ch chalk		a in ago
ā ape	ī idle	ou out	ng sing		e in happen
ah calm	o odd	u ugly	sh ship	ə =	i in capital
aw all	ō oats	ū rule	th think		o in occur
e end	oi oil	ur turn	th their		u in upon
ē easy			zh treasure		

shell—1. The hard outer covering of some animals and insects. Crabs, beetles, snails, and turtles have shells.   2. The hard outer covering of an egg or nut.   3. Any outer covering like this, such as a frame: *the* shell *of a building; a pie* shell. 4. A metal case filled with explosives, fired from a large gun. A shell explodes when it hits something. *Noun.*
—1. To take off an outer covering: *Father* shelled *the walnuts for us to eat.*   2. To hit over and over again with exploding devices: *The soldiers* shelled *the enemy's fort. Verb.*
shell (shel) *noun, plural* **shells;** *verb,* **shelled, shelling.**
■ **shell out:** To give something: *He* shelled out *a dollar for the raffle ticket.*
● See pictures at **lobster** and **peanut.**

she'll—The contraction of "she shall" or "she will."
she'll (shēl).

shellac—A clear liquid that is put on wood or metal to make them look smooth and shiny and to protect them from wear. It becomes very hard when it dries. *Noun.*
—To coat with this liquid: *We* shellacked *the new shelves. Verb.*
shel|lac (shə lak′) *noun, plural* **shellacs;** *verb,* **shellacked, shellacking.**

shellfish—An animal that has a hard outer covering and lives in water. Clams, lobsters, and crabs are all shellfish.
shell|fish (shel′fish′) *noun, plural* **shellfish** or **shellfishes.**

shelter—Something that protects or covers; refuge: *People ran to the house for* shelter *from the rain.*
—To give protection or cover: *The trees* sheltered *us from the hot sun. Verb.*
shel|ter (shel′tər) *noun, plural* **shelters;** *verb,* **sheltered, sheltering.**
● Synonyms: **defend, guard, shield,** for *verb.*

shelves—*See* **shelf.**
shelves (shelvz) *plural noun.*

shepherd—A person whose job is to care for sheep. *Noun.*
—1. To care for sheep or similar animals: *a farmer* shepherding *his flock.*   2. To guide or protect: *the minister* shepherding *her congregation. Verb.*
shep|herd (shep′ərd) *noun, plural* **shepherds;** *verb,* **shepherded, shepherding.**

sherbet—A frozen dessert that is made with fruit juice.
sher|bet (shur′bət) *noun, plural* **sherbets.**

sheriff—The most important law officer of a county: *The criminals surrendered when they saw the* sheriff *approach.*
sher|iff (sher′if) *noun, plural* **sheriffs.**

she's—The contraction of "she is" or "she has."
she's (shēz).

Shetland pony—A small, strong pony that has a rough coat and that children often ride for fun. Shetland ponies originally came from the Shetland Islands, near Scotland.
Shet|land po|ny (shet′lənd pō′nē) *noun, plural* **Shetland ponies.**

Shetland pony

Shetland sheepdog—A small working dog that looks very much like a collie. Originally bred in the Shetland Islands near Scotland, these dogs herd sheep.
Shet|land sheep|dog (shet′land shēp′dawg′) *noun, plural* **Shetland sheepdogs.**

shield—1. A large piece of metal or other hard material carried on the arm and used to protect oneself in battle.   2. A badge or other object that is shaped like such a piece of material. 3. Anything used as protection: *We used the umbrella as a* shield *against the strong sun. Noun.*
—To protect: *He* shielded *his head from the falling branch with his arm. Verb.*
shield (shēld) *noun, plural* **shields;** *verb,* **shielded, shielding.**
● Synonyms: **defend, guard, shelter,** for *verb.*

shift—To move or change the position or place of something: *to* shift *the furniture around in my bedroom. Verb.*
—1. A change of position, place, or direction: *a* shift *in the sun's rays as the day passes.*   2. A group of people who work at the same place at

the same time, or the time period when they work: *the night* shift. *Noun.*
shift (shift) *verb,* **shifted, shifting;** *noun, plural* **shifts.**

Shih Tzu—A very small dog with a long, thick coat and a short, square nose. It was originally bred in China long ago.
Shih Tzu (shēd zū) *noun, plural* **Shih Tzus.**

Shih Tzu

shilling—A British coin that is no longer used. Twenty shillings were equal to one pound.
shil|ling (shil′ing) *noun, plural* **shillings.**

shimmer—To shine faintly; glimmer: *The white swans* shimmered *in the moonlight.*
shim|mer (shim′ər) *verb,* **shimmered, shimmering.**

shin—The front part of the leg from the ankle to the knee. *Noun.*
—To climb by holding on with the arms and legs and pulling: *I* shinned *up the pole. Verb.*
shin (shin) *noun, plural* **shins;** *verb,* **shinned, shinning.**

shine—1. To give off light: *The moon* shines *through the clouds.* 2. To make bright; polish: *Father is* shining *his shoes.* 3. To do especially well: *She* shone *during her piano performance. Verb.*
—A light; brightness: *the* shine *of gold. Noun.*

shine (shīn) *verb,* **shone** or **shined, shining;** *noun.*

shingle—A thin piece of wood or other material used in overlapping rows to cover a roof or outside wall. *Noun.*
—To cover a roof or wall with these pieces of material. *Verb.*
shin|gle (shing′gəl) *noun, plural* **shingles;** *verb,* **shingled, shingling.**

Shinto—1. The national religion of Japan. It involves the worship of many gods. 2. A person who follows this religion.
Shin|to (shin′tō) *noun, plural* **Shintos.**

ship—1. A big boat. 2. A spacecraft or airplane. *Noun.*
—To transport by ship, airplane, truck, or train. *We* shipped *the package by train. Verb.*
ship (ship) *noun, plural* **ships;** *verb,* **shipped, shipping.**
• See Word Power at **boat** and at **nautical.**

-ship—A suffix that means "the condition of being." Leadership is the condition of being a leader.

Word Power

You can understand the meaning of many words that end in **-ship,** if you add the meaning of the suffix to the meaning of the rest of the word.
friendship: the condition of being a friend
partnership: the condition of being a partner

---

shipment—1. The act of sending products and other items: *The factory prepared the machines for* shipment *to the customer.* 2. The items that are sent: *The* shipment *arrived today.*
ship|ment (ship′mənt) *noun, plural* **shipments.**

shipshape—Neat and orderly: *They keep their house* shipshape *in case friends drop by.*
ship|shape (ship′shāp′) *adjective.*

shipwreck—The loss or destruction of a ship at sea.
ship|wreck (ship′rek′) *noun, plural* **shipwrecks.**

shipyard—A place where ships are built or repaired.
ship|yard (ship′yahrd′) *noun, plural* **shipyards.**

Shire—A large, strong workhorse first bred in England.
Shire (shīr) *noun, plural* **Shires.**

shirk—To avoid or neglect doing something one should do: *to* shirk *my daily chores in order to play.*
shirk (shurk) *verb,* **shirked, shirking.**

a at	i if	oo look	ch chalk		⌐ a in ago
ā ape	ī idle	ou out	ng sing		e in happen
ah calm	o odd	u ugly	sh ship	ə =	i in capital
aw all	ō oats	ū rule	th think		o in occur
e end	oi oil	ur turn	<u>th</u> their		⌐ u in upon
ē easy			zh treasure		

shirt—A piece of clothing with sleeves that is worn on the upper part of the body.
shirt (shurt) *noun, plural* **shirts.**

shiver—To shake because of fear, cold, or excitement: *He* shivered *in the icy water. Verb.* —The act of such shaking: *Noun.*
shiv|er (shiv′ər) *verb,* **shivered, shivering;** *noun, plural* **shivers.**

shoal—A shallow place in a body of water.
shoal (shōl) *noun, plural* **shoals.**

shock[1]—**1.** A sudden, violent hit or crash: *The* shock *of the falling tree made the ground shake.* **2.** Something that happens unexpectedly that upsets the emotions: *It was a* shock *to us when our vacation was canceled.* **3.** A physical weakness caused by a severe injury or emotional upset. **4.** The feeling when an electrical current passes through the body. *Noun.* —To surprise or upset: *The murder* shocked *the community. Verb.*
shock (shok) *noun, plural* **shocks;** *verb,* **shocked, shocking.**

shock[2]—A group of corn or other grain stalks that are gathered together and placed in a field to dry.
shock (shok) *noun, plural* **shocks.**

shoe—An outer covering for a foot: *I bought a new pair of leather* shoes *today.*
shoe (shū) *noun, plural* **shoes.**
■ **the shoe is on the other foot:** A situation that becomes the opposite of what it was before: *She would help me, too, if* the shoe were on the other foot.

shone—*See* **shine.**
shone (shōn) *verb.*

shook—*See* **shake.**
shook (shook) *verb.*

Shire

shoot—**1.** To hit with a bullet, arrow, or something similar: *The hunter* shot *the deer.* **2.** To send out from a weapon: *He* shot *a bullet from the gun.* **3.** To send forth forcefully: *She* shot *a stream of water from the hose.* **4.** To move quickly: *He* shot *out of the freezing water.* **5.** To come out of; grow: *The plants are* shooting *from the earth.* **6.** To take a picture; photograph: *Verb.* —A new plant growth: *The* shoots *came up green and strong. Noun.*
shoot (shūt) *verb,* **shot, shooting;** *noun, plural* **shoots.**
● A word that sounds the same is **chute.**

shop—**1.** A place where things are sold. **2.** A place where things are fixed or made: *The car door was fixed at the body* shop. *Noun.* —To go to stores to look at and buy things: *We* shopped *until the stores closed at night. Verb.*
shop (shop) *noun, plural* **shops;** *verb,* **shopped, shopping.**

shoplift—To steal something from a store while acting like a customer: *He* shoplifted *the earrings, but the sales clerk saw him do it.*
shop|lift (shop′lift′) *verb,* **shoplifted, shoplifting.**

shore—**1.** The land at the edge of a large body of water: *We waved to the people on the ship from the* shore. **2.** Land, as compared to sea: *The sailors had not been on* shore *for months.*
shore (shawr) *noun, plural* **shores.**

shoreline—The area where water and land come together: *The walls near the* shoreline *were washed away in the storm.*
shore|line (shawr′līn′) *noun, plural* **shorelines.**

short—**1.** Not long, far, or tall: *a* short *trip around the block.* **2.** Not having enough; not sufficient: *He is* short *on talent.* **3.** Taking only a little time to pronounce: *The "e" in "let" is a* short *vowel. Adjective.* —**1.** Not quite enough: *My allowance came up* short *of the cost of the record I wanted to buy.* **2.** Suddenly; quickly: *The runner stopped* short *when the horn blew. Adverb.* —**shorts:** **1.** Pants that reach from the waist to above the knees: *We wore our* shorts *for the summer walk.* **2.** Underpants for men and boys. *Noun.*
short (shawrt) *adjective,* **shorter, shortest;** *adverb; plural noun.*
■ **be caught short:** To not have something when it is needed: *She took extra food to the picnic because she did not want to* be caught short *if people were very hungry.*

shortage—Too little an amount of: *The* shortage *of snow made the skiers unhappy.*
short|age (shawr′tij) *noun, plural* **shortages.**

short circuit—A path followed by electrical current that has left the path it was meant to take. This may blow a fuse or cause a fire.
short cir|cuit (shawrt **sur′**kit) *noun, plural* **short circuits.**

shortcut—A shorter, quicker way: *We took a* shortcut *through the woods to save time.* Noun.
short|cut (shawrt′kut′) *noun, plural* **shortcuts.**

shorten—To make shorter; abbreviate: *He* shortened *his report at the teacher's request.*
short|en (shawr′tən) *verb,* **shortened, shortening.**
 • Synonyms: **abridge, trim**
   Antonyms: **enlarge, expand, lengthen**

shortening—Any of the kinds of fat used in cooking. Margarine and peanut oil are types of shortening.
short|en|ing (shawr′tə ning) *noun.*

shorthand—A method of writing quickly in which symbols and letters are used in place of words.
short|hand (shawrt′hand′) *noun.*

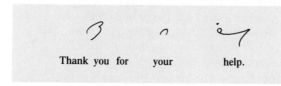

Thank you   for   your   help.

shorthand

shortly—Soon: *Please wait for me because I will finish supper* shortly.
short|ly (shawrt′lē) *adverb.*

shortstop—A baseball player in the position between second base and third base.
short|stop (shawrt′stop′) *noun, plural* **shortstops.**

shot[1]—1. The firing of a weapon, such as a gun. 2. Something that is fired from a weapon: *The gangster's* shot *missed his enemy.* 3. A person who shoots a weapon: *The army taught him to be a good* shot. 4. The sending of a spacecraft into space: *the moon* shot. 5. The range or distance over which something can be fired: *within* shot *of the target.* 6. An injection of a drug: *We went to the doctor's office for a flu* shot. 7. A photograph: *I took this* shot *with my new camera.* 8. An aimed stroke or throw in certain games: *The golfer took some practice* shots.
shot (shot) *noun, plural* **shots** or **shot.**
 ▪ **not by a long shot:** Not at all: *Did you do well in the race? Not by a long shot.*

shot[2]—*See* **shoot.**
shot (shot) *verb.*

shotgun—A type of gun that shoots many small balls of metal each time it is fired.
shot|gun (shot′gun′) *noun, plural* **shotguns.**

shot-put—An athletic event in which a very heavy ball is thrown through the air as far as possible.
shot-put (shot′poot′) *noun.*

shot-put

should—*See* **shall.**
should (shood) *verb.*

shoulder—1. The body part that connects the arm to the rest of the body. 2. The portion of a piece of clothing that covers this part of the body. 3. The edge along a road: *If the car breaks down, try to pull over to the* shoulder *to get it out of traffic.* Noun.
—To shove with the shoulder: *He* shouldered *his way past us.* Verb.
shoul|der (shōl′dər) *noun, plural* **shoulders;** *verb,* **shouldered, shouldering.**

shouldn't—The contraction of "should not."
should|n't (shood′ənt).

shout—To yell; cry out loudly: *He* shouted *for his dog to come back.* Verb.
—A loud cry or yell: *The lifeguard jumped up*

a at	i if	oo look	ch chalk		⌐a in ago
ā ape	ī idle	ou out	ng sing		e in happen
ah calm	o odd	u ugly	sh ship	ə =	i in capital
aw all	ō oats	ū rule	th think		o in occur
e end	oi oil	ur turn	th their		⌐u in upon
ē easy			zh treasure		

when she heard a shout *from a swimmer. Noun.*
shout (shout) *verb,* **shouted, shouting;** *noun,*
plural **shouts.**
- Synonyms: For *verb,* see Synonyms at **cry,**
verb 2.
Antonyms: **mumble, mutter, whisper,** for
verb.

shove—To push with force: *I will help you* shove
the box under the bed. Verb.
—A forceful push: *I think I will need a* shove *to*
start my sled down the hill. Noun.
shove (shuv) *verb,* **shoved, shoving;** *noun,*
plural **shoves.**

shovel—A long-handled tool with a broad blade,
used for digging and moving substances such as
dirt or snow. *Noun.*
—1. To dig and move with such a tool: *They*
shoveled *the cold ashes from the fireplace.*
2. To put or move in large amounts, usually in a
careless way: *The children* shoveled *the blocks*
back into the toy box. Verb.
shov|el (shuv′əl) *noun, plural* **shovels;** *verb,*
shoveled, shoveling.

show—1. To allow to be seen: *Please* show *your*
ticket at the door. 2. To display in public;
exhibit: *to* show *a movie.* 3. To reveal; make
known: *She* showed *her good manners when she*
let the elderly man have her seat. 4. To be in
sight: *Does the grass stain* show? 5. To point
out: *Our tour guide* showed *us all the historical*
sights of the city. 6. To explain to: *The artist is*
showing *the class how to draw.* 7. To give or
grant, often as a favor: *The queen* showed *mercy*
to the prisoners and set them free. Verb.
—1. A public display or exhibition: *an art* show.
2. A play, movie, television program, or other
entertainment: *We talked about the* show *all the*
way home from the theater. 3. A pretended
display: *She politely made a* show *of pleasure*
even though she did not like the dessert.
Noun.
show (shō) *verb,* **showed, showing;** *noun, plural*
shows.
- **show up:** To appear or arrive: *Their team never*
showed up *for the track meet.*
steal the show: To get the most attention: *The*
daring trapeze performers stole the show *at the*
circus.

shower—1. A brief fall of rain: *The weather*
forecast calls for showers *tomorrow.* 2. A large
amount of anything falling: *a* shower *of confetti.*
3. A bath in which water sprays down from
above: *I will need a* shower *when we finish*
cleaning the attic. Noun.

—1. To rain briefly: *It* showered *this morning,*
and then the sun came out. 2. To bathe by
spraying water from above: *I* showered *after the*
game. 3. To sprinkle or pour down upon: *Ash*
and soot showered *the city after the big fire.*
4. To give in large amounts. *Verb.*
show|er (shou′ər) *noun, plural* **showers;** *verb,*
showered, showering.

shown—*See* **show.**
shown (shōn) *verb.*
- A word that sounds the same is **shone.**

show-off—A person whose actions are done only
to attract attention: *After she crossed the finish*
line, she did two somersaults and a cartwheel,
just to be a show-off.
show-off (shō′awf′) *noun, plural* **show-offs.**

shrank—*See* **shrink.**
shrank (shrangk) *verb.*

shred—1. A small strip cut or torn off: *I need*
some shreds *of fabric to make a tail for my kite.*
2. A very small amount: *As the last* shred *of*
sunlight disappeared, the street lights came on.
Noun.
—To cut or tear into strips: *I need to* shred *some*
cheese for the pizza. Verb.
shred (shred) *noun, plural* **shreds;** *verb,*
shredded or **shred, shredding.**

shrewd—Having or showing careful thinking;
clever: *The salesperson was so* shrewd *that I*
ended up buying more than I had intended.
shrewd (shrūd) *adjective,* **shrewder,**
shrewdest.

Word History

Shrewd comes from an old English word and
once meant "wicked" or "with a bad temper."
People who do not like others can sometimes
find clever ways to be unkind. Today, shrewd
means "clever" or "with a sharp mind."

---

shriek—A loud, shrill cry or sound: *the* shriek *of*
a fire alarm; shrieks *of laughter. Noun.*
—To make a loud, shrill cry or sound: *We all*
shrieked *when the roller coaster sped down the*
track. Verb.
shriek (shrēk) *noun, plural* **shrieks;** *verb,*
shrieked, shrieking.

shrill—Having a sound that is high and piercing:
The shrill *sound of the bugle woke the sleeping*
soldiers.
shrill (shril) *adjective,* **shriller, shrillest.**

shrimp—A small shellfish that has a long tail and is eaten as food.
shrimp (shrimp) *noun, plural* **shrimps** or **shrimp.**

shrimp

shrine—A place, such as a tomb or chapel, where holy objects are kept.
shrine (shrīn) *noun, plural* **shrines.**

shrink—**1.** To become smaller or less: *My jeans shrank in the wash.* **2.** To move back, usually from fear: *Everyone shrank from the cage when the lions began to roar.*
shrink (shringk) *verb,* **shrank** or **shrunk, shrunk** or **shrunken, shrinking.**

shrub—A woody plant, smaller than a tree, that has many branching stems; bush.
shrub (shrub) *noun, plural* **shrubs.**

shrug—To raise the shoulders to show doubt or lack of interest: *She just shrugged her shoulders when we asked what she wanted to do. Verb.*
—The act of raising the shoulders to show doubt or lack of interest: *The farmer gave us a shrug when we asked her where a gas station was. Noun.*
shrug (shrug) *verb,* **shrugged, shrugging;** *noun, plural* **shrugs.**

shrunk—*See* **shrink.**
shrunk (shrungk) *verb.*

shudder—To tremble suddenly with cold or fear; shiver: *I held the puppy in my arms because the thunder made it shudder. Verb.*
—The act of trembling or shivering: *A shudder went through me when I went from a warm bath to the cold hallway. Noun.*

shud|der (shud′ər) *verb,* **shuddered, shuddering;** *noun, plural* **shudders.**

shuffle—**1.** To drag the feet on the ground while walking: *We shuffled across the lawn to try to get the mud off our shoes.* **2.** To change the order of: *It is my turn to be the dealer, so I will shuffle the cards.* **3.** To move about or mix together in a random way: *I shuffled record albums while trying to decide which ones to take to the party. Verb.*
—**1.** The act of dragging the feet while walking: *The weary girl set off for home in a shuffle.*
2. A turn to change the order of a deck of cards: *It is your shuffle. Noun.*
shuf|fle (shuf′əl) *verb,* **shuffled, shuffling;** *noun, plural* **shuffles.**

shuffleboard—A game in which heavy disks are pushed across a flat surface that has numbered spaces. Players stand on either end of the playing surface and use long wooden sticks to push the disks.
shuf|fle|board (shuf′əl bawrd′) *noun.*

shun—To avoid someone or something because of dislike, distrust, or caution: *Mother shuns the five o'clock traffic because it is always very heavy.*
shun (shun) *verb,* **shunned, shunning.**

shut—**1.** To move something into a closed position: *Please shut the door.* **2.** To close something by bringing its parts together: *Father shut the magazine and came to dinner.* **3.** To keep in or out by closing something: *to shut out the music; to shut the dog in the house for the night.*
shut (shut) *verb,* **shut, shutting.**

shutter—**1.** An attached window cover that can be opened and closed. **2.** A part on a camera that opens and closes to let in the right amount of light for taking a picture.
shut|ter (shut′ər) *noun, plural* **shutters.**

shuttle—**1.** A device used in weaving that carries the thread back and forth between the threads that are held in place. **2.** A device on a sewing machine that holds and moves the lower thread. **3.** A public vehicle, such as a bus, train, or airplane, that makes regular, short round trips. *Noun.*
—To make a short round trip: *We shuttled to the city for a business meeting. Verb.*
shut|tle (shut′əl) *noun, plural* **shuttles;** *verb,* **shuttled, shuttling.**

shy—**1.** Not comfortable around people; bashful: *Now that she is a cheerleader, it is hard to believe that she used to be shy.* **2.** Easily scared: *We tried to lure the shy rabbits into our yard.*

a at	i if	oo look	ch chalk		
ā ape	ī idle	ou out	ng sing		a in ago
ah calm	o odd	u ugly	sh ship	ə =	e in happen
aw all	ō oats	ū rule	th think		i in capital
e end	oi oil	ur turn	th their		o in occur
ē easy			zh treasure		u in upon

3. Short of a desired amount; not having enough: *We are one chair* shy *of the number we need. Adjective.*
—**1.** To move back or sideways suddenly: *The horse* shied *when it heard the loud noise.* **2.** To draw back to avoid: *The actor* shies *away from people who want his autograph. Verb.*
shy (shī) *adjective,* **shyer** or **shier, shyest** or **shiest;** *verb,* **shied, shying.**

Siamese cat—A short-haired cat that has blue eyes, a small, pointed face, large ears, and a long thin tail. It is tan or grayish white with darker markings around the face, ears, tail, and feet. These cats were originally bred in Thailand, once called Siam.
Si|a|mese cat (sī′ə mēz′ kat) *noun, plural* **Siamese cats.**

Siamese cat

Siberian husky—A medium-sized working dog with a soft, thick coat that can be tan, black, or gray with white markings. It has small ears and a thick tail that curves over its back. Originally bred in northern Russia, these dogs are used to pull sleds.
Si|be|ri|an husk|y (sī ber′ē ən hus′kē) *noun, plural* **Siberian huskies.**

sick—**1.** Not healthy; having an illness: *My grandmother is* sick *with the flu.* **2.** Likely to throw up: *Airplane trips make me feel* sick. **3.** Having had too much of something; disgusted: *By the end of winter, he is* sick *of cold weather.*
sick (sik) *adjective,* **sicker, sickest.**

sickle—A hand tool used for cutting tall grass, weeds, and grain. It has a sharp, curved blade on a short handle.
sick|le (sik′əl) *noun, plural* **sickles.**

sickness—**1.** The condition of poor health; illness: *There has been a lot of* sickness *in our school this year.* **2.** A particular illness.
sick|ness (sik′nis) *noun, plural* **sicknesses.**
• Synonyms: **ailment, disease,** for 2.
 Antonym: **health,** for 2.

side—**1.** A surface or line forming a boundary: *A square has four* sides. **2.** A surface that is not the top, bottom, back, or front: *Walk around to the left* side *of the barn.* **3.** One of the two surfaces of a flat object: *Write only on the front* side *of your paper.* **4.** One of two or more competing individuals, groups, teams, or views: *a* side *of a story; to pick* sides *in a football game.* **5.** A part of something away from the center: *my* side *of the bedroom; the north* side *of town.* **6.** Either the right or left half of a body: *I always go to sleep on my right* side. **7.** A line of relatives: *my mother's* side *of the family. Noun.*
—Being at or on a surface that forms a boundary: *I had to climb through a* side *window because we got locked out. Adjective.*
—**1.** To cover a surface that forms a boundary: *They are* siding *the garage with aluminum panels.* **2.** To take a position in a contest or argument; agree: *We* sided *with the governor's ideas on how to fight water pollution. Verb.*
side (sīd) *noun, plural* **sides;** *adjective; verb,* **sides, siding.**

sidesaddle—A saddle that lets a rider sit with both legs on the same side of a horse. *Noun.*
—With both legs on the same side of a horse: *The woman rode* sidesaddle. *Adverb.*
side|sad|dle (sīd′sad′əl) *noun, plural* **sidesaddles;** *adverb.*

sidetrack—To turn attention away from the main issue: *While I was doing my homework I was* sidetracked *when the phone rang.*
side|track (sīd′trak′) *verb,* **sidetracked, sidetracking.**

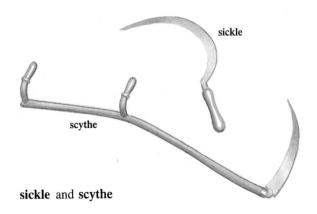

sickle and **scythe**

sidewalk—A path for walking that is often made of concrete; pavement.
side|walk (sīd′wawk′) *noun, plural* **sidewalks.**

sideways—1. To or from one side: *I turned* sideways *so I could see in the mirror how the pants fit me.* 2. With one side facing forward: *Turn the boxes* sideways *so they all fit on the shelf. Adverb.*
—Facing or directed toward one side: *I got a* sideways *view of the actor as he walked past me.*
side|ways (sīd′wāz′) *adverb, adjective.*

siege—The surrounding of an enemy fort or city by an army trying to capture it. A siege cuts off the supply of food and weapons in an attempt to force those inside to surrender.
siege (sēj) *noun, plural* **sieges.**

siesta—An afternoon rest. Siestas are often taken in countries where it gets too hot to work in the afternoon.
si|es|ta (sē es′tə) *noun, plural* **siestas.**

sieve—A kitchen tool with many small holes in the bottom. It lets liquids and very small pieces of material pass through but holds in larger pieces.
sieve (siv) *noun, plural* **sieves.**

sift—1. To separate large parts from small parts with a sieve or screen: *We sifted the rocks from the soil.* 2. To pass through a sieve or screen to make smoother or finer: *I sifted the flour to get rid of the lumps.* 3. To examine closely and carefully: *She sifted through many history books to prepare her report.*
sift (sift) *verb,* **sifted, sifting.**
• Synonyms: **filter, strain,** for 1.

sigh—1. To let out a long, deep breath because of sorrow, weariness, or relief: *I sighed when I found the lost money in the pocket of a dirty pair of pants.* 2. To make a sound like a long, deep breath: *Late at night, I can hear the old clock in the hall sighing and wheezing. Verb.*
—The act of taking a long, deep breath, or the sound of such a breath: *She let out a sigh as she snuggled in her bed. Noun.*
sigh (sī) *verb,* **sighed, sighing;** *noun, plural* **sighs.**

sight—1. The ability to see; vision: *The eye doctor told him that he had perfect* sight. 2. The act of viewing; seeing: *The baby got excited at the* sight *of her mother.* 3. The distance one is able to see: *They watched until the car drove out of* sight. 4. A display, scene, or other thing worthy of viewing: *The jewels at the museum are a wonderful* sight. 5. Something that is messed up or not pleasing to the eye: *The yard was a* sight *after the hurricane.* 6. A device on cameras, telescopes, and other instruments that helps the user to aim. *Noun.*
—To catch a view of; see: *The child* sighted *her grandparents and ran to meet them. Verb.*
sight (sīt) *noun, plural* **sights;** *verb,* **sighted, sighting.**
• A word that sounds the same is **site.**

sightseeing—The act of visiting and touring a place: *The book listed all the places for* sightseeing *in the city.*
sight|see|ing (sīt′sē′ing) *noun.*

sign—1. A board or the like with something written on it that informs, warns, or directs: *We followed highway* signs *to the airport.* 2. An indication of a state or condition; warning: *Her sniffling could be a* sign *of an allergy.* 3. A clue; evidence: *The footprints in the snow were a* sign *that someone had been there before them.* 4. A mark that represents something; symbol: *A picture of an airplane on a map is a* sign *that an airport is located in the area.* 5. A signal made by the movement of the body; gesture: *When the referee raised his arm, it was a* sign *to start the game. Noun.*
—To write one's name on: *Please* sign *at the end of the report. Verb.*
sign (sīn) *noun, plural* **signs;** *verb,* **signed, signing.**

signal—1. A device or object that warns, directs, or reminds: *The alarm was a* signal *to leave the building.* 2. A sign or sound that means the start of something: *The first note played by the band was the* signal *for the marchers to start walking. Noun.*
—1. To tell something to someone by a sign: *He* signaled *us to be silent by putting his finger on his lips.* 2. To tell or show something by giving off a sign: *The chiming of the bells* signals *the start of church services. Verb.*
sig|nal (sig′nəl) *noun, plural* **signals;** *verb,* **signaled, signaling.**

signature—1. The name of a person written by his or her own hand. 2. In music, a group of signs showing the exact key and timing used for

a at	i if	oo look	ch chalk		a in ago
ā ape	ī idle	ou out	ng sing		e in happen
ah calm	o odd	u ugly	sh ship	ə =	i in capital
aw all	ō oats	ū rule	th think		o in occur
e end	oi oil	ur turn	th their		u in upon
ē easy			zh treasure		

the music that follows. It usually appears at the beginning of a piece of music.

sig|na|ture (sig′nə chər) *noun, plural* **signatures.**

significance—**1.** Importance; seriousness: *When I saw the filthy river, I realized the* significance *of fighting pollution.* **2.** The meaning of something: *The teacher explained the* significance *of the poem to us.*

sig|nif|i|cance (sig nif′ə kəns) *noun.*

significant—Important; meaningful: *His first airplane ride had been a* significant *event in the pilot's life.*

sig|nif|i|cant (sig nif′ə kənt) *adjective.*

signify—**1.** To stand for; mean: *Red* signifies *stop.* **2.** To express something by words or signals: *to* signify *disapproval by shaking the head back and forth.*

sig|ni|fy (sig′nə fī) *verb,* **signified, signifying.**

sign language—A way of communicating without talking, by gesturing with the hands and arms to signify letters, words, or phrases.

sign lan|guage (sīn lang′gwij) *noun, plural* **sign languages.**

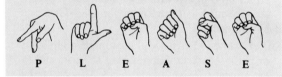

P L E A S E

sign language: In sign language, the manual, or finger, alphabet is used to spell words.

Sikhism—A religion of India, founded about 1500. It teaches that there is one God and that people live many times.

Sikh|ism (sē′kiz əm) *noun.*

silence—**1.** A lack of noise; total stillness; not a sound: *When there was* silence, *she began to read the story to the children.* **2.** The act of not speaking: *His* silences *often mean that he is thinking hard about what to say. Noun.*
—To make still, quiet, or soundless: *to* silence *the radio. Verb.*

si|lence (sī′ləns) *noun, plural* **silences;** *verb,* **silenced, silencing.**

• Synonyms: **quiet, still,** for *noun* **1.**
   Antonyms: **clamor, commotion, din, racket, uproar,** for *noun* **1.**

silent—**1.** Having no sound; making no noise: *Because the computer was* silent, *she did not realize it was turned on.* **2.** Without a word; not talking: *It is important to be* silent *when leaving the building during a fire drill.* **3.** Not pronounced; not given sound: *Some letters in words are called* silent *because they are not sounded when saying the word, such as the ''gh'' in ''sight.''*

si|lent (sī′lənt) *adjective.*

silhouette—**1.** An outline of something, usually the side view of a person's head, which is either cut out of black paper or drawn and filled in with black. **2.** The outline of something, easily seen because it is in front of a lighter, larger background: *We could see the* silhouette *of our house in the faint moonlight. Noun.*
—To show the shape or outline: *In the photograph, she was* silhouetted *against the white background. Verb.*

sil|hou|ette (sil′ū et′) *noun, plural* **silhouettes;** *verb,* **silhouetted, silhouetting.**

silhouette (noun, definition 1)

silicon—A chemical element that is always found with another chemical. It is found in such things as sand, rocks, and crystals, and it is used in making glass, computer parts, and steel.

sil|i|con (sil′ə kən) *noun.*

silk—**1.** A threadlike fiber that is made by silkworms. The silkworm uses this fiber to build its cocoon. **2.** Cloth made from this substance: *My blouse is smooth and soft because it is made from* silk. **3.** Something that looks or feels like this fiber or this cloth. *Noun.*

silk (silk) *noun, plural* **silks.**

silkworm—A type of caterpillar that produces silk with which to make its cocoon.

silk|worm (silk′wurm′) *noun, plural* **silkworms.**

silky terrier—A very small dog with small, pointed ears and a long, smooth, blue-tan coat. Its hair is parted in the middle on the top of its

head and down its back. Originally bred in Australia, this dog makes a good pet.
silk|y ter|ri|er (sil′kē ter′ē ər) *noun, plural* **silky terriers.**

sill—The long piece of wood or other hard material that lies beneath a door or window.
sill (sil) *noun, plural* **sills.**

silly—Lacking sense; ridiculous: *a silly face.*
sil|ly (sil′ē) *adjective,* **sillier, silliest.**

Word History

Silly comes from an old English word meaning "weak" or "to be pitied," which came from an even older English word meaning "happy." Some people who do not think well seem to be very happy, perhaps even happier than other people. But they also have problems that deserve pity. **Silly** has pointed to the happiness, then the pity. Now it is used for a kind of lack of sense that is foolish but cheerful.

---

silo—1. An airtight tower used by a farmer to store food for livestock. 2. A narrow, deep hole under the earth that is equipped to contain and fire a guided missile.
si|lo (sī′lō) *noun, plural* **silos.**

silo
(definition 1)

silt—1. Small pieces of dirt and other matter that are picked up and carried along by flowing water. 2. The layer of small pieces of dirt and other matter that builds up when these materials settle at the bottom of a river, lake, or other body of water.
silt (silt) *noun.*

silver—1. A precious metal that is pale gray and shiny. It is very soft, a good carrier of electricity and heat, and easy to shape. It is a chemical element. 2. Money that is made of this metal or made to look like it; coins: *When I counted the silver in my purse, I found that I had six dimes and two quarters.* 3. Eating and serving tools, such as knives, spoons, bowls, and dishes, that are made out of this metal or made to look like it. 4. A shiny, pale gray color: *The snow scattered silver on the dark green trees. Noun.*
—1. Made from this metal: *a silver bracelet; a silver dollar.* 2. Having a shiny, pale gray color: *a silver car; a silver crayon. Adjective.*
—To apply a coat of this metal: *The plate was made from copper and then silvered. Verb.*
sil|ver (sil′vər) *noun, plural* **silvers;** *adjective;* *verb,* **silvered, silvering.**

silversmith—A person whose job is to make or repair things of silver.
sil|ver|smith (sil′vər smith′) *noun, plural* **silversmiths.**

silverware—1. All the things made completely or partly of silver that are used to serve and to eat a meal. 2. Any metal forks, spoons, and knives used at a meal: *Please put the silverware on the table.*
sil|ver|ware (sil′vər wār′) *noun.*

similar—Alike; having a resemblance: *The earrings were similar in shape, but one pair was gold and the other was silver.*
sim|i|lar (sim′ə lər) *adjective.*

simile—A phrase that compares two things. "A shaggy dog with hair like a mop" and "muscles tough as steel" are two similes.
sim|i|le (sim′ə lē) *noun, plural* **similes.**

simmer—To heat liquid just to the point of boiling; cook with a low heat: *She simmered the vegetables in water.*
sim|mer (sim′ər) *verb,* **simmered, simmering.**

simple—1. Not complicated; not difficult; easy: *a simple puzzle;* simple *directions.* 2. Not having many pieces, parts, or steps: *a simple recipe; a* simple *machine.* 3. Not fancy or decorated: *She wore a simple green dress with a yellow scarf.* 4. Modest; plain; sincere: *My grandmother is a simple person and is always easy to be with.*

a at	i if	oo look	ch chalk		a in ago
ā ape	ī idle	ou out	ng sing		e in happen
ah calm	o odd	u ugly	sh ship	ə =	i in capital
aw all	ō oats	ū rule	th think		o in occur
e end	oi oil	ur turn	th their		u in upon
ē easy			zh treasure		

sim|ple (sim′pəl) *adjective,* **simpler, simplest.**

simplify—To make less complicated or difficult; put in a way that is easy to follow or understand: *When his mother* simplified *the directions, the child was able to make the cookies himself.* **sim|pli|fy** (sim′plə fī) *verb,* **simplified, simplifying.**

simply—1. In a way that is not complicated; easily: *Although the meal was put together* simply, *it was delicious.* 2. Plainly; without much added; in a modest way: *His room was furnished* simply, *with a bed, a dresser, and a table.* 3. No more than; just: *We* simply *went to the movies and came right home.* 4. Without doubt; definitely; thoroughly: *Our vacation was* simply *wonderful!* **sim|ply** (sim′plē) *adverb.*

sin—1. Something done on purpose that one believes is wrong in the eyes of God: *He knew that telling a lie was a* sin, *so he told the truth.* 2. Something that is not right and good: *It is a* sin *to waste food. Noun.* —To do something on purpose that one believes is wrong in the eyes of God. *Verb.* **sin** (sin) *noun, plural* **sins;** *verb,* **sinned, sinning.**

since—1. From a certain time in the past until the present time: *Dinner has been ready* since *six o'clock.* 2. In between a certain past time and now: *I have not seen her* since *last year. Preposition.* —1. In the time following a certain past time: *She has not gone swimming* since *she went to the beach last summer.* 2. Due to the fact that; because: *They will leave early,* since *traffic will be heavy later on. Conjunction.* —1. From then on; after then: *We got into the car early this morning and have been driving ever* since. 2. In the meantime: *At first he was not going to go, but he has changed his mind* since. *Adverb.* **since** (sins) *preposition, conjunction, adverb.*

sincere—Meaning what one says; truthful; not pretending: *She is* sincere *when she says she wants to help.* **sin|cere** (sin sēr′) *adjective,* **sincerer, sincerest.**

sing—1. To use the voice to perform music: *They all* sang *"Happy Birthday" when the cake was brought to the table.* 2. To make sounds like music: singing *birds.* **sing** (sing) *verb,* **sang** or **sung, sung, singing.**

singe—To almost burn; burn in a slight way, usually just at the edge; scorch: *He* singed *the napkin by putting it too near the stove.* **singe** (sinj) *verb,* **singed, singeing.**

single—1. One; individual: *There was a* single *chair by the window.* 2. Meant for one: *a* single *office; a game for a* single *player.* 3. Without a husband or wife; not married: *My aunt was* single *until her wedding last year. Adjective.* —1. One thing that is alone; a person or thing that is not attached to another; a person who is not married: *The chair is sold as a* single, *but you can buy two and put them together.* 2. In baseball, a hit that sends the batter to first base and no farther: *He hit a* single *in the first inning. Noun.* —1. To choose one from many: *She* singled *out the pink curtains for her room after seeing all the colors available.* 2. In baseball, to get a hit that sends the batter to first base and no farther: *She* singled *when the bases were loaded and drove home a run. Verb.* **sin|gle** (sing′gəl) *adjective; noun, plural* **singles;** *verb,* **singled, singling.**

singular—1. Not common; unique or rare: *A twenty-fifth anniversary celebration is a* singular *event.* 2. Meaning one person, place, or thing: singular *nouns, such as "cowgirl," "forest," and "spoon." Adjective.* —A word meaning one person, place, or thing: *The* singular *of "dogs" is "dog." Noun.* **sin|gu|lar** (sing′gyə lər) *adjective; noun, plural* **singulars.** Abbreviation: **sing.**

sinister—1. Looking like a threat; able to frighten people: *The pirate costume looked* sinister. 2. Wicked or evil: *a movie about* sinister *creatures from the swamp.* **sin|is|ter** (sin′ə stər) *adjective.*

Word History

Sinister comes from a Latin word meaning "left." Long ago, people believed in telling the future by signs and appearances. Something appearing on one's left side was a sign of bad luck.

---

sink—1. To go lower gradually; go down; descend: *Hold the spoon or it will* sink *into the gravy.* 2. To reduce or be reduced; lessen: *The number of students in the school* sank *to the lowest level in five years.* 3. To slip into a condition: *to* sink *into boredom.* 4. To dig or drill: *to* sink *an oil well.* 5. In certain sports, to cause the ball to go into something such as a basket or hole: *In last night's basketball game, I sank two free throws. Verb.*

—A bowl built into a frame, with faucets to put water in it and a drain to let water out. Kitchens and bathrooms have sinks. *Noun.*

sink (singk) *verb,* **sank** or **sunk, sunk, sinking;** *noun, plural* **sinks.**

sip—To drink very slowly, taking in small amounts at a time: *If you* sip *the soda, it will last longer. Verb.*

—A small drink: *a* sip *of hot cocoa. Noun.*

sip (sip) *verb,* **sipped, sipping;** *noun, plural* **sips.**

siphon—A device for moving liquids. One end of a tube is placed in a container filled with liquid, and the other end of the tube is set in another container on a lower level. Air pressure causes the liquid to flow from the higher container to the lower container. *Noun.*

—To transfer liquid in this way: *She* siphoned *the water from the fish tank into the bathtub so she could clean the tank. Verb.*

si|phon (sī′fən) *noun, plural* **siphons;** *verb,* **siphoned, siphoning.**

siphon
(noun)

sir—1. A name for a man that shows respect. 2. **Sir:** A title for a knight.

sir (sur) *noun, plural* **sirs.**

a at	i if	oo look	ch chalk	⎡ a in ago
ā ape	ī idle	ou out	ng sing	e in happen
ah calm	o odd	u ugly	sh ship	ə = ⎪ i in capital
aw all	ō oats	ū rule	th think	o in occur
e end	oi oil	ur turn	th their	⎣ u in upon
ē easy			zh treasure	

siren—A device, such as a horn, that makes a very loud sound as an alarm or warning: *Every day at noon, the* siren *at the fire station blows.*

si|ren (sī′rən) *noun, plural* **sirens.**

sister—1. A female with the same parents as another or others: *I have three* sisters *and one brother.* 2. A woman who is in the same group or has the same interests as other women. A nun is usually called a sister.

sis|ter (sis′tər) *noun, plural* **sisters.**

sisterhood—1. The special feeling that sisters, or women who feel as close as sisters, have for each other. 2. A group of women sharing the same beliefs or goals.

sis|ter|hood (sis′tər hood) *noun, plural* **sisterhoods.**

sister-in-law—1. A sister of one's wife or husband. 2. A brother's wife.

sis|ter-in-law (sis′tər in law′) *noun, plural* **sisters-in-law.**

sit—1. To bend the lower part of the body and rest upon something so that the weight is off the feet and settles on the lower back and upper legs: *Feel free to* sit *on the chair and rest your feet on the stool.* 2. To be on; rest on: *The sugar bowl* sits *on the table all the time.* 3. To be a part of a special group: *to* sit *on a jury.* 4. To stay still for a photograph or a portrait to be painted: *She made an appointment with the photographer for them to* sit *for a family picture.* 5. To take care of; watch over: *He* sits *for other people's children to earn money.*

sit (sit) *verb,* **sat, sitting.**

site—The spot where something is or will be located; setting: *The* site *for the carnival will be the town's park.*

site (sīt) *noun, plural* **sites.**

- Words that sound the same are **cite** and **sight**.
- Synonyms: **location, place, position, situation**

situation—**1.** The state of things at a particular time; facts that together create a particular condition: *The* situation *seemed hopeless until we came up with a great idea for raising money.* **2.** A job; work: *She hoped to find a* situation *for the summer months.* **3.** Location; site: *The cottage we'll be staying in has a scenic* situation, *on a hill overlooking the lake.*
sit|u|a|tion (sich′ū ā′shən) *noun, plural* **situations.**
- Synonyms: **place, position, spot,** for **3.**

six—One more than five; one less than seven; 6: **six** (siks) *adjective; noun, plural* **sixes.**

sixteen—Six more than ten; one more than fifteen; 16.
six|teen (siks′tēn′) *adjective; noun, plural* **sixteens.**

sixteenth—**1.** Next after the fifteenth. **2.** One of sixteen equal parts.
six|teenth (siks′tēnth′) *adjective; noun, plural* **sixteenths.**

sixth—**1.** Next after the fifth. **2.** One of six equal parts.
sixth (siksth) *adjective; noun, plural* **sixths.**

sixtieth—**1.** Next after the fifty-ninth. **2.** One of sixty equal parts.
six|ti|eth (siks′tē ith) *adjective; noun, plural* **sixtieths.**

sixty—Six times ten; one more than fifty-nine; 60.
six|ty (siks′tē) *noun, plural* **sixties;** *adjective.*

size—**1.** The amount of space that is filled by something: *The* size *of the new library is much larger than that of the old one.* **2.** The quantity or amount of something: *the* size *of my mother's pay check.* **3.** A measurement used in making things: *He wears a* size *9 shoe.*
size (sīz) *noun, plural* **sizes.**

sizzle—To become hot and make a hissing noise: *The hamburgers* sizzled *in the frying pan.*
siz|zle (siz′əl) *verb,* **sizzled, sizzling.**

skate¹—**1.** A boot or shoe with a metal blade, used as a device to enable one to move quickly on ice: *a pair of ice* skates. **2.** A boot or shoe with small wheels, used for moving quickly over a hard surface like wood or concrete: *a pair of roller* skates. *Noun.*
—To move over ice or a hard surface in special boots or shoes. *Verb.*
skate (skāt) *noun, plural* **skates;** *verb,* **skated, skating.**

skate²—A fish with a broad, flat body and a long tail. A skate is a type of ray.
skate (skāt) *noun, plural* **skates.**

skate²

skateboard—A short, narrow board with wheels on the bottom that is ridden over hard surfaces.
skate|board (skāt′bawrd′) *noun, plural* **skateboards.**

skeleton—**1.** The bones of a human or animal body. **2.** A framework that supports something: *Some houses have wooden* skeletons. *Noun.*
skel|e|ton (skel′ə tən) *noun, plural* **skeletons.**
- **skeleton in** (one's) **closet:** A secret fact that causes shame: *He does not talk much about his family because he is afraid people will find out about the* skeletons in *his* closet.

sketch—**1.** A quick, simple drawing of something: *She made a* sketch *of her dog.* **2.** A brief description or story: *He gave us a* sketch *of his vacation plans. Noun.*
—**1.** To draw quickly: *The artist* sketched *the model's face.* **2.** To give a brief description of: *She* sketched *out her plan to her friends. Verb.*
sketch (skech) *noun, plural* **sketches;** *verb,* **sketched, sketching.**

ski—One of a pair of long, thin pieces of wood or metal, used to move over snow or water. *Noun.*
—To move over snow or water: *We* skied *on the lake yesterday. Verb.*
ski (skē) *noun, plural* **skis** or **ski;** *verb,* **skied, skiing.**

skid—To slide on a slippery surface: *The boy's bike* skidded *on a patch of ice. Verb.*
—A slide on a slippery surface: *The motorcycle went into a* skid *when it tried to stop on a wet road. Noun.*
skid (skid) *verb,* **skidded, skidding;** *noun, plural* **skids.**
- **on the skids:** In the process of falling from a successful state: *That actor was once very popular, but now he is* on the skids.

skill—The ability to do something well: *He has a real* skill *at making new friends quickly.*
skill (skil) *noun, plural* **skills.**

skilled—**1.** Having the ability to do something well; expert: *He is a skilled musician.*
2. Needing a special ability or special training: *Teaching children to read is a skilled job.*
skilled (skild) *adjective.*
● Synonyms: **capable, competent,** for **1.**
Antonyms: **incompetent, unqualified,** for **1.**

skillet—A frying pan.
skil|let (skil′it) *noun, plural* **skillets.**

skillful—**1.** Having skill; expert: *a* skillful *carpenter.* **2.** Showing skill: *That rock wall is a* skillful *piece of work.*
skill|ful (skil′fəl) *adjective.*

skim—**1.** To take off something from the top of a liquid: *Mother* skimmed *the fat off the gravy.*
2. To move over quickly and lightly: *The dead leaves* skimmed *the ground as the wind blew them away.* **3.** To glance over; read quickly: *She* skimmed *the magazine while she waited in line.*
skim (skim) *verb,* **skimmed, skimming.**

skin—**1.** The covering around the body of a person or animal. **2.** The hide of an animal: *He has a rug made of bear* skin. *Noun.*
—To remove this covering from: *to* skin *a rabbit; to* skin *my knee on the sidewalk. Verb.*
skin (skin) *noun, plural* **skins;** *verb,* **skinned, skinning.**

■ **by the skin of** (one's) **teeth:** Just barely; by the smallest possible amount: *He passed the test* by the skin of *his* teeth.
get under (one's) **skin:** To anger or irritate someone: *She would not let her brother's teasing* get under *her* skin.
jump out of (one's) **skin:** To react with great delight or surprise: *I nearly* jumped out of my skin *when the cannon went off.*

skin diving—Underwater swimming using a face mask, flippers, and a breathing device.
skin div|ing (skin dī′ving) *noun.*
● See picture at **aqualung.**

skinny—Very thin; lean: *a* skinny *cat.*
skin|ny (skin′ē) *adjective,* **skinnier, skinniest.**
● Synonyms: **gaunt, scrawny, spare**
Antonyms: **fat, plump, stout**

skip—**1.** To move with light, hopping steps: *The girls* skipped *across the yard.* **2.** To bounce across a surface: *The stone* skipped *over the water.* **3.** To pay little or no attention to; leave out: *He* skipped *the math problems he did not understand.* **4.** To hop or spring over something: *She likes to* skip *rope.* **5.** To be promoted beyond the next regular grade: *He* skipped *third grade. Verb.*
—A light, hopping step: *The boy took a* skip *over the curb. Noun.*
skip (skip) *verb,* **skipped, skipping;** *noun, plural* **skips.**

skirt—**1.** A piece of woman's or girl's clothing that covers below the waist. It fastens around the waist and hangs down. **2.** Something like this piece of clothing that is part of a dress. *Noun.*
—**1.** To form a border around: *Trees* skirted *the camp ground.* **2.** To move around the border of: *We* skirted *the village on our bicycles. Verb.*
skirt (skurt) *noun, plural* **skirts;** *verb,* **skirted, skirting.**

skull—The bones of the head that surround and protect the brain.
skull (skul) *noun, plural* **skulls.**

skunk—An animal with black fur, a white stripe down its back, and a tail that looks like a little bush. When it is frightened, it sprays a liquid that smells bad.
skunk (skungk) *noun, plural* **skunks.**

skunk

sky—The space above the earth; the heavens: *We can see stars in the* sky *at night.*
sky (skī) *noun, plural* **skies.**
■ **out of a clear blue sky:** Without warning; all of a sudden: *Because she seemed to be doing very well, the candidate's withdrawal from the race for senator came* out of a clear blue sky.

sky diving or **skydiving**—An amusement or sport that involves leaping from an airplane in flight and falling some distance before opening the parachute one is wearing.

a at	i if	oo look	ch chalk		a in ago
ā ape	ī idle	ou out	ng sing		e in happen
ah calm	o odd	u ugly	sh ship	ə =	i in capital
aw all	ō oats	ū rule	th think		o in occur
e end	oi oil	ur turn	th their		u in upon
ē easy			zh treasure		

sky div|ing or **sky|div|ing** (skī′dī ving) *noun.*

Skye terrier—A small dog with a long, shaggy coat, a beard, and hair covering its eyes. It has short, stubby legs and a long body. Originally bred in Scotland, this dog is popular as a pet. **Skye ter|ri|er** (skī ter′ē ər) *noun, plural* **Skye terriers.**

skylark—A small, mostly brown bird that is known for the beautiful song it sings as it flies and for its steep upward flight. **sky|lark** (skī′lahrk′) *noun, plural* **skylarks.**

skylark

skylight—A window in a roof or ceiling for letting in light. **sky|light** (skī′līt′) *noun, plural* **skylights.**

skyline—**1.** The line along which the sky seems to touch the earth; the horizon: *They watched as the sun sank beneath the* skyline. **2.** The outline of buildings or other large objects, viewed with the sky as a background: *In a boat on the bay, the tourists viewed the* skyline *of the city.* **sky|line** (skī′līn′) *noun, plural* **skylines.**

skyrocket—A firecracker that shoots up into the air and explodes, throwing out sparks that light up the sky in a colorful display. *Noun.*
—To rise rapidly: *The cost of new houses* skyrocketed *last spring. Verb.*
sky|rock|et (skī′rok′it) *noun, plural* **skyrockets;** *verb,* **skyrocketed, skyrocketing.**

skyscraper—A very tall building. **sky|scrap|er** (skī′skrā′pər) *noun, plural* **skyscrapers.**

slab—A thick, wide slice or piece of something: *a* slab *of concrete; a* slab *of bacon.* **slab** (slab) *noun, plural* **slabs.**

slack—**1.** Loose or relaxed; not firm or taut: *a* slack *rope; a* slack *grip.* **2.** Not being careful or strict; sloppy: *The man was* slack *about how he dressed.* **3.** Not in a hurry; slow or listless: *The*

sad child walked at a slack pace. **4.** Not busy or active: *Summer is a* slack *season at many winter resorts. Adjective.*
—A loose, hanging part: *Take up the* slack *in the rope before you tie it. Noun.*
slack (slak) *adjective,* **slacker, slackest;** *noun, plural* **slacks.**

slacks—Long pants for everyday wear. **slacks** (slaks) *plural noun.*

slain—*See* **slay.** **slain** (slān) *verb.*

slam—**1.** To shut hard, making a loud sound: *The angry woman* slammed *the door.* **2.** To hit, set down, or hurl something with a strong motion, making a loud sound: *He* slammed *his fist on the table to get the crowd's attention. Verb.*
—The act of shutting or hitting with force, making a loud sound: *With a* slam *of the door, he stormed out of the house. Noun.*
slam (slam) *verb,* **slammed, slamming;** *noun, plural* **slams.**

slang—Words and expressions used in everyday speech that are usually popular for only brief periods of time. Slang may be new meanings for words already in use or totally new words and phrases. **slang** (slang) *noun.*

slant—To lie at an angle; slope: *A dirt road* slants *down to the left off the highway. Verb.*
—A sloping position: *The picture hung at a* slant *after she dusted it. Noun.*
slant (slant) *verb,* **slanted, slanting;** *noun, plural* **slants.**

slap—A smack with the palm of the hand or with a flat object: *a* slap *on the face. Noun.*
—**1.** To smack with the palm or with a flat object: *He* slapped *his friend on the back to congratulate her.* **2.** To put down hard: *He* slapped *coins on the counter to pay for the newspaper. Verb.*
slap (slap) *noun, plural* **slaps;** *verb,* **slapped, slapping.**

slash—**1.** To cut with a swinging movement: *He* slashed *at the tall weeds with a long knife.*
2. To reduce or lower greatly: *The factory* slashed *the costs of its cars in October to sell them faster. Verb.*
—**1.** A swinging movement that cuts or tears: *He cut the rope with a single* slash *of his sword.*
2. A cut: *The girl got a* slash *on her foot from climbing up the rocky cliff.* **3.** The act of lowering; a great reduction: *The store announced*

a slash in the prices of its furniture. Noun.
slash (slash) *verb,* **slashed, slashing;** *noun,*
plural **slashes.**

slat—**1.** A narrow strip of wood or metal: *The
slats on the shutters were dusty.*
slat (slat) *noun, plural* **slats.**

slate—**1.** A smooth, blue-gray rock that can easily
be cracked into flat layers. It is used in making
blackboards and tiles for construction.   **2.** A list
of candidates for public office: *Eleven people are
on the Republican* slate *for the town elections.*
slate (slāt) *noun, plural* **slates.**

slaughter—**1.** The putting of animals to death so
they can be used as food: *The farmer raised
livestock for* slaughter.   **2.** The fierce or violent
murder of numerous people or animals: *a bloody*
slaughter *of the prisoners. Noun.*
—1. To put animals to death so they can be used
as food.   **2.** To murder in a fierce or violent way
numerous people or animals. *Verb.*
slaughter (slaw'tər) *noun, plural* **slaughters;**
verb, **slaughtered, slaughtering.**

slave—**1.** A person who belongs to and works for
another person.   **2.** A person who works very
hard for little pay or reward: *The actors got all
the applause but the* slaves *who made the scenery
and costumes were just as important. Noun.*
—To work very hard for hours at a time: *He*
slaved *all day chopping down trees. Verb.*
slave (slāv) *noun, plural* **slaves;** *verb,* **slaved,
slaving.**

slavery—**1.** The condition of being a person who
belongs to and works for another: *to live in*
slavery.   **2.** The custom or practice of owning
people: Slavery *is against the law.*
slav|er|y (slā'vər ē) *noun.*

slay—To kill using violence: *to* slay *an enemy in
battle.*
slay (slā) *verb,* **slew, slain, slaying.**
● A word that sounds the same is **sleigh.**

sled—A vehicle for coasting or being pulled on
snow or ice. It has metal runners under a flat
surface that is often made of wood. *Noun.*
—To ride on such a vehicle: *The children had
fun as they* sledded *down the slope. Verb.*
sled (sled) *noun, plural* **sleds;** *verb,* **sledded,
sledding.**

a at	**i** if	**oo** look	**ch** chalk		**a** in ago
ā ape	**ī** idle	**ou** out	**ng** sing		**e** in happen
ah calm	**o** odd	**u** ugly	**sh** ship	**ə** =	**i** in capital
aw all	**ō** oats	**ū** rule	**th** think		**o** in occur
e end	**oi** oil	**ur** turn	**th** their		**u** in upon
ē easy			**zh** treasure		

sledge—A heavy vehicle with runners that is
pulled by horses.
sledge (slej) *noun, plural* **sledges.**
● See picture at **sled.**

sledgehammer—A big, heavy hammer that is
used by gripping the handle with both hands. It
is swung above the head and then brought down
with force upon the object being hit.
sledge|ham|mer (slej'ham'ər) *noun, plural*
sledgehammers.
● See picture at **wedge.**

sleek—**1.** Having a smooth, shiny appearance: *Her*
sleek *hair was tied with a ribbon.*   **2.** Smooth
and trim in design or form; having clean, simple
lines: *The metal chair was* sleek *and modern in
style.*
sleek (slēk) *adjective,* **sleeker, sleekest.**

sleep—**1.** To cease being awake; be in a state of
rest in which the mind relaxes its conscious
control over thoughts and bodily movements: *He*
slept *soundly all night and woke up feeling
refreshed.*   **2.** To have room or provide the
means for such rest: *Our tent* sleeps *six people.
Verb.*
—A natural state of rest of the mind and body
that happens at regular times in people and
animals. It helps the body to renew its energies:
Extra sleep *helped him to feel better when he had
a cold. Noun.*
sleep (slēp) *verb,* **slept, sleeping;** *noun.*

sleeping bag—A warm cloth bag that a person
gets into, from feet to neck, for the purpose of

sled

sledge

sleigh

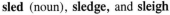

sled (noun), **sledge,** and **sleigh**

sleeping, usually when camping outdoors.
sleep|ing bag (slēp′ing bag) *noun, plural*
sleeping bags.

sleepy—**1.** Tired enough to go to sleep: *She was so* sleepy *that she could barely keep her eyes open.* **2.** Peaceful and quiet; without activity: *The* sleepy *village has not changed much over the years.*
sleep|y (slē′pē) *adjective,* **sleepier, sleepiest.**

sleet—**1.** Rain that is partly frozen or mixed with snow. *Noun.*
—To shower partly frozen rain: *It began to* sleet *rather than rain as the weather turned colder. Verb.*
sleet (slēt) *noun; verb,* **sleeted, sleeting.**

sleeve—**1.** The part of a piece of clothing that covers the arm or the upper part of the arm. **2.** An envelope of paper or plastic that holds and protects a phonograph record.
sleeve (slēv) *noun, plural* **sleeves.**

sleigh—A light vehicle with metal runners that is usually pulled by one or more horses and is used to transport people and things across snow or ice.
sleigh (slā) *noun, plural* **sleighs.**
 • A word that sounds the same is **slay.**
 • See picture at **sled.**

slender—**1.** Narrow; thin: *the* slender *tree swaying in the wind; a* slender *child slipping through the narrow opening in the fence.* **2.** Small; little: *There is only a* slender *chance of having our picnic unless it stops raining soon.*
slen|der (slen′dər) *adjective,* **slenderer, slenderest.**
 • Synonyms: **slight, slim,** for **1.**

slept—*See* **sleep.**
slept (slept) *verb.*

slew—*See* **slay.**
slew (slū) *verb.*

slice—A portion or piece cut from a whole: *a* slice *of roast beef; a* slice *of pie. Noun.*
—**1.** To cut into portions or pieces: *He* sliced *the watermelon.* **2.** To go through as if cutting: *The masts of the sailboat* sliced *the thick fog. Verb.*
slice (slīs) *noun, plural* **slices;** *verb,* **sliced, slicing.**

slick—**1.** Having a smooth, shiny surface: *She used the* slick *blue wrapping paper as a book cover.* **2.** So smooth as to cause people or things to slide; slippery: *The car skidded on the* slick *road. Adjective.*
—A slippery area on a surface: *The water froze into an icy* slick *on the driveway. Noun.*
slick (slik) *adjective,* **slicker, slickest;** *noun, plural* **slicks.**

slid—*See* **slide.**
slid (slid) *verb.*

slide—**1.** To glide or cause to glide on a slippery surface: *the new window* sliding *up and down easily; to* slide *the book across the table to his friend.* **2.** To move quietly with ease: *She* slid *behind the door so we wouldn't see her.* **3.** To lose one's footing or grip on a surface; slip: *He* slid *on the loose pebbles and fell down. Verb.*
—**1.** The act of moving smoothly over a surface: *The children had a good* slide *across the slippery ice.* **2.** A smooth sheet or board set on a slant upon which people may sit and move quickly in a downward direction: *My sister and I played on the* slide *in our yard.* **3.** The sudden downward movement of a mass of snow, ice, dirt, mud, or rocks: *When all the winter ice began to melt, there was a danger of* slides *on the sides of the mountains.* **4.** A small, transparent sheet, often made of glass, upon which something is set for viewing under a microscope. **5.** A transparent photograph that is put in a projector and shown on a screen. *Noun.*
slide (slīd) *verb,* **slid, slid** or **slidden, sliding;** *noun, plural* **slides.**

slight—**1.** Of little importance or significance; trivial: *The difference between the two kittens is so* slight *that it is hard to tell them apart.* **2.** Narrow; thin: *His waist is too* slight *for that pair of pants. Adjective.*
—To show indifference to; ignore; neglect: *She* slighted *her younger sister when her friend came to visit. Verb.*
slight (slīt) *adjective,* **slighter, slightest;** *verb,* **slighted, slighting.**
 • Synonyms: **slender, slim,** for *adjective* **2.**

slim—**1.** Thin; skinny: *The jacket looked loose and baggy on the* slim *boy.* **2.** Small; little: *There is only a* slim *chance that it will snow unless the weather turns colder. Adjective.*
—To reduce in size; lose weight: *Exercise helped her to* slim *her waist and legs. Verb.*
slim (slim) *adjective,* **slimmer, slimmest;** *verb,* **slimmed, slimming.**
 • Synonyms: **slender, slight,** for *adjective* **1.**

slime—**1.** A soft, sticky substance such as mud. **2.** The slippery, sticky substance given off by snails, slugs, and certain other animals.
slime (slīm) *noun, plural* **slimes.**

sling—**1.** A primitive weapon used to hurl rocks at an enemy. It is made of a leather strap that has a string attached to each end. It works by spinning it around by the strings and then releasing a rock held in the strap. **2.** A hanging loop used to lift

or hold up something, such as a loop of cloth draped around the neck to support an injured arm or hand. *Noun.*
—**1.** To throw something by whirling and releasing it from a leather strip: *He* slung *a stone and hit the target.* **2.** To hurl; fling: *He likes to* sling *pebbles into the pond to hear them splash.*
3. To hang something so that it swings loosely: *She* slung *the pocketbook over her shoulder and dashed out the door. Verb.*
sling (sling) *noun, plural* **slings;** *verb,* **slung, slinging.**

slingshot—A wooden or metal device in the shape of a Y, fitted with a piece of elastic that is connected to the tips of its two arms. A small object, such as a stone, that can be shot from it by stretching and releasing the elastic.
sling|shot (sling′shot′) *noun, plural* **slingshots.**

slink—To move in silence, as though hiding some bad deed; sneak: *The child* slunk *out of the kitchen leaving a trail of cookie crumbs.*
slink (slingk) *verb,* **slunk, slinking.**

slip[1]—**1.** To move in a smooth and quiet way; slide: *to* slip *out of bed; the snake* slipping *through the grass.* **2.** To slide without warning out of place, out of control, or out of one's grasp: *She* slipped *on the newly waxed floor.*
3. To make a mistake; do something wrong: *I got two of the problems right but* slipped *up on the third.* **4.** To escape or pass by without notice: *Before we realized it, the whole afternoon had* slipped *by.* **5.** To cause something to slide smoothly and easily: *He* slipped *a rubber band around the papers.* **6.** To get into or out of clothing quickly and easily: *She* slipped *out of her jacket. Verb.*
—**1.** The act of sliding without warning: *A* slip *on the sidewalk caused my fall.* **2.** A piece of girls' or women's underwear with a skirt and shoulder straps. **3.** A small mistake: *Pronouncing your name wrong was just a* slip *of the tongue. Noun.*
slip (slip) *verb,* **slipped, slipping;** *noun, plural* **slips.**
■ **give** (one) **the slip:** To escape from some authority's grasp: *The child ducked around the corner of the house and* gave *her mother* the slip.

slip one over on: To trick; deceive: *She tried to* slip one over on *her teacher when she said she lost her homework.*
● Synonyms: **blunder, error,** for *noun* **3.**

slip[2]—**1.** A narrow strip of paper, wood, or other material: *The boy handed his teacher a* slip *of paper when she asked for his doctor's excuse.*
2. A growth or cutting from a plant, used to start a new plant. It is placed in soil or water until it takes root.
slip (slip) *noun, plural* **slips.**

slipper—A light indoor shoe with a very low heel or no heel, which can be put on and taken off easily: *a bedroom* slipper; *a ballet* slipper.
slip|per (slip′ər) *noun, plural* **slippers.**

slippery—**1.** Likely to cause a person or thing to slide and fall down: *The path was* slippery *with wet leaves.* **2.** Likely to slip away; hard to hold onto: *The* slippery *spaghetti kept falling off my fork.*
slip|per|y (slip′ər ē) *adjective,* **slipperier, slipperiest.**

slit—To cut or cut open along a straight line: *The cook* slit *the biscuits and buttered each half. Verb.*
—A thin opening, cut, or tear: *a* slit *for putting envelopes in;* slits *in paper. Noun.*
slit (slit) *verb,* **slit, slitting;** *noun, plural* **slits.**

sliver—A small, narrow piece cut or split away from something; splinter: *a* sliver *of cake; a* sliver *in my finger.*
sliv|er (sliv′ər) *noun, plural* **slivers.**

slogan—A word, phrase, or short sentence used to advertise a product or to promote a cause; motto: *''The people's choice''* is the slogan *of the candidate for mayor.*
slo|gan (slō′gən) *noun, plural* **slogans.**

sloop—A sailboat having one mast and two or more sails that are set lengthwise.
sloop (slūp) *noun, plural* **sloops.**

slope—To lie on a slant: *The trail* sloped *steeply up from the canyon floor. Verb.*
—A line or surface that slants up or down: *This gentle ski* slope *is for beginners. Noun.*
slope (slōp) *verb,* **sloped, sloping;** *noun, plural* **slopes.**

sloppy—**1.** Not done or made with care: *Her handwriting is so* sloppy *that it is hard to read.*
2. Wet enough to splash and make slush or mud: *Three days of rain made the ground* sloppy.
slop|py (slop′ē) *adjective,* **sloppier, sloppiest.**

slot—A straight, narrow hole or groove: *His piggy bank has a* slot *on its back to receive coins.*
slot (slot) *noun, plural* **slots.**

a at	i if	oo look	ch chalk		a in ago
ā ape	ī idle	ou out	ng sing		e in happen
ah calm	o odd	u ugly	sh ship	ə =	i in capital
aw all	ō oats	ū rule	th think		o in occur
e end	oi oil	ur turn	<u>th</u> their		u in upon
ē easy			zh treasure		

sloth—A slow-moving, tree-dwelling animal that lives in Central and South America. Sloths hang upside down from tree branches and eat leaves and fruit.
sloth (slawth *or* slōth) *noun, plural* **sloths.**

sloth

slouch—1. To sit, stand, or move with the back bent, the head and shoulders drooping forward, and the muscles relaxed: *Tired and discouraged, she* slouched *toward home.* **2.** To droop or cause to droop down: *As she walked through the rain, her straw hat began to* slouch *over one eye.* *Verb.*

—A way of sitting, standing, or walking with the back bent, the head and shoulders drooping forward, and the muscles relaxed: *She thought she was too tall, so she walked with a* slouch. *Noun.*
slouch (slouch) *verb,* **slouched, slouching;** *noun, plural* **slouches.**

slow—1. Taking a long time to move, act, or happen; not fast: *Shall we take the jet airplane or the* slow *boat?* **2.** Moving at or displaying a time earlier than the correct time: *My watch is ten minutes* slow. **3.** Not smart; stupid: *I tried to teach my dog to fetch, but he is rather* slow. **4.** Not busy, active, or interesting: *The boss wants everyone to take vacation time during our* slow *season.* *Adjective.*
—Without haste or speed: *We had to drive* slow *in the heavy traffic.* *Adverb.*
—To go or cause to go at a more gradual pace; reduce one's speed: *We* slowed *down so he could catch up with us.* *Verb.*
slow (slō) *adjective,* **slower, slowest;** *adverb; verb,* **slowed, slowing.**

slug¹—1. A small, snaillike animal that has either no shell or one that can barely be seen. It lives in damp places and moves slowly. It is considered a garden pest because it eats plants. **2.** A metal object designed to be fired from a gun; bullet. **3.** An illegal, coin-shaped piece of metal used in place of a coin to operate a machine.
slug (slug) *noun, plural* **slugs.**

slug²—To strike a hard blow, especially with a fist or a bat: *She* slugged *the punching bag.*
slug (slug) *verb,* **slugged, slugging.**
• Synonyms: **hit, smack, whack**

sluggish—Slow to move, act, or respond; lazy: *My brain felt* sluggish, *and I could not think of the answer.*
slug|gish (slug′ish) *adjective.*

slum—A usually old and always dirty part of a town or city where the buildings are not cared for and where very poor people live in crowded conditions.
slum (slum) *noun, plural* **slums.**

slumber—1. To nap or sleep in a peaceful way: *The children* slumbered *in the back seat during the long drive.* **2.** To be still and serene: *All winter, the garden* slumbered *under its blanket of snow.* *Verb.*
—A period of sleep: *The alarm clock woke him from his* slumber. *Noun.*
slum|ber (slum′bər) *verb,* **slumbered, slumbering;** *noun, plural* **slumbers.**

sloop

slump—**1.** To collapse or fall without warning: *He fainted and* slumped *to the ground.* **2.** To go into a decline: *I was sick so much this month that my grades have* slumped. *Verb.*

—An unexpected collapse or decline: *Our team hit a* slump *and lost three in a row. Noun.*

slump (slump) *verb,* **slumped, slumping;** *noun, plural* **slumps.**

slung—*See* **sling.**

slung (slung) *verb.*

slur—To pronounce a syllable or a word in a careless way so that the sounds run together.

slur (slur) *verb,* **slurred, slurring.**

slush—Snow or ice that has begun to melt or is mixed with water: *Today's warm temperature has turned the snow to* slush.

slush (slush) *noun.*

sly—**1.** Clever at concealing what one is planning or doing; tricky: *A* sly *pickpocket pretended to bump into people while he stole their wallets.* **2.** Full of mischief; meant to tease: *"I think he likes you,"* she said with a sly wink.

sly (slī) *adjective,* **slier** or **slyer, sliest** or **slyest.**

smack—**1.** To close and open the lips noisily: *The smell of cookies baking made him* smack *his lips.* **2.** To kiss noisily: *He* smacked *his lips against the baby's cheek to make her laugh.* **3.** To hit hard and with a sharp sound: *to* smack *a mosquito; to* smack *a home run. Verb.*

—**1.** A sharp sound made with the lips, or a noisy kiss. **2.** A hard, loud hit: *She gave the ball a* smack *that knocked it over the fence. Noun.*

—In a direct way; headlong: *I could not stop and ran* smack *into the fence. Adverb.*

smack (smak) *verb,* **smacked, smacking;** *noun, plural* **smacks;** *adverb.*

● Synonyms: **slug**[2], **whack,** for *noun* **2.**

small—**1.** Not large; little: *Golf is played with a* small *ball.* **2.** Not grown up; young: *Kindergarten is for* small *children.* **3.** Not great in amount, value, or degree: *Could I ask you for a* small *favor?* **4.** Soft, low, or weak: *When we tried to move him after his fall, he gave a* small *cry. Adjective.*

—A part that is narrower than the rest, usually of the back: *Support the* small *of your back with a pillow when you exercise. Noun.*

small (smawl) *adjective,* **smaller, smallest:** *noun.* Abbreviation: **s.** or **sm.**

● Synonyms: **miniature, minute**[2]**, tiny, wee,** for *adjective* **1.**

Antonyms: For *adjective* **1,** see Synonyms at **big.**

small intestine—The part of the digestive system that connects the stomach with the large intestine. It is a very long and narrow tube in which the breaking down of food that was begun by the stomach is completed. Valuable food parts are absorbed into the blood, and waste material is passed on to the large intestine.

small in|tes|tine (smawl in tes′tən) *noun, plural* **small intestines.**

● See picture at **alimentary canal** and at **appendix.**

smallpox—A serious disease that spreads easily. People with smallpox have a high fever and blisters that can leave scars on the skin. Smallpox is now very rare.

small|pox (smawl′poks′) *noun.*

smart—**1.** To cause or feel a sharp pain: *The bee sting on my ankle* smarts. **2.** To suffer from hurt feelings: *He* smarted *when his friend insulted him. Verb.*

—**1.** Quick to learn; bright: *He is* smart *and always does well in school.* **2.** Sharp; stinging: *a* smart *slap; a* smart *kick in the shins.* **3.** Lively; brisk: *We had to work at a* smart *pace to finish the test on time.* **4.** In style; in fashion; elegant: *They have a big house in a* smart *neighborhood. Adjective.*

smart (smahrt) *verb,* **smarted, smarting;** *adjective,* **smarter, smartest.**

● Synonyms: **brilliant, clever,** for *adjective* **1.**

Antonyms: **dumb, stupid,** for *adjective* **1.**

smash—**1.** To shatter or crack into small parts with great force: *The egg rolled off the table and* smashed *on the floor.* **2.** To hit something in a violent way; crash: *The ship* smashed *into an iceberg. Verb.*

—A crash; the sound of something shattering: *I dropped the bottle, and it landed with a* smash. *Noun.*

smash (smash) *verb,* **smashed, smashing;** *noun, plural* **smashes.**

● Synonyms: **break, fracture,** for *verb* **1.**

smear—**1.** To smudge or stain with something sticky, dirty, or greasy: *Paint* smeared *the front of the artist's smock.* **2.** To spread something oily or sticky: *He* smeared *peanut butter on his*

a at	i if	oo look	ch chalk		a in ago
ā ape	ī idle	ou out	ng sing		e in happen
ah calm	o odd	u ugly	sh ship	ə =	i in capital
aw all	ō oats	ū rule	th think		o in occur
e end	oi oil	ur turn	th their		u in upon
ē easy			zh treasure		

toast.   **3.** To become or cause to become smudged or blurred: *If your face gets wet, your makeup will* smear.   **4.** To spoil or try to spoil someone's reputation: *Someone she works with* smeared *her with the boss by making nasty remarks about her attendance. Verb.*
—A smudge or stain: *There was a* smear *of gravy on the tablecloth. Noun.*
smear (smēr) *verb,* **smeared, smearing;** *noun, plural* **smears.**

Word History

Smear comes from an old English word meaning "grease." While it was used at first only when referring to fat or grease, in time **smear** came to mean a stain of any kind.

---

smell—**1.** To recognize or discover an odor by using one's nose: *I knew she had arrived when I smelled her perfume.*   **2.** To use the sense that recognizes odors to learn about something; sniff: *Please* smell *this milk to see if it is sour.*   **3.** To give off a good or bad odor: *That cheese really* smells. *Verb.*
—**1.** The sense that allows a person or animal to recognize or discover odors: *Some animals find their prey by* smell.   **2.** An odor: *Onions have a strong* smell. *Noun.*
smell (smel) *verb,* **smelled** or **smelt, smelling;** *noun, plural* **smells.**
● Synonyms: **fragrance, aroma, scent,** for *noun* 2.

smelt[1]—To melt ore in order to remove the metal that is in it.
smelt (smelt) *verb,* **smelted, smelting.**

smelt[2]—*See* **smell.**
smelt (smelt) *verb.*

smile—To let others know one is friendly, agreeable, or happy by curving up the corners of the mouth: *The boys* smiled *at the puppies in the pet store window. Verb.*
—An upward curve of the corners of the mouth that shows happiness, pleasure, or amusement: *She greeted her old friend with a happy* smile. *Noun.*
smile (smīl) *verb,* **smiled, smiling;** *noun, plural* **smiles.**

smock—A loose jacket or shirt, usually with long sleeves, that is worn to protect clothing underneath it. Artists and cooks often wear smocks to keep from soiling or staining their other clothes.
smock (smok) *noun, plural* **smocks.**

smog—A mixture of smoke and fog in the air.
smog (smog) *noun.*

smoke—The gray or white cloud that rises above a fire: Smoke *poured from the factory chimney. Noun.*
—**1.** To give off this cloud: *The damp wood* smoked *when we lit the fire.*   **2.** To breathe in this cloud from a cigarette, pipe, or cigar and then exhale it: *No one is allowed to* smoke *on the bus.*   **3.** To preserve meat or fish by exposing it to this cloud: *Sausage is* smoked *at the plant where my mother works. Verb.*
smoke (smōk) *noun; verb,* **smoked, smoking.**

smooth—**1.** Free from rough or uneven spots and flaws; slick; flat: *The lake was as* smooth *as glass.*   **2.** Having a flow or movement that is calm and without interruption: *We enjoyed a* smooth *boat ride because there was hardly any wind.*   **3.** Lacking difficulties or problems: *Now that I understand the work, I am making* smooth *progress in arithmetic.*   **4.** Having good manners or being pleasant, sometimes too much so: *The sales clerk was such a* smooth *talker that I bought more than I needed. Adjective.*
—**1.** To make even; level; flatten out: *She* smoothed *her hair with a brush.*   **2.** To remove all trouble or difficulties; ease: *Reading an extra book* smoothed *her way through the history course. Verb.*
smooth (smū̱th) *adjective,* **smoother, smoothest;** *verb,* **smoothed, smoothing.**

smooth fox terrier—A smooth-coated, short-haired fox terrier.
smooth fox ter|ri|er (smū̱th foks ter′ē ər) *noun, plural* **smooth fox terriers.**

smother—**1.** To kill by keeping a person or animal from breathing in air; suffocate: *The hot, thick smoke in the burning barn nearly* smothered

smooth fox terrier

several animals trapped inside.   **2.** To cover a thing with a thick layer of something else: *She* smothered *her hamburger with ketchup.*   **3.** To soften, lessen, or put out by covering: *We threw a blanket over the fire to* smother *it.*   **4.** To keep from showing or expressing something: *He was very angry but managed to* smother *his rage.*
smoth|er (smu<u>th</u> ər) *verb,* **smothered, smothering.**

smudge—A dirty spot; smear: *The artist had* smudges *of paint on her sweater. Noun.*
—To smear something with grease, dirt, or some other substance: *Paint* smudged *the child's fingers. Verb.*
smudge (smuj) *noun, plural* **smudges;** *verb,* **smudged, smudging.**

smug—Too pleased or satisfied with oneself: *Because he was* smug *about his ability to spell and did not study for the test, he failed it.*
smug (smug) *adjective,* **smugger, smuggest.**

smuggle—**1.** To break the law by carrying something in secret across a country's border: *The government is making a special effort to stop groups that are trying to* smuggle *guns into the country.*   **2.** To bring in or take out in secret: *A student tried to* smuggle *a dog into the classroom.*
smug|gle (smug'əl) *verb,* **smuggled, smuggling.**

snack—A small portion or quantity of food eaten at a time other than when a regular meal is served: *I had an apple for an afternoon* snack.
snack (snak) *noun, plural* **snacks.**

snag—**1.** Something sharp or jagged that sticks up in the air or out of water, such as a branch or a rock.   **2.** A rip or tear made by something sharp: *A branch made a* snag *in the kite when the wind blew it into the tree.*   **3.** An unexpected obstacle: *Our movie plans hit a* snag *because none of us had any money. Noun.*
—To catch on something sharp: *She* snagged *her sweater on a thorn. Verb.*
snag (snag) *noun, plural* **snags;** *verb,* **snagged, snagging.**

snail—A small animal that creeps slowly along a surface. It usually has a spiral shell into which it can pull its soft body for safety. Some snails live on land while others make their homes in water.
snail (snāl) *noun, plural* **snails.**

snake—A long, thin animal with a body covered in scales, no legs, and a forked tongue.
snake (snāk) *noun, plural* **snakes.**

snake doctor—See dragonfly.
snake doc|tor (snāk dok'tər) *noun, plural* snake doctors.

snake feeder—*See* dragonfly.
snake feed|er (snāk fē'dər) *noun, plural* snake feeders.

snap—**1.** To make or cause to make a sudden, sharp sound like a crack: *the flag* snapping *in the strong wind; to* snap *a rubber band around the box.*   **2.** To act, speak, or move in a quick, sharp manner: *When he heard the shot, his head* snapped *around.*   **3.** To break into pieces with a sharp sound like a crack: *The cook was* snapping *green beans into a bowl.*   **4.** To lose one's courage, temper, or patience: *Her temper* snapped *when she was caught in a traffic jam for two hours.*   **5.** To grasp something eagerly; pounce upon suddenly: *The shark* snapped *up the little fish.*   **6.** To photograph; take a snapshot: *Father* snapped *our pictures for the family album. Verb.*
—**1.** A sudden, sharp sound like a crack: *He signaled for quiet with a* snap *of his fingers.*
2. A sudden grab or bite: *The turtle caught the fly with a* snap *of its jaws.*   **3.** A brief spell of cold weather: *The cold* snap *sent the temperature below freezing.*   **4.** A fastener, catch, or clasp: *The baby's coat had* snaps *down the front.*
5. A flat, crisp, or brittle cookie: *Milk and ginger* snaps *make a good snack.*   **6.** Something that is easily done: *Reading the blackboard is a* snap *now that I have my glasses. Noun.*
—Made or done suddenly and without careful thought: *a* snap *judgment; a* snap *decision. Adjective.*
snap (snap) *verb,* **snapped, snapping;** *noun, plural* **snaps;** *adjective.*

a at	i if	oo look	ch chalk		
ā ape	ī idle	ou out	ng sing		a in ago
ah calm	o odd	u ugly	sh ship	ə =	e in happen
aw all	ō oats	ū rule	th think		i in capital
e end	oi oil	ur turn	<u>th</u> their		o in occur
ē easy			zh treasure		u in upon

snail

snapdragon—A popular garden plant with red, yellow, pink, orange, or white flowers that grow along tall stalks.
snap|drag|on (snap′drag′ən) *noun, plural* **snapdragons.**

snapshot—A quick photograph taken with a simple camera.
snap|shot (snap′shot′) *noun, plural* **snapshots.**

snare—A device used by trappers and hunters to capture small animals. When the animal applies pressure to a certain point, a loop of rope or string tightens around the animal's body and keeps it from escaping. *Noun.*
—**1.** To use such a trap: *We* snared *a squirrel but let it go.* **2.** To catch as if in such a trap: *Our team* snared *five of the best players in the class. Verb.*
snare (snâr) *noun, plural* **snares;** *verb,* **snared, snaring.**

snare drum—A small drum with string or wires stretched across the bottom. When the drum is struck with a drumstick, it makes a rattling sound.
snare drum (snâr drum) *noun, plural* **snare drums.**

snarl[1]—**1.** To growl angrily with the teeth showing: *The tiger* snarled *and paced around its cage.* **2.** To speak sharply and angrily: *"Hurry up!"* snarled *the boss at his lazy helper. Verb.*
—An angry growl: *The watchdog bared its teeth in a* snarl *at the robber. Noun.*
snarl (snahrl) *verb,* **snarled, snarling;** *noun, plural* **snarls.**

snarl[2]—**1.** A tangle or knot: *The horse's mane and tail were full of* snarls. **2.** A state of disorder or confusion: *Her history notes were in such a* snarl *that she could not make sense of them. Noun.*
—**1.** To tangle or become caught in a tangle: *A tree branch* snarled *the kite string.* **2.** To cause disorder or confusion; upset: *The accident damaged a traffic light and* snarled *traffic for hours. Verb.*
snarl (snahrl) *noun, plural* **snarls;** *verb,* **snarled, snarling.**

snatch—To take or grab in a quick or violent way: *The left fielder* snatched *the ball out of the air. Verb.*
—**1.** The act of taking something in a violent way or with a quick motion: *He made a* snatch *at his hat as the wind blew it off.* **2.** A little bit: *We heard* snatches *of music when the parade was still far away. Noun.*

snatch (snach) *verb,* **snatched, snatching;** *noun, plural* **snatches.**

sneak—To do or get something in a hidden way: *a few latecomers* sneaking *into the room after class had begun; to* sneak *his birthday presents into the closet. Verb.*
—A person who does something mean or dishonest in secrecy: *Some* sneak *took my bicycle without permission. Noun.*
sneak (snēk) *verb,* **sneaked, sneaking;** *noun, plural* **sneaks.**

sneaker—A shoe made for sports or informal wear. It has a rubber bottom that bends easily and a top made of canvas or leather.
sneak|er (snē′kər) *noun, plural* **sneakers.**

sneer—To look or speak with scorn: *The old miser* sneered *at people who were not rich. Verb.*
—An expression of scorn made by curling the upper lip: *The outlaw greeted the sheriff's warning with a* sneer. *Noun.*
sneer (snēr) *verb,* **sneered, sneering;** *noun, plural* **sneers.**

sneeze—To expel air in a sudden and violent way through the mouth and nose without being able to stop oneself. *Verb.*
—A sudden, violent burst of air from the mouth and nose: *He stayed in bed today with sniffles and* sneezes. *Noun.*
sneeze (snēz) *verb,* **sneezed, sneezing;** *noun, plural* **sneezes.**

snicker—A laugh that is partly held in and that shows one lacks respect or is being silly: *I heard* snickers *from the stands when I dropped the ball. Noun.*
—To laugh in such a way: *Please do not* snicker *if the actor forgets a line because he is doing his best. Verb.*
snick|er (snik′ər) *noun, plural* **snickers;** *verb,* **snickered, snickering.**
• Synonyms: **chuckle, giggle,** for *verb.*
  Antonyms: For *verb,* see Synonyms at **cry,** *verb* **1.**

sniff—**1.** To inhale through the nose quickly, in a way that can be heard: *She stepped outside and* sniffed *the cool night air.* **2.** To smell by inhaling quickly through the nose: *He took a cookie out of the box and* sniffed *it happily. Verb.*
—Something smelled in this way; an odor or scent: *He caught a* sniff *of her perfume as she walked by. Noun.*
sniff (snif) *verb,* **sniffed, sniffing;** *noun, plural* **sniffs.**

sniffle—To try to draw in air through a partly clogged nose; sniff in a noisy way: *People* sniffle *when they have a cold or are trying not to cry.* *Verb.*

snip—To cut quickly or into little bits with scissors or shears: *He* snipped *a small piece from the roll of tape.* *Verb.*
—**1.** An act of cutting in this way: *The gardener took a few* snips *at the hedge.* **2.** A small piece of something that has been cut off: *The floor was littered with* snips *of paper.* *Noun.*
snip (snip) *verb,* **snipped, snipping;** *noun,* *plural* **snips.**

snipe—A brown bird with a striped back and a very long bill. It lives on the edges of streams and marshes and is often hunted as game.
snipe (snīp) *noun, plural* **snipes** or **snipe.**

snipe

sniper—A person with a gun who fires from a hiding place at an enemy.
snip|er (snī′pər) *noun, plural* **snipers.**

snob—A person who admires people who have money or high social position, and who dislikes people who do not have these.
snob (snob) *noun, plural* **snobs.**

snoop—To sneak about prying into others' privacy: *She* snooped *in her brother's room while he was out.* *Verb.*

—Someone who acts this way: *He bought a telescope and became the neighborhood* snoop. *Noun.*
snoop (snūp) *verb,* **snooped, snooping;** *noun,* *plural* **snoops.**

snooze—To sleep lightly; take a nap: *The cat* snoozed *in front of the fire.* *Verb.*
—A short sleep: *She curled up on the sofa to take a* snooze. *Noun.*
snooze (snūz) *verb,* **snoozed, snoozing;** *noun,* *plural* **snoozes.**

snore—To breathe in a noisy way while asleep: *The dog* snored *so loudly he woke himself up.*
snore (snawr) *verb,* **snored, snoring.**

snorkel—A curved tube that allows a swimmer to breathe air while his or her face is under water.
snor|kel (snawr′kəl) *noun, plural* **snorkels.**

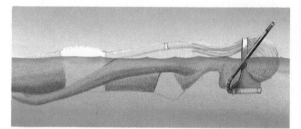

snorkel

snort—To force air loudly and violently out through the nose: *The old man* snorted *with laughter at the boy's ideas.*
snort (snawrt) *verb,* **snorted, snorting.**

snout—The long nose, mouth, and jaws of certain animals, such as pigs, anteaters, sharks, and alligators.
snout (snout) *noun, plural* **snouts.**

snow—**1.** Crystals of frozen water that fall to earth as light, white flakes. **2.** A mass of fallen snow: *The* snow *was so heavy it bent the trees.* *Noun.*
—To fall from the sky as this substance: *It* snowed *hard last night.* *Verb.*
snow (snō) *noun, plural* **snows;** *verb,* **snowed, snowing.**

snowball—A ball made by packing snow together.
snow|ball (snō′bawl′) *noun, plural* **snowballs.**

snowflake—One small, white crystal of frozen water. Many of these drop from the sky when the snow falls.
snow|flake (snō′flāk′) *noun, plural* **snowflakes.**

a at	i if	oo look	ch chalk		a in ago
ã ape	ī idle	ou out	ng sing		e in happen
ah calm	o odd	u ugly	sh ship	ə =	i in capital
aw all	ō oats	ū rule	th think		o in occur
e end	oi oil	ur turn	th their		u in upon
ē easy			zh treasure		

snowman—Snow packed tight and rolled or shaped to look somewhat like a person.
snow|man (snō′man′) *noun, plural* **snowmen.**

snowmobile—A motor vehicle with skis or runners for moving over snow.
snow|mo|bile (snō′mə bēl′) *noun, plural* **snowmobiles.**

snowplow—A truck or other vehicle with a broad metal blade mounted in front, used to clear roads and highways of snow.
snow|plow (snō′plou′) *noun, plural* **snowplows.**

snowshoe—One of a pair of broad, flat wooden frames strung with woven leather laces. Snowshoes are worn on the feet so that one can walk across deep snow without sinking into it.
snow|shoe (snō′shū′) *noun, plural* **snowshoes.**

snowy—1. Having snow or covered with snow: *We walked across a* snowy *field.* 2. Resembling snow; white: *He dried his hands on a* snowy *towel.*
snow|y (snō′ē) *adjective,* **snowier, snowiest.**

snub—To act scornfully toward; refuse to notice: *Now that she is famous, she* snubs *all her old friends. Verb.*
—An act of deliberate scorn: *I believe his refusal to shake hands with me was a* snub. *Noun.*
snub (snub) *verb,* **snubbed, snubbing;** *noun, plural* **snubs.**

snug—1. Offering comfort and security: *A storm raged outside, but we were* snug *by the fire.* 2. Covering something with little or no room to spare; tight: *He had grown so much that all his clothes were too short and* snug.
snug (snug) *adjective,* **snugger, snuggest.**

snuggle—To lean or press against so as to feel comfortable and secure, or so as to express love: *The baby* snuggled *against his mother.*
snug|gle (snug′əl) *verb,* **snuggled, snuggling.**
● Synonyms: **cuddle, nestle**

so—1. To this or that extent; in this or that degree: *We had never walked* so *far before.* 2. For this or that reason; therefore: *It is late,* so *I must go now.* 3. Also: *You like pizza, and* so *do I. Adverb.*
—In order that; with the result that: *She drove me into town* so *I could go shopping. Conjunction.*
—Such as has been said; this; that: *You told me this would be a funny movie, and it really is* so. *Pronoun.*

so (sō) *adverb, conjunction, pronoun.*
● Words that sound the same are **sew** and **sow**[1].

so-called—Named or thought of as something, but not really so: *My* so-called *friend lied about what I had said.*
so-called (sō′kawld′) *adjective.*

soak—1. To make or become completely wet: *The spilled milk* soaked *the tablecloth.* 2. To let remain in liquid until completely wet: *The laundry has been* soaking *all morning. Verb.*
—The act of making completely wet; the state of being made wet: *I gave my feet a warm* soak *after our long hike. Noun.*
soak (sōk) *verb,* **soaked, soaking;** *noun, plural* **soaks.**

soap—A material used for washing and cleaning. *Noun.*
—To rub this material into or on: *He* soaped *and rinsed the dog, then rubbed it dry. Verb.*
soap (sōp) *noun, plural* **soaps;** *verb,* **soaped, soaping.**
■ **no soap:** Absolutely not: *My parents said "no soap" when I asked about having a party this weekend.*

soar—1. To fly or sail high in the air: *The eagle* soared *over the tree tops.* 2. To rise very high: *mountains that* soar *above the valley; temperatures* soaring *during a heat wave.*
soar (sawr) *verb,* **soared, soaring.**
● A word that sounds the same is **sore.**
● Synonyms: **ascend, climb,** for 2.
Antonyms: **descend, sink,** for 2.

sob—To cry with a sound made by catching one's breath: *I heard the lost child as he* sobbed. *Verb.*
—The act of or the noises made when crying while catching one's breath: *The baby's* sobs *kept up until he fell asleep. Noun.*
sob (sob) *verb,* **sobbed, sobbing;** *noun, plural* **sobs.**
● Synonyms: **bawl, wail, weep**
Antonyms: See Antonyms at **cry.**

sober—1. Not drunk. 2. Serious; grave; solemn: *She looked very* sober *when she told us the bad news. Adjective.*
—To make or become serious or solemn: *His father's speech* sobered *him. Verb.*
so|ber (sō′bər) *adjective,* **soberer, soberest;** *verb,* **sobered, sobering.**

soccer—A game for two teams of eleven players each. Players move a round ball toward the other team's goal by striking it with any part of the body except the hands and arms. The person

guarding the goal may use hands and arms to move the ball away from the goal.
soc|cer (sok′ər) *noun*.

Word History

Soccer comes from the phrase "association football." In many countries, soccer is called "football." The rules of soccer were first set in 1848 by an association of English schools. An abbreviation for **association** is "assoc." People called the game "assoc. football." From "assoc." came **soccer**.

---

sociable—Friendly; fond of company: *He enjoys being alone, but his sister is* sociable.
so|cia|ble (sō′shə bəl) *adjective*.

social—1. Having to do with the lives and relationships of human beings: *We are very grateful for the fire department and other* social *services in our town.* 2. Having to do with friendliness and company: *The party was a most enjoyable* social *gathering.* 3. Having to do with fashionable or wealthy society: *local business people and* social *leaders.* 4. Having to do with animals and insects that live together in organized groups: *Some bees live alone, but others are* social. *Adjective*.
—A party or other informal gathering: *The young people organized an ice cream* social. *Noun*.
so|cial (sō′shəl) *adjective; noun, plural* **socials**.

socialism—An economic or political system in which the government owns the major businesses, decides what products these businesses make, and controls what is done with the products.
so|cial|ism (sō′shə liz′əm) *noun*.

socialist—A person who believes in or practices socialism.
so|cial|ist (sō′shə list) *noun, plural* **socialists**.

social security—In the United States, a government program that provides money and medical care for people who are old, orphaned, sick, or disabled. The money to do this is collected by the government from people who work or who employ workers.
so|cial se|cu|ri|ty (sō′shəl si kyoor′ə tē) *noun*.

social studies—A course of study that includes geography, history, government, economics, and other fields having to do with human society and relationships.
so|cial stud|ies (sō′shəl stud′ēz) *noun*.

society—1. A group of people organized because of a shared interest in the group's purpose: *a literary* society; *an animal welfare* society. 2. The people as a whole; everybody: *Society, she says, has a responsibility to help its less fortunate members.* 3. The people who live in a community, culture, century, or other particular place or time: *urban* society; *medieval* society. 4. Fashionable or well known people: *All of* society *turned out for the charity benefit dinner.*
so|ci|e|ty (sə sī′ə tē) *noun, plural* **societies**.

sock[1]—A knitted article of clothing that snugly covers the foot and lower leg.
sock (sok) *noun, plural* **socks**.
■ **sock away:** To save, especially money: *She has* socked away *enough cash for a new jacket.*

sock[2]—To hit with force; punch: *The hero of the movie* socked *the villain in the eye.*
sock (sok) *verb*, **socked**, **socking**.

socket—1. A hollow place into which something is put. 2. An electrical outlet.
sock|et (sok′it) *noun, plural* **sockets**.

sod—Earth with grass growing from it; upper part of the ground: *To start a garden, you must first remove the* sod. *Noun*.
—To cover with grassy earth: *We* sodded *the worn spots in our backyard last weekend. Verb*.
sod (sod) *noun; verb*, **sodded**, **sodding**.

soda—1. Any of several substances, such as baking soda and washing soda, that contain sodium. 2. Water that has been made bubbly by adding gas to it. It is often flavored. 3. A drink of bubbly water mixed with ice cream or fruit flavoring.
so|da (sō′də) *noun, plural* **sodas**.

Language Fact

Soda is one word for a kind of drink that is called by many words. It is also known as **pop**, as **soda pop**, and as **soft drink**. What people call this kind of drink may depend on where they live, but many people use more than one of these names.

---

sodium—A chemical element that is found only in combination with other elements. Table salt is sodium combined with chlorine.
so|di|um (sō′dē əm) *noun*.

a at	i if	oo look	ch chalk		a in ago
ā ape	ī idle	ou out	ng sing		e in happen
ah calm	o odd	u ugly	sh ship	ə =	i in capital
aw all	ō oats	ū rule	th think		o in occur
e end	oi oil	ur turn	th their		u in upon
ē easy			zh treasure		

sofa—A cushioned piece of furniture that seats two or more people; couch.
so|fa (sō′fə) *noun, plural* **sofas.**

soft—1. Not hard; easily pressed or crushed: *a* soft *tissue;* soft *clay.* 2. Not rough; smooth: *a kitten's* soft *fur.* 3. Not loud; quiet: *a* soft *echo.* 4. Not strong or powerful; weak: *a lazy person's* soft *muscles; the* soft *light of dawn; a* soft *breeze.*
soft (sawft) *adjective.*

softball—1. A team sport that is similar to baseball but uses a larger, softer ball that is thrown underhand by the pitcher. 2. The ball used in this sport.
soft|ball (sawft′bawl′) *noun, plural* **softballs.**

soft-coated wheaten terrier—A medium-sized dog with a thick, soft, curly coat of the color of wheat, and short ears and tail. Originally bred in Ireland, these dogs are used to herd cattle and hunt rats. They are also good watch dogs.
soft-coat|ed wheat|en ter|ri|er (sawft′kō′tid hwē′tən ter′ē ər) *noun, plural* **soft-coated wheaten terriers.**

soft drink—A flavored drink made with soda water. It has no alcohol in it.
soft drink (sawft dringk) *noun, plural* **soft drinks.**
● See Language Fact at **soda.**

software—The instructions that tell a computer what to do; program.
soft|ware (sawft′wār′) *noun.*

soggy—Full of water; soaked: *The rain made a* soggy *mess of our paper streamers.*
sog|gy (sog′ē) *adjective,* **soggier, soggiest.**

soil[1]—1. The surface layer of earth where plants grow; dirt: *Fertile* soil *produces good crops.*

soft-coated wheaten terrier

2. Geographical area; nation or country: *fighting a war on foreign* soil; *returning to their native* soil.
soil (soil) *noun, plural* **soils.**

soil[2]—To stain or get dirty: *We had* soiled *our baseball uniforms badly by the end of the game.*
soil (soil) *verb,* **soiled, soiling.**

solar—From or of the sun: solar *energy; a* solar *eclipse.*
so|lar (sō′lər) *adjective.*

solar system—The sun and the planets and other heavenly bodies that orbit around the sun.
so|lar sys|tem (sō′lər sis′təm) *noun, plural* **solar systems.**

solar system

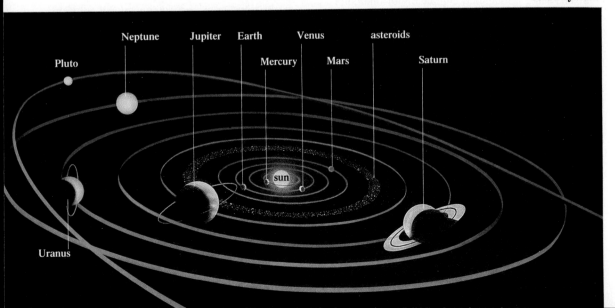

sold—*See* **sell.**
  sold (sōld) *verb.*

soldier—A member of an army.
  sol|dier (sōl′jər) *noun, plural* **soldiers.**

sole[1]—The one and only; single: *the sole boat to finish the race.*
  sole (sōl) *adjective.*
  • A word that sounds the same is **soul.**

sole[2]—The bottom surface of a foot or a shoe: *The rubber soles of my tennis shoes were worn smooth.*
  sole (sōl) *noun, plural* **soles.**
  • A word that sounds the same is **soul.**

sole[3]—A kind of fish used for food. It is flat and has small eyes set close together.
  sole (sōl) *noun, plural* **soles** or **sole.**
  • A word that sounds the same is **soul.**

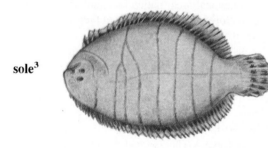

sole[3]

solemn—Very serious or formal; earnest: *a worried parent having a* solemn *expression; to make a* solemn *promise to study harder.*
  sol|emn (sol′əm) *adjective.*

solid—1. Being neither a liquid nor a gas: *Ice is the* solid *form of water.* 2. Not loose or hollow; compact; hard; firm: *a solid mass of rock.* 3. The same throughout; completely of one color or material: *a solid sliver chain; a solid red shirt.* 4. Real; reliable; dependable: *a solid reputation for good work; a solid citizen.* 5. Complete or continuing with no interruption: *I exercised for a solid hour.* 6. Having length, width, and height: *A cylinder is a solid figure. Adjective.*
  —A substance that is firm and keeps its shape, unlike liquids and gases. Metals, rocks, and wood are solids.
  sol|id (sol′id) *adjective; noun, plural* **solids.**

solitaire—1. A kind of card game having just one player. 2. Any precious stone set alone in a piece of jewelry.
  sol|i|taire (sol′ə tār) *noun, plural* **solitaires.**

solitary—1. Living or being apart from others: *There was a* solitary *house on the hill.* 2. Done or passed alone: *a* solitary *afternoon at home.*
  sol|i|tar|y (sol′ə tēr′ē) *adjective.*

solitude—The condition of being alone: *Some people like crowds, but I prefer* solitude.
  sol|i|tude (sol′ə tūd *or* sol′ə tyūd) *noun.*

solo—A piece of music for singing or playing by one person: *Each piano student played a* solo *at the final concert. Noun.*
  —Done or performed alone: *Her* solo *voyage around the world made her famous. Adjective.*
  so|lo (sō′lō) *noun, plural* **solos;** *adjective.*

soloist—A person who performs a solo.
  so|lo|ist (sō′lō ist) *noun, plural* **soloists.**

solstice—The moment each year when the sun is at either its most northern or its most southern position. In the United States and other places north of the equator, the summer solstice occurs on about June 21 and the winter solstice occurs on about December 21.
  sol|stice (sol′stis) *noun.*
  • See picture at **equinox.**

solution—1. The process of finding the answer to a problem: *You can work together in the* solution *of the math questions.* 2. The answer to a problem: *The detective found the* solution *to the crime.* 3. A mixture formed by dissolving one or more substances in a liquid: *a saltwater* solution.
  so|lu|tion (sə lū′shən) *noun, plural* **solutions.**

solve—To find a solution to: *She* solved *the mystery.*
  solve (solv) *verb,* **solved, solving.**

Somali—A medium-sized cat with a long, thick coat. It was first bred in the United States from the Abyssinian cat.
  So|ma|li (sə mah′lē) *noun, plural* **Somalis.**

somber—1. Dark and gloomy: *The empty house had a* somber *look.* 2. Sad or dejected: *to be in a* somber *mood after bad news.*
  som|ber (som′bər) *adjective.*

sombrero—A big hat with a wide brim that is worn especially in the southwest United States and Mexico.
  som|bre|ro (som brār′ō) *noun, plural* **sombreros.**

a at	i if	oo look	ch chalk		a in ago
ā ape	ī idle	ou out	ng sing		e in happen
ah calm	o odd	u ugly	sh ship	ə =	i in capital
aw all	ō oats	ū rule	th think		o in occur
e end	oi oil	ur turn	th their		u in upon
ē easy			zh treasure		

sombrero

Word History

Sombrero comes from two Latin words meaning "under shade." When a person wears a sombrero, his or her face and head are protected from the sun by being under the shade of the hat.

some—Of a number that is not known or named: *There were* some *boats anchored nearby.* Some *of the children were sick.*
some (sum) *adjective; pronoun.*
● A word that sounds the same is **sum.**

somebody—An unknown or unnamed person; someone: Somebody *was here before you.*
some│bod│y (sum′bod′ē) *pronoun.*

someday—At a future time: *I want to go around the world* someday.
some│day (sum′dā′) *adverb.*

somehow—In one way or another: *We will get across the river* somehow.
some│how (sum′hou) *adverb.*

someone—An unknown or unnamed person; somebody: *There is* someone *at the door.*
some│one (sum′wun) *pronoun.*

somersault—A leap or roll in which the feet make a complete circle up and over the head: *We practiced* somersaults *on a soft mat. Noun.*
—To do such a leap or roll: *circus clowns* somersaulting *around the ring. Verb.*
som│er│sault (sum′ər sawlt) *noun, plural* somersaults; *verb,* somersaulted, somersaulting.

something—A thing that is not known or named: *I knew there would be* something *to eat in the kitchen. Pronoun.*
—In some way or to some degree; a little bit: *The cartoon looked* something *like a dog. Adverb.*
some│thing (sum′thing) *pronoun, adverb.*

sometime—**1.** At a future time yet to be decided: *My grandfather asked me if I would like to go fishing with him* sometime.   **2.** At a time that is not known or specified: *I caught a cold* sometime *last winter.*
some│time (sum′tīm) *adverb.*

sometimes—On certain occasions; from time to time: *My brothers and I* sometimes *take long walks through the woods.*
some│times (sum′tīmz) *adverb.*

somewhat—To some degree: *His hair is* somewhat *like mine. Adverb.*
—Some amount: *It was* somewhat *of a surprise to me to hear I had won. Noun.*
some│what (sum′hwot) *adverb, noun.*
● Synonyms: **approximately, roughly,** for *adverb.*
Antonyms: **exactly, just, precisely,** for *adverb.*

somewhere—In, to, or at a place that is not named or known: *The plan is to meet* somewhere *between my house and his house. Adverb.*
—Some place: *We had to find* somewhere *to hide the kitten. Noun.*
some│where (sum′hwār) *adverb, noun.*

son—A male child.
son (sun) *noun, plural* sons.
● A word that sounds the same is **sun.**

sonar—A system used to locate underwater objects, such as reefs or submarines, by picking up sound waves reflected off their surfaces.
so│nar (sō′nahr) *noun, plural* sonars.

song—**1.** A musical piece that is sung.   **2.** The musical sound that is made by a bird.
song (sawng) *noun, plural* songs.
■ **for a song:** At a very low price: *At the church fair, mother got an old clock* for a song.

songbird—A bird that has a musical call.
song│bird (sawng′burd) *noun, plural* songbirds.

sonic—Having to do with sound or the speed at which sound travels.
son│ic (son′ik) *adjective.*

son-in-law—The husband of one's daughter.
son-in-law (sun′in law′) *noun, plural* sons-in-law.

sonnet—A poem that has fourteen lines and a set arrangement of rhymes.
son│net (son′it) *noun, plural* sonnets.

soon—**1.** In a short while: *The bus driver said we would be arriving* soon.   **2.** Ahead of the expected time; early: *The man at the garden center says it is too* soon *to plant flowers.*   **3.** In a quick manner; promptly: *Mother asked the plumber to come as* soon *as possible.*

4. Willingly: *Our camp counselor would just as soon have hiked farther, but we were too tired.*
soon (sūn) *adverb*, **sooner**, **soonest.**

soot—The black powder that forms when material such as wood or coal is burned.
soot (soot *or* sŭt) *noun.*

soothe—To make quiet and relaxed; calm: *Her lullaby soothed the baby during the thunderstorm.*
soothe (sū<u>th</u>) *verb*, **soothed**, **soothing.**

sophomore—A student in the second year of high school or college.
soph|o|more (sof′ə mawr) *noun, plural* **sophomores.**

soprano—**1.** The highest singing voice. **2.** A singer with this voice. **3.** Any musical instrument with a range like that of such a voice.
so|pran|o (sə pran′ō) *noun, plural* **sopranos.**

sore—**1.** Painful; tender: *The runner's feet were sore after the long race.* **2.** Feeling anger; upset: *He is sore because he lost a bet. Adjective.*
—A spot on the body that has been injured: *The little boy cried because he had a sore on his finger. Noun.*
sore (sawr) *adjective*, **sorer**, **sorest;** *noun, plural* **sores.**
• A word that sounds the same is **soar.**

sorority—A club that is only for girls or women. Usually these clubs are at colleges and universities.
so|ror|i|ty (sə rawr′ə tē) *noun, plural* **sororities.**

sorrow—Great sadness or regret; grief: *The children felt sorrow when their dog ran away.*
sor|row (sor′ō) *noun, plural* **sorrows.**
• Synonyms: **misery, woe**
Antonyms: See Synonyms at **bliss.**

sorry—**1.** Feeling regret, pity, or sadness: *I'm sorry I made fun of you.* **2.** Not very good; poor: *That old chair was in sorry shape.*
sor|ry (sor′ē) *adjective*, **sorrier**, **sorriest.**

sort—A group of people or things that have some of the same qualities; kind: *There are many sorts of trees. Noun.*
—To put in order by type, size, or class: *She sorted the marbles by color. Verb.*

sort (sawrt) *noun, plural* **sorts;** *verb*, **sorted**, **sorting.**
• Synonyms: For *noun*, see Synonyms at **class.**

SOS—A call or signal for rescue or other kind of help: *The boat sent out an SOS when it hit an iceberg.*
SOS (es′ō′es′) *noun, plural* **SOS's.**

sought—*See* **seek.**
sought (sawt) *verb.*

soul—**1.** The part of a person that is believed to cause that person to think, choose, and act. Many religions believe that the soul lives forever. **2.** A person: *There was not a soul on the beach.*
soul (sōl) *noun, plural* **souls.**
• A word that sounds the same is **sole.**

sound¹—**1.** That which can be heard; the vibrations that travel through the air to cause the sensation of hearing. **2.** The distance from which something can be heard: *We had a picnic within sound of the bubbling brook.* **3.** One of the noises that makes up human speech: *the "b" sound in "boy." Noun.*
—**1.** To make or cause a noise: *The alarm sounded when the fire broke out.* **2.** To pronounce or be pronounced: *"Their" and "there" sound alike.* **3.** To seem; appear: *He sounds as if he knows what he is doing. Verb.*
sound (sound) *noun, plural* **sounds;** *verb*, **sounded, sounding.**

sound²—**1.** Free from disease; healthy: *The athlete had a sound body.* **2.** Firm and solid: *a sound building.* **3.** Sensible: *Get some sound advice before you decide which college to attend.* **4.** Deep; peaceful: *a sound sleep. Adjective.*
—Deeply; thoroughly: *The tired children were sound asleep. Adverb.*
sound (sound) *adjective*, **sounder**, **soundest;** *adverb.*

sound³—**1.** To measure the depth of a body of water, usually by letting down a line with a weight on the end. **2.** To try to find out another's feelings or opinions: *I will sound her out before I ask to borrow some money. Verb.*
sound (sound) *verb*, **sounded, sounding.**

sound⁴—A long stretch of water that connects two larger bodies of water or separates an island from the mainland.
sound (sound) *noun, plural* **sounds.**

soundproof—Letting little or no sound pass through: *The band practices in a soundproof room. Adjective.*
—To make so that little or no sound passes through: *They soundproofed the walls of the*

a at	i if	oo look	ch chalk		
ā ape	ī idle	ou out	ng sing		a in ago
ah calm	o odd	u ugly	sh ship	ə =	e in happen
aw all	ō oats	ū rule	th think		i in capital
e end	oi oil	ur turn	<u>th</u> their		o in occur
ē easy			zh treasure		u in upon

theater to keep noise out. Verb.
sound|proof (sound′prūf′) *adjective; verb,*
soundproofed, soundproofing.

soundtrack—The part of a motion picture film
that carries a recording of the sound.
sound|track (sound′trak) *noun, plural*
soundtracks.

soup—A liquid food made from cooking meat,
fish, or vegetables in water or milk.
soup (sūp) *noun, plural* **soups.**

sour—1. Having a sharp and bitter taste: *Lemon
juice is* sour. 2. Unpleasant; disagreeable: *His*
sour *remarks made me angry. Adjective.*
—To make or become sour. *Verb.*
sour (sour) *adjective,* **sourer, sourest;** *verb,*
soured, souring.

source—1. The point or place from which
something comes: *The sea is the* source *of many
types of food.* 2. The beginning of a river or
stream.
source (sawrs) *noun, plural* **sources.**

south—1. The direction to the right of someone
watching the sun rise. 2. **South:** The part of any
country or area that is in or toward this direction.
Noun.
—Facing or in the south: *the* south *side of town.
Adjective.*
—Toward the south: *We drove* south *all day.
Adverb.*
south (south) *noun, adjective, adverb.*
Abbreviation: **S.**

southeast—The direction midway between south
and east. *Noun.*
—1. In the direction between south and east.
2. Coming out of this direction: *a* southeast *wind.
Adjective.*
south|east (south′ēst′) *noun, adjective.*
Abbreviation: **S.E.**

southern—1. Toward, in, or of the south: *a*
southern *climate.* 2. Coming from the south: *The*
southern *breeze brought warm weather.*
south|ern (suth̲′ərn) *adjective.*

South Pole—The most southern part of the
earth, where one end of the earth's axis is
located.
South Pole (south pōl) *noun.*
● See picture at **Antarctic Circle.**

southward—Toward the south: *This window has
a* southward *view. We drove* southward *all day.*
south|ward (south′wərd) *adjective, adverb.*

southwest—The direction midway between south
and west. *Noun.*
—1. In the direction between south and west.

2. Coming from that direction: *A* southwest *wind
brought stormy weather. Adjective.*
south|west (south′west′) *noun, adjective.*
Abbreviation: **S.W.**

southwester—A waterproof hat with a broad
brim in the back that protects the neck.
south|west|er (south′wes′tər *or* sou′wes′tər)
noun, plural **southwesters.**

southwester

souvenir—Something kept in order to remember
a person, place, or happening: *The girls had
shirts with the town's name on them as* souvenirs
of their vacation.
sou|ve|nir (sū′və nēr′ *or* sū′və nēr) *noun,
plural* **souvenirs.**
● Synonyms: **keepsake, memento, reminder,
token**

sovereign—A king or queen. *Noun.*
—1. Having the power of a king or queen: *The*
sovereign *leader led his country to many
victories.* 2. Not under the control of another
government: *The United States has been a*
sovereign *nation for more than 200 years.
Adjective.*
sov|er|eign (sov′rən) *noun, plural* **sovereigns;**
adjective.

sow[1]—To scatter and plant seeds in the ground:
They sowed *wheat and corn this year.*
sow (sō) *verb,* **sowed, sown** or **sowed, sowing.**
● Words that sound the same are **sew** and **so.**

sow[2]—An adult female pig.
sow (sou) *noun, plural* **sows.**

soybean—A bean plant from Asia that is now
grown in other places because of its nutritious
seeds. The seeds are eaten as food and are rich in
protein.
soy|bean (soi′bēn′) *noun, plural* **soybeans.**

space—1. The limitless area in which everything
and everyone exists. 2. The area beyond the
earth and its atmosphere; outer space: *The
satellite traveled through* space. 3. A limited
area set aside for a specific purpose: *It is hard to
find a parking* space. 4. A distance between two

or more things: *Leave a* space *as wide as your hand between the plants.* **5.** A certain amount of time: *She ate dinner and changed her clothes in the* space *of 15 minutes. Noun.*

—To arrange, leaving room between: *The farmer spaced the fence posts far apart. Verb.*

space (spās) *noun, plural* **spaces;** *verb,* **spaced, spacing.**

Word Power

If you are interested in space travel, here are some useful words for you to know. You can find these words in this dictionary. You can also find many other words having to do with outer space, such as the names of the planets.

aerospace	nosecone	spacecraft
astronaut	orbit	space shuttle
blastoff	rocket	space suit
countdown	satellite	sputnik
launching pad		

spacecraft—Any vehicle used for travel in outer space.

space|craft (spās′kraft′) *noun, plural* **spacecraft.**

space shuttle—A spacecraft that looks something like an airplane and can be used over and over.

space shut|tle (spās shut′əl) *noun, plural* **space shuttles.**

space suit—A sealed, protective outfit worn by a person traveling in outer space. It keeps out heat, cold, and radiation. It supplies the person with the proper amount of oxygen needed to live.

space suit (spās sūt) *noun, plural* **space suits.**

spade¹—A kind of shovel that has a flat metal blade on a long handle. When digging with a spade, a person presses the blade into the ground with a foot.

spade (spād) *noun, plural* **spades.**

spade²—**1.** A black shape that looks like an upside-down heart with a stem, used as a design on playing cards. **2.** A playing card that has one or more of these black shapes printed on it.

spade (spād) *noun, plural* **spades.**

spaghetti—A food that is a dried mixture of flour and water cut into long, thin sticks. Before being eaten, the sticks are cooked in boiling water until they become soft.

spa|ghet|ti (spə get′ē) *noun.*

span—**1.** The section or distance between two supports of a bridge or similar structure: *We rowed our boat under the widest* span *of the bridge.* **2.** The full extent or length of anything: *a person's life* span; *a long* span *of memory; an attention* span.

—To extend or stretch across: *a log that* spans *a stream. Verb.*

span (span) *noun, plural* **spans;** *verb,* **spanned, spanning.**

spaniel—A dog belonging to the group of medium-sized or small dogs that have a long, smooth coat and large, drooping ears.

span|iel (span′yəl) *noun, plural* **spaniels.**

spank—To punish by hitting with a flat object or open hand.

spank (spangk) *verb,* **spanked, spanking.**

spare—**1.** To treat with mercy; save from harm: *They* spared *the prisoners and set them free.* **2.** To show consideration to; save from unkindness: *Please* spare *her feelings and do not tell her about her mistake.* **3.** To give up something; do without: *Can you* spare *some time to help me clean the garage? Verb.*

—**1.** Not planned for other use; free: *to have some* spare *time.* **2.** Extra; not needed or used now: *some* spare *change; a* spare *tire.* **3.** Small; scanty; poor in amount or quality: *He was still hungry after his* spare *breakfast.* **4.** Skinny, thin: *Much exercise has given her a* spare *figure. Adjective.*

—**1.** Something extra or saved for later use: *The*

a at	i if	oo look	ch chalk		⌈ a in ago
ā ape	ī idle	ou out	ng sing		e in happen
ah calm	o odd	u ugly	sh ship	ə =	i in capital
aw all	ō oats	ū rule	th think		o in occur
e end	oi oil	ur turn	th their		⌊ u in upon
ē easy			zh treasure		

spade¹ and spade²

package had enough batteries to put in the radio as well as a couple of spares.   **2.** In bowling, the knocking down of all ten pins with two throws of the ball, one right after the other. *Noun.*
spare (spār) *verb,* **spared, sparing;** *adjective,* **sparer, sparest;** *noun, plural* **spares.**
● Synonyms: **gaunt, lean², scrawny,** for *adjective* **4.**
  Antonyms: **fat, plump, stout,** for *adjective* **4.**

spark—**1.** A small bit of burning material: *The screen keeps* sparks *in the fireplace.*   **2.** A small flash of light given off by electricity when it moves through the air.   **3.** A trace; little bit: *He does not like baseball very much and showed only a* spark *of interest in the game. Noun.*
—**1.** To send out small burning bits of material or flashes of light: *The fire* sparked *so much that we had to move back.*   **2.** To get something started: *to* spark *a discussion. Verb.*
spark (spahrk) *noun, plural* **sparks;** *verb,* **sparked, sparking.**

sparkle—**1.** To shine as brightly as bits of fire; glitter: *The sea* sparkled *in the sun.*   **2.** To bubble like ginger ale. *Verb.*
—A number of flashes of light; glitter: *the* sparkle *of diamonds. Noun.*
spar|kle (spahr′kəl) *verb,* **sparkled, sparkling;** *noun, plural* **sparkles.**
● Synonyms: **gleam, glint, glisten,** for *verb* **1.**

spark plug—A device that ignites fuel in an automobile engine or similar engine.
spark plug (spahrk plug) *noun, plural* **spark plugs.**

sparrow—Any of several small, common birds that have brownish feathers. Sparrows live in most parts of the world.
spar|row (spar′ō) *noun, plural* **sparrows.**

sparrow hawk—**1.** A hawk found in Africa, Asia, and Europe. It eats sparrows and other small birds.   **2.** A small falcon that lives in North America. It eats large insects, small birds, and other small animals.
spar|row hawk (spar′ō hawk) *noun, plural* **sparrow hawks.**

spat¹—A small fight or quarrel: *The sisters had a* spat *over whose turn it was to wash the dishes.*
spat (spat) *noun, plural* **spats.**

spat²—*See* spit.
spat (spat) *verb.*

spatter—To scatter or splash in small drops: *Grease* spattered *as the bacon cooked.*
spat|ter (spat′ər) *verb,* **spattered, spattering.**

speak—**1.** To say words; talk: *to* speak *on the*

phone.   **2.** To give a speech: *He was nervous about* speaking *at the meeting.*
speak (spēk) *verb,* **spoke, spoken, speaking.**
■ **so to speak:** To use an expression; in a manner of speaking: *Our pet hamster is quiet as a mouse,* so to speak.

speaker—**1.** A person who talks to an audience or gives a speech: *Our* speaker *tonight is a famous author.*   **2.** A device for reproducing sound from electrical signals.
speak|er (spē′kər) *noun, plural* **speakers.**

spear—**1.** A weapon that has a sharp point atop a long pole.   **2.** A thin stalk or stem of a plant, such as asparagus. *Noun.*
—To stab with a sharp object: *They* speared *marshmallows to cook over the campfire. Verb.*
spear (spēr) *noun, plural* **spears;** *verb,* **speared, spearing.**
● See picture at **asparagus.**

a spear from about 400 B.C.

a spear from the 1400's

a spear from the 1700's

spear (noun, definition 1)

spearmint—A common garden plant whose leaves are used for flavoring foods.
spear|mint (spēr′mint′) *noun, plural* **spearmints.**

sparrow hawk (definition 1)

special—Different from others; out of the ordinary; unusual: special *shoes for dancing;* special *care for a sick puppy. Adjective.*
—A product or service that is on sale: *Today's* special *at the restaurant is a ham and cheese sandwich. Noun.*
spe|cial (spesh′əl) *adjective; noun, plural* **specials.**
• Synonyms: **individual, particular, specific, unique,** for *adjective.*

specialist—A person who is an expert in a particular subject of study: *a* specialist *in the history of art.*
spe|cial|ist (spesh′ə list) *noun, plural* **specialists.**

specialize—To study and become an expert in a particular area or subject: *Some doctors* specialize *in the care of burn victims.*
spe|cial|ize (spesh′ə līz) *verb,* **specialized, specializing.**

specialty—**1.** Something in particular that a person gives a great deal of attention to and knows a lot about: *The lawyer's* specialty *is business law.* **2.** A product or service for which a place is known: *The* specialty *of that bakery is raisin bread.*
spe|cial|ty (spesh′əl tē) *noun, plural* **specialties.**

species—A group of living things having certain similar characteristics. Members of the same species can breed with one another. Wolves and dogs are different species. All breeds of dogs belong to a single species.
spe|cies (spē′shēz) *noun, plural* **species.**

specific—Particular; special: *Why do you want this* specific *dress and not the others?*
spe|cif|ic (spi sif′ik) *adjective.*
• Synonyms: **individual, unique**

specimen—One of a group of people or things that is used to show what the rest are like; sample: *She keeps dried* specimens *of various garden flowers in a book.*
spec|i|men (spes′ə mən) *noun, plural* **specimens.**

speck—**1.** A small spot or stain: *There are* specks *of gravy on the tablecloth.* **2.** A small bit or tiny piece: *She cleaned the* specks *of dust off the record before she played it.*
speck (spek) *noun, plural* **specks.**

spectacle—**1.** A grand or unusual thing to see; striking display or show: *The hundreds of bright red tulips in the park made quite a* spectacle. **2.** spectacles: Eyeglasses.
spec|ta|cle (spek′tə kəl) *noun, plural* **spectacles.**

spectacular—Making a striking or unusual display; impressive: *The fireworks were* spectacular.
spec|tac|u|lar (spek tak′yə lər) *adjective.*

spectator—A person who watches a show, game, or other activity but does not take part in it: *Most of the* spectators *at the spelling bee were parents of the students who were competing.*
spec|ta|tor (spek′tā tər *or* spek tā′tər) *noun, plural* **spectators.**

spectrum—The band of colors that is seen when white light separates as it passes through a prism or through something similar. The colors of the spectrum are the colors of the rainbow.
spec|trum (spek′trəm) *noun, plural* **spectra** (spek′trə) *or* **spectrums.**

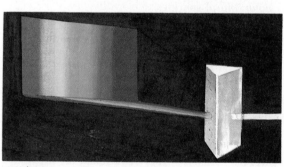

spectrum

Language Fact

The colors of the spectrum tend to blend into one another. Some people consider the spectrum to consist of seven colors—violet, indigo, blue, green, yellow, orange, and red. Others do not include indigo as a separate color. These people consider the spectrum to be made up of six colors.

sped—*See* **speed.**
sped (sped) *verb.*

speech—**1.** The act of saying words or sentences: *She burst out in* speech *when she got a good*

a at	i if	oo look	ch chalk		a in ago
ā ape	ī idle	ou out	ng sing		e in happen
ah calm	o odd	u ugly	sh ship	ə =	i in capital
aw all	ō oats	ū rule	th think		o in occur
e end	oi oil	ur turn	th their		u in upon
ē easy			zh treasure		

idea. **2.** The power or ability to speak: *He lost his* speech *when his throat got so sore.* **3.** A way of speaking: *His* speech *tells me he is from another part of the country.* **4.** A public talk or lecture: *The mayor is going to give a* speech *at our school on Friday.*
speech (spēch) *noun, plural* **speeches.**

speed—**1.** Fast movement; quickness: *The reporter worked with great* speed *to get the story done on time.* **2.** The rate at which something moves: *a* speed *allowed by traffic laws. Noun.*
—**1.** To move or make something move fast: *The runners* sped *around the track.* **2.** To drive at a faster rate than is safe or allowed by law: *The police officer told us we were* speeding. *Verb.*
speed (spēd) *noun, plural* **speeds;** *verb,* **sped** or **speeded, speeding.**
• Synonyms: **hasten, hurry, rush,** for *verb* **1.**
Antonyms: For *verb* **1,** see Synonyms at **dawdle.**

speedometer—A device that shows how fast a vehicle, such as an automobile, is moving.
speed|om|e|ter (spē dom′ə tər) *noun, plural* **speedometers.**

spell[1]—To say or write the letters of a word in their proper order.
spell (spel) *verb,* **spelled, spelling.**

spell[2]—**1.** A word or group of words thought to have magical power: *The wizard in the story cast a* spell *on the queen that turned her into a cow.* **2.** An attraction that seems magical; fascination: *the* spell *of moonlight on the sea.*
spell (spel) *noun, plural* **spells.**

speller—**1.** A person who says or writes the letters of a word in their proper order. **2.** A book used to help people learn the proper order of letters for various words.
spell|er (spel′ər) *noun, plural* **spellers.**

spelling—**1.** The saying or writing of the letters of a word in their proper order: *We practice our* spelling *when we write stories.* **2.** The proper order of letters to make a certain word: *''Programmer'' and ''programer'' are both correct* spellings *of the same word.*
spell|ing (spel′ing) *noun, plural* **spellings.**

spend—**1.** To pay money: *How much did you* spend *on your new skateboard?* **2.** To pass time in a certain way or place: *We* spent *the holidays at my grandparents' house.* **3.** To use up or wear out: *The crowd* spent *its excitement at the beginning of the game and was quiet by the end.*
spend (spend) *verb,* **spent, spending.**

spent—See **spend.**
spent (spent) *verb.*

sperm—The male cell of reproduction.
sperm (spurm) *noun, plural* **sperm** or **sperms.**

sperm whale—A large whale whose square-shaped head contains wax and oil that were formerly used to make medicines and cosmetics.
sperm whale (spurm hwāl) *noun, plural* **sperm whales.**

sperm whale

sphere—**1.** Any object, such as a globe or an orange, that is round like a ball. All the points on the surface of a sphere are the same distance from its center. **2.** An area of activity or a field of interest or study: *a small country within a larger country's* sphere *of influence; a subject outside her* sphere *of knowledge.*
sphere (sfēr) *noun, plural* **spheres.**

Sphinx—A large statue in Egypt. It has the body of a lion and the head of a man. It is carved out of stone and was made in ancient times.
Sphinx (sfingks) *noun.*

spice—A food flavoring that comes from one of various plants. Spices include pepper, ginger, and nutmeg. *Noun.*
—To add such a flavoring to food: *The hot cider was* spiced *with cinnamon. Verb.*
spice (spīs) *noun, plural* **spices;** *verb,* **spiced, spicing,**

spider—A small animal with eight thin legs that spread out from its central body. Spiders spin threads produced inside their bodies into webs, in

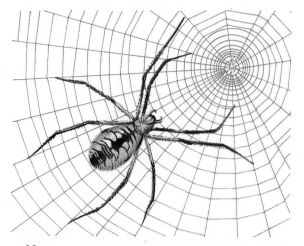

spider

which they catch insects for food.
spi|der (spī′dər) *noun, plural* **spiders**.

spied—*See* spy.
spied (spīd) *verb*.

spigot—A faucet.
spig|ot (spig′ət) *noun, plural* **spigots**.
● See Language Fact at **faucet**.

spike—**1.** A large, heavy metal nail.
2. Anything that is pointed and sticks straight up
or out of something: *the* spikes *on top of a wall;
the* spikes *on baseball shoes. Noun.*
—To hold together with a heavy metal nail.
Verb.
spike (spīk) *noun, plural* **spikes**; *verb*, **spiked,
spiking**.

spill—**1.** To cause or allow to run out or flow,
usually by accident; overturn: *He knocked over
the jar and* spilled *all the peanuts.* **2.** To flow
out or over: *The water* spilled *over the edge of
the pot. Verb.*
—A tumble or fall: *The wagon took a* spill *and
scattered the vegetables all over the road.
Noun.*
spill (spil) *verb*, **spilled** or **spilt**, **spilling**; *noun,
plural* **spills**.

spin—**1.** To keep turning around and around: *The
figure skater* spun *faster and faster.* **2.** To twist
long, thin pieces of fiber into yarn or thread.

3. To build a cocoon, nest, or web with a
hardened threadlike substance produced in the
body, as spiders do. *Verb.*
—**1.** A rapid turning: *The* spin *of the tires on the
ice made a loud, whining sound.* **2.** A short ride
or walk: *They took a* spin *around the block in the
new car. Noun.*
spin (spin) *verb*, **spun**, **spinning**; *noun, plural*
spins.

spinach—A green, leafy vegetable. Its leaves can
be eaten raw or cooked.
spin|ach (spin′ich *or* spin′ij) *noun*.

spinach

spinal column—The bones that run down the
center of the back; backbone; spine.
spi|nal col|umn (spī′nəl kol′əm) *noun, plural*
spinal columns.

spinal cord—A long, ropelike set of nerve
tissue that runs along and through the backbone.
Nerves extend from this cord to various parts of
the body. It is connected to the brain.
spi|nal cord (spī′nəl kawrd) *noun, plural*
spinal cords.

spindle—A long, thin rod that is used to spin
fibers into thread. It is the part of a spinning
wheel that holds and winds the thread.
spin|dle (spin′dəl) *noun, plural* **spindles**.

spine—**1.** The bones that run down the center of
the back; spinal column; backbone.
2. Something that looks like a backbone: *the*
spine *of a book.* **3.** Sharp spikes that grow on a
plant or animal.
spine (spīn) *noun, plural* **spines**.
● See picture at **vertebrae**.

spinning wheel—A device used to spin fiber
into yarn or thread. It consists of a large wheel
and a spindle set on a frame.
spin|ning wheel (spin′ing hwēl) *noun, plural*
spinning wheels.

a at	i if	oo look	ch chalk		⎡a in ago
ā ape	ī idle	ou out	ng sing		e in happen
ah calm	o odd	u ugly	sh ship	ə =	i in capital
aw all	ō oats	ū rule	th think		o in occur
e end	oi oil	ur turn	th their		⎣u in upon
ē easy			zh treasure		

spinster—A woman, especially an older woman, who is not married, has never been married, and is not likely to get married.
spin|ster (spin′stər) *noun, plural* **spinsters.**

Word History

Spinster at first referred to a woman whose occupation was to spin yarn for fabrics. Beginning in the 1600's, the word came to mean "an unmarried woman." Today, the term is rarely used in everyday speech and is considered old-fashioned. Many people also think it is insulting.

spiral—Something that curls around and around, in circles inside each other, or above each other. Coils and springs are spirals. *Noun.*
—Having a coiled shape; going around and around: *a* spiral *lock of hair; the* spiral *thread on a bottle cap; a* spiral *staircase. Adjective.*
—To move in a way that resembles such a shape; make into such a shape: *smoke* spiraling *out of the chimney. Verb.*
spi|ral (spī′rəl) *noun, plural* **spirals;** *adjective;* *verb,* **spiraled, spiraling.**

spire—A structure that is built on a tower and that comes to a point at the top.
spire (spīr) *noun, plural* **spires.**

spirit—1. The part of a human being that is believed to control thoughts, feelings, and choices; soul; mind. 2. A being such as an angel or ghost that does not have a body but is thought

spinning wheel

sometimes to become visible. 3. Courage: *It took* spirit *to rescue the kitten from that high tree.* 4. Lively energy: *the* spirit *of the crowd in the football stadium.* 5. **spirits:** Mood or attitude: *He had been feeling sad, but his* spirits *lifted when his dog met him at the door.*
spir|it (spēr′it) *noun, plural* **spirits.**
• Synonyms: **grit, heart, pluck,** for 3.

spiritual—Having to do with the spirit; religious: *Monks lead very* spiritual *lives. Adjective.*
—A religious piece of music, especially one that was first sung by blacks in the southern part of the United States. *Noun.*
spir|i|tu|al (spēr′ə chū əl) *adjective; noun, plural* **spirituals.**

spit—To push or thrust liquid or something else out of the mouth: *He bit into the rotten apple by mistake and had to* spit *it out. Verb.*
—The liquid that flows constantly into the mouth; saliva: *Noun.*
spit (spit) *verb,* **spat** or **spit, spitting;** *noun.*
■ **spitting image:** An exact likeness: *The twins were the* spitting image *of each other.*

spite—A bitter feeling toward someone: *Her brother broke her favorite doll, so she tore up his baseball cards out of* spite. *Noun.*
—To show bitter feelings toward someone; annoy: *He ignored her questions just to* spite *her. Verb.*
spite (spīt) *noun; verb,* **spited, spiting.**
■ **in spite of:** Not stopped by; regardless of: *He wore a sweater* in spite of *the hot weather.*

splash—To scatter a liquid all over; splatter: *He splashed milk on his friends when he dropped his glass. Verb.*
—1. The act of splattering a liquid all over: *a diver making a* splash *in a pool.* 2. The sound made by a splattered liquid: *the* splash *of rain on a roof.* 3. A mark made by a splattered liquid: *There were* splashes *of paint on the window.* 4. A mark of a different color: *Her brown hair had* splashes *of blonde in it. Noun.*
splash (splash) *verb,* **splashed, splashing;** *noun, plural* **splashes.**

splendid—1. Very beautiful or brilliant; grand: *a* splendid *gown; a* splendid *painting.* 2. Very good; excellent: *We had* splendid *weather on our vacation.*
splen|did (splen′did) *adjective.*
• Synonyms: **magnificent, majestic, stately,** for 1.

splendor—1. Great beauty or brilliance: *the* splendor *of a rainbow; the* splendor *of a diamond.* 2. A magnificent show; great display

of wealth: *the splendor of a royal palace.*
splen|dor (splen´dər) *noun, plural*
splendors.

splint—A thin strip of wood, metal, or plastic
that is used to keep a broken bone in place.
splint (splint) *noun, plural* **splints.**

splinter—A thin, pointed piece that has split off
from a hard material such as wood, glass, or
metal; sliver: *She got a splinter in her finger
from picking up the broken glass. Noun.*
—To break into such thin, pointed pieces: *The
wood splintered when he chopped it with an ax.
Verb.*
splin|ter (splin´tər) *noun, plural* **splinters;** *verb,*
splintered, splintering.

split—**1.** To burst or separate into parts or layers:
*a pair of jeans splitting at the seam; a river that
splits into several channels.* **2.** To divide or
break up into parts: *to split a class into two
groups. Verb.*
—**1.** A crack, break, or tear: *a split in the old
wooden chair; a split in his jacket.* **2.** A
dividing within a group: *There was a split in the
hiking club over which trail to take. Noun.*
split (split) *verb,* **split, splitting;** *noun, plural*
splits.

spoil—**1.** to cause damage or injury to something;
ruin: *A fall on the ice spoiled the skater's
performance.* **2.** To harm the character of
someone by too much praise or pampering: *They
spoiled the child so badly that he cried whenever
he did not get his way.* **3.** To decay; rot;
decompose: *Because no one picked up the apples
around the tree, they soon spoiled. Verb.*
—**spoils:** Goods or property taken by force: *The
pirates carried off spoils from the conquered
ship. Noun.*
spoil (spoil) *verb,* **spoiled** or **spoilt, spoiling;**
plural noun.
● Synonyms: **coddle, humor, indulge,** for *verb* 2.

spoke[1]—*See* **speak.**
spoke (spōk) *verb.*

spoke[2]—Any of the bars connecting the hub to
the rim of a wheel.
spoke (spōk) *noun, plural* **spokes.**

spoken—*See* **speak.** *Verb.*
—Said out loud and not written: *The lawyers*

gave spoken *arguments before the judge.
Adjective.*
spo|ken (spō´kən) *verb, adjective.*

sponge—**1.** An underwater animal with a skeleton
that has many holes and absorbs water. **2.** A pad
that has many holes in it and is used for
cleaning. Most such pads are made of rubber or
plastic, but some are made from the dried
skeletons of sponges. *Noun.*
—To clean with a pad that quickly absorbs
liquids: *Mother sponged up the spilled milk.
Verb.*
sponge (spunj) *noun, plural* **sponges;** *verb,*
sponged, sponging.
■ **throw in the sponge:** To give up: *After failing
to win the race for governor, the candidate
decided to throw in the sponge and leave
politics.*

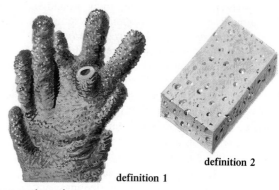

definition 2

definition 1

sponge (noun)

sponsor—**1.** A person or group of people taking
responsibility for someone or something: *The
garden club is the sponsor of a flower show.*
2. A company that pays the costs of a radio or
television show and then advertises its products
during it. *Noun.*
—To take responsibility or pay for something:
*Our school band sponsored the magazine drive.
Verb.*
spon|sor (spon´sər) *noun, plural* **sponsors;** *verb,*
sponsored, sponsoring.

spontaneous—Occurring without any plan;
happening freely or naturally: *The crowd burst
into spontaneous applause during the mayor's
speech.*
spon|ta|ne|ous (spon tā´nē əs) *adjective.*

spool—A wooden, plastic, or metal cylinder on
which thread or wire is wound.
spool (spūl) *noun, plural* **spools.**

spoon—A kitchen tool that has a handle with a
small, shallow bowl at the end. It is used for

a at	i if	oo look	ch chalk		a in ago
ā ape	ī idle	ou out	ng sing		e in happen
ah calm	o odd	u ugly	sh ship	ə =	i in capital
aw all	ō oats	ū rule	th think		o in occur
e end	oi oil	ur turn	th their		u in upon
ē easy			zh treasure		

eating, stirring, measuring, or serving food. *Noun.*
—To lift up something with this tool: *He spooned the vegetables onto his plate. Verb.*
spoon (spūn) *noun, plural* **spoons;** *verb,* **spooned, spooning.**

spore—A tiny part produced by fungi, plants, and some animals that can grow into a new plant or animal of its kind. Most spores consist of a single cell.
spore (spawr) *noun, plural* **spores.**

sport—**1.** A game that requires physical activity. Most sports involve competition. Baseball, bowling, football, and golf are sports. **2.** Any activity that is fun: *Skipping rope was her favorite sport.* **3.** A person who plays fairly and is a good winner or loser: *He was a good sport about losing the tennis match and shook hands with his opponent.*
sport (spawrt) *noun, plural* **sports.**
● Synonyms: **amusement, entertainment, pastime, play, recreation,** for **2.**
Antonyms: **chore, duty, task,** for **2.**

sportsmanship—The quality or behavior of a person or persons who play fairly and are good winners or losers: *The football player showed good* sportsmanship *when he helped the quarterback to his feet after tackling him.*
sports|man|ship (spawrts′mən ship) *noun.*

spot—**1.** A stain, mark, or blemish: *She got grease* spots *on her blouse while frying bacon.* **2.** A small part of something that is different from the rest, especially in color: *Her kitten is brown except for a white* spot *on the tip of its tail.* **3.** A location: *That field would be a good* spot *for our softball game. Noun.*
—**1.** To stain or mark: *Her boots* spotted *the rug with mud.* **2.** To locate; pick out; see and recognize: *He* spotted *his friend in the parking lot and called to him. Verb.*
spot (spot) *noun, plural* **spots;** *verb,* **spotted, spotting.**
■ **hit the spot:** To be just what is needed: *A cup of hot chocolate is sure to* hit the spot *after a day of ice-skating.*
put (someone) **on the spot:** To place someone in a difficult or dangerous situation: *He put me* on the spot *when he asked me if I had voted for him for club president.*
● Synonyms: **place, position, site, situation,** for *noun* **3.**

spouse—A husband or wife.
spouse (spous) *noun, plural* **spouses.**

spout—To spray out forcefully, usually through a narrow opening: *Water* spouted *from the hole in the hose.*
—A narrow opening through which liquid flows: *the* spout *of a coffee pot; the* spout *of a faucet. Noun.*
spout (spout) *verb,* **spouted, spouting;** *noun, plural* **spouts.**

sprain—To injure a muscle or joint by twisting it: *She fell while playing tennis and* sprained *her wrist. Verb.*
—An injury to a muscle or joint caused by twisting: *He got an ankle* sprain *from stepping in a hole in the street. Noun.*
sprain (sprān) *verb,* **sprained, spraining;** *noun, plural* **sprains.**

sprang—*See* **spring.**
sprang (sprang) *verb.*

sprawl—**1.** To spread out one's arms and legs in a relaxed way while sitting or lying down; stretch out ungracefully: *There was no room for me on the couch, because my brother was* sprawled *on it.* **2.** To spread out in a careless way: *Her room was neat except that her clothes were* sprawled *all over the bed.*
sprawl (sprawl) *verb,* **sprawled, sprawling.**

spray—A liquid that moves through the air in small drops: *the* spray *from a fountain. Noun.*
—To scatter or sprinkle a liquid or mist in the form of small drops: *to* spray *the grass; to* spray *paint on a fence. Verb.*
spray (sprā) *noun, plural* **sprays;** *verb,* **sprayed, spraying.**

spread—**1.** To stretch out; open out; unfold: *He* spread *the road map on the table.* **2.** To open wide; push or pull apart: *to* spread *one's arms to give a hug; to* spread *a ship's sails.* **3.** To scatter throughout an area: *to* spread *balloons about a room; to* spread *flower seeds in a garden.* **4.** To make or become known by many people: *to* spread *gossip; information about a scientist's discovery* spreading *quickly.* **5.** To cover by smearing with something: *She* spread *lotion on her hands. Verb.*
—**1.** The act or process of stretching, reaching, opening, or scattering: *the* spread *of rumor; the* spread *of a disease.* **2.** The amount that something stretches out: *The* spread *of the eagle's wings was wider than most people are tall.* **3.** A covering for a table or bed. **4.** A soft food, such as peanut butter or jelly, that is put in a layer on such other foods as bread or crackers. *Noun.*
spread (spred) *verb,* **spread, spreading;** *noun, plural* **spreads.**

spree—A joyful, happy time: *The children went on a* spree *at the carnival and rode on every ride.*
spree (sprē) *noun, plural* **sprees.**

sprig—A small branch; twig.
sprig (sprig) *noun, plural* **sprigs.**

sprightly—Merry; full of energy and spirit: *a* sprightly *dance.*
spright|ly (sprīt′lē) *adjective,* **sprightlier, sprightliest.**

spring—1. To move upward and forward quickly; jump or leap: *We saw a deer* spring *across the road.* 2. To snap like elastic: *The gate will* spring *shut if you let go of it.* 3. To happen or grow suddenly: *Thunderstorms sometimes* spring *up on hot summer days.* 4. To bring out, make happen, or announce suddenly: *to* spring *a surprise party on a friend; to* spring *bad news on someone. Verb.*
—1. The season of the year that comes between winter and summer. 2. A jump or leap: *She made a* spring *for the plate to try to catch it before it hit the floor.* 3. A device, usually made of bent or coiled metal, that returns to its normal shape after it is pushed in or stretched out: *the* springs *in a mattress.* 4. A flow of water from underground. *Noun.*
spring (spring) *verb,* **sprang** or **sprung, sprung, springing;** *noun, plural* **springs.**

springboard—A board used for diving or gymnastics that helps a person jump into the air.
spring|board (spring′bawrd′) *noun, plural* **springboards.**

sprinkle—1. To scatter in small amounts or drops: *He* sprinkled *salt and pepper on his eggs.* 2. To rain very lightly.
sprin|kle (spring′kəl) *verb,* **sprinkled, sprinkling.**

sprinkler—A device used for spraying water, usually on a lawn or garden.
sprin|kler (spring′klər) *noun, plural* **sprinklers.**

sprint—To run a short, fast race. *Verb.*
—A short race that is run at top speed. *Noun.*
sprint (sprint) *verb,* **sprinted, sprinting;** *noun, plural* **sprints.**

sprout—To start growing; produce buds or shoots: *The wheat is* sprouting. *Verb.*

—1. a bud or shoot on a plant. 2. **sprouts:** Young shoots of plants eaten as vegetables: *bean* sprouts, *alfalfa* sprouts. *Noun.*
sprout (sprout) *verb,* **sprouted, sprouting;** *noun, plural* **sprouts.**

spruce—An evergreen tree that has cones and needlelike leaves.
spruce (sprūs) *noun, plural* **spruces.**

spruce

needles

tree   cone

sprung—*See* **spring.**
sprung (sprung) *verb.*

spun—*See* **spin.**
spun (spun) *verb.*

spur—1. A small, pointed metal device fastened to the heel of a rider's boot. It is used to urge a horse to go forward or faster. 2. Something that urges one to action: *Pride in himself was the* spur *that made him always try his best. Noun.*
—1. To urge on a horse with this device: *to* spur *a horse to a gallop.* 2. To urge into action: *Her parents' faith in her* spurred *her to go to college. Verb.*
spur (spur) *noun, plural* **spurs;** *verb,* **spurred, spurring.**
■ **on the spur of the moment:** Without thinking about or preparing for something; on a spontaneous urge: *It turned out to be such a beautiful day that we decided to go fishing* on the spur of the moment.

spurt—To gush out or cause to gush out suddenly in a stream; spout: *The elephant* spurted *water from its trunk. Verb.*

—**1.** A sudden gush: Spurts *of flames came from the volcano.* **2.** A sudden, brief effort: *He reads a book in* spurts *rather than at a long sitting. Noun.*

spurt (spurt) *verb,* **spurted, spurting:** *noun, plural* **spurts.**

sputnik—Any of a series of artificial earth satellites launched by the Soviet Union from 1957 to 1961.

sput|nik (**sput′**nik *or* **spoot′**nik) *noun, plural* **sputniks.**

sputter—**1.** To make hissing or popping sounds: *The old tractor* sputtered *as it climbed the hill.* **2.** To speak in a hasty or confused manner: *The excited bank clerk* sputtered *to the police about the robbery.*

sput|ter (**sput′**ər) *verb,* **sputtered, sputtering.**

spy—**1.** Someone who observes others in secret: *A* spy *for the other team tried to watch us practice for the big game.* **2.** A government agent who tries secretly to get information about an enemy country. *Noun.*
—**1.** To observe others secretly: *That nosy woman hides behind her curtains and* spies *on her neighbors.* **2.** To act as a secret agent. **3.** To notice; get a quick glimpse of: *Mother* spied *dust under the chair. Verb.*

spy (spī) *noun, plural* **spies;** *verb,* **spied, spying.**

sq.—The abbreviation for **square.**

squad—**1.** A small group of soldiers. **2.** A small group of people who share a purpose or function: *a baseball* squad.

squad (skwod) *noun, plural* **squads.**

squadron—A group of military ships, airplanes, or other vehicles.

squad|ron (**skwod′**rən) *noun, plural* **squadrons.**

squall—A sudden, forceful gust of wind, often with rain, sleet, or snow.

squall (skwawl) *noun, plural* **squalls.**

square—**1.** A shape that has four equal sides and four equal angles. **2.** Something having this shape: *a* square *of paper; a* square *of cake.* **3.** An open area surrounded by streets or buildings on all sides: *a town* square; *a public* square. **4.** The number that results when a number is multiplied by itself: *The* square *of three is nine. Noun.*
—**1.** Having four equal sides and four equal angles: *a* square *tile; a* square *cushion.* **2.** Forming a right angle; perpendicular: *the* square *corners of a rug.* **3.** Truthful; fair: *He is always* square *with his friends, so they know they can count on him.* **4.** Measured by multiplying the length of an area by the width of the area: square *feet;* square *meters. Adjective.*
—**1.** To make into a shape with four equal sides: *He* squared *the napkin by folding it.* **2.** To mark or divide into shapes that have four equal sides: *Mother* squared *off the pan of brownies with a knife.* **3.** To make a right angle: *The carpenter sanded the window frame to* square *its corners.* **4.** To match or agree: *His figures on the cost of buying new uniforms for the band do not* square *with mine.* **5.** To multiply a number by itself: *Two* squared *equals four. Verb.*
—Solidly or directly: *The boy was not looking and ran* square *into a tree. Adverb.*

square (skwãr) *noun, plural* **squares;** *adjective,* **squarer, squarest;** *verb,* **squared, squaring;** *adverb.* Abbreviation: **sq.**

■ **all square:** All paid up or even: *She owed me two dollars and gave me five, so when I pay her three dollars we shall be* all square.
  square away: To make ready; put in order: *She is trying to get her house* squared away *before the weekend guests arrive.*

square	rectangle

square (noun, definition 1)

squash[1]—**1.** To press firmly on something and flatten it: *to* squash *a can with his foot.* **2.** To become flattened: *Please pack my groceries carefully because the bread and vegetables* squash *easily. Verb.*
—A game in which a hard rubber ball is hit with a racket against the walls of an indoor court. *Noun.*

squash (skwosh) *verb,* **squashed, squashing;** *noun.*

● Synonyms: **crush, mash,** for *verb* **1.**

an old-fashioned spur

a modern spur

spur (noun, definition 1)

squash²—Any one of a number of vegetables that have a yellow or green skin. Squashes are closely related to pumpkins.
squash (skwosh) *noun, plural* **squashes.**

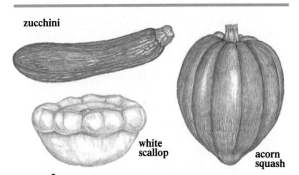

zucchini

white scallop

acorn squash

squash²: three kinds of squash

Word History

Squash¹ comes from a Latin word meaning "shake." **Squash²** comes from an American Indian word for these vegetables. When European settlers came to America, they found many vegetables, such as squash, that they had never seen before. In many cases, they simply used the American Indian name for such vegetables, because they did not have one of their own.

squat—1. To bend one's legs and sit on one's heels: *She* squatted *to pick up the papers she dropped.* 2. To live on an area of land without owning it: *The campers* squatted *on the ranch for a week.* 3. To live on public land in order to obtain ownership of it. *Verb.*
—Having a flattened look; short and wide: *a* squat *chair. Adjective.*
squat (skwot) *verb,* **squatted** or **squat, squatting;** *adjective,* **squatter, squattest.**

squawk—To make a harsh cry; screech: *The parrot* squawked *when it was frightened. Verb.*
—A harsh cry; screech: *the* squawk *of a hen. Noun.*
squawk (skwawk) *verb,* **squawked, squawking;** *noun, plural* **squawks.**

a at	i if	oo look	ch chalk		a in ago
ā ape	ī idle	ou out	ng sing		e in happen
ah calm	o odd	u ugly	sh ship	ə =	i in capital
aw all	ō oats	ū rule	th think		o in occur
e end	oi oil	ur turn	th their		u in upon
ē easy			zh treasure		

squeak—To make a brief, high, thin noise: *The drawer* squeaked *when I opened it. Verb.*
—A brief, high, thin noise: *We heard the* squeak *of his shoes as he walked down the hallway. Noun.*
squeak (skwēk) *verb,* **squeaked, squeaking;** *noun, plural* **squeaks.**

squeal—To make a loud, high cry or sound: *a pig* squealing; *the children* squealing *as they ride the roller coaster. Verb.*
—A loud, high cry or sound: *the* squeal *of tires when a car stops suddenly. Noun.*
squeal (skwēl) *verb,* **squealed, squealing;** *noun, plural* **squeals.**

squeeze—1. To press firmly: *to* squeeze *an orange to get juice; to* squeeze *my arm to get my attention.* 2. To hold tightly; hug; clasp: *She* squeezed *her son as he got off the train.* 3. To push into or through something by pressing firmly: *They* squeezed *into the crowded hotel lobby to see the movie actress.* 4. To force out or get something by pressing firmly: *Mother* squeezed *water out of the mop. Verb.*
—The act of pressing firmly: *He gave the tube a* squeeze *to get out the last of the toothpaste. Noun.*
squeeze (skwēz) *verb,* **squeezed, squeezing;** *noun, plural* **squeezes.**

squid—A sea animal similar to an octopus. It has ten arms and no shell.
squid (skwid) *noun, plural* **squids** or **squid.**

squid

squint—To close the eyes partly while looking: *He* squinted *to read the small print on the label.*
squint (skwint) *verb,* **squinted, squinting.**

squire—1. An English country gentleman and landowner. 2. In the Middle Ages, a young man from a noble family who served a knight in preparation for becoming a knight himself.
squire (skwīr) *noun, plural* **squires.**

squirm—1. To twist about or wriggle: *She squirmed as the water in the shower suddenly turned cold.* 2. To feel uneasy: *He squirmed when the teacher asked him a question. Verb.*
—*A twisting about or wriggling: The sudden squirm of the snake frightened the children. Noun.*
squirm (skwurm) *verb,* **squirmed, squirming;** *noun, plural* **squirms.**
• Synonyms: **fidget, wiggle,** for *verb* **1.**

squirrel—A bushy-tailed animal with gray, black, reddish, or dark brown fur. It lives in trees and eats mainly nuts.
squir|rel (skwur′əl *or* skwir′əl) *noun, plural* **squirrels.**

squirrel

Language Fact

Squirrel is pronounced in different ways, and the way people pronounce the word may depend on where they come from. In the eastern United States, and in large cities, people often say **skwir′əl**. In the rest of the country, it is more common to say **skwur′əl**.

squirt—1. To shoot out a liquid in a narrow stream: *The hose* squirted *water.* 2. To make wet by shooting out a liquid. *He* squirted *his wagon with water to wash it.* 3. To come out in a narrow stream: *Water* squirted *from the fountain. Verb.*
—A small amount of a liquid shot out in a narrow stream: *I like a few* squirts *of mustard on my hot dog. Noun.*
squirt (skwurt) *verb,* **squirted, squirting;** *noun, plural* **squirts.**

Sr.—The abbreviation for **senior.**

SS.—The abbreviation for **saints.**

St.—The abbreviation for **saint** and **street.**

stab—1. To injure by jabbing with a sharp weapon: *At the end of the story, the knight* stabbed *the dragon with his sword.* 2. To poke with something sharp: *She stopped the paper from blowing off the desk by* stabbing *it with her pencil. Verb.*
—1. An act of poking with something sharp: *With a* stab *of the pitchfork, the farmer lifted the hay.* 2. An injury made by a sharp weapon: *The pirate in the movie got a* stab *in the chest from a knife.* 3. A brief, sharp feeling: *a* stab *of guilt; a* stab *of sadness.* 4. An effort or attempt: *She took a* stab *at answering the question. Noun.*
stab (stab) *verb,* **stabbed, stabbing;** *noun, plural* **stabs.**
• Synonyms: **pierce, stick,** for *verb* **2.**

stable¹—A building with stalls for sheltering and feeding livestock, especially horses. *Noun.*
—To keep or shelter livestock in a place like this: *The horses were* stabled *after a day in the pasture. Verb.*
sta|ble (stā′bəl) *noun, plural* **stables;** *verb,* **stabled, stabling.**

stable²—Firm, constant, or steady; hard to move or change: stable *prices;* a stable *person;* a stable *environment.*
sta|ble (stā′bəl) *adjective.*

stack—A pile or large quantity of something: *a* stack *of hay; a* stack *of dishes. Noun.*
—To make into a pile or pack together: *She* stacked *the books on the shelf. Verb.*
stack (stak) *noun, plural* **stacks;** *verb,* **stacked, stacking.**
• Synonyms: **heap, mass¹, mound,** for *noun.*

stadium—A large structure for spectators. It consists of rows of seats built around a playing field. It is used for watching athletic contests and other public events.
sta|di|um (stā′dē əm) *noun, plural* **stadiums.**

staff—1. A pole, stick, rod, or bar used for supporting something: *a flag flying on its* staff; *hikers carrying* staffs *to help them walk along a rugged trail.* 2. People who work at a place or for a person: *the* staff *at the bank; the candidate's* staff. 3. The five lines and four spaces on which musical notes are written.
staff (staf) *noun, plural* **staffs.**

Staffordshire bull terrier—A medium-sized dog that has a large chest and a short coat with markings like those of a bulldog. Originally bred in England, these dogs were developed as fighters and are very fast.
Staf|ford|shire bull ter|ri|er (staf′ərd shēr bool ter′ē ər) *noun, plural* **Staffordshire bull terriers.**

Staffordshire bull terrier

stag—A male deer that is completely grown; buck.
stag (stag) *noun, plural* **stags.**
• See picture at **deer.**

stage—1. The raised platform in a theater or auditorium on which actors and other entertainers perform. **2.** The scene of some important event or action: *The countryside around the bridge was* the stage *for many important battles in the war.* **3.** A single step, period, point, or degree in a process, undertaking, or development: *Learning how to talk is an important* stage *in one's life.* **4.** A stagecoach. **5.** A section of a rocket or missile that has its own engine and fuel supply. As the fuel in each stage is used up, that part separates from the rest of the rocket or missile. *Noun.*
—To arrange, carry out, or present: *angry citizens who* stage *a protest; a science fair that was* staged *by our school. Verb.*
stage (stāj) *noun, plural* **stages;** *verb,* **staged, staging.**

stagecoach—An enclosed, horse-drawn coach for carrying passengers, mail, and freight regularly between stations along a fixed route. Stagecoaches were once a major means of transportation in many countries.
stage|coach (stāj′kōch′) *noun, plural* **stagecoaches.**

stagger—1. To move or cause to move with an unsteady, swaying motion: *He felt sick and faint on the field but managed to* stagger *back to the bench.* **2.** To shock, overwhelm, or amaze; astonish: *The amount of work still needing to be done* staggers *me.* **3.** To rearrange so as to overlap or alternate positions or times: *The closing hours at the three schools were* staggered *so the buses could handle their routes easily. Verb.*
—An unsteady, swaying walk. *Noun.*
stag|ger (stag′ər) *verb,* **staggered, staggering;** *noun, plural* **staggers.**

stagnant—1. Not flowing; having no current or motion: *The air was so* stagnant *that not a single leaf or branch moved on the trees.* **2.** Foul or stale from being motionless: *Water collected in* stagnant *pools in the ditch.*
stag|nant (stag′nənt) *adjective.*

stain—1. To spot or streak: *Tears* stained *her cheeks.* **2.** To bring dishonor upon; disgrace: *He refused to* stain *his reputation by accepting a bribe.* **3.** To color with a dye or pigment that penetrates the surface: *The old rocking chair was* stained *a dark brown. Verb.*
—1. A spot or streak: *The jelly left a* stain *on the napkin.* **2.** A mark of dishonor or disgrace: *His cowardly act was a* stain *on his family name.* **3.** A dye, pigment, or other substance used for coloring a surface: *He put a blue* stain *on the cabinet he uses for storing his records. Noun.*
stain (stān) *verb,* **stained, staining;** *noun, plural* **stains.**

stair—1. One of a set of steps for going from one story or level to another: *The second* stair *squeaked when I stepped on it.* **2.** An entire set of these steps; staircase: *A narrow* stair *led to the attic.* **3.** stairs: The set of steps for going from one story or level to another: *He ran down the* stairs *to answer the telephone.*
stair (stâr) *noun, plural* **stairs.**
• A word that sounds the same is **stare.**

a at	i if	oo look	ch chalk		a in ago
ā ape	ī idle	ou out	ng sing		e in happen
ah calm	o odd	u ugly	sh ship	ə =	i in capital
aw all	ō oats	ū rule	th think		o in occur
e end	oi oil	ur turn	th their		u in upon
ē easy			zh treasure		

staircase—One or more sets of stairs with their supporting framework and railings.
stair│case (stãr′kās′) *noun, plural* **staircases.**

stake—**1.** A pointed stick or post that is driven into the ground as a marker or a support: *She set stakes in the garden to mark where she planted the various vegetables.* **2.** Money or something valuable that is risked in a bet or gamble: *The stakes were high in the card game.* **3.** An interest; share: *Of course I am concerned about what you study in school, because I have a stake in your future. Noun.*
—**1.** To fasten, support, or secure with a pointed stick or post: *The gardener staked the little trees so they would not be blown over.* **2.** To mark boundaries with pointed sticks or posts: *The police staked off the scene of the crime.* **3.** To risk in a bet or gamble: *He staked five dollars on his last hand of cards. Verb.*
stake (stāk) *noun, plural* **stakes;** *verb,* **staked, staking.**
- **pull up stakes:** To move away; leave a place with all one's belongings: *Her grandparents pulled up stakes and moved to a place that has warmer weather.*
- A word that sounds the same is **steak.**

stalactite—A rock formation that hangs from the ceiling of a cave. It looks something like an icicle. It is formed by dripping water.
sta│lac│tite (stə lak′tīt) *noun, plural* **stalactites.**

Word Power

Stalactite and **stalagmite** sound alike, and it can be hard to remember which is which. Here is a way that you can keep their meanings in mind. Stalactites grow down from the top of a cave. Think of the "c" in **stalactite** as standing for "ceiling." Stalagmites grow up from the floor of a cave. Think of the "g" in **stalagmite** as standing for "ground."

---

stalagmite—A cone-shaped rock formation that sticks up from the floor of a cave. It is built up little by little as water drips from above.
sta│lag│mite (stə lag′mīt) *noun, plural* **stalagmites.**

stale—**1.** Not fresh; dry, hard, or flat from age: *That piece of toast has been there since breakfast and is probably stale by now.* **2.** Too familiar to be interesting: *The story of his winning goal has grown so stale that I do not think I can stand to hear it one more time.*
stale (stāl) *adjective,* **staler, stalest.**

stalk¹—The stem that supports a plant.
stalk (stawk) *noun, plural* **stalks.**

stalk²—**1.** To pursue or follow silently while staying out of sight: *The cat stalked the mouse.* **2.** To walk in a stiff or proud way: *Feeling that he had been insulted, the candidate stalked off the stage.*
stalk (stawk) *verb,* **stalked, stalking.**

stall¹—**1.** An enclosed space in a barn or stable for holding an animal. **2.** A small space where things for sale are displayed; booth; stand: *She sold her quilts from a stall at the fair. Noun.*
—To stop because of engine failure or because of getting stuck in mud or snow: *A truck stalled on the highway and caused a traffic jam. Verb.*
stall (stawl) *noun, plural* **stalls;** *verb,* **stalled, stalling.**

stall²—To speak or act in such a way as to prevent or delay something from happening: *When the teacher called on me, I stalled as long as I could but finally admitted I did not know the answer. Verb.*
—An excuse or activity meant to prevent or delay something from happening: *The child tried one stall after another to put off going to bed. Noun.*
stall (stawl) *verb,* **stalled, stalling;** *noun, plural* **stalls.**

stallion—An adult male horse.
stal│lion (stal′yən) *noun, plural* **stallions.**

stamen—The part of a flower in which pollen is made, surrounded by the petals. Each stamen has a slender stem with the pollen-bearing part at the top.
sta│men (stā′mən) *noun, plural* **stamens.**

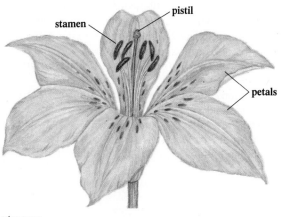

stamen

stammer—To hesitate or stumble in speaking; stutter: *People stammer when they are nervous,*

frightened, or embarrassed. Verb.
—Such a manner of speaking: *She was so nervous that she spoke with a* stammer. *Noun.*

stam|mer (stam′ər) *verb,* **stammered, stammering;** *noun, plural* **stammers.**

stamp—1. A small, usually square or rectangular piece of paper that is used on letters and packages to show that the required amount of postage has been paid: *a postage* stamp. **2.** The act of thrusting the foot down to strike or beat: *With a* stamp *of his boot, he crushed the can.* **3.** A device for marking a design, numbers, or letters on a surface, such as on paper, leather, or metal: *She has a rubber* stamp *with her name and address on it. Noun.*
—1. To put postage on: *He sealed the birthday card and* stamped *it.* **2.** To thrust the foot down to strike or beat: *The cheering crowd clapped their hands and* stamped *their feet.* **3.** To mark with a device that makes a design, numbers, or letters on a surface: *''This end up'' was* stamped *on the top of the crate.* **4.** To work to put out, put down, or put an end to: *to* stamp *out a fire; to* stamp *out a disease. Verb.*

stamp (stamp) *noun, plural* **stamps;** *verb,* **stamped, stamping.**

stampede—1. A sudden rush of a herd of startled animals, moving together: *The thunder started a cattle* stampede. **2.** A sudden rush of people running together or scattering in panic: *The earthquake caused a* stampede *of people in the streets. Noun.*
—To rush or scatter in panic: *When they saw the lion, the zebras* stampeded. *Verb.*

stam|pede (stam pēd′) *noun, plural* **stampedes;** *verb,* **stampeded, stampeding.**

stand—1. To get up or stay up on one's feet: *I* stood *and offered the woman my seat.* **2.** To set or be placed in an upright position: *to* stand *the books on the shelf; the table that* stands *in the center of the room.* **3.** To be in a certain position, place, degree, or condition: *The closet door* stood *open.* **4.** To continue to be in effect: *The ''no smoking'' rule still* stands. **5.** To put up with: *I cannot* stand *liars.* **6.** To have a certain opinion or belief about something: *Where do you* stand *on the issue of smoking in public? Verb.*
—1. A stop made in order to defend oneself from attack, as in a battle: *The troops made their last* stand *on the hill.* **2.** A place or position where a person is supposed to do something: *The clerk took his* stand *at the checkout counter.* **3.** A strong belief or opinion about something: *to take a* stand *against drugs.* **4.** A raised structure, usually with seats, where people can easily see or be seen: *The* stands *were full for the championship football game.* **5.** A small structure, such as a counter or stall, where items for sale are displayed: *The farmer set up a* stand *to sell her vegetables by the roadside.* **6.** A rack, table, or other such structure to hold or support something: *a plant* stand; *a music* stand. *Noun.*

stand (stand) *verb,* **stood, standing;** *noun, plural* **stands.**
• Synonyms: **abide, bear², endure, tolerate,** for *verb* **5.**

standard—1. A basis for measuring or an example to be followed: *The government sets* standards *for the quality of meat.* **2.** A flag, banner, or figure used as an emblem by a group of people: *The army raised its* standard *high and marched into battle. Noun.*
—1. Serving as, or widely used as, a common rule, measurement, example, or the like: *The inch, foot, and yard are* standard *measurements in the United States.* **2.** Being the most typical or accepted of its kind: *a* standard *model of car; the* standard *spelling of a word.* **3.** Viewed by many people as excellent or very dependable: *the* standard *reference book on breeds of dogs. Adjective.*

stand|ard (stan′dərd) *noun, plural* **standards;** *adjective.*
• Synonyms: **ideal, model, pattern,** for *noun* **1.**

Standardbred—A breed of horse developed in the United States and used mostly for harness racing. These horses look like thoroughbreds but are slightly smaller, and their racing gait is a fast trot or pace.

Stand|ard|bred (stan′dərd bred′) *noun, plural* **Standardbreds.**

standard schnauzer—A medium-sized working dog with a short, wiry coat, small pointed ears, and a short tail. This dog also has bushy eyebrows and whiskers on its face. Standard schnauzers were originally bred in Germany and are related to terriers.

stand|ard schnau|zer (stan′dərd shnou′zər) *noun, plural* **standard schnauzers.**

a at	i if	oo look	ch chalk		a in ago
ā ape	ī idle	ou out	ng sing		e in happen
ah calm	o odd	u ugly	sh ship	ə =	i in capital
aw all	ō oats	ū rule	th think		o in occur
e end	oi oil	ur turn	th their		u in upon
ē easy			zh treasure		

standing—A person's position or rank in a group, class, community, or the like: *Her grades give her the highest* standing *in the class. Noun.* —**1.** Upright; straight up and down: *Choose a pair of skis from that* standing *group.* **2.** Done from an upright position: *a* standing *jump off the diving board.* **3.** Lasting; long-term: *Mother has a* standing *order at the florist's to deliver fresh flowers every Friday.* **4.** Not moving or flowing; still: *A puddle is full of* standing *water. Adjective.*
stand|ing (stan′ding) *noun, plural* **standings;** *adjective.*

stank—*See* **stink.**
stank (stangk) *verb.*

stanza—Three or more lines that are grouped together in a poem; verse.
stan|za (stan′zə) *noun, plural* **stanzas.**

staple—A U-shaped piece of wire or metal with pointed ends. Staples are used to fasten together paper, cardboard, and such materials, or to hold a bolt or hook in place on wood or the like. *Noun.* —To hold together with a thin, U-shaped piece of wire or metal: *He* stapled *his homework papers together.*
sta|ple (stā′pəl) *noun, plural* **staples;** *verb,* **stapled, stapling.**

star—**1.** One of many huge balls of burning gases that are located in outer space. Unlike a planet or moon, which reflects light, a star gives off its own light. The sun is a star. **2.** A shape that has five or sometimes six points: *The cookie cutter is shaped as a* star. **3.** A person who is very good at doing something: *a tennis* star; *a basketball* star. **4.** A famous actor or actress, or one who has the most important part in a play, movie, or television program: *the* star *of the show. Noun.* —**1.** To mark or decorate with a shape having five or six points: *She* starred *the right answer on her test paper.* **2.** To have the most important part in a play, movie, or television program: *He* starred *in the school play. Verb.* —Best; outstanding: *She is the* star *player on the soccer team. Adjective.*
star (stahr) *noun, plural* **stars;** *verb,* **starred, starring.**
■ **see stars:** To be dizzy and see tiny flashes of light, as from a blow to the head: *I saw* stars *after I fell from the tree.*

starboard—The side of a ship or aircraft on the right of a person facing toward the front: *turning to* starboard. *Noun.* —On or at this side of a ship or aircraft: *Please*
sit on the starboard *side. Adjective.*
star|board (stahr′bərd) *noun, adjective.*

starch—**1.** An important white food substance that is found in many plants. Sources of starch include potatoes, rice, wheat, and corn. **2.** A mixture containing this substance that is used to make cloth stiff: *The cleaners put* starch *in Dad's white shirts. Noun.* —To apply this substance to cloth to stiffen it: *Mother* starched *and ironed the dining room tablecloth. Verb.*
starch (stahrch) *noun, plural* **starches;** *verb,* **starched, starching.**

stare—To look at carefully for a long time with wide-open eyes: *He* stared *at a spider that was spinning its web. Verb.* —A long, steady look with eyes opened wide: *She watched the magician with a curious* stare. *Noun.*
stare (stār) *verb,* **stared, staring;** *noun, plural* **stares.**
● A word that sounds the same is **stair.**

starfish—A sea animal whose flat body has five or more arms spreading out in a star shape from its center. The starfish is not a true fish.
star|fish (stahr′fish′) *noun, plural* **starfishes** or **starfish.**

starfish

starling—A bird with shiny black feathers and a short tail.
star|ling (stahr′ling) *noun, plural* **starlings.**

Star of David—A star with six points that is

Star of David

the emblem of the country of Israel and of the Jewish religion.
Star of Da|vid (stahr əv dā′vid) *noun, plural* **Stars of David.**

Stars and Stripes—A name for the flag of the United States.
Stars and Stripes (stahrz and strīps) *noun.*

Star-Spangled Banner—The national anthem of the United States.
Star-Span|gled Ban|ner (stahr′spang′gəld ban′ər) *noun.*

start—1. To cause something to move, act, be, or operate: *to start a lawn mower; to start a business.* 2. To begin: *It started to rain.* 3. To make a sudden movement, as from surprise: *She started out of bed when the alarm clock rang. Verb.*
—1. The beginning of something: *We didn't want to miss the start of the movie.* 2. A sudden movement, as from surprise: *I jumped with a start when the cat leaped from behind a chair. Noun.*
start (stahrt) *verb,* **started, starting;** *noun, plural* **starts.**
• Synonyms: **begin, commence, initiate,** for *verb* 1.
Antonyms: **end, finish, stop,** for *verb* 1.

startle—To cause to make a sudden movement from surprise or fear: *It startled the baby when the balloon popped.*
star|tle (stahr′təl) *verb,* **startled, startling.**

starve—1. To die from or kill with hunger: *Keep the bird feeder filled all winter long or the birds may starve.* 2. To have a great feeling of hunger: *Because the boy forgot his lunchbox, he starved all afternoon.*
starve (stahrv) *verb,* **starved, starving.**

state—1. The condition of someone or something at a certain time: *the state of one's health; a state of emergency after an earthquake.* 2. A country; nation: *The prime minister is our head of state.* 3. One of the sections into which a country is divided: *governor of a large state; the coast states. Noun.*
—1. Of or having to do with part or all of a nation or its government: *the state police; state secrets.* 2. Having to do with ceremonies or special occasions: *a state dinner. Adjective.*
—To declare; say: *Please state your name and address. Verb.*
state (stāt) *noun, plural* **states;** *adjective; verb,* **stated, stating.**

stately—Showing great dignity; grand in appearance or behavior: *a stately castle; a stately procession of soldiers marching in uniform.*
state|ly (stāt′lē) *adjective,* **statelier, stateliest.**
• Synonyms: **magnificent, majestic, splendid**
Antonym: **humble**

statement—Something that is said or written, such as a report or a record of an account: *a false statement; a charge account statement.*
state|ment (stāt′mənt) *noun, plural* **statements.**

statesman—A person who is very good at managing the work of national government or at dealing with issues of great public interest: *The statesman was able to get the two countries to agree to a peace treaty.*
states|man (stāts′mən) *noun, plural* **statesmen.**

static—Not moving, growing, or changing: *The price of school lunches has been static for two years. Adjective.*
—A problem with the sound coming from a radio, or with the sound or picture of a television, caused by electricity in the air. Static may be spots and streaks in a picture or crackling and squeaking noises. *Noun.*
stat|ic (stat′ik) *adjective, noun.*

station—1. A certain place where a person stands in order to do his or her job: *The school-crossing guard was at her station every morning and afternoon.* 2. A building for a certain job or purpose: *a fire station; a police station.* 3. A regular stop on a route: *a train station.* 4. A place from which television or radio signals are sent out. *Noun.*
—To put or place for a purpose: *She stationed herself on the curb to watch the parade. Verb.*

a at	i if	oo look	ch chalk	⎡ a in ago
ā ape	ī idle	ou out	ng sing	e in happen
ah calm	o odd	u ugly	sh ship	ə = i in capital
aw all	ō oats	ū rule	th think	o in occur
e end	oi oil	ur turn	th their	⎣ u in upon
ē easy			zh treasure	

sta|tion (stā′shən) *noun, plural* **stations;** *verb,* **stationed, stationing.**

stationary—1. Not moving or not able to move: *A house is* stationary. **2.** Not changing in any way: *The price of a movie ticket remained* stationary *this year.*
sta|tion|ar|y (stā′shə när′ē) *adjective.*
• A word that sounds the same is **stationery.**

stationery—Paper, envelopes, and cards that are used for writing or typing letters, notes, and the like.
sta|tion|er|y (stā′shə när′ē) *noun.*
• A word that sounds the same is **stationary.**

Stations of the Cross—A series of 14 paintings or sculptures that show scenes from the final days in the life of Jesus Christ. Prayers are said at each station.
Sta|tions of the Cross (stā′shənz əv thə kraws) *plural noun.*

station wagon—An automobile with an extra seat that can be folded down for a flat area in the rear instead of a separate, closed trunk. A station wagon has a back door so that cargo and passengers can be loaded and unloaded from the rear.
sta|tion wag|on (stā′shən wag′ən) *noun, plural* **station wagons.**

statistics—Facts that are given as numbers: *The* statistics *show that pizza is the most popular item on the school menu.*
sta|tis|tics (stə tis′tiks) *plural noun.*

statue—A sculpture of a person, animal, or mythical being, such as a unicorn or mermaid. Statues are usually made of marble, bronze, wood, clay, or similar materials.
stat|ue (stach′ū) *noun, plural* **statues.**

status—1. A person's rank or position in relation to others: *Her* status *as ambassador gives her many opportunities to meet people.* **2.** A condition; situation: *He listed his* status *as "married."*
sta|tus (stā′təs *or* stat′əs) *noun.*

stay¹—1. To not leave; remain: *Can you* stay *for supper?* **2.** To keep the same; not change: *Stay nice as you are.* **3.** To be a guest at; visit: *He* stayed *at a camp near the mountains. Verb.*
—A short time spent living somewhere; visit: *He had a pleasant* stay *at his grandfather's farm last summer. Noun.*
stay (stā) *verb,* **stayed, staying;** *noun, plural* **stays.**

stay²—A rope or wire that supports or holds something up: *Mother used several* stays *to keep up the tent.*
stay (stā) *noun, plural* **stays.**

steadfast—Loyal; unchanging: *She is a* steadfast *friend.*
stead|fast (sted′fast′) *adjective.*

steady—1. Without change; stable: *He has a* steady *job as a paper boy.* **2.** Not shaky or wobbling; firm: *A person needs a* steady *hand to thread a needle.* **3.** Not easily bothered or excited; even-tempered: *She has a* steady *mind and always thinks before doing something.* **4.** Moving, acting, or happening in an even, regular way: *There was a* steady *rise in prices this year. Adjective.*
—To stop from shaking or wobbling: *The girl* steadied *herself by holding the handrail as she walked across the bridge. Verb.*
stead|y (sted′ē) *adjective,* **steadier, steadiest;** *verb,* **steadied, steadying.**
■ **go steady:** To date someone on a regular basis and not date anyone else: *My sister and her boyfriend have been* going steady *for a year.*

steak—A thick slice of beef, pork, or fish that is cooked by broiling or frying.
steak (stāk) *noun, plural* **steaks.**
• A word that sounds the same is **stake.**

steal—1. To take something that belongs to another person without permission: *to* steal *apples from a neighbor's tree.* **2.** To do something enjoyable in secret: *He* stole *a look at the birthday gifts that were hidden in the closet.* **3.** To get by being charming or delightful: *The rabbit at the pet store* stole *our hearts.* **4.** To go slowly or quietly so as not to be noticed; sneak: *She* stole *out of the baby's room when it had fallen asleep.* **5.** In baseball, to run to the next base without being tagged, when a pitch is thrown to the batter.
steal (stēl) *verb,* **stole, stolen, stealing.**
• A word that sounds the same is **steel.**

steam—Water in the form of hot gas: *Steam came from the boiling water in the teakettle. Noun.*
—1. To give off water in the form of hot gas: *The cup of hot chocolate* steamed. **2.** To be covered with a mist: *His eyeglasses* steamed *up when he came in from the cold.* **3.** To use water in the form of a hot gas: *She* steamed *the carrots.*
4. To use hot gas for power: *The ship* steamed *across the river. Verb.*
steam (stēm) *noun; verb,* **steamed, steaming.**

steamboat—A boat whose engine is powered by water in the form of hot gas.
steam|boat (stēm′bōt′) *noun, plural* **steamboats.**

steam engine—A machine that is powered by water in the form of hot gas and that is used to run other machines.
steam en|gine (stēm en′jin) *noun, plural* **steam engines.**

steamroller—A large machine that has a heavy roller on the front to smooth and flatten a road surface. These machines used to have steam engines.
steam|roll|er (stēm′rō′lər) *noun, plural* **steamrollers.**

steamship—A large ship whose engines are powered by water in the form of hot gas.
steam|ship (stēm′ship′) *noun, plural* **steamships.**

steam shovel—A large digging machine that has a big bucket for scooping out dirt and rocks. These machines used to have steam engines.
steam shov|el (stēm shuv′əl) *noun, plural* **steam shovels.**

steel—A hard, strong metal that is made from iron and carbon. It is used in automobiles, tools, machinery, and the supports of large buildings.
steel (stēl) *noun.*
● A word that sounds the same is **steal.**

steep—Rising or falling sharply: *The children sledded down the* steep *slope.*
steep (stēp) *adjective,* **steeper, steepest.**

steeple—A high tower, usually with a pointed top, that is often seen on the roof of a church. It may have one or more bells inside.
stee|ple (stē′pəl) *noun, plural* **steeples.**

steer[1]—**1.** To guide or control: *to* steer *a ship; to* steer *a car:* **2.** To be guided or controlled: *This bicycle* steers *easily.* **3.** To set and hold to a path or the like: *The skier* steered *a course that led her away from the rocks.*
steer (stēr) *verb,* **steered, steering.**

steer[2]—A young male of cattle that is raised for beef.
steer (stēr) *noun, plural* **steers.**

stegosaurus—A large, plant-eating dinosaur that had a row of large, upright, bony plates down the center of its back and tail.
steg|o|sau|rus (steg′ə sawr′əs) *noun, plural* **stegosauri** (steg′ə sawr′ī).

stem[1]—**1.** The main trunk or stalk of a tree, bush, or other plant, to which the branches, leaves, fruit, and flowers are attached. **2.** Something that is long and slender, like this part of a plant: *The* stem *of a wine glass.*
stem (stem) *noun, plural* **stems.**

stem[2]—To plug up; stop: *The doctor soon* stemmed *the flow of blood from the victim's wound.*
stem (stem) *verb,* **stemmed, stemming.**

stench—A horrible smell: *the* stench *of garbage; the* stench *of a rotten egg.*
stench (stench) *noun, plural* **stenches.**

stencil—A thin piece of metal, paper, plastic, or cardboard in which letters or designs have been cut out. The stencil is placed on a wall, floor, cloth, piece of paper, or the like and then painted or inked to transfer the cut-out image onto the new surface. *Noun.*
—To decorate or print with letters or designs in this way. *Verb.*
sten|cil (sten′səl) *noun, plural* **stencils;** *verb,* **stenciled, stenciling.**

step—**1.** The action of raising the foot and putting it down in a different spot: *The baby took his first* steps *when he was a year old.* **2.** The distance covered by this action; a short way: *It's only a few* steps *from the back porch to the pool.* **3.** A place to put the foot when climbing up or down: *a stair* step. **4.** The sound a foot makes when it is put down while walking: *She thought that she heard* steps *coming down the attic stairs.* **5.** An action that is part of a larger group of actions taken for a certain purpose: *Losing a fear of the water is the first* step *in learning to swim. Noun.*
—**1.** To lift the foot and put it down in a different spot: *He* stepped *over the sleeping dog.* **2.** To press on something with the foot: *to* step *on the gas pedal; to* step *on someone's toes. Verb.*

a at	i if	oo look	ch chalk		a in ago
ā ape	ī idle	ou out	ng sing		e in happen
ah calm	o odd	u ugly	sh ship	ə =	i in capital
aw all	ō oats	ū rule	th think		o in occur
e end	oi oil	ur turn	th their		u in upon
ē easy			zh treasure		

stegosaurus

step (step) *noun, plural* **steps;** *verb,* **stepped,**
stepping.
- **step on it:** To hurry: *You'd better* step on it *or*
  you'll be late for school.

stepfather—The man a person's mother marries
after the person's real father has died or
divorced.
step|fa|ther (step′fah′thər) *noun, plural*
stepfathers.

stepladder—A short folding ladder that has flat
steps instead of round rungs for climbing.
step|lad|der (step′lad′ər) *noun, plural*
stepladders.

stepmother—The woman a person's father
marries after the person's real mother has died or
divorced.
step|moth|er (step′muth′ər) *noun, plural*
stepmothers.

stereo—Equipment that reproduces sound using
more than one speaker, giving it a realistic effect:
Let's play our new record album on the stereo.
ster|e|o (ster′ē ō′ *or* stēr′ē ō′) *noun, plural*
stereos.

stereophonic—Reproducing sound through the
use of more than one speaker to give it a realistic
effect: *a* stereophonic *record.*
ster|e|o|phon|ic (ster′ē ə fon′ik *or* stēr′ē ə
fon′ik) *adjective.*

sterilize—To rid of germs, often by heating:
Doctors sterilize *their medical instruments before*
each use.
ster|i|lize (ster′ə līz) *verb,* **sterilized,**
sterilizing.

sterling—1. Made of high-quality silver; being at
least 92.5 percent silver: *a* sterling *knife; a*
sterling *teapot.* 2. Excellent: *Everyone*
applauded the actor's sterling *performance.*
Adjective.
—1. Such high-quality silver, or things made
from it: *a table set with* sterling. 2. British
money: *a pound* sterling. *Noun.*
ster|ling (stur′ling) *adjective, noun.*

stern¹—1. Harsh; not kindly: *The teacher gave*
the noisy girls a stern *look.* 2. Sturdy or firm;
not yielding easily: *With* stern *determination, the*
pioneers continued moving west.
stern (sturn) *adjective,* **sterner, sternest.**

stern²—The back part of a ship or airplane.
stern (sturn) *noun, plural* **sterns.**

stethoscope—A medical instrument used for
listening to a heartbeat, breathing, or other body
sounds.

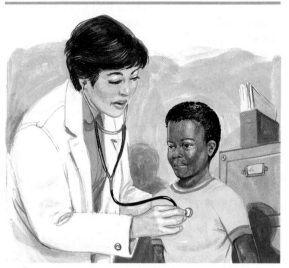

stethoscope

Word History

Stethoscope comes from a Greek word meaning
"chest" and another Greek word meaning
"examine." A doctor uses a stethoscope to
examine the chest area by listening to sounds
that come from this part of the body.

steth|o|scope (steth′ə skōp′) *noun, plural*
stethoscopes.

stew—To boil slowly in a covered pot; simmer: *to*
stew *chicken. Verb.*
—A kind of thick soup of meat and vegetables
that is cooked slowly with liquid in a covered
pot: *beef* stew; *lamb* stew. *Noun.*
stew (stū *or* styū) *verb,* **stewed, stewing;** *noun,*
plural **stews.**

steward—1. A man who takes care of the needs
of passengers on a ship, train, or airplane.
2. Someone who takes care of another person's
property: *The business executive has a* steward *to*
manage her mansion.
stew|ard (stū′ərd *or* styū′ərd) *noun, plural*
stewards.

stewardess—A woman who takes care of the
needs of passengers on a ship, train, or airplane.
stew|ard|ess (stū′ərd dis *or* styū′ər dis) *noun,*
plural **stewardesses.**

stick¹—1. A long, thin piece of wood, as from
the branch of a tree: *to use* sticks *for roasting*
marshmallows. 2. Something that has such a
long, thin shape: *a* stick *of chewing gum; a* stick

of butter; a stick *of candy; a hockey* stick.
stick (stik) *noun, plural* **sticks.**

stick²—1. To put the pointed end of something into or through an object: *to stick a balloon with a pin.* 2. To put or place: *I stuck my old toys in a box.* 3. To attach with glue or the like: *to stick a stamp on a letter.* 4. To become fastened; cling: *Bubble gum stuck to the bottom of his shoe.* 5. To keep from moving; jam or block: *The door is stuck and won't open.* 6. To thrust; extend: *I stuck my tongue out at her.* 7. To keep on with; continue: *She stuck with the job of raking the yard until it was finished.* 8. To puzzle; confuse; bring into uncertainty: *He was stuck on a long division problem.*
stick (stik) *verb,* **stuck, sticking.**
■ **stick up for:** To defend: *He stuck up for his sister when some older girls teased her.*
● Synonyms: **pierce, stab,** for 1.

sticky—1. Able to keep things fastened or attached: *The paste is sticky.* 2. Covered with something that can make things cling: *The floor is sticky where the soda pop spilled.*
stick|y (stik′ē) *adjective,* **stickier, stickiest.**

stiff—1. Not easy to bend: *These new shoes are stiff.* 2. Not easy to move: *The muscles in my leg are stiff from exercising.* 3. Not relaxed or natural; formal: *He gave a stiff handshake to his enemy.* 4. Very high or great; severe: *a stiff fine for speeding.* 5. Hard to do or put up with: *We had a stiff test in English but an easy one in science. Adjective.*
—Greatly; completely: *He was scared stiff on the roller coaster ride. Adverb.*
stiff (stif) *adjective,* **stiffer, stiffest;** *adverb.*

still—1. Not in motion; at rest: *The sleeping cat was still.* 2. Peaceful and free from noise: *The woods were still as the snow fell. Adjective.*
—To make or become calm or peaceful: *The bedtime story stilled the noisy child. Verb.*
—A condition of calm and freedom from noise: *You can hear leaves rustling in the still of the forest. Noun.*
—1. Yet; even; further: *That riddle is hard, but this one is harder still.* 2. All the same; nevertheless: *Although our family moved away, our old neighbor is still my best friend.* 3. Now

as before; yet: *He is still in high school.* 4. Without moving: *Stand still. Adverb.*
—And yet; nevertheless: *It was a breezy day; still, the sun was warm. Conjunction.*
still (stil) *adjective,* **stiller, stillest;** *verb,* **stilled, stilling;** *noun; adverb; conjunction.*
● Synonyms: **quiet, silence,** for *noun.*
Antonyms: **clamor, commotion, din, racket, uproar,** for *noun.*

stilt—One of a pair of long, slim pieces of wood to which a foot support is attached so that a person can walk raised above the ground.
stilt (stilt) *noun, plural* **stilts.**

stimulate—To arouse or stir up; make active or more active: *Seeing the movie about space travel stimulated my interest in becoming an astronaut.*
stim|u|late (stim′yə lāt′) *verb,* **stimulated, stimulating.**

sting—1. To pierce or hurt with something small and sharp: *Bees and wasps can sting.* 2. To have or cause a feeling of sharp pain or burning: *The shampoo stung when it got into his eyes. Verb.*
—1. The act of piercing or hurting with something small and sharp: *the sting of a needle.* 2. The injury caused by this action: *She put ice on the painful wasp sting on her leg.* 3. A sharp, pointed part of an animal, plant, or insect; stinger. *Noun.*
sting (sting) *verb,* **stung, stinging;** *noun, plural* **stings.**

stinger—The sharp, pointed part of an animal, plant, or insect that is used to pierce or hurt; sting.
sting|er (sting′ər) *noun, plural* **stingers.**

stingray—A wide, flat ocean fish with sharp spines on its long, whiplike tail. These spines can cause a painful injury to a person or animal that touches them.
sting|ray (sting′rā′) *noun, plural* **stingrays.**

stingy—Not generous; selfish: *Don't be stingy with your bag of popcorn; share some with me.*
stin|gy (stin′jē) *adjective,* **stingier, stingiest.**

stink—A strong, bad smell: *the stink of a rotten egg. Noun.*
—To have or give forth such a smell: *When a skunk sprays, it stinks. Verb.*
stink (stingk) *noun, plural* **stinks;** *verb,* **stank** or **stunk, stunk, stinking.**

stir—1. To move or cause to move slightly: *The breeze stirred the bedroom curtains.* 2. To use circular motions to mix together: *to stir a pot of spaghetti sauce.* 3. To excite or arouse: *The touchdown stirred the crowd to cheer wildly.*

a at	i if	oo look	ch chalk		a in ago
ā ape	ī idle	ou out	ng sing		e in happen
ah calm	o odd	u ugly	sh ship	ə =	i in capital
aw all	ō oats	ū rule	th think		o in occur
e end	oi oil	ur turn	th their		u in upon
ē easy			zh treasure		

4. To cause strong feelings in: *The sad, beautiful song* stirred *him. Verb.*
—**1.** Excited action; commotion: *There was a* stir *in the classroom when a bee flew in the window.*
2. The act of mixing together with circular motions: *The cook gave the cake batter one last* stir *before pouring it into the pan. Noun.*
stir (stur) *verb,* **stirred, stirring;** *noun, plural* **stirs.**

stirrup—A leather or metal loop that hangs down from the side of a saddle to hold a person's foot.
stir|rup (stur′əp *or* stēr′əp) *noun, plural* **stirrups.**
• See picture at **saddle.**

Word History

Stirrup comes from two old English words meaning "a rope for climbing." Stirrups, especially those made from leather, look like flat, U-shaped ropes. In old days, some stirrups were made from rope. They are used for helping a rider climb up onto or down from a horse or similar animal.

---

stitch—**1.** One of a series of loops formed by a needle and thread when sewing, embroidering, or closing wounds in surgery. **2.** One in a pattern of loops or knots made by a needle or hook and yarn in crochet or knitting. **3.** A burning pain especially in the area of the ribs: *Running up the hill gave him a* stitch *in his side. Noun.*
—To hold together, mend, or make with needle and thread; sew: *to* stitch *a hem. Verb.*
stitch (stich) *noun, plural* **stitches;** *verb,* **stitched, stitching.**
▪**in stitches:** Laughing very hard: *The circus clown left the audience* in stitches.

stock—**1.** Things to be used or sold; supply: *In*

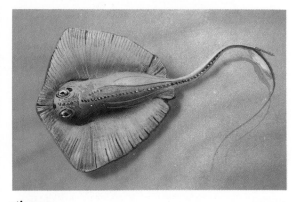

stingray

March, the store had a large stock *of kites.*
2. Farm or ranch animals, such as cattle: *The farmer fed his* stock *every morning and evening.* **3.** Shares of ownership in a business, that can be bought or sold: *She owns* stock *in the telephone company.* **4.** The group of ancestors from which one comes; nationality: *He is of peasant* stock. **5.** The wooden or metal part that is used as the handle of something, such as a rifle, whip, or fishing rod. **6.** Water in which meat or vegetables have been simmered for a long time, often then used to make sauces, soups, and gravies: *beef* stock; *chicken* stock.
7. stocks: A wooden frame with holes in which the ankles or the ankles and wrists of a person were locked for punishment of a crime. Stocks were once used in public places. *Noun.*
—**1.** Kept available for regular use or sale: *Light bulbs and soap are* stock *items in grocery stores.*
2. Having the job of taking care of the items for use or sale in a store: *He is a* stock *boy at the hardware store. Adjective.*
—**1.** To supply with: *We* stocked *the refrigerator with fresh vegetables from our garden.* **2.** To have available for use or sale: *Does this store* stock *suntan lotion? Verb.*
stock (stok) *noun, plural* **stocks;** *adjective; verb,* **stocked, stocking.**

stocking—A knitted covering that fits closely to the foot and leg.
stock|ing (stok′ing) *noun, plural* **stockings.**

stocky—Short and sturdy in build: *a* stocky *football player.*
stock|y (stok′ē) *adjective,* **stockier, stockiest.**

stole—*See* **steal.**
stole (stōl) *verb.*

stolen—*See* **steal.**
sto|len (stō′lən) *verb.*

stomach—**1.** The large organ like a bag or pouch into which food passes from the mouth and throat to begin the process of digestion. **2.** The area near the center of the body where this organ is located; belly: *The baby rolled over onto her* stomach. *Noun.*
—To bear; abide; endure: *He could no longer* stomach *her rude behavior and left the room. Verb.*
stom|ach (stum′ək) *noun, plural* **stomachs;** *verb,* **stomached, stomaching.**
• See picture at **alimentary canal.**

stone—**1.** The hard, solid material that is found in and under the soil, and that is used to make many walls and buildings; rock: *a* stone *house;* stone *with gold in it.* **2.** A piece of this material: *a grave* stone; *to throw a* stone *into a river.*

3. A more or less valuable piece of this material that has been cut and polished for use as a jewel; gem: *Rubies and emeralds are precious* stones. **4.** The hard seed of some kinds of fruit, such as peaches and cherries. *Noun.*
—To throw rocks at someone or something: *The people* stoned *the enemy soldiers. Verb.*
stone (stōn) *noun, plural* **stones;** *verb,* **stoned, stoning.**

stood—*See* **stand.**
stood (stood) *verb.*

stool—**1.** A seat without arms or a back. **2.** A low support or rest for the feet, such as a small bench.
stool (stūl) *noun, plural* **stools.**

stoop—**1.** To bend forward and down: *She* stooped *to pet the kitten.* **2.** To bend the head and shoulders forward when walking or standing: *Stand tall; don't* stoop. **3.** To do something that one knows is wrong; lower oneself: *He* stooped *to lying to his parents. Verb.*
—The act of bending forward the head and shoulders: *an old woman with a* stoop. *Noun.*
stoop (stūp) *verb,* **stooped, stooping;** *noun, plural* **stoops.**
• See picture at **posture.**

stop—**1.** To keep from acting, moving, or operating: *to* stop *a bicycle; to* stop *an elevator on the third floor; to* stop *the boy from throwing stones.* **2.** To cease or conclude; not continue: *Please* stop *whistling. The snow* stopped *falling.* **3.** To close an opening or the like by filling or covering: *to* stop *up a leak in the pool.* **4.** To block or halt: *The stone wall* stopped *the charging bull. Verb.*
—**1.** The act of not continuing or of keeping from acting, moving, or operating: *When the traffic light turned red, the truck came to a* stop. **2.** A place where a thing or person pauses or halts: *a bus* stop. **3.** A thing that halts, closes, plugs, or blocks something: *a bottle* stop; *a door* stop. **4.** A part of certain musical instruments that controls the sound. *Noun.*
stop (stop) *verb,* **stopped, stopping;** *noun, plural* **stops.**
• Synonyms: **end, finish,** for *verb* **2.**
Antonyms: **begin, commence, initiate, start,** for *verb* **2.**

stopper—A plug that is used to fill up an opening in a container: *Mother lifted the* stopper *on the bottle of perfume.*
stop|per (stop′ər) *noun, plural* **stoppers.**

storage—**1.** The storing of things, usually to keep them safe while not in use: *We use the attic for the* storage *of our winter clothes.* **2.** A place for keeping such things: *The library puts some older books in* storage. **3.** A part of a computer for keeping information; memory: *to retrieve a list of names from* storage.
stor|age (stawr′ij) *noun.*

store—**1.** A place where things are sold; shop: *A shoe* store; *a grocery* store. **2.** A supply of things to be used at a later time: *We baked a* store *of cookies for the holidays. Noun.*
—To put away for use at a later time: *squirrels* storing *nuts for the winter by burying them. Verb.*
store (stawr) *noun, plural* **stores;** *verb,* **stored, storing.**
• Synonyms: **collect, hoard, keep,** for *verb.*

storehouse—**1.** A building for storing goods or supplies. **2.** A person, book, or the like that has much information: *He is a* storehouse *of facts about his favorite baseball team.*
store|house (stawr′hous′) *noun, plural* **storehouses.**

stork—A wading bird with a long neck, a long bill, and long legs. Storks live in warm areas.
stork (stawrk) *noun, plural* **storks.**

stork

a at	**i** if	**oo** look	**ch** chalk		⌈ **a** in ago
ā ape	**ī** idle	**ou** out	**ng** sing		**e** in happen
ah calm	**o** odd	**u** ugly	**sh** ship	ə =	**i** in capital
aw all	**ō** oats	**ū** rule	**th** think		**o** in occur
e end	**oi** oil	**ur** turn	<u>**th**</u> their		⌊ **u** in upon
ē easy			**zh** treasure		

storm—**1.** A heavy fall of snow, rain, sleet, or hail together with high winds.   **2.** A huge, violent attack: *The knights took the castle by* storm.   **3.** A sudden, strong outbreak of emotion: *A* storm *of cheers came from the crowd when the batter hit a home run. Noun.*
—**1.** To blow with a strong wind and a heavy fall of snow, rain, sleet, or hail: *It* stormed *all afternoon, so we stayed inside.*   **2.** To rage or attack with great force: *Angry parents* stormed *over the school tax increase.*   **3.** To rush with fury: *She* stormed *out of the room after she lost the game. Verb.*
storm (stawrm) *noun, plural* **storms;** *verb,* **stormed, storming.**

story[1]—**1.** A report of something that really happened: *the boy's* story *of his fishing trip.*   **2.** A tale about something true or imagined, which is meant to entertain: *a ghost* story.   **3.** A tale meant to deceive; lie: *She told a* story *about how the dog chewed up her homework.*
sto|ry (stawr′ē) *noun, plural* **stories.**

story[2]—A floor of a house or other building, or the set of rooms on a floor: *She lives three* stories *up from me.*
sto|ry (stawr′ē) *noun, plural* **stories.**

stout—**1.** Heavy and thick: *a* stout *boy.*   **2.** Strong and sturdy: *a* stout *breed of horse.*   **3.** Brave; valiant: *a* stout *knight.*
stout (stout) *adjective,* **stouter, stoutest.**
• Synonyms: **fat, plump,** for **1.**
  Antonyms: For **1,** see Synonyms at **lean**[2].

stove—A device used for cooking or heating that uses electricity or burns fuel to provide heat: *a kitchen* stove; *a wood* stove.
stove (stōv) *noun, plural* **stoves.**

stow—**1.** To pack away, usually tightly; store: Stow *your fishing gear in the back of the boat.*   **2.** To fill by packing tightly: *The men* stowed *the warehouse with goods.*
stow (stō) *verb,* **stowed, stowing.**

stowaway—A person who sneaks aboard a ship, airplane, bus, or train.
stow|a|way (stō′ə wā′) *noun, plural* **stowaways.**

straddle—To spread the legs wide apart; have a leg on each side of something: *to* straddle *a horse; to* straddle *a bicycle.*
strad|dle (strad′əl) *verb,* **straddled, straddling.**

straggle—To stray away from the rest or from the direct course; wander: *The chicks* straggled *behind the mother hen.*
strag|gle (strag′əl) *verb,* **straggled, straggling.**

straight—**1.** Not curved, crooked, bent, or wavy: *a* straight *line;* straight *hair.*   **2.** Honest; truthful:

He gave his mother a straight *answer.*   **3.** Correctly arranged or ordered: *She could not keep their telephone numbers* straight. *Adjective.*
—**1.** In a direct line or way: *The arrow flew* straight *to the target.*   **2.** At once; immediately: *Come* straight *home after school. Adverb.*
straight (strāt) *adjective,* **straighter, straightest;** *adverb.*
• A word that sounds the same is **strait.**

straighten—**1.** To make or become even: *She* straightened *the crooked picture on the wall.*   **2.** To make neat or orderly: *He* straightened *up his desk.*
straight|en (strā′tən) *verb,* **straightened, straightening.**

straightforward—Truthful; honest: *She is* straightforward *and never hides her thoughts from anyone.*
straight|for|ward (strāt′fawr′wərd) *adjective.*
• Synonyms: **frank, open, outspoken**

strain—**1.** To pull tight or stretch to its limit; tug: *The rubber band* strained *to fit around the bundle of letters.*   **2.** To use as hard as possible: *She* strained *her eyes to read the tiny letters on the coin.*   **3.** To weaken, damage, or use up too much force or effort: *He* strained *his shoulder trying to lift the heavy box.*   **4.** To pass through a filter to remove solid matter from a liquid: *to* strain *tea before it is served; to* strain *lumps from gravy. Verb.*
—**1.** Any great pressure, force, or weight: *The* strain *on the shelf finally caused it to break.*   **2.** An injury caused by pulling or stretching a muscle too hard: *a leg* strain.   **3.** Too much worry, work, or other difficulty: *the* strain *of*

straddle

moving to a new neighborhood; the strain *of exam time at school. Noun.*
strain (strān) *verb,* **strained, straining;** *noun, plural* **strains.**
• Synonyms: **screen, sift,** for *verb* **4.**

strait—**1.** A narrow body of water that joins two larger bodies of water. **2. straits:** Great need or difficulty: *The town was in desperate* straits *after the tornado.*
strait (strāt) *noun, plural* **straits.**
• A word that sounds the same is **straight.**

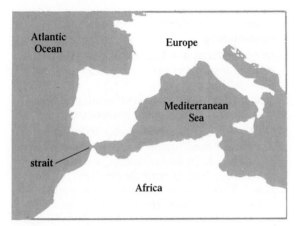

strait (definition 1)

strange—**1.** Odd; not usual or ordinary: *The lightning cast* strange *shadows on the wall.*
2. Not known before; not familiar: *He was nervous about going to a* strange, *new school.*
3. Out of place; uncomfortable: *She felt* strange *being the only one to wear shorts.*
strange (strānj) *adjective,* **stranger, strangest.**
• Synonyms: For **1,** see Synonyms at **curious.**

stranger—**1.** A person with whom one is not familiar: *A* stranger *knocked on the door and introduced himself as our new neighbor.* **2.** A person who is new to a country or place: *The country folk were* strangers *in the big city.*
stran|ger (strān′jər) *noun, plural* **strangers.**

strangle—**1.** To kill by squeezing the throat to stop a person or animal from breathing. **2.** To choke or cause to be choked: *The dog pulled at his leash so hard that it almost* strangled *him.*

a at	i if	oo look	ch chalk	⎡ a in ago
ā ape	ī idle	ou out	ng sing	e in happen
ah calm	o odd	u ugly	sh ship	ə = i in capital
aw all	ō oats	ū rule	th think	o in occur
e end	oi oil	ur turn	th their	⎣ u in upon
ē easy			zh treasure	

stran|gle (strang′gəl) *verb,* **strangled, strangling.**

strap—A long, narrow strip of leather or other material that bends easily, used to hold things together or in place: *a shoulder* strap *on a backpack; a* strap *to buckle a shoe. Noun.*
—To hold together or fasten with a long, narrow strip of leather or other material that bends: *Dad* strapped *our suitcases to the roof of the car. Verb.*
strap (strap) *noun, plural* **straps;** *verb,* **strapped, strapping.**

strategic—**1.** Of importance in military planning: *The bridge was in a* strategic *location for moving soldiers and supplies where they were needed.*
2. Of importance in planning any action: *She made a* strategic *move that caused her opponent to lose the game of checkers.*
stra|te|gic (strə tē′jik) *adjective.*

strategy—**1.** The careful planning needed to fight a battle or war successfully: *What is the general's* strategy *for winning the battle?* **2.** The careful planning, action, or method needed for achieving something: *They came up with a* strategy *for keeping the birthday party a surprise.*
strat|e|gy (strat′ə jē) *noun, plural* **strategies.**

straw—**1.** The stalks of plants such as wheat after the grain has been removed and the plants have dried. Straw is used to make brooms and hats.
2. A single dried stalk of such a plant. **3.** A narrow, hollow tube of paper, plastic, or glass that is made for sucking up drinks.
straw (straw) *noun, plural* **straws.**

strawberry—A sweet, red, juicy fruit that has lots of tiny yellow seeds on its surface and that is found on a low-growing plant.
straw|ber|ry (straw′ber′ē) *noun, plural* **strawberries.**

strawberry

stray—To wander away; roam: *The duckling* strayed *from the mother duck. Verb.*
—**1.** Lacking a home; lost: *The* stray *kitten hid under the parked car.* **2.** Appearing here and there: stray *wisps of hair;* stray *weeds in the lawn. Adjective.*
—An animal that is lost: *They took the* stray *to an animal shelter. Noun.*
stray (strā) *verb,* **strayed, straying;** *adjective; noun, plural* **strays.**

streak—**1.** A thin stripe or line, often uneven in shape: *In the dark, we could still see the skunk's white* streak. **2.** A bit or part; feature of someone's character: *That boy's angry* streak *may cause him trouble. Noun.*
—**1.** To mark or be marked with one or more thin lines: *Tears* streaked *his cheeks.* **2.** To move quickly: *The girls* streaked *to the swings. Verb.*
streak (strēk) *noun, plural* **streaks;** *verb,* **streaked, streaking.**

stream—**1.** A little river; a small body of flowing water. **2.** A continuous flow: *a* stream *of water from the faucet; a* stream *of people. Noun.*
—**1.** To flow or move continuously: *The runners* streamed *past the finish line.* **2.** To wave or flow at full length: *Ribbons* streamed *from her hair. Verb.*
stream (strēm) *noun, plural* **streams;** *verb,* **streamed, streaming.**

streamer—A long, thin flag or strip of material: *Colorful party* streamers *fluttered in the breeze.*
stream|er (strē′mər) *noun, plural* **streamers.**

streamline—**1.** To give something a smooth shape in order to reduce air or water resistance: *The designers worked to* streamline *the speed boat.* **2.** To make something run or work more smoothly and effectively: *We can* streamline *this job by using new, faster machines.*
stream|line (strēm′līn′) *verb,* **streamlined, streamlining.**

street—A public road that is maintained by a town or city: *Most of the town's shops are on the main* street.
street (strēt) *noun, plural* **streets.**

streetcar—A vehicle for public transportation that runs on electricity and moves along rails set into the streets; trolley car.
street|car (strēt′kahr′) *noun, plural* **streetcars.**

strength—**1.** Physical power: *Lifting weights is a test of* strength. **2.** Courage; good character: *It took* strength *to tell her parents the truth.* **3.** The power to withstand weight, force, or pressure: *We'll test the* strength *of the ice before we go*

skating. **4.** An amount of power or force: *Don't use this fertilizer at full* strength.
strength (strengkth *or* strength) *noun, plural* **strength.**

stress—**1.** Mental or physical strain: *Arguments cause a lot of* stress *between people.* **2.** Importance; emphasis: *The piano teacher places a lot of* stress *on practice.* **3.** The extra force or loudness used to say a certain syllable or word; accent: *Mom* stressed *the word "now" when she said, "Go to bed now." Noun.*
—To place emphasis on; give importance to: *The coach likes to* stress *team spirit. Verb.*
stress (stres) *noun, plural* **stresses;** *verb,* **stressed, stressing.**

stretch—**1.** To extend one or more parts of the body to full length: *The cat yawned and* stretched *when we woke it.* **2.** To reach from one point to another; continue across a space: *The sea* stretches *from the shore to the horizon.* **3.** To pull or expand; make longer or wider: *to* stretch *a rubber band; to* stretch *your imagination. Verb.*
—**1.** An unbroken length of land or time: *It's a long* stretch *from my house to yours.* **2.** The act of extending one or more parts of the body to full length or from one point to another: *With a* stretch *of her arm, she reached the bowl on the top shelf. Noun.*
stretch (strech) *verb,* **stretched, stretching;** *noun, plural* **stretches.**

stretcher—**1.** A canvas sheet with poles on each side, used to move injured or sick people. **2.** A light, portable bed with wheels, used to move injured or sick people.
stretch|er (strech′ər) *noun, plural* **stretchers.**

stricken—Hurt or upset by something: *We tried to soothe the* stricken *dog until help arrived. Adjective.*
—*See* **strike.** *Verb.*
strick|en (strik′ən) *adjective, verb.*

strict—**1.** Requiring that one stick closely to rules or limits: *Our parents are* strict *about our bedtimes.* **2.** Required of everyone, without exception; not changing: *The park has* strict *rules for those who use its swimming pool.* **3.** Complete; total: *in* strict *secrecy; in the* strictest *confidence.*
strict (strikt) *adjective,* **stricter, strictest.**

stride—**1.** To take long steps when walking: *He has to* stride *to keep up with his large dog.* **2.** To cross with a long step: *We'll have to* stride *over this puddle. Verb.*
—**1.** A long step or fast way of walking: *Her*

stride *kept her ahead of the other walkers.*
2. Good progress; advancement: *We've made great* strides *in finishing this difficult task. Noun.*
stride (strīd) *verb,* **strode, stridden, striding;** *noun, plural* **strides.**

■ **take in stride:** To accept or deal with something easily: *He took the bad grade in* stride *and worked harder.*

strike—**1.** To hit or slap, especially with the hand: *He was so angry he wanted to* strike *something.* **2.** To run into; collide with: *The bus* struck *a tree.* **3.** To set on fire by rubbing sharply: *to* strike *a match.* **4.** To have a strong effect on: *That* strikes *me as a great idea.* **5.** To announce by sound: *You must be back before the clock* strikes *six.* **6.** To come upon something: *to* strike *gold.* **7.** To stop work in protest of poor working conditions or low pay. *Verb.*
—**1.** The stopping of work in protest against poor working conditions or low pay. **2.** The finding of a valuable resource, such as gold or oil. **3.** In baseball, the batter's failure to hit a pitch or to swing when a good pitch is thrown. **4.** In bowling, the knocking down of all the pins with the first rolled ball. *Noun.*
strike (strīk) *verb,* **struck, struck,** or **stricken, striking;** *noun, plural* **strikes.**

string—**1.** A small cord with twisted threads; twine: *We need some* string *to tie on the balloons.* **2.** Something like such a small cord: *a* string *of pearls.* **3.** A series of events or things: *My uncle owns a* string *of restaurants.*
4. strings: Musical instruments that have strings and are played with a bow or by plucking. *Noun.*
—**1.** To put on a cord: *We like to* string *popcorn for the Christmas tree.* **2.** To furnish with cords: *to* string *a tennis racket.* **3.** To stretch from one point to another point: *I* strung *the line from wall to wall. Verb.*
string (string) *noun, plural* **strings;** *verb,* **strung, stringing.**

■ **pull strings:** To take advantage of one's position to get something: *The coach* pulled strings *to get the girl into basketball camp after the deadline.*

string bean—A long, thin green or yellow bean that is eaten as a vegetable.

string bean (string bēn) *noun, plural* **string beans.**

strip[1]—**1.** To remove one's clothing; undress. **2.** To pull off the covering from: *to* strip *the beds and put on clean sheets.*
strip (strip) *verb,* **stripped, stripping.**

strip[2]—A long, narrow piece of anything: *a* strip *of land.*
strip (strip) *noun, plural* **strips.**

stripe—A long thin line or band: *The road crew is painting* stripes *down the center of the road. Noun.*
—To mark or decorate with one or more of these lines: *The barber's pole was* striped *with red and white bands. Verb.*
stripe (strīp) *noun, plural* **stripes;** *verb,* **striped, striping.**

strive—To try hard: *to* strive *to win the contest.*
strive (strīv) *verb,* **strove** or **strived, striven** (striv′ən) **striving.**

strode—*See* **stride.**
strode (strōd) *verb.*

stroke—**1.** The act of striking; blow: *to nail the boards together with a few* strokes *of the hammer.* **2.** An unexpected happening: *The hikers found their way out of the woods by a* stroke *of good luck.* **3.** A mark or movement made by a pen or brush. **4.** A single complete movement that is repeated many times: *a swimming* stroke. **5.** A sudden paralyzing illness caused when a blood vessel in the brain gets broken or blocked. *Noun.*

plant   pods

string bean

a at	i if	oo look	ch chalk		a in ago
ā ape	ī idle	ou out	ng sing		e in happen
ah calm	o odd	u ugly	sh ship	ə =	i in capital
aw all	ō oats	ū rule	th think		o in occur
e end	oi oil	ur turn	<u>th</u> their		u in upon
ē easy			zh treasure		

—To rub gently with the hand: *The girl* stroked *the kitten. Verb.*
stroke (strōk) *noun, plural* **strokes;** *verb,* **stroked, stroking.**

stroll—To walk in an unhurried manner: *We* strolled *along the beach. Verb.*
—An unhurried walk: *She enjoys looking into the shop windows when she takes a* stroll *on the avenue. Noun.*
stroll (strōl) *verb,* **strolled, strolling;** *noun, plural* **strolls.**

strong—1. Having great power or force: *a* strong *horse pulling a heavy wagon.* 2. Not easily damaged or changed; sturdy: *a* strong *rope.*
strong (strawng) *adjective,* **stronger, strongest.**

strove—See **strive.**
strove (strōv) *verb.*

struck—*See* **strike.**
struck (struk) *verb.*

structure—1. Something that is built, such as a house or factory: *Many* structures *were damaged by the earthquake.* 2. The way that the parts of a thing are put together, arranged, or related: *the* structure *of a sentence.*
struc|ture (struk′chər) *noun, plural* **structures.**

struggle—1. To make a strong effort: *sailors* struggling *to sail the boat in the storm.* 2. To fight; battle: *The police officer* struggled *with the robber before arresting him. Verb.*
—1. A great effort: *Climbing the steep hill was a* struggle *for the tired child.* 2. A fight; battle: *When the* struggle *was over, the invading army had taken the city. Noun.*
strug|gle (strug′əl) *verb,* **struggled, struggling;** *noun, plural* **struggles.**

strung—*See* **string.**
strung (strung) *verb.*

stub—A short piece that is left after something has been used up or torn off: *she kept her ticket* stub. *Noun.*
—To bump one's toe or foot against something: *He* stubbed *his toe against the wall in the dark. Verb.*
stub (stub) *noun, plural* **stubs;** *verb,* **stubbed, stubbing.**

stubborn—1. Keeping firmly to a purpose or opinion; refusing to change or give in: *The* stubborn *boy would not come in for dinner.* 2. Hard to manage, deal with, or get rid of: *She could not get the* stubborn *spot off the pan no matter how hard she scrubbed it.*
stub|born (stub′ərn) *adjective.*

stuck—*See* **stick.**
stuck (stuk) *verb.*

student—1. A person who attends a school: *There are 20* students *in my class.* 2. A person who learns about something: *She is a* student *of painting.*
stu|dent (stū′dənt) *noun, plural* **students.**

studio—1. A place in which a painter, dancer, or other artist works or gives lessons. 2. A place where movies or television programs are filmed. 3. A place from which radio or television shows are broadcast.
stu|di|o (stū′dē o) *noun, plural* **studios.**

studious—Liking to study: *The* studious *girl quickly learned a great deal about science.*
stu|di|ous (stū′dē əs) *adjective.*

study—1. A use of one's mind to learn: *After careful* study, *he understood how to do the math problems.* 2. A careful examination: *She made a* study *of the flowers in the garden to see what kinds were there.* 3. A branch of knowledge: *history, arithmetic, and other* studies. 4. A room used for thinking, reading, or writing: *He worked on his report at the desk in his* study. *Noun.*
—1. To try to learn: *to* study *the history of our country.* 2. To look at carefully; examine: *The scientist* studied *the plant under the microscope. Verb.*
stud|y (stud′ē) *noun, plural* **studies;** *verb,* **studied, studying.**
• Synonyms: **analyze, inspect, investigate,** for *verb* 2.

stuff—1. The material that something is made of: *The* stuff *of the bird's nest is twigs and grass.* 2. Material that has no worth or use; junk: *Throw out that* stuff *in the basement. Noun.*
—1. To pack until full; cram: *We* stuffed *the bag with leaves.* 2. To plug or become stopped up: *Her nose was* stuffed. 3. To fill with food: *The dog* stuffed *itself until it could not eat any more.* 4. To fill the skin of a dead animal so that it looks as it did when living: *The museum had the bird* stuffed *and put on display.* 5. To put a mixture of ingredients into a chicken, fish, or other food to be cooked. *Verb.*
stuff (stuf) *noun; verb,* **stuffed, stuffing.**

stuffing—Material used to fill or pack something, especially a mixture of bread crumbs and other foods put inside a turkey, duck, or other animal to be cooked.
stuff|ing (stuf′ing) *noun, plural* **stuffings.**

stuffy—1. Lacking fresh air: *This room is* stuffy *unless a window is open.* 2. Not interesting;

dull: *I almost fell asleep during the* stuffy *lecture.*

stuff|y (stuf′ē) *adjective,* **stuffier, stuffiest.**

stumble—**1.** To trip or fall while walking. **2.** To walk or speak in an unsteady or clumsy way: *The sleepy child* stumbled *into her sister's bedroom.* **3.** To find by chance: *To her surprise, she* stumbled *upon the answer to the problem.*

stum|ble (stum′bəl) *verb,* **stumbled, stumbling.**

stump—**1.** The bottom part of a tree that is left standing after the rest of the tree has been cut down or broken off. **2.** What is left of anything after the main part has been broken or used up: *I had only the* stumps *of my crayons left. Noun.*
—To confuse or puzzle: *The difficult mathematics problem* stumped *me. Verb.*

stump (stump) *noun, plural* **stumps;** *verb,* **stumped, stumping.**

stun—**1.** To cause one to become dazed or unconscious: *The fall from his bicycle* stunned *him.* **2.** To shock: *We were* stunned *when we saw the damage done by the earthquake.*

stun (stun) *verb,* **stunned, stunning.**

stung—*See* **sting.**

stung (stung) *verb.*

stunk—*See* **stink.**

stunk (stungk) *verb.*

stunt—An unusual or difficult act done with great skill, to entertain or get attention: *Trick riders performed exciting* stunts *on horses at the rodeo.*

stunt (stunt) *noun, plural* **stunts.**

stupid—Having or showing little intelligence or sense: *a* stupid *answer.*

stu|pid (stū′pid) *adjective,* **stupider, stupidest.**

sturdy—**1.** Solid or strongly built: Sturdy *pillars supported the museum's roof.* **2.** Not giving in or giving up; unyielding: *the* sturdy *defenders.*

stur|dy (stur′dē) *adjective,* **sturdier, sturdiest.**

sturgeon—A large fish used as food, having pointed, bony scales along its sides.

stur|geon (stur′jən) *noun, plural* **sturgeons** or **sturgeon.**

stutter—To repeat certain sounds at the beginnings of words; stammer: *"D-d-d-don't shoot,"* the robber stuttered *as the police arrived. Verb.*

—The act or habit of speaking in such a way: *Some people have a* stutter *when they become nervous. Noun.*

stut|ter (stut′ər) *verb,* **stuttered, stuttering;** *noun.*

style—**1.** A certain manner or way in which something is done, written, or spoken: *to write a story in the* style *of your favorite author.* **2.** A way of dressing or behaving that is very fancy, fine, or elegant: *The family dressed in* style *for dinner at the expensive restaurant. Noun.*
—**1.** To make or shape in a certain way; design: *She* styled *her hair in curls.* **2.** To name or call; refer to as: *That amusement park is sometimes* styled *"Wonder World." Verb.*

style (stīl) *noun, plural* **styles;** *verb,* **styled, styling.**

sub-—A prefix that means "below." A subfreezing temperature is one that is below freezing.

Word Power

You can understand the meaning of many words that begin in **sub-,** if you add the meaning of the prefix to the meaning of the rest of the word.

subnormal: below normal

subzero: below zero

---

subject—**1.** A person or thing that is studied, discussed, or written about: *Science is her favorite* subject. **2.** A person or thing that is ruled, controlled, or governed by another: *The* subjects *had to pay taxes to their king.* **3.** A person or thing that is used for or undergoes something: *The lion was the* subject *of the animal trainer's instruction.* **4.** The word or group of words in a sentence that does or receives the action of the verb: *The mouse ate the cheese.* The subject of the sentence is "the mouse." *The cheese was eaten by the mouse.* The subject of the sentence is "the cheese." *Noun.*
— **1.** Under the power or control of another: *The moon is* subject *to the pull of the earth's gravity.* **2.** Likely to have or suffer from: *a desert* subject *to hot, dry winds.* **3.** Being dependent on: *The*

a at	i if	oo look	ch chalk		a in ago
ā ape	ī idle	ou out	ng sing		e in happen
ah calm	o odd	u ugly	sh ship	ə =	i in capital
aw all	ō oats	ū rule	th think		o in occur
e end	oi oil	ur turn	th their		u in upon
ē easy			zh treasure		

sturgeon

parade will take place on Saturday, subject *to good weather. Adjective.*
—**1.** To bring under control: *The village was* subjected *to the power of the invading army.* **2.** To cause to experience something: *to be* subjected *to medical tests. Verb.*
sub|ject (sub′jikt for *noun* and *adjective;* səb jekt′ for *verb*) *noun, plural* **subjects;** *adjective; verb,* **subjected, subjecting.**

submarine—**1.** A boat that can operate both on and under the surface of the water.   **2.** A large sandwich on a long roll.
sub|ma|rine (sub′mə rēn) *noun, plural* **submarines.**

submarine (definition 1)

submit—**1.** To give in to or obey the control of another; yield: *The soldier* submitted *to the orders of his captain.*   **2.** To give to another for approval: *The reporter* submitted *a story to the editor of the newspaper.*
sub|mit (səb mit′) *verb,* **submitted, submitting.**

subscribe—**1.** To agree to accept and pay for a certain number of issues of a publication: *My class* subscribes *to a magazine about animals.*   **2.** To approve; support; agree: *My teacher* subscribes *to the idea that all her students should be treated fairly.*
sub|scribe (səb skrīb′) *verb,* **subscribed, subscribing.**

subscription—The receiving of a certain publication in return for payment: *I gave my mother a* subscription *to a gardening magazine.*
sub|scrip|tion (səb skrip′shən) *noun, plural* **subscriptions.**

substance—**1.** A material; stuff; form of matter: substances *such as wood, clay, air, and water; the main* substances *of this wall are stone and cement.*   **2.** The most important part or real meaning of something; significance: *The* substance *of the principal's talk to the students was safety in the school.*

sub|stance (sub′stəns) *noun, plural* **substances.**

substantial—**1.** Having actual substance; real; truly existing: *He could not believe that the new bicycle in his driveway was* substantial *until he had touched it.*   **2.** Strongly built; firm or solid: *The dam must be* substantial *to hold back the flood waters.*   **3.** Large; extensive; great: *The hikers traveled a* substantial *distance during their first day on the trail.*
sub|stan|tial (səb stan′shəl) *adjective.*

substitute—A thing or person that takes the place of another: *We had a* substitute *because our teacher was ill. Noun.*
—**1.** To put in the place of something or someone else: *My mother* substitutes *honey for sugar when she bakes muffins.*   **2.** To serve in place of another; replace: *My brother* substituted *for me on my paper route when I was sick. Verb.*
sub|sti|tute (sub′stə tūt *or* sub′stə tyūt) *noun, plural* **substitutes;** *verb,* **substituted, substituting.**

subtle—So delicate and faint as to be hard to notice, recognize, or understand: *The difference between the two flavors is so* subtle *that it is hard to tell them apart.*
sub|tle (sut′əl) *adjective,* **subtler, subtlest.**

subtract—To take away: *When 3 is* subtracted *from 5, what is left is 2.*
sub|tract (səb trakt′) *verb,* **subtracted, subtracting.**

subtraction—The taking away of one number or amount from another to find the difference: $8 - 2 = 6$ *is an example of* subtraction.
sub|trac|tion (səb trak′shən) *noun, plural* **subtractions.**

suburb—A community, such as a town or village, that is just outside or close to a city.
sub|urb (sub′ərb) *noun, plural* **suburbs.**

suburban—Of or relating to a community that is just outside or close to a city: *The* suburban *stores are usually less crowded than those in the city.*
sub|ur|ban (sə bur′bən) *adjective.*

subway—An electric railroad that runs through tunnels under the streets of a city.
sub|way (sub′wā′) *noun, plural* **subways.**

succeed—**1.** To turn out favorably: *The sending of a spacecraft to the moon* succeeded.   **2.** To come next after another; take the place of: *The winter snows on the mountainside were* succeeded *by the green buds of spring.*
suc|ceed (sək sēd′) *verb* **succeeded, succeeding.**

success—1. A good outcome; fulfillment of one's hopes or efforts: *He had no* success *in opening the lock until he found the right key.* 2. A person or thing that fulfills a hope or effort: *His graceful movements made him a* success *as a dancer.*
suc|cess (sək ses′) *noun, plural* **successes.**

succession—1. A number of persons or things that follow each other in order: *A* succession *of rainy days made the ground very muddy.* 2. The following of one person or thing after another: *the* succession *to office of a new president; to lose three games in* succession.
suc|ces|sion (sək sesh′ən) *noun, plural* **successions.**

successive—Coming in order, one after another: *three* successive *weekends at the beach.*
suc|ces|sive (sək ses′iv) *adjective.*

succotash—A mixture of corn and Lima beans cooked together.
suc|co|tash (suk′ ə tash) *noun.*

such—1. Of this or that kind: *I find* such *stories as yours hard to believe.* 2. Of a certain kind that is like the others mentioned: *The children had ice cream, cookies, and other* such *treats at the party.* 3. To a great extent; very much: *The picnic was* such *fun! Adjective.*
—A thing or person of this or that kind: *The children put their hats, coats, and* such *in the closet. Pronoun.*
such (such) *adjective, pronoun.*

suck—1. To draw into the mouth: *The baby* sucked *the milk from the bottle.* 2. To use the mouth to draw up liquid from something: *She* sucked *a slice of orange.* 3. To lick while holding in the mouth: *My brother likes to* suck *icicles.* 4. To create a force that pulls: *The tornado* sucked *up the small trees in its path.*
suck (suk) *verb,* **sucked, sucking.**

sucker—1. A body part that pulls food into the mouth or that holds tightly to a surface: *The octopus gripped the stones with the* suckers *along its tentacles.* 2. A hard candy, usually on a stick, that is licked while being held in the mouth; lollipop. 3. A person who is easily tricked or fooled.
suck|er (suk′ər) *noun, plural* **suckers.**

suction—The act of drawing a liquid or gas into a space by removing the air in that space: *We used* suction *to drain the water from our fish tank.*
suc|tion (suk′shən) *noun.*

sudden—1. Happening quickly and without warning: *A* sudden *gust of wind pulled my umbrella out of my hand.* 2. Changing or happening all at once; abrupt; hasty: *With a* sudden *movement, she turned around and rushed out the door.*
sud|den (sud′ən) *adjective.*

suds—Soapy bubbles and foam on water.
suds (sudz) *plural noun.*

sue—To bring a case against in a court of law: *He* sued *the man whose car damaged his fence.*
sue (sū) *verb,* **sued, suing.**

suede—Leather that has a soft surface like velvet. It is used to make such items as shoes, purses, and jackets.
suede (swād) *noun.*

suffer—1. To feel pain, sorrow, or hurt: *He* suffered *from the disappointment of losing the game.* 2. To feel or experience: *She* suffered *loneliness when her friend moved away.* 3. To be harmed or get worse: *The garden will* suffer *if the plants are not watered.*
suf|fer (suf′ər) *verb,* **suffered, suffering.**

sufficient—As much as is needed; enough: *There is more than* sufficient *room at our table for six people.*
suf|fi|cient (sə fish′ənt) *adjective.*

suffix—One or more syllables joined to the end of a word to give that word another meaning or to form another word. In the word **artist,** the word **art** is joined with the suffix **-ist.**
suf|fix (suf′iks) *noun, plural* **suffixes.**

a at	i if	oo look	ch chalk		a in ago
ā ape	ī idle	ou out	ng sing		e in happen
ah calm	o odd	u ugly	sh ship	ə =	i in capital
aw all	ō oats	ū rule	th think		o in occur
e end	oi oil	ur turn	th their		u in upon
ē easy			zh treasure		

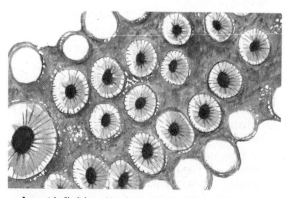

sucker (definition 1): An octopus has many suckers on the underside of its tentacles.

Word History

Suffix comes from a Latin word meaning "fasten upon." A suffix is fastened to the end of a word to change the meaning of the word or to form another word.

Often, when a suffix is added to a word, the spelling of the word is changed. When you add the suffix **-ing** to **write** to make **writing,** the "e" is dropped. When you add **-ing** to **stop** to make **stopping,** an extra "p" is added. When you add **-ing** to **die** to make **dying,** the "ie" is dropped and a "y" is added.

suffocate—1. To kill by not allowing to breathe; smother: *The plastic bag* suffocated *the moth that had flown inside it.* 2. To die from being unable to breathe: *The moth* suffocated *from the lack of air.* 3. To make uncomfortable by a lack of fresh air; stifle: *If we do not open a window, the stale air in this room will* suffocate *us.*
suf|fo|cate (suf′ə kāt) *verb,* **suffocated, suffocating.**

Suffolk—A horse that is bred in England as a work animal. It is chestnut-colored and has a strong body.
Suf|folk (suf′ək) *noun, plural* **Suffolks.**

sugar—A sweet substance that is gotten mostly from sugar cane or sugar beets. *Noun.*
—To put this substance in or on something: *I like lemonade when it has been lightly* sugared. *Verb.*
sug|ar (shoog′ər) *noun, plural* **sugars;** *verb,* **sugared, sugaring.**

sugar beet—A plant with a large white root from which sugar is made.
sug|ar beet (shoog′ər bēt) *noun, plural* **sugar beets.**

sugar cane—A tall grass with a thick stalk from which sugar is made.
sug|ar cane (shoog′ər kān) *noun.*

suggest—1. To bring to mind; recall: *One story* suggested *another as we sat around the fire.* 2. To propose for consideration; offer an idea or a way of doing something: *My sister* suggested *we build a sand castle.* 3. To express indirectly; hint: *The look on her face* suggested *that we had better stop teasing her.*
sug|gest (səg jest′) *verb,* **suggested, suggesting.**

suicide—An act by which a person kills himself or herself.
su|i|cide (sū′ə sīd) *noun, plural* **suicides.**

suit—1. Clothes of matching color and fabric that are worn together. 2. A legal action brought to court. 3. One of the four sets of playing cards, which are spades, hearts, diamonds, and clubs. *Noun.*
—1. To make fit; adapt: *The farmers* suit *their daily work to the weather.* 2. To be what is wanted; be agreeable to: *A hamburger would* suit *me fine.* 3. To be appropriate and attractive: *Mother says my new haircut* suits *me better. Verb.*
suit (sūt) *noun, plural* **suits;** *verb,* **suited, suiting.**
▪**follow suit:** To do as someone else does; follow an example: *Our teacher placed a flower at the foot of the statue, and the rest of the class* followed suit.

suitable—Appropriate; right for a situation: *The camp sent a list of* suitable *clothing to bring.*
suit|a|ble (sū′tə bəl) *adjective.*
• Synonyms: **correct, fit¹, proper**

suitcase—A travel bag used for carrying clothes and other belongings.
suit|case (sūt′kās′) *noun, plural* **suitcases.**

suite—1. Several connected rooms for use together: *Our* suite *at the hotel had two bedrooms, a living room, and a kitchen.* 2. A number of things that make a set or series: *a* suite *of furniture; a* suite *of ballet music.*
suite (swēt) *noun, plural* **suites.**
• A word that sounds the same is **sweet.**

suitor—A man who seeks a woman's company with the thought of romance.
suit|or (sū′tər) *noun, plural* **suitors.**

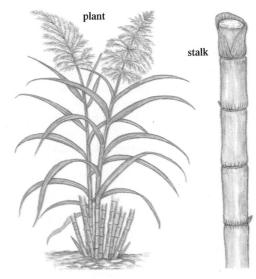

sugar cane

Sukkoth or **Sukkot**—A Jewish festival celebrated for eight or nine days in September or October. Small huts are built to recall the years during which the Jews wandered in the desert. **Suk|koth** or **Suk|kot** (soo kōth′ or soo kōt′) *noun.*

sulfur—A light yellow substance that is plentiful in nature and is used in matches, gunpowder, medicines, and insecticides. It is a chemical element. **sul|fur** (sul′fər) *noun.*

sulk—To be silent and gloomy; show resentment of a person, act, or remark by moody behavior: *Mother told my brother to stop* sulking *and help with the chores.* **sulk** (sulk) *verb,* **sulked, sulking.**

sullen—**1.** Silent in a gloomy way; in bad humor: *The coach was* sullen *because we did not play our best.* **2.** Dull; dreary: *With a lot of cleaning, we turned the* sullen *attic into a cheery room.* **sul|len** (sul′ən) *adjective.*

sultan—The title of the ruler in some Muslim countries. **sul|tan** (sul′tən) *noun, plural* **sultans.**

sum—**1.** A certain amount, especially of money: *We collected the* sum *of four hundred and sixty dollars for our class trip.* **2.** The total made by adding two or more numbers: *Twelve is the* sum *of five and seven.* **sum** (sum) *noun, plural* **sums.**
• A word that sounds the same is **some.**

sumac—Any of several kinds of small bushes and trees with long, narrow leaves. Most types of sumac have dense, upright clusters of red berries. **su|mac** (sū′mak or shū′mak) *noun, plural* **sumacs.**

summarize—To tell or write the main points of: *It was hard to* summarize *such a long book.* **sum|ma|rize** (sum′ə rīz) *verb,* **summarized, summarizing.**

summary—A brief written or spoken review of the main points of something. **sum|ma|ry** (sum′ər ē) *noun, plural* **summaries.**

summer—The season after spring and before autumn. It has the warmest weather and the longest days. *Noun.*
—To pass the time of this season: *We summered at home last year because we were tired of traveling. Verb.* **sum|mer** (sum′ər) *noun, plural* **summers;** *verb,* **summered, summering.**

summit—The highest part; top: *From the* summit *of the trail we could see for miles.* **sum|mit** (sum′it) *noun, plural* **summits.**

summon—**1.** To ask to come; send for: *Their neighbors saw smoke and* summoned *help before the fire spread.* **2.** To call upon and bring into action: *The runners* summoned *their strength for the last lap.* **sum|mon** (sum′ən) *verb,* **summoned, summoning.**

summons—An official notice to appear in court. **sum|mons** (sum′ənz) *noun, plural* **summonses.**

sun—**1.** The star closest to us. The earth and other planets revolve around the sun and get light and heat from it. **2.** The light and heat produced by this star: *Fruit can be dried in the* sun *for later eating. Noun.*
—To put in or be in the heat and light of this star: *The dog* sunned *itself on the porch. Verb.* **sun** (sun) *noun, plural* **suns;** *verb,* **sunned, sunning.**
• A word that sounds the same is **son.**

Sun.—The abbreviation for **Sunday.**

sunbathe—To relax in the light and warmth of the sun: *We sat around* sunbathing *by the pool.* **sun|bathe** (sun′bāth′) *verb,* **sunbathed, sunbathing.**

sunbeam—A small streak of light from the sun: Sunbeams *were breaking through the clouds.* **sun|beam** (sun′bēm′) *noun, plural* **sunbeams.**

sunburn—A painful redness of the skin caused by exposure to the rays of the sun: *The swimming*

a at	i if	oo look	ch chalk		a in ago
ā ape	ī idle	ou out	ng sing		e in happen
ah calm	o odd	u ugly	sh ship	ə =	i in capital
aw all	ō oats	ū rule	th think		o in occur
e end	oi oil	ur turn	th their		u in upon
ē easy			zh treasure		

sumac: Sumac as it appears in the fall.

coach got a bad sunburn *on her face. Noun.*
—To burn or become burned by the rays of the sun: *She* sunburns *very easily. Verb.*
sun|burn (sun′burn′) *noun, plural* **sunburns;** *verb,* **sunburned** *or* **sunburnt, sunburning.**

sundae—A dish of ice cream topped with syrup, fruit, nuts, or whipped cream.
sun|dae (sun′dā *or* sun′dē) *noun, plural* **sundaes.**
• A word that sounds the same is **Sunday.**

Sunday—The first day of the week; the day that is between Saturday and Monday.
Sun|day (sun′dē *or* sun′dā) *noun, plural* **Sundays.** *Abbreviation:* **Sun.**
• A word that sounds the same is **sundae.**

Word History

Sunday comes from an old English word meaning ''day of the sun.'' The day was also called ''day of the sun'' earlier, in Latin.

---

sundial—A device that shows the time of day by means of the shadow of a pointer, cast by the sun on a special marked plate.
sun|di|al (sun′dī′əl) *noun, plural* **sundials.**

sundial

sundown—The time of day when the sun moves below the horizon.
sun|down (sun′doun′) *noun, plural* **sundowns.**

sunflower—A tall plant that has large, yellow flowers with dark centers. A sunflower produces seeds that can be eaten or made into an oil for cooking. It is the state flower of Kansas.
sun|flow|er (sun′flou′ər) *noun, plural* **sunflowers.**

sung—*See* **sing.**
sung (sung) *verb.*

sunglasses—Eyeglasses with colored lenses that protect the eyes from the brightness of the sun.
sun|glass|es (sun′glas′iz) *plural noun.*

sunk—*See* **sink.**
sunk (sungk) *verb.*

sunken—1. Fallen underwater: *a sunken* treasure; *a sunken* ship. 2. Below the level of the surrounding area: *a sunken* room; *a sunken* bathtub. 3. Fallen in; hollow: *The sick woman has* sunken *eyes. Adjective.*
—*See* **sink.** *Verb.*
sunk|en (sung′kən) *adjective, verb.*

sunlight—The light of the sun: Sunlight *streamed in through the open window.*
sun|light (sun′līt′) *noun.*

sunny—1. Having plenty of sunshine: *a sunny day.* 2. Warmed or lighted by the sun: *the sunny side of a house; a sunny room.* 3. Cheerful; bright: *a sunny smile; a sunny personality.*
sun|ny (sun′ē) *adjective,* **sunnier, sunniest.**

sunrise—The time when the sun appears over the horizon each morning; beginning of the day: *The sky is filled with beautiful colors at* sunrise.
sun|rise (sun′rīz′) *noun, plural* **sunrises.**

sunset—The time of day when the sun moves below the horizon; sundown: *The park closes at* sunset.
sun|set (sun′set′) *noun, plural* **sunsets.**

sunshine—The light of the sun: *Mother told us to go out and play in the* sunshine.
sun|shine (sun′shīn′) *noun.*

sunflower

suntan—The reddish-brown color of a person's skin when it has been exposed to the sun: *She gets a dark* suntan *every summer.*
sun|tan (sun′tan′) *noun, plural* **suntans.**

super—A person who manages an apartment or office building; superintendent. *Noun.*
—Of extremely good quality; very pleasing: *a* super *outfit; a* super *party. Adjective.*
su|per (sū′pər) *noun, plural* **supers;** *adjective.*

super-—A prefix that means "beyond," or "more than," or "exceeding": A supernatural event is beyond what is natural. Supersonic speed is more speed than the speed of sound. A supermarket exceeds the size and variety of other food markets.

Word Power

You can understand the meanings of many words that begin with **super-,** if you add a meaning of the prefix to the meaning of the rest of the word.
supernormal: beyond normal
superhuman: more than human
superhighway: exceeding other highways

---

superb—**1.** Grand; rich; elegant: *The royal jewels are* superb. **2.** Excellent; of very good quality: *The class did a* superb *job on this art project.*
su|perb (sū purb′) *adjective.*
• Synonyms: **outstanding, wonderful**

superintendent—A person who manages the operation of an organization or a building: *the* superintendent *of schools; the* superintendent *of an apartment building.*
su|per|in|tend|ent (sū′pər in ten′dənt) *noun, plural* **superintendents.**

superior—**1.** Better than average: *The coach told us we played a* superior *game.* **2.** Having higher quality: *People are willing to spend more money for a* superior *product.* **3.** Higher in rank or position: *Soldiers must salute their* superior *officers.* **4.** Proud; acting as though one is better than others: *Once she got to know us, she dropped her* superior *attitude. Adjective.*
—A person of higher rank, position, or ability: *A principal is a teacher's* superior. *Noun.*

superior—su|pe|ri|or (sə pēr′ē ər) *adjective; noun, plural* **superiors.**

superlative—Of the highest degree or quality: *a musician of* superlative *talent. Adjective.*
—The form of an adjective or adverb showing the most of a quality. "Prettiest," "fastest," and "loudest" are superlatives of "pretty," "fast," and "loud." *Noun.*
su|per|la|tive (sə per′lə tiv) *adjective; noun, plural* **superlatives.**

supermarket—A large store that sells groceries and other household goods. Customers take items from shelves and pay for everything at once.
su|per|mar|ket (sū′pər mahr′kit) *noun, plural* **supermarkets.**

supernatural—Above or beyond what we know or understand; unable to be explained: *That comic strip character has* supernatural *powers.*
su|per|nat|u|ral (sū pər nach′ər əl) *adjective.*

supersonic—**1.** Able to move at a speed more than the speed of sound: *a* supersonic *jet.* **2.** Having to do with sounds that are too high to be heard by the human ear.
su|per|son|ic (sū′pər son′ik) *adjective.*

superstition—A belief that events can be caused or influenced by acts that have no real connection with them. One superstition is that if a black cat crosses a person's path, it causes bad luck. Another superstition is that it is bad luck to walk under a ladder.
su|per|sti|tion (sū′pər stish′ən) *noun, plural* **superstitions.**

superstitious—Believing that events can be caused or influenced by acts that have no real connection with them; believing in superstitions: *It is* superstitious *to feel that Friday the 13th is an unlucky day.*
su|per|sti|tious (sū′pər stish′əs) *adjective.*

supervise—To be in charge of; manage: *She* supervises *the work of 20 people at the factory.*
su|per|vise (sū′pər vīz′) *verb,* **supervised, supervising.**

supper—The evening meal: *We had roast beef, potatoes, and green beans for* supper.
sup|per (sup′ər) *noun, plural* **suppers.**

supply—To give what is needed or wanted; provide: *to* supply *food; to* supply *electricity. Verb.*
—An amount of something that is or can be provided: *The art teacher told us she would bring a fresh* supply *of clay to the next class. Noun.*
sup|ply (sə plī′) *verb,* **supplied, supplying;** *noun, plural* **supplies.**
• Synonyms: **equip, furnish,** for *verb.*

a at	i if	oo look	ch chalk		⌈ a in ago
ā ape	ī idle	ou out	ng sing		e in happen
ah calm	o odd	u ugly	sh ship	ə =	i in capital
aw all	ō oats	ū rule	th think		o in occur
e end	oi oil	ur turn	<u>th</u> their		⌊ u in upon
ē easy			zh treasure		

support—1. To hold the weight of; keep from falling: *Can the bookcase* support *a television set?* 2. To provide with confidence and strength: *His friends* support *him when he feels sad.* 3. To provide money and other things needed for life: *She* supports *herself and two children.* 4. To believe in a purpose or goal: *I* support *the law against loud music in the park.* 5. To help prove; confirm: *His experiments* support *his theory. Verb.*
—1. The act of holding up or helping: *The candidate asked for our* support. 2. Someone or something that holds up or provides help: *The bridge* supports *were checked for cracks. Noun.*
sup|port (sə pawrt′) *verb,* supported, supporting; *noun, plural* supports.

suppose—1. To imagine something as true in order to consider the effect: Suppose *we moved to the mountains.* 2. To consider likely: *I* suppose *he will ask her to the dance.* 3. To expect: *We were* supposed *to be home an hour ago.*
sup|pose (sə pōz′) *verb,* supposed, supposing.

supreme—1. Greatest in authority, rank, or power: *The head of the government is* supreme *commander of the armed forces.* 2. Highest in quality or degree: *a* supreme *actor;* supreme *courage.*
su|preme (sə prēm′) *adjective.*

Supreme Court—The highest court of law in the United States consisting of a chief justice and eight associate justices.
Su|preme Court (sə prēm′ kawrt) *noun, plural* Supreme Courts.

sure—1. Without doubt; positive: *Are you* sure *you turned the oven off?* 2. Safe; reliable; steady: *a* sure *grip; a* sure *shot.* 3. Certain to happen: *He felt that this debate would be a* sure *win. Adjective.*
—Certainly; of course: *I could* sure *use a glass of water. Adverb.*
sure (shoor) *adjective,* surer, surest; *adverb.*

surely—Certainly; truly; without a doubt: *That was* surely *the best roast I have ever tasted.*
sure|ly (shoor′lē) *adverb.*

surf—The waves of the ocean as they crash near the shore: *The* surf *makes swimming in the ocean a lot of fun. Noun.*
—To ride a surfboard on a wave: *His brother* surfs *every afternoon. Verb.*
surf (surf) *noun; verb,* surfed, surfing.
• A word that sounds the same is **serf**.

surface—1. The outside of an object: *Someone had written on the desk's* surface. 2. The top layer of the ground or of water: *The* surface *of the pond was covered with oil.* 3. Any of the sides of an object: *A sheet of paper has two writing* surfaces, *front and back.* 4. The outward appearance; what seems to be: *On the* surface, *he is shy, but in fact he loves company. Noun.*
—Of, on, or at the top of something: *The* surface *temperature of the lake is still chilly in May. Adjective.*
—1. To make smooth; cover the top of: *Dad* surfaced *our driveway with concrete for a basketball court.* 2. To rise or come to the top: *The diver* surfaced *after an hour underwater. Verb.*
sur|face (sur′fis) *noun, plural* surfaces; *adjective; verb,* surfaced, surfacing.

surfboard—A long, narrow board used for riding waves to the shore.
surf|board (surf′bawrd′) *noun, plural* surfboards.

superstition and **superstitious**

surfboard

surfing—The sport of riding waves to the shore on a surfboard.
surf|ing (sur′fing) *noun.*

surge—1. To move powerfully: *The tropical storm* surged *over the small island.* 2. To rush forward as a wave does: *The runners* surged *toward the finish line. Verb.*
—1. A swelling or rushing of waves: *The* surge *of the ocean made me seasick.* 2. Something that moves like a wave: *the* surge *of the crowd through the city streets.* 3. A sudden swell of emotion: *He felt a* surge *of confidence. Noun.*
surge (surj) *verb,* surged, surging; *noun, plural* surges.

surgeon—A doctor who treats injuries and illness by performing operations; specialist in surgery.
sur|geon (sur′jən) *noun, plural* surgeons.

Language Fact

Surgeon, doctor, and **physician** all mean people who cure injuries or illnesses. **Surgeon** comes from a Greek word that means "hand work." Surgeons are specially trained medical doctors who actually fix people with their hands. **Doctor** comes from a Latin word meaning "teacher" and can be used for a highly educated person in any of several professions. Usually it means a medical doctor. **Physician** comes from a Latin word meaning "natural science." Physicians are medical doctors of various kinds.

---

surgery—The medical treatment of diseases and injuries by performing operations. The body is cut open, and the damaged parts are repaired or removed.
sur|ger|y (sur′jər ē) *noun, plural* surgeries.

surname—A person's last name: *All students whose* surnames *begin with "A" sat in the front row.*
sur|name (sur′nām′) *noun, plural* surnames.

surplus—An amount that is more than is needed or wanted; excess: *The store is having a sale because it has a* surplus *of goods. Noun.*
—More than is needed: *Pioneers stored* surplus *food for the long winters. Adjective.*

sur|plus (sur′plus′) *noun, plural* surpluses; *adjective.*

surprise—1. A feeling of astonishment caused by something unexpected: *She was filled with* surprise *when she won the race.* 2. Something that astonishes: *Children love* surprises. 3. The act of catching someone or something unprepared: *The sudden storm took us by* surprise. *Noun.*
—1. To cause astonishment: *He* surprised *her with flowers.* 2. To catch unprepared; come without warning: *The teacher* surprised *the class with a quiz. Verb.*
—Coming unexpectedly: *a* surprise *party; a* surprise *attack. Adjective.*
sur|prise (sər prīz′) *noun, plural* surprises; *verb,* surprised, surprising; *adjective.*

surrender—1. To stop fighting or resisting and turn oneself in: *The rebels* surrendered *to the army.* 2. To give in to an emotion: *She* surrendered *to her amusement and laughed out loud. Verb.*
—The act of giving in: *The* surrender *of the fort came after a long night of fighting. Noun.*
sur|ren|der (sə ren′dər) *verb,* surrendered, surrendering; *noun, plural* surrenders.

surround—To enclose on all sides; make a boundary or circle around: *A high fence* surrounds *the lion's cage at the zoo.*
sur|round (sə round′) *verb,* surrounded, surrounding.

surroundings—The conditions in which a person or thing lives: *He wants his children to grow up in happy* surroundings.
sur|round|ings (sə roun′dingz) *noun.*

survey—1. To examine and study all of: *The judge* surveyed *the facts of the case.* 2. To measure the shape, size, location, and borders of land: *The town will* survey *the field before they build a park there. Verb.*
—1. A general look at something: *The librarian led the children on a* survey *of the library.* 2. A formal study or poll: *The newspaper held a* survey *of people's opinions on pollution control.* 3. The measuring of land to identify its features: *A* survey *of the property showed it to be much wider than we thought. Noun.*
sur|vey (sər vā′ for *verb;* sur′vā or sər vā′ for *noun) verb,* surveyed, surveying; *noun, plural* surveys.

surveyor—A person whose job is to measure land to identify its features.
sur|vey|or (sər vā′ər) *noun, plural* surveyors.

a at	i if	oo look	ch chalk		a in ago
ā ape	ī idle	ou out	ng sing		e in happen
ah calm	o odd	u ugly	sh ship	ə =	i in capital
aw all	ō oats	ū rule	th think		o in occur
e end	oi oil	ur turn	th their		u in upon
ē easy			zh treasure		

survival—1. The act or condition of continuing to live: *The guide teaches young hikers about survival in the wilderness.*   2. Something that continues to exist: *Some holiday traditions are survivals from earlier times.*
sur|viv|al (sər vī′vəl) *noun, plural* **survivals.**

survive—1. To live longer than: *Our dog survived our cat by one year.*   2. To live through; continue to live: *to survive an accident; to survive the cold winter.*
sur|vive (sər vīv′) *verb,* **served, surviving.**

Susan B. Anthony Day—February 15, the anniversary of Susan B. Anthony's birthday, is celebrated in memory of her efforts to gain rights for women, especially the right to vote.
Su|san B. An|tho|ny Day (sū′zən bē an′thə nē dā) *noun.*

suspect—1. To believe that something is likely or possible: *I suspect it may rain today.*   2. To believe someone is guilty, without having much proof: *They suspect him of taking the money.*
3. To have doubts about; mistrust: *Mother suspected my version of the story. Verb.*
—A person thought to have done something wrong: *The suspects were arrested this morning. Noun.*
sus|pect (sə spekt′ for *verb;* sus′pekt for *noun*) *verb,* **suspected, suspecting;** *noun, plural* **suspects.**

suspend—1. To hang down from above: *They suspended the decoration from the light.*   2. To hold in place without visible support: *The dancer seemed to be suspended in the air.*   3. To stop for a little while: *Work on the tree fort was suspended after dark.*   4. To take away a position, privilege, or job for a time: *Our coach said he would suspend us from games if we did not go to practice.*
sus|pend (sə spend′) *verb,* **suspended, suspending.**

suspenders—A pair of straps that are fastened to pants and fit over the shoulders to keep the pants from falling.
sus|pend|ers (sə spen′dərz) *plural noun.*

suspense—The condition of being anxious or worried about what will happen: *We watched the movie in suspense to see how the boy would escape.*
sus|pense (sə spens′) *noun.*

suspension—1. The act of taking away a position, privilege, or job: *the suspension of a driver's license; a suspension without pay from a*

job.   2. A mixture in which small pieces of a solid float throughout a liquid: *the suspension of vegetables in soup.*
sus|pen|sion (sə spen′shən) *noun, plural* **suspensions.**

suspension bridge—A bridge that is held up by strong cables that hang between large towers.
sus|pen|sion bridge (sə spen′shən brij) *noun, plural* **suspension bridges.**

suspension bridge

suspicion—1. The act of thinking something without having proof: *His suspicions were confirmed when the man turned out to be an old friend.*   2. The condition of being thought guilty without proof of guilt: *Somebody ate the last cookie, and my brother was under suspicion.*
3. A small amount: *This ice cream has a suspicion of peach flavor.*
sus|pi|cion (sə spish′ən) *noun, plural* **suspicions.**

suspicious—1. Causing doubt or mistrust: *My little sister's suspicious actions made me think she was up to something.*   2. Feeling doubt or mistrust: *He is suspicious of strangers.*
3. Showing suspicion: *My cousin gave me a suspicious look when I offered to hold his ice cream cone.*
sus|pi|cious (sə spish′əs) *adjective.*

Sussex spaniel—A medium-sized hunting dog with a small body and a large head and ears. Its golden coat is thick and smooth. Originally

Sussex spaniel

bred in England, these dogs hunt by smell.
Sus|sex span|iel (sus′iks span′yəl) *noun,*
plural Sussex spaniels.

sustain—**1.** To keep up; keep going: *Books,*
games, and songs sustained *the children's*
interest on the long airplane ride. **2.** To provide
with food or other essentials: *The mother bear*
sustained *her young with fish from the river.*
3. To hold up; support: *The old chair could no*
longer sustain *the weight of my father and*
collapsed. **4.** To suffer: *The man* sustained *a*
broken arm in the accident.
sus|tain (sə stān′) *verb,* sustained, sustaining.

S.W.—The abbreviation for **southwest**.

swagger—To walk in a proud or boastful
manner: *The boys on the winning team*
swaggered *into the locker room. Verb.*
—A proud or boastful way of walking: *The*
villain came on stage with a swagger. *Noun.*
swag|ger (swag′ər) *verb,* swaggered,
swaggering; *noun, plural* swaggers.

swallow[1]—**1.** To move food and liquid into the
stomach through the mouth and throat. **2.** To
take in and cover up completely: *The waves*
swallowed *up the sinking boat.* **3.** To hold back;
keep inside: *She* swallowed *her anger. Verb.*
—**1.** The act of moving into the stomach through
the mouth and throat: *He finished the glass of*
water in one large swallow. **2.** An amount that
can be taken in one such act: *Please take a*
swallow *of medicine. Noun.*

swal|low (swol′ō) *verb,* swallowed, swallowing;
noun, plural swallows.
swallow[2]—One of several kinds of small birds
with narrow, pointed wings and a forked tail.
swal|low (swol′ō) *noun, plural* swallows.

swallow[2]

swam—*See* **swim**.
swam (swam) *verb.*

swamp—An area of wet, muddy land covered by
plants: *The stream ends in a* swamp. *Noun.*
—**1.** To fill with water: *waves* swamping *a boat.*
2. To overwhelm by giving too much of
something: *The boss* swamped *me with work. Verb.*
swamp (swomp) *noun, plural* swamps; *verb,*
swamped, swamping.

swan—A large water bird, usually white, having
a long, slender neck.
swan (swon) *noun, plural* swans.

swan

swap—To exchange: *He* swapped *his old baseball*
glove for a collection of baseball cards. Verb.
—An exchange; trade: *I will make you a* swap *of*
my red sweater for your green one. Noun.
swap (swop) *verb,* swapped, swapping; *noun,*
plural swaps.
• Synonyms: **barter, trade,** for *verb.*

a at	i if	oo look	ch chalk		a in ago
ā ape	ī idle	ou out	ng sing		e in happen
ah calm	o odd	u ugly	sh ship	ə =	i in capital
aw all	ō oats	ū rule	th think		o in occur
e end	oi oil	ur turn	th their		u in upon
ē easy			zh treasure		

swarm—1. A large group of bees that leave one hive and fly away to start a new colony. 2. A large group of people or things that are moving around: *a swarm* of shoppers. *Noun.*
—1. To move about in large numbers: *Flies* swarmed *around our picnic basket.* 2. To be crowded or filled: *The park* swarms *with people on warm, sunny days. Verb.*
swarm (swawrm) *noun, plural* **swarms;** *verb,* **swarmed, swarming.**

swastika—A figure formed by a cross with bent arms.
swas|ti|ka (swos′tə kə) *noun, plural* **swastikas.**

swat—To hit hard; give a sharp blow to: *He* swatted *the bug. Verb.*
—A sharp, hard hit: *Give that mosquito a* swat. *Noun.*
swat (swot) *verb,* **swatted, swatting;** *noun, plural* **swats.**

sway—1. To move or cause to move back and forth or from side to side: *The strong wind made the man* sway *as he walked over the bridge.* 2. To change the thinking or feeling of: *The child would not be* swayed *and insisted on having chocolate ice cream. Verb.*
—1. The action of moving back and forth or from side to side: *The* sway *of the wagon made us hold on to our seats.* 2. Power; influence: *The company was under the* sway *of a greedy man. Noun.*
sway (swā) *verb,* **swayed, swaying;** *noun, plural* **sways.**
• Synonyms: reel², stagger, teeter, waver, for *verb* **1.**

swear—1. To make a solemn promise by God or by any person, being, or thing that is holy: *to* swear *on the Bible.* 2. To promise or take an oath to do something; vow: *to* swear *to be friends forever.* 3. To use bad language; curse.
swear (swâr) *verb,* **swore, sworn, swearing.**

sweat—1. Moisture coming through the skin, usually because of heat, hard work, worry, or exercise. 2. Moisture that collects in drops on the surface of something. *Noun.*
—1. To give off moisture through the skin: *He* sweated *as he cut the grass.* 2. To gather moisture from the air so that it collects in drops on the surface of something: *My soda bottle is* sweating *from this heat. Verb.*
sweat (swet) *noun; verb,* **sweated** or **sweat, sweating.**

sweater—A knitted piece of clothing, often made of wool or cotton, that is worn on the upper part of the body, usually over a shirt or blouse.
sweat|er (swet′ər) *noun, plural* **sweaters.**

sweep—1. To clean with a broom or brush: *He* swept *the basement.* 2. To clear away or remove with a broom or brush: *Please* sweep *the crumbs off the floor.* 3. To move or carry along with great force: *the sudden breeze* sweeping *off his hat.* 4. To pass over quickly and steadily: *His eyes* swept *over the audience in search of his friends. Verb.*
—1. The act of cleaning by brushing: *This floor needs a good* sweep. 2. A steady driving or sweeping motion: *The* sweep *of the water moved the pebbles along.* 3. A broad range or stretch: *We could see a wide* sweep *of wheat fields from the train window. Noun.*
sweep (swēp) *verb,* **swept, sweeping;** *noun, plural* **sweeps.**

sweet—1. Having a taste like that of sugar. 2. Pleasing to the ear, nose, or eye: *a* sweet *perfume.* 3. Kind or agreeable: *a* sweet *person.* 4. Not salted or spoiled: sweet *butter. Adjective.*
—Something that tastes like sugar: *She popped a* sweet *into her mouth. Noun.*
sweet (swēt) *adjective,* **sweeter, sweetest;** *noun, plural* **sweets.**
• A word that sounds the same is **suite.**

sweetheart—Someone who is loved and who returns that love: *He bought his* sweetheart *a Valentine.*
sweet|heart (swēt′hahrt′) *noun, plural* **sweethearts.**

sweet pea—A climbing plant with sweet-smelling flowers.
sweet pea (swēt′pē) *noun, plural* **sweet peas.**

sweet pea

sweet potato—The large, sweet, yellow or orange root of a vine that is cooked and eaten as a vegetable.
sweet potato (swēt pə tā′tō) *noun, plural* **sweet potatoes.**

swell—1. To increase in size; expand: *The bubble* swelled *until it suddenly popped.* **2.** To rise above a level or surface: *The hills* swelled *in the distance. Verb.*
—A long wave or series of waves: *The surfers rode the* swell *into shore. Noun.*
—Fine; wonderful: *We had a* swell *time at the circus. Adjective.*
swell (swel) *verb,* **swelled, swelled** or **swollen, swelling;** *noun, plural* **swells;** *adjective,* **sweller, swellest.**

swept—*See* **sweep.**
swept (swept) *verb.*

swerve—To turn to the side suddenly: *She* swerved *her bike to avoid the puddle in the road.*
swerve (swurv) *verb,* **swerved, swerving.**

swift—1. Moving or able to move with great speed: *a* swift *runner.* **2.** Happening quickly: *a* swift *answer. Adjective.*
—A small bird with long wings. It is related to the hummingbird. *Noun.*
swift (swift) *adjective,* **swifter, swiftest;** *noun, plural* **swifts.**

swift (noun)

swim—1. To move through water using legs, arms, or fins: *Fish* swim. **2.** To move across something in this manner: *They* swam *the river.* **3.** To float in liquid or be covered by liquid: *mashed potatoes* swimming *in gravy.* **4.** To feel dizzy: *The roller coaster ride made my head* swim. *Verb.*
—The act of swimming or time spent swimming: *We will have a nice* swim *in the pool. Noun.*
swim (swim) *verb,* **swam, swum, swimming;** *noun, plural* **swims.**

swindle—To cheat of money or other valuables: *He tried to* swindle *her out of her savings. Verb.*
—The act of such cheating. *Noun.*
swin|dle (swin′dəl) *verb,* **swindled, swindling;** *noun, plural* **swindles.**

swine—A pig.
swine (swīn) *noun, plural* **swine.**
• See picture at **pig.**

swing—1. To move or cause to move back and forth: *She* swings *her arms as she runs.* **2.** To make move in a curving motion: *to* swing *our bicycles around the corner. Verb.*
—1. The act of moving back and forth or in a curving motion: *A mighty* swing *sent the baseball out of the park.* **2.** A hanging seat on which one can move back and forth. *Noun.*
swing (swing) *verb,* **swung, swinging;** *noun, plural* **swings.**
■ **in full swing:** At its highest or most active point: *She could not back out when the campaign was* in full swing.

swirl—To move with a twisting or circular motion: *Her skirt* swirled *as they danced around the room. Verb.*
—1. A twisting or circular movement: *the* swirl *of water going down the drain.* **2.** A twist or curl: *a* swirl *of syrup on the pancakes. Noun.*
swirl (swurl) *verb,* **swirled, swirling;** *noun, plural* **swirls.**

swish—To move with a rustling sound: *The basketball* swished *through the net. Verb.*
—A rustling sound. *Noun.*
swish (swish) *verb,* **swished, swishing;** *noun, plural* **swishes.**

switch—1. A change or exchange: *a* switch *of clothes.* **2.** A device for stopping or starting an electric current. **3.** A swift stroke or lash: *The horse swatted the fly with a* switch *of its tail.* **4.** A thin stick used to deliver stinging blows. **5.** A device used for shifting a train from one track to another. *Noun.*
—1. To change or exchange: *I* switched *tennis rackets with my sister.* **2.** To turn an electric current on or off: *Please* switch *on the radio.* **3.** To strike a blow with a thin stick or the like: *a farmer* switching *his team of horses to pull harder.* **4.** To move with a swinging motion: *He* switched *his finger to get our attention. Verb.*

a at	i if	oo look	ch chalk		a in ago
ā ape	ī idle	ou out	ng sing		e in happen
ah calm	o odd	u ugly	sh ship	ə =	i in capital
aw all	ō oats	ū rule	th think		o in occur
e end	oi oil	ur turn	th their		u in upon
ē easy			zh treasure		

switch (swich) *noun, plural* **switches;** *verb,* **switched, switching.**

switchboard—A control panel with electric switches or plugs used to connect telephone lines.
switch|board (swich′bawrd′) *noun, plural* **switchboards.**

swivel—A device that allows something to turn freely: *the swivel on an office chair. Noun.*
—To turn freely: *The bird cage swiveled from a hook in the ceiling. Verb.*
swiv|el (swiv′əl) *noun, plural* **swivels;** *verb,* **swiveled, swiveling.**

swollen—Enlarged from swelling: *Her ring would not fit on her swollen finger. Adjective.*
—*See* **swell.** *Verb.*
swol|len (swō′lən) *adjective, verb.*

swoop—1. To come down with a rush: *The kite swooped when I gave it a strong pull.* 2. To grab or clutch suddenly: *She swooped up her books and dashed off to school. Verb.*
—A quick downward movement: *It took three swoops for the sea gull to catch the tiny fish. Noun.*
swoop (swūp) *verb,* **swooped, swooping;** *noun, plural* **swoops.**
■ **in one fell swoop:** With one dramatic act or stroke: *She dropped an empty pot and got everyone's attention in one fell swoop.*

sword—A weapon made of a long, sharp metal blade attached to a handle.
sword (sawrd) *noun, plural* **swords.**

swordfish—A large ocean fish with a long, swordlike bone that sticks out from its upper jaw.
sword|fish (sawrd′fish′) *noun, plural* **swordfish** or **swordfishes.**

swordfish

swore—*See* **swear.**
swore (swawr) *verb.*

sworn—*See* **swear.**
sworn (swawrn) *verb.*

swum—*See* **swim.**
swum (swum) *verb.*

swung—*See* **swing.**
swung (swung) *verb.*

sycamore—A tall tree with smooth bark that peels off in thin brown pieces.
syc|a|more (sik′ə mawr) *noun, plural* **sycamores.**

leaf

tree

fruit

sycamore

syllabify—To break a word into syllables.
syl|lab|i|fy (sə lab′ə fī) *verb,* **syllabified, syllabifying.**

syllable—1. A group of letters that is spoken as a single sound: *The word "cat" has one syllable, while the word "kitten" has two.* 2. The word or part of a word that such a group of letters spells.
syl|la|ble (sil′ə bəl) *noun, plural* **syllables.**

symbol—Something that stands for another thing: *The color red is often a symbol for "stop."*
sym|bol (sim′bəl) *noun, plural* **symbols.**
● A word that sounds the same is **cymbal.**

female   male

symbol: These symbols are used to stand for male and female.

symbolic—Used as a symbol; standing for something: *Robins are* symbolic *of spring.*
sym|bol|ic (sim bol′ik) *adjective.*

symbolize—To stand for something; be a symbol of: *The white dove* symbolizes *peace.*
sym|bol|ize (sim′bə līz) *verb,* **symbolized, symbolizing.**

symmetrical—Having a balanced arrangement on opposite sides of a line or around a center; *a* symmetrical *garden.*
sym|met|ri|cal (si met′rə kəl) *adjective.*

symmetry—A regular, balanced arrangement on either side of a line or around a center: *Your garden has lovely* symmetry.
sym|me|try (sim′ə trē) *noun, plural* **symmetries.**

sympathetic—1. Having or showing kindness and understanding toward others: *a* sympathetic *friend who visited me when I was ill.* 2. In favor of; agreeable: *My parents are* sympathetic *to my desire to become a writer.*
sym|pa|thet|ic (sim′pə thet′ik) *adjective.*

sympathize—1. To have or show kindness and understanding: *He* sympathized *with me when I broke my leg.* 2. To agree with the feelings of another: *I* sympathize *with your wish to be a track star.*
sym|pa|thize (sim′pə thīz) *verb,* **sympathized, sympathizing.**

sympathy—1. A feeling of kindness and of understanding for the problems of others. 2. Agreement; favor: *We are in* sympathy *with your decision to spend more time in piano practice.*
sym|pa|thy (sim′pə thē) *noun, plural* **sympathies.**

symphony—1. A long piece of music written for an orchestra. 2. An orchestra that plays this type of music.
sym|pho|ny (sim′fə nē) *noun, plural* **symphonies.**

symptom—A sign of something: *Sneezing may be a* symptom *of a cold.*
symp|tom (simp′təm) *noun, plural* **symptoms.**

synagogue—A place used by Jews for worship and religious education.
syn|a|gogue (sin′ə gog) *noun, plural* **synagogues.**

synonym—A word whose meaning is the same as, or very similar to, the meaning of another word: *"Unhappy" is a* synonym *of "sad."*
syn|o|nym (sin′ə nim) *noun, plural* **synonyms.**

Word History

Synonym comes from a Greek prefix meaning "together" and a Greek word meaning "name." Words that are synonyms are names for the same thing. Because they have the same meaning, they go together. You can find many of these words together in the lists of synonyms in this dictionary.

---

synonymous—Having the same meaning or a similar meaning: *The words "big" and "large" are* synonymous.
syn|on|y|mous (si non′ə məs) *adjective.*

synthetic—Not natural; artificial: *Plastic is* synthetic.
syn|thet|ic (sin thet′ik) *adjective.*

syringa—A bush with bunches of white flowers that bloom in the summer; mock orange. One kind of syringa is the state flower of Idaho.
sy|rin|ga (sə ring′gə) *noun, plural* **syringas.**

syringa

syringe—A narrow tube fitted with a piston or rubber bulb for drawing in and then forcing out a liquid. Syringes are used to inject fluids into the body and to clean wounds. *Noun.*
—To clean or inject with a syringe. *Verb.*
sy|ringe (sə rinj′) *noun, plural* **syringes;** *verb,* **syringed, syringing.**

syrup—A sweet, thick liquid, such as maple syrup or molasses.
syr|up (sēr′əp *or* sur′əp) *noun, plural* **syrups.**

system—1. A set of parts that form a whole: *the railroad* system. 2. A group of facts, rules, or beliefs: *a* system *of religion.* 3. An organized plan or method: *We need a dependable* system *for getting our project finished on time.*
sys|tem (sis′təm) *noun, plural* **systems.**

a at	**i** if	**oo** look	**ch** chalk		**a** in ago
ā ape	**ī** idle	**ou** out	**ng** sing		**e** in happen
ah calm	**o** odd	**u** ugly	**sh** ship	ə =	**i** in capital
aw all	**ō** oats	**ū** rule	**th** think		**o** in occur
e end	**oi** oil	**ur** turn	**th** their		**u** in upon
ē easy			**zh** treasure		

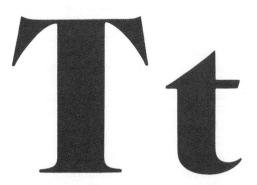

About 1,900 years ago, the Romans gave the captial T its present form. The small letter t was first used about 1,500 years ago. It reached its present form about 500 years ago.

About 5,000 years ago, the ancient Egyptians used a mark that looked like this.

About 3,500 years ago, people in the Middle East used a cross-shaped letter. They called it *taw*, their word for "mark."

About 3,000 years ago, other people in the Middle East used a similar form.

About 2,600 years ago, the Greeks gave the letter this form. They called it *tau*.

T or **t**—The 20th letter of the alphabet: *There are two* t's *in the word "matter."*
T, t (tē) *noun, plural* **T's** or **Ts**, **t's** or **ts**.

T. or **T**—1. An abbreviation for **tablespoon** or **tablespoons**. 2. The abbreviation for **ton** or **tons**.

tab—A small flap that sticks out from something: *The* tab *on the top made it easy to open the box.*
tab (tab) *noun, plural* **tabs**.
• Synonyms: **label, tag¹**

tabernacle—1. A place of worship. 2. A place where something holy is kept.
tab|er|nac|le (tab′ər nak′əl) *noun, plural* **tabernacles**.

table—1. A piece of furniture that has legs and a flat top. 2. Food that is served: *We put on a good* table *for the birthday party.* 3. A chart of numbers or a list of information: *a price* table; *a multiplication* table; *the* table *of contents at the front of a book.*
ta|ble (tā′bəl) *noun, plural* **tables**.
■ **turn the tables:** To reverse a situation: *At first, the younger player was losing, but she* turned the tables *and won the match.*

tablecloth—A protective covering placed over a table.
ta|ble|cloth (tā′bəl klawth′) *noun, plural* **tablecloths**.

tablespoon—1. A large spoon that is used for serving and eating. 2. A unit of measure, especially for ingredients used in cooking. It is equal to three teaspoons (0.015 liter).
ta|ble|spoon (tā′bəl spūn′) *noun, plural* **tablespoons**. Abbreviation: **T.** or **T** or **tbsp.**

table tennis—*See* **ping-pong**.
ta|ble ten|nis (tā′bəl ten′is) *noun*.

tack—1. A small pin or nail with a sharp point and a wide, flat head. 2. A method or course of action: *If this plan fails, we shall try a different* tack. *Noun.*
—1. To fasten with flat-headed, short nails: *We* tacked *down the rug to hold it in place.* 2. To add or attach: *She* tacked *a birthday card onto his present.* 3. To sew with loose stitches. *Verb.*
tack (tak) *noun, plural* **tacks**; *verb*, **tacked, tacking**.

tackle—1. Equipment or supplies for an activity: *I carried the fishing* tackle *to the lake.* 2. A device made of ropes and pulleys. Tackles are used to lift heavy things. 3. The act of throwing someone to the ground: *His* tackle *stopped the quarterback after a short run. Noun.*
—1. To deal with; try to solve; face: *I guess it is about time that I* tackle *this mess in my room.* 2. To grab and throw someone to the ground. *Verb.*
tack|le (tak′əl) *noun, plural* **tackles**; *verb*, **tackled, tackling**.

taco—A fried tortilla filled with one or more of such ingredients as beef, chicken, cheese, beans, tomatoes, lettuce, and spicy sauce.
ta|co (tah′kō) *noun, plural* **tacos**.

tact—The ability to do and say the proper things in any given situation: *She thought his painting was ugly, but she showed such* tact *in her comments about it that she avoided hurting his feelings.*
tact (takt) *noun*.

tactics—1. The science of how to use military forces in battle. 2. Carefully planned methods used to achieve something; strategy: *These* tactics *should help us win the game.*
tac|tics (tak′tiks) *noun.*

tadpole—A very young frog or toad; polliwog. It lives in water and has gills and a long tail.
tad|pole (tad′pōl′) *noun, plural* **tadpoles.**

tadpole

taffy—A chewy, sticky candy made from boiled brown sugar or molasses.
taf|fy (taf′ē) *noun, plural* **taffies.**

tag¹—A small card or piece of material that is attached to something: *Directions on how to wash this shirt are on the* tag *sewn inside it. Noun.*
—1. To attach a small card or piece of material to something: *We* tagged *my clothes with my name and address before I went to camp.* 2. To stay nearby so as to follow: *My little brother* tagged *after me when I went on a walk. Verb.*
tag (tag) *noun, plural* **tags;** *verb,* **tagged, tagging.**
• Synonyms: **label, tab,** for *noun* 1.

tag²—A game in which one player is called "it" and chases other players until one is touched. He or she then becomes "it" and tries to catch another player. *Noun.*
—To touch briefly: *The shortstop* tagged *the runner at second base. Verb.*
tag (tag) *noun; verb,* **tagged, tagging.**

tail—1. The part of an animal's body that sticks out past its back end: *The cat sticks its long, furry* tail *straight up in the air when it walks.* 2. Something that is long and shaped like such a body part: *the* tail *of a kite.* 3. The back part of

something: *the* tail *of a long line of cars; the* tail *of an airplane. Noun.*
—To follow secretly: *The police* tailed *the suspected criminal. Verb.*
tail (tāl) *noun, plural* **tails;** *verb,* **tailed, tailing.**
■ **turn tail:** To run away from a dangerous or unpleasant situation: *When it started to get dark in the woods, we* turned tail *and ran home.*
• A word that sounds the same is **tale.**

tailor—A person who earns a living by making, altering, or mending clothes. *Noun.*
—To make, alter, or mend clothes: *He* tailored *the suit so that it fit perfectly. Verb.*
tai|lor (tā′lər) *noun, plural* **tailors;** *verb,* **tailored, tailoring.**

take—1. To get hold of; grasp: *Please* take *the dog's leash so he does not run away.* 2. To capture: *The enemy* took *the fort at dawn.* 3. To accept or receive: *to* take *someone's advice; to* take *medicine.* 4. To have or get: *Please* take *a piece of candy.* 5. To carry: *The porter at the hotel* took *our bags to the car.* 6. To use: *He* took *this chance to thank his parents.* 7. To require: *It* takes *patience and practice to learn to play the piano.* 8. To choose: *I want you to* take *the one you like best.* 9. To subtract: *If you* take *7 from 11 you get 4.* 10. To steal or remove: *Who* took *my pencil?* 11. To understand or interpret: *I* take *the poem to be about the beauty of earth.*
take (tāk) *verb,* **took, taken, taking.**
■ **take after:** To be or act like: *When it comes to artistic talent, she* takes after *her grandfather.*
• See Language Fact at **bring.**

taken—*See* **take.**
tak|en (tā′kən) *verb.*

takeoff—The act of rising into the air: *Her* takeoff *from the diving board was perfect.*
take|off (tāk′awf′) *noun, plural* **takeoffs.**

tale—1. A story: *Grandfather told many* tales *about what life was like when he was a child.* 2. A false story; fib; lie: *He told a* tale *about how his sister had broken the vase when he had really broken it himself.*
tale (tāl) *noun, plural* **tales.**
• A word that sounds the same is **tail.**

talent—1. A natural ability to do a certain thing; gift: *She has a* talent *for mathematics and gets good grades without studying much.* 2. One who has a natural ability: *The writer's first book was excellent and proved she was a genuine* talent.
tal|ent (tal′ənt) *noun, plural* **talents.**

talented—Having a natural ability to do something; being very good at what one does: *a*

a at	i if	oo look	ch chalk		a in ago
ā ape	ī idle	ou out	ng sing		e in happen
ah calm	o odd	u ugly	sh ship	ə =	i in capital
aw all	ō oats	ū rule	th think		o in occur
e end	oi oil	ur turn	th their		u in upon
ē easy			zh treasure		

talented *musician; a* talented *mechanic.*
tal|ent|ed (**tal′**ən tid) *adjective.*

talk—1. To speak; say words: *Her throat was so sore that she could not talk.* 2. To have a conversation: *When her brother came home from college, they* talked *for hours.* 3. To get someone to do something by speaking; persuade; influence: *He was* talked *into bringing his collection of records to the party. Verb.*
—1. A conversation: *They had a nice* talk *on the telephone.* 2. A short, casual speech: *The writer is going to give a* talk *at the library. Noun.*
talk (tawk) *verb,* **talked, talking;** *noun, plural* **talks.**
■ **talk back:** To answer someone in a rude way: *She was sent to the principal's office because she* talked back *to the teacher when she was told to be quiet.*
talk big: To speak in a bragging way; praise oneself or one's things: *He always* talks big, *but he never does anything worth noticing.*

tall—1. Having a greater height than what is standard; higher than other things: *a* tall *building.* 2. Having a certain height; high: *That bookcase stands several feet* tall. 3. Not believable; incredible; exaggerated: *There were many* tall *tales told about the famous cowboy.*
tall (tawl) *adjective,* **taller, tallest.**

talon—A claw of an eagle or similar bird. Talons are long and very sharp and are used for catching animals.
tal|on (**tal′**ən) *noun, plural* **talons.**
● See picture at **claw.**

tambourine—A round, flat, hand-held drum with metal disks around the edge. It is played by beating it with the fingers and by shaking it to make the disks produce a ringing sound.
tam|bou|rine (tam′bə **rēn′**) *noun, plural* **tambourines.**

tambourine

tame—1. Gentle; calm: *Our dog is so* tame *that it does not bark when people come to the door.* 2. Made calm, obedient, and not fearful of people; not wild: *Some of the animals at the zoo were* tame *enough for children to pet them. Adjective.*
—To train to overcome wildness: *The circus performer* tamed *the tigers. Verb.*
tame (tām) *adjective,* **tamer, tamest;** *verb,* **tamed, taming.**

tamper—To meddle improperly: *He* tampered *with the toaster and broke it.*
tam|per (**tam′**pər) *verb,* **tampered, tampering.**

tan—1. A light yellowish brown color. 2. The darkened color of a person's skin after it has been exposed to the sun. *Noun.*
—Having a light yellowish brown color: tan *shoes. Adjective.*
—1. To have one's skin become a darker color because it was exposed to the sun: *My arms* tanned *when I mowed the lawn.* 2. To change animal skin into leather: *We cannot make the saddle until we finish* tanning *the hide. Verb.*
tan (tan) *noun, plural* **tans;** *adjective; verb,* **tanned, tanning.**

tang—A strong taste, especially one that has a slight sting to it: *What did you put in this sauce to give it such a* tang?
tang (tang) *noun, plural* **tangs.**

tangerine—1. A reddish orange fruit that looks and tastes like an orange but generally is smaller and has a looser peel. 2. A reddish orange color.
—Having a reddish orange color. *Adjective.*
tan|ge|rine (tan′jə **rēn′**) *noun, plural* **tangerines;** *adjective.*

tangle—To knot or become knotted together in a twisted mess; snarl: *The kite string became* tangled *in a tree. Verb.*
—A knotted, twisted mess: *Her hair was in such a* tangle *when she woke up that it hurt to brush it. Noun.*
tan|gle (**tang′**gəl) *verb,* **tangled, tangling;** *noun, plural* **tangles.**

tank¹—A large container for a liquid or a gas: *a water* tank *for trained porpoises; an air* tank *that a skin diver wears.*
tank (tangk) *noun, plural* **tanks.**

tank²—An armored military vehicle that travels on continuous metal tracks. It is equipped with a

Word History

Tank² comes from **tank**¹—in a way. When these vehicles were first introduced, they were meant to be a secret weapon that would take the enemy by surprise. The crates that were used for shipping the vehicles were labeled ''tank'' as a disguise. After people had called the vehicles ''tanks'' for a while, the name stayed.

cannon, machine guns, and other weapons.
tank (tangk) *noun, plural* **tanks.**

tanker—A large ship or other vehicle that is specially equipped to transport liquids: *an oil* tanker; *a milk* tanker.
tank|er (**tang′**kər) *noun, plural* **tankers.**

tantrum—An outburst of bad temper; fit of anger: *He had a* tantrum *when his parents told him he could not go out and play.*
tan|trum (**tan′**trəm) *noun, plural* **tantrums.**

Taoism—One of the main religions of China. People who practice it believe in leading very simple, peaceful, and humble lives.
Tao|ism (**tou′**iz əm *or* **dou′**iz əm) *noun.*

tap¹—1. To touch or hit in a soft, light way: *I* tapped *him on the shoulder to get his attention.* 2. To make a soft but sharp sound by continually hitting something lightly: *She* tapped *her fingernails on the table. Verb.*
—A soft blow or touch, especially one that makes a light but sharp sound: *a* tap *on the door; the* tap *of a branch against a window. Noun.*
tap (tap) *verb,* **tapped, tapping;** *noun, plural* **taps.**

tap²—A device that can be opened and closed to allow water or other liquids to flow out of pipes or containers; faucet. *Noun.*
—1. To make an opening in something to allow liquid to flow out; unplug: *to* tap *a barrel of apple cider; to* tap *a maple tree to get sap to make syrup.* 2. To connect a device to a telephone in order to listen in secretly on others' phone calls: *They* tapped *his telephone in order to obtain evidence. Verb.*
tap (tap) *noun, plural* **taps;** *verb,* **tapped, tapping.**
• For noun, see Language Fact at **faucet.**

a at	i if	oo look	ch chalk	⌐a in ago
ā ape	ī idle	ou out	ng sing	e in happen
ah calm	o odd	u ugly	sh ship	ə = i in capital
aw all	ō oats	ū rule	th think	o in occur
e end	oi oil	ur turn	th̲ their	⌐u in upon
ē easy			zh treasure	

tape—1. A long, thin piece of cloth, plastic, or other material: *to seal a package with a piece of* tape; *to measure the length of a room with a* tape. 2. A strip of specially treated plastic on which sound or pictures and sound are recorded: *The album is available on record and on* tape. *Noun.*
—1. To fasten with a thin strip of cloth, plastic, or other material; attach one thing to another: *to* tape *a box closed for storage; to* tape *a poster to the wall.* 2. To use a strip of specially treated plastic to record sound or pictures and sound: *He* taped *the football game so he could watch it later. Verb.*
tape (tāp) *noun, plural* **tapes;** *verb,* **taped, taping.**

taper—1. To make or become gradually narrower at one end: *an ice cream cone that* tapers *at the bottom.* 2. To lessen: *The storm* tapered *off as it blew out to sea.*
ta|per (**tā′**pər) *verb,* **tapered, tapering.**
• A word that sounds the same is **tapir.**

tape recorder—A device that records sounds on a specially treated plastic tape.
tape re|cord|er (tāp ri **kawr′**dər) *noun, plural* **tape recorders.**

tapioca—A food starch that is widely used to make puddings. It comes from the roots of a tropical plant.
tap|i|o|ca (tap′ē ō′kə) *noun, plural* **tapiocas.**

tapir—A large tropical animal that looks like a pig but is related to the rhinoceros and the horse. It has a short, heavy body and a very long,

tap² (noun)

tapir

thick nose that acts as a movable trunk.
ta|pir (tā′pər) *noun, plural* **tapirs** or **tapir.**
• A word that sounds the same is **taper.**

taps—A bugle call that is played to mark the end of a waking day in the military services. It means that all lights should be put out. It is also played during the burial services of a military person.
taps (taps) *plural noun.*

tar—A thick, sticky, black or dark brown substance that is made from wood or coal. It is used for paving roads and as a waterproof material on roofs. *Noun.*
—To cover with this substance: *The workers* tarred *the roof to keep it from leaking. Verb.*
tar (tahr) *noun, plural* **tars;** *verb,* **tarred, tarring.**

tarantula—A spider with a large, hairy body and hairy legs. Its bite can be very painful but is not poisonous. Tarantulas live in warm climates.
ta|ran|tu|la (tə ran′chə lə) *noun, plural* **tarantulas.**

tarantula

tardy—Not on time; late; overdue: *He was* tardy *for school because he missed his bus.*
tar|dy (tahr′dē) *adjective,* **tardier, tardiest.**

target—1. Something that is aimed or shot at: *a* target *for an archery contest; a town as the* target

of an artillery attack.   **2.** Anything that is made fun of, laughed at, or disliked: *The clown was the* target *of the ringmaster's jokes.*   **3.** A purpose for doing something; goal; end: *The cookie sale was very successful, and we made much more money that the* target *we had set.*
tar|get (tahr′git) *noun, plural* **targets.**

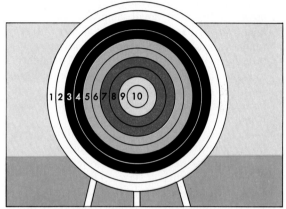

target (definition 1)

tariff—A tax that one country places on goods imported from another country.
tar|iff (tar′if) *noun, plural* **tariffs.**

tarnish—To lose or cause to lose shine or color: *We had not polished the silver bowl for some time, and it* tarnished. *Verb.*
—A coating that dulls the shine or color of a metal object: *The brass piggy bank looked dirty because it was covered with* tarnish. *Noun.*
tar|nish (tahr′nish) *verb,* **tarnished, tarnishing;** *noun, plural* **tarnishes.**

tart[1]—Having a sharp and sour taste: *The* tart *lemonade needed more sugar.*
tart (tahrt) *adjective,* **tarter, tartest.**

tart[2]—A small pie with filling of fruit or other sweet, and with no crust on top. It is meant for one person to eat.
tart (tahrt) *noun, plural* **tarts.**

tartan—A plaid design on woolen cloth that developed in Scotland. Each Scottish clan has its own tartan.
tar|tan (tahr′tən) *noun, plural* **tartans.**

task—A piece of work that needs to be done: *Cleaning his room is his main* task *for the day.*
task (task) *noun, plural* **tasks.**
• Synonyms: **chore, duty**
  Antonyms: See Synonyms at **amusement.**

tassel—1. A bunch of threads or cords that are tied securely at one end and are hanging free at

the other. Tassels are found on blankets, pillows, rugs, and hats.   **2.** Anything that looks like this: *a tassel of hair pulled together with a ribbon.*
tas|sel (tas′əl) *noun, plural* **tassels.**

taste—**1.** The flavor of something that is taken into the mouth: *The candy had a sweet* taste.
2. The sense that tells the flavor of something taken into the mouth: *The hot sauce burned his mouth and ruined his* taste *for the rest of the meal.* **3.** Just a bit; small sample: *a* taste *of honey for my oatmeal; a* taste *of victory.* **4.** A fondness or liking; preference: *She has more of a* taste *for tennis than for football.* **5.** The ability to know and appreciate what is good or beautiful: *I always read the books she recommends, because she has good* taste *in such matters.* *Noun.*
—**1.** To see what the flavor of something is by taking it into the mouth: *The chef* tasted *the sauce to make sure it had enough lemon flavor.*
2. To have a particular flavor: *The glue on the back of the stamps* tasted *like spearmint.* **3.** To feel something briefly: *He* tasted *life in the big city when he visited his cousin. Verb.*
taste (tāst) *noun, plural* **tastes;** *verb,* **tasted, tasting.**

tasty—Full of good flavor; pleasing in flavor: *The children finished eating the* tasty *birthday cake in no time at all.*
tast|y (tās′tē) *adjective,* **tastier, tastiest.**

tatter—A hanging piece of torn or shredded material: *The cuff of his pants was in* tatters *from having been caught in the bicycle chain.*
tat|ter (tat′ər) *noun, plural* **tatters.**

tattle—To tell on someone; give away a secret: *After she saw her brother break the window, she ran to* tattle *to their parents.*
tat|tle (tat′əl) *verb,* **tattled, tattling.**

tattletale—One who tells on someone else or gives away secrets: *The* tattletale *told everyone the club's secret password.*
tat|tle|tale (tat′əl tāl′) *noun, plural* **tattletales.**

tattoo—To put a permanent, colored picture or other design on the skin. The skin is tattooed by pricking small, deep holes in it and then placing colors in the holes: *The circus performer was* tattooed *all over his chest. Verb.*

—A permanent picture or other design put on the skin: *He has a* tattoo *of a lion on his arm. Noun.*
tat|too (ta tū′) *verb,* **tattooed, tattooing;** *noun, plural* **tattoos.**

taught—*See* **teach.**
taught (tawt) *verb.*

tavern—**1.** A place where a person can buy and drink alcoholic beverages; bar.   **2.** A place where a traveler can take a room for the night; inn.
tav|ern (tav′ərn) *noun, plural* **taverns.**

tawny—Having a brownish yellow color: *a* tawny *leather purse.*
taw|ny (taw′nē) *adjective.*

tax—**1.** Money that citizens and businesses are required to pay to a government. It is used to pay for the cost of running the government and its programs.   **2.** A serious and continuing difficulty; burden: *Having a job after school was a* tax *on his ability to keep up with his studies.* *Noun.*
—**1.** To put a tax on: *to* tax *certain purchases.*
2. To require a tax from: *The town* taxed *its citizens heavily to pay for the new school.* **3.** To overburden, overload, or overwork: *Please hurry up, because you are really* taxing *my patience.* *Verb.*
tax (taks) *noun, plural* **taxes;** *verb,* **taxed, taxing.**

taxi—A car that transports people in exchange for money; taxicab; cab. *Noun.*
—**1.** To transport or be transported in a car for pay: *They had to* taxi *to school when their family's car broke down.* **2.** To move slowly along the ground, as an airplane does before and after takeoff: *The plane* taxied *out to the runway.* *Verb.*
tax|i (tak′sē) *noun, plural* **taxis;** *verb,* **taxied, taxiing** or **taxying.**

taxicab—A car that transports people in exchange for money; cab; taxi.
tax|i|cab (tak′sē kab′) *noun, plural* **taxicabs.**

TB—The abbreviation for **tuberculosis.**

tbsp.—The abbreviation for **tablespoon** or **tablespoons.**

tea—**1.** A drink made by soaking the dried leaves of a certain plant in water. It is served hot or cold and often has sugar, milk, or lemon added to it.   **2.** This plant or its leaves.   **3.** An afternoon meal at which this drink is served.
tea (tē) *noun, plural* **teas.**

teach—**1.** To help a person to know, understand, or learn; train: *to* teach *a child to cook; to* teach *a dog a trick.* **2.** To give instruction or classes

a at	i if	oo look	ch chalk		a in ago
ā ape	ī idle	ou out	ng sing		e in happen
ah calm	o odd	u ugly	sh ship	ə =	i in capital
aw all	ō oats	ū rule	th think		o in occur
e end	oi oil	ur turn	th their		u in upon
ē easy			zh treasure		

in: *She* teaches *sewing and music in her home.*
teach (tēch) *verb,* **taught, teaching.**

teacher—A person who helps others know, understand, or learn; person who gives classes or lessons.
teach|er (tē′chər) *noun, plural* **teachers.**

teakettle—A covered kettle that has a spout and a handle and is used for boiling water.
tea|ket|tle (tē′ket′əl) *noun, plural* **teakettles.**

team—1. Two or more people doing work together, especially a group on one side in a sport or game: *a team of doctors operating on a patient; a soccer team.* 2. Two or more animals harnessed to a vehicle or piece of equipment: *A team of horses pulled the hay wagon. Noun.*
—To join together to do work: *The mothers* teamed *up to raise money for new band uniforms. Verb.*
team (tēm) *noun, plural* **teams;** *verb,* **teamed, teaming.**

teammate—A fellow member of a team.
team|mate (tēm′māt′) *noun, plural* **teammates.**

teamster—Someone whose job is driving a truck or a team of animals.
team|ster (tēm′stər) *noun, plural* **teamsters.**

teamwork—The activity of a group of people working together to accomplish the same goal; cooperation: *The* teamwork *of the parents helped make the school fair a big success.*
team|work (tēm′wurk′) *noun.*

teapot—A small, covered container with a handle and spout. It is used to brew and serve tea.
tea|pot (tē′pot′) *noun, plural* **teapots.**

tear[1]—1. A clear drop of a salty fluid that comes from the eye. Tears form when something, such as smoke, irritates the eye or when a person is upset. 2. **tears:** The act of crying; weeping: *He broke into* tears *when he fell off his bicycle.*
tear (tēr) *noun, plural* **tears.**

tear[2]—1. To split or become split apart: *She* tears *up letters after she reads them.* 2. To put a hole in something: *The cat* tore *the curtains with its claws.* 3. To remove forcefully: *to* tear *a story out of a magazine.* 4. To injure by cutting: *The board he was holding slipped and* tore *his finger.* 5. To divide into sides: *The city was* torn *by riots.* 6. To move with great speed or force: *The fire engines* tore *down the street. Verb.*
—A hole caused by ripping: *She slipped on the ice and got a* tear *in her skirt. Noun.*
tear (tār) *verb,* **tore, torn, tearing;** *noun, plural* **tears.**

■ **be torn between:** To have trouble choosing between two separate desires: *We* were torn between *going to the circus and going to the amusement park.*

tease—1. To bother; annoy; make fun of: *to* tease *the cat by pulling its tail; to* tease *someone about the way she walks.* 2. To joke playfully and affectionately with: *Her father* teased *her about how grown-up she looked in her new dress. Verb.*
—Someone who bothers or makes fun of others: *He had been such a* tease *about her new hat that she did not talk to him for a week. Noun.*
tease (tēz) *verb,* **teased, teasing;** *noun, plural* **teases.**

teaspoon—1. A small spoon used for serving and eating. 2. A unit of measure, especially for ingredients used in cooking. It is equal to one-third of a tablespoon (0.005 liter).
tea|spoon (tē′spūn′) *noun, plural* **teaspoons.** Abbreviation: **tsp.**

technical—1. Having to do with special knowledge of a scientific subject or an art: *Most of the audience did not understand the chemist's speech, because it was too* technical. 2. Having to do with industrial or mechanical arts: *He is going to* technical *school to train for a job as an automobile mechanic.*
tech|ni|cal (tek′nə kəl) *adjective.*

technician—A person who has special skill in a particular subject, especially a mechanical one: *a computer* technician.
tech|ni|cian (tek nish′ən) *noun, plural* **technicians.**

technique—A manner of doing things well in a science, art, or profession; technical method: *The dentist is using a new* technique *to clean teeth.*
tech|nique (tek nēk′) *noun, plural* **techniques.**

technology—1. The science that deals with the industrial and mechanical arts: *a school for radio* technology. 2. All the methods and machines that people have developed and used to satisfy their needs and desires: *a book about the history of* technology; *modern* technology.
tech|nol|o|gy (tek nol′ə jē) *noun, plural* **technologies.**

teenager—Someone who is older than 12 years of age and younger than 20.
teen|ag|er (tēn′ā jər) *noun, plural* **teenagers.**

teens—The years in someone's life from the age of 13 to the age of 19.
teens (tēnz) *plural noun.*

teeter—1. To rock back and forth in an unsteady manner; sway: *The boy* teetered *as he walked on* the log across the stream.   **2.** To go up and down on a seesaw.

tee|ter (tē′tər) *verb,* teetered, teetering.
●Synonyms: **reel², stagger, waver,** for **1.**

teeter-totter—A seesaw.

tee|ter-tot|ter (tē′tər tot′ər) *noun, plural* **teeter-totters.**
●See picture at **fulcrum.**

teeth—*See* **tooth.**

teeth (tēth) *plural noun.*
■**cut (one's) teeth:** To learn or be trained by experiencing something for the first time: *The new artist was assigned to* cut *her* teeth *on a simple cartoon project.*
in the teeth of: Directly against: *He was cold when he got home, because he had walked* in the teeth of *the strong wind.*
to the teeth: Entirely; to an extreme degree: *She has furnished her new apartment* to the teeth.

teethe—To grow teeth: *a baby that is* teething.

teethe (tēth) *verb,* teethed, teething.

tel- or **tele-**—A prefix that means ''working over a long distance'' or ''having to do with television.'' A telephoto lens allows photographs to be taken at a distance from the subject. A telecast is a television broadcast.

Word Power

You can tell the meanings of many words that begin with **tel-** or **tele-,** if you add a meaning of the prefix to the meaning of the rest of the word.
telecommunication: communication over a long distance
teleplay: a play written for television

---

telegram—A message sent by telegraph: *The mayor sent the governor a* telegram *to congratulate her on winning the election.*

tel|e|gram (tel′ə gram) *noun, plural* **telegrams.**

telegraph—The system or equipment for sending messages in code through electrical wires. *Noun.* —To send a message by means of this system or equipment: *The toy store ran out of the popular dolls and had to* telegraph *a rush order to the factory. Verb.*

tel|e|graph (tel′ə graf) *noun, plural* **telegraphs;** *verb,* **telegraphed, telegraphing.**

telephone—A device or system for sending and receiving speech through electrical wires. *Noun.* —**1.** To call or speak to a person by using this device: *She* telephoned *the florist to order flowers for her mother.*   **2.** To send a message by this device: *He* telephoned *his acceptance of the dinner invitation. Verb.*

tel|e|phone (tel′ə fōn) *noun, plural* **telephones;** *verb,* **telephoned, telephoning.**

telescope—An instrument that consists of lenses and a tube and is used to make distant objects seem closer and larger.

tel|e|scope (tel′ə skōp) *noun, plural* **telescopes.**

telescope

television—**1.** The process or system used for sending pictures and sounds by means of electrical signals.   **2.** The device used to view these pictures and hear these sounds.

tel|e|vi|sion (tel′ə vizh′ən) *noun, plural* **televisions.**

tell—**1.** To say to someone; express in words: *He found it hard to* tell *how he felt at hearing the news.*   **2.** To give a report or account of something: *She* told *us about her childhood on a farm.*   **3.** To let someone know; inform: *to* tell *me your secret; to* tell *us your name.*   **4.** To answer: *What did he* tell *you when you asked him where he had been?*   **5.** To command; order: *She* told *him to leave.*   **6.** To find out or recognize: *The hikers could* tell *what time it was by the position of the sun in the sky.*

tell (tel) *verb,* **told, telling.**
■ **tell me another:** I don't believe you: *You forgot your book report?* Tell me another.

a at	i if	oo look	ch chalk		a in ago
ā ape	ī idle	ou out	ng sing		e in happen
ah calm	o odd	u ugly	sh ship	ə =	i in capital
aw all	ō oats	ū rule	th think		o in occur
e end	oi oil	ur turn	th their		u in upon
ē easy			zh treasure		

tell off: To talk angrily to; scold: *She told her brother off for leaving her bicycle in the rain.*

• Synonyms: **reply, respond,** for **4.**
Antonyms: **ask, inquire, question,** for **4.**

teller—**1.** Someone who tells something: *Our camp counselor was a good* teller *of ghost stories.* **2.** Someone whose job is to receive and give out money at a bank.
tell|er (tel′ər) *noun, plural* **tellers.**

temper—**1.** A person's usual mood or state of mind: *My sister has a pleasant* temper *and rarely gets upset.* **2.** A tendency to become angry: *We have to be careful what we say around her, because she has such a* temper. **3.** A calm mood: *He never loses his* temper *when we tease him but instead teases us right back. Noun.*
—To make softer or more pleasant: *Mother's smile* tempered *her criticism about how my room looked.*
tem|per (tem′pər) *noun, plural* **tempers;** *verb,* **tempered, tempering.**

temperament—One's usual way of acting, thinking, or feeling; temper: *That nurse has a gentle* temperament.
tem|per|a|ment (tem′pər mənt) *noun, plural* **temperaments.**

temperate—Not extreme in temperature; neither too hot nor too cold: *We are moving to a* temperate *climate because we do not like the bitter cold winters here.*
tem|per|ate (tem′pər it) *adjective.*

temperature—The measure of how cold or how hot someone or something is: *an outside* temperature *of 45 degrees; a body* temperature *of 100 degrees.*
tem|per|a|ture (tem′pər ə chər) *noun, plural* **temperatures.**

temple[1]—A place of worship: *an ancient* temple.
tem|ple (tem′pəl) *noun, plural* **temples.**

temple[2]—The flattened area on each side of the forehead.
tem|ple (tem′pəl) *noun, plural* **temples.**

tempo—The speed at which a piece of music is played.
tem|po (tem′pō) *noun, plural* **tempos** or **tempi** (tem′pē).

temporary—Not lasting or staying very long: *The store hired* temporary *workers for the holiday season.*
tem|po|rar|y (tem′pə rãr ē) *adjective.*
Abbreviation: **temp.**

tempt—**1.** To try to get someone to do something wrong or unwise: *The hope of getting a job tempted* him *to lie about his age.* **2.** To appeal strongly to; attract: *The plate of cookies* tempted *the child.* **3.** To put to the test in a bold or foolish way; risk; provoke: *to* tempt *fate; to* tempt *one's luck.*
tempt (tempt) *verb,* **tempted, tempting.**

ten—One more than nine; one less than eleven; 10.
ten (ten) *adjective; noun, plural* **tens.**

Ten Commandments—The ten laws for correct living that are listed in the Bible. According to the Bible, God gave the Ten Commandments to the Jewish people.
Ten Com|mand|ments (ten kə mand′mənts) *noun.*

tenant—Someone who pays money for the use of another person's land or building: *the* tenants *of an apartment building.*
ten|ant (ten′ənt) *noun, plural* **tenants.**

tend[1]—**1.** To be inclined; have as a habit: *Kittens* tend *to sleep often.* **2.** To go or move in a certain direction: *This trail* tends *to the right after you pass the lake.*
tend (tend) *verb,* **tended, tending.**

tend[2]—**1.** To take care of; look after; watch over: *doctors* tending *their patients; to* tend *a garden; a worker* tending *a machine.* **2.** To apply oneself; pay attention: *to* tend *to his homework; an artist who* tends *to the details in her paintings.*
tend (tend) *verb,* **tended, tending.**

tendency—An inclination; habit: *My little brother has a* tendency *to giggle.*
tend|en|cy (ten′dən sē) *noun, plural* **tendencies.**

tender—**1.** Not hard, rough, or tough; soft: *Potatoes and carrots become* tender *when they are cooked.* **2.** Delicate or fragile: *The newborn kittens are* tender *and must be handled carefully.* **3.** Showing love; fond: *His grandfather gave him a* tender *pat on the head.* **4.** Sensitive; sore; painful: *The bump on his head is still* tender.
ten|der (ten′dər) *adjective.*
• Synonyms: **gentle, kind[1],** for **3.**
Antonyms: **bloodthirsty, brutal, cruel, violent,** for **3.**

tendon—A strong band or cord of tissue that joins a muscle to a bone or to some other body part.
ten|don (ten′dən) *noun, plural* **tendons.**

tenement—An apartment building that is in a poor part of a city, in bad condition, and too crowded.
ten|e|ment (ten′ə mənt) *noun, plural* **tenements.**

Tennessee walking horse—A breed of horse with an easy and comfortable manner of walking that makes it pleasant to ride. This horse was first bred in Tennessee, for riding.
Ten|nes|see walk|ing horse
(ten′ə sē waw′king hawrs) *noun, plural*
Tennessee walking horses.

tennis—A game in which two players or two pairs of players hit a ball back and forth over a net with rackets. It is played on a flat court made of clay, grass, or some other material.
ten|nis (ten′is) *noun.*
• See picture at **forehand** and at **backhand.**

tenor—1. A man's singing voice that is higher than bass and lower than alto. 2. A singer having such a voice. 3. Any musical instrument with a range like that of such a voice.
ten|or (ten′ər) *noun, plural* **tenors.**

tense[1]—The form of a verb that shows the time of the action or of the condition that it indicates. "She walked" is in the past tense. "She walks" is in the present tense. "She will walk" is in the future tense.
tense (tens) *noun, plural* **tenses.**

tense[2]—1. Stretched tight; strained: *He pulled on the rubber band until it was* tense *and ready to snap*. 2. Anxious; worried: *My aunt is afraid of flying and feels* tense *whenever she travels by airplane*. 3. Filled with or creating much suspense or nervousness: *We had a* tense *moment when we thought we had forgotten our keys.*
Adjective.
—To make or become tight or strained: *Every muscle in his body* tensed *as he listened to the strange noise in the darkness. Verb.*
tense (tens) *adjective,* **tenser, tensest;** *verb,*
tensed, tensing.
• Synonyms: **nervous, upset,** for *adjective* **2.**
Antonyms: **placid, tranquil,** for *adjective* **2.**

tent—A shelter that can be folded up and moved. It is made of a waterproof material, such as canvas or nylon, that is held up by one or more poles.
tent (tent) *noun, plural* **tents.**

tentacle—A long, thin, flexible limb of certain animals. It is used for feeling, grasping, or moving. The eight arms of an octopus are tentacles.
ten|ta|cle (ten′tə kəl) *noun, plural* **tentacles.**
• See picture at **octopus.**

tenth—1. Next after the ninth. 2. One of ten equal parts.
tenth (tenth) *adjective; noun, plural* **tenths.**

tepee—A cone-shaped tent made by stretching animal hides or tree bark over tall poles. Tepees were a common form of shelter for some North American Indians.
te|pee (tē′pē) *noun, plural* **tepees.**

tepee

term—1. A word or group of words that has a special meaning in connection with a certain subject: *"Base," "inning," and "home run" are baseball* terms. 2. The set period of time that a thing lasts: *She served as president of the club for a one-year* term. 3. **terms: a.** The conditions of an agreement: *The* terms *of the sale made it clear that nothing could be returned to the store.* **b.** A relationship; way of treating one another: *The three boys have been on friendly* terms *with one another for years. Noun.*
—To call; name: *The lion is often* termed *the king of beasts. Verb.*
term (turm) *noun, plural* **terms;** *verb,* **termed, terming.**

terminal—1. A station at either end of a transportation line: *an airline* terminal; *a bus* terminal. 2. A keyboard and video display unit for entering information and receiving it from a computer: *a computer* terminal.
ter|mi|nal (tur′mə nəl) *noun, plural* **terminals.**

a at	i if	oo look	ch chalk	⎧ a in ago
ā ape	ī idle	ou out	ng sing	e in happen
ah calm	o odd	u ugly	sh ship	ə = i in capital
aw all	ō oats	ū rule	th think	o in occur
e end	oi oil	ur turn	th their	⎩ u in upon
ē easy			zh treasure	

termite—A pale insect with a dark head, which looks somewhat like an ant. Termites live in large groups and eat wood, paper, and other material. They can cause much damage to books, buildings, furniture, and certain crops.
ter|mite (tur′mīt) *noun, plural* **termites**.

tern—One of a number of small sea gulls. Terns are graceful flyers and have thin bodies, long bills, pointed wings, and forked tails.
tern (turn) *noun, plural* **terns**.
● A word that sounds the same is **turn**.

terrace—1. A flat, outdoor area next to a house. It is used for relaxing or dining and is usually paved.   2. A balcony on an apartment building.   3. A flat, raised section of earth with sides that are either sloping or straight up and down. Terraces are often built one above another on a hillside for farming.
ter|race (ter′is) *noun, plural* **terraces**.

terrain—An area of land having certain natural features: *The hikers crossed the thickly wooded terrain between the lake and the mountains.*
ter|rain (tə rān′) *noun, plural* **terrains**.

terrapin—A kind of medium-sized turtle that lives in fresh water or at the edge of the sea. The meat of some terrapins is used as food.
ter|ra|pin (ter′ə pin) *noun, plural* **terrapins**.

terrarium—A container, such as a glass bowl, in which small plants are grown and in which small animals, such as salamanders or snails, may be kept.
ter|rar|i|um (tə rār′ē əm) *noun, plural* **terrariums** or **terraria** (tə rār′e ə).

terrarium

terrestrial—1. Of or having to do with the earth, considered separately from outer space: *At the museum, we saw a lunar rock and many types of terrestrial ones.*   2. Of or living on the land rather than in water or in the air: *a terrestrial animal; a terrestrial plant.*
ter|res|tri|al (tə res′trē əl) *adjective*.

terrible—1. Bringing about great fear or terror; awful: *A terrible fire swept through the city.*   2. Very bad; unpleasant: *His terrible table manners ruined our meal.*
ter|ri|ble (ter′ə bəl) *adjective*.
● Synonyms: **dreadful, horrible**, for **1**.

terrier—Any one of several species of small, energetic dogs. These dogs were originally bred to hunt small animals by driving them from their burrows.
ter|ri|er (ter′ē ər) *noun, plural* **terriers**.

terrific—1. Very great, severe, or frightful: *The terrific winds of the hurricane knocked down trees and damaged houses.*   2. Unusually good; wonderful: *We all enjoyed the terrific singing and dancing in the show.*
ter|rif|ic (tə rif′ik) *adjective*.
● Synonyms: **delightful, heavenly, marvelous, sensational**, for **2**.

terrify—To cause great terror; scare: *The loud clap of thunder terrified my dog.*
ter|ri|fy (ter′ə fī) *verb*, **terrified, terrifying**.

territory—1. An area of land; region: *unexplored territory; enemy territory.*   2. Land that is owned and ruled by a distant government.   3. An area controlled by the United States or Canada that does not have the same rights and privileges as states and provinces.
ter|ri|to|ry (ter′ə tawr′ē) *noun, plural* **territories**. Abbreviation: ter. or terr.

terror—1. Extreme fear: *The movie about the monster filled him with terror.*   2. A thing or person that creates extreme fear: *The fierce tiger is the terror of the jungle.*
ter|ror (ter′ər) *noun, plural* **terrors**.

terrorist—A person who does acts of violence in order to frighten or control people, or in order to force a government to give in to certain demands: *The newspaper said that terrorists set off a bomb in a department store yesterday.*
ter|ror|ist (ter′ər ist) *noun, plural* **terrorists**.

terse—Short and without unnecessary words or details; brief: *After his long, vague question, she gave him a terse reply, "Not today, tomorrow."*
terse (turs) *adjective*, **terser, tersest**.

test—1. A group of questions or exercises designed to measure knowledge or ability.

2. Any trial, examination, or measurement: *a scientific* test; *a test of strength. Noun.*
—To measure or examine: *This quiz will* test *your knowledge of history. Verb.*
test (test) *noun, plural* **tests;** *verb,* **tested, testing.**

testament—**1.** Written instructions regarding what to do with one's property after one dies; will. **2. Testament:** One of the two main parts of the Bible. The Christian Bible consists of the Old Testament and the New Testament. The Jewish Bible consists only of the writings in the Old Testament.
tes|ta|ment (tes′tə mənt) *noun, plural* **testaments.**

testify—To offer evidence as proof either in court or informally; state to be true: *My friends will* testify *that I left when they did.*
tes|ti|fy (tes′tə fī) *verb,* **testified, testifying**

testimony—**1.** A statement made by a witness under oath in a court of law: *Her* testimony *at the trial helped convict the criminal.* **2.** Proof of something; evidence: *Her tears were clear* testimony *of her sorrow.*
tes|ti|mo|ny (tes′tə mō′nē) *noun, plural* **testimonies.**

test tube—A thin tube of glass that is closed at one end. It is used for laboratory experiments.
test tube (test tūb) *noun, plural* **test tubes.**

tetanus—A serious disease in which the muscles get extremely stiff. It is caused by certain germs that enter the body through a wound. It can be prevented or cured through receiving a shot or medicine. Another name for this disease is **lockjaw.**
tet|a|nus (tet′ə nəs) *noun.*

tether—A length of rope or chain used as a leash to keep an animal in a certain area. *Noun.*
—To fasten with a length of rope or chain: *We* tethered *the dog to the fence post while we went for a swim. Verb.*
teth|er (teth′ər) *noun, plural* **tethers;** *verb,* **tethered, tethering.**
- **at the end of** (one's) **tether:** At the end of one's patience or strength: *He was already* at the end of *his* tether *when the chain came off his bicycle; and so he started to cry.*

text—**1.** The main part of a printed work, considered separately from such other parts as the illustrations, the table of contents, and the glossary. **2.** The actual words in a speech or written work: *The pamphlet contained the entire* text *of the state constitution.* **3.** A topic; subject; theme: *The* text *of the sermon was based on a psalm.*
text (tekst) *noun, plural* **texts.**

textbook—A book that is used for classroom study: *a science* textbook.
text|book (tekst′book′) *noun, plural* **textbooks.**

textile—**1.** A fabric; cloth. **2.** A material that is used to make a fabric. *Noun.*
—Having to do with fabrics: *My uncle sells raw cotton to the* textile *mill. Adjective.*
tex|tile (teks′təl *or* teks′tīl) *noun, plural* **textiles;** *adjective.*

texture—The look and feel of something; quality of a surface: *the smooth* texture *of leather; the sticky, lumpy* texture *of oatmeal.*
tex|ture (teks′chər) *noun, plural* **textures.**

-th—A suffix used for numbers, four and above, to indicate position in a series or one of a number of equal parts. The seventh person in line holds position number seven in the line. An eighth of a pie is one of eight equal pieces of a pie.

a at	i if	oo look	ch chalk		a in ago
ā ape	ī idle	ou out	ng sing		e in happen
ah calm	o odd	u ugly	sh ship	ə =	i in capital
aw all	ō oats	ū rule	th think		o in occur
e end	oi oil	ur turn	<u>th</u> their		u in upon
ē easy			zh treasure		

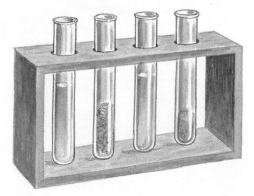

test tube

You can understand the meanings of many words that end with **-th**, if you add a meaning of the suffix to the meaning of the rest of the word.
twenty-fourth: number 24 in a series
fifth: one of five equal parts

than—1. In relation to; in comparison with: *This is a longer book* than *that one.* 2. Except: *I cannot write any other way* than *this.*
than (<u>than</u> *or* <u>thən</u>) *conjunction.*

thank—To express appreciation or gratitude to: *I want to* thank *you for your help.*
thank (thangk) *verb,* **thanked, thanking.**

thanks—1. Thank you: Thanks *for the pretty dress.* 2. Appreciation or gratitude: *How may we show our* thanks *to you?*
thanks (thangks) *noun.*

Thanksgiving Day—A national holiday in the United States and Canada. On this day, people give thanks with feasting and prayer for the good things they have received during the year. In the United States, Thanksgiving Day is celebrated on the fourth Thursday of November. In Canada, it is celebrated on the second Monday of October.
Thanks|giv|ing Day (thangks′giv′ing dā) *noun, plural* **Thanksgiving Days.**

that—1. Being the particular person, place, or thing mentioned: *I like* that *shirt you are wearing.* 2. Being the one farther away: *I will sit in this seat near the door, and you may sit in* that *one near the window. Adjective.*
—1. A particular person, place, or thing: *I think* that *is a good idea.* 2. Who or whom: *She was one of the spectators that left early.* 3. When; in which: *Do you remember the time* that *we went to the carnival? Pronoun.*
—1. **That** is used to introduce an idea which is said, thought, wished, or the like: *I think* that *he is telling the truth.* 2. **That** is used to show purpose or result: *She studied so late* that *she fell asleep in her chair. Conjunction.*
—So; to the degree, extent, or amount mentioned or indicated earlier: *I did not think the movie was* that *funny. Adverb.*
that (that *or* <u>thət</u>) *adjective; pronoun, plural* **those;** *conjunction; adverb.*

that'll—The contraction of "that will" or "that shall."
that'll (<u>that</u>′əl).

that's—The contraction of "that is" or "that has."
that's (<u>thats</u>).

thaw—1. To melt: *The sun* thawed *the snowman.* 2. To become warm until no longer frozen: *The meat did not* thaw *in time for dinner. Verb.*
—Warm weather that follows freezing weather: *the spring* thaw. *Noun.*
thaw (thaw) *verb,* **thawed, thawing;** *noun, plural* **thaws.**

the[1]—A particular one meant or shown: *Please hand me* the *pencil I just sharpened.*
the (<u>thə</u> *or* <u>thē</u>) *definite article.*

the[2]—Which one, when people or things are compared: *Our parents got to bed* the *soonest of us all.*
the (<u>thə</u> *or* <u>thē</u>) *adverb.*

theater or **theatre**—A place where movies or plays are presented.
the|a|ter or **the|a|tre** (thē′ə tər) *noun, plural* **theaters** or **theatres.**

thee—A form of the word **you** that is rarely used today: *I shall visit* thee *soon.*
thee (<u>thē</u>) *pronoun.*

theft—The act or an instance of stealing.
theft (theft) *noun, plural* **thefts.**

their—Belonging to or having to do with the ones mentioned: *It was* their *turn to take in the laundry.*
their (<u>thār</u>) *adjective.*
• Words that sound the same are **there** and **they're.**

theirs—The one or ones that belong to the people or things mentioned: *I took my books home, but they left* theirs *in school.*
theirs (<u>thārz</u>) *pronoun.*
• A word that sounds the same is **there's.**

them—The ones already mentioned: *I told my friends that I would meet* them *at the park.*
them (<u>them</u>) *pronoun.*

theme—1. The main idea in a speech or a piece of writing or art; subject: *The* theme *of the book was that small misunderstandings can lead to big problems.* 2. A written composition, such as a school assignment; essay. 3. A melody in a piece of music.
theme (thēm) *noun, plural* **themes.**

themselves—1. The people or things mentioned, when acting alone or experiencing the results of their own action: *painting the room* themselves; *no one to blame but* themselves. 2. Their real or true selves: *The children are not* themselves

when they are as tired and cranky as tonight.
them|selves (<u>them</u> selvz') *pronoun.*

then—**1.** At that time: *I remembered how shy he was* then. **2.** Soon after that: *We finished clearing the table and* then *began to wash the dishes.* **3.** Next in order of time or place: *On our street, you will see my house,* then *my neighbor's house, and* then *an open field.* **4.** In that case: *If you cannot find your mittens,* then *wear your gloves. Adverb.*
—That time: *I saw him last week, but I have not seen him since* then. *Noun.*
then (<u>then</u>) *adverb, noun.*

theology—The study of God and of religious beliefs.
the|ol|o|gy (thē ol'ə jē) *noun.*

theory—**1.** An explanation that comes from thought or observation: *a theory of why there are no more dinosaurs; the theory of evolution.* **2.** The ideas of a science or art, considered separately from the practice of it: *He could not play an instrument himself, but he enjoyed studying music theory.*
the|o|ry (the'ər ē) *noun, plural* **theories.**

therapy—The treatment of a sickness or a disability: *He rode a bicycle each day as* therapy *for his weakened leg muscles.*
ther|a|py (ther'ə pē) *noun, plural* **therapies.**

there—**1.** In or at that place: *He opened the closet and hung his coat* there. **2.** To or toward that place: *My grandmother's house is not far from mine, and I often walk* there *to see her.* **3. There** is also used in sentences in which the subject comes after the verb: *Are* there *any fish in this pond? Adverb.*
—That place: *She left the store and walked from* there *to the bus stop. Noun.*
—An expression showing feeling: *"There! The work is all finished!" Interjection.*
there (<u>th</u>ār) *adverb, noun, interjection.*
• Words that sound the same are **their** and **they're.**

thereabouts—Near that place, time, or amount: *He lost his hat in the park, or* thereabouts.
there|a|bouts (<u>th</u>ār'ə bouts') *adverb.*

therefore—Because of that: *She ate a big lunch and* therefore *was not hungry at dinner time.*
there|fore (<u>th</u>ār'fawr) *adverb.*
• Synonyms: **consequently, hence, thus**

there's—The contraction of "there is" or "there has."
there's (<u>th</u>ārz).

thermal—Of or having to do with heat: thermal *underwear to keep you warm.*
ther|mal (thur'məl) *adjective.*

thermometer—A device used to measure temperature. A thermometer is usually a glass tube containing mercury or alcohol that rises or falls in the tube as the temperature around it goes up or down.
ther|mom|e|ter (thər mom'ə tər) *noun, plural* **thermometers.**
• See Word History at **thermos.**

thermos—A container that keeps its contents hot or cold for many hours.
ther|mos (thur'məs) *noun, plural* **thermoses.**

Word History

Thermos comes from a Greek word meaning "hot." A thermos is made to prevent heat from passing in or out. Hot liquids stay hot and cold liquids stay cold for a long time inside a thermos. When a word begins with "therm-," the word usually has something to do with heat. A **thermometer** measures how hot a place, a person, or a thing is. A **thermostat** controls how hot a place, a room, or a building is.

---

thermostat—An automatic device that controls temperature. Thermostats are used in many kinds of equipment, such as ovens, refrigerators, and air conditioners.
ther|mo|stat (thur'mə stat) *noun, plural* **thermostats.**
• See Word History at **thermos.**

thesaurus—A kind of dictionary that lists groups of words that have the same meaning or opposite meanings.
the|sau|rus (thi sawr'əs) *noun, plural* **thesauruses** or **thesauri** (thi sawr'ī).

these—Nearby, or shown, or just mentioned: These *gloves are mine. Adjective.*
—The ones nearby, or shown, or just mentioned: These *are my favorite cookies. Pronoun.*
these (<u>th</u>ēz) *plural adjective, plural pronoun.*

a at	i if	oo look	ch chalk		a in ago
ā ape	ī idle	ou out	ng sing		e in happen
ah calm	o odd	u ugly	sh ship	ə =	i in capital
aw all	ō oats	ū rule	th think		o in occur
e end	oi oil	ur turn	<u>th</u> their		u in upon
ē easy			zh treasure		

they—1. The persons, animals, or things last mentioned: *The boxes are easy to carry because they are not heavy.*   2. People in general; some people: *Did they say it may rain tomorrow?*
they (th̄ā) *plural pronoun.*

they'd—The contraction of "they had" and "they would."
they'd (th̄ad).

they'll—The contraction of "they will" and "they shall."
they'll (th̄al).

they're—The contraction of "they are."
they're (th̄ar).
● Words that sound the same are **their** and **there.**

they've—The contraction of "they have."
they've (th̄av).

thick—1. Having much between the two opposite sides or surfaces; not thin: *The heavy truck rode on* thick *tires.*   2. Having a certain distance or amount between the two opposite sides or surfaces: *The pile of papers is several inches* thick.   3. Having a large number of things close together; dense: *a forest* thick *with trees.*   4. Not flowing easily: *The milk shake was so* thick *that I could hardly suck it through the straw.* *Adjective.*
—In a way that has much between opposite sides or surfaces, or that is dense: *The pie was sliced* thick. *Adverb.*
—The place that has the most activity or danger: *The boat was tossed as it sailed through the* thick *of the storm. Noun.*
thick (thik) *adjective,* **thicker, thickest;** *adverb; noun.*
■ **through thick and thin:** In both good and bad times: *The family found joy in one another through thick and thin.*

thicken—To make or become thick or thicker: *The fog* thickened *until we could barely see the road.*
thick|en (thik′ən) *verb,* **thickened, thickening.**

thicket—A group of bushes, shrubs, or small trees that grow close together.
thick|et (thik′it) *noun, plural* **thickets.**

thief—One who steals.
thief (th̄ēf) *noun, plural* **thieves.**

thieves—See **thief.**
thieves (th̄ēvz) *plural noun.*

thigh—The part of the leg that is between the knee and the hip.
thigh (th̄ī) *noun, plural* **thighs.**

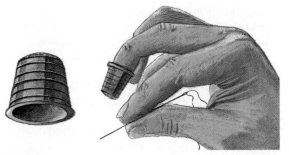

thimble

thimble—A small metal or plastic cap that is worn over a fingertip to protect it when pushing a needle in sewing.
thim|ble (thim′bəl) *noun, plural* **thimbles.**

thin—1. Having little between the two opposite sides or surfaces; not thick: *Sunlight came into the room through the* thin *curtains.*   2. Not fat; trim; slender: *The pants looked big and loose on the* thin *boy.*   3. Not set close together: *The leaves on the trees become* thin *in the fall.*
4. Not dense: *The cloud was so* thin *that I could see through it.*   5. That flows or pours easily; like water: *The paint was so* thin *that it kept dripping from the brush.*   6. Having a weak sound: *The shy girl made her speech in a* thin *voice.*   7. Easy not to believe; not convincing: *a* thin *excuse. Adjective.*
—In a way that has little between opposite sides or surfaces, or that is not dense. *She cut the slices of turkey* thin. *Adverb.*
—To make or become less thick: *The gardener* thinned *the bush by cutting some of its branches. Verb.*
thin (thin) *adjective,* **thinner, thinnest;** *adverb; verb,* **thinned, thinning.**
● Synonyms: **lean², scrawny, skinny, slender, slim,** for *adjective* 2.

thing—1. An object or a substance that can be seen, touched, heard, smelled, or tasted: *There were many good* things *to eat at the picnic.*
2. Whatever is done, spoken of, or thought of: *She laughed at the funny* things *he said.*
3. Matter; business: *At the pet show,* things *went very well.*   4. A person or animal: *That puppy is a cute* thing.   5. **things:** Personal belongings: *When he finished his work, he put his* things *away in his desk.*
thing (thing) *noun, plural* **things.**

think—1. To use the mind to have ideas or make judgments: *If you* think *carefully, you will know the right thing to do.*   2. To have an idea, opinion, or belief: *I will* think *of a way to*

surprise my brother on his birthday. **3.** To consider thoroughly; examine in the mind with care: *I need a moment to* think *the problem through.* **4.** To believe likely; expect: *I* think *it might snow.*
think (thingk) *verb,* **thought, thinking.**

third—**1.** Next after the second. **2.** One of three equal parts.
third (thurd) *adjective; noun, plural* **thirds.**

thirst—**1.** A feeling of dryness in the mouth or throat caused by the need for a drink. **2.** A wanting of something to drink: *A glass of lemonade satisfied her* thirst. *Noun.*
—To feel this sensation or this wanting. *Verb.*
thirst (thurst) *noun, plural* **thirsts;** *verb,* **thirsted, thirsting.**

thirteen—Three more than ten; one more than twelve: 13.
thir|teen (thur′tēn′) *adjective; noun, plural* **thirteens.**

thirteenth—**1.** Next after the twelfth. **2.** One of thirteen equal parts.
thir|teenth (thur′tēnth′) *adjective; noun, plural* **thirteenths.**

thirtieth—**1.** Next after the twenty-ninth. **2.** One of thirty equal parts.
thir|ti|eth (thur′tē ith) *adjective; noun, plural* **thirtieths.**

thirty—Three times ten; 30.
thir|ty (thur′tē) *adjective; noun, plural* **thirties.**

this—Nearby, shown, or just mentioned: *I hope you like* this *record. Adjective.*
—**1.** The one that is nearby, shown, or just mentioned: This *is my mother. Pronoun.*
—To the amount, degree, or extent that has been indicated: *If I had know it would be* this *cold, I would have worn a coat. Adverb.*
this (this) *adjective, plural* **these;** *pronoun, plural* **these;** *adverb.*

thistle—A plant whose stems and leaves are covered with sharp spines. The blossoms of most thistles are some shade of purple.
this|tle (this′əl) *noun, plural* **thistles.**

thorax—**1.** The part of the human body between the neck and the abdomen; chest. **2.** The part of the body of an insect between the head and the abdomen, including the legs and wings.
tho|rax (thawr′aks) *noun, plural* **thoraxes.**

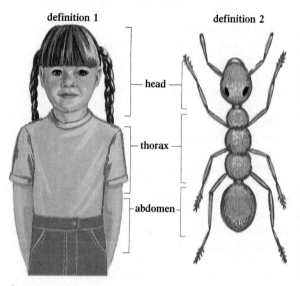

definition 1   definition 2

head

thorax

abdomen

thorax

thorn—**1.** A sharp point on a stem or branch of a plant. *Be careful of* thorns *when you cut the roses.* **2.** A plant that has such points.
thorn (thawrn) *noun, plural* **thorns.**

thorough—Being or doing all that is necessary; complete: *He did a* thorough *job of cleaning his room.*
thor|ough (thur′ō) *adjective.*

Thoroughbred—A breed of horses that is used mostly in racing. These horses were first bred in Europe in the 1600's and 1700's.
Thor|ough|bred (thur′ō bred′) *noun, plural* **Thoroughbreds.**

those—Being the persons, places, or things mentioned: *Put* those *papers on the desk. Adjective.*

thistle

a at	i if	oo look	ch chalk		a in ago
ā ape	ī idle	ou out	ng sing		e in happen
ah calm	o odd	u ugly	sh ship	ə =	i in capital
aw all	ō oats	ū rule	th think		o in occur
e end	oi oil	ur turn	th their		u in upon
ē easy			zh treasure		

—The persons, places, or things mentioned: *Are those your shoes?* Pronoun.
those (<u>th</u>ōz) *plural adjective, plural pronoun.*

thou—A form of the word **you** that is rarely used today: *"Thou shall not kill."*
thou (<u>th</u>ou) *pronoun.*

though—Despite the fact that; although: *The school play was a success, though we had expected a bigger audience. Conjunction.*
—Nevertheless; however: *Painting the fence took many hours of hard work; it was fun, though. Adverb.*
though (<u>th</u>ō) *conjunction, adverb.*

thought—1. The act of thinking: *Give the question some* thought. 2. What a person thinks; idea: *His* thought *was to go fishing. Noun.*
—See **think.** *Verb.*
thought (thawt) *noun, plural* **thoughts;** *verb.*

thousand—A hundred times ten; 1,000.
thou|sand (thou′zənd) *adjective; noun, plural* **thousands.**

thousandth—1. The last in a series of 1,000; following the 999th. 2. One of a thousand equal parts.
thou|sandth (thou′zəndth) *adjective; noun, plural* **thousandths.**

thrash—1. To beat or whip: *The man said he would* thrash *the boy if he kept missing school.* 2. To make quick, violent movements back and forth: *After thrashing around in the net, the dolphin freed itself.*
thrash (thrash) *verb,* **thrashed, thrashing.**
   Synonyms: **batter[1], maul, pelt[1],** for 1.

thread—1. A thin cord made of silk, cotton, or similar material for use in sewing. 2. A long, thin stream of water or other liquid: *a thread of water trickling down the rock.* 3. The main idea that joins together the different parts of a story or discussion: *The* thread *of the story was the friendship of the two farmers.* 4. The ridge or groove that winds around a screw. *Noun.*
—1. To put a thin cord through the eye of a needle. 2. To pass through something by going in and out in a winding, weaving manner: *We threaded our way through the thick forest. Verb.*
thread (thred) *noun, plural* **threads;** *verb,* **threaded, threading.**

threat—1. A statement that one intends to hurt or punish another: *Her* threat *to keep us after school stopped the giggling in the classroom.* 2. A warning of possible trouble: *Those dark clouds are a* threat *of rain.*
threat (thret) *noun, plural* **threats.**

threaten—1. To say that one intends to hurt or punish: *The pirate* threatened *to sink the ship.* 2. To be the cause of danger to: *Strong winds* threatened *the sailors.* 3. To be a sign or warning of: *Those dark clouds* threaten *a storm.*
threat|en (thret′ən) *verb,* **threatened, threatening.**

three—1. One more than two; one less than four; 3.
three (thrē) *adjective; noun, plural* **threes.**

thresh—To remove the grain from wheat, rye, or other cereal plants by beating.
thresh (thresh) *verb,* **threshed, threshing.**

threshold—1. The piece of wood or stone placed beneath a door. 2. A beginning point: *Space scientists believe we are at the* threshold *of travel to other planets.*
thresh|old (thresh′ōld) *noun, plural* **thresholds.**

threw—See **throw.**
threw (thrū) *verb.*
  • A word that sounds the same is **through.**

thrice—Three times: *The magician waved the wand* thrice *over the black box.*
thrice (thrīs) *adverb.*

thrifty—Careful about spending money; not wasteful: *Having to buy the things he wanted from his allowance taught him to be* thrifty.
thrift|y (thrif′tē) *adjective,* **thriftier, thriftiest.**

thrill—A strong feeling of happiness or excitement: *the* thrill *of riding the roller coaster. Noun.*
—To have or produce this feeling: *The rock star* thrilled *his fans. Verb.*
thrill (thril) *noun, plural* **thrills;** *verb,* **thrilled, thrilling.**

thrive—To grow or develop in a lively or successful way; flourish; prosper: *the puppy* thriving *in his new home; the tourist business* thriving *in the summer.*
thrive (thrīv) *verb,* **throve** or **thrived, thrived** or **thriven, thriving.**

throat—1. The front part of the neck: *She had a necklace around her* throat. 2. The passage through which food moves on its way from the mouth to the stomach: *I had a sore* throat. 3. The narrowest part of something: *The funnel had a long* throat.
throat (thrōt) *noun, plural* **throats.**
  ■ **jump down (one's) throat:** To criticize or scold in a sudden and severe way: *The manager would* jump down *her* throat *for the slightest mistake.*
  stick in (one's) throat: To be difficult to say

or accept: *The defeat in the tennis match* stuck in *my* throat *because I had expected to win.*

throb—To beat or pound, especially in a rapid or heavy way: *Her heart* throbbed *with excitement as the judge handed her the first prize.* Verb.
—A beat, especially a forceful one: *The patient suddenly felt a* throb *of pain in his shoulder.* Noun.
throb (throb) *verb,* **throbbed, throbbing;** *noun,* plural **throbs.**

throne—1. An official chair for a king, queen, bishop, or other important person that is used during ceremonies. 2. The power and authority of a king, queen, or other ruler: *Knights swore loyalty to the* throne *before going off to battle.*
throne (thrōn) *noun,* plural **thrones.**
• A word that sounds the same is **thrown.**

throng—Many people together; crowd: *A* throng *of customers were in the store. Noun.*
—To move in a crowd; fill: *We* thronged *the ice-cream shop on the hot day.*
throng (throng) *noun,* plural **throngs;** *verb,* **thronged, thronging.**
• Synonyms: **crush, multitude,** for *noun.*

throttle—A valve that controls the flow of fuel to an engine: *The pilot opened the* throttle *to get more power for takeoff.*
throt|tle (throt′əl) *noun,* plural **throttles.**

Word History

Throttle comes from an old English word meaning "throat." The throttle of an engine works in a way that is somewhat like the way the throat of a person or animal works. The engine's throttle opens and closes to control the flow of gas to the engine, just as a throat opens and closes to control the passage of food to the stomach or air to the lungs.

---

through—1. In one end or side and out the other, or from beginning to end: *an old path winding* through *the woods; to see* through *a window; to sit* through *a good movie twice.* 2. From place to place in a particular location; around: *We spent* hours wandering through *the science museum.* 3. Because of or by means of; with: *Only* through *practice will you learn to sing the song.* Preposition.
—1. From one end or side to the other: *You can go around, but not* through. 2. Finished; complete: *Everybody raced outside as soon as class was* through. 3. From its beginning to end or all the way: *to see a project* through; *to drive* through *without stopping. Adverb.*
—1. Going from one place to another without changing or stopping: *a* through *flight.*
2. Allowing free movement: *Trucks take the* through *road because it has no traffic lights.* Adjective.
through (thrū) *preposition, adverb, adjective.*
• This word is also spelled **thru.**
• A word that sounds the same is **threw.**

throughout—Everywhere; in all parts: *I looked* throughout *the house for my missing book.*
through|out (thrū out′) *preposition.*

throve—*See* **thrive.**
throve (thrōv) *verb.*

throw—1. To hurl something so that it travels a distance through the air: *She* threw *the ball to first base.* 2. To force from its place; make fall: *The earthquake caused the furniture to shake,* throwing *all the books off the table.* 3. To move fast: *He* threw *himself into the project and finished it in less than an hour.* 4. To fling aside in a careless way: *She* threw *her books on the desk and went to get a snack.* 5. To give, as an act of entertaining: *They* threw *a dinner to honor their coach.* 6. To allow someone else to win, sometimes for money and sometimes out of kindness: *His older sister* threw *the last game, allowing him to win. Verb.*
—1. The act of hurling something through the air: *The pitcher's* throw *was called a strike. Noun.* 2. A blanket or similar covering that is used to keep someone or something warm: *There was always a* throw *on the chair if someone wanted to take a nap. Noun.*
throw (thrō) *verb,* **threw, thrown, throwing;** *noun,* plural **throws.**
• Synonyms: For *verb* 1, see Synonyms at **cast.**

thrown—*See* **throw.**
thrown (thrōn) *verb.*
• A word that sounds the same is **throne.**

thru—*See* **through.**
thru (thrū) *preposition.*
• A word that sounds the same is **threw.**

a at	i if	oo look	ch chalk		a in ago
ā ape	ī idle	ou out	ng sing		e in happen
ah calm	o odd	u ugly	sh ship	ə =	i in capital
aw all	ō oats	ū rule	th think		o in occur
e end	oi oil	ur turn	<u>th</u> their		u in upon
ē easy			zh treasure		

thrush—One of a family of singing birds that includes bluebirds and robins.
thrush (thrush) *noun, plural* **thrushes.**

thrush: The wood thrush is the largest North American thrush, except for the robin.

thrust—To push forcefully: *She always* thrusts *her way to the head of the line. Verb.*
—**1.** A forceful push: *The* thrust *of the wind knocked over the chairs.* **2.** The power to drive an airplane, ship, or other vehicle. *Noun.*
thrust (thrust) *verb,* **thrust, thrusting;** *noun, plural* **thrusts.**

thud—A muffled, heavy sound: *the* thud *of a footstep on the floor above. Noun.*
—To hit with a muffled, heavy sound: *He let his notebook drop, and it* thudded *on the desk. Verb.*
thud (thud) *noun, plural* **thuds;** *verb,* **thudded, thudding.**

thug—A tough, rough person, usually one who commits crimes: *The* thug *was caught by the police and arrested for robbing the old man.*
thug (thug) *noun, plural* **thugs.**

thumb—**1.** The shortest and most separate finger on the hand. It enables a person to do many things, such as grasping and picking up objects, when it is used with the other fingers. **2.** The part of a glove or other covering for the hand that goes over this finger. *Noun.*
—To turn the pages fast with this finger: *The boy* thumbed *through the newspaper to find the sports page. Verb.*
thumb (thum) *noun, plural* **thumbs;** *verb,* **thumbed, thumbing.**
■ **all thumbs:** Very clumsy; unable to do something or unable to do it well and easily: *She was all thumbs when it came to sewing.*
stick out like a sore thumb: To be different from others, usually in a bad way: *The overgrown grass* stuck out like a sore thumb *in the neighborhood of well-trimmed lawns.*

under (one's) **thumb:** Under the direction, authority, or control of someone else: *He has them* under *his* thumb, *and they will do anything he says.*

thumbnail—The fingernail on the thumb. *Noun.*
—Very short or small; brief: *Their assignment was to write a* thumbnail *summary of five books they had read. Adjective.*
thumb|nail (thum′nāl′) *noun, plural* **thumbnails;** *adjective.*

thumbtack—A thin nail like a short pin with a large, round, flat head. *Noun.*
—To attach something with this kind of nail: *The best papers were* thumbtacked *to the bulletin board. Verb.*
thumb|tack (thum′tak′) *noun, plural* **thumbtacks;** *verb,* **thumbtacked, thumbtacking.**

thump—**1.** To make a loud, dull sound by hitting or falling on something: *The dog jumped from the bed and* thumped *onto the floor.* **2.** To go back and forth very fast; pound: *After the race, my heart was* thumping. *Verb.*
—A loud, dull sound: *the* thump *of the horse's hoof hitting the firm ground. Noun.*
thump (thump) *verb,* **thumped, thumping;** *noun, plural* **thumps.**

thunder—**1.** The loud boom and sharp crack heard when lightning strikes. **2.** A noise like this: *the* thunder *of the excited crowd; the* thunder *of running cattle. Noun.*
—**1.** To make a loud boom and sharp crack when lightning strikes: *Did you hear it* thunder *last night during the rain?* **2.** To make a noise like this: *When their father is upset, his voice* thunders *from room to room. Verb.*
thun|der (thun′dər) *noun; verb,* **thundered, thundering.**
■ **steal** (one's) **thunder: 1.** To take another's thought, idea, or plan and call it one's own: *She certainly* stole *my* thunder *when she sang the same song I was going to sing in the talent show.* **2.** To do something to earn praise that would otherwise have gone to another: *When he brought his horse to the science fair, he* stole *everyone's* thunder.

thunderstorm—Rain with lightning and thunder.
thun|der|storm (thun′dər stawrm′) *noun, plural* **thunderstorms.**

Thurs.—The abbreviation for **Thursday.**

Word History

Thursday comes from the name of a god of thunder. The ancient Romans named this day of the week for their thunder god. Then the people who lived long ago in Germany, Denmark, Sweden, and Norway changed the name. They named it for their own thunder god. That is the name we use today.

Thursday—The day of the week that follows Wednesday and comes before Friday.
Thurs|day (**thurz′**dē *or* **thurz′**dā) *noun, plural* **Thursdays.** Abbreviation: **Thurs.**

thus—1. In a certain way; as described: *There was no time to change my dirty clothes, and I had to go* thus *to dinner.* 2. And so; as a result: *Marching and playing music at the same time will be hard to do;* thus *we will need to practice.*
thus (thus) *adverb.*
   • Synonyms: **consequently, hence, therefore,** for 2.

thy—A form of the word **your** that is rarely used today: *Where is* thy *horse, Sir Knight?*
thy (thī) *adjective.*

thyme—An herb that is used to season foods.
thyme (tīm) *noun, plural* **thymes.**
   • A word that sounds the same is **time.**

Tibetan spaniel—A small dog much like the Pekingese but with a longer nose, longer legs, and less hair. It has a soft coat that feels like silk. Originally bred in Tibet, these dogs were used as watch dogs.
Ti|bet|an span|iel (ti **bet′**ən **span′**yəl) *noun, plural* **Tibetan spaniels.**

Tibetan terrier—A medium-sized dog with a long, shaggy coat, drooping ears, and a long-haired tail that curves up and over the back. These dogs were originally bred in Tibet as pets.
Ti|bet|an ter|ri|er (ti **bet′**ən **ter′**ē ər) *noun, plural* **Tibetan terriers.**

tick¹—A short, slight sound; click: *the* tick *of the clock on the stove. Noun.*
—1. To make a short, slight sound: *a watch* ticking. 2. To operate; work: *Good service is what makes this business* tick. 3. To pass along; go on: *The seconds* ticked *by slowly when he had to wait to see the dentist. Verb.*
tick (tik) *noun, plural* **ticks;** *verb,* **ticked, ticking.**

tick²—A small animal that attaches itself to the skin of other animals and uses their blood for food. It has eight legs, is related to a spider, and can carry diseases.
tick (tik) *noun, plural* **ticks.**

tick²

ticket—1. A card or similar object that lets the holder enter a certain place or see or do a certain thing: *All the* tickets *for the rock concert were sold out weeks early.* 2. A notice that one has broken a law and must pay a fine or appear in court: *a* ticket *for not stopping at a stop sign; a* ticket *for littering.* 3. A tag that gives information about something: *The sale* ticket *showed that the price had been cut in half.* 4. A group of candidates from the same political party running for office. *Noun.*
—1. To put a tag on something: *The salesperson* ticketed *the new shipment of skirts.* 2. To give notice that one has broken a law and must pay a fine or appear in court: *The police* ticketed *all the illegally parked cars. Verb.*
tick|et (**tik′**it) *noun, plural* **tickets;** *verb,* **ticketed, ticketing.**

a at	i if	oo look	ch chalk		┌ a in ago
ā ape	ī idle	ou out	ng sing		e in happen
ah calm	o odd	u ugly	sh ship	ə =	i in capital
aw all	ō oats	ū rule	th think		o in occur
e end	oi oil	ur turn	th̲ their		u in upon └
ē easy			zh treasure		

Tibetan spaniel

tickle—1. To cause someone to laugh by touching: *to tickle the child's cheek.*   2. To make happy; cause joy or delight: *Their unexpected visit* tickled *their grandmother. Verb.*
—1. A light touch: *the tickle of a feather on his nose. Noun.*
tick|le (tik′əl) *verb,* **tickled, tickling;** *noun, plural* **tickles.**
■ **tickled pink:** Extremely pleased; very excited: *She was* tickled pink *when she saw her high mark on the test.*

tidal wave—1. A huge ocean wave caused by an underwater earthquake or volcanic eruption. Such a wave is more properly called a **tsunami.** 2. An overwhelming expression of feeling or opinion: *A tidal wave of popular support swept the new mayor into office.*
tid|al wave (tī′dəl wāv) *noun, plural* **tidal waves.**

tide—1. The alternate rise and fall of oceans and other large bodies of water, caused by the pull of gravity of the sun and the moon. High and low tides each happen about twice a day.
2. Something that goes up or down in a similar way: *As vacation time approaches, there is a rising* tide *of excitement among the students.*
tide (tīd) *noun, plural* **tides.**

tidy—1. In a neat arrangement: *His* tidy *little garden had vegetables all in rows.*   2. Rather large; impressive: *She has a* tidy *sum in the bank. Adjective.*
—To straighten up; make neat: *We can have the party if we* tidy *up afterwards. Verb.*
ti|dy (tī′dē) *adjective,* **tidier, tidiest;** *verb,* **tidied, tidying.**

tie—1. To attach or fasten with a knot or bow of string, ribbon, or rope: *The sailor* tied *the boat to the dock.*   2. To connect; join together: *Love of the outdoors and things that grow* tied *the farmer to his land.*   3. To cause to have an equal score: *The game is* tied *at 32 points for each side. Verb.*
—1. Something that fastens or holds things together: *undoing the* ties *and opening the box; breaking the* ties *to my old neighborhood because of having to move away.*   2. A piece of cloth worn knotted around the neck; necktie.   3. An even score: *If the game ends in a* tie, *we must keep playing until someone scores.*   4. One of the heavy wood beams placed across and under a railroad track as support for the rails. *Noun.*
tie (tī) *verb,* **tied, tying;** *noun, plural* **ties.**

tiger—A large, meat-eating animal of the cat family. It has a yellow coat with black stripes.

Tigers are found in some parts of Asia.
ti|ger (tī′gər) *noun, plural* **tigers.**

tiger

tight—1. Firmly in place; not loose: *I can't budge the* tight *lid on this jar.*   2. Firmly drawn together: *This cloth has a* tight *weave.*   3. Fitting too snugly: *Last year's clothes are* tight *now.*
4. Hard to manage or get out of: *Owing him a big favor will put us in a* tight *spot.*   5. Not far apart; almost even: *The competition for first place is* tight.   6. Stingy; miserly: *Although she is rich, she is* tight *with her money. Adjective.*
—In a way that is firm or fixed; not to be moved easily: *closing the window* tight; *holding on* tight *to the railing. Adverb.*
tight (tīt) *adjective,* **tighter, tightest;** *adverb.*
■ **up tight:** Tense; nervous; anxious: *He would have more fun if he would relax and be less* up tight.

tightrope—A rope or wire pulled tight in the air for acrobats to balance on when performing.
tight|rope (tīt′rōp′) *noun, plural* **tightropes.**

tightrope

tights—A close-fitting, knitted covering for the lower body and legs. They are worn by dancers and acrobats and also by girls and women as regular clothes.
tights (tīts) *plural noun.*

tigress—A female tiger.
ti|gress (tī′gris) *noun, plural* **tigresses.**

tile—A piece of baked clay, plastic, or other material that is thin and flat or curved. It is used as a covering for roofs, floors, and walls, and for decoration. *Noun.*
—To put such pieces on: *They* tiled *the bottom of the swimming pool. Verb.*
tile (tīl) *noun, plural* **tiles;** *verb,* **tiled, tiling.**

till¹—Between now and a later time; between one time and another; until: *not to come back* till *Friday; staying out* till *midnight. Preposition.*
—From now to a later time; from one time to another; until: *We must work on the project* till *it is finished. Conjunction.*
till (til) *preposition, conjunction.*

till²—To plow up the soil in order to grow crops.
till (til) *verb,* **tilled, tilling.**

till³—A box, drawer, tray, or other place where money is kept in a store or bank: *An employee was caught stealing money from the* till.
till (til) *noun, plural* **tills.**

tiller—A lever at the rear of a boat attached to the rudder. Turning it from side to side steers the boat.
till|er (til′ər) *noun, plural* **tillers.**

tiller

rudder

tiller

tilt—To lean or cause to lean; slant: *to tilt the ladder against the wall; the boat* tilting *when the wave struck it. Verb.*
—A position in which one end of something is higher than the other: *The* tilt *of the table caused the pencil to roll off. Noun.*
tilt (tilt) *verb,* **tilted, tilting;** *noun, plural* **tilts.**

timber—1. Wood used in buildings, furniture, and other things; lumber. 2. A strong wood beam that is used as a support in a building: *Oak* timbers *held up the roof.* 3. A wooded area; forest: *Many acres of* timber *were burned in the forest fire.*
tim|ber (tim′bər) *noun, plural* **timbers.**

time—1. A period during which something happens or continues: *She left a short* time *ago.* 2. A historical period; age: *the* time *of knights and castles.* 3. A particular point in a period; hour and minute by the clock: *Can you tell me the* time? 4. The period needed or wanted to do something: *Do we have* time *for another game?* 5. An event or occasion; a doing or happening: *Play that song one more* time. 6. The feelings one has while experiencing something: *He had a bad* time *when his dog died. Noun.*
—1. To measure a period: *The teacher* timed *us while we took the test.* 2. To set or plan the moment or period of: *She* timed *dinner for six o'clock. Verb.*
time (tīm) *noun, plural* **times;** *verb,* **timed, timing.**
  ▪ **behind the times:** Not modern; not up-to-date: *My father's taste in music is twenty years* behind the times.
  kill time: To do something just to make time pass: *She* killed time *in the dentist's waiting room by reading a magazine.*
  mark time: To do little; get little done: *He* marked time *in a dull job for a year.*

time line—A kind of chart that shows certain events in order along a line, with the dates when the events happened.
time line (tīm līn) *noun, plural* **time lines.**

times—Multiplied by: *Two* times *three is six.*
times (tīmz) *preposition.*

timid—Lacking courage; not bold: *A rabbit is a* timid *animal.*
tim|id (tim′id) *adjective.*
  • Synonyms: **afraid, fearful**
  Antonyms: See Synonyms at **brave.**

tin—1. A soft, silver-colored metal. It is used to make other metals, such as bronze and pewter. It is a chemical element. 2. A container made of or coated with this metal: *The cook put the pie*

a at	i if	oo look	ch chalk		⌐a in ago
ā ape	ī idle	ou out	ng sing		e in happen
ah calm	o odd	u ugly	sh ship	ə =	i in capital
aw all	ō oats	ū rule	th think		o in occur
e end	oi oil	ur turn	th their		⌐u in upon
ē easy			zh treasure		

into a tin *and baked it in the oven. Noun.*
tin (tin) *noun, plural* **tins.**

tingle—To have a prickly feeling: *My fingers and toes* tingled *after being in the cold air so long. Verb.*
—A prickly feeling: *Fear caused* tingles *up and down my spine. Noun.*
tin|gle (ting′gəl) *verb,* **tingled, tingling;** *noun, plural* **tingles.**

tinker—A person whose work is to mend pots and pans. *Noun.*
—To work at something in a clumsy or useless way: *I* tinkered *with my broken radio but could not fix it. Verb.*
tink|er (ting′kər) *noun, plural* **tinkers;** *verb,* **tinkered, tinkering.**

tinkle—To make a short, high sound like a bell ringing: *Ice cubes* tinkled *in the pitcher of lemonade. Verb.*
—A short, high sound similar to the ringing of a bell: *I heard the* tinkle *of broken glass. Noun.*
tin|kle (ting′kəl) *verb,* **tinkled, tinkling;** *noun, plural* **tinkles.**

tint—**1.** A color or a shade of a color: *The man's beard was brown with several* tints *of red appearing throughout. Noun.*
—To put a little color in or on: *Our outing in the sun* tinted *my cheeks pink. Verb.*
tint (tint) *noun, plural* **tints;** *verb,* **tinted, tinting.**

tiny—Very little: *The beach is made of* tiny *grains of sand.*
ti|ny (tī′nē) *adjective,* **tinier, tiniest.**
• Synonyms: See Synonyms at **small.**
  Antonyms: See Synonyms at **big.**

-tion—A suffix that means "the act of," or "the condition of," or "the result of": Graduation is the act of graduating. Perfection is the condition of being perfect. A definition is the result of defining.

Word Power

You can understand the meanings of many words that end in **-tion,** if you add a meaning of the suffix to the meaning of the rest of the word.
  origination: the act of originating
  corruption: the condition of being corrupt
  substitution: the result of substituting

---

tip[1]—**1.** The pointed or narrow end of something: *I pressed the button with the* tip *of my finger.*
2. A small object designed to fit onto the end of

something: *The laces on my shoes have plastic* tips.
tip (tip) *noun, plural* **tips.**

tip[2]—**1.** To cause to lean or slant; tilt: *She* tipped *the box to pour out some cereal.* **2.** To fall over or cause to fall over: *the boat* tipping *and throwing us into the water; the dog* tipping *over his water dish.* **3.** To lift one's hat in greeting: *When they met on the street, he* tipped *his hat.*
tip (tip) *verb,* **tipped, tipping.**

tip[3]—**1.** Money given as a reward for service: *We gave the taxi driver a* tip *when we left her cab.*
2. A piece of important information or helpful advice: *The dentist gave me some* tips *on how to care for my teeth. Noun.*
—**1.** To give money in return for service: *She* tipped *the person who delivered our pizza a dollar.* **2.** To give a piece of information or advice: *A friend* tipped *me off that you have a skateboard for sale. Verb.*
tip (tip) *noun, plural* **tips;** *verb,* **tipped, tipping.**

tiptoe—To walk in a soft way on the toes: *He* tiptoed *through the room where his father was taking a nap. Verb.*
—The very end of the feet: *I had to stand on* tiptoe *to see over the fence. Noun.*
tip|toe (tip′tō′) *verb,* **tiptoed, tiptoeing;** *noun, plural* **tiptoes.**

tiptop—Extremely good; excellent: *She always gets* tiptop *marks in science.*
tip|top (tip′top′) *adjective.*

tire[1]—To exhaust; make weary: *The long climb up the hill* tired *us.*
tire (tīr) *verb,* **tired, tiring.**

tire[2]—A ring that surrounds a wheel, made of rubber or other material. It can be solid or inflated with air. *Automobiles have four* tires.
tire (tīr) *noun, plural* **tires.**

tired—Needing rest; lacking energy: *He was* tired *from running up all those steps.*
tired (tīrd) *adjective.*

tiresome—Boring; dull: *He thinks washing dishes is a* tiresome *task.*
tire|some (tīr′səm) *adjective.*

tissue—**1.** A large number of living cells that are alike and that together form a certain part of a living thing: *Muscle* tissue *moves the bodies of animals.* **2.** A piece of soft paper that can absorb liquid and that serves as a handkerchief: *He blew his nose on a* tissue.
tis|sue (tish′ū) *noun, plural* **tissues.**

title—1. The name of a book, film, play, piece of music, or the like: *The title of my poem is "Clouds."* 2. A word or phrase, often attached to someone's name, that shows the person's official position: *His titles are "Professor" and "Doctor."* 3. In sports, the position of first place: *She won the women's tennis title.* 4. The legal ownership of property.
ti|tle (tī′təl) *noun, plural* **titles.**

tn.—The abbreviation for **ton** or **tons.**

to—1. Toward; in the direction of: *He drove to the city.* 2. Until something is reached; as far as: *He was dressed in black from head to toe.* 3. Until; as long as: *school from nine to three.* 4. Into the state or condition of: *The wind tore the flag to ribbons.* 5. Belonging with; accompanied by: *Here is the top to the box.* 6. Against; compared to: *They won, 21 to 14.* 7. **To** shows one that receives, or that something is done for: *He handed his homework to the teacher.* 8. **To** is used with verbs: *She wants to be a doctor.*
to (tū *or* tə) *preposition.*
• Words that sound the same are **too** and **two.**

toad—A small animal that looks like a frog but has a bumpy skin and short hind legs. Toads lay their eggs in water, but live mostly on land.
toad (tōd) *noun, plural* **toads.**

toad

toadstool—A mushroom, especially a poisonous one or one that cannot be eaten.
toad|stool (tōd′stūl′) *noun, plural* **toadstools.**

toast¹—Bread heated until it turns brown. *Noun.*
—1. To heat a food until it turns brown: *She*

toasted *a cheese sandwich for lunch.* 2. To warm; heat: *We toasted ourselves in the sunshine after swimming. Verb.*
toast (tōst) *noun; verb,* **toasted, toasting.**

toast²—An act of drinking performed as a way of showing good wishes, respect, or celebration: *We drank a toast to him on his birthday. Noun.*
—To drink in honor or celebration of someone or something: *We toasted her graduation. Verb.*
toast (tōst) *noun, plural* **toasts;** *verb,* **toasted, toasting.**

Word History

Toast¹ comes from a Latin word meaning "to dry out." **Toast²** comes from an old custom. At one time, drinks were flavored with little pieces of spiced toast.

---

toaster—A small kitchen appliance used for heating bread and other foods.
toast|er (tōs′tər) *noun, plural* **toasters.**

tobacco—The leaves of a plant that are made into products for smoking or chewing. Tobacco is smoked in cigars, cigarettes, and pipes.
to|bac|co (tə bak′ō) *noun, plural* **tobaccos** or **tobaccoes.**

toboggan—A long, flat-bottomed sled with no runners, designed to seat more than one person. Its front end curves up, and there are often low rails along each side. *Noun.*
—To ride on such a sled: *We spent the afternoon tobogganing with friends. Verb.*
to|bog|gan (tə bog′ən) *noun, plural* **toboggans;** *verb,* **tobogganed, tobogganing.**

a at	i if	oo look	ch chalk		a in ago
ā ape	ī idle	ou out	ng sing		e in happen
ah calm	o odd	u ugly	sh ship	ə =	i in capital
aw all	ō oats	ū rule	th think		o in occur
e end	oi oil	ur turn	th their		u in upon
ē easy			zh treasure		

toboggan

today—1. This present 24-hour period: *Is today Monday?*   2. The present time: *Today many people have radios.* Noun.
—1. On or for this present 24-hour period: *My report is due today.*   2. At the present time; now: *Today robots do that job.* Adverb.
to|day (tə dā′) *noun; adverb.*

toddler—A child who is learning to walk or who has just learned to walk.
tod|dler (tod′lər) *noun, plural* **toddlers.**

toe—1. One of the small parts at the front end of a foot.   2. The section of a shoe or stocking that covers the front end of a foot: *You scuffed the toe of your shoe when you kicked the ball.*
toe (tō) *noun, plural* **toes.**
■ **on (one's) toes:** Ready to act; alert: *The teacher gives quizzes to keep us on our toes.*
toe the line or **toe the mark:** To keep strictly to the rules: *Our team has to toe the line.*
● A word that sounds the same is **tow.**

toenail—The thin, hard layer growing at the top of the end of a toe.
toe|nail (tō′nāl′) *noun, plural* **toenails.**

toffee—Candy made of sugar and butter, boiled together. When it hardens, it becomes crisp.
tof|fee (tawf′ē) *noun, plural* **toffees.**

tofu—A soft food, somewhat like cheese, made from soybeans. Tofu is used in Oriental and vegetarian cooking.
to|fu (tō′fū) *noun.*

toga—An outer garment draped in a loose fashion that was worn by men in ancient Rome.
to|ga (tō′gə) *noun, plural* **togas.**

toga

together—1. With each other: *He and I ride to work* together.   2. With cooperation; in an agreeable way: *We worked* together *to plan the party.*   3. Into a group, mass, or body: *putting a puzzle* together.   4. Taken or thought of as a whole: *I like you better than all my other friends put* together.
to|geth|er (tə geth′ər) *adverb.*

toil—Hard labor; steady hard work or effort: *It took many years of* toil *to build that dam.* Noun.
—To work hard; make a great effort: *The farmers* toiled *in the hot sun to bring in the harvest.* Verb.
toil (toil) *noun; verb,* **toiled, toiling.**

toilet—A bathroom bowl with a seat. The toilet is used for body wastes, which are washed away with water.
toi|let (toi′lit) *noun, plural* **toilets.**

token—1. Something that is a sign of another thing: *The groom gave the bride a ring as a* token *of his love.*   2. Something that is used to help remember: *I kept one shell as a* token *of my summer by the ocean.*   3. A small, flat piece of metal or plastic. Tokens are sold for use in place of money to pay train, bus, or subway fares.
to|ken (tō′kən) *noun, plural* **tokens.**
● Synonyms: **keepsake, memento, reminder, souvenir,** for 2.

told—*See* **tell.**
told (tōld) *verb.*

tolerant—Willing to let others hold to beliefs or practices that are different from or opposed to one's own: *She was* tolerant *of his opinion even though she didn't agree with him.*
tol|er|ant (tol′ər ənt) *adjective.*

tolerate—To put up with; endure: *He couldn't* tolerate *her teasing any longer.*
tol|er|ate (tol′ə rāt′) *verb,* **tolerated, tolerating.**
● Synonyms: **abide, bear², stand**

toll¹—To sound a series of slow, regular chimes: *The great bell in the tower clock* tolled *eleven.* Verb.
—A chime made by ringing a bell: *The* toll *of the lighthouse bell could be heard throughout the village.* Noun.
toll (tōl) *verb,* **tolled, tolling;** *noun, plural* **tolls.**

toll²—A payment collected for the right to do or use something. Tolls are sometimes charged for the use of roads, bridges, or tunnels.
toll (tōl) *noun, plural* **tolls.**

tomahawk—A hatchet carried by some North

tomahawk

American Indians as a weapon or tool.
tom|a|hawk (tom′ə hawk) *noun, plural*
tomahawks.

tomato—A juicy, red or yellow fruit that is eaten
raw or cooked. Tomatoes grow on vines.
to|ma|to (tə mā′tō *or* tə **mah**′tō) *noun, plural*
tomatoes.

tomb—A grave, building, or special room in
which a dead body is placed. It can be either
under or above the ground.
tomb (tūm) *noun, plural* **tombs.**

tombstone—A stone, usually with words carved
in it, placed to mark a tomb.
tomb|stone (tūm′stōn′) *noun, plural*
tombstones.

tomcat—A male cat.
tom|cat (tom′kat′) *noun, plural* **tomcats.**

tomorrow—**1.** The day following today: *It is
raining tonight, but* tomorrow *should be sunny.*
2. The future: *the world of* tomorrow. *Noun.*
—On the day following today: *I hope to see you
again* tomorrow. *Adverb.*
to|mor|row (tə mawr′ō *or* tə mor′ō) *noun,
plural* **tomorrows;** *adverb.*

Word History

Tomorrow comes from two old English words
that mean ''to the morning.'' Tomorrow is the
day that begins the next morning after today.

---

tom-tom—A small drum.
tom|tom (tom′tom′) *noun, plural* **tom-toms.**

ton—A unit of weight equal to 2,000 pounds (907
kilograms) in the United States and Canada. In
the United Kingdom, a ton is equal to 2,240
pounds (1,016 kilograms). A metric ton is equal
to 1,000 kilograms (2,205 pounds).
ton (tun) *noun, plural* **tons.**

tone—**1.** A noise described by how it sounds: *a
whining* tone; *soft* tones *of the singer.* **2.** In
music, the difference in pitch between two notes.
3. A particular style or quality: *Paper decorations
and bowls of pink punch gave a festive* tone *to
the room.* **4.** A shade of a color: *an outfit in*
tones *of blue.*
tone (tōn) *noun, plural* **tones.**

tongs—A tool with two arms that open and close
to grip something: *ice-cube* tongs.
tongs (tongz *or* tawngz) *plural noun.*

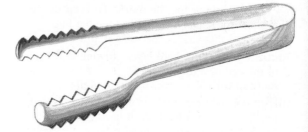

tongs

tongue—**1.** The movable body part attached to the
bottom of the mouth. In humans, it is used to
help in tasting and swallowing food and drink,
and to form sounds. **2.** This part of an animal
cooked and eaten as meat. **3.** The power of
speech: *She suffered from stage fright but
suddenly found her* tongue *and spoke her lines.*
4. A language, especially a spoken language: *My
native* tongue *is English.*
tongue (tung) *noun, plural* **tongues.**

tom-tom

tom-tom

a at	i if	oo look	ch chalk	⎡ a in ago
ā ape	ī idle	ou out	ng sing	e in happen
ah calm	o odd	u ugly	sh ship	ə = i in capital
aw all	ō oats	ū rule	th think	o in occur
e end	oi oil	ur turn	th their	⎣ u in upon
ē easy			zh treasure	

■ **hold** (one's) **tongue:** To keep quiet: *He wanted to argue with her but managed to* hold *his* tongue.

on the tip of (one's) **tongue:** About to be spoken; ready to be said at any moment: *My cousin has hundreds of baseball facts* on the tip of *his* tongue.

tongue in cheek: Not seriously or sincerely; with humor or exaggeration: *Did she really like my hat, or was she saying that* tongue in cheek?

tongue-tied—Unable to speak, usually because of shyness, embarrassment, or surprise: *When I finally stood face to face with my favorite actress, I was too* tongue-tied *to say a word.*
tongue|tied (tung′tīd′) *adjective.*

tonight—This present night; the night following this present day: *Did you forget that* tonight *is Saturday? Noun.*
—On or during this present night or the night following this present day: *I want to read this book* tonight. *Adverb.*
to|night (tə nīt′) *noun, adverb.*

tonsil—One of two oval lumps of body tissue, located one on each side of the back of the throat, behind the tongue.
ton|sil (ton′səl) *noun, plural* **tonsils.**

tonsillitis—A condition in which the tonsils become swollen and painful.
ton|sil|li|tis (ton′sə lī′tis) *noun.*

too—**1.** Also; besides: *There are apples in that bowl, and there are some bananas,* too. **2.** More than what is good or right; more than should be: *I am* too *tired to go bowling.*
too (tū) *adverb.*
● Words that sound the same are **to** and **two.**
● Synonyms: **furthermore, likewise, moreover,** for **1.**

took—*See* **take.**
took (took) *verb.*

tool—**1.** A device powered by hand or by electricity, used to do some kind of work; instrument: *She knows how to use a saw, a hammer, a drill, and other* tools. **2.** A thing, person, or group used to do some kind of work: *A dictionary is a* tool *for learning about words. Noun.*
—To make, shape, or decorate with such a device: *She carefully* tooled *a design on the top of the wooden box. Verb.*
tool (tūl) *noun, plural* **tools;** *verb,* **tooled, tooling.**

toot—A short blast on a horn or whistle. *Noun.*
—To blow or sound a horn or whistle in short blasts: *She* tooted *on the trumpet to awaken the other campers. Verb.*
toot (tūt) *noun, plural* **toots;** *verb,* **tooted, tooting.**

tooth—**1.** Any one of several hard objects like bones along the edges of the mouth, used for biting and chewing. **2.** Something that looks or works like this body part: *the* teeth *of a comb; a* tooth *of a rake.*
tooth (tūth) *noun, plural* **teeth.**
■ **tooth and nail:** With every available weapon; with every resource at one's command: *The doctors fought* tooth and nail *to save the patient's life.*

toothache—A pain in or near a tooth.
tooth|ache (tūth′āk′) *noun, plural* **toothaches.**

toothbrush—A small brush with a handle, used to clean the teeth.
tooth|brush (tūth′brush′) *noun, plural* **toothbrushes.**

toothpaste—A soft, thick substance made for use in cleaning the teeth.
tooth|paste (tūth′pāst′) *noun, plural* **toothpastes.**

toothpick—A small, pointed piece of wood or plastic used to remove bits of food from between the teeth.
tooth|pick (tūth′pik′) *noun, plural* **toothpicks.**

top¹—**1.** The part or piece that is above the rest of something: *the* top *of the hill; the* top *of my desk.* **2.** The position or rank above all others: *Her bowling score put her at the* top *of the league.* **3.** The greatest degree possible: *quarreling at the* top *of their voices.* **4.** A garment, or the part of a garment, worn on the upper half of the body: *the* top *of the overalls; a* top *to match her skirt. Noun.*
—**1.** About, at, or forming the part or piece above the rest: *the* top *rung of the ladder.* **2.** Greatest in amount or degree: *The baker set the oven at its* top *temperature. Adjective.*
—**1.** To supply with an upper surface or add something to an upper surface: *He* topped *the pizza with cheese and sausage.* **2.** To be on or at the upper part or to form such a part: *whipped cream* topping *the ice cream.* **3.** To achieve more or be better than: *He* topped *my story with a better one. Verb.*
top (top) *noun, plural* **tops;** *adjective; verb,* **topped, topping.**

top²—A child's toy that has a point at the bottom on which it spins.
top (top) *noun, plural* **tops.**

topic—A subject; matter; theme: *The topic of space travel interests most people.*
top|ic (top′ik) *noun, plural* **topics.**

topple—To fall or cause to fall: *A big wave toppled my sand castle.*
top|ple (top′əl) *verb,* **toppled, toppling.**

tops—The best or greatest: *He thinks that singer is tops, and he owns all her records.*
tops (tops) *adjective.*

topsoil—The top layer of soil, which is the richest for growing crops.
top|soil (top′soil′) *noun.*

topsy-turvy—1. Upside down: *The acrobat hung topsy-turvy from the trapeze.* 2. In a condition of confusion: *Everything on my desk is piled topsy-turvy.*
top|sy-tur|vy (top′sē tur′vē) *adverb.*

Torah—1. The Old Testament in the Bible. 2. The first five books of the Old Testament.
To|rah (tawr′ə) *noun.*

torch—1. A piece of wood or another object that is burned to give light, often held in the hand. 2. A tool that throws out a hot flame that can soften or melt metal.
torch (tawrch) *noun, plural* **torches.**

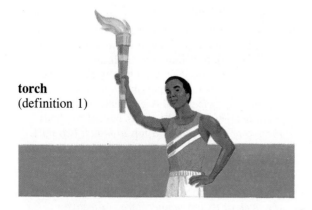

torch
(definition 1)

tore—*See* **tear.**
tore (tawr) *verb.*

torment—To cause severe pain or suffering to: *Flies* tormented *the old horse. Verb.*
—Severe pain or suffering: *His infected ear*

caused him several days of extreme torment. *Noun.*
tor|ment (tawr ment′ for *verb;* **tawr**′ment for *noun) verb,* **tormented, tormenting;** *noun, plural* **torments.**

torn—*See* **tear.**
torn (tawrn) *verb.*

tornado—A violent wind that spins around in a funnel-shaped column. When its narrow end moves across the ground, it can destroy anything in its path.
tor|na|do (tawr nā′dō) *noun, plural* **tornadoes** or **tornados.**

torpedo—A large cylinder shaped like a bullet that is filled with explosives and is designed to move underwater by its own power. Torpedoes are fired at enemy ships from ships, submarines, or low-flying airplanes. *Noun.*
—To hit with one or more of these weapons: *Enemy aircraft* torpedoed *the submarine. Verb.*
tor|pe|do (tawr pē′dō) *noun, plural* **torpedoes;** *verb,* **torpedoed, torpedoing.**

torrent—A strong rush or downpour of water or other liquid: *The rain came down in* torrents.
tor|rent (tawr′ənt) *noun, plural* **torrents.**

tortilla—A baked bread made from corn meal or flour that is shaped like a very thin pancake.
tor|til|la (tawr tē′yə) *noun, plural* **tortillas.**

tortoise—A land turtle with a high rounded shell and short, thick legs.
tor|toise (tawr′təs) *noun, plural* **tortoises** or **tortoise.**

tortoise

torture—1. The act of causing great pain on purpose. 2. Severe physical or emotional pain. *Noun.*
—To cause great pain on purpose. *Verb.*
tor|ture (tawr′chər) *noun, plural* **tortures;** *verb,* **tortured, torturing.**

toss—1. To throw in an easy way; fling: *We* tossed *the ball around while we waited.* 2. To throw around or be thrown around: *The equipment in the back of the truck* tossed *and*

a at	i if	oo look	ch chalk		a in ago
ā ape	ī idle	ou out	ng sing		e in happen
ah calm	o odd	u ugly	sh ship	ə =	i in capital
aw all	ō oats	ū rule	th think		o in occur
e end	oi oil	ur turn	th their		u in upon
ē easy			zh treasure		

turned as we drove up the bumpy road. **3.** To mix with a few light strokes: *Use the wooden spoons to* toss *the salad.* **4.** To flip a coin to settle something: *We* tossed *to see who would pay. Verb.*

—**1.** A throw: *She caught the* toss, *and the runner was out.* **2.** The flip of a coin to settle something: *Our team won the* toss. *Noun.*

toss (taws) *verb,* **tossed, tossing;** *noun, plural* **tosses.**

• Synonyms: See Synonyms at **cast.**

total—Whole; complete: *It took four weeks to finish the* total *project. Adjective.*

—Sum; whole amount: *Our club has a* total *of $25 in its treasury. Noun.*

—**1.** To figure the sum of; add: *After we* total *these figures, we can draw up a budget.* **2.** To be an amount that results from adding figures together: *With tax, the cost* totals *eight dollars exactly. Verb.*

to|tal (tō′təl) *adjective; noun, plural* **totals;** *verb,* **totaled, totaling.**

totem—An animal or other natural thing used as a symbol of a family or tribe, especially among American Indians.

to|tem (tō′təm) *noun, plural* **totems.**

toucan—A colorful bird with a very large brightly colored beak.

tou|can (tū′kan) *noun, plural* **toucans.**

toucan

touch—**1.** To feel with some part of the body: *The radiator was too hot to* touch. **2.** To make contact; bring against or be against: touching *his handkerchief to his face; leaves* touching *as they fall.* **3.** To affect emotionally; move: *His story was very sad and* touched *everyone who read it. Verb.*

—**1.** Contact, especially when feeling something

with part of the body: *Her gentle* touch *calmed the frightened animal.* **2.** The sense that works by contact with the body: *The old coat was rough to the* touch. **3.** A little bit; trace: *She felt a* touch *of envy when she saw her sister wearing a new outfit.* **4.** Communication; closeness: *He calls every week to stay in* touch *with his grandmother. Noun.*

touch (tuch) *verb,* **touched, touching;** *noun, plural* **touches.**

touchdown—In football, the act of getting the ball over the other team's goal line, by which six points are scored.

touch|down (tuch′doun′) *noun, plural* **touchdowns.**

tough—**1.** Difficult to cut, tear, break, or damage: *The puppy chewed on the* tough *bone.* **2.** Able to endure difficulty; strong: *Explorers need to be brave and* tough. **3.** Difficult; hard: *Even though I studied, this test is still* tough. **4.** Rough; likely to get into trouble: *The* tough *student was suspended from school after the fight. Adjective.*

tough (tuf) *adjective,* **tougher, toughest.**

tour—To visit several different places: *We enjoyed* touring *your city. Verb.*

—A trip to several places: *Their* tour *took them to seven countries. Noun.*

tour (toor) *verb,* **toured, touring;** *noun, plural* **tours.**

tourist—One who travels for enjoyment.

tour|ist (toor′ist) *noun, plural* **tourists.**

tournament—A sporting event involving a series of matches.

tour|na|ment (tur′nə mənt *or* toor′nə mənt) *noun, plural* **tournaments.**

tourniquet—Something that is pressed tightly to stop bleeding. A common tourniquet for an arm or leg is a bandage tightened with a stick.

tour|ni|quet (tur′nə ket) *noun, plural* **tourniquets.**

tow—To haul by attaching a rope or cable to something and pulling it along: *We will have to* tow *the car home if it will not start.*

tow (tō) *verb,* **towed, towing.**

• A word that sounds the same is **toe.**

toward or **towards**—**1.** In the direction of: *She pointed the telescope* toward *the evening star.* **2.** Regarding; in connection with: *How do you feel* toward *summer school?* **3.** Near in time; close to: *She arrived* toward *the end of class.* **4.** As part of; for: *raising money* toward *a new church building.*

to|ward *or* to|wards (tawrd *or* tawrdz *or* tə **wawrd**′ *or* tə **wawrdz**′) *preposition.*

towel—A piece of cloth or paper used for wiping or drying: *a hand* towel; *a dish* towel. *Noun.*
—To wipe or dry with such a piece: *Dad* toweled *the baby after her bath. Verb.*
tow|el (tou′əl) *noun, plural* **towels**; *verb,* **toweled, toweling.**

tower—A high, thin structure that stands alone or is part of a building. *Noun.*
—To rise high; be very tall: *The mountains* towered *over the village below. Verb.*
tow|er (tou′ər) *noun, plural* **towers**; *verb,* **towered, towering.**

town—A place where a number of people live, larger than a village but smaller than a city. *Noun.*
town (toun) *noun, plural* **towns**; *adjective.*

toxic—Very bad for health; poisonous: toxic *fumes*; toxic *wastes.*
tox|ic (tok′sik) *adjective.*

toy—Something made to be played with. *Noun.*
—To play carelessly: toying *with her dinner. Verb.*
toy (toi) *noun, plural* **toys**; *verb,* **toyed, toying.**

trace—1. A sign of something that is now gone: *You can still see* traces *of last year's fire in the woods.* **2.** A little amount; tiny bit: *Just a* trace *of ice cream remained in the bowl. Noun.*
—**1.** To find by following tracks or other signs: *They used the ripples to* trace *the fish through the water.* **2.** To make a copy by drawing lines on a second piece of paper laid on top: *She* traced *the picture so she could color it again. Verb.*
trace (trās) *noun, plural* **traces**; *verb,* **traced, tracing.**

track—1. Metal bars on which railroad trains run. **2.** A mark left by something or someone, such as a footprint: *We followed their* tracks *in the mud.* **3.** A trail or path: *a* track *through the forest.* **4.** A way like a road, made for racing: *a horse* track. **5.** A group of sports including contests of running, jumping, and throwing: *The pole vault is his favorite event in* track. *Noun.*
—**1.** To follow prints of an animal or person: *The hunters were unable to* track *the deer.* **2.** To mark with footprints: *She* tracked *mud all over*

the clean floor and had to wash it again. Verb.
track (trak) *noun, plural* **tracks**; *verb,* **tracked, tracking.**

tract—1. An area of land or water. **2.** A system of organs and other parts of the body that are related because they carry out a certain function: *the digestive* tract.
tract (trakt) *noun, plural* **tracts.**

traction—Friction between something and the surface it moves on, which prevents slipping: *We put sand on the icy road to give the car wheels better* traction.
trac|tion (trak′shən) *noun.*

tractor—1. A powerful vehicle with large, heavy rear tires or two continuous metal belts for moving. It is used to pull farm machinery or other heavy loads. **2.** A small similar vehicle used for lawn and garden work.
trac|tor (trak′tər) *noun, plural* **tractors.**

tractor (definition 2)

trade—1. The exchange of goods for money or other goods in a society; commerce. **2.** A giving of one thing in return for another: *The girls made a* trade *of their bicycles for a day.* **3.** A type of work or business: *I have a brother whose* trade *is plumbing. Noun.*
—**1.** To exchange goods for money or other goods: *This country* trades *with many foreign countries.* **2.** To exchange: *I will* trade *you my comic books for your hamster cage. Verb.*
trade (trād) *noun, plural* **trades**; *verb,* **traded, trading.**
• Synonyms: **career, occupation, profession, vocation,** for *noun* 3; **barter, exchange, swap,** for *verb* 2.

trademark—A symbol put on a product to show who made it. It is registered with the government

a at	i if	oo look	ch chalk		ə =	a in ago
ā ape	ī idle	ou out	ng sing			e in happen
ah calm	o odd	u ugly	sh ship			i in capital
aw all	ō oats	ū rule	th think			o in occur
e end	oi oil	ur turn	<u>th</u> their			u in upon
ē easy			zh treasure			

to protect it from illegal use by others.

trade|mark (trād′mahrk′) *noun, plural* **trademarks.**

tradition—Beliefs, stories, or customs taught by each generation to the next. *Eating turkey is my favorite Thanksgiving* tradition.

tra|di|tion (trə dish′ən) *noun, plural* **traditions.**

Word History

Tradition comes from a Latin word meaning "to hand over." Traditions are passed from one generation to the next as though they were objects handed over from parent to child. However, "to hand over" can have another meaning, and **treason** also comes from the same Latin word. To hand over a fort or information to an enemy is treason to one's country.

---

traditional—Following traditions: *a traditional holiday feast.*

tra|di|tion|al (trə dish′ə nəl) *adjective.*

traffic—1. People or vehicles traveling close together: *Traffic is slow today because it is raining.* 2. The act of buying and selling: *Traffic in smuggled goods is illegal. Noun.*
—To trade in; buy and sell: *They* traffic *in fruits and vegetables at this market. Verb.*

traf|fic (traf′ik) *noun; verb,* **trafficked, trafficking.**

tragedy—1. A play, movie, novel, or other story that has a sad ending. 2. A very sad event; disaster.

trag|e|dy (traj′ə dē) *noun, plural* **tragedies.**
• Synonyms: **calamity, catastrophe,** for **2.**

tragic—1. Having to do with a written or performed tragedy: *He is a good* tragic *actor.* 2. Very sad; bringing disaster: *a* tragic *accident; a* tragic *mistake.*

trag|ic (traj′ik) *adjective.*

trail—1. A path in the country: *a trail through the mountains.* 2. A track of any sort left by a person or animal that has passed by: *a trail of peanut shells.* 3. A scent left by a person or animal that has passed by: *The dogs were on the* trail *of the rabbit.* 4. Something that follows: *a* trail *of dust behind a wagon. Noun.*
—1. To follow a track or scent left by an animal or person: *hunters* trailing *a leopard.* 2. To follow behind: *to* trail *the leader in a race; smoke* trailing *the locomotive.* 3. To drag or be dragged along: *The boy* trailed *his jacket into his room.* 4. To move along slowly: *hikers* trailing

back toward the camp. 5. To be losing to another player or team: *We* trail *by ten points.* 6. To grow along the ground or another surface: *Vines* trailed *over the door of the deserted cottage. Verb.*

trail (trāl) *noun, plural* **trails;** *verb,* **trailed, trailing.**

trailer—A vehicle that moves by being pulled by a truck or a car.

trail|er (trā′lər) *noun, plural* **trailers.**

train—1. A locomotive and the railroad cars connected to it. 2. A line of traveling people, animals, or vehicles: *a train of covered wagons.* 3. The part that drags behind something such as a gown or a robe. 4. A series in order; sequence: *the train of thought leading to my decision. Noun.*
—1. To guide someone's actions and ideas: *The teacher* trained *his students not to interrupt each other.* 2. To teach or study: *He* trained *to be an electrician.* 3. To make or become fit for an athletic event: *She* trained *hard for the track meet.* 4. To get something to turn in a certain direction: *a vine* trained *to grow up a wall. Verb.*

train (trān) *noun, plural* **trains;** *verb,* **trained, training.**

training—1. Education in a certain profession, art, or trade: *His training was in classical music.* 2. The development of physical fitness through diet and exercise: *Her training is to run for an hour every day. Noun.*

train|ing (trān′ing) *noun, plural* **trainings.**

trait—A special way that someone or something is, looks, or behaves; special quality: *One of her best* traits *is her courage.*

trait (trāt) *noun, plural* **traits.**
• Synonyms: **characteristic, feature**

traitor—A person who betrays a country, a person, or a group.

trai|tor (trā′tər) *noun, plural* **traitors.**

tramp—1. To walk with a heavy step: *She got angry and* tramped *up the stairs.* 2. To step on something heavily; trample: *The children were careless and* tramped *on the flowers in the garden.* 3. To go by foot; hike: *The soldiers* tramped *through the fields. Verb.*
—1. A loud sound of feet: *the* tramp *of the marching band.* 2. A person without a home or a job, who wanders about begging for food and other needs. *Noun.*

tramp (tramp) *verb,* **tramped, tramping;** *noun, plural* **tramps.**

trample—To walk with heavy steps on something: *The grass cannot grow there because*

too many people trample *it as they pass.*
tram|ple (tram′pəl) *verb,* **trampled, trampling.**

trampoline—A sheet of canvas or similar material that is stretched and held by large springs fastened to a metal frame. It is used for jumping and exercises.
tram|po|line (tram′pə lēn′ *or* tram′pə lin) *noun, plural* **trampolines.**

trampoline

trance—1. A condition similar to sleep, in which a person's mind seems not to be in control of the body: *He was hypnotized and went into a* trance. 2. A dreamy condition in which a person is full of thought.
trance (trans) *noun, plural* **trances.**

tranquil—Peaceful; calm; placid: *Mornings at the lake are very* tranquil.
tran|quil (trang′kwəl *or* tran′kwəl) *adjective,* **tranquiler, tranquilest.**

tranquilizer—A drug used to make a person or animal feel calm and less nervous.
tran|quil|iz|er (trang′kwə lī′zər *or* tran′kwə lī′zər) *noun, plural* **tranquilizers.**

transaction—The process of carrying on: *the* transaction *of business.*

trans|ac|tion (tran zak′shən) *noun, plural* **transactions.**

transfer—To shift from one to another: *I transfer to a different bus here. Verb.*
—1. The act of shifting from one to another: *a* transfer *to a new school; a* transfer *of cargo from a ship to a train.* 2. A piece of paper that lets one change to another public vehicle: *Did you get a* transfer *from the bus driver? Noun.*
trans|fer (trans fur′ *or* trans′fur for *verb;* trans′fur for *noun*) *verb,* **transferred, transferring;** *noun, plural* **transfers.**

transform—1. To change; turn something to another form: *Exercise* transformed *him from a weak, fat man to a strong, thin one.*
trans|form (trans fawrm′) *verb,* **transformed, transforming.**

transfusion—The act of transferring blood from one person or animal to another.
trans|fu|sion (trans fyū′zhən) *noun, plural* **transfusions.**

transistor—A tiny device used in electronic equipment, such as computers, radios, and televisions.
tran|sis|tor (tran zis′tər) *noun, plural* **transistors.**

transit—1. The process of going from one place to another: *The clerk marked our suitcases so they would not be lost in* transit. 2. Public transportation: *The* transit *system has raised fares on the buses.*
tran|sit (tran′zit) *noun.*

transition—A change from one condition, thing, place, activity, or idea to another: *The* transition *from a rainy day to a sunny one took only one hour.*
tran|si|tion (tran zish′ən) *noun, plural* **transitions.**

translate—To change from one language into another: *That popular Spanish novel has just been* translated *into English, so now I can read it.*
trans|late (trans lāt′) *verb,* **translated, translating.**

translation—1. The process of changing from one language into another: *The* translation *of that huge book from English into Japanese may take years.* 2. Something that has been changed from one language into another: *The English* translation *is not as good as the original French version of the book.*
trans|la|tion (trans lā′shən) *noun, plural* **translations.**

a at	i if	oo look	ch chalk		⌈ a in ago
ā ape	ī idle	ou out	ng sing		e in happen
ah calm	o odd	u ugly	sh ship	ə =	i in capital
aw all	ō oats	ū rule	th think		o in occur
e end	oi oil	ur turn	th their		⌊ u in upon
ē easy			zh treasure		

transmission—**1.** The process of sending along: *the* transmission *of electricity through wires.* **2.** The part of an automobile, bus, or truck that sends power from the engine to the wheels. **3.** The broadcasting of radio or television. trans|mis|sion (trans **mish′**ən) *noun, plural* **transmissions.**

transmit—**1.** To send along: *to* transmit *a message; to* transmit *a disease.* **2.** To send out by radio, television, or wire: *The television station* transmits *my favorite show at 8 P.M.* trans|mit (trans **mit′**) *verb,* **transmitted, transmitting.**

transom—A small window set in a wall over another window or a door: *On hot days, our teacher opens the* transom. tran|som (tran′səm) *noun, plural* **transoms.**

transom

transparent—**1.** Able to be seen through: *The toys were wrapped in* transparent *plastic.* **2.** So weak that its real meaning is easily understood; feeble: *Mother's reason for going shopping alone was so* transparent *that I knew she was buying me a birthday present.* trans|par|ent (trans **par′**ənt) *adjective.*

transplant—**1.** To move a growing plant to a new container or spot: *She* transplanted *the seedling to a larger pot.* **2.** To transfer skin or another body part to a different place on the body or to a different person's body. *Verb.* —A transfer of skin or another body part to a different place on the body or to a different person's body: *The heart* transplant *was a success. Noun.* trans|plant (trans **plant′** for *verb;* **trans′**plant

for *noun) verb,* **transplanted, transplanting;** *noun, plural* **transplants.**

transport—To carry from one place to another: *Large trucks* transport *logs from the forest to the sawmill. Verb.* —**1.** The process of carrying from one place to another: *The* transport *of the soldiers was done by helicopters.* **2.** A ship or aircraft built to carry people and things from one place to another. *Noun.* trans|port (trans **pawrt′** for *verb;* **trans′**pawrt for *noun) verb,* **transported, transporting;** *plural* **transports.**

transportation—The process or means of carrying people or things from one place to another: *the* transportation *of children to school.* trans|por|ta|tion (trans′pər **tā′**shən) *noun.*

trap—**1.** A device for catching or killing animals. **2.** A means of tricking someone into doing or saying something: *Her question was a* trap *to make me give away the surprise. Noun.* —**1.** To catch an animal in a device for that purpose: *We* trapped *the mouse and put it outside.* **2.** To trick someone into doing or saying something: *With a clever question, the lawyer* trapped *her into admitting her guilt. Verb.* trap (trap) *noun, plural* **traps;** *verb,* **trapped, trapping.**

trap door—A door in a floor, ceiling, or roof: *You get into our attic through a* trap door. trap door (trap dawr) *noun, plural* **trap doors.**

trapeze—A short bar hung between two ropes or wires. It swings back and forth and is used for acrobatics. tra|peze (tra **pēz′**) *noun, plural* **trapezes.**

trapeze

trash—Stuff that is of no use; rubbish: *The dump is filled with* trash. *Noun.*
trash (trash) *noun.*
• Synonyms: See Synonyms at **garbage.**

travel—To go from one place to another; move: *to* travel *through several countries; airplanes traveling through the sky. Verb.*
—The act of going from one place to another: *She hopes to spend the summer in* travel. *Noun.*
trav|el (trav′əl) *verb,* **traveled** *or* **travelled, traveling** or **travelling;** *noun, plural* **travels.**

tray—A dish with a flat bottom and a raised edge, used to hold or carry things: *The waitress brought our dinners on a* tray.
tray (trā) *noun, plural* **trays.**

treacherous—**1.** Not trustworthy, loyal, or faithful; quick to betray or deceive: *The* treacherous *soldier gave secret information to the enemy.* **2.** Not reliable or safe: *The icy roads are* treacherous.
treach|er|ous (trech′ər əs) *adjective.*

tread—**1.** To step; walk along: *We saw someone* treading *up the path.* **2.** To stamp on; crush: *If too many people* tread *on the grass, it will die. Verb.*
—**1.** The sound of walking or a way of walking: *the heavy* tread *of a large man; the quick, light* tread *of a cat.* **2.** The part of a stair step that one walks on: *The* treads *were covered with carpet.* **3.** The part of a tire that has grooves and rolls on the ground: *The tire* treads *left a pattern in the soft dirt. Noun.*
tread (tred) *verb,* **trod, trodden** *or* **trod, treading;** *noun, plural* **treads.**

treason—The betrayal of a person's country, especially by giving aid to an enemy: *It will be* treason *if someone lets the enemy into the fort.*
trea|son (trē′zən) *noun.*
• See Word History at **tradition.**

treasure—Valuables such as gold and precious stones; riches: *The king's* treasure *is locked away in the tower. Noun.*
—To value greatly: *I* treasured *the long summer days on my grandparents' farm. Verb.*
treas|ure (trezh′ər) *noun, plural* **treasures;** *verb,* **treasured, treasuring.**

treasurer—Someone whose job is to manage the money of a club, a business, or a government.
treas|ur|er (trezh′ər ər) *noun, plural* **treasurers.**

treasury—**1.** The money that an organization has: *We can pay for the supplies out of the company* treasury. **2. Treasury:** The department of a government in charge of the money matters for the country.
treas|ur|y (trezh′ər ē) *noun, plural* **treasuries.**

treat—**1.** To behave toward; act toward; deal with: *He* treats *his new bicycle like a treasure.* **2.** To provide medical service: *The doctor* treated *him for a broken arm.* **3.** To buy something for another person: *She* treated *me to a movie. Verb.*
—**1.** The act of buying something for another, or the thing bought: *He delighted his friends when he told them that the meal would be his* treat. **2.** Something that gives pleasure: *A day at the beach was a* treat *for the children. Noun.*
treat (trēt) *verb,* **treated, treating;** *noun, plural* **treats.**

treatment—**1.** A way of dealing with someone or something: *special* treatment; *unkind* treatment. **2.** Something used or done to cure: *The* treatment *is to stay in bed and drink plenty of liquid.*
treat|ment (trēt′mənt) *noun, plural* **treatments.**

treaty—An agreement between nations to act in a certain way: *a peace* treaty.
trea|ty (trē′tē) *noun, plural* **treaties.**

tree—A large plant having a single, thick, woody trunk and many branches. *Noun.*
—To chase up a tree: *The cat has* treed *a squirrel. Verb.*
tree (trē) *noun, plural* **trees;** *verb,* **treed, treeing.**
■ **bark up the wrong tree:** To try for the wrong thing, or go about getting something in the wrong way: *The students thought they had the solution to the problem, but the teacher told them they were* barking up the wrong tree.
up a tree: Stuck in a difficult situation: *The boy found himself* up a tree *because he promised to get 100 signatures on the petition and could get only 10.*

trek—To make a long journey; migrate: *The mountain villagers* trekked *to the city with all their belongings. Verb.*
—A journey, especially a long, slow, difficult one: *a* trek *through the desert. Noun.*
trek (trek) *verb,* **trekked, trekking;** *noun, plural* **treks.**

a at	i if	oo look	ch chalk	a in ago
ā ape	ī idle	ou out	ng sing	e in happen
ah calm	o odd	u ugly	sh ship	ə = i in capital
aw all	ō oats	ū rule	th think	o in occur
e end	oi oil	ur turn	th their	u in upon
ē easy			zh treasure	

trellis

trellis—A structure made of thin pieces of wood or metal bars that cross each other. It is used to support climbing plants.
trel|lis (trel′is) *noun, plural* **trellises.**

tremble—To shiver or shake because of cold or a strong emotion such as fright or anger: *The young dancer* trembled *when she heard the applause.*
trem|ble (trem′bəl) *verb,* **trembled, trembling.**

tremendous—1. Enormous; huge: *A hippopotamus is a* tremendous *animal.*
2. Wonderful; excellent: *a* tremendous *work of art; a* tremendous *party.*
tre|men|dous (tri men′dəs) *adjective.*
• Synonyms: For **1**, see Synonyms at **big.**
Antonyms: For **1**, see Synonyms at **small.**

tremor—1. A shaking or trembling of the body: *There was a* tremor *in her voice as she spoke to the large crowd.* **2.** A shaking movement; vibration: *Passing trains send* tremors *through houses near the tracks.*
trem|or (trem′ər) *noun, plural* **tremors.**

trench—A deep, narrow ditch: *They dug a* trench *to drain the water from the pond.*
trench (trench) *noun, plural* **trenches.**

trend—The general direction of something; tendency: *a* trend *toward smaller families; a new* trend *in clothes.*
trend (trend) *noun, plural* **trends.**

trespass—To go on property without the owner's permission: *The woman yelled at us for* trespassing *in her yard. Verb.*
—A sin; offense: *She felt bad about her* trespasses *and tried to be better. Noun.*
tres|pass (tres′pəs *or* tres′pas) *verb,* **trespassed, trespassing;** *noun, plural* **trespasses.**

trestle—A framework bridge of wood or metal, built to hold up railroad tracks or a road.
tres|tle (tres′əl) *noun, plural* **trestles.**

tri-—A prefix that means "three." A triangle has three angles.

trial—1. The examining and deciding of the facts of a law case in a court. **2.** The trying or testing of something: *We drove the car as a* trial *before we bought it.* **3.** Troubles; suffering: *He has faced many* trials *in his long life.*
tri|al (trī′əl) *noun, plural* **trials.**

triangle—1. A figure that has three angles and three sides. **2.** Something shaped like this. **3.** A musical instrument in this shape that is made of a bent steel bar. It rings when struck with a small steel rod.
tri|an|gle (trī′ang′gəl) *noun, plural* **triangles.**

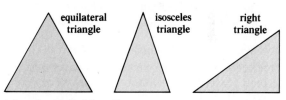

triangle (definition 1)

triangular—1. Shaped like a triangle; having three sides and three angles: *a* triangular *piece of cheese.* **2.** Having to do with a group of three: *a* triangular *agreement; a* triangular *contest.*
tri|an|gu|lar (trī ang′gyə lər) *adjective.*

tribal—Of a tribe: *a* tribal *village;* tribal *customs.*
trib|al (trī′bəl) *adjective.*

tribe—A group of people with shared ancestors, customs, language, and other characteristics: *Some* tribes *of American Indians lived in tepees.*
tribe (trīb) *noun, plural* **tribes.**

tributary—A river or stream that flows into a larger river or other body of water.
trib|u|tar|y (trib′yə tār′ē) *noun, plural* **tributaries.**

tribute—Something given to show thanks, respect, or admiration: *A moment of silence was observed as a* tribute *to the brave astronauts.*
trib|ute (trib′yūt) *noun, plural* **tributes.**

triceratops

triceratops—A dinosaur with a very large head, a big horn above each eye and a smaller one on the nose, a bony collar around the neck, and a powerful tail.
tri|cer|a|tops (trī ser′ə tops) *noun.*

trick—1. Something done to deceive or fool: *The telephone call was a* trick *to get her to the surprise party.* 2. A clever act of skill: *The seals and dolphins at the zoo are trained to do many* tricks. 3. A practical joke: *The boys like to play* tricks *on each other. Noun.*
—To deceive or fool: *Mother* tricked *me into eating broccoli. Verb.*
trick (trik) *noun, plural* **tricks**; *verb,* **tricked, tricking.**
■ **do the trick:** To accomplish what one wants: *Some wood, some nails, and a hammer should* do the trick.
● Synonyms: **bluff², mislead,** for *verb.*

trickery—The use of methods that deceive or fool: *My brother used* trickery *to get me to rake his part of the yard.*
trick|er|y (trik′ər ē) *noun, plural* **trickeries.**

trickle—1. To flow in small drops or a small stream: *Water* trickled *from the leaky faucet.* 2. To come, go, or move slowly: *People* trickled *into the new store when it opened. Verb.*
—A small flow or stream: *A* trickle *of ice cream ran down her chin. Noun.*
trick|le (trik′əl) *verb,* **trickled, trickling;** *noun, plural* **trickles.**
● Synonyms: **dribble, drip,** for *verb* 1.
Antonym: **gush,** for *verb* 1.

tricky—1. Using ways that fool; deceitful: *Our* tricky *cat always gets out of the house.* 2. Difficult to manage; requiring skill and care: *a*
tricky *lock; a* tricky *road with sharp turns.*
trick|y (trik′ē) *adjective,* **trickier, trickiest.**

tricycle—A small vehicle, usually for young children, with one big wheel in the front and two smaller wheels in back. It is moved by pedals and steered by handlebars.
tri|cy|cle (trī′sə kəl *or* trī′sik′əl) *noun, plural* **tricycles.**

tried—Proved trustworthy: *She is a* tried *and true employee. Adjective.*
—See **try.** *Verb.*
tried (trīd) *adjective, verb.*

trifle—1. Something that is not very important: *Stop arguing over* trifles *and get to work.* 2. A small amount; bit: *a* trifle *hot; a* trifle *early. Noun.*
—To behave or talk foolishly or carelessly: *Do not* trifle *with the computer. Verb.*
tri|fle (trī′fəl) *noun, plural* **trifles;** *verb,* **trifled, trifling.**

trigger—A small lever that is pulled back by the finger to fire a gun. *Noun.*
—To set off or cause something: *His angry remark* triggered *a long and noisy argument. Verb.*
trig|ger (trig′ər) *noun, plural* **triggers;** *verb,* **triggered, triggering.**

trim—1. To make neat and tidy by cutting away parts: *Dad* trimmed *the bushes in our front yard.* 2. To shorten by taking parts out: *I* trimmed *my long speech to five minutes.* 3. To add ornaments to; adorn; decorate: *We* trim *our Christmas tree will bells and glass balls. Verb.*
—Neat and tidy; in order: *She has the* trimmest *yard on our street. Adjective.*
—1. Something used as an ornament or decoration. 2. A good, strong condition: *The horse is in* trim *for the race. Noun.*
trim (trim) *verb,* **trimmed, trimming;** *adjective,* **trimmer, trimmest;** *noun, plural* **trims.**
● Synonyms: **abridge, abbreviate, condense,** for *verb* 2.
Antonyms: **enlarge, expand, lengthen,** for *verb* 2.

trimming—1. Something used to ornament or decorate: *The* trimming *on the cake was so pretty we hated to cut it.* 2. **trimmings:** Things added to a meal or event to make it complete or better: *Our holiday dinner was turkey and all the* trimmings.
trim|ming (trim′ing) *noun, plural* **trimmings.**

a at	i if	oo look	ch chalk		a in ago
ā ape	ī idle	ou out	ng sing		e in happen
ah calm	o odd	u ugly	sh ship	ə =	i in capital
aw all	ō oats	ū rule	th think		o in occur
e end	oi oil	ur turn	th their		u in upon
ē easy			zh treasure		

trinket—A small, often fancy, ornament, such as a piece of jewelry.
trin|ket (**tring′**kit) *noun, plural* **trinkets.**

trio—1. A group of three. 2. A piece of music to be performed by three singers or musicians.
tri|o (**trē′**ō) *noun, plural* **trios.**

trip—A process of going from one place to another place; journey. *Noun.*
—1. To catch one's foot against something and then stumble or fall: *I tripped over my brother's foot.* 2. To cause to stumble or fall: *The books I left on the floor tripped me.* 3. To make or cause to make an error: *She tripped up her friend with the riddle. Verb.*
trip (trip) *noun, plural* **trips;** *verb,* **tripped, tripping.**

triple—1. Three times as much or as many; three times the basic amount: *She ate no meat but took a triple serving of vegetables.* 2. Having three parts: *He tied his shoelace into a triple knot. Adjective.*
—To increase or be increased by three times: *We tripled the recipe to serve the extra guests. Verb.*
—A baseball hit that allows the batter to reach third base safely. *Noun.*
tri|ple (**trip′**əl) *adjective; verb,* **tripled, tripling;** *noun, plural* **triples.**

triplet—One of three persons born to the same mother at the same time.
tri|plet (**trip′**lit) *noun, plural* **triplets.**

tripod—A stand with three legs, used to support a camera, telescope, or other object.
tri|pod (**trī′**pod′) *noun, plural* **tripods.**

tripod

triumph—1. A victory; an important success or accomplishment: *Her speech was a triumph, admired by everyone.* 2. The feeling one has after victory or success: *shouts of triumph. Noun.*

—To have success; win: *The hikers triumphed over wind and snow to reach the top of the mountain. Verb.*
tri|umph (**trī′**umf) *noun, plural* **triumphs;** *verb* **triumphed, triumphing.**

trivia—Things or facts of little importance.
triv|i|a (**triv′**ē ə) *plural noun.*

trivial—Unimportant: *He wrote only the main ideas and left out the trivial details.*
triv|i|al (**triv′**ē əl) *adjective.*

trod—*See* **tread.**
trod (trod) *verb.*

trodden—*See* **tread.**
trod|den (**trod′**ən) *verb.*

troll—An imaginary dwarf or giant that is unpleasant and ugly. Trolls are supposed to live in caves or hills and have magical powers.
troll (trōl) *noun, plural* **trolls.**

trolley—1. A kind of streetcar that runs on tracks and is powered by electricity. 2. A small wheel at the end of a pole that carries electricity to the motor of a streetcar, bus, or train.
trol|ley (**trol′**ē) *noun, plural* **trolleys.**

trombone—A brass musical instrument with a U-shaped tube that slides in and out. This sliding controls the sounds made by the instrument.
trom|bone (**trom′**bōn *or* trom **bōn′**) *noun, plural* **trombones.**

trombone

troop—1. A large group of people or animals: *A troop of children crowded onto the bus.*
2. **troops:** Soldiers. *Noun.*
—To move, walk, or march together: *We all trooped into the house when it started to rain. Verb.*
troop (trūp) *noun, plural* **troops;** *verb,* **trooped, trooping.**

Language Fact

Trooper used to mean a soldier on a horse or a policeman on a horse. Today, police officers who work for state governments are often called troopers, because many state police forces used to ride horses in their work.

trooper—A police officer.
troop|er (trū′pər) *noun, plural* **troopers.**

trophy—An object, usually a cup or small statue, that is awarded to someone who wins a contest or game or who makes a great accomplishment.
tro|phy (trō′fē) *noun, plural* **trophies.**

tropical—Having to do with the tropics: *Parrots are* tropical *birds.*
trop|i|cal (trop′ə kəl) *adjective.*

tropics—The regions of the earth that are near the equator, where it is hot all year.
trop|ics (trop′iks) *plural noun.*

trot—1. To ride a horse or to move at a speed between a walk and a run. 2. To run slowly: *I trotted to the store because it was too far to run fast. Verb.*
—The pace of an animal when it moves its feet at a speed between a walk and a run. *Noun.*
trot (trot) *verb,* **trotted, trotting;** *noun, plural* **trots.**

trouble—1. A dangerous, unpleasant, or difficult condition: *He got in* trouble *by climbing the tree too high.* 2. Extra work or bother: *He took the* trouble *to wrap the package neatly.* 3. An illness; ailment: *My brother got glasses after his eye* trouble *began. Noun.*
—1. To cause worry or discomfort: *She was* troubled *by a toothache.* 2. To cause extra work or bother: *Would it* trouble *you to answer a few questions? Verb.*
trou|ble (trub′əl) *noun, plural* **troubles;** *verb,* **troubled, troubling.**
■ **ask for trouble:** To do something that is likely to cause a harmful or unpleasant condition: *Playing with matches is* asking for trouble.
borrow trouble: To be upset about something that may not happen: *You are* borrowing trouble *if you worry about losing the next game.*

troublesome—Causing trouble; making problems: *The puppy would not stop its* troublesome *barking.*
trou|ble|some (trub′əl səm) *adjective.*

trough—A long, narrow container that holds food or water for farm animals.
trough (trawf) *noun, plural* **troughs.**

trousers—A pair of pants; slacks.
trou|sers (trou′zərz) *plural noun.*

trout—A freshwater fish, often with spots on its body, used for food.
trout (trout) *noun, plural* **trouts** or **trout.**

trowel—1. A tool that has a flat, wide blade for spreading or smoothing plaster or cement. 2. A small garden shovel with a short handle.
trow|el (trou′əl) *noun, plural* **trowels.**

truce—A stop in fighting; a short time of peace: *The two nations wanted a* truce *in order to discuss a peace agreement.*
truce (trūs) *noun, plural* **truces.**

truck—A large motor vehicle that is used to carry heavy loads. *Noun.*
—To carry things in such a motor vehicle: *Fresh vegetables are* trucked *to the city from the country. Verb.*
truck (truk) *noun, plural* **trucks;** *verb,* **trucked, trucking.**

trudge—To walk with slow, heavy steps: *She* trudged *through the deep snow. Verb.*
—A slow, difficult walk: *a* trudge *across wet fields. Noun.*
trudge (truj) *verb,* **trudged, trudging;** *noun, plural* **trudges.**

true—1. Not false or wrong; right: *It is* true *that we are moving.* 2. Real; actual: *My mom has a* true *diamond in her ring.* 3. Loyal; faithful: *Her dog is a* true *pal.* 4. A real or correct example of: *A starfish is not a* true *fish.*
true (trū) *adjective,* **truer, truest.**
● Synonyms: **authentic, genuine, original,** for **2.**
Antonyms: **counterfeit, false,** for **2.**

truly—1. In a sincere or true manner; honestly: *I am* truly *sorry that I forgot your birthday.* 2. In fact; really: *The mountains are* truly *amazing.*
tru|ly (trū′lē) *adverb.*

trumpet—1. A small brass musical instrument with three valves on top. The valves control the sounds made by the instrument. 2. A sound like that made by such a musical instrument. *Noun.*
—To make a sound like the sound of this musical instrument: *The swans were* trumpeting *as they flew overhead. Verb.*

				a in ago
a at	**i** if	**oo** look	**ch** chalk	
ā ape	**ī** idle	**ou** out	**ng** sing	e in happen
ah calm	**o** odd	**u** ugly	**sh** ship	ə = i in capital
aw all	**ō** oats	**ū** rule	**th** think	o in occur
e end	**oi** oil	**ur** turn	**th** their	u in upon
ē easy			**zh** treasure	

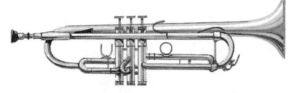

trumpet (noun, definition 1)

trum|pet (trum′pit) *noun, plural* **trumpets;**
verb, **trumpeted, trumpeting.**

trunk—**1.** The stem of a tree, from which the
roots and branches grow. **2.** A large, covered
box that is used to carry and store things. **3.** A
boxlike area in an automobile that is used to
carry and store things. **4.** A person's or animal's
body, not including the head, arms, and legs.
5. The long nose of an elephant. **6. trunks:**
Short pants that are worn in many sports.
trunk (trungk) *noun, plural* **trunks.**

Word History

Trunk comes from a Latin word meaning "to
damage by cutting." A tree trunk is what is left
after the branches are cut away. People used to
believe that trunks for carrying things were made
from hollow tree trunks. The trunk of a body is
like a tree trunk because arms and legs grow
from it like branches and roots.

trust—**1.** Belief or faith in someone or something:
She had trust *in her doctor.* **2.** Care; keeping:
Our neighbors left their dog in our trust *when
they went on vacation. Noun.*
—**1.** To believe in someone or something;
depend on: *He* trusted *the police officer to give
him good directions.* **2.** To hope or expect: *I*
trust *you sent Grandma a thank-you note. Verb.*
trust (trust) *noun, plural* **trusts;** *verb,* **trusted,
trusting.**

trustee—A person or group of people responsible
by law for taking care of something for another
person: *A* trustee *managed his farm while he was
ill.*
trus|tee (trus tē′) *noun, plural* **trustees.**

truth—**1.** A thing that is true; fact: *It is the* truth
that I have never seen her before. **2.** The
condition of being true: *They believe in the* truth
of my explanation.
truth (trūth) *noun, plural* **truths.**

try—**1.** To make an effort or attempt: *She* tried *to
reach the top shelf.* **2.** To examine or test:
Please try *this new cereal.* **3.** In a court of law,
to examine and decide the facts: *The factory*

owner *was* tried *and found guilty of polluting the
river. Verb.*
—An attempt or effort: *She gave the doorbell
another* try *before leaving. Noun.*
try (trī) *verb,* **tried, trying;** *noun, plural* **tries.**

trying—Not easy to bear; annoying: *It was very*
trying *when his shoelace kept breaking.*
try|ing (trī′ing) *adjective.*

tryout—A test to see if a person is good enough
to become a member of a team or group: *Tryouts
for the swim team were held last week.*
try|out (trī′out′) *noun, plural* **tryouts.**

T-shirt—A light, knitted piece of clothing that
has short sleeves and no collar. It can be worn as
a casual shirt or as underwear.
T-shirt (tē′shurt′) *noun, plural* **T-shirts.**

tsp.—An abbreviation for **teaspoon** or **teaspoons.**

tsunami—A huge ocean wave caused by an
underwater earthquake or volcanic eruption. It is
sometimes called a tidal wave.
tsu|na|mi (tsu nah′mē) *noun, plural* **tsunamis.**

tub—**1.** A big, open container used for washing or
bathing. **2.** A round container used to hold food:
a tub *of margarine.*
tub (tub) *noun, plural* **tubs.**

tuba—A large brass musical instrument with three
valves on the side. The valves control the very
low sounds made by the instrument.
tu|ba (tū′ba) *noun, plural* **tubas.**

tuba

tube—**1.** A long, hollow pipe made of glass or
other material, used to hold or carry liquids or
gases. **2.** A small, easily bent container that has
a cap at one end: *a* tube *of toothpaste; a* tube *of
glue.* **3.** Anything with a long, hollow shape.
tube (tūb) *noun, plural* **tubes.**

tuberculosis—A disease caused by certain bacteria that usually infects the lungs.
tu|ber|cu|lo|sis (tū bur′ky lō′sis) *noun.* Abbreviation: **TB**

tuck—1. To put into a safe place: *She* tucked *a handkerchief into her pocket.*   2. To put the end or edge of something under or in: *He* tucked *the sheet under the mattress.*   3. To sew small folds in a piece of clothing: *The tailor* tucked *the waist of the dress. Verb.*
   —A small fold sewed into a piece of clothing. *Noun.*
tuck (tuk) *verb,* **tucked, tucking;** *noun, plural* **tucks.**

Tues.—The abbreviation for **Tuesday.**

Tuesday—The third day of the week; day between Monday and Wednesday.
Tues|day (tūz′dē, tūz′dā, tyūz′dē *or* tyūz′dā) *noun, plural* **Tuesdays.** Abbreviation: **Tues.**

Word History

Tuesday comes from the name of a god of war. The ancient Romans called the day after their war god. Then the people who lived in Germany, Denmark, Sweden, and Norway changed the name and called the day after their war god.

---

tuft—A bunch of something that grows or is held together at one end: *The bird has a* tuft *of feathers on its head.*
tuft (tuft) *noun, plural* **tufts.**

tug—To pull hard; yank: *He* tugged *at the weed until it came out of the ground. Verb.*
   —A hard pull: *There was a* tug *on the kite string as the wind blew harder. Noun.*
tug (tug) *verb,* **tugged, tugging;** *noun, plural* **tugs.**

tugboat—A small, powerful boat that pushes or pulls larger boats or barges.
tug|boat (tug′bōt′) *noun, plural* **tugboats.**

tuition—Money paid for schooling or instruction.
tu|i|tion (tū ish′ən *or* tyū ish′ən) *noun, plural* **tuitions.**

tulip

tulip—A large, cup-shaped flower that grows from a bulb. Tulips grow in many bright colors.
tu|lip (tū′lip *or* tyū′lip) *noun, plural* **tulips.**

tumble—1. To roll or fall over, usually in a clumsy manner: *She* tumbled *down the snowy hill.*   2. To do somersaults, headstands, leaps, or other such acrobatic acts: *The gymnast* tumbled *across the mat. Verb.*
   —1. The act of rolling or falling in a clumsy manner: *He took a* tumble *down the cellar stairs.*   2. A somersault or other such acrobatic feat. *Noun.*
tum|ble (tum′bəl) *verb,* **tumbled, tumbling;** *noun, plural* **tumbles.**

tumbleweed—A plant that grows in the western United States. When it dies in autumn, the wind breaks it from its roots and the plant is blown about, scattering its seeds as it goes.
tum|ble|weed (tum′bəl wēd′) *noun, plural* **tumbleweeds.**

tumbling—The performing of acrobatic acts, such as somersaults and leaps.
tum|bling (tum′bling) *noun.*

tumor—A swelling in the body, caused by an unusual growth of the body's cells.
tu|mor (tū′mər *or* tyū′mər) *noun, plural* **tumors.**

tuna—A large fish found in most warm seas. It is a popular food.
tu|na (tū′nə) *noun, plural* **tunas** *or* **tuna.**

tundra—A huge, flat area of land in arctic regions. Tundras have no trees because the earth below the surface is always frozen.
tun|dra (tun′drə) *noun, plural* **tundras.**

tune—1. A series of musical notes; melody.   2. The correct musical pitch: *The guitar was out of* tune. *Noun.*
   —To adjust to the correct musical pitch: *to* tune *a piano. Verb.*
tune (tūn *or* tyūn) *noun, plural* **tunes;** *verb,* **tuned, tuning.**

a at	**i** if	**oo** look	**ch** chalk	⌈ **a** in ago
ā ape	**ī** idle	**ou** out	**ng** sing	**e** in happen
ah calm	**o** odd	**u** ugly	**sh** ship	ə = **i** in capital
aw all	**ō** oats	**ū** rule	**th** think	**o** in occur
e end	**oi** oil	**ur** turn	**th** their	⌊ **u** in upon
ē easy			**zh** treasure	

tunnel—A long underground or underwater passage. *Noun.*
—To dig a long underground or underwater passage. *Verb.*
tun|nel (tun′əl) *noun, plural* **tunnels;** *verb,* **tunneled, tunneling.**

turban—A long scarf that is wrapped around the head like a hat by men in some countries.
tur|ban (tur′bən) *noun, plural* **turbans.**

turf—The top part of the soil where the roots of grass and small plants grow.
turf (turf) *noun.*

turkey—A large bird with a bare head and reddish brown or white feathers. Turkeys are raised by farmers for food.
tur|key (tur′kē) *noun, plural* **turkeys.**

turkey

Word History

Turkey comes from the name of a country, Turkey. But the bird has nothing to do with the country! Another kind of bird was known as a "turkey cock" because people in Europe got it by way of Turkey. When turkeys reached Europe from North America, people got the two kinds of birds confused. So they called the North American bird after the country in Asia.
● See also Word History at **turquoise.**

Turkish angora—A long-haired, medium-sized cat that has a long body and tail and long, silky white hair. It has a wedge-shaped face and blue or amber eyes. These cats were originally bred in Turkey.
Turk|ish an|go|ra (tur′kish ang gawr′ə) *noun, plural* **Turkish angoras.**

turn—1. To move around in a circle; rotate: *The pinwheel turned.* 2. To change direction: *She turned to wave at a friend.* 3. To become changed or cause to be changed: *The roads turned slippery.* 4. To take a path around or about: *We turned the corner.* 5. To feel or cause to feel sick: *Eating all that ice cream made his stomach turn.* 6. To change or cause to change one's feelings or opinions: *He turned all my friends from me when I made him mad. Verb.*
—1. A spinning around; rotation: *a turn of the handle; two full turns of the dial.* 2. A change of direction: *a turn to the right.* 3. A time or chance to do something: *It is not my turn to take out the garbage. Noun.*
turn (turn) *verb,* **turned, turning;** *noun, plural* **turns.**
● A word that sounds the same is **tern.**

turnip—A plant whose large, round root can be cooked and eaten as a vegetable.
tur|nip (tur′nəp) *noun, plural* **turnips.**

turnout—A gathering of people: *There was a large turnout for the parade.*
turn|out (turn′out′) *noun, plural* **turnouts.**

turnpike—A wide road or highway. Some turnpikes charge a toll to drivers.
turn|pike (turn′pīk′) *noun, plural* **turnpikes.**

turnstile—A gate with bars that turn. Only one person at a time can pass through it.
turn|stile (turn′stīl′) *noun, plural* **turnstiles.**

turntable—A round, flat surface that turns around, such as one on which phonograph records are played.
turn|ta|ble (turn′tā′bəl) *noun, plural* **turntables.**

turpentine—A liquid that is made from the wood or gum of some pine trees. It is used to thin some paints and to clean paint brushes.
tur|pen|tine (tur′pən tīn) *noun.*

turquoise—1. A greenish blue stone used as a gem. 2. A greenish blue color. *Noun.*
—Having a greenish-blue color. *Adjective.*
tur|quoise (tur′koiz *or* tur′kwoiz) *noun, plural* **turquoises;** *adjective.*

Word History

Turquoise comes from a French word meaning "from Turkey." People in Europe used to get this stone from the people who lived in Turkey.
● See also Word History at **turkey.**

turret—1. A small tower, usually built on the corner of a building.   2. The machine that holds and turns a big gun, as in a tank or a ship.
tur|ret (tur′it) *noun, plural* **turrets.**

turtle—1. A four-legged animal with a hard, rounded shell. Turtles live in salt water, in fresh water, and on land.   2. A movable mark on a computer screen, used with the computer language LOGO.
tur|tle (tur′təl) *noun, plural* **turtles.**

turtleneck—1. A high collar that is folded down and fits closely to the neck.   2. A piece of clothing with such a collar.
tur|tle|neck (tur′təl nek′) *noun, plural* **turtlenecks.**

tusk—A long, curving tooth. It sticks out of the side of the mouth and usually grows in pairs, as in the elephant and walrus.
tusk (tusk) *noun, plural* **tusks.**
● See picture at **ivory.**

tutor—One who teaches a pupil or pupils in a private arrangement rather than in school. *Noun.*
—To give individual, private instruction: *Please tutor him in the subjects he failed. Verb.*
tu|tor (tū′tər *or* tyū′tər) *noun, plural* **tutors;** *verb,* **tutored, tutoring.**

TV or **T.V.**—The abbreviation for **television.**

tweed—A coarse wool cloth made by weaving yarns of two or more colors.
tweed (twēd) *noun, plural* **tweeds.**

twelfth—1. Next after the eleventh.   2. One of twelve equal parts.
twelfth (twelfth) *adjective; noun, plural* **twelfths.**

twelve—One more than eleven; one less than thirteen; 12.
twelve (twelv) *adjective; noun, plural* **twelves.**

twentieth—1. Next after the nineteenth.   2. One of twenty equal parts.
twen|ti|eth (twen′tē ith) *adjective; noun, plural* **twentieths.**

twenty—One more than nineteen; one less than twenty-one; 20.
twen|ty (twen′tē) *adjective; noun, plural* **twenties.**

turtle (definition 1)

twice—1. Two times: *I have already seen this movie* twice.   2. Double; times two: *I bought* twice *as many pencils as I need.*
twice (twīs) *adverb.*

twig—A tiny branch of a tree or bush.
twig (twig) *noun, plural* **twigs.**

twilight—1. The pale light seen in the sky just before sunrise and just after sunset.   2. The time of day when this light is seen, especially the hours between sunset and darkness.
twi|light (twī′līt′) *noun, plural* **twilights.**

twin—1. One of two persons born to the same mother at the same time.   2. One of a pair of closely similar things: *The gems looked like* twins *but only one was a real diamond. Noun.*
—1. Being one or both of two persons born to the same mother at the same time: *My* twin *brother is a good swimmer.*   2. Being a pair, or one of a pair, that are closely similar: *The* twin *statues stood on each side of the entrance. Adjective.*
twin (twin) *noun, plural* **twins;** *adjective.*

twine—A strong cord made of two or more strings twisted together. *Noun.*
—To coil together; wind around something: *Let me* twine *these ribbons in your hair. Verb.*
twine (twīn) *noun, plural* **twines;** *verb,* **twined, twining.**
● Synonyms: **curl, twist,** for *verb.*

twinge—A sharp pain that comes and goes suddenly. *Noun.*
—To have or cause this feeling: *The pitcher's elbow* twinged *after the game. Verb.*
twinge (twinj) *noun, plural* **twinges;** *verb,* **twinged, twinging.**

twinkle—To sparkle; flash: *The tiny bulbs on the Christmas tree* twinkled. *Verb.*
—A sparkling light: *the* twinkle *of the star-filled sky. Noun.*

a at	i if	oo look	ch chalk		⌈ a in ago
ā ape	ī idle	ou out	ng sing		e in happen
ah calm	o odd	u ugly	sh ship	ə =	i in capital
aw all	ō oats	ū rule	th think		o in occur
e end	oi oil	ur turn	th their		⌊ u in upon
ē easy			zh treasure		

twin|kle (twing′kəl) *verb,* **twinkled, twinkling;**
noun, plural **twinkles.**
• Synonyms: **blink, flicker**[1]**, glimmer,** for *verb.*

twirl—To spin; rotate rapidly: *The skater* twirled
upon the tip of her skate.
twirl (twurl) *verb,* **twirled, twirling.**

twist—1. To wind; turn; coil: *She* twisted *her hair
into a braid.* 2. To change the normal shape of:
*We could not use the fork after the garbage
disposal* twisted *it.* 3. To change the true
meaning of: *He* twisted *the facts to avoid getting
into trouble.* 4. To curve around; follow a
crooked path: *The river* twisted *through the
town.* 5. To injure a part of the body by turning:
I twisted *my ankle while playing soccer. Verb.*
—1. A bend; curve: *He hammered the* twist *out
of the damaged bicycle frame.* 2. An unexpected
change or event: *The peculiar* twist *of the story
made it a very exciting mystery. Noun.*
twist (twist) *verb,* **twisted, twisting;** *noun,*
plural **twists.**
• Synonyms: **curl, twine,** for *verb* 1.

twister—A tornado; cyclone.
twist|er (twis′tər) *noun, plural* **twisters.**

twitch—To move or cause to move in a quick,
jerking manner: *I knew I had a fish on the hook
when I saw the fishing rod* twitch. *Verb.*
—A quick, jerking movement: *She gets a* twitch
in her eyelids whenever she is very tired. Noun.
twitch (twich) *verb,* **twitched, twitching;** *noun,*
plural **twitches.**

twitter—1. A rapid series of peeping sounds
made by birds. 2. A condition of nervous
excitement: *in a* twitter *about a party. Noun.*
—To make a rapid series of peeping sounds: *The
birds* twittered *outside my window. Verb.*
twit|ter (twit′ər) *noun, plural* **twitters;** *verb,*
twittered, twittering.

two—One more than one; one less than three; 2.
two (tū) *adjective; noun, plural* **twos.**
• Words that sound the same are **to** and **too.**

-ty—1. A suffix that means "ten times." Ninety is
ten times nine. 2. A suffix that means "a
quality or a condition of being." Loyalty is the
quality of being loyal.

Word Power

You can understand the meanings of many words
that end with **-ty,** if you add a meaning of the
suffix to the meaning of the rest of the word.
  seventy: seven times ten
  cruelty: the quality of being cruel

---

tying—*See* **tie.**
ty|ing (tī′ing) *verb.*

type—1. A sort; kind; class: *There are three
different* types *of cactus in this pot.* 2. The
raised letters, numbers, and symbols used to print
books, magazines, and newspapers. *Noun.*
—1. To use a typewriter: *Please* type *this
report.* 2. To determine what kind something
belongs to; classify: *We must* type *these shells for
our collection. Verb.*
type (tīp) *noun, plural* **types;** *verb,* **typed,**
typing.
• Synonyms: For *noun* 1, see Synonyms at **class,**
  noun 1.

typewriter—A machine that is worked by hand
and that prints letters, numbers, and symbols
onto paper. A typewriter is operated by pressing
marked keys with the fingers.
type|writ|er (tīp′rī′tər) *noun, plural*
typewriters.

typhoon—A violent storm that occurs in certain
tropical areas.
ty|phoon (tī fūn′) *noun, plural* **typhoons.**

typical—Like most of a particular kind;
representative: *a* typical, *common dog.*
typ|i|cal (tip′ə kəl) *adjective.*
• Synonyms: **common, regular**
  Antonyms: See Synonyms at **odd.**

tyrannosaurus—A large, meat-eating dinosaur
that walked upright on its two hind legs and had
two front legs like arms.
ty|ran|no|sau|rus (ti ran′ə sawr′əs *or*
tī ran′ə sawr′əs) *noun, plural* **tyrannosauri**
(ti ran′ə sawr′ī *or* tī ran′ə sawr′ī).

tyrannosaurus

tyranny—The use of power in a cruel and unjust
manner: *the* tyranny *of an evil government.*
tyr|an|ny (tēr′ə nē) *noun, plural* **tyrannies.**

tyrant—A cruel, unjust person in authority: *She
was a* tyrant *to the people who worked for her.*
ty|rant (tī′rənt) *noun, plural* **tyrants.**

About 1,900 years ago, the Romans used the letter **V** for both U and V sounds. During the Middle Ages, scholars used the letter **U** for a vowel and **V** for a consonant. The small letter **u** was first used about 1,500 years ago. It did not come into regular use as a vowel until about 500 years ago.

About 5,000 years ago, the ancient Egyptians used this symbol. Later, people in the Middle East used the same symbol. They called it *waw,* their word for ''hook.''

About 3,000 years ago, other people in the Middle East used a similar symbol.

About 2,600 years ago, the Greeks gave the letter this form. They called it *upsilon.*

U or **u**—The twenty-first letter of the alphabet: *There are two* u's *in the word ''useful.''*
U, u (yū) *noun, plural* **U's** or **Us, u's** or **us.**
 • A word that sounds the same is **you.**

ugh—A word used to express disgust or horror: Ugh! *a spider!*
ugh (ug *or* u) *interjection.*

ugly—**1.** Not pleasing to look at: *an* ugly *dress.* **2.** Not pleasing to hear: ugly *music; an* ugly *word.* **3.** Violent or dangerous: *an* ugly *temper; an* ugly *storm.*
ug|ly (ug′lē) *adjective,* **uglier, ugliest.**
 • Synonyms: **hideous, homely, plain, unsightly,** for **1.**
Antonyms: **gorgeous, lovely, pretty,** for **1.**

ukulele—A small guitar that has four strings.
u|ku|le|le (yū′kə lā′lē) *noun, plural* **ukuleles.**

ultimate—**1.** Last in a process or series; final: *The* ultimate *step in putting up a tent is fastening the ropes.* **2.** Most basic: *The* ultimate *reason for exercising is to stay healthy.*
ul|ti|mate (ul′tə mit) *adjective.*

umbrella—A device made of a round piece of cloth or plastic on a metal frame of several rods that fold in or out from the top of a central pole.

ukulele

Word History

Ukulele comes from two Hawaiian words meaning ''jumping flea.'' This musical instrument is named after a British army officer, Edward Putvis, who made it popular in Hawaii in the 1800's. His nickname was ''jumping flea.''

a at	i if	oo look	ch chalk		⟨ a in ago
ā ape	ī idle	ou out	ng sing		e in happen
ah calm	o odd	u ugly	sh ship	ə =	i in capital
aw all	ō oats	ū rule	th think		o in occur
e end	oi oil	ur turn	th their		u in upon
ē easy			zh treasure		

Word History

Umbrella comes from an Italian word meaning "shade." In hot, sunny places, umbrellas are used to give shade from sunlight. So **parasol** comes from two Spanish words meaning "for the sun." A parasol is a small umbrella.

An umbrella protects a person from the sun or rain. **um|brel|la** (um **brel′**ə) *noun, plural* **umbrellas.**

umpire—A person who decides the results of plays made in certain sports, such as baseball, and who makes sure that the rules of the game are followed correctly. *Noun.*
—To decide the results of plays and make sure the rules are followed, in certain sports: *My father* umpires *our park's evening baseball games. Verb.*
um|pire (um′pīr) *noun, plural* **umpires;** *verb,* **umpired, umpiring.**

un-—A prefix that means "not." An uncertain person is someone who is not certain.

Word Power

You can understand the meanings of many words that begin with **un-**, if you add the meaning of the prefix to the meaning of the rest of the word.
   undeclared: not declared
   unfound: not found

UN or **U.N.**—The abbreviation for **United Nations.**

unaccented—Not said forcefully or loudly: *The "a" in the word "alone" is* unaccented.
un|ac|cent|ed (un **ak′**sen tid *or* un′ak **sen′**tid) *adjective.*

unanimous—1. With everyone agreeing: *She was elected to head the club by a* unanimous *vote.* 2. In complete agreement: *The three friends were* unanimous *in wanting to visit the zoo.*
u|nan|i|mous (yū **nan′**ə məs) *adjective.*

Word History

Unanimous comes from two Latin words meaning "one mind." People who are unanimous in having an opinion are all alike in their thinking about that subject, so they are said to be of "one mind."

unbearable—Not able to be put up with; past enduring: *This cold weather is almost* unbearable.
un|bear|a|ble (un **bār′**ə bəl) *adjective.*

unbecoming—Not proper or attractive: unbecoming *behavior; an* unbecoming *hair style.*
un|be|com|ing (un′bi **kum′**ing) *adjective.*

unbelievable—Hard to accept as true; incredible: *His story about a hidden treasure is* unbelievable.
un|be|liev|a|ble (un′bi **lē′**və bəl) *adjective.*

unbreakable—Not easily broken, or impossible to break: *This toy is* unbreakable.
un|break|a|ble (un **brā′**kə bəl) *adjective.*

unbroken—1. Not in pieces; whole: *an* unbroken *window.* 2. Not interrupted: *I drew an* unbroken *line across the page.* 3. Not passed in excellence; not beaten: *an athlete's* unbroken *running record.* 4. Not tamed: *an* unbroken *horse.*
un|bro|ken (un **brō′**kən) *adjective.*

uncalled-for—Unsuitable; not proper; rude: *an* uncalled-for *remark.*
un|called-for (un **kawld′**fawr′) *adjective.*

uncanny—Mysterious and strange; eerie: *an* uncanny *ability to find lost objects; an* uncanny *light in the window of the empty cabin.*
un|can|ny (un **kan′**ē) *adjective.*

uncertain—1. Not known; in doubt: *It's* uncertain *whether I'll go on the trip.* 2. Not dependable; changeable: *an* uncertain *mood;* uncertain *weather.*
un|cer|tain (un **sur′**tən) *adjective.*

uncle—1. The brother of one's father or mother. 2. The husband of one's aunt.
un|cle (ung′kəl) *noun, plural* **uncles.**
■ **cry uncle** or **say uncle:** To give up in defeat; surrender: *The bully wouldn't leave the boy alone until he* cried uncle.

unconscious—1. Not able to think, feel, or see for a time; not awake: *She ran so hard into the pole that she was knocked* unconscious. 2. Not aware: *My sister is* unconscious *of my having borrowed her radio.* 3. Not done or said on purpose: *an* unconscious *choice; an* unconscious *belief.*
un|con|scious (un **kon′**shəs) *adjective.*

uncover—1. To remove a cover from: *to* uncover *a bed; to* uncover *a jar.* 2. To make known; reveal: *to* uncover *the truth; to* uncover *a hiding place.*
un|cov|er (un **kuv′**ər) *verb,* **uncovered, uncovering.**

under—1. Below: *Your shoes are* under *the chair*. 2. Beneath or covered by: *a stream that runs* under *the ground; a lawn that is* under *the snow*. 3. Less than: *The toy costs* under *seven dollars*. 4. Governed by; within the authority or control of: *The school attracted many students* under *the new principal*. 5. In a certain group or class of things: *The phone book lists chairs* under *the word "furniture."* 6. Because of; considering: Under *the circumstances, I have changed my mind*. Preposition.
—In or to a place that is below something; down: *Her toy boat quickly went* under *when she pulled the plug in the bathtub*. Adverb.
—Lower: *the* under *side of a table; an* under *level of government*. Adjective.
un|der (un′dər) *preposition, adverb, adjective.*

under-—A prefix that means "beneath" or "less." Something underground is beneath the ground. Something underdeveloped is less developed than it might be.

Word Power

You can understand the meanings of many words that begin with **under-**, if you add a meaning of the prefix to the meaning of the rest of the word.
underarm: the part of the body beneath the arm
underachiever: one who achieves less than is possible

---

underbrush—Small trees, bushes, shrubs, and other plants that grow beneath tall trees in a forest.
un|der|brush (un′dər brush′) *noun.*

underdeveloped—1. Not so large or mature as possible: *an* underdeveloped *plant; an* underdeveloped *body*. 2. Lacking in economic, social, scientific, or similar growth: *That* underdeveloped *country has many poor people*.
un|der|de|vel|oped (un′dər di **vel**′əpt) *adjective.*

underdog—A person or group that is thought to have little chance of winning a contest or doing well in life: *His lack of popularity made him an* underdog *in the election for mayor*.

a at	i if	oo look	ch chalk		a in ago	
ā ape	ī idle	ou out	ng sing		e in happen	
ah calm	o odd	u ugly	sh ship	ə =	i in capital	
aw all	ō oats	ū rule	th think		o in occur	
e end	oi oil	ur turn	th their		u in upon	
ē easy			zh treasure			

un|der|dog (un′dər dawg′) *noun, plural* **underdogs.**

underfoot—1. In the way: *My sister is often* underfoot *when I want to be alone*. 2. Beneath the feet; on the ground: *They trampled the newspapers that were dropped* underfoot.
un|der|foot (un′dər foot′) *adjective, adverb.*

undergo—To experience; go through; have happen: *Babies* undergo *many changes as they grow*.
un|der|go (un′dər gō′) *verb,* **underwent, undergone, undergoing.**

underground—1. Below the surface of the earth: *an* underground *tunnel*. 2. Secret or illegal: *an* underground *movement to overthrow the government*. Adjective.
—1. A place below the surface of the earth. 2. A group or organization that works in secret to accomplish something: *The* underground *attacked the invading soldiers from ambush*. Noun.
—Below the surface of the earth: *The engineers worked* underground *to build a new pipeline*. Adverb.
un|der|ground (un′dər **ground**′ for *adjective* and *adverb;* un′dər ground′ for *noun*) *adjective; noun, plural* **undergrounds;** *adverb.*

undergrowth—Small bushes and other plants that grow close together beneath the trees in a forest or other wooded area; underbrush.
un|der|growth (un′dər grōth′) *noun.*

underhand—With the hand facing upward and the arm swinging upward and forward: *an* underhand *pitch; to throw a ball* underhand.
un|der|hand (un′dər hand′) *adjective, adverb.*

underhand

underline—To draw a line below something: *I underlined my name on the list.*
un|der|line (un′dər līn′ *or* un′dər līn′) *verb,* **underlined, underlining.**

underneath—Below; beneath: *I sat on the chair and petted the dog that lay* underneath. *The boy hid the note* underneath *his book.*
un|der|neath (un′dər nēth′) *adverb, preposition.*

underpass—A road or way that goes under a road, bridge, or the like.
un|der|pass (un′dər pas′) *noun, plural* **underpasses.**

underpass

underprivileged—Lacking the opportunities or advantages that other people have, especially because one is poor: *an* underprivileged *community.*
un|der|priv|i|leged (un′dər priv′ə lijd) *adjective.*

undersea—Used, done, or being below the surface of the sea: undersea *travel; an* undersea *cave.*
un|der|sea (un′dər sē′) *adjective.*

undershirt—A light-weight garment that is worn beneath a shirt or next to the skin on the upper part of the body, usually by males.
un|der|shirt (un′dər shurt′) *noun, plural* **undershirts.**

underside—The bottom surface: *He lay down on the ground so that he could look at the* underside *of the car.*
un|der|side (un′dər sīd′) *noun, plural* **undersides.**

understand—1. To get the meaning of: *She doesn't* understand *your question.* 2. To have much experience with and know very well: *I* understand *arithmetic.* 3. To sympathize with another's feelings, ideas, or the like: *My mother*

understands *when I'm sad.* 4. To have learned; know: *I* understand *that you bought a new dog.* 5. To believe; assume: *I* understand *that children under six are admitted free.*
un|der|stand (un′dər stand′) *verb,* **understood, understanding.**

understanding—1. The getting hold of the meaning of something: *My* understanding *of what your remark suggested.* 2. Knowledge based on experience or study: *an* understanding *of cars.* 3. A belief held because of something that was agreed upon: *It's my* understanding *that you were going to feed the cat.* 4. The ability to sympathize with another's feelings, ideas, or the like: *We admire the* understanding *he has for lonely people.* 5. An agreement: *The angry neighbors finally reached an* understanding *and settled their differences. Noun.*
—Showing or having kind and sympathetic feelings: *The father gave his upset son an* understanding *pat on the back. Adjective.*
un|der|stand|ing (un′dər stan′ding) *noun, plural* **understandings;** *adjective.*

understood—*See* understand.
un|der|stood (un′dər stood′) *verb.*

undertake—1. To try; attempt: *She will* undertake *to learn how to ice-skate.* 2. To choose or agree to do something, such as a task: *I* undertook *to cut the lawn.*
un|der|take (un′dər tāk′) *verb,* **undertook, undertaken, undertaking.**

undertaker—A person whose job is to prepare the dead for burial and to arrange funerals.
un|der|tak|er (un′dər tā′kər) *noun, plural* **undertakers.**

undertaking—1. Something that is done or attempted: *Climbing the mountain was a difficult* undertaking. 2. The business of arranging funerals and preparing dead people for burial.
un|der|tak|ing (un′dər tā′king for 1; un′dər tā′king for 2) *noun, plural* **undertakings.**

undertook—*See* undertake.
un|der|took (un′dər took′) *verb.*

undertow—A strong current below the surface of a body of water, which moves in the direction opposite to the current at the surface of the water: *The sea's* undertow *kept pulling the boat away from shore.*
un|der|tow (un′dər tō′) *noun, plural* **undertows.**

underwater—Below the surface of the water: *an* underwater *rescue; to swim* underwater.
un|der|wa|ter (un′dər wawt′ər *or* un′dər wot′ər) *adjective, adverb.*

underway—Already being done; in progress: *The construction of the new road has been* underway *for a week.*
un|der|way (un′dər wā′) *adverb.*

underwear—Light-weight garments that are worn beneath a person's clothing and next to the skin.
un|der|wear (un′dər wār′) *noun.*

underweight—Weighing less than is needed or usual: *That skinny girl is very* underweight.
un|der|weight (un′dər wāt′) *adjective.*

underwent—*See* undergo.
un|der|went (un′dər went′) *verb.*

undo—1. To untie or unwrap: *to* undo *a ribbon; to* undo *a package.* 2. To do away with; produce the opposite effect of what has already been done: *You can* undo *a lie by telling the truth.*
un|do (un dū′) *verb,* undid, undone, undoing.

undone—Not completed; not finished: *I colored half of the picture and left the rest* undone.
un|done (un dun′) *adjective.*

unearth—1. To dig something up out of the ground: *to* unearth *a buried treasure.* 2. To discover, especially after much searching: *to* unearth *a clue to a mystery; to* unearth *a letter in a stack of papers.*
un|earth (un urth′) *verb,* unearthed, unearthing.

uneasy—1. Nervous or worried: *I felt* uneasy *about diving into the water.* 2. Not comfortable: *Her anger made us* uneasy.
un|eas|y (un ē′zē) *adjective,* uneasier, uneasiest.

unequal—1. Not the same in size, degree, amount, or the like: unequal *stacks of wood; an* unequal *number of boys and girls in a classroom.* 2. Not fairly matched; not balanced: *A spelling contest between first grade students and fifth grade students is* unequal. 3. Not having the abilities or skills to do something: *A baby is* unequal *to the task of tying shoes.*
un|e|qual (un ē′kwəl) *adjective.*

uneven—1. Not smooth or straight; bumpy or crooked: *an* uneven *path; an* uneven *line.* 2. Not able to be divided by two without one left over: *Three is an* uneven *number.* 3. Not fairly matched; unequal: *an* uneven *race.*

un|e|ven (un ē′vən) *adjective,* unevener, unevenest.

unexpected—Happening without warning; surprising: *an* unexpected *visit; an* unexpected *turn in the road.*
un|ex|pect|ed (un′ek spek′tid) *adjective.*
• Synonyms: abrupt, sudden
Antonyms: gradual, slow

unfortunate—Having or marked by bad luck: *It's* unfortunate *that you lost your glasses.*
un|for|tu|nate (un fawr′chə nit) *adjective.*

unhealthy—1. Not having good health; not well; sick: *She has been* unhealthy *lately and has missed several days of school.* 2. Resulting from bad health: *an* unhealthy *cough;* unhealthy *fatigue.* 3. Bad for one's health: *an* unhealthy *diet; an* unhealthy *habit.*
un|health|y (un hel′thē) *adjective,* unhealthier, unhealthiest.

UNICEF—The commonly used name for the United Nations Children's Fund. This agency of the Untied Nations aids children in more than 100 countries by helping to solve problems of health, hunger, and education.
UNICEF (yū′nə sef) *noun.*

Word History

UNICEF comes from the first letters of the words in the original name of this agency. When the agency was started in 1946, it was called the *United Nations International Children's Emergency Fund.*

---

unicorn—An imaginary animal that looks like a horse but has a single, cone-shaped horn in the middle of its forehead.
u|ni|corn (yū′nə kawrn′) *noun, plural* unicorns.

unicorn

a at	i if	oo look	ch chalk		a in ago
ā ape	ī idle	ou out	ng sing		e in happen
ah calm	o odd	u ugly	sh ship	ə =	i in capital
aw all	ō oats	ū rule	th think		o in occur
e end	oi oil	ur turn	th their		u in upon
ē easy			zh treasure		

unicycle

unicycle—A vehicle that has pedals and a seat like a bicycle but has only one wheel. It is mainly used by acrobats, circus performers, and other entertainers.
u|ni|cy|cle (yū′nə sī′kəl) *noun, plural* **unicycles.**

uniform—The special or official clothing that is worn by members of a particular group. People who wear uniforms include nurses, police officers, soldiers, and baseball players. *Noun.*
—**1.** Always the same; not changing: *a phonograph record spinning at a* uniform *speed.* **2.** Having little or no difference; alike: *We cut the pie so that all the pieces were of a* uniform *size. Adjective.*
u|ni|form (yū′nə fawrm) *noun, plural* **uniforms;** *adjective.*

unimportant—Not important; trivial: *You could make your story shorter by leaving out the* unimportant *details.*
un|im|por|tant (un′im pawr′tənt) *adjective.*

union—**1.** A uniting or joining together of two or more people or things: *The large club was formed by the* union *of the two smaller clubs.* **2.** A group of workers joined together to improve their pay, hours, and other working conditions; labor union. **3. the Union:** The United States of America.
un|ion (yūn′yən) *noun, plural* **unions.**

unique—Being the only one of its kind; special: *a singer with a* unique *voice; a kind of tree* unique *to this part of the country.*
u|nique (yū′nēk′) *adjective.*
● Synonyms: **individual, particular, specific**
Antonym: **general**

unison—Total agreement: *There was* unison *among the members of the class about the theme for the dance.*
u|ni|son (yū′nə sən *or* yū′nə zən) *noun.*
■ **in unison:** Together: *police officers and fire fighters working* in unison; *fans doing a cheer* in unison.

unit—**1.** An individual person, group, or thing that is part of a larger group or thing: *We just finished a* unit *on butterflies in science class.* **2.** A piece of equipment that has a particular purpose: *a heating* unit *on a stove.* **3.** A fixed quantity used as a standard of measurement or value: *a* unit *of distance; a* unit *of money.* **4.** The smallest whole number; one.
u|nit (yū′nit) *noun, plural* **units.**

Unitarian—A member of a church that accepts the teachings of Jesus Christ as a guide for living but does not believe that Jesus was divine.
U|ni|tar|i|an (yū′nə tār′ē ən) *noun, plural* **Unitarians.**

unite—To join or bring together: *an agreement to* unite *the two companies under a single name.*
u|nite (yū nīt′) *verb,* **united, uniting.**

United Nations—An international organization that was set up in 1945 to work for world peace, understanding, and economic development. Nearly every country in the world belongs to the United Nations.
U|nit|ed Na|tions (yū nī′tid nā′shənz) *noun.* Abbreviations: **UN** or **U.N.**

United Nations: The United Nations flag has a map of the world inside a wreath of olive branches. The olive branches are a symbol of peace.

universal—**1.** Of, for, or shared by all: *There was* universal *support for the treaty.* **2.** Being or occurring everywhere: universal *space; a* universal *truth, that matter is made of atoms.*
u|ni|ver|sal (yū′nə vur′səl) *adjective.*

universe—Everything that exists, including the earth, the planets, the stars, and outer space.
u|ni|verse (yū′nə vurs′) *noun, plural* **universes.**

university—A college and other schools of higher learning, such as schools of law and medicine.
u|ni|ver|si|ty (yū′nə vur′sə tē) *noun, plural* **universities.** Abbreviation: **univ.** or **U.**

unknown—Not known or familiar: *a scientist discovering an* unknown *planet; an actor who was once* unknown *but is now a star.*
un|known (un nōn′) *adjective.*

unless—**1.** Except when: *He tends to be in a good mood* unless *he is tired.* **2.** Except on the condition that; if not: *She said she would like some ice cream* unless *it is chocolate.*
un|less (un les′) *conjunction.*

unlike—Not alike; different: *Although the twins looked the same, they were very much* unlike *in other ways. Adjective.*
—Different from: *He writes books* unlike *any others I have read. Preposition.*
un|like (un līk′) *adjective, preposition.*

unlikely—**1.** Not likely: *It is* unlikely *that she will pass the test unless she studies.* **2.** Not likely to succeed; likely to fail: *an* unlikely *plan; an* unlikely *project.*
un|like|ly (un līk′lē) *adjective,* **unlikelier, unlikeliest.**

unmanned—Without a crew: *an* unmanned *spacecraft.*
un|manned (un mand′) *adjective.*

unqualified—Not qualified; not fitted; incompetent: *She is* unqualified *for the job, because she lacks the proper training.*
un|qual|i|fied (un kwol′ə fīd) *adjective.*

unreasonable—**1.** Not having, showing, or using good sense: *It was* unreasonable *of him to want to play outside when it was raining.* **2.** Too great: *The theater charged an* unreasonable *price for admission.*
un|rea|son|a|ble (un rē′zən ə bəl) *adjective.*

unreliable—Not to be relied on, depended on, or trusted: *an* unreliable *car that is difficult to start;*

an unreliable *source of information.*
un|re|li|a|ble (un′ri lī′ə bəl) *adjective.*

unruly—Hard to control; boisterous: *The crowd became* unruly *when the performance did not start on time.*
un|ru|ly (un rū′lē) *adjective.*

unsatisfactory—Not satisfactory or acceptable: *He did an* unsatisfactory *job on the test and got a low grade.*
un|sat|is|fac|to|ry (un′sat is fak′tər ē) *adjective.*

unsettled—**1.** Not peaceful or orderly: *The city remained* unsettled *even after the riots stopped.* **2.** Not decided or cleared up: *an* unsettled *argument; an* unsettled *question.* **3.** Not lived in: *The explorers traveled deep into the* unsettled *forest.*
un|set|tled (un set′əld) *adjective.*

unsightly—Not pleasing to look at; ugly: *She pulled the* unsightly *weeds from the garden.*
un|sight|ly (un sīt′lē) *adjective,* **unsightlier, unsightliest.**
• Synonyms: See Synonyms at **ugly.**
Antonyms: **gorgeous, lovely, pretty**

unskilled—**1.** Not having skill or special training: *an* unskilled *worker.* **2.** Not requiring a special skill or training: *an* unskilled *job.*
un|skilled (un skild′) *adjective.*

unsound—**1.** In bad condition: *The tires on that bicycle are* unsound *and should be replaced.* **2.** Not based on clear thinking, good judgment, or fact: unsound *advice; an* unsound *plan; an* unsound *idea.*
un|sound (un sound′) *adjective.*

unsteady—Not steady or firm; shaky: *He had an* unsteady *walk for several months after he hurt his leg.*
un|stead|y (un sted′ē) *adjective,* **unsteadier, unsteadiest.**

unthinkable—Impossible to think of, consider, or imagine: *the* unthinkable *results of a nuclear war.*
un|think|a|ble (un thing′kə bəl) *adjective.*

until—**1.** Up to the time of: *She is staying with her grandparents* until *Sunday.* **2.** Before: *Our teacher said we shall not get our tests back* until *tomorrow. Preposition.*
—**1.** Up to the time that: *He played outside* until *it got dark.* **2.** Before: *We did not get to the game* until *it was nearly over.* **3.** To the point or degree that: *He was so interested in the book that he read* until *he could hardly keep his eyes open. Conjunction.*
un|til (un til′) *preposition, conjunction.*

a at	i if	oo look	ch chalk		a in ago
ā ape	ī idle	ou out	ng sing		e in happen
ah calm	o odd	u ugly	sh ship	ə =	i in capital
aw all	ō oats	ū rule	th think		o in occur
e end	oi oil	ur turn	th their		u in upon
ē easy			zh treasure		

unusual—Not usual; different; rare: *to take an* unusual *way home; an* unusual *sense of humor; an* unusual *old coin.*
un|u|su|al (un yū′zhū əl) *adjective.*
• Synonyms: **abnormal, odd, uncommon**
Antonyms: **common, regular, typical**

up—1. From a lower to a higher position: *The smoke from the campfire rose* up *into the sky.*
2. In, at, or on a higher level: *You will find the book you want* up *on the top shelf.* 3. In or into an upright position: *It is hard to stand* up *after sitting for so long.* 4. Out of bed: *Father is the first one to get* up *in the morning.* 5. Above the horizon: *Did you see the moon come* up *last night?* 6. In or into notice, view, or discussion: *I am glad you brought* up *that question.* 7. At bat in baseball: *He came* up *with the bases loaded. Adverb.*
—1. Going or directed upward: *The temperature is* up *from this morning.* 2. Being in a raised or high position: *After the storm, the water in the lake was* up. 3. Out of bed: *Why are you* up *so early?* 4. Above the horizon: *The sun was* up *by the time we started our trip.* 5. At bat in baseball: *The pitcher is* up *after the catcher. Adjective.*
—1. To a higher place on or in: *He climbed* up *the ladder to paint the ceiling.* 2. To or at a farther place: *My best friend lives* up *the block from me. Preposition.*
up (up) *adverb, adjective, preposition.*
▪ **on the up and up:** Honest; sincere: *The popular mayor was always* on the up and up *with the people of the town.*
up against: Faced by something to be dealt with: *She was doing fine on the test until she came* up against *the division problems.*
up to: 1. Doing: *She wrote a paper about what she had been* up to *during summer vacation.*
2. Capable of; able to do: *Do you really feel that you are* up to *a project that difficult?*

upbringing—The care and training given to a person during childhood.
up|bring|ing (up′bring′ing) *noun.*

uphill—Toward the top of a hill; upward: *The trail is easy except for one* uphill *climb. The road to the cabin winds* uphill *the rest of the way.*
up|hill (up′hil′ for *adjective;* up′**hil**′ for *adverb*) *adjective, adverb.*

upholster—To fit furniture with coverings, stuffing, cushions, or springs: *The arms of the chair were badly worn, so we sent it out to be* upholstered.

up|hol|ster (up hōl′stər) *verb,* **upholstered, upholstering.**

upholstery—The material used for covering a piece of furniture; stuffing, cushions, or springs for a piece of furniture: *a stain on the couch's* upholstery.
up|hol|ster|y (up hōl′stər ē) *noun, plural* **upholsteries.**

upkeep—The putting or keeping of something in proper condition; maintenance: *The money was to go toward the* upkeep *of the historic buildings in the town.*
up|keep (up′kēp′) *noun.*

upon—On: *The clown wore a silly hat* upon *his head.*
up|on (ə pon′) *preposition.*

upper—Higher: *an* upper *shelf in a cabinet; an* upper *floor of a skyscraper.*
up|per (up′ər) *adjective.*

upper hand—A position of advantage or control: *to gain the* upper hand *in a game.*
up|per hand (up′ər hand) *noun.*

uppermost—Having the highest position or rank: *His apartment was on the* uppermost *floor, and we had to take an elevator to reach it. Adjective.*
—In the highest position or rank: *When she got lost, she held* uppermost *in her mind the belief that she would get home safely. Adverb.*
up|per|most (up′ər mōst′) *adjective, adverb.*

upright—1. Straight up and down; erect; vertical: *Workers put the telephone pole back into an* upright *position after the strong winds had knocked it over.* 2. Good or honest: *All my friends are* upright *and would never cheat on a test. Adjective.*
—In a straight up and down position: *The small tree was held* upright *by several wires. Adverb.*
up|right (up′rīt′) *adjective, adverb.*

uprising—A revolt or rebellion: *The leaders of the* uprising *against the government were captured and put in jail.*
up|ris|ing (up′rī′zing) *noun, plural* **uprisings.**

uproar—A noisy and excited disturbance: *The audience created an* uproar *when the singer finished her most famous song.*
up|roar (up′rawr′) *noun, plural* **uproars.**
• Synonyms: **clamor, commotion, din, racket**
Antonyms: **quiet, silence, still**

uproot—1. To tear or pull out a plant and its roots: *The strong winds* uprooted *several trees on*

our block.   **2.** To force to leave: *The war uprooted many people from their homes.*
up|root (up **root'** *or* up **rŭt'**) *verb,* **uprooted, uprooting.**

upset—**1.** To tip or knock over; overturn: *He upset the pitcher of lemonade, and it fell to the floor.*   **2.** To interfere with or disturb: *The flat tire on her bicycle upset her plans to go for a ride.*   **3.** To make worried or nervous: *His cat's illness upset him.*   **4.** To make sick: *All the food I ate at the game upset my stomach.*   **5.** To defeat unexpectedly: *She upset last year's champion in the spelling bee. Verb.*
—**1.** Knocked, tipped, or turned over: *an upset salt shaker.*   **2.** Worried; anxious: *He was upset about his bad grade in science.*   **3.** Sick: *an upset stomach. Adjective.*
—An unexpected victory: *Our team won an upset over the first-place team. Noun.*
up|set (up **set'** for *verb;* up **set'** *or* **up'set'** for *adjective;* **up'set'** for *noun*) *verb,* **upset, upsetting;** *adjective; noun, plural* **upsets.**
• Synonyms: **nervous, tense²,** for *adjective* 2.
  Antonyms: **placid, tranquil,** for *adjective* 2.

upside down—**1.** With the top at the bottom: *The acrobat hung* upside down *from the trapeze.*   **2.** In or into disorder or confusion: *He turned his room* upside down *looking for his keys.*
up|side down (**up'**sīd doun') *adverb.*

upside-down—Having the top at the bottom: *He was in an* upside-down *position during part of his dive.*
up|side-down (**up'**sīd doun') *adjective.*

upstairs—**1.** Up the stairs: *Be careful going upstairs, because the carpet on the steps is loose.*   **2.** On or to an upper floor: *My sister is asleep upstairs. Adverb.*
—Being on an upper floor: *an upstairs bathroom; an upstairs hallway. Adjective.*
—The upper floor of a building: *He cleaned the basement while his brother vacuumed the upstairs. Noun.*
up|stairs (**up'stārz'**) *adverb, adjective, noun.*

upstream—Toward or at the source of a river or stream; against the current: *During our canoe trip, we ate lunch at an* upstream *picnic area.*

We went upstream *as far as the waterfall.*
up|stream (**up'strēm'**) *adjective, adverb.*

up-to-date—Using or showing the latest developments or style; modern; current: *an* up-to-date *science book with all the recent discoveries; wearing an* up-to-date *outfit to the dance.*
up-to-date (**up'**tə **dāt'**) *adjective.*

upward or **upwards**—Toward a higher place: *The* upward *flight of the bird took it above the trees. The train began to climb* upward *when it reached the mountains.*
up|ward or **up|wards** (**up'**wərd *or* **up'**wərdz) *adjective, adverb.*

uranium—A silver-white, radioactive metal that is used as a source of nuclear energy. It is a chemical element.
u|ra|ni|um (yū **rā'**nē əm) *noun.*

Word History

Uranium is named after the planet Uranus. The discovery of Uranus came only a few years before the discovery of uranium.

Uranus—The third largest planet and the seventh farthest from the sun. It has five moons and at least nine thin rings around it.
U|ra|nus (yoo **rā'**nəs *or* **yoor'**ə nəs) *noun.*
• See picture at **solar system.**

urban—Having to do with a city; civic: *He grew up in the city and has always liked* urban *life.*
ur|ban (**ur'**bən) *adjective.*

urge—**1.** To try to convince; plead with; ask earnestly: *His friends* urged *him to try out for the school play.*   **2.** To force or drive onward: *The farmer* urged *the cattle toward the barn.*   **3.** To argue strongly for or recommend: *The union* urged *better working conditions for its members. Verb.*
—A strong desire or impulse: *I have an* urge *to dance whenever I hear my favorite song. Noun.*
urge (urj) *verb,* **urged, urging;** *noun, plural* **urges.**

urgent—Needing or demanding immediate attention: *an* urgent *message; an* urgent *problem.*
ur|gent (**ur'**jənt) *adjective.*

urine—A clear, yellowish fluid that is produced by the kidneys and given off as waste from the body.
u|rine (**yoor'**ən) *noun.*

a at	i if	oo look	ch chalk		a in ago
ā ape	ī idle	ou out	ng sing		e in happen
ah calm	o odd	u ugly	sh ship	ə =	i in capital
aw all	ō oats	ū rule	th think		o in occur
e end	oi oil	ur turn	th their		u in upon
ē easy			zh treasure		

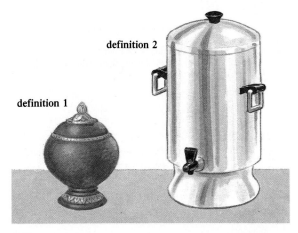

definition 2

definition 1

urn

urn—1. A vase set on a base. Urns are used mainly for decoration, but some are used to hold the ashes of the dead.   2. A container with a faucet, used to make and serve coffee or tea.
urn (urn) *noun, plural* **urns.**
  ● A word that sounds the same is **earn.**

us—The group including the person or people speaking, when that group is acted on, or when other words are joined to it by such words as **by** or **from:** *father telling* us *a story; our dog running to meet* us; *the other girls looking at* us.
us (us) *pronoun.*

usage—1. A way of handling something; treatment: *With the proper* usage, *that tape recorder will last a long time.*   2. The way that people commonly use words: *a dictionary that explains* usage.
us|age (yū′sij) *noun, plural* **usages.**

use—1. To bring or put into service for a particular purpose: *to* use *a straw for drinking a soda; to* use *one's imagination when reading a story.*   2. To spend or consume: *We* used *all our money at the carnival. Verb.*
  —1. The act of serving or the state of being in service: *to get one's hands clean through the* use *of soap and water; an elevator that is in* use.
  2. A way in which something serves; the purpose for which something serves: *to learn the* use *of a computer.*   3. The right to have the service of something: *She gave her friend the* use *of her pencil for the test.*   4. The ability to have the service of something: *I lost the* use *of my arm for a moment after I bumped my elbow.*   5. A need to have the service of something: *Do you have any* use *for this ragged old sweater? Noun.*

use (yūz for *verb;* yūs for *noun*) *verb,* **used, using;** *noun, plural* **uses.**
  ■ **used to: 1.** Accustomed to: *When the lights went out, it took me a minute to get* used to *the dark.*   **2.** Did in the past; formerly did: *She* used to *get home before her brother, but now he gets home before she does.*

used—Having been owned by someone else; not new; secondhand: *The family bought a* used *piano at the auction.*
used (yūzd) *adjective.*

useful—Being of good service; helpful: *a bus that is a* useful *form of transportation; a* useful *recipe; a* useful *tool.*
use|ful (yūs′fəl) *adjective.*

user-friendly—Designed or made to be easy: *He was nervous about working with the computer until he was shown how* user-friendly *it is.*
u|ser-friend|ly (yū′zər frend′lē) *adjective.*

usher—A person who leads people to their seats in such places as a church or theater. *Noun.*
  —To lead people to their seats in such places. *Verb.*
ush|er (ush′ər) *noun, plural* **ushers;** *verb,* **ushered, ushering.**

usual—Regular, ordinary, or expected: *the* usual *time for dinner; an actor who gives his* usual *fine performance.*
u|su|al (yū′zhū əl) *adjective.*

utensil—A container, tool, or instrument that is used for a particular purpose. Pots and pans are cooking utensils.
u|ten|sil (yū ten′səl) *noun, plural* **utensils.**

utility—1. A company that provides a public service. Electric companies are utilities.   2. The quality of being useful or practical: *Your invention has an interesting design, but does it have* utility?
u|til|i|ty (yū til′ə tē) *noun, plural* **utilities.**

utmost—Greatest or highest: *She has the* utmost *admiration for that writer. Adjective.*
  —The most, greatest, or best that is possible: *The fire fighters did their* utmost *to rescue people from the burning building. Noun.*
ut|most (ut′most′) *adjective, noun.*

utter¹—Complete; total: *The house has suffered years of* utter *neglect and is falling apart.*
ut|ter (ut′ər) *adjective.*

utter²—To let out or speak: *to* utter *words of thanks; to* utter *a sigh of relief.*
ut|ter (ut′ər) *verb,* **uttered, uttering.**

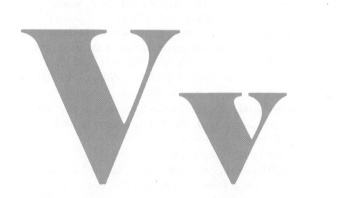

About 1,900 years ago, the Romans gave the capital V its present form. The small letter v was first used about 1,500 years ago. It reached its present form about 500 years ago.

About 5,000 years ago, the ancient Egyptians used this symbol. Later, people in the Middle East used the same symbol. They called it *waw,* their word for "hook."

About 3,000 years ago, other people in the Middle East used a similar symbol.

About 2,600 years ago, the Greeks gave the letter this form. They called it *upsilon.*

V or v—**1.** The twenty-second letter of the alphabet: *There are two v's in the word "valve."* **2.** The Roman numeral for the number 5.
V, v (vē) *noun, plural* **V's** or **Vs, v's** or **vs.**

v.—The abbreviation for **verb** and for **volt** or **volts.**

vacant—Not filled; empty: *a* vacant *building; a* vacant *seat on a bus.*
va|cant (vā′kənt) *adjective.*

vacation—A time of rest and recreation from school, work, or other responsibilities: *We went camping for two weeks during summer* vacation. *Noun.*
—To spend time away from school, work, or other responsibilities in order to rest and enjoy oneself: *We* vacationed *near a lake. Verb.*
va|ca|tion (vā kā′shən) *noun, plural* **vacations;** *verb,* **vacationed, vacationing.**

vaccinate—To give someone a vaccine to protect him or her from a certain disease: *The doctor* vaccinated *the girl against measles.*
vac|ci|nate (vak′sə nāt′) *verb,* **vaccinated, vaccinating.**

vaccination—The act of giving someone a vaccine: *We went to the doctor for our flu* vaccination.
vac|ci|na|tion (vak′sə nā′shən) *noun, plural* **vaccinations.**

vaccine—A special mixture containing certain weak or dead germs that is given to people or animals to protect them from the disease that those germs can cause.
vac|cine (vak sēn′ *or* vak′sēn) *noun, plural* **vaccines.**

Word History

Vaccine comes from a Latin word meaning "from cows." The first vaccine was made from a virus that was found in cows. When this virus was given in small amounts to humans, it protected them from a disease called smallpox. This discovery led scientists to make vaccines against many other diseases, such as mumps and polio.

---

vacuum—**1.** An empty space that does not have anything in it, not even air. **2.** A cleaning machine that sucks dirt and dust from floors, carpets, and furniture. *Noun.*
—To use such a cleaning machine: *I* vacuumed *the carpet. Verb.*
vac|u|um (vak′yūm *or* vak′yū əm) *noun, plural* **vacuums;** *verb,* **vacuumed, vacuuming.**

vague—Not clear; lacking a definite outline: *a*

a at	i if	oo look	ch chalk		a in ago
ā ape	ī idle	ou out	ng sing		e in happen
ah calm	o odd	u ugly	sh ship	ə =	i in capital
aw all	ō oats	ū rule	th think		o in occur
e end	oi oil	ur turn	th their		u in upon
ē easy			zh treasure		

vague *idea of what you mean; the* vague *shape of the tree in the mist.*
vague (vāg) *adjective,* **vaguer, vaguest.**
• Synonyms: **hazy, obscure**
  Antonyms: **apparent, clear, evident, obvious, plain**

vain—1. Caring or thinking too much about one's looks, talents, achievements, or similar qualities: *When she fell, the* vain *girl worried more about the dirt on her face than about the damage to her books.* 2. Having no success; useless: *We made a* vain *attempt to grow vegetables in our garden, but the rabbits ate them all.*
vain (vān) *adjective,* **vainer, vainest.**
• Words that sound the same are **vane** and **vein.**

valentine—1. A greeting card or a small gift that is sent to a sweetheart, relative, or friend on Valentine's Day. 2. A person chosen to be someone's sweetheart on Valentine's Day: *The boy asked the girl in the house next door to be his* valentine.
val|en|tine (val′ən tīn′) *noun, plural* **valentines.**

Valentine's Day—A holiday celebrated on February 14 by exchanging cards and gifts.
Val|en|tine's Day (val′ən tīnz′ dā) *noun.*
• This holiday is also called **Saint Valentine's Day.**

valiant—Having or showing courage; brave: *a* valiant *knight; a* valiant *attempt to put out a fire.*
val|iant (val′yənt) *adjective.*

valid—1. Based on facts or evidence; true: *a* valid *answer; a* valid *excuse for being late.* 2. Acceptable under certain rules or by law: *a* valid *library card; a* valid *birth certificate.*
val|id (val′id) *adjective.*

valley—An area of low land between mountains or hills, often with a stream or river flowing through it.
val|ley (val′ē) *noun, plural* **valleys.**

valuable—1. Worth lots of money: *a* valuable *painting.* 2. Very useful or important: *a* valuable *device;* valuable *clues to a crime. Adjective.*
—**valuables:** Small possessions that are worth lots of money: *My parents keep their coin collection, jewelry, and other* valuables *safely hidden. Noun.*
val|u|a|ble (val′yū ə bəl *or* val′yə bəl) *adjective; plural noun.*

value—1. The amount of money something is worth: *The* value *of this car is many thousands of dollars.* 2. The degree of importance or usefulness something has: *the* value *of good health; the* value *of knowledge. Noun.*

—1. To figure out how much money something is worth: *This watch is* valued *at one hundred dollars.* 2. To think of something as being very important or useful: *I* value *my friends' kindness. Verb.*
val|ue (val′yū) *noun, plural* **values;** *verb,* **valued, valuing.**

valve—1. A device that opens or closes to control the flow of gas or liquid through a channel: *The* valve *on the water heater allows steam to escape.* 2. One half of the hinged shell of a clam, oyster, or similar sea animal.
valve (valv) *noun, plural* **valves.**

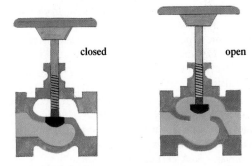

valve (definition 1)

van—A motor vehicle for moving equipment, animals, furniture, or other heavy goods. Some vans are the size of large trucks. Some vans are not much larger than cars.
van (van) *noun, plural* **vans.**

vane—A thin metal or wood blade that turns on a rod when the wind blows and shows which way the wind is blowing: *a weather* vane.
vane (vān) *noun, plural* **vanes.**
• Words that sound the same are **vain** and **vein.**

vane

vanilla—A flavoring used in cake, candy, ice cream, and other sweet foods. Vanilla is made from a tropical orchid plant.
va|nil|la (və nil′ə) *noun.*

vanish—1. To disappear suddenly: *The kite* vanished *behind a tall tree.* 2. To stop existing; to be no more: *Certain types of animals have* vanished *from the earth.*
van|ish (van′ish) *verb,* **vanished, vanishing.**

vapor—Very small bits of something in the air, especially water in the form of clouds, mist, or fog: *The boiling water turned into* vapor.
va|por (vā′pər) *noun.*

variation—1. A change in something: *There was little* variation *in her cheerful mood from day to day.* 2. Something that is slightly different from the same type of thing: *That excuse is a* variation *of her last excuse.*
var|i|a|tion (vār′ē ā′shən) *noun, plural* **variations.**

variety—1. The fact or quality of not being the same: *I like* variety *in the people I meet.* 2. A number of different kinds of similar things: *a* variety *of buildings; a* variety *of pens and pencils.* 3. A certain kind of something: *What* variety *of car do your parents drive?*
va|ri|e|ty (və rī′ə tē) *noun, plural* **varieties.**
• Synonyms: For definition **3**, see Synonyms at **class**, *noun¹.*

various—1. Of different kinds: *We saw* various *animals at the zoo.* 2. More than one; several: *I tried on* various *coats to see which fit best.*
var|i|ous (vār′ē əs) *adjective.*

varnish—A thin, clear liquid that is painted on metal, wood, or a similar material and that leaves a hard, shiny coating when it dries. *Noun.*
—To paint or coat with such a liquid: *My father* varnished *the bedroom door. Verb.*
var|nish (vahr′nish) *noun, plural* **varnishes;** *verb,* **varnished, varnishing.**

varsity—The team that represents a school, college, or university in a certain sport: *the basketball* varsity. *Noun.*
—Of or played by such a team: varsity *football. Adjective.*
var|si|ty (vahr′sə te) *noun, plural* **varsities;** *adjective.*

vary—1. To become or make different: *days* varying *in length from one season to another; to* vary *a recipe.* 2. To be different or of different kinds: *The dresses* vary *in color and length.*
var|y (vār′ē) *verb,* **varied, varying.**
• Synonyms: **alter, change, modify,** for **1.**
Antonyms: **conserve, maintain, preserve,** for **1.**

vase—A tall container, often made of glass or pottery, for holding flowers or for decorating a room.
vase (vās, vāz, *or* vahz) *noun, plural* **vases.**

vast—Very great in size, area, or amount: *a* vast *mountain; a* vast *forest; a* vast *number of cars on the street.*
vast (vast) *adjective,* **vaster, vastest.**

vat—A large tank that is used for holding or storing liquids.
vat (vat) *noun, plural* **vats.**

Vatican—1. The group of buildings where the pope lives and works. 2. The government of the pope over the Roman Catholic Church.
Vat|i|can (vat′ə kən) *noun.*

vault¹—1. An arched structure that serves as a roof or ceiling. 2. A room with very strong walls, floor, and ceiling, used to keep money and valuable items safe.
vault (vawlt) *noun, plural* **vaults.**

vault¹ (definition 1)

vault²—To jump over something, especially with the help of a pole or one's hands: *The girl* vaulted *over the fallen tree trunk. Verb.*
—A jump made with the help of a pole or one's hands. *Noun.*
vault (vawlt) *verb,* **vaulted, vaulting;** *noun, plural* **vaults.**

a at	i if	oo look	ch chalk		⌈ a in ago
ā ape	ī idle	ou out	ng sing		e in happen
ah calm	o odd	u ugly	sh ship	ə =	i in capital
aw all	ō oats	ū rule	th think		o in occur
e end	oi oil	ur turn	th their		⌊ u in upon
ē easy			zh treasure		

VCR—The abbreviation for **videocassette recorder**.

veal—The meat of a calf.
veal (vēl) *noun*.
• See Language Fact at **pork**.

vegetable—A plant whose leaves, roots, fruit, or other parts are used as food: *Corn, tomatoes, lettuce, potatoes, and broccoli are some of my favorite* vegetables. *Noun.*
—Of or having to do with such a plant: vegetable *soup. Adjective.*
veg|e|ta|ble (vej′tə bəl *or* vej′ə tə bəl) *noun, plural* **vegetables;** *adjective.*

vegetarian—A person who does not eat meat, fish, or other animal foods. *Noun.*
—Eating or having no meat: *a vegetarian* meal; vegetarian *restaurants. Adjective.*
veg|e|tar|i|an (vej′ə tār′ē ən) *noun, plural* **vegetarians;** *adjective.*

vegetation—Plants: *The forest has lots of* vegetation.
veg|e|ta|tion (vej′ə tā′shən) *noun.*

vehicle—A device for carrying things or people from place to place, especially on wheels or runners. Cars, trains, sleds, and airplanes are vehicles.
ve|hi|cle (vē′ə kəl) *noun, plural* **vehicles.**

veil—1. A very thin piece of cloth that is worn by women over the head, face, and shoulders: *a wedding* veil. 2. Anything that hides or covers something: *a veil of secrecy; a veil of smoke. Noun.*
—To hide or cover with or as if with such cloth: *to* veil *one's face; to* veil *one's true intentions. Verb.*
veil (vāl) *noun, plural* **veils;** *verb,* **veiled, veiling.**

vein—1. One of the blood vessels through which blood flows to the heart from all parts of the body. 2. One of the stiff, threadlike channels that form the framework of a leaf or an insect's wing. 3. A long, thin deposit of mineral or ore in rock: *a vein of gold.* 4. A streak having a different color from the marble or wood in which it appears: *This tan door has some dark brown* veins. 5. A mood or manner: *Her words were funny, but she said them in a serious* vein.
vein (vān) *noun, plural* **veins.**
• Words that sound the same are **vain** and **vane**.

velocity—How fast something moves, especially in one certain direction; speed: *The* velocity *of the wind today is twenty miles per hour.*
ve|loc|i|ty (və los′ə tē) *noun, plural* **velocities.**

velvet—A soft cloth with short, thick, raised fibers on its surface. Velvet is very soft and has a faint shine. *Noun.*
—Soft, smooth, and having a shine like this cloth: *the* velvet *fur of a white rabbit. Adjective.*
vel|vet (vel′vit) *noun, adjective.*

vendor—A person who sells something: *a peanut* vendor.
ven|dor (ven′dər) *noun, plural* **vendors.**

venison—The meat of a deer.
ven|i|son (ven′ə sən *or* ven′ə zen) *noun.*

venom—Poison. Some snakes, lizards, spiders, and other animals have venom in their bite or sting.
ven|om (ven′əm) *noun, plural* **venoms.**

vent—An opening that lets a gas or liquid pass in or out of a closed space: *We opened the heating* vent *to make the room warmer. Noun.*
—To express or release: *to* vent *anger. Verb.*
vent (vent) *noun, plural* **vents;** *verb,* **vented, venting.**

ventilation—The circulation of fresh air: *Its many windows give our house good* ventilation *in the summer.*
ven|ti|la|tion (ven′tə lā′shən) *noun.*

ventriloquist—A person who can make voice sounds so that they seem to come from somewhere else, especially from a wooden puppet.
ven|tril|o|quist (ven tril′ə kwist) *noun, plural* **ventriloquists.**

venture—An activity that involves danger or risk: *His* venture *into the jungle to catch a wild tiger was successful. Noun.*
—1. To do something that involves danger or risk: *He* ventured *into the lake to save the drowning dog.* 2. To say or do something, at the

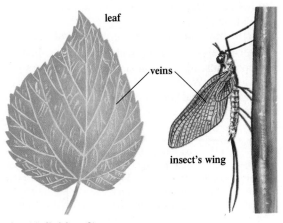

leaf
veins
insect's wing

vein (definition 2)

risk of being embarrassed: *She* ventured *her opinion about who was the better dancer. Verb.*
ven|ture (ven′chər) *noun, plural* **ventures;** *verb,* **ventured, venturing.**

Venus—The second planet from the sun.
Ve|nus (vē′nəs) *noun.*
● See picture at **solar system.**

verb—A word that expresses an action or a state of being: *"Eat," "be," "love," "run,"* and *"think"* are verbs.
verb (vurb) *noun, plural* **verbs.**

verbal—In or of words, especially spoken words: *They gave us* verbal *directions and also a map of the route.*
ver|bal (vur′bəl) *adjective.*

verdict—The decision made by a jury at the end of a trial: *a verdict of "not guilty."*
ver|dict (vur′dikt) *noun, plural* **verdicts.**

verify—To prove to be correct or true: *to verify today's date; to verify that she really did arrive home on time.*
ver|i|fy (ver′ə fī′) *verb,* **verified, verifying.**
● Synonyms: **confirm, establish**

verse—**1.** Words that are put together in a certain pattern of sounds, usually in rhyme: *The song is written in* verse. **2.** A group of lines of words that forms one section of a song or poem: *This poem has four* verses. **3.** A short, numbered section of a chapter in the Bible.
verse (vurs) *noun, plural* **verses.**

version—**1.** A description or report from a certain point of view: *Each witness told a different* version *of the crime.* **2.** A translation into another language: *the English* version *of a German song.*
ver|sion (vur′zhən) *noun, plural* **versions.**

versus—Against: *our school's team* versus *theirs.*
ver|sus (vur′səs) *preposition.* Abbreviation: **vs.**

vertebra—One of the small bones that form the backbone.
ver|te|bra (vur′tə brə) *noun, plural* **vertebras.**

vertebrate—An animal with a backbone. Fish, amphibians, reptiles, birds, and mammals are vertebrates. *Noun.*
—Having a backbone: *a* vertebrate *animal. Adjective.*

ver|te|brate (vur′tə brāt′ *or* vur′tə brit) *noun, plural* **vertebrates;** *adjective.*

vertical—Straight up and down: *The fence is in a* vertical *position.*
ver|ti|cal (vur′tə kəl) *adjective.*

very—**1.** Extremely; greatly; highly: *a* very *cold day; a* very *pretty girl.* **2.** Truly; really: *a* very *good price.* **3.** Exactly: *We saw the* very *same movie. Adverb.*
—**1.** Same: *That's the* very *toy I bought yesterday.* **2.** Simple; bare: *The* very *idea of speaking in public makes me nervous.* **3.** Exact: *the* very *middle of the yard.* **4.** Absolute; complete: *the* very *end of the day. Adjective.*
ver|y (ver′ē) *adverb; adjective,* **verier, veriest.**

vessel—**1.** A ship or large boat. **2.** A hollow holder or container, such as a bowl or vase. **3.** A narrow tube that carries fluids in the body: *a blood* vessel.
ves|sel (ves′əl) *noun, plural* **vessels.**

vest—A short, sleeveless piece of clothing that is worn over a shirt or blouse. *Noun.*
—To give as a right or as a form of authority: *The police are* vested *with the power to arrest law breakers. Verb.*
vest (vest) *noun, plural* **vests;** *verb,* **vested, vesting.**
■ **close to the vest:** In a very careful, clever, and secret way so as to gain an advantage: *She played* close to the vest *in planning her new restaurant so no one would copy her idea.*

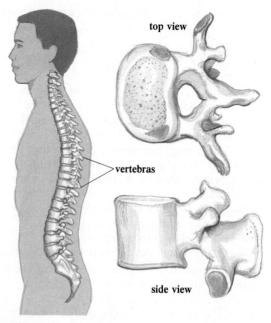

top view

vertebras

side view

vertebra

veteran—**1.** A person who has had many years of experience: *My teacher is a* veteran *of this elementary school.*   **2.** A person who has served in the armed forces: *a war* veteran. *Noun.*
—Having had many years of experience: *a* veteran *musician;* veteran *fire fighters. Adjective.*
vet|er|an (vet′ər ən) *noun, plural* **veterans;** *adjective.*

Veterans Day—November 11, a holiday in honor of all who have served in the United States armed forces.
Vet|er|ans Day (vet′ər ənz dā) *noun.*

veterinarian—A doctor who treats animals.
vet|er|i|nar|i|an (vet′ər ə nãr′ē ən) *noun, plural* **veterinarians.** Abbreviation: **vet.**

veto—**1.** The power of a president, governor, or other official to reject an act passed by a legislature and stop it from becoming a law.
2. A refusal to give consent: *My brother's idea of having only ice cream for dinner met with a* veto *from our parents. Noun.*
—**1.** To stop an act from becoming a law: *The President did not like the tax bill passed by Congress and* vetoed *it.*   **2.** To refuse consent; prohibit: *Her mother* vetoed *her plan to stay overnight at a friend's house. Verb.*
ve|to (vē′tō) *noun, plural* **vetoes;** *verb,* **vetoed, vetoing.**

Word History

Veto comes from a Latin word meaning "I forbid." In ancient Rome, a government official was appointed to protect the interests of the common people. If this official thought a proposed law was unfair to the common people, he could stop it from being passed by saying, "Veto."

---

via—By way of: *It was a beautiful day, so she walked home* via *the park.*
vi|a (vī′ə *or* vē′ə) *preposition.*

viaduct—A bridge used for carrying a road or railroad over such things as a valley or a highway.
vi|a|duct (vī′ə dukt′) *noun, plural* **viaducts.**

vibrate—To move or cause to move rapidly up and down or back and forth; quiver: *The powerful wind made the windows* vibrate.
vi|brate (vī′brāt) *verb,* **vibrated, vibrating.**

vibration—Rapid movement back and forth or up and down: *the* vibration *of a banjo string when it is plucked.*

vi|bra|tion (vī brā′shən) *noun, plural* **vibrations.**

vice-—A prefix meaning "one that takes the place of" or "second in rank to." A vice-mayor takes the place of a mayor when necessary. A vice-admiral is second in rank to an admiral.

Word Power

You can understand the meanings of many words that begin with **vice-,** if you add a meaning of the prefix to the meaning of the rest of the word.
vice-chairman: one that takes the place of a chairman
vice-principal: second in rank to a principal

---

vice-president—**1.** An officer who ranks second to a president.   **2. Vice-President:** The government official who ranks second to the President of the United States.
vice-pres|i|dent (vīs′prez′ə dənt) *noun, plural* **vice-presidents.** Abbreviation: **V.P.**

vice versa—The other way around: *Do you want to go to the grocery store first and then have lunch, or* vice versa?
vi|ce ver|sa (vī′sə vur′sə) *adverb.*

vicinity—A nearby or surrounding area or region; neighborhood: *The radio reported that a tornado had been seen in the* vicinity *of our town, so we took shelter.*
vi|cin|i|ty (və sin′ə tē) *noun, plural* **vicinities**

vicious—**1.** Evil; wicked: *a robber's* vicious *urge to steal.*   **2.** Cruel or mean; full of spite: vicious *laughter at another's misfortune.*   **3.** Savage; fierce: *a* vicious *tiger.*
vi|cious (vish′əs) *adjective.*
• Synonyms: **ferocious, wild,** for **3.**

victim—**1.** A person or animal that is injured, killed, or made to suffer: *a victim of the flu; a* victim *of a fire.*   **2.** A person who is taken advantage of, cheated, or tricked: *the victim of a hoax.*
vic|tim (vik′təm) *noun, plural* **victims.**

victorious—**1.** Having won a victory: *The* victorious *player leaped over the tennis net.*
2. Having to do with victory: *an army's* victorious *march into a conquered town.*
vic|to|ri|ous (vik tawr′ē əs) *adjective.*

victory—The defeat of an enemy or opponent: *The town held a parade to celebrate the team's* victory *in the championship game.*
vic|to|ry (vik′tər ē) *noun, plural* **victories.**

vicuña (definition 1)

vicuña—1. An animal related to the camel. It looks like a llama and lives in South America. It has fine, soft wool. 2. The wool from this animal.
vi|cu|ña (vi kūn′yə) *noun, plural* **vicuñas.**

video—Having to do with the picture part of a television broadcast: *There were problems with the* video *portion of the broadcast, but we were still able to listen to the game. Adjective.*
—1. The picture part of a television broadcast. 2. A videotaped performance of a popular song, often showing lively dancing: *a rock* video. *Noun.*
vid|e|o (vid′ē ō′) *adjective; noun, plural* **videos.**

videocassette—A small plastic case that contains videotape.
vid|e|o|cas|sette (vid′ē ō kə set′) *noun, plural* **videocassettes.**

videocassette recorder—A device for recording television programs onto videocassettes of videotape and then playing them back on a television set. It is also used for playing prerecorded videocassettes, which can be bought or rented.

videocassette recorder
vid|e|o|cas|sette re|cord|er (vid′ē ō kə set′ ri **kawr**′dər) *noun, plural*
videocassette recorders. Abbreviation: **VCR**

videotape—A type of magnetic tape that is used to record pictures and sounds. *Noun.*
—To make a recording with such a tape: *We* videotaped *my brother's graduation from high school. Verb.*
vid|e|o|tape (vid′ē ō tāp′) *noun, plural* **videotapes;** *verb,* **videotaped, videotaping.**

view—1. The act of seeing; sight: *His* view *of the performance was blocked by a post.* 2. The range of sight: *We watched our grandparents' car until it disappeared from* view. 3. Something that can be seen: *a room with a* view *of the mountains.* 4. A way of thinking; opinion: *In her* view, *that was the best book the author ever wrote. Noun.*
—1. To look at or see; watch: *We* viewed *the parade from our porch.* 2. To think about; consider: *She* viewed *her brother's plan for a picnic with excitement. Verb.*
view (vyū) *noun, plural* **views;** *verb,* **viewed, viewing.**
■ **take a dim view of:** To regard with doubt or disapproval: *He took a dim view of his chances of becoming a member of the choir, but he tried out anyway.*

vigor—Active strength or force; vim: *to be filled with* vigor *and finish one's chores quickly; to argue with* vigor.
vig|or (vig′ər) *noun.*

vigorous—Full of or done with energy and spirit: *a* vigorous *teacher; a* vigorous *run around the block.*
vig|or|ous (vig′ər əs) *adjective.*
● Synonyms: **brisk, energetic, lively**

Viking or **viking**—Any one of a group of fierce northern pirates who raided the coasts of Europe from the A.D. 700's to the A.D. 1000's.
Vi|king or vi|king (vī′king) *noun, plural* **Vikings** or **vikings.**

village—A small group of houses that form a community. A village is smaller than a town.
vil|lage (vil′ij) *noun, plural* **villages.**

villain—An evil person: *The* villain *in the movie was always dressed in black.*
vil|lain (vil′ən) *noun, plural* **villains.**

vim—Energy; vigor: *He was filled with* vim *after his nap.*
vim (vim) *noun.*

vine—A plant with a long, bending stem. Vines grow along the ground or climb walls, fences, or

a at	i if	oo look	ch chalk		ə =	a in ago
ā ape	ī idle	ou out	ng sing			e in happen
ah calm	o odd	u ugly	sh ship			i in capital
aw all	ō oats	ū rule	th think			o in occur
e end	oi oil	ur turn	th their			u in upon
ē easy			zh treasure			

other plants. Grapes, melons, and beans grow on vines.
vine (vīn) *noun, plural* **vines.**

vinegar—A sour liquid used in salad dressings and in flavoring and preserving food.
vin|e|gar (vin′ə gər) *noun, plural* **vinegars.**

Word History

Vinegar comes from a French word meaning "sour wine." Some kinds of vinegar are made from wine. But other kinds are made from cider, the juice of berries, and other liquids.

---

vineyard—A piece of land where grapes are grown.
vine|yard (vin′yərd) *noun, plural* **vineyards.**

vinyl—Any one of a number of strong plastics. Vinyls are used to make a wide variety of products, including floor tiles, leatherlike clothing, and toys. *Noun.*
vi|nyl (vī′nəl) *noun, plural* **vinyls.**

viola—A musical instrument that has four strings and is played with a bow. It looks like a violin but is a little larger and lower in tone.
vi|o|la (vē ō′lə) *noun, plural* **violas.**

viola

violin

viola and **violin**

violate—To fail to obey or keep; break: *to* violate *a treaty; to* violate *a law; to* violate *a trust.*
vi|o|late (vī′ə lāt′) *verb,* **violated, violating.**

violence—Strong or rough force: *the* violence *of a storm; the* violence *of war.*
vi|o|lence (vī′ə ləns) *noun.*

violent—**1.** Done with strong physical force; brutal: *a violent* attack. **2.** Showing or caused by strong feelings: *a violent* argument; *a violent* temper.
vi|o|lent (vī′ə lənt) *adjective.*
• Synonyms: **bloodthirsty, cruel,** for **1.**
  Antonyms: **gentle, kind**[1], **tender,** for **1.**

violet—**1.** Any of many small flowers. Most violets are purple or blue, but some are white or yellow. The violet is the state flower of Illinois, New Jersey, Rhode Island, and Wisconsin. **2.** A bluish purple color. *Noun.*
—Having a bluish purple color: *a violet* sweater. *Adjective.*
vi|o|let (vī′ə lit) *noun, plural* **violets;** *adjective.*

violet (noun, definition 1)

violin—A musical instrument that has four strings and is played with a bow.
vi|o|lin (vī′ə lin′) *noun, plural* **violins.**
• See picture at **viola.**

virgin—Not yet changed or used; in the original state; pure: *to be the first to plant crops in* virgin *soil; finding rabbit tracks in the* virgin *snow.*
vir|gin (vur′jin) *adjective.*

virtue—**1.** Moral goodness in how one thinks and behaves: *Our minister is a person of great* virtue. **2.** A particular kind of moral goodness. *Patience is her best* virtue. **3.** Any good quality: *He has the* virtue *of being a good listener.*
vir|tue (vur′chū) *noun, plural* **virtues.**
■ **make a virtue of necessity:** To make the best of a bad situation; do what one has to do without complaining: *During the thunderstorm, I made a virtue of necessity by staying indoors and reading a book.*

virus—A tiny germ that lives in the cells of other living things. Viruses cause many diseases in

human beings, animals, and plants. Measles, colds, and polio are caused by viruses.
vi|rus (vī′rəs) *noun, plural* **viruses.**

vise—A tool with a pair of jaws that are opened and closed by means of a screw or lever. It is used to hold an object firmly in place while it is being worked on.
vise (vīs) *noun, plural* **vises.**

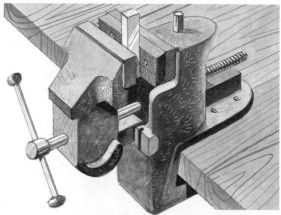

vise

visible—1. Able to be seen: *When the fog cleared, the mountains became* visible *in the distance.* 2. Easily seen, noticed, or understood: *There was* visible *improvement in her handwriting when she started to hold her pencil differently.*
vis|i|ble (viz′ə bəl) *adjective.*

vision—1. The ability to see; sense of sight: *Her* vision *used to be perfect, but now she needs to wear glasses when she reads.* 2. The ability to look or plan ahead: *The mayor was a person of great* vision *and often solved problems before they even occurred.* 3. Something that is seen in one's imagination or dreams: *When she daydreamed, she often had* visions *of being a famous ballet dancer.*
vi|sion (vizh′ən) *noun, plural* **visions.**

visit—1. To go or come to see: *Many of her friends* visited *her when she was in the hospital.* 2. To stay with as a guest: *My cousins are* visiting *us for a week. Verb.*
—A short stay or call: *The class paid a* visit *to the museum to see the new exhibit. Noun.*
vis|it (viz′it) *verb,* **visited, visiting;** *noun, plural* **visits.**

visitor—A person who goes to see another; guest.
vis|i|tor (viz′i tər) *noun, plural* **visitors.**

visor—The part that sticks out on the front of a cap and shades the eyes from the sun; brim.
vi|sor (vī′zər) *noun, plural* **visors.**

visual—Having to do with sight: *maps and other* visual *aids; eyeglasses used for correcting a* visual *problem.*
vis|u|al (vizh′ū əl) *adjective.*

vital—1. Having to do with or necessary for life: *a person's heartbeat and other* vital *signs; food* vital *to survival.* 2. Very important: *It is* vital *that I get a good grade on this test, or I will fail this subject.* 3. Full of life: *a* vital *person who takes part in many activities.*
vi|tal (vī′təl) *adjective.*

vitamin—Any one of a group of substances that the body needs in small amounts to be healthy and work normally. A balanced diet provides the body with the vitamins it needs.
vi|ta|min (vī′tə min) *noun, plural* **vitamins.**

vivid—1. Very bright and strong; brilliant: *His new bicycle is a* vivid *red.* 2. Clear and sharp: *That book includes a* vivid *description of pioneer life.* 3. Active; full of life: *Her* vivid *personality affects those around her and makes them all livelier.*
viv|id (viv′id) *adjective.*

Vizsla—A short-haired hunting dog that has a rusty gold coat. Originally bred in central Europe, these dogs were used to hunt with falcons.
Vizs|la (vēz′lah) *noun, plural* **Vizslas.**

a at	i if	oo look	ch chalk	⎡ a in ago
ā ape	ī idle	ou out	ng sing	e in happen
ah calm	o odd	u ugly	sh ship	ə = i in capital
aw all	ō oats	ū rule	th think	o in occur
e end	oi oil	ur turn	th their	⎣ u in upon
ē easy			zh treasure	

Vizsla

vocabulary—1. All the words in a language. 2. All the words used or understood by a particular person or group: *reading to improve one's vocabulary; the vocabulary of lawyers.* 3. A list of words and their meanings in alphabetical order; glossary: *If you do not understand a word in the book, check the vocabulary in the back.*
vo|cab|u|lar|y (vō kab′yə lār′ē) *noun, plural* **vocabularies.**

vocal—Having to do with or produced by the voice: vocal *music;* vocal *approval for a plan.*
vo|cal (vō′kəl) *adjective.*

vocal cords—Two bands of tissue in the throat. Sound is produced when the cords are close together and air from the lungs causes them to vibrate.
vo|cal cords (vō′kəl kawrdz) *plural noun.*

vocation—A particular job, career, or trade: *to prepare for a vocation as a lawyer.*
vo|ca|tion (vō kā′shən) *noun, plural* **vocations.**
• Synonyms: **occupation, profession**

voice—1. The sound that is made through the mouth by speaking, singing, or shouting: *the voices of children on the playground; glad to hear a friend's voice on the telephone.* 2. The ability to speak: *He had a sore throat and lost his voice.* 3. The right to express a choice or opinion: *My sister and I have a voice in deciding what to do on family outings. Noun.*
—To express or say: *to voice an idea. Verb.*
voice (vois) *noun, plural* **voices;** *verb,* **voiced, voicing.**
■ **with one voice:** With complete agreement; all together: *The children answered* with one voice *when they were asked if they wanted ice cream.*

volcano—1. An opening in the earth's surface through which fire, lava, dust, ashes, and hot gases burst forth. 2. A mountain formed by the material forced out of such an opening.
vol|ca|no (vol kā′nō) *noun, plural* **volcanoes** or **volcanos.**

Word History

Volcano comes from the name of a Roman god, Vulcan. Vulcan was the god of fire.

---

volleyball—1. A game in which two teams hit a ball back and forth across a net. The players hit the ball with their hands or arms and try to keep it from touching the ground. 2. The ball used in this game.

vol|ley|ball (vol′ē bawl′) *noun, plural* **volleyballs.**

volt—A unit for measuring the force of an electric current.
volt (vōlt) *noun, plural* **volts.** Abbreviation: **v.**

Word History

Volt comes from a man's name. Count Alessandro Volta was an Italian scientist of the 1700's and 1800's. Volta did many experiments with electricity and invented the electric battery.

---

voltage—The amount of force of an electric current, as measured in volts.
volt|age (vōl′tij) *noun, plural* **voltages.**

volume—1. A book: *a volume of poetry; a library with thousands of volumes.* 2. One of a set or series of books, magazines, or newspapers: *two volumes of the encyclopedia.* 3. The amount of space that something occupies: *the volume of a room; the volume of a box.* 4. The amount of loudness of sound: *Please turn down the volume on the radio.*
vol|ume (vol′yūm) *noun, plural* **volumes.** Abbreviations: **v.** or **vol.**
■ **speak volumes:** To be very expressive; be full of meaning: *His parents did not even have to ask him if he broke the dish, because the look on his face* spoke volumes.

voluntary—1. Done, made, or given by one's own free will: *a voluntary decision; a voluntary contribution.* 2. Controlled by the will: *We use voluntary muscles in the arm, hand, and fingers when we write.*
vol|un|tar|y (vol′ən tār′ē) *adjective.*

volunteer—1. A person who does something by his or her own free will and usually without pay: *volunteers at a church bake sale; volunteers working for a candidate for President.* 2. A person who chooses to join the armed forces. *Noun.*
—1. To offer to do something by one's own free will: *My sister volunteered to wash the dishes, even though it was my turn to do them.* 2. To offer or give something by one's own free will: *to volunteer a suggestion; to volunteer an answer to a question. Verb.*
—Acting as a volunteer; made up of volunteers: *a volunteer army; a volunteer fire department. Adjective.*
vol|un|teer (vol′ən tēr′) *noun, plural* **volunteers;** *verb,* **volunteered, volunteering;** *adjective.*

vote—1. The formal expression of a choice: *Have you cast your* vote *for class president yet?*
2. The right to give such an expression of choice: *The people in that country are ruled by a dictator and do not have the* vote.   3. The number for and against: *The* vote *was 25 in favor of the plan and 15 against. Noun.*
—1. To express a choice formally: *I* voted *for him to be captain of the team.*   2. To make available or give by a formal choice: *The board members* voted *funds for the repair of the church roof. Verb.*
vote (vōt) *noun, plural* **votes;** *verb,* **voted, voting.**

vow—A solemn pledge; formal promise: *marriage* vows. *Noun.*
—To make a solemn pledge; promise formally: *She* vowed *that she would not tell the secret. Verb.*
vow (vou) *noun, plural* **vows;** *verb,* **vowed, vowing.**

vowel—Any one of the letters *a, e, i, o,* and *u.* The letter *y* is sometimes a vowel.
vow|el (vou′əl) *noun, plural* **vowels.**

voyage—A long journey by water or through space: *a* voyage *across the ocean; a* voyage *to the moon.*
—To make such a journey: voyaging to distant islands.
voy|age (voi′ij) *noun, plural* **voyages;** *verb,* **voyaged, voyaging.**

vs.—The abbreviation for **versus.**

vulgar—Showing or having bad manners or taste; coarse; crude: *He has the* vulgar *habit of talking when his mouth is full of food.*
vul|gar (vul′gər) *adjective.*

vulture—Any one of several large birds that feed on dead animals. Vultures have no feathers on their heads and necks. They have dark feathers on the rest of their bodies.
vul|ture (vul′chər) *noun, plural* **vultures.**

vulture

a at	i if	oo look	ch chalk		a in ago
ā ape	ī idle	ou out	ng sing		e in happen
ah calm	o odd	u ugly	sh ship	ə =	i in capital
aw all	ō oats	ū rule	th think		o in occur
e end	oi oil	ur turn	th their		u in upon
ē easy			zh treasure		

About 5,000 years ago, the ancient Egyptians used this symbol. Later, people of the Middle East used the same symbol. They called it *waw*, their word for "hook."

About 3,000 years ago, other people in the Middle East used a similar symbol.

About 1,900 years ago, the Romans gave the capital **V** its present form. About 1,000 years ago, writers used **VV** as a letter. **VV** was also written **UU**, and the letter became known as "double U." The letter became the present form of **W**. The small letter **w** was first used about 1,000 years ago. It reached its present form about 500 years ago.

About 2,600 years ago, the Greeks gave the letter this form. They called it *upsilon*.

W or **w**—The twenty-third letter of the alphabet: *There are two w's in the word "window."*
W, w (dub′əl yū′) *noun, plural* **W's** or **Ws, w's** or **ws.**

W. or **W**—The abbreviations for **west.**

wad—**1.** A small, tightly packed mass of soft material: *a wad of cotton; a wad of gum.* **2.** A tight roll of papers or paper money: *a wad of five-dollar bills. Noun.*
—To form into a tightly packed mass: *After she finished with the grocery list, she* wadded *it up and threw it away. Verb.*
wad (wahd) *noun, plural* **wads;** *verb,* **wadded, wadding.** .

waddle—To walk with short steps, swaying the body from side to side, as a duck does. *Verb.*
—A walk in which a person or animal takes short steps and sways from side to side: *She walked with a bit of a* waddle *to try to keep her balance on the ice. Noun.*
wad|dle (wahd′əl) *verb,* **waddled, waddling;** *noun, plural* **waddles.**

wade—**1.** To walk in or through water, mud, or anything else that keeps the feet from moving freely: *He had to* wade *through the deep snow to get to the bus stop.* **2.** To make one's way slowly and with difficulty: *The teacher* waded *through a stack of students' essays before he went home.*
wade (wād) *verb,* **waded, wading.**

wafer—**1.** A thin cookie, cracker, or piece of candy. **2.** A Host used in a communion service.
wa|fer (wā′fər) *noun, plural* **wafers.**

waffle—A light, crisp cake made of batter. A waffle is cooked in a special appliance that presses a pattern of squares into it.
waf|fle (wahf′əl) *noun, plural* **waffles.**

wag—To move or cause to move up and down or from side to side: *My dog always* wags *her tail when she sees me coming. Verb.*
—The act of moving up and down or from side to side: *a wag of the head; a wag of a finger. Noun.*
wag (wag) *verb,* **wagged, wagging;** *noun, plural* **wags.**

wage—A payment for work: *She changed jobs in order to get a higher* wage. *Noun.*
—To carry on: *The President announced a plan to* wage *a war against drug abuse. Verb.*
wage (wāj) *noun, plural* **wages;** *verb,* **waged, waging.**
• Synonyms: **earnings, pay, salary,** for *noun.*

wager—A bet: *The friends made a small* wager *on which one of them would become class president. Noun.*
—To bet: *I* wagered *my brother a quarter that I could beat him home. Verb.*
wa|ger (wā′jər) *noun, plural* **wagers;** *verb,* **wagered, wagering.**

wagon—1. A four-wheeled vehicle used for carrying loads or passengers. A wagon is usually drawn by a horse or a team of horses. 2. A four-wheeled, toy cart: *She put her dolls in her wagon to take them to her friend's house.* wag|on (wag′ən) *noun, plural* **wagons.**

wail—1. To make a long cry of sadness or pain: *Her baby brother* wailed *when he bumped his head.* 2. To make a sound like a long, sad cry: *The sirens* wailed *as the fire trucks rushed to the burning building. Verb.*
—A long, sad cry or a sound like one: *a* wail *of grief. Noun.*
wail (wāl) *verb,* **wailed, wailing;** *noun, plural* **wails.**
• Synonyms: **bawl, sob, weep,** for *verb* 1.
Antonyms: For *verb* 1, see Antonyms at **cry.**

waist—1. The part of the body between the ribs and the hips. 2. The part of a piece of clothing that fits around this part of the body: *I do not have to wear a belt with these pants, because the waist is elastic.*
waist (wāst) *noun, plural* **waists.**
• A word that sounds the same is **waste.**

wait—1. To stay in a place until someone comes or something happens: *to* wait *for a bus at a bus stop; to* wait *for a friend to call.* 2. To put something off or be put off; delay or be delayed: *to* wait *until the last moment to study; to let a job* wait. *Verb.*
—The act of spending time until something happens, or the time spent: *We had a long* wait *in line before we could get tickets to the movie. Noun.*
wait (wāt) *verb,* **waited, waiting;** *noun, plural* **waits.**
■ **lie in wait:** To stay hidden and ready to ambush or attack: *The army approached the forest where the enemy was* lying in wait.
• A word that sounds the same is **weight.**

waiter—A man who serves food and drink to people in a restaurant or other place.
wait|er (wā′tər) *noun, plural* **waiters.**

waitress—A woman who serves food and drink to people in a restaurant or other place.
wait|ress (wā′tris) *noun, plural* **waitresses.**

wake¹—1. To stop sleeping: *He plans to* wake *up early tomorrow to go fishing.* 2. To cause to stop sleeping: *The thunderstorm last night* woke *my whole family.* 3. To become or cause to become active; stir up: *The movie* waked *a desire in him to become a dancer. Verb.*
—A watch kept over the body of a dead person before burial. *Noun.*
wake (wāk) *verb,* **waked** or **woke, waked, waking;** *noun, plural* **wakes.**

wake²—The track a boat, ship, or other thing makes as it moves through water.
wake (wāk) *noun, plural* **wakes.**
■ **in the wake of:** After; behind: *Roads were flooded* in the wake of *the storm.*

waken—1. To cause to stop sleeping: *The alarm clock* wakened *him.* 2. To stop sleeping: *She* wakened *from her nap.* 3. To become or cause to become active; stir up: *The book* wakened *her interest in history.*
wak|en (wā′kən) *verb,* **wakened, wakening.**

walk—1. To move or travel on foot; go by steps. When walking, a person always has one foot on the ground. 2. To go over, through, or across on foot: *She* walked *the fields looking for flowers.* 3. To go with someone on foot: *He* walked *his friend home after school.* 4. To cause to go on foot: *to* walk *a dog.* 5. In baseball, to allow a batter to go to first base by pitching four balls, or to go to first base after being pitched four balls: *a pitcher* walking *the first batter he faces; a batter* walking *to load the bases. Verb.*
—1. An act of going on foot: *She took a* walk *around the block.* 2. The distance to be covered in going on foot, or the time it takes to cover a certain distance on foot: *a short* walk *to a friend's house; a five-minute* walk *to the train.* 3. A place set apart or designed for going on foot; path; sidewalk: *The large garden has a gravel* walk *through it.* 4. A way of stepping; gait: *He has a little hop in his* walk. 5. In baseball, the advance of a batter to first base after having been pitched four balls. *Noun.*
walk (wawk) *verb,* **walked, walking;** *noun, plural* **walks.**
■ **win in a walk:** To win easily: *The popular candidate won the election* in a walk.
• Synonyms: **stroll** for *noun* 1; **pace, stride** for *noun* 4.

walkie-talkie—A portable two-way radio.
walk|ie-talk|ie (waw′kē taw′kē) *noun, plural* **walkie-talkies.**

wall—1. A solid structure that forms the side of a building or room. 2. A solid structure that

a at	i if	oo look	ch chalk	⎡ a in ago
ā ape	ī idle	ou out	ng sing	e in happen
ah calm	o odd	u ugly	sh ship	ə = i in capital
aw all	ō oats	ū rule	th think	o in occur
e end	oi oil	ur turn	th their	⎣ u in upon
ē easy			zh treasure	

divides or protects an area: *We took a walk along the old stone* wall *that surrounds the town.*
3. Something that looks or acts like such a structure: *The fields were separated by a* wall *of trees. Noun.*
—To divide, surround, protect, or block with such a structure or something like it: *The rocks from the avalanche* walled *up the entrance to the cave. Verb.*
wall (wawl) *noun, plural* **walls;** *verb,* **walled, walling.**
- **drive** (someone) **up the wall:** To annoy; irritate: *The sound of fingernails scratching against a blackboard* drives *her up the wall.*

wallet—A flat, folding case for carrying money, cards, and photographs.
wal|let (wahl′it *or* waw′lit) *noun, plural* **wallets.**

wallop—**1.** To hit hard: *She* walloped *the ball, and it went flying over the fence.* **2.** To beat completely: *Our team* walloped *theirs. Verb.*
—A hard blow: *It took only two* wallops *with the hammer to drive the nail into the wall. Noun.*
wal|lop (wahl′əp) *verb,* **walloped, walloping;** *noun, plural* **wallops.**

wallow—To roll about in mud, as pigs do.
wal|low (wahl′lō) *verb,* **wallowed, wallowing.**

wallpaper—Paper that has colors and patterns printed on it, used to decorate the walls of rooms. *Noun.*
—To put such paper on the walls of a room: *We are going to* wallpaper *my bedroom this weekend. Verb.*
wall|pa|per (wawl′pā′pər) *noun, plural* **wallpapers;** *verb,* **wallpapered, wallpapering.**

walnut—**1.** A sweet nut that grows on a tall tree and has a hard shell. **2.** The tree on which such nuts grow. **3.** A dark wood that comes from this

walkie-talkie

tree and is sometimes used to make furniture.
wal|nut (wawl′nut) *noun, plural* **walnuts.**

walrus—A large sea animal that lives in Arctic regions. It has a pair of long, ivory tusks and a tough, wrinkled skin.
wal|rus (wawl′rəs *or* wahl′rəs) *noun, plural* **walruses.**

walrus

Word History

Walrus comes from the Dutch name for the animal. The Dutch name came from two Dutch words. One meant "whale," and the other meant "horse." A walrus is like a whale, but it is not much like a horse. Experts believe that a form of this name was earlier used for some other animal.

waltz—**1.** A smooth dance in which a couple glides and whirls across the floor. **2.** The music for this dance. *Noun.*
—To do this dance. *Verb.*
waltz (wawlts) *noun, plural* **waltzes;** *verb,* **waltzed, waltzing.**

wampum—Small beads made from polished shells. Some tribes of North American Indians used wampum for money and for decoration.
wam|pum (wahm′pəm) *noun.*

wand—A thin rod or stick: *a magic* wand.
wand (wahnd) *noun, plural* **wands.**

wander—**1.** To move about from place to place without having a goal: *to be bored and* wander *through the house; a dog* wandering *the streets.*
2. To stray from a place, group, or subject: *to have one's mind* wander *while listening to a long speech; to* wander *off from a picnic in search of flowers.* **3.** To follow a winding course: *The river* wanders *through the valley.*
wan|der (wahn′dər) *verb,* **wandered, wandering.**

wane—To become smaller in size or importance: *That actor's popularity has* waned *since he made that awful movie.*
wane (wān) *verb,* **waned, waning.**

want—**1.** To wish for; desire: *He* wants *to go swimming.* **2.** To need; require: *The floor really* wanted *cleaning after I walked on it with my muddy shoes.* **3.** To be without; lack: *She is a fairly good singer but* wants *the talent to be a great one. Verb.*
—**1.** A need or desire: *She has* want *of a nap, because she did not sleep well last night.* **2.** A lack: *The charity went bankrupt for* want *of contributions. Noun.*
want (wahnt *or* wawnt) *verb,* **wanted, wanting;** *noun, plural* **wants.**
■ **want for:** To be in need of: *She is happy as she is and* wants for *nothing.*

wanting—Lacking; missing: *There is a button* wanting *on that shirt, so I cannot wear it.*
want|ing (wahn′ting *or* wawn′ting) *adjective.*

war—**1.** Fighting between nations or groups of people within a nation: *He fought overseas during the last* war. **2.** Any fight or struggle: *the* war *against hunger; the* war *against drug abuse. Noun.*
—To fight; battle: *The rebels have* warred *against the government for several years. Verb.*
war (wawr) *noun, plural* **wars;** *verb,* **warred, warring.**
● A word that sounds the same is **wore.**

warble—To sing with many, rapidly changing notes: *a* warbling *bird. Verb.*
—**1.** The act of singing in this way. **2.** A song sung in this way. *Noun.*
war|ble (wawr′bəl) *verb,* **warbled, warbling;** *noun, plural* **warbles.**

warbler—Any of several small songbirds. Most warblers have brightly colored feathers.
war|bler (wawr′blər) *noun, plural* **warblers.**

ward—**1.** A section of a hospital: *the emergency* ward. **2.** A person who is under the control or care of a court or a guardian. **3.** A division of a city or town.
ward (wawrd) *noun, plural* **wards.**

-ward—A suffix that means "in the direction of" or "toward." If a car is traveling seaward, it is traveling in the direction of the sea. If you look skyward, you look toward the sky.

You can understand the meanings of many words that end with **-ward,** if you add a meaning of the suffix to the meaning of the rest of the word.
schoolward: in the direction of school
leftward: toward the left

warden—**1.** A person whose job is making sure that certain laws, especially hunting and fishing laws, are obeyed: *The game* warden *checked the hunter's license.* **2.** The head of a prison.
ward|en (wawrd′ən) *noun, plural* **wardens.**

wardrobe—**1.** A person's clothes: *a summer* wardrobe. **2.** A closet or tall piece of furniture where clothes are kept.
ward|robe (wawr′drōb′) *noun, plural* **wardrobes.**

Word History

Wardrobe comes from an old French word for a place to keep clothes. That word came from two old French words. One meant "to guard," and the other meant "a piece of clothing." So a wardrobe is a place where clothes are guarded or protected.

warehouse—A large building where merchandise is stored.
ware|house (wār′hous′) *noun, plural* **warehouses.**

wares—Goods for sale; merchandise: *During the festival, many merchants displayed their* wares *on the sidewalk in front of their stores.*
wares (wārz) *plural noun.*

a at	i if	oo look	ch chalk		⌈ a in ago
ā ape	ī idle	ou out	ng sing		e in happen
ah calm	o odd	u ugly	sh ship	ə =	i in capital
aw all	ō oats	ū rule	th think		o in occur
e end	oi oil	ur turn	th their		⌊ u in upon
ē easy			zh treasure		

warbler

warfare—Fighting; combat: *That book describes how* warfare *has changed since the time when soldiers fought with swords and bows and arrows.*
war|fare (wawr′fār′) *noun.*

warlike—1. Fond of fighting: *They were a* warlike *people who preferred to settle disputes by battle instead of talking.*   2. Threatening war; possibly leading to war: *The president considered the boycott of his country's goods to be a* warlike *act.*
war|like (wawr′līk′) *adjective.*

warm—1. Somewhat hot: *a* warm *bath;* warm *milk; the* warm *days of spring.*   2. Giving or keeping heat: *a* warm *fire; a* warm *jacket.*
3. Having a feeling of heat: *We were* warm *after running around the block.*   4. Full of kindness or showing kindness; friendly; affectionate: *a* warm *greeting; a* warm *letter; a* warm *person. Adjective.*
—1. To make or become somewhat hot: *We* warmed *ourselves by the fire.*   2. To fill with pleasing or friendly feelings: *The music had a special charm that* warmed *the hearts of all who heard it. Verb.*
warm (wawrm) *adjective,* **warmer, warmest;** *verb,* **warmed, warming.**

warm-blooded—Having blood that stays close to one temperature, regardless of the temperature in the air or other surroundings. Human beings, other mammals, and birds are warm-blooded. Nearly all other kinds of animals are cold-blooded.
warm-blood|ed (wawrm′blud′id) *adjective.*

warmth—1. The condition of being somewhat hot: *the* warmth *of the sun; the* warmth *of a fire.*
2. Friendly or lively feelings: *to welcome a friend with* warmth; *to speak with* warmth *about a trip.*
warmth (wawrmth) *noun.*

warn—1. To give notice beforehand of possible danger, harm, or evil; put on guard: *Mother* warned *us not to swim in the river.*   2. To advise or caution; inform: *The label on the bottle* warned *that certain people should not take the medicine.*
warn (wawrn) *verb,* **warned, warning.**
• A word that sounds the same is **worn.**

warning—A notice or advice given beforehand: *a* warning *that the ice on the lake is too thin for skating; a* warning *not to eat too many snacks before dinner.*
warn|ing (wawr′ning) *noun, plural* **warnings.**

warp—1. To bend, curve, or twist out of shape: *Years of sun and rain have* warped *the boards on the floor of the porch.*   2. To become bent, curved, or twisted out of shape: *The record* warped *when we left it in the hot car.*
warp (wawrp) *verb,* **warped, warping.**

warrant—An official paper that gives the right to arrest or to search. *Noun.*
—1. To justify; deserve: *Her performance on the piano* warrants *special praise.*   2. To guarantee: *The new toaster is* warranted *for a year. Verb.*
war|rant (wawr′ənt *or* wahr′ənt) *noun, plural* **warrants;** *verb,* **warranted, warranting.**

warrior—A person who is used to fighting in war.
war|ri|or (wawr′ē ər *or* wahr′ē ər) *noun, plural* **warriors.**

warship—A ship that is built with weapons for fighting battles.
war|ship (wawr′ship′) *noun, plural* **warships.**

wart—A small, hard lump that grows on the skin. It is caused by a virus.
wart (wawrt) *noun, plural* **warts.**

was—The form of **be** used with **I, he, she,** or **it** to show the past: *I* was *sick last night and went to bed early.*
was (wahz *or* wuz) *verb.*

wash—1. To clean by using water or soap and water: *I just finished* washing *the floor, and it is still wet.*   2. To remove by using water or soap and water: *He* washed *the mud off his bicycle.*
3. To make oneself clean: *She got dusty during the softball game, so she had to* wash *afterward.*
4. To carry away or destroy by water: *The waves* washed *sand from the beach. Verb.*
—1. The act of cleaning: *He gave his hands and face a* wash *before dinner.*   2. A batch of clothes or other items to clean with soap and water, or cleaned with soap and water; laundry: *I put my dirty jeans in the* wash.   3. The flow or sound of moving water: *the* wash *of a stream over pebbles. Noun.*
wash (wahsh *or* wawsh) *verb,* **washed, washing;** *noun, plural* **washes.**
■ **come out in the wash:** To become known in the end: *The truth about whether he is really her friend will* come out in the wash.
wash up: To finish; ruin: *If we lose one more game, our chance of winning the prize is* washed up.

washcloth—A small piece of cloth used for washing oneself.
wash|cloth (wahsh′klawth′, wahsh′klahth′, wawsh′klawth′, *or* wawsh′klahth′) *noun, plural* **washcloths.**

washer—1. A person or machine that washes. 2. A flat ring placed between a nut and a bolt to give a tighter fit. Most washers are made of rubber or metal.
wash|er (wawsh′ər *or* wahsh′ər) *noun, plural* washers.

washing—A group of clothes or other items that are to be cleaned with soap and water or that have been cleaned with soap and water; laundry.
wash|ing (wahsh′ing *or* wawsh′ing) *noun.*

Washington's Birthday—February 22. The birthday of the first President of the United States used to be celebrated on this date. It is now celebrated on the third Monday in February.
Wash|ing|ton's Birth|day (wosh′ing tənz burth′dā) *noun.*
• See also **President's Day.**

wasn't—The contraction of "was not."
was|n't (wahz′ənt *or* wuz′ənt).

wasp—A flying insect that has a narrow waist. A wasp can give a painful sting.
wasp (wahsp) *noun, plural* wasps.

wasp

waste—1. To use or spend carelessly or needlessly: *He* wasted *his time staring out of the window, when he should have been writing his report.* 2. To ruin or damage; destroy: *The tornado* wasted *the town.* 3. To lose strength, health, or energy: *to* waste *away because of disease. Verb.*
—1. The act of wasting or condition of being wasted: *It would be a real* waste *of your singing talent if you do not try out for the choir.* 2. Worthless or useless material; garbage. 3. Useless or wild land: *desert* waste. *Noun.*
—1. Left over; worthless; useless: waste *paper.* 2. Having to do with or used for garbage: *a* waste *bag; a* waste *dump. Adjective.*

waste (wāst) *verb,* **wasted, wasting;** *noun, plural* **wastes;** *adjective.*
• A word that sounds the same is **waist.**
• Synonyms: For *noun* 2, see Synonyms at **garbage.**

wastebasket—A basket or other open container used to hold things to be thrown away: *She put the crumpled paper in the* wastebasket.
waste|bas|ket (wāst′bas′kit) *noun, plural* wastebaskets.

wasteful—Spending or using something carelessly or uselessly: *She was* wasteful *of water and often ran the shower for several minutes before getting into it.*
waste|ful (wāst′fəl) *adjective.*

wasteland—An area, such as a desert, where few or no plants and animals live.
waste|land (wāst′land′) *noun, plural* wastelands.

watch—1. To look at with attention: *They* watched *the movie from the balcony.* 2. To take care of; keep guard over: *My friend asked if I would* watch *his bicycle while he went in the store.* 3. To look for or wait for; be alert: *We went to* watch *for the train. Verb.*
—1. The act of guarding or looking at with attention: *a teacher keeping a* watch *on the children on the playground.* 2. A person or group of people who guard or protect something: *the night* watch *at a bank.* 3. A small device used for telling time. It is worn on the wrist or carried in a pocket. *Noun.*
watch (wahch) *verb,* **watched, watching;** *noun, plural* **watches.**

watchdog—A dog that guards property.
watch|dog (wahch′dawg′) *noun, plural* watchdogs.

watchful—On the lookout; alert: *The teacher was* watchful *to see that the class was not bored.*
watch|ful (wahch′fəl) *adjective.*

watchword—A word used to prove that a person belongs to a group and should be allowed past a guard; password.
watch|word (wahch′wurd) *noun, plural* watchwords.

water—The liquid that forms lakes, oceans, rivers, and rain. *Noun.*
—1. To put this liquid on or into: *I need to* water *the garden, because the weather has been so dry lately.* 2. To give an animal a drink of this liquid: *They* watered *the horses at the lake.* 3. To form tears or saliva: *onions making the eyes* water; *the smell of chocolate cake making the mouth* water. *Verb.*

a at	i if	oo look	ch chalk		a in ago
ā ape	ī idle	ou out	ng sing		e in happen
ah calm	o odd	u ugly	sh ship	ə =	i in capital
aw all	ō oats	ū rule	th think		o in occur
e end	oi oil	ur turn	th their		u in upon
ē easy			zh treasure		

wa|ter (waw′tər) *noun, plural* **waters;** *verb,*
watered, watering.

■ **in deep water:** In great trouble or difficulty:
She was in deep water *for lying to her parents.*
like water off a duck's back: Without having
any effect: *Our pleas to him to be on time were*
like water off a duck's back, *and he showed up
late as usual.*
water over the dam: Something that is past
and cannot be changed: *My poor grade on the
last test is* water over the dam.

water buffalo—A large ox that has long,
curved horns, and that likes to be in water or
mud. Water buffaloes live in Asia. They are used
to pull or carry heavy loads.
wa|ter buf|fa|lo (waw′tər buf′ə lō′) *noun,
plural* **water buffaloes, water buffalos,** or
water buffalo.

water buffalo

water color—1. A paint that is made by mixing
the coloring material with water. 2. A picture or
design made with such a paint.
wa|ter col|or (waw′tər kul′ər) *noun, plural*
water colors.

watercress—A plant that grows in water. Its
leaves are used in salads.
wa|ter|cress (waw′tər kres′) *noun, plural*
watercresses.

waterfall—A stream of water that falls from a
high place.
wa|ter|fall (waw′tər fawl′) *noun, plural*
waterfalls.

waterfront—The part of a city or town that is
near a body of water, or any land near a body of
water: *to go to the* waterfront *to watch a sailboat
race; a cabin on the* waterfront *that makes it
easy to go fishing.*
wa|ter|front (waw′tər frunt′) *noun, plural*
waterfronts.

water lily

water lily—A plant that grows in water. Its
leaves and flowers float on top of the water.
wa|ter lil|y (waw′tər lil′ē) *noun, plural*
water lilies.

watermelon—A large, sweet fruit. It has a
thick, green rind and juicy, red or pink pulp. It
grows on a vine.
wa|ter|mel|on (waw′tər mel′ən) *noun, plural*
watermelons.
● See picture at **melon.**

water moccasin—A poisonous snake that lives
in watery areas of the southeast United States.
wa|ter moc|ca|sin (waw′tər mok′ə sin) *noun,
plural* **water moccasins.**
● Another name for this snake is **cottonmouth.**

water moccasin

water polo—A water sport played by two teams
that try to score by throwing or pushing a ball
into the opponent's goal.
wa|ter po|lo (waw′tər pō′lō) *noun.*

water power—The energy produced by falling
or flowing water. Water power is used to run
machines and generate electricity.
wa|ter pow|er (waw′tər pou′ər) *noun.*

waterproof—Able to keep water from passing
through: *a* waterproof *hat;* waterproof *paper.
Adjective.*
—To treat with a special substance that keeps
water from passing through: *This umbrella has
been* waterproofed. *Verb.*
wa|ter|proof (waw′tər prūf′) *adjective; verb,*
waterproofed, waterproofing.

water ski—One of a pair of short, wide skis for gliding over water.
wa|ter ski (waw′tər skē) *noun, plural* **water skis.**

water-ski—To glide over water while wearing a pair of short, wide skis by holding a rope that is attached to a motorboat.
wa|ter-ski (waw′tər skē′) *verb,* **water-skied, water-skiing.**

waterway—A narrow body of water, such as a river or a canal, that ships and boats use.
wa|ter|way (waw′tər wā′) *noun, plural* **waterways.**

water wheel—A very large wheel that is turned by water flowing onto it. Water wheels provide power for machines, especially at mills.
wa|ter wheel (waw′tər hwēl) *noun, plural* **water wheels.**

water wheel

watery—1. Filled with water or moisture: watery *eyes.* 2. Having or containing too much water: watery *stew;* watery *pie.*
wa|ter|y (waw′tər ē) *adjective,* **waterier, wateriest.**

watt—A unit for measuring electric power: *This light bulb uses 75 watts.*
watt (wot) *noun, plural* **watts.** Abbreviation: w

wave—1. To move back and forth or up and down; flutter or sway: *to wave a banner; tall flowers waving in the breeze.* 2. To greet or signal by moving the hand or something else back and forth: *to wave hello; to wave a flashlight in warning.* 3. To give curves or curls to: *to wave hair. Verb.*
—1. A ridge or curve moving on the surface of a body of water: *The ocean waves broke against the shore.* 2. Anything like such a ridge or curve: *Sound and light move in waves.* 3. The act of greeting or signaling by moving the hand or something else back and forth: *a wave of the hand.* 4. A curve or curl: *waves in her hair.* 5. A sudden rise or drop in the temperature, which lasts for a time: *a heat wave. Noun.*
wave (wāv) *verb,* **waved, waving;** *noun, plural* **waves.**
■ **make waves:** To disturb the usual way of doing something; cause trouble: *Even though you don't like what the group is doing, you agreed to it, so don't make waves now.*

wavelength—The distance between the peak of one wave and the peak of the wave that is next to it.
wave|length (wāv′lengkth′ *or* wāv′length′) *noun, plural* **wavelengths.**
■ **on the same wavelength:** Thinking or feeling the same way; in agreement: *My friend and I must be on the same wavelength, because we bought the same bicycles.*

waver—To move in an unsteady way; sway: *He wavered back and forth as he tried to cross the slippery ice.*
wa|ver (wā′vər) *verb,* **wavered, wavering.**
• Synonyms: reel², stagger, teeter

wavy—Full of curves or curls: wavy *hair.*
wav|y (wā′vē) *adjective,* **wavier, waviest.**

wax¹—1. A sticky, yellowish substance made by bees for building honeycombs. 2. Any similar substance: *candle* wax; *ear* wax. 3. A substance that is used for polishing furniture, shoes, cars, or floors. *Noun.*
—To polish with this substance: *to wax a car. Verb.*
wax (waks) *noun, plural* **waxes;** *verb,* **waxed, waxing.**

wax²—1. To increase in size, strength, or intensity: *The moon waxes until it is full.* 2. To become: *The boy waxed silly as he told more jokes.*
wax (waks) *verb,* **waxed, waxing.**

way—1. A means or method: *We know several ways of cooking food.* 2. A road, path, or similar means of going from one place to another: *The bridge gave us a way across the river.* 3. A direction: *Do you know which way he went?* 4. Movement or travel along a certain

a at	i if	oo look	ch chalk		⎡ a in ago
ā ape	ī idle	ou out	ng sing		e in happen
ah calm	o odd	u ugly	sh ship	ə =	i in capital
aw all	ō oats	ū rule	th think		o in occur
e end	oi oil	ur turn	<u>th</u> their		⎣ u in upon
ē easy			zh treasure		

route: *I found a dollar on my* way *to the store.*
5. Distance: *It's only a short* way *from my house to yours.* **6.** What one wants or wishes: *Our aunt always lets my brother get his* way. **7.** A detail, manner, or respect: *In many* ways, *I'm glad to be going back to school. Noun.*
—Far: *She threw the ball* way *down the street. Adverb.*
way (wā) *noun, plural* **ways;** *adverb.*
■ **give way: 1.** To give in; submit; yield: *The mayor* gave way *to the people's demands for more parks.* **2.** To fall or break under force or pressure: *The old shelf finally* gave way *when she put the heavy box on it.*
• A word that sounds the same is **weigh.**

we—The people who are speaking or writing: We *ate at the new restaurant.*
we (wē) *plural pronoun.*
• A word that sounds the same is **wee.**

weak—**1.** Likely to break or fall under pressure: *a* weak *table.* **2.** Lacking strength, energy, or power: *a* weak *old woman; a* weak *voice.*
weak (wēk) *adjective,* **weaker, weakest.**
• A word that sounds the same is **week.**
• Synonyms: **feeble, lame, poor,** for **2.**

weaken—To make less strong: *The team was* weakened *when its two best players left.*
weak|en (wē′kən) *verb,* **weakened, weakening.**

weakling—A person or animal that lacks strength or energy.
weak|ling (wēk′ling) *noun, plural* **weaklings.**

weakly—In a way that lacks strength or energy: *to struggle* weakly; *pretending* weakly *to help. Adverb.*
—Lacking health or strength; feeble: *a* weakly *person. Adjective.*
weak|ly (wēk′lē) *adverb; adjective,* **weaklier, weakliest.**
• A word that sounds the same is **weekly.**

weakness—**1.** The condition or quality of lacking strength, energy, or intensity: *The* weakness *of the light made it difficult to see.* **2.** A fault; flaw: *His* weakness *is that he doesn't keep his room clean.* **3.** A special liking: *Her* weakness *for candy may make her put on weight.*
weak|ness (wēk′nis) *noun, plural* **weaknesses.**

wealth—**1.** A great amount of money or valuable possessions; riches: *The king is a man of* wealth. **2.** A very large amount: *a* wealth *of knowledge; a* wealth *of food.*
wealth (welth) *noun.*

wealthy—Having a great amount of money or valuable possessions; rich: *That* wealthy *woman owns several cars and houses.*

wealth|y (wel′thē) *adjective,* **wealthier, wealthiest.**

weapon—**1.** An object or machine that is used to attack or defend. Guns, cannons, knives, and clubs are weapons. **2.** Any action or means that is used to attack or defend: *We used a special spray in our garden as a* weapon *against insects.*
weap|on (wep′ən) *noun, plural* **weapons.**

wear—**1.** To have on the body: *to* wear *a hat; to* wear *jewelry.* **2.** To show: *to* wear *a frown.* **3.** To use up or damage by much use or rubbing: *The initials on my suitcase have been* worn *away.* **4.** To make by rubbing: *to* wear *a hole in a mitten.* **5.** To last, even after much use: *This sweater has* worn *well. Verb.*
—**1.** The act of using or the condition of being used: *I gave away my dress after two years of* wear. **2.** Damage that comes from much use: *Our old couch shows signs of* wear. **3.** Clothing: *That store doesn't sell men's* wear. *Noun.*
wear (wār) *verb,* **wore, worn, wearing;** *noun.*
■ **wear off:** To disappear slowly: *The effects of the medicine* wore off.
wear thin: 1. To grow weak; decrease: *My fear of the dog* wore thin *after I got to know him better.* **2.** To become less interesting: *That old story is* wearing thin.

weariness—The condition of being very tired: *After the long run, my* weariness *made it hard to stand up.*
wea|ri|ness (wēr′ē nis) *noun.*
• Synonyms: **exhaustion, fatigue**

weary—Very tired: *Studying so hard made her* weary. *Adjective.*
—To make or become very tired: *Painting the house* wearied *us. Verb.*
wea|ry (wēr′ē) *adjective,* **wearier, weariest;** *verb* **wearied, wearying.**

weasel—A quick, small animal with a long, narrow body, short legs, and soft brown fur. Weasels eat small animals, birds, and eggs.
wea|sel (wē′zəl) *noun, plural* **weasels** or **weasel.**
■ **weasel out:** To get out of an agreement or a

weasel

responsibility in a sneaky way: *She* weaseled out *of helping me clean up the yard.*

weather—The condition of the sky at a certain place and time: *the* weather *has been sunny, hot, and dry here this past month. Noun.*
—**1.** To become dried, worn, or faded from being outside: *The wind, rain, and sun* weathered *our wooden fence.* **2.** To come through safely; survive: *to* weather *a storm. Verb.*
weath|er (we<u>th</u>′ ər) *noun; verb,* **weathered, weathering.**
■ **under the weather:** Not feeling well; sick: *The girl stayed home from school because she was* under the weather.

Word Power

If you are interested in weather, here are some words for you to know. They are words used in the scientific study of weather. You can find these words in this dictionary.

barometer	Fahrenheit	squall
blizzard	humidity	temperature
Celsius	hurricane	thermometer
centigrade	meteorology	tornado
cyclone	monsoon	typhoon
drought	precipitation	vane

---

weather vane—A device that turns to show which way the wind is blowing; vane.
weath|er vane (we<u>th</u>′ ər vān) *noun, plural* **weather vanes.**
● See picture at **vane.**

weave—**1.** To make by passing threads or strips of material over and under one another in a crisscross pattern: *to* weave *a basket; to* weave *a rug.* **2.** To make a web: *The spider is* weaving *a web.* **3.** To move from side to side while making one's way forward: *The boy had to* weave *through the line of customers to reach his mother. Verb.*
—A pattern or way in which threads or strips of material are passed over and under one another: *a loose* weave. *Noun.*
weave (wēv) *verb,* **wove, woven, weaving** for

definitions 1 and 2, **weaved, weaving** for definition 3; *noun, plural* **weaves.**
● A word that sounds the same is **we've.**

web—**1.** A network of fine, silky threads spun by a spider; cobweb. **2.** Any network like a spider's web: *a* web *of paths in the forest.* **3.** The skin that connects the toes of certain water animals, such as ducks and frogs.
web (web) *noun, plural* **webs.**

webbed—Having or connected by a web: *Frogs have* webbed *feet.*
webbed (webd) *adjective.*

web-footed—Having toes that are connected by skin: *Geese are* web-footed.
web-foot|ed (web′ foot′ id) *adjective.*

wed—**1.** To take as a husband or wife; marry: *My aunt* wedded *my uncle 10 years ago.* **2.** To join in marriage: *A priest will* wed *the couple.*
wed (wed) *verb,* **wedded, wedded** or **wed, wedding.**

Wed.—The abbreviation for **Wednesday.**

we'd—The contraction of "we had," "we should," or "we would."
we'd (wēd).
● A word that sounds the same is **weed.**

wedding—**1.** A marriage ceremony. **2.** The anniversary of a marriage: *Our parents celebrated 25 years of marriage on their silver* wedding.
wed|ding (wed′ ing) *noun, plural* **weddings.**

wedge—**1.** A block of metal, wood, or other material that is thick at one end and that narrows to a thin edge at the other end. A wedge is used to split, separate, or lift objects, or to hold things in place. **2.** Something that is shaped like such a block: *a* wedge *of pie. Noun.*
—**1.** To split or separate with such a block: *to* wedge *a cabinet away from the wall.* **2.** To hold in place with such a block: *to* wedge *a door open.* **3.** To crowd, force, or squeeze, in or through a limited space: *to* wedge *a way between two closely parked cars. Verb.*
wedge (wej) *noun, plural* **wedges;** *verb,* **wedged, wedging.**

wedlock—The state of being married: *The couple was joined in* wedlock.
wed|lock (wed′ lok′) *noun.*

Wednesday—The fourth day of the week.
Wednes|day (wenz′ dē *or* wenz′ dā′) *noun, plural* **Wednesdays.** Abbreviation: **Wed.**

a at	i if	oo look	ch chalk		a in ago
ā ape	ī idle	ou out	ng sing		e in happen
ah calm	o odd	u ugly	sh ship	ə =	i in capital
aw all	ō oats	ū rule	th think		o in occur
e end	oi oil	ur turn	<u>th</u> their		u in upon
ē easy			zh treasure		

Word History

Wednesday comes from the name of a god. Long ago in Germany, Denmark, Sweden, and Norway, people believed that this god was the leader of all their gods and goddesses.

wee—1. Very little; tiny: *a wee puppy.* 2. Very early: *the wee hours of the morning.*
wee (wē) *adjective,* **weer, weest.**
  • A word that sounds the same is **we.**
  • Synonyms: For **1**, see Synonyms at **small.**
  Antonyms: For **1**, see Synonyms at **big.**

weed—A plant that grows where it is useless or harmful: *We pulled the* weeds *out of our flower garden. Noun.*
  —1. To rid of useless or harmful plants: *to* weed *a garden.* 2. To rid of anything that is unwanted, useless, or harmful: *to* weed *out the bad workers from the good ones. Verb.*
weed (wēd) *noun, plural* **weeds;** *verb,* **weeded, weeding.**
  • A word that sounds the same is **we'd.**

week—1. A period of seven days: *We spent two* weeks *in a cabin by a lake.* 2. The five days from Monday to Friday, during which a person works or attends school: *the work* week.
week (wēk) *noun, plural* **weeks.** Abbreviation: wk.
  • A word that sounds the same is **weak.**

weekday—Any day of the week except Saturday and Sunday.
week|day (wēk′dā′) *noun, plural* **weekdays.**

weekend—The period of time between Friday night and Monday morning.
week|end (wēk′end′) *noun, plural* **weekends.**

wedge (noun, definition 1)

weekly—1. Done, appearing, or happening once each week: *a weekly magazine.* 2. Having to do with a week or weekdays: *a weekly salary. Adjective.*
  —A newspaper or magazine that is published once each week. *Noun.*
  —Once each week; every week: *She visits her grandmother* weekly. *Adverb.*
week|ly (wēk′lē) *adjective; noun, plural* **weeklies;** *adverb.*
  • A word that sounds the same is **weakly.**

weep—To shed tears; cry: *He* wept *with joy when he heard the good news.*
weep (wēp) *verb,* **wept, weeping.**
  • Synonyms: **bawl, sob, wail**
  Antonyms: See Antonyms at **cry.**

weevil—A kind of small beetle that feeds on and destroys farm crops, such as grain and cotton.
wee|vil (wē′vəl) *noun, plural* **weevils.**
  • See picture at **boll weevil.**

weigh—1. To find out how heavy someone or something is: *to* weigh *vegetables.* 2. To have a certain amount of heaviness: *Some trucks* weigh *several tons.* 3. To think about carefully: *He* weighed *the advantages and disadvantages of moving to a new city.* 4. To press down on and cause to bend or sag: *The heavy books* weighed *down the shelf.* 5. To be a burden: *Regret for her rudeness* weighed *on her mind.*
weigh (wā) *verb,* **weighed, weighing.**
  • A word that sounds the same is **way.**

weight—1. How heavy someone or something is: *He is trying to lose* weight. 2. The force that the pull of gravity has on something: *A person's* weight *is six times larger on earth than on the moon.* 3. A unit or system of units for measuring how heavy something or someone is: *A gram is a unit of metric* weight. 4. Something heavy: *a paper* weight; *exercise* weights. 5. A burden; load: *the* weight *of responsibility.*
6. Value or importance: *the* weight *of someone's opinion.*
weight (wāt) *noun, plural* **weights.** Abbreviation: wt.
  ■ **pull** (one's) **weight:** To do one's fair share of work: *She* pulled *her* weight *in helping us set up camp.*
  throw (one's) **weight around:** To make a show of one's importance or influence: *The famous actress* threw *her* weight around *to get a good seat at the restaurant.*
  • A word that sounds the same is **wait.**

weightless—1. Barely heavy; very light: *a* weightless *balloon.* 2. Not experiencing the pull

of gravity: *Astronauts can float in outer space because they're* weightless.
weight|less (wāt′lis) *adjective.*

Weimaraner—A large dog with a smooth gray coat, pale eyes, and a tail that is cut short. Originally bred in Germany, Weimaraners were used as hunting dogs.
Wei|ma|ra|ner (wī′mə rah′nər) *noun, plural* **Weimaraners.**

Weimaraner

weird—**1.** Mysterious; eerie: *A weird light was shining in the abandoned cottage.* **2.** Unusual; very odd: *Her hair was arranged in a weird manner.*
weird (wērd) *adjective.*
• Synonyms: For **2**, see Synonyms at **curious.**

welcome—**1.** To greet with pleasure, friendliness, or ceremony: *The mayor welcomed the famous astronaut into town with a parade.* **2.** To be glad to accept or receive: *We welcome your invitation. Verb.*
—A kind and friendly greeting: *Our neighbor gave us a warm welcome. Noun.*
—**1.** Accepted or received with warmth and pleasure: *a welcome friend; a welcome sight.* **2.** Freely and warmly permitted: *You're welcome to eat some cookies.* **3.** A polite reply to the words "Thank you," said as "You're welcome." *Adjective.*
wel|come (wel′kəm) *verb,* **welcomed, welcoming;** *noun, plural* **welcomes;** *adjective.*

Word History

Welcome comes from an old English word meaning "wanted guest." A welcome visitor is someone that people are glad to see and want to be with.

weld—To join pieces of metal by softening them with heat and pressing them together. The pieces cool and harden into one: *to weld metal bars into a fence.*
weld (weld) *verb,* **welded, welding.**

welfare—**1.** Health, happiness, and prosperity; well-being: *Parents care about their children's welfare.* **2.** Money and other help that the government gives to those who are in need: *Poor families often receive welfare.*
wel|fare (wel′fār′) *noun.*

well¹—**1.** In a way that is good or satisfactory; all right: *to sing well; to do well at school.* **2.** Completely; thoroughly: *Clean your room well.* **3.** Much; quite a lot: *He jogged well over three miles today.* **4.** Closely; personally: *We know her well. Adverb.*
—**1.** Not sick; healthy: *Is your grandmother well?* **2.** Good; satisfactory: *All is well. Adjective.*
—**Well¹** expresses surprise, relief, or the beginning of a new thought: *Well! Look who's here. Well, he should have known better. Interjection.*
well (wel) *adverb,* **better, best;** *adjective; interjection.*

well²—**1.** A deep hole that is made in the ground by digging or drilling and from which oil, water, or gas is obtained. **2.** A spring or other natural source of water. **3.** Anything like such a hole or spring, that is used as a source of something: *An encyclopedia is a well of facts. Noun.*
—To rise or flow to the surface from a deeper source: *Tears welled in his eyes. Verb.*
well (wel) *noun, plural* **wells;** *verb,* **welled, welling.**

we'll—The contraction of "we will" or "we shall."
we'll (wēl).

well-balanced—Properly matched; reasonable: *a well-balanced meal; well-balanced plans.*
well-bal|anced (wel′bal′ənst) *adjective.*

well-behaved—Having good manners or behavior; polite: *a well-behaved child.*
well-be|haved (wel′bi hāvd′) *adjective.*

a at	**i** if	**oo** look	**ch** chalk		a in ago
ā ape	**ī** idle	**ou** out	**ng** sing		e in happen
ah calm	**o** odd	**u** ugly	**sh** ship	ə =	i in capital
aw all	**ō** oats	**ū** rule	**th** think		o in occur
e end	**oi** oil	**ur** turn	**th** their		u in upon
ē easy			**zh** treasure		

well-being—The condition of being healthy, happy, and prosperous; welfare: *Success at work and then a long vacation gave her a strong feeling of* well-being.
well-be|ing (wel′bē′ing) *noun.*

well-bred—Brought up to have good manners; polite: *We could see by his concern for others that he was* well-bred.
well-bred (wel′bred′) *adjective.*

well-known—Known to many people; famous: *a* well-known *book; a* well-known *city.*
well-known (wel′nōn′) *adjective.*

well-to-do—Having enough money to live comfortably; fairly rich; prosperous: *that* well-to-do *family takes a nice vacation every year.*
well-to-do (wel′tə dū′) *adjective.*

Welsh corgi—*See* **Cardigan Welsh corgi** and **Pembroke Welsh corgi.**
Welsh cor|gi (welsh cawr′gē) *noun, plural* Welsh corgis.

Welsh pony—A very strong work pony that was originally bred in Wales.
Welsh po|ny (welsh pō′nē) *noun, plural* Welsh ponies.

Welsh pony

Welsh springer spaniel—A large hunting dog with drooping ears, white and red markings, and a long, silky coat. Originally bred in Wales, these dogs were trained to spring at game in order to force it from hiding.
Welsh spring|er span|iel
(Welsh spring′ər span′yəl) *noun, plural* Welsh springer spaniels.

Welsh terrier—A medium-sized dog with a square snout, a short, upright tail, and a wiry black and tan coat. These dogs were originally bred in Wales for fox hunting.
Welsh ter|ri|er (welsh ter′ē ər) *noun, plural* Welsh terriers.

went—*See* **go.**
went (went) *verb.*

wept—*See* **weep.**
wept (wept) *verb.*

were—*See* **be.**
were (wur) *verb.*

we're—The contraction of "we are."
we're (wēr).

weren't—The contraction of "were not."
weren't (wurnt).

west—1. The direction in which the sun sets. 2. West: a. Any place that is in this direction. b. The part of the United States that is in this direction from the Mississippi River. *Noun.*
—1. Toward or in this direction: *on the* west *side of town.* 2. From this direction: *a* west *wind. Adjective.*
—Toward this direction: *to walk* west. *Adverb.*
west (west) *noun, adjective, adverb.*
Abbreviation: **W.** or **W**

western—1. Of, in or toward the direction in which the sun sets: *a* western *state.* 2. Coming from this direction: *a* western *storm.* 3. Western: a. of or in the part of the United States that is in this direction from the Mississippi River. b. Of or in the part of the world that is in this direction from Asia. *Adjective.*
—A story, book, television program, or movie

Welsh springer spaniel

about frontier life in this part of the United States. *Noun.*
west|ern (wes′tərn) *adjective; noun, plural* **westerns.**

westerner—1. Someone who lives in or was born in the western part of a country.
2. Westerner: Someone who lives in or was born in the western part of the United States.
west|ern|er (wes′tər nər) *noun, plural* **westerners.**

West Highland white terrier—A small dog with a wiry white coat, straight ears, and a short, upright tail. These dogs were originally bred in Scotland.
West High|land white ter|ri|er (west hī′lənd hwīt ter′ē ər) *noun, plural* **West Highland white terriers.**

westward—Toward the west: *A* westward *mountain cliff; a ship that sails* westward.
west|ward (west′wərd) *adjective, adverb.*

wet—1. Covered, dampened, or soaked with a liquid such as water: *a* wet *towel;* wet *fingers.*
2. Not yet dry or hard: wet *paint;* wet *clay.*
3. Rainy: wet *weather. Adjective.*
—To cover, dampen, or soak with a liquid such as water: *to* wet *one's hair. Verb.*
wet (wet) *adjective,* **wetter, wettest;** *verb,* **wet** or **wetted, wetting.**
　■ **all wet:** Entirely mistaken; wrong: *You're* all wet *if you think that one plus one equals three.*
　wet behind the ears: Lacking experience: *The new delivery person was* wet behind the ears *and easily got lost.*

we've—The contraction of "we have."
we've (wēv).
　● A word that sounds the same is **weave.**

whack—To strike with a sharp, swift blow: *to* whack *a stick against a fence; to* whack *a ball. Verb.*
—**1.** A sharp, swift blow: *She gave the rug a* whack.　**2.** The loud, echoing sound made by such a blow: *We could hear the* whacks *of the hammer. Noun.*
whack (hwak) *verb,* **whacked, whacking;** *noun, plural* **whacks.**

　■ **to have a whack at** or **to take a whack at:** To make an attempt; try: *Let me* take a whack at *lighting the campfire.*
　out of whack: Not working properly: *My radio is* out of whack.
　● Synonyms: **hit, slug², smack,** for *noun* 1.

whale—A very large sea animal that has a fishlike body with a broad, horizontal tail. Whales are mammals that breathe air.
whale (hwāl) *noun, plural* **whales.**

whaling—The hunting of whales for their flesh and oil.
whal|ing (hwā′ling) *noun.*

wharf—A landing place, such as a platform, that is built along a shore for ships to load and unload goods; dock.
wharf (hwawrf) *noun, plural* **wharves** (hwawrvz) or **wharfs.**

what—1. A word that is used to ask questions about things or people: What *would you like to play?*　**2.** The thing that; that which: *Did she do* what *you asked her to?*　**3.** Anything that: *My brother does* what *he wants. Pronoun.*
—**1.** A word that is used to ask questions about things or people: What *city do you live in?*
2. Any that: *Use* what *crayons you need.*
3. How great, surprising, or remarkable: What *a game! Adjective.*
—In which way; how: What *does that matter? Adverb.*
—A word that is used to show surprise, disbelief, or some other strong emotion: What! *It's bedtime already? Interjection.*
what (hwut *or* hwaht) *pronoun, adjective, adverb, interjection.*
　■ **so what?:** Why should anyone care?: *If he likes that one better than this one,* so what?
　what's what: The important details about something; true state or condition: *I heard that the neighbors may be moving. Do you know* what's what?

whatever—1. Anything that: *Wear* whatever *you want.*　**2.** No matter what: Whatever *he does, I'm sure he'll do it well.*　**3.** Which thing or things; what: Whatever *made him choose that color? Pronoun.*
—**1.** Any that: *You may borrow* whatever *tools you need.*　**2.** All of: *She spent* whatever *money she had left.*　**3.** Of any kind at all: *No pets* whatever *are allowed here.*　**4.** No matter what; any: Whatever *choice she makes will be fine. Adjective.*
what|ev|er (hwət ev′ər) *pronoun, adjective.*

a at	i if	oo look	ch chalk		a in ago
ā ape	ī idle	ou out	ng sing		e in happen
ah calm	o odd	u ugly	sh ship	ə =	i in capital
aw all	ō oats	ū rule	th think		o in occur
e end	oi oil	ur turn	th their		u in upon
ē easy			zh treasure		

what's—The contraction of "what is" or "what has."
   what's (hwuts *or* hwahts).

wheat—A tall grass with slender leaves and hollow stems that produces grain. The grain is used to make flour for bread and pasta products.
   wheat (hwēt) *noun.*

wheat

wheel—1. A round device that turns on a rod in its center. Wheels are used to move automobiles and other vehicles, and to provide power to certain machines. **2.** Anything that is shaped like or uses such a device: *a car's steering* wheel. *Noun.*
   —**1.** To more or roll on such a device: *The movers* wheeled *the furniture into our house.*
   2. To turn suddenly; spin: *She* wheeled *around at the sound of the bell. Verb.*
   wheel (hwēl) *noun, plural* **wheels;** *verb,* **wheeled, wheeling.**

wheelbarrow—A cart that has handles in the back for pushing by hand and one or two wheels underneath in the front. Wheelbarrows are used for moving small loads, such as dirt.
   wheel|bar|row (hwēl′bar′ō) *noun, plural* **wheelbarrows.**

wheelchair—A chair, usually made mostly of metal, on wheels. Wheelchairs are used for moving people who are ill or have handicaps.
   wheel|chair (hwēl′chār′) *noun, plural* **wheelchairs.**

wheeze—To breathe with difficulty, producing a hoarse, whistling sound: *The old man coughed and* wheezed.
   wheeze (hwēz) *verb,* **wheezed, wheezing.**

whelk—A large sea snail that has a spiral shell and is sometimes used for food.
   whelk (hwelk) *noun, plural* **whelks.**

when—At what time: When *does the store open? Adverb.*
   —**1.** At the time that: *I used to have a cat* when *I was five years old.* **2.** At any time that: *I get nervous* when *I speak in front of a group of people.* **3.** As soon as: *She'll pay the bill* when *it arrives.* **4.** At which time: *She slept until 8 A.M.,* when *the alarm rang.* **5.** Although: *He visited a friend* when *he should have stayed at home.* **6.** Considering that; if: *Why are you joining that club* when *you already belong to too many? Conjunction.*
   —What or which time: *Since* when *have you worn glasses? Pronoun.*
   when (hwen) *adverb, conjunction, pronoun.*

whenever—At whatever time: *I exercise* whenever *possible. We can leave* whenever *he arrives.*
   when|ev|er (hwen ev′ər) *adverb, conjunction.*

where—**1.** At or in what place: Where *is my sweater?* **2.** To what place: Where *is he going?* **3.** From what place: Where *did you buy that toy?* **4.** In what way: Where *is the humor in what he said? Adverb.*
   —**1.** At or in which place: *We're going to the zoo,* where *we can see lots of animals.* **2.** In any place in which; wherever: *Plant the flowers* where *the garden is empty.* **3.** Any place to which: *I'll go* where *she goes. Conjunction.*
   where (hwār) *adverb, conjunction.*

whereabouts—At or near what place: Whereabouts *do you live? Adverb.*
   —The place where someone or something is: *We don't know our dog's* whereabouts. *Noun.*
   where|a|bouts (hwār′ə bouts′) *adverb, noun.*

whereupon—At which time; after which: *We waited until the rain stopped,* whereupon *we went outside to play.*
   where|up|on (hwār′ə **pon**′ *or* hwār′ə **pawn**′) *conjunction.*

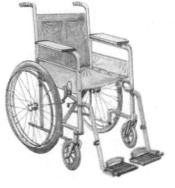

wheelchair

wherever—At, in, or to what place; where: Wherever *did she get that idea? Adverb.*
—To or in whatever place; anywhere: *He travels* wherever *he likes. Conjunction.*
wher|ev|er (hwār ev′ər) *adverb, conjunction.*

whether—1. A word that is used to show a choice between things: *I don't know* whether *to buy that game or this one.* 2. If: *She asked* whether *she could visit her friend.*
wheth|er (hwe<u>th</u>′ər) *conjunction.*

whew—A word that is used to show surprise, relief, or disappointment: Whew! *We arrived just in time for the movie.*
whew (hwyū) *interjection.*

whey—The watery part of milk that separates from the curds in making cheese or when milk sours.
whey (hwā) *noun.*

which—1. What one or ones: Which *is your favorite color?* 2. The one or ones that; any that: *List those* which *we named in class.* 3. The one or ones already talked or written about: *My parents like that house,* which *used to belong to my aunt. Pronoun.*
—1. What particular one or ones: Which *athlete won the race?* 2. Being the one or ones that are named: *You can eat* which *dessert you like. Adjective.*
which (hwich) *pronoun, adjective.*

whichever—1. Any one that; any that: *You can have* whichever *coat you like best. Take* whichever *you like.* 2. No matter what or which: Whichever *house we move to will be fine.* Whichever *you choose, we'll be glad to get it for you.*
which|ev|er (hwich ev′ər) *adjective, pronoun.*

whiff—A slight puff or smell: *a* whiff *of smoke; a* whiff *of grilled hamburgers.*
whiff (hwif) *noun, plural* **whiffs.**

while—A period of time: *a short* while. *Noun.*
—1. During the time that: while *someone is sleeping.* 2. At the same time that; although: While *we like winter, we prefer summer. Conjunction.*
—To spend time in a pleasant and relaxed way: *to* while *away the afternoon playing games. Verb.*

while (hwīl) *noun; conjunction; verb,* **whiled, whiling.**
- **worth** (one's) **while:** Worth one's effort, time, or trouble: *You'll find exercising to be* worth *your* while.

whim—A sudden wish or idea: *He had a* whim *to go swimming.*
whim (hwim) *noun, plural* **whims.**

whimper—To cry with soft, broken, whining sounds: *The hurt puppy* whimpered. *Verb.*
—The sound made by such a cry: *We heard her sad* whimpers. *Noun.*
whim|per (hwim′pər) *verb,* **whimpered, whimpering;** *noun, plural* **whimpers.**

whine—1. To make a long, shrill cry of complaint: *The baby* whined *for more ice cream.* 2. To complain in an annoying way: *to* whine *about having to mow the lawn. Verb.*
—The sound made by such a cry: *The dog's* whines *grew louder. Noun.*
whine (hwīn) *verb,* **whined, whining;** *noun, plural* **whines.**
• Synonyms: **fuss, gripe, grumble,** for *verb* 2.

whinny—A gentle or joyful neigh: *a horse's* whinny. *Noun.*
—To make such a sound: *We heard the horses* whinnying *in the stable. Verb.*
whin|ny (hwin′ē) *noun, plural* **whinnies;** *verb,* **whinnied, whinnying.**

whip—1. To hit with or as if with a stick, strap, or the like: *The strong wind* whipped *against the trees.* 2. To move or pull quickly and suddenly: *to see a person* whip *around; to* whip *a comb out of a pocket.* 3. To beat something, such as cream, until it is foamy: *We* whipped *the eggs for breakfast.* 4. To defeat: *We* whipped *the other school's baseball team. Verb.*
—A rod or stick, often with a leather strap at the end, used to drive cattle and horses. *Noun.*
whip (hwip) *verb,* **whipped, whipping;** *noun, plural* **whips.**
• Synonyms: **batter[1], beat, maul, pelt[1], thrash,** for *verb* 1.

whippet—A medium-sized, swift-running dog with very slender legs, a long thin tail, and a short, smooth coat. Whippets look like small greyhounds and are believed to have been bred in England for racing.
whip|pet (hwip′it) *noun, plural* **whippets.**

whippoorwill—A plump North American bird with brownish feathers. The call of the whippoorwill sounds like this bird's name.
whip|poor|will (hwip′ər wil′) *noun, plural* **whippoorwills.**

a at	i if	oo look	ch chalk		a in ago
ā ape	ī idle	ou out	ng sing		e in happen
ah calm	o odd	u ugly	sh ship	ə =	i in capital
aw all	ō oats	ū rule	th think		o in occur
e end	oi oil	ur turn	<u>th</u> their		u in upon
ē easy			zh treasure		

whippoorwill

whir—To make a low, steady buzzing sound: *The machine's wheels* whirred. *Verb.*
—A low, steady buzzing sound: *the* whir *of the clothes dryer. Noun.*
whir (hwur) *verb,* **whirred, whirring;** *noun,* *plural* **whirs.**

whirl—**1.** To spin or cause to spin quickly; rotate: *The wind made the loose papers* whirl *around us.* **2.** To turn around suddenly; wheel: *He* whirled *when I called his name.* **3.** To feel dizzy: *The girl's head* whirled *with delight when she saw all of her birthday gifts. Verb.*
—**1.** A quick spin or rotating movement: *She gave the wheel a* whirl. **2.** A dizzy or confused condition: *Her thoughts are in a* whirl *from all the new places she visited. Noun.*
whirl (hwurl) *verb,* **whirled, whirling;** *noun,* *plural* **whirls.**
■ **give (something) a whirl:** To try something new: *Why don't you give this dance a* whirl?

whirlpool—A current of water that spins very quickly: *The river's dangerous* whirlpool *sank*

whippet

the canoe, pulling it down in a few seconds.
whirl|pool (hwurl′pūl′) *noun, plural* **whirlpools.**

whirlwind—A current of air that spins very quickly and violently: *Several trees toppled in the storm's* whirlwind.
whirl|wind (hwurl′wind′) *noun, plural* **whirlwinds.**

whisk—**1.** To sweep or brush quickly and lightly: *to* whisk *crumbs from the chair.* **2.** To move quickly: *to* whisk *oneself out the door; to be* whisked *away in a car.*
whisk (hwisk) *verb,* **whisked, whisking.**

whisker—**1.** A stiff, long hair that grows on the faces of cats, mice, dogs, and certain other animals. **2. whiskers:** The hair on a man's face; beard and mustache.
whisk|er (hwis′kər) *noun, plural* **whiskers.**

whiskey—A strong alcoholic drink made from grain, such as corn, rye, or barley.
whis|key (hwis′kē) *noun, plural* **whiskeys.**

whisper—**1.** To say very softly and quietly, using the breath but not the vocal cords: *He* whispered *the secret to me.* **2.** To make a soft, rustling sound: *The wind* whispered *through the trees. Verb.*
—A low, soft, rustling or hissing sound: *We heard* whispers *in the audience. Noun.*
whis|per (hwis′pər) *verb,* **whispered, whispering;** *noun, plural* **whispers.**
● Synonyms: **mumble, mutter,** for *verb* **1.**
Antonyms: For *verb* **1,** see Synonyms at **cry,** *verb* **2.**

whistle—**1.** To make a clear, shrill sound by forcing air out between the teeth or between partly closed and rounded lips: *to* whistle *a tune.* **2.** To make or move with a sound like this: *The wind* whistled *through gaps in the cabin's boards.* **3.** To signal or call with a clear, shrill sound: *The train* whistled *that it was about to leave. Verb.*
—**1.** A device that makes a clear, shrill sound when air is forced through it: *a police officer's* whistle. **2.** A clear, shrill sound made by forced air: *the* whistle *of the tea kettle. Noun.*
whis|tle (hwis′əl) *verb,* **whistled, whistling;** *noun, plural* **whistles.**
■ **as clean as a whistle:** Completely clean and shiny; having no dirt or mess: *We washed the dishes until there were* as clean as a whistle.
blow the whistle: To reveal so as to stop or punish: *I* blew the whistle *on the boys who cheated on the test.*

white—**1.** The very lightest color; color of salt or fresh snow. **2.** Something that is light in color:

egg whites.   **3.** A person who is a member of a race that has light skin. *Noun.*
—**1.** Of the very lightest color; having the color of salt or fresh snow: *That car is* white.   **2.** Light in color: *Her fingers were* white *with cold.*
3. Pale gray or silver: white *hair.*   **4.** Having to do with a race of people that has light skin.
5. Filled with snow: *a* white *Christmas. Adjective.*
white (hwīt) *noun, plural* **whites;** *adjective,* **whiter, whitest.**
  ■ **white lie:** A harmless lie, usually told in an effort to be polite: *I told a* white lie *about why I couldn't go to her party so I wouldn't hurt her feelings.*

whitecap—A sea wave with a foaming white crest.
white|cap (hwīt′cap′) *noun, plural* **whitecaps.**

White House—**1.** The official home of the President of the United States, in Washington, D.C.   **2.** The power or office of the President of the United States: *The* White House *held a meeting with an important foreign official.*
White House (hwīt hous) *noun.*

whiten—To make or become the lightest color possible: *to* whiten *clothes with bleach.*
whit|en (hwīt′ən) *verb,* **whitened, whitening.**

white scallop—A white squash shaped something like the shell of a scallop.
white scal|lop (hwīt skol′əp *or* skal′əp) *noun, plural,* **white scallops.**
  ● See picture at **squash²**.

whitewash—A liquid containing water and white coloring, used to whiten wood fences, walls, and similar surfaces.
white|wash (hwīt′wawsh′ *or* hwīt′wahsh′) *noun.*

whittle—**1.** To cut small pieces from wood or another substance with a knife: *She* whittled *a fallen tree branch to pass the time.*   **2.** To make or shape in this way; carve: *to* whittle *a statue out of soap.*
whit|tle (hwit′əl) *verb,* **whittled, whittling.**

whiz—To move quickly with a low buzzing or humming sound: *The ball* whizzed *past my shoulder.*
whiz (hwiz) *verb,* **whizzed, whizzing.**
  ■ **whiz kid:** A young person who has talent or

knowledge that is outstanding for someone his or her age: *My sister is a* whiz kid *at chess.*

who—**1.** Which person or persons: Who *left the door open?*   **2.** The person or persons; that: *This is the woman* who *helped me find our dog.*
who (hū) *pronoun.*
  ● See Language Fact at **whom**.

whoa—Stop: *"*Whoa!*" she said to the speeding horse.*
whoa (hwō *or* wō) *interjection.*

who'd—The contraction of "who would" or "who had."
who'd (hūd).

whoever—**1.** Anyone that: Whoever *likes green can have my green pen.*   **2.** No matter who: Whoever *wants this dog, I plan to keep it.*
3. What person; who: Whoever *said you could eat the whole cake?*
who|ev|er (hū ev′ər) *pronoun.*

whole—With no part left out or missing; complete: *the* whole *day; a* whole *set of toy blocks. Adjective.*
—All of the parts of something; the complete thing: *the* whole *of the week. Noun.*
whole (hōl) *adjective, noun.*
  ■ **on the whole:** In general; with few exceptions: On the whole, *I like school.*
  ● A word that sounds the same is **hole**.

wholehearted—Warm and enthusiastic; sincere: *a* wholehearted *welcome.*
whole|heart|ed (hōl′hahr′tid) *adjective.*

whole number—A number that refers to whole things, not to parts of things like a fraction: *2, 5, 20, and 83 are* whole numbers, *but 2/3 and 5/10 are fractions.*
whole num|ber (hōl num′bər) *noun, plural* **whole numbers.**

wholesale—The sale of goods in large quantities, to be sold in small quantities by others such as store owners: *This table was bought at* wholesale *and sold to us at retail.*
whole|sale (hōl′sāl′) *noun.*

wholesome—**1.** Good for the health: wholesome *food.*   **2.** Showing good health; healthy: *His suntan gives him a* wholesome *appearance.*
whole|some (hōl′səm) *adjective.*

who'll—The contraction of "who will" or "who shall."
who'll (hūl).

wholly—Completely; totally: *I agree with you* wholly.
whol|ly (hō′lē) *adverb.*
  ● A word that sounds the same is **holy**.

a at	i if	oo look	ch chalk		a in ago
ā ape	ī idle	ou out	ng sing		e in happen
ah calm	o odd	u ugly	sh ship	ə =	i in capital
aw all	ō oats	ū rule	th think		o in occur
e end	oi oil	ur turn	<u>th</u> their		u in upon
ē easy			zh treasure		

whom—1. Which person or persons: *For* whom *did you buy that gift?* 2. The person or persons: *The woman* whom *I saw before has gone away.* **whom** (hūm) *pronoun.*

Language Fact

Whom is used to show that a person receives the action of a verb: Whom *did you see?* It is also used with prepositions: *He is the one with* whom *I spoke.* **Who** is used to show that a person performs the action of a verb: *She is the one who helped me.* It is also used to ask questions: Who *is there?*

---

whoop—A loud cry or shout: *She let out a* whoop *of excitement at seeing her friend again. Noun.* —To make a loud cry or shout: *to* whoop *with joy. Verb.* **whoop** (hūp *or* hwūp) *noun, plural* **whoops;** *verb,* **whooped, whooping.**
 • A word that sounds the same is **hoop.**

whooping crane—A large, very rare North American crane with white feathers, a red face, and a loud cry. **whoop|ing crane** (hū′ping krān *or* hwū′ping krān) *noun, plural* **whooping cranes.**

whooping crane

who's—The contraction of ''who is'' or ''who has.'' **who's** (hūz).
 • A word that sounds the same is **whose.**

whose—Of which or of whom: *a house* whose *door is painted red; the girl* whose *dress is blue.* **whose** (hūz) *pronoun.*
 • A word that sounds the same is **who's.**

why—1. For what reason: Why *did you miss school yesterday?* 2. Because of which: *Her friendliness is the reason* why *I like her. Adverb.* —A word that is used to show surprise, doubt, or some other feeling: Why, *maybe we should leave now. Interjection.* **why** (hwī) *adverb, interjection.*

wick—A length of cord or woven fibers in a candle or oil lamp that draws up oil or melted wax to be burned as fuel. **wick** (wik) *noun, plural* **wicks.**

wicked—Evil; vicious: *a wicked* witch; *wicked thoughts.* **wick|ed** (wik′id) *adjective,* **wickeder, wickedest.**
 • Synonyms: **bad, naughty, wrong** Antonyms: **good, moral, right**

wicker—Thin, bending branches or twigs, usually of willow. Wicker is woven together to make furniture, mats, baskets, and such items. **wick|er** (wik′ər) *noun.*

wide—1. Covering a large amount of space from side to side; broad: *a wide* lawn; *a wide* road. 2. Measuring a certain distance from side to side: *The window is three feet (one meter)* wide. 3. Having many different kinds; having a large range: *a wide* selection of toys. 4. Far from the point that is aimed at: *She threw the dart* wide *of its target.* 5. Completely open: *Her eyes were* wide *with wonder. Adjective.* —1. Throughout a large area: *to be known far and* wide. 2. All the way; fully: *a window that is open* wide. *Adverb.* **wide** (wīd) *adjective,* **wider, widest;** *adverb.*

widen—To make or become more broad: *to* widen *a sidewalk; a street that* widens *farther down.* **wid|en** (wīd′ən) *verb,* **widened, widening.**

widespread—1. Happening in many places or involving many people: *a widespread* disease; *a widespread* tradition. 2. Fully open: *to fly with* widespread *wings.* **wide|spread** (wīd′spred′) *adjective.*

widow—A woman whose husband has died and who has not married again. **wid|ow** (wid′ō) *noun, plural* **widows.**

widower—A man whose wife has died and who has not married again. **wid|ow|er** (wid′ō ər) *noun, plural* **widowers.**

width—The measurement of something from side to side: *The* width *of the door is three feet (one meter).* **width** (width) *noun, plural* **widths.**
 • See picture at **dimension.**

wife—A woman who is married.
wife (wīf) *noun, plural* **wives.**

Word History

Wife comes from an old English word meaning "woman." Hundreds of years ago, all women were called "wives," whether or not they were married.

wig—A covering made of real or artificial hair, worn on the head.
wig (wig) *noun, plural* **wigs.**

wiggle—To move from side to side or twist with short, quick motions: *The worm* wiggled *on the sidewalk.*
wig|gle (wig′əl) *verb,* **wiggled, wiggling.**
• Synonyms: **fidget, squirm, wriggle.**

wigwam—An Indian dwelling made of poles covered with hides, bark, or mats.
wig|wam (wig′wom′) *noun, plural* **wigwams.**

wigwam

wild—1. Living or growing in a natural state; not controlled: *a wild rabbit; wild flowers.*
2. Fierce; violent: *a wild wind; a wild battle.*
3. Lacking in discipline or control: *The wild girl pulled the other girls' hair to be mean.*
4. Fantastic; silly; unbelievable: *a wild idea. Adjective.*
—In a natural state; not under control: *Weeds grow wild. Adverb.*

—A large area of land that is in its natural state; wilderness: *Bears live in the wild. Noun.*
wild (wīld) *adjective,* **wilder, wildest;** *adverb; noun, plural* **wilds.**
• Synonyms: **ferocious, savage, vicious,** for *adjective* 2.

wildcat—A medium-sized animal that is related to the domestic cat but is larger and untamed. Wildcats are smaller than lions and tigers, and include lynxes, bobcats, and ocelots.
wild|cat (wīld′kat′) *noun, plural* **wildcats.**

wildebeest—*See* **gnu.**
wil|de|beest (wil′də bēst′), *noun, plural* **wildebeests.**

wilderness—A large area of land that is in its natural state and has few or no people living on it: *We camped in the wilderness.*
wil|der|ness (wil′dər nis) *noun, plural* **wildernesses.**

wildlife—Wild plants and animals that live in their natural surroundings: *Jungles have lots of wildlife.*
wild|life (wīld′līf′) *noun.*

will[1]—**1.** To be going to; be about to: *She will wash the dishes.* **2.** To have to; must: *"You will eat all your vegetables," said the boy's father.* **3.** To be able to; can: *This table will seat six.*
will (wil) *verb.*
• See Language Fact at **shall.**

will[2]—**1.** The power of the mind to decide and control what one does: *His strong will helps him to study hard.* **2.** A legal paper that says what a person wants to have done with his or her property after death: *My parents inherited my uncle's house in his will. Noun.*
—**1.** To use the power of the mind to decide and control what one does: *The girl willed herself to eat fewer sweets.* **2.** To give away one's property after death by means of a legal paper: *The woman willed her jewelry to her daughter. Verb.*
will (wil) *noun, plural* **wills;** *verb,* **willed, willing.**
▪ **with a will:** With energy and strong purpose: *He ran with a will and won the race.*

willing—Wanting to do something or content to do something: *He is willing to go if we wait.*
will|ing (wil′ing) *adjective.*

willow—A tree with narrow leaves and thin branches that bend easily.
wil|low (wil′ō) *noun, plural* **willows.**

wilt—To lose freshness and firmness; droop: *Plants wilt if they are not watered enough.*
wilt (wilt) *verb,* **wilted, wilting.**

a at	i if	oo look	ch chalk		a in ago
ā ape	ī idle	ou out	ng sing		e in happen
ah calm	o odd	u ugly	sh ship	ə =	i in capital
aw all	ō oats	ū rule	th think		o in occur
e end	oi oil	ur turn	th their		u in upon
ē easy			zh treasure		

wimp—A person who is weak or cowardly: *They called her a* wimp *because she was afraid to disagree with anyone.*
wimp (wimp) *noun, plural* **wimps.**

win—1. To do better than the other side in a game, contest, or battle: *That painting should* win *first place.* 2. To get as a reward or prize: *He bought a skateboard after he* won *$50 in the raffle.* 3. To earn by hard work or skill: *Women* won *the right to vote many years ago. Verb.*
—A victory; the result of doing better than another: *a record of 13 straight* wins. *Noun.*
win (win) *verb,* **won, winning;** *noun, plural* **wins.**

wince—To jerk quickly away from something painful or unpleasant; flinch; recoil: *She* winced *when the thorn stuck her hand.*
wince (wins) *verb,* **winced, wincing.**

winch—A machine for lifting or pulling heavy objects.
winch (winch) *noun, plural* **winches.**

wind[1]—1. Any air that moves: *A gentle* wind *feels good in the summer.* 2. The breath: *She got the* wind *knocked out of her when she fell. Noun.*
—To cause difficulty in breathing: *The jog around the block* winded *me. Verb.*
wind (wind) *noun, plural* **winds;** *verb,* **winded, winding.**

■ **get wind of:** To discover or hear about something: *The other team* got wind of *our game plan, so we had to change it.*
in the wind: Going to happen; about to occur: *She has been asking questions about my birthday, so I think something is* in the wind.
take the wind out of (one's) **sails:** To take away another's good position or advantage: *She took the* wind out of *my* sails *when she told me that I missed the deadline.*

wind[2]—1. To wrap around or be wrapped around something: *He went to* wind *a bandage around his scraped knee.* 2. To change directions several times: *The road* winds *along the river.* 3. To twist a handle or similar device that causes something to work: *Please* wind *the music box.*
wind (wīnd) *verb,* **wound, winding.**
● Synonyms: **curl, twine, twist** for 1.

windbreaker—A sports jacket that fits tight around the waist and wrists to keep the wind out.
wind|break|er (wind′brā′kər) *noun, plural* **windbreakers.**

wind instrument—A musical instrument that is played by blowing air through it. Flutes and trumpets are wind instruments.
wind in|stru|ment (wind in′strə mənt) *noun, plural* **wind instruments.**

windmill—A machine with large arms at the top that turn in a circle when the wind blows. Windmills can pump water or produce electricity.
wind|mill (wind′mill′) *noun, plural* **windmills.**

windmill

window—An open space in a wall that can let light and air into a room. Most windows are filled with glass and can be open or closed: *Let's open a* window *and air this room out.*
win|dow (win′dō) *noun, plural* **windows.**

windowpane—One section of glass in a window: *a ball next to the broken* windowpane.
win|dow|pane (win′dō pān′) *noun, plural* **windowpanes.**

windowsill—A piece of wood or stone right beneath a window.
win|dow|sill (win′dō sil′) *noun, plural* **windowsills.**

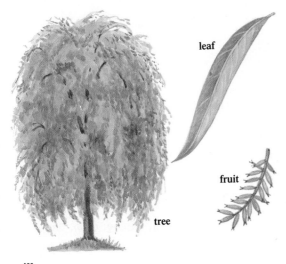
leaf

fruit

tree

willow

windpipe—The tube that carries air from the throat to the lungs.
wind|pipe (wind′pīp′) *noun, plural* **windpipes.**

windshield—A piece of glass or special plastic at the front of an automobile or other vehicle. It protects people from being hit by wind, rocks, or rain.
wind|shield (wind′shēld′) *noun, plural* **windshields.**

windsurfing—The sport in which people use the power of the wind to ride across water on a surfboard that has a sail.
wind|surf|ing (wind′sur′fing) *noun.*

windy—Having strong wind: *a* windy *day; a* windy *place.*
wind|y (win′dē) *adjective,* **windier, windiest.**

wine—A drink that contains alcohol and is made from the juice of certain fruits, such as grapes or plums.
wine (wīn) *noun, plural* **wines.**
  ● A word that sounds the same is **whine.**

wing—1. The movable body parts on birds, insects, or other animals that allows them to fly. 2. Something like this body part in shape or use: *an airplane's* wings. 3. A part of a building that sticks out from the main section: *The hospital added a new* wing *to have more room.*
4. wings: The parts of a theater that are on either side of the stage: *The actor left the stage through the* wings. *Noun.*
—To fly: *Ducks* wing *south for the winter. Verb.*
wing (wing) *noun, plural* **wings;** *verb,* **winged, winging.**
  ■ **on the wing: 1.** Flying: *The birds were on the* wing *as soon as we walked near the nest.*
  2. Busy; active: *I hardly see her anymore since she's always on the wing.*
  take wing: To fly away; to leave: *birds taking* wing; *people taking* wing *after the show.*

wingspread—The distance between the tips of an animal's wings when they are spread as if for flying: *A crow has a larger* wingspread *than a sparrow.*
wing|spread (wing′spred′) *noun, plural* **wingspreads.**

wink—To quickly close and open one eye, as a sign of affection or as a signal: *She* winked *at me when her brother started to tease us. Verb.*
—The act of quickly closing and opening one eye: *The coach gave her a* wink *as a sign to bunt. Noun.*
wink (wingk) *verb,* **winked, winking;** *noun, plural* **winks.**
  ■ **wink at:** To pretend not to see something, so that someone can continue without punishment: *Dad* winked *at our water balloon fight on the hot day.*

winner—The person or side that does better than others: *The* winner *gets to keep that big trophy.*
win|ner (win′ər) *noun, plural* **winners.**

winning—1. Doing better than others; successful: *a* winning *team; a* winning *ticket.* 2. Pleasant; charming: *a* winning *smile; a* winning *personality. Adjective.*
—**winnings:** The reward for having won: *The gambler's* winnings *were small. Noun.*
win|ning (win′ing) *adjective, plural noun.*

winter—The season of the year that comes between fall and spring; the coldest season of the year: *The days grow shorter in the* winter.
win|ter (win′tər) *noun, plural* **winters.**

wintergreen—A plant with red berries and white flowers. Its oil is used as a flavoring.
win|ter|green (win′tər grēn′) *noun, plural* **wintergreens.**

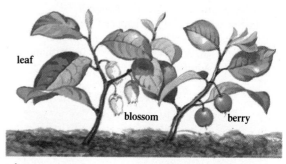

leaf　blossom　berry

wintergreen

wintry—Having to do with winter or like winter: wintry *weather; a* wintry *day.*
win|try (win′trē) *adjective,* **wintrier, wintriest.**

wipe—To dry or clean by rubbing with something: *to* wipe *up a spill; to* wipe *one's mouth. Verb.*
—The act of drying or cleaning by rubbing: *He gave the table a quick* wipe *to clean off the dust. Noun.*
wipe (wīp) *verb,* **wiped, wiping;** *noun, plural* **wipes.**

a at	i if	oo look	ch chalk	a in ago
ā ape	ī idle	ou out	ng sing	e in happen
ah calm	o odd	u ugly	sh ship	ə = i in capital
aw all	ō oats	ū rule	th think	o in occur
e end	oi oil	ur turn	th their	u in upon
ē easy			zh treasure	

wire—**1.** A thin, flexible piece of metal. **2.** A telegram: *She got a* wire *announcing the baby's birth. Noun.*
—**1.** To fasten with a thin piece of metal: *Mom had to* wire *the bird cage shut after the door broke.* **2.** To send a telegram: *He* wired *home for money when his wallet was stolen.* **3.** To install electricity: *People who* wire *houses are trained specialists. Verb.*
wire (wīr) *noun, plural* **wires;** *verb,* **wired, wiring.**

■ **down to the wire:** To the last minute possible; to the end: *The race was so close that it was* down to the wire *before we knew who won.*
under the wire: Just before the last minute possible; not quite too late: *The deadline for the contest is in two hours, so your entry is just* under the wire.

wire fox terrier—A small dog with a square face and a rough, wiry coat that is usually white with black or tan markings. Originally bred in England to hunt foxes, it makes a good watchdog.
wire fox ter|ri|er (wīr foks **ter′**ē ər) *noun, plural* **wire fox terriers.**

wirehaired pointing griffon—A medium-sized hunting dog with a rough, gray and brown coat. This dog points to and retrieves game. It was originally bred in France and the Netherlands.
wire|haired point|ing grif|fon (**wir′**hārd′ **point′**ing **grif′**ən) *noun, plural* **wirehaired pointing griffons.**

wireless—Using or having no wires: *a* wireless *telephone: a* wireless *radio. Adjective.*

—Another word for radio in some countries, such as the United Kingdom: *a program on the* wireless. *Noun.*
wire|less (**wīr′**lis) *adjective; noun, plural* **wirelesses.**

wiretap—To attach an electronic device to a telephone wire to listen to conversations or to record them.
wire|tap (**wīr′**tap) *verb,* **wiretapped, wiretapping.**

wiring—A set of wires that carries electricity: *The* wiring *in this lamp is bad, so it won't light.*
wir|ing (**wīr′**ing) *noun.*

wiry—**1.** Like wire, or made of wire: wiry *hair; a* wiry *brush.* **2.** Thin but strong: *a* wiry *body.*
wir|y (**wīr′**e) *adjective,* **wirier, wiriest.**

wisdom—Knowledge of what is right; good judgment in what is moral and true: *People who live long often have much* wisdom.
wis|dom (**wiz′**dəm) *noun.*

wise—Having or showing knowledge of what is right; with good judgment: *A* wise *person learns from mistakes.*
wise (wīz) *adjective,* **wiser, wisest.**

-wise—A suffix that means ''in the manner of,'' or ''in the direction of.'' Likewise is in a manner like something else. Lengthwise is in the direction of length.

Word Power

You can understand the meanings of many words that end in **-wise,** if you add a meaning of the suffix to the meaning of the rest of the word.
nowise: in no manner
widthwise: in the direction of the width

---

wisecrack—A smart remark, sometimes insulting: *She made some* wisecrack *about his new glasses.*
wise|crack (**wīz′**krak′) *noun, plural* **wisecracks.**

wish—**1.** A strong desire or hope for something: *If you could have a* wish *come true, what would it be?* **2.** A pleasant expression for someone: *best* wishes *for a happy birthday. Noun.*
—**1.** To want something; desire: *He* wished *for good weather on their vacation.* **2.** To express a desire: *I* wish *you a merry Christmas. Verb.*
wish (wish) *noun, plural* **wishes;** *verb,* **wished, wishing.**

wishbone—A bone in the breast of chickens and

wirehaired pointing griffon

Language Fact

Wishbone is not the scientific name for this part of a bird, but people use this name because of the custom of making a wish on this bone. Two people take hold of the wishbone and pull it until it breaks. Whoever has the larger piece gets to make a wish.

other birds that is shaped somewhat like the letter Y.
wishbone (wish′bōn′) *noun, plural* **wishbones.**

wishful—Having or showing a desire; longing: *His* wishful *face told me how much he missed his friend.*
wish|ful (wish′fəl) *adjective.*

wisp—**1.** A small scrap or piece of something: wisps *of hair in my face.* **2.** A small amount of smoke: wisps *of smoke blowing into the air.*
wisp (wisp) *noun, plural* **wisps.**

wisteria—A climbing plant with a woody stem and groups of purple, blue, or white flowers that droop from the branches.
wis|te|ri|a (wi stēr′ē ə) *noun.*

wisteria

wistful—Sadly longing for something: *The* wistful *dog stared at the meat on the table.*
wist|ful (wist′fəl) *adjective.*

a at	i if	oo look	ch chalk		a in ago
ā ape	ī idle	ou out	ng sing		e in happen
ah calm	o odd	u ugly	sh ship	ə =	i in capital
aw all	ō oats	ū rule	th think		o in occur
e end	oi oil	ur turn	th their		u in upon
ē easy			zh treasure		

wit—**1.** The ability to make clever, funny observations about life: *Her* wit *kept us all entertained during the bus ride.* **2.** A person who can make clever, funny observations: *Our history teacher is such a* wit *that class is never boring.* **3.** The ability to think clearly, especially during a rough situation: *The man struggled to keep his* wits *during the traffic jam.*
wit (wit) *noun, plural* **wits.**

witch—A person thought to have magic powers and who uses the powers to do bad or evil things.
witch (wich) *noun, plural* **witches.**

with—**1.** In the company of another: *May I go* with *you?* **2.** Added to: *Mom likes cream* with *her coffee.* **3.** Having or wearing: *the man* with *the dog; the woman* with *the hat.* **4.** In a certain way: *He spoke* with *haste.* **5.** In the opinion of: *This idea is okay* with *me.* **6.** On the same side; in support of: *He is* with *me on my neighborhood cleanup plan.* **7.** Using: *She wiped her cut* with *a tissue.* **8.** Because of; as a result of: *He cried* with *joy at the movie's happy ending.* **9.** In regard to: *She is unhappy* with *her test score.* **10.** In the same direction as: *The raft is drifting* with *the river's tide.* **11.** Against: *I wouldn't want to fight* with *that big man.*
with (with *or* with) *preposition.*

withdraw—**1.** To take away or remove: *The senator will* withdraw *her objection to the plan if it is worded differently.* **2.** To back off; retreat: *We* withdrew *when the other side threw a bunch of snowballs.*
with|draw (with **draw′** *or* with **draw′**) *verb,* **withdrew, withdrawn, withdrawing.**

withdrawn—*See* **withdraw.** *Verb.*
—Shy; quiet: *He was* withdrawn *until he got to know us. Adjective.*
with|drawn (with **drawn′** *or* with **drawn′**) *verb, adjective.*

wither—To dry up or cause to dry up: *The lack of rain* withered *the lawn and garden.*
with|er (with′er) *verb,* **withered, withering.**

withhold—**1.** To refuse to give or allow: *The newspaper is* withholding *the names of the victims.* **2.** To control; restrain: *The audience* withheld *their applause until the end of the ceremony.*
with|hold (with **hōld′** *or* with **hōld′**) *verb,* **withheld, withholding.**

within—**1.** Inside of something: Within *this chest are my most precious souvenirs.* **2.** Not past; not beyond: *I live* within *20 miles of the lake.*
with|in (with **in′** *or* with **in′**) *preposition.*

without—1. Lacking; not having: *a sandwich without fries; a tree without leaves.* 2. In a way that leaves something out; not doing or making: *I crept in without making noise.*
with|out (with out′ *or* with out′) *preposition.*

withstand—To resist some kind of pressure; to hold out successfully: *Tall buildings are made to withstand strong winds.*
with|stand (with stand′ *or* with stand′) *verb,* **withstood, withstanding.**

witness—1. Someone who has seen or heard something: *Are you a witness to the robbery?* 2. A person who is asked to give evidence in a court of law: *That doctor has been a medical witness in several trials. Noun.*
—1. To see or hear something: *We witnessed the car accident from across the street.* 2. To sign a legal document as someone who was present: *to witness a marriage license. Verb.*
wit|ness (wit′nis) *noun, plural* **witnesses;** *verb,* **witnessed, witnessing.**

witty—Clever and funny: *a witty person; a witty remark.*
wit|ty (wit′ē) *adjective,* **wittier, wittiest.**

wives—*See* **wife.**
wives (wīvz) *plural noun.*

wizard—1. A man thought to have magic powers; a magician: *The king asked his wizard to tell him the future.* 2. A clever, talented person: *He's a wizard in the kitchen and makes many good dishes.*
wiz|ard (wiz′ərd) *noun, plural* **wizards.**

Word History

Wizard comes from an old English word meaning "wise person." When people believed in magic, they thought of it as something needing to be studied carefully. Only a wise person, they thought, would be able to use magical powers.

---

wobble—To move from side to side in a shaky or unsteady way: *That old cart wobbles, so don't set anything heavy on it.*
wob|ble (wob′əl) *verb,* **wobbled, wobbling.**

woe—Great sadness or trouble: *The family in the story suffered many woes after being shipwrecked.*
woe (wō) *noun, plural* **woes.**
• Synonyms: **misery, sorrow**
 Antonyms: See Synonyms at **bliss.**

woeful—Showing great sadness or trouble, or filled with sadness and trouble: *a woeful face; a woeful day.*
woe|ful (wō′fəl) *adjective.*

woke—*See* **wake.**
woke (wōk) *verb.*

wolf—A wild animal that looks like a dog and lives in northern areas. *Noun.*
—To gobble food quickly: *Don't wolf your food down, or you'll get sick. Verb.*
wolf (woolf) *noun, plural* **wolves** (woolvz); *verb,* **wolfed, wolfing.**
■ **cry wolf:** To announce that there is a problem when no problem really exists: *When she claimed to be sick but had no sign of illness, her father decided she was* crying wolf.
keep the wolf from the door: To protect oneself from poverty and hunger: *The poor man had to work night and day just to* keep the wolf from the door.
throw to the wolves: To give someone or something up to an unpleasant situation: *She told me she would help, but she* threw me to the wolves *the day before my project was due.*
wolf in sheep's clothing: Someone who hides bad intentions behind a polite appearance: *The family friend turned out to be a* wolf in sheep's clothing *when he stole the television.*

wolf (noun)

wolfhound—Any dog belonging to a group of large dogs that were originally bred to hunt wolves. Borzois, Irish wolfhounds, and Scottish deer hounds are wolfhounds.
wolf|hound (woolf′hound′) *noun, plural* **wolfhounds.**
• See pictures at **borzoi** and **Irish wolfhound.**

wolverine—A wild animal with short legs and

wolverine

dark, bushy fur. It is related to the weasel.
wol|ver|ine (wool′və rēn′) *noun, plural*
wolverines.

wolves—*See* **wolf.**
wolves (woolvz) *plural noun.*

woman—1. An adult person that is female. 2. All
adult female people.
wom|an (woom′ən) *noun, plural* **women**
(wim′ən).

womb—The part of the body of most female
mammals that holds and nourishes young before
they are born.
womb (wūm) *noun, plural* **wombs.**

wombat—An animal that looks like a small bear
and lives in Australia. Female wombats carry
their young in a pouch, like kangaroos.
wom|bat (wom′bat) *noun, plural* **wombats.**

wombat

women—*See* **woman.**
women (wim′ən) *plural noun.*

won—*See* **win.**
won (wun) *verb.*
• A word that sounds the same is **one.**

a at	**i** if	**oo** look	**ch** chalk		a in ago
ā ape	**ī** idle	**ou** out	**ng** sing		e in happen
ah calm	**o** odd	**u** ugly	**sh** ship	ə =	i in capital
aw all	**ō** oats	**ū** rule	**th** think		o in occur
e end	**oi** oil	**ur** turn	<u>th</u> their		u in upon
ē easy			**zh** treasure		

wonder—1. To want to know something; to be
curious: *I wonder why he didn't come.* 2. To be
amazed: *I wonder that she can even stand after
jogging 10 miles. Verb.*
—1. An unusual or awesome sight: *His magic is
a* wonder *that everyone should see.* 2. Surprise;
amazement: *She asked with* wonder *if the rumor
was true. Noun.*
won|der (wun′dər) *verb,* **wondered, wondering:**
noun, plural **wonders.**

wonderful—Very good or remarkable: *a*
wonderful *surprise; a* wonderful *job.*
won|der|ful (won′dər fəl) *adjective.*
• Synonyms: **excellent, outstanding, superb**

won't—The contraction of "will not."
won't (wōnt).

wood—1. The hard material that is the trunk and
branches of a tree. 2. This material cut up and
used for building: *Most of the furniture in our
house is made of* wood. 3. **woods:** A large
number of trees growing close together; forest:
We hiked through the woods.
wood (wood) *noun, plural* **woods.**
■ **touch wood** or **knock on wood:** To touch
something made of wood in the belief that this
act makes good luck continue or prevents bad
luck: *She's doing well in science class,* knock
on wood.
• A word that sounds the same is **would.**

woodchuck—A wild animal with short legs,
brown fur, and a bushy tail. A woodchuck digs
tunnels in the ground and lives in them.
wood|chuck (wood′chuk′) *noun, plural*
woodchucks.
• Another name for this animal is **groundhog.**

woodchuck

wooded—Covered with trees: wooded *country; a* wooded *area.*
wood|ed (wood′id) *adjective.*

wooden—Made from wood: *a* wooden *chest; a* wooden *door.*
wood|en (wood′ən) *adjective.*

woodland—Land that is covered with trees.
wood|land (wood′land′) *noun, plural* **woodlands.**

woodpecker—A bird that has a strong, sharp bill. A woodpecker drills tiny holes in trees to find insects for food.
wood|peck|er (wood′pek′ər) *noun, plural* **woodpeckers.**

woodpecker

woodwind—A musical instrument that is played by blowing air through it, but that is not a horn. Clarinets and saxophones are woodwinds. Trumpets and trombones are not.
wood|wind (wood′wind′) *noun, plural* **woodwinds.**

woodwork—Things that are made of wood, especially parts of a house, such as doors and stairs.
wood|work (wood′wurk′) *noun.*
■ **come out of the woodwork:** To come out of hiding; seem to come from nowhere: *At first no one thought he would win the election, but now he has votes* coming out of the woodwork.

woodworking—The skill of making things from wood.
wood|work|ing (wood′wur′king) *noun.*

woody—1. Having several trees: *a* woody *field.* 2. Made of wood or like wood.
wood|y (wood′ē) *adjective,* **woodier, woodiest.**

woof—A dog's bark: *That small dog has a funny* woof. *Noun.*
—To make the sound of a dog barking; bark: *Our dog* woofs *loudly when the doorbell rings. Verb.*
woof (woof) *noun, plural* **woofs;** *verb,* **woofed, woofing.**

wool—1. The thick, curly hair of sheep or some other animals that is made into cloth. 2. Cloth or yarn made from the fur of sheep or certain other animals.
wool (wool) *noun, plural* **wools.**
■ **pull the wool over** (one's) **eyes:** To trick or deceive someone: *She* pulled the wool over *my* eyes *by making me think she left and then hiding.*

woolen—Made of wool: Woolen *sweaters can be itchy.*
wool|en (wool′ən) *adjective.*

woolly—1. Made of wool: *This* woolly *hat keeps me warm on windy days.* 2. Soft and fuzzy: woolly *fur.*
wool|ly (wool′ē) *adjective,* **woollier, woolliest.**

word—1. A sound or group of sounds that has a meaning: *He couldn't understand a* word *she said.* 2. A letter or group of letters that means such a sound: *We have a quiz next week on our spelling* words. 3. A short conversation or comment: *Mom asked to have a* word *with me about my grades.* 4. A promise: *I give you my* word *that I didn't tell anyone.* 5. News; information: *Have you received any* word *from the contest judge?* 6. words: Angry remarks: *They had* words *about who started the rumor. Noun.*
—To express ideas with sounds or letters: *He* worded *his opinion mildly so that he did not hurt his friend. Verb.*
word (wurd) *noun, plural* **words;** *verb,* **worded, wording.**
■ **as good as** (one's) **word:** Dependable; doing what one promises: *If she said she'll call, she will, since she's* as good as *her* word.
eat (one's) **words:** To take back what one has said; admit error: *If you are too quick in judging him, you may have to* eat *your* words.
● Synonyms: **assurance, pledge, guarantee,** for *noun* **4.**

wording—The way that something is said or written; words used to express a thought: *The* wording *of her comment was polite, but the meaning was rude.*
word|ing (wur′ding) *noun, plural* **wordings.**

word processor—A computer that does the work of a typewriter better and faster. It has a keyboard and a screen. People see on the screen the words that they have typed, and can change mistakes before the machine prints the words on paper.
word pro|ces|sor (wurd pros′es′ər) *noun, plural* **word processors.**

wordy—Using too many words: *The speaker was so wordy that our class ended ten minutes late.*
word|y (**wur′**dē) *adjective,* **wordier, wordiest.**

wore—*See* **wear.**
wore (wawr) *verb.*
● A word that sounds the same is **war.**

work—1. The effort required to do something; labor: *The teacher said our essays should take about two hours' work.* 2. How a person earns money; job: *His* work *as a nurse sounds exciting.* 3. Tasks that are done or need to be done: *Dad saved some household* work *for us to do this weekend.* 4. Something that has resulted from effort: *He doesn't consider that novel one of his better* works. 5. **works:** The moving parts of a machine: *She examined the* works *of the typewriter before trying to fix it. Noun.*
—1. To put forth effort to do something; labor: *He* worked *on the painting until it was finished.* 2. To earn money; have a job: *She* works *before school delivering papers.* 3. To use; manage: *Dad says I'm too young to* work *the lawn mower.* 4. To perform a function; go; run: *The car doesn't* work, *so we must take the bus. Verb.*
work (wurk) *noun, plural* **works;** *verb,* **worked, working.**

workbench—A sturdy table where physical labor is done and where tools are often stored.
work|bench (**wurk′**bench′) *noun, plural* **workbenches.**

workbook—A book for students that has questions and exercises and that can be written in.
work|book (**wurk′**book′) *noun, plural* **workbooks.**

worker—1. Someone who works: *The* workers *take their breaks in the afternoon.* 2. A female bee, ant, or other insect that cannot have young. These females do the work of their hive or nest.
work|er (**wur′**kər) *noun, plural* **workers.**

workhorse—1. A horse that is used mainly for working rather than for riding or racing. 2. A person who does much work quickly: *When it comes to his homework, he is a* workhorse.
work|horse (**wurk′**hors′) *noun, plural* **workhorses.**

workmanship—The talent and skill used to make something: *The handmade pottery showed fine* workmanship.
work|man|ship (**wurk′**mən ship) *noun.*

workout—Exercise, especially of a regular sort: *My* workout *is to swim every afternoon.*
work|out (**wurk′**out′) *noun, plural* **workouts.**

workshop—1. A room or area where physical labor is done and where machines are often stored and used. 2. People who study or work together to learn about a certain subject: *a* workshop *in writing that meets in the library.*
work|shop (**wurk′**shop′) *noun, plural* **workshops.**

world—1. The earth: *People used to think that the* world *was flat.* 2. A part of the earth: *In history we studied people of the eastern* world. 3. All the people living on the earth: *He thinks that hunger is the* world's *biggest problem.* 4. An area of interest or study: *The* world *of science was excited about her discovery of a new star.* 5. A large quantity; lots: *His talk with his parents did all three of them a* world *of good.*
world (wurld) *noun, plural* **worlds.**

worldwide—Being or happening all over the world: *She thinks there should be a* worldwide *effort to stop all wars.*
world|wide (**wurld′wīd′**) *adjective.*

worm—A kind of animal like a snake but smaller and without scales. Worms have no backbone and live in the ground. *Noun.*
—1. To wriggle or crawl like this animal: *She* wormed *her way through the crowded lobby to the door.* 2. To get in a cunning, sly way: *He* wormed *the answer from us. Verb.*
worm (wurm) *noun, plural* **worms;** *verb,* **wormed, worming.**

worn—*See* **wear.** *Verb.*
—Shabby from much use; frayed: *This blanket is so* worn *it's barely in one piece. Adjective.*
worn (wawrn) *verb, adjective.*
● A word that sounds the same is **warn.**

worn-out—1. In poor condition from much use; not able to be used anymore: *Dad says that our television is* worn-out *and we need a new one.* 2. Tired; weary: *He was* worn-out *from his long day at work.*
worn|out (**worn′out′**) *adjective.*

a at	i if	oo look	ch chalk		a in ago
ā ape	ī idle	ou out	ng sing		e in happen
ah calm	o odd	u ugly	sh ship	ə =	i in capital
aw all	ō oats	ū rule	th think		o in occur
e end	oi oil	ur turn	th their		u in upon
ē easy			zh treasure		

worry—1. To feel or cause to feel troubled or restless: *He* worried *about his sick friend.* 2. To grasp and pull again and again: *a dog* worrying *a bone. Verb.*
—Something that causes a troubled or restless feeling; concern: *Their biggest* worry *was how to explain the broken glass. Noun.*
wor|ry (wur′ē) *verb,* worried, worrying; *noun, plural* worries.

worse—1. More than bad; not so good as another; not so good as before: *He is a bad swimmer, but you are even* worse. 2. More than ill: *If you do not rest, you will feel* worse. *Adjective.*
—More than badly; less well than another or before: *This shirt fits* worse *than that. Adverb.*
worse (wurs) *adjective, adverb.*

worship—Devotion to a holy being, especially God, shown by prayer and ceremonies. *Noun.*
—1. To pray to God or another sacred being. 2. To love and respect: *She* worships *her older brother. Verb.*
wor|ship (wur′ship) *noun; verb,* worshiped or worshipped, worshiping or worshipping.

worst—1. Most bad; less good than any other: *the* worst *grade in the class.* 2. Most ill: *She felt* worst *when her fever was highest. Adjective.*
—Most badly; less well than any other: *The old car works* worst *right after it is started. Adverb.*
worst (wurst) *adjective, adverb.*

worth—1. Having a certain value: *Mom didn't think that shirt was* worth *$22.* 2. Good or important enough: *He thought the play was* worth *seeing twice.* 3. Having wealth that amounts to: *He is* worth *a million dollars. Adjective.*
—1. Value, importance: *Her dad says friendship can't be measured in* worth. 2. The amount that a sum of money will buy: *We bought $25* worth *of food for our picnic. Noun.*
worth (wurth) *adjective, noun.*

worthwhile—Useful or good enough to spend time or effort on; worthy: *Practicing the piano takes time, but I think the results are* worthwhile.
worth|while (wurth′hwīl′) *adjective.*

worthy—1. Good or valuable; worthwhile: *Helping stray animals is a* worthy *cause.* 2. Deserving praise or honor: *She feels that nursing is a* worthy *profession.*
wor|thy (wur′thē) *adjective,* worthier, worthiest.

would—*See* will.
would (wood) *verb.*
• A word that sounds the same is **wood.**

wouldn't—The contraction of "would not."
wouldn't (wood′ənt).

wound[1]—An injury to some part of the body, especially a cut: *a knife* wound. *Noun.*
—1. To injure or hurt: *His hand was* wounded *when he fell off the swing.* 2. To hurt someone's feelings: *Their remarks* wounded *her. Verb.*
wound (wūnd) *noun, plural* wounds; *verb,* wounded, wounding.

wound[2]—*See* wind.
wound (wound) *verb.*

wove—*See* weave.
wove (wōv) *verb.*

woven—*See* weave.
wo|ven (wō′vən) *verb.*

wow—A word that shows surprise, wonder, or excitement: Wow! *I can't believe I actually won.*
wow (wou) *interjection.*

wrap—1. To wind or fold a cover around: *She* wrapped *a towel around her wet hair.* 2. To clasp; hold: *He* wrapped *his arm around his sister during the scary movie.* 3. To disguise by covering with something: *Please* wrap *Mom's birthday present before she gets home from work.*
wrap (rap) *verb,* wrapped, wrapping.
• A word that sounds the same is **rap.**

wrapper—A piece of paper, cloth, or other material that covers something: *a candy* wrapper.
wrap|per (rap′ər) *noun, plural* wrappers.

wrapping—Paper or other material used to cover something: *The* wrapping *on this present is lovely.*
wrap|ping (rap′ing) *noun, plural* wrappings.

wrath—Strong anger: *Her* wrath *lessened when we explained that it was an accident.*
wrath (rath) *noun.*
• Synonyms: **fury, rage**
Antonyms: **calm, peace**

wreath—A circle of flowers or leaves that is used as a decoration, especially at Christmas or at funerals.
wreath (rēth) *noun, plural* wreaths (rēthz).

wreck—To damage badly; destroy; ruin: *to* wreck *a car; to* wreck *a chance. Verb.*
—1. Damaging accident; crash: *This winding road is the scene of many car* wrecks. 2. What remains after something has been damaged or ruined: *The people set to cleaning up the* wreck *of their town after the tornado. Noun.*
wreck (rek) *verb,* wrecked, wrecking; *noun, plural* wrecks.

wreckage—What remains after something has been damaged or destroyed.
wreck|age (rek′ij) *noun.*

wren

wren—A small, brown or gray songbird that often points its tail up in the air.
wren (ren) *noun, plural* **wrens.**

wrench—**1.** A tool that is used for gripping something tightly so that it can be turned. **2.** A sudden, hard twist. *Noun.*
—**1.** To twist or pull with force: *He* wrenched *the book out of my hands.* **2.** To hurt part of the body by twisting: *to* wrench *an ankle. Verb.*
wrench (rench) *noun, plural* **wrenches;** *verb,* **wrenched, wrenching.**

wrestle—**1.** To fight by holding, pulling, leaning, and such actions, in close physical contact: *kittens* wrestling *on the rug.* **2.** To take part in a sport that is like such fighting. **3.** To struggle to solve or do something: wrestling *with a problem.*
wres|tle (res′əl) *verb,* **wrestled, wrestling.**

wretched—**1.** Uncomfortable and miserable: *The flu left him feeling* wretched. **2.** Wicked; vicious: *The* wretched *killer was imprisoned.*
wretch|ed (rech′id) *adjective.*

wriggle—To twist and turn from side to side; wiggle: *Don't* wriggle *while getting a hair cut.*
wrig|gle (rig′əl) *verb,* **wriggled, wriggling.**
• Synonyms: **fidget, squirm**

wring—**1.** To twist something and squeeze: *Please help me* wring *out these wet blankets.* **2.** To get something by force or effort.
wring (ring) *verb,* **wrung, wringing.**
• A word that sounds the same is **ring.**

wrinkle—A fold or crease in the surface of something: *My sister is very neat and makes sure that all the* wrinkles *are out of her bedspread. Noun.*
—To have or cause to have creases or folds: *The shirts* wrinkled *from the heat in the dryer. Verb.*
wrin|kle (ring′kəl) *noun, plural* **wrinkles;** *verb,* **wrinkled, wrinkling.**

wrist—The part of the body that connects the hand to the arm.
wrist (rist) *noun, plural* **wrists.**

wristwatch—A small watch connected to a band or strap and worn on the wrist.
wrist|watch (rist′woch′) *noun, plural* **wristwatches.**

write—**1.** To form letters or words with a pencil, a pen, or another writing tool: *The teacher told us to* write *our answers in the test booklet.* **2.** To send a letter: *Her friend* wrote *to her every week from summer camp.* **3.** To be the author of: *to* write *a story; to* write *a letter.*
write (rīte) *verb,* **wrote, written, writing.**
• Words that sound the same are **right** and **rite.**

writing—**1.** Letters or words that have been made by hand: *His* writing *is hard to read.* **2.** writings: The works of an author; stories, poems or plays that a person has written: *Her* writings *have been collected together into one book.*
writ|ing (rī′ting) *noun, plural* **writings.**

written—*See* **write.**
writ|ten (rit′ən) *verb.*

wrong—**1.** Not true or right; incorrect: *He followed the* wrong *directions and got lost.* **2.** Not good; unfair; evil: *It is* wrong *to cheat on tests.* **3.** Not working correctly: *Something is* wrong *with this phone.* **4.** Not proper; unsuitable: *This blouse is* wrong *for that skirt. Adjective.*
—In an incorrect way; badly: *She dialed* wrong *and didn't reach her friend. Adverb.*
—Something that is not good; bad act: *Dad said laughing at the crippled man was a* wrong. *Noun.*
—To treat badly: *I* wronged *him by starting that rumor about him. Verb.*
wrong (rong) *adjective; adverb; noun, plural* **wrongs;** *verb,* **wronged, wronging.**
• Synonyms: **bad, naughty, wicked,** for *adjective* 2.
Antonyms: **moral, right,** for *adjective* 2.

wrote—*See* **write.**
wrote (rōte) *verb.*

wrung—*See* **wring.**
wrung (rung) *verb.*
• A word that sounds the same is **rung.**

a at	i if	oo look	ch chalk		a in ago
ā ape	ī idle	ou out	ng sing		e in happen
ah calm	o odd	u ugly	sh ship	ə =	i in capital
aw all	ō oats	ū rule	th think		o in occur
e end	oi oil	ur turn	th their		u in upon
ē easy			zh treasure		

About 1,900 years ago, the Romans gave the capital **X** its present form. The small letter **x** was first used about 1,200 years ago. It reached its present form about 500 years ago.

About 3,500 years ago, people in the Middle East had a letter called *samekh*, but historians are not sure what symbol they used for this letter. About 3,000 years ago, other people in the Middle East used this symbol for the letter *samekh*.

About 2,600 years ago, the Greeks gave the letter this form. They called it *chi*.

X or **x**—1. The twenty-fourth letter of the alphabet: *There is one* x *in the word "ox."*
2. The Roman numeral for the number 10.   **3.** A scientific symbol for something that is unknown.
X, x (eks) *noun, plural* **X's** *or* **Xs, x's** *or* **xs.**

Xerox—A trademark for a process of making photographic copies of written or printed material.
Xe|rox (zēr′oks) *noun.*

Xmas—Christmas.
X|mas (kris′məs *or* eks′məs) *noun, plural* **Xmases.**

X ray—1. A powerful type of radiation that can pass through substances which ordinary light cannot pass through. Doctors use X rays to take pictures of parts of the body that cannot be seen from the outside, such as the lungs and bones.
2. A picture made with such radiation: *The dentist looked at an X ray of the girl's tooth to see if she had a cavity.*
X ray (eks rā) *noun, plural* **X rays.**

Word History

X rays were named by a German scientist, Wilhelm Roentgen. He discovered X rays in 1895. When he named them, Roentgen did not understand what the rays were. X is a scientific symbol for something that is unknown.

X-ray—To look at, photograph, or treat with the powerful type of radiation called X rays: *The*

guards at the airport X-rayed *the luggage to check for weapons.* Verb.
—Producing or having to do with this type of radiation: *an* X-ray *machine.* Adjective.
X-ray (eks′rā′) *verb,* **X-rayed, X-raying;** *adjective.*

xylophone—A musical instrument that is made up of two rows of different-sized, wooden bars. It is played by striking the bars with a small wooden hammer.
xy|lo|phone (zī′lə fōn′) *noun, plural* **xylophones.**

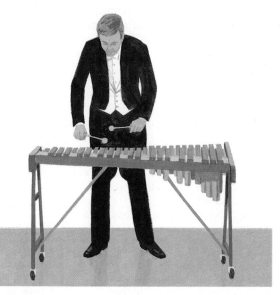

xylophone

About 1,900 years ago, the Romans gave the capital **Y** its present form. The small letter **y** was first used about 1,700 years ago. It reached its present form about 500 years ago.

About 5,000 years ago, the ancient Egyptians used this symbol. Later people in the Middle East used the same symbol. They called it *waw*, their word for ''hook.''

About 3,000 years ago, other people in the Middle East used a similar symbol.

About 2,600 years ago, the Greeks gave the letter this form. They called it *upsilon*.

Y or **y**—The twenty-fifth letter of the alphabet: *There are two* y's *in the word ''yearly.''*
Y, y (wī) *noun, plural* **Y's** or **Ys, y's** or **ys.**

-y—A suffix that means ''full of,'' ''resembling,'' or ''tending to.'' A dirty shirt is one that is full of dirt. A fish that has a silvery color has a color resembling silver. A weepy person tends to weep easily.

Word Power

You can understand the meanings of many words that end in **-y**, if you add a meaning of the suffix to the meaning of the rest of the word.
  salty: full of salt
  waxy: resembling wax
  chatty: tending to chat

---

yacht—A small ship used for pleasure trips or racing.
yacht (yaht) *noun, plural* **yachts.**

yak—A long-haired ox that lives in Asia. It is raised for its milk and meat, and it is used as a work animal.
yak (yak) *noun, plural* **yaks.**

a at	i if	oo look	ch chalk		a in ago
ā ape	ī idle	ou out	ng sing		e in happen
ah calm	o odd	u ugly	sh ship	ə =	i in capital
aw all	ō oats	ū rule	th think		o in occur
e end	oi oil	ur turn	th their		u in upon
ē easy			zh treasure		

yam—**1.** The thick root of a plant that grows in tropical regions. It is ground into flour or eaten as a vegetable.   **2.** A type of sweet potato.
yam (yam) *noun, plural* **yams.**

yank—To pull with a sharp, sudden movement; jerk: *to* yank *weeds from a garden; to* yank *a door open. Verb.*
—A sudden, sharp movement: *She gave the leash a* yank *to keep her dog from getting into the wet cement. Noun.*
yank (yangk) *verb,* **yanked, yanking;** *noun, plural* **yanks.**

Yankee—**1.** A person born or living in the United States.   **2.** A person born or living in the northern United States.
Yan|kee (yang′kē) *noun, plural* **Yankees.**

yak

yap—A quick, sharp bark. *Noun.*
—To give a quick, sharp bark: *The dog* yapped *when we knocked on the door. Verb.*
yap (yap) *noun, plural* **yaps**; *verb,* **yapped, yapping.**
• Synonyms: **yelp, yip**

yard[1]—**1.** An area of ground next to or around a building: *My brother and I take turns mowing the* yard *at our house.* **2.** A place where railroad cars are kept.
yard (yahrd) *noun, plural* **yards.**

yard[2]—A unit of length equal to 36 inches or 3 feet (0.9 meter).
yard (yahrd) *noun, plural* **yards.** Abbreviation: **yd.**

yard

meter

foot

yard[2]

yardstick—A measuring stick that is one yard long.
yard|stick (yahrd′stik′) *noun, plural* **yardsticks.**

yarmulka—A small, close-fitting cap worn by Jewish men and boys, especially for prayer and certain ceremonies.
yar|mul|ka (yahr′məl kə) *noun, plural* **yarmulkas.**

yarn—**1.** Thick thread made of twisted or spun fibers of cotton, wool, silk, nylon, or other material. It is used in knitting and weaving. **2.** A story, especially one that is long or made up: *He told several* yarns *about what life was like in the army.*
yarn (yahrn) *noun, plural* **yarns.**

yawl—A type of sailboat with two masts. The rear mast is shorter than the other.
yawl (yawl) *noun, plural* **yawls.**

yawn—**1.** To open the mouth wide and take a deep breath. People yawn when they are tired or bored. **2.** To open wide: *The pit* yawned *at our feet. Verb.*
—The act of opening the mouth wide and taking a deep breath: *He gave a big* yawn *before going to bed. Noun.*
yawn (yawn) *verb,* **yawned, yawning;** *noun, plural* **yawns.**

yd.—The abbreviation for **yard[2]** and **yards[2].**

ye—You. Ye was commonly used in the past but is rarely used today.
ye (yē) *pronoun.*

yea—Yes. *Adverb.*
—A vote or voter in favor of something: *The bill passed by a vote of 15* yeas *to 10 nays. Noun.*
yea (yā) *adverb; noun, plural* **yeas.**

year—**1.** The period from January 1 to December 31. A year is made up of 12 months. A normal year has 365 days, and a leap year has 366 days. **2.** Any period of 12 months: *seven* years *old; an appliance that is guaranteed for a* year *from the time it was bought.* **3.** A period of time, usually less than 12 months, that is spent in a certain activity: *the school* year.
year (yēr) *noun, plural* **years.** Abbreviation: **yr.**

yearling—An animal that is one year old.
year|ling (yēr′ling) *noun, plural* **yearlings.**

yearly—**1.** Happening once every 12 months; annual: *We are looking forward to our town's* yearly *Memorial Day parade.* **2.** For or during a 12-month period: yearly *income;* yearly *rainfall. Adjective.*
—Once a year or every year: *to do spring cleaning* yearly. *Adverb.*
year|ly (yēr′lē) *adjective; adverb.*

yearn—To have a longing: *to* yearn *to hear a friendly voice.*
yearn (yurn) *verb,* **yearned, yearning.**
• Synonyms: **crave, long[2]**

yeast—A substance that is used in baking to make dough rise. Yeast is tiny, one-celled fungi that grow quickly.
yeast (yēst) *noun, plural* **yeasts.**

yell—To shout; cry out loudly: *We screamed and* yelled *as we rode the roller coaster. Verb.*
—A loud cry or shout: *She gave a* yell *when she stubbed her toe. Noun.*
yell (yel) *verb,* **yelled, yelling;** *noun, plural* **yells.**
• Synonyms: For *verb,* see Synonyms at **cry,** *verb* 2.
Antonyms: **mumble, mutter, whisper,** for *verb.*

yellow—**1.** The color of butter or ripe lemons. **2.** The yolk of an egg. *Noun.*
—Having the color of butter or ripe lemons: *a* yellow *sweater. Adjective.*
—To become this color: *The pages of the old magazines had* yellowed *with age. Verb.*
yel|low (yel′ō) *noun, plural* **yellows;** *adjective,* **yellower, yellowest;** *verb,* **yellowed, yellowing.**

yellowhammer

yellowhammer—A woodpecker that lives in North America. It has yellow patches on the undersides of its wings.
yel|low|ham|mer (yel′ō ham′ər) *noun, plural* **yellowhammers.**

yellow jacket—A kind of wasp that has yellow and black bands on its body.
yel|low jack|et (yel′ō jak′it) *noun, plural* **yellow jackets.**

yelp—A quick, sharp bark. *Noun.*
—To give a quick, sharp bark: *The dog* yelped *when I stepped on its tail. Verb.*
yelp (yelp) *noun, plural* **yelps;** *verb,* **yelped, yelping.**
 • Synonyms: **yap, yip**

yen¹—The basic unit of money used in Japan.
yen (yen) *noun, plural* **yen.** Abbreviation: Y

yen²—A strong desire or hunger: *to get a sudden* yen *to take a walk; to have a* yen *for a sundae.*
yen (yen) *noun, plural* **yens.**

yes—A word that is used to show that one agrees with something, or approves of something, or thinks that something is true: Yes, *I think you are right. Adverb.*
—1. An answer that shows one agrees with something, or approves of something, or thinks that something is true: *They said* yes *to the offer of ice cream.* 2. A vote or voter in favor of something: *We can count on her to be a* yes *when the vote on our bill is taken. Noun.*
yes (yes) *adverb; noun, plural* **yeses.**

yesterday—1. The day before today: Yesterday *was the last day of summer vacation, and we are* back in school today. 2. The recent past: *Many books of* yesterday *are still popular now. Noun.*
—On the day before today: *I had a cold* yesterday, *but I am feeling better today. Adverb.*
yes|ter|day (yes′tər dē *or* yes′tər dā′) *noun, plural* **yesterdays;** *adverb.*

yet—1. Up to now; so far: *It has not snowed* yet *this winter.* 2. At this time; now; still: *It is not dark* yet, *so we can keep playing outside for a while.* 3. At that time; then: *He had not finished his speech* yet *when the bell rang.* 4. At some time in the future; eventually: *He practices the piano several hours a day in the hope of* yet *becoming a famous pianist.* 5. In addition; also: *She is a good athlete and* yet *a good student.* 6. Nevertheless; but: *The test was short* yet *difficult. Adverb.*
—Nevertheless; but; however: *I thought she looked familiar,* yet *I could not remember her name. Conjunction.*
yet (yet) *adverb, conjunction.*

yew—An evergreen tree that has dark green needles and reddish brown bark. Its wood is used to make bows for archery.
yew (yū) *noun, plural* **yews.**
 • Words that sound the same are **ewe** and **you.**

yield—1. To give forth; produce: *The orchard* yielded *many types of apples.* 2. To give up; surrender: *After a long battle, the town finally* yielded *to the enemy.* 3. To give way to pressure or force: *to* yield *to a demand; a gate* yielding *to someone pushing against it. Verb.*
—An amount produced: *a large* yield *of wheat. Noun.*
yield (yēld) *verb,* **yielded, yielding;** *noun, plural* **yields.**

yip—A quick, sharp bark. *Noun.*
—To give a quick, sharp bark: *The dog* yipped *and wagged its tail when it saw its owner coming. Verb.*
yip (yip) *noun, plural* **yips;** *verb,* **yipped, yipping.**
 • Synonyms: **yap, yelp**

Y.M.C.A. or YMCA—An organization that promotes the development of the body, mind, and spirit of young men and boys. Its name comes from the first letters of the words Young Men's Christian Association.
Y.M.C.A. *or* YMCA (wī′em′sē′ā′) *noun, plural* **Y.M.C.A.'s** *or* **Y.M.C.A.s, YMCA's** *or* **YMCAs.**

Y.M.H.A. or YMHA—An organization that promotes the development of the body, mind, and spirit of young Jewish men and boys. Its

a at	**i** if	**oo** look	**ch** chalk		**a** in ago
ā ape	**ī** idle	**ou** out	**ng** sing		**e** in happen
ah calm	**o** odd	**u** ugly	**sh** ship	ə =	**i** in capital
aw all	**ō** oats	**ū** rule	**th** think		**o** in occur
e end	**oi** oil	**ur** turn	**th** their		**u** in upon
ē easy			**zh** treasure		

name comes from the first letters of the words Young Men's Hebrew Association.

Y.M.H.A. or **YMHA** (wī'em'āch'ā') *noun,* *plural* **Y.M.H.A.'s** or **Y.M.H.A.s, YMHA's** or **YMHAs.**

yogurt—A thick, soft food that is made by adding certain bacteria to milk. Most yogurt is sour, though some is sweetened with fruit flavoring.
yo|gurt (yō'gərt) *noun, plural* **yogurts.**

Word History

Yogurt comes from the Turkish name for this food. People in Turkey and some other countries of the Middle East have eaten yogurt for thousands of years.

---

yoke—**1.** A wooden frame used to join two oxen or other work animals together.   **2.** A pair of animals joined together with such a frame: *a yoke of oxen.*   **3.** The part of a dress or other piece of clothing that fits around the neck and shoulders. *Noun.*
—To join together with such a frame: *to yoke oxen to a cart. Verb.*
yoke (yōk) *noun, plural* **yokes** for definitions **1** and **3, yoke** for definition **2;** *verb,* **yoked, yoking.**
• A word that sounds the same is **yolk.**

yolk—The yellow part of an egg.
yolk (yōk) *noun, plural* **yolks.**
• A word that sounds the same is **yoke.**

Yom Kippur—The most important and sacred Jewish holy day. It occurs 10 days after Rosh Hashanah in September or October. It is observed with fasting and worship.
Yom Kip|pur (yom **kip'**ər *or* yōm ki'pūr) *noun.*

yonder—Over there; in that place: *The town lies yonder, past the river. Adverb.*
—Being within sight; located over there: *Yonder fields are green with ripening corn. Adjective.*
yon|der (yon'dər) *adverb, adjective.*

Yorkshire terrier—A small dog with long, silky hair. Its coat is steel blue and golden tan. Originally bred in England, these dogs were used to hunt and kill rats.
York|shire ter|ri|er (yawrk'shər ter'ē ər) *noun, plural* **Yorkshire terriers.**

you—**1.** The person or persons spoken to: *nice to hear from* you; *some good news for all of* you.
2. Anybody at all; one: *One thing about that book is that* you *never know what will happen next.*
you (yū) *pronoun.*
• Words that sound the same are **ewe** and **yew.**

you'd—The contraction of "you had" or "you would."
you'd (yūd).

you'll—The contraction of "you will" or "you shall."
you'll (yūl).
• A word that sounds the same is **Yule.**

young—**1.** Being in an early stage of life or development; not old: *a young child; a* young *kitten; a* young *project.*   **2.** Having the look or qualities of youth: *Her uncle is* young *for his years and has very little gray hair.*   **3.** Having to do with or belonging to youth; early: *He liked to tell stories about his* young *days when he was in college. Adjective.*
—Offspring in an early stage of development: *a lioness protecting her* young. *Noun.*
young (yung) *adjective,* **younger, youngest;** *plural noun.*

youngster—A child or young person: *The* youngsters *put on a show for their parents.*
young|ster (yung'stər) *noun, plural* **youngsters.**

your—Having to do with or belonging to you: *May I borrow one of* your *pencils?*
your (yoor) *adjective.*
• A word that sounds the same is **you're.**

you're—The contraction of "you are."
you're (yoor).
• A word that sounds the same is **your.**

yours—The one or ones that belong to you: *My coat and* yours *look alike.*
yours (yoorz) *pronoun.*

Yorkshire terrier

yourself—**1.** A word used to refer to the person spoken or written of: *You have only* yourself *to blame if you are late.* **2.** Your true or usual self: *You are not* yourself *on days when you need more sleep.*
  your|self (yoor self′) *pronoun, plural* **yourselves.**

yourselves—*See* **yourself.**
  your|selves (yoor selvz′) *pronoun.*

youth—**1.** The condition or quality of being young: *the spirit of* youth; *the freshness of* youth. **2.** The time of life between being a child and being an adult: *She was a dancer in her* youth. **3.** The first or early stage of something: *Many people think the computer is still in its* youth. **4.** A young man: *Her father played football when he was a* youth. **5.** Young people in general: *What will the future be like for the* youth *of this country?*
  youth (yūth) *noun, plural* **youths** or **youth.**

you've—The contraction of "you have."
  you've (yūv).

yowl—A long cry; howl. *Noun.*
  —To make a long cry or howl: *He yowled when he closed the drawer on his finger. Verb.*
  yowl (youl) *noun, plural* **yowls;** *verb,* **yowled, yowling.**
  • Synonyms: For *verb,* see Synonyms at **cry,** *verb* 2.
  Antonyms: **mumble, mutter, whisper**

yo-yo—A small spinning toy. It is made up of a disklike spool that has a string wound through its center. The string is tied to a finger and used to move the yo-yo up and down.
  yo-yo (yō′yō′) *noun, plural* **yo-yos.**

yr.—The abbreviation for **year.**

yuan—A unit of money in China. Its symbol is $.
  yu|an (yū ahn′) *noun, plural* **yuan.**

a at	i if	oo look	ch chalk		⎡ a in ago
ā ape	ī idle	ou out	ng sing		e in happen
ah calm	o odd	u ugly	sh ship	ə =	i in capital
aw all	ō oats	ū rule	th think		o in occur
e end	oi oil	ur turn	th their		⎣ u in upon
ē easy			zh treasure		

plant   flower

yucca

yucca—A plant that grows in the warm, dry regions of the United States and Mexico. It has pointed leaves and white, bell-shaped flowers. The yucca is the state flower of New Mexico.
  yuc|ca (yuk′ə) *noun, plural* **yuccas.**

Yule or **yule**—Christmas or the Christmas season.
  Yule or **yule** (yūl) *noun, plural* **Yules** or **yules.**
  • A word that sounds the same is **you'll.**

Yuletide or **yuletide**—The Christmas season.
  Yule|tide or **yule|tide** (yūl′tīd′) *noun, plural* **Yuletides** or **yuletides.**

Y.W.C.A. or **YWCA**—An organization that promotes the development of the body, mind, and spirit of young women and girls. The name comes from the first letters of the words Young Women's Christian Association.
  Y.W.C.A. or **YWCA** (wī′dub′əl yū sē′ā′) *noun, plural* **Y.W.C.A.'s** or **Y.W.C.A.s, YWCA's** or **YWCAs.**

Y.W.H.A. or **YWHA**—An organization that promotes the development of the body, mind, and spirit of young Jewish women and girls. The name comes from the first letters of the words Young Women's Hebrew Association.
  Y.W.H.A. or **YWHA** (wī′dub′əl yū āch′ā′) *noun, plural* **Y.W.H.A.'s** or **Y.W.H.A.s, YWHA's** or **YWHAs.**

About 1,900 years ago, the Romans gave the capital Z its present form. The small letter z was first used about 1,200 years ago. It reached its present form about 500 years ago.

About 5,000 years ago, the ancient Egyptians used a symbol of an arrow.

About 3,500 years ago, people in the Middle East made a simpler symbol. They called it *zayin*, their word for "weapon."

About 3,000 years ago, other people in the Middle East used this symbol of a weapon.

About 2,600 years ago, the Greeks gave the letter this form. They called it *zeta*.

Z or **z**—The twenty-sixth and last letter of the alphabet: *There are two z's in the word "zigzag."*
Z, z (zē) *noun, plural* **Z's** *or* **Zs, z's** *or* **zs.**

zebra—A wild animal that has black and white stripes on its body and looks like a horse. It lives in Africa.
ze|bra (zē′brə) *noun, plural* **zebras** *or* **zebra.**

zebra

zenith—1. The point in the sky directly overhead. 2. The highest or best point: *The* zenith *of our trip to the museum was seeing the dinosaur exhibit.*
ze|nith (zē′nith) *noun, plural* **zeniths.**

zephyr—1. A soft breeze: *A cool* zephyr *blew through the open window.* 2. The west wind.
zeph|yr (zef′ər) *noun, plural* **zephyrs.**

Zeppelin—A large airship shaped like a cigar. It was designed to carry passengers and cargo.
Zep|pe|lin (zep′ə lən) *noun, plural* **Zeppelins.**
• See Language Fact at **airship.**

zero—1. The number that leaves any number the same if it is added or subtracted; 0. 2. The point on a scale from which something is measured: *It has been so cold lately that the temperature has only risen above* zero *once in the last week.* 3. Nothing: *Unless it rains soon, all our work in the garden will amount to* zero. *Noun.*
—1. Of or at this number or point: *the* zero *mark;* zero *degrees.* 2. None at all; not any: *She had* zero *luck in getting her brother to drive her to the game. Adjective.*
ze|ro (zēr′ō) *noun, plural* **zeros** *or* **zeroes;** *adjective.*
• See picture at **Fahrenheit.**

Word History

Zero probably comes from the Italian form of an Arabic word meaning "empty."

zest—A keen enjoyment; spirit; zing: *to have a* zest *for reading; to play a game with* zest.
zest (zest) *noun.*

zigzag—A line or pattern that goes from one side to another in short, sharp turns: *He drew a*

zigzag *in his picture to represent lightning.*
Noun.
—To move in short, sharp turns from one side to
another: *The river follows a straight course*
through town, but then it starts to zigzag. *Verb.*
—Having short, sharp turns from one side to
another: *a sweater with a* zigzag *design on it.*
Adjective.
—With short, sharp turns from one side to
another: *He ran* zigzag *through the garden to*
avoid stepping on the flowers. Adverb.
zig|zag (**zig′**zag′) *noun, plural* **zigzags;** *verb,*
zigzagged, zigzagging; *adjective; adverb.*

zing—Liveliness; zest: *The young cheerleaders*
performed their routine with a lot of zing.
zing (zing) *noun.*

zinnia—A garden flower that grows in many
colors.
zin|ni|a (zin′ē ə) *noun, plural* **zinnias.**

zip—To fasten or close with a zipper: *It is getting*
cold, so you had better zip *up your jacket.*
zip (zip) *verb,* **zipped, zipping.**

Zip Code—A number that identifies a postal
delivery area in the United States. It is written
after the name of the state in an address on a
piece of mail.
Zip Code (zip cōd) *noun, plural* **Zip Codes.**

Word History

Zip in **Zip Code** comes from the first letters of
the words *Z*oning *I*mprovement *P*lan. Zip Codes
were introduced in 1963 as a way to improve
mail delivery in the United States.

---

zipper—A fastener that is made of two rows of
pieces that fit together snugly. The pieces are
joined or separated by pulling a sliding device up
or down. Zippers are used on clothing and
luggage.
zip|per (zip′ər) *noun, plural* **zippers.**

zither—A musical instrument that is a flat
wooden box with 32 or more strings stretched

zither

across it. A zither is played by plucking the
strings.
zith|er (zith′ər *or* zi<u>th</u>′ər) *noun, plural* **zithers.**

zloty—A unit of money in Poland. Abbreviation:
Z1.
zlo|ty (zlaw′tē) *noun, plural* **zlotys.**

zodiac—The section of the sky in which the sun
rises throughout the year. It is divided into 12
parts called ''signs'' which are named after
constellations in them.
zo|di|ac (zō′dē ak) *noun.*

zone—**1.** An area or region that has a special
quality or use: *a loading* zone *for trucks; a*
no-parking zone. **2.** Any of the five regions into
which the surface of the earth is divided
according to climate. *Noun.*
—To set off an area or region for a special
purpose or use: *The people who live in that part*
of town do not want their neighborhood to be
zoned *for business. Verb.*
zone (zōn) *noun, plural* **zones;** *verb,* **zoned,**
zoning.

zoo—A park or other place where wild animals
are kept and displayed.
zoo (zū) *noun, plural* **zoos.**

zoologist—A scientist who studies animal life.
zo|ol|o|gist (zō ol′ə jist) *noun, plural*
zoologists.

zoology—The scientific study of all types of
animal life.
zo|ol|o|gy (zō ol′ə jē) *noun.*

zoom—To move or climb suddenly and quickly:
race cars zooming *from the starting line; a jet*
zooming *into the sky.*
zoom (zūm) *verb,* **zoomed, zooming.**

zucchini—A long squash that has a green skin.
zuc|chi|ni (zū ke′nē) *noun, plural* **zucchini** or
zucchinis.
• See picture at **squash²**.

---

a at	i if	oo look	ch chalk		a in ago
ā ape	ī idle	ou out	ng sing		e in happen
ah calm	o odd	u ugly	sh ship	ə =	i in capital
aw all	ō oats	ū rule	th think		o in occur
e end	oi oil	ur turn	<u>th</u> their		u in upon
ē easy			zh treasure		

REFERENCE SECTION

CONTENTS

Word Power Exercises

GRADES 3–6

For each of the numbered words shown in heavy black type, choose the lettered word or group of words that means the same or nearly the same thing. Thus, for "**1. note**" the correct answer is "b. short letter." If you need to look up a meaning, most of these words are in this dictionary.

Words that you may not find in this dictionary are those that are formed with a prefix, such as in- (incorrect), or with a suffix, such as -ness (wickedness). To find the meanings of such words, look up the meaning of the main part of the word and the meaning of the prefix or suffix.

Answer Key on pages 844–846

GRADE 3

1. note
a. good grade
b. short letter
c. funny joke

2. hike
a. small rocket
b. nickname
c. long walk

3. mash
a. cut
b. crush
c. peel

4. cab
a. bus
b. ship
c. taxi

5. pitch
a. throw
b. trip
c. run

6. club
a. deep cut
b. heavy stick
c. good deed

7. land
a. go ashore
b. rent
c. use

8. bill
a. great sea wave
b. large rock
c. bird's beak

9. pack
a. barrel
b. route
c. bundle

10. snack
a. hiding place
b. small meal
c. low stool

11. melon
a. fruit
b. tree
c. road

12. merry
a. very red
b. good to eat
c. full of fun

13. often
a. never
b. many times
c. sometimes

14. silent
a. strong
b. quiet
c. noisy

15. trip
a. stumble
b. catch
c. laugh

16. plain
a. wooden
b. funny
c. simple

17. green
a. not ripe
b. very sweet
c. melted

18. weak
a. not happy
b. not sleepy
c. not strong

19. lower
a. make noise
b. let down
c. make strong

20. whip
a. beat
b. smell
c. hop

21. clearing
a. small forest
b. open space
c. large flock

22. gift
a. tooth
b. seed
c. present

23. tablet
a. writing pad
b. picnic table
c. small bag

24. choose
a. talk about
b. give up
c. pick out

25. explain
a. make clear
b. discover
c. mix up

26. act
a. part of a play
b. part of a song
c. part of a war

27. wink
a. hand signal
b. horn signal
c. eye signal

28. simple
a. hard
b. wrong
c. easy

29. fluffy
a. long and wide
b. bright and shiny
c. soft and light

30. boast
a. complain
b. ask
c. brag

31. chilly
a. quite warm
b. very hot
c. rather cold

32. glad
a. happy
b. sad
c. angry

33. lumber
a. rolls of cloth
b. pieces of wood
c. piles of dirt

34. crippled
a. huge
b. small
c. lame

35. tornado
a. brave soldier
b. strong wind
c. calm weather

36. measure
a. find money
b. find size
c. find fun

37. cartoon
a. funny picture
b. funny song
c. heavy box

38. arrive
a. stay
b. begin
c. come

39. jig
a. lively dance
b. sad song
c. hunting dog

40. escape
a. get free
b. go up
c. come in

41. cozy
a. dark
b. comfortable
c. dirty

42. wrench
a. tool
b. dish
c. key

43. missing
a. hungry
b. tired
c. absent

44. false
a. quite small
b. growing wild
c. not real

45. nurse
a. depend on
b. take care of
c. give away

46. magnet
a. catches birds
b. attracts iron
c. fixes glass

47. leap
a. walk
b. see
c. jump

48. nightmare
a. bad dream
b. white horse
c. warm room

49. mermaid
a. farm girl
b. older lady
c. fishlike woman

50. moccasin
a. Indian shoe
b. pirate flag
c. Eskimo dog

51. branch
a. mark on cattle
b. part of tree
c. water on grass

52. bitter
a. sharp-tasting
b. bright-looking
c. rough-feeling

53. swallow
a. building
b. tree
c. bird

54. hockey
a. flower
b. game
c. fish

55. lullaby
a. cage for bird
b. dish for food
c. song for baby

56. repay
a. give back
b. take from
c. wish for

57. timber
a. wood
b. leather
c. metal

58. invent
a. make something new
b. fill a hole
c. hunt all around

59. verse
a. pail of water
b. part of poem
c. long story

60. gem
a. horn
b. glove
c. jewel

GRADE 4

1. ability
a. learning
b. skill
c. hope

2. bashful
a. shy
b. bold
c. harmful

3. incorrect
a. uncertain
b. wrong
c. probably right

4. fake
a. not loyal
b. false
c. unhealthy

5. forgetful
a. failing to do
b. unable to remember
c. meaning to do

6. frown
a. appear busy
b. look angry
c. be ready

7. suffer
a. get excited
b. complain
c. have pain

8. clue
a. reason
b. riddle
c. helpful fact

9. fret
a. worry
b. rejoice
c. celebrate

10. marvelous
a. wonderful
b. dull
c. sparkling

11. visible
a. torn
b. can be seen
c. brave

12. confess
a. admit
b. describe
c. brag

13. ordinary
a. different
b. common
c. strange

14. halt
a. stop
b. avoid
c. rise

15. locate
a. cut off
b. bring about
c. find

16. imagine
a. try to explain
b. put in order
c. picture in one's mind

17. lengthen
a. make longer
b. take away
c. shrink

18. pretend
a. tend toward
b. make believe
c. hide something

19. solve
a. find the answer
b. make a riddle
c. look for facts

20. wept
a. cleaned
b. brushed off
c. cried

21. decision
a. good deed
b. mistake
c. judgment reached

22. miss
a. grab something
b. capture
c. fail to hit

23. obedience
a. lack of discipline
b. following orders
c. power to enforce

24. pride
a. being careless
b. being understanding
c. being proud

25. smear
a. paint
b. throw out
c. mark or stain

26. surround
a. follow
b. shut in on all sides
c. be near

27. active
a. motionless
b. hasty
c. lively

28. brave
a. foolish
b. calm
c. fearless

29. convince
a. make a person believe
b. speak softly
c. trick a person into

30. retire
a. exchange
b. go back again
c. stop working

31. disapprove
a. be sorry for
b. refuse to reply
c. show dislike of

32. signature
a. your name in writing
b. stamp of approval
c. heavy truck

33. talent
a. attitude
b. natural ability
c. understanding

34. earnings
a. leftovers
b. food supplies
c. pay for work

35. glamorous
a. ragged
b. shy
c. fascinating

36. wickedness
a. being playful
b. being bad
c. being sorry

37. nonsense
a. lack of skill
b. need to be clear
c. foolishness

38. replace
a. put back
b. renew
c. treat badly

39. splendid
a. round
b. very good
c. narrow

40. unkind
a. cruel
b. not known
c. jealous

41. awkward
a. awful
b. playful
c. clumsy

42. downhearted
a. discouraged
b. ill
c. excited

43. fantastic
a. simple
b. harmful
c. strange

44. liberty
a. patriotism
b. goodness
c. freedom

45. mystery
a. secret
b. cause
c. untrue event

46. self-confidence
a. being shy
b. belief in yourself
c. selfishness

47. tender
a. soft
b. clear
c. thin

48. income
a. money earned
b. money spent
c. invitation

49. uncomfortable
a. unkind
b. unwilling
c. uneasy

50. voyage
a. warehouse
b. ocean trip
c. pirate

51. aid
a. help
b. try
c. repair

52. habit
a. lack of method
b. usual way of doing
c. reason for doing

53. press
a. teachers
b. farmers
c. newspapers

54. recount
a. reorder
b. repay
c. count again

55. section
a. smallest slice
b. more than half
c. part

56. perfect
a. without fault
b. almost right
c. very difficult

57. uncertain
a. proven
b. not sure
c. very certain

58. unexpected
a. not interested
b. amazing
c. without warning

59. unimportant
a. of special value
b. not important
c. unable to be carried

60. drowsy
a. filthy
b. sleepy
c. bored

61. statement
a. something said
b. proof
c. harsh word

62. disgraceful
a. harmful
b. sorrowful
c. shameful

63. dungeon
a. office
b. store
c. cell

64. roam
a. run slowly
b. wander
c. walk with a purpose

65. shortage
a. too small an amount
b. part that shrinks
c. early death

66. password
a. correct answer
b. secret word
c. warning

67. stupid
a. smart but slow
b. lazy
c. without good sense

68. useless
a. of no value
b. of some value
c. of great value

69. elastic
a. will not bend
b. breaks easily
c. springs back

70. display
a. show
b. hide
c. stop

71. misplace
a. lose
b. enjoy
c. ruin

72. comedian
a. hard worker
b. funny person
c. popular singer

73. slender
a. quick
b. long and thin
c. weak

74. theft
a. mystery
b. robbery
c. what remains

75. echo
a. repeated sound
b. loud explosion
c. steady beat

76. festival
a. trip
b. serious event
c. entertainment

77. result
a. what happens
b. purpose
c. cause of something

78. uninvited
a. not difficult
b. not reasonable
c. not asked

79. permission
a. amount to be paid
b. approval to do
c. way through

80. disaster
a. great misfortune
b. wrong guess
c. drama

GRADE 5

1. outstanding
a. important
b. difficult
c. certain

2. forbidden
a. not allowed
b. not clear
c. not thoughtful

3. bleach
a. rip apart
b. rub together
c. make whiter

4. nasty
a. not pleasant
b. rainy
c. healthy

5. sorrowful
a. sad
b. alone
c. mean

6. suggestion
a. weak excuse
b. strict order
c. possible idea

7. transfer
a. change over
b. rub out
c. buy

8. vanish
a. miss
b. disappear
c. paint

9. enjoyable
a. pleasant
b. nasty
c. hopeful

10. penalty
a. gain
b. rule
c. punishment

11. truthful
a. honest
b. frightened
c. guilty

12. unsafe
a. unlocked
b. dangerous
c. free of charge

13. zone
a. shiny metal
b. definite place
c. cold air

14. advice
a. helpful opinion
b. unwanted information
c. bad decision

15. combine
a. discuss in detail
b. join together
c. cut apart

16. difficult
a. unusual
b. simple
c. hard

17. effort
a. sharp tool
b. hard try
c. small insult

18. consult
a. behave well
b. eat up
c. seek advice

19. normal
a. insane
b. funny
c. usual

20. notice
a. skip
b. speak
c. see

21. press
a. repair
b. squeeze
c. turn

22. recall
a. misplace
b. remember
c. forget

23. equip
a. sell
b. give
c. furnish

24. greedy
a. needing to be cleaned
b. wanting too much
c. going too fast

25. similar
a. alike
b. distant
c. well-dressed

26. adulthood
a. average size
b. full growth
c. admission price

27. modern
a. up-to-date
b. official
c. regular

28. rude
a. not polite
b. not sincere
c. too proud

29. cruelty
a. dishonesty
b. deep regret
c. unkind treatment

30. defend
a. refuse to attend
b. search for weapons
c. guard from harm

31. forgiveness
a. shame
b. pardon
c. approval

32. furious
a. careless
b. angry
c. sad

33. identify
a. try
b. guess
c. recognize

34. luxury
a. bad bargain
b. extra comfort
c. necessary purchase

35. anxious
a. inactive
b. sure
c. eager

36. excellence
a. average height
b. one of many
c. rare goodness

37. flexible
a. very strong
b. easily bent
c. higher than others

38. expand
a. make larger
b. release pressure
c. tighten up

39. gossip
a. unfriendly talk
b. happy event
c. complete explanation

40. paralyze
a. act slowly
b. make powerless
c. speed up

41. pledge
a. promise
b. request
c. faith

42. replacement
a. ruined material
b. substitute
c. worn part

43. unfamiliar
a. not well-known
b. much the same
c. connected to another

44. unsatisfactory
a. not good enough
b. artificial
c. more than needed

45. clatter
a. evil talk
b. slow movement
c. confused noise

46. carefree
a. without authority
b. honest
c. without worry

47. delay
a. tie together
b. shake slowly
c. put off until later

48. powerless
a. unsure
b. tired
c. weak

49. postpone
a. delay
b. send
c. quit

50. threat
a. reasonable request
b. helpful offer
c. possible harm

51. amuse
a. make smile
b. make angry
c. make mistakes

52. boldness
a. seriousness
b. good sense
c. courage

53. compress
a. squeeze together
b. take prisoner
c. stretch out

54. grief
a. sorrow
b. fear
c. excitement

55. account
a. something extra
b. short term
c. business record

56. deadline
a. end of a race
b. time limit
c. fishing equipment

57. quiver
a. hold tight
b. shake
c. scream

58. billboard
a. large sign
b. horse-drawn cart
c. steam engine

59. attractive
a. different
b. pleasing
c. unusual

60. opinion
a. purpose
b. belief
c. test

61. discourage
a. spend foolishly
b. talk at length
c. lessen hope

62. generally
a. in part
b. usually
c. entirely

63. ambition
a. desire for success
b. fear of others
c. lack of confidence

64. advisable
a. honest
b. useless
c. wise

65. bagpipe
a. large insect
b. musical instrument
c. colorful robe

66. motto
a. nickname
b. story
c. saying

67. victorious
a. has won
b. has fought
c. has watched

68. pace
a. price
b. silence
c. rate

69. escort
a. shout
b. cover the head
c. go along with

70. intelligence
a. ability to learn
b. blame
c. great happiness

71. advertisement
a. polite act
b. paid announcement
c. rare condition

72. blunder
a. stupid mistake
b. loud noise
c. low hedge

73. brutal
a. cruel
b. large
c. clever

74. visual
a. can be divided
b. can be heard
c. can be seen

75. fragile
a. heavy
b. easily broken
c. disagreeable

76. eternal
a. ending quickly
b. rushing wildly
c. lasting forever

77. column
a. vertical part of a page
b. frying pan
c. long coat

78. navigate
a. go to the movies
b. run a ship
c. peel an apple

79. mold
a. growth on bread
b. glass pot
c. secret meeting

80. confused
a. set apart
b. mixed up
c. acting natural

GRADE 6

1. allowable
a. more than usual
b. strange
c. permitted

2. bonus
a. center part
b. important paper
c. something extra

3. just
a. fair
b. harsh
c. selfish

4. admirer
a. wild animal
b. one who approves
c. one who dislikes

5. anniversary
a. bitter enemy
b. musical composition
c. yearly event

6. brilliance
a. brightness
b. confidence
c. rudeness

7. capable
a. not needed
b. having great value
c. able to do

8. frequent
a. careless
b. polite
c. happening often

9. leadership
a. necessary action
b. willingness to give
c. ability to guide

10. portable
a. easily carried
b. forbidden
c. told in secret

11. abolish
a. eat rapidly
b. do away with
c. take prisoner

12. estimate
a. wander off course
b. follow close behind
c. judge approximately

13. loyalty
a. being uncertain
b. being faithful
c. being hopeful

14. magical
a. mysterious
b. successful
c. silent

15. majority
a. smallest group
b. greater part
c. amount less than half

16. supreme
a. clear
b. weak
c. highest

17. symbol
a. cloak
b. emblem
c. waterway

18. vow
a. deep wound
b. tool for drawing
c. solemn promise

19. absentee
a. something ordinary
b. escaped prisoner
c. person not present

20. combat
a. game
b. riddle
c. fight

21. counterfeit
a. false
b. below average
c. incomplete

22. disciple
a. follower
b. leader
c. director

23. disregard
a. treat with care
b. wear down
c. pay no attention to

24. document
a. furnish written proof
b. find a mistake
c. act a story

25. insert
a. put in
b. erase
c. force apart

26. wisdom
a. distant land
b. great learning
c. religion

27. deserve
a. receive punishment
b. be worthy of
c. take care of

28. fiction
a. great discovery
b. made-up story
c. historic event

29. minor
a. less important
b. very certain
c. fully grown

30. panic
a. uncontrolled fear
b. childhood disease
c. funny event

31. ridiculous
a. stiff
b. laughable
c. artistic

32. slogan
a. motto
b. apartment
c. jacket

33. strict
a. light-weight
b. stern
c. fast

34. voluntary
a. done by choice
b. done by force
c. done by accident

35. accustomed
a. far away
b. usual
c. exact

36. advantageous
a. helpful
b. errorless
c. confused

37. annual
a. with flowers
b. yearly
c. part-time

38. grant
a. hold back
b. give
c. tell a secret

39. hesitate
a. remain firm
b. offer an excuse
c. be undecided

40. radar
a. large telescope
b. sun's energy
c. radio wave locator

41. ruling
a. joke
b. mistake
c. decision

42. abbreviation
a. short form of word
b. folk song
c. dramatic play

43. eliminate
a. number
b. get rid of
c. light up

44. thigh
a. part of arm
b. part of leg
c. part of neck

45. yearn
a. long for
b. be jealous over
c. be afraid of

46. shatter
a. break into pieces
b. nail down tightly
c. handle quietly

47. blueprint
a. blue flower
b. famous painting
c. building plan

48. item
a. one dozen
b. separate thing
c. pile of goods

49. site
a. location
b. tent
c. battlefield

50. kindling
a. entrance hall
b. firewood
c. small boat

51. mishap
a. planned event
b. unlucky accident
c. repaired object

52. playwright
a. writes plays
b. plans contests
c. teaches school

53. raid
a. quick death
b. long war
c. sudden attack

54. gong
a. wind instrument
b. saucer-shaped bell
c. small drum

55. thump
a. sharp scream
b. dull sound
c. low whistle

56. halo
a. ring of light
b. leafy crown
c. silken robe

57. tamper
a. suggest calmly
b. meddle improperly
c. speak honestly

58. severe
a. raw
b. thin
c. harsh

59. stupidity
a. lack of intelligence
b. sudden hunger
c. weakened condition

60. concern
a. worry
b. courage
c. regret

61. deceive
a. split
b. lie
c. promise

62. illegal
a. against law
b. not desirable
c. secret

63. vicinity
a. amusement park
b. region nearby
c. sticky liquid

64. associate
a. connect
b. figure out
c. avoid

65. collision
a. expensive mistake
b. hitting together
c. hard work

66. foresight
a. looking ahead
b. failing to remember
c. offering to help

67. reliable
a. dependable
b. dangerous
c. repeating

68. solution
a. answer
b. clue
c. mystery

69. eclipse
a. cut off light
b. carry messages
c. wash with chemicals

70. jagged
a. square
b. rattling
c. uneven

71. opponent
a. teammate
b. house guest
c. person on other side

72. absorbing
a. very interesting
b. very difficult
c. tired out

73. conduct
a. reason
b. explanation
c. behavior

74. transform
a. make larger
b. change
c. heal

75. rampage
a. decayed leaves
b. wild outbreak
c. act of heroism

76. secrecy
a. sharing knowledge
b. concealing from others
c. finding out

77. approximately
a. accurately
b. nearly
c. usually

78. core
a. unit of measurement
b. inner part
c. ruined piece

79. dignity
a. lack of importance
b. poor judgment
c. serious worth

80. migrate
a. sleep a long time
b. suffer a headache
c. move to another place

81. plywood
a. large tree
b. type of oven
c. board made of thin layers

82. benefit
a. game
b. help
c. duty

83. confide
a. mark off with lines
b. set on fire
c. tell as a secret

84. content
a. serious thought
b. satisfaction
c. enclosed area

85. part
a. join
b. seek
c. separate

86. pose
a. agree
b. protect
c. pretend

87. adviser
a. tennis player
b. heating lamp
c. person who gives opinion

88. persuade
a. win over
b. cover up
c. pass by

89. pursuit
a. chase
b. warm clothing
c. cause of trouble

90. endorse
a. approve
b. waste
c. avoid

91. landscape
a. mine
b. area fenced in
c. scenery

92. nuisance
a. long story
b. something that annoys
c. famous person

93. humid
a. damp
b. cool
c. breezy

94. nominate
a. forget completely
b. put up for election
c. repeat aloud

95. amateur
a. not a professional
b. not working
c. house guest

96. incinerator
a. gentle breeze
b. waste burner
c. long trip

97. hoarse
a. sounding rough and dee
b. sticky
c. old and weary

98. finance
a. provide money for
b. dance around a tree
c. open a store

99. urgent
a. unable to last
b. demanding immediate attention
c. helpless in defeat

100. occasional
a. very seldom
b. now and then
c. very unusual

Answer Key

3rd grade	4th and 5th grades	6th grade
54 to 60, above average	71 to 80, above average	88 to 100, above average
42 to 53, average	62 to 70, average	64 to 87, average
41 or under, below average	61 or under, below average	63 or under, below average

GRADE 3

1. **note** (b) short letter
2. **hike** (c) long walk
3. **mash** (b) crush
4. **cab** (c) taxi
5. **pitch** (a) throw
6. **club** (b) heavy stick
7. **land** (a) go ashore
8. **bill** (c) bird's beak
9. **pack** (c) bundle
10. **snack** (b) small meal
11. **melon** (a) fruit
12. **merry** (c) full of fun
13. **often** (b) many times
14. **silent** (b) quiet
15. **trip** (a) stumble
16. **plain** (c) simple
17. **green** (a) not ripe
18. **weak** (c) not strong
19. **lower** (b) let down
20. **whip** (a) beat
21. **clearing** (b) open space
22. **gift** (c) present
23. **tablet** (a) writing pad
24. **choose** (c) pick out
25. **explain** (a) make clear
26. **act** (a) part of a play
27. **wink** (c) eye signal
28. **simple** (c) easy
29. **fluffy** (c) soft and light
30. **boast** (c) brag
31. **chilly** (c) rather cold
32. **glad** (a) happy
33. **lumber** (b) pieces of wood
34. **crippled** (c) lame
35. **tornado** (b) strong windstorm
36. **measure** (b) find size

37. **cartoon** (a) funny picture
38. **arrive** (c) come
39. **jig** (a) lively dance
40. **escape** (a) get free
41. **cozy** (b) comfortable
42. **wrench** (a) tool
43. **missing** (c) absent
44. **false** (c) not real

45. **nurse** (b) take care of
46. **magnet** (b) attracts iron
47. **leap** (c) jump
48. **nightmare** (a) bad dream
49. **mermaid** (c) fishlike woman
50. **moccasin** (a) Indian shoe
51. **branch** (b) part of tree
52. **bitter** (a) sharp-tasting

53. **swallow** (c) bird
54. **hockey** (b) game
55. **lullaby** (c) song for baby
56. **repay** (a) give back
57. **timber** (a) wood
58. **invent** (a) make something new
59. **verse** (b) part of poem
60. **gem** (c) jewel

GRADE 4

1. **ability** (b) skill
2. **bashful** (a) shy
3. **incorrect** (b) wrong
4. **fake** (b) false
5. **forgetful** (b) unable to remember
6. **frown** (b) look angry
7. **suffer** (c) have pain
8. **clue** (c) helpful fact
9. **fret** (a) worry
10. **marvelous** (a) wonderful
11. **visible** (b) can be seen
12. **confess** (a) admit
13. **ordinary** (b) common
14. **halt** (a) stop
15. **locate** (c) find
16. **imagine** (c) picture in one's mind
17. **lengthen** (a) make longer
18. **pretend** (b) make believe
19. **solve** (a) find the answer
20. **wept** (c) cried
21. **decision** (c) judgment reached
22. **miss** (c) fail to hit
23. **obedience** (b) following orders
24. **pride** (c) being proud
25. **smear** (c) mark or stain
26. **surround** (b) shut in on all sides
27. **active** (c) lively

28. **brave** (c) fearless
29. **convince** (a) make a person believe
30. **retire** (c) stop working
31. **disapprove** (c) show dislike of
32. **signature** (a) your name in writing
33. **talent** (b) natural ability
34. **earnings** (c) pay for work
35. **glamorous** (c) fascinating
36. **wickedness** (b) being bad
37. **nonsense** (c) foolishness
38. **replace** (a) put back
39. **splendid** (b) very good
40. **unkind** (a) cruel
41. **awkward** (c) clumsy
42. **downhearted** (a) discouraged
43. **fantastic** (c) strange
44. **liberty** (c) freedom
45. **mystery** (a) secret
46. **self-confidence** (b) belief in yourself
47. **tender** (a) soft
48. **income** (a) money earned
49. **uncomfortable** (c) uneasy
50. **voyage** (b) ocean trip
51. **aid** (a) help
52. **habit** (b) usual way of doing

53. **press** (c) newspapers
54. **recount** (c) count again
55. **section** (c) part
56. **perfect** (a) without fault
57. **uncertain** (b) not sure
58. **unexpected** (c) without warning
59. **unimportant** (b) not important
60. **drowsy** (b) sleepy
61. **statement** (a) something said
62. **disgraceful** (c) shameful
63. **dungeon** (c) cell
64. **roam** (b) wander
65. **shortage** (a) too small an amount
66. **password** (b) secret word
67. **stupid** (c) without good sense
68. **useless** (a) of no value
69. **elastic** (c) springs back
70. **display** (a) show
71. **misplace** (c) lose
72. **comedian** (b) funny person
73. **slender** (b) long and thin
74. **theft** (b) robbery
75. **echo** (a) repeated sound
76. **festival** (c) entertainment
77. **result** (a) what happens
78. **uninvited** (c) not asked
79. **permission** (b) approval to do
80. **disaster** (a) great misfortune

GRADE 5

1. **outstanding** (a) important
2. **forbidden** (a) not allowed
3. **bleach** (c) make whiter
4. **nasty** (a) not pleasant
5. **sorrowful** (a) sad
6. **suggestion** (c) possible idea
7. **transfer** (a) change over
8. **vanish** (b) disappear
9. **enjoyable** (a) pleasant
10. **penalty** (c) punishment
11. **truthful** (a) honest
12. **unsafe** (c) dangerous
13. **zone** (b) definite place
14. **advice** (a) helpful opinion
15. **combine** (b) join together
16. **difficult** (c) hard
17. **effort** (b) hard try
18. **consult** (c) seek advice
19. **normal** (c) usual
20. **notice** (c) see
21. **press** (b) squeeze
22. **recall** (b) remember
23. **equip** (c) furnish
24. **greedy** (b) wanting too much
25. **similar** (a) alike
26. **adulthood** (b) full growth
27. **modern** (a) up-to-date

28. **rude** (a) not polite
29. **cruelty** (c) unkind treatment
30. **defend** (c) guard from harm
31. **forgiveness** (b) pardon
32. **furious** (b) angry
33. **identify** (c) recognize
34. **luxury** (b) extra comfort
35. **anxious** (a) eager
36. **excellence** (c) rare goodness
37. **flexible** (b) easily bent
38. **expand** (a) make larger
39. **gossip** (a) unfriendly talk
40. **paralyze** (b) make powerless
41. **pledge** (a) promise
42. **replacement** (b) substitute
43. **unfamiliar** (a) not well-known
44. **unsatisfactory** (a) not good enough
45. **clatter** (c) confused noise
46. **carefree** (a) without worry
47. **delay** (c) put off until later
48. **powerless** (c) weak
49. **postpone** (a) delay
50. **threat** (c) possible harm
51. **amuse** (a) make smile
52. **boldness** (c) courage
53. **compress** (a) squeeze together

54. **grief** (a) sorrow
55. **account** (c) business record
56. **deadline** (b) time limit
57. **quiver** (b) shake
58. **billboard** (a) large sign
59. **attractive** (b) pleasing
60. **opinion** (b) belief
61. **discourage** (c) lessen hope
62. **generally** (b) usually
63. **ambition** (a) desire for success
64. **advisable** (c) wise
65. **bagpipe** (b) musical instrument
66. **motto** (c) saying
67. **victorious** (a) has won
68. **pace** (c) rate
69. **escort** (c) go along with
70. **intelligence** (a) ability to learn
71. **advertisement** (b) paid announcement
72. **blunder** (a) stupid mistake
73. **brutal** (a) cruel
74. **visual** (c) can be seen
75. **fragile** (b) easily broken
76. **eternal** (c) lasting forever
77. **column** (a) vertical part of a page
78. **navigate** (b) run a ship
79. **mold** (a) growth on bread
80. **confused** (b) mixed up

GRADE 6

1. **allowable** (c) permitted
2. **bonus** (c) something extra
3. **just** (a) fair

4. **admirer** (b) one who approves
5. **anniversary** (c) yearly event
6. **brilliance** (a) brightness

7. **capable** (c) able to do
8. **frequent** (c) happening often
9. **leadership** (c) ability to guide

10. **portable** (a) easily carried
11. **abolish** (b) do away with
12. **estimate** (c) judge approximately
13. **loyalty** (b) being faithful
14. **magical** (a) mysterious
15. **majority** (b) greater part
16. **supreme** (c) highest
17. **symbol** (b) emblem
18. **vow** (c) solemn promise
19. **absentee** (c) person not present
20. **combat** (c) fight
21. **counterfeit** (a) false
22. **disciple** (a) follower
23. **disregard** (c) pay no attention to
24. **document** (a) furnish written proof
25. **insert** (a) put in
26. **wisdom** (b) great learning
27. **deserve** (b) be worthy of
28. **fiction** (b) made-up story
29. **minor** (a) less important
30. **panic** (a) uncontrolled fear
31. **ridiculous** (b) laughable
32. **slogan** (a) motto
33. **strict** (b) stern
34. **voluntary** (a) done by choice
35. **accustomed** (b) usual
36. **advantageous** (a) helpful
37. **annual** (b) yearly
38. **grant** (b) give
39. **hesitate** (c) be undecided
40. **radar** (c) radio wave locator
41. **ruling** (c) decision
42. **abbreviation** (a) short form of word

43. **eliminate** (b) get rid of
44. **thigh** (b) part of leg
45. **yearn** (a) long for
46. **shatter** (a) break into pieces
47. **blueprint** (c) building plan
48. **item** (b) separate thing
49. **site** (a) location
50. **kindling** (b) firewood
51. **mishap** (b) unlucky accident
52. **playwright** (a) writes plays
53. **raid** (c) sudden attack
54. **gong** (b) saucer-shaped bell
55. **thump** (b) dull sound
56. **halo** (a) ring of light
57. **tamper** (b) meddle improperly
58. **severe** (c) harsh
59. **stupidity** (a) lack of intelligence
60. **concern** (a) worry
61. **deceive** (b) lie
62. **illegal** (a) against law
63. **vicinity** (b) region nearby
64. **associate** (a) connect
65. **collision** (b) hitting together
66. **foresight** (a) looking ahead
67. **reliable** (a) dependable
68. **solution** (a) answer
69. **eclipse** (a) cut off light
70. **jagged** (c) uneven
71. **opponent** (c) person on other side
72. **absorbing** (a) very interesting
73. **conduct** (c) behavior
74. **transform** (b) change

75. **rampage** (b) wild outbreak
76. **secrecy** (b) concealing from others
77. **approximately** (b) nearly
78. **core** (b) inner part
79. **dignity** (c) serious worth
80. **migrate** (c) move to another place
81. **plywood** (c) board made of thin layers
82. **benefit** (b) help
83. **confide** (c) tell as a secret
84. **content** (b) satisfaction
85. **part** (c) separate
86. **pose** (c) pretend
87. **adviser** (c) person who gives opinion
88. **persuade** (a) win over
89. **pursuit** (a) chase
90. **endorse** (a) approve
91. **landscape** (c) scenery
92. **nuisance** (b) something that annoys
93. **humid** (a) damp
94. **nominate** (b) put up for election
95. **amateur** (a) not a professional
96. **incinerator** (b) waste burner
97. **hoarse** (a) sounding rough and deep
98. **finance** (a) provide money for
99. **urgent** (b) demanding immediate attention
100. **occasional** (b) happening now and then

Presidents of the United States

President	Served	State of birth	Born	Died
1. George Washington	1789–1797	Virginia	Feb. 22, 1732	Dec. 14, 1799
2. John Adams	1797–1801	Massachusetts	Oct. 30, 1735	July 4, 1826
3. Thomas Jefferson	1801–1809	Virginia	Apr. 13, 1743	July 4, 1826
4. James Madison	1809–1817	Virginia	Mar. 16, 1751	June 28, 1836
5. James Monroe	1817–1825	Virginia	Apr. 28, 1758	July 4, 1831
6. John Quincy Adams	1825–1829	Massachusetts	July 11, 1767	Feb. 23, 1848
7. Andrew Jackson	1829–1837	South Carolina	Mar. 15, 1767	June 8, 1845
8. Martin Van Buren	1837–1841	New York	Dec. 5, 1782	July 24, 1862
9. William H. Harrison	1841	Virginia	Feb. 9, 1773	Apr. 4, 1841
10. John Tyler	1841–1845	Virginia	Mar. 29, 1790	Jan. 18, 1862
11. James K. Polk	1845–1849	North Carolina	Nov. 2, 1795	June 15, 1849
12. Zachary Taylor	1849–1850	Virginia	Nov. 24, 1784	July 9, 1850
13. Millard Fillmore	1850–1853	New York	Jan. 7, 1800	Mar. 8, 1874
14. Franklin Pierce	1853–1857	New Hampshire	Nov. 23, 1804	Oct. 8, 1869
15. James Buchanan	1857–1861	Pennsylvania	Apr. 23, 1791	June 1, 1868
16. Abraham Lincoln	1861–1865	Kentucky	Feb. 12, 1809	Apr. 15, 1865
17. Andrew Johnson	1865–1869	North Carolina	Dec. 29, 1808	July 31, 1875
18. Ulysses S. Grant	1869–1877	Ohio	Apr. 27, 1822	July 23, 1885
19. Rutherford B. Hayes	1877–1881	Ohio	Oct. 4, 1822	Jan. 17, 1893
20. James A. Garfield	1881	Ohio	Nov. 19, 1831	Sept. 19, 1881
21. Chester A. Arthur	1881–1885	Vermont	Oct. 5, 1829	Nov. 18, 1886
22. Grover Cleveland	1885–1889	New Jersey	Mar. 18, 1837	June 24, 1908
23. Benjamin Harrison	1889–1893	Ohio	Aug. 20, 1833	Mar. 13, 1901
24. Grover Cleveland	1893–1897	New Jersey	Mar. 18, 1837	June 24, 1908
25. William McKinley	1897–1901	Ohio	Jan. 29, 1843	Sept. 14, 1901
26. Theodore Roosevelt	1901–1909	New York	Oct. 27, 1858	Jan. 6, 1919
27. William H. Taft	1909–1913	Ohio	Sept. 15, 1857	Mar. 8, 1930
28. Woodrow Wilson	1913–1921	Virginia	Dec. 29, 1856	Feb. 3, 1924
29. Warren G. Harding	1921–1923	Ohio	Nov. 2, 1865	Aug. 2, 1923
30. Calvin Coolidge	1923–1929	Vermont	July 4, 1872	Jan. 5, 1933
31. Herbert C. Hoover	1929–1933	Iowa	Aug. 10, 1874	Oct. 20, 1964
32. Franklin D. Roosevelt	1933–1945	New York	Jan. 30, 1882	Apr. 12, 1945
33. Harry S. Truman	1945–1953	Missouri	May 8, 1884	Dec. 26, 1972
34. Dwight D. Eisenhower	1953–1961	Texas	Oct. 14, 1890	Mar. 28, 1969
35. John F. Kennedy	1961–1963	Massachusetts	May 29, 1917	Nov. 22, 1963
36. Lyndon B. Johnson	1963–1969	Texas	Aug. 27, 1908	Jan. 22, 1973
37. Richard M. Nixon	1969–1974	California	Jan. 9, 1913	
38. Gerald R. Ford	1974–1977	Nebraska	July 14, 1913	
39. James E. Carter, Jr.	1977–1981	Georgia	Oct. 1, 1924	
40. Ronald W. Reagan	1981–1989	Illinois	Feb. 6, 1911	
41. George H. W. Bush	1989–1993	Massachusetts	June 12, 1924	
42. William J. (Bill) Clinton	1993–	Arkansas	Aug. 19, 1946	

Prime Ministers of Canada

Prime Minister	Served	Place of birth	Born	Died
1. Sir John A. Macdonald	1867–1873	United Kingdom	Jan. 11, 1815	June 6, 1891
2. Alexander Mackenzie	1873–1878	United Kingdom	Jan. 28, 1822	Apr. 17, 1892
3. Sir John A. Macdonald	1878–1891	United Kingdom	Jan. 11, 1815	June 6, 1891
4. Sir John J. C. Abbott	1891–1892	Quebec	Mar. 12, 1821	Oct. 30, 1893
5. Sir John S. D. Thompson	1892–1894	Nova Scotia	Nov. 10, 1844	Dec. 12, 1894
6. Sir Mackenzie Bowell	1894–1896	United Kingdom	Dec. 27, 1823	Dec. 10, 1917
7. Sir Charles Tupper	1896	Nova Scotia	July 2, 1821	Oct. 30, 1915
8. Sir Wilfrid Laurier	1896–1911	Quebec	Nov. 20, 1841	Feb. 17, 1919
9. Sir Robert L. Borden	1911–1920	Nova Scotia	June 26, 1854	June 10, 1937
10. Arthur Meighen	1920–1921	Ontario	June 16, 1874	Aug. 5, 1960
11. W. L. Mackenzie King	1921–1926	Ontario	Dec. 17, 1874	July 22, 1950
12. Arthur Meighen	1926	Ontario	June 16, 1874	Aug. 5, 1960
13. W. L. Mackenzie King	1926–1930	Ontario	Dec. 17, 1874	July 22, 1950
14. Richard B. Bennett	1930–1935	New Brunswick	July 3, 1870	June 26, 1947
15. W. L. Mackenzie King	1935–1948	Ontario	Dec. 17, 1874	July 22, 1950
16. Louis S. St. Laurent	1948–1957	Quebec	Feb. 1, 1882	July 25, 1973
17. John G. Diefenbaker	1957–1963	Ontario	Sept. 18, 1895	Aug. 16, 1979
18. Lester B. Pearson	1963–1968	Ontario	Apr. 23, 1897	Dec. 27, 1972
19. Pierre E. Trudeau	1968–1979	Quebec	Oct. 18, 1919	
20. Charles Joseph Clark	1979–1980	Alberta	June 5, 1939	
21. Pierre E. Trudeau	1980–1984	Quebec	Oct. 18, 1919	
22. John N. Turner	1984	United Kingdom	June 7, 1929	
23. Martin Brian Mulroney	1984–	Quebec	Mar. 20, 1939	

The Fifty States and Their Capitals*

Alabama—Al|a|bam|a (al′ə **bam**′ə). CAPITAL:
Montgomery—Mont|gom|er|y (mont **gum**′ər ē).
Abbreviation: Ala. *or* AL

Alaska—A|las|ka (ə **las**′kə). CAPITAL: Juneau—Ju|neau
(**ju**′nō). *Abbreviation:* AK

Arizona—Ar|i|zo|na (ar′ə **zō**′nə). CAPITAL: Phoenix—
Phoe|nix (**fē**′niks). *Abbreviation:* Ariz. *or* AZ

Arkansas—Ar|kan|sas (**ahr**′kən saw′). CAPITAL:
Little Rock—Lit|tle Rock (**lit**′əl rok). *Abbreviation:*
Ark. *or* AR

California—Cal|i|for|ni|a (kal′ə **fawr**′nyə). CAPITAL:
Sacramento—Sac|ra|men|to (sak′rə **men**′tō).
Abbreviation: Calif. *or* CA

Colorado—Col|o|ra|do (kol′ə **rad**′ō *or* kol′ə **rah**′dō).
CAPITAL: Denver—Den|ver (**den**′vər). *Abbreviation:*
Colo. *or* CO

Connecticut—Con|nect|i|cut (kə **net**′ə kət). CAPITAL:
Hartford—Hart|ford (**hahrt**′fərd). *Abbreviation:* Conn.
or CT

Delaware—Del|a|ware (**del**′ə wār). CAPITAL: Dover—
Do|ver (**dō**′vər). *Abbreviation:* Del. *or* DE

Florida—Flor|i|da (**flawr**′ə də *or* **flahr**′ə də). CAPITAL:
Tallahassee—Tal|la|has|see (tal′ə **has**′ē).
Abbreviation: Fla. *or* FL

Georgia—Geor|gia (**jawr**′jə). CAPITAL: Atlanta—
At|lan|ta (at **lan**′tə). *Abbreviation:* Ga. *or* GA

Hawaii—Ha|wai|i (hə **wī**′ē). CAPITAL: Honolulu—
Hon|o|lu|lu (hon′ə **lū**′lū). *Abbreviation:* HI

Idaho—I|da|ho (**ī**′də hō). CAPITAL: Boise—Boi|se
(**boi**′sē *or* **boi**′zē). *Abbreviation:* Id. *or* ID

Illinois—Il|li|nois (il′ə **noi**′). CAPITAL: Springfield—
Spring|field (**spring**′fēld′). *Abbreviation:* Ill. *or* IL

Indiana—In|di|an|a (in′dē **an**′ə). CAPITAL: Indianapolis
—In|di|a|nap|o|lis (in′dē ə **nap**′ə lis). *Abbreviation:*
Ind. *or* IN

Iowa—I|o|wa (**ī**′ə wə). CAPITAL: Des Moines—
Des Moines (də **moin**). *Abbreviation:* Ia. *or* IA

Kansas—Kan|sas (**kan**′zəs). CAPITAL: Topeka—
To|pe|ka (tə **pe**′kə). *Abbreviation:* Kans. *or* KS

Kentucky—Ken|tuck|y (kən **tuk**′ē). CAPITAL: Frankfort
—Frank|fort (**frangk**′fərt). *Abbreviation:* Ky. *or* KY

Louisiana—Lou|i|si|an|a (lū ē′zē **an**′ə). CAPITAL:
Baton Rouge—Ba|ton Rouge (**bat**′ən rūzh).
Abbreviation: La. *or* LA

Maine—Maine (mān). CAPITAL: Augusta—Au|gus|ta
(aw **gus**′tə). *Abbreviation:* Me. *or* ME

Maryland—Mar|y|land (**mār**′ə lənd). CAPITAL:
Annapolis—An|nap|o|lis (ə **nap**′ə lis). *Abbreviation:*
Md. *or* MD

Massachusetts—Mas|sa|chu|setts (mas′ə **chū**′səts).
CAPITAL: Boston—Bos|ton (**baw**′stən). *Abbreviation:*
Mass. *or* MA

Michigan—Mich|i|gan (**mish**′i gən). CAPITAL: Lansing
—Lan|sing (**lan**′sing). *Abbreviation:* Mich. *or* MI

Minnesota—Min|ne|so|ta (min′ə **sō**′tə). CAPITAL:
St. Paul—St. Paul (sānt pawl). *Abbreviation:* Minn.
or MN

Mississippi—Mis|sis|sip|pi (mis′ə **sip**′ē). CAPITAL:
Jackson—Jack|son (**jak**′sən). *Abbreviation:* Miss. *or*
MS

Missouri—Mis|sou|ri (mə **zoor**′ē *or* mə **zoor**′ə).
CAPITAL: Jefferson City—Jef|fer|son Cit|y
(**jef**′ər sən **sit**′ē). *Abbreviation:* Mo. *or* MO

Montana—Mon|tan|a (mon **tan**′ə). CAPITAL:
Helena—Hel|e|na (**hel**′ə nə). *Abbreviation:* Mont. *or*
MT

Nebraska—Ne|bras|ka (nə **bras**′kə). CAPITAL:
Lincoln—Lin|coln (**ling**′kən). *Abbreviation:* Neb. *or*
NE

Nevada—Ne|va|da (nə **vad**′ə *or* nə **vahd**′ə). CAPITAL:
Carson City—Car|son Cit|y (**kahr**′sən **sit**′ē).
Abbreviation: Nev. *or* NV

New Hampshire—New Hamp|shire (nū
hamp′shər). CAPITAL: Concord—Con|cord
(**kong**′kərd). *Abbreviation:* N.H. *or* NH

New Jersey—New Jer|sey (nū **jur**′zē). CAPITAL:
Trenton—Tren|ton (**tren**′tən). *Abbreviation:* N.J. *or*
NJ

New Mexico—New Mex|i|co (nū **mek**′si kō′).
CAPITAL: Santa Fe—San|ta Fe (**san**′tə fā).
Abbreviation: N.Mex. *or* NM

New York—New York (nū yawrk). CAPITAL: Albany
—Al|ba|ny (**awl**′bə nē). *Abbreviation:* N.Y. *or* NY

North Carolina—North Car|o|li|na (nawrth
kar′ə **lī**′nə). CAPITAL: Raleigh—Ra|leigh (**raw**′lē *or*
rahl′ē). *Abbreviation:* N.C. *or* NC

North Dakota—North Da|ko|ta (nawrth də **kō**′tə).
CAPITAL: Bismarck—Bis|marck (**biz**′mahrk′).
Abbreviation: N.Dak. *or* ND

Ohio—O|hi|o (ō **hī**′ō). CAPITAL: Columbus—
Co|lum|bus (kə **lum**′bəs). *Abbreviation:* O. *or* OH

Oklahoma—O|kla|ho|ma (ō′klə **hō**′mə). CAPITAL:
Oklahoma City—O|kla|ho|ma Cit|y
(ō′klə **hō**′mə **sit**′ē). *Abbreviation:* Okla. *or* OK

Oregon—Or|e|gon (**awr**′i gən *or* **ahr**′i gən). CAPITAL:
Salem—Sa|lem (**sā**′ləm). *Abbreviation:* Ore. *or* OR

Pennsylvania—Penn|syl|va|ni|a (pen′səl **vān**′yə).
CAPITAL: Harrisburg—Har|ris|burg (**har**′əs burg′).
Abbreviation: Penn. *or* PA

Rhode Island—Rhode Is|land (rōd **ī**′lənd). CAPITAL:
Providence—Prov|i|dence (**prov**′ə dəns).
Abbreviation: R.I. *or* RI

South Carolina—South Car|o|li|na (south
kar′ə **lī**′nə). CAPITAL: Columbia—Co|lum|bi|a
(kə **lum**′bē ə). *Abbreviation:* S.C. *or* SC

South Dakota—South Da|ko|ta (south də **kō**′tə).
CAPITAL: Pierre—Pierre (pēr). *Abbreviation:* S.Dak. *or*
SD

*Where two abbreviations are listed, the first is the traditional
abbreviation, and the second is the abbreviation now used for mail.

Tennessee—Ten|nes|see (ten′ə sē′). CAPITAL: Nashville—Nash|ville (**nash**′vil′). *Abbreviation:* Tenn. *or* TN

Texas—Tex|as (**tek**′səs). CAPITAL: Austin—Aus|tin (**aw**′stən). *Abbreviation:* Tex. *or* TX

Utah—Utah (yū′taw′ *or* yū′tah′). CAPITAL: Salt Lake City—Salt Lake Cit|y (sawlt lāk **sit**′ē). *Abbreviation:* Ut. *or* UT

Vermont—Ver|mont (vər **mont**′). CAPITAL: Montpelier —Mont|pe|li|er (mont **pēl**′yər). *Abbreviation:* Vt. *or* VT

Virginia—Vir|gin|i|a (vər **jin**′yə). CAPITAL: Richmond —Rich|mond (**rich**′mənd). *Abbreviation:* Va. *or* VA

Washington—Wash|ing|ton (**wawsh**′ing tən *or* **wahsh**′ing tən). CAPITAL: Olympia—O|lym|pi|a (ə **lim**′pē ə). *Abbreviation:* Wash. *or* WA

West Virginia—West Vir|gin|i|a (west vər **jin**′yə). CAPITAL: Charleston—Charles|ton (**chahrlz**′tən). *Abbreviation:* W.Va. *or* WV

Wisconsin—Wis|con|sin (wis **kon**′sən). CAPITAL: Madison—Mad|i|son (**mad**′ə sən). *Abbreviation:* Wis. *or* WI

Wyoming—Wy|o|ming (wī ō′ming). CAPITAL: Cheyenne —Chey|enne (shī **an**′ *or* **shī**′en). *Abbreviation:* Wyo. *or* WY

The Provinces and Territories of Canada and Their Capitals

Provinces

Alberta—Al|ber|ta (al **bur**′tə). CAPITAL: Edmonton—Ed|mon|ton (**ed**′mən tən). *Abbreviation:* Alta.

British Columbia—Brit|ish Co|lum|bi|a (**brit**′ish kə **lum**′bē ə). CAPITAL: Victoria—Vic|to|ri|a (vik **tawr**′ē ə). *Abbreviation:* B.C.

Manitoba—Man|i|to|ba (man′ə **tō**′bə). CAPITAL: Winnipeg—Win|ni|peg (**win**′ə peg′). *Abbreviation:* Man.

New Brunswick—New Bruns|wick (nū **brunz**′wik). CAPITAL: Fredericton—Fred|er|ic|ton (**fred**′rik tən). *Abbreviation:* N.B.

Newfoundland—New|found|land (**nū**′fən lənd). CAPITAL: St. John's—St. John's (sānt jonz). *Abbreviation:* Nfld.

Nova Scotia—No|va Sco|ti|a (nō′və **skō**′shə). CAPITAL: Halifax—Hal|i|fax (**hal**′ə faks′). *Abbreviation:* N.S.

Ontario—On|tar|i|o (on **tār**′ē ō). CAPITAL: Toronto—To|ron|to (tə **ron**′tō). *Abbreviation:* Ont.

Prince Edward Island—Prince Ed|ward Is|land (prins **ed**′wərd **ī**′lənd). CAPITAL: Charlottetown—Char|lotte|town (**shahr**′lət toun′). *Abbreviation:* P.E.I.

Quebec—Quebec (kwi **bek**′ *or* ki **bek**′). CAPITAL: Quebec—Que|bec (kwi **bek**′ *or* ki **bek**′). *Abbreviation:* Que.

Saskatchewan—Sas|katch|e|wan (sə **skach**′ə wahn′). CAPITAL: Regina—Re|gi|na (ri **jī**′nə). *Abbreviation:* Sask.

Territories

Northwest Territories—North|west Ter|ri|to|ries (nawrth**′west**′ **ter**′ə tawr′ēz). CAPITAL: Yellowknife—Yel|low|knife (**yel**′ə nīf′). *Abbreviation:* N.W.Ter.

Yukon Territory—Yu|kon Ter|ri|to|ry (**yū**′kon′ **ter**′ə tawr′ē). CAPITAL: Whitehorse—White|horse (**hwīt**′hawrs′). *Abbreviation:* Y.T.

Independent Countries of the World and Their Capitals

Afghanistan—Af|ghan|i|stan (af gan′ə stan′). CAPITAL: Kabul—Ka|bul (kah′bul).

Albania—Al|ba|ni|a (al bā′nē ə). CAPITAL: Tiranë—Ti|ra|në (ti rahn′ə).

Algeria—Al|ge|ri|a (al jēr′ē ə). CAPITAL: Algiers—Al|giers (al jērz′).

Andorra—An|dor|ra (an dawr′ə). CAPITAL: Andorra—An|dor|ra (an dawr′ə).

Angola—An|go|la (ang gō′lə). CAPITAL: Luanda—Lu|an|da (lū ahn′də).

Antigua and Barbuda—An|ti|gua and Bar|bu|da (an tē′gwə and bahr bū′də). CAPITAL: St. John's—St. John's (sānt jahnz).

Argentina—Ar|gen|ti|na (ahr′jən tē′nə). CAPITAL: Buenos Aires—Bue|nos Ai|res (bwā′nos īr′ās).

Armenia—Ar|me|ni|a (ahr mē′nē ə *or* ahr mēn′yə). CAPITAL: Yerevan—Ye|re|van (yer′ə vahn′).

Australia—Aus|tra|li|a (aw strāl′yə). CAPITAL: Canberra—Can|ber|ra (kan′bər ə).

Austria—Aus|tri|a (aws′trē ə). CAPITAL: Vienna—Vi|en|na (vē en′ə).

Azerbaijan—Az|er|bai|jan (ah′zər bī jahn′ *or* ahz′ər bī jan′). CAPITAL: Baku—Ba|ku (bah kū′).

Bahamas—Ba|ha|mas (bə hah′məz). CAPITAL: Nassau—Nas|sau (nas′aw′).

Bahrain—Bah|rain (bah rān′). CAPITAL: Manama—Ma|na|ma (mə nam′ə).

Bangladesh—Ban|gla|desh (bahng′glə desh′ *or* bang′glə desh′). CAPITAL: Dhaka—Dha|ka (dak′ə).

Barbados—Bar|ba|dos (bahr bā′dōz). CAPITAL: Bridgetown—Bridge|town (brij′toun).

Belarus—Be|la|rus (bel′ə rūs′). CAPITAL: Minsk—Minsk (minsk).

Belgium—Bel|gium (bel′jəm). CAPITAL: Brussels—Brus|sels (brus′əlz).

Belize—Be|lize (bə lēz′). CAPITAL: Belmopan—Bel|mo|pan (bel′mō pan′).

Benin—Be|nin (be nēn′). CAPITAL: Porto-Novo—Por|to-No|vo (pawr′tō nō′vō).

Bhutan—Bhu|tan (bū tahn′). CAPITAL: Thimphu—Thim|phu (thim′bū).

Bolivia—Bo|liv|i|a (be liv′ē ə). CAPITALS: La Paz—La Paz (lə paz); Sucre—Su|cre (sū′krā).

Bosnia and Hercegovina—Bos|ni|a and Her|ce|go|vi|na (bahz′nē ə and hert′sə gō vē′nə). CAPITAL: Sarajevo—Sa|ra|je|vo (sahr ə ye′vō).

Botswana—Bot|swa|na (bōt swah′nah). CAPITAL: Gaborone—Ga|bo|ro|ne (gahb′ə rō′nē).

Brazil—Bra|zil (brə zil′). CAPITAL: Brasília—Bra|sí|li|a (brə sēl′yə).

Brunei—Bru|nei (brū′nī′). CAPITAL: Bandar Seri Begawan—Ban|dar Se|ri Be|ga|wan (bun′dər ser′ē bə gah′wən).

Bulgaria—Bul|gar|i|a (bul gār′ē ə). CAPITAL: Sofia—So|fi|a (sō′fē ə *or* sō fē′ə).

Burkina Faso—Bur|ki|na Fa|so (boor kē′nə fah′sō). CAPITAL: Ouagadougou—Oua|ga|dou|gou (wah′gə dū′gū).

Burma—Bur|ma (bur′mə). CAPITAL: Rangoon—Ran|goon (ran gūn′).

Burundi—Bu|run|di (boo rūn′dē). CAPITAL: Bujumbura—Bu|jum|bu|ra (bū′jəm boor′ə).

Cambodia—Cam|bo|di|a (kam bō′dē ə). CAPITAL: Phnom Penh—Phnom Penh (Pə nom′ pen).

Cameroon—Cam|er|oon (kam′ə rūn′). CAPITAL: Yaoundé—Ya|oun|dé (yah ūn dā′).

Canada—Can|a|da (kan′ə də). CAPITAL: Ottawa—Ot|ta|wa (ot′ə wə).

Cape Verde—Cape Verde (kāp vurd). CAPITAL: Praia—Prai|a (prī′ə).

Central African Republic—Cen|tral Af|ri|can Re|pub|lic (sen′trəl af′ri kən ri pub′lik). CAPITAL: Bangui—Ban|gui (bahng gē′).

Chad—Chad (chad). CAPITAL: N'Djamena—N'Dja|me|na (en jahm′ə nə).

Chile—Chi|le (chil′ē). CAPITAL: Santiago—San|ti|a|go (san′tē ah′gō).

China—Chi|na (chī′nə). CAPITAL: Beijing—Bei|jing (bā′jing′), also called Peking—Pé|king (pē king′).

Colombia—Co|lom|bi|a (kə lum′bē ə). CAPITAL: Bogotá—Bo|go|tá (bō′gə tah′).

Comoros—Com|o|ros (kahm′ə rōz′). CAPITAL: Moroni—Mo|ro|ni (maw rō′nē).

Congo—Con|go (kahng′gō). CAPITAL: Brazzaville—Braz|za|ville (braz′ə vil′).

Costa Rica—Cos|ta Ri|ca (kōs′tə rē′kə). CAPITAL: San José—San Jo|sé (san hō zā′).

Croatia—Cro|a|tia (krō ā′shə). CAPITAL: Zagreb—Za|greb (zah′greb).

Cuba—Cu|ba (kyū′bə). CAPITAL: Havana—Ha|va|na (hə van′ə).

Cyprus—Cy|prus (sī′prəs). CAPITAL: Nicosia—Nic|o|si|a (nik′ə sē′ə).

Czechoslovakia—Czech|o|slo|va|ki|a (chek′ə slō vahk′ē ə). CAPITAL: Prague—Prague (prahg).

Denmark—Den|mark (den′mahrk′). CAPITAL: Copenhagen—Co|pen|ha|gen (kō′pən hā′gən *or* kō′pən hah′gən).

Djibouti—Dji|bou|ti (ji bū′tē). CAPITAL: Djibouti—Dji|bou|ti (ji bū′tē).

Dominica—Dom|i|ni|ca (dahm′ə nē′kə). CAPITAL: Roseau—Ro|seau (rō zō′).

Dominican Republic—Do|min|i|can Re|pub|lic (də min′i kən ri pub′lik). CAPITAL: Santo Domingo—San|to Do|min|go (sahn′tō dō ming′gō).

Ecuador—Ec|ua|dor (ek′wə dawr′). CAPITAL: Quito—Qui|to (kē′tō).

Egypt—E|gypt (ē′jəpt). CAPITAL: Cairo—Cai|ro (kī′rō).

El Salvador—El Sal|va|dor (el sal′və dawr′). CAPITAL: San Salvador—San Sal|va|dor (san sal′və dawr′).

Equatorial Guinea—E|qua|to|ri|al Guin|ea (ē′kwə tawr′ē əl gin′ē). CAPITAL: Malabo—Ma|la|bo (mah lah′bō).

Estonia—Es|to|ni|a (e **sto**′nē ə). CAPITAL: Tallinn—Tal|linn (**tah**′lin).

Ethiopia—E|thi|o|pi|a (ē′thē **ō**′pē ə). CAPITAL: Addis Ababa—Ad|dis A|ba|ba (**ad**′is **ab**′ə bə).

Fiji—Fi|ji (**fē**′jē). CAPITAL: Suva—Su|va (**sū**′və).

Finland—Fin|land (**fin**′lənd). CAPITAL: Helsinki—Hel|sin|ki (**hel**′sing′kē).

France—France (frans). CAPITAL: Paris—Par|is (**par**′əs).

Gabon—Ga|bon (ga **bōn**′). CAPITAL: Libreville—Li|bre|ville (**lē**′brə vil′).

Gambia—Gam|bi|a (**gam**′bē ə). CAPITAL: Banjul—Ban|jul (**bahn**′jūl′).

Georgia—Geor|gia (**jawr**′jə). CAPITAL: Tbilisi—Tbi|li|si (tə bə **lē**′sē).

Germany—Ger|ma|ny (**jur**′mə nē). CAPITAL: Berlin—Ber|lin (bər **lin**′).

Ghana—Gha|na (**gahn**′ə). CAPITAL: Accra—Ac|cra (ə **krah**′ or **ak**′rə).

Great Britain—Great Brit|ain (grāt **brit**′ən). See United Kingdom.

Greece—Greece (grēs). CAPITAL: Athens—Ath|ens (**ath**′ənz).

Grenada—Gre|na|da (grə **nā**′də). CAPITAL: St. George's—St. George's (sānt **jorj**′əz).

Guatemala—Gua|te|ma|la (gwah′tə **mah**′lə). CAPITAL: Guatemala City—Gua|te|ma|la Cit|y (gwah′tə **mah**′lə **sit**′ē).

Guinea—Guin|ea (**gin**′ē). CAPITAL: Conakry—Con|a|kry (**kon**′ə krē).

Guinea-Bissau—Guin|ea-Bis|sau (**gin**′ē bis **ou**′). CAPITAL: Bissau—Bis|sau (bis **ou**′).

Guyana—Guy|an|a (gī **an**′ə). CAPITAL: Georgetown—George|town (**jorj**′toun).

Haiti—Hai|ti (**hā**′tē). CAPITAL: Port-au-Prince—Port-au-Prince (pawrt′ō **prins**′).

Honduras—Hon|du|ras (hon **dū**′rəs). CAPITAL: Tegucigalpa—Te|gu|ci|gal|pa (tə gū′sə **gal**′pə).

Hungary—Hun|ga|ry (**hung**′gə rē). CAPITAL: Budapest—Bu|da|pest (**bū**′də pest′).

Iceland—Ice|land (**īs**′lənd) CAPITAL: Reykjavík—Reyk|ja|vík (**rāk**′yə vēk′).

India—In|di|a (**in**′dē ə). CAPITAL: New Delhi—New Del|hi (nū **del**′ē).

Indonesia—In|do|ne|si|a (in′də **nē**′zhə). CAPITAL: Jakarta—Ja|kar|ta (jə **kahrt**′ə).

Iran—I|ran (i **rahn**′ or ī **ran**′). CAPITAL: Teheran—Te|he|ran (te′ə **rahn**′).

Iraq—I|raq (i **rahk**′ or i **rak**′). CAPITAL: Baghdad—Bagh|dad (**bag**′dad′).

Ireland—Ire|land (**īr**′lənd). CAPITAL: Dublin—Dub|lin (**dub**′lən).

Israel—Is|ra|el (**iz**′rē əl or **iz**′rā əl). CAPITAL: Jerusalem—Je|ru|sa|lem (jə **rū**′sə ləm).

Italy—It|a|ly (**it**′əl ē). CAPITAL: Rome—Rome (rōm).

Ivory Coast—I|vo|ry Coast (**ī**′və rē kōst). CAPITAL: Abidjan—Ab|i|djan (ab′i **jahn**′).

Jamaica—Ja|mai|ca (jə **mā**′kə). CAPITAL: Kingston—Kings|ton (**king**′stən).

Japan—Ja|pan (jə **pan**′). CAPITAL: Tokyo—To|ky|o (**tō**′kē ō′).

Jordan—Jor|dan (**jawr**′dən). CAPITAL: Amman—Am|man (**ah**′mahn).

Kazakhstan—Ka|zakh|stan (kah′zahk **stahn**′). CAPITAL: Alma-Ata—Al|ma-A|ta (al′mə ə **tah**′).

Kenya—Ke|nya (**ken**′yə or **kēn**′yə). CAPITAL: Nairobi—Nai|ro|bi (nī **rō**′bē).

Kiribati—Ki|ri|bati (**kēr**′ə bahs′). CAPITAL: Tarawa—Ta|ra|wa (tə **rah**′wə).

Korea, North—North Ko|re|a (nawrth kə **rē**′ə). CAPITAL: Pyongyang—Pyong|yang (**pyong**′yahng′).

Korea, South—South Ko|re|a (south kə **rē**′ə). CAPITAL: Seoul—Seoul (sōl).

Kuwait—Ku|wait (kū **wāt**′ or kū **wīt**′). CAPITAL: Kuwait—Ku|wait (kū **wāt**′ or kū **wīt**′).

Kyrgyzstan—Kyr|gyz|stan (kir gi **stahn**′). CAPITAL: Bishkek—Bish|kek (bish **kek**′).

Laos—Laos (**lah**′ōs). CAPITAL: Vientiane—Vien|tiane (vyen **tyahn**′).

Latvia—Lat|vi|a (**lat**′vē ə). CAPITAL: Riga Ri|ga (**rē**′gə).

Lebanon—Leb|a|non (**leb**′ə nən). CAPITAL: Beirut—Bei|rut (bā **rūt**′).

Lesotho—Le|so|tho (lə **sō**′tō). CAPITAL: Maseru—Mas|e|ru (**maz**′ə rū′).

Liberia—Li|be|ri|a (lī **bēr**′ē ə). CAPITAL: Monrovia—Mon|ro|vi|a (mun **rō**′vē ə).

Libya—Lib|y|a (**lib**′ē ə). CAPITAL: Tripoli—Trip|o|li (**trip**′ə lē).

Liechtenstein—Liech|ten|stein (**lik**′tən stīn′). CAPITAL: Vaduz—Va|duz (vah **dūts**′).

Lithuania—Lith|u|a|ni|a (lith′ū **a**′nē ə). CAPITAL: Vilnius—Vil|ni|us (**vil**′nē oos).

Luxembourg—Lux|em|bourg (**luk**′səm burg′). CAPITAL: Luxembourg—Lux|em|bourg (**luk**′səm burg′).

Macedonia—Mac|e|do|ni|a (mas′ ə **dō**′ nē ə). CAPITAL: Skopjie—Skop|jie (**skawp**′ ya).

Madagascar—Mad|a|gas|car (mad′ə **gas**′kər). CAPITAL: Antananarivo—An|ta|na|na|ri|vo (ahn′tah nah′nah **rē**′vō).

Malawi—Ma|la|wi (mah **lah**′wē). CAPITAL: Lilongwe—Li|long|we (li **lawng**′wā).

Malaysia—Ma|lay|si|a (mə **lā**′zhə). CAPITAL: Kuala Lumpur—Kua|la Lum|pur (**kwah**′lə **loom**′poor).

Maldives—Mal|dives (**mal**′dīvz′). CAPITAL: Male—Ma|le (**mah**′lē).

Mali—Ma|li (**mah**′lē). CAPITAL: Bamako—Ba|ma|ko (**bam**′ə kō).

Malta—Mal|ta (**mawl**′tə). CAPITAL: Valletta—Val|let|ta (və **let**′ə).

Mauritania—Mau|ri|ta|ni|a (mawr′ə **tā**′nē ə). CAPITAL: Nouakchott—Nouak|chott (nwahk **shot**′).

Mauritius—Mau|ri|ti|us (maw **rish**′əs). CAPITAL: Port Louis—Port Louis (pawrt **lū**′əs or pawrt **lū**′ē).

Mexico—Mex|i|co (**mek**′si kō′). CAPITAL: Mexico City—Mex|i|co Cit|y (**mek**′si kō′ **sit**′ē).

Moldova—Mol|do|va (mol **do**′və). CAPITAL: Chisinau—Chi|si|nau (kē shi **nou**′).

Monaco—Mo|na|co (**mon'**ə kō'). CAPITAL: Monaco—Mo|na|co (**mon'**ə kō').

Mongolia—Mon|go|li|a (mon **gō'**lē ə). CAPITAL: Ulan Bator—Ulan Ba|tor (ū lahn' **bah'**tawr').

Morocco—Mo|roc|co (mə **rok'**ō). CAPITAL: Rabat—Ra|bat (rə **baht'**).

Mozambique—Mo|zam|bique (mō'zəm **bēk'**). CAPITAL: Maputo—Ma|pu|to (mah **pū'**tō).

Namibia—Na|mib|i|a (nə mib'ē ə). CAPITAL: Windhoek—Wind|hoek (**vint'**hūk).

Nauru—Na|u|ru (nah'**rū**). No capital.

Nepal—Ne|pal (nə **pawl'**). CAPITAL: Kathmandu—Kath|man|du (kat'man **du'**).

Netherlands—Neth|er|lands (**neth'**ər ləndz). CAPITAL: Amsterdam—Am|ster|dam (**am'**stər dam').

New Zealand—New Zea|land (nū **zē'**lənd). CAPITAL: Wellington—Wel|ling|ton (**wel'**ing tən).

Nicaragua—Nic|a|ra|gu|a (nik'ə **rahg'**wə). CAPITAL: Managua—Ma|na|gu|a (mə **nahg'**wə).

Niger—Ni|ger (**nī'**jər). CAPITAL: Niamey—Nia|mey (nyah **mā'**).

Nigeria—Ni|ge|ri|a (nī **jēr'**ē ə). CAPITAL: Abuja—A|bu|ja (ah **bu'** jah).

Norway—Nor|way (**nawr'**wā'). CAPITAL: Oslo—Os|lo (**oz'**lō or **os'**lō).

Oman—Oman (ō **mahn'**). CAPITAL: Muscat—Mus|cat (**mus'**kat').

Pakistan—Pa|ki|stan (**pak'**i stan' or pahk'i **stahn'**). CAPITAL: Islamabad—Is|lam|a|bad (is **lahm'**ə bahd').

Panama—Pan|a|ma (**pan'**ə mah'). CAPITAL: Panama City—Pan|a|ma Cit|y (**pan'**ə mah' **sit'**ē).

Papua New Guinea—Pa|pu|a New Guin|ea (**pap'**yū ə nū **gin'**ē). CAPITAL: Port Moresby—Port Mores|by (pawrt **mawrz'**bē).

Paraguay—Par|a|guay (**pār'**ə gwī' or **pār'**ə gwā'). CAPITAL: Asunción—A|sun|ci|ón (ah sūn'**syawn'**).

Peru—Pe|ru (pə **rū'**). CAPITAL: Lima—Li|ma (**lē'**mə).

Philippines—Phil|ip|pines (**fil'**ə pēnz'). CAPITAL: Manila—Ma|nil|a (mə **nil'**ə).

Poland—Po|land (**pō'**lənd). CAPITAL: Warsaw—War|saw (**wawr'**saw').

Portugal—Por|tu|gal (**pawr'**chə gəl). CAPITAL: Lisbon—Lis|bon (**liz'**bən).

Qatar—Qa|tar (**kaht'**ahr or **gaht'**ahr). CAPITAL: Doha—Do|ha (**dō'**hah').

Romania—Ro|ma|ni|a (rō **mā'**nē ə). CAPITAL: Bucharest—Bu|cha|rest (**bū'**kə rest').

Russia—Rus|sia (**rush'**ə). CAPITAL: Moscow—Mos|cow (**mos'**kō or **mos'**kou).

Rwanda—Rwan|da (rū ahn'də). CAPITAL: Kigali—Ki|ga|li (ki **gahl'**ē).

St. Christopher and Nevis—St. Chris|to|pher and Ne|vis (sānt **kris'**tə fer and **nē'**vəs). CAPITAL: Basseterre—Basse|terre (bahs **tār'**).

St. Lucia—St. Lu|ci|a (sānt **lū'**shə). CAPITAL: Castries—Cas|tries (**kas'**trēz).

St. Vincent and the Grenadines—St. Vin|cent and the Gren|a|dines (sānt **vin'**sənt and thə gren'ə **dēnz'**). CAPITAL: Kingstown—Kings|town (**kingz'**toun).

San Marino—San Ma|ri|no (san mə **rē'**nō). CAPITAL: San Marino—San Ma|ri|no (san mə **rē'**nō).

São Tomé and Príncipe—São To|mé and Prín|ci|pe (soun taw **me'** and **prēn'**sē pə). CAPITAL: São Tomé—São To|mé (soun taw **me'**).

Saudi Arabia—Sau|di Arabia (**soud'**ē ə **rā'**bē ə or **sawd'**ē ə **rā'**bē ə). CAPITAL: Riyadh—Ri|yadh (rē **yahd'**).

Senegal—Sen|e|gal (sen'ə **gawl'**). CAPITAL: Dakar—Da|kar (dah **kahr'**).

Seychelles—Sey|chelles (sā **shelz'** or sā **shel'**). CAPITAL: Victoria—Vic|to|ri|a (vik **tawr'**ē ə).

Sierra Leone—Si|er|ra Le|one (sē **ār'**ə lē **ōn'**). CAPITAL: Freetown—Free|town (**frē'**toun').

Singapore—Sing|a|pore (**sing'**ə pawr'). CAPITAL: Singapore—Sing|a|pore (**sing'**ə pawr').

Slovenia—Slo|ve|ni|a (slō **vē'**nē ə or slo **ven'**yə). CAPITAL: Ljubljana—Lju|blja|na (lū'blē **ah'**nə).

Solomon Islands—Sol|o|mon Is|lands (**sol'**ə mən ī'ləndz). CAPITAL: Honiara—Ho|ni|a|ra (hō'nē **ahr'**ə).

Somalia—So|ma|li|a (sō **mahl'**ē ə). CAPITAL: Mogadishu—Mog|a|di|shu (maw'gah dē'shū).

South Africa—South Af|ri|ca (south **af'**ri kə). CAPITALS: Cape Town—Cape Town (kāp toun); Pretoria—Pre|to|ri|a (pri **tawr'**ē ə); Bloemfontein—Bloem|fon|tein (**blūm'**fon tān).

Spain—Spain (spān). CAPITAL: Madrid—Ma|drid (mə **drid'**).

Sri Lanka—Sri Lan|ka (srē **lahng'**kə). CAPITAL: Colombo—Co|lom|bo (kə **lum'**bō).

Sudan—Su|dan (sū **dan'**). CAPITAL: Khartoum—Khar|toum (kahr **tūm'**).

Suriname—Su|ri|na|me (sur'rē **nahm'**ə). CAPITAL: Paramaribo—Par|a|mar|i|bo (pār'ə **mār'**ə bō').

Swaziland—Swa|zi|land (**swah'**zē land'). CAPITAL: Mbabane—M|ba|bane (em'bə **bahn'**).

Sweden—Swe|den (**swē'**dən). CAPITAL: Stockholm—Stock|holm (**stok'**hōm or **stok'**hōlm).

Switzerland—Swit|zer|land (**swit'**sər lənd). CAPITAL: Bern—Bern (burn or bārn).

Syria—Syr|i|a (**sēr'**ē ə). CAPITAL: Damascus—Da|mas|cus (də **mas'**kəs).

Taiwan—Tai|wan (tī **wahn'**). CAPITAL: Taipei—Tai|pei (tī **pā'**).

Tajikistan—Ta|jik|i|stan (tə jik'ə **stan'**). CAPITAL: Dushanbe—Du|shan|be (dū **shahn'** bə).

Tanzania—Tan|za|ni|a (tan'zə **nē'**ə). CAPITAL: Dar es Salaam—Dar es Sa|laam (dahr es sə **lahm'**).

Thailand—Thai|land (**tī'**land). CAPITAL: Bangkok—Bang|kok (**bang'**kok').

Togo—To|go (**tō'**gō). CAPITAL: Lomé—Lo|mé (law **mā'**).

Tonga—Ton|ga (**tong'**gə). CAPITAL: Nukualofa—Nu|ku|a|lo|fa (nū'kū ah lō'fah).

Trinidad and Tobago—Trin|i|dad and To|ba|go (**trin'**ə dad' and tə **bā'**gō). CAPITAL: Port-of-Spain—Port-of-Spain (pawrt ov **spān'**).

Tunisia—Tu|ni|si|a (tū nē′zhə). CAPITAL: Tunis—Tu|nis (tū′nəs).

Turkey—Tur|key (tur′kē). CAPITAL: Ankara—An|ka|ra (ang′kə rə).

Turkmenistan—Turk|me|ni|stan (turk′mə nə stan′). CAPITAL: Ashkhabad—Ash|kha|bad (ahsh′kə bahd′).

Tuvalu—Tu|va|lu (tū vah′lū). CAPITAL: Funafuti—Fu|na|fu|ti (fū′nah fū′tē).

Uganda—U|gan|da (yū gan′də or yū gahn′də). CAPITAL: Kampala—Kam|pa|la (kahm pah′lə).

Ukraine—U|kraine (yū krān′). CAPITAL: Kiev—Ki|ev (kē′ef or kē′ev).

United Arab Emirates—U|nit|ed Ar|ab E|mir|ates (yū nīt′əd ar′əb i mēr′ətz). CAPITAL: Abu Dhabi—A|bu Dha|bi (ah′bū dah′bē).

United Kingdom—U|nit|ed King|dom (yū nīt′əd king′dəm). CAPITAL: London—Lon|don (lun′dən). [Also known as Great Britain—Great Brit|ain (grāt brit′ən). Includes: England—Eng|land (ing′glənd); Wales—Wales (wālz); Scotland—Scot|land (skot′lənd); and Northern Ireland—North|ern Ire|land (north′ərn īr′lənd).]

United States—U|nit|ed States (yū nīt′əd stāts). CAPITAL: Washington, D.C.—Wash|ing|ton, D.C. (waw′shing tən dē cē or wah′shing tən dē cē).

Uruguay—U|ru|guay (yur′ə gwī′ or yur′ə gwā′). CAPITAL: Montevideo—Mon|te|vi|de|o (mon′tə və dā′ō).

Uzbekistan—Uz|bek|i|stan (ooz bek′ə stan′). CAPITAL: Tashkent—Tash|kent (tahsh kent′).

Vanuatu—Van|u|a|tu (vah′nū ah′tū). CAPITAL: Port-Vila—Port-Vi|la (pawrt vē′lə).

Vatican City—Vat|i|can Cit|y (vat′i kən sit′ē). No capital.

Venezuela—Ven|e|zu|e|la (ven′ə zə wā′lə). CAPITAL: Caracas—Ca|ra|cas (kə rah′kəs).

Vietnam—Vi|et|nam (vē′et nahm′ or vē′et nam′). CAPITAL: Hanoi—Ha|noi (hah noi′).

Western Samoa—West|ern Sa|mo|a (wes′tərn sə mō′ə). CAPITAL: Apia—A|pi|a (ah pē′ah or ah′pē ah′).

Yemen—Ye|men (yem′ən). CAPITAL: Sana—Sa|na (sah nah′).

Yugoslavia—Yu|go|sla|vi|a (yū′gō slah′vē ə). CAPITAL: Belgrade—Bel|grade (bel grād′ or bel′grād).

Zaire—Za|ire (zah ēr′). CAPITAL: Kinshasa—Kin|sha|sa (kin shah′sə).

Zambia—Zam|bi|a (zam′bē ə). CAPITAL: Lusaka—Lu|sa|ka (lū sah′kə).

Zimbabwe—Zim|ba|bwe (zim bahb′wä). CAPITAL: Harare—Ha|ra|re (hah rah′rä).

Major Languages

Arabic—Ar|a|bic (ar′ə bik).
Chinese—Chi|nese (chī nēz′).
Czech—Czech (chek).
Danish—Dan|ish (dā′nish).
Dutch—Dutch (duch).
English—Eng|lish (ing′glish).
French—French (french).
German—Ger|man (jur′mən).
Greek—Greek (grēk).
Hebrew—He|brew (hē′brū).
Hindi—Hin|di (hin′dē).

Hungarian—Hun|gar|i|an (hung gār′ē ən).
Italian—I|tal|i|an (i tal′yən).
Japanese—Jap|a|nese (jap′ə nēz′).
Latin—Lat|in (lat′ən).
Norwegian—Nor|we|gi|an (nawr wē′jən).
Polish—Pol|ish (pō′lish).
Portuguese—Por|tu|guese (pawr′chə gēz′).
Russian—Rus|sian (rush′ən).
Spanish—Span|ish (span′ish).
Swedish—Swed|ish (swē′dish).
Turkish—Turk|ish (tur′kish).

Continents of the World

Africa—Af|ri|ca (af′ri kə).
Antarctica—Ant|arc|ti|ca (ant ahrk′ti kə or ant ahr′ti kə).
Asia—A|sia (ā′zhə).
Australia—Aus|tra|li|a (aw strāl′yə).

Europe—Eu|rope (yoor′əp).
North America—North A|mer|i|ca (nawrth ə mer′ə kə).
South America—South A|mer|i|ca (south ə mer′ə kə).

Oceans and Seas

Adriatic Sea—A|dri|at|ic Sea (ā′drē at′ik sē).
Aegean Sea—Ae|ge|an Sea (i jē′ən sē).
Antarctic Ocean—Ant|arc|tic O|cean (ant ahrk′tik ō′shən or ant ahrt′ik ō′shən).
Arctic Ocean—Arc|tic O|cean (ahrk′tik ō′shən or ahrt′ik ō′shən).
Atlantic Ocean—At|lan|tic O|cean (at lan′tik ō′shən).
Baltic Sea—Bal|tic Sea (bawl′tik sē).

Black Sea—Black Sea (blak sē).
Caribbean Sea—Ca|rib|be|an Sea (kar′ə bē′ən sē or kə rib′ē ən sē).
Indian Ocean—In|di|an O|cean (in′dē ən ō′shən).
Mediterranean Sea—Med|i|ter|ra|ne|an Sea (med′ə tə rā′nē ən sē).
North Sea—North Sea (nawrth sē).
Pacific Ocean—Pa|cif|ic O|cean (pə sif′ik ō′shən).
Red Sea—Red Sea (red sē).

Longest Rivers

Amazon—Am|a|zon (**am′** ə zon). South America.

Arkansas—Ar|kan|sas (**ahr′**kən saw). United States.

Colorado—Col|o|rad|o (kol ə **rad′**ō or kol ə **rah′**dō). United States.

Congo—Con|go (**kong′**gō). Africa.

Danube—Dan|ube (**dan′**yūb). Europe.

Ganges—Gan|ges (**gan′**jēz). India-Bangladesh.

Huang He—Huang He (hwahng hu). The name means Yellow River. China.

Indus—In|dus (**in′**dəs). China-Pakistan.

Mackenzie—Mac|ken|zie (mə ken′zē). Canada.

Mekong—Me|kong (**mā′kong′**). Asia.

Mississippi—Mis|sis|sip|pi (mis′ə **sip′**ē). United States.

Missouri—Mis|sou|ri (mə **zoor′**ē or mə **zoor′**ə). United States.

Niger—Ni|ger (**nī′**jər). Africa.

Nile—Nile (nīl). Africa.

Rhine—Rhine (rīn). Europe.

Rio Grande—Ri|o Grande (rē′ō grand). The name means Large River. United States-Mexico.

St. Lawrence—Saint Law|rence (sānt **lawr′**əns or sānt **lahr′**əns). Canada-United States.

Volga—Vol|ga (**vol′**gə or **vōl′**gə). Union of Soviet Socialist Republics.

Yangtze—Yang|tze (**yahngt′zu′** or **yank′sē′**). China.

Zambezi—Zam|be|zi (zam **bē′**zē). Africa.

Gods and Goddesses

Greek and Roman

Aphrodite—Aph|ro|di|te (af′rə **dī′**tē). See **Venus.**

Apollo—A|pol|lo (ə **pol′**ō). The Greek and Roman god of the sun, poetry, music, and archery.

Ares—Ar|es (**ār′**ēz). See **Mars.**

Athena—A|the|na (ə **thē′**nə). See **Minerva.**

Cronus—Cro|nus (**krō′**nəs). See **Saturn.**

Hades—Ha|des (**hā′**dēz). See **Pluto.**

Hephaestus—He|phaes|tus (hi **fes′** təs). See **Vulcan.**

Hera—He|ra (**hēr′**ə). See **Juno.**

Hermes—Her|mes (**hur′**mēz). See **Mercury.**

Janus—Ja|nus (**jā′**nəs). The Roman god of beginnings and endings and of gates and doors. January is named for him.

Juno—Ju|no (**jū′**nō). The Roman goddess of women and marriage and the wife of **Jupiter.** Some people believe the month of June is named for her. The Greeks called her **Hera.**

Jupiter—Ju|pi|ter (**jū′**pə tər). In Roman mythology, the king of all the gods. **Juno** was his wife. The planet Jupiter is named for him. The Greeks called him **Zeus.**

Mars—Mars (mahrz). The Roman god of war. Both March and the planet Mars are named for him. The Greeks called him **Ares.**

Mercury—Mer|cu|ry (**mur′**kyər ē). The messenger of the gods in Roman mythology. The planet Mercury is named for him. The Greeks called him **Hermes.**

Minerva—Mi|ner|va (mə **nur′**və). The Roman goddess of wisdom, the arts, and war. The Greeks called her **Athena.**

Neptune—Nep|tune (**nep′**tūn or **nep′**tyūn). The Roman god of the sea. The planet Neptune is named for him. The Greeks called him **Poseidon.**

Pluto—Plu|to (**plū′**tō). The Roman god of the dead. The planet Pluto is named for him. The Greeks called him **Hades.**

Poseidon—Po|sei|don (pə **sī′**dən). See **Neptune.**

Saturn—Sat|urn (**sat′**ərn). The Roman god of planting and harvest. Both Saturday and the planet Saturn are named for him. The Greeks called him **Cronus.**

Uranus—U|ra|nus (yoo **rā′**nəs or **yoor′**ə nəs). In both Greek and Roman mythology, the first god of the sky. The planet Uranus is named for him.

Venus—Ve|nus (**vē′**nəs). The Roman goddess of love and beauty. The planet Venus is named for her. The Greeks called her **Aphrodite.**

Vulcan—Vul|can (**vul′**kən). The Roman god of fire. The Greeks called him **Hephaestus.**

Zeus—Zeus (zūs). See **Jupiter.**

Norse*

Balder—Bal|der (**bawl′**dər). The Norse god of light, goodness, wisdom, and peace.

Freya—Frey|a (**frā′**ə). The Norse goddess of love and beauty.

Frigg—Frigg (frig). The Norse goddess of the sky and the wife of **Odin.** Friday is named for her.

Hel—Hel (hel). The Norse goddess of the lower world and the daughter of **Loki.**

Loki—Lo|ki (**lō′**kē). The Norse god of destruction and mischief and the brother of **Odin.**

Odin—O|din (**ō′**din). The ruler of all the Norse gods. He was also called **Woden.** Wednesday is named for him.

Thor—Thor (thawr). The Norse god of thunder and lightning and war. Thursday is named for him.

Tyr—Tyr (tēr). A Norse god of war and victory and a son of **Odin** and **Frigg.** Tuesday is named for him.

Woden—Wo|den (**wō′**dən). See **Odin.**

*The Norse (nawrs) gods and goddesses were worshiped by people who lived in what are now Germany, Denmark, Norway, and Sweden, and later by people who lived in what is now England.

Metric Conversion Tables

From Customary Units to Metric Units
(approximate)

	Multiply number of:	By:	To find how many:
Length	inches (in.)	25.0	millimeters (mm)
	inches (in.)	2.5	centimeters (cm)
	feet (ft.)	30.0	centimeters (cm)
	feet (ft.)	0.3	meters (m)
	yards (yds.)	0.9	meters (m)
	miles (mi.)	1.6	kilometers (km)
Weight	ounces (oz.)	28.	grams (g)
	pounds (lbs.)	0.45	kilograms (kg)
	tons (t.)	0.9	metric tons (t)
Volume (liquid)	fluid ounces (fl. oz.)	30.0	milliliters (ml)
	pints (pts.)	0.47	liters (l)
	quarts (qts.)	0.95	liters (l)
	gallons (gals.)	3.8	liters (l)
Area	square inches (sq. in.)	6.5	square centimeters (cm^2)
	square feet (sq. ft.)	0.09	square meters (m^2)
	square yards (sq. yds.)	0.8	square meters (m^2)
	square miles (sq. mi.)	2.6	square kilometers (km^2)
Temperature (exact)	degrees Fahrenheit (°F.) (after subtracting 32)	0.55	degrees Celsius (°C)

From Metric Units to Customary Units
(approximate)

	Multiply number of:	By:	To find how many:
Length	millimeters (mm)	0.04	inches (in.)
	centimeters (cm)	0.4	inches (in.)
	centimeters (cm)	0.033	feet (ft.)
	meters (m)	3.3	feet (ft.)
	meters (m)	1.1	yards (yds.)
	kilometers (km)	0.6	miles (mi.)
Weight	grams (g)	0.035	ounces (oz.)
	kilograms (kg)	2.2	pounds (lbs.)
	metric tons (t)	1.1	tons (t.)
Volume (liquid)	milliliters (ml)	0.03	fluid ounces (fl. oz.)
	liters (l)	2.1	pints (pts.)
	liters (l)	1.06	quarts (qts.)
	liters (l)	0.26	gallons (gals.)
Area	square centimeters (cm^2)	0.16	square inches (sq. in.)
	square meters (m^2)	11.1	square feet (sq. ft.)
	square meters (m^2)	1.2	square yards (sq. yds.)
	square kilometers (km^2)	0.4	square miles (sq. mi.)
Temperature (exact)	degrees Celsius (°C)	1.8	degrees Fahrenheit (°F.) (then add 32)

The Magic of Words

You Can Make Magic!

Say the word *dog*. That word is just a noise that you make with your tongue and throat. But anyone who hears it will think of a four-footed animal that barks and wags its tail. So, with nothing but a noise, you can put a picture of a dog in other peoples' minds. And that's a sort of magic—the magic of words!

With words, people can share ideas, and knowledge, and fun. No other creature on earth can do such things. Only humans have the magic of words.

Did you ever wonder where these noises we call words came from—how they began? Most of them have stories to tell. Many of the words you use come from long ago. They've been through many adventures. You use words that sailed with the hardy Vikings and rode with the armored knights of Normandy. You use words that were made up by Greek explorers in Egypt thousands of years ago. There's a tale behind most words—a tale that may be surprising, amusing, or exciting.

Come now, and find out about these wonderful things called words. Find out what some of the words you use really mean—why you call a certain kind of dog a *poodle*, and why the top of a house is called a *roof*. Find out what names mean, for names are words, too. Find out the many ways you can use words for fun and entertainment. You're in for a real treat, learning about *The Magic of Words!*

Fun with Words

Did you ever stop to think how many games, puzzles, and other ways of having fun depend on words? Here's a collection of riddles, tongue twisters, puns, and many other kinds of word games. See for yourself how much fun you can have with words! And how much you can learn while having fun.

Mr. Fister's Tongue Twister

Read this story aloud. You won't believe what happens.

Mr. Fister's sister Sue enjoys  .

She should! Sue sells ____. The store Sue sells

____ in is near the ____ .

It's simply called Sue's ____ ____ Store.

Naturally, Sue searches the ____ for the

____ she sells. Some say Sue's silly for selling

____ in a ____ store. But Sue's smart.

She ____ .

Sometimes, Mr. Fister helps his sister Sue search

for ____ on the ____ .

He enjoys ____ , too. But he doesn't sell

____ . He sells ____ .

The store he sells ____ in is near Sue's

____ ____ Store.

It's called Mr. Fister's  Store.

One day, Mr. Fister told his sister Sue, "I sold six

to six who came into my

Store !"

Mr. Fister's sister Sue . "Those

must be the same six I sold sixty

!"

"Shucks," said Mr. Fister, "the same six

must have visited your

Store after buying six in my store."

"Yesh," Sue.

Mr. Fister chuckled. "Selling **shix** silk **seets**

to the **shame** six sheiks

who bought **shixty she sells**

seems to have twisted your tongue, my dear **Shue** !"

And that was Mr. Fister's  .

Read a riddle

A riddle is a puzzling question that is usually answered with a guess. Or, there may be a hidden meaning that you have to think out.

Riddles have always been popular. Long ago, people took riddles seriously. But today, most riddles are silly questions with silly answers. This kind of riddle is called a conundrum.

What's a conundrum? It's a riddle based on an imaginary likeness between two very different things.

The answer to a conundrum is a play on words that usually makes people laugh—or at least smile or grin. See how often you laugh, smile, or grin when you learn the answers to these conundrums:

What tree:
1. has many friends? (poplar)
2. sighs a lot?
3. cries a lot?
4. is a couple?
5. does everyone carry in their hands?

What flower is:
1. a dairy product and a dish?
2. a country with many cars?
3. a cow's mistake?
4. watched over by shepherds?
5. what he did when he sat on a tack?

What letter of the alphabet is:

1. an insect that makes money for people who sell honey?
2. where "The Owl and the Pussycat" went to?
3. in your head?
4. a bird that chatters?
5. a small, round, green vegetable?

What two letters of the alphabet form a:

1. number between 75 and 85?
2. word that means "to rot"?
3. word that means "simple"?
4. word that means "frozen"?
5. word that means "an Indian tent"?

What part of your body is:

1. part of a clock?
2. a tropical tree?
3. a cut of meat?
4. bent macaroni?
5. a student?
6. a flower?
7. a pot cover?
8. corn on the cob?
9. first part of a rocket?
10. part of a river?
11. a bed of spring flowers?
12. part of a shoe?
13. the edge of a saw?
14. a young cow?

Answers: (tree) 1. poplar 2. pine 3. weeping willow 4. pear 5. palm (flower) 1. buttercup 2. carnation 3. cowslip 4. phlox 5. rose (one letter) 1. B 2. C 3. I 4. J 5. P (two letters) 1. A-T 2. D-K 3. E-Z 4. I-C 5. T-P (body) 1. hands 2. palm 3. shoulder 4. elbow 5. pupil 6. iris 7. lid 8. ear 9. nose 10. mouth 11. two lips—tulips 12. tongue 13. teeth 14. calf

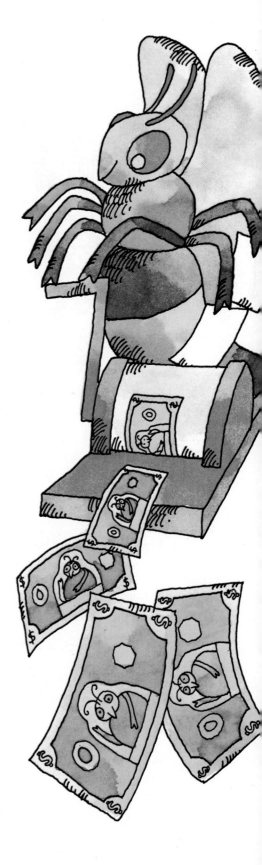

Just for p(h)un

Snow White has a father named Egg—Egg White. Get the yolk?

That is a pun, and puns are another way to have fun with language.

What's a pun? It's a funny way of saying something while meaning something else. You "play" with words.

Pun words sound alike, but are usually spelled differently. And they mean different things.

Words such as *ant* and *aunt*, *flower* and *flour*, *hair* and *hare* sound alike but are spelled differently and have different meanings. Such words are called homonyms. Homonym is the name for two or more words that sound alike but mean different things. The words may or may not be spelled the same. The word *homonym* comes from the Greek. It means "same name." Homonyms are a good source of puns. Here are a few examples:

Eight famous mathematicians ate dinner together, so the headline read, "Eight ate eight dinners at eight."	**eight-ate**
A poison berry can bury you unless, of course, it's really a boysenberry.	**berry-bury**
It can cost a lot of dough to shoot a doe out of season.	**dough-doe**
The ecologist bought his wife a fir for Christmas. He thought it was fur enough.	**fir-fur**
A horse is a horse, but a sick pony is a little hoarse.	**horse-hoarse**
A pair of trees may grow pears—unless the pair are pines.	**pair-pear**

Running back again

"Otto, the pup," said Mom, "has lots of pep at noon!"

How many palindromes can you find in that sentence? The word *palindrome* comes from a Greek word and means "running back again." So, a palindrome is a word, a group of words, or a sentence that "runs back again" the same way it started. That's the fun of a palindrome. The first sentence has five palindromes: Otto, pup, Mom, pep, and noon.

Here are some famous palindromes. They make as much sense when you read them backward as they do when you read them forward:

MADAM, I'M ADAM.

NAME NO ONE MAN.

ABLE WAS I ERE I SAW ELBA.

A MAN, A PLAN, A CANAL—PANAMA!

Word games

Calling All Cities!

The leader calls out the name of any
big city. The next player must name
another city before the leader can count
to ten. The name of this city must start
with the last letter in the name of the
city just called. Otherwise, the player is
out. The winner is the last remaining
player.

Word Snap!

The leader needs two or more sets of alphabet cards. The leader calls out a category, such as animals, and holds up one of the alphabet cards.

The first player to call out an animal name that begins with the letter shown, gets the card. The winner is the player who ends up with the most cards.

Snip!

"It" stands inside a circle of players and tosses a knotted handkerchief to any player. At the same time, "It" calls out a three-letter word, spells the word, counts to twelve, and says, "Snip!"

The player who catches the handkerchief must say three words that begin with the letters in the word.

Let's say "It" calls, "Dog, d-o-g." The player with the handkerchief might yell, "Doctor, Oats, Ginger." If he does this before "It" counts to twelve and says "Snip!" he's safe.

But if "It" counts to twelve and says "Snip!" first, the player is out, o-u-t.

The last one out is the winner.

Birds, Beasts, Fishes, or Flowers

Two teams line up opposite each other, with a good running distance between them.

Team 1 picks one of the categories in the title, and an example, such as: Bird—cardinal. This team then crosses to face Team 2. They shout out the category —in this example—"Bird" and the first letter of the bird they chose—"C."

When Team 2 guesses "cardinal," the players on Team 1 run for their side.

Team 2 chases them. Any player tagged before reaching his side must join Team 2.

Then Team 2 gets a turn. The team that loses the most players loses the game.

Deborah

Thomas

Brian

Eric

Ellen

Names are Words

Do you know that both your first and last names are *words* that have special meanings? They are. On the next few pages you'll find many first and last names and what they mean. Perhaps you'll find your names, or the names of some of your friends. And you may be surprised to learn what some of the names mean!

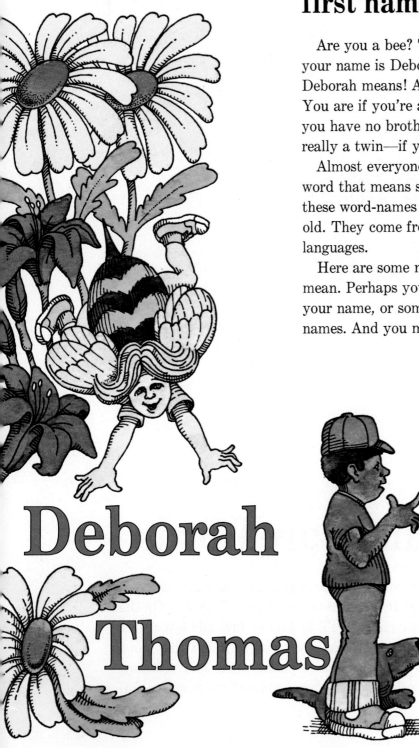

What does your first name mean?

Are you a bee? That's what you are if your name is Deborah—for that's what Deborah means! Are you a wise advisor? You are if you're an Alfred! And even if you have no brothers or sisters, you're really a twin—if your name is Thomas!

Almost everyone's first name is a word that means something. Many of these word-names are thousands of years old. They come from many different languages.

Here are some names and what they mean. Perhaps you'll find the meaning of your name, or some of your friends' names. And you may be surprised!

Deborah

Thomas

Albert, Alberta, Bert, Bertha, Elaine, Eleanor, Ellen, Elena, Helen, Helene, Helena, and Lenore mean *bright*. Robert and Roberta mean *bright fame*.

Ellen

Enid, Catherine, Karen, Katherine, Kathleen, Kathryn, Kay, and Kitty mean *pure*.

Bess, Beth, Betsy, Betty, Elisa, Elsie, Elizabeth, and Lisa mean *belongs to God*.

Alice, Alicia, and Alison mean *truth*.

Russell

Rufus, Russell, and Rory mean *red-haired*.

Earl, Ethel, Patricia, Patrick, and Patsy mean *noble*.

Greta, Maggie, Mamie, Margaret, Margot, Marguerite, Marjorie, Meg, Peggy, and Rita mean *pearl*.

Greta

Debbie, Deborah, and Melissa mean *bee*.

Andrew, Carl, Carlo, Carol, Caroline, Carrie, Charles, Charlotte, and Karl mean *man* or *manly*.

Enrico, Hal, Harriet, Harry, Henry, and Henrietta, mean *master of a house.*

Enrico

Anthony, Antoinette, Antonia, Antonio, Antony, Toni, and Tony mean *great value*.

Esther, Ettie, Hester, and Stella mean *star*.

Brian

Brian and Ramsey mean *strong*.

Evan, Hans, Ian, Ivan, Jack, Jan, Jane, Janet, Janice, Jean, Jenny, Joan, Joanna, Johanna, John, Juan, Juanita, and Sean mean *God is gracious*.

Clarissa

Claire, Clara, Clarence, Clarice, Clarissa, and Rodney mean *famous*.

Barbara and Barbie mean *stranger*.

Basil, Eric, and Erica mean *royal*. Rex and Roy mean *king*. Riccardo and Richard mean *harsh king*.

Eric

Ann, Anna, Anne, Annette, Annie, and Hannah mean *grace*.

Sue, Susan, Susanna, Suzie, and Suzanne mean *graceful white lily*.

Errol and Wendy mean *wanderer*.

Wendy

Abigail, Abby, Gail, and Gayle mean *father's joy*.

Bartholomew, Bart, George, Georgette, and Georgina mean *farmer*.

George

Lewis, Lew, Louis, Louise, Luther, and Lulu mean *great warrior*.

Dee, Dora, Doreen, Dorothea, Dorothy, Ted, and Theodore mean *a gift of God*.

Mari, Maria, Marie, Marilyn, Marion, Marlene, Mary, Maureen, and Molly are thought to mean either *rebel* or *bitter*.

Alfreda

Alfred, Alfreda, and Conrad mean *wise advisor*.

Alastair, Alexander, Alexandra, Sandra, and Sandy mean *defender of man*.

How last names were invented

Once upon a time, four men lived on the same street in a little town. They all had the same name—Tom. And that was the only name any of them had. In those days, only kings and nobles had last names. Most men and women had only first names.

Because the men had the same name, you might think people would get them mixed up. But there was a way of telling them apart. One Tom had a father named John, so he was called *Tom, John's son.* Another Tom, a baker, was called *Tom the Baker.* The third Tom had light-colored hair. He was known as

Tom the White. And the fourth Tom lived next to a park called the village green, so he was known to everyone as *Tom of the Green.*

Tom the Baker married a girl named Meg. She became known as *Meg, Tom the Baker's wife.* They had a little boy named John, and he was known as *John, the Baker's son.* But after a while, people got tired of saying all those words. So they simply called Tom the Baker, *Tom Baker.* His wife became *Meg Baker,* and his son was *John Baker.*

That's how last names came to be. People took their father's first name, or the name of their job, or the name of the place where they lived, or a name that told how they looked. They put these names after their first names. When a man married, his wife and children took his last name. Sometimes, a widow or single woman might adopt children and give them her last name.

So, today, our last names can tell us something about the people we got them from, long ago—as you'll see in the next few pages.

Before there were last names, children were often known by their father's name. If a man named Robert had a boy named John, the boy might be known as *John, Robert's*—meaning that he was Robert's son. If Robert had a daughter named Poll, she might be called *Poll, Robert's.* After a while, these became regular last names. When a boy grew up and married, he would give his last name to his wife and children. So, if your name ends with *s,* as in Roberts, Thomas, Adams, or Rogers, it came from someone who, long ago, had a father named Robert, Thomas, Adam, or Roger.

When people began to write last names, they often turned an *'s* ending of a name into *es, is,* or *ez.* Thus, names such as Jones and Hughes mean John's and

Hugh's. Names such as Davis, Harris, and Willis mean Davey's, Harry's, and Wil's. And Rodriguez and Hernandez mean Rodrigo's and Hernando's.

Boys were often called by their father's name with the word "son" added. If Wil had a son called Jack, the boy might be known as *Jack, Wil's son*. These kinds of names became regular last names, too. So if your last name ends in *son* or *sen*, as in Wilson, Johnson, Andersen, or Nelsen, you got it from someone whose father was named Wil, John, Anders, or Nels.

People who spoke other languages added "son" to their fathers' names, too. If your name ends in *sohn*, *wicz*, *vich*, or *ak*, those endings all mean "son."

People in some countries put their word for "son" in *front* of their fathers' names. *Mac*, *Mc*, and *Fitz* all mean "son of."

**Jack, Wil's son,
and the Wilson family**

Iron pounders and clothes makers

Lots of last names come from the kind of work people did.

For hundreds of years, one of the most important jobs was making things out of metal—tools, weapons, horseshoes, and so on. To make these things, metalworkers heated the metal until it was soft and then hammered it into shape. In the Old English language, a person who hammered metal was called a *smith*. Metalworkers in other countries were usually also called by a name that meant "to hammer metal." When people began to take last names, many metalworkers took the name of their job. So if your name is Smith, Schmitt, Herrera, Ferrar, Ferraro, Kowalski, Kovacs, or MacGowan, you probably had an ancestor who was a metalworker.

The word *mill* means "grind," and people who ground flour were called millers. That's where the names Miller, Mueller, and Molinaro come from.

Men who make clothes are tailors. The names Taylor, Snider, Schneider, and Sarto all mean "tailor."

People once drove carts and wagons for a living, just as they drive trucks today. If your name is Carter, Porter, Wagner, or Schroeder, you probably got the name from someone who drove a cart or wagon.

Is your name Baker, Baxter, Fournier, Piekarz, or Boulanger? If so, you may have had an ancestor who was a baker.

Hills, brooks, and woods

Many last names come from places where people lived. A man named Robert, who lived on a hill, might call himself "Robert o' the Hill." A woman whose house was beside a brook might be known as "Nell of the Brook." After a while, these names were shortened to Robert Hill and Nell Brook.

Hill, Hull, Hillman, Downs, Downing, Lowe, Law, Knapp, Knowles, Peck, and Barrows are all names that come from people who lived on top of, on the side of, or at the bottom of a hill.

Brooks, Burns, Beck, Rivera, and Arroyo are names that come from people who lived beside a stream.

Wood, Woods, Atwood, Smallwood, Boyce, DuBois, Holt, Hurst, Shaw, and Silva are names that come from people who lived near small forests.

Marsh, Morse, Moore, Mosher, Carr, Carson, Kerr, Slaughter, and Tanaka are names that come from people who lived near a marsh, or swampy place.

Castle, Castillo, Castello, Zamecki, Burke, Burk, Borg, Burris, and Burr lived near a castle. Streeter, Lane, Strass, and Estrada lived near a road.

Lake, Lynn, Poole, and Pollard are all names that come from people who lived near lakes, ponds, or pools.

And Meadows, Mead, Field, Fields, Lee, Pratt, Vega, Murawski, and Campos are names that were given to people who lived near grassy fields.

Are any of your friends nicknamed "Red," "Whitey," or "Curly"? These are common nicknames for people with red hair, very light blond hair, and curly hair.

Hundreds of years ago, many people took such nicknames for their last names. A man might call himself "John White Head," or "Will the Red," or "Tom Curly." If your last name is White, Wise,

Weiss, Whitehead, Whitlock, Whitman, Blanchard, Blount, or Bannon, your name may come from someone who had very light hair. If you are a Reed, Reid, Read, Roth, Russell, or Flynn, your name means "red." And if you are a Krause, Kruse, Cassidy, or Rizzo, you probably had an ancestor who was a "Curly."

Many other nicknames also became last names. Names such as Long, Lang, Hoch, and Longfellow were nicknames for tall people. Little, Short, Small, Bass, Basset, Kline, Klein, Cline, Kurtz, Block, and Grubb were nicknames for people who were short. If your last name is Gay, Bliss, Murray, Froh, Merriman, Blaha, or Allegretti, you got your name from a good-natured person, for these names all mean "happy" or "cheerful."

In long-ago times, when last names were first used, most people seldom left the little towns where they were born. Everyone in a town knew everyone else. If a new person came to town to live, the people called him "new man," or "newcomer." After a while, he might take that for his last name. That's what Newman, Newcomb, Doyle, Doran, and Dowell mean.

Some last names are the names of animals. This came about in one of several ways.

Hundreds of years ago, most signs had no writing on them—just a picture. Many of the signs in front of inns had a picture of an animal—a wolf, a bear, a lion, or some kind of bird. People who worked at inns, or lived near them, often took the name of the animal on the inn sign as their last name.

Other last names that are the names of animals come from nicknames. A man who was said to be "as smart as a fox" might have become known as Fox. And a very brave man might have been called Lion.

So, if your last name is the name of an animal, your name may have come from an ancestor who took the

name from a sign in front of an inn. Or, it may have been a nickname. Or, it may have been the name given to a man because he hunted a certain kind of animal.

The names Wolf, Wolfe, Wolff, and Lupo all mean *wolf*. Fox, Fuchs, Todd, and Volpe are all names that mean *fox*. Names such as Lyon, Lyons, Loewe, and Leon mean *lion*. And the names Buck, Hart, Hirsch, and Roe mean *deer*.

Last names such as Bird, Byrd, Crow, Crowe, Hahn, Fink, Crane, Coe, Cox, Ortega, Garza, Aguilar, Adler, and Vogel come from the word *bird* or the names of different kinds of birds.

The names Haas and Hare both mean *rabbit*. As you might guess, the name Baer means *bear*. And it might surprise you to learn that the name Drake is from the word *draca*, which means—*dragon!*

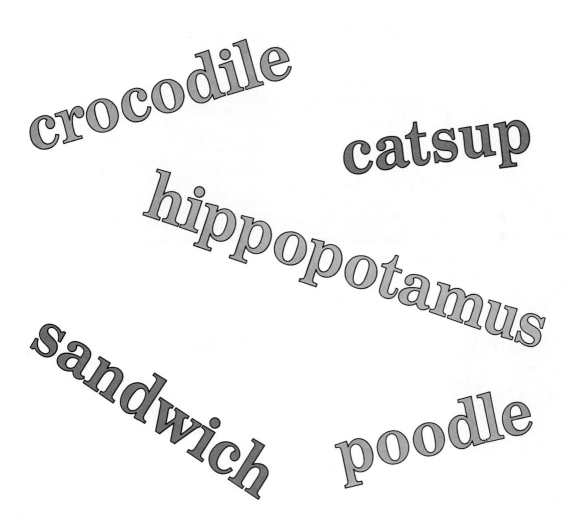

crocodile

catsup

hippopotamus

sandwich

poodle

Word Stories

Most words are names of things—creatures, objects, or actions. But why do we call things by certain names? You know that a hippopotamus is a certain kind of animal—but *why* is it called a hippopotamus? You know what an attic is, and what a sandwich is. But how did they get these names? There's a wonderful story behind most words—and here are some of the stories.

hippopotamus

Splash dogs and river horses

Did you ever hear of an animal called a river horse—or a pebble worm—or a splash dog? Probably not. But these are the *meanings* of the names of three animals you know very well.

Most names are words that mean something. Sometimes, the things they mean are funny or surprising.

The hippopotamus was named by the ancient Greeks. The first Greeks who saw a hippopotamus snorting and splashing in a river must have thought it looked like a fat horse, because the word *hippopotamus* means "river horse" in Greek.

The ancient Greeks also gave the

crocodile

poodle

crocodile its name. The first crocodile they saw must have been lying with its feet tucked under it on a gravel beach, so that it looked like a legless worm. The Greeks put together their words for *pebble* and *worm* to make the word *krokodilos*, which means "pebble worm."

Poodle comes from the German word *Pudelhund*. In German, *pudeln* means "to splash water," and *hund* means "dog." So a poodle is a "splash dog."

Our name for the bug called a beetle comes from the Old English word *bitula*, which means "biter."

Spider also comes from an Old English word, *spithre*, which means "spinner."

Duck is from the Old English word *duce*. Pronounced *dook uh*, it means "diver." This is a good name, because ducks dive down in the water to get their food.

The names of many North American animals come from Indian words. The word *moose* is almost like the Algonkian word *moos-u*, which means "he strips off bark." The Indians gave this big animal that name because when he's very hungry he eats bark that he strips off young trees.

The name *octopus* comes from two Greek words—*okto*, meaning "eight," and *pous*, meaning "foot." So *octopus* means "eight-footed," because this animal has eight wiggly tentacles.

spider

duck

menu
Clam Chowder
Hamburger
Sandwich
coleslaw
French Fries
Chocolate Sundae

That looks like a pretty good lunch, doesn't it! But where did these rather strange names come from? Why do we call a lump of ground beef a *hamburger*? What in the world does *coleslaw* mean? And why is a dish of ice cream with chocolate syrup called a *sundae*?

Here's how each of the foods on this menu got its name.

Clam chowder is a soup made out of clams and vegetables. Soup is usually cooked in a big pot. And our word *chowder* comes from the French word *chaudiere*, which means "pot."

There is no ham at all in hamburger. It's made of ground beef. Americans think of hamburger as being an American food, but it really came from Germany. Long ago, many German people came to America to live. They brought with them a lot of recipes for their favorite foods. One of these foods was a kind of meat ball made of ground beef. These meat balls were supposed to have been invented in the German city of Hamburg, so they became known as hamburgers.

But why should a hamburger between two pieces of bread be called a *sandwich*?

The word *sandwich* comes from the name of an English town. Long ago, the town of Sandwich was owned by a nobleman called the Earl of Sandwich. The earl loved to

sandwich

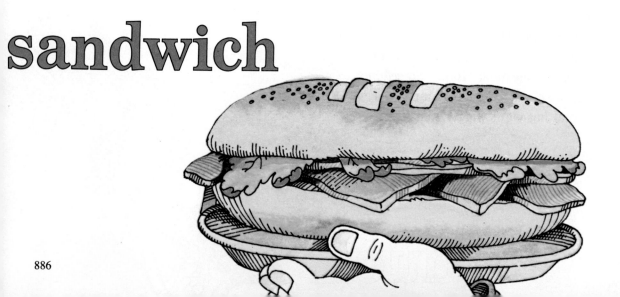

play cards. One day, he was playing cards and didn't want to stop for dinner, even though he was hungry. So he told a servant to bring him some slices of meat between two pieces of toasted bread. Others tried this new way of eating bread and meat together. They called it a *sandwich,* in honor of the earl. To this day, any kind of food that is served between slices of bread is called a sandwich.

Coleslaw is a spicy salad made of chopped cabbage. This salad comes from Holland, and its name is made up of two Dutch words—*kool* meaning "cabbage," and *sla,* meaning "salad." So *coleslaw* simply means "cabbage salad"—just what it is.

You might think that French fried potatoes got their name because they were first made in France. But that's not the reason. Cooks at restaurants and hotels often cut meat and vegetables into long strips, and this used to be called *Frenching.* When American cooks first began to fry potatoes that had been Frenched, they called them Frenched fried potatoes. Now, we just call them French fries.

french fries

Do you like ketchup on your French fries? Lots of people do. Ketchup, or catchup, or catsup as it is also spelled, is a tomato sauce. The name comes from the Chinese word *ke-tsiap,* which means "taste." So, when you put tomato ketchup on your French fries, you're just putting tomato taste on them.

Wind-eyes in the posts

It's spring-cleaning time at your house. You're going to wash the wind-eyes in the elegant room. Then you're going to help your mother paint the posts in the cooking place.

That sounds strange, doesn't it? But, as a matter of fact, every house really does have lots of "wind-eyes," "posts" in every room, a "cooking place," and, usually, an "elegant room," too. It also has "pieces" in the windows and "splits" on its "cover"!

What are wind-eyes? Well, long ago, Vikings living in Britain had openings in the walls of their houses to let in light and air. To the Vikings, the openings seemed like eyes looking out at the wind. So they called them "wind-eyes." Their word for "wind-eye" was *vindauga*—and that's where our word *window* comes from. So *window* really means "wind-eye."

And what about the glass in a window—the panes? How did they get this name? At one time, people used pieces of cloth to cover the window openings in walls.

Coquina!

Long ago, in England, such a piece of cloth was called a *pannus*, meaning "a piece of cloth." Later, that word was changed to *pan*, and then *pane*, and simply meant "piece." Thus, a windowpane is a window "piece."

The "posts" in every room in a house are the walls. Long ago, when a Roman army made camp, the soldiers put walls around the camp's four sides. The walls were made of wooden posts pounded into the ground. The Roman word for *post* was *vallus*, and the wall of posts was called a *vallum*. So, our word *wall*, which comes from *vallum*, means "a row of posts."

We could call the attic of a house the "elegant room." This seems a strange name for a room that's usually full of junk. But here's how it works out.

Many people in England once thought the ancient Greek city of Athens must have been the most elegant and beautiful place in the world. They changed the Greek word *Attikos*, which means "of Athens" to *Attic*, and used it to mean something that was truly elegant. They built houses with rows of pillars along the top, as the Greeks had done. These pillars were said to be "Attic style." After a while, people called the whole top part of such a house an *attic*. So, the word *attic*,

Cooking place!

our name for the dusty, junk-filled room at the top of a house, really means something fine and elegant, like ancient Athens.

The part of a house where cooking is done is the kitchen. Why not just call this room the "cooking room"? How did it get the odd name *kitchen?*

The word *kitchen* comes from the Latin word *coquina,* which means "cooking." Roman soldiers took that word into Britain, where it became *cychene,* and meant a place where cooking was done. *Cychene* became *kuchene,* and finally *kitchen.* So kitchen really means "a cooking place."

And, last of all, every house has a cover with splits on it. Our word *roof* comes from the Old English word *hrof,* meaning "cover." Roofs have shingles, and shingles used to be made of pieces of wood that had been split. The Latin word *scindula* means "split." In English, this word was changed to *shindle* and then to *shingle.* So a house with a shingle roof has a "cover" with "splits."

And that's the story of the wind-eyes, elegant room, posts, cover, and splits of your house.

A break, a lump, and a sip

Have you ever broken a fast?

Yes, you have, lots of times. And you were never blamed for breaking it!

Fast doesn't only mean "quick," it also means to go without eating. You fast all night long, while you're asleep. Then, when you wake up in the morning and eat, you *break* your fast—that is, you stop fasting. And that's why we call our morning meal breakfast.

At noontime you eat a lump! The word *lunch* first meant a lump of bread. There was also an old word, *nuncheon*, which meant a noontime drink. Word experts think this was changed to *luncheon*, meaning a lump of food at noontime.

Evening is suppertime. Supper is usually your biggest meal, so you'd be surprised if your mother gave you only soup and told you to "sip it." But that's what *supper* really means. It comes from the older word *sup*, which meant to sip a liquid. Nowadays, people usually say, "Let's have supper." Long ago, they were more likely to say, "Let us sup."

Wear words

Pants is a funny-sounding word. Where did such a word come from?

A long time ago, many plays had a character called Pantalone. And Pantalone usually wore long, red tights. The first kind of long trousers that men wore were quite tight-fitting, so they became known as *pantaloons*, after Pantalone's long tights. But because *pantaloons* is such a long word, it was soon shortened to *pants*. And that's what it has been, ever since.

Lots of people wear pants called *jeans, denims, dungarees,* or *Levi's*. These are all pants made out of strong cotton cloth, usually dyed blue. How did they get all these strange names?

Jeans comes from the name *Genes,* which is the

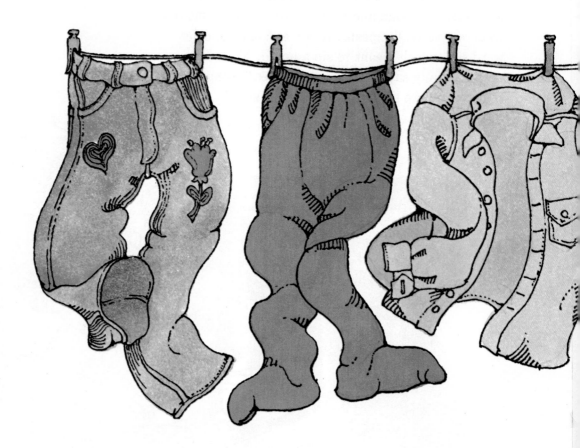

French name for the city of Genoa, Italy, where a lot of cotton cloth was made. French people called the cloth by their name for the city. We use the French name as our word for the pants.

Another kind of strong cotton cloth was made in the city of Nimes, France. The cloth was called *serge de Nimes*. And, of course, *denims* comes from *de Nimes*.

Dungarees comes from the East Indian word *dungri*. Long ago, English traders brought coarse cotton cloth called *dungri* back from India. In time, the English people changed the word to dungaree.

Levi's are named after a man, Levi Strauss. He was a clothing merchant who put metal fasteners on the pockets of pants to keep them from tearing.

Perhaps you've wondered about the word *clothes*. *Clothes* simply means "cloths"—the cloths you wear.

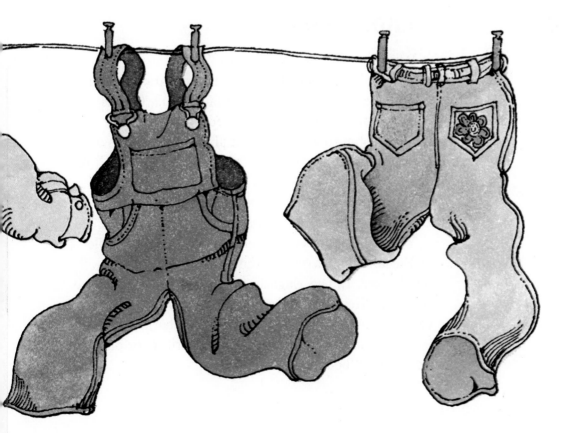

School words

Believe it or not, *school* means "spare time!"

The ancient Greeks believed that education was one of the most important things in life. Young Greeks would even use their spare time for learning. They liked to listen to wise men talk about science and other things. The Greek word *schole*, means "spare time." A group of young Greeks who listened to teachers in their spare time was called a *schole*. And, of course, that's where our word *school* comes from.

Your schoolbooks owe their name to a tree. People in England once wrote on the thin, inner bark of beech trees. In Old English, the name of the beech tree was *boc*. After a while, *boc*, then *bok*, and finally *book* came to mean the writing on a sheet of bark. Now it means many sheets of paper, with writing or printing on them, all bound together.

The pen that you do your schoolwork with is named after a feather. For hundreds of years people wrote with feathers. They cut the quills to a point and dipped them in ink. The Latin word for feather is *penna,* and so the feathers used for writing became known as *pens.* And to this day, we still call any writing tool that uses ink a *pen.*

The word *pencil* comes from a Latin word, too. The word is *penicillus,* and means "brush" or "little tail." Artists used to call their smallest, pointed brushes pencils, because the brush looked like a little pointed tail. In time, the name came to be used for the pointed writing tool we call a pencil.

And why are you and your schoolmates called pupils? The Latin word *pupillae* means "little dolls." Long ago, that word came to mean children who were in the care of a teacher. It is from this word that we got the English word, *pupil.*

Lazy Words

Most of us don't like to take the time to say long words. So we shorten the words by using only part of them. Our language is full of such parts-of-words. We call them "lazy words," but we are really the lazy ones.

Gun is really part of the word *dragon*. The first guns were sometimes called dragons because they shot out smoke and fire, the way dragons are supposed to.

Cab is short for the French word *cabriolet*, which comes from a word meaning "to leap or caper." And a cabriolet was a light, two-wheeled carriage that bounced a lot, so the name was a good one.

Are you a baseball or football fan? This kind of fan comes from the word *fanatic*. A fanatic is someone who gets wildly excited about something he or she believes in.

Bus is part of a word, too. Big carriages once traveled back and forth on city streets, picking up people who wanted to go somewhere. Because these carriages were for everybody to use, they were called omnibuses, from a Latin word that means "for all." After a while, *omnibus* got shortened to *bus*.

Mathematics, photograph, advertisement, telephone, airplane, and *examination* are all words that we often shorten—such as saying *ad* for *advertisement*. What "lazy words" have been made from the others?

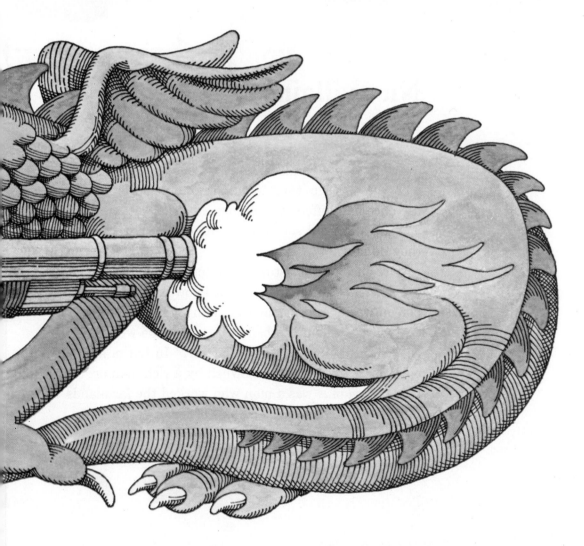

Nice villains
and naughty chairs

Can a villain be nice? Can a chair be naughty?

Once, long ago, they could. Many of the words we
use once had different meanings. *Nice*, *villain*, and
naughty all meant something quite different from what
they do now.

Nice once meant "stupid." It comes from the Latin
word *nescius*, which means "not knowing." A nice
person was once someone who didn't know anything!

Today, a villain is a bad person. But the word
villain once simply meant "a farmer." In Latin, a
villa was a big farmhouse, owned by a rich man or
noble. A *vilanus* was a man who worked the farmlands
that belonged to the *villa*. The word *vilanus* got
changed to *villein* in French, and then to *villain* in

English. Because the villains had poor manners and no education, the nobles looked down on them, as if they were bad people. So, slowly, the word *villain* came to mean someone who was wicked.

Long ago, someone might have said that a chair was naughty. A naughty chair would have been a chair that wasn't much good. *Naughty* meant "good for nothing." It comes from the word *naught*, which we still use to mean "nothing."

Quick used to mean "alive" instead of "fast," as it does now. It comes from the Old English word *cwic*. When people said someone was quick, they meant that he was alive. When they wanted someone to do something in a hurry, they said, "be quick," meaning "be alive, move fast, like a live person." After a while, *quick* came to mean "fast," as it does now.

And if someone calls you "silly," you shouldn't care. *Silly* used to mean "happy."

Howls, thumps, and creaks

It was midnight, and the sky was black and stormy! The wind *howled,* and there were *crashes* of thunder. Rain *pattered* sharply on the roof of the old haunted house. A shutter, swinging in the wind, went *bang-bang, bang-bang* against the side of the house.

"I'm not afraid," the boy who had gone into the house on a dare said to himself.

But suddenly, he heard another noise. From down in the cellar there came the long, slow *creak* of a door opening. The boy's hair stood up with fright as he heard the *clank* of dragging chains. Then—*thump* . . . *thump* . . . *thump.* Something was coming up the stairs! With a *shriek,* the boy rushed out of the house.

One reason why ghost stories are so much fun is because they use words that help us imagine the spooky sounds of a haunted house at night. For words such as *howl, crash, patter, bang, creak, clank, thump,* and *shriek* are really imitations of sounds.

Our language is full of words that imitate sounds. *Thud* is a word that imitates the sound something heavy makes when it falls to the ground. *Squish* sounds like the noise your feet make when you walk through mud. *Squawk, bark, croak, purr, buzz,* and *grunt* sound like noises certain animals make. How many other noise-words can you think of?